Auditing
and Other Assurance Services

Canadian Tenth Edition

Alvin A. Arens
PricewaterhouseCoopers Auditing Professor
Michigan State University

Randal J. Elder
Syracuse University

Mark S. Beasley
North Carolina State University

Ingrid B. Splettstoesser-Hogeterp
York University

Contributions to Chapter 10,
Fraud Auditing, were made by
Linda A. Robinson
University of Waterloo

PEARSON
Prentice
Hall

Toronto

Library and Archives Canada Cataloguing in Publication

  Auditing and other assurance services / Alvin A. Arens ... [et al.]. –
Canadian 10th ed.

Includes index.
Canadian 5th–Canadian 7th eds. published under title: Auditing : an integrated approach / W. Morley Lemon, Alvin A. Arens, James K. Loebbecke.
ISBN 0-13-129615-9

  1. Auditing—Textbooks. I. Arens, Alvin A.
HF5667.A69 2006   657'.45   C2005-906755-1

The publisher gratefully acknowledges the Canadian Institute of Chartered Accountants for permission to reprint published material.

ISBN 0-13-126915-9

Vice President, Editorial Director: Michael J. Young
Editor-in-Chief, Business and Economics: Gary Bennett
Executive Acquisitions Editor: Samantha Scully
Executive Marketing Manager: Cas Shields
Developmental Editor: Eleanor MacKay
Production Editor: Avivah Wargon
Copy Editor: Jennifer Therriault
Production Manager: Deborah Starks
Page Layout: Bill Renaud
Art Director: Julia Hall
Interior Design: Michelle Bellemare
Cover Design: David Cheung
Cover Image: Getty Images/Jack Hollingsworth

4 5   11 10 09 08

Printed and bound in the United States of America.

BRIEF CONTENTS

CONTENTS

PREFACE

Welcome to the Canadian Tenth Edition of *Auditing and Other Assurance Services.* It is with great pleasure that I bring forward this tenth edition, after having read through mountains of exposure drafts and numerous web pages. It was a wonderful challenge to provide you with new materials that highlight the changes that have taken place because of Sarbanes-Oxley in the U.S. and the many evolving standards in Canada. The most recent changes are the massive June 2005 revisions to the *CICA Handbook,* reflecting a more risk-based approach in auditing.

OBJECTIVES

As with any profession, auditing has its highs and its lows. The lows are the high-profile failures and management manipulation of financial statements, such as Nortel in Canada, and Enron and Worldcom in the United States. The highs are the thousands of qualified and brilliant professionals who conduct professional engagements and serve their clients every year. This text describes the highs and lows in vignettes and focus boxes, while providing the basic materials that you need to learn.

This book is intended for use in a first auditing course, for one-semester or two-semester instruction at the undergraduate or graduate level. Using a risk-based approach, it focuses on the auditor's decision-making process. It is important to keep the underlying objective in mind—the auditor needs to collect evidence to enable the statement of an opinion with respect to financial statements (and other types of information, as discussed in the later chapters). Assessing and documenting the risks associated with the client's business and the various components of the financial statements allows the auditor to target the fieldwork to specific objectives called audit assertions. If a student in auditing understands the objectives to be accomplished in a given audit area, the circumstances of the engagement, and the decisions to be made, he or she should be able to determine the appropriate evidence to gather and how to evaluate the evidence obtained.

The title of this book reflects the reality that auditing goes beyond financial statement auditing to other assurance services. In incorporating some new material from the U.S. tenth edition, my primary purpose is to integrate the most important concepts of financial statement auditing and the general assurance engagement framework. New problems and focus boxes highlight electronic commerce, non-profit businesses, and topics that engage professional judgment.

ORGANIZATION

This text is divided into five parts.

Part 1, The Auditing Profession (Chapters 1–4)

We begin with a description of assurance services, including auditing, and the role of public accounting firms and other organizations, such as the Office of the Auditor General of Canada, in doing audits. The impact of Sarbanes-Oxley, new Canadian quality control standards, and the formation of the Canadian Public Accountability Board on the standards of audits is explained. Chapter 2, Professional Relationships, has been renamed to reflect the fact that the professional rules of conduct govern the behaviour of the public accountant in the context of relationships with corporations, other business entities, and the users of reports. New independence standards using a threat-based model are applied to public and non-public engagements. Chapter 3 describes audit reports and variations to such reports. The impact of electronic filing is considered, as well as a sample report of assurance with respect to internal control over financial reporting, currently being considered as a requirement in Canada. (This type of report is required by public companies under Section 404 of the *Sarbanes-Oxley Act of 2002* in the United States.) Part 1 concludes with Chapter 4, an investigation of the auditor's legal liability and the profession's response.

Part 2, The Audit Process (Chapters 5–12)

Chapter 5 explains the auditor's and management's responsibilities and the key role of the audit committee in corporate governance. Transaction cycles are explained with a new black-and-white insert, the annual report and financial statements of Hillsburg Hardware Limited, a fictitious public company located in eastern Canada. Chapter 6 discusses evidence decisions and the general concepts of evidence accumulation. The risk-based audit approach with its large investment in up-front planning and the development of a client risk profile are explained in Chapter 7, while Chapter 8 explains the concepts of materiality and the audit risk model. Chapter 9, Internal Controls and Control Risk, uses the components of internal control that are consistent with international and U.S. standards. Fraud Auditing, the new Chapter 10, examines the nature of fraud and the auditor's responsibilities with respect to fraud. Chapter 11 proves an overall risk-based audit plan, linking planning to assertion-based audit programs, while Chapter 12 discusses sampling concepts relevant to the audit process.

Part 3, Application of the Audit Process to the Sales and Collection Cycle (Chapters 13 and 14)

These chapters apply the concepts from Part 2 to the audit of sales, cash receipts, and the related income statement and balance sheet accounts, using further details from Hillsburg Hardware Limited as examples. In Chapter 13, the audit procedures for sales and cash receipts are related to internal control and audit objectives for tests of controls. Chapter 14 continues to use audit objectives and the results of internal controls tests to formulate tests of details of balances. You will learn to apply audit sampling to the audit of sales, cash receipts, and accounts receivable by incorporating sampling into the appropriate test, showing the design, conduct, and evaluation of the sample.

Part 4, Application of the Audit Process to Other Cycles (Chapters 15–20)

Each of the chapters in Part 4 deals with a specific transaction cycle or part of a transaction cycle in much the same manner as Chapters 13 and 14 deal with the sales and collection cycle. Each chapter is meant to demonstrate the relationship of internal control and tests of controls for each broad category of transactions to the related balance sheet and income statement accounts. Cash in bank is the first chapter studied, since the audit of cash balances is related to most other audit areas.

Part 5, Completing the Audit and Offering Other Services (Chapters 21–24)

The quality of the audit depends on evaluating whether sufficient audit evidence has been gathered, in the context of the client risk profile and the audit risk model, to state an opinion on the financial statements. This final phase is explained in Chapter 21. Chapter 22 focuses on review and compilation engagements, a common service for small- and medium-sized businesses, both profit-oriented and non-profit. Chapter 23 looks at engagements where accountants require advanced skills. These are specialized assurance engagements, such as environmental audits, WebTrust and SysTrust, and business valuations. The need for expertise in the financial statement audit, including each of the transaction cycles, is discussed by examining advanced information systems, service centre audits, and tax complexities. The final chapter, Chapter 24, covers services performed most often by governmental and internal auditors, including risk assessment and systems control design, training and education on risk management and internal controls, specialized audits such as operational audits, and financial statement audits.

CHAPTER OUTLINE

Each chapter contains the following:

- Learning objectives, listing the questions that you should be able to answer after reading the chapter
- An opening vignette discussing a real-world topic to highlight a theme and the importance of the chapter
- Figures and tables to illustrate, summarize, or clarify topics covered
- Focus boxes and website links identifying relevant research, key current topics, or recent events in the area
- Essential terms in the margin, for easy reference, with an alphabetic list at the end of the chapter for review
- A summary providing brief answers to the learning objective questions
- A list of *CICA Assurance Handbook* sections referenced in the chapter, targeting additional readings
- Review questions for students to assess comprehension of chapter material
- Five multiple-choice questions. Additional questions in the same format are included on the Companion Website as another resource for students.
- Discussion questions and a professional judgment problem offering real-world topics to apply chapter content to
- One or more integrated cases useful for practising judgment and decision skills, which can be used to develop teamwork and presentation skills when done as a group

STUDENT RESOURCES

Companion Website *Auditing and Other Assurance Services,* Canadian Tenth Edition, is supported by an excellent Companion Website at **www.pearsoned.ca/arens** that truly reinforces and enhances the text material.

INSTRUCTIONAL SUPPORT MATERIALS

Instructor's Resource CD-ROM The Instructor's Resource CD-ROM contains a rich collection of materials to facilitate the teaching of the course. Some of the material presented on the CD-ROM can also be downloaded from a secure password-protected instructor's area of the Pearson Education Canada online catalogue. The CD-ROM includes the following items:

INSTRUCTOR'S RESOURCE MANUAL AND TRANSPARENCY MASTERS The Instructor's Resource Manual assists the instructor in teaching the course more efficiently. The features include instructions for assignments, practical examples to help the students understand the material, and helpful suggestions on how to effectively teach each chapter. This manual includes numerous enlarged transparency masters, including key tables and figures from the book.

INSTRUCTOR'S SOLUTIONS MANUAL This comprehensive resource provides detailed solutions to all the end-of-chapter review questions, multiple choice questions, problems, and cases.

PEARSON TESTGEN A comprehensive testbank of questions has been prepared to accompany the new edition. The questions are rated by difficulty level, and the answers are referenced by section. The test bank is presented in a special computerized format known as Pearson TestGen. It enables instructors to view and edit the existing question, add questions, generate tests, and print the tests in a variety of formats. Powerful search and sort functions make it easy to locate questions and arrange them in any order desired. TestGen also enables instructors to administer tests on a local area network, have the tests graded electronically, and have the results prepared in electronic or printed reports. Issued on the Instructor's Resource CD-ROM, the Pearson TestGen is compatible with IBM or Macintosh systems.

POWERPOINT SLIDES Electronic colour slides are available in Microsoft PowerPoint. The slides illuminate and build on key concepts in the text.

IMAGE LIBRARY The Image Library is an impressive resource that helps instructors create vibrant lecture presentations. Almost every figure and table in the text is provided and organized by chapter for convenience. These images can easily be imported into Microsoft PowerPoint to create new presentations or to add to existing ones.

ACKNOWLEDGMENTS FOR THE CANADIAN TENTH EDITION

Our world is changing. This text reflects some of those changes in the auditing profession. Through these last two editions, I would like to thank the many medical professionals who enabled me to return to full-time work after adjusting to a permanent disability due to brain surgery in 1999, which changed the face of my work environment. Such changes certainly have spurred my creativity and the knowledge that we are all different, bringing a broad spectrum of skills to the work that we do.

I would like to thank the following individuals who contributed their time and energy in sharing their opinions and best practices, helping to make this book representative not only of sound theory, but of the actual work done in the field of audit and assurance:

David Lee, Office of the Auditor General of Ontario
Jim McCarter, Auditor General of Ontario
Brian Morgan, Osler Hoskin and Harcourt
David Scott, Canadian Public Accountability Board
Richard Smith, Office of the Auditor General of Canada
Frank Vandenhoven, Office of the Auditor General of Canada
Rick Wood, Grant Thornton
Larry Yarmolinsky, Internal Audit Division, Government of Ontario.

As well, very special thanks to Linda Robinson for her work on Chapter 10, Fraud Auditing.

Thanks are also due to the following reviewers for their valuable feedback:

Merridee Bujaki, University of Ottawa
Peggy Coady, Memorial University of Newfoundland
Patrick D. Coristine, Grande Prairie Regional College
Patrick Delaney, Concordia University
Vincent Durant, St. Lawrence College
Brian Friedrich, CGA-BC Lecturer
Laura Friedrich, CGA-BC Lecturer
Karim Jamal, University of Alberta
Marc Kampschuur, British Columbia Institute of Technology
Brad MacDonald, Saskatchewan Institute of Applied Science and Technology—
    Palliser Campus
Michael Malkoun, St. Clair College
Jennifer Nicholson, Saint Mary's University
Ted Nowak, Concordia University
Claudia Parker, Northern Alberta Institute of Technology
Sandra M. Robinson, Concordia University
D. Rand Rowlands, George Brown College
Brad Sacho, Kwantlen University College
Al Seaman, McMaster University
Glynes Sylvestre, University of Regina

In addition, thank you to all the editorial and production staff at Pearson Canada for putting together a high-quality product, including Gary Bennett, Editor-in-Chief, Business and Economics; Samantha Scully, Executive Acquisitions Editor; Eleanor MacKay, Developmental Editor; Avivah Wargon, Production Editor; and Deborah Starks, Production Manager.

This book is dedicated to my family—Jake, Pat, and Mike—who did the extra chores around the house and cooked dinner while I worked late. Thank you; without your love and support this book would not have been possible.

Ingrid B. Splettstoesser-Hogeterp

A Great Way to Learn and Instruct Online

The Pearson Education Canada Companion Website is easy to navigate and is organized to correspond to the chapters in this textbook. Whether you are a student in the classroom or a distance learner you will discover helpful resources for in-depth study and research that empower you in your quest for greater knowledge and maximize your potential for success in the course.

[**www.pearsoned.ca/arens**]

Jump to... http://www.pearsoned.ca/arens   Home | Search | Help | Profile

Home >

Companion Website

Auditing and Other Assurance Services, Canadian Tenth Edition, by Arens, Elder, Beasley, and Splettstoesser-Hogeterp

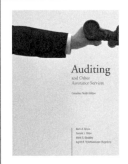

Student Resources

The modules in this section provide students with tools for learning course material. These modules include:

- Chapter Objectives
- Chapter Summaries
- Web Destinations
- Self-Test Quizzes
- Internet Exercises
- Application Exercises
- Glossary Flashcards
- PowerPoint Prentation Slides

In the quiz modules students can send answers to the grader and receive instant feedback on their progress through the Results Reporter. Coaching comments and references to the textbook may be available to ensure that students take advantage of all available resources to enhance their learning experience.

Instructor Resources

This module links directly to additional teaching tools. Downloadable PowerPoint Presentations and an Instructor's Manual are just some of the materials that may be available in this section.

PART 1

THE AUDITING PROFESSION

These first four chapters provide background for performing financial audits, which is our primary focus. This background will help you understand why auditors perform audits the way they do.

This book begins with a description of assurance services, including auditing, and the role of public accounting firms and other organizations in doing audits. The chapters in Part 1 emphasize the regulation and control of public accounting firms through auditing and ethical standards as well as the legal responsibilities of auditors. We also present a detailed discussion of audit reports, which are the final products of audits.

CHAPTER 1

THE DEMAND FOR AUDITING AND ASSURANCE SERVICES

Don't all accountants do the same thing? No, not really. There are accountants who do only accounting, accountants who do auditing (public accountants or internal auditors), and accountants who have many other specializations, such as financial planning or forensics.

LEARNING OBJECTIVES

After reading this chapter, you should be able to answer the following questions:

1. What are the different types of accountants, and what do they do? What are the different types of engagements completed by public accountants? What differentiates accounting from auditing and assurance services from nonassurance services? Why are audits so important?

2. How are public accounting firms organized? What are some of the largest public accounting firms?

3. What market forces ensure that audit and assurance engagements are completed to high standards of quality? Who develops and maintains the standards that public accountants use? How are these standards enforced?

CANADA'S AUDITOR GENERAL ILLUSTRATES HIGH ETHICAL STANDARDS

Sheila Fraser, FCA, was appointed Auditor General (AG) of Canada in 2001 for a 10-year term. Since then, the Office of the Auditor General has issued reports addressing important issues affecting all Canadians. Copies of these reports are available online at **www.oag-bvg.gc.ca**.

Office of the Auditor General
of Canada
www.oag-bvg.gc.ca

Chapter 3 of the March 2004 Report is titled "National Security in Canada—The 2001 Anti-Terrorism Initiative." The chapter provides background information on the security initiatives taken by Canada and then explains the scope of the audit. It concludes by saying that, although the "vast majority of funds . . . have been channelled to identified priority areas . . . needed improvements have been delayed by several years . . . We also found deficiencies in the management of intelligence." A team of nine people from the Auditor General's office, with a variety of expertise, conducted this audit of Canadian national security.

The National Security audit and the other audits undertaken by the Auditor General's office are conducted by preparing criteria against which the activities and actions of many departments and agencies are measured. Identification of needed improvements is made by comparing actual activity in the departments against the prepared criteria, as was done for the National Security audit.

Ms. Fraser, in public presentations and interviews, continues to state that most people (including those in the civil service) conduct their work with integrity and honesty, even though her office's audits discover weaknesses. Her department of about 400 auditors examines the

Sources: 1. Delacourt, Susan. 2004. "An auditor who doesn't sound like a bean-counter," Toronto Star, February 14, 2004, p. F4. 2. Fraser, Bruce. W. 2004. "Sheila Fraser—Cool Under Fire," Internal Auditor, Vol. LXI:IV, August 2004, pp. 72–77. 3. www. oag-bvg.bgc.ca, Office of the Auditor General of Canada, retrieved September 13, 2004.

What other types of audits might the Auditor General conduct? What about your provincial auditor general? What are some local issues that might need to be investigated?

Public Accountants (PAs) such as Ms. Fraser provide examinations of controls, audit financial statements, and also help businesses be more successful. As businesses become more complex and need more reliable information, PAs play a vital role, both in providing assurance on information other than financial statements and providing business advisory and tax services. For example, businesses and consumers who use information technology and electronic communication networks such as the Internet to conduct business and make decisions need independent assurances about the reliability and security of that electronic information. Auditors are valued because of their technical knowledge and independence in providing assurances, as well as their competence and experience in assisting companies to improve operations. Auditors often make and help implement recommendations that improve profitability by enhancing revenue or reducing costs, including the reduction of errors and fraud, and by improving operational controls.

→1.1 PROFESSIONAL ACCOUNTANTS AND THEIR WORK
Professional Accounting/Auditing Organizations

Before beginning a discussion of auditing, it is appropriate to disclose who performs the auditing function—external and internal—in Canada. There are five major organizations in Canada or represented in Canada that provide a professional designation relating to accounting and/or auditing. The organizations, the designation awarded, and the manner of qualifying for the designation are discussed below. All organizations require that individuals have a university degree and obtain relevant work experience.

The senior body is the **Canadian Institute of Chartered Accountants** (CICA) whose members are **chartered accountants** or CAs. The use of the title "chartered accountant" (CA) is regulated by provincial law. The educational requirements for becoming a CA vary among provinces, with a common experience requirement of 30 months. All provinces require that an individual, to qualify as a CA, pass a national uniform examination administered by the CICA. The CICA also assists CAs in the specialization process, by coordinating specialist designations, as described later in the chapter.

The use of the title "**certified general accountant**" (CGA), awarded by the **Certified General Accountants Association of Canada** (CGAAC), is also regulated by provincial law. Experience requirements are set at a minimum of two years in a combination of intermediate and senior positions in accounting or finance. Individuals, depending upon educational background, must pass a variety of subject-based examinations, with a capstone national examination.

The **Society of Management Accountants of Canada** (SMAC) administers the **Certified Management Accountant** (CMA) program, leading to the CMA designation. Provincial law restricts the use of this title to those persons earning the right to use it. Students must pass examinations in required subject areas as well as uniform national examinations after completing an SMAC course of study. It is possible to gain exemption

CANADIAN INSTITUTE OF CHARTERED ACCOUNTANTS—sets the accounting and auditing standards in the private and public sectors, which must be followed by public accountants in Canada; one of the three major accounting organizations in Canada providing a professional designation relating to accounting and auditing; umbrella organization of the provincial institutes and *ordre* that regulates the CA profession in Canada

Canadian Institute of Chartered Accountants
www.cica.ca

CHARTERED ACCOUNTANT—one of three professional designations in Canada relating to accounting and auditing

CERTIFIED GENERAL ACCOUNTANT—one of three professional designations in Canada relating to accounting and auditing

CERTIFIED GENERAL ACCOUNTANTS ASSOCIATION OF CANADA—one of the three major accounting organizations in Canada providing a professional designation relating to accounting and auditing; umbrella organization of the provincial associations that regulates the CGA profession in Canada

Certified General Accountants Association of Canada
www.cga-online.org

SOCIETY OF MANAGEMENT ACCOUNTANTS OF CANADA—one of the three major accounting organizations in Canada providing a professional designation relating to accounting and auditing; umbrella organization of the provincial societies that regulates the CMA profession in Canada

Society of Management Accountants of Canada
www.cma-canada.org

CERTIFIED MANAGEMENT ACCOUNTANT—one of three professional designations in Canada relating to accounting and auditing

---

[1] Each chapter's opening vignette illustrates important auditing principles.

from subject area examinations by taking appropriate university courses. Furthermore, students must meet experience requirements.

Internal auditors have a professional organization, the Institute of Internal Auditors (IIA), and a professional designation, "certified internal auditor" (CIA). The designation is earned by passing a set of examinations that are administered worldwide by the IIA and by meeting experience requirements. Unlike the professional organizations discussed above, the IIA membership includes persons not having a CIA designation.

The Information Systems Audit and Control Association (ISACA) awards the CISA (Certified Information Systems Auditor) designation to individuals passing an international examination and meeting experience requirements. Persons not having the CISA designation can join ISACA as associate members, much like persons not having a CIA can join the IIA.

Because of the dynamic nature of business environments, each organization offers continuing education programs, providing the opportunity for members to specialize in particular areas such as taxation, information systems, management consulting, or business valuations. Professional organizations in many of these specialized areas offer specific programs of study leading to further specialist designations.

Nature of Auditing

Auditing is the accumulation and evaluation of evidence about information to determine and report on the degree of correspondence between the information and established criteria. Auditing should be done by a competent, independent person.

This description of **auditing** includes several key words and phrases. Each is discussed in this section and analyzed more extensively in later chapters. For ease of understanding, the terms are discussed in a different order than they occur in the description.

Information and Established Criteria To do an audit, there must be information in a *verifiable form* and some standards (*criteria*) by which the auditor can evaluate the information. Information can and does take many forms. Auditors routinely perform audits of quantifiable information, including companies' financial statements and individuals' federal income tax returns. Auditors also perform audits of more subjective information, such as the effectiveness of computer systems and the efficiency of manufacturing operations.

The criteria against which information is evaluated vary depending on the information being audited. For example, in the audit of historical financial statements by public accounting firms, the criteria are generally accepted accounting principles. To illustrate, this means that in the audit of Magna International Inc.'s financial statements, Ernst & Young LLP, the CA firm, determines whether Magna International Inc.'s financial statements have been prepared in accordance with generally accepted accounting principles. The Canada Revenue Agency uses the provisions of the *Income Tax Act* to audit tax returns. In the audit of Magna's corporate tax return by the Canada Revenue Agency, the *Income Tax Act*, rather than generally accepted accounting principles, would provide the criteria for assessment.

For more subjective information, such as auditing the effectiveness of computer operations, it is more difficult to establish criteria. Typically, auditors and the entities being audited agree on the criteria well before the audit starts. For a computer application, the criteria might, for example, include the absence of input or output errors.

Accumulating and Evaluating Evidence **Evidence** is defined as any information used by the auditor to determine whether the information being audited is stated in accordance with the established criteria. Evidence takes many different forms, including oral testimony of the auditee (client), written communication with outsiders, and observations by the auditor. Certain evidence (from a third party) is considered more reliable than other evidence (from the client). It is important to obtain a sufficient quality and volume of evidence to satisfy the audit objectives. The process of determining the amount of evidence necessary and evaluating whether the information corresponds to the established criteria is a critical part of every audit. It is the primary subject of this book.

AUDITING—the accumulation and evaluation of evidence about information to determine and report on the degree of correspondence between the information and established criteria

Magna International Inc.
www.MagnaInt.com

Ernst & Young LLP
www.ey.com

EVIDENCE—any information used by the auditor to determine whether the information being audited is stated in accordance with established criteria

Competent, Independent Person The auditor must be *qualified* to understand the criteria used and *competent* to know the types and amount of evidence to accumulate to reach the proper conclusion after the evidence has been examined. The auditor also must have an *independent mental attitude*. The competence of the individual performing the audit is of little value if he or she is biased in the accumulation and evaluation of evidence.

Auditors reporting on company financial statements are often called *independent auditors*. Even though an auditor of published financial statements is paid a fee by a company, he or she is normally sufficiently independent to conduct audits that can be relied on by users. Although absolute independence is impossible, auditors strive to maintain a high level of independence to keep the confidence of users relying on their reports. Although internal auditors work for the company, they usually report directly to the audit committee to help maintain independence from the operating units being audited.

Reporting The final stage in the audit process is the **auditor's report**—the communication of the findings to users. Reports differ in nature, but in all cases they must inform readers of the degree of correspondence between information and established criteria. Reports also differ in form and can vary from the highly technical types usually associated with financial statements to a simple oral report in the case of an audit of a small department's effectiveness.

AUDITOR'S REPORT—the communication of audit findings to users

Figure 1-1 summarizes the important ideas in the description of auditing by illustrating an audit of an individual's tax return by a Canada Revenue Agency auditor. The objective is to determine whether the tax return was prepared in a manner consistent with the requirements of the *Income Tax Act*. The auditor examines supporting records provided by the taxpayer and from other sources, such as the taxpayer's employer. After completing the audit, the Canada Revenue Agency auditor will issue a report to the taxpayer assessing additional taxes, advising that a refund is due, or stating that there is no change in the status of his or her return.

Economic Demand for Auditing

Businesses, governments, and not-for-profit organizations use auditing services extensively. A brief study of the economic reasons for auditing highlights why auditing is so necessary, as well as some of the legal problems auditors face.

To illustrate the need for auditing, consider a bank manager's decision to make a loan to a business. The decision will be based on such factors as previous financial relations with the business and the financial condition of the business as reflected by its financial statements. Assuming the bank makes the loan, it will charge a rate of interest determined primarily by three factors:

Canada Revenue Agency
www.cra-arc.gc.ca

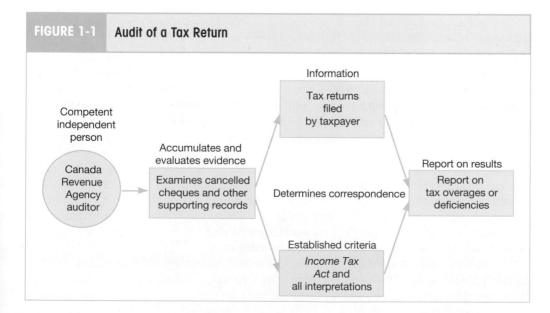

FIGURE 1-1   Audit of a Tax Return

1. *Risk-free interest rate.* This is approximately the rate the bank could earn by investing in Canada Treasury Bills for the same length of time as the business loan.
2. *Business risk for the customer.* This risk reflects the possibility that the business will not be able to repay its loan because of economic or business conditions such as a recession, poor management decisions, or unexpected competition in the industry.
3. *Information risk.* This risk reflects the possibility that the information upon which the business decision was made was inaccurate. A likely cause of the **information risk** is the possibility of inaccurate financial statements.

INFORMATION RISK—the risk that information upon which a business decision is made is inaccurate

Auditing has no effect on either the risk-free interest rate or business risk. It can have a significant effect on information risk. If the bank manager is satisfied that there is no information risk, the risk is eliminated and the overall interest rate to the borrower can be reduced. Even if information risk cannot be totally eliminated, its reduction can have a significant effect on the borrower's ability to obtain capital at a reasonable cost. For example, assume a large company has total interest-bearing debt of approximately $1 billion. If the interest rate on that debt is reduced by only 1 percent, the annual savings in interest is $10 million. Many lenders such as banks require annual audits for companies with large bank loans outstanding.

As society becomes more complex, there is an increased likelihood that unreliable information will be provided to decision makers. There are several reasons for this: remoteness of information, bias and motives of provider, voluminous data, and the existence of complex exchange transactions.

Managements of businesses and the users of their financial statements may conclude that the best way to deal with information risk is simply to have it remain reasonably high. A small company may find it less expensive to pay higher interest costs than to increase the costs of reducing information risk.

For larger businesses, it is usually practical to incur such costs to reduce information risk. There are three main ways to do so:

1. The user may go to the business premises to examine records and obtain information about the reliability of the statements.
2. Management is responsible for providing reliable information to users. Users may evaluate the likelihood of sharing their information risk loss with management.
3. The most common way for users to obtain reliable information is to have an independent audit performed. The audited information is then used in the decision-making process on the assumption that it is reasonably complete, accurate, and unbiased. Typically, management engages the auditor to provide assurances to users that the financial statements are reliable. If the financial statements are ultimately determined to be materially incorrect, the auditor can be sued by both the users and management.

Distinction between Auditing and Accounting

Many financial statement users and members of the general public confuse *auditing* and *accounting*. The confusion occurs because most auditing is concerned with accounting information, and many auditors have considerable expertise in accounting matters. The confusion is increased by giving the title "public accountant" to individuals who perform the external audit function. The term "public accountant" is discussed on page 12.

ACCOUNTING—the recording, classifying, and summarizing of economic events in a logical manner for the purpose of providing financial information for decision making

Accounting is the recording, classifying, and summarizing of economic events in a logical manner for the purpose of providing financial information for decision making. The function of accounting, both to an entity and to society as a whole, is to provide certain types of quantitative information that management and others can use to make decisions. To provide relevant information, accountants must have a thorough understanding of the principles and rules that provide the basis for preparing the accounting information. In addition, accountants must develop a system to ensure that the entity's economic events are properly recorded in a timely way and at a reasonable cost.

In *auditing* accounting data, the concern is with determining whether recorded information properly reflects the economic events that occurred during the accounting period. However, the auditor is not simply auditing data but must look at the organization's business dynamics, including its strategies and economic niches, as discussed further in Chapter 7. Since the accounting rules are the criteria for evaluating whether the accounting information is properly recorded, any auditor involved with these data must also thoroughly understand the rules. In the context of the audit of financial statements, these are generally accepted accounting principles. Throughout this text, the assumption is made that the reader has already studied generally accepted accounting principles.

In addition to understanding accounting, the auditor must also possess expertise in the accumulation and interpretation of audit evidence. It is this expertise that distinguishes auditors from accountants. Determining the proper audit procedures and the number and types of items to test, and evaluating the results are tasks that are unique to the auditor.

Types of Audits

Three types of audits are discussed in this section: financial statement audits, compliance audits, and operational audits.

Financial Statement Audits

A **financial statement audit** is conducted to determine whether the overall financial statements (the information being verified) are stated in accordance with specified criteria. Normally, the criteria are generally accepted accounting principles (GAAP), although it is also common to conduct audits of financial statements prepared using the cash basis or some other basis of accounting appropriate for the organization. The financial statements most often included are the balance sheet, income statement, statement of retained earnings, and statement of cash flows, including accompanying footnotes.

FINANCIAL STATEMENT AUDIT—an audit conducted to determine whether the overall financial statements of an entity are stated in accordance with specified criteria (usually GAAP)

In determining whether financial statements are fairly stated in accordance with GAAP, the auditor performs appropriate tests to determine whether the statements contain material errors or other misstatements. An integrated approach to auditing considers both the risk of errors and operating controls intended to prevent errors. Increasingly, this integrated approach incorporates a strategic perspective of the business entity.

As businesses increase in complexity, it is no longer sufficient for auditors to focus narrowly on accounting transactions. In a *strategic systems audit* approach, the auditor must have a thorough understanding of the entity and its environment. This holistic, top-level understanding includes knowledge of the client's industry and its regulatory and operating environment, including external relationships, such as suppliers, customers, and creditors. In addition, the auditor considers the client's business strategies and processes and measurement indicators for critical success factors related to those strategies. This analysis helps the auditor identify risks associated with the client's strategies that may affect whether the financial statements are fairly stated. Many of the skills necessary for the strategic systems audit approach are similar to those needed to provide other types of assurance services that can add value to the audit function.

Compliance Audits

The purpose of a **compliance audit** is to determine whether the auditee is following specific procedures or rules set down by a higher authority. A compliance audit for a private business could include determining whether accounting personnel are following the procedures prescribed by the company controller, reviewing wage rates for compliance with minimum wage laws, or examining contractual agreements with bankers and other lenders to be sure the company is complying with legal requirements. In the audit of governmental units such as school boards, there is increased compliance auditing due to extensive regulation by higher government authorities. In virtually every private and not-for-profit organization, there are prescribed policies, contractual agreements, and legal requirements that may call for compliance auditing.

COMPLIANCE AUDIT—(1) a review of an organization's financial records performed to determine whether the organization is following specific procedures, rules, or regulations set down by some higher authority; (2) an audit performed to determine whether an entity that receives financial assistance from a federal or provincial government has complied with specific laws and regulations

Results of compliance audits are generally reported to someone within the organizational unit being audited rather than to a broad spectrum of users. Management, as opposed to outside users, is the primary group concerned with the extent of compliance with certain prescribed procedures and regulations. Hence, a significant portion of work of this type is done by auditors employed by the organizational units themselves. There are exceptions. When an organization wants to determine whether individuals or organizations that are obliged to follow its requirements are actually complying, the auditor is employed by the organization issuing the requirements. An example is the auditing of taxpayers for compliance with the *Income Tax Act*—the auditor is employed by the government to audit the taxpayers' tax returns.

Operational Audits An **operational audit** is a review of any part of an organization's operating procedures and methods for the purpose of evaluating *economy, efficiency,* and *effectiveness.* At the completion of an operational audit, recommendations to management for improving operations are normally expected. An example of an operational audit is evaluating the efficiency and accuracy of processing payroll transactions by using a newly installed computer system. Another example, for which most accountants would feel less qualified, is evaluating the efficiency, accuracy, and customer satisfaction in processing the distribution of letters and packages by a company such as Canada Post. An example of an economy issue is whether goods and services are obtained at the best price.

Because of the many different areas in which operational effectiveness can be evaluated, it is impossible to characterize the conduct of a typical operational audit. In one organization, the auditor might evaluate the relevancy and sufficiency of the information used by management when acquiring new capital assets, while in a different organization the auditor might evaluate the efficiency of the paper flow in processing sales. In operational auditing, the reviews are not limited to accounting. They can include the evaluation of organization structure, computer operations, production methods, marketing, and any other area in which the audit team is qualified, such as national security in Canada, described on page 2.

The conduct of an operational audit and the reported results are less easily defined than either a financial statement audit or a compliance audit: Economy, efficiency, and effectiveness of operations are far more difficult to evaluate objectively than compliance or the presentation of financial statements in accordance with generally accepted accounting principles. Establishing criteria for evaluating the information in an operational audit is an extremely subjective matter. In this sense, operational auditing is more similar to management consulting than to what is generally regarded as auditing. Operational auditing has increased in importance in the past decade. We look at operational auditing in greater depth in Chapter 24.

Table 1-1 summarizes the three types of audits by providing an example of each type and illustrating the available evidence, information, and established criteria for each example.

Assurance Services

Assurance services, or *assurance engagements*, are independent professional services that improve the quality of information for decision makers. Individuals who are responsible for

TABLE 1-1	Examples of the Three Types of Audits			
Type of Audit	Example	Available Evidence	Information	Established Criteria
Financial Statement Audit	Annual audit of TransCanada Corporation's financial statements	Documents, records, and outside sources of evidence	TransCanada Corporation's financial statements	Canadian generally accepted accounting principles
Compliance Audit	Determine if bank requirements for loan continuation have been met	Financial statements and calculations by the auditor	Company records	Loan agreement provisions
Operational Audit	Evaluate whether the computerized payroll processing for subsidiary H is operating economically, efficiently, and effectively	Error reports, payroll records, and payroll processing costs	Number of payroll records processed in a month, costs of the department, and number of errors made	Company standards for economy, efficiency, and effectiveness in payroll department

making business decisions seek assurance services to help improve the reliability and relevance of the information to make their decisions. Assurance services are valued because the assurance engagement provider is independent and is perceived as unbiased with respect to the information examined.

A financial statement audit is an example of an assurance engagement. Section 5025 of the *CICA Assurance Handbook* defines an **assurance engagement** as:

> an engagement where, pursuant to an accountability relationship between two or more parties, a practitioner is engaged to issue a written communication expressing a conclusion concerning a subject matter for which the accountable party is responsible.

Assurance services can be performed by PAs or by a variety of other professionals. For example, companies that perform television ratings are performing an assurance engagement. BBM Canada, a non-profit television rating organization, and Nielsen Media Research Canada conduct television rating. These organizations provide assurance that a specified number of viewers are watching the identified television shows. Another example of a company that provides assurance services is the Canadian Council of Better Business Bureaus (CCBBB). The CCBBB collects information about Canadian businesses. Some of the information is not verified (so would be considered equivalent to a compilation engagement, discussed below), while other information, such as details about current business scams, are verified, providing assurance regarding the specifics of those illegal activities.

The need for assurance is not new. PAs have provided assurance services for years, particularly about historical financial statement information. PA firms have also performed assurance services related to lotteries and contests to provide assurance that winners were determined in an unbiased fashion in accordance with contest rules. More recently, PAs have been expanding the types of assurance services they perform, such as assurance engagements about company financial forecasts and web site controls. The demand for assurance services is expected to grow as the demand for forward-looking information increases and as more real-time information becomes available through the Internet.

Attestation Services The **attestation** service is an assurance service in which the PA issues a report about the reliability of an assertion prepared by another party. Compare this process to that of an assurance engagement, discussed above, where the auditor may actually prepare the report. The following discussion looks first at attestation services related to financial reporting and then at other attestation services.

AUDIT OF HISTORICAL FINANCIAL STATEMENTS Audits of historical cost financial statements are a major service provided by many of the larger public accounting firms. In the audit of financial statements, the responsible other party is the client who is making various assertions in the form of published financial statements. The auditor's report expresses an opinion on whether those financial statements are in conformity with Canadian generally accepted accounting principles or with another appropriate disclosed basis of accounting. External users of financial statements rely on the auditor's report for their decision-making purposes.

Many publicly traded companies in Canada are required to have audits. Auditor reports can be found in any public company's annual financial report, and many companies' audited financial statements can be accessed via the Internet from System for Electronic Document Analysis and Retrieval (SEDAR) at **sedar.com**. This web site, developed by the Canadian Securities Administrators (CSA) and CDS Inc., a subsidiary of the Canadian Depository for Securities Limited, has been available since 1997. It contains public filings, such as annual reports, management discussion and analysis, and press releases from public companies. Most public companies also have a web site where copies of financial statements are posted. However, sedar.com is particularly useful for examining information about public companies that do not have a web site, such as Jannock Properties Limited, headquartered in Streetsville, Ontario.

Many public companies voluntarily contract for audits to provide assurance to investors and to facilitate access to capital. Many privately held companies also have annual financial statement audits to obtain financing from banks and other institutions. Government and not-for-profit entities often have audits to meet the requirements of lenders or funding sources.

ASSURANCE ENGAGEMENT— issuance of a written communication expressing a conclusion on a subject matter where an accountable party is responsible as part of an accountability relationship

BBM Canada
www.bbm.ca

Nielsen Media Research Canada
www.nielsenmedia.ca

Canadian Council of Better Business Bureaus
www.canadiancouncilbbb.ca

ATTESTATION—a written communication regarding the reliability of another party's written assertion

System for Electronic Document Analysis and Retrieval (SEDAR)
www.sedar.com

REVIEW OF HISTORICAL FINANCIAL STATEMENTS Many smaller, non-public companies want to issue financial statements to various users but do not wish to incur the cost of an auditor's report. A review, which provides a much lower degree of assurance than an audit, is usually conducted in such a situation. The PA is required to do considerably less work than in an audit so the resulting cost is less. Reviews are discussed in more detail in Chapter 22.

ATTESTATION ON INTERNAL CONTROL OVER FINANCIAL REPORTING In the U.S., Certified Public Accountants (CPAs, the equivalent to CAs) also attest to management's assertion about the effectiveness of internal control over financial reporting. Publicly traded companies are required to include management's report on the effectiveness of internal control over financial reporting in their annual report, along with the audit firm's attestation on that report. The auditor's evaluation of the effectiveness of internal control over financial reporting is integrated with the audit of the financial statements. The report on the effectiveness of internal control provides forward-looking information because effective internal controls reduce the likelihood of future misstatements.

Some Canadian companies also need to comply with this internal control attestation process, as discussed further in Chapter 3.

OTHER ATTESTATION SERVICES Public accountants may also prepare special reports for clients where the PA audits and provides an opinion on financial information other than financial statements or on compliance with an agreement or regulations. For example, an auditor might provide an opinion on the sales at a Shoppers Drug Mart in a Saskatoon shopping mall because the store's rent is based on sales and the owner of the mall requires an audit opinion.

Assurance Services on Information Technology One of the major factors affecting the demand for other assurance services is the growth of the Internet and electronic commerce. Concern over privacy and security of information on the Internet has slowed the potential growth of electronic commerce. In addition, the volume of real-time information available on the Internet is shifting the need for assurance from historical information at a point in time, such as financial statements, to assurances about the reliability of processes generating information in a real-time format. For example, many business functions, such as ordering and making payments, are conducted over the Internet and directly between computers using electronic data interchange (EDI). As transactions and information are shared online and in real time, there is an even greater demand for assurances about computer controls surrounding information transacted electronically and the security of the information related to the transactions. PAs can help provide assurance about these functions.

To respond to the growing need for assurance related to business transacted over the Internet, the American Institute of Certified Public Accountants (AICPA) and the Canadian Institute of Chartered Accountants (CICA) developed two products. The *WebTrust* service is an electronic seal affixed to a web site to assure the user that established criteria related to business practices, transaction integrity, and information processes have been met. *SysTrust* provides assurance on information system reliability. These two services are discussed further in Chapter 23.

Other Assurance Services There are almost no limits to the types of services that PAs can provide. A survey of large CPA firms, performed by the AICPA Special Committee on Assurance Services, identified more than 200 assurance services currently provided. A selection of these will be discussed in Chapters 22 and 23.

Figure 1-2 reflects the relationship between assurance and nonassurance services. Assurance services are broader in scope and can also include some management consulting if assurance is provided. Attest services are a subset of assurance services. PAs can also help organizations assess risks within the organization and design procedures to mitigate those risks. Bookkeeping, tax, and many management consulting services provide needed services without adding assurance.

Nonassurance Services PA firms perform numerous other services that generally fall outside the scope of assurance services. Some of these are related to financial statements, while others would be considered financial planning or management advisory services.

COMPILATIONS A compilation involves the PA preparing financial statements from a client's records or from other information provided. A compilation is much less extensive than a review and the cost is much less. No assurance is provided by a compilation.

TAX SERVICES Public accounting firms prepare corporate and individual tax returns for both audit and non-audit clients. In addition, sales tax, tax planning, and other aspects of tax services are provided by most firms.

MANAGEMENT ADVISORY SERVICES Management advisory services handle things like retirement planning and personal financial planning. Most PA firms also provide certain services that enable businesses to operate more effectively including simple suggestions for improving accounting systems, help with marketing strategies, computer installations, and pension benefit consulting. The firm offering these types of services needs to be aware of independence rules that prohibit the provision of some of these services to audit clients, as discussed in the next chapter. Examples of such services, also called *business advisory services*, are discussed in Chapter 23.

ACCOUNTING AND BOOKKEEPING SERVICES Some small clients lack the personnel or expertise to prepare their own subsidiary records. Many small public accounting firms work with accounting software packages to help clients record their transactions. Often such clients proceed with a compilation engagement.

If a PA conducts a review or an audit after bookkeeping work, care must be taken to ensure that independence rules are properly followed. In particular, the PA must ensure that all transactions and journal entries are approved by management during the bookkeeping engagement.

Types of Auditors

This section will briefly discuss the four most widely known types of auditors. They are public accountants, government auditors, Canada Revenue Agency auditors, and internal auditors.

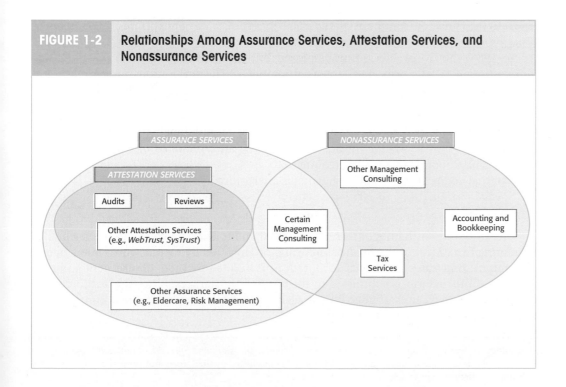

FIGURE 1-2 **Relationships Among Assurance Services, Attestation Services, and Nonassurance Services**

ASSURANCE SERVICES

NONASSURANCE SERVICES

ATTESTATION SERVICES

Audits

Reviews

Other Attestation Services (e.g., *WebTrust, SysTrust*)

Other Assurance Services (e.g., Eldercare, Risk Management)

Certain Management Consulting

Other Management Consulting

Accounting and Bookkeeping

Tax Services

Public Accountants Public accounting firms have, as a primary responsibility, the performance of the audit function on published financial statements of all publicly traded companies and most other large companies. Such an audit is known as an *attestation* engagement because the auditor attests to the fair presentation in the financial statements. If the audit is due to a size requirement, or required by law, the audit is a statutory audit. Because of the widespread use of audited financial statements in the Canadian economy, as well as businesses' and other users' familiarity with these statements, it is common to use the terms *auditor* and *public accounting firm* synonymously even though there are several types of auditors. Another term frequently used to describe a public accounting firm is **independent auditors**.

A number of Canadian provinces restrict the audit attest function to chartered accountants licensed in that province. Other provinces also license certified general accountants to perform the audit attest function, while still other provinces do not require a licence to perform an attest audit. The two bodies whose members perform most of the attest audits in Canada are the Canadian Institute of Chartered Accountants and the Certified General Accountants Association of Canada. The term *public accountant* is used frequently throughout this book to describe an individual who is licensed to perform the audit attest function.

Most young professionals who want to become public accountants start their careers working for a public accounting firm. After they become public accountants, many leave the firm to work in industry, government, or education. These people may continue to be members of a professional body but may lose their right to practise as independent auditors. CAs and CGAs must meet licensing requirements to maintain their right to practise in most provinces. It is common, therefore, to find people who are CAs or CGAs but who have not practised as independent auditors for a time.

Government Auditors The Government of Canada and the various provincial governments have **Auditors General** who are responsible for auditing the ministries, departments, and agencies who report to that government. These government auditors may be appointed by a bipartisan committee or by the government or party in power in that jurisdiction. They report to their respective legislatures and are responsible to the body appointing them. The primary responsibility of the government audit staff is to perform the audit function for government. The extent and scope of the audits performed are determined by legislation in the various jurisdictions. For example, in 1977, the federal parliament made a revision to existing legislation in passing the *Auditor General Act* that required the Auditor General to report to the House of Commons on the *efficiency* and *economy* of expenditures or whether *value for money* had been received.

In 1984, the House of Commons passed Bill C-24, which amended the *Financial Administration Act* with respect to Crown corporations.[2] The implications are significant for auditors in public practice and in the government. Included among its stipulations are the following:

1. Internal audits that look at financial matters or compliance with regulations, and audits that look at whether or not the operations are conducted in an efficient, effective, and economic manner are required.
2. External audits of the financial statements are required.
3. Special examinations of efficiency, effectiveness, and economy must be carried out every five years.

The audit responsibilities of these government auditors are much like those of a public accounting firm. Most of the financial information prepared by various government agencies and, in some cases, by Crown corporations is audited by these government auditors before the information is submitted to the various legislatures. Since the authority for expenditures and receipts of government agencies is defined by law, there is considerable emphasis on compliance in these audits.

INDEPENDENT AUDITOR—a public accountant or accounting firm that performs audits of commercial and noncommercial entities

AUDITOR GENERAL—responsible for auditing federal and provincial ministries, departments, and agencies, including Crown corporations

---

[2] The interested reader is referred to *A Director's Introduction to the Audit and Special Examination Provisions of the Financial Administration Act* (as amended by Bill C-24) published by the Canadian Comprehensive Auditing Foundation from which this material is taken.

An example of audit work in the public sector is the evaluation of the computer operations of a particular governmental unit. The auditor can review and evaluate any aspect of the computer system, but he or she is likely to emphasize the adequacy of the equipment, the efficiency of the operations, the adequacy and usefulness of the output, and similar matters with the objective of identifying means of providing the same services for less cost.

In many provinces, experience as a government auditor fulfills the experience requirement for a professional designation. In those provinces, if an individual passes the professional examination and fulfills the experience stipulations of the particular professional organization, he or she may then obtain the professional certification.

As a result of their great responsibility for auditing the expenditures of the various governments, their use of advanced auditing concepts, their eligibility to be professional accountants, and their opportunities for performing operational audits, government auditors are highly regarded in the auditing profession.

Canada Revenue Agency Auditors The Canada Revenue Agency has as its responsibility the enforcement of the federal tax laws as they have been defined by Parliament and interpreted by the courts. A major responsibility of this agency is to audit the returns of taxpayers to determine whether they have complied with the tax laws. The auditors who perform these examinations are referred to as **Canada Revenue Agency auditors**. These audits are solely compliance audits.

CANADA REVENUE AGENCY AUDITOR—an auditor who works for the Canada Revenue Agency and conducts examinations of taxpayers' returns

It might seem that the audit of returns for compliance with the federal tax laws would be a simple and straightforward problem, but nothing could be further from the truth. The tax laws are highly complicated, and there are hundreds of volumes of court interpretations. The tax returns being audited vary from the simple returns of individuals who work for only one employer and take the standard tax deductions to the highly complex returns of multinational corporations. There are taxation problems involving individual taxpayers, sales taxes, goods and services tax, corporate taxes, trusts, and so forth. An auditor involved in any of these areas must have considerable knowledge to conduct an audit.

Internal Auditors **Internal auditors**, many of whom are members of the IIA, are employed by individual companies to audit for management, much as the Auditor General does for Parliament. The internal audit group in some large firms can include over a hundred persons and typically reports directly to the audit committee of the board of directors or a senior executive.

INTERNAL AUDITOR—an auditor employed by a company to audit for the company's board of directors and management

Internal auditors' responsibilities vary considerably, depending upon the employer. Some internal audit staffs consist of only one or two employees who may spend most of their time doing routine compliance auditing. Other internal audit staffs consist of numerous employees who have diverse responsibilities, including many outside the accounting area. In recent years, many internal auditors have become involved in operational auditing or have developed expertise in evaluating computer systems. They also provide assistance in evaluating new systems prior to implementation and in assessing risks within the organization.

Modern internal auditing takes a proactive business advisory approach in contrast to traditional operational- and compliance-based audit. The need to emphasize consulting is evident from the Institute of Internal Auditors who define internal audit (**www.theiia.org**) as "an independent, objective assurance and consulting activity designed to add value and improve an organization's operations. It helps an organization accomplish its objectives by bringing a systematic, disciplined approach to evaluate and improve the effectiveness of risk management, control and governance processes."

To operate effectively, an internal auditor must be independent of the line functions in an organization but will not be independent of the entity as long as an employer-employee relationship exists. Internal auditors provide management with valuable information for making decisions concerning the efficient and effective operation of its business. Users from outside the entity, however, are unlikely to want to rely on information verified by internal auditors because of their lack of independence. This lack of independence is the major difference between internal auditors and public accounting firms.

→1.2 **ORGANIZATION OF PUBLIC ACCOUNTING FIRMS**

Public Accounting Firms

There are currently more than 1,000 public accounting firms in Canada. These firms range in size from a sole practitioner to the more than 4,000 professional staff employed by Canada's largest CA firm, Deloitte & Touche LLP. Four size categories can be used to describe public accounting firms: "Big Four" international firms, national firms, large local and regional firms, and small local firms.

International Firms The four largest accounting firms in the world, referred to as the "Big Four," include Deloitte & Touche, KPMG, PricewaterhouseCoopers, and Ernst & Young. In Canada, the seven largest firms include the Big Four plus Grant Thornton, BDO Dunwoody, and Meyers Norris Penny.[3] They audit most of the 1,000 largest companies in Canada. Their gross revenues ranged from $123 million to over $1 billion for 2004[4]; international revenues are more than $5 billion for the largest of these firms. These firms range in size from a staff of several hundred professionals in Toronto to smaller offices with fewer than 20 people.

These international firms are so large because they need to be able to serve all major international cities as the globalization of businesses increases. For example, if a Canadian company has branches in the United States, Brazil, and Spain, the public accounting firm doing the audit needs auditors in each of those countries. Each of the Big Four now has the capability to serve all major international markets.

National Firms Several other firms in Canada, such as Collins Barrow and BHD Association, are referred to as national firms because they have offices in most major cities. Their revenues range from $21 million to more than $98 million.[5] These firms perform the same services as international firms and compete directly with them for clients. In addition, each is affiliated with firms in other countries and therefore has an international capability.

Large Local and Regional Firms There are fewer than 40 public accounting firms with professional staffs of more than 50 people. Some have only one office and serve clients primarily within commuting distance. Others have several offices in a province or region and service a larger radius of clients. These firms compete with other public accounting firms, including the Big Four, for clients. Many of them become affiliated with associations of public accounting firms to share resources for such matters as technical information and continuing education. Firms in this category have revenues that range upwards to $21 million.[6]

Small Local Firms Most of these public accounting firms have fewer than 25 professionals in their single-office firm. They perform audits and related services primarily for smaller businesses and not-for-profit entities, although some do have one or two clients with public ownership. Many small firms are resigning from these public company audits, due to the need to register with the Canadian Public Accountability Board (CPAB). We discuss this trend later in the chapter.

Structure of Public Accounting Firms

Because of their responsibility for the audit of financial statements, it is essential that professionals working for public accounting firms have a high level of *independence* and *competence*. Independence permits the auditors to remain unbiased in drawing conclusions about the financial statements. Competence permits auditors to conduct the audit efficiently and

Deloitte & Touche
www.deloitte.com

KPMG International
www.kpmg.com

PricewaterhouseCoopers
www.pwcglobal.com

Ernst & Young LLP
www.ey.com

Grant Thornton
www.grantthornton.com

BDO Dunwoody
www.bdo.ca

Meyers Norris Penny
www.mnp.ca

---

[3] *The Bottom Line* (April 2005), p. 12.

[4] Ibid, p. 12.

[5] Ibid, p. 12.

[6] Ibid, p. 14.

effectively. Confidence in an auditor's independence and competence enables users to rely upon the statements. The large number of public accounting firms in Canada makes it impossible for users to evaluate the independence and competence of individual firms. Consequently, an organizational structure for public accounting firms has emerged that encourages, but certainly does not guarantee, these qualities.

The organizational form used by many public accounting firms is that of a *sole proprietorship* or a *partnership*, although some provinces allow special purpose limited liability partnerships. In a typical firm, several CAs or CGAs join together to practise as partners, offering auditing and other services to interested parties. The partners normally hire professional staff to assist them in their work. Most of these assistants for the assurance engagements are, or aspire to become, CAs or CGAs.

The existence of a separate entity to perform audits encourages independence by avoiding an employee–employer relationship between public accounting firms and their clients. A separate entity also enables a public accounting firm to become sufficiently large so that it is rare for any one client to represent a significant portion of a partner's total income, thereby endangering the firm's independence. Competence is encouraged by having a large number of professionals with related interests associated in one firm, which facilitates a professional attitude and continuing professional education.

The organizational hierarchy in a typical public accounting firm includes partners, managers, supervisors, seniors or in-charge auditors, and assistants, with a new employee usually starting as an assistant and spending two or three years in each classification before achieving partner status. The titles of the positions vary from firm to firm, but the basic structure is the same in all. When we refer in this text to the *auditor*, we mean the particular person performing some aspect of a financial statement audit. It is common to have one or more auditors from each level on larger engagements.

E-Commerce and PA Firm Operations

Like all industries, PA firms are using the Internet to market their services. Firms of all sizes use the Internet to highlight such things as office locations or affiliations, service lines, and industry specializations and provide reference tools and materials to existing and potential clients. Firm web sites feature news and insights about business issues, such as updates on changes in tax laws and interactive forms to determine which type of retirement account to choose. Firm web sites also feature online software tools and databases to subscribers who pay a fee. For example, Ernst & Young sells its *Accounting and Auditing Tool Kit* to subscribers through its Ernst & Young Online web site. PricewaterhouseCoopers LLP, through an alliance with Watchfire^{sm}, offers a privacy management software tool, *WatchfireWebCPO*, that provides protection to online information.

PA firms also use the Internet to connect their global professional staff. Firm personnel from around the world can contribute services to a client on a timely basis without having to be physically present at the client's location. Communicating electronically among firm personnel is especially advantageous for firms that serve multinational clients with operations around the globe. For example, personnel in Toronto, Tokyo, and London who have expertise in local regulations and business cultures can serve local clients and branches of international clients with operations in those cities, and can also communicate with engagement team personnel serving those clients in other locations.

PA firms are also taking advantage of online resources and databases that can be accessed through the Internet. These resources are useful to PAs for staying current on emerging business and standards-setting issues. Databases, such as *Standard and Poor's Net Advantage Database* and *Goldman Sachs Research Database*, provide extensive industry-specific information and coverage of companies that PAs use on a subscription basis to stay current on industry developments and to obtain industry data useful for auditing and consulting.

→ 1.3 RESPONDING TO THE PUBLIC CALL FOR HIGH-QUALITY AUDITS

Professional Accounting Organizations

Professional accounting organizations serve as umbrella organizations to which all certified members belong by virtue of their membership in a provincial institute/*ordre* or have joined as associate members (IIA and ISACA only). Depending upon the organization, they coordinate the examination processes, provide for continuing education activities, fund research projects, produce relevant publications, and engage in standard setting and peer review processes.

Research and Publications Each association has some form of monthly newsletter or national magazine. For example, in its role as representative of the CAs in Canada, the CICA publishes a wide range of materials. These include the monthly *CAmagazine*, accounting and auditing research studies, and the bi-annual *Financial Reporting in Canada*. It coordinates the Uniform Evaluation exam and publishes the Board of Evaluators' Report on each year's exam. It also coordinates the common activities of the provincial institutes and *ordre*.

Continuing Education The CICA is very active in continuing professional education, sponsoring seminars, and developing and providing material to the provincial institutes and *ordre* for use by their membership. The CICA established six specializations for Chartered Accountants, in cooperation with other professional organizations upon completion of their CA.

The Certified General Accountants Association of Canada plays a similar role in the professional lives of CGAs, as does the Society of Management Accountants of Canada in the lives of CMAs and the Institute of Internal Auditors in the lives of CIAs. For example, CGAAC publishes *CGA Magazine* and SMAC publishes *CMA*. In addition, CGAAC and SMAC administer exams and provide professional guidance and continuing professional education. They also conduct research and publish materials of interest to their members and students.

Establishing Standards and Rules The CICA has been given the authority by the *Canada Business Corporations Act* and the various provincial incorporating acts to set accounting and auditing standards that must be followed by public accountants doing audits of companies chartered under one of those acts. This is done by stating that the financial statements should be prepared in accordance with the standards as set out in the *CICA Handbooks*.

In its role as standard setter, the CICA supports research by its own research staff and, through grants, by others. It also sets the standards, which are called "Recommendations"

CAmagazine
www.camagazine.com

CGA Magazine
www.cga-online.org

CMA Management Magazine
www.managementmag.com

and are codified in the *CICA Handbooks*, and proposes guidelines and rules for members and other public accountants to follow. The *CICA Handbooks* are a four-volume set, with two volumes on accounting and two on assurance.

You learned in an earlier accounting course about the accounting standards or Recommendations issued by the Accounting Standards Board and about the Accounting Guidelines issued by the Accounting Standards Board of the CICA. You also learned about the Emerging Issues Committee (EIC) of the CICA, which issues abstracts on contemporary accounting issues.

This text will focus on standards or Recommendations issued by another body of the CICA, the **Auditing and Assurance Standards Board** (AASB). It will also focus on Assurance and Related Services Guidelines issued by the AASB. **Assurance Recommendations** are issued by the Auditing and Assurance Board, as explained in Section 5021, and are the rules underlying the audits, assurance engagements, and related services activities carried out by public accountants. Assurance Recommendations are the italicized portions of Sections 5000 to 9200 and Sections PS 5000 to PS 6420 of the *CICA Assurance Handbook*. Sections preceded by PS are specific to audits of public sector companies. These are considered to be authoritative rules. **Assurance and Related Services Guidelines** are also issued by the Auditing and Assurance Standards Board. They do not have the authority of Assurance Recommendations and are either interpretations of existing Recommendations or the views of the AASB on a particular matter of concern. An example is Assurance and Related Services Guideline 40 (AuG-40) issued in September 2003 entitled "Auditor's report on the financial statements of federally regulated financial institutions."

Ways Public Accountants Are Encouraged to Perform Effectively

Because public accounting firms play an important social role, it is essential for the management of those firms and their professional staff to conduct themselves appropriately and provide high-quality audits and other services. The various professional organizations (CICA and CGAAC) and other outside organizational influences have developed several mechanisms to increase the likelihood of appropriate audit quality and professional conduct. These are summarized in Figure 1-3 and discussed in the remainder of this and subsequent chapters. The codes of professional conduct of the various accounting bodies also have a significant influence on members. The codes are meant to provide a standard of conduct for members who are in public practice. The codes and related issues of professional conduct are examined in Chapter 2. Legal liability is studied in Chapter 4. Shaded circles indicate items discussed in this chapter.

AUDITING AND ASSURANCE STANDARDS BOARD—a committee of the CICA that has the responsibility for issuing Assurance Recommendations and Assurance and Related Services Guidelines

ASSURANCE RECOMMENDATIONS—a framework for the auditor to use to assist him or her in the conduct of an audit engagement; the rules underlying the audits and related services activities carried on by public accountants; the italicized portions of the *CICA Assurance Handbook*. They are issued by the Auditing and Assurance Standards Board.

ASSURANCE AND RELATED SERVICES GUIDELINES—Interpretations of Assurance Recommendations or views of the Auditing and Assurance Standards Board on particular matters of concern; less authoritative than Assurance Recommendations

FIGURE 1-3 Ways the Profession and Society Encourage Public Accountants to Conduct Themselves at a High Level

Generally Accepted Auditing Standards

Auditing or assurance standards are general guidelines to aid auditors in fulfilling their professional responsibilities in the audit of historical financial statements. They include consideration of professional qualities such as competence and independence, reporting requirements, and evidence.

The broadest guidelines available are the eight **generally accepted auditing standards** (GAAS) detailed in Section 5100. These standards are not sufficiently specific to provide any meaningful guide to practitioners, but they do represent a framework upon which the CICA can provide Recommendations. These eight standards, summarized in Figure 1-4, are:

GENERALLY ACCEPTED AUDITING STANDARDS—eight auditing standards, developed by the CICA, consisting of the general standard, examination standards, and reporting standards; often called auditing standards

General Standard The examination should be performed and the report prepared by a person or persons having adequate technical training and proficiency in auditing, with due care and with an objective state of mind.

Examination Standards

(i) The auditor should plan and perform the audit to reduce audit risk to an acceptably low level that is consistent with the objective of an audit. The auditor should plan the nature, timing and extent of direction and supervision of engagement team members and review their work.

(ii) The auditor should obtain an understanding of the entity and its environment, including internal control, sufficient to identify and assess the risks of material misstatement of the financial statements whether due to fraud or error, and sufficient to design and perform further audit procedures.

(iii) The auditor should obtain sufficient appropriate audit evidence to be able to draw reasonable conclusions on which to base the audit opinion.

Reporting Standards

(i) The report should identify the financial statements and distinguish between the responsibilities of management and the responsibilities of the auditor.

(ii) The report should describe the scope of the auditor's examination.

(iii) The report should contain either an expression of opinion on the financial statements or an assertion that an opinion cannot be expressed. In the latter case, the reasons therefore should be stated.

(iv) Where an opinion is expressed, it should indicate whether the financial statements present fairly, in all material respects, the financial position, results of operations and cash flows in accordance with Canadian generally accepted accounting principles, except when the financial statements: are prepared as described in *Auditor's Report on Financial Statements Prepared Using a Basis of Accounting other than Generally Accepted Accounting Principles*, paragraph 5600.09; or are financial statements of a

FIGURE 1-4 **Summary of Eight Generally Accepted Auditing Standards**

Generally Accepted Auditing Standards

General qualifications and conduct	*Examination* performance of the audit	*Reporting* results
Adequate technical training and proficiency in auditing, due care, and objective state of mind.	Adequate planning and execution to reduce risk to an acceptable level, and proper supervision	Identify the financial statements and responsibilities of management and the auditor
	Sufficient understanding of business and environment and of internal control; tests of controls required if control risk assessment below maximum	Refer to scope of examination
		Expression of opinion or assertion opinion cannot be expressed
	Sufficient appropriate audit evidence	Indicate whether financial statements present fairly in accordance with disclosed basis of accounting (usually Canadian GAAP)

federal, provincial, territorial or local government, and the auditor is required to express an opinion on the fair presentation of the financial statements in accordance with a disclosed basis of accounting, when the auditor would refer to *Audit of Government Financial Statements*, Section PS 5200, for guidance.

The report should provide adequate explanation with respect to any reservation contained in such opinion.

Auditing Recommendations

As was previously indicated, the Recommendations in the *CICA Assurance Handbook* are the most authoritative references available to public accountants performing financial statements audits of companies incorporated under the various federal or provincial incorporating acts or listed on one of the Canadian stock exchanges. In addition, CAs are required by their rules of professional conduct to follow the Recommendations of the *CICA Handbooks*. The Recommendations are a framework for the auditor to use to assist him or her in the conduct of the audit engagement. The framework is built upon the eight generally accepted auditing standards. Frequently, these Recommendations are referred to as auditing standards or GAAS, even though they are not one of the eight generally accepted auditing standards.

Auditing standards in the United States are issued by the American Institute of Certified Public Accountants (AICPA) and the Public Company Accounting Oversight Board, as described in Focus Box 1-2. Another authoritative source of standards would be International Standards on Auditing (ISAs) discussed on page 21.

Although GAAS and the Assurance and Related Services Recommendations are the authoritative auditing pronouncements for members of the profession, they provide less direction to auditors than might be assumed. There are almost no specific audit procedures required by the standards; and there are no specific requirements for auditors' decisions, such as determining sample size, selecting sample items from the population for testing, or evaluating results. Some practitioners believe the standards should provide more clearly defined guidelines for determining the extent of evidence to be accumulated. Such specificity would eliminate some difficult audit decisions and provide a line of defence for a public accounting firm charged with conducting an inadequate audit. However, highly specific requirements could turn auditing into mechanistic evidence gathering, devoid of professional judgment. From the point of view of both the profession and the users of auditing services, there is probably greater harm in defining authoritative guidelines too specifically than too broadly.

American Institute of Certified
Public Accountants
www.aicpa.org

Public Company Accounting
Oversight Board
www.pcaobus.org

Focus Box 1-2

CREATION OF PCAOB CHANGES AMERICAN STANDARD SETTING PROCESS

The *Sarbanes-Oxley Act of 2002*, signed into legislation on July 30, 2002, is considered by many observers to be the most important legislation affecting the American auditing profession since the 1933 and 1934 Securities Acts. The *Sarbanes-Oxley Act* was triggered by the bankruptcies and alleged audit failures involving Enron and WorldCom. The provisions of the Act apply to publicly held companies and their audit firms.

This Act established the Public Company Accounting Oversight Board (PCAOB), appointed and overseen by the Securities and Exchange Commission (SEC). The PCAOB will provide oversight for auditors of public companies, including establishing auditing and quality control standards for public company audits and performing inspections of the quality controls at audit firms performing those audits. These activities were formerly the responsibility of the AICPA. The U.S. Auditing Standards Board (ASB) is still responsible for issuing pronouncements on auditing matters for all entities other than public companies.

Although the PCAOB is responsible for setting standards, existing auditing standards remain in effect for public companies until the PCAOB develops specific guidance. The AICPA is responsible for standards in several areas, as follows: Pronouncements on auditing standards called *Statements on Auditing Standards* (SASs); compilation and review standards called *Statements on Standards for Accounting and Review Services* (SSARSs); attestation standards; consulting standards and a Code of Professional Conduct.

GAAS and the Assurance and Related Services Recommendations should be looked upon by practitioners as *minimum standards* of performance, rather than as maximum standards or ideals. Any professional auditor constantly seeking means of reducing the scope of the audit by relying only on the standards, rather than evaluating the substance of the situation, fails to satisfy the spirit of the standards. At the same time, the existence of auditing standards does not mean the auditor must always follow them blindly. If the requirement of a Recommendation is impossible to perform, the auditor might adopt some other course of action that allows adherence to the spirit of the Recommendation. Similarly, if the amount involved is not material, it is also unnecessary to follow the standard. It is important to note, however, that the burden of justifying departures from the standards falls upon the practitioner.

When the *CICA Handbooks* are silent on an issue, the auditor must turn to other authoritative sources. These include the SASs issued by the AICPA, the ISAs issued by the International Federation of Accountants, textbooks, journals, and technical publications. Materials published by the CICA, mentioned earlier in the chapter, such as audit technique studies, are particularly useful in furnishing assistance on specific questions.

In the remainder of this section, GAAS are discussed briefly. There is further study of the standards and frequent reference to General Assurance and Auditing Recommendations throughout the text.

Adequate Technical Training and Proficiency in Auditing The *general standard* stresses the important qualities the auditor should possess. The general standard is normally interpreted as requiring the auditor to have formal education in auditing and accounting, adequate practical experience for the work being performed, and continuing professional education. Recent court cases clearly demonstrate that the auditor must be technically qualified and experienced in those industries in which the auditor has clients.

In any case in which the public accountant or the accountant's assistants are not qualified to perform the work, a professional obligation exists to acquire the requisite knowledge and skills, suggest someone else who is qualified to perform the work, or decline the engagement.

Objective State of Mind The importance of an objective state of mind or independence was stressed earlier in the definition of auditing. The *Rules of Professional Conduct* of the various provincial institutes of CAs and the *ordre* as well as the GAAS in the *CICA Handbooks* stress the need for independence. The rules of conduct of CGAAC also stress the need for independence for CGAs engaged in public accounting. The *Canada Business Corporations Act* (*CBCA*), which is similar to several of the provincial incorporating acts, also requires the auditor to be independent. Public accounting firms are required to follow several practices to increase the likelihood of independence of all personnel. For example, there are established procedures for larger audits that utilize an audit committee whenever there is a dispute between management and the auditors.[7] Specific methods to ensure that auditors maintain their independence are studied in Chapter 2. An audit committee is a subcommittee of the board of directors of a company. The majority of the audit committee members should be composed of directors not belonging to management. The internal and external auditors usually report to the audit committee. Audit committees are discussed further in Chapter 2.

To assist the auditor, the CBCA specifies the auditor's qualifications in Section 161 but also provides the auditor with statutory rights and responsibilities. These give the auditor the right to attend shareholder meetings and the right to have access to the necessary records, information, and explanations necessary to conduct the audit. These rights afford the auditor the necessary access for completion of the audit.

Due Care The general standard involves *due care* in the performance of all aspects of auditing. Simply stated, this means that the auditor is a professional responsible for fulfilling his or her duties diligently and carefully. As an illustration, due care includes consideration of the

---

[7]An audit committee is a subcommittee of the board of directors of a company. The majority of the audit committee members should be composed of directors not belonging to management. The internal and external auditors usually report to the audit committee. Audit committees are discussed further in Chapter 2.

completeness of the working papers, the sufficiency of the audit evidence, and the appropriateness of the auditor's report. As a professional, the auditor must not be guilty of negligence or bad faith, but he or she is not expected to make perfect judgments in every instance.

Adequate Planning, Proper Execution, and Proper Supervision The *examination standards* concern planning, risk assessment, and evidence accumulation and other activities during the actual conduct of the audit in the field. The first standard deals with ascertaining that the engagement is sufficiently well planned and executed to ensure an adequate audit and that there is proper supervision of assistants. Supervision is essential in auditing because a considerable portion of the field work or examination is done by inexperienced staff members.

Sufficient Understanding of Environment and Internal Control The client must be assessed in the context of the business environment and the corporate governance process. One of the most widely accepted points in the theory and practice of auditing is the importance of the client's accounting systems and whether internal controls are sufficient to generate reliable financial information. If the auditor is convinced the client has excellent controls that provide reliable data and safeguard assets and records, the amount of audit evidence to be accumulated can be significantly less than for a system that is not adequate. In some instances, the controls may be so inadequate as to preclude reliance on the data in the records and an audit may not be possible.

Sufficient Appropriate Audit Evidence The decision as to how much evidence and of what quality to accumulate for a given set of circumstances is one requiring professional judgment. A major portion of this book is concerned with the study of evidence accumulation and the circumstances affecting the amount needed.

Four Reporting Standards The four reporting standards require the auditor to prepare a report on the financial statements identifying the financial statements and the responsibilities of management and the auditors, and indicating the scope of the auditor's examination. The report must contain either an expression of opinion or explain why no opinion can be expressed. The opinion should indicate whether or not the statements are in accordance with an appropriate disclosed basis of accounting (usually Canadian GAAP). Section 5400 of the *CICA Handbook*, which deals more specifically with the auditor's report, is discussed in Chapter 3. We also discuss acceptable alternatives to Canadian GAAP, such as using a different basis of accounting, in Chapter 3.

International Auditing Standards

The CICA, the CGAAC, and the SMAC are members of the International Federation of Accountants (IFAC), a body that seeks to harmonize auditing standards on a worldwide basis. IFAC, through the International Auditing and Assurance Standards Board (IAASB), issues International Standards on Auditing (ISAs) and International Auditing Practice Statements (IAPSs) for the guidance of accountants in member countries. ISAs are standards and are authoritative while IAPSs provide guidance and are not authoritative.

International Federation of Accountants
www.ifac.org

International Organization of Securities Commissions
www.iosco.org

Ontario Securities Commission
www.osc.gov.on.ca

Inco Limited
www.inco.com

U.S. Securities and Exchange Commission
www.sec.gov

In addition, the provincial securities commissions are members of the International Organization of Securities Commissions (IOSCO). IOSCO members are concerned with securities, which are issued by a company in one country and sold in a second country. For example, shares of Inco Limited, a Canadian company, are traded on the Toronto Stock Exchange (under the jurisdiction of the Ontario Securities Commission [OSC]) and on the New York Stock Exchange (under the jurisdiction of the U.S. Securities and Exchange Commission [SEC]); Inco's shares are said to be "cross-listed." Both the OSC and the SEC are members of IOSCO. IOSCO members are concerned about International Auditing and Assurance Standards as they have to decide on the quality, sufficiency, and appropriateness of evidence collected and the report issued for audits of financial statements submitted to them for cross-listing.

A Canadian auditor must conduct an audit of a Canadian or foreign company in accordance with Canadian GAAS (i.e., follow the *Handbooks*) and may, in addition, conduct the audit in accordance with international GAAS (i.e., the ISAs or the GAAS of another country such as the U.S.). In such a case, the auditor may report that the audit was conducted using Canadian and foreign GAAS. It is important to note that Canadian GAAS would be the floor in this case.

Where there are reporting differences between Canadian GAAS and the ISAs or foreign GAAS, the auditor should follow Canadian reporting standards. An example is the Auditing Guideline 21, "Canada–United States Reporting Differences." AuG-21 requires the auditor to issue an auditor's report in compliance with Canadian GAAS and to also issue a separate comment explaining the conflict between the reporting standards.

The *Handbooks* take precedence over the ISAs when there is a conflict. A Canadian auditor who is engaged to conduct an examination in accordance with International Standards on Auditing would consult the most recent version of the ISAs.

Quality Control

QUALITY CONTROLS—methods used by a public accounting firm to make sure that the firm meets its professional responsibilities

For a public accounting firm, quality control comprises the methods used to make sure that the firm meets its professional responsibilities to clients. These methods include the organizational structure of the public accounting firm and the procedures the firm sets up. For example, a public accounting firm might have an organizational structure that assures the technical review of every engagement by a partner who has expertise in the client's industry.

A public accounting firm must make sure that generally accepted auditing standards are followed on every audit. **Quality controls** are the methods used by the firm that help it meet those standards consistently on every engagement. Quality controls are therefore established for the entire public accounting firm and all the activities in which the firm is involved; GAAS require that these standards are applied to each engagement on an individual basis.

Elements of Quality Control In August 2004, the CICA adopted quality control standards for audits that are generally effective for December 1, 2005. The *CICA Assurance Handbook* Section GSF-QC describes general standards of quality control that are applied to firms performing assurance engagements. These are described in Table 1-2, where the components of quality control are listed under a series of headings called elements of quality control.

These standards clarify the minimum policies and procedures that firms should have in place. Also in August 2004, specific requirements were adopted in *CICA Assurance Handbook* Section 5030 for individual engagements and form part of GAAS. Public accountants need to ensure that they adequately apply quality control to each audit engagement. For example, there are specific procedures to help ensure that differences of opinion on an engagement are brought forward and cleared before finalizing the engagement. We will be looking at these quality control procedures in more detail when we talk about the various phases of the audit engagement throughout this text.

CANADIAN PUBLIC ACCOUNTABILITY BOARD—an oversight organization for the audit of publicly listed businesses that includes practice inspections

Canadian Public Accountability Board
www.cpab-ccrc.ca

These updated quality control standards complement the new independence rules that were implemented in 2003. After the *Sarbanes-Oxley Act of 2002* was passed in the U.S., creating the PCOAB, a similar body was implemented in Canada, called the **Canadian Public Accountability Board** (CPAB). Rather than being legislated, the CPAB was created by the provincial securities commissions, the Office of the Superintendent of Financial Institutions, and the CICA. The CPAB's purpose is to help improve the public's confidence in independent auditing. This is accomplished by promoting high quality audits. The CPAB has developed an oversight program that involves regular inspections of those PA firms that audit Canadian public companies.[8] One of the items absent from the CPAB's mission statement is the development of auditing standards. This is a key difference between the Canadian and the U.S. approach. Although the CPAB will provide feedback to the standard setting process, it is leaving these up to the existing standard setting bodies within Canada, namely the CICA, and coordination with international standard setting bodies.

PA firms that audit companies called "reporting issuers" are required to register with the CPAB and are subject to a quality control inspection by the CPAB. (This inspection process is discussed further in the next section, under the heading *practice inspection*.) The term "reporting issuers" is used to describe entities, such as profit-oriented businesses and mutual

---

[8]Source: Canadian Public Accountability Board, www.cpab-ccrc.ca, accessed November 13, 2004.

funds, that have raised capital from the public, are listed on a Canadian stock exchange, and are required to file annual audited financial statements with their listing exchange. A list of about 230 registered firms can be found on the CPAB web site. These include both CGA firms and CA firms. The registration documentation is public (except for fee information) and includes the quality control procedures that firms have in place for each of the quality control elements listed in Table 1-2. These registered firms were required to have the new quality control standards in place by January 1, 2005.

The CPAB web site is an excellent source describing the operationalization of quality control procedures. We will be discussing quality control specifics as we work through the audit process in this text.

PA firms that do not audit reporting issuers are not subject to the quality control inspection by the CPAB, but will still be required to have quality control standards in place. These standards specify that quality control needs to be considered during all phases of the engagement, including client acceptance, continuance, planning, and execution of the engagement.

TABLE 1-2	Elements of Quality Control at the Firm Level
Element	**Summary of Requirements**
1. Leadership and responsibilities within the firm:	An organizational culture that provides audit quality should be present. Quality control procedures should be developed, documented, implemented, and communicated. Management within a firm should ensure that qualified personnel monitor and address non-compliance with quality control procedures. A firm should establish a formal code of conduct that includes procedures for individuals to disclose differences of opinion or any inappropriate conduct.
2. General ethical requirements:	The general ethical principles of integrity, objectivity, professional competence and due care, confidentiality, and professionalism should be addressed at the policy level, promoted by firm personnel, and monitored.
3. Independence:	Policies and procedures should be developed, communicated, and monitored to ensure that the firm complies with the independence guidelines. Areas to be addressed are: extent of nonassurance services provided to audit clients, documentation of independence evaluations, partner rotation (where required), fee policies, partner compensation, and effects of litigation.
4. Client acceptance or continuance:	Documentation of annual risk assessment processes should be present, including an evaluation of a potential client's management integrity and auditor competence and independence.
5. General human resource policies:	Adequate hiring policies (and documentation of their implementation) that ensure competence and integrity of personnel should be in place. Ongoing professional development of personnel should exist, with assignment to work that matches employee competence, and performance evaluation related to audit quality.
6. Extent of professional development:	Employees should be adequately trained in the skills needed to conduct audits. Both instructors and attendees are to be evaluated, with documentation of that evaluation.
7. Engagement performance:	Adequate processes and procedures should be in place to ensure that the audit is conducted in accordance with GAAS, that quality control procedures are followed for each engagement, and appropriately documented. These include the use of software tools, supervision, review of work, use of internal or specialist consultation, and processes for handling differences of opinion.
8. Engagement quality control review:	Quality control review is to take place during the engagement and monitoring should occur after engagement completion. Policies in place should include use of second or independent partner review, technical review, documentation, and compliance with quality control processes. Processes should exist for following up internal and external complaints.
9. Documentation:	Policies should address extent of documentation, whether retained in hard copy or electronic format, file retention, storage, security and back-up for audit documentation, correspondence, policies, and procedures.

The quality control procedures that a public accounting firm employs will depend on the size of the firm, the number of practice offices, and the nature of the practice. The quality control procedures of a 150-office international firm with many complex multinational clients would vary considerably from those of a 5-person firm specializing in small audits in one or two industries.

Practice Inspection One of the ways in which the PA profession in Canada has dealt with quality control is through the establishment of *practice inspection* by the professional associations, provincial institutes, and *ordre*. Practice inspection as an example, for CAs, is administered by the provincial institute or *ordre* and is usually mandatory for CAs in public practice. A practice inspection of each practice unit (usually an office but it could be each partner in the office) is normally completed every three years but could be yearly if the practice unit is found not to maintain the level of practice standards set forth by the provincial practice inspection committee.

In addition to the provincial institutes, the CPAB will conduct practice inspections aimed at the quality of the audit process. The purpose of all practice inspections is to ensure the existence of and adherence to quality control standards. For those audit firms that have 50 or more reporting issuers, this inspection is done on an annual basis. For audit firms having fewer reporting issuers, they will be inspected at least once every three years. This inspection could be conducted by the CPAB or by provincial accounting bodies, with the CPAB providing direction and reviewing the results. The first report completed by the CPAB, dated October 6, 2004, is available from its web site. The report discusses the results of the audit of the four largest public accounting firms in Canada, which together audit more than 4,000 entities (all reporting issuers or public companies), representing more than 90 percent of market capitalization that is audited.[9]

The amount of work done by the practice inspection team depends on the degree of documentation the practice unit has on its quality control procedures. If the controls are well documented and the practice inspector finds that the controls are being complied with, the inspection will be much briefer than if there is no documentation or if the controls are not being complied with.

A Provincial Practice Inspection Committee does have sanctions it can impose. These include re-inspection the following year and referral to the Professional Conduct Committee, whose powers include requiring the member to take courses, removing the practice unit's right to train students, and expelling the member from the Institute and forfeiting the member's right to use the appellation Chartered Accountant.

The CPAB could impose additional sanctions or restrictions such as engaging an independent monitor or limiting the right to audit reporting issuers. It could also make the inspection reports public.

Practice inspection can be beneficial to the profession and individual firms. The profession gains if reviews result in practitioners doing higher quality audits. A firm can also gain if the practice inspection improves the firm's practices and thereby enhances its reputation and effectiveness and reduces the likelihood of lawsuits. Of course, practice inspection is costly. There is always a trade-off between costs and benefits.

Provincial Securities Commissions

Securities regulation in Canada is a provincial matter; therefore, companies that issue securities in Canada must abide by rules promulgated by the **provincial securities commissions**. The national umbrella organization, the Canadian Securities Administrators, sets policies to which the member commissions agree to adhere. The provincial securities commissions are responsible for administering the purchase and sale of securities within their jurisdictions.

Copies of the actual policy statements, which may include questions and answers and multimedia presentations about them are available at the web sites of the following provincial securities commissions' sites: British Columbia Securities Commission, Alberta Securities Commission, Ontario Securities Commission, and the Commission des valeurs mobilières du Québec.

---

[9] Source: Canadian Public Accountability Board, www.cpab-ccrc.ca, Accessed: November 14, 2004.

More specifics on some of these rules will be discussed in subsequent chapters. The Canadian Securities Administrators (CSA) was responsible for the rule that required listed companies' auditors to participate in the oversight program of the CPAB. It also implemented the requirement that the listing company's Chief Financial Officer and Chief Executive Officer provide certification of annual and interim financial statements (as well as the accompanying management discussion and analysis and information forms filed with the exchanges). Other recent requirements include: every listed company must have an audit committee, with specifics about the composition and responsibilities of those audit committees, and that auditors are to report on management's assertion about the quality of internal controls. We will be discussing how many of these requirements affect the audit process in subsequent chapters.

Securities and Exchange Commission

Since many Canadian companies sell their stocks and borrow money in the United States, they must meet the requirements of the **Securities and Exchange Commission** (SEC). It is therefore appropriate to review the functions and operations of that body.

The overall purpose of the Securities and Exchange Commission, an agency of the U.S. federal government, is to assist in providing investors with reliable information upon which to make investment decisions. To this end, the *Securities Act of 1933* requires most companies planning to issue new securities to the public to submit a registration statement to the SEC for approval. The *Securities Exchange Act of 1934* provides additional protection by requiring the same companies and others to file detailed annual reports with the commission. The commission examines these statements for completeness and adequacy before permitting a company to sell its securities through the securities exchanges.

Although the SEC requires considerable information that is not of direct interest to CPAs, the securities acts of 1933 and 1934 require financial statements, accompanied by the opinion of an independent certified public accountant, as part of a registration statement and subsequent reports.

Of special interest to auditors are several specific reports that are subject to the reporting provisions of the securities acts. The most important of these are the following:

- *Forms S-1 to S-16.* These forms must be completed and registered with the SEC whenever a company plans to issue new securities to the public. The S-1 form is the general form when there is no specifically prescribed form. The others are specialized forms. For example, S-11 is for registration of securities of certain real estate companies. All S forms apply to the *Securities Act of 1933*.
- *Form 8-K.* This report is filed at the end of any month in which significant events have occurred that are of interest to public investors. Such events include the acquisition or sale of a subsidiary, a change in officers or directors, an addition of a new product line, or a change in auditors.
- *Form 10-K.* This report must be filed annually within 60 days after the close of each fiscal year for companies with more than $75 million in public equity, and within 90 days for all other companies. Extensive detailed financial information is contained in this report, including audited financial statements.
- *Form 10-Q.* This report must be filed quarterly for all publicly held companies. It contains certain financial information and requires timely auditor reviews of the financial statements before filing with the commission.

Since large CPA firms usually have clients that must file one or more of these reports each year, and the rules and regulations affecting filings with the SEC are extremely complex, most CPA firms have specialists who spend a large portion of their time making sure their clients satisfy all SEC requirements.

The SEC has considerable influence in setting generally accepted accounting principles and disclosure requirements for financial statements as a result of its authority for specifying reporting requirements considered necessary for fair disclosure to investors. The SEC has power to establish rules for any CPA associated with audited financial statements submitted to the commission. Even though the commission has taken the position that accounting

SECURITIES AND EXCHANGE COMMISSION—a U.S. federal agency that oversees the orderly conduct of the securities markets; the SEC assists in providing investors in public corporations with reliable information upon which to make investment decisions

U.S. Securities and Exchange Commission (SEC)
www.sec.gov

principles and auditing standards should be set by the profession, the SEC's attitude is generally considered in any major change proposed by the Auditing Standards Board or equivalent U.S. standard setting bodies.

The SEC requirements of greatest interest to CPAs are set forth in the commission's *Regulation S-X* and Accounting Series Releases, and Accounting and Auditing Enforcement Releases. These publications constitute important regulations, as well as decisions and opinions on accounting and auditing issues affecting any CPA dealing with publicly held companies.

SUMMARY

1. *What are the different types of accountants, and what do they do?* Public accountants (PAs), who audit and perform other professional services, can be either CGAs or CAs in Canada. Although some CMAs provide assurance services, most CMAs are financial management professionals. CIAs and internal auditors often do operational audits and help management assess risks. There are also many specialist designations, such as the CISA.

   What are the different types of engagements completed by public accountants? PAs complete financial statement audits, compliance audits, operational audits, and perform reviews and compilations. They also do bookkeeping, accounting, tax work, and provide management advisory services.

   What differentiates accounting from auditing and assurance services from nonassurance services? Accounting involves the actual preparation of underlying records, while auditing helps determine whether that recorded information reflects actual economic events. An audit is an attest engagement, a subset of assurance engagements. For an attest engagement, the client prepares the materials (such as the financial statements), and the auditor provides a written report on it, while for an assurance engagement, the auditor may actually prepare the report (such as commenting on lottery processes).

   Why are audits so important? Audits provide added value to information since they provide independent assurance where the user of the report is remote from the provider, where the provider may be biased, or where data audited is voluminous or complex.

2. *How are public accounting firms organized?* Most accounting firms are set up as sole proprietorships or partnerships, although some are set up as limited liability partnerships.

   What are some of the largest public accounting firms? The four largest firms are Deloitte & Touche, KPMG International, PricewaterhouseCoopers, and Ernst & Young.

3. *What market forces ensure that audit and assurance engagements are completed to high standards of quality?* The biggest threat is that a PA firm will be forced out of business due to legal liability, such as the failure of Andersen, discussed on page 15. Provincial securities commissions and the CPAB are now involved to ensure that the quality of audits is high. Completion of audits to high ethical standards, such as those of the Auditor General, help maintain the positive image of auditors. The use of technology in auditing, just as information technology has been adopted by other businesses, helps ensure the effective and efficient completion of audits.

   Who develops and maintains the standards that public accountants use? In Canada, public accounting standards are the responsibility of the CICA. The CICA develops standards in consultation with many organizations and groups: other accounting organizations in Canada, CPAB, securities and exchange commissions, international or other national standard setting organizations, individual PAs, and the business community.

   How are these standards enforced? Quality control inspections called practice inspections are conducted by the professional associations, the provincial institutes/*ordre*, and the CPAB.

CICA ASSURANCE HANDBOOK SECTIONS REFERENCED IN THIS CHAPTER

GSF-QC – General standards of quality control for firms performing assurance engagements.
Section 5021 – Authority of auditing and assurance standards and other guidance.
Section 5025 – Standards for assurance engagements.
Section 5030 – Quality control procedures for assurance engagements.
Section 5100 – Generally accepted auditing standards.

Section 5400 – The auditor's standard report.
Section 5600 – Auditor's report on financial statements prepared using a basis of accounting other than generally accepted accounting principles.
AuG-21 – Canada–US reporting differences.
AuG-40 – Auditor's report on the financial statements of regulated financial institutions.
Section PS-5200 – Audit of government financial statements.

ESSENTIAL TERMS

Accounting—the recording, classifying, and summarizing of economic events in a logical manner for the purpose of providing financial information for decision making   (p. 6).

Assurance and Related Services Guidelines—interpretations of Assurance Recommendations or views of the Auditing and Assurance Standards Board on particular matters of concern; less authoritative than Assurance Recommendations   (p. 17).

Assurance engagement—issuance of a written communication expressing a conclusion on a subject matter where an accountable party is responsible as part of an accountability relationship; also called assurance service   (p. 9).

Assurance Recommendations—a framework for the auditor to use to assist him or her in the conduct of an audit engagement; the rules underlying the audits and related services activities carried on by public accountants; the italicized portions of the *CICA Assurance Handbook*. They are issued by the Auditing and Assurance Standards Board   (p. 17).

Assurance services—see assurance engagement.

Attestation—a written communication regarding the reliability of another party's written assertion   (p. 9).

Auditing—the accumulation and evaluation of evidence about information to determine and report on the degree of correspondence between the information and established criteria   (p. 4).

Auditing and Assurance Standards Board—a committee of the CICA that has the responsibility for issuing Assurance Recommendations and Assurance and Related Services Guidelines   (p. 17).

Auditor General—responsible for auditing federal and provincial ministries, departments, and agencies, including Crown corporations   (p. 12).

Auditor's report—the communication of audit findings to users   (p. 5).

Canada Revenue Agency auditor—an auditor who works for the Canada Revenue Agency and conducts examinations of taxpayers' returns   (p. 13).

Canadian Institute of Chartered Accountants (CICA)—sets the accounting and auditing standards in the private and public sectors, which must be followed by public accountants in Canada; one of the three major accounting organizations in Canada providing a professional designation relating to accounting and auditing; umbrella organization of the provincial institutes and *ordre* that regulates the CA profession in Canada   (p. 3).

Canadian Public Accountability Board—an oversight organization for the audit of publicly listed businesses that includes practice inspections   (p. 22).

Certified General Accountant—one of three professional designations in Canada relating to accounting and auditing   (p. 3).

Certified General Accountants Association of Canada (CGAAC)—one of the three major accounting organizations in Canada providing a professional designation relating to accounting and auditing; umbrella organization of the provincial associations that regulates the CGA profession in Canada   (p. 3).

Certified Management Accountant (CMA)—one of three professional designations in Canada relating to accounting and auditing   (p. 3).

Chartered Accountant (CA)—one of three professional designations in Canada relating to accounting and auditing   (p. 3).

Compliance audit—(1) a review of an organization's financial records performed to determine whether the organization is following specific procedures, rules, or regulations set down by some higher authority; (2) an audit performed to determine whether an entity that receives financial assistance from a federal or provincial government has complied with specific laws and regulations   (p. 7).

Evidence—any information used by the auditor to determine whether the information being audited is stated in accordance with established criteria   (p. 4).

Financial statement audit—an audit conducted to determine whether the overall financial statements of an entity are stated in accordance with specified criteria (usually GAAP)   (p. 7).

Generally accepted auditing standards—eight auditing standards, developed by the CICA, consisting of the general standard, examination standards, and reporting standards; often called auditing standards   (p. 18).

Independent auditor—a public accountant or accounting firm that performs audits of commercial and noncommercial entities   (p. 12).

Information risk—the risk that information upon which a business decision is made is inaccurate   (p. 6).

Internal auditor—an auditor employed by a company to audit for the company's board of directors and management   (p. 13).

Operational audit—a review of any part of an organization's operating procedures and methods for the purpose of evaluating economy, efficiency and effectiveness   (p. 8).

Provincial securities commissions—provincial organizations with quasi-legal status that administer securities regulations within their jurisdictions   (p. 24).

Quality control—methods used by a public accounting firm to make sure that the firm meets its professional responsibilities   (p. 22).

Securities and Exchange Commission (SEC)—a U.S. federal agency that oversees the orderly conduct of the securities markets; the SEC assists in providing investors in public corporations with reliable information upon which to make investment decisions   (p. 25).

Society of Management Accountants of Canada (SMAC)—one of the three major accounting organizations in Canada providing a professional designation relating to accounting and auditing; umbrella organization of the provincial societies that regulates the CMA profession in Canada   (p. 3).

1-1 Briefly describe the accounting organizations that exist in Canada and identify the professional designations they award.

1-2 Explain what is meant by determining the degree of correspondence between information and established criteria. What are the information and established criteria for the audit of Glickle Ltd.'s tax return by a Canada Revenue Agency auditor? What are they for the audit of Glickle Ltd.'s financial statements by a public accounting firm?

1-3 Describe the nature of evidence the Canada Revenue Agency auditor will use in the audit of Glickle Ltd.'s tax return.

1-4 In the conduct of audits of financial statements, it would be a serious breach of responsibility if the auditor did not thoroughly understand accounting. However, many competent accountants do not have an understanding of the auditing process. What causes this difference?

1-5 What are the differences and similarities among audits of financial statements, compliance audits, and operational audits?

1-6 List five examples of specific operational audits that could be conducted by an internal auditor in a manufacturing company.

1-7 What are the major differences in the scope of the audit responsibilities for public accountants, auditors from the Auditor General's office, Canada Revenue Agency auditors, and internal auditors?

1-8 Distinguish the following three risks: risk-free interest rate, business risk, and information risk. Which one or ones does the auditor reduce by performing an audit?

1-9 Although the *CICA Handbook* standards provide general guidance, the application of these standards is dependent upon particular circumstances. In practice, a professional accountant may encounter situations where *CICA Handbook* standards do not exist or may not apply. Since there is no substitute for the exercise of professional judgment in the determination of what constitutes fair presentation and good practice, it has been suggested that too much effort is being directed toward the development of standards. Discuss the issues raised in the above statements. (CICA adapted)

1-10 What major characteristics of the organization and conduct of public accounting firms permit them to fulfill their social function competently and independently?

1-11 What roles are played by the CICA, the CGAAC, and the SMAC for their members?

1-12 What role do the *CICA Handbooks* have in the professional activities of public accountants in Canada?

1-13 Distinguish between generally accepted auditing standards and generally accepted accounting principles, and give two examples of each.

1-14 Explain the relationship among audit services, attestation services, and assurance services, and give examples of each.

1-15 How did business failures by Enron and WorldCom affect quality control procedures over PA firms in Canada and the U.S.?

1-16 What is meant by the term "quality control" as it relates to a public accounting firm?

1-17 State what is meant by the term "practice inspection." What are the implications of the term for the CA profession?

1-18 Select the best response for each question.

a. Which of the following *best* describes why an independent auditor is asked to express an opinion on the fair presentation of financial statements?

  (1) It is a customary courtesy for all shareholders of a company to receive an independent report on management's stewardship of the affairs of the business.

  (2) It is management's responsibility to seek available independent aid in the appraisal of the financial information shown in its financial statements.

  (3) The opinion of an independent party is needed because a company may *not* be objective with respect to its own financial statements.

  (4) It is difficult to prepare financial statements that fairly present a company's financial position and cash flow without the expertise of an independent auditor.

(AICPA adapted)

b. Operational audits generally have been conducted by internal auditors and governmental audit agencies but may be performed by public accountants. A primary purpose of an operational audit is to provide

  (1) a means of assurance that internal accounting controls are functioning as planned.

  (2) aid to the independent auditor, who is conducting the examination of the financial statements.

  (3) the results of internal examinations of financial and accounting matters to a company's top-level management.

  (4) a measure of management performance in meeting organizational goals.

c. Which of the following professional services would be considered an attestation engagement?

  (1) A consulting service engagement to provide computer processing advice to a client.

(2) An engagement to report on statutory requirements.

(3) An income tax engagement to prepare federal tax returns.

(4) the compilation of financial statements from a client's financial records.

d. A PA firm is reasonably assured of meeting its responsibility to provide services that conform with professional standards by

(1) adhering to generally accepted auditing standards.

(2) having an appropriate system of quality control.

(3) joining professional societies that enforce ethical conduct.

(4) maintaining an attitude of independence in its engagements.

e. Which of the following is an element of a PA firm's quality control system that should be considered in establishing its quality control policies and procedures?

(1) Complying with laws and regulations.

(2) Using statistical sampling techniques.

(3) Managing personnel.

(4) Considering audit risk and materiality.

DISCUSSION QUESTIONS AND PROBLEMS

1-19 Daniel Charon is the loan officer of the Georgian Bay Bank. Georgian Bay Bank has a loan of $540,000 outstanding from Regional Delivery Service Ltd., a company specializing in the delivery of products of all types on behalf of smaller companies. Georgian Bay's collateral on the loan consists of 20 small delivery trucks with an average original cost of $45,000.

Charon is concerned about the collectibility of the outstanding loan and whether the trucks still exist. He therefore engages Susan Virms, public accountant, to count the trucks, using registration information held by Charon. She is engaged because she spends most of her time auditing used automobile and truck dealerships and has extensive specialized knowledge about used trucks. Charon requests that Virms issue a report stating

1. which of the 20 trucks is parked in Regional's parking lot on the night of June 30.

2. the condition of each truck, using the categories of poor, good, and excellent.

3. the fair market value of each truck using the current "blue book" for trucks, which states the approximate wholesale prices of all used truck models based on the poor, good, and excellent categories.

Required

a. Identify which aspects of this narrative fit each of the following parts of the definition of auditing:

(1) information.

(2) established criteria.

(3) accumulates and evaluates evidence.

(4) competent, independent person.

(5) report of results.

b. Identify the greatest difficulties Virms is likely to have doing this assurance engagement.

1-20 In the normal course of performing their responsibilities, auditors frequently conduct examinations or reviews of the following:

1. Federal income tax returns of an officer of a corporation to determine whether he or she has included all taxable income in the return

2. Disbursements of a branch of the Canadian government for a special research project to determine whether the project was conducted effectively and efficiently

3. Computer operations of a corporation to evaluate whether the computer centre is being operated as efficiently as possible

4. Annual statements for the use of management

5. Operations of the Canada Revenue Agency to determine whether Canada Revenue Agency auditors are using their time efficiently in conducting audits

6. Statements for bankers and other creditors when the client is too small to have an accounting staff

7. Financial statements of a branch of the Canadian government to make sure the statements present fairly the actual disbursements made during a certain period

8. Federal income tax returns of a corporation to determine whether the tax laws have been followed

9. Financial statements for the use of shareholders when there is an internal audit staff

10. A bond indenture agreement to make sure a company is following all requirements of the contract

11. The computer operations of a large corporation to evaluate whether the internal controls are likely to prevent misstatements in accounting and operating data

12. Disbursements of a branch of the Canadian government for a special research project to determine whether the expenditures were consistent with the legislative bill that authorized the project

Required

For each of the examples, state the type of auditor (public accountant, Auditor General, Canada Revenue Agency, or internal) that would most likely be used and the type of audit (audit of financial statements, compliance audit, or operational) that would take place.

1-21 The following comments summarize the beliefs of some practitioners about quality control and practice inspection:

Quality control and practice inspection are quasi-governmental methods of regulating the profession. There are two effects of such regulation. First, it gives a competitive advantage to national PA firms because they already need formal structures to administer their complex organizations. Quality control requirements do not significantly affect their structure. Smaller firms now need a more costly organizational structure, which has proven unnecessary because of existing partner involvement on engagements. The major advantage smaller PA firms have traditionally had is a simple and efficient organizational structure. Now that advantage has been eliminated because of quality con-

trol requirements. Second, quality control and practice inspection are not needed to regulate the profession. Elements of quality control have always existed, at least informally, for quality firms. Three things already provide sufficient assurance that informal quality control elements are followed without practice inspection. They are competitive pressures to do quality work, legal liability for inadequate performance, and a code of professional ethics requiring that PAs follow generally accepted auditing standards.

Required
a. State the pros and cons of these comments.
b. Evaluate whether control requirements and practice inspection are worth their cost.

1-22 Consumers' Union is a non-profit organization that provides information and counsel on consumer goods and services. A major part of its function is the testing of different brands of consumer products that are purchased on the open market and then reporting the results of the tests in *Consumer Reports*, a monthly publication. Examples of the types of products it tests are middle-sized automobiles, residential dehumidifiers, canned tuna, and boys' jeans.

Required
a. In what ways are the services provided by Consumers Union similar to assurance services provided by PA firms?

b. Compare the concept of information risk introduced in this chapter with the information risk problem faced by a buyer of an automobile.
c. Compare the causes of information risk faced by users of financial statements as discussed in this chapter with those faced by a buyer of an automobile.
d. Compare the ways users of financial statements can reduce information risk with those available to a buyer of an automobile.

1-23 A small, but expanding, specialty home-products retailer recently implemented an Internet portal that allows customers to order merchandise online. In the first few months of operation, their Internet site attracted a large number of visitors; however, very few placed orders online. The retailer conducted several focus-group sessions with potential shoppers to identify reasons why shoppers were visiting the web site without placing orders. Shoppers in the focus group made these comments:

1. "I am nervous about doing business with this retailer because it is relatively unknown in the marketplace. How do I know the product descriptions on the web site are accurate, and that the stated return policies are followed?"
2. "I am reluctant to provide my credit card information online. How do I know the transmission of my personal

credit card information to the retailer's web site is protected?"
3. "Retailers are notorious for selling information about customers to others. The last thing I want to do is enter personal information online, such as my name, address, telephone number, and e-mail address. I am afraid this retailer will sell that information to third parties and then I'll be bombarded with a bunch of junk e-mail messages!"
4. "Web sites go down all the time due to system failures. How do I know the retailer's web site will be operating when I need it?"

Required
Discuss whether this situation provides an opportunity for PAs to address these customer concerns. How could a PA provide assistance?

1-24 In light of recent business failures, the public has expressed concern about the usefulness of the financial statement audit and the auditor's report. Because of these concerns, the accounting faculty at a local university has organized a panel to discuss the function of the auditor's report and the possible expansion of the auditor's responsibilities.

The faculty has invited a representative from industry, the investment community, the banking community, and you, a professional accountant in public practice, to sit on the panel.

You have noted the following excerpts from presentations by the other participants.

Mr. Don Bogart, Vice-President, Finance, Casablanca Industries: Our audit fees, in my opinion, are already far too high. I believe you should reconsider the need for increased auditor

involvement and perhaps even the need for an annual audit, which has become an unnecessary evil. If the auditor's role is to be expanded, something must be done to reduce the costs and maximize the benefits.

Ms. Elizabeth Ashton, Financial Analyst: I would be more comfortable if the independent auditor attested to business viability, management credibility, and future-oriented data. We question the relevance of audited financial statements to the decisions we have to make.

Mr. Richard Shivas, Senior Corporate Loan Officer: I agree with Elizabeth. In addition to historical-cost financial statements, we need current value and prospective information on which to base our decision. We would like more assurance from the auditor than is presently conveyed with the financial statement audit that the company will be able to turn its assets into profits. We are tired of hearing about problems when it is too late.

Required
Present your comments.

(CICA adapted)

PROFESSIONAL JUDGMENT PROBLEM

1-25 The Mobile Home Manufacturing Company is audited by Rossi and Montgomery, PAs. Mobile Home has decided to issue stock to the public and wants Rossi and Montgomery to perform all the audit work necessary to satisfy the requirements for filing with the OSC. The PA firm has never had a client go public before.

Required
a. What are the implications of Rossi and Montgomery's accepting the engagement?
b. List the additional issues confronting the auditors when they file with the OSC as compared to dealing with a regular audit client.

CASE

1-26 Raymonde, the owner of a small company, asked Holmes, public accountant, to conduct an audit of the company's records. Raymonde told Holmes that an audit is to be completed in time to submit audited financial statements to a bank as part of a loan application. Holmes immediately accepted the engagement and agreed to provide an auditor's report within three weeks. Raymonde agreed to pay Holmes a fixed fee plus a bonus if the loan was granted.

Holmes hired two accounting students to conduct the audit and spent several hours telling them exactly what to do. Holmes told the students not to spend time reviewing the controls but instead to concentrate on proving the mathematical accuracy of the ledger accounts, and summarizing the data in the accounting records that supported Raymonde's financial statements. The students followed Holmes' instructions and after two weeks gave Holmes the financial statements, which did not include footnotes. Holmes reviewed the statements and prepared an unqualified auditor's report. The report did not refer to generally accepted accounting principles.

Required
Briefly describe each of the generally accepted auditing standards and indicate how the actions of Holmes resulted in a failure to comply with each standard. Organize your answer as follows: Brief Description of GAAS; Holmes' Actions Resulting in Failure to Comply with GAAS.

(AICPA adapted)

CHAPTER 2

PROFESSIONAL RELATIONSHIPS

The public accountant is a professional who works with the audit committee, board of directors, management, and other professionals such as lawyers. In addition to providing a high quality of work, the public accountant is expected to be free from bias and to behave in an ethical manner. In this chapter, we will look at some of the issues and rules affecting the public accountant's behaviours in relationship with others.

LEARNING OBJECTIVES

After reading this chapter, you should be able to answer the following questions:

1. What are ethics and why are they important? How can I work through an ethical conflict (known as an ethical dilemma)?

2. How are public accountants different from other professionals? What is the role of a code of professional conduct in encouraging public accountant professional behaviour?

3. What are the facets of independence? How does the auditor's relationship with the audit committee affect independence? What are some of the key rules of professional conduct and how are they enforced?

COMPANY RESTATES FINANCIAL INFORMATION AT AUDITOR REQUEST

Electronic Data Systems Corporation (EDS) is an information technology service provider with an estimated $24 billion in revenue for 2004. The company is required to file its financial information with the SEC in the United States. For its third quarter financial statements, effective September 30, 2004, EDS disagreed with its auditors, KPMG LLP about the timing and write-off amount for one of its major accounts. KPMG also raised issues with EDS' audit committee about the quarterly bonus plan accruals for 2003 and 2004. These disagreements were reported in the public press because the disagreement resulted in a delay in releasing the third quarter financial statements.

This situation illustrates how important the audit committee is to the public accountant when dealing with disputes with management about the amounts to be recorded in the published financial statements. The EDS audit committee was able to use expert assistance to help resolve this disagreement between KPMG and EDS management. Auditors have a difficult job and are expected to perform their work with a high level of technical competence and integrity. By taking a solid stand with respect to accuracy and disclosure in the financial statements of EDS, KPMG set an example showing how quality financial statements can be provided to the investing public.

Sources: 1. "EDS settles dispute with its auditor," Toronto Star, p. E5, November 17, 2004. 2. Electronic Data Systems Corporation, www.eds.com, Form 8-K (November 3, 2004 and November 15, 2004), Accessed: January 5, 2005.

How do you feel when someone disagrees with you? Are you able to sit back and discuss things reasonably? Have you ever prepared a tax return and included figures that were unsubstantiated? This would be against the rules of professional conduct. Do you believe there are "grey" areas of behaviour—where you are uncertain how you might behave in a given circumstance? Now is a good time to decide what you think is ethical and what is not.

In the previous chapter, we discussed the nature of auditing and the demand for audit and other assurance services. The value of the audit report and the demand for audit services depend on public confidence in the independence and integrity of PAs as they conduct their work. This chapter discusses ethics and the independence and other ethical requirements for CAs and CGAs under professional rules of conduct.

→2.1 ETHICAL BEHAVIOUR IS A CORNERSTONE OF TRUST
What Are Ethics?

Ethics can be defined broadly as a set of moral principles or values. Each of us has such a set of values, although we may or may not have considered them explicitly. Philosophers, religious organizations, and other groups have defined, in various ways, ideal sets of moral principles or values. Examples of prescribed sets of moral principles or values at the implementation level include laws and regulations, church doctrine, codes of business ethics for professional groups such as CAs, CGAs, and CMAs, and codes of conduct within individual organizations such as accounting firms, corporations, and universities.

ETHICS—a set of moral principles or values

An example of ethical principles is included in Figure 2-1 on page 34. These principles were developed by combining principles developed by the Josephson Institute of Ethics (a non-profit organization focused on ethical quality) with ethical standards published by both an international coaching organization and a technical journal. A search of the Internet will reveal thousands of sites with published ethical standards.

It is common for people to differ in their moral principles or values and the relative importance they attach to these principles. These differences reflect life experiences, successes and failures, and the influences of parents, teachers, religious organizations, and friends.

Need for Ethics Ethical behaviour is necessary for a society to function in an orderly manner. It can be argued that ethics is the glue that holds a society together. Imagine, for example, what would happen if we couldn't depend on the people we deal with to be honest. If parents, teachers, employers, siblings, coworkers, and friends all consistently lied, it would be almost impossible for effective communication to occur.

The need for ethics in society is sufficiently important that many commonly held ethical values are incorporated into laws. However, many of the ethical values found in Figure 2-1 cannot be incorporated into laws because of the judgmental nature of certain values. This does not imply, though, that the principles are less important for an orderly society.

Why People Act Unethically Most people define unethical behaviour as conduct that differs from what they believe would have been appropriate given the circumstances. Each of us decides what constitutes ethical behaviour. It is important to understand what causes people to act in a manner that we decide is unethical.

There are two primary reasons why people act unethically: the person's ethical standards are different from those of society as a whole, or the person chooses to act selfishly. In many instances, both reasons exist.

PERSON'S ETHICAL STANDARDS DIFFER FROM GENERAL SOCIETY Extreme examples of people whose behaviour violates almost everyone's ethical standards are drug dealers, bank robbers, and larcenists. Most people who commit such acts feel no remorse when they are apprehended because their ethical standards differ from those of society as a whole.

There are also many far less extreme examples where others violate our ethical values. When people cheat on their tax returns, treat other people with hostility, lie on employment applications, or perform below their competence level as employees, most of us regard that as unethical behaviour. If the other person has decided that this behaviour is ethical and acceptable, there is a conflict of ethical values that is unlikely to be resolved.

THE PERSON CHOOSES TO ACT SELFISHLY The difference between ethical standards that differ from general society's and acting selfishly is illustrated in the following example. Person A finds a briefcase in an airport containing important papers and $1,000. He tosses the briefcase and keeps the money. He brags to his family and friends about his good fortune. Person A's values probably differ from most of society's. Person B faces the same situation but responds differently. He keeps the money but leaves the briefcase in a conspicuous place. He tells nobody and spends the money on a new wardrobe. It is likely that Person B has violated his own ethical standards, but he has decided that the money was too important to pass up. He has chosen to act selfishly. What would you do? Shouldn't the briefcase in its entirety be returned?

A considerable portion of unethical behaviour results from selfish behaviour. Political scandals result from the desire for political power; cheating on tax returns and expense reports is motivated by financial greed; performing below one's competence and cheating on tests are typically due to laziness. In each case, the person knows that the behaviour is inappropriate but chooses to do it anyway because of the personal sacrifice needed to act ethically.

Ethical Dilemmas

ETHICAL DILEMMA—a situation in which a decision must be made about the appropriate behaviour

An **ethical dilemma** is a situation a person faces in which a decision must be made about the appropriate behaviour. A simple example of an ethical dilemma is finding a diamond ring, which necessitates deciding whether to attempt to find the owner or to keep it. A far more difficult ethical dilemma to resolve is the following one; it is the type of case that might be used in an ethics course:

Qin Zhang is the in-charge on the September 30, 2004 audit of Paquette Forest Products Inc., a forest products company that produces lumber and paper products in northern Manitoba. The company employs 375 people and is the main employer in the remote town of Duck Lake, Manitoba; the other businesses in Duck Lake provide goods and services to Paquette Forest Products and its employees. In the course of the audit, Qin discovers that the company has had a number of failures of the equipment that removes the sulphuric acid from the paper production process, and as a result, thousands of litres of untreated water have been dumped into the Loon River and Duck Lake. Qin learns that the cost of replacing the equipment so that no further spills are likely is much more than the company can afford and that if ordered to replace the equipment by the environment ministry, the company would be forced to cease operations. What should Qin do?

Auditors, accountants, and other business people face many ethical dilemmas in their business careers. Dealing with a client who threatens to seek a new auditor unless an unqualified opinion is issued presents a serious ethical dilemma if an unqualified opinion is inappropriate. Deciding whether to confront a supervisor who has materially overstated departmental revenues as a means of receiving a larger bonus is a difficult ethical dilemma. Continuing to be a part of the management of a company that harasses and mistreats employees or treats customers dishonestly is a moral dilemma, especially if the person has a family to support and the job market is tight. Deciding whether or not to report negligence of a supervisor to a partner is a problem young staff accountants may face.

Rationalizing Unethical Behaviour There are alternative ways to resolve ethical dilemmas, but care must be taken to avoid methods that are rationalizations of unethical behaviour. The following are rationalization methods commonly employed that can easily result in unethical conduct:

1. *Everybody does it.* The argument that it is acceptable to falsify tax returns, cheat on exams, or sell defective products is commonly based on the rationalization that everyone else is doing it and therefore it is acceptable.
2. *If it's legal, it's ethical.* Using the argument that all legal behaviour is ethical relies heavily on the perfection of laws. Under this philosophy, one would have no obligation to return a lost object unless the other person could prove that it was his or hers.
3. *Likelihood of discovery and consequences.* This philosophy relies on evaluating the likelihood that someone else will discover the behaviour. Typically, the person also assesses the severity of the penalty (consequences) if there is a discovery. An example is deciding whether to correct an unintentional overbilling to a customer when the customer has already paid the full billing. If the seller believes the customer will detect the error and respond by not buying in the future, the seller will inform the customer now; otherwise the seller will wait to see if the customer complains.

Resolving Ethical Dilemmas In recent years, formal frameworks have been developed to help people resolve ethical dilemmas. The purpose of such a framework is to identify the ethical issues and decide on an appropriate course of action using the person's own values. The six-step approach that follows is intended to be a relatively simple approach to resolving ethical dilemmas:

1. Obtain the relevant facts.
2. Identify the ethical issues from the facts.
3. Determine who is affected by the outcome of the dilemma and how each person or group is affected.
4. Identify the alternatives available to the person who must resolve the dilemma.
5. Identify the likely consequence of each alternative.
6. Decide on the appropriate action.

An illustration is used to demonstrate how a person might use this six-step approach to resolve an ethical dilemma.

Ethical Dilemma Bryan Longview has been working six months as a staff assistant for De Souza & Shah, public accountants. Currently he is assigned to the audit of Reyon Manufacturing Corp. under the supervision of Karen Van Staveren, an experienced audit senior. There are three auditors assigned to the audit, including Karen, Bryan, and a more experienced assistant, Martha Mills. During lunch on the first day, Karen says, "It will be necessary for us to work a few extra hours on our own time to make sure we come in on budget. This audit isn't very profitable anyway, and we don't want to hurt our firm by going over budget. We can accomplish this easily by coming in a half hour early, taking a short lunch break, and working an hour or so after normal quitting time. We just won't write that time down on our time report." Bryan recalls reading in the firm's policy manual that working hours and not charging for them on the time report is a violation of De Souza & Shah's employment policy. He also knows that seniors are paid bonuses, instead of overtime, whereas staff are paid for overtime but get no bonuses. Later, when discussing the issue with Martha, she says, "Karen does this on all of her jobs. She is likely to be our firm's next audit manager. The partners think she's great because her jobs always come in under budget. She rewards us by giving us good engagement evaluations, especially under the cooperative attitude category. Several of the other audit seniors follow the same practice."

Resolving the Ethical Dilemma Using the Six-Step Approach

RELEVANT FACTS There are three key facts in this situation that deal with the ethical issue and how the issue will likely be resolved:

- The staff person has been informed he will work hours without recording them as hours worked.
- Firm policy prohibits this practice.
- Another staff person has stated that this practice is common practice for Karen and also for other seniors in the firm.

ETHICAL ISSUE The ethical issue in this situation is not difficult to identify.

- Is it ethical for Bryan to work hours and not record them as hours worked in this situation?

WHO IS AFFECTED AND HOW IS EACH AFFECTED? There are typically more people affected in situations where ethical dilemmas occur than might be expected. The following are the key persons involved in this situation:

Who	How Affected
Bryan	Being asked to violate firm policy. Hours of work will be affected. Pay will be affected. Performance evaluations may be affected. Attitude about firm may be affected.
Martha	Same as Bryan.
Karen	Success on engagement and in firm may be affected. Hours of work will be affected.
De Souza & Shah	Stated firm policy is being violated. May result in underbilling clients in current and future engagements. May affect firm's ability to realistically budget engagements and bill clients, thus violating quality control procedures as specified in *CICA Handbook* Section 5030.23. May affect the firm's ability to motivate and retain employees.
Audit staff assigned to Reyon Manufacturing Corp. in the future	May result in unrealistic time budgets. May result in unfavourable time performance evaluations. May result in pressures to continue practice of not charging for hours worked.
Other staff in De Souza & Shah	Following the practice on this engagement may motivate others to follow the same practice on other engagements, resulting in a poor ethical climate at the firm.

- Refuse to work the additional hours.
- Perform in the manner requested.
- Inform Karen that he will work the additional hours and will charge the additional hours to the engagement.
- Talk to a manager or partner about Karen's request.
- Contact the designated whistle-blowing partner.
- Refuse to work on the engagement.
- Quit working for the firm.

Each of these options includes a potential consequence, the worst likely one being termination by the firm.

Focus Box 2-1

HELPING OUT THE WHISTLE BLOWER

Poor Bryan—in our ethical dilemma example, he is stuck in a quagmire of individuals who are not following his firm's policies. There is help in *CICA Handbook* Standards, though. Section GSF-QC, paragraphs 103 to 107 explain how situations of non-compliance with the firm's system of quality control should be handled to avoid reprisals.

Recording time worked accurately is a firm policy that directly affects quality of planning for an engagement, which would affect the ability of the firm to conduct a high quality audit. Employees need a risk-free way to report peer pressure or other forms of violations, such as field work disputes. This could be accomplished by having a designated standards partner available for anonymous discussion, or having a toll-free number or third-party organization handle the complaints and then notify the appropriate individuals in the organization for action.

The firm needs to establish a protocol, provide clear, risk-free reporting mechanisms, and have an oversight group or individual track and resolve items reported. The oversight group needs to have sufficient authority to query and resolve items that are brought to its attention. For example, with prompt action, Bryan's partner on this engagement could be asked to visit the client at 5:30 p.m., and remind Karen that the firm is taking a solid stand on its time recording policies given the new quality control standards that were implemented in 2004.

Sources: 1. Murdock, Hernan, "Early Warning System," *Internal Auditor*, August 2003, pp. 57–61. 2. Moulton, Gary, "Safe Disclosure," *CAmagazine*, October 2003, pp. 20–27.

CONSEQUENCES OF EACH ALTERNATIVE In deciding the consequences of each alternative, it is essential to evaluate both the short- and long-term effects. There is a natural tendency to emphasize the short term because those consequences will occur quickly, even when the long-term consequences may be more important. For example, consider the potential consequences if Bryan decides to work the additional hours and not report them. In the short term, he will likely get good evaluations for cooperation and perhaps a salary increase. In the longer term, what will be the effect of not reporting the hours this time when other ethical conflicts arise? Consider the following similar ethical dilemmas Bryan might face in his career as he advances:

- An audit firm supervisor asks Bryan to work three unreported hours daily and 15 each weekend.
- An audit firm supervisor asks Bryan to initial certain audit procedures as having been performed when they were not.
- Bryan concludes that he cannot be promoted to manager unless he persuades assistants to work hours that they do not record.
- Management of a client informs Bryan, who is now a partner, that either the company gets an unqualified opinion for a $40,000 audit fee or the company will change auditors.
- Management of a client informs Bryan that the audit fee will be increased by $25,000 if Bryan can find a plausible way to increase earnings by $1 million.

Notice how each dilemma is more serious than the one preceding it; the penalty that Bryan would face if he were to be caught grows more severe as the dilemma grows more serious. In short, if Bryan agrees to work the additional hours and not report them, he has put himself on a slippery slope that grows ever steeper.

APPROPRIATE ACTION Only Bryan can decide the appropriate option to select in the circumstances after considering his ethical values and the likely consequences of each option. At one extreme, Bryan could decide that the only relevant consequence is the potential impact on his career. Most of us would conclude that Bryan is an unethical person if he follows that course. At the other extreme, Bryan can decide to refuse to work for a firm that permits even one supervisor to violate firm policies. Many people would consider such an extreme reaction naive.

→2.2 PROFESSIONAL ETHICS AND PRINCIPLES OF CONDUCT
Special Need for Ethical Conduct in Professions

Our society has attached a special meaning to the term "professional." A professional is expected to conduct himself or herself at a higher level than most other members of society. For example, when the press reports that a physician, clergyperson, member of Parliament, or CA, CGA, or CMA has been indicted for a crime, most people feel more disappointment than when the same thing happens to people who are not labelled as professionals.

The term "professional" carries a responsibility for conduct that extends beyond satisfying the person's responsibilities to himself or herself and beyond the requirements of our society's laws and regulations. A CA, CGA, or CMA in public practice, as a professional, recognizes a responsibility to the public, to the client, and to fellow practitioners, including honourable behaviour, even if that means personal sacrifice.

The underlying reason for a high level of professional conduct by any profession is the need for *public confidence* in the quality of service by the profession, regardless of the individual providing it. For the professional public accountant, it is essential that the client and external financial statement users have confidence in the quality of audits and other services. If users of services do not have confidence in physicians, judges, or public accountants, the ability of those professionals to serve clients and the public effectively is diminished.

It is not practical for users to evaluate the performance of professional services because of their *complexity*. A patient cannot be expected to evaluate whether an operation was properly performed. A financial statement user cannot be expected to evaluate audit performance. Most users have neither the competence nor the time for such an evaluation. Public confidence in the quality of professional services is enhanced when the profession encourages high standards of performance and conduct on the part of all practitioners.

In recent years, increased competition has made it more difficult for public accountants and many other professionals to conduct themselves in a professional manner. Increased competition sometimes makes public accounting firms more concerned about keeping clients and maintaining a reasonable profit. Because of the increased competition, many public accounting firms have implemented philosophies and practices that are frequently referred to as *improved business practices*. These include such things as improved recruiting and personnel practices, better office management, and more effective advertising and other promotional methods. Public accounting firms are also attempting to become more efficient in doing audits in a variety of ways, for example, through the use of computers, effective audit planning, and careful assignment of staff.

These changes are desirable as long as they do not interfere with the conduct of CAs, CGAs, or CMAs as professionals.

Difference Between Public Accounting Firms and Other Professionals
Public accounting firms have a different relationship with users of financial statements than most other professionals have with the users of their services. Lawyers, for example, are typically engaged and paid by a client and have primary responsibility to be an advocate for that client. Public accounting firms are engaged by management for private companies and the audit committee for public companies and are paid by the company issuing the financial statements,

but the primary beneficiaries of the audit are statement users. Often, the auditor doesn't know or have contact with the statement users but has frequent meetings and ongoing relationships with client personnel.

It is essential that users regard such public accounting firms as competent and unbiased. If users were to believe that such public accounting firms do not perform a valuable service (reduce information risk), the value of and demand for those firms' audit and other attestation reports would be reduced. There is, therefore, considerable incentive for public accounting firms to conduct themselves at a high professional level.

Ways Professional Accountants in Public Practice Are Encouraged to Conduct Themselves Professionally

There are several ways in which society and the public accounting professions encourage those in public practice to conduct themselves appropriately and to do high-quality audits and related services. Figure 2-2 shows the most important ways. Several of these were discussed in Chapter 1, including GAAS requirements and the Recommendations of the *CICA Handbooks*, professional examinations, quality control, the CPAB and provincial securities commissions, practice inspection, and continuing education. The ability of individuals to sue public accounting firms also exerts considerable influence on the way practitioners conduct themselves and audits. Legal liability is studied in Chapter 4. The *code of professional conduct* of the public accountant's respective accounting body also has a significant influence on the practitioner. It is meant to provide a standard of conduct for members of that body. These codes, some of their more important tenets, and related issues of professional conduct are the content of the remainder of this chapter.

Code of Professional Conduct

A code of conduct can consist of *general statements* of ideal conduct or *specific rules* that define unacceptable behaviour. The advantage of general statements is the emphasis on positive activities that encourage a high level of performance. The disadvantage is the difficulty of enforcing general ideals because there are no minimum standards of behaviour. The advantage of carefully defined specific rules is the enforceability of minimum behaviour and performance standards. The disadvantage is the tendency of some practitioners to define the rules as maximum rather than minimum standards. A second disadvantage is that some practitioners may view the code as the law and conclude that if some action is not prohibited, it must be ethical. A practitioner must consider the intent of the code in addressing whether a particular action is acceptable or not.

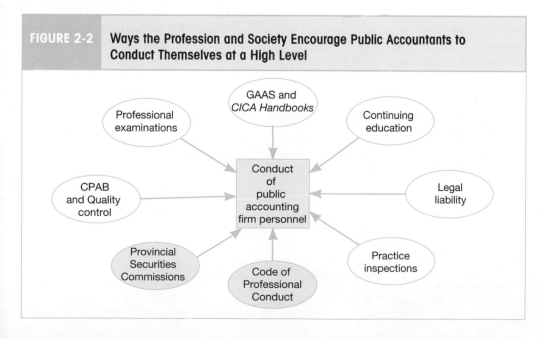

FIGURE 2-2   Ways the Profession and Society Encourage Public Accountants to Conduct Themselves at a High Level

A professional code of conduct serves both the members of the body promulgating the code and the public. It serves members by setting standards the members must meet and providing a benchmark against which the members will be measured by their peers. The public is served because the code provides a list of the standards to which the members of the body should adhere and helps determine expectations of members' behaviour.

The provincial institutes and Quebec *ordre* of chartered accountants determine the rules of professional conduct for members and students of that provincial institute or *ordre*. The provincial institutes and *ordre* have harmonized their rules of professional conduct so that, generally, the same set of rules applies to all CAs in Canada. Certain rules (e.g., confidentiality, which is discussed below) apply to students as well as to members. All of the rules apply to members in public practice, while a smaller number also apply to members who are not engaged in the practice of public accounting.

The rules of conduct for certified general accountants are determined by the CGAAC and apply to all CGAs and CGA students in Canada; the provincial associations are charged with administering the code and have the power to amend and add to this national code of conduct. The principles and rules of conduct apply to all members, although certain rules are specific to public practitioners. We will restrict the remainder of our discussion to rules of conduct of CGAs and Ontario CAs (as an example of provincial rules of conduct).

Generally the codes of conduct have attempted to accomplish both the objectives of general statements of ideal conduct and of specific rules. For example, there are three parts to the *Rules of Professional Conduct* of the Institute of Chartered Accountants of Ontario: principles that are stated in broad terms, the rules themselves, and interpretation of the rules. Figure 2-3 is illustrative. The parts are listed in order of increasing specificity: the principles provide ideal standards of conduct, whereas ethical rulings are more specific, and the interpretations are very specific.

Principles of Professional Conduct The principles generally are characteristics that the professional body deems desirable in its members. An organization is judged by the behaviour of its members; therefore, one principle would be that members behave in a way that enhances the reputation of all the members. Members should act *ethically* and in a way that will serve the *public interest.* When the courts discipline a member of a profession, the profession's reputation suffers along with that of the member. It is a mistake to think that only the member loses his or her reputation in such a situation.

Other common principles are that members act with *integrity and due care* in the performance of their professional activities, that they maintain (i.e., keep current) their professional competence, that they do not undertake work for which they lack the necessary competence, and that they behave in a professional way toward colleagues. The accountant must maintain *confidentiality* with respect to the affairs and business of the client. There is one principle that relates more specifically to public accountants: the accountant should ensure that he or she maintains an *independent or objective state of mind* when providing assurance services (e.g., audits or reviews) for clients.

FIGURE 2-3	Code of Professional Conduct

Principles	Ideal standards of ethical conduct stated in philosophical terms. They are not enforceable.
Rules of conduct	Minimum standards of ethical conduct stated as specific rules. They are enforceable.
Interpretations	Interpretations of the rules of conduct. They are not enforceable, but a practitioner must justify departure.

A careful examination of these principles will indicate that most are applicable to any professional, not just professional accountants. For example, physicians should behave in a way that is not discreditable to their profession, they should act ethically and in a way that serves the public interest, and they should exercise integrity and due care. Physicians should maintain their professional competence and behave in a professional way toward their colleagues. They should not breach their clients' confidentiality. One difference between auditors and other professionals, as discussed earlier, is that most professionals need not be concerned about remaining independent.

These principles will be explored more fully in the balance of this chapter.

Rules of Conduct The discussion that follows will consider some of the more important rules of conduct followed by public accountants in Canada. A student interested in obtaining a particular professional designation (e.g., CA, CGA, or CMA) should refer to and become familiar with the specific rules of conduct of the body to which he or she seeks admission.

As was mentioned previously, while all the rules discussed below apply to members of the professional accounting bodies in public practice, some of the rules discussed do not apply to members who are not engaged in the practice of public accounting.

Figure 2-3 indicated that while principles are not enforceable, the rules of conduct are. For that reason, the rules of conduct of the accounting bodies are stated in more precise language than the principles can be. Because of their enforceability, the rules are often called *Rules* or *Code of Professional Conduct*.

At what level do practitioners conduct themselves in practice? As in any profession, the level varies among practitioners. Some operate at high levels, whereas others operate as close to the minimum level as possible. Unfortunately, some also conduct themselves below the minimum level set by the profession.

Interpretations of Rules of Conduct The need for published interpretations of the rules of conduct arises when there are frequent questions from practitioners about a particular rule. The various institutes and *ordre* of chartered accountants issue interpretations of certain rules of conduct together with the rules themselves. Interpretations are not officially enforceable, but a departure from the interpretations would be difficult, if not impossible, for a practitioner to justify in a disciplinary hearing.

Applicability of the Rules of Conduct As was mentioned previously, the rules of conduct for CAs and CGAs specifically state that while the rules are for all CAs and CGAs respectively, certain rules, because of their nature, may not apply to members who are not in public practice.

It would be a violation of the rules if someone did something on behalf of a member that would have been a violation if the member had done it. An example is a banker who states in a newsletter that Johnson and Able, public accountants, have the best tax department in the province and consistently get large refunds for their tax clients. This is likely to create false or unjustified expectations and is a violation of both the CA and CGA rules of conduct.

A member is also responsible for compliance with the rules by employees and partners.

Definitions A few definitions must be understood to minimize misinterpretation of the rules to be discussed shortly.

- *Client*—the person(s) or entity that retains a member or his or her firm, engaged in the practice of public accounting, for the performance of professional services.
- *Firm*—a proprietorship or partnership engaged in the practice of public accounting, including individual partners thereof.
- *Member*—a member of the Canadian Institute of Chartered Accountants (and a provincial institute or *ordre*) or of the Certified General Accountants Association of Canada (and a provincial association).
- *Practice of public accounting*—holding out to be a public accountant and at the same time performing for a client one or more types of services rendered by public accountants.

Summary of the Basic Components of a Code of Conduct The intent of this section is to discuss several rules of conduct that are fundamental to the practice of public accounting. As such, they are found in differing forms and to differing degrees in the rules of professional conduct of CAs and CGAs. It must be pointed out that the rules of conduct governing the behaviour of these two groups of professionals are much more extensive and detailed than the ensuing discussion. For more detail, refer to the specific rules of conduct of these associations.

→ 2.3 PROFESSIONAL RULES OF CONDUCT FOR THE PUBLIC ACCOUNTANT

Independence

Generally, the rules of conduct promulgated by the accounting bodies require their members who are engaged in the practice of public accounting to be independent when they perform certain functions. For example, the rules require that auditors of historical financial statements be independent. **Independence** is also required for other types of attestation engagements such as review engagements.

INDEPENDENCE—impartiality in performing professional services

Independence in auditing means taking an *unbiased viewpoint* in the performance of audit tests, the evaluation of the results, and the issuance of the auditor's report. If the auditor is an advocate for the client, a particular banker, or anyone else, he or she cannot be considered independent. Independence must certainly be regarded as the auditor's most critical characteristic. The reason that many diverse users are willing to rely upon the professional public accountant's reports as to the fairness of financial statements is their expectation of an unbiased viewpoint.

Not only is it essential that professional public accountants maintain an independent attitude in fulfilling their responsibilities, but it is also important that the users of financial statements have confidence in that independence. These two objectives are frequently identified as independence in fact and independence in appearance. **Independence in fact** exists when the auditor is actually able to maintain an unbiased attitude throughout the audit, whereas **independence in appearance** is the result of others' interpretation of this independence. If auditors are independent in fact but users believe them to be advocates for the client, most of the benefit of the audit function will be lost.

INDEPENDENCE IN FACT—the auditor's ability to take an unbiased viewpoint in the performance of professional services

INDEPENDENCE IN APPEARANCE—the auditor's ability to maintain an unbiased viewpoint *in the eyes of others*

The Facets of Independence

In response to the recent financial statement and management frauds, the CA provincial and *ordre* professional codes of conduct have adopted very specific rules of conduct with respect to independence, while the CGA rules remain more general. These rules are considered a foundation of having public trust, since objectivity in an engagement relies upon auditor independence. We will discuss more specific rules where they exist.

When deciding to accept a client or whether to continue an existing engagement, the PA is required to examine five facets of independence: *self-interest threat, self-review threat, advocacy threat, familiarity threat,* and *intimidation threat.* The PA is to assess threats to the facets when they exist and document the safeguards that were used to reduce the threats to an acceptable level. Table 2-1 lists threats to the five facets of independence with examples. Table 2-2 on page 44 describes safeguards that the firm can implement to either eliminate the threats or reduce them to an acceptable level.

SELF-INTEREST THREAT—A threat to independence where the member has a financial interest in the client or in the financial results of the client

ADVOCACY THREAT—A threat to independence where the firm or member is perceived to promote (or actually does promote) the client's position

SELF-REVIEW THREAT—A threat to independence where the public accountant is in the position of having to audit his or her own work during the period

It is obvious that some of the threats affect overall independence—if you own shares in your client's business (**self-interest threat**) or are trying to help them obtain financing (**advocacy threat**) you stand to gain from the result of the financial statement audit.

Some people have more difficulty seeing the impact of other threats. With the **self-review threat** you are auditing your own work. Imagine that you have assisted the client in designing an information system that calculates the costs for an inventory system. The new system seems to be working well and there are excellent reports that track inventory movement and out-of-stock situations. However, during the design phase, you neglected to put in controls to highlight when the system creates a negative inventory situation, either due to clerical error or programming error.

TABLE 2-1	Facets of independence

Threat to Facet	Examples
Self-interest threat—when the member has a financial interest in the client or in the financial results of the client.	The firm or member owns shares in or has a loan to the client. The client fees are significant in relation to the total fee base of the PA or of the firm.
Self-review threat—when the PA is placed in the position of having to audit his or her own work during the audit.	PA prepared original data or records for the client as part of a bookkeeping engagement. PA designed and implemented an accounting information system used to process client records.
Advocacy threat—when the firm or member is perceived to promote (or actually does promote) the client's position.	PA is acting as an advocate in resolving a dispute with a major creditor of the client. The firm or PA is promoting the sale of shares or other securities for the client, or is receiving a commission for such sales.
Familiarity threat—occurs when it is difficult to behave with professional skepticism during the engagement.	There is a long association of senior staff with the client (e.g., being on the engagement for ten years). A former partner of the firm is now the chief financial officer of the client.
Intimidation threat—the client intimidates the firm or its staff with respect to the content of the financial statements or with respect to the conduct of the audit.	The client threatens to replace the audit firm over a disclosure disagreement. The client places a maximum upon the audit fee that is unrealistic with respect to the amount of work that needs to be completed.

What would you do during the audit? Perhaps you would be less likely to point this error out to the client in a management letter because it would imply that you did not properly perform your work during the system design. Alternatively, you might not detect the system inadequacy during your analysis of internal controls because you believe that it is such an excellent system that you do not complete a detailed analysis of internal controls. This example shows how a self-review threat can be very dangerous to the completion of a quality audit engagement.

With a **familiarity threat**, it may be that you were the audit junior on a job, worked as an assistant, then were promoted to supervisor and manager, and are now a partner. You've worked with the client for fifteen years, and it seems that you know the strengths and weaknesses of all of the employees, junior and executive alike. You may take it for granted that they are doing their job just as well this year as they did last year. However, you do not know that the Controller is going through a messy divorce and the vice-president of Finance has started gambling. They are both short of money, giving them an incentive to manipulate the records and steal money from the company. The actual financial manipulation could lead to **intimidation threat**—where the senior accounting personnel expect you to overlook their manipulation or lose the audit. You have known these individuals for fifteen years and think of them as friends, so what is a little financial statement manipulation among friends?

The independence rule situations listed in Table 2-3 on page 45 help prevent independence threats from occurring. Some rules apply to all assurance engagements (e.g., financial statement audit and review for businesses of all sizes) while others apply only to an entity listed on a stock exchange with total market capitalization greater than $10 million, called a **listed entity**.

In addition to the specifics described in Table 2-3, where the member or firm is not allowed to complete the engagement, there are situations where only the person affected is to be excluded from the engagement team. These situations include where the student or member:

FAMILIARITY THREAT—A threat to independence that occurs when it is difficult to behave with professional skepticism during the engagement

INTIMIDATION THREAT—A threat to independence that occurs when the client intimidates the firm or its staff with respect to the content of the financial statements or with respect to the conduct of the audit.

LISTED ENTITY—an entity whose debt or shares is listed on a stock exchange and that has market capitalization and total assets greater than $10 million

TABLE 2-2	Safeguards to Independence	
Safeguard Category	**Examples**	
Created by the profession, or provided in legislation or securities exchange regulation	Education and training provided by the professional accounting body. Practice review provided by the professional accounting body or by the CPAB.	
Provided by the client	A qualified, independent audit committee. A corporate code of ethics that provides for disclosure and resolution of conflicts. Competent client personnel.	
Available within the firm's systems and procedures	Firm policies and procedures that promote awareness and ensure compliance for independence. Rotation of senior personnel on client engagements.	

- has a loan to or guarantees a loan to the client;
- has an immediate family member as a director, officer, or employee that can exert control over the engagement, or is in an accounting role; or
- was an employee in a financial oversight position with the client during the duration of the audit.

At the engagement level, independence rules for listed clients include the mandatory rotation of senior personnel (with reinstatement provisions after two years) as follows: the engagement partner and quality control partner after five years; other partners who provide more than ten hours of service after seven years. All services to a listed client must be approved by the audit committee.

A practical way for a PA to document the independence rules for each engagement is to fill in a checklist. A checklist actively states that the rules have been followed for the engagement and clearly identifies action taken where threats exist with a conclusion stated for each engagement. This helps ensure that the assessment of independence is part of the quality assurance process for each engagement.

It seems from the above list that it would be difficult for a PA to provide comprehensive services to a client! What if you work for a small practice where the bulk of the work is accounting, bookkeeping, and review engagements? How is your work affected? Assuming that you and the other members of the firm have adequately addressed the five facets of independence, the primary practical concerns would be familiarity and self-review. There should be periodic change of staff at a client, where possible, and all transactions and journal entries should be discussed with and approved by the client before being processed.

Independence is far broader than simply preventing a financial interest, such as owning shares in a client. For the PA to be truly independent, all five facets must be considered and addressed for each engagement.

AUDIT COMMITTEE—selected members of a client's board of directors, who provide a forum for the auditors to remain independent of management

Audit Committee An **audit committee** is a selected number of members of a company's board of directors who provide a forum that is independent of management for both the external and internal auditors. Most audit committees are made up of three to five or sometimes as many as seven directors. Incorporating acts generally require that the majority of the committee must be outside directors (i.e., not part of company management).

A typical audit committee decides such things as which public accounting firm to retain and the scope of services the public accounting firm is to perform. The audit committee also meets with the public accounting firm to discuss the progress and findings of the audit and helps resolve conflicts between the public accounting firm and management. Many of the same comments could be made about the audit committee and the internal auditors.

Most organizations that have debt or securities listed on a Canadian or American stock exchange (regardless of size) are required to have an audit committee consisting of at least three independent members who are also directors of the organization. Members of the audit committee are also required to be financially literate.

	Applicability of Independence Rules			

TABLE 2-3   **Applicability of Independence Rules**

Independence Rule Situation	Prohibited Engagements if Situation Applies During Term of Engagement			
	Audit of Listed Entity	Audit of Non-listed Entity	Other Assurance Engagement (e.g., review)	Non-assurance Service
Direct or indirect financial interest	X	X	X	X
Exerts control over the entity	X	X	X	
Has a loan from or has a loan guaranteed by the entity (except in normal course of business; e.g., a bank)	X	X	X	
Close business relationship	X	X	X	
Engagement staff accepted financial related position at client within the last year	X			
Member of firm is officer or director	X	X	X	
Management decisions were made	X	X	X	
Prepared or changed originating source data or journal entry without management approval	X	X	X	
Accounting or bookkeeping services	X			
Valuation services provided	X			
Actuarial services provided	X			
Internal audit services provided	X			
Financial information systems design or implementation	X			
Expert opinion or service	X			
Legal services	X	X	X	
Human resources for senior positions	X			
Corporate finance services	X	X	X	

Note: Not all situations are listed. Please consult the rules of conduct at www.icao.on.ca for more details.

The auditor has the right to attend meetings of the audit committee and to call meetings if he or she feels they are necessary. Directors who become aware of *any* misstatements in issued financial statements must notify the auditor and the audit committee of the misstatements.

Aids to Maintaining Independence The accounting profession and society, especially in the past decade, have been concerned about ensuring that (1) auditors maintain an unbiased attitude in performing their work (independence in fact) and (2) users perceive auditors as being independent (independence in appearance). Many of the elements shown in Figure 2-2 and other requirements or inducements encourage public accountants to maintain independence in fact and appearance. These are now briefly summarized.

LEGAL LIABILITY The penalty involved when a court concludes that a practitioner is not independent can be severe, including criminal action. The courts have certainly provided major incentives for auditors to remain independent. Legal liability is studied in Chapter 4.

RULES OF PROFESSIONAL CONDUCT The existing rules of conduct restrict public accountants in their financial and business relationships with clients.

GENERALLY ACCEPTED AUDITING STANDARDS The general standards require the auditor to maintain an objective state of mind in all matters related to the assignment.

PUBLIC ACCOUNTING FIRM QUALITY CONTROL STANDARDS Most public accounting firms establish policies and procedures to provide reasonable assurance that all personnel are independent.

AUDIT COMMITTEE An audit committee, as was recently discussed, can help auditors remain independent of management.

SHOPPING FOR ACCOUNTING PRINCIPLES Management may consult with other accountants on the application of accounting principles. Although consultation with other accountants is an appropriate practice, it can lead to a loss of independence in certain circumstances. For example, suppose one public accounting firm replaces the existing auditors on the strength of accounting advice offered but later finds facts and circumstances that require the public accounting firm to change its stance. It may be difficult for the new public accounting firm to remain independent in such a situation. The Auditing and Assurance Standards Board issued Section 7600, "Reports on the Application of Accounting Principles," setting out requirements that must be met when a public accounting firm is requested to provide a written opinion on the application of accounting principles or auditing standards by a party other than the client (also discussed in Chapter 22). Such an opinion would be issued for specific circumstances or transactions relating to an audit, review, or compilation client of another public accounting firm. It applies if the public accountant is asked to provide a generic or hypothetical opinion on the application of accounting principles.

The purpose of Section 7600 is to minimize the likelihood of management following the practice commonly called "opinion shopping," which could result in a potential intimidation threat to independence. Primary among the requirements is that the consulted or "reporting" accounting firm should communicate with the entity's incumbent accountant to obtain all the available facts to form a professional judgment on the matters the firm has been requested to report on.

APPROVAL OF AUDITOR BY SHAREHOLDERS The *Canada Business Corporations Act* and other incorporating acts require shareholders to approve the selection of a new auditor or continuation of the existing one. Shareholders are usually a more objective group than management. It is questionable, however, whether they are in a position to evaluate the performance of previous or potential auditors.

CONCLUSION Regardless of the rules set forth by the rules of conduct of the various accounting bodies, it is essential that the public accountant maintain an unbiased relationship with management and all other parties affected by the performance of the public accountant's responsibilities. In every engagement, including those involving management advisory and tax services, the public accountant must not subordinate his or her professional judgment to that of others. Even though pressures on the public accountant's objectivity and integrity are frequent, the long-run standing of the profession in the financial community demands resisting those pressures. If the conflicts are sufficiently serious to compromise the public accountant's independence, it may be necessary for the public accounting firm to resign from the engagement.

Confidentiality

The rules of conduct for PAs state that members shall not disclose any confidential client or employer information without the specific consent of the client or employer. The rules also prohibit using **confidential** or **inside information** to earn profits or benefits.

The rule against disclosure does not apply if the member is called upon to disclose the information by the courts. Communication between an auditor and client is not privileged as it is between lawyer and client; a court can require a PA to produce all files and documents held including confidential advice provided. For this reason, the auditor must be careful what information is put into the file, recognizing that the file could appear as a court

CONFIDENTIAL INFORMATION—
client information that may not be disclosed without the specific consent of the client except under authoritative professional or legal investigation

document. The rule against disclosure also does not apply if the member's professional body requires the confidentiality rule to be waived in connection with the body's exercise of its duties (e.g., when an auditor is called upon to produce working papers in connection with the disciplinary process, or when an auditor is required to produce files as part of practice inspection).

While the rules of professional conduct with respect to confidentiality are quite clear, as you will discover in Chapter 4, the auditor may be confronted with a situation where he or she must choose between confidentiality and other rules of conduct or another course of action. For example, Chapter 4 discusses the auditor's legal responsibilities for client confidentiality. A situation is described where an auditor has two clients who deal with each other; the auditor must choose between violating the rule respecting confidentiality or the rule respecting association with false or misleading financial information. Chapter 4 also illustrates the conflict that arises when an auditor has information about one client that could be beneficial to a second client. This demonstrates how auditors face ethical dilemmas where they cannot rely on the rules of conduct to provide a solution.

Need for Confidentiality During an audit or other type of engagement, practitioners obtain a considerable amount of information of a confidential nature, including officers' salaries, product pricing and advertising plans, and product cost data. If auditors divulged this information to outsiders or to client employees who have been denied access to the information, their relationship with management would be strained and, in extreme cases, would cause the client harm. The confidentiality requirement applies to all services provided by public accounting firms, including tax and management services.

Ordinarily, the public accounting firm's working papers can be provided to someone else only with the express permission of the client. This is the case even if a public accountant sells his or her practice to another public accounting firm or is willing to permit a successor auditor to examine the working papers prepared for a former client. Permission is not required from the client, however, if the working papers are subpoenaed by a court or are used as part of practice inspection. If the working papers are subpoenaed, the client should be informed immediately. The client and the client's lawyer may wish to challenge the subpoena.

Maintenance of the Reputation of the Profession

The rules of accounting bodies in Canada require their members to behave in the best interest of their profession and the public. This means accountants should not take advantage of the trust placed in them. An accountant should not be publicly critical of a colleague (i.e., by making a complaint about the colleague's behaviour to their professional body or by being critical, as a successor auditor, to the new client) without giving the colleague a chance to explain his or her actions first.

Actions by a member of a professional body—in law, medicine, or any other profession—reflect not only on the member but also on the body. For example, a lawyer who steals trust monies sullies not only his or her own reputation but also that of the law profession; the theft brings all lawyers into disrepute. Reputation is affected by anti-social behaviour such as harassment and discrimination since such behaviour is considered abhorrent, resulting in professional disciplinary actions. Therefore, it is essential that an accountant behave in an exemplary manner as a member of the professional body.

Integrity and Due Care

The rules of conduct for professional accountants require members to act with integrity and due care. Integrity is one of the hallmarks of the profession. One of a professional accountant's most important assets is his or her reputation for honesty and fair dealing; if users of financial statements audited by or prepared by an accountant do not believe in the practitioner's honesty or fairness, the value of the financial statements or the audit is diminished. The professional accountant's behaviour with clients, colleagues, employers, and employees must be above reproach.

Due care in the performance of duties is also a hallmark of a professional. The public accountant has a legal duty of care to certain users of financial statements, as will be seen in

Chapter 4. Due care means the application by a professional of a level of care and skill in accordance with what would reasonably be expected of a person of his or her rank and training. Note that due care is mentioned in the general standard of GAAS in Section 5100 of the *CICA Assurance Handbook.*

Competence

A PA has a responsibility to maintain his or her professional competence. The rules of conduct require practitioners to maintain competence; similarly the GAAS state the necessity of "adequate technical training and proficiency in auditing." The public expects that all professionals will strive to keep abreast of the latest techniques and methodologies.

The accounting associations offer continuing professional education courses in a variety of subject areas to assist members in maintaining competence. In addition, a number of other organizations provide courses.

Members are encouraged to keep current in a variety of ways. The various institutes and the *ordre* of chartered accountants have practice inspections (discussed in Chapter 1) over a three-year period of all public practice units. Certified general accountants and many CAs, such as those in Ontario, are required to attend a certain number of continuing professional education courses a year. Primarily, however, it is a PA's professionalism that dictates that he or she keep current.

The general standard, of GAAS explicitly and of the rules of conduct of the various professional accounting bodies implicitly, requires the auditor to have the necessary technical knowledge and competence to conduct the audit. This is especially true as businesses—and accounting for them—increase in complexity. An auditor should not undertake an audit of a client unless that auditor has both knowledge of that client's business and industry and of the technical aspects of the audit. For example, the audit of an insurance company requires knowledge of auditing the policy reserves that form a significant part of the insurance company's liabilities. Many larger accounting firms form industry specialization groups within the firm that are responsible for all audits within their specialty.

An audit firm should decline a new audit if the firm either lacks or does not have access to the technical knowledge required to complete the audit. Similarly, an auditor within a firm should ensure that he or she has access to the technical knowledge required to complete the audit.

Adherence to GAAP and GAAS

Professional accounting bodies require their members in practice as public accountants and working in industry not to associate with false or misleading information or to fail to reveal material omissions from financial statements. Users of financial statements prepared by or audited by professional accountants are entitled to believe that the financial statements are complete and fairly present the financial position of the company. They are entitled to believe that the financial statements are not false and misleading. They are entitled to rely on the integrity of the accountants involved.

Given that public trust of professional accountants does exist, if an accountant betrayed this trust and provided a clean opinion on financial statements known to be misleading, users would accept the statements as correct and would suffer a loss. Discovery that the public accountant was associated with false and misleading financial information or failed to reveal a material fact would destroy the accountant's reputation for integrity.

PAs are required to comply with professional standards when preparing and auditing financial statements. These standards would include the standards of the professional body but, more importantly, GAAP and GAAS as set out in the *CICA Handbooks*. As you learned in Chapter 1, the *Canada Business Corporations Act* and the incorporating acts of many of the provinces require financial statements to be prepared according to GAAP as specified by the *CICA Accounting Handbooks* and also require the auditor's report to be in accordance with the standards of the *CICA Assurance Handbook.* The Canadian Securities Administrators, who set policy for the securities commissions and stock exchanges in Canada, also specify the *Handbooks* as the source of GAAP.

Advertising and Solicitation

A profession's reputation is not enhanced if the members openly solicit one another's clients or engage in advertising that is overly aggressive, self-laudatory, or critical of other members of the profession, or that makes claims that cannot be substantiated. As a consequence, the professional accounting bodies in Canada either explicitly or implicitly prohibit solicitation of another public accountant's client and advertising that is not in keeping with the profession's high standards.

Responding to a request for information from a client of another public accounting firm is not solicitation, nor is responding to an invitation to tender from another firm's client. Rather, solicitation is approaching the client of another public accounting firm to convince him or her to switch to one's own firm: It is a targeted act of seeking a specific professional engagement.

Advertising that is in good taste is acceptable. It may include complimentary material about the accounting firm but should not claim any superior skills or make promises that can't be kept (e.g., a promise that certain favourable results will be achieved). Advertising is a general process of informing potential users of the availability of services.

There has been a gradual change over the past few years as the rules regarding solicitation and advertising have been made less stringent. As a consequence, advertising in the various media is much more common. There is an increased emphasis on marketing and more competitive pricing of services. Many public accounting firms have developed sophisticated advertising for national journals read by business people and for local newspapers.

Has the quality of audits become endangered by these changes? The existing legal exposure of public accountants, the disciplinary processes of the professional accounting bodies, practice inspection requirements, and the potential for interference by the securities commissions and government has kept audit quality high. In the opinion of the authors, the changes in the rules have caused greater competition in the profession but not so much that high-quality, efficiently run public accounting firms have been harmed.

Other Rules

BREACHES OF THE RULES The rules of conduct of the professional accounting bodies require members who are aware of a breach of the rules by another member to report that member to the profession's discipline committee after first advising the member of the intent to make a report. The bodies are self-regulating. It is important that the member be notified of the intent to report the breach in case there are mitigating circumstances of which the reporting member is not aware.

CONTINGENT FEES The charging of a fee based on the outcome of an audit, such as the granting of a loan by a bank, could easily impair the auditor's independence. Contingent fees are prohibited for audits, reviews, and any other engagements that require the auditor to be objective.

COMMUNICATION WITH PREDECESSOR AUDITOR The rules of conduct of the PAs and incorporating acts such as the *Canada Business Corporations Act* require a (potential) successor auditor, prior to accepting an appointment as auditor, to communicate with the incumbent auditor to enquire if there are any circumstances of which the incumbent is aware that might preclude the successor from accepting the appointment. The successor would ask the potential client to authorize the incumbent to provide the information requested. If the client refuses to do so, the successor should be reluctant to accept the appointment because it is likely that the client is hiding something.

The rules also require that the incumbent respond to the successor's request and be candid in responding. The communication between the incumbent and the successor is important because it prevents a successor from unknowingly accepting an appointment that might, if all the facts were known, be rejected. For example, if the incumbent resigned after finding that management of the client was dishonest and was engaged in fraud, it is unlikely any public accounting firm would accept the client if the incumbent passed on that knowledge. In short, the required communication protects prospective successors, and thus the profession, from getting involved with undesirable clients. Review of the previous auditor's working papers is an important part of the audit process, as discussed further in audit planning.

PROFESSIONAL LIABILITY INSURANCE In several provinces, members practising public accounting are required to carry professional liability insurance. Two issues arise that can cause confusion: defining public accounting and the extent of work being done without remuneration.

For example, during tax season, individuals may prepare tax returns for family and friends at no charge. Since basic advice such as maximization of RRSP contributions is often included, this process is considered to be practising public accounting. However, if only a limited number of returns are being prepared for no remuneration, a public practice is not being carried on. If more than a handful of returns are being prepared and fees are being charged, either on a full- or part-time basis, then professional liability insurance is required.

OTHER RULES The rules of conduct of the professional accounting bodies include many more rules than have been described here; an aspiring professional accountant should be aware of the rules of conduct of the professional body to which membership is sought. The rules not covered, and those described above, may be categorized as general rules, rules that deal with protection of the public, rules that deal with relations with other accountants, and rules that relate to the conduct of a professional practice.

Enforcement

The rules of conduct for CAs are established and administered provincially. The rules of conduct for CGAs are promulgated by CGA-Canada. The provincial CGA associations have the power to add rules and have the responsibility for enforcing the rules.

The various professional bodies have the power to impose penalties ranging from public censure in the body's newsletter or requiring courses to be taken to upgrade skills to levying fines or expulsion. CPAB has the power to restrict a firm's ability to audit a listed entity. As previously mentioned, the professional accounting bodies are self-regulating; that is, they have the responsibility for developing their own rules of conduct and for disciplining members who violate the rules. There is a danger that the public will perceive the disciplinary process as not being as stringent as it should be and that there is a reluctance to punish members who break the rules. This issue is being dealt with by including laypersons on the disciplinary committees and by the inspections supervised by CPAB. Information is also available to the public about findings of the discipline committees and punishments meted out by them.

SUMMARY

1. *What are ethics and why are they important?* Ethics are broad moral principles or values that help guide our behaviour and establish trustworthy, responsible, and fair relationships.

    How can I work through an ethical conflict (known as an ethical dilemma)? A six-step framework that walks through information collection, analysis, and a decision is provided in the chapter (see p. 35).

2. *How are public accountants different from other professionals?* The clients of PAs are individuals, as well as management of corporations. In addition, PAs have a responsibility to users of financial statements, such as shareholders and creditors. This is a more expanded responsibility than that of other professionals.

    What is the role of a code of professional conduct in encouraging public accountant professional behaviour? Such a code of conduct can have general statements of ideal conduct and specific rules that define unacceptable behaviour.

3. *What are the facets of independence?* There are five areas where independence must be considered: self-interest, self-review, advocacy, familiarity, and intimidation.

    How does the auditor's relationship with the audit committee affect independence? The audit committee can help the auditor remain independent of management by making the auditor retention decision, approving the services provided by the PA, discussing the audit progress and findings, and by helping to resolve conflicts between the PA firm and management.

    What are some of the key rules of professional conduct and how are they enforced? There are rules of professional conduct covering independence, confidentiality, maintenance of the reputation of the profession, integrity and due care, competence, adherence to professional standards, and advertising and solicitation. Rules of conduct are enforced by the professional accounting associations and by CPAB.

GSF-QC – General standards of quality control for firms performing assurance engagements.

Section 5030 – Quality control procedures for assurance engagements.

Section 5100 – Generally accepted auditing standards.

Section 7600 – Reports on the application of accounting principles.

ESSENTIAL TERMS

Advocacy threat—A threat to independence where the firm or member is perceived to promote (or actually does promote) the client's position   (p. 42).

Audit committee—selected members of a client's board of directors, who provide a forum for the auditors to remain independent of management   (p. 44).

Confidential information—client information that may not be disclosed without the specific consent of the client except under authoritative professional or legal investigation   (p. 46).

Ethical dilemma—a situation in which a decision must be made about the appropriate behaviour   (p. 34).

Ethics—a set of moral principles or values   (p. 33).

Familiarity threat—A threat to independence that occurs when it is difficult to behave with professional skepticism during the engagement   (p. 43).

Independence—impartiality in performing professional services (p. 42).

Independence in appearance—the auditor's ability to maintain an unbiased viewpoint *in the eyes of others*   (p. 42).

Independence in fact—the auditor's ability to take an unbiased viewpoint in the performance of professional services   (p. 42).

Intimidation threat—a threat to independence that occurs when the client intimidates the firm or its staff with respect to the content of the financial statements or with respect to the conduct of the audit   (p. 43).

Listed entity—an entity whose debt or shares is listed on a stock exchange and that has market capitalization and total assets greater than $10 million   (p. 43).

Self-interest threat—a threat to independence where the member has a financial interest in the client or in the financial results of the client   (p. 42).

Self-review threat—a threat to independence where the public accountant is in the position of having to audit his or her own work during the period   (p. 42).

REVIEW QUESTIONS

2-1   Explain the need for a code of professional ethics for public accountants. In which ways should the public accountants' code of ethics be similar to and different from that of other professional groups, such as lawyers or dentists?

2-2   List the three parts which normally comprise a code of professional conduct, and state the purpose of each.

2-3   What is meant by the statement, "The rules of professional conduct of a professional accounting organization should be regarded as a minimum standard?"

2-4   Distinguish between independence in fact and independence in appearance. State three activities that may not affect independence in fact but are likely to affect independence in appearance.

2-5   Why is an auditor's independence so essential?

2-6   What are the five facets of independence discussed in the chapter? Explain why each is a necessary component of a public accountant's independence.

2-7   Many people believe that a public accountant cannot be truly independent when payment of fees is dependent on the management of the client. Explain a way of reducing this appearance of lack of independence.

2-8   The auditor's working papers usually can be provided to someone else only with the permission of the client. What is the rationale for such a rule?

2-9   The rules of conduct of PAs require them to report a breach of the rules of conduct by a member to their profession's disciplinary body. What should they do before making such a report?

2-10   After accepting an engagement, a public accountant discovers that the client's industry is more technical than at first realized and that he or she (i.e., the accountant) is not competent in certain areas of the operation. What should the public accountant do in this situation?

2-11   Identify and explain factors that should keep the quality of audits high even though advertising and tendering are allowed.

2-12   Why do you think the rules of conduct of the professional accounting bodies ban contingent fees for audits?

2-13   Why is it so important that a successor auditor communicate with the incumbent before accepting an appointment as auditor? What should the successor do if the incumbent doesn't reply?

MULTIPLE CHOICE QUESTIONS

2-14 Select the best response for each question.

a. What is the meaning of the generally accepted auditing standard that requires the auditor to be independent?

   (1) The auditor must be without bias with respect to the client under audit.
   (2) The auditor's sole obligation is to third parties.
   (3) The auditor may have a direct ownership interest in his or her client's business if it is not material.
   (4) The auditor must adopt a critical attitude during the audit.

b. The independent audit is important to readers of financial statements because it

   (1) measures and communicates financial and business data included in financial statements.
   (2) determines the future stewardship of the management of the company whose financial statements are audited.
   (3) involves the objective examination of and reporting on management-prepared statements.
   (4) reports on the accuracy of all information in the financial statements.

(AICPA adapted)

c. An auditor strives to achieve independence in appearance to

   (1) maintain public confidence in the profession.
   (2) become independent in fact.
   (3) comply with the generally accepted standards of field work.
   (4) maintain an unbiased mental attitude.

d. In which one of the following situations would a public accountant be in violation of the rules of conduct in determining his or her audit fee?

   (1) A fee equal to last year's fee plus 10 percent.
   (2) A fee based on the nature of the service rendered and the public accountant's particular expertise instead of the actual time spent on the engagement.
   (3) A fee based on whether the public accountant's report on the client's financial statements results in the approval of a bank loan.
   (4) A fee based on the fee charged by the prior auditor.

e. The rules of conduct state that a public accountant shall not disclose any confidential information obtained in the course of a professional engagement except with the consent of his or her client. In which one of the situations given below would disclosure by a public accountant be in violation of the rules?

   (1) Disclosing confidential information in compliance with a subpoena issued by a court.
   (2) Disclosing confidential information to another accountant interested in purchasing the public accountant's practice.
   (3) Disclosing confidential information in connection with a disciplinary hearing by the public accountant's professional conduct committee.
   (4) Disclosing confidential information in order to properly discharge the public accountant's responsibilities in accordance with his or her profession's standards.

(AICPA adapted)

DISCUSSION QUESTIONS AND PROBLEMS

2-15 Trish Mulcahy, a new junior in your office, says that she doesn't understand why she can't work on the audit of a company that is a client of your firm and that is owned by her uncle. Trish says she knows she must have an independent attitude and she will; her relationship to the owner is not important.

Required

What would you say in answer to her question? Would you let her work on the audit?

2-16 Each of the following scenarios involves a possible violation of the rules of conduct. Indicate whether each is a violation and explain why if you think it is.

a. John Brown is a public accountant, but not a partner, with three years of professional experience with Lyle and Lyle, Public Accountants, a one-office public accounting firm. He owns 25 shares of stock in an audit client of the firm, but he does not take part in the audit of the client and the amount of stock is not material in relation to his total wealth.

b. In preparing the corporate tax returns for a client, Phyllis Allen, public accountant, observed that the deductions for contributions and interest were unusually large. When she asked the client for backup information to support the deductions, she was told, "Ask me no questions, and I will tell you no lies." Allen completed the return on the basis of the information acquired from the client.

c. A client requested assistance of Kim Tanabe, public accountant, in the installation of a computer system for maintaining production records. Tanabe had no experience in this type of work and no knowledge of the client's production records, so he obtained assistance from a computer consultant. The consultant is not in the practice of public accounting, but Tanabe is confident of her professional skills. Because of the highly technical nature of the work, Tanabe is not able to review the consultant's work.

d. Five small Moncton public accounting firms have become involved in an information project by taking part in an interfirm working paper review program. Under the program, each firm designates two partners to review the working papers, including the tax returns and the financial statements, of another public accounting firm taking part in the program. At the end of each review, the auditors who prepared the working papers and the reviewers have a conference to discuss the strengths and weaknesses of the audit. They do not obtain the authorization from the audit client before the review takes place.

e. George Thorty, PA, was having a matrimonial dispute with his wife, and he got so angry that he threatened to kill her. His wife obtained a court injunction requiring that he stay away from her home and place of work. George violated the injunction and was sent to jail after being found in contempt of court.

f. Bill Wendal, public accountant, set up a casualty and fire insurance agency to complement his auditing and tax ser-

vices. He does not use his own name on anything pertaining to the insurance agency and has a highly competent manager, Renate Jones, who runs it. Wendal frequently requests Jones to review with the management of an audit client the adequacy of the client's insurance if it seems underinsured. He feels that he provides a valuable service to clients by informing them when they are underinsured.

g. Michelle Rankin, public accountant, provides tax services, management advisory services, and bookkeeping services and conducts audits for the same client. She requires management to approve, in writing, transactions, and journal entries. Since her firm is small, the same person frequently provides all the services.

2-17 Each of the following situations involves possible violations of the rules of conduct that apply to professional accountants. For each situation, state whether it is a violation. Where there is a violation, explain the nature of the violation and the rationale for the existing rule.

a. Mario Danielli is the partner on the audit of a charitable organization. He is also a member of the board of directors, but this position is honorary and does not involve performing a management function.

b. Martha Painter, CA, was appointed as the trustee of the So family trust. The So family trust owned the shares of the So Manufacturing Company, which is audited by another partner in Ms. Painter's office. Ms. Painter owns 15 percent of the shares of the So Manufacturing Company, and is also a director of the company, in the position of Treasurer.

c. Marie Godette, LLB, has a law practice. Godette has recommended one of her clients to Sean O'Doyle, public accountant. O'Doyle has agreed to pay Godette 10 percent of the fee O'Doyle receives from Godette's client.

d. Theresa Barnes, CA, has an audit client, Choi, Inc., which uses another public accounting firm for management services work. Barnes sends her firm's literature covering its

management services capabilities to Choi on a monthly basis unsolicited.

e. Alan Goldenberg leased several vehicles from his friend Norm. Norm said that he would give Alan a $200 commission for each referral. Alan referred several clients to Norm that were interested in leasing vehicles. After a few months, Alan was pleased to receive a cheque for $3,000 in the mail. Several of his clients had decided to change automobile leasing companies.

f. Edward Golikowski completed financial projections for his client that covered a period of three years. Edward was in a hurry, inadvertently stated that they covered five years and redid the client's calculations, rather than checking assumptions and doing field work, even though he attached an assurance report.

g. Marcel Poust, public accountant, has sold his public accounting practice, which includes bookkeeping, tax services, and auditing to Sheila Lyons, public accountant. Poust obtained permission from all audit clients for audit-related working papers before making them available to Lyons. He did not get permission before releasing tax- and management services-related working papers.

2-18 The *Canada Business Corporations Act* requires all companies incorporated under it to have audit committees.

Required

a. Describe an audit committee.
b. What are the typical functions performed by an audit committee?

c. Explain how an audit committee can help an auditor be more independent.
d. Your friend's mother, who is chair of an audit committee of a large publicly traded company, knows that you are studying auditing and has asked you for advice on how she can make the audit committee she chairs more effective. Your response should consider both sides of each recommendation you make.

2-19 Diane Harris, public accountant, is the auditor of Fine Deal Furniture, Inc. In the course of her audit for the year ended December 31, 2004, she discovered that Fine Deal had serious going concern problems. Henri Fine, the owner of Fine Deal, asked Harris to delay completing her audit.

Harris is also the auditor of Master Furniture Builders Ltd., whose year end is January 31. The largest receivable on Master Furniture's list of receivables is Fine Deal Furniture; the amount owing represents about 45 percent of Master Furniture's total receivables, which in turn are 60 percent of Master Furniture's net

assets. The management of Master Furniture is not aware of Fine Deal's problems and is certain the amount will be collected in full.

Master Furniture is in a hurry to get the January 31, 2005, audit finished because the company has made an application for a sizable loan from their bank to expand their operations. The bank has informally agreed to advance the funds based on draft financial statements submitted by Master Furniture just after the year end.

Required

What action should Harris take and why?

2-20 Marie Janes encounters the following situations in doing the audit of a large auto dealership. Janes is not a partner.

1. The sales manager tells her that there is a sale on new cars (at a substantial discount) that is limited to long-established customers of the dealership. Because her firm has been doing the audit for several years, the sales manager has decided that Janes should also be eligible for the discount.
2. The auto dealership has an executive lunchroom that is available free to employees above a certain level. The controller informs Janes that she can also eat there any time.

3. Janes is invited to and attends the company's annual Christmas party. When presents are handed out, she is surprised to find herself included. The present has a value of approximately $200.

Required
a. Assuming Janes accepts the offer or gift in each situation, has she violated the rules of conduct?
b. Discuss what Janes should do in each situation.

2-21 The following are situations that may violate the general rules of conduct of professional accountants. Assume in each case that the public accountant is a partner.

1. Simone Able, public accountant, owns a substantial limited partnership interest in an apartment building. Juan Rodriquez is a 100 percent owner in Rodriquez Marine Ltd. Rodriquez also owns a substantial interest in the same limited partnership as Able. Able does the audit of Rodriquez Marine Ltd.
2. Horst Baker, public accountant, approaches a new audit client and tells the president that he has an idea that could result in a substantial tax refund in the prior year's tax return by application of a technical provision in a tax law that the client had overlooked. Baker adds that the fee will be 50 percent of the tax refund after it has been resolved by Canada Revenue Agency. The client agrees to the proposal.
3. Chantal Contel, public accountant, advertises in the local paper that her firm does the audit of 14 of the 36 largest drugstores in the city. The advertisement also states that the average audit fee, as a percentage of total assets for the drug-

stores she audits, is lower than any other public accounting firm's in the city.
4. Olaf Gustafson, public accountant, sets up a small loan company specializing in loans to business executives and small companies. Gustafson does not spend much time in the business because he works full time with his public accounting practice. No employees of Gustafson's public accounting firm are involved in the small loan company.
5. Louise Elbert, public accountant, owns a material amount of stock in a mutual fund investment company, which in turn owns stock in Elbert's largest audit client. Reading the investment company's most recent financial report, Elbert is surprised to learn that the company's ownership in her client has increased dramatically.

Required
Discuss whether the facts in any of the situations indicate violations of the rules of conduct for professional accountants. If so, identify the nature of the violation(s).

PROFESSIONAL JUDGMENT PROBLEM

2-22 Joseph Smith is the chairman and chief operating officer of Maximum Software Limited, providing software solutions to companies in Manitoba. Mr. Smith owns 40 percent of the company, and has several silent partners, who sit on the board of directors, but who do not participate in the company's operations. The chief financial officer of Maximum is Barbara Black, who has been with the company since its inception ten years ago.

Joseph is short of money, so he created a fictitious company and requested that Barbara send monthly cheques of $10,000 to this company, called Network Best, for consulting fees. Barbara

agreed since Joseph approves the invoices. The controller, Samuel Chu, is a single parent with three children. Samuel did a normal credit check on Network Best, then told Barbara that the company did not exist and the invoices should not be paid. Barbara berated Samuel and told him to be quiet or he would lose his job. Joseph billed amounts through Network Best for three years.

Required
Assuming that all of the individuals described are qualified accountants, what rules of professional conduct have been violated? What should Barbara or Samuel have done?

CASES

2-23 Gilbert and Bradley formed a corporation called Financial Services, Inc., each man taking 50 percent of the authorized common stock. Gilbert is a public accountant and a member of one of the professional accounting bodies in Canada. Bradley is a CPCU (Chartered Property Casualty Underwriter). The corporation performs auditing and tax services under Gilbert's direction and insurance services under Bradley's supervision. The opening of the corporation's office was announced by an 8 cm, two-column "card" in the local newspaper.

One of the corporation's first audit clients was Grandtime Corp. Grandtime had total assets of $600,000 and total liabilities of $270,000. In the course of his examination, Gilbert found that Grandtime's building, with a book value of $240,000, was pledged as security for a 10-year term note in the amount of $200,000. The client's statements did not mention that the building was pledged as security for the note. However, as the failure to disclose the lien did not affect either the value of the assets or the amount of the liabilities and his examination was satisfactory in all other respects, Gilbert rendered an unqualified opinion on Grandtime's financial statements. About two months after the date of his opinion, Gilbert learned that an insurance company was planning to loan Grandtime $150,000 in the form of a first mortgage note on the building. Realizing that the insurance company was unaware of the existing lien on the building, Gilbert had Bradley notify the insurance company of the fact that Grandtime's building was pledged as security for the term note.

Required

Identify and discuss the ethical implications of those acts by Gilbert that were in violation of the rules of conduct.

2-24 Barbara Whitley had great expectations about her future as she sat at her graduation ceremony in May 2004. She was about to receive her Masters of Accountancy degree, and the following week she would begin her career on the audit staff of Green, Thresher & Co., a public accounting firm. Things looked a little different to Barbara in February 2005. She was working on the audit of Delancey Fabrics Ltd., a textile manufacturer with a calendar year end. The pressure was enormous. Everyone on the audit team was putting in 70-hour weeks, and it still looked as if the audit wouldn't be done on time. Barbara was doing work in the property area, vouching additions for the year. The audit program indicated that a sample of all items over $10,000 should be selected, plus a judgmental sample of smaller items. When Barbara went to take the sample, Jack Bean, the senior, had left the client's office and couldn't answer her questions about the appropriate size of the judgmental sample. Barbara forged ahead with her own judgment and selected 50 smaller items. Her basis for doing this was that there were about 250 such items, so 50 was a reasonably good proportion of such additions. Barbara audited the additions with the following results: the items over $10,000 contained no errors; however, the 50 small items contained a large number of errors. In fact, when Barbara projected them to all such additions, the amount seemed quite significant.

A couple of days later, Jack Bean returned to the client's office. Barbara brought her work to Jack in order to inform him of the problems she found, and got the following response: "My God, Barbara, why did you do this? You were only supposed to look at the items over $10,000 plus 5 or 10 little ones. You've wasted a whole day on that work, and we can't afford to spend any more time on it. I want you to throw away the schedules where you tested the last 40 small items and forget you ever did them."

When Barbara asked about the possible audit adjustment regarding the small items, none of which arose from the first 10 items, Jack responded, "Don't worry, it's not material anyway. You just forget it; it's my concern, not yours."

Required

a. In what way is this an ethical dilemma for Barbara?
b. Use the six-step approach discussed in the book to resolve the ethical dilemma.

CHAPTER 3

THE AUDITOR'S REPORT

Reports are essential to the audit or other attestation process because they provide information about what is being attested to, what the public accountant did, and the conclusions reached. Standard wording and rules about the types of report guide their preparation.

LEARNING OBJECTIVES

After reading this chapter, you should be able to answer the following questions:

1. When can the PA issue a *standard unqualified audit report*? How many parts are there in this report and why are they significant?

2. How can we categorize the auditor's report when there are variations in wording? Under what conditions would modified wording occur or an additional explanatory paragraph be added?

3. What two types of situations would cause problems with issuing an opinion on financial statements? How is materiality related to the wording changes used for these *departures* in audit opinion?

4. What type of report is issued when the auditor provides an opinion on management's report on internal control? Is the auditor responsible for financial information posted on a client's web site?

A QUALIFIED AUDIT REPORT—PROBLEMS WITH MANAGEMENT INTEGRITY

Halvorson & Co., public accountants, had been the auditors of Fine Furniture, Inc. (FFI) for many years. Halvorson was a top-tier accounting firm with national offices across the country. It was proud of the quality of its staff and the type of service it provided to its clients. FFI was a medium-sized client that had been with the firm for over 20 years, a great accomplishment given the volatility of the furniture industry, and the local partners knew the owners well. Recently, Al Trent, one of the firm's senior qualified accountants, had joined Fine Furniture, Inc. as the chief financial officer. Al was well liked, and had been with the firm since he left university.

Bruce Marks, the partner in charge of the FFI audit, was livid as Steve Smith, a newly hired qualified accountant, left his office with a dejected look on his face. Samantha, one of the audit seniors in the office, spoke to Bruce later in the day after he had calmed down. Bruce was steaming about a situation that had arisen the previous day. Fine Furniture, Inc. was going to receive a qualified audit report this year, with respect to inventory. Bruce used phrases like "unable to determine the quantity of inventory on hand at year end" and "potential overstatement of expenses" as he explained what was going to happen to the audit report. Bruce was particularly angry because he was now faced with having to report Al Trent to the provincial institute of chartered accountants for unethical behaviour and having to discipline Steve Smith due to the events at FFI. He exclaimed that both of these highly qualified and competent men should have known better.

Steve had gone first to the east end location of FFI to count inventory. The furniture inventory was well organized and labelled, and it had taken him only an hour to complete his test counts and gather necessary documentation. The inventory count had gone well. Al had shown him around and then offered to take Steve to lunch and for a round of golf. Steve did not know Al at all, except by reputation, and had felt this was a good way to get to know the senior financial officer at the company, while also getting in a round of golf.

About five hours later, Steve finally made it to the west end location of FFI. Unfortunately, here, inventory was not that well organized. It was simply a storage location operated by part-time staff, who looked particularly harried. The location was very busy, with shipments constantly leaving and arriving. It was almost as if the staff were not aware there was an inventory count that afternoon. Even though Steve was tired, he managed to jot down very specific details of inventory, including serial numbers. At that point he realized several of the items had the same serial numbers as those he had seen in the east end location. It was like being hit with a ton of bricks.

Without communicating his concerns to FFI staff, Steve methodically went through the contents of the warehouse, staying late into the evening. Fully two-thirds of the items he had counted at the east end location were also here at the west end. Steve also grimaced as he realized what Al had done when he filled up his car with gasoline that afternoon. Al had purchased several food items at the gas bar and had asked the attendant to just "include it with the gas" as he paid for the bill with what looked like a company credit card. It must be routine if he did it even with Steve there in his presence—not material transactions but clearly an indication of Al's ethics with respect to business practices.

Steve went home, and wrote up what had happened that day, knowing that it was partially his own behaviour that had given FFI the opportunity to ship inventory from the east to the west end. If he had not noted down serial numbers, the attempt to inflate inventory values would not have been detected.

Users of financial statements rely on the auditor's report to provide assurance on the company's financial statements. What if Steve had not detected FFI's attempt to inflate inventory? Think about the impact this would have had on Halvorson & Co. and the users of both FFI's financial statements and the auditor's report attached to those statements.

The auditor's report is the final step in the entire audit process. By studying it now, we will be able to refer to different auditor's reports as evidence accumulation is studied throughout the text. These evidence concepts are more meaningful after you understand the form and content of the final product of the audit. We begin by describing the content of the standard auditor's report.

→3.1 THE STANDARD AUDIT REPORT

Standard Unqualified Auditor's Report

The most common type of audit report is the **standard unqualified auditor's report**. It is also often referred to as the *auditor's standard report*. It is used when the following conditions have been met:

Conditions for Standard Unqualified Report

1. An audit engagement has been undertaken to express an opinion on financial statements.
2. The general standard has been followed by the auditor in all respects on the engagement.
3. Sufficient appropriate audit evidence has been accumulated, and the auditor has conducted the engagement in a manner that concludes that the examination standards have been met.
4. The financial statements, which include the balance sheet, the income statement, the statement of retained earnings, the cash flow statement, and the notes to the financial

STANDARD UNQUALIFIED AUDITOR'S REPORT—the report a public accountant issues when all auditing conditions have been met, no significant misstatements have been discovered and left uncorrected, and it is the auditor's opinion that the financial statements are fairly stated in accordance with generally accepted accounting principles statements, are fairly presented in accordance with an appropriate disclosed basis of accounting, usually generally accepted accounting principles.

5. There are no circumstances which, in the opinion of the auditor, would require modifying the wording of the report or adding an additional explanatory paragraph.

When these conditions are met, the standard unqualified auditor's report on the financial statements, as shown in Figure 3-1, is issued. Different auditors may vary the wording slightly in the standard report, but the meaning will be the same.

Parts of Standard Unqualified Auditor's Report Each standard unqualified auditor's report includes eight distinct parts. These parts are labelled in bold letters in Figure 3-1.

1. *Report Title.* Paragraph 5400.07 states that the auditor's report should be titled.
2. *Addressee.* Paragraph 5400.35 requires that the addressee of the auditor's report be disclosed. Normally, the addressees are the shareholders since it is usually they who appoint the auditor.
3. *Introductory Paragraph.* The first paragraph of the auditor's report does three things. First, it makes the simple statement that the public accounting firm has done an *audit*. The scope paragraph clarifies what is meant by an audit.

 Second, it lists the financial statements that were audited, including the balance sheet date and the period for the income statement, the statement of retained earnings, and the cash flow statement. While the notes to the financial statements are not mentioned specifically, they are an integral part of the financial statements and their inclusion is implicit.

 Third, the introductory paragraph states that the financial statements are the responsibility of management and that the auditor's responsibility is to express an opinion on the financial statements. In this way, the introductory paragraph (a) communicates that management is responsible for selecting the appropriate generally

FIGURE 3-1	The Standard Auditor's Report

	AUDITOR'S REPORT
Report Title	
Addressee	To the Shareholders of Hillsburg Hardware Ltd.
Introductory Paragraph (factual statement)	We have audited the balance sheet of Hillsburg Hardware Ltd. as at December 31, 2005, and the statements of income, retained earnings, and cash flows for the year then ended. These financial statements are the responsibility of the company's management. Our responsibility is to express an opinion on these financial statements based on our audit.
Scope Paragraph (factual statement)	We conducted our audit in accordance with Canadian generally accepted auditing standards. Those standards require that we plan and perform an audit to obtain reasonable assurance whether the financial statements are free of material misstatement. An audit includes examining, on a test basis, evidence supporting the amounts and disclosures in the financial statements. An audit also includes assessing the accounting principles used and significant estimates made by management, as well as evaluating the overall financial statement presentation.
Opinion Paragraph (conclusions)	In our opinion, these financial statements present fairly, in all material respects, the financial position of the company as at December 31, 2005, and the results of its operations and cash flows for the year then ended in accordance with Canadian generally accepted accounting principles.
Name of Public Accounting Firm	*Berity, Kao, Kadous & Co.* Chartered Accountants
Place of Issue	Halifax, Nova Scotia
Auditor's Report Date	February 15, 2006

accepted accounting principles and for making the measurement decisions and disclosures in applying those principles, and (b) clarifies the respective roles of management and the auditor.

4. *Scope Paragraph.* The scope paragraph is a factual statement about what the auditor did in the audit. This paragraph first states that the auditor followed generally accepted auditing standards. The remainder briefly describes important aspects of an audit.

The scope paragraph states that the audit is designed to obtain *reasonable assurance* about whether the statements are free of *material* misstatement. The inclusion of the word "material" conveys the meaning that auditors search for significant misstatements, not minor errors that do not affect users' decisions. The use of the term "reasonable assurance" is intended to indicate that an audit cannot be expected to eliminate completely the possibility that a material error or fraud or other irregularity will exist in the financial statements. In other words, an audit provides a high level of assurance, but it is not a guarantee.

The remainder of the scope paragraph discusses the audit evidence accumulated and states that the auditor believes the evidence accumulated was appropriate for the circumstances to express the opinion presented. The words "test basis" indicate that sampling was used rather than an audit of every transaction and amount on the statements. Whereas the introductory paragraph of the report states that management is responsible for the preparation and content of the financial statements, the scope paragraph states that the auditor has the responsibility to evaluate the appropriateness of those accounting principles, estimates, and financial statement disclosures and presentations given. The auditor cannot simply accept management's representations about appropriateness.

5. *Opinion Paragraph.* The final paragraph in the standard auditor's report states the auditor's conclusions based on the results of the audit. This part of the auditor's report is so important that often the entire report is referred to as simply the *auditor's opinion.* The opinion paragraph is stated as an opinion rather than as a statement of absolute fact or a guarantee. The intent is to indicate that the conclusions are based on professional judgment. The phrase "in our opinion" indicates that there may be some information risk associated with the financial statements, even though the statements have been audited.

The opinion paragraph is directly related to the three generally accepted auditing reporting standards described in Figure 1-4, page 18. The auditor is required to state an opinion about the financial statements taken as a whole, including a conclusion about whether the company followed an appropriate disclosed basis of accounting, usually Canadian generally accepted accounting principles.

One of the most controversial parts of the auditor's report is the meaning of the term *presents fairly.* The auditor means that the financial statements are fairly presented in accordance with the accounting principles described in the opinion paragraph. A layperson may mistake "presents fairly" to mean that the values in the financial statements represent the realizable values of the assets. It is important that lay people understand the auditor's message. The auditor cannot and does not check every transaction.

6. *Name of Public Accounting Firm.* The name identifies the public accounting firm or practitioner that has performed the audit. Typically, the firm's name is used since the entire firm has the legal and professional responsibility to make certain the quality of the audit meets professional standards as illustrated in Figure 3-1.

7. *Place of Issue.* Paragraph 5400.36 suggests that the place of issue may be identified in the letterhead on which the auditor's report is printed or at the foot of the report as is illustrated in Figure 3-1.

8. *Auditor's Report Date.* The appropriate date for the report as illustrated in Figure 3-1 is the one on which the auditor has completed the most important auditing procedures in the field. Section 5405.06 refers to "... substantial completion of examination. ... " This date is important to users because it indicates the last day of the auditor's responsibility for the review of significant events that occurred after the date of the financial

statements. For example, if the balance sheet is dated December 31, 2005, and the audit report is dated March 6, 2006, the implication is that the auditor has searched for material, unrecorded transactions, and events that occurred up to March 6, 2006, that may have had an effect on the 2005 statements.

Section 5405 discusses, among other things, double dating of the auditor's report. Double dating is done when a material event occurs after the completion of fieldwork and after the date of the auditor's report and before the date the report is issued. The auditor will then double date the report as follows:

March 6, 2006
except for Note 17 which is
as of April 2, 2006

If the effect of the event was so material as to change the 2005 financial statements significantly, the auditor would probably extend the audit for the financial statements as a whole and date the report with the revised date for completion of fieldwork. In the example provided, the new date of the auditor's report would be April 2, 2006.

→ 3.2 HOW THE PA PROVIDES ADDITIONAL INFORMATION

Categories of Auditor's Reports

Most users of financial statements read the auditor's report. When the report consists of three standard paragraphs, they conclude that the five conditions listed on pages 57 and 58 have been met.

A deviation from the standard unqualified report will cause knowledgeable users of financial statements to recognize that the auditor intends to communicate additional or limiting information. In extreme cases, the auditor may conclude that the financial statements are materially misstated, but usually the cause of the deviation is less significant.

The categorization of audit reports in Figure 3-2 is used throughout the remainder of the chapter. The departures from a standard unqualified report are considered increasingly severe as one follows down the figure. A denial or adverse opinion is normally far more important to users than an unqualified report with an explanatory paragraph or modified wording.

Unqualified Auditor's Report with Explanatory Paragraph or Modified Wording

In certain situations, an unqualified auditor's report is issued, but the wording deviates from the standard unqualified report. The *unqualified report with explanatory paragraph or modified wording* meets the criteria of a complete audit with satisfactory results and financial statements that are fairly presented, but the auditor believes it is necessary to provide additional

FIGURE 3-2	Four Categories of Auditor's Reports
Standard unqualified	The five conditions stated on pages 57 and 58 have been met.
Unqualified with explanatory paragraph or modified wording	A complete audit took place and financial statements are fairly presented in accordance with disclosed accounting principles, but the auditor believes that it is important or required to provide additional information.
Qualified	The auditor concludes that the financial statements are fairly presented "except for," but the scope of the auditor's examination has been restricted or there has been failure to comply with GAAP.
Adverse or denial	The auditor concludes that the scope limitation is so significant that the auditor is unable to form an opinion as to whether the financial statements are fairly presented (denial) or that the deviation from GAAP is so significant that the financial statements are not fairly presented (adverse).

information. In a *qualified, adverse,* or *denial report,* the auditor either has not performed a complete audit or is not satisfied that the financial statements are fairly presented.

Unqualified Auditor's Report When the Appropriate Disclosed Basis of Accounting Is Not GAAP In certain situations, an unqualified auditor's report is issued when the disclosed basis of accounting is not generally accepted accounting principles.

Reporting standard (iv) (see page 18) requires the auditor's report to state "whether the financial statements present fairly, in all material respects, the financial position, results of operations and cash flows in accordance with Canadian generally accepted accounting principles." Section 5600 covers non-GAAP statements that might include financial statements prepared in accordance with regulatory legislation or with contractual requirements. In such circumstances, the auditor would express the opinion that the financial statements presented fairly the financial position, results of operations, and cash flows in accordance with the disclosed basis of accounting.

Modifications in the Standard Unqualified Auditor's Report The auditor may be reporting under a statute that requires the inclusion of information in addition to that provided in the auditor's report. Normally, such explanatory information should be included after the opinion paragraph. For example, Assurance and Related Services Guideline 40 (AuG-40), "Auditor's Report on the Financial Statements of Federally Regulated Financial Institutions," provides guidance on the wording of the auditor's report of a financial institution governed by a federal statute such as the *Bank Act* or the *Insurance Companies Act.* Similarly, AuG-10, "Legislative Requirements to Report on the Consistent Application of Generally Accepted Accounting Principles," allows the auditor to state that accounting principles have been applied on a basis consistent with the preceding year.

Paragraph 5701.05 also suggests that if the auditor wishes to expand his or her report to include other information and explanations, such information should be included in a paragraph following the opinion paragraph. For example, when comparative financial statements are presented that were not audited or were audited by another auditor, that information would be disclosed in a paragraph following the opinion paragraph.

Reporting on Comparative Financial Statements AuG-8, "Auditor's Report on Comparative Financial Statements," affects those companies filing financial statements with the Ontario Securities Commission (OSC). The *CICA Handbooks* normally require the auditor to report only on the current year's financial statements. Publicly listed organizations must refer to both periods under audit. AuG-8 provides examples of wording that would be used for the standard unqualified report, and examples of opinions with reservations.

Canada–United States Reporting Differences Cross-listed organizations are those companies that are listed on multiple stock exchanges. AuG-21, "Canada–United States Reporting Differences," provides guidance to the auditor on report preparation for Canadian companies where the audit report would differ under Canadian and U.S. GAAP due to treatment differences for disclosures of going concern problems and of changes in generally accepted accounting principles between periods.

The guideline requires that the report be prepared in accordance with Canadian GAAS and that any additional comments required be attached but be distinct from the auditor's report.

Changes in GAAP or the Application Thereof Paragraph 5400.17 requires the auditor to evaluate a change in accounting principle or in the application of an accounting principle in the financial statements being reported on and to assess whether or not the new principle, or the application, is in accordance with generally accepted accounting principles. In addition, the auditor must assess whether the method of accounting for the change, which may be retroactive or prospective, and the disclosure of the change are also in accordance with GAAP.

If the change, its application, and its disclosure are in accordance with GAAP, the auditor should express an unqualified opinion. On the other hand, if the change or its application or its disclosure in the financial statements is not in accordance with GAAP, the auditor should issue a qualified or adverse opinion.

Certain changes in the financial statements may not be changes in a principle or in its application. Examples of such changes include:

1. Changes in an estimate, such as a decrease in the life of an asset for amortization purposes.
2. Error corrections not involving principles, such as a previous year's mathematical error.
3. Variations in format and presentation of financial information.
4. Changes because of substantially different transactions or events, such as new endeavours in research and development or the sale of a subsidiary.

A change in estimate need not be disclosed in the notes although disclosure may be desirable. An error correction, on the other hand, must be fully disclosed.

Unusual Uncertainties Affecting the Financial Statements

Management customarily makes a number of estimates in the preparation of financial statements, including the useful lives of amortizable assets, the collectibility of receivables, and the realizability of inventory and other assets. There is usually enough evidence to permit reasonable estimation of these items. Sometimes, the auditor encounters a situation in which the outcome of a matter cannot be reasonably estimated at the time the statements are being issued. These matters are defined as contingencies. Examples include threats of the expropriation of assets, income tax or litigation contingencies (collectible or payable), and guarantees of the indebtedness of others.

There are also less specific situations in which the ability of the company to continue as a going concern is open to question.[1] Paragraphs 5510.51–53 of the *CICA Assurance Handbook* address this problem. The going concern assumption and potential liquidity issues are discussed further in the audit planning and evidence chapters.

The appropriate type of opinion to issue when either specific or general uncertainties exist depends on the materiality of the items in question and on the disclosure of the items by management in the notes. An unqualified opinion is appropriate if the uncertainty is not disclosed but is immaterial. If the amount involved is material but the accounting treatment, disclosure, and presentation of either a contingency or going concern problem are in accordance with GAAP, the auditor would not refer to the uncertainty in the auditor's report. The auditor must be very sure that the disclosure is such that it draws attention to the uncertainty. If the going concern problem is adequately disclosed, the auditor makes no mention of it in the auditor's report.

What makes an annual report informative? One aspect is transparency—having information that is easy to understand and clear in its communication. It also needs to be specific, explaining what a company is doing well, or doing poorly, with plans for remedial action. Potash Corporation of Saskatchewan Inc. earned awards of excellence in 2004 in the *CICA Corporate Reporting Awards*. Management discussion and analysis (MD&A) standards provided by the CICA provide a floor for presentation, but the way information is presented, including the use of graphics and images, as shown on Potash's web site, help improve clarity. Annual information presented to shareholders includes much more than the financial statements and the auditor's report—yet without the financial statements to provide point-in-time information and the auditor's report to provide assurance, MD&A would be less meaningful to shareholders and other users of financial information.

Sources: 1. Colapinto, Robert, 2005. "The Winners' Circle," *CAmagazine*, January/February 2005, pp. 24-28. 2. www.potashcorp.com, PotashCorp, Accessed: January 26, 2005.

---

[1]For a thorough and interesting discussion of this topic see Boritz, J. E., *The "Going Concern" Assumption: Accounting and Auditing Implications*, Toronto: CICA, 1991.

3.3 CHANGES TO THE AUDIT OPINION

Conditions Requiring a Departure from an Unqualified Auditor's Report

It is essential that auditors and readers of auditor's reports understand the circumstances when a standard unqualified report is not appropriate (there is a reservation of opinion) and the type of auditor's report issued in each circumstance. In the study of auditor's reports that depart from an unqualified report, there are three closely related topics: the conditions requiring a departure from an unqualified opinion, the types of opinions other than unqualified, and materiality.

First, the two conditions requiring a departure are briefly summarized. Each is discussed in greater depth later in the chapter.

1. SCOPE RESTRICTION: THE SCOPE OF THE AUDITOR'S EXAMINATION HAS BEEN RESTRICTED When the auditor has not accumulated sufficient evidence to determine if financial statements are stated in accordance with GAAP, a scope restriction exists. There are two major causes of scope restrictions: restrictions imposed by the client and those caused by circumstances beyond either the client's or auditor's control. An example of a client restriction is management's refusal to permit the auditor to confirm material receivables or to physically examine material inventory. An example of a restriction caused by circumstances is when the engagement is not agreed upon until after the client's year end. It may not be possible to physically observe inventories, do certain cut-off tests, or perform other important procedures after the balance sheet date.

2. GAAP DEPARTURE: THE FINANCIAL STATEMENTS HAVE NOT BEEN PREPARED IN ACCORDANCE WITH GAAP Paragraph 5510.06 lists three examples of departures from generally accepted accounting principles:

1. An inappropriate accounting treatment; for example, failure to capitalize a capital lease.
2. An inappropriate valuation of an item in the financial statements; for example, failure to provide an adequate allowance for doubtful accounts.
3. A failure to disclose essential information in an informative manner; for example, failure to adequately disclose a going concern problem or a material contingency.

Auditor's Reports Other Than Unqualified

Whenever either of the two conditions requiring a departure from an unqualified report exists and is material, a report other than an unqualified report must be issued. Three main types of auditor's reports are issued under these conditions: *qualified opinion, adverse opinion*, and *denial of opinion*.

Qualified Opinion A **qualified opinion** or reservation of opinion can result from a limitation on the scope of the audit or failure to follow generally accepted accounting principles. A qualified opinion can be used only:

1. For a scope limitation: The auditor's fieldwork has been restricted, but the restriction is confined to a specific area such as opening inventory.
2. For a GAAP departure: The financial statements are fairly presented except for failure to comply with one or more GAAP and the effect can be quantified or isolated.

An adverse opinion or a denial must be used if the auditor believes the condition being reported upon is extremely material. For this reason, the qualified opinion is considered a less severe type of report for disclosing departures than an adverse opinion or a denial.

Whenever an auditor issues a qualified opinion, he or she must use the term *except for* or, less frequently, *except that* or *except as* in the opinion paragraph. The implication is that the auditor is satisfied that the overall financial statements are correctly stated "except for" a particular part. Examples of qualifications are given later in the chapter. It is unacceptable to use these phrases with any type of audit opinion other than a qualified one.

Qualified opinions are fairly rare in practice. The provincial securities commissions will

QUALIFIED OPINION—a report issued when the auditor believes that financial statements are fairly stated but that either there was a material, but not pervasive, limitation in the scope of the audit, or there was a failure to follow GAAP that resulted in a material, but not pervasive, misstatement in the financial statements accept qualified statements from a public company only in rare circumstances. Lenders or creditors may not accept qualified statements from private companies. Consequently the conditions giving rise to the qualifications are often corrected.

Adverse Opinion An **adverse opinion** is used only when the auditor concludes the overall financial statements are **materially misstated** *or misleading* so that they do not present fairly the financial position or results of operations and changes in cash flows in conformity with generally accepted accounting principles because of a GAAP departure.

Denial of Opinion A **denial of opinion** is issued whenever the auditor has been *unable to satisfy himself or herself* that the overall financial statements are fairly presented. The necessity for denying an opinion may arise because of a *severe limitation on the scope* of the audit examination, which would prevent the auditor from expressing an opinion on the financial statements as a whole.

The denial is distinguished from an adverse opinion in that it can arise only from a *lack of knowledge* by the auditor, whereas to express an adverse opinion, the auditor must have knowledge that the financial statements are not fairly stated. Both denials and adverse opinions are used only when the extent of the scope limitation or the effects of noncompliance with GAAP are material and pervasive.

Materiality

Materiality is an essential consideration in determining the appropriate type of report for a given set of circumstances. For example, if a misstatement is immaterial relative to the financial statements of the entity for the current period and is not expected to have a material effect in future periods, it is appropriate to issue an unqualified report.

Another consideration is the pervasiveness of the scope limitation or the departure from GAAP. If the scope limitation is pervasive, a denial is appropriate; if the departure from GAAP is pervasive, an adverse opinion is appropriate. If the limitation or non-GAAP conditions are material but not pervasive, a qualified opinion is appropriate.

Definition The common definition of materiality as it applies to accounting and, therefore, to audit reporting is provided in paragraph 5142.04 and is

A misstatement... in financial statements is considered to be material if... the decision of a person who is relying on the financial statements... will be changed or influenced.

In applying this definition, three levels are used for determining the type of opinion to issue. The relationship of level to type of opinion is presented in Table 3-1.

AMOUNTS ARE IMMATERIAL When a misstatement in the financial statements exists but is unlikely to affect the decisions of a reasonable user, it is considered to be immaterial. An unqualified opinion is therefore appropriate. For example, assume management recorded unexpired insurance as an asset in the previous year and decided to expense it in the current year to reduce record-keeping costs. Management failed to follow GAAP, but if the amounts are small, the misstatement would be immaterial, and a standard unqualified auditor's report would be appropriate.

AMOUNTS ARE MATERIAL BUT NOT PERVASIVE The second level of materiality exists when a misstatement in the financial statements would affect a user's decision, but the overall statements are still useful. For example, knowledge of a large misstatement in capital assets might affect a user's willingness to loan money to a company if the assets were the collateral. A misstatement of inventory does not mean that cash, accounts receivable, and other elements of the financial statements, or the financial statements as a whole, are materially incorrect.

To make materiality decisions when a condition requiring a departure from an unqualified report exists, the auditor must evaluate all effects on the financial statements. Assume the auditor is unable to satisfy himself or herself whether inventory is fairly stated (scope limitation) in deciding on the appropriate type of opinion. Because of the effect of a misstatement in inventory on other accounts and on totals in the statements, the auditor needs to consider the materiality of the combined effect on inventory, total current assets, total

TABLE 3-1	Relationship of Materiality to Type of Opinion and Significance in Terms of Reasonable User's Decision		
		Type of Audit Report	
		Auditing related	Accounting Related
Materiality Level	Significance in Terms of Reasonable User's Decisions	Scope restricted by client or conditions	Financial statements not prepared in accordance with GAAP*
Immaterial	Decisions are unlikely to be affected.	Unqualified: Standard report	Unqualified: Standard report
Material	Decisions are likely to be affected only if the information in question is important to the specific decisions being made. The overall financial statements are considered fairly stated. Thus, there is a material error, but it does not overshadow the financial statements as a whole.	Qualified: Additional paragraph and qualified opinion (*except for*)	Qualified: Qualified scope, additional paragraph, and qualified opinion (*except for*)
Material and pervasive	Most or all decisions based on the financial statements are likely to be significantly affected. The overall fairness of the financial statements is in question.	Denial of opinion	Adverse opinion

*or an appropriate disclosed basis of accounting

working capital, total assets, income taxes, income taxes payable, total current liabilities, cost of goods sold, net income before taxes, and net income after taxes.

When the auditor concludes that a misstatement is material but does not overshadow the financial statements as a whole, a qualified opinion (using "except for") is appropriate.

AMOUNTS ARE MATERIAL AND PERVASIVE SUCH THAT OVERALL FAIRNESS OF STATEMENTS IS IN QUESTION The highest level of misstatement exists when users are likely to make incorrect decisions if they rely on the overall financial statements. Using the previous example of inventory, a large misstatement could be so material to the financial statements as a whole that the auditor's report should indicate the financial statements taken as a whole cannot be considered fairly stated. When the highest level of misstatement exists, the auditor must issue either a denial of opinion or an adverse opinion.

When determining whether an exception is material and pervasive, the extent to which the exception affects different parts of the financial statements must be considered. This is referred to as *pervasiveness*. A misclassification between cash and accounts receivable affects only those two accounts and is therefore not pervasive. On the other hand, failure to record a material sale could be pervasive because it affects sales, accounts receivable, income tax expense, accrued income taxes, and retained earnings, which in turn affect current assets, total assets, current liabilities, total liabilities, owners' equity, gross margin, and operating income.

As misstatements become more pervasive, the likelihood of issuing an adverse opinion rather than a qualified opinion is increased. For example, suppose the auditor decides a misclassification between cash and accounts receivable should result in a qualified opinion because it is material; the failure to record a sale of the same dollar amount may result in an adverse opinion because of pervasiveness.

Materiality Decisions In concept, the effect of materiality on the type of opinion to issue is straightforward. In application, deciding upon actual materiality in a given situation is a difficult judgment. There are no simple, well-defined guidelines that enable auditors to decide when something is immaterial, material, or material and pervasive.

There are differences in applying materiality for deciding whether failure to follow GAAP is material compared to deciding whether a scope limitation is material.

MATERIALITY DECISIONS—GAAP DEPARTURE When a client has failed to follow GAAP, the audit report will be unqualified, qualified opinion only, or adverse, depending on the materiality and pervasiveness of the departure. Several aspects of materiality must be considered.

Dollar amounts compared with a base. The primary concern in measuring materiality when a client has failed to follow GAAP is usually the total dollar misstatement in the accounts involved, compared to some base. A $10,000 misstatement might be material for a small company but not for a larger one. Misstatements must, therefore, be compared with some measurement base before a decision can be made about the materiality of the failure to follow GAAP. Common bases include net income before taxes, total assets, revenue, gross profit, and shareholders' equity.

To evaluate overall materiality, the auditor must combine all unadjusted errors and judge whether there may be individually immaterial errors that, when combined, significantly affect the statements. When comparing potential misstatements with a base, the auditor must carefully consider all accounts affected by a misstatement (pervasiveness). It is, for example, important not to overlook the effect of an understatement of ending inventory on cost of goods sold, income before taxes, income tax expense, and accrued income taxes payable.

Measurability. The dollar error of some misstatements cannot be accurately measured. For example, a client's unwillingness to disclose an existing lawsuit or the acquisition of a new company subsequent to the balance sheet date is difficult, if not impossible, to measure in terms of dollar amounts. The materiality question the auditor must evaluate in such a situation is the effect on statement users of the failure to make the disclosure.

Nature of the item. The decision of a user may also be affected by the kind of misstatement in the financial statements. The following may affect the user's decision and, therefore, the auditor's opinion in a different way than most misstatements.

1. Transactions are illegal or fraudulent.
2. An item may materially affect some future period even though it is immaterial when only the current period is considered.
3. An item has a "psychic" effect (e.g., small profit versus small loss or cash balance versus overdraft).
4. An item may be important in terms of possible consequences arising from contractual obligations (e.g., the effect of failure to comply with a debt restriction may result in a material loan being called).

MATERIALITY DECISIONS—SCOPE LIMITATIONS When there is a scope limitation in an audit, the audit report will be unqualified, qualified scope and opinion, or denial, depending on the materiality and pervasiveness of the scope limitation. The auditor will consider the same three factors included in the previous discussion, but they will be considered differently. The size of *potential misstatements*, where there are scope limitations, is important in determining whether an unqualified report, a qualified report, or a denial of opinion is appropriate. For example, if recorded accounts payable of $400,000 was not audited, the auditor must evaluate the potential misstatement in accounts payable and decide how materially the financial statements could be affected. The pervasiveness of these potential misstatements must also be considered.

It is typically more difficult to evaluate the materiality of potential misstatements resulting from scope limitations than for failure to follow GAAP. Misstatements resulting from failure to follow GAAP are known. Those resulting from scope limitations must usually be subjectively measured in terms of potential or likely misstatements. For example, the recorded accounts payable of $400,000 might be understated by more than a million dollars, which may affect several totals including gross margin, net earnings, and total liabilities.

Discussion of Conditions Requiring a Departure

This part of the chapter examines the conditions requiring a departure from an unqualified report in greater detail and shows examples of reports.

Auditor's Scope Has Been Restricted There are two major categories of scope restrictions: those caused by a client and those caused by conditions beyond the control of either the client or the auditor. The effect on the auditor's report is the same for either, but the interpretation of materiality is likely to be different. Whenever there is a scope restriction, the appropriate response is to issue an unqualified report, a qualification of scope and opinion, or a denial of opinion, depending on materiality and pervasiveness.

For client-imposed restrictions, the auditor should be concerned about the possibility that management is trying to prevent discovery of misstated information. In such cases, it would be appropriate to issue a denial of opinion whenever materiality and pervasiveness are in question. When restrictions are due to conditions beyond the client's control, a qualification of scope and opinion is more likely.

Two restrictions occasionally imposed by clients on the auditor's scope relate to the observation of physical inventory and the confirmation of accounts receivable, but other restrictions may also occur. Reasons for client-imposed scope restrictions may be a desire to save audit fees and, in the case of confirming receivables, to prevent possible conflicts between the client and customer when amounts differ.

A qualified report or denial of opinion resulting from a client restriction requires a reservation paragraph to describe the restriction; the reservation paragraph is located between the scope and opinion paragraph. In addition, the opinion paragraph must be modified.

The most common case in which conditions beyond the client's and auditor's control cause a scope restriction is an engagement agreed upon after the client's balance sheet date. Certain cut-off procedures, physical examination of inventory, and other important procedures may not be possible under those circumstances. When the auditor cannot perform desired procedures but can be satisfied with alternative procedures that verify the information is fairly stated, an unqualified report is appropriate. If alternative procedures cannot be performed, a scope qualification and, depending on the materiality and pervasiveness, either an opinion qualification or a denial of opinion is necessary. A reservation paragraph would describe the restriction.

For example, the report in Figure 3-3 would be appropriate for an audit in which the amounts were material but not pervasive, and the auditor was unable to audit the financial statements of a company's foreign affiliate and could not satisfy himself or herself by alternative procedures. The first paragraph is omitted from the example because it contains standard wording.

When the amounts are so material that a denial of opinion is required, the introductory and scope paragraphs could remain the same, but the opinion paragraph might be as shown in Figure 3-4. The middle paragraph shows the serious deficiencies that result in a denial.

Statements Are Not in Conformity with GAAP When the auditor knows that the financial statements may be misleading because they were not prepared in conformity with generally

---

FIGURE 3-3	Qualified Scope and Opinion Report Due to Scope Restriction

AUDITOR'S REPORT

(Same introductory paragraph as standard report)	Introductory Paragraph
Except as explained in the following paragraph, we conducted our audit . . . (remainder is the same as the scope paragraph in the standard report).	Scope Paragraph—Qualified
We were unable to obtain audited financial statements supporting the Company's investment in a foreign affiliate stated at $475,000, or its equity in earnings of that affiliate of $365,000, which is included in net income, as described in Note X to the financial statements. Because of the nature of the Company's records, we were unable to satisfy ourselves as to the carrying value of the investment or the equity in its earnings by means of other auditing procedures.	Third Paragraph—Added
In our opinion, except for the effects of such adjustments, if any, as might have been determined to be necessary had we been able to examine evidence regarding the foreign affiliate investment and earnings, these financial statements present fairly, in all material respects, the financial position of Laughlin Corporation as of December 31, 2005, and the results of its operations and cash flows for the year then ended in accordance with Canadian generally accepted accounting principles.	Opinion Paragraph—Qualified

| | **FIGURE 3-4** | **Denial of Opinion Due to Scope Restriction** |

AUDITOR'S REPORT

Introductory Paragraph

(Same introductory paragraph as standard report)

Scope Paragraph—Qualified

(Same scope paragraph as Figure 3-3)

Third Paragraph—Added

Our examination indicated serious deficiences in internal control of general fund transactions. As a consequence, we were unable to satisfy ourselves that all revenues and expenditures of the organization had been recorded nor were we able to satisfy ourselves that the recorded transactions were proper. As a result, we were unable to determine whether adjustments were required in respect of recorded and unrecorded assets, recorded and unrecorded liabilities and the components making up the statements of revenue and expense, accumulated surplus (deficit) and changes in cash flow.

Opinion Paragraph—Denial

In view of the possible material effects on the financial statements of the matters described in the preceding paragraph, we are unable to express an opinion as to whether these financial statements are presented fairly in accordance with Canadian generally accepted accounting principles.

accepted accounting principles, he or she must issue a qualified or an adverse opinion, depending on the materiality and pervasiveness of the item in question. The opinion must clearly state the nature of the deviation from accepted principles and the amount of the misstatement, if it is known. Figure 3-5 shows an example of a qualified opinion when a client did not capitalize leases as required by GAAP. The first and second paragraphs in the example are omitted because they include standard wording.

When the amounts are so material and pervasive that an adverse opinion is required, the scope would still be unqualified, the reservation paragraph could remain the same, but the opinion paragraph might be as shown in Figure 3-6.

When the client fails to include information that is necessary for the fair presentation of financial statements in the body of the statements or in the related footnotes, it is the responsibility of the auditor to present information in the auditor's report and to issue a qualified or an adverse opinion. It is common to put this type of qualification in an added paragraph (the scope paragraph will remain unqualified) and to refer to the added paragraph in the opinion paragraph. Figure 3-7 shows an example of an auditor's report in which the auditor considered the financial statement disclosure inadequate.

Existence of More Than One Condition Requiring a Qualification Auditors may encounter situations involving more than one of the conditions requiring modification of the unqual-

| | **FIGURE 3-5** | **Qualified Opinion Report Due to Non-GAAP** |

AUDITOR'S REPORT

Introductory and Scope Paragraphs

(Same introductory and scope paragraphs as standard report)

Third Paragraph—Added

The Company has excluded from property and debt in the accompanying balance sheet certain lease obligations that, in our opinion, should be capitalized in order to conform with Canadian generally accepted accounting principles. If these lease obligations were capitalized, property would be increased by $4,600,000, long-term debt by $4,200,000, and retained earnings by $400,000 as of December 31, 2005, and net income and earnings per share would be increased by $400,000 and $1.75, respectively, for the year then ended.

Opinion Paragraph—Qualified

In our opinion, except for the effects of not capitalizing lease obligations, as discussed in the preceding paragraph, these financial statements present fairly, in all material respects, the financial position of Ajax, Inc. as of December 31, 2005, and the results of its operations and cash flows for the year then ended in accordance with Canadian generally accepted accounting principles.

FIGURE 3-6	Adverse Opinion Due to Non-GAAP	

AUDITOR'S REPORT

(Same introductory and scope paragraphs as standard report)

Introductory and Scope Paragraphs

(Same third paragraph as that used for the third paragraph in Figure 3-5)

Third Paragraph—Added

In our opinion, because of the effects of the matters discussed in the preceding paragraph, these financial statements do not present fairly, in accordance with Canadian generally accepted accounting principles, the financial position of Ajax, Inc. as of December 31, 2005, or the results of its operations and cash flows for the year then ended.

Opinion Paragraph—Adverse

FIGURE 3-7	Qualified Opinion Due to Inadequate Disclosure	

AUDITOR'S REPORT

(Same introductory and scope paragraphs as standard report)

Introductory and Scope Paragraphs

On January 15, 2006, the company issued debentures in the amount of $3,600,000 for the purpose of financing plant expansion. The debenture agreement restricts the payment of future cash dividends to earnings after December 31, 2007. In our opinion, disclosure of this information is required to conform with Canadian generally accepted accounting principles.

Third Paragraph—Added

In our opinion, except for the omission of the information discussed in the preceding paragraph, these financial statements present fairly . . . (remainder is the same as the opinion in the standard report).

Opinion Paragraph—Qualified

ified report. In these circumstances, the auditor should qualify his or her opinion for each condition. Paragraph 5510.33 states that "[it] is essential that all reservations be disclosed because the reader of an auditor's report should be able to assume that the financial statements, except with respect to matters on which the auditor has expressed a reservation of opinion, are presented fairly in accordance with generally accepted accounting principles." An example is presented in Figure 3-8.

FIGURE 3-8	Qualified Opinion (Departure from GAAP and a Scope Limitation)	

AUDITOR'S REPORT

(Same introductory paragraph as standard report)

Introductory Paragraph

Except as explained in the following paragraph, we conducted our audit . . . (remainder is the same as the scope paragraph in the standard report).

Scope Paragraph—Modified Wording

Management has advised us that the company may become liable with respect to guarantees given for indebtedness of a subsidiary located in another country. However, management has declined to provide us with further information and will not permit us to contact the subsidiary as management believes disclosure is not in the company's best interests. As a result, we have been unable to obtain sufficient audit evidence to form an opinion with respect to the possible liability. Furthermore, the matter has not been disclosed in the notes to the financial statements. In our opinion, such disclosure is required under Canadian generally accepted accounting principles.

Third Paragraph—Added

In our opinion, except that disclosure has not been made with respect to the contingent liability referred to in the preceding paragraph and except for the effect of adjustments, if any, which we may have determined to be necessary had we been able to obtain sufficient information regarding this matter, these financial statements present fairly, in all material respects, . . . (remainder is the same as the opinion in the standard report).

Opinion Paragraph—Modified Wording

Reports Involving Reliance on Another Auditor Or a Specialist In Canada, although the main or primary auditor may rely on another auditor or a specialist in determining the appropriate opinion to issue on the financial statements, the primary auditor takes responsibility for that opinion, and only the name of the primary auditor appears on the auditor's report. *CICA Assurance Handbook* Sections 6930 and 5049 deal with the (primary) auditor's reliance on another auditor and on a specialist respectively. Inability to rely on the work of another auditor or a specialist is a scope limitation issue.

The auditor may rely on another auditor because the client's business is either too complex or widespread and the primary auditor either does not have the personnel or the proximity to all the client locations to do the audits with his or her own personnel. For example, the primary auditor, a public accounting firm located in Halifax, may rely on another public accounting firm located in Regina as the secondary auditor to audit the Halifax client's subsidiary located in Regina.

Section 6930 requires the primary auditor to assess the secondary auditor's professional qualifications, competence, and integrity in determining whether or not to rely on the secondary auditor. As you will discover in Chapter 4, the primary auditor who does rely on a secondary auditor is responsible for any deficiencies in the secondary auditor's work. The decision on whether or not to rely on that work is based on the primary auditor's judgment.

If the primary auditor decides that an unqualified opinion is appropriate, the name of the secondary auditor is not mentioned. If however, the primary auditor decides that a qualified or denial of opinion is appropriate *and the qualification arises because of inability to rely on the work of the secondary auditor*, the explanation of the qualification in the third paragraph could mention the name of the secondary auditor in explaining the reason for the qualification (scope limitation).

The auditor may have to rely on a specialist, such as an actuary, in completing the audit. Normally the auditor would not mention the specialist or reliance on the specialist. However, if the auditor believes that a qualified or denial of opinion is appropriate *and the qualification arises because of inability to rely on the work of the specialist*, the explanation of the qualification in the third paragraph would mention the name of the specialist in explaining the reason for the qualification.

Negative Assurance

It is inappropriate to include in the auditor's report any additional comments that counterbalance the auditor's opinion. For example, the use of such terminology as "However, nothing came to our attention that would lead us to question the fairness of the presentations" as a part of a denial of opinion is inappropriate and a violation of the standards of reporting. A statement of this kind, which is referred to as *negative assurance*, tends to confuse readers about the nature of the auditor's examination and the degree of responsibility he or she is assuming.

The use of negative assurance is considered appropriate only in the case of review engagements and prospectuses (Sections 7110 and 7115). Review engagements are considered in Chapter 22.

→3.4 INTERNAL CONTROL AND ELECTRONIC FILING

Combined Reports on Financial Statements and Internal Control over Financial Reporting

The *Sarbanes–Oxley Act of 2002* requires the auditor of a public company to attest to management's report on the effectiveness of internal control over financial reporting. Similar requirements exist in Canada for large listed entities and apply to Canadian subsidiaries of American companies. The audit of internal control is integrated with the audit of the financial statements. However, the auditor may choose to issue separate reports on the financial statements and internal control over financial reporting or issue a combined report. Figure 3-9 includes an example of a combined report on the financial statements and management's report on internal control over financial reporting. Although the audit opinion on the financial statements addresses multiple reporting periods, management's assertion about the effectiveness of internal control is as of the end of the most recent fiscal year.

The introductory, scope, and opinion paragraphs are modified to include reference to management's report on internal control over financial reporting and the scope of the auditor's work and opinion on internal control over financial reporting. The introductory and opinion paragraphs also refer to the framework used to evaluate internal control. Note that the report includes an additional definition of internal control over financial reporting paragraph between the introductory and scope paragraphs. The report also includes an

---

FIGURE 3-9   **Auditor's Report**

To the Shareholders of Westbrook Company, Inc.

We have audited the accompanying balance sheet of Westbrook Company, Inc. as at December 31, 2005, and the related statements of income, retained earnings, and cash flows for the year then ended. We have also audited the effectiveness of Westbrook Company, Inc.'s internal control over financial reporting as at December 31, 2005, in accordance with criteria established in *Internal Control—Integrated Framework*, as issued by the Committee of Sponsoring Organizations of the Treadway Commission (COSO), and management's assessment thereof included in the accompanying report, *Management's Report on Internal Control, 2005*. Westbrook Company, Inc.'s management is responsible for these financial statements, for maintaining effective internal control over financial reporting, and for its assessment of the effectiveness of internal control over financial reporting. Our responsibility is to express an opinion on these financial statements, an opinion on management's assessment, and an opinion on the effectiveness of the company's internal control over financial reporting based on our audits.
Introductory Paragraph

A company's internal control over financial reporting is a process designed to provide reasonable assurance regarding the reliability of financial reporting and the preparation of financial statements for external purposes in accordance with generally accepted accounting principles. A company's internal control over financial reporting includes those policies and procedures that (1) pertain to the maintenance of records that, in reasonable detail, accurately and fairly reflect the transactions and dispositions of the assets of the company; (2) provide reasonable assurance that transactions are recorded as necessary to permit preparation of financial statements in accordance with generally accepted accounting principles, and that receipts and expenditures of the company are being made only in accordance with authorizations of management and directors of the company; and (3) provide reasonable assurance regarding prevention or timely detection of unauthorized acquisition, use, or disposition of the company's assets that could have a material effect on the financial statements.
Definition Paragraph

We conducted our audit of Westbrook Company, Inc.'s financial statements in accordance with Canadian generally accepted auditing standards. Those standards require that we plan and perform an audit to obtain reasonable assurance whether the financial statements are free of material misstatement. An audit of financial statements includes examining, on a test basis, evidence supporting the amounts and disclosures in the financial statements. A financial statement audit also includes assessing the accounting principles used and significant estimates made by management, and evaluating the overall financial statement presentation. We conducted our audit of the effectiveness of the Company's internal control over financial reporting, and management assessment thereof, in accordance with the standards established by the Canadian Institute of Chartered Accountants (CICA) for audits of internal control over financial reporting. Those standards require that we plan and perform our audit to obtain reasonable assurance about whether effective internal control over financial reporting was maintained in all material respects. Our audit of internal control over financial reporting included obtaining an understanding of internal control over financial reporting, testing and evaluating the design and operating effectiveness of internal control over financial reporting, and performing such other procedures as we considered necessary in the circumstances. We believe that our audits provide a reasonable basis for our opinions.
Scope Paragraph

In our opinion, the financial statements referred to above present fairly, in all material respects, the financial position of Westbrook Company, Inc. as at December 31, 2005, and the results of its operations and its cash flows for the year then ended in accordance with Canadian generally accepted accounting principles. Also, in our opinion, management's assessment that Westbrook Company, Inc. maintained effective internal control over financial reporting as at December 31, 2005, is fairly stated, in all material respects, in accordance with criteria established in *Internal Control—Integrated Framework* issued by the Committee of Sponsoring Organizations of the Treadway Commission (COSO). Furthermore, in our opinion, Westbrook Company, Inc. maintained, in all material respects, effective internal control over financial reporting as at December 31, 2005, in accordance with criteria established in *Internal Control—Integrated Framework* issued by the Committee of Sponsoring Organizations of the Treadway Commission (COSO).
Opinion Paragraph

Because of its inherent limitations, internal control over financial reporting may not prevent or detect misstatements. Also, projections of any evaluation of effectiveness to future periods are subject to the risk that controls may become inadequate because of changes in conditions, or that the degree of compliance with the policies or procedures may deteriorate.
Inherent Limitations Paragraph

additional paragraph following the opinion that addresses the inherent limitations of internal control.

Impact of E-Commerce on Audit Reporting

Most public companies provide access to financial information through their home web page. Visitors to a company's web site can view the company's most recent audited financial statements, including the auditor's report. In addition, it is common for the company to include such information as unaudited quarterly financial statements, other selected financial information, and press releases often labelled as "About the Company" or "Investor Relations" on its web site.

Even before the widespread use of the Internet, companies often published documents that contained information in addition to audited financial statements and the independent auditor's report. The most common example was and still is the company's annual report. Under generally accepted auditing standards, the auditor has no obligation to perform any procedures to corroborate the other information. The auditor is, however, responsible for reading the other information to determine whether it is materially consistent with information in the audited financial statements.

However, under current auditing standards, auditors are not required to read information contained in electronic sites, such as the company's web site, that also contain the company's audited financial statements and the auditor's report. Auditing standards note that electronic sites are a means of distributing information and are not considered "documents," as that term is used in GAAS.

SUMMARY

1. *When can the PA issue a standard unqualified audit report?* It can be issued for an audit engagement where sufficient evidence has been collected using GAAS, where the financial statements are fairly presented in accordance with GAAP.

   How many parts are there in this report and why are they significant? Figure 3-1, page 58 shows the eight parts to the audit report: title the report; identify the addressee; describe what has been audited and how; list the responsibilities of the auditor and management; and provide an opinion on the financial statements. It also identifies the audit firm, the place of issue, and the date of the report.

2. *How can we categorize the auditor's report when there are variations in wording?* In addition to the standard unqualified report, there is the unqualified report with an explanatory paragraph or modified wording, a qualified, adverse, or denial of opinion.

   Under what conditions would modified wording occur or an additional explanatory paragraph be added? Such a report would be issued when a complete audit with satisfactory results has been completed, but the auditor believes it is necessary to provide additional information.

3. *What two types of situations would cause problems with issu-* *ing an opinion on financial statements?* When either the scope of the auditor's examination has been restricted, or the financial statements have not been prepared in accordance with GAAP, the auditor may be unable to issue a standard unqualified report.

   How is materiality related to the wording changes used for these departures in audit opinion? A qualified report is likely to be used when the issue is material but does not overshadow the financial statements as a whole. If problems are material and pervasive, then a denial of opinion or an adverse opinion would result.

4. *What type of report is issued when the auditor provides an opinion on management's report on internal control?* The auditor can provide a report titled "Auditor's report" that is a combined report on the financial statements and on management's report on internal control over financial reporting.

   Is the auditor responsible for financial information posted on a client's web site? No, the auditor is not responsible. However, the auditor could review this material to ensure it is materially consistent with the financial statements.

CICA ASSURANCE HANDBOOK SECTIONS REFERENCED IN THIS CHAPTER

Section 5049 – Use of specialists in assurance engagements.
Section 5142 – Materiality.
Section 5400 – The auditor's standard report.
Section 5405 – Date of the auditor's report.
Section 5510 – Reservations in the auditor's report.
Section 5600 – Auditor's report on financial statements prepared

using a basis of accounting other than generally accepted accounting principles.
Section 5701 – Other reporting matters.
Section 6930 – Reliance on another auditor.
Section 7110 – Auditor involvement with offering documents of public and private entities.

Section 7115 – Auditor involvement with offering documents of public and private entities—current legislative and regulatory requirements.

AuG-8 – Auditor's report on comparative financial statements.

AuG-10 – Legislative requirements to report on the consistent application of generally accepted accounting principles.

AuG-21 – Canada–US reporting differences.

AuG-40 – Auditor's report on the financial statements of federally regulated financial institutions.

ESSENTIAL TERMS

Adverse opinion—a report issued when the auditor believes the financial statements are materially misstated or misleading as a whole so that they do not present fairly the entity's financial position or the results of its operations and cash flows in conformity with generally accepted accounting principles   (p. 64).

Denial of opinion—a report issued when the auditor has not been satisfied that the overall financial statements are fairly presented   (p. 64).

Material misstatement—a misstatement in the financial statements, knowledge of which would affect a decision of a reasonable user of the statements   (p. 64).

Qualified opinion—a report issued when the auditor believes that financial statements are fairly stated but that either there was a material, but not pervasive, limitation in scope of the audit, or there was a failure to follow GAAP that resulted in a material, but not pervasive, misstatement in the financial statements   (p. 63).

Standard unqualified auditor's report—the report a public accountant issues when all auditing conditions have been met, no significant misstatements have been discovered and left uncorrected, and it is the auditor's opinion that the financial statements are fairly stated in accordance with generally accepted accounting principles   (p. 57).

REVIEW QUESTIONS

3-1   Explain why auditor's reports are important to users of financial statements.

3-2   What five circumstances are required for a standard unqualified report to be issued?

3-3   List the eight parts of an unqualified auditor's report and explain the meaning of each part. How do the parts compare with those found in a qualified report?

3-4   What are the purposes of the introductory paragraph in the auditor's report? Identify the most important information included in the introductory paragraph.

3-5   What are the purposes of the scope paragraph in the auditor's report? Identify the most important information included in the scope paragraph.

3-6   What are the purposes of the opinion paragraph in the auditor's report? Identify the most important information included in the opinion paragraph.

3-7   What is meant by the term "appropriate disclosed basis of accounting"? How does such a basis differ from GAAP? When is such a basis acceptable?

3-8   On February 17, 2006, a public accountant completed the examination of the financial statements for Buckheizer Corporation for the year ended December 31, 2005. The audit is satisfactory in all respects. On February 26, the auditor completed the tax return and the pencil draft of the financial statements. The final auditor's report was completed, attached to the financial statements, and delivered to the client on March 7. What is the appropriate date on the auditor's report?

3-9   Explain what is meant by "contingencies." Give an example of a contingency and discuss its appropriate disclosure in the financial statements.

3-10   List the conditions requiring a departure from an unqualified opinion, and give one specific example of each of those conditions.

3-11   Distinguish between a qualified opinion, an adverse opinion, and a denial of opinion, and explain the circumstances under which each is appropriate.

3-12   Define "materiality" as it is used in audit reporting. What conditions will affect the auditor's determination of materiality?

3-13   Distinguish between the levels of materiality and pervasiveness an auditor considers when assessing how to deal with a non-GAAP condition in the financial statements.

3-14   How does an auditor's opinion differ between scope limitations caused by client restrictions and limitations resulting from conditions beyond the client's control? What is the effect of each on the auditor's work?

3-15   Munroe Corp. had a bad year financially and the president, Jan de Boer, instructed the controller not to amortize the capital assets so that the company would show a small profit. The controller argued that GAAP required Munroe to amortize the capital assets on a regular basis and a qualified auditor's report would likely result. De Boer told the controller to disclose the failure to record amortization in the notes to the financial statements. You are the in-charge auditor on the Munroe audit. Write a memo to de Boer in response to the controller's suggestion.

3-16   At times, for a variety of reasons, an auditor must rely on another firm of auditors to perform part of an audit. What reference does the primary auditor make to the secondary auditor in the auditor's report?

3-17   Describe the additional information included in the introductory, scope, and opinion paragraphs in a combined audit report on financial statements and management's report on the effectiveness of internal control over financial reporting. What is the nature of the additional paragraphs in the audit report?

3-18 What responsibility does the auditor have for information on the company's web site that may be linked to electronic versions of the company's annual financial statements and auditor's report? How does this differ from the auditor's responsibility for other information in the company's annual report that includes the financial statements and auditor's report?

MULTIPLE CHOICE QUESTIONS

3-19 The following questions concern unqualified auditor's reports. Choose the best response.

a. An auditor's unqualified standard report

   (1) implies only that items disclosed in the financial statements and footnotes are properly presented and takes no position on the adequacy of disclosure.

   (2) implies that disclosure is adequate in the financial statements and footnotes.

   (3) explicitly states that all material items have been disclosed in conformity with generally accepted accounting principles.

   (4) explicitly states that disclosure is adequate in the financial statements and footnotes.

The following question concerns auditor's reports other than unqualified reports. Choose the best response.

b. If an auditor issues an adverse auditor's report when there is a very material contingency, the reader of the auditor's report should conclude that

   (1) the auditor was not able to form an opinion on the outcome of the contingency.

   (2) the auditor became aware of the contingency after the balance sheet date but prior to the audit report date.

   (3) there were no audit procedures available to the auditor by which he or she could obtain satisfaction concerning the outcome of the uncertainty.

   (4) the note disclosure with respect to the contingency was not adequate.

c. A public accountant will issue an adverse auditor's opinion if

   (1) the scope of his or her examination is limited by the client.

   (2) his or her exception to the fairness of presentation is so material and pervasive such that an "except for" opinion is not justified.

   (3) he or she did not perform sufficient auditing procedures to form an opinion on the financial statements taken as a whole.

   (4) major uncertainties exist concerning the company's future such that an "except for" opinion is not justified.

d. An auditor will express an "except for" opinion if

   (1) the client refuses to provide for a probable income tax liability that is very material and pervasive.

   (2) there is a high degree of uncertainty associated with the client company's future.

   (3) he or she did not perform procedures sufficient to form an opinion on the valuation of accounts receivable, which are material.

   (4) the auditor is basing his or her opinion in part upon work done by another auditor.

e. Under which of the following circumstances should an auditor issue a qualified or adverse opinion?

   (1) The financial statements contain a departure from generally accepted accounting principles, the effect of which is material.

   (2) The primary auditor decides to make reference to the report of another auditor who audited a subsidiary.

   (3) There has been a material change between periods in the method of the application of accounting principles.

   (4) Note disclosure describing significant uncertainties affecting the financial statements is provided.

(AICPA adapted)

DISCUSSION QUESTIONS AND PROBLEMS

3-20 A careful reading of a standard unqualified auditor's report indicates several important phrases. Explain why each of the following phrases or clauses is used rather than the alternative provided.

a. "In our opinion, these financial statements present fairly" rather than "These financial statements present fairly."

b. "We conducted our audit in accordance with Canadian generally accepted auditing standards" rather than "Our audit was performed to detect material misstatements in the financial statements."

c. "These financial statements present fairly, in all material respects, the financial position" rather than "These financial statements are correctly stated."

d. "In accordance with Canadian generally accepted accounting principles" rather than "are properly stated to represent the true economic conditions."

e. "Brown & Phillips, CAs (firm name)," rather than "James E. Brown, CA (individual partner's name)."

3-21 Roscoe, public accountant, has completed the examination of the financial statements of Excelsior Corporation as of and for the year ended December 31, 2005. Roscoe also examined and reported on the Excelsior financial statements for the prior year. Roscoe drafted the following report for 2005:

> We have audited the balance sheet and statements of income and retained earnings of Excelsior Corporation as of December 31, 2005. We conducted our audit in accordance with Canadian generally accepted accounting standards. Those standards require that we plan and perform the audit to obtain reasonable assurance about whether the financial statements are free of misstatement.
>
> We believe that our audits provide a reasonable basis for our opinion.
>
> In our opinion, the financial statements referred to above present fairly the financial position of Excelsior Corporation as of December 31, 2005, and the results of its operations for the year then ended in conformity with Canadian generally accepted auditing standards, applied on a basis consistent with those of the preceding year.
>
> (Signed)
>
> Roscoe, Public Accountant

Other Information:

- Excelsior is presenting comparative financial statements.
- Excelsior does not wish to present a cash flow statement for either year.
- During 2005, Excelsior changed its method of accounting for long-term construction contracts, properly reflected the effect of the change in the current year's financial statements, and restated the prior year's statements. Roscoe is satisfied with Excelsior's justification for making the change. The change is discussed in footnote 12.
- Roscoe was unable to perform normal accounts receivable confirmation procedures, but alternate procedures were used to satisfy Roscoe as to the existence of the receivables.
- Excelsior Corporation is the defendant in a lawsuit, the outcome of which is highly uncertain. If the case is settled in favour of the plaintiff, Excelsior will be required to pay a substantial amount of cash, which might require the sale of certain capital assets. The litigation and the possible effects have been properly disclosed in footnote 11.
- Excelsior issued debentures on January 31, 2003, in the amount of $10,000,000. The funds obtained from the issuance were used to finance the expansion of plant facilities. The debenture agreement restricts the payment of future cash dividends to earnings after December 31, 2004. Excelsior declined to disclose this essential data in the footnotes to the financial statements.

Required

a. Identify and explain any items included in "Other Information" that need not be part of the auditor's report.

b. Explain the deficiencies in Roscoe's auditor's report as drafted.

(AICPA adapted)

3-22 For the following independent situations, assume you are the audit partner on the engagement.

1. During your examination of Debold Batteries Ltd., you conclude there is a possibility that inventory is materially overstated. The client refuses to allow you to expand the scope of your examination sufficiently to verify whether the balance is actually misstated.
2. You are auditing Woodcolt Linen Services, Inc. for the first time. Woodcolt has been in business for several years but has never had an audit before. After the audit is completed, you conclude that the current year balance sheet is stated correctly in accordance with GAAP. The client did not authorize you to do test work for any of the previous years.
3. You were engaged to examine Cutter Steel Corp.'s financial statements after the close of the corporation's fiscal year. Because you were not engaged until after the balance sheet date, you were not able to physically observe inventory, which is very material. On the completion of your audit, you are satisfied that Cutter's financial statements are presented fairly, including inventory about which you were able to satisfy yourself by the use of alternative audit procedures.
4. Four weeks after the year-end date, a major customer of

Prince Construction Ltd. declared bankruptcy. Because the customer had confirmed the balance due to Prince at the balance sheet date, management refuses to charge off the account or otherwise disclose the information. The receivable represents approximately 10 percent of accounts receivable and 20 percent of net earnings before taxes.

5. You complete the audit of Johnson Department Store Ltd., and, in your opinion, the financial statements are fairly presented. On the last day of the examination, you discover that one of your supervisors assigned to the audit had a material investment in Johnson.
6. Auto Delivery Company Ltd. has a fleet of several delivery trucks. In the past, Auto Delivery had followed the policy of purchasing all equipment. In the current year, they decided to lease the trucks. This change in policy is fully disclosed in footnotes.

Required

For each situation, state the type of auditor's report that should be issued. If your decision depends on additional information, state the alternative reports you are considering and the additional information you need to make the decision.

3-23 For the following independent situations, assume you are the audit partner on the engagement.

1. Kieko Corporation has prepared financial statements but has decided to exclude the cash flow statement. Management explains to you that the users of their financial statements find that particular statement confusing and prefer not to have it included.

2. HardwareFromHome.com is an Internet-based start-up company created to sell home hardware supplies online. Although the company had a promising start, a downturn in e-commerce retailing has negatively affected the company. The company's sales and cash position have deteriorated significantly, and you have reservations about the ability of the company to continue in operation for the next year.

3. Approximately 20 percent of the audit for Furtney Farms, Inc. was performed by a different public accounting firm, selected by you. You have reviewed its working papers and believe it did an excellent job on its portion of the audit. Nevertheless, you are unwilling to take complete responsibility for its work.

4. The controller of Fair City Hotels Co. Ltd. will not allow you to confirm the receivable balance from two of its major customers. The amount of the receivable is material in relation to Fair City's financial statements. You are unable to satisfy yourself as to the receivable balance by alternative procedures.

5. In the last three months of the current year, Oil Refining Corp. decided to change direction and go significantly into the oil-drilling business. Management recognizes that this business is exceptionally risky and could jeopardize the success of its existing refining business, but there are significant potential rewards. During the short period of operation in drilling, the company has had three dry wells and no successes. The facts are adequately disclosed in footnotes.

Required

a. For each situation, identify which of the conditions requiring modification of or a deviation from an unqualified standard report is applicable.

b. State the level of materiality as immaterial, material, or material and pervasive. If you cannot decide the level of materiality, state the additional information needed to make a decision.

c. Given your answers in parts (a) and (b), identify the appropriate auditor's report from the following choices:

1. Unqualified—standard wording
2. Qualified opinion—GAAP departure
3. Qualified opinion—scope limitation
4. Denial
5. Adverse

3-24 The following are independent situations for which you will recommend an appropriate auditor's report:

1. Subsequent to the date of the financial statements as part of the post-balance sheet date audit procedures, a public accountant learned of heavy damage to one of a client's two plants due to a recent fire; the loss will not be reimbursed by insurance. The newspapers described the event in detail. The financial statements and appended notes as prepared by the client did not disclose the loss caused by the fire.

2. A public accountant is engaged in the examination of the financial statements of a large manufacturing company with branch offices in many widely separate cities. The public accountant was not able to count the substantial undeposited cash receipts at the close of business on the last day of the fiscal year at all branch offices.

   As an alternative to this auditing procedure used to verify the accurate cutoff of cash receipts, the public accountant observed that deposits in transit as shown on the year-end bank reconciliation appeared as credits on the bank statement on the first business day of the new year. The public accountant was satisfied as to the cutoff of cash receipts by the use of the alternative procedure.

3. On January 2, 2006, the Retail Auto Parts Company Limited received a notice from its primary supplier that, effective immediately, all wholesale prices would be increased by 10 percent. On the basis of the notice, Retail Auto Parts revalued its December 31, 2005, inventory to reflect the higher costs. The inventory constituted a material proportion of total assets; however, the effect of the revaluation was material to current assets but not to total assets or net income. The increase in valuation is adequately disclosed in the footnotes.

4. E-lotions.com, Inc. is an online retailer of body lotions and other bath and body supplies. The company records revenues at the time customer orders are placed on the web site, rather than when the goods are shipped, which is usually two days after the order is placed. The auditor determined that the amount of orders placed but not shipped as of the balance sheet date is not material.

5. During the course of the examination of the financial statements of a corporation for the purpose of expressing an opinion on the statements, a public accountant is refused permission to inspect the minute books. The corporate secretary instead offers to give the public accountant a certified copy of all resolutions and actions relating to accounting matters.

Required

a. For each situation, identify which of the conditions requiring a deviation from or modification of an unqualified standard report is applicable.

b. State the level of materiality as immaterial, material, or material and pervasive. If you cannot decide the level of materiality, state the additional information needed to make a decision.

c. Given your answers in parts (a) and (b), identify the appropriate auditor's report from the following alternatives:

(1) Unqualified—standard wording
(2) Qualified opinion—GAAP departure
(3) Qualified opinion—scope limitation
(4) Denial
(5) Adverse

(AICPA adapted)

3-25 You are the in-charge on the audit of Saskatoon Building Products Limited (SBP), a company listed on the Vancouver Stock Exchange. In the course of your audit, you discover that SBP's working capital ratio is below 2:1 and that, therefore, the company is in default on a substantial loan from Prairie Bank. Management announces to you its intention to sell a large block of provincial bonds, which were included in long-term investments, and some land that had been purchased for expansion, which was included in capital assets. Management proposes including the bonds and land as current assets pending disposition. Such inclusion would increase the current ratio to 2.2:1.

Prairie Bank and your client have not enjoyed cordial relations of late, and you have been advised by Avril Chui, the manager of the Saskatoon branch, that they "are looking forward to receiving the audited statements because they are concerned that SBP has been having problems."

Required
a. Draft the memo to your partner outlining the problem.
b. Draft the auditor's report.

3-26 The following are two unrelated situations:
1. You are the auditor of Xact Ltd., a company which at December 31, 2005, had working capital of $200,000, total assets of $2,500,000, and total liabilities of $2,200,000. During the three years ended December 31, 2005, the company sustained operating losses totalling $700,000.

    Management has been informed that Butler Inc. will not renew a debenture they hold issued by Xact in the amount of $500,000 and maturing September 30, 2006. The debenture is presently classed as a long-term liability. Although preliminary discussions have already been held with various commercial lenders, it presently appears uncertain as to whether Xact will be able to refinance this debt. In addition, it appears doubtful that Xact will be able to obtain short-term borrowing to finance the debt.
2. Your client, Bat Ltd., owns 15 percent of the shares of Bird Ltd. The 2005 pre-tax net income of Bat is $1,000,000 and its shareholder's equity is $3,000,000.

    The investment in Bird is carried on Bat's balance sheet (as of December 31, 2005) at $250,000, which represents original cost. Bird has incurred significant losses in the past few years. A current appraisal by a qualified business valuator indicates that the current market value of 100 percent of the issued and outstanding shares of Bird is $1,000,000. You are also aware that an investor who held 20 percent of the shares of Bird recently sold those shares for $180,000.

    Your client, Bat Ltd., insists that the shares be shown at their original cost of $250,000 but is willing to expand note disclosure.

Required
a. Outline possible deviations (if any) from a standard auditor's report that may be necessary, and give reasons. State your assumptions.
b. Outline the minimum note disclosure you would consider adequate in the circumstances. What additional disclosure would be desirable?

(CICA adapted)

3-27 The following tentative auditor's report was drafted by a staff accountant and submitted to a partner in the public accounting firm of Bettrioni & Bee.

Auditor's Report
To the Audit Committee of Athabaska Widgets, Inc.

We have examined the consolidated balance sheet of Athabaska Widgets, Inc., and subsidiaries as of December 31, 2005, and the related consolidated statement of income, retained earnings, and cash flow for the year then ended. These financial statements are the responsibility of the company's management. Our responsibility is to express an opinion on these financial statements based on our audit.

Our examinations were made in accordance with Canadian generally accepted auditing standards as we considered necessary in the circumstances. Other auditors examined the financial statements of certain subsidiaries and have furnished us with reports thereon containing no exceptions. Our opinion expressed herein, insofar as it relates to the amounts included for those subsidiaries, is based solely upon the reports of the other auditors.

As discussed in note 4 to the financial statements, on January 8, 2006, the company halted the production of certain medical equipment as a result of enquiries by the Alberta Medical Association, which raised questions as to the adequacy of some of the company's sterilization equipment and related procedures. Management is not in a position to evaluate the effect of this production halt and the ensuing litigation, which may have an adverse effect on the financial position of Athabaska Widgets, Inc.

As fully discussed in note 7 to the financial statements, in 2005 the company extended the use of the average cost method of accounting to include all inventories. In examining inventories, we engaged Dr. Irwin Same to test check the technical requirements and specifications of certain items of equipment manufactured by the company.

In our opinion, except for the effects, if any, on the financial statements of the ultimate resolution of the matter discussed in the second preceding paragraph, the financial statements referred to above present fairly the financial position of Athabaska Widgets, Inc., as of December 31, 2005, the results of operations for the year then ended, in conformity with Canadian generally accepted accounting principles.

To be signed by
Bettrioni & Bee

March 1, 2006, except for note 4 for which the date is January 8, 2006

Required

Identify deficiencies in the staff accountant's tentative report that constitute departures from the generally accepted standards of reporting.

(AICPA adapted)

PROFESSIONAL JUDGMENT PROBLEM

3-28 Jeffrey Simms, a qualified accountant, is a supervisor with a public accounting firm, and is a close friend of yours. You regularly have lunch together, and share both personal and business information.

Today, you had asked Jeffrey why he looked so tired, even when it is not busy season. Jeffrey responded, "Well, it's great to be a qualified accountant right now. Not only is there work for my own firm, but because I have so much experience designing internal control systems, I can provide consulting for clients advising them how to beef up their internal controls before the auditors come in. Everyone wants to get a clean combined audit report now that the large public companies have to report on their internal controls. With a consulting company that a few of us have set up, I can work through my holidays and my weekends while the going is hot!"

Your mind in a turmoil, you make some noncommittal remark and change the subject.

Required
What should you do?

CASES

3-29 Grogus Limited (GL) is a private company, incorporated in 1997 under federal legislation. GL was audited for the first time for the year ended July 31, 2005, by a CA who issued a qualified audit opinion because GL did not record amortization. According to the CA's estimate, the amount not recorded last year was $125,000 or approximately 20 percent of last year's income. During the current year, the vice-president of finance approached the CA indicating that he wanted an unqualified opinion for the year ending July 31, 2006, as he anticipates that the company will become a public company in the near future.

The vice-president of finance has presented the CA with the following contentious accounting issues facing the company:
1. GL has not in the past recorded amortization on its fixed assets. The president's feelings about this subject were noted in last year's report to the shareholders as follows: "Our capital assets are increasing, not decreasing in value. In my opinion, the recording of this fictitious expense (amortization) will make our financial statements misleading."

    The Board of Directors, however, has agreed that amortization will be recorded this year in order to obtain an unqualified opinion. The computation of the amortization expense would take into consideration residual value of the capital assets and a remaining asset life of 12 years, which the CA agrees is the maximum remaining life of the assets. According to the Board of Directors, residual values have been estimated after giving effect to expected increases of $1,000,000 in those values over the next 12 years.
2. During the year, the company has incurred expenditures of $400,000 related to the development of a refinement on one of its existing products. The large majority of the costs were related to the design, construction, and testing of pre-production prototypes. The technical feasibility of the refinement has been clearly established and management is now optimistic that it will be a profitable product for the company.

Similar expenditures of $200,000 had been written off last year because, at that time, it was management's opinion that they would not continue with the project. Management has reinstated the $200,000 of expenditures incurred last year by a credit to miscellaneous income and intends to write off the total development costs incurred of $600,000 over a period of five years.
3. In connection with the installation of a new computer system during the year, software costs of $270,000 were incurred and capitalized. GL is willing to amortize such costs over this year and the next five years to the end of the computer lease.
4. Last year GL capitalized $60,000 of interest on debt during the period of construction of one of its manufacturing buildings. The $60,000 was expensed for income tax purposes, but no future income tax liability was recorded. GL is willing to amortize the capitalized sums over a period of 20 years, commencing in the current year.
5. In both this and the previous year, GL has received approximately 40 percent of its revenue from one customer. The loss of this customer would result in significant excess capacity for the company.

    GL's net income for the current year was $1,500,000 prior to recording any adjustment(s) required to resolve the contentious accounting issues.

Required
a. What do these situations indicate about management competence and attitudes?
b. Discuss the audit report considerations for each issue presented. Describe the alternative methods available for resolving each contentious issue.
c. Assume management has agreed with all your recommendations. Draft your auditor's report, omitting the scope paragraph.

(CICA adapted)

3-30 Raven Limited is a Canadian company engaged in a wholesaling business and currently distributes three major product lines. Over the years, the company has distributed several other product lines, only to discontinue them when the competition became too intense. During the past three years, one of its product lines, the carbon filtering systems, has suffered a continual decline in sales volume and has had a negative effect on the company's operating profits. At December 31, 2004, a significant portion of the inventory of carbon filtering systems was about two years old.

In October 2005, management decided to discontinue distribution of carbon filtering systems, and notified the company's customers that it would continue to sell the inventory on hand but would no longer accept orders for items that would have to be purchased from a manufacturer. After this notice was sent to the company's customers, the sales volume of carbon filtering systems declined even further. Therefore, management decided in early 2006 to sell this inventory in bulk to one of the company's competitors.

Management informs you in February 2006 that it is currently negotiating the sale with one competitor and that the asking price is $1,100,000, which it is confident it will get. It is unwilling to permit you to review any documentation supporting the current negotiations because of a commitment made not to disclose the purchaser's identity. It also informs you that the only firm written offer received so far is from a second competitor and the amount of this offer is $800,000. It is prepared to provide you with a copy of this offer.

Based on these facts, management concludes that a write-down of $500,000 (i.e., to the amount of $1,100,000 currently being negotiated) is all that is required. Management believes that this should be treated as an extraordinary item and will make any disclosure you request but will not change its position on this item.

Required
Discuss the effect of this issue on the auditor's report.

(CICA adapted)

CHAPTER 4

LEGAL LIABILITY

Why can the auditor be sued when a business goes bankrupt? Isn't it management's responsibility to run the business? In this chapter, we will explore terminology associated with legal liability, and look at how lawsuits and legislation have framed the legal environment.

LEARNING OBJECTIVES

After reading this chapter, you should be able to answer the following questions:

1. What are an auditor's sources of legal liability? How is this related to a distinction between business failure and audit failure?

2. Do accountants have the right of privileged communication? What other concepts or terms are associated with auditor's legal liability? What should auditors do if a client sues them?

3. Who else can sue the auditor, besides the client? How would the auditor defend against such suits? Can the auditor go to jail because of criminal liability?

4. If the auditor has access to confidential information that would help a different business avoid financial hardship, can this information be disclosed? What are individual accountants and the profession doing to respond to legal liability?

PHANTOM INVENTORY

Mickey Monus was the local hero in Youngstown, Ohio. He acquired a local drugstore and, within 10 years, added 299 more stores to form the U.S. national deep-discount retail chain, Phar-Mor, Inc. The company was viewed as the rising star by some retail experts and was considered to be the next Wal-Mart. Even Sam Walton announced that the only company he feared in the expansion of Wal-Mart was Phar-Mor.

Phar-Mor sold a variety of household products and prescription drugs at substantially lower prices than other discount stores. Monus described the company's strategy as "power buying," whereby Phar-Mor loaded up on products when suppliers were selling at rock-bottom prices.

Actually, Phar-Mor's prices were so low that the company was selling goods for less than their cost, causing the company to lose money. However, Monus continued to argue internally that through Phar-Mor's power buying, it would get so large that it could sell its way out of trouble. Unwilling to allow these shortfalls to damage Phar-Mor's appearance of success, Monus and his team began to engage in creative accounting so that Phar-Mor never reported these losses in its financial statements.

Management dumped the losses into "bucket accounts," only to reallocate those amounts to the company's hundreds of stores in the form of phantom increases in inventory costs. Monus's team issued fake invoices for merchandise purchases, made fraudulent journal entries to increase inventory and decrease cost of goods sold, and overcounted and double-counted inventory items.

Unfortunately, the auditors never uncovered the fraud. They allegedly observed inventory in only four stores out of 300, and they informed Phar-Mor management months in advance about the stores they would visit. Phar-Mor executives fully stocked the four selected stores but allocated the false inventory increases to the other 296 stores.

The fraud was ultimately uncovered when a travel agent received a Phar-Mor cheque signed by Monus paying for expenses that were unrelated to Phar-Mor. The agent showed the cheque to her landlord, who happened to be a Phar-Mor investor, and he contacted David Shapiro, Phar-Mor's CEO. Subsequent investigation of the invalid expenditure eventually led to the discovery of the inventory fraud.

Monus was eventually convicted and went to jail for 5 years. The CFO, who did not profit personally, was sentenced to 33 months in prison. The audit failure cost the audit firm over $300 million in civil judgments.

Sources: Adapted from Beasley, Buckless, Glover, and Prawitt, Auditing Cases: An Interactive Learning Approach, 2nd Edition, Prentice-Hall, 2003, pp. 25–41 and Joseph T. Wells, "Ghost Goods: How to Spot Phantom Inventory," Journal of Accountancy (June 2001), pp. 33–36.

How do you feel about legal liability? Does it worry you that you might be sued if you become a public accountant? How does it feel to know that you might be called upon to be an expert witness? Legal liability (and its consequences) can be significant and is the reason accountants carry liability insurance—to enable them to conduct their work in a professional manner, and deal with lawsuits from clients and others. Sound quality control practices and adherence to independence rules and other professional standards and rules of conduct assist firms in preventing lawsuits.

This chapter discusses the nature of **legal liability** of public accountants. First, the reasons for increased litigation against public accountants are discussed. This is followed by a detailed examination of the nature of the lawsuits and the sources of potential liability. Significant lawsuits involving public accountants that relate to the various issues are presented in summary form. You will note that the cases discussed come from the United States, the United Kingdom, and Canada; the legal systems in all three countries (except in Quebec, whose private law is based on French civil law[1]) are based on English common law; as a consequence, when judges in all three countries hand down decisions, while they have no obligation to follow decisions in the other countries, they will often refer to those decisions in the course of giving their own judgment. The chapter ends with a discussion of the options available to the profession and individual practitioners to minimize liability while meeting society's needs.

LEGAL LIABILITY—the professional's obligation under the law to provide a reasonable level of care while performing work for those he or she serves

→4.1 APPRECIATING THE LEGAL ENVIRONMENT

Changed Legal Environment

Professionals have always had a duty to provide a reasonable level of care while performing work for those they serve. Audit professionals have a responsibility under common law to fulfill implied or expressed contracts with clients. They are liable to their clients for negligence and/or breach of contract should they fail to provide the services or should they fail to exercise due care in their performance. Auditors may also be held liable under the tort of negligence or due to provincial securities acts to parties other than their clients in certain circumstances. Although the precise legal definition of the auditor's *third-party* (people who

---

[1] Smyth, J. E., D. A Soberman, and A. J. Easson, *The Law and Business Administration in Canada*, Seventh Edition, Toronto, Ontario: Prentice Hall Canada Inc., 1995, pp. 46–47.

do not have a contract with the auditor) liability continues to evolve, the position of the Supreme Court of Canada, at this time, remains that the auditor owes a duty of care to third parties who are part of a limited group of persons whom the auditor knows will use and rely on the audit, and that the auditor's knowledge extends to the purpose or transaction for which the financial statements would be used.

Note the use of the term "evolve" here; in Canada, as in other countries, lower courts are presenting other definitions. You will see further discussion of this shortly. Finally, in rare cases, auditors have also been held liable for criminal acts. A criminal conviction against an auditor can result only when it is demonstrated that the auditor acted with criminal intent.

A relatively new area of liability is fiduciary duty. **Fiduciary duty** is a growing body of Canadian law that has affected accountants and may also affect auditors. The Supreme Court of Canada case of *Robert L. Hodgkinson v. David L. Sims and Jerry S. Waldman* (File No. 23033, 1997) summarized many of the then current definitions of a fiduciary. On page 385 of the case, the court indicates that "the hallmark of a fiduciary relationship is that one party is dependent upon or in the power of the other." It then looks to three conditions: (1) the fiduciary has the ability to exercise discretion or power, (2) discretion or power can be unilaterally exercised, and (3) the beneficiary is peculiarly vulnerable. The court then goes on to say that this is not an absolute test. It is not further discussed in this text since in an ordinary auditor–client relationship, no fiduciary duty would arise.[2]

The five sources of auditor's legal liability identified in the previous paragraphs are the main focus of this chapter. They are summarized in Table 4-1, with an example of a potential claim from each source.

In recent years, both the number of lawsuits and size of awards to plaintiffs have significantly increased in both Canada and the United States, although the increase in the United States has been more significant because of a number of factors, including the more litigious climate in that country. Many of the lawsuits brought against auditors are brought by third parties. There are no simple reasons for this increase, but the following are major factors:

- The growing awareness of the responsibilities of public accountants by users of financial statements.
- An increased consciousness on the part of the provincial securities commissions regarding their responsibility for protecting investors' interests.

FIDUCIARY DUTY—a party (such as an accountant) has an obligation to act for the benefit of another, and that obligation includes discretionary power

TABLE 4-1	Five Major Sources of Auditor's Legal Liability
Source of Liability	**Example of Potential Claim**
Client—liability to client under common law	Client sues auditor for not discovering a defalcation during the audit.
Third party—liability to third parties under common law	Bank sues auditor for not discovering materially misstated financial statements.
Liability under provincial securities acts	A purchaser of stock issued by a company sues the auditor for not discovering materially misstated financial statements in a prospectus.
Criminal liability	Court prosecutes auditor under the *Criminal Code of Canada* for knowingly issuing an incorrect auditor's report.
Fiduciary duty—one party has an obligation to act for the benefit of another, and that obligation includes discretionary power	An accountant acting as trustee for a client invests in inappropriate investment vehicles and otherwise squanders the assets of the trust.

---

[2]See also: Paskell-Mede, Mindy, "Fiduciary duty," *CAmagazine* (April 2004), pp. 43–44, 49.

- Increased market volatility, resulting in losses to third parties such as shareholders and institutional investors.
- The greater complexity of auditing and accounting due to such factors as the increasing size of business, the sophistication of computer-based systems, and the intricacies of business operations.
- Society's increasing acceptance of lawsuits by injured parties against anyone who might be able to provide compensation and who appears to be at least partially responsible for the loss. This is frequently called the "deep-pocket" concept of liability.
- The willingness of public accounting firms to settle their legal problems out of court in an attempt to avoid costly legal fees and adverse publicity rather than resolving them through the judicial process.
- The difficulty courts have in understanding and interpreting technical accounting and auditing matters.

Distinction Among Business Failure, Audit Failure, and Audit Risk

Many accounting and legal professionals believe that a major cause of lawsuits against public accounting firms is the lack of understanding by financial statement users of the difference between a *business failure* and an *audit failure* and between an *audit failure* and *audit risk*. These terms are first defined then followed by a discussion of how misunderstanding in the differences between the terms often results in lawsuits against auditors.

BUSINESS FAILURE A **business failure** occurs when a business is unable to repay its lenders or meet the expectations of its investors, due to economic or business conditions such as a recession, poor management decisions, or unexpected competition in the industry. The extreme case of business failure is filing for bankruptcy. As stated in Chapter 1, there is always some risk that a business will fail.

AUDIT FAILURE An **audit failure** occurs when the auditor issues an erroneous audit opinion as the result of an underlying failure to comply with the requirements of generally accepted auditing standards. For example, the auditor may have assigned unqualified assistants to perform audit tasks, and because of their lack of competence and inappropriate supervision, they failed to find material misstatements that qualified auditors would have discovered.

AUDIT RISK An **audit risk** is the risk that the auditor will conclude that the financial statements are fairly stated and an unqualified opinion can therefore be issued when, in fact, they are materially misstated. As will be shown in subsequent chapters, auditing cannot be expected to uncover all material financial statement misstatements. Auditing is limited by sampling, and certain misstatements and well-concealed frauds are extremely difficult to detect; therefore, there is always some risk that the audit will not uncover a material financial statement misstatement even when the auditor has complied with generally accepted auditing standards.

Most accounting professionals agree that in most cases when an audit has failed to uncover material misstatements, and the wrong type of audit opinion is issued, a legitimate question may be raised as to whether the auditor followed due care. If the auditor failed to use due care in the conduct of the audit, then there is an audit failure. In such cases, the law often allows parties who suffered losses as a result of the auditor's breach of duty of care owed to them to recover some or all of the losses proximately caused by the audit failure. It is difficult in practice to determine when the auditor has failed to follow due care because of the complexity of auditing. It is also not always clear who has a right to expect the benefits of an audit because of the evolving nature of the law. Nevertheless, an auditor's failure to follow due care can be expected to result in a claim of negligence and, where appropriate, damages against the public accounting firm.

The difficulty arises when there has been a business failure, but not an audit failure. For example, when a company goes bankrupt or cannot pay its debts, it is common for statement users to claim there was an audit failure, particularly when the most recently issued auditor's opinion indicates the financial statements were fairly stated. This conflict between statement users and auditors often arises because of what is referred to as the **expectation gap** *between users and auditors*. Most auditors believe that conducting an audit in

BUSINESS FAILURE—the situation when a business is unable to repay its lenders, or meet the expectations of its investors because of economic or business conditions

AUDIT FAILURE—a situation in which the auditor issues an erroneous audit opinion as the result of an underlying failure to comply with the requirements of generally accepted auditing standards

AUDIT RISK—the risk that the auditor will conclude that the financial statements are fairly stated and an unqualified opinion can therefore be issued when in fact they are materially misstated

EXPECTATION GAP—the conflict between what some users expect from an auditor's report and what the auditor's report is designed to deliver; some users believe that an auditor's report is a guarantee as to the accuracy of the financial statements, although the report is in fact an opinion based on an audit conducted according to generally accepted auditing standards accordance with generally accepted auditing standards is all that can be expected of auditors. Many users believe auditors guarantee the accuracy of financial statements, and some users even believe the auditor guarantees the financial viability of the business. Fortunately for the profession, the courts continue to support the auditor's view.

→4.2 LEGAL TERMS AFFECTING PAs AND THEIR CLIENTS

Legal Concepts Affecting Liability

The public accountant is responsible for every aspect of his or her public accounting work, including auditing, taxes, management advisory services, and accounting and bookkeeping services. Section 5020 of the *CICA Assurance Handbook*, "Association," helps explain the public accountant's involvement with an enterprise or with information issued by that enterprise. For example, if a public accountant negligently failed to properly prepare and file a client's tax return, the public accountant can be held liable for any penalties and interest the client was required to pay plus the tax preparation fee charged.

Most of the major lawsuits against public accounting firms have dealt with audited or unaudited financial statements. The discussion in this chapter deals primarily with these two aspects of public accounting. The areas of liability in auditing can be classified as (1) liability to clients, (2) liability to third parties under common law and statute law, and (3) criminal liability. Several legal concepts apply to these types of lawsuits against public accountants: the *prudent person concept, liability for the acts of others,* and the *lack of privileged communication.*

Prudent Person Concept There is agreement within the profession and the courts that the auditor is not a guarantor or insurer of financial statements. The auditor is only expected to conduct the audit with due care. Even then, the auditor cannot be expected to be perfect.

The standard of due care to which the auditor is expected to be held is often referred to as the **prudent person concept.** It is expressed in *Cooley on Torts* as follows:

> Every man who offers his service to another and is employed assumes the duty to exercise in the employment such skill as he possesses with reasonable care and diligence. In all these employments where peculiar skill is prerequisite, if one offers his service, he is understood as holding himself out to the public as possessing the degree of skill commonly possessed by others in the same employment, and, if his pretensions are unfounded, he commits a species of fraud upon every man who employs him in reliance on his public profession. But no man, whether skilled or unskilled, undertakes that the task he assumes shall be performed successfully, and without fault or error. *He undertakes for good faith and integrity, but not for infallibility,* and he is liable to his employer for negligence, bad faith, or dishonesty, but not for losses consequent upon pure errors of judgment.

Liability for Acts of Others The partners of a public accounting firm may have *joint and several liability* if a suit for tort or negligence is brought against the partnership. In other

PRUDENT PERSON CONCEPT—the legal concept that a person has a duty to exercise reasonable care and diligence in the performance of his or her obligations to another words, each partner may be held liable in a civil action for the tort or negligent actions of each of the other partners and employees in the partnership. Ontario provincial legislation has given accounting firms the ability to reduce their liability by forming **limited liability partnerships** (LLPs). Under this organizational form, individual partners who had nothing to do with the engagement or with the supervision of the staff who carried out the engagement would not be liable on their personal assets. In the absence of fraud or actual knowledge, only the person who did the work and those who supervised that person, as well as the firm itself, would be liable. The auditor can also be held responsible for damages of others using the concept of joint and several liability. If an auditor is partially responsible but none of the other defendants have assets or insurance, then there will be an attempt to collect all damages from the auditor.

LIMITED LIABILITY PARTNERSHIP (LLP)—an organizational structure whereby only the person who does the work, those who supervise that person, and the firm itself are liable, but not other individual partners within the firm

The partners may also be liable for the work of others on whom they rely. The groups an auditor is most likely to rely on are *other public accounting firms* engaged to do part of the work, *internal auditors*, and *specialists* called upon to provide technical information. Where a primary–secondary auditor relationship exists, the primary auditor would be entitled to rely upon the work of the secondary auditor, assuming that the primary auditor had conducted sufficient quality control work with respect to that secondary auditor. If the auditor proved that there was appropriate reliance on the work of a specialist, there would be an extremely strong defence that the auditor was not negligent and would not be liable to the plaintiff, assuming that GAAS were followed.

Focus Box 4-2
CHANGING THE RULES FOR CIVIL LIABILITY

The Ontario government enacted legislation in 2002 as part of Bill 198, the *Ontario Securities Act*, that both increases legal liability and reduces the amounts that auditors could be liable for. The legislation has not yet been proclaimed—revisions were still being considered and made as of this writing. The proposed legislation provides that investors could sue (with court permission) where they relied upon information that was misrepresented (such as incorrect financial statements). Changes that would affect public accountants are proportional liability (they could be sued for only the portion that they are judged to be at fault) and a cap on

liability based upon a formula that is the greater of $1 million and the earnings from the client (and its affiliates) from the twelve months preceding the misrepresentation. These changes could potentially mean that more parties could sue the auditor, but that the amount liable would be less.

Sources: 1. Morgan, Brian, "New liabilities," *CAmagazine* (June/July 2003), pp. 34–36. 2. Alas-Sevillanao, Manual, "Civil liability for secondary market disclosure," Ontario Management Board Secretariat, 2004, www.mbs.gov.on.ca/MBS/english/mbs/releases/general/nov2204-background.html, Accessed: October 2005.

Lack of Privileged Communication Public accountants do not have the right under common law to withhold information from the courts on the grounds that the information is privileged. As stated in Chapter 2, a court can subpoena information in an auditor's working papers. Confidential discussions between the client and auditor cannot be withheld from the courts. In the very specific situation where an accountant prepares documentation as a result of a lawyer's request to be used in existing or potential litigation, that documentation could be considered privileged (e.g., *Cineplex Odeon v. MNR* [Ministry of National Revenue], 1994).

Definitions of Legal Terms

The material in the rest of the chapter can be covered more effectively if the most common legal terms affecting public accountants' liability are understood.

Negligence and Fraud The first four terms deal with the auditor's negligence or fraud. The distinctions are useful for discussing the application of the law to various types of lawsuits against auditors because they affect the outcome of many suits.

NEGLIGENCE—failure to exercise reasonable care in the performance of one's obligations to another

NEGLIGENCE Absence of reasonable care that can be expected of a person in a set of circumstances. When **negligence** of an auditor is being evaluated, it is in terms of what other competent auditors would have done in the same situation.

TORT ACTION FOR NEGLIGENCE Failure of a party to meet its social or professional obligations, contractual or otherwise, thereby causing injury to another party to whom a duty was owed is **tort action for negligence**. A typical negligence action against a public accountant is a bank's claim that an auditor had a duty to uncover material errors in financial statements that had been relied on in making a loan.

TORT ACTION FOR NEGLIGENCE—a legal action taken by an injured party against the party whose negligence resulted in the injury

A plaintiff in a tort action (i.e., a case brought by a plaintiff for an alleged wrong suffered at the hands of the defendant) for negligence against a public accountant must prove all of the following to succeed:

1. The accountant (defendant) must owe a duty of care to the plaintiff.
2. The defendant must have been negligent in the performance of that duty (i.e., did not act in accordance with the prudent person concept).
3. The plaintiff must have suffered a loss.
4. There must be a connection between the defendant's negligence and the plaintiff's loss. For example, the plaintiff relied on financial statements audited by the defendant, who was negligent in the performance of the audit, and the plaintiff suffered a loss because of that reliance.

FRAUD A false assertion that has been made knowingly, or without belief in its truth, or recklessly without caring whether or not it is true. To prove **fraud**, the plaintiff must also be able to prove that the accountant intended the plaintiff to act on the assertion, that the plaintiff did act on it, and that, as a consequence, the plaintiff suffered a loss. An example is an auditor giving a standard (unqualified) opinion on financial statements that will be used to obtain a loan when the auditor *knows* the financial statements contain a material misstatement.

FRAUD—a false assertion that has been made knowingly, without belief in its truth, or recklessly without caring whether it is true or not

CONSTRUCTIVE FRAUD Existence of such recklessness that, even though there was no actual intent to defraud, a court will impute or construe fraud to the action. For example, if a public accountant failed to follow most of the generally accepted auditing standards, he or she may be found to have committed **constructive fraud** even though no intent to deceive statement users has been proved. This concept has been used in foreign court cases but has not been used in Canadian cases. It is therefore not discussed further in this chapter. We will focus instead on negligence and fraud.

CONSTRUCTIVE FRAUD—conduct that the law construes as fraud even though there was no actual intent to deceive; considered to be so reckless that the courts decide it is tantamount to fraud

Contract Law

BREACH OF CONTRACT Failure of one or both parties in a contract to fulfill the requirements of the contract. An example is the failure of a public accounting firm to deliver a tax return on the agreed-upon date. Parties who have a relationship that is established by a contract are said to have *privity of contract.*

Typically, public accounting firms and clients sign an *engagement letter* to formalize their agreement about the services to be provided, fees, and timing. There can be privity of contract without a written agreement, but an engagement letter defines the contract more clearly.

THIRD-PARTY BENEFICIARY A third party who does not have privity of contract but is known to the contracting parties and is intended to have certain rights and benefits under the contract. A common example is a bank that has a large loan outstanding at the balance sheet date and requires an audit as a part of its loan agreement.

Common and Statutory Law

COMMON LAW, JUDGE-MADE LAW, OR CASE LAW Law that has been developed through court decisions rather than through government statutes. The bulk of the law of negligence has been created in this fashion. An example is an auditor's liability to a bank related to the auditor's failure to discover material misstatements in financial statements that were relied on in issuing a loan. This law is continually evolving as new decisions are handed down by the courts; what might be used as a successful defence by an auditor today may not be successful tomorrow, while a defence that was not successful in the past might now be successful. The thing to remember is that **common law** is always evolving as new precedents are set by the courts.

STATUTORY LAW Laws and regulations that have been passed by a Canadian government body, either federal or provincial. The *Canada Business Corporations Act* is an important statutory law affecting auditors of companies incorporated under its jurisdiction.

COMMON LAW—laws developed through court decisions rather than through government statutes; also called *judge-made law* or *case law*

Other Terms

CIVIL ACTION An action between individuals such as those that may be brought for breach of contract or tort.

CRIMINAL ACTION An action brought under a provision of criminal statute law, for example, the *Criminal Code of Canada*.

CONTRIBUTORY NEGLIGENCE When a person injured by a public accountant's negligence has also been negligent, and this negligence has also caused or contributed to the person's loss or injuries, this is known as **contributory negligence**. A common example of such negligence is failure to give a public accountant information requested during the preparation of a tax return. The client later sues the accountant for improper preparation of the return. The court may hold that there was contributory negligence by the client, and any damages that the client is awarded would be reduced in proportion to the amount that the client's own negligence was responsible for the loss. This defence is also used to reduce the effects of joint and several liability.

CONTRIBUTORY NEGLIGENCE—a legal defence under which the professional claims that the client failed to perform certain obligations and that it is the client's failure to perform those obligations that brought about the claimed damages

Liability to Clients

The term *client* refers to the entity being audited and not to its owners or shareholders. Although the shareholders vote to appoint the auditors, the contract is between the enterprise and the auditors. In effect, shareholders are third parties and are discussed further, together with liability to other third parties, on page 91.

Lawsuits against public accountants from clients vary widely, including such claims as failure to complete an audit engagement on the agreed-upon date, inappropriate withdrawal from an audit, failure to discover a *defalcation*, and breach of the confidentiality requirements of public accountants. Typically, these lawsuits are relatively rare, and they do not receive the publicity often given to third-party suits. *Cameron v. Piers*, Figure 4-4 on page 90, is a case in this area.

A typical lawsuit involves a claim that the auditor did not discover an employee **defalcation** (theft of assets) as a result of negligence in the conduct of the audit. The lawsuit can be for breach of contract, a tort action for negligence, or both. Tort actions can be based on ordinary negligence or fraud. Note that, while it might sound odd for plaintiffs to claim under both breach of contract and negligence, the way each is proven and the amount of damages available under each might be different. By claiming under both, the plaintiff is thus covering all bases. The plaintiff cannot, however, be awarded damages twice for one event or loss.

DEFALCATION—theft of assets

The principal issue in cases involving alleged negligence is usually the level of care required. Although it is generally agreed that nobody is perfect, not even a professional, in most instances any significant misstatement will create a doubt regarding competence. In the auditing environment, failure to meet generally accepted auditing standards is often strong evidence of negligence. An example of an audit case raising the question of negligent performance by a public accounting firm is the case of *Haig v. Bamford* (see Figure 4-7 on page 93). The reader should remember from the study of generally accepted auditing standards in Chapter 1 that determining due care and the amount and type of evidence to be obtained on an audit are subjective decisions. In a suit where negligence by an auditor was alleged, the court would hear evidence from one or more expert (auditing) witnesses as to the decision they would have reached in similar circumstances. From this evidence, a judge or jury would decide what the average public accountant would do and, therefore, what the accountant being sued should have done. In this way, the determination of negligence occurs.

The question of level of care becomes more difficult in the environment of unaudited financial statements (i.e., a review or compilation) in which there are few accepted standards to evaluate performance. An example of a lawsuit dealing with the failure to uncover fraud in unaudited financial statements is the *Multi Graphics* case, summarized in Figure 4-1. Figure 4-2 addresses a key standard of review engagements (plausibility, Chapter 23) in *Italian Gifts v. Dixon,* 2000.

Auditor's Defences Against Client Suits for Negligence The public accounting firm normally uses one of or a combination of six defences when there are legal claims of negligence by clients: lack of duty to perform the service, absence of misstatement, absence of negligence, contributory negligence, no damages, and absence of causal connection.

LACK OF DUTY The **lack of duty to perform** the service means that the public accounting firm claims there was no duty owed to the client to perform the task that is now said to have been negligently performed. For example, the public accounting firm might claim that errors were not uncovered because the firm did a review engagement, not an audit. A common way for a public accounting firm to demonstrate a lack of duty to perform is by use of an *engagement letter.*[3] Many litigation experts believe well-written engagement letters are one of the most important ways public accounting firms can reduce the likelihood of adverse legal actions.

Harry Kuziw et al. v. James W. Abbott et al. (Figure 4-3) illustrates reliance and a lack of duty.

ABSENCE OF MISSTATEMENT Prior to addressing negligence, the defendant accountants could provide evidence that the financial statements were in accordance with GAAP, that is, that there were no material errors. Thus, even if the auditors had been negligent, the

FIGURE 4-1	*466715 Ontario Limited Operating as Multi Graphics Print & Litho v. Helen Proulx and Doane Raymond* (1998)[4]

Doane Raymond (now Grant Thornton) carried out review engagements between 1985 and 1993 for Multi Graphics Print and Litho for an annual fee of about $1,500. Helen Proulx, the sole bookkeeper, commenced fraudulent activity in 1988, when she was given signing authority. Shortly afterwards, a computerized ACCPAC Bedford system was installed. The fraud involved Proulx preparing cheques to herself, signing and cashing them (the cheques were recorded as payable to suppliers or to reimbursement of petty cash), pocketing money for C.O.D. orders and issuing fictitious invoices, and having a differential between the amount deposited and the amount recorded and pocketing the difference. Over $100,000 was stolen. The owners signed cheques over $1,000 and did not handle mail or review source documents or bank statements.

When the fraud was discovered, Multi Graphics sued the accountants, claiming that the accountants ought to have known of the control problems at Multi Graphics and should have alerted the owners to the related dangers. The accountants countered by saying that they were retained to provide review services. The engagement letter explicitly described a review engagement, stating that there was no responsibility to consider internal controls or to detect fraud. The accountants were not consulted on issues of internal controls, the change in the computerized accounting system, or the change in signing authority.

The court ruled in favour of Doane Raymond, finding that the accountants had fulfilled their professional and contractual obligations, and that the agreement between the parties specifically excluded responsibility to detect fraud and error. The court added that the duty of care in a review engagement would not create the obligation to go any further than the accountants did.

[3]Two types of letters that are commonly used by auditors to reduce potential liability to clients are an engagement letter and a management representation letter. An engagement letter is a signed agreement between the public accounting firm and the client identifying such items as whether an audit is to be done, other services to be provided, the date by which the work is to be completed, and the fees. The representation letter documents oral communication between auditors and management, and states management's responsibilities for fair presentation in the financial statements.

[4]Kulig, P., "Doane Raymond Absolved of Wrongdoing," *The Bottom Line* (November 1, 1998), p. 14, and trial judgment, Ontario Court (General Division), 95-CU-87608, August 20, 1998.

appropriate financial statements would not have differed from those on which the plaintiff relied. Therefore, no grounds exist for suing the auditors, since the financial statements appropriately portray the financial situation of the organization and there was an *absence of misstatement*.

FIGURE 4-2   *Italian Gifts v. Dixon (2000)*[5]

Dixon, a chartered accountant firm, was hired to conduct a review engagement for Italian Gifts. The firm did not detect an underremittance of sales taxes with a corresponding overremittance of income taxes. In one particular month, only $1.68 in sales taxes was remitted on more than $19,000 of sales. The client was claiming damages that included the penalties and interest on the unremitted sales tax, as well as income tax overpayments that could not be recovered, interest on overpaid income taxes, and professional fees.

Two lower courts had rejected this claim for three reasons:

1. no duty was owed since the client was not relying on the accountants for tax remittances
2. the nature of a review engagement would not have included the duty of preparing sales tax remittances
3. the bookkeeping [review engagement] function was not of a nature to require an analysis of the remittances

The Ontario Court of Appeal overturned this rejection, by stating that the accountants' failure to inquire into the plausibility of the sales tax remittances fell below the standards set out in the *CICA Handbooks*. This reference reinforces the importance of this CICA publication. A simple analysis (calculating sales tax as a percentage of sales, for example) would have revealed the inadequacy of these amounts. An engagement letter with exclusions for responsibility on the detection of errors and irregularities was not considered an acceptable defense, due to the accountants' negligence.

Given the client's own errors, which caused the original problem, and that clients are clearly responsible for their own financial statements, the Court of Appeal reduced the damages by 50% due to contributory negligence.

FIGURE 4-3   *Kuziw et al. v. Abbott et al. (1984)*

Abbott *et al.* provided accounting services to Graf-Tech Publication Services Ltd. for several years. William J. Hemenway, a member of the firm of Abbott *et al.*, who had done work for Harry Kuziw in connection with other investments that Kuziw had made, introduced Kuziw to Graf-Tech in early 1980 in response to Kuziw's request for information about "business opportunities."

Graf-Tech was suffering from cash shortages and was being pressed by Canada Customs and Revenue Agency for overdue payroll deductions. It was also suffering from managerial weaknesses. Hemenway explained both the positive and negative aspects of Graf-Tech to Kuziw and provided him with statements with "Accountant's Comments" dated June 30, 1979, and with statements for January and February 1980 that had each been prepared with a "Notice to Reader." Kuziw knew that no audit had been done and appeared to understand the implications of work done under then Section 8100 (now Section 9200) of the *CICA Assurance Handbook*. The court found that Kuziw had conducted an extensive investigation on his own including discussions with the senior management of Graf-Tech and with the manager of the bank where Graf-Tech banked. Kuziw's lawyer suggested outside accounting advice but Kuziw demurred.

Kuziw made two investments and gave guarantees totalling $235,000 over the next several months. In addition, he became active in Graf-Tech's management. Despite this assistance, the company went into receivership in late 1980. Among the reasons for the receivership was the fact that Graf-Tech's principal contract was much less profitable than had been believed and than had been indicated by the financial statements prepared by Hemenway's firm some months earlier.

The Court of the Queen's Bench of Manitoba, upheld on appeal by the Court of Appeal of Manitoba, found that while Hemenway had known that Kuziw planned to rely on the financial statements he had prepared, Kuziw had not relied to any significant degree on the information. Accordingly, Kuziw could not succeed. The court went on to state that it believed that Hemenway had "discharged his professional responsibility."

This case is of interest, in addition to its finding, because the judgment discusses at some length the difference between an audit and a compilation, as well as the responsibility of the accountant.

---

[5]Paskell-Mede, Mindy, "A Limitation of Liability," *CAmagazine* (November 2000), pp. 47–48.

ABSENCE OF NEGLIGENCE Evidence to refute a claim would be that the audit was performed in accordance with generally accepted auditing standards. Even if there were undiscovered unintentional misstatements (errors) or intentional misstatements or misrepresentations (fraud and other irregularities), the auditors would argue that they are not responsible if the audit was properly conducted; the **absence of negligence**. The public accounting firm is not expected to be infallible.

It is likely that the courts will accept the *CICA Assurance Handbooks* as evidence of appropriate standards of behaviour for the auditor, but it is possible that the courts could decide that an auditor who complied with the *Handbooks* had been negligent. Such circumstances would be rare, but they could occur if the court thought the auditor had complied with the letter and not the spirit of the rules, or if GAAP was not sufficiently informative.

The courts recognize that it is possible to make a valid exercise of judgment that, nonetheless, has an unfavourable outcome. In that case, the auditor would not be found negligent. The auditor would want expert testimony that he or she had made a valid exercise of judgment. For example, the auditor might have selected a sample from a population for testing that was not representative of that population and, hence, had not found a material misstatement that was present in the population. The courts would likely determine that the auditor had not been negligent since the auditor had made a valid exercise in judgment in selecting the sample.

Requiring auditors to discover all material misstatements would, in essence, make them insurers or guarantors of the accuracy of the financial statements. The courts do not require that. *Cameron v. Piers, Conrod & Allen* (Figure 4-4) is an example of a case where the public accountant was not negligent; the court ruled that the auditor had satisfied the prudent person concept.

CONTRIBUTORY NEGLIGENCE A defence of contributory negligence means that the public accounting firm claims that part or all of the loss arose because of the claimant's own negligence. For example, suppose the client is the claimant and argues that the public accounting firm was negligent in not uncovering an employee theft of cash. A likely contributory negligence defence is the auditor's claim that the public accounting firm informed management of a weakness in the internal controls that enhanced the likelihood of the fraud, but management did not correct it. Management often does not correct internal control weaknesses because of cost considerations, attitudes about employee honesty, or procrastination. In the event of a lawsuit of the nature described, the auditor is unlikely to lose the suit, assuming a

---

FIGURE 4-4	*Cameron v. Piers, Conrod & Allen* (1985)[6]

Piers, Conrod & Allen (PCA) were the auditors for Cameron Limited and its subsidiary, Kentville Publishing Company Limited. The year end of the latter company was October 31, while that of the former company was December 31. Kentville was run by a competent accountant who was in frequent contact with and highly regarded by the owner of Cameron Limited.

PCA was unable to gain access to Kentville books for the year ended October 31, 1979, until several months after the year end.

The auditor from PCA and his staff went to the offices of Kentville and did what work was considered necessary to complete the audit of Cameron. At that time, there was no indication of any serious problems at Kentville. The Cameron December 31, 1979, financial statements were issued with an unqualified opinion. The notes to the financial statements indicated that the accounts of Kentville and other subsidiaries were not consolidated but were carried at cost.

Subsequently, the manager of Kentville was hospitalized. It was discovered that the reports that the manager had been giving to the owner of Cameron and to the auditor were not accurate.

Cameron Limited sued PCA on the grounds that PCA had been negligent in evaluating Cameron's investment in Kentville as at December 31, 1979. The court found (sustained on appeal) that the auditor had not been negligent in that he had exercised reasonable care and skill in attempting to evaluate Cameron's investment in Kentville.

---

[6]Rowan, Hugh, Q.C., "Stymied by Management: A Case of Negligence?" *CAmagazine* (April 1986), pp. 80–87.

strong contributory negligence defence, if the client was informed in writing of internal control weaknesses. Figure 4-2, *Italian Gifts v. Dixon* is an example of contributory negligence.

NO DAMAGES (OR REDUCED DAMAGES) It is possible that the financial statements were misstated and that the audit was negligently performed but that the plaintiff did not suffer any damages. This was one of the issues addressed by the Supreme Court of Canada in the case of *Hercules Managements v. Ernst & Young* (Figure 4-9 on page 94). A third party, the shareholders, claimed damages, but the Supreme Court stated that the damages were suffered by the corporate entity itself rather than by the shareholders. Thus, those plaintiffs (the shareholders) had no standing in law to claim the damages.

ABSENCE OF CAUSAL CONNECTION To succeed in an action against the auditor, the client must be able to show that there is a close causal connection between the auditor's breach of the standard of due care and the damages suffered by the client. For example, assume an auditor failed to complete an audit on the agreed-upon date. The client alleges that this caused a bank not to renew an outstanding loan, which caused damages. A potential auditor defence is that the bank refused to renew the loan for other reasons, such as the weakening financial condition of the client. The case of *Kuziw et al. v. Abbott et al.*, discussed in Figure 4-3 on page 89, illustrates **absence of causal connection**; the court ruled that the purchaser, Kuziw, did not rely on an incorrect auditor's report but rather had decided to purchase Graf-Tech based on other information.

ABSENCE OF CAUSAL CONNECTION—a legal defence under which the professional contends that the damages claimed by the client were not brought about by any act of the professional

→4.3 LIABILITY TO NON-CLIENTS
Liability to Third Parties Under Common Law

A public accounting firm may be potentially liable to third parties if a loss was incurred by the claimant due to reliance on misleading financial statements. Third parties are any people with whom the auditor did *not* enter into a contract and include actual and potential shareholders, vendors, bankers, and other creditors or investors, employees, and customers. A typical suit might occur when a bank is unable to collect a major loan from an insolvent customer. The bank will claim that misleading audited financial statements were relied upon in making the loan, and that the public accounting firm should be held responsible because it failed to perform the audit with due care. Understanding when the auditor will be held liable calls for an understanding of the continuing evolution of this area of the law.

Evolution of Liability The leading precedent-setting auditing case in third-party liability was a 1931 U.S. case, *Ultramares Corporation v. Touche*. It established the traditional common law approach known as the *Ultramares* doctrine. The case has been cited many times in England and Canada. It is summarized in Figure 4-5.

FIGURE 4-5	*Ultramares Corporation v. Touche* (1931)

The creditors of an insolvent corporation (Ultramares) relied on the audited financials and subsequently sued the accountants, alleging that they were guilty of negligence and fraudulent misrepresentation. The accounts receivable had been falsified by adding to approximately $650,000 in accounts receivable another item of over $700,000. The creditors alleged that careful investigation would have shown the $700,000 to be fraudulent. The accounts payable contained similar discrepancies. The court held that the accountants had been negligent but ruled that accountants would not be liable to third parties for honest blunders beyond the bounds of the original contract unless they were third-party beneficiaries. The court held that only one who enters into a contract with an accountant for services can sue if those services are rendered negligently.

The court went on, however, to order a new trial on the issue of fraudulent misstatement. The form of certificate then used said, "We further certify that subject to provisions for federal taxes on income the said statement in our opinion presents a true and correct view of the financial condition." The court pointed out that to make such a representation if one did not have an honest belief in its truth would be fraudulent misrepresentation.

The key aspect of the *Ultramares* doctrine is that ordinary negligence is insufficient for liability to third parties because of the lack of privity of contract between the third party and the auditor. The judge commented that it would be inappropriate to hold the auditors liable to third parties in the circumstances since this would open the doors to indeterminate liability of an indeterminate amount to an indeterminate number of people. The case was followed by other jurisdictions on the basis of the policy considerations underlying this judgment. In addition, *Ultramares* also held that if there had been fraud or constructive fraud, the auditor could be held liable to more general third parties.

Traditionally, third parties in Canada were in a similar position to those in the United States: they were effectively prevented from suing successfully for negligent misstatements if they had no contract with the auditor. The situation began to change in 1963 with an English case, *Hedley Byrne & Co. Ltd. v. Heller & Partners Ltd.* (Figure 4-6). This case too was a landmark case. Although the case was British, not Canadian, and did not deal specifically with accountants, it contained very real implications for them. In the United Kingdom, it was viewed as the long-awaited statement about the law of negligent misstatement and it came from the most senior court of that country, the House of Lords. All common law countries were naturally interested in its outcome. The defence of lack of privity enunciated in *Ultramares* was said by the House of Lords to be no longer relevant. The various opinions of the law lords on the case did not make it clear to whom those providing opinions on statements would owe a duty of care. The notion of foreseeable third parties was introduced as a possible test of the extent of duty. The law lords said that those uttering negligent misstatements may be liable to third parties but did not make it clear precisely under what circumstances. Courts in a number of countries have been grappling with the issue ever since.

The Supreme Court of Canada decided the next case of importance on this issue in 1976. The case was *Gordon T. Haig v. Ralph L. Bamford et al.*; see Figure 4-7.

This case confirms the finding in *Hedley Byrne v. Heller* that lack of privity is not necessarily a valid defence. However, the Supreme Court decided it should not consider the foreseeability test (i.e., test 1) as it was not relevant to the particular circumstances. Instead, the narrower test of actual knowledge of the limited class was deemed to be appropriate; that is, in Canada, persons making negligent misstatements (in this case, auditors) are potentially liable to all those third parties who were members of a limited group of whom the auditors had knowledge at the time the audit was performed and to whom the audited financial statements were issued. For example, the test of actual knowledge would apply if an auditor were asked to give an opinion on financial statements to be shown to several local banks for purposes of obtaining a loan. The narrowest of the three tests, that the auditor must know the actual individual, was rejected as being too narrow.

At about the same time, another case of interest was unfolding; it was *Toromont Industrial Holdings Limited v. Thorne, Gunn, Helliwell & Christenson*. This case, summarized in Figure 4-8, reached its final resolution in the High Court of Justice in Ontario.

The *Toromont* case raises several interesting issues. The judgment, which referred both to *Hedley Byrne* and a lower court decision on *Haig v. Bamford*, confirmed the broadening of an auditor's liability to third parties known to be using the audited financial statements. In the

| FIGURE 4-6 | *Hedley Byrne v. Heller & Partners* (1963) |

Hedley Byrne was an advertising agency that was about to incur a liability for advertising for a client. They asked their bankers to find out from the client's bankers, Heller & Partners, if the client was credit-worthy. Heller replied in the affirmative to the banker, who passed the information on to Hedley Byrne, and so Hedley Byrne, a third party, incurred the liability. Subsequently, the client was unable to pay its accounts, and Hedley Byrne sued Heller for negligence.

Heller & Partners had issued a disclaimer together with their opinion and thus the House of Lords ruled in their favour. However, with respect to the lack of privity, the Lords found that not to be a bar to success by the plaintiff, Hedley Byrne. Some of the law lords argued that despite the lack of privity, Heller owed a duty of care to Hedley Byrne and that Heller should have foreseen that Hedley Byrne would rely on their statement about the client.

Scholler Furniture & Fixtures Ltd. needed additional working capital and approached Saskatchewan Economic Development Corporation (SEDCO) for further advances. SEDCO agreed to grant the advances providing Scholler would produce satisfactory audited financial statements for the fiscal period ended March 31, 1965.

Scholler told his accountants, Bamford *et al.,* that he needed audited financial statements for SEDCO, his bank, and a potential but then unknown investor. The statements were prepared, with an auditor's report appended and shown to Haig who invested $20,000.

Subsequently, the company again foundered, and investigation revealed that the financial statements included $28,000 of revenue received in advance as earned revenue; the corrected statements showed that the company had lost money and not earned a sizable profit as shown by the earlier statements. It was discovered that Bamford *et al.,* although they were told an audit was required and although they appended an auditor's report, had not done an audit.

Later Haig advanced additional funds but the company went into receivership. Haig sued the accountants for negligence and sought to recover both his original investment and later advance.

The Supreme Court, in their decision, concurred with lower courts that Bamford *et al.* had been negligent. Insofar as the extent of the duty of care on the part of the accountants to third parties, the court said there were three possible tests:

1. Foreseeability of the use of audited financial statements by the plaintiff
2. Actual knowledge of the limited class who will rely on the audited statements
3. Actual knowledge of the person who will rely on the audited statements

The appropriate test was deemed to be 2. The court decided that Haig was entitled to recover his original investment from the auditors because he had relied on the financial statements that had been negligently prepared. He was not entitled to recover subsequent investments because he made them based on his own information.

case of *Toromont v. Thorne,* Toromont was able to prove that Thorne *et al.* owed a duty of care to Toromont and that Thorne *et al.* had been negligent in the performance of that duty, but Toromont was not able to prove that it suffered a loss. As a consequence, Toromont did not succeed.

In 1997, in *Hercules Managements v. Ernst & Young,*[8] as mentioned earlier, the court ruled that the auditors had no special knowledge that the shareholders planned to use the

Toromont proposed to acquire all of the shares of Cimco Ltd. for cash and Toromont shares. The purchase price was based on Cimco's assets, liabilities, and financial position at that date. Prior to purchase, a partner from the accounting firm that did Toromont's audit talked to a partner of Thorne, Cimco's auditors, about the work the latter had done with regard to the December 31, 1968, financial statements. Cimco's financial statements at this point were in draft form. In other words, Thorne *et al.* were aware of Toromont's interest in the financial statements prior to their being issued.

The court decided that the financial statements did present fairly the financial position at December 31, 1968, but that the auditors, Thorne *et al.,* had been negligent in their performance of the 1968 audit. The reasons given were as follows:

1. They did not obtain sufficient evidence about certain contracts.
2. They relied too heavily on oral evidence from management.
3. They did not adequately check the system of internal control in force although they relied on it.
4. The accounts included goodwill with respect to a company sold two years previously.

The court concluded that Thorne *et al.* had been negligent and that Toromont did have a right of action as Thorne knew Toromont would be relying on the financial statements. The court, however, also concluded that Toromont did not suffer any loss from the negligence, and so the case was dismissed.

---

[7]The *Haig v. Bamford* case first decided in a lower court in 1972 for the plaintiff. The decision was appealed and reversed by the Saskatchewan Court of Appeal in 1974. Haig appealed that decision and was successful in the Supreme Court of Canada in 1976.

[8]Paskell-Mede, Mindy, "What Liability Crisis?" *CAmagazine* (May 1996), pp. 47–48.

financial statements for investment decisions and that there was no privity of contract. The auditors relied on *Caparo* in their defence that they owed no duty of care to the shareholders. Figure 4-9 describes this case further, and shows that the Supreme Court of Canada agreed with the lower court.

Auditor Defences Against Third-Party Suits The defences available to auditors in suits by clients are also available in third-party lawsuits (Figure 4-10).

The previous section outlined the lack of duty of care defence. As the preceding discussion has suggested, the court, in *Ultramares*, limited the auditor's liability for negligence to parties being in privity with the auditor. *Hedley Byrne* introduced the notion of the auditor having a duty of care to foreseeable third parties; *Haig v. Bamford* narrowed the responsibility for duty of care by the auditor to the limited class whom the auditor actually knew would use and rely on the financial statements. The more recent cases in both the United Kingdom

FIGURE 4-9	***Hercules Managements Ltd. v. Ernst & Young (1997)*[9]**

Hercules Managements Ltd. and other shareholders of Northguard Acceptance Ltd. (NGA) and of Northguard Holdings Ltd. (NGH) sued Ernst and Young in 1988 after both NGA and NGH went into receivership in 1984. The plaintiffs argued that the audit reports for the years 1980, 1981, and 1982 were negligently prepared and that the shareholders suffered financial losses due to reliance on these reports.

This action was dismissed both by the Manitoba Court of Queen's Bench and by the Manitoba Appeal Court on the grounds that (1) the defendants did not owe the plaintiffs a duty of care and (2) the claims should be brought by the corporations and not by the shareholders individually, since a shareholder cannot succeed for a reduction in value of equity, even if a duty of care was owed, because the loss of equity is really the loss suffered by the company.

In May 1997, the Supreme Court of Canada generally agreed. The court said audited financial reports call for "a duty of care" by auditors when they are used "as a guide for the shareholders, as a group, in supervising or overseeing management." Thus, there appears to be no direct liability to the shareholders for any reduction in the value of their equity.

This case has entrenched the principle of no general auditor liability where this might give rise to an indeterminate amount of such liability in the absence of any evidence that the auditor knew of a specific purpose, other than corporate governance, to which the financial statements would be put. Such liability, though, could be legislated, as described in Focus Box 4-2 on page 85.

FIGURE 4-10	**Five Auditor Defences Against Third-Party Suits**

Defence	Description
Duty of care	Liability is limited to foreseeable known users [see Note].
Absence of misstatement	Also known as 'no error'—the financial statements as relied upon are accurate in all material respects.
Non-negligent performance	The auditor conducted the audit in accordance with GAAS.
Absence of causal connection	a) It is irrelevant that the financial statements are materially misstated, as the user did not rely upon them; or b) The auditor is only liable for losses due to fraud after a time when they could or should have detected the fraud.
Contributory negligence	The party suing is also negligent.

Note: This defence is subject to legislation. For example, in Ontario, it is proposed that auditors would have liability to investors, which is presently not the case under common law.

---

[9]From Mathias, Philip, "Auditors Not Legally Liable to Investors, Top Court Rules," *The Financial Post* (May 24, 1997), p. 3; and Paskell-Mede, Mindy and Don Selman, "Point, Counterpoint," *CAmagazine* (September 1997), pp. 39–40.

and Canada suggest that we now know that the limited class is to be defined in relation to the known purpose of the financial statements and that, therefore, each case should be decided on its own factual context.

The second defence in third-party suits, absence of misstatement, is also known as "no error" in the financial statements. Thus, a plaintiff's damages would be inappropriately calculated because the financial statements on which they relied would have been accurate.

Next is non-negligent performance. If the auditor conducted the audit in accordance with GAAS, there is a strong inference of no negligence. Recognize, however, that non-negligent performance is difficult to demonstrate to a court. Proving lack of negligence normally involves a debate between experts hired by both sides. The judge, who is a layperson with respect to accounting and auditing, then assesses the credibility of the experts from both sides in order to make an independent decision based upon legal, accounting, and auditing concepts.

Absence of causal connection in third-party suits has two variations. The first occurs when there is a material misstatement in the financial statements, the second when there is a defalcation at the client or plaintiff's place of business. When there is a misstatement in the financial statements, it usually means nonreliance on the financial statements by the user. For example, assume the auditor can demonstrate that a lender relied upon an ongoing banking relationship with a customer, rather than the financial statements, in making a loan. The fact that the auditor was negligent in the conduct of the audit would not be relevant in that situation. In the case of a defalcation, the auditors would not be liable for the entire loss caused by the culprit (e.g., if there had been a certain amount of defalcation that had already taken place before the auditors could have been expected to detect it). Normally, the auditor is only held liable for additional fraud committed after the first date on which the whistle could have been blown. Another good example of "no causal connection" arises in tax cases. Sometimes misfired tax planning results in the client paying additional taxes. The accountant would not be liable to reimburse the client for taxes paid, but only for the interest and penalties, since nothing could have been done legitimately to avoid payment of the taxes.

Finally, it is possible to find contributory negligence if it could be said the claimants were themselves negligent, say, by ignoring other relevant information. It would be more common, however, for the auditor to defend on one of the other bases outlined above.

Criminal Liability

Fraud by anyone can be a criminal act and the perpetrator can be subject to criminal prosecution.[10] The criminal action would be brought by the Attorney General; conviction of a professional accountant for **criminal liability** would likely result in a charge of criminal misconduct by the professional accountant's institute (or *ordre*). In addition, a civil action for damages could be brought by the person(s) suffering a loss from the fraudulent act.

Fraud may include an auditor's association with financial statements he or she knows are materially misstated or false. For example, if the auditor of a company gave an unqualified auditor's report on the company's financial statements knowing that inventory was grossly overvalued, it is possible the auditor would be found guilty of criminal fraud and could be sued in a civil action.

Suppose in this case that inventory was to be valued at the lower of cost or market but the auditor deliberately did not include drastic decreases in market value that occurred in the second month following the balance sheet date. Failure to reflect all the information in the auditor's possession in the financial statements would make them misleading *despite their being in accordance with GAAP*. This occurs when there are multiple alternatives under GAAP or where GAAP requires limited disclosure. The auditor could be judged guilty of fraud.

While there are almost no Canadian cases involving fraud, there have been several U.S. cases. Fraud, however, is interpreted more liberally in the U.S. There the term "fraud" is used in civil cases, where errors in financial statement disclosures occur, which benefit management or others. Although not great in absolute number, these U.S. fraud cases damage the

CRIMINAL LIABILITY FOR AUDITORS—the possibility of being found guilty under criminal law; defrauding a person through knowing involvement with false financial statements

---

[10]Section 338 of the *Criminal Code of Canada*.

integrity of the profession, both in Canada and the U.S., due to their high profile, and reduce the profession's ability to attract and retain outstanding people. On the positive side, these court actions encourage practitioners to use extreme care and exercise good faith in their activities.

The leading case of criminal action against CPAs is *United States v. Simon*, which occurred in 1969. In this case, three auditors were prosecuted for filing false financial statements of a client with the government and held to be criminally liable. The consequences for these three men were significant. They lost their CPA certificates under the U.S. Rule 501 of the *Code of Professional Conduct* (acts discreditable) and were forced to leave the profession. Simon has been followed by three additional major criminal cases. In *United States v. Natelli* (1975), two auditors were convicted of criminal liability for certifying the financial statements of National Student Marketing Corporation that contained inadequate disclosures pertaining to accounts receivable.

In *United States v. Weiner* (1975), three auditors were convicted of securities fraud in connection with their audit of Equity Funding Corporation of America. Equity Funding was a financial conglomerate the financial statements of which had been overstated through a massive fraud by management. The fraud was so extensive and the audit work so poor that the court concluded the auditors must have been aware of the fraud and were therefore guilty of complicity. In Canada, these auditors would likely have been found guilty of negligence.

In *ESM Government Securities v. Alexander Grant & Co.* (1986), an American case, it was revealed by management to the partner in charge of the audit of ESM that the previous year's audited financial statements contained a material misstatement. Rather than complying with professional and firm standards in such circumstances, the partner agreed to say nothing in the hope that management would work its way out of the problem during the current year. Instead, the situation worsened, eventually to the point where losses exceeded $300 million. The partner was subsequently convicted of criminal charges for his role in sustaining the fraud and was handed a 12-year prison term. In this case, the partner personally benefited from the fraud and would likely also have been found guilty of fraud in Canada.

Figure 4-11 describes *United States v. Andersen* (2002). This case is another example of criminal liability.

Several practical lessons can be learned from these five cases:

- An investigation of the integrity of management is an important part of deciding on the acceptability of clients and the extent of work to perform.
- Independence in appearance and fact by all individuals on the engagement is essential, especially in a defence involving criminal actions.
- Transactions with related parties require special scrutiny because of the potential for misstatement.
- Generally accepted accounting principles cannot be relied upon exclusively in deciding whether financial statements are fairly presented.
- Good documentation may be just as important in the auditor's defence of criminal charges as in a civil suit.

FIGURE 4-11 United States v. Andersen (2002)—Criminal Liability

In this case, the government charged Andersen with destruction of documents related to the firm's audit of Enron. During the period between October 19, 2001, when Enron alerted Andersen that the SEC had begun an enquiry into Enron's accounting for certain special purpose entities, and November 8, 2001, when the SEC served Andersen with a subpoena in connection with its work for Enron, Andersen personnel shredded extensive amounts of physical documentation and deleted computer files related to Enron.

The firm was ultimately convicted of one count of obstruction of justice. The conviction was not based on the document shredding, but was based on the alteration of a memo related to Enron's characterization of charges as nonrecurring in its third quarter 2001 earnings release, in which the company announced a loss of $618 million.

As a result of the conviction, Andersen was no longer able to audit publicly traded U.S. companies, which sealed the fate of the Andersen firm. This conviction was overturned in May 2005 by the U.S. Supreme Court.

- The potential consequences of the auditor knowingly committing a wrongful act are so severe that it is unlikely that the potential benefits could ever justify the actions.

Money Laundering Part XII.2 of the *Criminal Code*, Bill C-61, is known informally as the "proceeds of crime" legislation. In *R. v. Loewen* (1996), an accountant was convicted of laundering $125,000. The accountant stated to an undercover officer that he had a "few companies" through which he could move money. He then transferred the money through various accounts, retaining a commission. If this accountant was a professionally designated accountant, actions by the accountant's professional organization would have followed, likely expelling the accountant from the organization.

This case clearly demonstrates the accountant undertaking a criminal act. However, the legislation also applies to individuals who accept property (including fees), should they know or be wilfully blind to the fact that the property was obtained illegally. Such individuals could be charged with possession or laundering. This is an additional incentive for accountants to be cautious when they have any doubts regarding management integrity.

→4.4 AUDITOR CONFIDENTIALITY AND LIABILITY PREVENTION

Conflict Between Confidentiality and Association with False and Misleading Information

The issue here is whether a public accountant has greater responsibility for the rule of professional conduct regarding confidentiality or for the rule regarding association with false and misleading financial information.

Consider the following scenario that could easily occur in a public accounting firm. PA & Co., public accountants, is the auditor for both BG Construction Inc. (BG) and Carter Building Supplies Ltd. (CBS). BG, whose year end is January 31, 2006, owes a large amount of money to CBS, whose year end is February 28, 2006. Suppose an audit of BG is completed but the statements have not been issued. As BG's auditor, you are concerned about whether the company will be able to continue to operate or will become insolvent.

As auditor of BG, you are aware during your audit of CBS that a material asset of CBS (the receivable from BG) may be worthless. How do you ensure that CBS's February 28, 2006, financial statements are not misleading? There is a conflict between the confidentiality due BG and the association with CBS's financial statements (potentially false and misleading if the receivable from BG is not reserved) if you provide a clean opinion. If the auditor cannot persuade BG to disclose the problem to CBS either directly or through the issue of BG's financial statements, the auditor should probably resign from the CBS audit. The BG confidentiality issue is a common problem because a public accounting firm often has clients who conduct business with one another.

Consolidata Services, Inc., Figure 4-12 on page 98, addresses the question of public accounting firms' responsibility to inform users when they have information normally considered confidential under the public accounting profession's rules of conduct. A recent Canadian case, *Transamerica Commercial Finance Corporation,* addressed this issue in the context of an auditor's responsibility to disclose normally confidential information to a major creditor when the financial statements are not misstated. This case is outlined in Figure 4-13.

In the Consolidata Services case, the information had or would have had a significant effect on the plaintiff client or other clients of the same CPA firm. The CPA firm informed other clients of confidential information that was obtained during a conference with Consolidata Services. The CPA firm did so on the advice of legal counsel and contended it had a professional duty to inform other clients and help them avoid losses. This points to a dilemma facing public accounting firms in both Canada and the U.S. It is difficult to do the "right thing" even when there are good intentions.

The *Transamerica* case illustrates how accountants could be in possession of information that would be important for creditors in lending decisions. In this particular case, it supports the view that the auditor is justified in maintaining client information as confidential when the financial statements are not misleading.

The Profession's Response to Legal Liability

There are a number of things the CICA, the CGAAC, and the public accounting profession as a whole can do to reduce the practitioner's exposure to lawsuits. The instituting of practice inspection by the provincial institute, CPABs, and *ordre* of members in public practice

---

FIGURE 4-12	*Consolidata Services, Inc. v. Alexander Grant & Company* (1981)

Consolidata Services Inc. was a payroll services company that prepared payroll cheques and disbursed payroll moneys to clients, employees, and taxing authorities. The CPA firm's relationship with Consolidata involved tax work rather than auditing or accounting services. In addition, the CPA firm recommended the payroll services to existing clients, and Consolidata, in return, recommended the CPA firm to its clients.

In a meeting between representatives of the CPA firm and Consolidata, it was determined that Consolidata was insolvent. After discussion with its legal counsel, the CPA firm requested that Consolidata notify its customers about the insolvency, but management refused to do so. The president then informed the CPA firm that he had resigned. The CPA firm informed management of its intent to inform its customers of Consolidata's insolvency. Consolidata requested the CPA firm to wait ten days to enable them to borrow money to correct their solvency problem.

The CPA firm partners decided to call all twelve of its clients that used Consolidata's payroll services to advise them not to send in any more money. No one informed Consolidata's other 24 customers.

The client sued for negligence and breach of contract for breaking an obligation of confidentiality. The court found in favour of Consolidata Services, Inc., in the amount of $1.3 million.

FIGURE 4-13	*Transamerica Commercial Finance Corporation, Canada v. Dunwoody & Company and F. S. Hirtle* (1996)[11]

Dunwoody and Company was the auditor for the years ended January 31,1984 to 1987 for a Toyota car dealership called Robin Hood Holdings Ltd. The partner responsible for the engagement was F. S. Hirtle, named as a co-defendant. Transamerica financed the Toyota dealership by providing a credit line of $1.1 million, $500,000 of which was for used vehicle inventory and $200,000 for a capital loan.

Because of decreasing liquidity, Robin Hood Holdings Ltd. engaged in dubious financial practices. For the year ending January 31, 1986, the company used inter-company financial transfers to obtain unauthorized borrowing from the bank (known as "kiting"). The auditors detected this, advised the client in writing to discontinue this practice, and ensured that the financial statements accurately reflected cash balances. In January 1986, Transamerica conducted a surprise vehicle inventory and found several used vehicles missing. The vehicles had already been sold.

This resulted in a credit review, and a representative of Transamerica held a meeting with the auditors in March 1987 while the audit was in progress. During this meeting, Mr. Hirtle discussed financial reorganization issues with Transamerica but did not disclose the kiting (which continued) or the fact that, during the audit, two fictitious vehicles were discovered in inventory. The auditors again warned Robin Hood Holdings Ltd. to discontinue the kiting.

Transamerica concluded that credit should continue to be extended but that Robin Hood required careful monitoring (which Transamerica did not do). In January 1988, the auditors discovered 15 to 20 fictitious vehicles, and continuing financial irregularities. After consulting with legal counsel, Dunwoody advised that it would not be providing Robin Hood with an auditor's opinion.

Transamerica put Robin Hood into receivership, operated the dealership in an attempt to reduce its losses, and eventually sold it as a going concern. Transamerica calculated its losses at over $1 million and sued Dunwoody to recover these losses on the basis that Dunwoody should have disclosed the financial irregularities and the fictitious inventory in March 1987.

Both the Supreme Court of British Columbia in 1994 and the Court of Appeal for British Columbia dismissed the plaintiff's action, awarding the defendant some costs. The courts found that the defendant owed a professional duty of confidentiality to its client. They also found that the plaintiff did not rely on the defendants and that its losses arose solely from its own business and management decisions made during the course of its dealings with Robin Hood.

---

[11]Trial judgment, Supreme Court of British Columbia, No. C902491 (February 18, 1994), and trial judgment, Court of Appeal for British Columbia, CA018550 (April 18, 1996).

(discussed in Chapter 1) is one positive step in recognizing additional responsibility that the public demands of professionals. Some of the others are discussed briefly.

1. *Conduct research in auditing.* Continued research is important in finding better ways to do such things as uncover unintentional material misstatements or management and employee fraud, communicate audit results to statement users, and make sure that auditors are independent. Significant research already takes place through the professional accounting associations, public accounting firms, and universities. For example, the University of Waterloo Centre for Information Systems Assurance (UWCISA) has a variety of research and educational activities, including information systems assurance research.

University of Waterloo Centre for Information Systems Assurance (UWCISA)
www.arts.uwaterloo.ca/ACCT/uwcisa

2. *Set standards and rules.* The CICA must constantly set standards and revise them to meet the changing needs of auditing. New Assurance and Related Services Recommendations, Assurance and Related Services Guidelines, revisions of the rules of conduct of the various professional accounting bodies, and other pronouncements must be issued as society's needs change and as new technology arises from experience and research. Focus Box 4-3 provides an example of the role of standards.

3. *Set requirements to protect auditors.* The CICA can help protect public accountants by setting certain requirements that better practitioners already follow. Naturally, these requirements should not be in conflict with meeting users' needs.

4. *Establish practice inspection requirements.* The periodic examination of a firm's practices and procedures is a way to educate practitioners and identify firms not meeting the standards of the profession.

5. *Defend unjustified lawsuits.* It is important that public accounting firms continue to oppose unwarranted lawsuits even if, in the short run, the costs of winning exceed the costs of settling.

6. *Educate users.* It is important to educate investors and others who read financial statements as to the meaning of the auditor's opinion and the extent and nature of the auditor's work. Users must be educated to understand that auditors do not test 100 percent of all records and do not guarantee the accuracy of the financial records or the future prosperity of the company. It is also important to educate users to understand that accounting and auditing are arts, not sciences, and that perfection and precision are unachievable.

7. *Sanction members for improper conduct and performance.* One characteristic of a profession is its responsibility for policing its own membership. The professional accounting bodies have disciplinary procedures that are designed to deal with the problems of inadequate performance by members.

8. *Lobby for changes in laws.* If the risk exposure of auditors to legal liability becomes too high, insurance will either be prohibitively expensive or unobtainable, and self-insurance is not an option. If the risk exposure does start to approach an unacceptable level,

---

Focus Box 4-3

WHAT RELATIONSHIP DO THE STANDARDS OF THE FORUM OF FIRMS HAVE WITH NORTEL?

Nortel Networks Corp. was in the news for many months, from the summer of 2004 through the early part of 2005, as financial statement misstatements were discovered—apparently because executives needed specific figures to obtain their management bonuses. Since Nortel stock is traded on many exchanges around the world, it is considered an international audit.

The Forum of Firms (FOF) is a small group—international public accounting firms that perform audits of financial statements of international companies where financial statements may be used in multiple countries. These firms are required to comply with international auditing standards. They also identify audit practice issues, discuss best practices, and offer a voluntary global inspection program—cooperation on an international scale intended to improve the quality of audit engagements.

Sources: 1. Bruser, David, "Nortel targets bogus bonuses," *Toronto Star*, July 3, 2004, pp. D1, D10. 2. Hamilton, Tyler, "Driving from a profit to a loss," *Toronto Star*, January 13, 2005, pp. D1, D7. 3. "The Forum of Firms" and "Transnational Auditors Committee," www.ifac.org, Accessed: February 8, 2005.

governments should be lobbied at least to ensure viable insurance coverage exists. Lobbying can produce results such as the June 1998 law permitting limited liability partnerships (LLPs) in Ontario.

The Individual Professional Accountant's Response to Legal Liability

Practising auditors may also take specific action to minimize their liability. Most of this book deals with that subject. A summary of several of these practices is included at this point.

1. *Deal only with clients possessing integrity.* The auditor needs to be alert to risk factors that may result in lawsuits. There is an increased likelihood of having legal problems when a client lacks integrity in dealing with customers, employees, units of government, and others. A public accounting firm needs procedures to evaluate the integrity of clients and should dissociate itself from clients found lacking.
2. *Hire qualified personnel and train and supervise them properly.* A considerable portion of most audits is done by young professionals with relatively little experience. Given the high degree of risk public accounting firms have in doing audits, it is important that these young professionals be qualified and well trained. Supervision of their work by experienced and qualified professionals is also essential.
3. *Follow the standards of the profession.* A firm must implement procedures to make sure that all firm members understand and follow the Recommendations of the *CICA Handbooks* and other authoritative sources of GAAP and GAAS, their profession's rules of conduct, and other professional guidelines.
4. *Maintain independence.* Independence is more than merely financial. Independence, in fact, requires an attitude of responsibility separate from the client's interest. Much litigation has arisen from a too willing acceptance by an auditor of a client's representation or of a client's pressures. The auditor must maintain an attitude of *healthy professional skepticism.*
5. *Understand the client's business.* The lack of knowledge of industry practices and client operations has been a major factor in auditors failing to uncover errors in several cases. It is important that the audit team be educated in these areas.
6. *Perform quality audits.* Quality audits require that appropriate evidence be obtained and appropriate judgments be made about the evidence. It is essential, for example, that the auditor evaluate a client's internal controls and modify the quantity and quality of evidence obtained to reflect the findings. Well-documented and monitored quality control procedures help provide quality audits.
7. *Document the work properly.* The preparation of good working papers helps in organizing and performing quality audits. Quality working papers are essential if an auditor has to defend an audit in court.
8. *Obtain an engagement letter and a representation letter.* These two letters are essential in defining the respective obligations of client and auditor. They are helpful especially in lawsuits between the client and auditor, but also in third-party lawsuits.
9. *Maintain confidential relations.* Auditors are under an ethical and sometimes legal obligation not to disclose client matters to outsiders.
10. *Carry adequate insurance.* It is essential for a public accounting firm to have adequate insurance protection in the event of a lawsuit. Although insurance rates have risen considerably in the past few years as a result of increasing litigation, professional liability insurance is still available for all public accountants.
11. *Seek legal counsel.* Whenever serious problems occur during an audit, a public accountant would be wise to consult experienced counsel. In the event of a potential or actual lawsuit, the auditor should immediately seek an experienced lawyer.

APPENDIX A
SECURITIES LEGISLATION

In Chapter 1, it was pointed out that a number of Canadian companies were listed on American stock exchanges or sold securities in the United States or both, and that these companies were therefore subject to the requirements of the *Securities Act of 1933* and the *Securities Exchange Act of 1934*. The following discussion pertains to the civil liability of accountants under a typical Canadian securities act—the *Ontario Securities Act*—and relevant U.S. acts.

Ontario Securities Act Part XXIII, Civil Liability, deals with liability for misrepresentation in a prospectus. It applies not only to auditors, but issuers, those selling securities, underwriters, and directors. Auditors are not referred to directly but are described in Section 130(1) as those "whose consent has been filed pursuant to a requirement of the regulations but only with respect to reports, opinions, or statements that have been made by them." The section states that the purchaser who purchases the security based on the prospectus is deemed to be relying on representations with respect to that prospectus. Thus, the issue of privity would be automatically dealt with in the event that the purchaser sued the auditor or others.

Section 130(8) goes on to state that all persons or companies specified in the first section are jointly and severally liable, but the amount recoverable (specified in the next paragraph of the Act) would not exceed the price at which the securities were offered to the public.

Section 131 specifies the same deemed reliance, liability, and amount recoverable in the context of a take-over bid circular.

U.S. Laws

SECURITIES ACT OF 1933 This act deals with the information in registration statements and prospectuses. It concerns only the reporting requirements for companies issuing new securities. The only parties that can recover from auditors under the 1933 act are original purchasers of securities. The amount of the potential recovery is the original purchase price less the value of the securities at the time of the suit. If the securities have been sold, users can recover the amount of the loss incurred.

The Securities Act of 1933 imposes an unusual burden on the auditor. Section 11 of the 1933 act defines the rights of third parties and auditors. These are summarized as follows:

- Any third party who purchased securities described in the registration statement may sue the auditor for material misrepresentations or omissions in audited financial statements included in the registration statement.
- The third-party user does not have the burden of proof that he or she relied on the financial statements or that the auditor was negligent or fraudulent in doing the audit. The user must prove only that the audited financial statements contained a material misrepresentation or omission.
- The auditor has the burden of demonstrating as a defence that (1) an adequate audit was conducted in the circumstances or (2) all or a portion of the plaintiff's loss was caused by factors other than the misleading financial statements. The 1933 act is the only common or statutory law where the burden of proof is on the defendant.
- The auditor has responsibility for making sure the financial statements were fairly stated beyond the date of issuance, up to the date the registration statement became effective, which could be several months later. For example, assume the audit report date for December 31, 2004, financial statements is February 10, 2005, but the registration statement is dated November 1, 2005. In a typical audit, the auditor must review transactions through the audit report date, February 10, 2005. In statements filed under the 1933 act, the auditor is responsible to review transactions through the registration statement date, November 1, 2005.

Although the burden may appear harsh to auditors, there have been few cases tried under the 1933 act.

SECURITIES EXCHANGE ACT OF 1934 The liability of auditors under the *Securities Exchange Act of 1934* frequently centres on the audited financial statements issued to the public in annual reports or submitted to the SEC as a part of annual 10-K reports.

Every company with securities traded on national and over-the-counter exchanges is required to submit audited statements annually. There are obviously a much larger number of statements falling under the 1934 act than under the 1933 act.

In addition to annual audited financial statements, there is potential legal exposure to auditors for quarterly (10-Q), monthly (8-K), or other reporting information. The auditor is frequently involved in reviewing the information in these other reports; therefore, there may be legal responsibility. However, few cases have involved auditors for reports other than auditor's reports.

SEC SANCTIONS Closely related to auditor's liability is the Security and Exchange Commission's (SEC's) authority to sanction. The SEC has the power in certain circumstances to sanction or suspend practitioners from doing audits for SEC companies. Rule 2(e) of the SEC's *Rules of Practice* says:

> The commission may deny, temporarily or permanently, the privilege of appearing or practising before it in any way to any person who is found by the commission... (1) not to possess the requisite qualifications to represent others, or (2) to be lacking in character or integrity or to have engaged in unethical or improper professional conduct.

The SEC has temporarily suspended a number of individual CPAs from doing any audits of SEC clients in recent years. It has similarly prohibited a number of CPA firms from accepting any new SEC clients for a period, such as six months. At times, the SEC has required an extensive review of a major CPA firm's practices by another CPA firm. In some cases, individual CPAs and their firms have been required to participate in continuing education programs and to make changes in their practice. Sanctions such as these are published by the SEC and are often reported in the business press, making them a significant embarrassment to those involved.

FOREIGN CORRUPT PRACTICES ACT OF 1977 Another significant congressional action affecting both CPA firms and their clients was the passage of the *Foreign Corrupt Practices Act of 1977*. The act makes it illegal to offer a bribe to an official of a foreign country for the purpose of exerting influence and obtaining or retaining business. The prohibition against payments to foreign officials is applicable to all U.S. domestic firms, regardless of whether they are publicly or privately held, and to foreign companies filing with the SEC.

Apart from the bribery provisions that affect all companies, the law also requires SEC registrants under the *Securities Exchange Act of 1934* to meet additional requirements. These include the maintenance of reasonably complete and accurate records and an adequate system of internal control. The law significantly affects all SEC companies and may affect auditors through their responsibility to review and evaluate systems of internal control as a part of doing the audit.

SUMMARY

1. *What are an auditor's sources of legal liability?* Auditors could be liable to clients or third parties such as shareholders and debt holders.

   How is this related to a distinction between business failure and audit failure? Financial statement users might confuse business failures, for example due to bankruptcy, with an audit failure, where an audit was not conducted in accordance with GAAS, resulting in more frequent lawsuits.

2. *Do accountants have the right of privileged communication?* No. Accountants must disclose their working papers to the courts when subpoenaed.

   What other concepts or terms are associated with auditor's legal liability? The prudent person concept (p. 84) is an important concept, as are distinctions between negligence and fraud (p. 86) and distinctions between contract and common law (p. 87).

   What should auditors do if a client sues them? With the assistance of legal counsel, assuming the conduct of an audit in accordance with GAAS, the auditor would likely pursue one of the defences listed in the chapter commencing on page 88.

3. *Who else can sue the auditor, besides the client?* Non-clients such as actual and potential shareholders, vendors, bankers, creditors, investors, employees, or customers can sue an auditor.

   How would the auditor defend against such suits? The auditor would use a series of defences used with clients, summarized in Figure 4-10 (page 94).

   Can the auditor go to jail because of criminal liability? Yes. This would likely only occur, though, where the auditor was deliberately involved with materially incorrect financial statements and intended to mislead.

4. *If the auditor has access to confidential information that would help a different business avoid financial hardship, can this information be disclosed?* No. The auditor has a duty to hold client information confidential. It can be disclosed only with client permission.

What are individual accountants and the profession doing to respond to legal liability? Individual accountants can undertake many actions (listed on page 100) to help prevent lawsuits. The profession has made changes in the recent past, including the formation of the Forum of Firms, participation with the CPAB, and numerous activities such as research (listed commencing on page 99).

CICA ASSURANCE HANDBOOK SECTIONS REFERENCED IN THIS CHAPTER

Section 5020 – Association.

Section 9200 – Compilation engagements.

ESSENTIAL TERMS

Absence of causal connection—a legal defence under which the professional contends that the damages claimed by the client were not brought about by any act of the professional   (p. 91).

Absence of negligence—a legal defence under which the professional claims that the disputed service was properly performed; an auditor would claim that the audit was performed according to generally accepted auditing standards   (p. 90).

Audit failure—a situation in which the auditor issues an erroneous audit opinion as the result of an underlying failure to comply with the requirements of generally accepted auditing standards   (p. 83).

Audit risk—the risk that the auditor will conclude that the financial statements are fairly stated and an unqualified opinion can therefore be issued when in fact they are materially misstated (p. 83).

Business failure—the situation when a business is unable to repay its lenders, or meet the expectations of its investors because of economic or business conditions   (p. 83).

Common law—laws developed through court decisions rather than through government statutes; also called *judge-made law* or *case law*   (p. 87).

Constructive fraud—conduct that the law construes as fraud even though there was no actual intent to deceive; considered to be so reckless that the courts decide it is tantamount to fraud (p. 86).

Contributory negligence—a legal defence under which the professional claims that the client failed to perform certain obligations and that it is the client's failure to perform those obligations that brought about the claimed damages   (p. 87).

Criminal liability for auditors—the possibility of being found guilty under criminal law; defrauding a person through knowing involvement with false financial statements   (p. 95).

Defalcation—theft of assets   (p. 87).

Expectation gap—the conflict between what some users expect from an auditor's report and what the auditor's report is designed to deliver; some users believe that an auditor's report is a guarantee as to the accuracy of the financial statements, although the report is in fact an opinion based on an audit conducted according to generally accepted auditing standards   (p. 83).

Fiduciary duty—a party (such as an accountant) has an obligation to act for the benefit of another, and that obligation includes discretionary power   (p. 82).

Fraud—a false assertion that has been made knowingly, without belief in its truth, or recklessly without caring whether it is true or not   (p. 86).

Lack of duty to perform—a legal defence under which the professional claims that no contract existed with the plaintiff; therefore no duty existed to perform the disputed service   (p. 88).

Legal liability—the professional's obligation under the law to provide a reasonable level of care while performing work for those he or she serves   (p. 81).

Limited liability partnership (LLP)—an organizational structure whereby only the person who does the work, those who supervise that person, and the firm itself are liable, but not other individual partners within the firm   (p. 85).

Negligence—failure to exercise reasonable care in the performance of one's obligations to another   (p. 86).

Prudent person concept—the legal concept that a person has a duty to exercise reasonable care and diligence in the performance of his or her obligations to another   (p. 84).

Tort action for negligence—a legal action taken by an injured party against the party whose negligence resulted in the injury (p. 86).

REVIEW QUESTIONS

4-1   The legal environment in which a public accountant in Canada operates is changing. Discuss some of the reasons for the changes.

4-2   Distinguish between business risk and audit risk. Why is business risk a concern to auditors?

4-3   How does the *prudent person concept* affect the liability of the auditor?

4-4   A partner in a public accounting firm may be held liable for errors in the work of others. Identify at least two groups of such others and explain why the partner might be liable.

4-5   Differentiate between a "criminal action" and a "civil action."

4-6   A common type of lawsuit against public accountants is for the failure to detect a defalcation. State the auditor's responsibility for such discovery. Give authoritative support for your answer.

4-7 What is meant by "contributory negligence"? Under what conditions will this likely be a successful defence?

4-8 Is the auditor's liability affected if the third party was unknown rather than known? Explain.

4-9 Distinguish between the auditor's potential liability to the client, liability to third parties under common law, and criminal liability. Describe one situation for each type of liability in which the auditor could be held legally responsible.

4-10 In what ways can the profession positively respond and reduce liability in auditing?

4-11 In what ways can an individual public accountant positively respond and reduce liability in auditing?

MULTIPLE CHOICE QUESTIONS

4-12 The following questions concern public accounting firms' liability under common law. Choose the best response.

a. Natasha Sharp, a public accountant, was engaged by Peters & Sons, a partnership, to give an opinion on the financial statements that were to be submitted to several prospective partners as part of a planned expansion of the firm. Sharp's fee was fixed on a per diem basis. After a period of intensive work, Sharp completed about half of the necessary fieldwork. Then, due to unanticipated demands upon her time by other clients, Sharp was forced to abandon the work. The planned expansion of the firm failed to materialize because the prospective partners lost interest when the auditor's report was not promptly available. Sharp offered to complete the task at a later date. This offer was refused. Peters & Sons suffered damages of $40,000 as a result. Under the circumstances, what is the probable outcome of a lawsuit between Sharp and Peters & Sons?

(1) Peters & Sons will recover damages for breach of contract.
(2) Sharp will recover damages for breach of contract.
(3) Sharp will be compensated for the reasonable value of the services actually performed.
(4) Neither Sharp nor Peters & Sons will recover against the other.

b. Wilhelm Corporation orally engaged Humm & Dawson to audit its year-end financial statements. The engagement was to be completed within two months after the close of Wilhelm's fiscal year for a fixed fee of $22,500. Under these circumstances, what obligation is assumed by Humm & Dawson?

(1) None, because the contract is unenforceable since it is not in writing.
(2) An implied obligation to take extraordinary steps to discover all defalcations.
(3) The obligation of an insurer of its work, which is liability without fault.
(4) An implied promise to exercise reasonable standards of competence and care.

c. The most significant aspect of the Haig v. Bamford case was that it

(1) defined the auditor's responsibilities in tort law to third parties.
(2) extended the auditor's responsibility for events after the end of the audit period.
(3) defined foreseeable third parties.
(4) created a more general awareness of the auditor's responsibility for discovering misstatements.

d. If a public accounting firm is being sued for civil fraud by a third party based upon materially false financial statements, which of the following is the best defence the accountants could assert?

(1) Lack of privity.
(2) Lack of reliance.
(3) Contributory negligence on the part of the client.
(4) A disclaimer contained in the engagement letter.

(AICPA adapted)

e. Major, Major, & Sharpe, PAs, are the auditors of MacLain Technologies. In connection with the public offering of $10 million of MacLain securities, Major expressed an unqualified opinion as to the financial statements. Subsequent to the offering, certain misstatements were revealed. Major has been sued by the purchasers of the stock offered pursuant to the registration statement that included the financial statements audited by Major. In the ensuing lawsuit by the MacLain investors, Major will be able to avoid liability if

(1) the misstatements were caused primarily by MacLain.
(2) it can be shown that at least some of the investors did not actually read the audited financial statements.
(3) it can prove due diligence in the audit of the financial statements of MacLain.
(4) MacLain had expressly assumed any liability in connection with the public offering.

DISCUSSION QUESTIONS AND PROBLEMS

4-13 Helmut & Co., a public accounting firm, was the new auditor of Mountain Ltd., a private company in the farm equipment and supply business.

In early February 2005, Helmut & Co. began the audit for the year ended December 31, 2004. The audit was to be run by Frost, a senior who had just joined Helmut from another firm. Frost was to be assisted by two juniors.

Sara Mountain, the president of Mountain Ltd., approached Frost and said that the Bank of Trail was prepared to increase their loan to Mountain upon receipt of the 2004 financial statements.

The juniors were assigned the accounts receivable and inventory sections, both of which were significant in relation to total assets, while Frost concentrated on the income statement and the remaining balance sheet accounts. The audit was finished quickly, and after a cursory review of the file and statements by Martin Helmut, senior partner of Helmut & Co., the signed auditor's report was appended to the financial statements, which were delivered to Mountain, who in turn sent them to the bank.

The bank increased the bank loan significantly based principally on the very successful year the company had enjoyed, despite the fact that the farm supply business was depressed. Several months later, Mountain Ltd. made an assignment in bankruptcy. The trustee found that many accounts receivable were still outstanding from the balance sheet date and that inventory on hand included substantial quantities of obsolete and damaged goods that had been included in the year-end inventory at cost. In addition, the year-end inventory amount included inventory that had been sold prior to the year end.

Bank of Trail sued Helmut & Co. for negligence.

Required

Discuss Helmut & Co.'s defence. Is lack of privity a defence in this case? Was Helmut & Co. negligent? Explain your answer fully.

4-14 Watts and Williams, a firm of PAs, audited the accounts of Sampson Skins, Inc., a corporation that imports and deals in fine furs. Upon completion of the audit, the auditors supplied Sampson Skins with 20 copies of the audited financial statements. The firm knew in a general way that Sampson Skins wanted that number of copies of the auditor's report to furnish to banks and other potential lenders.

The balance sheet in question was misstated by approximately $800,000. Instead of having a $600,000 net worth, the corporation was insolvent. The management of Sampson Skins had doctored the books to avoid bankruptcy. The assets had been overstated by $500,000 of fictitious and nonexistent accounts receivable and $300,000 of nonexistent skins listed as inventory when in fact Sampson Skins had only empty boxes. The audit failed to detect these fraudulent entries. Martinson, relying on the audited financial statements, loaned Sampson Skins $200,000. He seeks to recover his loss from Watts and Williams.

Required

State whether each of the following is true or false and give your reasons:

a. If Martinson alleges and proves negligence on the part of Watts and Williams, he will be able to recover his loss.
b. If Martinson alleges and proves constructive fraud (that is, gross negligence on the part of Watts and Williams), he will be able to recover his loss.
c. Martinson does not have a contract with Watts and Williams.
d. Unless actual fraud on the part of Watts and Williams could be shown, Martinson could not recover.
e. Martinson is a third-party beneficiary of the contract Watts and Williams made with Sampson Skins.

4-15 The public accounting firm of André, Mathieu & Paquette (AMP) was expanding very rapidly. Consequently, it hired several junior accountants, including Jim Small. The partners of the firm eventually became dissatisfied with Small's production and warned him that they would be forced to terminate him unless his output increased significantly.

At that time, Small was engaged in audits of several clients. He decided that to avoid being fired, he would reduce or omit entirely some of the standard auditing procedures listed in audit programs prepared by the partners. One of the public accounting firm's clients, Newell Corporation, was in serious financial difficulty and had adjusted several of the accounts being examined by Small to appear financially sound. Small prepared fictitious working papers in his home at night to support purported completion of auditing procedures assigned to him, although he in fact did not examine the adjusting entries. The public accounting firm rendered an unqualified opinion on Newell's financial statements, which were grossly misstated. Several creditors, relying on the audited financial statements, subsequently extended large sums of money to Newell Corporation.

Required

Would the public accounting firm be liable to the creditors who extended the money because of their reliance on the erroneous financial statements if Newell Corporation should fail to pay them? Explain.

(AICPA adapted)

4-16 Jan Sharpe recently joined the public accounting firm of Spark, Watts, and Wilcox. On her third audit for the firm, Sharpe examined the underlying documentation of 200 disbursements as a test of purchasing, receiving, vouchers payable, and cash disbursement procedures. In the process, she found 12 disbursements for the purchase of materials with no receiving reports in the documentation. She noted the exceptions in her working papers and called them to the attention of the audit supervisor. Relying on prior experience with the client, the audit supervisor disregarded Sharpe's comments, and nothing further was done about the exceptions.

Subsequently, it was learned that one of the client's purchasing agents and a member of its accounting department were engaged in a fraudulent scheme whereby they diverted the receipt of materials to a public warehouse while sending the invoices to the client. When the client discovered the fraud, the conspirators had obtained approximately $70,000, $50,000 of which was recovered after the completion of the audit.

Required

Discuss the legal implications and liabilities to Spark, Watts, and Wilcox as a result of the facts just described.

(AICPA adapted)

4-17 In confirming accounts receivable on December 31, 2003, the auditor found 15 discrepancies between the customer's records and the recorded amounts in the subsidiary ledger. A copy of all confirmations that had exceptions was turned over to the company controller to investigate the reason for the difference. He, in turn, had the bookkeeper perform the analysis. The bookkeeper analyzed each exception, determined its cause, and prepared an elaborate working paper explaining each difference. Most of the differences in the bookkeeper's report indicated that the errors were caused by timing differences in the client's and customer's records. The auditor reviewed the working paper and concluded that there were no material exceptions in accounts receivable.

Two years subsequent to the audit, it was determined that the bookkeeper had stolen thousands of dollars in the previous three years by taking cash and overstating accounts receivable. In a lawsuit by the client against the public accountant, an examination of the auditor's December 31, 2003, accounts receivable working papers, which were subpoenaed by the court, indicated that one of the explanations in the bookkeeper's analysis of the exceptions was fictitious. The analysis stated the error was caused by a sales allowance granted to the customer for defective merchandise the day before the end of the year. The difference was actually caused by the bookkeeper's theft.

Required
a. What are the legal issues involved in this situation? What should the auditor use as a defence in the event that she is sued?
b. What was the public accountant's deficiency in conducting the audit of accounts receivable?

4-18 Marino Rossi, a public accountant, audited the financial statements of Newfoundland Rugs Ltd. Cooke, the president of Newfoundland Rugs, told Rossi that the company was planning a private placement of company bonds to raise $500,000 of needed capital. The audit proceeded smoothly, and the audited financial statements were issued.

Unbeknownst to Rossi, several significant receivables represented consignment accounts and not receivables, but Cooke had persuaded the companies involved to sign the receivable confirmations Rossi had sent out, indicating they agreed that they owed the balances reported at the balance sheet date. In addition, a large number of rolls of low quality interior carpeting had been classed as first quality. The effect of these two fraudulent acts resulted in a profit of $150,000 (instead of a loss of $480,000) and a positive net worth (instead of a negative net worth).

Newfoundland Rugs borrowed the money on the private placement and then went bankrupt several months later.

Required
a. Could the lenders on the private placement succeed in a suit against Rossi? If so, what must they prove?
b. What defence would Rossi use?

PROFESSIONAL JUDGMENT PROBLEM

4-19 In 2004, the Board of Directors of Lively Plays, Inc. fired George Drewerson, the co-founder and another senior management representative of the company, claiming that they had engaged in fraudulent financial activities and had defrauded the company of $4 million. Payley and Karson, PAs, have been the auditors of Lively Plays, Inc. for many years, and were the personal tax advisors of Mr. Drewerson during that time.

Lively Plays, Inc. engaged personnel from another office of Payley and Karson to conduct a forensic audit (a special investigation of the fraud). The forensic audit discovered that Drewerson was engaged in a fraudulent kickback scheme whereby he received directly, or through a company owned by him, about $6 million. About $3.5 million was capitalized as pre-production costs, resulting in materially misstated financial statements. Mr. Drewerson obtained a court injunction delaying the release of the forensic report on the grounds that Payley and Karson owed him a fiduciary duty. Mr. Drewerson claimed he should have had the right to review the forensic report before it was released to determine whether any confidential information had been released.

Required
a. Describe the role of Payley and Karson, and discuss any apparent conflicts of interest in this situation.
b. Based upon the facts provided, is it likely that Payley and Karson would be considered as having a fiduciary duty with respect to Mr. Drewerson's financial affairs?
c. If Mr. Drewerson were found to be guilty of fraud, and had declared the income from the fraud on his income tax return, what would be the potential liability of Payley and Karson with respect to the audited financial statements of Lively Plays, Inc.?

CASE

4-20 In late 1998 and early 1999, Your Best Magnets Inc. (YBM) offices in New York and Toronto were raided by the U.S. Organized Strike Force and the Royal Canadian Mounted Police. Records were seized, and the public company and its officers were charged with money laundering. The company has since been delisted and court proceedings continue. One newspaper article showed the flow of a single YBM transaction of $2.3 million being split into different amounts, moving between 10 different banks and as many different companies. Connections were shown with Russian organized crime.

The auditors of YBM, Delskiny and Lather, CPAs, were subpoenaed to appear before a grand jury in the United States.

Required
a. What are the auditor's normal responsibilities during an audit engagement with respect to assessing management integrity?

b. How does the assessment of management integrity tie in to the nature of evidence to be collected during the audit?

c. Assume that one of the directors of YBM was a member of Russian organized crime, known to local and international police forces but not publicly known. What is the auditor's normal responsibility regarding detection of criminal affiliations of directors?

d. How does crime affiliation by directors or other management affect the fair presentation of financial statements?

e. The company's financial statements in 1996 showed $13.6 million worth of North American magnet sales—a figure that exceeded total magnet imports to the continent that year. YBM officials created fictitious sales lists and destroyed banking records. Auditors identified questionable transactions, demanded explanations from management, and received supporting evidence. A clean auditor's report was issued in 1996. Discuss the potential legal liability of the auditors should it be discovered that several sales on the sales lists were for fictitious companies.

PART 2 CHAPTERS 5-12

THE AUDIT PROCESS

Part 2 presents the audit process in a manner that will enable you to apply the concepts developed in these chapters to any audit area. It is essential to understand the material in these chapters because the information will be used extensively in almost all chapters throughout the rest of the book. We also highlight the importance of audit planning.

Chapters 5 and 6 deal with auditors' and managements' responsibilities, audit objectives, and general concepts of evidence accumulation. The remaining chapters study various aspects of audit planning in depth, including auditors' responsibility for detecting fraud. Chapter 11 summarizes and integrates audit planning and audit evidence. You will use these planning concepts throughout the rest of the book.

Many of the concepts throughout the remainder of the book are illustrated with examples based on the Hillsburg Hardware company. The financial statements and other information from the company's annual report are included in the black and white insert on pages 136–151.

CHAPTER 5

AUDIT RESPONSIBILITIES AND OBJECTIVES

Now that you have an understanding of the environment within which an auditor functions, as well as the type of report produced, we can begin to look at the specifics of the financial statement audit.

LEARNING OBJECTIVES

After reading this chapter, you should be able to answer the following questions:

1. What is the objective of conducting an audit of financial statements? Explain the difference between management and auditor responsibilities with respect to the financial statements and the discovery and correction of material misstatements or illegal acts.

2. How are financial statements divided into cycles? How is this cycle approach related to the financial statement audit? What is the relationship among cycles? Between the cycle approach and entity level controls?

3. Describe management assertions about financial information. Relate management assertions to general transaction-related audit objectives and general balance-related audit objectives.

4. List the four phases of a financial statement audit and provide an overview of the audit process.

HERE COME THE AUDIT DETECTIVES!

Lawsuits, lawsuits everywhere! Risks of management fraud! What do you do? You either send away your risky client or you send in the audit detectives, auditors that are experts in forensic investigation.

As of late 2004, research statistics indicated that the top four accounting firms were dropping clients considered to be high risk. For example, Audit Analytics reported that, in the first three quarters of 2004, the top four accounting firms resigned from 157 audits. The reasons for these resignations do not have to be stated by the firms, but a likely conclusion is that the engagement was high risk or could affect the firm's perception of independence.

For those high-risk engagements that a PA firm decides to keep, it is necessary to assign additional expertise to the audit team to evaluate risky or complex information. Such assignment does not necessarily mean that the auditor suspects fraud, but it would help ensure that high quality evidence is obtained for areas that are difficult to audit or that could involve professional judgment due to the need for estimates or evaluation. *The Globe and Mail* reported, in November 2004, that at least two Canadian accounting firms—KPMG and Deloitte and Touche—were using forensic auditors on audit teams to help evaluate risks. The Office of the Auditor General of Canada also has specialized forensic auditors who assist with the risk assessment and the evidence-gathering process for high risk engagements.

Sources: 1. Crosariol, B., "Audit detectives walking the beat at accountancies," The Globe and Mail, November 29, 2004, p. B13. 2. Jensen, B., "Bob Jensen's threads on professional practice, fees, choosing accountants, financial advisors and consultants," www.trinity.edu/rjensen/fees.htm, Accessed: February 26, 2005. 3. Interview with: Rick Smith, Assistant Auditor General, Office of the Auditor General of Canada, January 13, 2005.

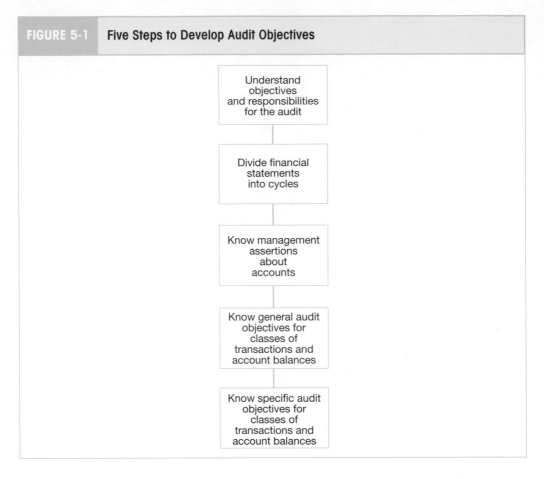

FIGURE 5-1   Five Steps to Develop Audit Objectives

Understand objectives and responsibilities for the audit

Divide financial statements into cycles

Know management assertions about accounts

Know general audit objectives for classes of transactions and account balances

Know specific audit objectives for classes of transactions and account balances

Forensic auditors are PAs who have had training in fraud detection and gathering of documentation, often obtaining a professional designation such as Certified Fraud Examiner (CFE). Does this sound exciting to you? Although the possibility of tension and secrecy are present, sifting through information to support potential fraud requires meticulous attention to detail and skills in information technology. Think about what might make an audit engagement risky and keep your ideas in mind as we go through the next few chapters.

Before beginning the study of how to conduct an audit, it is necessary first to understand the objectives of an audit and the way the auditor approaches accumulating evidence. Those are the most important topics covered in this chapter. Figure 5-1 summarizes the five topics that provide keys to understanding evidence accumulation; these are the steps used to develop specific audit objectives.

→5.1   THE OBJECTIVE OF THE AUDIT—MANAGEMENT AND AUDITOR RESPONSIBILITIES

Objective of Conducting an Audit of Financial Statements

Paragraph 5090.01 of the *CICA Assurance Handbook* states (in part):

> The objective of an audit of financial statements is to express an opinion whether the financial statements present fairly, in all material respects, the financial position, results of operations and cash flows in accordance with generally accepted accounting principles. ...

Paragraph 5090.01 appropriately emphasizes the expression of an opinion on *financial statements*. The only reason auditors accumulate evidence is to enable them to reach conclusions about whether financial statements are fairly stated in all material respects and to issue an appropriate auditor's report.

When, on the basis of adequate evidence, the auditor concludes that the financial statements are unlikely to mislead a prudent user, the auditor gives an audit opinion on their fair presentation and associates his or her name with the statements. If facts or evidence discovered subsequent to their issuance indicate that the statements were not actually fairly presented, the auditor is likely to have to demonstrate to the courts or regulatory agencies that he or she conducted the audit in a proper manner and drew reasonable conclusions. Although not an insurer or a guarantor of the fairness of the presentations in the statements, the auditor has considerable responsibility for notifying users as to whether or not the statements are properly stated. If the auditor believes the statements are not fairly presented or is unable to reach a conclusion because of insufficient evidence or prevailing conditions, the auditor has the responsibility to notify the users through the auditor's report.

Management's Responsibilities

The responsibility for adopting sound accounting policies, maintaining adequate internal control, and making fair representations in the financial statements *rests with management* rather than with the auditor. The primary responsibility for internal control and the financial statements appropriately rests with management given that the entity's transactions and related assets, liabilities, and equity are within the direct knowledge and control of management throughout the year. In contrast, the auditor's knowledge of these matters and internal control is limited to that acquired during the audit.

In recent years, the annual reports of many public companies have included a statement about management's responsibilities and relationship with the public accounting firm. Page 144 (black-and-white insert) presents a report of management's responsibility by the management of a large retail hardware distributor, Hillsburg Hardware Limited. The first paragraph states management's responsibilities for the fair presentation of the financial statements, while the second paragraph discusses management's responsibilities with respect to internal control. The third paragraph comments on the Audit Committee, the Board of Directors, and their role with respect to the financial statements.

Management's responsibility for the fairness of the representations (assertions) in the financial statements carries with it the privilege of determining which disclosures it considers necessary. Although management has the responsibility for the preparation of the financial statements and the accompanying footnotes, it is acceptable for an auditor to draft this material for the client or to offer suggestions for clarification. In the event that management insists on financial statement disclosure that the auditor finds unacceptable, the auditor can either issue an adverse or qualified opinion or, as a last resort, withdraw from the engagement. These responsibilities are described in detail in Section 5110.18–5110.20.

The Canadian Securities Administrators (CSA), Canada's securities regulators, have filed rules that impose requirements similar to those of the U.S. *Sarbanes-Oxley Act of 2002* for most companies listed on Canadian stock exchanges. The chief executive officer (CEO) and chief financial officer (CFO) of such companies must certify annual and interim financial statements as well as management discussion and analysis (MD & A) and certain information forms that are filed with the stock exchanges. Management is required to certify that they have reviewed the documents, that they do not contain any misrepresentations or material omissions and present fairly the financial condition of the company, and that disclosure controls and procedures or internal control over financial reporting have been designed, evaluated, and disclosed. If companies do not adhere to these rules, they will not be allowed to sell their shares or debt via Canadian stock exchanges.

Auditor's Responsibilities

Paragraph 5090.05 of the *CICA Assurance Handbook* states that, "The auditor should plan and perform an audit with an attitude of professional skepticism, recognizing that circumstances may exist that cause the financial statements to be materially misstated."

The requirement for an attitude of skepticism does not mean that the auditor should conduct the audit with an attitude of disbelief or of distrust in management. Rather, it means that the auditor should not be blind to evidence that suggests that documents, books, or records have been altered or are incorrect. The auditor should not assume that management

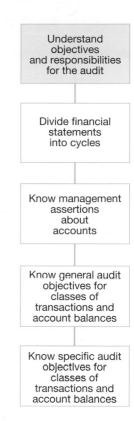

Understand objectives and responsibilities for the audit

Divide financial statements into cycles

Know management assertions about accounts

Know general audit objectives for classes of transactions and account balances

Know specific audit objectives for classes of transactions and account balances is dishonest, but the possibility of dishonesty must be considered. The concept of reasonable assurance indicates that the auditor is not an insurer or guarantor of the correctness of the financial statements.

There are several reasons why the auditor is responsible for reasonable but not absolute assurance. First, most audit evidence results from testing a sample of a population such as accounts receivable or inventory. Sampling inevitably includes some risk of not uncovering a material misstatement. Also, the areas to be tested; the type, extent, and timing of those tests; and the evaluation of test results require significant judgment on the part of the auditor. Even with good faith and integrity, auditors can make mistakes and errors in judgment. Second, accounting presentations contain complex estimates, which inherently involve uncertainty and can be affected by future events. Third, fraudulently prepared financial statements are often extremely difficult, if not impossible, for the auditor to detect, especially when there is collusion among management.

The *CICA Assurance Handbook*, in Section 5135 "The Auditor's Responsibility to Consider Fraud," details how the auditor should utilize professional skepticism when considering the risk of the financial statements containing material error or fraud and other irregularities. Section 5135 distinguishes between two types of misstatements, *errors* and *fraud and other irregularities*. An **error** is an *unintentional* misstatement of the financial statements, whereas **fraud and other irregularities** are *intentional*. Two examples of errors are a mistake in extending price times quantity on a sales invoice and overlooking older raw materials in determining lower of cost or market for inventory.

For fraud and other irregularities, a distinction can be drawn between *theft of assets*, often called "defalcation" or "employee fraud," and *fraudulent financial reporting*, often called "management fraud." Another way of characterizing the difference is that employee fraud is perpetrated against the company while management fraud is perpetrated for the company (i.e., for the company's benefit). An example of theft of assets is a clerk taking cash at the time a sale is made and not entering the sale in the cash register. An example of fraudulent financial reporting is the intentional overstatement of sales near the balance sheet date to increase reported earnings. In the case of the former, the company loses the money stolen; in the case of the latter, the company appears more profitable and, presumably, its stock rises in price.

It is usually more difficult for auditors to uncover fraud and other irregularities than errors. This is because of the intended deception associated with fraud and other irregularities. The auditor's responsibility for uncovering fraud and other irregularities deserves special attention. Not only the auditors, but also professional accountants employed by management, should be alert to errors, fraud, and other irregularities. These issues are also discussed in Chapter 10. Section 5110.14 describes specific responsibilities of the auditor (i.e., keeping the client's information confidential, maintaining independence, and communicating (where required) with management or the audit committee).

Management Fraud Management fraud is inherently difficult to uncover because (1) it is possible for one or more members of management to override internal controls, and (2) there is typically an effort to conceal the misstatement. Instances of **management fraud** may include omission of transactions or disclosures, fraudulent amounts, or misstatements of recorded amounts.

Audits cannot be expected to provide the same degree of assurance for the detection of material management fraud as is provided for an equally material error. Concealment by management makes fraud more difficult for auditors to find. The cost of providing equally high assurance for management fraud and for errors is economically impractical for both auditors and society.

FACTORS INDICATING POTENTIAL MANAGEMENT FRAUD Due to criticism of the profession resulting from auditors' nondiscovery of several large management frauds, auditors now have greater responsibility for discovering management fraud than they did previously. The most important change has been increased emphasis on auditors' responsibility to evaluate factors that may indicate an increased likelihood of management fraud. These are discussed further in Chapter 10.

ERROR—an unintentional misstatement of the financial statements

FRAUD OR OTHER IRREGULARITY—an intentional misstatement of the financial statements

MANAGEMENT FRAUD—a fraud or other irregularity resulting in fraudulent financial reporting

Employee Fraud The profession has also been emphatic that the auditor has less responsibility for the discovery of employee fraud than for errors. If auditors were responsible for the discovery of all employee fraud, auditing tests would have to be greatly expanded because many types of employee fraud are extremely difficult if not impossible to detect. The procedures that would be necessary to uncover all cases of fraud would certainly be more expensive than the benefits would justify. For example, if there is fraud involving the collusion of several employees that includes the falsification of documents, it is unlikely that such a fraud would be uncovered in a normal audit.

As the auditor assessed the likelihood of material management fraud, he or she should also evaluate the likelihood of material employee fraud. This is normally done initially as a part of understanding the entity's internal control and assessing control risk. Audit evidence should be expanded when the auditor finds an absence of adequate controls or failure to follow prescribed procedures, if he or she believes material employee fraud could exist.

Computer Fraud Computer fraud consists of fraud conducted with the assistance of computer software or hardware. This could include deliberately programming functions into a computer program so that it incorrectly calculates interest, placing unauthorized employees ("horses") on a computerized payroll system, falsifying an electronic mail message, obtaining "free" long distance telephone services, or creating fraudulent electronic cash transactions.

As with other forms of error or fraud, the auditor cannot be expected to always detect immaterial fraud but should investigate unusual relationships or patterns. Good internal controls spanning the development, acquisition, or use of automated systems help to prevent computer fraud.

Illegal Acts **Illegal acts** are defined in Section 5136 as "a violation of a domestic or foreign statutory law or government regulation attributable to the entity under audit, or to management or employees acting on the entity's behalf." Two examples of illegal acts are a violation of income tax laws and a violation of an environmental protection law. Section 5136 points out that an auditor's responsibility is to comply with GAAS and, as a result, the auditor may not detect an illegal act or become aware that an illegal act has occurred.

The performance of an illegal act by management or an employee of a company may affect the company (and the financial statements) in a variety of ways. For example, the payment of a bribe by a subsidiary in a foreign country could lead to expulsion of the company and/or expropriation of the company's assets; the balance sheet could be affected. Failing to properly dispose of untreated waste products could make the company liable for fines and penalties; the income statement could be affected. Even if the magnitude of the illegal act itself is not material, the consequences could well be so. As such, the auditor must be interested in illegal acts so that their potential impact may be properly evaluated.

When an illegal act is discovered, the auditor must consider whether such an act is a reflection of the company's corporate culture. Are such acts condoned or encouraged by management? If management does not promote ethical behaviour, the auditor should question management's good faith and consider whether continued association with the client is desirable.

Section 5136.21 recommends that the auditor "obtain written representation from management" with respect to illegal acts or possible illegal acts that would affect the financial statements or notes thereto. The section goes on to say that, other than enquiry of management, the auditor should not search for illegal acts unless there is reason to believe they may exist.

DIRECT-EFFECT ILLEGAL ACTS Certain violations of laws and regulations have a direct financial effect on specific account balances in the financial statements. For example, a violation of income tax laws directly affects income tax expense and income taxes payable. The auditor's responsibilities under Section 5136 for these direct-effect illegal acts are the same as for errors or fraud and other irregularities. On each audit, the auditor will, therefore, normally evaluate whether there is evidence available to indicate material violations of federal or provincial tax laws. This might be done by discussions with client personnel and examination of reports issued by Canada Revenue Agency after it has completed an examination of the client's tax return.

> **ILLEGAL ACTS**—violations of laws or government regulations other than irregularities

INDIRECT-EFFECT ILLEGAL ACTS Most illegal acts affect the financial statements only indirectly. For example, if a company violates environmental protection laws, there is an effect on the financial statements only if there is a fine or sanction. Potential material fines and sanctions indirectly affect financial statements by creating the need to disclose a contingent liability for the potential amount that might ultimately be paid. This is called an *indirect-effect illegal act.* Other examples of illegal acts that are likely to have only an indirect effect are violations of insider securities trading regulations, employment equity laws, and employee safety requirements.

Auditing standards clearly state that the auditor provides *no assurance* that indirect-effect illegal acts will be detected. Auditors lack legal expertise, and the frequent indirect relationship between illegal acts and the financial statements makes it impractical for auditors to assume responsibility for discovering those illegal acts.

There are three levels of responsibility that the auditor has for finding and reporting illegal acts.

- *Evidence accumulation when there is no reason to believe indirect-effect illegal acts exist.* Many audit procedures normally performed on audits to search for errors or fraud and other irregularities may also uncover illegal acts. Examples include reading the minutes of the board of directors and enquiring of the client's lawyers about litigation. The auditor should also enquire of management about policies it has established to prevent illegal acts and whether management knows of any laws or regulations that the company has violated. Other than these procedures, the auditor should not search for indirect-effect illegal acts unless there is reason to believe they may exist.
- *Evidence accumulation and other actions when there is reason to believe direct- or indirect-effect illegal acts may exist.* The auditor may find indications of possible illegal acts in a variety of ways. For example, the minutes may indicate that an investigation by a government agency is in progress, or the auditor may identify unusually large payments to consultants or government officials.

  When the auditor believes an illegal act has occurred, it is necessary to take several actions. First, the auditor should enquire of management at a level above those likely to be involved in the potential illegal act. Second, the auditor should consult with the client's lawyers or another specialist who is knowledgeable about the potential illegal act. Third, the auditor should consider accumulating additional evidence to determine if there actually is an illegal act. All three of these actions are intended to provide the auditor information about whether the suspected illegal act actually exists.
- *Actions when the auditor knows of an illegal act.* The first course of action when an illegal act has been identified is to consider the effects on the financial statements, including the adequacy of disclosures. These effects may be complex and difficult to resolve. For example, a violation of equal opportunity laws could involve significant fines, but it could also result in the loss of customers or key employees, which could materially affect future revenues and expenses. If the auditor concludes that the disclosures relative to an illegal act are inadequate, the auditor should modify the auditor's report accordingly. The auditor must also ensure that the audit committee or an appropriate level of management has been informed of the illegal act.

The auditor should also consider the effect of such illegal acts on his or her relationship with management. If management knew of the illegal act and failed to inform the auditor, it is questionable whether management can be believed in other discussions.

→5.2 FINANCIAL STATEMENT CYCLES AND ENTITY LEVEL CONTROLS

Financial Statement Cycles

Audits are performed by dividing the financial statements into smaller segments or components. The division makes the audit more manageable and aids in the assignment of tasks to different members of the audit team. For example, most auditors treat capital assets and notes payable as different segments. Each segment is audited separately but not completely independently (e.g., the audit of capital assets may reveal an unrecorded note payable.) After the audit of each segment is completed, including interrelationships with other segments, the results are combined. A conclusion can then be reached about the financial statements taken as a whole.

There are different ways of segmenting an audit. One approach would be to treat every account balance on the statements as a separate segment. Segmenting that way is usually inefficient. It would result in the independent audit of such closely related accounts as inventory and cost of goods sold.

The Cycle Approach to Segmenting an Audit A more common way to divide an audit is to keep closely related types (or classes) of transactions and account balances in the same segment. This is called the **cycle approach**. For example, sales, sales returns, cash receipts, and charge-offs of uncollectible accounts are four classes of transactions that cause accounts receivable to increase and decrease. They are therefore all part of the sales and collection cycle. Similarly, payroll transactions and accrued payroll are a part of the payroll and personnel cycle.

The logic of using the cycle approach can be seen by thinking about the way transactions are recorded in journals, data files, or databases and summarized in the general ledger and financial statements. Figure 5-2A shows that flow for manual, paper-based systems. Transactions are written into journals, the totals posted to the general ledger, and financial statements prepared from the general ledger. Figure 5-2B shows the flow for batch processing systems. Transactions are entered into subsystems, resulting in transactions being retained in history files for each subsystem. The transactions are used to update the appropriate master files. Each subsystem is used to print a report summarizing the transactions entered (called a "history report," or often still a "journal"). The general ledger subsystem is used to prepare the financial statements. Figure 5-2C, which depicts database processing, looks deceptively simple since all transactions are updated against a single database containing all company data. Such systems are normally more complex than batch processing systems, however.

To the extent that it is practical, the cycle approach combines transactions recorded in different journals or subsystems with the general ledger balances that result from those transactions.

CYCLE APPROACH—a method of dividing an audit by keeping closely related types of transactions and account balances in the same segment

- Understand objectives and responsibilities for the audit
- Divide financial statements into cycles
- Know management assertions about accounts
- Know general audit objectives for classes of transactions and account balances
- Know specific audit objectives for classes of transactions and account balances

FIGURE 5-2A	Transaction Flow from Journals to Financial Statements for Manual Systems*

Transactions	Journals	Ledgers, Trial Balance, and Financial Statements
Sales	Sales journal	General ledger and subsidiary records
Cash receipts	Cash receipts journal	General ledger trial balance
Acquisition of goods and services	Acquisitions journal	Financial statements
Cash disbursements	Cash disbursements journal	
Payroll services and disbursements	Payroll journal	
Allocation and adjustments	General journal	

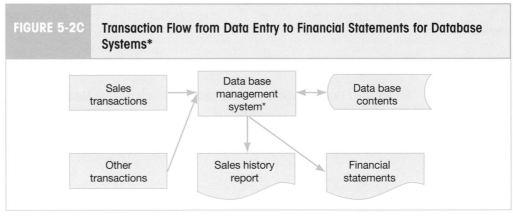

FIGURE 5-2C   Transaction Flow from Data Entry to Financial Statements for Database Systems*

*The structure and complexity depend upon the type of database used.

The cycles used in this text follow and are then explained in detail.

- Sales and collection cycle
- Acquisition and payment cycle
- Payroll and personnel cycle
- Inventory and warehousing cycle
- Capital acquisition and repayment cycle

Each of these cycles is so important that is part of the title of one or more chapters in the remainder of this book.

To illustrate the application of cycles to audits, Figure 5-3 presents the December 31, 2004 trial balance of Hillsburg Hardware Limited. The financial statements prepared from

FIGURE 5-3 Hillsburg Hardware Limited Adjusted Trial Balance

HILLSBURG HARDWARE LIMITED
TRIAL BALANCE
December 31, 2004

		Debit	Credit
S,A,P,C	Cash in bank	$ 827,568	
S	Trade accounts receivable	20,196,800	
S	Allowance for uncollectible accounts		$ 1,240,000
S	Other accounts receivable	945,020	
A,I	Inventories	29,864,621	
A	Prepaid expenses	431,558	
A	Land	3,456,420	
A	Buildings	32,500,000	
A	Computer and delivery equipment	3,758,347	
A	Furniture and fixtures	2,546,421	
A	Accumulated amortization		31,920,126
A	Trade accounts payable (1)		4,483,995
C	Notes payable		4,179,620
P	Accrued payroll		1,349,800
P	Accrued payroll expenses		119,663
C	Accrued interest		149,560
C	Dividends payable		1,900,000
A	Goods and services tax payable (net) (1)		235,994
A	Accrued income tax		795,442
C	Long-term notes payable		24,120,000
A	Deferred tax		738,240
A	Other accrued payables		829,989
C	Capital stock		8,500,000
C	Retained earnings		11,929,075
S	Sales		144,327,789
S	Sales returns and allowances	1,241,663	
I	Cost of goods sold	103,240,768	
P	Salaries and commissions	7,738,900	
P	Sales payroll benefits	1,422,100	
A	Travel and entertainment selling	1,110,347	
A	Advertising	2,611,263	
A	Sales and promotional literature	321,620	
A	Sales meetings and training	924,480	
A	Miscellaneous sales expense	681,041	
P	Executive and office salaries	5,523,960	
P	Administrative payroll benefits	682,315	
A	Travel and entertainment—administrative	561,680	
A	Computer maintenance and supplies	860,260	
A	Stationery and supplies	762,568	
A	Postage	244,420	
A	Telephone and fax	722,315	
A	Rent	312,140	
A	Legal fees and retainers	383,060	
A	Auditing and related services	302,840	
A	Amortization	1,452,080	
S	Bad debt expense	3,323,084	
A	Insurance	722,684	
A	Office repairs and maintenance	843,926	
A	Miscellaneous office expense	643,680	
A	Miscellaneous general expense	323,842	
A	Gain on sale of assets		719,740
A	Income taxes	1,746,600	
C	Interest expense	2,408,642	
C	Dividends	1,900,000	
		$237,539,033	$237,539,033

(1) These accounts were grouped together on the financial statements

Note: Letters in the left-hand column refer to the following transaction cycles: S = Sales and collection, A = Acquisition and payment, P = Payroll and personnel, I = Inventory and warehousing, C = Capital acquisition and repayment.

this trial balance are included in the black-and-white insert on pages 136–151. Prior-year figures usually included for comparative purposes are excluded from Figure 5-3 in order to focus on transaction cycles. A trial balance is used to prepare financial statements and is a primary focus of every audit. The letter representing a cycle is shown for each account in the left column beside the account name. Each account has at least one cycle associated with it, and only cash and inventories are a part of two or more cycles.

The cycles used in this text are shown again in Table 5-1. The accounts for Hillsburg Hardware Limited are summarized in Table 5-1 by cycle and include the transaction types that typically appear in each cycle. The following observations expand the information contained in Table 5-1.

All general ledger accounts and transaction types for Hillsburg Hardware Limited are included at least once. For a different company, the number and types of transactions and general ledger accounts would differ, but all would be included.

Some transaction types and general ledger accounts are included in more than one cycle. When that occurs, it means the transaction type is used to record transactions from more than one cycle and indicates a tie-in between the cycles. The most important general ledger account included in and affecting several cycles is the general cash (cash in bank). General cash connects most cycles.

The capital acquisition and repayment cycle is closely related to the acquisition and payment cycle. The acquisition of goods and services includes the purchase of inventory, supplies, and general services in performing the main business operations. Transactions in the capital acquisitions cycle are related to financing the business, such as issuing stock or debt, paying dividends, and repaying of debt. The same transaction type is used to record transactions for both cycles, and the transactions are similar. There are two reasons for treating capital acquisition and repayment separately from the acquisition of goods and services. First, the transactions are related to financing a company rather than to its operations. Second, most capital acquisition and repayment cycle accounts involve few transactions, but each is often highly material and therefore should be audited extensively. Considering both reasons, it is more convenient to separate the two cycles.

The inventory and warehousing cycle is closely related to all other cycles, especially for a manufacturing company. The cost of inventory includes raw materials (acquisition and payment cycle), direct labour (payroll and personnel cycle), and manufacturing overhead (acquisition and payment and payroll and personnel cycles). The sale of finished goods involves the sales and collection cycle. Because inventory is material for most manufacturing companies, it is common to borrow money using inventory as security. In those cases, the capital acquisition and repayment cycle is also related to inventory and warehousing.

Relationships Among Cycles Figure 5-4 on page 120 illustrates the relationship of the cycles to one another. In addition to the five cycles, general cash is also shown. Each cycle is studied in detail in later chapters.

Figure 5-4 shows that cycles have no beginning or end except at the origin and final disposition of a company. A company begins by obtaining capital, usually in the form of cash. In a manufacturing company, cash is used to acquire raw materials, capital assets, and related goods and services to produce inventory (acquisition and payment cycle). Cash is also used to acquire labour for the same reason (payroll and personnel cycle). Acquisition and payment and payroll and personnel are similar in nature, but the functions are sufficiently different to justify separate cycles. The combined result of these two cycles is inventory (inventory and warehousing cycle). At a subsequent point, the inventory is sold and billings and collections result (sales and collection cycle). The cash generated is used to pay dividends and interest and to start the cycles again. The cycles interrelate in much the same way in a service company, where there will be no inventory, but there may be unbilled receivables.

Relationships Among Transaction Cycles Transaction cycles are of major importance in the conduct of the audit. For the most part, auditors treat each cycle separately during the audit. Although auditors should take care to interrelate different cycles at different times and be aware of the interrelationships among the cycles, they must treat the cycles somewhat independently in order to manage complex audits effectively.

TABLE 5-1	Cycles Applied to Hillsburg Hardware Limited

Cycle	Transaction Types Included in the Cycle (See Figures 5-2A, B, C)	General Ledger Account Included in the Cycle	
		Balance Sheet	Income Statement
Sales and collection	Sales Cash receipts Journal entries	Cash in bank Trade accounts receivable Allowance for uncollectible accounts Other accounts receivable	Sales Sales returns and allowances Bad debt expense
Acquisition and payment	Acquisitions Cash disbursements Journal entries	Cash in bank Inventories Prepaid expenses Land Buildings Computer and delivery equipment Furniture and fixtures Accumulated amortization Trade accounts payable Goods and services tax payable Accrued income tax Deferred tax Other accrued payables	Advertising[S] Amortization Auditing[A] and related services Computer maintenance and supplies Gain on sale of assets Income taxes Insurance[A] Legal fees and retainers[A] Miscellaneous general expense[A] Miscellaneous office expense[A] Miscellaneous sales expense[S] Office repairs and maintenance Postage[A] Rent[A] Sales and promotional literature[S] Sales meetings and training[S] Stationery and supplies[A] Taxes[A] Telephone and fax[A] Travel and entertainment—selling[S] Travel and entertainment—administrative[A]
Payroll and personnel	Payroll Journal entries	Cash in bank Accrued payroll Accrued payroll benefits	Salaries and commissions[S] Sales payroll benefits[S] Executive and office salaries[A] Administrative payroll benefits[A]
Inventory and warehousing	Acquisitions Sales Journal entries	Inventories	Cost of goods sold
Capital acquisition and repayment	Acquisitions Cash disbursements Journal entries	Cash in bank Notes payable Accrued interest Long-term notes payable Accrued interest Capital stock Retained earnings Dividends Dividends payable	Interest expense

S = Selling expense
A = General and administrative expense

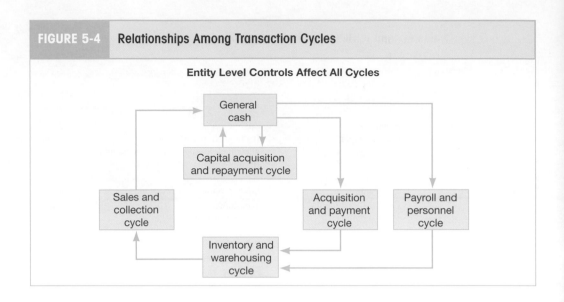

FIGURE 5-4 Relationships Among Transaction Cycles

Corporate Governance and Entity Level Systems

Prior to looking at specific cycles, the auditor will enquire about and document corporate governance systems, such as the policies and procedures employed by the Board of Directors, the Audit Committee, and Senior Management. As you will discover in later chapters, actions at the corporate governance level have a significant impact upon the level of risk assigned to the audit of the organization.

There are also many entity level controls, such as supervision policies and information technology general controls that affect multiple or all transaction cycles. For example, controls over program changes affect all systems that have automated information systems, as do security and access controls. Prior to working with individual transaction cycles, the auditor would document, evaluate, and test (where reliance is warranted) these entity level controls. Chapter 9 looks at the study and assessment of internal controls.

Setting Audit Objectives

Auditors conduct audits consistent with the cycle approach by performing audit tests of the transactions making up ending balances and also by performing audit tests of the account balances themselves. Figure 5-5 illustrates this important concept by showing the four classes of transactions that determine the ending balance in accounts receivable. Assume that the beginning balance of $17,521 was audited in the prior year and is therefore considered reliable. If the auditor could be completely sure that each of the four classes of transactions was correctly stated, the auditor could also be sure that the ending balance of $20,197 was correctly stated. However, it may be impractical for the auditor to obtain complete assurance about the correctness of each class of transactions resulting in less than complete assurance about the ending balance in accounts receivable. In such a case, overall assurance can be increased by auditing the ending balance of accounts receivable. Auditors have found that, generally, the most efficient way to conduct audits is to *obtain some combination of assurance for each class of transactions and for the ending balance in the related account.*

For any given class of transactions, there are several audit objectives that must be met before the auditor can conclude that the transactions are properly recorded. They are called *transaction-related audit objectives* in the remainder of this book. For example, there are specific sales transaction-related audit objectives and specific sales returns and allowances transaction-related audit objectives.

Similarly, there are several audit objectives that must be met for each account balance. They are called *balance-related audit objectives*. For example, there are specific accounts receivable balance-related audit objectives and specific accounts payable balance-related audit objectives. It will be shown later that the transaction-related and balance-related audit

FIGURE 5-5

FIGURE 5-5 **Balances and Transactions Affecting Those Balances for Accounts Receivable**

Accounts Receivable (in thousands)

Beginning balance	$ 17,521		
Sales	$144,328	$137,087	Cash receipts
		$ 1,242	Sales returns and allowances
		$ 3,323	Charge-off of uncollectible accounts
Ending balance	$ 20,197		

objectives, called **specific audit objectives**, are somewhat different but closely related. Throughout the remainder of this text, the term "audit objectives" refers to both transaction-related and balance-related audit objectives.

Before examining audit objectives in more detail, it is necessary to understand management assertions. These are studied next.

→5.3 MANAGEMENT ASSERTIONS AND AUDIT OBJECTIVES

Management Assertions

Assertions are implied or expressed representations by management about classes of transactions and the related accounts in the financial statements. As an illustration, the management of Hillsburg Hardware Limited asserts that cash of $827,568 (see Figure 5-3) was present in the company's bank accounts or on the premises as of the balance sheet date. Unless otherwise disclosed in the financial statements, management also asserts that the cash was unrestricted and available for normal use. Similar assertions exist for each asset, liability, equity, revenue, and expense item in the financial statements. These assertions apply to both classes of transactions and account balances.

Management assertions are directly related to generally accepted accounting principles. These assertions are part of the *criteria management uses to record and disclose accounting information in financial statements*. Return to the definition of auditing in Chapter 1, on page 4. It states, in part, that auditing is a comparison of information (financial statements) to established criteria (assertions established according to generally accepted accounting principles). Auditors must therefore understand the assertions to do adequate audits.

Section 5300.21 of the *CICA Assurance Handbook* lists and describes assertions that management makes with respect to items in the financial statements. This text generally uses these same assertions, except that "ownership" has been extended to "rights and obligations," affecting both assets and liabilities, as described below.

ASSERTIONS ABOUT EXISTENCE Assertions about existence deal with whether assets, obligations, and equities included in the balance sheet actually existed on the balance sheet date. For example, management asserts that merchandise inventory included in the balance sheet exists and is available for sale at the balance sheet date.

ASSERTIONS ABOUT OCCURRENCE Assertions about occurrence concern whether recorded transactions included in the financial statements actually occurred during the accounting period.

SPECIFIC AUDIT OBJECTIVES— transaction-related or balance-related audit objectives for each class of transactions and account balance

MANAGEMENT ASSERTIONS— implied or expressed representations by management about classes of transactions and related accounts in the financial statements

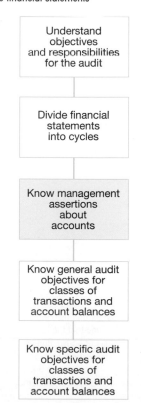

Management asserts that sales in the income statement represent exchanges of goods or services that actually took place.

ASSERTIONS ABOUT COMPLETENESS These management assertions state that all transactions and accounts that should be presented in the financial statements are included. For example, management asserts that all sales of goods and services are recorded and included in the financial statements. Similarly, management asserts that notes payable in the balance sheet include all such obligations of the entity.

The completeness assertion deals with matters opposite from those of the existence or occurrence assertions. The completeness assertion is concerned with the possibility of omitting items from the financial statements that should have been included, whereas the existence or occurrence assertions are concerned with inclusion of amounts that should not have been included.

Thus, recording a sale that did not take place would be a violation of the occurrence assertion, whereas the failure to record a sale that did occur would be a violation of the completeness assertion.

ASSERTIONS ABOUT VALUATION An asset or liability is asserted as being recorded at an appropriate carrying value. This involves the use of management judgment to determine whether the value is accurately recorded originally (normally at cost) and whether the current carrying value is appropriate. For capital assets, this includes determining the amount of amortization that should be recorded against the asset, and whether the asset value has been impaired or not, thus requiring a writedown. Inventory should be examined for potential obsolescence, and accounts receivable should be assessed for collectibility. Management asserts that its estimates and conclusions on valuation are those that should be used for the financial statements.

ASSERTIONS ABOUT ACCURACY, MEASUREMENT, OR ALLOCATION These assertions deal with whether the asset, liability, equity, revenue, and expense accounts have been included in the financial statements at appropriate amounts and in the proper period. For example, management asserts that property is recorded at historical cost equal to the invoice amount and that such cost is accurately allocated to appropriate accounting periods using the amortization rate that has been determined. Similarly, management states that the correct quantities and prices were used to calculate ending inventory amounts, and that only the inventory on hand at the end of the year was included in inventory.

ASSERTIONS ABOUT OWNERSHIP: RIGHTS AND OBLIGATIONS These management assertions deal with whether assets are the rights of the entity and liabilities are the obligations of the entity at a given date. For example, management asserts that assets are owned by the company or amounts capitalized for leases in the balance sheet represent the cost of the entity's rights to leased property, and that the corresponding lease liability represents an obligation of the entity.

ASSERTIONS ABOUT STATEMENT PRESENTATION (AND DISCLOSURE) These assertions deal with whether components of the financial statements are properly combined or separated, described, and disclosed. Disclosures should be clearly expressed. For example, management asserts that obligations classified as long-term liabilities on the balance sheet will not mature within one year. Similarly, management asserts that amounts presented as extraordinary items in the income statement are properly classified and described.

Transaction-Related Audit Objectives

The auditor's transaction-related audit objectives follow and are closely related to management assertions. This is not surprising since the auditor's primary responsibility is to determine whether management assertions about financial statements are justified.

These **transaction-related audit objectives** are intended to provide a *framework* to help the auditor accumulate sufficient competent audit evidence required by the third examination standard and decide the proper evidence to accumulate for classes of transactions given the circumstances of the engagement. The objectives remain the same from audit to audit, but the evidence varies depending on the circumstances.

TRANSACTION-RELATED AUDIT OBJECTIVES—six audit objectives that must be met before the auditor can conclude that the total for any given class of transactions is fairly stated. The general transaction-related audit objectives are occurrence, completeness, accuracy, classification, timing, and posting and summarization

A distinction must be made between *general transaction-related audit objectives* and *specific transaction-related audit objectives* for each class of transactions. The general transaction-related audit objectives discussed here are applicable to every class of transactions but are stated in broad terms. Specific transaction-related audit objectives are also applied to each class of transactions but are stated in terms tailored to a class of transactions, such as sales transactions. Once you know the general transaction-related audit objectives, they can be used to develop specific transaction-related audit objectives for each class of transactions being audited. The six general transaction-related audit objectives are discussed next.

General Transaction-Related Audit Objectives

OCCURRENCE—RECORDED TRANSACTIONS OCCURRED This objective deals with whether recorded transactions have actually occurred. Inclusion of a sale in the sales journal when no sale occurred violates the occurrence objective. This objective is the auditor's counterpart to the management assertion of occurrence.

COMPLETENESS—EXISTING TRANSACTIONS ARE RECORDED This objective deals with whether all transactions that should be included in the journals have actually been included. Failure to enter a sale into a computer system and thus into the general ledger when a sale occurred violates the completeness objective. The objective is the counterpart to the management assertion of completeness.

The occurrence and completeness objectives emphasize opposite audit concerns; occurrence deals with potential overstatement and completeness with unrecorded transactions (understatement).

ACCURACY—RECORDED TRANSACTIONS ARE STATED AT THE CORRECT AMOUNTS This objective deals with the accuracy of information for accounting transactions. For sales transactions, there would be a violation of the accuracy objective if the quantity of goods shipped was different from the quantity billed, the wrong selling price was used for billing, extension or adding errors (perhaps due to program errors) occurred in billing, or the wrong amount was updated to the master file. Accuracy is one part of the measurement assertion.

CLASSIFICATION—TRANSACTIONS INCLUDED IN THE CLIENT'S RECORDS ARE PROPERLY CLASSIFIED Examples of misclassifications for sales are including cash sales as credit sales, recording a sale of operating capital assets as revenue, and misclassifying commercial sales as residential sales. Classification is also a part of the measurement assertion.

TIMING—TRANSACTIONS ARE RECORDED ON THE CORRECT DATES A timing error occurs if transactions are not recorded on the dates the transactions took place. A sales transaction, for example, should be recorded on the date of shipment. Timing is also a part of the measurement assertion.

POSTING AND SUMMARIZATION—RECORDED TRANSACTIONS ARE UPDATED TO THE MASTER FILES AND ARE CORRECTLY SUMMARIZED This objective deals with the accuracy of the transfer of information from recorded transactions to subsidiary records (or master files) and summarization to the general ledger. For example, if a sales transaction is recorded in the wrong customer's record and thus to the wrong customer in the master file, it is a violation of this objective. Posting and summarization is also a part of the measurement assertion.

Since the posting of transactions to subsidiary records, the general ledger, and other related master files is typically accomplished automatically by computerized accounting systems, the risk of random human error in posting is minimal. Once the auditor has established that the computer is functioning properly, there is a reduced concern about posting or summarization errors.

Specific Transaction-Related Audit Objectives
The general transaction-related audit objectives must be applied to each material type (class) of transaction in the audit. Such transactions typically include sales, cash receipts, acquisitions of goods and services, payroll, and so on. Table 5-2 on page 125 summarizes the six transaction-related audit objectives. It includes the general form of the objectives, the application of the objectives to sales transactions, and the assertions. Notice that only three general assertions are associated with transaction-related audit objectives. This shows that four of the assertions are not satisfied by performing tests of controls, but instead are satisfied by substantive tests of transactions.

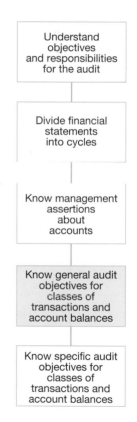

Understand objectives and responsibilities for the audit

Divide financial statements into cycles

Know management assertions about accounts

Know general audit objectives for classes of transactions and account balances

Know specific audit objectives for classes of transactions and account balances

Balance-Related Audit Objectives

BALANCE-RELATED AUDIT OBJEC-
TIVES—nine audit objectives that
must be met before the auditor can
conclude that any given account
balance is fairly stated. The general
balance-related audit objectives are
existence, completeness, valuation,
accuracy, classification, cutoff,
detail tie-in, rights and obligations,
and presentation and disclosure

Balance-related audit objectives are similar to the transaction-related audit objectives just discussed. They also follow from management assertions and they provide a framework to help the auditor accumulate sufficient appropriate evidence. There are also both general and specific balance-related audit objectives.

There are two differences between balance-related and transaction-related audit objectives. First, as the terms imply, balance-related audit objectives are applied to account balances, whereas transaction-related audit objectives are applied to classes of transactions such as sales transactions and cash disbursements transactions. Second, there are more audit objectives for account balances than for classes of transactions. There are nine balance-related audit objectives compared to six transaction-related audit objectives. These are also shown on Table 5-2.

Because of the way audits are done, balance-related audit objectives are almost *always* applied to the ending balance in balance sheet accounts, such as accounts receivable, inventory, and notes payable. Balance-related objectives are also applied to certain income statement accounts. These usually involve non-routine transactions and unpredictable expenses, such as a legal expense or repairs and maintenance. Other income statement accounts are closely related to balance sheet accounts and are tested simultaneously (e.g., amortization expense with accumulated amortization, interest expense with notes payable).

When using the balance-related audit objectives as a framework for auditing balance sheet account balances, the auditor accumulates evidence to verify detail that supports the account balance, rather than verifying the account balance itself. For example, in auditing accounts receivable, the auditor obtains a listing of the aged accounts receivable balances from the client that agrees to the general ledger balance (see page 424 for an illustration). The accounts receivable balance-related audit objectives are applied to the customer accounts in that listing.

Following is a brief discussion of the nine general balance-related audit objectives. Throughout the discussion, there is reference to a supporting schedule, which refers to client-provided working papers or reports such as the accounts receivable listing just described.

General Balance-Related Audit Objectives

EXISTENCE—AMOUNTS INCLUDED EXIST This objective deals with whether the amounts included in the financial statements should actually be included. For example, inclusion of an account receivable from a customer in the accounts receivable trial balance when there is no receivable from that customer violates the existence objective. Similarly, if the same inventory is accidentally counted twice and thus inventory is inflated, the existence objective has been violated. This objective is the auditor's counterpart to the management assertion of existence or occurrence.

COMPLETENESS—EXISTING AMOUNTS ARE INCLUDED This objective deals with whether all amounts that should be included have actually been included. Failure to include an account receivable from a customer when the receivable exists violates the completeness objective. Forgetting to count and include certain types of inventory does the same. This objective is the counterpart to the management assertion of completeness.

The existence and completeness objectives emphasize opposite audit concerns; existence deals with potential overstatement and completeness deals with unrecorded transactions and amounts (understatement).

VALUATION (REALIZABLE VALUE)—ASSETS ARE INCLUDED AT THE AMOUNTS ESTIMATED TO BE REALIZED This objective concerns whether an account balance has been reduced for declines from historical cost to net realizable value. Examples of when this objective applies are considering the adequacy of the allowance for uncollectible accounts receivable and writedowns of inventory for obsolescence. The objective applies only to asset accounts and is part of the valuation assertion.

ACCURACY—AMOUNTS INCLUDED ARE STATED AT THE CORRECT AMOUNTS The accuracy objective refers to amounts being included at the correct arithmetic amount. An inventory item on a client's inventory listing could be incorrect because the number of units of inventory on hand was

| | TABLE 5-2 | Management Assertions, General Audit Objectives, and Specific Audit Objectives |

Management Assertion	General Transaction-Related Audit Objectives	Specific Sales Transaction-Related Audit Objectives	General Balance-Related Audit Objectives	Specific Balance-Related Audit Objectives Applied to Inventory
Existence	N/A	N/A	Existence	All recorded inventories exist at the balance sheet date.
Occurrence	Occurrence	Recorded sales are for shipments made to nonfictitious customers.	N/A	N/A
Completeness	Completeness	Existing sales transactions are recorded.	Completeness	All existing inventory has been counted and included in inventory.
Valuation	N/A	N/A	Valuation	Inventories have been written down where net realizable value is less than book value.
Measurement	Accuracy	Recorded sales are for the amount of goods shipped and are correctly billed and recorded.	Accuracy	Inventory quantities agree with items physically on hand. Prices used to extend inventory cost are materially correct. Extensions of price times quantity are correct and details are correctly added.
Measurement	Classification	Sales transactions are classified to the correct account.	Classification	Inventory items are properly classified as raw materials, work in process, or finished goods.
Allocation	Timing	Sales are recorded on the correct dates.	Cutoff	Purchases at year end are recorded in the correct period. Sales at year end are recorded in the correct period.
Measurement	Posting and summarization	Sales transactions are updated correctly to the customer master file, and the posting to the general ledger summed these transactions correctly.	Detail tie-in	Total of inventory items agrees with general ledger.
Rights and obligations	N/A	N/A	Rights and obligations	The company has title to all inventory items listed. Inventories are not pledged as collateral.
Presentation and disclosure	N/A	N/A	Presentation and disclosure	Major categories of inventories and their bases of valuation are disclosed. The pledge or assignment of any inventories is disclosed.

misstated, the unit price was incorrect, or the total was incorrectly extended due to a programming error. Each of these violates the accuracy objective. Accuracy is one part of the measurement assertion.

CLASSIFICATION—AMOUNTS INCLUDED IN THE CLIENT'S LISTING ARE PROPERLY CLASSIFIED Classification involves determining whether items on a client's listing are included in the correct accounts. For example, on the accounts receivable listing, receivables must be separated into short-term and long-term, and amounts due from affiliates, officers, and directors must be classified separately from amounts due from customers. Inventory should be correctly classified by type. Classification is also a part of the measurement assertion.

CUTOFF—TRANSACTIONS NEAR THE BALANCE SHEET DATE ARE RECORDED IN THE PROPER PERIOD In testing for cutoff, the objective is to determine whether transactions are recorded in the proper period. The transactions that are most likely to be misstated are those recorded near the end of the accounting period. It is proper to think of cutoff tests as a part of verifying either the balance sheet accounts or the related transactions but, for convenience, auditors usually perform them as a part of auditing balance sheet accounts. Cutoff is also part of the measurement assertion.

DETAIL TIE-IN—TRANSACTION DETAILS SUM TO THE MASTER FILES AMOUNTS, AND SUBSIDIARY RECORDS (MANUAL OR AUTOMATED) AGREE WITH THE TOTAL IN THE ACCOUNT BALANCE IN THE GENERAL LEDGER Account balances on financial statements are supported by details in data files and schedules prepared by clients. The detail tie-in objective is concerned that the details are accurately prepared, correctly added, and agree with the general ledger. For example, individual accounts receivable on a listing of accounts receivable should agree with the customer master file and the total should equal the general ledger control account. Detail tie-in is also a part of the measurement assertion.

RIGHTS AND OBLIGATIONS In addition to existing, most assets must be owned before they can be included in the financial statements. Similarly, liabilities must belong to the entity. Rights are always associated with assets and obligations with liabilities. This objective is the auditor's counterpart to the management assertion of rights and obligations (ownership).

PRESENTATION AND DISCLOSURE—ACCOUNT BALANCES AND RELATED DISCLOSURE REQUIREMENTS ARE PROPERLY PRESENTED IN THE FINANCIAL STATEMENTS In fulfilling the presentation and disclosure objective, the auditor tests to make certain that all balance sheet and income statement accounts and related information are correctly set forth in the financial statements and properly described in the body and footnotes of the statements. This objective has its counterpart in the management assertion of presentation and disclosure.

Presentation and disclosure is closely related to, but distinct from, classification. Accounting information for balance-related audit objectives is correctly classified if all information on a report or in a data file supporting an account balance is summarized in the appropriate accounts. The information is correctly disclosed if those account balances and related footnote information are properly combined, described, and presented in the financial statements. For example, if a long-term note receivable is included on an accounts receivable listing, there is a violation of the classification objective. If the long-term note receivable is correctly classified but combined with accounts receivable on the financial statements, there is a violation of the presentation and disclosure objective.

Specific Balance-Related Audit Objectives After the general balance-related audit objectives are understood, specific balance-related audit objectives for each account balance on the financial statements can be developed. There should be at least one specific balance-related audit objective for each general balance-related audit objective unless the auditor believes that the general balance-related audit objective is not relevant or is unimportant in the circumstances. There may be more than one specific balance-related audit objective for a general balance-related audit objective. For example, specific balance-related audit objectives for rights and obligations of the inventory of Hillsburg Hardware Limited could include that (1) the company has title to all inventory items listed and (2) inventories are not pledged as collateral unless it is disclosed.

Relationships Among Management Assertions and Balance-Related Audit Objectives The reason there are more general balance-related audit objectives than management assertions is to provide additional guidance to auditors in deciding what evidence to accumulate. Table 5-2 illustrates this by showing the relationships among management assertions, the general balance-related audit objectives, and specific balance-related audit objectives as applied to inventory for a company such as Hillsburg Hardware Limited.

How Audit Objectives Are Met

The auditor must obtain sufficient appropriate audit evidence to support all management assertions in the financial statements. As stated earlier, this is done by accumulating evidence in support of some appropriate combination of transaction-related audit objectives and balance-related audit objectives. Table 5-2 shows a significant overlap between the two types of audit objectives. The only assertions that must be addressed through balance-related audit objectives, rather than some combination of balance- and transaction-related audit objectives, are rights and obligations and presentation and disclosure.

The auditor plans the appropriate combination of audit objectives and the evidence that must be accumulated to meet them by following an audit process. An audit process is a well-defined methodology for organizing an audit to ensure that the evidence gathered is both sufficient and appropriate, and that all required audit objectives are both specified and met. The audit process described in this text has four specific phases. These are shown in Figure 5-6. An expanded summary of the audit process is presented in Figure 11-7 on page 330. The remainder of this chapter provides a brief introduction to each of the four phases.

→5.4 AUDIT PHASES

Prior to the audit evidence assessment and collection process, the auditor determines whether there are any threats to independence. If threats exist, they must be dealt with or the audit engagement must be declined. Then, the auditor develops an overview risk profile for the audit engagement. This risk profile is prepared by considering the business environment, the industry sector in which the client operates, and by having sufficient knowledge of the client's business. The auditor would also obtain information about the management oversight process, part of the control environment, to decide on the client risk profile. Many additional activities are considered part of the audit plan and are considered further in Chapter 7.

Risk Assessment and Audit Planning (Phase I) For any given audit, there are many ways an auditor can accumulate evidence to meet the overall audit objectives. Two overriding considerations affect the approach the auditor selects: *sufficient appropriate audit evidence must be accumulated to meet the auditor's professional responsibility*, and *the cost of accumulating the evidence should be minimized*. The first consideration is the more important, but cost minimization is necessary if public accounting firms are to be competitive and profitable. If there were no concern for controlling costs, decision making about the types and amounts of evidence to select would be easy. Auditors would keep adding evidence, without concern for efficiency, until they were sufficiently certain there were no material misstatements.

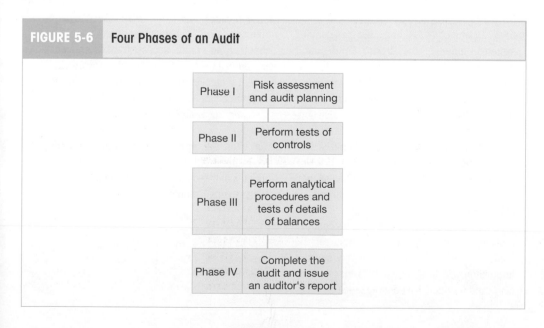

FIGURE 5-6	Four Phases of an Audit

Phase I — Risk assessment and audit planning

Phase II — Perform tests of controls

Phase III — Perform analytical procedures and tests of details of balances

Phase IV — Complete the audit and issue an auditor's report

Concern for sufficient appropriate audit evidence and cost control necessitates planning the engagement. The plan should result in an effective audit approach at reasonable cost. Planning and designing an audit approach can be broken down into several parts. Two are addressed briefly here. Others are discussed in later chapters.

OBTAINING KNOWLEDGE OF THE CLIENT'S BUSINESS To adequately interpret the meaning of information obtained throughout the audit, an *understanding of the client's business and industry* is essential. Unique aspects of different businesses are reflected in the financial statements. An audit of a life insurance company could not be performed with due care without an understanding of the unique characteristics of that business. Imagine attempting to audit a client in the bridge construction industry without understanding the construction business and the percentage-of-completion method of accounting. Neither audit could be effectively conducted without an awareness of the business environment or regulatory environment within which these businesses function. Examination Standard (ii) of generally accepted auditing standards in paragraph 5100.02 *requires* the auditor to "obtain an understanding of the entity and its environment" as a basis for planning the audit.

UNDERSTANDING THE CLIENT'S INTERNAL CONTROL AND ASSESSING CONTROL RISK It was pointed out in Chapter 1 that the ability of the client's internal controls to generate reliable financial information and safeguard assets and records is one of the most important and widely accepted concepts in the theory and practice of auditing. If the client has excellent internal controls, *control risk* will be low and the amount of audit evidence to be accumulated can be significantly less than when internal controls are inadequate.

Examination Standard (ii) of generally accepted auditing standards in paragraph 5100.02 *requires* the auditor to gain a sufficient understanding of internal control to plan the audit. This understanding is obtained by reviewing organization charts and procedural manuals, by discussions with client personnel, by completing internal control questionnaires and flowcharts, and by observing client activities. Many firms have software that assists in the evaluation process by prompting the auditor to answer specific questions and then providing a summary of the likely effects of the responses on control risk. Software also helps the auditor link controls to specific assertions.

After the auditor gains an understanding of internal control, he or she is in a position to evaluate how effective controls should be in preventing and detecting errors or fraud and other irregularities. This evaluation involves identifying specific controls that reduce the likelihood that errors or fraud and other irregularities will occur and not be detected

---

Focus Box 5-1

UNDERSTANDING THE CLIENT'S BUSINESS INCLUDES INFORMATION SYSTEMS

Do you know what operating system your client uses? Or when they last upgraded it? Operating systems manage the basic input/output processes of computer systems and also manage access to the computer system by providing for validation (such as a password and user ID that must be entered to access application software). If an operating system has vulnerabilities, these can be exploited by external hackers as well as internal employees intent on mischief. Auditors need to determine versions in use, procedures for upgrading, and control processes, such as management of activity logs.

Where there are inadequate access controls, malicious programs such as "bots" can be loaded onto computers. Bots are very effective in monitoring activity, so much so that they are also used for authorized activity (such as tracking web usage). Malicious bots create copies of themselves and set up procedures to enable unauthorized system access. It takes only one computer in a network with old software (i.e. current protection mechanisms do not exist) to make an entire network vulnerable.

As part of knowledge of the client, the auditor would ask about procedures in place to prevent virus, bot, or worm infection in a network. For example, frequency of anti-virus program updates and regular patching (updating of operating systems) should occur.

Sources: 1. Dunham, Ken, 2005. "On Malicious Code," *Information Systems Security.* May/Jun 2005, Vol. 14 (2). 2. Silltow, John, 2005. "Operating Systems: Basic Information Auditors Need to Know," *ITAudit,* June 1, 2005. Vol. 9.

and corrected on a timely basis. Supervisory, managing, or monitoring controls are specifically identified as having important effects. This process is referred to as *assessing control risk.*

Perform Tests of Controls (Phase II) Where the auditor has assessed control risk at a level below maximum based on the identification of controls, he or she may then reduce the extent to which the accuracy of the financial statement information related directly to those controls must be validated through the accumulation of evidence. However, to justify using a control risk assessment below maximum, the auditor must test the effectiveness of the controls. The procedures involved in this type of testing are commonly referred to as **tests of controls**. For example, assume that the client's order entry software requires that all amounts over $10,000 must be entered twice. This control is directly related to the accuracy transaction-related audit objective for sales. One possible test of the effectiveness of this control is for the auditor to enter a transaction over $10,000 and observe whether the system requests a second entry.

TESTS OF CONTROLS—audit procedures to test the effectiveness of control policies and procedures in support of a reduced assessed control risk

Auditors also evaluate the client's recording of transactions by verifying the dollar amounts of transactions. An example is for the auditor to compare the unit selling price on a duplicate sales invoice with the approved sales price in the inventory master file as a test of the accuracy objective for sales transactions. Like the test of control in the previous paragraph, this test satisfies the accuracy transaction-related audit objective for sales.

Perform Analytical Procedures and Tests of Details of Balances (Phase III) Phase III procedures are described as substantive procedures; there are two general categories of phase III procedures: analytical procedures and tests of details of balances. **Analytical procedures** are those that assess the overall reasonableness of transactions and balances. An example of an analytical procedure that would provide some assurance for the accuracy objective for both sales transactions (transaction-related audit objective) and accounts receivable (balance-related audit objective) is to have the auditor run an exception report (using audit software) of sales transactions for unusually large amounts and compare total monthly sales to prior years. If a company is consistently using incorrect sales prices, significant differences are likely.

ANALYTICAL PROCEDURES—use of comparisons and relationships to determine whether account balances or other data appear reasonable

TEST OF DETAILS OF BALANCES— an auditor's tests for monetary errors or fraud and other irregularities in the details of balance sheet and income statement accounts

Tests of details of balances are specific procedures intended to test for monetary misstatements in the balances in the financial statements. An example related to the accuracy objective for accounts receivable (balance-related audit objective) is direct written communication with the client's customers. Tests of ending balances are essential to the conduct of the audit because most of the evidence is obtained from a source independent of the client and therefore considered to be of high quality.

There is a close relationship among the general review of the client's circumstances, results of understanding internal control and assessing control risk, analytical procedures, and the tests of details of the financial statement account balances. If the auditor has obtained a reasonable level of assurance for any given audit objective by performing tests of controls and analytical procedures, the tests of details for that objective can be significantly reduced. In most instances, however, some tests of details of significant financial statement account balances are necessary.

Complete the Audit and Issue an Auditor's Report (Phase IV) After the auditor has completed all the procedures for each audit objective and for each financial statement account, it is necessary to combine the information obtained to reach an *overall conclusion* as to whether the financial statements are fairly presented. This is a highly subjective process that relies heavily on the auditor's professional judgment. In practice, the auditor continuously combines the information obtained as he or she proceeds through the audit. The final combination is a summation at the completion of the engagement. When the audit is completed, the public accountant must issue an auditor's report to accompany the client's published financial statements. The report must meet well-defined technical requirements that are affected by the scope of the audit and the nature of the findings. These reports have already been studied in Chapter 3.

SUMMARY

1. *What is the objective of conducting an audit of financial statements?* The auditor expresses an opinion about the fairness of presentation of the financial statements.

   Explain the difference between management and auditor responsibilities with respect to the financial statements and the discovery and correction of material misstatements or illegal acts. Management is responsible for designing internal controls to prevent and detect errors, fraud, or illegal acts. These controls should be concerned with errors of all sizes, not just material errors. Auditors are concerned with material misstatements, as they consider the financial statements in the context of users. Auditors express an opinion on the financial statements that have been prepared by management.

2. *How are financial statements divided into cycles?* The smaller segments or components are: cash; capital acquisition and repayment; acquisition and payment; payroll and personnel; inventory and warehousing; and sales and collection.

   How is this cycle approach related to the financial statement audit? One aspect of evidence gathering is the auditor testing classes of transactions that are part of the transaction cycles.

   What is the relationship among cycles? The cycles show that transactions are related to each other, since the cycles interrelate. For example, cash has a role in each of the cycles—payment of sales, purchase of materials, and acquisition of debt.

   What is the relationship between the cycle approach and entity level controls? Entity level controls affect all cycles, as the corporate governance structure includes policies and procedures over all transactions.

3. *Describe management assertions about financial information.* Management assertions are implied or expressed representations about classes of transactions and accounts in the financial statements.

   Relate management assertions to general transaction-related audit objectives and general balance-related audit objectives. Transaction-related and balance-related audit objectives follow from and are closely related to management assertions and provide a framework to help the auditor collect audit evidence.

4. *List the four phases of a financial statement audit and provide an overview of the audit process.* The four phases are: risk assessment and audit planning; performing tests of controls; performing analytical procedures and tests of details of balances; completing the audit and issuing an auditor's report. These phases allow the auditor to collect sufficient, appropriate audit evidence to state an opinion on the financial statements.

CICA ASSURANCE HANDBOOK SECTIONS REFERENCED IN THIS CHAPTER

Section 5090 – Audit of financial statements – an introduction.
Section 5100 – Generally accepted auditing standards.
Section 5110 – Terms of the engagement.
Section 5135 – The auditor's responsibility to consider fraud.

Section 5136 – Misstatements – illegal acts.
Section 5300 – Audit evidence.

ESSENTIAL TERMS

Analytical procedures—use of comparisons and relationships to determine whether account balances or other data appear reasonable   (p. 129).

Balance-related audit objectives—nine audit objectives that must be met before the auditor can conclude that any given account balance is fairly stated. The general balance-related audit objectives are existence, completeness, valuation, accuracy, classification, cutoff, detail tie-in, rights and obligations, and presentation and disclosure   (p. 124).

Cycle approach—a method of dividing an audit by keeping closely related types of transactions and account balances in the same segment   (p. 115).

Error—an unintentional misstatement of the financial statements   (p. 112).

Fraud or other irregularity—an intentional misstatement of the financial statements   (p. 112).

Illegal acts—violations of laws or government regulations other than irregularities   (p. 113).

Management assertions—implied or expressed representations by management about classes of transactions and related accounts in the financial statements   (p. 121).

Management fraud—a fraud or other irregularity resulting in fraudulent financial reporting   (p. 112).

Specific audit objectives—transaction-related or balance-related audit objectives for each class of transactions and account balance   (p. 121).

Tests of controls—audit procedures to test the effectiveness of control policies and procedures in support of a reduced assessed control risk   (p. 129).

Tests of details of balances—an auditor's tests for monetary errors or fraud and other irregularities in the details of balance sheet and income statement accounts   (p. 129).

Transaction-related audit objectives—six audit objectives that must be met before the auditor can conclude that the total for any given class of transactions is fairly stated. The general trans-action-related audit objectives are occurrence, completeness, accuracy, classification, timing, and posting and summarization (p. 122).

REVIEW QUESTIONS

5-1 State the objective of the audit of financial statements. In general terms, how do auditors meet that objective?

5-2 Distinguish between management's and the auditor's responsibility for the financial statements being audited.

5-3 Distinguish between the terms "errors" and "fraud and other irregularities." What is the auditor's responsibility for finding each?

5-4 Distinguish between management fraud and employee fraud. Discuss the likely difference between these two types of fraud on the fair presentation of financial statements.

5-5 Define the term "illegal act." What is the auditor's responsibility with respect to illegal acts by clients?

5-6 Describe what is meant by the cycle approach to auditing. What are the advantages of dividing the audit into different cycles?

5-7 Why are sales, sales returns and allowances, bad debts, cash discounts, accounts receivable, and allowance for uncollectible accounts all included in the same cycle?

5-8 How are entity level controls related to cycles?

5-9 Distinguish between the general audit objectives and management assertions. Why are the general audit objectives more useful to auditors?

5-10 An acquisition of equipment repairs by a construction company is recorded in the incorrect accounting period. Which transaction-related audit objective has been violated? Which transaction-related objective has been violated if the acquisition has been capitalized as a capital asset rather than expensed?

5-11 Distinguish between the existence and completeness balance-related audit objectives. State the effect on the financial statements (overstatement or understatement) of a violation of each in the audit of accounts receivable.

5-12 Identify the management assertion and general balance-related audit objective for the specific balance-related audit objective: All recorded capital assets exist at the balance sheet date.

5-13 Identify the four phases of the audit. What is the relationship of the four phases to the objective of the audit of financial statements?

MULTIPLE CHOICE QUESTIONS

5-14 Choose the best response for each question.

a. Which of the following best describes the reason why an independent auditor reports on financial statements?

(1) A management fraud may exist, and it is more likely to be detected by independent auditors.
(2) Poorly designed internal controls may be in existence.
(3) Different interests may exist between the company preparing the statements and the persons using the statements.
(4) A misstatement of account balances may exist and is generally corrected as the result of the independent auditor's work.

b. The major reason an independent auditor gathers audit evidence is to

(1) form an opinion on the financial statements.
(2) detect fraud.
(3) assess control risk.
(4) evaluate management.

(AICPA adapted)

c. The primary responsibility for the adequacy of disclosure in the financial statements and footnotes rests with the

(1) partner assigned to the engagement.
(2) staff member who drafts the statements and footnotes.

(3) auditor in charge of fieldwork.
(4) client.

(AICPA adapted)

d. An independent auditor has the responsibility to design the audit examination to provide reasonable assurance of detecting errors or fraud and other irregularities that might have a material effect on the financial statements. Which of the following, if material, would be a *fraud* as defined in the *CICA Assurance Handbook*?

(1) Misinterpretation of facts that existed when the financial statements were prepared.
(2) Misappropriation of an asset or groups of assets.
(3) Clerical mistakes in the accounting data underlying the financial statements.
(4) Mistakes in the application of accounting principles.

e. Although the discovery of fraud is not the objective of the public accountant's ordinary audit engagement, the public accountant would be responsible for the detection of fraud if it is material and the public accountant failed to detect it due to

(1) management's failure to disclose an unrecorded transaction. The documents pertaining to the transaction are kept in a confidential file.
(2) management's description of internal control.

(3) management's misstatement of the value of an inventory of precious gems.

(4) the amount of fidelity bond coverage for certain employees not being compatible with the amount of potential defalcation that might be committed.

DISCUSSION QUESTIONS AND PROBLEMS

5-15 Frequently, questions have been raised regarding the responsibility of the independent auditor for the discovery of fraud (including defalcations and other similar irregularities), and concerning the proper course of conduct of the independent auditor when his or her examination discloses specific circumstances that arouse suspicion about the existence of fraud.

Required

a. What are (1) the function and (2) the responsibilities of the independent auditor in the examination of financial state-

ments? Discuss fully, but in this part, do not include fraud in the discussion.

b. What are the responsibilities of the independent auditor for the detection of fraud and other irregularities? Discuss fully.

c. What is the independent auditor's proper course of conduct when his or her examination discloses specific circumstances that arouse his or her suspicion as to the existence of fraud and other irregularities?

(AICPA adapted)

- -

5-16 The classes of transactions and the titles of the journals used for Phillips Equipment Rental Co. Ltd. are shown in the following chart.

CLASSES OF TRANSACTIONS	TITLES OF JOURNALS
Purchase returns	Cash receipts register
Rental revenue	Cash disbursements journal
Charge-off of uncollectible accounts	Acquisitions journal
Acquisitions of goods and services (except payroll)	Revenue history
Collection of goods and services tax	Payroll journal
Adjusting entries (for payroll)	Adjustments history
Payroll service and payments	
Cash disbursements (except payroll)	
Cash receipts	

Required

a. Identify one financial statement balance that is likely to be affected by each of the nine classes of transactions.

b. For each class of transactions, identify the journal that is likely to be used to record the transactions.

c. Identify the transaction cycle that is likely to be affected by each of the nine classes of transactions.

d. Explain how total rental revenue, as cited on the financial statements of Phillips Equipment Rental Co. Ltd., is accumulated in journals and summarized on the financial statements. Assume there are several adjusting entries for rental revenue at the balance sheet date.

- -

5-17 It is well accepted that throughout the conduct of the ordinary audit, it is essential to obtain large amounts of information from management and to rely heavily on management's judgments. After all, the financial statements are management's representations, and the primary responsibility for their fair presentation rests with management, not the auditor. For example, it is extremely difficult, if not impossible, for the auditor to evaluate the obsolescence of inventory as well as management can in

a highly complex business. Similarly, the collectibility of accounts receivable and the continued usefulness of machinery and equipment are heavily dependent on management's willingness to provide truthful responses to questions.

Required

Reconcile the auditor's responsibility for discovering material misrepresentations by management with these comments.

- -

5-18 The following general ledger accounts are included in the trial balance for an audit client, Jones Wholesale Stationery Store.

Income tax expense	Allowance for doubtful accounts
Income tax payable	Inventory
Accounts receivable	Property tax expense
Advertising expense	Interest expense
Travel expense	Amortization expense—furniture and equipment
Bonds payable	Retained earnings
Common stock	Sales
Unexpired insurance	Salaries, office and general
Furniture and equipment	Telephone and fax expense
Cash	

Notes receivable trade	Bad debt expense
Purchases	Insurance expense
Sales salaries expense	Interest receivable
Accumulated amortization of furniture and equipment	Interest income
	Accrued sales salaries
Notes payable	Rent expense
Property tax payable	Prepaid interest expense

Required

a. Identify the accounts in the trial balance that are likely to be included in each transaction cycle. Some accounts will be included in more than one cycle. Use the format that follows.

Sales and collection
Acquisition and payment
Payroll and personnel
Inventory and warehousing
Capital acquisition and repayment

b. How would the general ledger accounts in the trial balance most likely differ if the company were a retail store rather than a wholesale company? How would they differ for a hospital or a government unit?

5-19 The following are specific balance-related audit objectives applied to the audit of accounts receivable (a through h) and management assertions (1 through 7). The list referred to in the specific balance-related audit objectives is the list of the accounts receivable from each customer at the balance sheet date.

Specific Balance-Related Audit Objective

a. There are no unrecorded receivables.
b. Receivables have not been sold or discounted.
c. Uncollectible accounts have been provided for.
d. Receivables that have become uncollectible have been written off.
e. All accounts on the list are expected to be collected within one year.
f. Any agreement or condition that restricts the nature of trade receivables is known and disclosed.

g. All accounts on the list arose from the normal course of business and are not due from related parties.
h. Sales cutoff at year end is proper.

Management Assertion

1. Existence
2. Occurrence
3. Completeness
4. Valuation
5. Measurement
6. Rights and obligations
7. Presentation and disclosure

Required

For each specific balance-related audit objective, identify the appropriate management assertion.

5-20 The following are specific transaction-related audit objectives applied to the audit of cash disbursements (a through f), management assertions (1 through 7), and general transaction-related audit objectives (8 through 13).

Specific Transaction-Related Audit Objective

a. Recorded cash disbursement transactions are for the amount of goods or services received and are correctly recorded.
b. Cash disbursement transactions are properly included in the accounts payable master file and are correctly summarized.
c. Recorded cash disbursements are for goods and services actually received.
d. Cash disbursement transactions are properly classified.
e. Existing cash disbursement transactions are recorded.
f. Cash disbursement transactions are recorded on the correct dates.

Management Assertion

1. Existence
2. Occurrence
3. Completeness
4. Valuation

5. Measurement
6. Rights and obligations
7. Presentation and disclosure

General Transaction-Related Audit Objective

8. Occurrence
9. Completeness
10. Accuracy
11. Classification
12. Timing
13. Posting and summarization

Required

a. Explain the differences among management assertions, general transaction-related audit objectives, and specific transaction-related audit objectives and their relationships to one another.
b. For each specific transaction-related audit objective, identify the appropriate management assertion.
c. For each specific transaction-related audit objective, identify the appropriate general transaction-related audit objective.

5-21 The following are two specific balance-related audit objectives in the audit of accounts payable. The list referred to in the objectives is the aged accounts payable trial balance produced using the supplier master file. The total of the list equals the accounts payable balance on the general ledger.

1. All accounts payable included on the list represent amounts due to valid vendors.

2. There are no unrecorded accounts payable.

Required

a. Explain the difference between these two specific balance-related audit objectives.
b. For the audit of accounts payable, which of these two specific balance-related audit objectives would usually be more important? Explain.

5-22 The following are nine general balance-related audit objectives for the audit of any balance sheet account (1 through 9) and eleven specific balance-related audit objectives for the audit of property, plant, and equipment (a through k).

General Balance-Related Audit Objective

1. Existence
2. Completeness
3. Valuation
4. Accuracy
5. Classification
6. Cutoff
7. Detail tie-in
8. Rights and obligations
9. Presentation and disclosure

Specific Balance-Related Audit Objective

a. There are no unrecorded capital assets in use.
b. The company has valid title to the assets owned.
c. Details of property, plant, and equipment agree with the general ledger.
d. Capital assets physically exist and are being used for the purpose intended.
e. Property, plant, and equipment are recorded at the correct amount.
f. The company has a contractual right for use of assets leased.
g. Liens or other encumbrances on property, plant, and equipment items are known and disclosed.
h. Cash disbursements and/or accrual cutoff for property, plant, and equipment items are proper.
i. Expense accounts do not contain amounts that should have been capitalized.
j. Amortization is determined in accordance with an acceptable method and is materially correct as computed.
k. Capital asset accounts have been properly adjusted for declines in historical cost.

Required

a. What are the purposes of the general balance-related audit objectives and the specific balance-related audit objectives? Explain the relationship between these two sets of objectives.
b. For each general balance-related objective, identify one or more specific balance-related audit objectives. No letter can be used for more than one general balance-related audit objective.

PROFESSIONAL JUDGMENT PROBLEM

5-23 PA has been the auditor for several years of Widget Limited, a widely owned public company that operates a wholesaling business. During the last few years, the company's net income has been declining steadily and its management has been criticized severely by some influential shareholders.

At the commencement of the current year's audit, PA was given draft financial statements that showed a large increase in net income over the previous year. Suspecting that income may have been overstated for the current year's audit, PA has determined that

- The company's method of operating and level of efficiency are unchanged.
- Sales volume was the same this year as for the past several years.
- Unit selling prices and purchasing costs have not changed.
- The company's nonwholesaling revenues have remained at the same low level.

Required

a. List the methods that could have been used by management to overstate net income for the year.
b. What would need to occur at the corporate governance level to enable management to misstate the financial statements?

(CICA adapted)

CASE

5-24 Leslie Donald is the audit manager responsible for the annual audit of ABC Electronics Ltd. (ABC), a Canadian public company involved in the manufacture and distribution of highly competitive electronic products. He has completed his review of the audit files and has discussed a number of issues with the audit senior. Since the partner in charge of the engagement has arranged to meet with the chairman of ABC's audit committee three days from now, Leslie has decided to write a memo to the partner to outline a number of matters that bother him. These concerns arise as a result of the following information that has come to his attention:

1. Based on results for the first three quarters of the year, ABC management estimated annual net income of $1,000,000. Primarily as a result of audit adjustments to provide for obsolete inventory, net income has been reduced to slightly more than $300,000.

2. The senior had written short audit notes throughout the files, including the following:

Testing of controls over disbursements showed that, out of a sample of 150 cheques tested, 24 cases of incomplete supporting documentation were discovered.

Twelve of the 24 exceptions found in our disbursement tests were payments totalling $50,000 to some freelance management consultants who traditionally have been paid without an invoice. These payments have been satisfactorily verified by telephone conversations. The other 12 cheques were issued to Sales Promotion Enterprises Ltd., and, although not supported by invoices, were approved by Bill Rogerson, the general manager. These cheques total $85,000 and all bear a second endorsement by I. B. Graten. They have been charged to account 809, Inventory on Consignment, and the inventory has been confirmed by Sales Promotion Enterprises Ltd. as being on hand at year end.

Our tests of sales invoices disclosed no errors or unusual conditions except that invoices to Global Galaxy Stores (Global) are priced at 5 percent over the approved price list. The invoicing clerk's explanation was that this policy was established verbally by Bill Rogerson, and Global was the only customer to which this price applied.

3. Leslie asked Bill Rogerson for an explanation for payments to Sales Promotion Enterprises Ltd. Bill claimed that he could not remember the transaction well but, in view of the immaterial amount involved and his approval for each payment, suggested that the payments were of no audit significance. Later, Leslie and Bill had lunch together, and Bill offered some additional information on a confidential basis. He said that Sales Promotion Enterprises Ltd. was owned by a buyer for one of ABC's largest customers, Global. The payments guaranteed orders from Global at prices favourable to ABC, and orders in the past year had exceeded $8,000,000. Bill explained that the arrangements were made by ABC's president and, for obvious reasons, were to be considered highly confidential. Bill claimed to have no knowledge of the management consultants.

Required

Assume the role of Leslie Donald, the audit manager, and prepare the memo to the audit partner. Identify potential problems. For each problem, indicate the parties affected by the problem, alternative methods of dealing with the problem, reporting responsibilities, and a recommended course of action.

(CICA adapted)

Rick Chulick, President and Chief Operating Officer

DEAR SHAREHOLDERS: **March 29, 2005**

We are proud to announce another year of noticeable improvement.

In last year's letter we stated, "We are committed to increasing the efficiency and effectiveness of operations through cost savings and productivity improvements. In addition, we intend to maintain and further develop our customer base through recently implemented post-sale service programs." The operating results in this report demonstrate that our objectives have been achieved, resulting in a net income increase of $740,000 from 2003 to 2004. This amounts to 15 cents per share, a 23.2% increase from last year. Our goal in the current year is to further improve the results of operations and create value for shareholders. In doing so, we will focus primarily on the following three strategic components of our business plan:

1. Post-sale service arrangements designed to further develop and maintain our customer base.

2. Aggressive advertising campaigns that allow us to penetrate markets dominated by national wholesale hardware store chains.

3. Implementation of new warehouse technology designed to increase productivity and reduce stocking and distribution costs.

We will report our progress throughout the year.

Christopher J. Kurran
Chief Executive Officer

Rick Chulick
President and Chief Operating Officer

2

HISTORY

Hillsburg Stores Ltd. began operations in 1980 in Halifax, Nova Scotia, as a retail hardware store chain. On September 25, 1986, Hillsburg merged with Handy Hardware and Lumber Company, which established the concept of selling high-quality hardware through wholesale distribution outlets in 1981, to form Handy-Hillsburg, Inc., a provincial corporation. On June 5, 1990, after spinning off all of its lumber-related assets to Handy Corporation, the company changed its name to Hillsburg Hardware, Ltd. On October 22, 1992, the company reincorporated as a federal company and changed its name to Hillsburg Hardware Limited (heareafter referred to as "the Company"), which trades on the TSX under the symbol "HLSB."

OVERVIEW

Hillsburg Hardware Limited is a wholesale distributor of hardware equipment to a variety of independent, high-quality hardware stores in the eastern part of Canada. The primary products are power and hand tools, landscaping equipment, electrical equipment, residential and commercial construction equipment, and a wide selection of paint products.

More than 90% of the Company's products are purchased from manufacturers and shipped either directly to customers or to the main warehouse in Halifax, Nova Scotia, where shipments are combined to minimize the costs of freight and handling.

Hardware retailers, now more than ever, find it advantageous to purchase from us rather than directly from manufacturers. We make it possible for smaller, independent retailers to purchase on an as-needed basis, rather than in bulk. Moreover, we offer our customers a range of high-quality products that cannot be found at most national chains.

We also offer far more post-sale services to customers than are offered by manufacturers and other national distributors. We simplify the purchasing process by assigning each customer a permanent salesperson. Each salesperson becomes involved in the sales process,

and also acts as a liaison between the customer and post-sale service areas. For example, when customers experience technical problems with recently purchased hardware, their salesperson has the responsibility to coordinate both exchanges and warranty repairs with the manufacturer. This process adds value for customers and makes post-sales service more efficient and less problematic. Low turnover and extensive training of our salespeople enhance this service.

To further encourage customer loyalty, each customer is given access to our internal database system—ONHAND (Online Niche-Hardware Availability Notification Database). The ONHAND system lets customers check the availability of hard-to-find products instantly over the Internet. Moreover, the system includes data such as expected restock dates for items that are currently sold out and expected availability dates for items that will soon be introduced to the market.

Because of the two aforementioned processes, we have managed to maintain a repeat-customer base. Nearly 75% of all first-time customers make at least one additional purchase within one year of their first purchase.

Recently, there have been major consolidations in the wholesale hardware industry. We believe this consolidation trend is advantageous to our operations as a distributor of hard-to-find, high-quality hardware equipment. The recent consolidation of Builder's Plus Hardware, Inc., one of the top ten largest national hardware store chains, is a case in point. One month after the consolidation, Builder's Plus decided not to carry high-end construction and landscaping equipment in order to focus on what it called the "typical hardware customer."

PRODUCTS

To more effectively manage inventory, we carefully monitor the composition of net sales by category of items sold. The following chart indicates the percentage of net sales by class of merchandise sold during the years 2004, 2003, and 2002:

BUSINESS

MARKETING PROGRAM

This year, the Company made a significant investment in a new advertising campaign. Various radio, newspaper, magazine, and television advertisements were purchased at the local and regional levels using the Company's new catchphrase, "Hardware for Hard Workers." The new jingle has been partially responsible for the fiscal 2004 increase in sales of 9%.

CUSTOMERS

The majority of our customers are located in Nova Scotia, Prince Edward Island, New Brunswick, and Newfoundland and Labrador. Our current customer base consists of more than 400 independently owned hardware stores. Approximately 25% of our customers make up more than 80% of total sales revenue. To promote long-standing relationships with customers, we offer an array of incentive and customer appreciation programs. Since these programs were implemented in 1997, customer satisfaction ratings have improved steadily in each subsequent year.

SUPPLIERS

We purchase hardware and other products from more than 300 manufacturers in Canada. No single vendor accounted for more than 5% of our purchases during fiscal 2004, but our 25 largest vendors accounted for nearly 35%. We currently have long-term supply agreements with two vendors: Mechanical Tools and Painter's Paradise. These agreements are in effect until the end of fiscal year 2005. The combined dollar amount of each contract is not expected to exceed 5% of total purchases for the year.

COMPETITORS

There are other regional wholesale hardware distributors that compete with the Company, but national wholesale hardware store chains dominate the industry. Most of our competitors are not only larger, but have greater financial resources than our company. Ten national chains exist in the geographic area in which Hillsburg Hardware Limited operates. Of the ten national chains, Hardware Bros., Tools & Paint, and Construction City account for a significant portion of the wholesale hardware market share and also carry the hard-to-find and high-quality items we provide. The success of our business depends on our ability to keep distribution costs to a minimum and our customers satisfied through superior customer service.

The chart that follows is a breakdown of market share in the wholesale hardware market by competitor category, including the 2% market share held by the Company. The chart illustrates that we have considerable opportunity for sales growth.

EMPLOYEES

Hillsburg Hardware currently employs 319 individuals. The majority of our employees are involved in day-to-day sales. Because of our marketing and customer relations strategy, we make significant investments in ongoing training and professional development activities. Each year employees are required to attend 75 hours of professional training. Each employee receives a performance evaluation at least four times per year, usually once each quarter. Our turnover is among the lowest in the industry because of our compensation, training, and evaluation programs. We regard our employees as our most valuable asset.

Hillsburg Hardware Limited
2%

Other Regional Wholesale Hardware Distrbutors
5%

Tools & Paint
17%

Construction City
15%

Hardware Bros.
22%

Other National Wholesale Hardware Store Chains
39%

4

BUSINESS

PROPERTIES

The Company owns and operates its main warehouse and an administrative office. The main warehouse and administrative office are in the same 475,000 square-foot building. We also rent a second warehouse for $312,000 annually. The building, located in Sydney, Nova Scotia, serves as an off-site storage facility.

LEGAL PROCEEDINGS

On September 3, 2003, a suit was filed in the Municipal Court in Yarmouth, Nova Scotia against the Company. The product liability suit, "*Don Richards* v. *Hillsburg Hardware Limited*" is related to injuries that resulted from an alleged defective design of a tractor manufactured by Silo-Tractor, a Canadian corporation. The suit is currently in pretrial proceedings. In the opinion of our legal counsel, the suit is without merit. We intend to vigorously defend our position.

The Company does not believe any other legal issues materially affect its finances.

EXECUTIVE OFFICERS

The following list provides names and present positions of the Company's officers:

NAME		POSITION
John P. Higgins		Chairman of the Board
Rick Chulick	54	President and Chief Operating Officer (a)
Christopher J. Kurran		Chief Executive Officer (b)
Avis A. Zomer		Chief Financial Officer
Brandon S. Mack		Vice-President, Sales and Marketing
Mary R. Moses		Vice-President, Merchandising
Vanessa M. Namie		Vice-President, Operations (c)
Joseph A. Akuroi		Vice-President, Quality Assurance (d)

(a) Mr. Chulick has been President and Chief Operating Officer of the Company since November 1993. Mr. Chulick was Chairman of the Board from 1996 to 1998.

(b) Mr. Kurran has been Chief Executive Officer of the Company since September 1999. Prior to his role as CEO, Mr. Kurran was employed from 1990 to 1998 by Trini Enterprises, an industrial distributor.

(c) Ms. Namie has been employed by the Company since its inception in 1992. She has held her current position since 1998 and served as an operations manager from 1992 to 1998.

(d) Mr. Akuroi was Chief Operating Officer and President of Hardware Bros., one of the ten largest wholesale hardware chains in the country, from 1996 to 2001.

5

BUSINESS

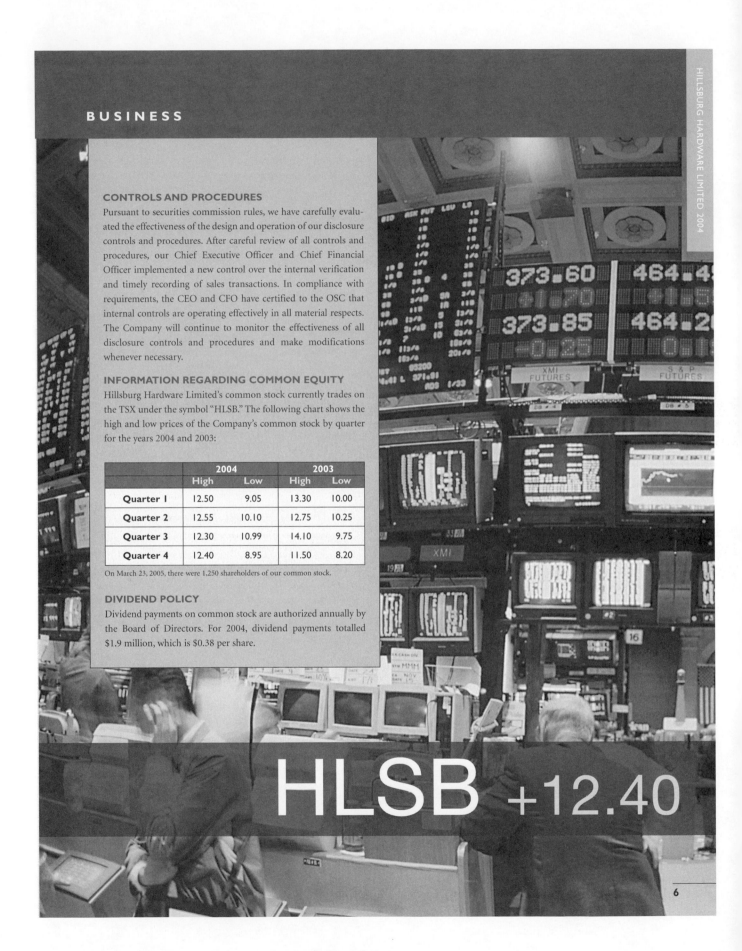

CONTROLS AND PROCEDURES

Pursuant to securities commission rules, we have carefully evaluated the effectiveness of the design and operation of our disclosure controls and procedures. After careful review of all controls and procedures, our Chief Executive Officer and Chief Financial Officer implemented a new control over the internal verification and timely recording of sales transactions. In compliance with requirements, the CEO and CFO have certified to the OSC that internal controls are operating effectively in all material respects. The Company will continue to monitor the effectiveness of all disclosure controls and procedures and make modifications whenever necessary.

INFORMATION REGARDING COMMON EQUITY

Hillsburg Hardware Limited's common stock currently trades on the TSX under the symbol "HLSB." The following chart shows the high and low prices of the Company's common stock by quarter for the years 2004 and 2003:

	2004		2003	
	High	Low	High	Low
Quarter 1	12.50	9.05	13.30	10.00
Quarter 2	12.55	10.10	12.75	10.25
Quarter 3	12.30	10.99	14.10	9.75
Quarter 4	12.40	8.95	11.50	8.20

On March 23, 2005, there were 1,250 shareholders of our common stock.

DIVIDEND POLICY

Dividend payments on common stock are authorized annually by the Board of Directors. For 2004, dividend payments totalled $1.9 million, which is $0.38 per share.

HLSB +12.40

To the Shareholders of Hillsburg Hardware Limited

We have audited the accompanying balance sheets of Hillsburg Hardware Limited as at December 31, 2004 and 2003, and the related statements of income, retained earnings, and cash flows for each of the years in the three-year period ended December 31, 2004. We have also audited the effectiveness of Hillsburg Hardware Limited's internal control over financial reporting as at December 31, 2004, in accordance with criteria established in *Internal Control—Integrated Framework*, as issued by the Committee of Sponsoring Organizations of the Treadway Commission (COSO), and management's assessment thereof included in the accompanying report, *Management's Report on Internal Control, 2005*. Hillsburg Hardware Limited's management is responsible for these financial statements, for maintaining effective internal control over financial reporting, and for its assessment of the effectiveness of internal control over financial reporting. Our responsibility is to express an opinion on these financial statements, an opinion on management's assessment, and an opinion on the effectiveness of the company's internal control over financial reporting based on our audits.

A company's internal control over financial reporting is a process designed to provide reasonable assurance regarding the reliability of financial reporting and the preparation of financial statements for external purposes in accordance with generally accepted accounting principles. A company's internal control over financial reporting includes those policies and procedures that (1) pertain to the maintenance of records that, in reasonable detail, accurately and fairly reflect the transactions and dispositions of the assets of the company; (2) provide reasonable assurance that transactions are recorded as necessary to permit preparation of financial statements in accordance with generally accepted accounting principles, and that receipts and expenditures of the company are being made only in accordance with authorizations of management and directors of the company; and (3) provide reasonable assurance regarding prevention or timely detection of unauthorized acquisition, use, or disposition of the company's assets that could have a material effect on the financial statements.

We conducted our audit of Hillsburg Hardware Limited's financial statements in accordance with Canadian generally accepted auditing standards. Those standards require that we plan and perform an audit to obtain reasonable assurance whether the financial statements are free of material misstatement. An audit of financial statements includes examining, on a test basis, evidence supporting the amounts and disclosures in the financial statements. A financial statement audit also includes assessing the accounting principles used and significant estimates made by management, and evaluating the overall financial statement presentation. We conducted our audit of the effectiveness of the Company's internal control over financial reporting, and management assessment thereof, in accordance with the standards established by the Canadian Institute of Chartered Accountants (CICA) for audits of internal control over financial reporting. Those standards require that we plan and perform our audit to obtain reasonable assurance about whether effective internal control over financial reporting was maintained in all material respects. Our audit of internal control over financial reporting included obtaining an understanding of internal control over financial reporting, testing, and evaluating the design and operating effectiveness of internal control over financial reporting, and performing such other procedures as we considered necessary in the circumstances. We believe that our audits provide a reasonable basis for our opinions.

In our opinion, the financial statements referred to above present fairly, in all material respects, the financial position of Hillsburg Hardware Limited as at December 31, 2004 and 2003, and the results of its operations and its cash flows for each of the years in the three-year period ended December 31, 2004 in accordance with Canadian generally accepted accounting principles. Also, in our opinion, management's assessment that Hillsburg Hardware Limited maintained effective internal control over financial reporting as at December 31, 2004, is fairly stated, in all material respects, in accordance with criteria established in *Internal Control—Integrated Framework* issued by the Committee of Sponsoring Organizations of the Treadway Commission (COSO). Furthermore, in our opinion, Hillsburg Hardware Limited maintained, in all material respects, effective internal control over financial reporting as at December 31, 2004, in accordance with criteria established in *Internal Control—Integrated Framework* issued by the Committee of Sponsoring Organizations of the Treadway Commission (COSO).

Because of its inherent limitations, internal control over financial reporting may not prevent or detect misstatements. Also, projections of any evaluation of effectiveness to future periods are subject to the risk that controls may become inadequate because of changes in conditions, or that the degree of compliance with the policies or procedures may deteriorate.

Berger, Kao, Kadous & Co., LLP

Berger, Kao, Kadous & Co., LLP
Halifax, Nova Scotia
March 21, 2005

7

FINANCIAL STATEMENTS

Management's Accountability

To Our Shareholders:

The management of Hillsburg Hardware Limited is responsible for the accompanying Financial Statements and all other information in the annual report. The financial statements have been prepared by management in accordance with Canadian generally accepted accounting principles, which recognize the necessity of relying on some best estimates and informed judgments. All financial information in the annual report is consistent with the Financial Statements.

To discharge its responsibilities for financial reporting and safeguarding of assets, management depends on the Company's systems of internal accounting control. These systems are designed to provide reasonable assurance that the financial records are reliable and form a proper basis for the timely and accurate preparation of financial statements. Management meets the objectives of internal accounting control on a cost-effective basis through the prudent selection and training of personnel, adoption and communication of appropriate policies, and employment of an internal audit program.

The Board of Directors oversees management's responsibilities for financial statements primarily through the activities of its Audit Committee, which is composed solely of Directors who are neither officers nor employees of the Company. This Committee meets with management and the Company's independent auditors, Berger, Kao, Kadous & Co., LLP, to review the financial statements and recommend approval by the Board of Directors. The Audit Committee is also responsible for making recommendations with respect to the appointment and remuneration of the Company's auditors. The Audit Committee also meets with the auditors, without the presence of management, to discuss the results of their audit, their opinion on internal accounting controls, and the quality of financial reporting.

The financial statements have been audited by Berger, Kao, Kadous & Co., LLP, whose appointment was ratified by shareholder vote at the annual shareholders' meeting.

John P. Higgins	Christopher J. Kurran	Avis A. Zomer
Chairman of the Board	Chief Executive Officer	Chief Financial Officer

8

HILLSBURG HARDWARE LIMITED
BALANCE SHEETS (in thousands)
December 31

ASSETS	2004	2003
Current assets		
Cash and cash equivalents	$ 828	$ 743
Trade receivables (net of allowances of $1,240 and $1,311)	18,957	16,210
Other receivables	945	915
Merchandise inventory	29,865	31,600
Prepaid expenses	432	427
Total current assets	51,027	49,895
Property and equipment		
Land	3,456	3,456
Buildings	32,500	32,000
Equipment, furniture, and fixtures	6,304	8,660
Less: accumulated amortization	(31,920)	(33,220)
Total property and equipment (net)	10,340	10,896
Total assets	$ 61,367	$ 60,791
LIABILITIES AND SHAREHOLDERS' EQUITY		
Current liabilities		
Trade accounts payable	$ 4,720	$ 4,432
Notes payable	4,180	4,589
Accrued payroll	1,350	715
Accrued payroll taxes	120	116
Accrued interest and dividends payable	2,050	1,975
Accrued income tax	796	523
Total current liabilities	13,216	12,350
Long-term notes payable	24,120	26,520
Deferred income taxes	738	722
Other long-term payables	830	770
Total liabilities	38,904	40,362
SHAREHOLDERS' EQUITY		
Common stock (5,000,000 shares issued)	8,500	8,500
Retained earnings	13,963	11,929
Total shareholders' equity	22,463	20,429
Total liabilities and shareholders' equity	$ 61,367	$ 60,791

See Notes to Financial Statements.

"We offer our customers a range of high-quality products that cannot be found at most national chains."

9

INCOME STATEMENT

HILLSBURG HARDWARE LIMITED
INCOME STATEMENT (in thousands)
Year Ended December 31

	2004	2003	2002
Net sales	$143,086	$131,226	$122,685
Cost of sales	103,241	94,876	88,724
Gross profit	39,845	36,350	33,961
Selling, general and administrative expenses	32,475	29,656	28,437
Operating income	7,370	6,694	5,524
Other income and expense			
Interest expense	2,409	2,035	2,173
Gain on sale of assets	(720)	—	—
Total other expense (income)	1,689	2,035	2,173
Earnings before income taxes	5,681	4,659	3,351
Provision for income taxes	1,747	1,465	1,072
Net income	$3,934	$3,194	$2,279
Earnings per share	$0.79	$0.64	$0.46

See Notes to Financial Statements.

STATEMENTS OF RETAINED EARNINGS

HILLSBURG HARDWARE LIMITED
STATEMENTS OF RETAINED EARNINGS (in thousands)

	Common Stock		Paid-in Capital	Retained Earnings	Total Shareholders' Equity
	Shares	Par value			
Balance as of December 31, 2001	5,000	$5,000	$3,500	$10,256	$18,756
Net income				2,279	2,279
Dividends paid				(1,900)	(1,900)
Balance as of December 31, 2002	5,000	5,000	3,500	10,635	19,135
Net income				3,194	3,194
Dividends paid				(1,900)	(1,900)
Balance as of December 31, 2003	5,000	5,000	3,500	11,929	20,129
Net income				3,934	3,934
Dividends paid				(1,900)	(1,900)
Balance as of December 31, 2004	5,000	$5,000	$3,500	$13,963	$22,463

See Notes to Financial Statements.

10

CASH FLOWS

HILLSBURG HARDWARE LIMITED STATEMENTS OF CASH FLOWS (in thousands) Year Ended December 31			
Operating activities	**2004**	**2003**	**2002**
Cash flows provided by (used in) operating activities:			
Net income	$ 3,934	$ 3,194	$ 2,279
Amortization	1,452	1,443	1,505
(Gain) loss on sale of assets	(720)	—	—
Deferred income taxes increase (decrease)	16	(8)	43
Changes in non-cash working capital:			
Trade and other receivables	(2,777)	(393)	(918)
Merchandise inventory	1,735	(295)	(430)
Prepaid expenses	(5)	(27)	(55)
Accounts payable	288	132	76
Accrued liabilities	714	77	142
Income taxes payable	273	23	13
Net cash provided by operating activities	4,910	4,146	2,655
Investing activities			
Capital expenditures	(10,500)	(1,800)	(2,292)
Sale of equipment	10,324	—	—
Net cash used in investing activities	(176)	(1,800)	(2,292)
Financing activities			
Dividend payment	(1,900)	(1,900)	(1,900)
Proceeds (repayments) from borrowings (net)	(2,749)	(423)	1,602
Net cash used in financing activities	(4,649)	(2,323)	(298)
Net increase in cash and cash equivalents	85	23	65
Cash and cash equivalents at beginning of year	743	720	655
Cash and cash equivalents at end of year	$ 828	$ 743	$ 720

See Notes to Financial Statements.

1. DESCRIPTION OF SIGNIFICANT ACCOUNTING POLICIES AND BUSINESS

We are a wholesale distributor of high-quality power tools, hand tools, electrical equipment, landscaping equipment, residential and commercial construction equipment, and paint products. The majority of our customers are smaller, independent hardware stores located in Nova Scotia, Prince Edward Island, New Brunswick, and Newfoundland and Labrador.

Allowance for Doubtful Accounts: Our allowance for doubtful accounts is maintained to account for expected credit losses. Estimates of bad debts are based on individual customer risks and historical collection trends. Allowances are evaluated and updated when conditions occur that give rise to collection issues.

Merchandise Inventory: Merchandise inventory is presented at the lower of average cost or market. To present accurately the estimated net realizable value of the accounts, we adjust inventory balances when current and expected future market conditions, as well as recent and historical turnover trends, indicate adjustments are necessary.

Property and Equipment: Land, buildings, computers and other equipment, and furniture and fixtures are stated at historical cost. Depreciation is calculated on a straight-line basis over estimated useful lives of the assets. Estimated useful lives are 20 to 35 years for buildings and 2 to 10 years for equipment and furniture and fixtures.

Revenue Recognition: Revenues are recognized when goods are shipped, title has passed, the sales price is fixed, and collectibility is reasonably assured. A sales returns and allowance account is maintained to reflect estimated future returns and allowances. Adjustments to the sales returns and allowance account are made in the same period as the related sales are recorded and are based on historical trends, as well as analyses of other relevant factors. Sales are recorded net of returns and allowances in the statements referred to in this report.

Income Taxes: The deferred income tax account includes temporary differences between financial accounting income and taxable income. The account consists largely of temporary differences related to (1) the valuation of inventory, (2) depreciation, and (3) other accruals.

2. OTHER RECEIVABLES

The other receivables balance consists largely of vendor allowances and vendor rebates. When vendor allowances and vendor rebates are recognized (all activities required by the supplier are completed, the amount is determinable, and collectibility is reasonably certain), they are recorded as reductions of costs of goods sold.

3. NOTES PAYABLE

Notes payable for the year ended December 31, 2004 consists of three notes payable to the bank. Each note carries a fixed interest rate of 8.5%. One note for $4,180,000 matures in June 2005 and the other two

mature on December 31, 2007. During 2004, there was an additional note outstanding in the amount of $4,400,000, which was paid off during October 2004.

4. COMMITMENTS

The Company is currently committed to an operating lease that expires in 2008. Rental payments for the remainder of the lease are set at $312,000 per annum.

5. SEGMENT REPORTING

The Company operates in one segment. The breakdown of revenues (in thousands) from different products is listed in the chart below:

SEGMENT REPORTING			
	2004	2003	2002
Power Tools	$ 31,479	$ 27,557	$ 26,991
Hand Tools	21,463	19,684	18,403
Landscaping Equipment	14,309	15,645	13,494
Electrical Goods	17,170	15,849	11,042
Residential Construction Equipment	21,463	18,372	15,949
Commercial Construction Equipment	11,447	10,498	9,815
Paint Products	25,755	23,621	26,991
	$143,086	**$131,226**	**$122,685**

6. EARNINGS PER SHARE

Earnings per share calculations for 2004, 2003, and 2002 were computed as follows:

Numerators
(net income in thousands): $3,934, $3,194, and $2,279

Denominators
(shares of common stock): 5,000,000
(unchanged for all years)

Diluted earnings per share was the same as basic earnings per share for all years.

**Management's Discussion and Analysis
of Financial Condition and Results of Operations**

The following discussion and analysis of the results of our operations and our financial condition are based on the financial statements and related notes included in this report. When preparing the financial statements, we are frequently required to use our best estimates and judgments. These estimates and judgments affect certain asset, liability, revenue, and expense account balances. Therefore, estimates are evaluated constantly based on our analyses of historical trends and our understanding of the general business environment in which we operate. There are times, however, when different circumstances and assumptions cause actual results to differ from those expected when judgments were originally made. The accounting policies referred to in Note 1 to the financial statements, in our opinion, influence the judgments and estimates we use to prepare our financial statements.

RESULTS OF OPERATIONS

For the year ended December 31, 2004, gross profit increased by 9.6% or $3,495,000 from 2003. This increase in gross profit more than offsets the increase in operating expenses from 2003 to 2004 of $2,819,000 or 9.5%. The increase in gross margin largely explains the operating income increase of $676,000.

For the year ended December 31, 2003, gross profit increased by $2,389,000 or 7% from 2002. Total operating expenses increased by $1,219,000 or approximately 4.3% from 2002. The increase in gross profit offset the total operating expense increase, and the net result was a $1,170,000 increase in operating income.

Net Sales: From 2003 to 2004 net sales increased by $11,860,000 or 9%. The increase in net sales can be explained largely by an aggressive advertising campaign that the Company organized during the second half of 2004. Net sales for 2003 increased by $8,541,000 or 7% from 2002, which is consistent with industry-wide average revenue growth of 7% from 2002 to 2003.

Gross Profit: Gross profit as a percentage of net sales stayed relatively stable at 27.68% and 27.70% in 2002 and 2003, respectively, but increased to 27.85% in 2004. The 2004 increase is mostly due to improved vendor incentive programs, our focus on cost containment, and increases in the resale values of certain commodities such as PVC piping material and certain types of metal wiring. While gross profit percentages in the industry have declined somewhat, our position as a niche provider in the overall hardware market allows us to charge premium prices without losing customers.

Selling, General and Administrative Expenses: Selling expenses increased by $1,911,000 or 14.8% from 2003 to 2004 and by $805,000 or 6.7% from 2002 to 2003. As a percentage of net sales, selling expenses increased by 0.52% since 2003 and decreased by 0.03% from 2002 to 2003. The increase in selling expenses as a percentage of net sales from 2003 to 2004 is due to our new advertising campaign and increased expenditures on sales meetings and training.

General and administrative expenses increased by $908,000 or 5.4% from 2003 to 2004 and by $414,000 or 2.5% from 2002 to 2003. As a percentage of net sales, general and administrative expenses decreased by 0.42% since 2003 and decreased by 0.55% from 2002 to 2003. The overall increase from 2003 to 2004 was caused mostly by unexpected repairs needed to reattach and replace damaged shelving units in our main warehouse building.

Interest Expense : In 2004, interest expense increased by $374,000, or approximately 18.4%, compared to 2003. The increase was due to an overall interest rate increase and the restructuring of debt covenants that are less restrictive but demand higher interest rates. In 2003 interest expense decreased by $138,000 or 6.4% compared to 2002. The 2003 decrease was mainly due to the Company's decision to decrease the level of long-term debt. The average interest rates on short- and long-term debt during 2004 were approximately 10.5% and 8.5% respectively.

LIQUIDITY

During 2004, our working capital requirements were primarily financed through our line of credit, under which we are permitted to borrow up to the lesser of $7,000,000 or 75% of accounts receivable outstanding less than 30 days. The average interest rate on these short-term borrowings in 2004 was approximately 10.5%.

Cash provided by operating activities for 2004 and 2003 was $4,910,000 and $4,146,000 respectively. The change from 2003 to 2004 is primarily due to the increase in net income. Increases in receivables were largely offset by decreases in inventories and increases in payables and other current liabilities. The increase in cash provided from operating activities of $1,491,000 from 2002 to 2003 is largely the result of the increase in net income and smaller increases in receivables and merchandise inventory in 2003 compared to 2002. We believe that cash flow from operations and the available short-term line of credit will continue to allow us to finance operations throughout the current year.

STATEMENT OF CONDITION

Merchandise inventory and trade accounts receivable together accounted for over 95% of current assets in both 2004 and 2003. Merchandise inventory turned over approximately 3.4 times in 2004 and 3.0 times in 2003. Average days to sell inventory were 108.6 and 120.9 in 2004 and 2003 respectively. Net trade receivables turned over approximately 7.6 times in 2004 and in 2003. Days to collect accounts receivable computations were 48.1 and 48.0 in 2004 and 2003 respectively. Both inventory and accounts receivable turnover are lower than industry averages. We plan for this difference to satisfy the market in which we operate. Our market consists of smaller, independent hardware stores that need more favourable receivable collection terms and immediate delivery of inventory. Because we hold large amounts of inventory, we are able to fill orders quicker than most of our competitors even during the busiest times of the year.

OUTLOOK

During 2004 we experienced another year of noticeable improvement. The Company's financial performance can largely be attributed to (1) a continued focus on cost containment, (2) productivity improvements, (3) aggressive advertising, and (4) the implementation of programs designed to enhance customer satisfaction.

During 2005, we will continue to apply the same strategic efforts that improved 2004 performance. We are also implementing a new warehouse information system designed to increase productivity and reduce stocking and distribution costs. Management believes that earnings growth will be primarily driven by (1) continued focus on

customer satisfaction, (2) penetration into markets currently dominated by national wholesale hardware store chains, and (3) the use of technology to attract additional customers and promote more efficient operations.

INFORMATION CONCERNING FORWARD-LOOKING STATEMENTS

This report contains certain forward-looking statements (referenced by such terms as "expects" or "believes") that are subject to the effects of various factors including (1) changes in wholesale hardware prices, (2) changes in the general business environment, (3) the intensity of the competitive arena, (4) new national wholesale hardware chain openings, and (5) certain other matters influencing the Company's ability to react to changing market conditions. Therefore, management wishes to make readers aware that the aforementioned factors could cause the actual results of our operations to differ considerably from those indicated by any forward-looking statements included in this report.

HILLSBURG HARDWARE LIMITED
FIVE-YEAR FINANCIAL SUMMARY (in thousands, except for per share amounts)

BALANCE SHEET DATA:	2004	2003	2002	2001	2000
Current assets	$ 51,027	$ 49,895	$ 49,157	$ 47,689	$ 46,504
Total assets	61,367	60,791	59,696	57,441	51,580
Current liabilities	13,216	12,350	12,173	12,166	9,628
Long-term notes payable	24,120	26,520	26,938	25,432	25,223
Total shareholders' equity	22,463	20,429	19,135	18,756	15,764
INCOME STATEMENT DATA:					
Net sales	$ 143,086	$ 131,226	$ 122,685	$ 120,221	$ 117,115
Cost of sales	103,241	94,876	88,724	88,112	85,663
Gross profit	39,845	36,350	33,961	32,109	31,452
Earnings before income taxes	5,681	4,659	3,351	3,124	1,450
Net income	3,934	3,194	2,279	2,142	994
Cash provided by operating activities	4,910	4,146	2,655	1,811	1,232
Per common share data:					
Net income	$ 0.79	$ 0.64	$ 0.46	$ 0.43	$ 0.22
Cash dividends per share	$ 0.38	$ 0.38	$ 0.38	$ —	$ —
Common shares outstanding	5,000	5,000	5,000	5,000	4,500
KEY OPERATING RESULTS AND FINANCIAL POSITION RATIOS:					
Gross profit (%)	27.85%	27.70%	27.68%	26.71%	26.86%
Return on assets (%)	9.30%	7.73%	5.72%	5.73%	2.86%
Return on common equity (%)	26.49%	23.55%	17.69%	18.10%	9.50%

14

AUDIT EVIDENCE

What does an auditor examine to provide assurance about the quality of the financial statements? When has enough information been collected? These are difficult questions and this chapter examines the nature of evidence that is collected. It is important to understand evidence before we go on to talk about the audit process in more detail in later chapters.

LEARNING OBJECTIVES

After reading this chapter, you should be able to answer the following questions:

1. What are the four evidence decisions that need to be made? What does the auditor mean by the phrase "sufficient appropriate audit evidence?"

2. List and explain the seven general methods of evidence collection.

3. How does the auditor choose which type of evidence to collect?

4. What are analytical procedures? What is their role in the evidence collection process? Describe five major types of analytical procedures.

THE ILLUSION OF EXISTENCE

His neighbours had not seen him for two years. Canada Post kept emptying the full mailbox and then stopped delivering his mail. Family knocked on the door to say hello, but he did not answer—they thought he just wasn't home.

The condominium corporation president assumed that everything was in order because his monthly fees were being paid. Jim Sulkers had died two years earlier, in November 2002, but his monthly disability pension continued to be deposited into his bank account. Then, electronic banking systems ensured that his bills were paid—utilities and condo fees, and possibly other expenses, were paid automatically. His death was discovered on August 25, 2004 when police climbed through his window and discovered a calendar turned to November 2002.

Is this the perfect neighbour and tenant—someone who pays his bills and is not seen or heard?

Sources: 1. Canadian Press, "Man lay dead in bed for two years," Toronto Star, August 27, 2004, www.thestar.com/ NASApp/cs/ContentSe . . . ol=968350116467, Accessed: March 4, 2005. 2. George, Lianne, "A High-Tech Ghost Story," Macleans, September 20, 2004, www.macleans.ca/shared/print.jsp?content=20040920_88654 88654, Accessed: March 4, 2005.

Think about Jim Sulker's disability company—why did they continue to pay his pension for two years? Why did Canada Post stop mail delivery without contacting a person? As an auditor, can you rely on the regular payment of bills to verify the existence of an entity? This story seems to indicate that regular payment does not necessarily mean that a person is alive. What alternative sources of evidence are required, in addition to electronic bill payments, to confirm the existence of a person or entity?

→6.1 AUDIT EVIDENCE AND ASSOCIATED DECISIONS

Nature of Evidence

Evidence was defined in Chapter 1 as *any information used by the auditor* to determine whether the information being audited is stated in accordance with the established criterion. The information varies widely in the extent to which it persuades the auditor whether financial statements are stated in accordance with generally accepted accounting principles. Evidence includes persuasive information, such as the auditor's count of marketable securities, and less persuasive information, such as responses to questions by the client's employees.

Audit Evidence Contrasted with Legal and Scientific Evidence The use of evidence is not unique to auditors. Evidence is also used extensively by scientists, lawyers, and historians.

Through television, most people are familiar with the use of evidence in legal cases dealing with the guilt or innocence of a party charged with a crime such as robbery. In legal cases, there are well-defined rules of evidence enforced by a judge for the protection of the innocent. It is common, for example, for legal evidence to be judged inadmissible on the grounds that it is irrelevant, prejudicial, or based on hearsay.

Similarly, in scientific experiments, the scientist obtains evidence to draw conclusions about a theory. Assume, for example, a medical scientist is evaluating a new medicine that may provide relief for asthma sufferers. The scientist will gather evidence from a large number of controlled experiments over an extended period of time to determine the effectiveness of the medicine.

The auditor also gathers evidence to draw conclusions. Different evidence is used by auditors than by scientists or lawyers, and it is used in different ways, but in all three cases, evidence is used to reach conclusions. Table 6-1 illustrates key characteristics of evidence from the perspective of a scientist doing an experiment, a legal case involving an accused thief, and an auditor of financial statements. There are six bases of comparison. Note the similarities and differences among the three professions.

Audit Evidence Decisions

A major decision facing every auditor is determining the appropriate types and *amount of evidence* to accumulate to be satisfied that the components of the client's financial statements and the overall statements are fairly stated. This judgment is important because of the prohibitive cost of examining and evaluating all available evidence. For example, in an audit of financial statements of most organizations, it is impossible for the public accountant to examine the contents of all computer files or available evidence such as cancelled cheques, vendors' invoices, customer orders, payroll time cards, and the many other types of documents and records.

The auditor's *decisions* on evidence accumulation can be broken into the following four subdecisions:

1.   Which audit procedures to use (their "nature," Section 5143.10)
2.   What sample size to select for a given procedure (the "extent" of a test, Section 5143.18)
3.   Which particular items to select from the population
4.   When to perform the procedures (the "timing," Section 5143.14).

Audit Procedures An **audit procedure** is the detailed instruction for the collection of a particular type of audit evidence that is to be obtained at some time during the audit. For example, evidence such as physical inventory counts, comparisons of cancelled cheques

AUDIT PROCEDURE—detailed instruction for the collection of a type of audit evidence

	Scientific Experiment Involving Testing a Medicine	Legal Case Involving an Accused Thief	Audit of Financial Statements
TABLE 6-1	**Characteristics of Evidence for a Scientific Experiment, a Legal Case, and an Audit of Financial Statements**		
Basis of Comparison			
Use of the evidence	Determine effects of using the medicine	Decide guilt or innocence of accused	Determine if statements are fairly presented
Nature of evidence	Results of repeated experiments	Direct evidence and testimony by witnesses and party involved	Various types of audit evidence generated by the auditor, third parties, and the client
Party or parties evaluating evidence	Scientist	Jury and judge	Auditor
Certainty of conclusions from evidence	Vary from uncertain to near certainty	Requires guilt beyond a reasonable doubt	High level of assurance
Nature of conclusions	Recommend or not recommend use of medicine	Innocence or guilt of party	Issue one of several alternative types of auditor's reports
Typical consequences of incorrect conclusions from evidence	Society uses ineffective or harmful medicine	Guilty party is not penalized or innocent party found guilty	Statement users make incorrect decisions and auditor may be sued

with cash disbursements, journal entries, and shipping document details is collected using audit procedures.

In designing audit procedures, it is common to spell them out in sufficiently specific terms to permit their use as instructions during the audit. For example, the following is an audit procedure for the verification of cash disbursements:

- Obtain the cash disbursements report and compare the payee name, amount, and date on the cancelled cheque with the cash disbursement report.

Several commonly used audit procedure terms are defined and illustrated with examples later in this chapter.

Sample Size Once an audit procedure is selected, it is possible to vary the sample size from one to all the items in the population being tested. In the audit procedure above, suppose there are 6,600 cheques recorded in the cash disbursements report. The auditor might select a sample size of 40 cheques for comparison with the cash disbursements report. The decision of how many items to test must be made by the auditor for each audit procedure. The sample size for any given procedure is likely to vary from audit to audit.

Items to Select After the sample size has been determined for a particular audit procedure, it is still necessary to decide the particular items to test. If the auditor decides, for example, to select 40 cancelled cheques from a population of 6,600 for comparison with the cash disbursements journal, several different methods can be used to select the specific cheques to be examined. The auditor could (1) select a week and examine the first 40 cheques, (2) select the 40 cheques with the largest amounts (also known as "key items"), (3) select the cheques randomly, or (4) select those cheques the auditor thinks are most likely to be in error. A combination of these methods could also be used.

Timing An audit of financial statements usually covers a period such as a year, and an audit is usually not completed until several weeks or months after the end of the period. The timing of audit procedures can therefore vary from early in the accounting period to long after it has ended. In the audit of financial statements, the client normally wants the audit completed one to three months after year end.

Audit procedures often incorporate sample size, items to select, and timing into the procedure. The following is a modification of the audit procedure previously used to include all four audit evidence decisions. (Italics identify the timing, items to select, and sample size decisions.)

- Obtain the *October* cash disbursements report and compare the payee name, amount, and date on the cancelled cheque with the cash disbursements report for a *randomly selected sample of 40* cheque numbers.

Audit Program The detailed instructions for the entire collection of evidence for an audit area is called an **audit program**. The audit program always includes a list of the audit procedures. It usually also includes the sample sizes, items to select, and the timing of the tests. Normally, there is an audit program for each component of the audit. Therefore, there will be an audit program for accounts receivable, for sales, and so on. An example of an audit program that includes audit procedures, sample size, items to select, and timing is given on page 327 in Table 11-4. The right side of the audit program also includes the audit objectives for each procedure, as studied in Chapter 5.

Most auditors use computers to facilitate the preparation of audit programs. The simplest application of computers involves typing the audit program in a word processor and saving it from one year to the next to facilitate changes and updating. A more sophisticated application involves the use of a specialized program designed to help the auditor think through the planning considerations of the audit and select appropriate procedures using audit program generator software or other audit planning database templates.

Persuasiveness of Evidence

The third examination standard requires the auditor to obtain *sufficient appropriate audit evidence to be able to draw reasonable conclusions on which to base the audit opinion*. Because of the nature of audit evidence and the cost considerations of doing an audit, it is unlikely that the auditor will be completely convinced that the opinion is correct. However, the auditor must be persuaded that his or her opinion is correct with a high level of assurance. By combining all evidence from the entire audit, the auditor is able to decide when he or she is sufficiently persuaded to issue an auditor's report.

The three determinants of the **persuasiveness of evidence** are *sufficiency*, *appropriateness*, and *timeliness*. Notice that the first two are taken directly from the third examination standard.

Sufficiency The *quantity* of evidence obtained determines its **sufficiency** (Section 5300.07). Quantity is measured primarily by the sample size the auditor selects. For a given audit procedure, the evidence obtained from a sample of 50 would ordinarily be more sufficient than from a sample of 25.

There are several factors that determine the appropriate sample size in audits. The two most important ones are the auditor's expectation of errors and the effectiveness of the client's internal controls. To illustrate, assume that during the audit of Lau Computer Parts Inc., the auditor concludes that there is a high likelihood of obsolete inventory due to the nature of the client's industry. The auditor would sample more inventory items for obsolescence in an audit such as this than in one where the likelihood of obsolescence was low. Similarly, if the auditor concludes that a client has effective rather than ineffective internal controls over recording capital assets, a smaller sample size in the audit of purchases of capital assets is warranted. Expectation of errors and internal controls and their effect on sample size are critical topics in this book and are studied in depth in subsequent chapters, starting with Chapter 8.

In addition to affecting sample size, the particular items tested affect the sufficiency of evidence. Samples containing population items with large dollar values, items with a high likelihood of error, and items that are representative of the population are usually considered sufficient. In contrast, most auditors would usually consider samples insufficient that contain only the largest dollar items from the population, unless these items make up a large portion of the total population.

APPROPRIATENESS OF
EVIDENCE—the degree to which
evidence can be considered relevant
and reliable

Appropriateness **Appropriateness** refers to the quality of evidence, to the degree to which the evidence can be considered believable or worthy of trust. If evidence is considered to be highly appropriate, it is a great help in persuading the auditor that the financial statements are fairly stated. For example, if an auditor counted inventory, that evidence would be more appropriate than if management gave the auditor its own figures. Generally, the more appropriate the evidence, the less evidence is needed. Evidence is appropriate when it is both relevant and reliable.

Appropriateness of evidence deals with the audit procedures selected. Appropriateness cannot be improved by selecting a larger sample size or different population items. It can only be improved by selecting audit procedures that contain a higher quality of one or more of the following six characteristics of appropriate evidence.

Relevance Evidence must *pertain to or be relevant to the objective* the auditor is testing before it can be persuasive. For example, assume the auditor is concerned that a client is failing to bill customers for shipments (completeness transaction-related audit objective). If the auditor selected a sample of duplicate sales invoices and traced each to related shipping documents, the evidence would *not be relevant* for the completeness objective. A relevant procedure would be to compare a sample of shipping documents with related duplicate sales invoices to determine if each shipping document had been billed. The reason the second audit procedure is relevant and the first is not is because the shipment of goods is the normal criteria used for determining whether a sale has occurred and should have been billed. By tracing from shipping documents to duplicate sales invoices, the auditor can determine if shipments have been billed to customers. When the auditor traces from duplicate sales invoices to shipping documents, it is impossible to find unbilled shipments.

RELEVANCE OF EVIDENCE—the
pertinence of the evidence to the
audit objective being tested

Relevance can only be considered in terms of specific audit objectives. Evidence may be relevant to one objective but not to a different one. In the previous example, when the auditor traced from the duplicate sales invoices to related shipping documents, the evidence was relevant to the existence transaction-related audit objective. Most evidence is relevant to more than one, but not all, objectives.

Reliability The following five issues affect **reliability of evidence**.

RELIABILITY OF EVIDENCE—evidence is reliable when it is obtained
from (1) the auditor's direct knowledge, (2) an independent provider,
(3) a client with effective internal
controls, (4) qualified providers
such as law firms and banks, or
(5) objective sources

Auditor's direct knowledge Evidence obtained directly by the auditor through physical examination, observation, reperformance, and inspection is more appropriate than information obtained indirectly. For example, if the auditor calculates the gross margin as a percentage of sales and compares it with previous periods using an audit software program, the evidence would be more reliable than if the auditor relied on the calculations of the controller.

Independence of provider Evidence obtained from a source outside the entity is more reliable than that obtained from within. For example, external evidence such as communications from banks, lawyers, or customers is generally regarded as more reliable than answers obtained from enquiries of the client. Similarly, documents that originate from outside the client's organization are considered more reliable than those that originate within the company and have never left the client's organization. An example of external evidence is an insurance policy, while a purchase requisition is internal evidence.

Effectiveness of client's internal controls When a client's internal controls are effective, evidence obtained therefrom is more reliable than when they are weak. For example, if internal controls over sales and billing are effective, the auditor can obtain more appropriate evidence from sales invoices and shipping documents than if the controls are inadequate.

Qualifications of individuals providing the information Although the source of information is independent, the evidence will not be reliable unless the individual providing it is qualified to do so. For this reason, communications from law firms and bank confirmations are typically more highly regarded than accounts receivable confirmations from persons not familiar with the business world. Also, evidence obtained directly by the auditor may not be reliable if he or she lacks the qualifications to evaluate the evidence. For example, examination of an inventory of diamonds by an auditor who is not trained to distinguish between diamonds and glass would not provide reliable evidence of the existence of diamonds.

Degree of objectivity Objective evidence is more reliable than evidence that requires considerable judgment to determine whether it is correct. Examples of objective evidence include confirmation of accounts receivable and bank balances, the physical count of securities and cash, and the adding (footing) of a list of accounts payable to determine if it is the same as the balance in the general ledger. Examples of subjective evidence include communication from a client's lawyers as to the likely outcome of outstanding lawsuits against the client, observation of obsolescence of inventory during physical examination, and enquiries of the credit manager about the collectibility of noncurrent accounts receivable. In evaluating the reliability of subjective evidence, the qualifications of the person providing the evidence is important.

Timeliness The **timeliness** of audit evidence can refer either to when it was accumulated or to the period covered by the audit. Evidence is usually more persuasive for balance sheet accounts when it is obtained as close to the balance sheet date as possible. For example, the auditor's count of marketable securities on the balance sheet date would be more persuasive than a count two months earlier. For income statement accounts, evidence is more persuasive if there is a sample from the entire period under audit rather than from only a part of the period. For example, a random sample of sales transactions for the entire year would be more persuasive than a sample from only the first six months.

TIMELINESS—the timing of audit evidence in relation to the period covered by the audit

Combined Effect The persuasiveness of evidence can be evaluated only after considering the combination of sufficiency, appropriateness, and timeliness. A large sample of evidence is not persuasive unless it is relevant to the audit objective being tested. A large sample of evidence that is neither appropriate nor timely is also not persuasive. Similarly, a small sample of only one or two pieces of appropriate and timely evidence also lacks persuasiveness. The auditor must evaluate the degree to which all three qualities have been met in deciding persuasiveness.

There are direct relationships among the four evidence decisions and the three qualities that determine the persuasiveness of evidence. Table 6-2 shows those relationships.

To illustrate the relationships shown in Table 6-2, assume an auditor is verifying inventory that is a major item in the financial statements. Generally accepted auditing standards require that the auditor be reasonably persuaded that inventory is not materially misstated. The auditor must therefore obtain a sufficient amount of appropriate and timely evidence about inventory. This means deciding which procedures to use for auditing inventory to satisfy the appropriateness requirement, as well as determining the proper sample size and items to select from the population to satisfy the sufficiency requirement. Finally, the auditor

TABLE 6-2	Relationships Among Evidence Decisions and Persuasiveness
Audit Evidence Decisions	**Qualities Affecting Persuasiveness of Evidence**

Audit procedures	Appropriateness
	   Relevance
	   Reliability
	      Auditor's direct knowledge
	      Independence of provider
	      Effectiveness of internal controls
	      Qualifications of provider
	      Objectivity of evidence

Sample size and items to select	Sufficiency
	   Adequate sample size
	   Selecting appropriate population items

Timing	Timeliness
	   When procedures are performed
	   Portion of period audited

must determine the timing of these procedures. The combination of these four evidence decisions must result in sufficiently persuasive evidence to satisfy the auditor that inventory is materially correct. The audit program for inventory will reflect these decisions. In practice, the auditor applies the four evidence decisions to specific audit objectives in deciding sufficient appropriate evidence.

Persuasiveness and Cost In making decisions about evidence for a given audit, both persuasiveness and cost must be considered. It is rare when only one type of evidence is available for verifying information. The persuasiveness and cost of all alternatives should be considered before selecting the best type or types. The auditor's goal is to obtain a sufficient amount of timely, reliable evidence that is relevant to the information being verified, and to do so at the lowest possible total cost. However, cost is never an adequate justification for omitting a necessary procedure.

Focus Box 6–1

CONTRADICTORY DATA AFFECTS OVER 3,000 TAXPAYERS

How would you feel if you received a tax assessment that was based on incorrect information? Now imagine you were required to pay additional taxes. CIBC's Amicus unit, administering 3,061 customers of President's Choice Financial, sent incorrect tax information to Canada Revenue Agency (CRA), while sending different (correct) information to the customers. The incorrect information sent to CRA stated that the customers had cashed in some of their 2003 RRSPs, resulting in tax reassessments.

How is it possible that computer systems could send different information to two different parties? The *Toronto Star* reported that the cause was the switch from a manual to a computer-based system. This would mean that there was either a large-scale programming error or data entry error. It was likely a human-caused error. What kinds of checks and balances should be in place? It would seem reasonable that a company compare paper-based information to electronic information before placing a new system into production.

Sources: 1. Laidlaw, Stuart, 2005, "Tax error blamed on systems update," *Toronto Star*, January 27, 2005, p. D3. 2. Olive, David, 2005. "CIBC is really, really sorry," *Toronto Star*, January 27, 2005, p. D3.

→6.2 METHODS OF EVIDENCE COLLECTION

Types of Audit Evidence

The *CICA Assurance Handbook*, in the third examination standard, specifies that audit evidence may be obtained through the methods of inspection, observation, enquiry, confirmation, recalculation or reperformance, and analytical procedures and then defines and explains the terms in Section 5300. We use the following categories of evidence gathering, as shown in the second column:

Evidence Methods in *CICA Assurance Handbook*	Seven Types of Evidence
• Inspection	• Physical examination
• Observation	• Confirmation
• Enquiry	• Documentation
• Confirmation	• Observation
• Recalculation	• Inquiries of the client
• Reperformance	• Reperformance
• Analytical review	• Analytical procedures

The seven broad categories are defined and discussed shortly. The order in which the categories are listed and discussed should not be interpreted as signifying the relative strengths of the types or categories of evidence. In other words, the fact that "physical examination" appears at the top of the list does not mean that any evidence belonging to that category is automatically stronger than evidence belonging to another category. The quality of each type of evidence, regardless of type, must be evaluated according to the criteria of its type.

Before beginning the study of types of evidence, it is useful to show the relationships among auditing standards, which were studied in Chapter 1, types of evidence, and the four evidence decisions discussed earlier in this chapter. These relationships are shown in Figure 6-1. Notice that the standards are general, whereas audit procedures are specific. Types of evidence are broader than procedures and narrower than the standards. Every audit procedure obtains one or more types of evidence.

Physical Examination **Physical examination** is the inspection or count by the auditor of a *tangible asset.* This type of evidence is most often associated with inventory and cash, but is also applicable to the verification of securities, notes receivable, and tangible capital assets. The distinction between the physical examination of assets, such as marketable securities and cash, and the examination of documents, such as cancelled cheques and sales documents, is important for auditing purposes. If the object being examined, such as a sales invoice, has no inherent value, the evidence is called *documentation.* For example, before a cheque is signed, it is a document; after it is signed, it becomes an asset; and when it is cancelled, it becomes a document again. Technically, physical examination of the cheque can only occur while the cheque is an asset.

Physical examination, which is a direct means of verifying that an asset actually exists (existence objective), is regarded as one of the most reliable and useful types of audit evidence. Generally, physical examination is an objective means of ascertaining both the quantity and the description of the asset. In some cases, it is also a useful method for evaluating an asset's condition or quality. However, physical examination is not sufficient evidence to verify that existing assets are owned by the client (rights and obligations objective), and in many cases the auditor is not qualified to judge such qualitative factors as obsolescence or authenticity (net realizable value for the valuation objective). Proper valuation for financial statement purposes usually cannot be determined by physical examination.

PHYSICAL EXAMINATION—the auditor's inspection or count of a tangible asset

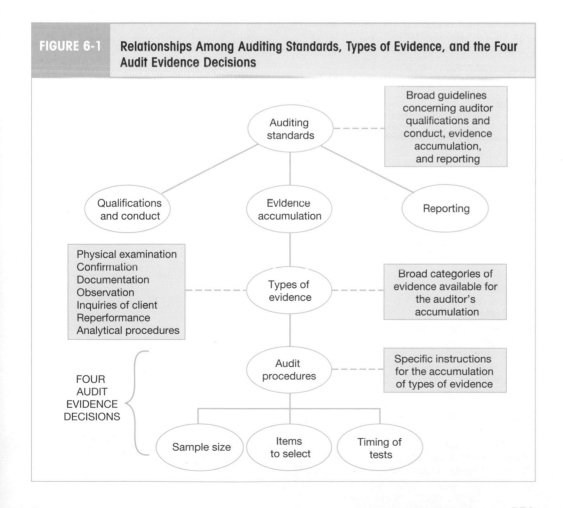

FIGURE 6-1   **Relationships Among Auditing Standards, Types of Evidence, and the Four Audit Evidence Decisions**

Confirmation **Confirmation** describes the *receipt* of a *written or oral response* from an *independent third party* verifying the accuracy of information that was *requested by the auditor.* The request is made to the client, and the client asks the independent third party to respond directly to the auditor. Since confirmations come from sources that are independent of the client, they are a highly regarded and often-used type of evidence. However, confirmations are relatively costly to obtain and may cause some inconvenience to those asked to supply them. Therefore, they are not used in every instance in which they are applicable. Because of the high reliability of confirmations, auditors typically obtain written responses rather than oral ones whenever it is practical. Written confirmations are easier for supervisors to review and provide more support if it is necessary to demonstrate that a confirmation was received.

Whether or not confirmations should be used depends on the reliability needs of the situation as well as the alternative evidence available. Traditionally, confirmations are not used to verify individual transactions between organizations, such as sales transactions, because the auditor can use documents for that purpose. Similarly, confirmations are seldom used in the audit of capital-asset additions because these can be verified adequately by documentation and physical examination. While confirmations are generally a very reliable form of evidence, the auditor must be aware that the third party providing the confirmation may be careless or may not have the correct information; the auditor should not automatically assume the confirmation is correct, especially if the response is unexpected or contradicts other evidence. In addition, the third party may not be independent of the client.

The *CICA Assurance Handbook* requires confirmation of accounts receivable except: when combined inherent risk and control risk (defined on page 219) and other substantive procedures would provide sufficient appropriate evidence; or when confirmation would be ineffective in providing reliable audit evidence. This requirement exists because accounts receivable usually represent a significant balance on the financial statements, and confirmations are a highly reliable type of evidence about them.

Although confirmation is not required for any account other than accounts receivable, this type of evidence is useful in verifying many types of information as explained in

TABLE 6-3	Information Frequently Confirmed
Information	**Source**
Assets	
Cash in bank	Bank
Accounts receivable	Customer
Notes receivable	Maker
Owned inventory out on consignment	Consignee
Inventory held in public warehouses	Public warehouse
Cash surrender value of life insurance	Insurance company
Liabilities	
Accounts payable	Creditor
Notes payable	Lender
Advances from customers	Customer
Mortgages payable	Mortgagor
Bonds payable	Bondholder
Owners' Equity	
Shares outstanding	Registrar and transfer agent
Other Information	
Insurance coverage	Insurance company
Contingent liabilities	Company law firm(s), bank, and others
Bond indenture agreements	Bondholder
Collateral held by creditors	Creditor

Section 5303, "Confirmation." The major types of information that are frequently confirmed, along with the source of the confirmation, are indicated in Table 6-3.

To be considered reliable evidence, confirmations must be controlled by the auditor from the time they are prepared until they are returned. If the client controls the preparation of the confirmation, performs the mailing, or receives the responses, the auditor has lost control and with it independence; thus the reliability of the evidence is reduced.

Documentation **Documentation** is the auditor's examination of the *client's documents and records* to substantiate the information that is or should be included in the financial statements. The documents examined by the auditor are the records used by the client to provide information for conducting its business in an organized manner. Since each transaction in the client's organization is normally supported by at least one document, there is a large volume of this type of evidence available. For example, the client often retains a customer order, a shipping document, and a duplicate sales invoice for each sales transaction. These same documents, whether in paper or electronic form, are useful evidence for verification by the auditor of the accuracy of the client's records for sales transactions. Documentation is a form of evidence widely used in every audit because it is usually readily available to the auditor at a relatively low cost. Sometimes it is the only reasonable type of evidence available.

DOCUMENTATION—the auditor's examination of the client's documents and records to substantiate the information that is or should be included in the financial statements

Documents can be conveniently classified as internal or external. An **internal document** is one that has been prepared and used within the client's organization and is retained without ever going to an outside party such as a customer or a vendor. Examples of internal documents include duplicate sales invoices, employees' time reports, exception reports, and inventory receiving reports. An **external document** is one that has been in the hands of someone outside the client's organization who is a party to the transaction being documented, but that is either currently in the hands of the client or readily accessible. In some cases, external documents originate outside the client's organization and end up in the hands of the client. Examples of this type of external document are vendors' invoices, cancelled notes payable, and insurance policies. Other documents, such as cancelled cheques, originate with the client, go to an outsider, and are finally returned to the client.

INTERNAL DOCUMENT—a document, such as an employee time report, that is prepared and used within the client's organization

EXTERNAL DOCUMENT—a document, such as a vendor's invoice, that has been used by an outside party to the transaction being documented, and that the client now has or can easily obtain

The primary determinant of the auditor's willingness to accept a document as reliable evidence is whether it is internal or external, and when internal, whether it was created and processed under conditions of good internal control. Internal documents created and processed under conditions of weak internal control may not constitute reliable evidence.

Since external documents have been in the hands of both the client and another party to the transaction, there is some indication that both members are in agreement about the information and the conditions stated on the document. Therefore, external documents are regarded as more reliable evidence than internal ones. Some external documents have exceptional reliability because they are prepared with considerable care and, frequently, have been reviewed by lawyers or other qualified experts. Examples include title papers to property such as land, insurance policies, indenture agreements, and contracts.

When auditors use documentation to support recorded transactions or amounts, it is often referred to as **vouching**. To vouch recorded acquisition transactions, the auditor might, for example, trace from the acquisitions report to supporting vendors' invoices and receiving reports and thereby satisfy the existence objective. If the auditor traces from receiving reports to the acquisitions report to satisfy the completeness objective, it would not be appropriate to call it vouching.

VOUCHING—the use of documentation to support recorded transactions or amounts

It is common, in many companies, for a portion of clients' documentation to be available only in electronic form. For example, many companies use EDI (Electronic Data Interchange—the electronic exchange of standardized business transactions). This change in business practices increases the dependence of organizations on computer-based information systems. Purchase, shipping, billing, cash receipt, and cash disbursement transactions may be available only in electronic form. Financial statement assertions most affected by EDI are completeness, accuracy, and authorization of transactions, resulting in a need for new audit techniques.

Other forms of automation, such as image processing systems, where documents are scanned and converted into electronic images rather than being stored in paper format, also require changes in audit techniques. Auditors need to assess the strength of such electronic evidence based upon controls in place over changes to such documents, just as they would assess the strength of internal paper documentation.

OBSERVATION—the use of the senses to assess certain activities

Observation Observation is the use of the senses to assess certain activities. Throughout the audit, there are many opportunities to exercise sight, hearing, touch, and smell to evaluate a wide range of things. For example, the auditor may tour a plant to obtain a general impression of a client's facilities, observe whether equipment is rusty to evaluate whether it is obsolete, and watch individuals perform accounting tasks to determine whether the person assigned a responsibility is performing it. Observation is rarely sufficient by itself because there is the risk that the client's personnel involved in accounting activities are aware of the auditor's presence. They may, therefore, perform their responsibilities in accordance with company policy but resume other activities once the auditor is out of sight. It is necessary to follow up initial impressions with other kinds of corroborative evidence. Nevertheless, observation is useful in most parts of the audit.

ENQUIRY OF THE CLIENT—the obtaining of written or oral information from the client in response to questions during the audit

Enquiries of the Client **Enquiry of the client** is the obtaining of *written* or *oral information* from the client in response to questions from the auditor. Although considerable evidence is obtained from the client through enquiry, it usually cannot be regarded as conclusive because it is not from an independent source and may be biased in the client's favour. Therefore, when the auditor obtains evidence through enquiry, it is normally necessary to obtain further corroborating evidence through other procedures. As an illustration, when the auditor wants to obtain information about the client's method of recording and controlling accounting transactions, he or she usually begins by asking the client how internal controls operate. Later, the auditor performs tests of controls to determine if the transactions are recorded (completeness objective) and authorized in the manner stated.

REPERFORMANCE—the rechecking of the computations and transfers of information made by the client during the period under audit

Reperformance As the word implies, **reperformance** involves rechecking the computations and transfers of information made by the client during the period under audit. Rechecking of computations consists of testing the client's arithmetical accuracy. It includes such procedures as extending sales invoices and inventory, adding reports and subsidiary ledgers, and checking the calculation of amortization expense and prepaid expenses. Rechecking of transfers of information consists of tracing amounts to be confident that when the same information is included in more than one place, it is recorded at the same amount each time. For example, the auditor normally makes limited tests to ascertain that the information in the sales history report has been included for the proper customer and at the correct amount in the subsidiary accounts receivable files and is accurately summarized in the general ledger.

When done manually, reperformance involves selecting a sample of transactions. However, many auditors use computer-assisted audit techniques so that reperformance can occur for a whole class of transactions. For example, in the inventory file, quantity on hand times unit price can be extended, added, and agreed to the general ledger control total.

ANALYTICAL PROCEDURES—use of comparisons and relationships to determine whether account balances or other data appear reasonable

Analytical Procedures Analysis is used to identify the components of a financial statement item so that its characteristics can be considered during planning. **Analytical procedures** use comparisons and relationships between financial and nonfinancial information to determine whether account balances appear reasonable. An example is comparing the gross margin percent in the current year with the preceding year's. For certain audit objectives or small account balances, analytical procedures may be the only evidence needed. For other accounts, other types of evidence may be reduced when analytical procedures indicate that an account balance appears reasonable. In some cases, analytical procedures are also used to isolate accounts or transactions that should be investigated more extensively to help in deciding whether additional verification is needed. An example is comparison of the current period's total repair expense with previous years' and investigation of the difference, if it is significant, to determine the cause of the increase or decrease.

Section 5301 of the *CICA Assurance Handbook* states that analytical procedures should be used *on all audits to conduct risk assessments and at or near the end of the audit when assessing the financial statements as a whole.* For certain audit objectives or small account balances, analytical procedures alone may be sufficient evidence. In most cases, however, additional evidence beyond analytical procedures is also necessary to satisfy the requirement for sufficient competent evidence.

Because analytical procedures are an important part of planning audits, performing tests of each cycle, and completing audits, their use is studied more extensively at the end of this chapter, and in most remaining chapters of this book. Normally, specialized software or spreadsheet templates are used to perform analytical procedures.

→ 6.3 CHOOSING THE RIGHT TYPE OF EVIDENCE

Reliability of Types of Evidence

The criteria discussed earlier in the chapter for determining the reliability of evidence are related to the seven types of evidence in Table 6-4. Several observations are apparent from a study of Table 6-4.

First, the effectiveness of the client's internal controls has a significant effect on the reliability of most types of evidence. For example, internal documentation from a company with effective internal controls is more reliable because the documents or electronic data are more likely to be accurate. Similarly, analytical procedures will not be appropriate evidence if the internal controls that produced the data provide information of questionable accuracy.

Second, both physical examination and reperformance are likely to be highly reliable if internal controls are effective, but their use differs considerably. These two types of evidence effectively illustrate that equally reliable evidence may be completely different.

Third, a specific type of evidence is rarely sufficient by itself to provide competent evidence to satisfy any objective. It is apparent from examining Table 6-4 that observation, enquiries of the client, and analytical procedures are examples of this.

Cost of Types of Evidence

The two most expensive types of evidence are physical examination and confirmation. Physical examination is costly because it normally requires the auditor's presence when the client is counting the asset, often on the balance sheet date. For example, physical examination of inventory can result in several auditors travelling to widely separated geographical

TABLE 6-4	Reliability of Types of Evidence				
	Criteria to Determine Reliability				
Type of Evidence	Independence of Provider	Effectiveness of Client's Internal Control	Auditor's Direct Knowledge	Qualifications of Provider	Objectivity of Evidence
Physical examination	High (auditor does)	Varies	High	Normally high (auditor does)	High
Confirmation	High	Not applicable	Low	Varies—usually high	High
Documentation	Varies—external more independent than internal	Varies	Low	Varies	High
Observation	High (auditor does)	Varies	High	Normally high (auditor does)	Medium
Enquiries of the client	Low (client provides)	Not applicable	Low	Varies	Varies—low to high
Reperformance	High (auditor does)	Varies	High	High (auditor does)	High
Analytical procedures	High/low (auditor does/client responds)	Varies	High	Not applicable	Low

locations. Confirmation is costly because the auditor must follow careful procedures in the confirmation preparation, mailing, and receipt, and in the follow-up of nonresponses and exceptions.

Documentation and analytical procedures are moderately costly. If client personnel locate documents for the auditor and organize them for convenient use, documentation usually has a fairly low cost. When auditors must find those documents themselves, documentation can be extremely costly. Even under ideal circumstances, information and data on documents are sometimes complex and require interpretation and analysis. For example, it is usually time-consuming to read and evaluate a client's contracts, lease agreements, and minutes of the board of directors' meetings. Analytical procedures require the auditor to decide which analytical procedures to use, enter, or transfer data to make the calculations, and evaluate the results. Doing so may take considerable time.

The three least expensive types of evidence are observation, enquiries of the client, and reperformance. Observation is normally done concurrently with other audit procedures. An auditor can easily observe whether client personnel are following appropriate inventory counting procedures at the same time he or she counts a sample of inventory (physical examination). Enquiries of clients are done extensively on every audit and normally have a low cost. Certain enquiries may be costly, such as obtaining written statements from the client documenting discussions throughout the audit.

Reperformance can vary in cost. It can be low when it involves simple calculations and tracing that can be done at the auditor's convenience. Costs per transaction are reduced when the auditor's computer software is used to perform these tests after obtaining a copy of the client data files.

Application of Types of Evidence to Evidence Decisions

An application of three types of evidence to the four evidence decisions for one audit objective is shown in Table 6-5. First, examine column 5 in Table 5-2 on page 125. These are the specific objectives of the audit of inventory for Hillsburg Hardware Limited. The overall objective is to obtain persuasive evidence (sufficient, appropriate, and timely), at reasonable cost, that inventory is materially correct. The auditor must therefore decide which audit procedures to use to satisfy each objective, what the sample size should be for each procedure, which items from the population to include in the sample, and when to perform each procedure.

TABLE 6-5	Types of Evidence and Decisions for a Specific Audit Objective*			
		Evidence Decisions		
Type of Evidence	Audit Procedure	Sample Size	Items to Select	Timing
Observation	Observe client's personnel counting inventory to determine whether they are properly following instructions	All count teams	Not applicable	Balance sheet date
Physical examination	Count a sample of inventory and compare quantity and description to client's counts	120 items	40 items with large dollar value, plus 80 randomly selected	Balance sheet date
Documentation	Compare quantity on client's perpetual records to quantity on client's counts	70 items	30 items with large dollar value, plus 40 randomly selected	Balance sheet date

*Balance-related audit objective: Inventory quantities agree with items physically on hand.

One objective from Table 5-2 is selected for further study: inventory quantities agree with items physically on hand. Several types of evidence are available to satisfy this objective. Table 6-5 lists three types of evidence and gives examples of the four evidence decisions for each type.

Special Terms

Audit procedures are the detailed steps, usually written in the form of instructions, for the accumulation of the seven types of audit evidence. They should be sufficiently clear to enable members of the audit team to understand what is to be done.

Several different terms are commonly used to describe audit procedures. These are presented and defined in Table 6-6. To help you understand the terms, an illustrative audit procedure and the type of evidence with which it is associated are shown.

TABLE 6-6	Terms, Audit Procedures, and Types of Evidence	
Term and Definition	**Illustrative Audit Procedure**	**Type of Evidence**
Examine—A reasonably detailed study of a document or record to determine specific facts about it.	*Examine* a sample of vendors' invoices or data to determine whether the goods or services received are reasonable and of the type normally used by the client's business.	Documentation
Scan—A less detailed examination of a document or record to determine if there is something unusual warranting further investigation.	*Scan* the sales report, looking for large and unusual transactions. For large sales history files, run an exception report using audit software of large amounts.	Analytical procedures
Read—An examination of written information to determine facts pertinent to the audit and the recording of those facts in a working paper.	*Read* the minutes of a board of directors' meeting and summarize all information that is pertinent to the financial statements in a working paper.	Documentation
Compute—A calculation done by the auditor independent of the client.	*Compute* the inventory turnover ratios and compare to previous years as a test of inventory.	Analytical procedures
Recompute—A calculation done to determine whether a client's calculation is correct.	*Recompute* the unit sales price times the number of units for a sample of duplicate sales invoices and compare the totals to the client's calculations.	Reperformance
Foot—Addition of a column of numbers to determine if the total is the same as the client's.	*Foot* the sales history files using audit software and compare all totals to the general ledger.	Reperformance
Trace—An instruction normally associated with documentation or reperformance. The instruction should state what the auditor is tracing and where it is being traced from and to. Frequently, an audit procedure that includes the term *trace* will also include a second instruction, such as *compare* or *recompute*.	*Trace* a sample of sales transactions from the sales reports to sales invoices and *compare* customer name, date, and the total dollar value of the sale.	Documentation
	Trace postings from the sales reports to the general ledger accounts.	Reperformance
Compare—A comparison of information in two different locations. The instruction should state which information is being compared in as much detail as practical.	Select a sample of sales invoices and *compare* the unit selling price as stated on the invoice to the master files of unit selling prices authorized by management.	Documentation
Count—A determination of assets on hand at a given time. This term should only be associated with the type of evidence defined as physical examination.	*Count* petty cash on hand at the balance sheet date.	Physical examination
Observe—The act of observation should be associated with the type of evidence defined as observation.	*Observe* whether the two inventory count teams independently count and record inventory quantities.	Observation
Enquire—The act of enquiry should be associated with the type of evidence defined as enquiry.	*Enquire* of management whether there is any obsolete inventory on hand at the balance sheet date.	Enquiries of client

→ 6.4 ANALYTICAL PROCEDURES AND THEIR ROLE

Analytical Procedures

ANALYSIS—identification of components of financial statements and analytical procedures

The Auditing and Assurance Standards Board (AASB) defines **analysis** (Section 5301.02) as including (1) the process of identifying elements or components of financial statement items so that their characteristics can be considered during the design of audit procedures, and (2) the process of performing analytical procedures. Auditors utilize *analytical procedures*, which use financial and nonfinancial data in meaningful comparisons and relationships to determine whether account balances or other data appear reasonable. The results of the analytical procedures can be used to help in designing the nature, timing, and extent of other audit procedures so that sufficient appropriate audit evidence may be obtained and the appropriate opinion given in the auditor's report.

For example, the auditor might compare current year recorded commissions expense to total recorded sales multiplied by the average commission rate as a test of the overall reasonableness of recorded commissions. For this analytical procedure to be relevant, the auditor has likely concluded that recorded sales are correctly stated, all sales earn a commission, and there is an average actual commission rate that is readily determined.

As will be discussed below, the AASB, in Section 5301, recommends that the auditor use analysis in planning the audit and may use analysis as a substantive procedure. The section concludes by recommending that the auditor use analytical procedures in his or her overall evaluation of the financial statements.

Purposes and Timing of Analytical Procedures

The most important reasons for utilizing analytical procedures are discussed in this section. As a part of that discussion, the appropriate timing is also examined.

Understanding the Client's Business In the next chapter, there is a discussion of the need to obtain knowledge about the client's industry and business. Analytical procedures are one of the techniques commonly used in obtaining that knowledge.

Generally, an auditor considers knowledge and experience about a client company obtained in prior years as a starting point for planning the examination for the current year. By conducting analytical procedures where the current year's unaudited information is compared to prior years' audited information, changes are highlighted. These changes can represent important trends or specific events, all of which will influence audit planning. For example, a decline in gross margin percentages over time may indicate increasing competition in the company's market area and the need to consider inventory pricing more carefully during the audit. Similarly, an increase in the balance in capital assets may indicate a significant acquisition that must be reviewed.

Assessment of the Entity's Ability to Continue as a Going Concern Analytical procedures are often useful as an indication that the client company is encountering severe financial difficulty. The likelihood of financial failure must be considered by the auditor in the assessment of audit-related risks (discussed further in Chapter 8) as well as in connection with management's use of the going concern assumption in preparing the financial statements. Certain analytical procedures can be helpful in that regard. For example, if a higher than normal ratio of long-term debt to net worth is combined with a lower than average ratio of profits to total assets, a relatively high risk of financial failure may be indicated. Not only would such conditions affect the audit plan, they may indicate that substantial doubt exists about the entity's ability to continue as a going concern, which would require disclosure in the notes to the financial statements.

UNUSUAL FLUCTUATIONS—significant unexpected differences indicated by analytical procedures between the current year's unaudited financial data and other data used in comparisons

Indication of the Presence of Possible Misstatements in the Financial Statements Significant unexpected differences between the current year's unaudited financial data and other data used in comparisons are commonly referred to as **unusual fluctuations**. Unusual fluctuations occur when significant differences are not expected but do exist, or when significant differences are expected but do not exist. In either case, one of the possible reasons for an unusual fluctuation is the presence of an accounting error or fraud and other irregularities. If the unusual fluctuation is large, the auditor must determine the reason for it and satisfy himself or herself that the cause is a valid economic event and not an error or fraud. For example, in comparing the ratio of the allowance for uncollectible accounts receivable to gross accounts receivable with that of the previous year, suppose the ratio had decreased while, at the same time, accounts receivable turnover also decreased. The combination of these two pieces of information would indicate a possible understatement of the allowance. This aspect of analytical procedures is often referred to as *attention directing* because it results in the performance of more detailed procedures by the auditor in the specific audit areas where errors or fraud and other irregularities might be found.

Reduction of Detailed Audit Tests When an analytical procedure reveals no unusual fluctuations, the implication is that the possibility of a material misstatement is minimized. In that case, the analytical procedure constitutes substantive evidence in support of the fair statement of the related account balances, and it is possible to perform fewer detailed tests in connection with those accounts. For example, if analytical procedure results of a small account balance such as prepaid insurance are favourable, no detailed tests may be necessary. In other cases, certain audit procedures can be eliminated, sample sizes can be reduced, or the timing of the procedures can be moved farther away from the balance sheet date.

Analytical procedures are usually inexpensive compared with tests of details since, in many cases, they can be automated. Most auditors therefore prefer to reduce tests of details with analytical procedures whenever possible. To illustrate, it may be far less expensive to calculate and review sales and accounts receivable ratios than to confirm accounts receivable. If it is possible to reduce confirmations by doing analytical procedures, considerable cost savings can occur.

The extent to which analytical procedures provide useful substantive evidence depends on their reliability in the circumstances. For some audit objectives and in some circumstances, they may be the most effective procedure to apply. These objectives might include proper classification of transactions, completeness of recording transactions, and accuracy of management's judgments and estimates in certain areas, such as the allowance for uncollectible accounts. For other audit objectives and circumstances, analytical procedures may be considered attention directing at best, and not relied on for gathering substantive evidence. An example is determining the validity of sales transactions.

Timing Analytical procedures are performed principally at any of three times during an engagement. Paragraph 5301.03 states that analysis should be used in the *planning phase* as risk assessment procedures to assist in determining the nature, extent, and timing of other auditing procedures to be performed. Performance of analytical procedures during planning helps the auditor identify significant matters requiring special consideration later in the engagement. For example, the calculation of inventory turnover before inventory price tests are done may indicate the need for special care during those tests.

Analytical procedures are often done *during the testing phase* of the examination in conjunction with other audit procedures. For example, the prepaid portion of each insurance policy might be compared with the same policy for the previous year as a part of doing tests of prepaid insurance.

Paragraph 5301.25 states that analytical procedures should be used *during the completion phase* of the audit. Such tests are useful at that point as a final review for material misstatements or financial problems, and to help the auditor take a final "objective look" at the financial statements that have been audited. It is common for a partner to do a detailed review of the analytical procedures during the final review of working papers and financial statements. Typically, a partner has a good understanding of the client and its business because of ongoing relationships. Knowledge about the client's business combined with effective analytical procedures is a way to identify possible oversights in an audit.

The purposes of analytical procedures for each of the three different times they are performed is shown in Figure 6-2. The shaded boxes in the matrix indicate that certain purposes are applicable to a certain phase. Notice that purposes vary for different phases of the

FIGURE 6-2 Timing and Purposes of Analytical Procedures

Purpose	Phase		
	(Required) Planning Phase	Testing Phase	(Required) Completion Phase
Understand client's industry and business and assess risks			
Assess going concern			
Indicate possible misstatements (attention directing)			
Reduce detailed tests			

audit. Analytical procedures are performed during the planning phase for all four purposes, whereas the other two phases are used primarily to determine appropriate audit evidence and to reach conclusions about the fair presentation of financial statements.

Five Types of Analytical Procedures

An important part of using analytical procedures is selecting the most appropriate procedures. There are five major types of analytical procedures:

1. Compare client and industry data.
2. Compare client data with similar prior-period data.
3. Compare client data with client-determined expected results.
4. Compare client data with auditor-determined expected results.
5. Compare client data with expected results using nonfinancial data.

These procedures are facilitated by many of the firm's software tools that provide direct linkages to client data.

Compare Client and Industry Data Suppose you are doing an audit and obtain the following information about the client and the average company in the client's industry:

	Client		Industry	
	2004	2003	2004	2003
Inventory turnover	3.4	3.5	3.9	3.4
Gross margin percent	26.3%	26.4%	27.3%	26.2%

If we look only at client information for the two ratios shown, the company appears to be stable with no apparent indication of difficulties. However, compared with the industry, the client's position has worsened. In 2003, the client did slightly better than the industry in both ratios. In 2004, it did not do nearly as well. Although these two ratios by themselves may not indicate significant problems, the example illustrates how comparison of client data with industry data may provide useful information about the client's performance. For example, the company may have lost market share, its pricing may not be competitive, it may have incurred abnormal costs, or it may have obsolete items in inventory.

The Financial Post Company and Dun & Bradstreet Canada Limited accumulate financial information for thousands of larger companies and compile the data for different lines of business; local credit bureaus compile data for companies in their community. Many public accounting firms purchase these publications for use as a basis for industry comparisons in their audits.

The Financial Post
www.financialpost.com

Dun & Bradstreet Canada Limited
www.dnb.ca

The most important benefits of industry comparisons are as an aid to understanding the client's business and as an indication of the likelihood of financial failure. The ratios in Dun & Bradstreet Canada, for example, are primarily of a type that bankers and other credit executives use in evaluating whether a company will be able to repay a loan. The same information is useful to auditors in assessing the relative strength of the client's capital structure, its borrowing capacity, and its likelihood of financial failure.

A major weakness in using industry ratios for auditing is the difference between the nature of the client's financial information and that of the firms making up the industry totals. Since the industry data are broad averages, the comparisons may not be meaningful. Frequently, the client's line of business is not the same as the industry standards. In addition, different companies follow different accounting methods, and this affects the comparability of data. This does not mean that industry comparisons should not be made. Rather, it is an indication of the need for care in interpreting the results.

Compare Client Data with Similar Prior-Period Data Suppose the gross margin percentage for a company has been between 26 and 27 percent for each of the past four years but is 23 percent in the current year. This decline in gross margin should be a concern to the auditor. The cause of the decline could be a change in economic conditions. However, it could also be caused by misstatements in the financial statements, such as sales or purchase cutoff errors, unrecorded sales, overstated accounts payable, or inventory costing errors. The auditor should determine the cause of the decline in gross margin and consider the effect, if any, on evidence accumulation.

There are a wide variety of analytical procedures where client data are compared with similar data from one or more prior periods. The following are common examples.

COMPARE THE CURRENT YEAR'S BALANCE WITH THAT FOR THE PRECEDING YEAR One of the easiest ways to make this test is to include the preceding year's adjusted trial balance results in a separate column of the current year's trial balance spreadsheet. The auditor can easily compare the current year's and previous year's balance to decide early in the audit whether a particular account should receive more than the normal amount of attention because of a significant change in the balance. For example, if the auditor observes a substantial increase in supplies expense, the auditor should determine whether the cause was an increased use of supplies, a misstatement in the account due to a misclassification, or a misstatement in supplies inventory.

COMPARE THE DETAIL OF A TOTAL BALANCE WITH SIMILAR DETAIL FOR THE PRECEDING YEAR If there have been no significant changes in the client's operations in the current year, much of the detail making up the totals in the financial statements should also remain unchanged. By briefly comparing the detail of the current period with similar detail of the preceding period, it is often possible to isolate information that needs further examination. Comparison of details may take the form of details over time or details at a point in time. A common example of the former is comparing the monthly totals for the current and preceding year for sales, repairs, and other accounts. An example of the latter is comparing the details of loans payable at the end of the current year with those at the end of the preceding year.

COMPUTE RATIOS AND PERCENTAGE RELATIONSHIPS FOR COMPARISON WITH PREVIOUS YEARS The comparison of totals or details with previous years as described in the two preceding paragraphs has two shortcomings. First, it fails to consider growth or decline in business activity. Second, relationships of data to other data, such as sales to cost of goods sold, are ignored. Ratio and percentage relationships overcome both shortcomings. The example discussed earlier about the decline in gross margin is a common percentage relationship used by auditors.

A few types of ratios and internal comparisons are included in Table 6-7 to show the widespread use of ratio analysis. In all cases, the comparisons should be with calculations

TABLE 6-7	Internal Comparisons and Relationships
Ratio or Comparison	**Possible Misstatement**
Raw material turnover for a manufacturing company.	Misstatement of inventory or cost of goods sold or obsolescence of raw material inventory.
Sales commissions divided by net sales.	Misstatement of sales commissions.
Sales returns and allowances divided by gross sales.	Misclassified sales returns and allowances or unrecorded returns or allowances subsequent to year end.
Goods and services tax payable (current year) divided by goods and services tax payable (preceding year).	Failure to properly accrue the goods and services tax owing at year end.
Each of the individual manufacturing expenses as a percentage of total manufacturing expense.	Significant misstatement of individual expenses within a total.

made in previous years for the same client. There are many potential ratios and comparisons available for use by an auditor. Subsequent chapters dealing with specific audit areas describe other examples. Normally, the auditor will arrange to have trial balance information entered annually into audit software that calculates a range of ratios and comparisons automatically.

Many of the ratios and percentages used for comparison with previous years are the same ones used for comparison with industry data. For example, it is useful to compare current year gross margin with industry averages and previous years. The same can be said for most of the ratios described in Appendix B beginning on page 172.

There are also numerous potential comparisons of current- and prior-period data beyond those normally available from industry data. For example, the percent of each expense category to total sales can be compared with that of previous years. Similarly, in a multiunit operation (e.g., a retail chain), internal comparisons for each unit can be made with previous periods (e.g., the revenue and expenses for individual retail outlets in a chain of stores can be compared).

Compare Client Data with Client-Determined Expected Results Most companies prepare **budgets** for various aspects of their operations and financial results. Since budgets represent the client's expectations for the period, an investigation of the most significant areas in which differences exist between budgeted and actual results may indicate potential misstatements. The absence of differences may also indicate that misstatements are unlikely. It is common, for example, in the audit of local, provincial, and federal governmental units to use this type of analytical procedure.

Whenever client data are compared with budgets, there are two special concerns. First, the auditor must evaluate whether the budgets were realistic plans. In some organizations, budgets are prepared with little thought or care and therefore are not realistic expectations. Such information has little value as audit evidence. The second concern is the possibility that current financial information was changed by client personnel to conform to the budget. If that has occurred, the auditor will find no differences in comparing actual data with the budget even if there are misstatements in the financial statements. Discussing budget procedures with client personnel is used to satisfy the first concern. Assessment of control risk and detailed audit tests of actual data are usually done to minimize the likelihood of the latter concern.

Compare Client Data with Auditor-Determined Expected Results A second common type of comparison of client data with expected results occurs when the *auditor calculates the expected balance for comparison with the actual balance*. In this type of analytical procedure, the auditor makes an estimate of what an account balance should be by relating it to some other balance sheet or income statement account or accounts, or by making a projection

BUDGETS—written records of the client's expectations for the period; a comparison of budgets with actual results may indicate whether or not misstatements are likely based on some historical trend. An example of calculating an expected value based on relationships of accounts is the independent calculation of interest expense on long-term notes payable by multiplying the ending monthly balance in notes payable by the average monthly interest rate. An example of using a historical trend would be where the moving average of the allowance for uncollectible accounts receivable as a percent of gross accounts receivable is applied to the balance of gross accounts receivable at the end of the audit year to determine an expected value for the current allowance.

Compare Client Data with Expected Results Using Nonfinancial Data Suppose that in auditing a hotel, you can determine the number of rooms, room rate for each room, and occupancy rate. Using those data, it is relatively easy to estimate total revenue from rooms to compare with recorded revenue. The same approach can sometimes be used to estimate such accounts as tuition revenue at universities (average tuition times enrolment), factory payroll (total hours worked times wage rate), and cost of materials sold (units times materials cost per unit).

The major concern in using nonfinancial data is the accuracy of the data. In the previous illustration, it is appropriate to use an estimated calculation of hotel revenue as audit evidence unless the auditor is not satisfied with the reasonableness of the count of the number of rooms, room rate, and occupancy rate. It would be more difficult for the auditor to evaluate the accuracy of the occupancy rate than the other two items.

Using Statistical Techniques and Computer Software

The use of statistical techniques is desirable to make analytical procedures more relevant. Many auditors use computer software to make statistical and nonstatistical calculations easier. These two auditors' tools are discussed briefly.

Statistical Techniques Several statistical techniques that aid in interpreting results can be applied to analytical procedures. The advantages of using statistical techniques are the ability to make more sophisticated calculations and their objectivity.

The most common statistical technique for analytical procedures is regression analysis. Regression analysis is used to evaluate the reasonableness of a recorded balance by relating (regressing) the total to other relevant information. For example, the auditor might conclude that total selling expenses should be related to total sales, the previous year's selling expenses, and the number of salespeople. The auditor would then use regression analysis to statistically determine an estimated value of selling expenses for comparison with recorded values, or to assess the profitability of different product lines. Regression and other statistical methods commonly used for analytical procedures can be found in several advanced auditing texts dealing with statistical sampling techniques for auditing.

Auditor's Computer Software Computer-based **audit software** can be used to perform extensive analytical procedures as a byproduct of other audit testing. In the past several years, most public accounting firms have implemented a variety of computer software as tools for doing more efficient and effective audits. One feature common to all such software is the ability to input or import the client's general ledger into the auditor's computer system. Adjusting entries and financial statements are thereby computerized to save time. These are linked to working papers and cross-referenced, saving many hours of tedious working-paper referencing. Some systems also link directly to client data.

The general ledger information for the client is saved and carried forward in the auditor's computerized data file year after year. The existence of current and previous years' general ledger information on the auditor's computer files permits extensive and inexpensive computerized analytical calculations. The analytical information can also be shown in different forms such as graphs and charts to help interpret the data.

A major benefit of computerized analytical procedures is the ease of updating the calculations when adjusting entries to the client's statements are made. If there are several adjusting entries to the clients' records, the analytical procedures calculations can be quickly revised. For example, a change in inventory and cost of goods sold affects a large number of ratios. All affected ratios can be recalculated immediately.

AUDIT SOFTWARE—software used to automate preparation of audit working papers or the analysis of client data files

APPENDIX B
COMMON FINANCIAL RATIOS

Auditors' analytical procedures often include the use of general financial ratios during planning and final review of the audited financial statements. These are useful for understanding the most recent events and financial status of the business, and for viewing the statements from the perspective of a user. The general financial analysis may be effective for identifying possible problem areas for additional analysis and audit testing, as well as business problem areas for which the auditor can provide other assistance. This appendix presents a number of widely used general financial ratios.

Short-Term Debt-Paying Ability

$$\text{Current ratio} = \frac{\text{current assets}}{\text{current liabilities}}$$

$$\text{Quick ratio} = \frac{\text{cash + marketable securities + net accounts receivable}}{\text{current liabilities}}$$

$$\text{Cash ratio} = \frac{\text{cash + marketable securities}}{\text{current liabilities}}$$

Many companies follow an operating cycle whereby production inputs are obtained and converted into finished goods, and then sold and converted into cash. This requires an investment in working capital; that is, funds are needed to finance inventories and accounts receivable. A majority of these funds come from trade creditors and the balance comes from initial capitalization, bank borrowings, and positive net cash flow from operations.

At any given time, a company can attain a net working capital position. This is the excess of current assets over current liabilities and is also measured by the current ratio. Presumably, if net working capital is positive (i.e., the current ratio is greater than 1.0), the company has sufficient available assets to pay its immediate debts; and the greater the excess (the larger the ratio), the better off the company is in this regard. Thus, companies with a comfortable net working capital position are considered preferred customers by their bankers and trade creditors and are given favourable treatment. Companies with inadequate net working capital are in danger of not being able to obtain credit.

However, this is a somewhat simplistic view. The current assets of companies will differ in terms of both valuation and liquidity, and these aspects will affect a company's ability to meet its current obligations. One way to examine this problem is to restrict the analysis to the most available and objective current assets. Thus, the quick ratio eliminates inventories from the computation, and the cash ratio further eliminates accounts receivable. Usually, if the cash ratio is greater than 1.0, the company has excellent short-term debt-paying ability. In some cases, it is appropriate to state marketable securities at market value rather than cost in computing these ratios.

Short-Term Liquidity

If a company does not have sufficient cash and cash-like items to meet its obligations, the key to its debt-paying ability will be the length of time it takes the company to convert less liquid current assets into cash. This is measured by the short-term liquidity ratios.

The two turnover ratios—accounts receivable and inventory—are very useful to auditors. Trends in the accounts receivable turnover ratio are frequently used in assessing the reasonableness of the allowance for uncollectible accounts. Trends in the inventory turnover ratio are used in identifying a potential inventory obsolescence problem.

$$\text{Average accounts receivable turnover} = \frac{\text{gross credit sales net of returns}}{\text{average gross receivables}}$$

$$\text{Average days to collect (or number of days' sales in accounts receivable)} = \frac{\text{average gross receivables} \times 365}{\text{gross credit sales net of returns}}$$

$$\text{Average inventory turnover} = \frac{\text{cost of goods sold}}{\text{average inventory}}$$

$$\text{Average days to sell (or average days' sales in inventory)} = \frac{\text{average inventory} \times 365}{\text{cost of goods sold}}$$

$$\text{Average days to convert inventory to cash} = \text{average days to sell} + \text{average days to collect}$$

When the short-term liquidity ratios (and the current ratio) are used to examine a company's performance over time or to compare performance among companies, differences in inventory accounting methods, fiscal year ends, and cash-credit sales mix can have a significant effect. With regard to inventories, a few companies have adopted the LIFO method. This can cause inventory values to differ significantly from FIFO values. When companies with different valuation methods are being compared, the company's LIFO value inventory can be adjusted to FIFO to obtain a better comparison.

When two companies have different fiscal year ends, such that one is on a natural business year and the other is not, the simple average gross receivables and inventory figures for the former will be lower. This will tend to cause the natural business year company to appear more liquid than it really is. If this is a problem, an averaging computation with quarterly data can be used.

Finally, the use of net sales per the financial statements in the receivables liquidity ratios can be a problem when a significant portion of sales is for cash. This will be somewhat mitigated when the proportions are fairly constant among periods or companies for which comparisons are being made.

Ability to Meet Long-Term Debt Obligations and Preferred Dividends

$$\text{Debt to equity ratio} = \frac{\text{total liabilities}}{\text{total equity}}$$

$$\text{Tangible net assets to equity ratio} = \frac{\text{total equity} - \text{intangible assets}}{\text{total equity}}$$

$$\text{Times interest earned} = \frac{\text{operating income}}{\text{interest expense}}$$

$$\text{Times interest and preferred dividends earned} = \frac{\text{operating income}}{\text{interest expense} + [\text{preferred dividends}/(1 - \text{tax rate})]}$$

A company's long-run solvency depends on the success of its operations and on its ability to raise capital for expansion or even survival over periods of temporary difficulty. From another point of view, common shareholders will benefit from the leverage obtained from borrowed capital that earns a positive net return.

A key measure in evaluating this long-term structure and capacity is the debt-to-equity ratio. If this ratio is too high, it may indicate the company has used up its borrowing capacity and has no cushion for future events. If it is too low, it may mean available leverage is not being used to the owner's benefit. If the ratio is trending up, it may mean earnings are too low to support the needs of the enterprise. And, if it is trending down, it may mean the company is doing well and setting the stage for future expansion.

The tangible net assets–to-equity ratio indicates the current quality of the company's equity by removing those assets of which the realization is wholly dependent on future operations, such as goodwill. This ratio can be used to better interpret the debt-to-equity ratio.

Lenders are generally concerned about a company's ability to meet interest payments as well as its ability to repay principal amounts. The latter will be appraised by evaluating the company's long-term prospects as well as its net asset position. The realizable value of assets will be important in this regard and may involve specific assets that collateralize the debt.

The ability to make interest payments is more a function of the company's ability to generate positive cash flows from operations in the short run, as well as over time. Thus, times interest earned shows how comfortably the company should be able to make interest (and preferred dividend) payments, assuming earnings trends are stable.

Operating and Performance Ratios

The key to remedying many financial ills is to improve operations. All creditors and investors, therefore, are interested in the results of operations of a business enterprise, and it is not surprising that a number of operating and performance ratios are in use. The most widely used operating and performance ratio is earnings per share, which is an integral part of the basic financial statements for most companies. Several additional ratios can be calculated and will give further insights into operations.

The first of these is the efficiency ratio. This shows the relative volume of business generated from the company's operating asset base. In other words, it shows whether sufficient revenues are being generated to justify the assets employed. When the efficiency ratio is low, there is an indication that additional volume should be sought before more assets are obtained. When the ratio is high, it may be an indication that assets are being fully utilized (i.e., there is little excess capacity) and an investment in additional assets will soon be necessary.

$$\text{Earnings per share} = \frac{\text{earnings} - \text{preferred dividends}}{\text{number of common shares}}$$

$$\text{Efficiency ratio} = \frac{\text{gross sales net of returns}}{\text{tangible operating assets}}$$

$$\text{Profit margin ratio} = \frac{\text{operating income}}{\text{gross sales net of returns}}$$

$$\text{Profitability ratio} = \frac{\text{operating income}}{\text{tangible operating assets}}$$

$$\text{Return on total assets ratio} = \frac{\text{income before interest} + \text{taxes}}{\text{total assets}}$$

$$\text{Return on common equity ratio} = \frac{\text{income before taxes} - (\text{preferred dividends}/1 - \text{tax rate})}{\text{common equity}}$$

Leverage ratios (computed separately for each source of capital other than common equity, for example, short-term debt, long-term debt, deferred taxes) =
$$\frac{(\text{return on total assets} \times \text{amount of source}) - \text{cost attributable to source}}{\text{common equity}}$$

$$\text{Book value per common share} = \frac{\text{common equity}}{\text{number of common shares}}$$

The second ratio is the profit margin ratio. This shows the portion of sales that exceeds cost (both variable and fixed). When there is weakness in this ratio, it is generally an indication that either (1) gross margins (revenues in excess of variable costs) are too low or (2) volume is too low with respect to fixed costs.

Two ratios that indicate the adequacy of earnings relative to the asset base are the profitability ratio and the return on total assets ratio. In effect, these ratios show the efficiency and profit margin ratios combined.

An important perspective on the earnings of the company is what kind of return is provided to the owners. This is reflected in the return (before taxes) on common equity. If this ratio is below prevailing long-term interest rates or returns on alternative investments, owners will perceive that they should convert the company's assets to some other use, or perhaps liquidate, unless return can be improved.

An interesting supplemental analysis is provided through leverage analysis. Here, the proportionate share of assets for each source of capital is multiplied by the company's return on total assets. This determines the return on each source of capital. The result is compared to the cost of each source of capital (e.g., interest expense), and a net contribution by capital source is derived. If this amount is positive for a capital source, it may be an indication that additional capital should be sought. If the leverage is negative from a capital source, recapitalization alternatives and/or earnings improvements should be investigated. It is also helpful to use this leverage analysis when considering the debt-to-equity ratio.

The final operating and performance ratio is book value per common share. This shows the combined effect of equity transactions over time.

The use of operating and performance ratios is subject to the same accounting inconsistencies mentioned for the liquidity ratios previously identified. The usefulness of these ratios in making comparisons over time or among companies may be affected by the classification of operating versus nonoperating items, inventory methods, amortization methods, research and development costs, and off-balance-sheet financing.

Illustration

Computation of the various ratios is illustrated using the financial statements of Hillsburg Hardware Limited introduced in Chapter 5.

$$\text{Earnings per share} = \frac{3,934 - 0}{5,000} = \$0.79$$

$$\text{Current ratio} = \frac{51,027}{13,216} = 3.86$$

$$\text{Quick ratio} = \frac{828 + 0 + 18,957}{13,216} = 1.50$$

$$\text{Cash ratio} = \frac{828}{13,216} = 0.06$$

$$\text{Accounts receivable turnover} = \frac{143,086}{(20,197 + 17,521)/2} = 7.59 \text{ times}$$

$$\text{Days to collect} = \frac{18,859 \times 365}{143,086} = 48.11 \text{ days}$$

$$\text{Inventory turnover} = \frac{103,241}{(29,865 + 31,600)/2} = 3.36 \text{ times}$$

$$\text{Days to sell} = \frac{30,733 \times 365}{103,241} = 108.65 \text{ days}$$

$$\text{Days to convert to cash} = 108.65 + 48.11 = 156.76 \text{ days}$$

$$\text{Debt to equity} = \frac{38,904}{22,463} = 1.73$$

$$\text{Tangible net assets to equity} = \frac{22,463}{22,463} = 1.00$$

$$\text{Times interest earned} = \frac{7,370}{2,409} = 3.06 \text{ times}$$

$$\text{Times interest and preferred dividends earned} = \frac{7,370}{2,409 + 0/(1 - 0.31)} = 3.06 \text{ times}$$

$$\text{Efficiency ratio} = \frac{143,086}{29,865 + 10,340} = 3.56$$

$$\text{Profit margin ratio} = \frac{7{,}370}{143{,}086} = 0.05$$

$$\text{Profitability ratio} = \frac{7{,}370}{29{,}865 + 10{,}340} = 0.18$$

$$\text{Return on total assets} = \frac{5{,}681 + 2{,}409}{61{,}367} = 0.13$$

$$\text{Return on common equity} = \frac{5{,}681 - 0/(1 - 0.31)}{22{,}463} = 0.25$$

Leverage ratios:

$$\text{Current liabilities} = \frac{(0.13 \times 13{,}216) - 0}{22{,}463} = 0.08$$

$$\text{Notes payable} = \frac{(0.13 \times 28{,}300) - 2{,}409}{22{,}463} = 0.06$$

$$\text{Book value per common share} = \frac{22{,}463}{5{,}000} = \$4.49$$

SUMMARY

1. *What are the four evidence decisions that need to be made?* The auditor needs to select audit procedures, choose sample size, decide on items to select, and determine the timing of the actual conduct of the procedures.

   What does the auditor mean by the phrase "sufficient appropriate audit evidence?" The auditor needs to have enough evidence that is relevant to the financial statement accounts to state an opinion on the financial statements.

2. *List and explain the seven general methods of evidence collection.* These are: physical examination (inspecting a tangible asset); confirmation (written or oral response from an independent third party); documentation (examining client documents and records); observation (using senses, such as watching); enquiries of the client (obtaining written or oral details); reperformance (redoing the work); and analytical procedures (use of comparisons and relationships).

3. *How does the auditor choose the type of evidence to collect?* The auditor considers the independence of the provider, the effectiveness of internal controls, the qualifications of the provider (including the auditor), and the objectivity of the evidence in the context of the specific financial statement assertions that are being examined, as well as the overall risk of the engagement and the materiality of the account or balance.

4. *What are analytical procedures?* It is the use of financial and nonfinancial data in meaningful comparisons and relationships to assess the reasonableness of account balances or other data.

   What is their role in the evidence collection process? They are used in all phases of the audit, and are required during the planning and completion phase.

   Describe five major types of analytical procedures. Client data can be compared to industry data, prior-period data, client-determined or auditor-determined expected results, or to nonfinancial data.

CICA ASSURANCE HANDBOOK SECTIONS REFERENCED IN THIS CHAPTER

Section 5143 – The auditor's procedures in response to assessed risks.
Section 5300 – Audit evidence.

Section 5301 – Analysis.
Section 5303 – Confirmation.

ESSENTIAL TERMS

Analysis—identification of components of financial statements and analytical procedures (p. 166).

Analytical procedures—use of comparisons and relationships to determine whether account balances or other data appear reasonable (p. 162).

Appropriateness of evidence—the degree to which evidence can be considered relevant and reliable (p. 156).

Audit procedure—detailed instruction for the collection of a type of audit evidence (p. 153).

Audit program—detailed instructions for the entire collection of evidence for an audit area or an entire audit; always includes audit procedures and may also include sample sizes, items to select, and timing of the tests (p. 155).

Audit software—software used to automate preparation of audit working papers or the analysis of client data files (p. 171).

Budgets—written records of the client's expectations for the period; a comparison of budgets with actual results may indicate whether or not misstatements are likely (p. 170).

Confirmation—the auditor's receipt of a written or oral response from an independent third party verifying the accuracy of information requested (p. 160).

Documentation—the auditor's examination of the client's documents and records to substantiate the information that is or should be included in the financial statements (p. 161).

Enquiry of the client—the obtaining of written or oral information from the client in response to questions during the audit (p. 162).

External document—a document, such as a vendor's invoice, that has been used by an outside party to the transaction being documented, and that the client now has or can easily obtain (p. 161).

Internal document—a document, such as an employee time report, that is prepared and used within the client's organization (p. 161).

Observation—the use of the senses to assess certain activities (p. 162).

Persuasiveness of evidence—the degree to which the auditor is convinced that the evidence supports the audit opinion; the three determinants of persuasiveness are the sufficiency, appropriateness, and timeliness of the evidence (p. 155).

Physical examination—the auditor's inspection or count of a tangible asset (p. 159).

Relevance of evidence—the pertinence of the evidence to the audit objective being tested (p. 156).

Reliability of evidence—evidence is reliable when it is obtained from (1) the auditor's direct knowledge, (2) an independent provider, (3) a client with effective internal controls, (4) qualified providers such as law firms and banks, or (5) objective sources (p. 156).

Reperformance—the rechecking of the computations and transfers of information made by the client during the period under audit (p. 162).

Sufficiency of evidence—the quantity of evidence; appropriate sample size (p. 155).

Timeliness—the timing of audit evidence in relation to the period covered by the audit (p. 157).

Unusual fluctuations—significant unexpected differences indicated by analytical procedures between the current year's unaudited financial data and other data used in comparisons (p. 166).

Vouching—the use of documentation to support recorded transactions or amounts (p. 161).

REVIEW QUESTIONS

6-1 Discuss the similarities and differences between evidence in a legal case and evidence in the audit of financial statements.

6-2 List the four major evidence decisions that must be made on every audit.

6-3 Describe what is meant by an audit procedure. Why is it important for audit procedures to be carefully worded?

6-4 Describe what is meant by an audit program for accounts receivable. What four things should be included in an audit program?

6-5 Explain why the auditor can only be persuaded with a reasonable level of assurance, rather than convinced, that the financial statements are correct.

6-6 Identify the three factors that determine the persuasiveness of evidence. How are these three factors related to audit procedures, sample size, items to select, and timing?

6-7 Identify the characteristics that determine the appropriateness of evidence. For each characteristic, provide one example of a type of evidence that is likely to be appropriate.

6-8 List the seven types of audit evidence included in this chapter, and give two examples of each.

6-9 What are the four characteristics of the definition of a confirmation? Distinguish between a confirmation and external documentation.

6-10 Distinguish between internal documentation and external documentation as audit evidence and give three examples of each.

6-11 Explain the importance of analytical procedures as evidence in determining the fair presentation of the financial statements.

6-12 Your client, Harper Ltd., has a contractual commitment as a part of a bond indenture to maintain a current ratio of 2.0. If the ratio falls below that level on the balance sheet date, the entire bond becomes payable immediately. In the current year, the client's financial statements show that the ratio has dropped from 2.6:1 or 2.6 to 2.05:1 or 2.05 over the past year. How should this situation affect your audit plan?

6-13 Distinguish between attention-directing analytical procedures and those intended to reduce detailed substantive procedures.

6-14 Gail Gordon, a public accountant, has found ratio and trend analysis relatively useless as a tool in conducting audits. For several engagements, she computed the industry ratios included in publications by The Financial Post Company and compared them with client ratios. For most engagements, the client's business was significantly different from the industry data in the publication, and the client would automatically explain away any discrepancies by attributing them to the unique nature of its operations. In cases in which the client had more than one branch in different industries, Gordon found the ratio analysis no help at all. How could Gordon improve the quality of her analytical procedures?

6-15 It is imperative that the auditor follow up on all material differences discovered through analytical procedures. What factors affect such investigations?

MULTIPLE CHOICE QUESTIONS

6-16 Choose the best response.

a. Which of the following types of documentary evidence should the auditor consider to be the most reliable?

(1) A sales invoice issued by the client and supported by a delivery receipt from an outside trucker.
(2) A cheque, issued by the company and bearing the payee's endorsement, that is included with the bank statements mailed directly to the auditor.
(3) A working paper prepared by the client's controller and reviewed by the client's treasurer.
(4) Confirmation of an account payable balance mailed by and returned directly to the auditor.

b. The most reliable type of documentary audit evidence that an auditor can obtain is

(1) calculations by the auditor from company records.
(2) confirmations received directly from third parties.
(3) physical examination by the auditor.
(4) external documents.

c. Significant unexpected fluctuations identified by analytical procedures will usually necessitate a(n)

(1) consistency qualification.
(2) understanding of the client's internal controls.
(3) explanation in the representation letter.
(4) auditor investigation.

d. Which of the following situations has the best chance of being detected when a public accountant compares revenues and expenses with the prior year and investigates all changes exceeding a fixed percentage?

(1) The company changed its capitalization policy for small tools in the current year.
(2) An increase in property tax rates has not been recognized in the company's current accrual.
(3) The cashier began lapping accounts receivable in the current year.
(4) Because of worsening economic conditions, the current provision for uncollectible accounts was inadequate.

e. The auditor is concerned that a client is failing to bill customers for shipments. An audit procedure that would gather relevent evidence would be to:

(1) Select a sample of duplicate sales invoices and trace each to related shipping documents.
(2) Trace a sample of shipping documents to related duplicate sales invoices.
(3) Trace a sample of Sales Journal entries to the Accounts Receivable transaction history file.
(4) Compare the total of the Accounts Receivable master file with the balance of the Accounts Receivable in the general ledger.

DISCUSSION QUESTIONS AND PROBLEMS

6-17 The following are examples of documentation typically obtained by auditors:

1. Vendors' invoices
2. General ledgers
3. Bank statements
4. Cancelled payroll cheques
5. Payroll time cards
6. Purchase requisitions
7. Receiving reports (documents prepared when merchandise is received)
8. Minutes of the board of directors' meetings
9. Remittance advices
10. Signed TD-1s (Employees' Income Tax Withholding Exemption Certificates)
11. Signed lease agreements
12. Duplicate copies of bills of lading
13. Accounts receivable transaction history file
14. Cancelled notes payable
15. Sales invoices history file
16. Articles of incorporation
17. Notes receivable

Required

a. Classify each of the preceding items according to type of documentation: (1) internal or (2) external.
b. Explain why external evidence is more reliable than internal evidence.

6-18 The following are examples of audit procedures:

1. Review the accounts receivable with the credit manager to evaluate their collectibility.
2. Stand by the payroll time clock to determine whether any employee "swipes in" more than one time.
3. Count inventory items and record the amount in the audit working papers.
4. Obtain a letter from the client's law firm addressed to the public accounting firm stating that the law firm is not aware of any existing lawsuits.
5. Extend the cost of inventory times the quantity in an inventory transaction file to test whether it is accurate.
6. Obtain a letter from an insurance company to the public accounting firm stating the amount of the fire insurance coverage on buildings and equipment.
7. Examine an insurance policy stating the amount of the fire insurance coverage on buildings and equipment.
8. Calculate the ratio of cost of goods sold to sales as a test of overall reasonableness of gross margin relative to the preceding year.
9. Obtain information about the system of internal controls by asking the client to fill out a questionnaire.
10. Trace the total on the cash disbursements journal to the general ledger.
11. Watch employees count inventory to determine whether company procedures are being followed.
12. Examine a piece of equipment to make sure a major acquisition was actually received and is in operation.
13. Calculate the ratio of sales commissions expense to sales as a test of sales commissions.
14. Examine corporate minutes of directors' meetings to determine the authorization of the issue of bonds.
15. Obtain a letter from management stating there are no unrecorded liabilities.
16. Review the total of repairs and maintenance for each month to determine whether any month's total was unusually large.
17. Compare a duplicate sales invoice with the sales history file for customer name and amount.
18. Add the sales journal entries to determine whether they were correctly totalled.
19. Make a petty cash count to make sure the amount of the petty cash fund is intact.
20. Obtain a written statement from a bank stating the client has $15,671 on deposit and liabilities of $50,000 on a demand note.

Required

Classify each of the preceding items according to the seven types of audit evidence: (1) physical examination, (2) confirmation, (3) documentation, (4) observation, (5) enquiries of the client, (6) reperformance, and (7) analytical procedures.

6-19 List two examples of audit evidence that the auditor can use in support of each of the following:

a. Recorded amount of entries in the purchase journal

b. Physical existence of inventory

c. Accuracy of accounts receivable

d. Ownership of capital assets

e. Liability for accounts payable

f. Obsolescence of inventory

g. Existence of petty cash.

6-20 As auditor of Star Manufacturing Corp., you have obtained a trial balance taken from the books of Star one month prior to year end:

	DR. (CR.)
Cash in bank	$87,000
Trade accounts receivable	345,000
Notes receivable	125,000
Inventories	317,000
Land	66,000
Buildings, net	350,000
Furniture, fixtures, and equipment, net	325,000
Trade accounts payable	(213,000)
Goods and services tax payable	(22,000)
Mortgages payable	(400,000)
Capital stock	(300,000)
Retained earnings	(510,000)
Sales (net)	(3,130,000)
Cost of sales	$2,300,000
General administrative expenses	622,000
Legal and professional fees	3,000
Interest expense	35,000

Notes: There are no inventories consigned either in or out. All notes receivable are due from outsiders and held by Star.

Required

Which accounts should be confirmed with outside sources? Briefly describe from whom they should be confirmed and the information that should be confirmed. Organize your answer in the following format:

ACCOUNT NAME	FROM WHOM CONFIRMED	INFORMATION TO BE CONFIRMED

(AICPA adapted)

6-21 The following audit procedures were performed in the audit of inventory to satisfy specific balance-related audit objectives as discussed in Chapter 5. The audit procedures assume the auditor has obtained the inventory count records that list the client's inventory. The general balance-related audit objectives from Chapter 5 are also included.

Audit Procedures

1. Using audit software, extend unit prices times quantity, foot the extensions, and compare the total to the general ledger.
2. Trace selected quantities from the inventory listing to the physical inventory to make sure the items exist and the quantities are the same.

3. Question operating personnel about the possibility of obsolete or slow-moving inventory.

4. Select a sample of quantities of inventory in the factory warehouse, and trace each item to the inventory count sheets to determine if it has been included and if the quantity and description are correct.

5. Using both this year's and last year's inventory data files, compare quantities on hand and unit prices, printing any with greater than a 30 percent or $15,000 variation from one year to the next.

6. Examine sales invoices and contracts with customers to determine if any goods are out on consignment with customers. Similarly, examine vendors' invoices and contracts with vendors to determine if any goods on the inventory listing are owned by vendors.

7. Send letters directly to third parties who hold the client's inventory and request that they respond directly to us.

General Balance-Related Audit Objectives

Existence
Completeness
Valuation
Accuracy
Classification
Cutoff
Detail tie-in
Rights and obligations
Presentation and disclosure

Required

a. Identify the type of audit evidence used for each audit procedure.
b. Identify the general balance-related audit objective or objectives satisfied by each audit procedure.

6-22 The following are eight situations, each containing two means of accumulating evidence.

1. Confirm accounts receivable with business organizations versus confirming receivables with consumers.
2. Physically examine 8-cm steel plates versus examining electronic parts.
3. Examine duplicate sales invoices when several competent people are checking one another's work versus examining documents prepared by a competent person in a one-person staff.
4. Physically examine inventory of parts for the number of units on hand versus examining them for the likelihood of inventory being obsolete.
5. Confirm a bank balance versus confirming the oil and gas reserves with a geologist specializing in oil and gas.
6. Confirm a bank balance versus examining the client's bank statements.
7. Physically count the client's inventory held by an independent party versus confirming the count with an independent party.
8. Physically count the client's inventory versus obtaining a count from the company president.

Required

a. For each of the eight situations, state whether the first or second type of evidence is more reliable.
b. For each situation, state which of the factors discussed in the chapter affect the appropriateness of the evidence.

6-23 In auditing the financial statements of a manufacturing company, the public accountant has found that the traditional audit trail has been replaced by an electronic one. As a result, the public accountant may place increased emphasis on analytical procedures of the data under audit. These tests, which are also applied in auditing visibly posted accounting records, include the computation of ratios that are compared with prior-year ratios or with industry-wide norms. Examples of analytical procedures are the computation of the rate of inventory turnover and the computation of the number of days' sales in receivables.

Required

a. Discuss the advantages to the public accountant of the use of analytical procedures in an audit.
b. In addition to the computations given in part (c), list five ratios that an auditor may compute during an audit on balance sheet accounts and related income accounts. For each ratio listed, name the two (or more) accounts used in its computation.
c. When an auditor discovers that there has been a significant change in a ratio when compared with the preceding year's, he or she considers the possible reasons for the change. Give the possible reasons for the following significant changes in ratios:

(1) The rate of inventory turnover (ratio of cost of sales to average inventory) has decreased from the preceding year's rate.
(2) The number of days' sales in receivables (ratio of average daily accounts receivable to sales) has increased over the prior year.

(AICPA adapted)

6-24 Your comparison of the gross margin percentage for Singh Drugs Ltd. for the years 2001 through 2004 indicates a significant decline.

A discussion with Marilyn Adams, the controller, brings to light two possible explanations. She informs you that the industry gross profit percentage in the retail drug industry declined fairly steadily for three years, which accounts for part of the decline. A second factor was the declining percentage of the total volume resulting from the pharmacy part of the business. The pharmacy sales represent the most profitable portion of the business, yet the competition from discount drugstores prevents these sales from expanding as fast as the non-drug items such as magazines, candy, and many other items sold. Adams feels strongly that these two factors are the cause of the decline.

	2004	2003	2002	2001
Sales (thousands)	$14,211	$12,916	$11,462	$10,351
COGS (thousands)	9,223	8,266	7,313	6,573
Gross margin	$4,988	$4,650	$4,149	$3,778
Percentage	35.1	36.0	36.2	36.5

The additional information shown at left and below is obtained from independent sources and the client's records as a means of investigating the controller's explanations.

Required

a. Evaluate the explanation provided by Adams. Show calculations to support your conclusions.
b. Which specific aspects of the client's financial statements require intensive investigation in this audit?

SINGH DRUGS LTD.					
Year	Drug Sales	Non-Drug Sales	Drug Cost of Goods Sold	Non-Drug Cost of Goods Sold	Industry Gross Profit Percentage for Retailers of Drugs and Related Products
2004	$5,126	$9,085	$3,045	$6,178	32.7
2003	$5,051	$7,865	$2,919	$5,347	32.9
2002	$4,821	$6,641	$2,791	$4,522	33.0
2001	$4,619	$5,732	$2,665	$3,908	33.2

6-25 In the audit of Worldwide Wholesale Inc., you performed extensive ratio and trend analysis. No material exceptions were discovered except for the following:

1. Commission expense as a percentage of sales had stayed constant for several years but has increased significantly in the current year. Commission rates have not changed.
2. The rate of inventory turnover has steadily decreased for four years.
3. Inventory as a percentage of current assets had steadily increased for four years.
4. The number of days' sales in accounts receivable has steadily increased for three years.

5. Allowance for uncollectible accounts as a percentage of accounts receivable has steadily decreased for three years.
6. The absolute amounts of amortization expense and amortization expense as a percentage of gross fixed assets are significantly smaller than in the preceding year.

Required

a. Evaluate the potential significance of each of the exceptions above for the fair presentation of financial statements.
b. State the follow-up procedures you would use to determine the possibility of material misstatements.
c. What do these changes indicate about the overall financial position of Worldwide Wholesale Inc.?

6-26 As part of the analytical procedures of Mahogany Products, Inc., you perform calculations of the following ratios:

	Industry Averages		Mahogany Products, Inc.	
Ratio	2004	2003	2004	2003
1. Current ratio	3.30	3.80	2.20	2.60
2. Days to collect receivables	87.00	93.00	67.00	60.00
3. Days to sell inventory	126.00	121.00	93.00	89.00
4. Purchases divided by accounts payable	11.70	11.60	8.50	8.60
5. Inventory divided by current assets	0.56	0.51	0.49	0.48
6. Operating earnings divided by tangible assets	0.08	0.06	0.14	0.12

	Industry Averages		Mahogany Products, Inc.	
Ratio	2004	2003	2004	2003
7. Operating earnings divided by net sales	0.06	0.06	0.04	0.04
8. Gross margin percentage	0.21	0.27	0.21	0.19
9. Earnings per share	$14.27	$13.91	$2.09	$1.93

Required

For each of the preceding ratios:

a. State whether there is a need to investigate the results further and, if so, the reason for further investigation.
b. State the approach you would use in the investigation.
c. Explain how the operations of Mahogany Products, Inc. appear to differ from those of the industry.

6-27 Following are the auditor's calculations of several key ratios for Cragston Star Products Ltd. The primary purpose of this information is to assess the risk of financial failure, but any other relevant conclusions are also desirable.

RATIO	2004	2003	2002	2001	2000
Current ratio	2.08	2.26	2.51	2.43	2.50
Quick ratio	0.97	1.34	1.82	1.76	1.64
Earnings before taxes divided by interest expense	3.50	3.20	4.10	5.30	7.10
Accounts receivable turnover	4.20	5.50	4.10	5.40	5.60
Days to collect receivables	86.90	66.40	89.00	67.60	65.20
Inventory turnover	2.03	1.84	2.68	3.34	3.36
Days to sell inventory	179.80	198.40	136.20	109.30	108.60
Net sales divided by tangible assets	0.68	0.64	0.73	0.69	0.67

RATIO	2004	2003	2002	2001	2000
Operating income divided by net sales	0.13	0.14	0.16	0.15	0.14
Operating income divided by tangible assets	0.09	0.09	0.12	0.10	0.09
Net income divided by common equity	0.05	0.06	0.10	0.10	0.11
Earnings per share	$4.30	$4.26	$4.49	$4.26	$4.14

Required

a. What major conclusions can be drawn from this information about the company's future?
b. What additional information would be helpful in your assessment of this company's financial condition?
c. Based on the ratios above, which particular aspects of the company do you believe should receive special emphasis in the audit?

PROFESSIONAL JUDGMENT PROBLEM

6-28 Your province administers standardized tests to public students in public schools and high schools on the subjects of reading, writing, and mathematics. Reports are produced both by school and for the province overall describing how students fared in these tests. Recently, the Annual Report of the Office of the provincial Auditor General evaluated this testing process. The report was thorough, describing the process and how it was audited and providing some observations and recommendations. One observation related to the methods of monitoring and comparing student progress. Issues raised were as follows:

• Not enough information is collected in student information systems about student practices, such as homework assignment, homework completion, and whether remedial assistance was provided or available.
• There were questions about the accuracy of information recorded about students.

• Concerns were raised about the comparability of data for students from school to school.
• Information systems may not be capable of retaining sufficient student data.

Required

a. Using the seven different types of evidence listed in Table 6-4, identify the evidence that the provincial auditor's office might have collected to reach the conclusions described above. For each type of evidence, explain who would have provided the evidence, and note the level of objectivity of such evidence. Justify your answer.
b. What would be the relevant transaction-related audit objectives considered during this audit? List at least one audit procedure that could have been conducted for each of the transaction-related audit objectives that you consider to be relevant.

CASE

6-29 A lawyer you know is working on a case for one of his clients who has commenced legal proceedings against an industrial company and its auditor in connection with the company's failure. The auditor, ironically, had precipitated the failure by refusing to issue an unqualified auditor's opinion on the most recent annual financial statements. The CA's professional judgment is being questioned, not because of this refusal and its consequences, but because the lawyer's client claims that the financial statements for prior years should not have received unqualified auditor's opinions.

The lawyer will be reviewing the audit files before the case goes to court. He will also have the opportunity to cross-examine the company's auditor in court.

The lawyer has come to Janet Brown, CA, for assistance in the preparation of his case. He has asked her to describe the general characteristics of good professional judgment and, in particular, the steps she would expect the CA to have taken to ensure that he was exercising good professional judgment in this situation.

Required

a. Assume the role of Janet Brown and draft a response to the lawyer.
b. What are the characteristics of working papers that should be present in the defendant CA's working papers?

(CICA adapted)

CHAPTER 7

AUDIT PLANNING AND DOCUMENTATION

How does an auditor decide whether to accept a client or take on a new client? What is involved in the risk analysis process? This chapter identifies many parts to the audit planning and client risk profile process. The auditor not only needs to examine the industry and the business environment but also many details about the client and its governance process before deciding upon the nature of the audit plan.

LEARNING OBJECTIVES

After reading this chapter you should be able to answer the following questions:

1. Why is adequate planning essential to the audit planning process?

2. What are the preplanning steps that the auditor completes before obtaining an engagement letter? Why is an engagement letter important?

3. How is a client risk profile developed? How does the quality of the control environment contribute to an assessment of risks of fraud?

Describe the additional resources that an auditor may use for clients with high-risk profiles.

4. What working papers does the auditor retain to document the planning and risk profile process? Explain the purposes of working papers. What are the common characteristics of high quality working papers?

PSSST—WOULD YOU LIKE TO BUY A TOWN?

The aerial photographs of the town show lush greenery and ocean frontage. Other photos show a deserted shopping mall and deserted suburban streets, complete with mowed lawns. The American-owned mining town of Kitsault, B.C. had an asking price of $7 million according to the October 2, 2004 *Toronto Star*. The town was abandoned two years after completion, in 1983, when the prices for molybdenum (used to strengthen steel) dropped, making the mine unprofitable.

Stelco had an opposite dilemma in spring 2005. Placed into receivership in early 2004 to protect it from creditors, Stelco started making excellent profits as steel prices rose in spring 2005. Stelco's CEO, Courtney Pratt, in order to maintain creditor protection, had to justify the original entry into receivership.

These two cases illustrate how many businesses are vulnerable to raw material market prices and the importance of understanding the marketplace within which a business operates. Some companies can increase their prices for finished goods when raw materials increase, others cannot. As market prices drop, companies may be forced to shed assets or change the way they run their operations to stay profitable.

Sources: 1. Berman, David, 2005. "Stelco's resurrection," National Post, March 4, 2005, p. FP9. 2. Foster, Peter, 2004. "Why Stelco is no bargain . . . yet," Financial Post, November 12, 2004, p. FP11. 3. Girard, Daniel, 2004. "Modern-day ghost town on the block," The Toronto Star, October 2, 2004, pp. H1, H3.

Think about the appliances in your kitchen—refrigerators, stoves, microwaves, or toasters. Many raw materials are in these products—aluminum, plastics, and steel. If the cost of raw materials rose, what would happen to the companies that produce these appliances when raw materials go up? Can they increase their prices? How does raw material price volatility affect companies that produce appliances? How would raw material price volatility affect the risk profile of your client, a major refrigerator producer?

→7.1   THE IMPORTANCE OF AUDIT PLANNING

Planning

The first generally accepted auditing examination standard in Section 5100 requires adequate planning.

> The auditor should plan and perform the audit to reduce audit risk to an acceptably low level that is consistent with the objective of an audit. If assistants are employed, they should be properly supervised.

Section 5150.05 of the *CICA Assurance Handbook* defines audit planning as "developing a general strategy and a detailed approach for the expected nature, extent, and timing of the audit."

There are three main reasons why the auditor should properly plan engagements: to enable the auditor to obtain sufficient appropriate audit evidence for the circumstances, to help keep audit costs reasonable, and to avoid misunderstandings with the client. Obtaining sufficient appropriate audit evidence is essential if the public accounting firm is to minimize legal liability and maintain a good reputation in the professional community. Keeping costs reasonable helps the firm remain competitive and thereby retain its clients, assuming the firm has a reputation for doing quality work. Avoiding misunderstandings with the client is important for good client relations and for facilitating quality work at reasonable costs. For example, suppose the auditor informs the client that the audit will be completed before June 30 but is unable to finish it until August because of inadequate scheduling of staff. The client is likely to be upset with the public accounting firm and may even sue for breach of contract.

Figure 7-1 presents the major parts of audit planning. The figure also indicates the steps that we consider in this chapter and identifies when we will cover the remaining steps.

Before beginning the discussion of preplanning, it is useful to briefly introduce two risk terms that are discussed in depth in the next chapter: audit risk and inherent risk. These two risks have a significant effect on the conduct and cost of audits. Much of the early planning on audits deals with obtaining information to help auditors assess these risks.

AUDIT RISK—a measure of how willing the auditor is to accept that the financial statements may be materially misstated after the audit is completed and an unqualified opinion has been issued

Audit risk is a measure of how willing the auditor is to accept that the financial statements may be materially misstated after the audit is completed and an unqualified opinion has been issued. When the auditor decides on a lower audit risk, it means that the auditor wants to be more certain that the financial statements are *not* materially misstated. Zero risk would be certainty, and a 100 percent risk would be complete uncertainty.

When the auditor decides that a lower audit risk on an audit is appropriate, there are three potential effects:

- More evidence is required to increase audit assurance that there are no material misstatements. It is difficult to implement increased evidence accumulation after the fieldwork has commenced because audit risk applies to the entire audit. It is expensive and often impractical to increase evidence in every part of an audit.
- The engagement may require more experienced staff. Public accounting firms should staff all engagements with qualified staff, but for low audit risk clients, special care is appropriate in staffing.
- The engagement will be reviewed more carefully than usual. Public accounting firms need to be sure that the working papers and other matters on all audits are adequately reviewed. When audit risk is low, there is often more extensive review, including a review by personnel who were not assigned to the engagement.

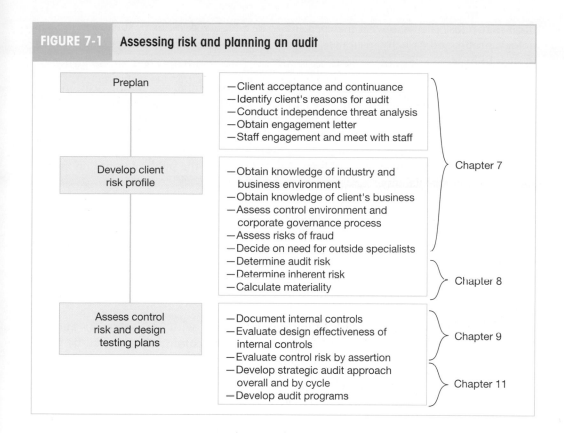

FIGURE 7-1 | **Assessing risk and planning an audit**

Preplan	—Client acceptance and continuance —Identify client's reasons for audit —Conduct independence threat analysis —Obtain engagement letter —Staff engagement and meet with staff	} Chapter 7
Develop client risk profile	—Obtain knowledge of industry and business environment —Obtain knowledge of client's business —Assess control environment and corporate governance process —Assess risks of fraud —Decide on need for outside specialists —Determine audit risk —Determine inherent risk —Calculate materiality	} Chapter 8
Assess control risk and design testing plans	—Document internal controls —Evaluate design effectiveness of internal controls —Evaluate control risk by assertion —Develop strategic audit approach overall and by cycle —Develop audit programs	} Chapter 9 } Chapter 11

Inherent risk is a measure of the auditor's assessment of the likelihood that there are material misstatements in a segment before considering the effectiveness of the internal controls. If, for example, the auditor concludes that there is a high likelihood of material misstatement in an account such as accounts receivable, the auditor would conclude that inherent risk for accounts receivable is high.

When the auditor concludes that there is a high inherent risk for an account or a class of transactions, the same three potential effects are appropriate as for the lower audit risk. However, it is easier and more common to implement increased evidence accumulation for inherent risk than for audit risk because inherent risk can usually be isolated to one or two accounts or a class of transactions. For example, if inherent risk is high only for accounts receivable, the auditor can restrict the evidence expansion to the audit of accounts receivable.

INHERENT RISK—a measure of the auditor's assessment of the likelihood that there are material misstatements in a segment before considering the effectiveness of the internal controls

→ 7.2 BEFORE ACCEPTING AN ENGAGEMENT, PREPLANNING TAKES PLACE

Preplan the Audit

Most preplanning takes place early in the engagement, frequently in the client's office, to the extent that this is practical. **Preplanning the audit** involves the following steps: decide whether to accept or continue doing the audit for the client, identify the client's reasons for the audit, conduct an independence threat analysis, obtain an engagement letter, and select staff for the engagement.

Client Acceptance and Continuance Even though obtaining and retaining clients is not easy in a competitive profession such as public accounting, a public accounting firm must use care in deciding which clients are acceptable. The firm's legal and professional responsibilities are such that clients who lack integrity or argue constantly about the proper conduct of the audit and fees can cause more problems than they are worth. Some public accounting

PREPLANNING THE AUDIT— involves deciding whether to accept or continue doing the audit for the client, identifying the client's reasons for the audit, conducting an independence threat analysis, obtaining an engagement letter, and selecting staff for the engagement firms may refuse clients in what they perceive to be a high-risk industry such as high technology, health, and casualty insurance, and may even discontinue auditing existing clients in such industries.

NEW CLIENT INVESTIGATION Before accepting a new client, most public accounting firms investigate the company to determine its acceptability. To the extent possible, the prospective client's standing in the business community, financial stability, and relations with its previous public accounting firm should be evaluated. For example, many public accounting firms use considerable caution in accepting new clients from newly formed, rapidly growing businesses. Many of these businesses fail financially and expose the public accounting firm to significant potential liability.

For prospective clients that have previously been audited by another public accounting firm, the new (successor) auditor is *required* by the rules of conduct of the institutes and *ordre* of chartered accountants, by the rules of conduct of CGAAC, and by incorporating acts such as the *Canada Business Corporations Act* to communicate with the predecessor auditor. The purpose of the requirement is to help the successor auditor evaluate whether to accept the engagement. The communication may, for example, inform the successor auditor that the client lacks integrity or that there have been disputes over accounting principles, audit procedures, or fees.

The burden of initiating the communication rests with the successor auditor. Permission must be obtained from the client before the communication can be made because of the confidentiality requirement in the rules of conduct of the professional accounting bodies. The predecessor auditor is required to respond to the request for information. In the event there are legal problems or disputes between the client and the predecessor, the latter's response can be limited to stating that no information will be provided. The successor should seriously consider the desirability of accepting a prospective engagement, without considerable investigation, if a client will not permit the communication or the predecessor will not provide a comprehensive response.

Even when a prospective client has been audited by another public accounting firm, other investigations are needed. Sources of information include local lawyers, other public accountants, banks, and other businesses.

Many practitioners take advantage of the Internet as a search tool to learn more about the potential new client and its key operations by studying available client web sites and by using search engines for other sites that discuss the potential client. In addition, they use database search tools or customized search engines to examine financial data or recent publications about the client. This information is useful in the client acceptance decision and throughout the audit if the client is accepted.

CONTINUING CLIENTS Considering whether or not to continue doing the audit of an existing client is as important a decision as deciding whether or not to accept a new client. For that reason, many public accounting firms evaluate existing clients annually to determine whether there are reasons for not continuing to do the audit. Previous conflicts over such things as the appropriate scope of the audit, the type of opinion to issue, or fees may cause the auditor to discontinue association. The auditor may also determine that the client lacks basic integrity and therefore should no longer be a client. If there is a lawsuit against a public accounting firm by a client or a suit against the client by the public accounting firm, the firm probably should not do the audit because its independence could be questioned.

Even if none of the previously discussed conditions exist, the public accounting firm may decide not to continue doing audits for a client because of excessive risk. For example, a public accounting firm might decide that there is considerable risk of a regulatory conflict between a governmental agency and a client, which could result in financial failure of the client and ultimately, lawsuits against the public accounting firm. Even if the engagement is profitable, the risk may exceed the short-term benefits of doing the audit.

Investigation of new clients and re-evaluation of existing ones are an essential part of deciding audit risk. Assume that a potential client is in a reasonably risky industry and has management with a reputation of integrity but also known to take aggressive financial risks. If the public accounting firm decides that audit risk is extremely low, it may choose not to accept the engagement. If the public accounting firm concludes that audit risk is low but the client is still acceptable, it is likely to affect the fee proposed to the client. Audits with a low audit risk will normally result in higher audit costs, which should be reflected in higher audit fees.

Identify Client's Reasons for Audit Two major factors affecting the appropriate evidence to accumulate are the likely statement users and their intended uses of the statements. It will be shown in Chapter 8 that the auditor is likely to accumulate more evidence when the statements are to be used extensively. This is often the case for publicly held companies, those with extensive indebtedness, and companies that are to be sold in the near future.

The most likely uses of the statements can be determined from previous experience in the engagement and discussion with management. Throughout the engagement, the auditor may get additional information as to why the client is having an audit and the likely uses of the financial statements. This information may affect the auditor's assessment of acceptable audit risk.

Conduct Independence Threat Analysis The rules of conduct state that an auditor may conduct an audit only if he or she is independent. The five threats to independence (i.e., self-interest, self-review, advocacy, familiarity, and intimidation) must be explicitly assessed, and any potential threats described. The auditor then determines whether it is possible to institute safeguards to mitigate the threat (e.g., as changing the partner in charge of an engagement to deal with the familiarity threat). If such safeguards can be put into place, or there are no threats, the engagement can be accepted. The auditor would communicate to the Audit Committee any such threats and how they had been dealt with.

If there are threats without compensating safeguards available, or the safeguards do not adequately mitigate the threat, the engagement must be declined.

Obtain an Engagement Letter A clear understanding of the terms of the engagement should exist between the client and the public accounting firm. The terms should be in writing (Section 5110) to minimize misunderstandings. This is done using an engagement letter.

The **engagement letter** is an agreement between the public accounting firm and the client for the conduct of the audit and related services. It should specify whether the auditor will perform an audit, a review, or a compilation, plus any other services such as tax returns or management services. It should also state any restrictions to be imposed on the auditor's work, deadlines for completing the audit, assistance to be provided by the client's personnel in obtaining records and documents, and schedules to be prepared for the auditor. If the client has an internal audit department, it will also specify the role of that department during the audit. It often includes an agreement on fees. The engagement letter is also a means of informing the client that the auditor is not responsible for the discovery of all acts of fraud.

The engagement letter does not affect the public accounting firm's responsibility to external users of audited financial statements, but it can affect legal responsibilities to the client. For example, if the client sued the public accounting firm for failing to find a material misstatement, one defence a public accounting firm could use would be a signed engagement letter stating that a review, rather than an audit, was agreed upon.

Engagement letter information is important in planning the audit principally because it affects the timing of the tests and the total amount of time the audit and other services will take. If the deadline for submitting the audit report is soon after the balance sheet date, a significant portion of the audit must be done before the end of the year. When the auditor is preparing tax returns and a management letter, or if client assistance is not available, arrangements must be made to extend the amount of time for the engagement. Client-imposed restrictions on the audit could affect the procedures performed and possibly even the type of audit opinion issued. An example of an engagement letter for the audit of Hillsburg Hardware Limited is given in Figure 7-2. The financial statements for Hillsburg Hardware Limited are included on pages 136–151.

ENGAGEMENT LETTER—an agreement between the public accounting firm and the client as to the terms of the engagement for the conduct of the audit and related services

FIGURE 7-2   Engagement Letter

Boritz, Kao, Kadous & Co., LLP
Halifax, Nova Scotia, B3M 3JP

June 14, 2004

Mr. Rick Chulick, President
Hillsburg Hardware Limited
2146 Willow Street
Halifax, Nova Scotia
B3H 3F9

Dear Mr. Chulick:

The purpose of this letter is to outline the terms of our engagement to audit the financial statements of Hillsburg Hardware Limited for the year ending December 31, 2004.

Objective, scope, and limitations

Our statutory function as auditor of Hillsburg Hardware Limited is to report to the shareholders by expressing an opinion on Hillsburg Hardware Limited's financial statements. We will conduct our audit in accordance with Canadian generally accepted auditing standards and will issue an audit report.

It is important to recognize that there are inherent limitations in the auditing process. Since audits are based on the concept of selective testing of the data underlying the financial statements, they are subject to the limitation that material misstatements, if they exist, may not be detected. Because of the nature of fraud, including attempts at concealment through collusion and forgery, an audit designed and executed in accordance with Canadian generally accepted auditing standards may not detect a material fraud. Further, while effective internal control reduces the likelihood that misstatements will occur and remain undetected, it does not eliminate the possibility. For these reasons, we cannot guarantee that misstatements or other illegal acts, if present, will be detected.

Our responsibilities

We will be responsible for performing the audit in accordance with Canadian generally accepted auditing standards. These standards require that we plan and perform the audit to obtain reasonable assurance about whether the financial statements present fairly, in all material respects, the financial position, results of operations, and cash flows in accordance with Canadian generally accepted accounting principles. Accordingly, we will design our audit to provide reasonable, but not absolute, assurance of detecting fraud, errors, and other irregularities that have a material effect on the financial statements taken as a whole, including illegal acts the consequences of which have a material effect on the financial statements.

One of the underlying principles of the profession is a duty of confidentiality with respect to client affairs. Accordingly, except for information that is in or enters the public domain, we will not provide any third party with information related to Hillsburg Hardware Limited without Hillsburg Hardware Limited's permission, unless required to do so by legal authority, the rules of professional conduct/code of ethics, or to satisfy the requirements of the Canadian Public Accountability Board.

We will communicate in writing to the Audit Committee the relationships between our ourselves and Hillsburg Hardware Limited that, in our professional judgment, may reasonably be thought to bear on our independence. Further, we will confirm our independence with respect to Hillsburg Hardware Limited

The objective of our audit is to obtain reasonable assurance that the financial statements are free of material misstatement. However, if we identify any of the following matters, they will be communicated to the appropriate level of management, including the Audit Committee:
  (a) misstatements, other than trivial errors;
  (b) fraud;
  (c) misstatements that may cause future financial statements to be materially misstated;
  (d) illegal or possibly illegal acts, other than ones considered inconsequential;
  (e) significant weakness in internal control; and
  (f) certain related party transactions.
The matters communicated will be those that we identify during the course of our audit. Audits do not usually identify all matters that may be of interest to management in discharging its responsibilities. The type and significance of the matter to be communicated will determine the level of management to which the communication is directed.

We will consider Hillsburg Hardware Limited's internal control over financial reporting solely for the purpose of determining the nature, timing, and extent of auditing procedures necessary for expressing our opinion on the financial statements. This consideration will not be sufficient for us to render an opinion on the effectiveness of internal control over financial reporting.

Management's responsibilities

Management is responsible for:
(a) The fair presentation of Hillsburg Hardware Limited's financial statements in accordance with generally accepted accounting principles;

Completeness of information:
(b) providing us with and making available complete financial records and related data and copies of all minutes of meetings of shareholders, directors, and committees of directors;
(c) providing us with information relating to any known or probable instances of non-compliance with legislative or regulatory requirements, including financial reporting requirements;
(d) providing us with information relating to any illegal or possibly illegal acts, and all facts related thereto;
(e) providing us with information regarding all related parties and related party transactions;

Fraud and error:
(f) the design and implementation of internal controls to prevent and detect fraud and error;
(g) an assessment of the risk that the financial statements may be materially misstated as a result of fraud;
(h) providing us with information relating to fraud or suspected fraud affecting the entity involving: (i) management, (ii) employees who have significant roles in internal control; or (iii) others, where the fraud could have a material effect on the financial statements;
(i) providing us with information relating to any allegations of fraud or suspected fraud affecting the entity's financial statements communicated by employees, former employees, analysts, regulators, or others;
(j) communicating its belief that the effects of any uncorrected financial statement misstatements aggregated during the audit are immaterial, both individually and in the aggregate, to the financial statements taken as a whole;

Recognition, measurement, and disclosure:
(k) providing us with an assessment of the reasonableness of significant assumptions underlying fair value measurements and disclosures in the financial statements;
(l) providing us with any plans or intentions that may affect the carrying value or classification of assets or liabilities
(m) providing us with the measurement and disclosure of transactions with related parties;
(n) providing us with an assessment of significant estimates and all known areas of measurement uncertainty;
(o) providing us with claims and possible claims, whether or not they have been discussed with Hillsburg Hardware Limited legal counsel;
(p) providing us with information relating to other liabilities and gain or loss contingencies, including those associated with guarantees, whether written or oral, under which Hillsburg Hardware Limited is contingently liable;
(q) providing us with information on whether or not Hillsburg Hardware Limited has satisfactory title to assets, liens, or encumbrances on assets, and assets pledged as collateral;
(r) providing us with information relating to compliance with aspects of contractual agreements that may affect the financial statements;
(s) providing us with information concerning subsequent events, and
(t) providing us with written confirmation of significant representations provided to us during the engagement on matters that are:
  (i) directly related to items that are material, either individually or in the aggregate, to the financial statements;
  (ii) not directly related to items that are material to the financial statements but are significant, either individually or in the aggregate, to the engagement; and
  (iii) relevant to your judgments or estimates that are material, either individually or in the aggregate, to the financial statements.

Coordination of the Audit

Assistance is to be supplied by your personnel, including preparation of schedules and analysis of accounts, as described in a separate attachment.

Fees

Our fees are based on the amount of time required at various levels of responsibility, plus out-of-pocket expenses (i.e., travel, printing, telephone, and communications) payable upon presentation of billing. We will notify you immediately of any circumstances we encounter that could significantly affect our estimate of total fees.

We appreciate the opportunity to be of service to Hillsburg Hardware Limited The above terms of our engagement shall remain operative until amended, terminated, or superceded in writing.

If you have any questions about the contents of this letter, please raise them. If the services as outlined are in accordance with your requirements and if the above terms are acceptable, please sign the copy of this letter in the space provided and return it to us.

Yours very truly,

J.E. Boritz
Boritz, Kao, Kadous & Co., LLP

Accepted by:
Title: President
Date: June 21, 2004

Selecting Staff for the Engagement Assigning the appropriate staff to the engagement is important to meet the generally accepted auditing standards of Section 5100 and to promote audit efficiency. The general standard states in part:

> The examination should be performed and the report prepared by a person or persons having adequate technical training and proficiency in auditing...

Staff must, therefore, be assigned with that standard in mind. On larger engagements, there are likely to be one or more partners and staff at several experience levels doing the audit. Specialists in such technical areas as statistical sampling and computer auditing may also be assigned. On smaller audits, there may be only one or two staff members.

A major consideration affecting staffing is the need for continuity from year to year. An inexperienced staff assistant is likely to become the most experienced nonpartner on the engagement within a few years. Continuity helps the public accounting firm maintain familiarity with the technical requirements and closer interpersonal relations with the client's personnel. The extent of assistance provided by the client, including work done by the internal audit department also affects staffing. Throughout the planning and conduct of the audit, the entire team meets to share information and to ensure awareness of risks.

→ 7.3   THE RELEVANCE OF A CLIENT RISK PROFILE

Develop Client Risk Profile

An extensive understanding of the client's business and industry and knowledge about the company's operations are essential for doing an adequate audit. This allows the auditor to assess the client's business risk (see page 6).

Obtain Knowledge of Client's Industry and Business Environment There are three primary reasons for obtaining a good understanding of the client's industry. First, many industries have unique accounting requirements that the auditor must understand to evaluate whether the client's financial statements are in accordance with generally accepted accounting principles. For example, if an auditor is doing an audit of a city, the auditor must understand municipal accounting requirements. There are also unique accounting requirements for construction companies, railroads, not-for-profit organizations, financial institutions, and many other organizations.

Second, the auditor can often identify risks in the industry that may affect the auditor's assessment of audit risk, or even whether auditing companies in the industry is advisable. As stated earlier, certain industries are riskier than others, such as the high-tech and biomedical industries.

Finally, there are inherent risks that are typically common to all clients in certain industries. Understanding those risks aids the auditor in identifying the client's business and inherent risks. Examples include potential inventory obsolescence in the fashion clothes industry, accounts receivable collection problems in the consumer loan industry, and reserve for loss risks in the casualty insurance industry.

Knowledge of the client's industry can be obtained in different ways. These include discussions with the auditor in the firm who was responsible for the engagement in previous years and other auditors in the firm currently on similar engagements, as well as conferences with the client's personnel, including internal auditors. Many of the larger public accounting firms have industry specialists who can be consulted for their expertise. Smaller firms that do not have the expertise can consult the practice advisory service of their professional body. There are often industry audit guides, textbooks, and technical magazines available for the auditor to study in most major industries. Some auditors follow the practice of subscribing to specialized journals for those industries to which they devote a large amount of time. Considerable knowledge can also be obtained by participating actively in industry associations and training programs.

Obtain Knowledge of Client's Business Knowledge about the client's business that differentiates it from other companies in its industry is also needed. This knowledge will help the auditor more effectively assess audit risk and inherent risk, and will also be useful in designing analytical procedures (Table 7-1).

Section 5141 of the *CICA Assurance Handbook* requires the auditor to obtain knowledge of the entity's business and environment in order to assess risks and conduct the audit. The section goes on to indicate that the auditor's knowledge of the business is a basis for helping the auditor plan and carry out the audit, including:

- Assessing risks of error or fraud
- Determining materiality levels and assessing inherent risk
- Obtaining an understanding of internal control
- Identifying the sources and nature of audit evidence available
- Designing audit procedures
- Understanding the substance of transactions
- Assessing whether sufficient appropriate evidence is available
- Assessing the appropriateness of management's selection and application of accounting principles
- Evaluating management's overall financial statement presentation

Companies filing their financial statements with a securities commission or whose securities are traded in a public market and all life insurance enterprises are required under paragraph 1701.16 of the *CICA Accounting Handbook* to disclose segment information by industry and by geographic area and the amount of export sales. Auditors must have sufficient knowledge of a company's business to enable them to evaluate whether segmented information should be disclosed and to determine whether the client's disclosure of segmented information is appropriate.

The auditor's *permanent files* frequently include the history of the company, a list of the major lines of business, and a record of the most important accounting policies in previous years. Study of this information and discussions with the client's personnel aid in understanding the business.

A tour of the client's facilities is helpful in obtaining a better understanding of the client's business and operations because it provides an opportunity to observe operations first-hand and to meet key personnel. The actual viewing of the physical facilities aids in understanding physical safeguards over assets and in interpreting accounting data by providing a frame of reference in which to visualize such assets as inventory in process, data processing equipment, and factory equipment. A knowledge of the physical layout also facilitates getting answers to questions later in the audit.

Transactions with related parties are important to auditors because they must be *disclosed in the financial statements* if they are material. Generally accepted accounting principles require disclosure of the nature of the related-party relationship; a description of transactions, including dollar amounts; and amounts due from and to related parties. Transactions with related parties are not arms-length transactions. There is, therefore, a risk that they were not valued at the same amount as they would have been if the transactions had been with an independent party. Most auditors assess inherent risk as high for related parties and related party transactions, both because of the accounting disclosure requirements and the lack of independence between the parties involved in the transactions.

A party is considered to be a **related party** in Section 3840 of the *CICA Accounting Handbook* when it "has the ability to exercise, directly or indirectly, control, joint control or significant influence over [the operating and financial decisions of another party]." A **related party transaction** is any transaction between the client and a related party. Common examples include sales or purchase transactions between a parent company and its subsidiary, exchanges of equipment between two companies owned by the same person, and loans to officers. A less common example, called *economic dependence*, is the potential for exercise of significant influence on an audit client by, for example, its most important supplier or customer, lender or borrower.

Because related party transactions must be disclosed, it is important that all related parties be *identified and included in the permanent files* early in the engagement. Finding undisclosed related party transactions is thereby facilitated. Common ways of identifying related

RELATED PARTY—affiliated company, principal owner of the client company, or any other party with which the client deals such that one of the parties can influence the management or operating policies of the other

RELATED PARTY TRANSACTION—any transaction between the client and a related party

TABLE 7–1   Obtain Knowledge of Client's Business

Task	Example Applied to Hillsburg Hardware Limited
Tour the plant and offices	Done by Fran Moore and assistant during a second client visit. Fran made notes of significant observations for later follow-up.
Identify related parties	Fran Moore reviewed information in permanent file with Chief Executive Officer, President, and Chief Financial Officer, and updated files.
Articles of incorporation and bylaws	Fran Moore attended the offices of legal counsel and reviewed the corporate articles and bylaws for changes. The fact that there were no changes from the prior year was reported in the permanent file.
Minutes of meetings	At the offices of legal counsel, Fran Moore read all minutes. Minutes recording key decisions were copied for the working papers, noting items requiring follow-up during the audit.
Review significant contracts	Fran Moore reviewed continuing contracts for changes and summarized new contracts that were relevant to the audit.
Perform preliminary analytical procedures	Fran Moore used audit software to compare current year unaudited balances to the prior year, highlighting significant changes. Key ratios were examined and compared to prior years and industry averages. Results were discussed with management and used to identify potential audit issues.
Document control environment and corporate governance processes	The audit partner and Fran Moore met with the Audit Committee to discuss management's response to audit recommendations from the previous year. The Audit Committee minutes were reviewed and discussions were held with the Audit Committee and senior management to discuss changes in policies and obtain an overview of key management decisions. Discussions were summarized in the audit working papers.

parties include enquiry of management, review of filings with regulatory bodies such as securities commissions, and examination of shareholders' listings to identify principal shareholders. Section 6010 describes in further detail both the audit planning and the more procedural issues associated with the audit of related party transactions.

Three closely related types of legal documents and records should be examined early in the engagement: articles of incorporation and bylaws, minutes of board of directors' and shareholders' meetings, and contracts. Some information, such as contracts, must be disclosed in the financial statements. Other information, such as authorizations in the board of directors' minutes, is useful in other parts of the audit. Early knowledge of these legal documents and records enables auditors to interpret related evidence throughout the engagement and to make sure there is proper disclosure in the financial statements.

The **articles of incorporation**, granted by the federal government or by the province in which the company is incorporated, is the legal document necessary for recognizing a corporation as a separate entity. It includes the exact name of the corporation, the date of incorporation, the kinds and amounts of capital stock the corporation is authorized to issue, and the types of business activities the corporation is authorized to conduct. In specifying the kinds of capital stock, it also includes such information as the voting rights of each class of stock, preferences and conditions necessary for dividends, and prior rights in liquidation.

The **bylaws** include the rules and procedures adopted by the shareholders of the corporation. They specify such things as the fiscal year of the corporation, the frequency of shareholder meetings, the method of voting for directors, and the duties and powers of the corporate officers.

The auditor must understand the requirements of the articles of incorporation and the bylaws in order to determine whether the financial statements are properly presented. The

ARTICLES OF INCORPORATION—a legal document granted by the federal or provincial jurisdiction in which a company is incorporated that recognizes a corporation as a separate entity. It includes the name of the corporation, the date of incorporation, capital stock the corporation is authorized to issue, and the types of business activities the corporation is authorized to conduct

BYLAWS—the rules and procedures adopted by a corporation's shareholders, including the corporation's fiscal year and the duties and powers of its officers correct disclosure of the shareholders' equity, including the proper payment of dividends, depends heavily on these requirements.

The **corporate minutes** are the official record of the meetings of the board of directors and shareholders. They include summaries of the most important topics discussed at these meetings and the decisions made by the directors and shareholders. The auditor should read the minutes to obtain information that is relevant to performing the audit. There are two categories of relevant information in minutes: authorizations and discussions by the board of directors affecting inherent risk.

CORPORATE MINUTES—the official record of the meetings of a corporation's board of directors and shareholders, in which corporate issues such as the declaration of dividends and the approval of contracts are documented

Common authorizations in the minutes include compensation of officers, new contracts and agreements, acquisitions of property, loans, and dividend payments. While reading the minutes, the auditor should identify relevant authorizations and include the information in the working papers by making an abstract of the minutes or by obtaining a copy and underlining significant portions. Some time before the audit is completed, there must be a follow-up of this information to be sure that management has complied with actions taken by the shareholders and the board of directors. As an illustration, the authorized compensation of officers should be traced to each individual officer's payroll record as a test of whether the correct total compensation was paid. Similarly, the auditor should compare the authorizations of loans with notes payable to make certain that these liabilities are recorded.

Information included in the minutes affecting the auditor's assessment of inherent risk are likely to involve more general discussions. To illustrate, assume that the minutes state that the board of directors discussed two topics: changes in its industry that affect the usefulness of existing machinery and equipment, and a possible lawsuit by Environment Canada for chemical seepage at a plant in Ontario. The first discussion is likely to affect the inherent risk of obsolete equipment and the second one the inherent risk of an illegal act.

Clients become involved in different types of contracts that are of interest to the auditor. These can include such diverse items as long-term notes and bonds payable, stock options, pension plans, contracts with vendors for future delivery of supplies, software usage and maintenance contracts, government contracts for completion and delivery of manufactured products, royalty agreements, union contracts, and leases.

Most contracts are of primary interest in individual parts of the audit and, in practice, receive special attention during the different phases of the detailed tests. For example, the provisions of a pension plan would receive substantial emphasis as a part of the audit of the unfunded liability for pensions. The auditor should review and abstract the documents early in the engagement to gain a better perspective of the organization and to become familiar with potential problem areas. Later these documents can be examined more carefully as a part of the tests of individual audit areas.

The existence of contracts often affects the auditor's assessed inherent risk. To illustrate, assume that the auditor determines early in the audit that the client has signed several sales contracts with severe nonperformance clauses committing the company to deliver specified quantities of its product at agreed-upon prices during the current and next five years. The inherent risk for total sales, liabilities for penalties, and sales commitment disclosures are likely to be assessed as high in this situation.

Chapter 6 discussed the timing of analytical procedures and the four purposes of performing them. Doing analytical procedures during the planning phase is an essential part of conducting both efficient and effective audits. For a brief review, you should examine the four purposes of analytical procedures on pages 166–168 and especially Figure 6-2 on page 168.

Instead of restating the importance of analytical procedures during the planning phase, one example of analytical procedures typically done during planning is provided for each of the four purposes shown in Table 7-2.

Chapter 9 explains that internal controls are logically grouped into several levels or categories. The first level discussed is the control environment, the level of controls established by senior management. Since senior management, the board of directors, and the Audit Committee have a pervasive effect on the company, it is important that their policies, procedures, and key decisions be considered when developing a client risk profile. Previous material collected, such as minutes of directors' meetings and information about related parties, help build a profile of the control environment. Discussions with the audit committee and

TABLE 7-2	Examples of Analytical Procedures Performed During Planning
Purpose	**Analytical Procedure Performed During the Planning Phase**
Understand the client's industry and business	Calculate key ratios for the client's business and compare them to industry averages.
Assess going concern	Calculate the debt-to-equity ratio and compare it to previous years and successful companies in the industry.
Indicate possible misstatements	Compare the gross margin to prior years, looking for large fluctuations.
Reduce detailed tests	Compare prepaid expenses and related expense accounts to prior years.

with senior management about their decision-making processes and the ways that policies are implemented help to complete the picture.

Assess Control Environment and Corporate Governance Processes Using knowledge about the industry, the business environment, and the client's business, the auditor will assess the effect that the control environment and corporate governance structure has upon inherent and control risks. In a well run business with a corporate code of ethics that is demonstrated and enforced by management, the auditor will conclude that these risks are reduced. Where management does not pay attention to the ethical environment in the business, or even condones poor business practices, the risks are increased.

Assess Risks of Fraud Section 5135.048 of the *CICA Assurance Handbook* requires that the auditor use the knowledge of the client's business to consider whether there are fraud risk factors present. These factors are considered further in Chapter 10. For example, unusual fluctuations in the preliminary analytical procedures could point the auditor to accounts that need to be queried, while a poor control environment could leave lower levels of management unsupervised. Management remuneration based upon profits could bias management toward overstating income. The relevant risks would be documented and the impact upon inherent and control risks and audit procedures at the assertion level noted.

Decide on Need for Outside Specialists When the auditor encounters situations requiring specialized knowledge, it may be necessary to consult a specialist. Section 5049 of the *CICA Assurance Handbook*, "Use of Specialists in Assurance Engagements," establishes the requirements for selecting specialists and reviewing their work. Examples include using a diamond expert in evaluating the replacement costs of diamonds and an actuary for determining the appropriateness of the recorded value of insurance loss reserves or the company pension plan assets. Another common use of specialists is consulting with lawyers on the legal interpretation of contracts and titles and in dealing with paperless systems.

In the previously discussed example of a large inventory of computers and computer parts, the public accounting firm may decide to engage a specialist if no one within the firm is qualified to evaluate whether the inventory is obsolete. The auditor should evaluate the specialist's professional qualifications and understand the objectives and scope of the specialist's work. The auditor should also consider the specialist's relationship to the client, including circumstances that might impair the specialist's objectivity.

Summary of the Purposes of Audit Planning

There are several purposes of the planning procedures discussed in this section. A major purpose is to provide information to aid the auditor in assessing audit risk and inherent risk. These assessments will affect the auditor's client acceptance or continuation decision, the proposed audit fee, and the auditor's evidence decisions. A second purpose is to obtain information that requires follow-up during the audit. Doing so is one step in obtaining sufficient appropriate audit evidence. Other purposes include staffing the engagement and obtaining an engagement letter.

Rhonda McMillan had been the in-charge auditor on the audit of Blaine Construction Corp. in 2001. Now she is sitting here, in 2004, in a room full of lawyers who are asking her questions about the 2001 audit. Blaine was sold to another company in 2002 at a purchase price that was based primarily on the 2001 audited financial statements. Several of the large construction contracts showed a profit in 2001 using the percentage-of-completion method but ultimately resulted in large losses for the buyer. Since Rhonda's firm audited the 2001 financial statements, the buyer is trying to make the case that Rhonda's firm failed in its audit of contract costs and revenues.

The buyer's lawyer is taking Rhonda's deposition and is asking her about the audit work she did on contracts. Referring to the working papers, his examination goes like this:

Lawyer: Do you recognize this exhibit and, if you do, would you please identify it for us?

Rhonda: Yes, this is the summary of contracts in progress at the end of 2001.

Lawyer: Did you prepare this document?

Rhonda: I believe the client prepared it, but I audited it. My initials are right here in the upper right-hand corner.

Lawyer: When did you do this audit work?

Rhonda: I'm not sure; I forgot to date this one. But it must have been about the second week in March because that's when we did the fieldwork.

Lawyer: Now I'd like to turn your attention to this tick mark next to the Baldwin contract. You see where it shows Baldwin, and then the red sort of cross-like mark?

Rhonda: Yes.

Lawyer: In the explanation for that mark, it says: "Discussed status of job with Elton Burgess. Job is going according to schedule and he believes that the expected profit will be earned." Now my question is, Ms. McMillan, what exactly was the nature and content of your discussion with Mr. Burgess?

Rhonda: Other than what is in the explanation to this tick mark, I have no idea. I mean, this all took place three years ago. I only worked on the engagement that one year, and I can hardly even remember that.

→ 7.4 THE NATURE OF AUDIT WORKING PAPERS

Working Papers

According to the *CICA Assurance Handbook*, paragraph 5145.02,

> Working papers are the [written or electronic] records kept by the auditor of procedures applied and the results thereof, information obtained and conclusions reached in performing his or her examination [in accordance with Canadian GAAS] and preparing his or her report.

Working papers should include all the information the auditor considers necessary to conduct the examination adequately and to provide support for the auditor's report.

WORKING PAPERS—the records kept by the auditor of the procedures applied, the tests performed, the information obtained, and the pertinent conclusions reached in the engagement

Purposes of Working Papers The overall objective of working papers is to aid the auditor in providing reasonable assurance that an adequate audit was conducted in accordance with generally accepted auditing standards. More specifically, the working papers, as they pertain to the current year's audit, provide a basis for planning the audit, a record of the evidence accumulated and the results of the tests, data for determining the proper type of auditor's report, and a basis for review by supervisors and partners. Increasingly, working papers are maintained in computerized files, with the only paper component consisting of documentation provided by the client or external parties.

BASIS FOR PLANNING THE AUDIT If the auditor is to plan the current year's audit adequately, the necessary reference information must be available in the working papers. The papers include such diverse planning information as conclusions on client risk analysis, descriptive information about internal control, a time budget for individual audit areas, the audit program, and the results of the preceding year's audit.

RECORD OF THE EVIDENCE ACCUMULATED AND THE RESULTS OF THE TESTS The working papers are the primary means of documenting that an adequate audit was conducted in accordance with Canadian GAAS. If the need arises, the auditor must be able to demonstrate to regulatory agencies, such as the British Columbia Securities Commission, and to the courts, that the audit was well planned and adequately supervised; the evidence accumulated was appropriate, sufficient, and timely; and the auditor's report was proper considering the results of the examination.

DATA FOR DETERMINING THE PROPER TYPE OF AUDITOR'S REPORT The working papers provide an important source of information to assist the auditor in deciding the appropriate auditor's report to issue in a given set of circumstances. The data in the papers are useful for evaluating the adequacy of audit scope and the fairness of the financial statements. In addition, the working papers contain information needed to assist the client in the preparation of the financial statements.

BASIS FOR REVIEW The working papers are the primary frame of reference used by supervisory personnel to evaluate whether sufficient appropriate evidence was accumulated to justify the auditor's report.

In addition to the purposes directly related to the auditor's report, the working papers can also serve as the basis for preparing tax returns, filings with the provincial securities commissions, and other reports. They are a source of information for issuing communications to the audit committee and management concerning various matters, such as internal control weaknesses or operations recommendations. Working papers also provide a frame of reference for training personnel and aid in planning and coordinating subsequent audits.

Contents and Organization Each public accounting firm establishes its own approach to preparing and organizing working papers, and the beginning auditor must adopt his or her firm's approach. The emphasis in this text is on the general concepts common to all working papers.

Figure 7-3 illustrates the contents and organization of a typical set of papers. They contain virtually everything involved in the examination. There is a definite logic to the type of working papers prepared for an audit and the way they are arranged in the files, even though different firms may follow somewhat different approaches. In the figure, the working papers start with more general information, such as corporate data in the permanent files, and end with the financial statements and auditor's report. In between are the working papers supporting the auditor's tests.

PERMANENT FILES—auditors' working papers that contain data of a *historical or continuing nature* pertinent to the current audit, such as copies of articles of incorporation, bylaws, bond indentures, and contracts

Permanent Files **Permanent files** are intended to contain data of a *historical or continuing nature* pertinent to the current examination. These files provide a convenient source of information about the audit that is of continuing interest from year to year. The permanent files typically include the following:

- Extracts or copies of such company documents of continuing importance as the articles of incorporation, bylaws, bond indentures, and contracts. The contracts are pension plans, leases, software usage and maintenance agreements, stock options, and so on. Each of these documents is of significance to the auditor for as many years as it is in effect.
- Analyses, from previous years, of accounts that have continuing importance to the auditor. These include accounts such as long-term debt, shareholders' equity accounts, goodwill, and capital assets. Having this information in the permanent files enables the auditor to concentrate on analyzing only the changes in the current year's balance while retaining the results of previous years' audits in a form accessible for review.

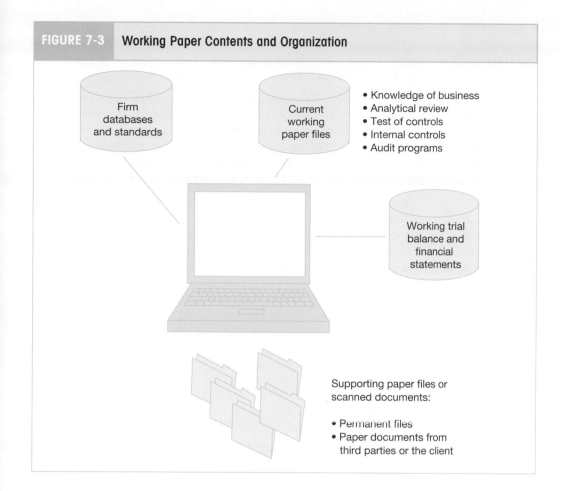

FIGURE 7-3 Working Paper Contents and Organization

Firm databases and standards

Current working paper files

• Knowledge of business
• Analytical review
• Test of controls
• Internal controls
• Audit programs

Working trial balance and financial statements

Supporting paper files or scanned documents:

• Permanent files
• Paper documents from third parties or the client

- Information related to the understanding of internal control and assessment of control risk. This includes organization charts, flowcharts, questionnaires, and other internal control information, including enumeration of controls and weaknesses in the system.
- The results of analytical procedures from previous years' audits. Among these data are ratios and percentages computed by the auditor, and the total balance or the balance by month for selected accounts. This information is useful in helping the auditor decide whether there are unusual changes in the current year's account balances that should be investigated more extensively.

Analytical procedures and the understanding of internal control and assessment of control risk are included in the current period working papers rather than in the permanent file by many public accounting firms.

Current Files The **current files** include all working papers applicable to the year under audit. There is one set of permanent files for each client and a set of current files for each year's audit. The types of information included in the current file are briefly discussed in the sections that follow. As firms strive toward a paperless environment, much of this information is prepared and stored electronically on secure systems.

CURRENT FILES—all working papers applicable to the year under audit

RISK ASSESSMENT AND MATERIALITY Prior to commencing controls testing or detail testing, conclusions need to be reached on the client risk profile, materiality, audit risk, inherent risks, and control risks. Reasoning and conclusions are documented, and the resulting overall audit approach is documented. Analytical procedures for planning purposes may also be included in this section.

AUDIT PROGRAM The *audit program* is kept in the relevant section with that section's working papers (e.g., accounts receivable), although some firms may also keep the audit program in a separate file. As the audit progresses, each auditor initials the program (or enters their password) for the audit procedures performed and records the date of completion. The inclusion in the working papers of a well-designed audit program completed in a conscientious manner is evidence of a high-quality audit.

GENERAL INFORMATION Some working papers include current period information that is of a general nature rather than designed to support specific financial statement amounts. This includes such items as staff scheduling and budgets, abstracts or copies of minutes of the board of directors' meetings, abstracts of contracts or agreements not included in the permanent files, notes on discussions with the client, working-paper review comments, subsequent events analysis, and summary documentation indicating audit conclusions by section.

WORKING TRIAL BALANCE Since the basis for preparing the financial statements is the general ledger, the amounts included in that record are the focal point of the examination. As early as possible after the balance sheet date, the auditor obtains or prepares a copy of the general ledger accounts and their year-end balances (frequently in electronic form). Once incorporated into working papers, this schedule is the **working trial balance**.

WORKING TRIAL BALANCE—a listing of the general ledger accounts and their year-end balances

LEAD SCHEDULE—a working paper that contains the detailed accounts from the general ledger making up a line item total in the working trial balance

The technique used by many firms is to have the auditor's working trial balance in the same grouping format as the financial statements. Each line item on the trial balance is supported by a **lead schedule**, containing the detailed accounts from the general ledger making up the line item total. Each detailed account on the lead schedule is, in turn, supported by appropriate schedules evidencing the audit work performed and the conclusions reached. As an example, the relationship between cash as it is stated on the financial statements, the working trial balance, the lead schedule for cash, and the supporting working papers is presented in Figure 7-4. As the figure indicates, cash on the financial statements is the same as on the working trial balance and the total of the detail on the cash lead schedule. Initially, figures for the lead schedule were taken from the general ledger. The audit work performed resulted in an adjustment to cash that would be evidenced in the detail schedules and reflected on the lead schedule, the working trial balance, and the financial statements.

ADJUSTING AND RECLASSIFICATION ENTRIES When the auditor discovers material misstatements in the accounting records, the financial statements must be corrected. For example, if the client failed to reduce inventory properly for obsolete raw materials, an adjusting entry can be suggested by the auditor to reflect the realizable value of the inventory. Even though adjusting entries discovered in the audit are typically prepared by the auditor, they must be approved and made by the client because the books and records are the client's and management has primary responsibility for the fair presentation of the statements. It is therefore important to remember that when the auditor believes that an adjusting or reclassification entry is required, the auditor must ask management to make the entry. Figure 7-4 illustrates an adjustment of the general cash account for $90. Use of automated working-paper software facilitates the necessary posting of such entries to multiple levels of working papers, from the working paper where the adjustment was described, to the lead schedule, to the working trial balance, and through to the financial statements.

Reclassification entries are frequently made in the statements to present accounting information properly, even when the general ledger balances are correct. A common example is the reclassification for financial statement purposes of material credit balances in accounts receivable to accounts payable. Because the balance in accounts receivable on the general ledger reflects the accounts receivable properly from the point of view of operating the company on a day-to-day basis, the reclassification entry is not included in the client's general ledger.

Only those adjusting and reclassification entries that significantly affect the fair presentation of financial statements must be made. The determination of when a misstatement should be adjusted is based on *materiality*. The auditor should keep in mind that several immaterial misstatements that are not adjusted could result in an overall material misstatement when the misstatements are combined. It is common for auditors to summarize on a separate working paper all adjusting and reclassification entries that have not been recorded or posted to the accounts in the books or the working papers as a means of determining their cumulative effect.

FIGURE 7-4 | **Relationship of Working Papers to Financial Statements**

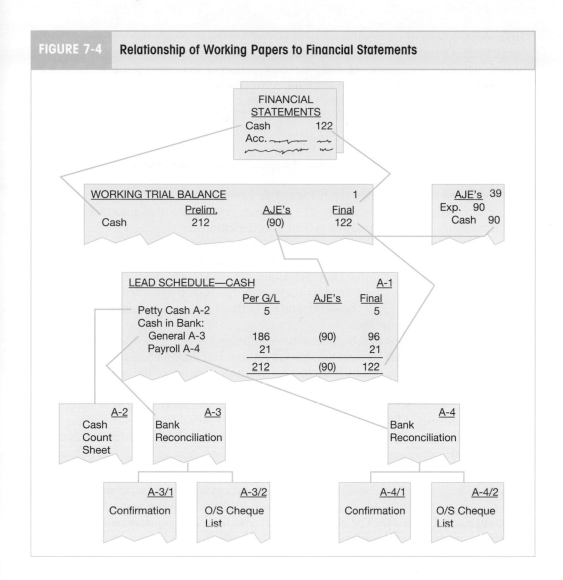

SUPPORTING SCHEDULES The largest portion of **supporting schedule working papers** includes the detailed schedules prepared by the client or the auditors in support of specific amounts on the financial statements. Many different types of schedules are used. Use of the appropriate type for a given aspect of the audit is necessary to document the adequacy of the audit and to fulfill the other objectives of working papers. Following are the major types of supporting schedule:

- *Analysis.* An analysis is designed to show the *activity in a general ledger account* during the entire period under examination, tying together the beginning and ending balances. This type of schedule is normally used for accounts such as marketable securities, notes receivable, allowance for doubtful accounts, capital assets, long-term debt, and all equity accounts. The common characteristic of these accounts is the significance of the activity in the account during the year. In most cases, the **analysis working papers** have cross-references to other working papers or are automatically linked as electronic files.
- *Trial balance or list.* This type of schedule consists of the *details that make up a year-end balance* of a general ledger account. It differs from an analysis in that it includes only those items constituting the end-of-the-period balance. Common examples of **trial balance or list working papers** include aged trial balances or lists in support of trade accounts receivable, trade accounts payable, repairs and maintenance expenses, legal expense, and miscellaneous income. An example is included in Figure 7-5 on page 201.
- *Reconciliation of amounts.* A **reconciliation of amounts working paper** *supports a specific amount* and is normally expected to tie the amount recorded in the client's records

SUPPORTING SCHEDULE WORKING PAPER—a detailed schedule prepared by the client or the auditor in support of a specific amount on the financial statements

ANALYSIS WORKING PAPER—a supporting schedule that shows the activity in a general ledger account during the entire period under audit

TRIAL BALANCE OR LIST WORKING PAPER—a supporting schedule of the details that make up the year-end balance of a general ledger account

RECONCILIATION OF AMOUNTS WORKING PAPER—a schedule that supports a specific amount; it normally ties the amount recorded in the client's records to another source of information, such as a bank statement or a confirmation to another source of information. Examples include the reconciliation of bank balances with bank statements, the reconciliation of subsidiary accounts receivable balances with confirmations from customers, and the reconciliation of accounts payable balances with vendors' statements. An example of a bank reconciliation is shown in Figure 15-4, p.460.

- *Tests of reasonableness.* A test of reasonableness schedule, as the name implies, contains information that enables the auditor to evaluate whether the client's balance appears to include a misstatement considering the circumstances in the engagement. Frequently, auditors test amortization expense, the provision for income taxes, and the allowance for doubtful accounts by tests of reasonableness. These tests are primarily analytical procedures.

- *Summary procedures.* Another type of schedule *summarizes the results* of a specific audit procedure performed. Examples are the summary of the results of accounts receivable confirmation and the summary of inventory observations.

- *Examination of supporting documents.* A number of special-purpose schedules are designed to *show detailed tests performed*, such as examination of documents during tests of transactions or cutoffs. These schedules show no totals, and they do not tie in to the general ledger because they document only the tests performed and the results found. The schedules must, however, state a definite positive or negative conclusion about the objective of the test.

- *Informational.* This type of schedule contains information as opposed to audit evidence. These schedules include information for tax returns and data such as time budgets and the client's working hours, which are helpful in administration of the engagement.

- *Outside documentation.* Much of the content of the working papers consists of the outside documentation gathered by auditors, such as confirmation replies and copies of client agreements. Although not "schedules" in the real sense, these are indexed and interfiled or scanned as images. Procedures are indicated on them in the same manner as on the other schedules.

Preparation of Working Papers The proper preparation of schedules to document the audit evidence accumulated, the results found, and the conclusions reached are an important part of the audit. The auditor must recognize the circumstances requiring the need for a schedule and the appropriate design of schedules to be included in the files. Although the design depends on the objectives involved, working papers should possess certain characteristics:

- Each working paper should be properly identified with such information as the client's name, the period covered, a description of the contents, the initials of the preparer, the date of preparation, and an index code. Where automated working-paper software is used, defaults can be set up in the software, simplifying this process.

- Working papers should be indexed and cross-referenced to aid in organizing and filing. One type of indexing is illustrated in Figure 7-4. The lead schedule for cash has been indexed as A-1, and the individual general ledger accounts making up the total cash on the financial statements are indexed as A-2 through A-4. The final indexing is for the schedules supporting A-3 and A-4.

- Completed working papers must clearly indicate the audit work performed. This is accomplished in three ways: by a written statement in the form of a memorandum, by initials on the audit procedures in the audit program, and by notations directly on the working paper schedules. Notations on working papers are accomplished by the use of *tick marks*, which are *symbols* written adjacent to the detail on the body of the schedule. These notations must be clearly explained at the bottom of the working paper.

- Each working paper should include sufficient information to fulfill the objectives for which it was designed. If the auditor is to prepare working papers properly, the auditor must be aware of his or her goals. For example, if a working paper is designed to list the detail and show the verification of support of a balance sheet account, such as prepaid insurance, it is essential that the detail on the working paper reconcile with the trial balance.

- The conclusions that were reached about the segment of the audit under consideration should be plainly stated.

The common characteristics of proper working-paper preparation are indicated in Figure 7-5.

Ownership of Working Papers The working papers prepared during the engagement, including those prepared by the client for the auditor, are the *property of the auditor*. The only time anyone else, including the client, has a legal right to examine the papers is when the papers are subpoenaed by a court as legal evidence or when they are required by the public accountant's professional organization in connection with disciplinary proceedings or practice inspection. At the completion of the engagement, working papers are retained on the public accounting firm's premises for future reference. Many firms follow the practice of microfilming the working papers after several years to reduce storage costs.

Confidentiality of Working Papers The need to maintain a confidential relationship with the client was discussed in Chapter 2. It was noted that the rules of conduct of the professional accounting bodies require their members not to disclose any confidential information obtained in the course of a professional engagement except with the consent of the client or, as was noted above, when required by the courts or by the professional accounting associations.

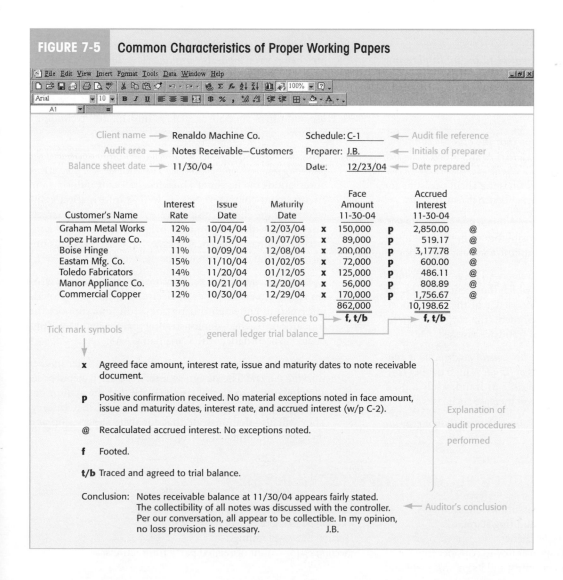

FIGURE 7-5   Common Characteristics of Proper Working Papers

Client name → Renaldo Machine Co.	Schedule: C-1 ← Audit file reference
Audit area → Notes Receivable—Customers	Preparer: J.B. ← Initials of preparer
Balance sheet date → 11/30/04	Date: 12/23/04 ← Date prepared

Customer's Name	Interest Rate	Issue Date	Maturity Date		Face Amount 11-30-04		Accrued Interest 11-30-04	
Graham Metal Works	12%	10/04/04	12/03/04	x	150,000	p	2,850.00	@
Lopez Hardware Co.	14%	11/15/04	01/07/05	x	89,000	p	519.17	@
Boise Hinge	11%	10/09/04	12/08/04	x	200,000	p	3,177.78	@
Eastam Mfg. Co.	15%	11/10/04	01/02/05	x	72,000	p	600.00	@
Toledo Fabricators	14%	11/20/04	01/12/05	x	125,000	p	486.11	@
Manor Appliance Co.	13%	10/21/04	12/20/04	x	56,000	p	808.89	@
Commercial Copper	12%	10/30/04	12/29/04	x	170,000	p	1,756.67	@
					862,000		10,198.62	

Cross-reference to → **f, t/b**   → **f, t/b**
general ledger trial balance

Tick mark symbols ↓

x   Agreed face amount, interest rate, issue and maturity dates to note receivable document.

p   Positive confirmation received. No material exceptions noted in face amount, issue and maturity dates, interest rate, and accrued interest (w/p C-2).

@   Recalculated accrued interest. No exceptions noted.

f   Footed.

t/b Traced and agreed to trial balance.

Explanation of audit procedures performed

Conclusion: Notes receivable balance at 11/30/04 appears fairly stated. The collectibility of all notes was discussed with the controller. ← Auditor's conclusion
Per our conversation, all appear to be collectible. In my opinion, no loss provision is necessary.   J.B.

During the course of the examination, auditors obtain a considerable amount of information of a confidential nature, including officer salaries, product pricing and advertising plans, and product cost data. If auditors divulged this information to outsiders or to client employees who have been denied access, their relationship with management would be seriously strained. Furthermore, having access to the working papers would give employees an opportunity to alter information on them. For these reasons, care must be taken to protect the working papers at all times.

Ordinarily, the working papers can be provided to someone else only with the express permission of the client; the client owns the data on the working papers. This is the case even if a public accountant sells his or her practice to another public accounting firm. Permission is not required from the client, however, if the working papers are subpoenaed by a court or are used in connection with disciplinary hearings or practice inspection conducted by the auditor's professional body.

Summary of Working Papers Working papers are an essential part of every audit for effectively planning the audit, providing a record of the evidence accumulated and the results of the tests, deciding the proper type of auditor's report, and reviewing the work of assistants. Public accounting firms establish their own policies and approaches for working-paper preparation to make sure that these objectives are met. Public accounting firms make sure that working papers are properly prepared and are appropriate for the circumstances in the audit.

SUMMARY

1. *Why is adequate planning essential to the audit planning process?* Planning helps ensure that the auditor gathers enough evidence of suitable quality, assists in keeping audit costs reasonable, and helps avoid misunderstandings with the client.

2. *What are the preplanning steps that the auditor completes before obtaining an engagement letter?* As described in Figure 7-1, the auditor goes through a client acceptance and continuance decision process, identifies the client's reasons for an audit, and conducts an independence threat analysis.

   Why is an engagement letter important? The engagement letter clarifies the responsibilities of both the auditor and the client and is used to minimize misunderstandings.

3. *How is a client risk profile developed?* The auditor obtains knowledge of the industry in which the client operates, the business environment, and knowledge of the client's business. Then, the control environment, the corporate governance process, and the risks of fraud are assessed.

   How does the quality of the control environment contribute to an assessment of risks of fraud? A high quality control environment will reduce risks of fraud, while a poor quality control environment will increase such risks.

   Describe the additional resources that an auditor may use

for clients with high-risk profiles. The auditor could use external specialists (e.g., an actuary, a lawyer, or a specialist in valuing client inventory, such as diamonds, computer equipment, or other types of assets). The auditor could also use audit firm specialists, such as information technology auditors.

4. *What working papers does the auditor retain to document the planning and risk profile process?* The auditor will document observations of the client's business, relevant industry and environment characteristics, as well as information gathered about the client's business (e.g., related parties, extracts from articles of incorporation, bylaws, minutes), and conduct preliminary analytical review. Supported conclusions for each of the risk factors will be included.

   Explain the purposes of working papers. They are a written record (in either paper or electronic form) that provide information collected during the audit and support the conclusions reached, demonstrating that the audit was conducted in accordance with Canadian GAAS.

   What are the common characteristics of high-quality working papers? The design will reflect clarity of purpose, allowing others to clearly see the work that the auditor has completed so that it could be reperformed if necessary. They will also demonstrate that adequate supervision and review were completed during the audit.

CICA ASSURANCE HANDBOOK SECTIONS REFERENCED IN THIS CHAPTER

Section 5049 – Use of specialists in assurance engagements.
Section 5100 – Generally accepted auditing standards.
Section 5110 – Terms of the engagement.
Section 5135 – The auditor's responsibility to consider fraud.
Section 5141 – Understanding the entity and its environment and

assessing the risks of material misstatement.
Section 5145 – Documentation.
Section 5150 – Planning.
Section 6010 – Audit of related party transactions.

ESSENTIAL TERMS

Analysis working paper—a supporting schedule that shows the activity in a general ledger account during the entire period under audit   (p. 199).

Articles of incorporation—a legal document granted by the federal or provincial jurisdiction in which a company is incorporated that recognizes a corporation as a separate entity. It includes the name of the corporation, the date of incorporation, capital stock the corporation is authorized to issue, and the types of business activities the corporation is authorized to conduct (p. 192).

Audit risk—a measure of how willing the auditor is to accept that the financial statements may be materially misstated after the audit is completed and an unqualified opinion has been issued   (p. 184).

Bylaws—the rules and procedures adopted by a corporation's shareholders, including the corporation's fiscal year and the duties and powers of its officers   (p. 192).

Corporate minutes—the official record of the meetings of a corporation's board of directors and shareholders in which corporate issues such as the declaration of dividends and the approval of contracts are documented   (p. 193).

Current files—all working papers applicable to the year under audit   (p. 197).

Engagement letter—an agreement between the public accounting firm and the client as to the terms of the engagement for the conduct of the audit and related services   (p. 187).

Inherent risk—a measure of the auditor's assessment of the likelihood that there are material misstatements in a segment before considering the effectiveness of the internal controls   (p. 185).

Lead schedule—a working paper that contains the detailed accounts from the general ledger making up a line item total in the working trial balance   (p. 198).

Permanent files—auditors' working papers that contain data of a *historical or continuing nature* pertinent to the current audit, such as copies of articles of incorporation, bylaws, bond indentures, and contracts   (p. 196).

Preplanning the audit—involves deciding whether to accept or continue doing the audit for the client, identifying the client's reasons for the audit, conducting an independence threat analysis, obtaining an engagement letter, and selecting staff for the engagement   (p. 185).

Reconciliation of amounts working paper—a schedule that supports a specific amount; it normally ties the amount recorded in the client's records to another source of information, such as a bank statement or a confirmation   (p. 199).

Related party—affiliated company, principal owner of the client company, or any other party with which the client deals such that one of the parties can influence the management or operating policies of the other   (p. 191).

Related party transaction—any transaction between the client and a related party   (p. 191).

Supporting schedule working papers—a detailed schedule prepared by the client or the auditor in support of a specific amount on the financial statements   (p. 199).

Trial balance or list working paper—a supporting schedule of the details that make up the year-end balance of a general ledger account   (p. 199).

Working papers—the records kept by the auditor of the procedures applied, the tests performed, the information obtained, and the pertinent conclusions reached in the engagement   (p. 195).

Working trial balance—a listing of the general ledger accounts and their year-end balances   (p. 198).

REVIEW QUESTIONS

7-1   What benefits does the auditor derive from planning audits?

7-2   Identify the major steps in planning audits.

7-3   What are the responsibilities of the successor and predecessor auditors when a company is changing auditors?

7-4   What factors should an auditor consider prior to accepting an engagement?

7-5   What is the purpose of an engagement letter? What subjects should be covered in such a letter?

7-6   List the four types of information the auditor should obtain or review as a part of gaining background information for the audit, and provide one specific example of how the information will be useful in conducting an audit.

7-7   When a public accountant has accepted an engagement from a new client that is a manufacturer, it is customary for the public accountant to tour the client's plant facilities. Discuss the ways in which the public accountant's observations made during the course of the plant tour will be of help as he or she plans and conducts the audit.

7-8   An auditor acquires background knowledge of the client's industry as an aid to his or her audit work. How does the acquisition of this knowledge aid the auditor in distinguishing between obsolete and current inventory?

7-9   Define what is meant by a "related party." What are the auditor's responsibilities for related parties and related party transactions?

7-10   Jennifer Bailey has many clients in the manufacturing business. She has worked in this sector for many years and believes that she knows the industry well. Explain why it is important for Jennifer to conduct a client risk analysis every year. For each step of the client risk analysis, list the benefits to the inclusion of this task as part of the client risk analysis process.

7-11 Your firm has performed the audit of Danko Inc. for several years, and you have been assigned the responsibility for the current audit. How would your review of the articles of incorporation and bylaws for this audit differ from that of the audit of a client that was audited by a different public accounting firm in the preceding year?

7-12 Identify four types of information in the client's minutes of the board of directors' meetings that are likely to be relevant to the auditor. Explain why it is important to read the minutes early in the engagement.

7-13 Explain why it is important for working papers to include each of the following: identification of the name of the client, period covered, description of the contents, initials of the preparer, date of the preparation, and an index code.

7-14 Why is it essential that the auditor not leave questions or exceptions in the working papers without an adequate explanation?

7-15 What type of working papers can be prepared by the client and used by the auditor as a part of the working-paper file? When client assistance is obtained in preparing working papers, describe the proper precautions the auditor should take.

7-16 Who owns the working papers? Under what circumstances can they be used by other people?

MULTIPLE CHOICE QUESTIONS

7-17 Select the best response for the following questions.

a. Which of the following is an effective audit planning and control procedure that helps prevent misunderstandings and inefficient use of audit personnel? Arranging

   (1) to provide the client with copies of the audit programs to be used during the audit.
   (2) a preliminary conference with the client to discuss audit objectives, fees, timing, and other information.
   (3) to have the auditor prepare and post any necessary adjusting or reclassification entries prior to final closing.
   (4) to make copies, for inclusion in the working papers, of those client-supporting documents examined by the auditor.

b. The independent auditor should acquire an understanding of a client's internal audit function to determine whether the work of internal auditors will be a factor in determining the nature, timing, and extent of the independent auditor's procedures. The work performed by internal auditors might be such a factor when the internal auditor's work includes

   (1) presence on an information systems steering committee.
   (2) review of administrative practices to improve efficiency and achieve management objectives.
   (3) study and evaluation of internal controls.
   (4) preparation of internal financial reports for management purposes.

   (AICPA adapted)

c. When approached to perform an audit for the first time, the public accountant should make enquiries of the predecessor auditor. This is a necessary procedure because the predecessor may be able to provide the successor with information that will assist the successor in determining whether

   (1) the company follows the policy of rotating its auditors.
   (2) in the predecessor's opinion, internal control of the company has been satisfactory.
   (3) the predecessor's work should be used.
   (4) the engagement should be accepted.

d. Audit working papers are used to record the results of the auditor's evidence-gathering procedures. When preparing working papers, the auditor should remember that working papers should be

   (1) kept on the client's premises so that the client can have access to them for reference purposes.
   (2) the primary support for the financial statements being examined.
   (3) considered as a part of the client's accounting records that are retained by the auditor.
   (4) designed to meet the circumstances and the auditor's needs on each engagement.

e. A basic premise underlying the application of analytical procedures is that

   (1) the study of financial ratios is an acceptable alternative to the investigation of unusual fluctuations.
   (2) plausible relationships among data may reasonably be expected to exist and continue in the absence of known conditions to the contrary.
   (3) these procedures *cannot* replace tests of controls and tests of details of balances.
   (4) statistical tests of financial information may lead to the discovery of material errors or fraud and other irregularities in the financial statements.

DISCUSSION QUESTIONS AND PROBLEMS

7-18 Two public accountants were talking about their profession while golfing one day. One commented that she thought that the decision to continue as auditor for a client was as important as the decision whether to accept a company as a new client.

Her golfing partner asked her what she meant.

Required
Explain to the second golfer what the first golfer meant.

7-19 In late spring, you are advised of a new assignment as the in-charge accountant of your public accounting firm's recurring annual audit of a major client, Lancer Inc. You are given the engagement letter for the audit covering the current fiscal year and a list of personnel assigned to this engagement. It is your responsibility to plan and supervise the fieldwork for the engagement.

Discuss the necessary preparation and planning for the Lancer Inc. annual audit *prior* to beginning fieldwork at the client's office. In your discussion, include the sources you should consult, the type of information you should seek, the preliminary plans and preparation you should make for the fieldwork, and any actions you should take relative to the staff assigned to the engagement.

(AICPA adapted)

7-20 The minutes of the board of directors of Marygold Catalogue Company Ltd. for the year ended December 31, 2004, were provided to you.

Meeting of February 16, 2004

Ruth Ho, chair of the board, called the meeting to order at 4:00 p.m. The following directors were in attendance:

Margaret Aronson	Claude La Rose
Fred Brick	Lucille Renolds
Henri Chapdelaine	J.T. Schmidt
Ruth Ho	Marie Titard
Homer Jackson	Roald Asko

The minutes of the meeting of October 11, 2003, were read and approved.

Marie Titard, president, discussed the new marketing plan for wider distribution of catalogues in the western market. She made a motion for approval of increased expenditures of approximately $50,000 for distribution costs, which was seconded by Asko and unanimously passed.

The unresolved dispute with the Canada Revenue Agency over the tax treatment of leased office buildings was discussed with Harold Moss, the tax partner from Marygold's public accounting firm, Moss & Lawson. In Mr. Moss's opinion, the matter would not be resolved for several months and could result in an unfavourable settlement.

J. T. Schmidt moved that the computer equipment that was no longer being used in the Kingston office, since new equipment had been acquired in 2003, be donated to the Kingston Vocational School for use in their repair and training program. Margaret Aronson seconded the motion and it unanimously passed.

Annual cash dividends were unanimously approved as being payable April 30, 2004 for shareholders of record April 15, 2004, as follows:

Class A common—$10 per share
Class B common—$5 per share

Officers' bonuses for the year ended December 31, 2003, were approved for payment March 1, 2004, as follows:

Marie Titard—President $26,000
Lucille Renolds—Vice-President $12,000
Roald Asko—Controller $12,000
Fred Brick—Secretary-Treasurer $9,000

Meeting adjourned 6:30 p.m.

Fred Brick, Secretary

Meeting of September 15, 2004

Ruth Ho, chair of the board, called the meeting to order at 4:00 p.m. The following directors were in attendance:

Margaret Aronson	Claude La Rose
Fred Brick	Lucille Renolds
Henri Chapdelaine	J. T. Schmidt
Ruth Ho	Marie Titard
Homer Jackson	Roald Asko

The minutes of the meeting of February 16, 2004, were read and approved. Marie Titard, president, discussed the improved sales and financial condition for 2004. She was pleased with the results of the catalogue distribution and cost control for the company. No action was taken.

The nominations for officers were made as follows:

President—Marie Titard
Vice-President—Lucille Renolds
Controller—Roald Asko
Secretary-Treasurer—Fred Brick

The nominees were elected by unanimous voice vote.

Salary increases of 6 percent, exclusive of bonuses, were recommended for all officers for 2005. Marie Titard moved that such salary increases be approved, seconded by J. T. Schmidt, and unanimously approved.

	Salary	
	2004	**2005**
Marie Titard, President	$90,000	$95,400
Lucille Renolds, Vice-President	$60,000	$63,600
Roald Asko, Controller	$60,000	$63,600
Fred Brick, Secretary-Treasurer	$40,000	$42,400

Roald Asko moved that the company consider adopting a pension/profit-sharing plan for all employees as a way to provide greater incentive for employees to stay with the company. Considerable discussion ensued. It was agreed without adoption that Asko should discuss the legal and tax implications with lawyer Cecil Makay and a public accounting firm reputed to be knowledgeable about pension and profit-sharing plans, Able and Bark.

Roald Asko discussed the expenditure of $58,000 for acquisition of a new computer for the Kingston office to replace equipment that was purchased in 2003 and has proven ineffective. Asko moved that the transaction be approved, seconded by Jackson, and unanimously adopted. Fred Brick moved that a loan of $36,000, from the Kingston Bank, be approved. The interest is floating at 2 percent above prime. The collateral is to be the new computer equipment being installed in the Kingston office. A chequing account, with a minimum balance of $2,000 at all times until the loan is repaid, must be opened and maintained if the loan is granted. Seconded by La Rose and unanimously approved.

Lucille Renolds, chair of the audit committee, moved that the public accounting firm of Moss & Lawson be selected again for the company's annual audit and related tax work for the year ended December 31, 2005. Seconded by Aronson and unanimously approved.

Meeting adjourned 6:40 p.m.

Fred Brick, Secretary

a. How do you, as the auditor, know that all minutes have been made available to you?

b. Read the minutes of the meetings of February 16 and September 15. Use the following format to list and explain information that is relevant for the 2004 audit:

INFORMATION RELEVANT TO 2004 AUDIT	AUDIT ACTION REQUIRED
1.	
2.	

c. Read the minutes of the meeting of February 16, 2004. Did any of that information pertain to the December 31, 2003, audit? Explain what the auditor should have done during the December 31, 2003, audit with respect to 2004 minutes.

7-21 CA has been the auditor of Niles Ltd., a medium-sized manufacturing company, for just over two years. After CA billed the company for the first year audit, Mr. Hiles, the president, called CA to his office to discuss the audit fee, expressing surprise and concern as to its size. CA pointed out that an audit fee for a first-time audit is always higher than normal and gave Mr. Hiles several examples of the work he had to do that would not be required in subsequent years.

CA reminded Mr. Hiles that they had previously discussed this point in broad terms and Mr. Hiles accepted the explanation. CA suggested that the audit fee for subsequent years could be reduced if the staff of Niles Ltd. were to prepare some of the schedules for CA's working papers. Mr. Hiles agreed with this suggestion.

For the second year audit, Niles Ltd.'s staff prepared several of the schedules, and CA was able to reduce his fee. However, Mr. Hiles, on receiving the billing for the second year's audit fee, was still concerned as to its size.

When discussing the results of the audit with CA, Mr. Hiles expressed surprise as to the quantity of schedules that had to be prepared by his staff, particularly considering the fact that CA and his staff prepared additional working papers themselves. He asked CA what were the purposes of audit working papers. Mr. Hiles also expressed concern about all the information in the working papers on his company being in CA's files and asked who owned the working papers.

Required

a. What are the purposes or functions of audit working papers? (Include the benefits to the client and the auditor.)
b. What records may be included in audit working papers?
c. What factors affect the public accountant's judgment of the type and content of the working papers for a particular engagement?
d. Who owns or has access to audit working papers?
e. What can CA do to improve Mr. Hiles' understanding of the audit fee billings?

(CICA adapted)

ABC Company Inc.
Notes Receivable
31/12/04

Schedule _____ Date
Prepared by __JD__ 21/1/05
Approved by __PP__ 5/2/05

Acct 110

	Apex Co.	Ajax, Inc.	J.J. Co.	P. Smith	Martin-Peterson	Tent Co.
					Maker	
Date						
Made	15/6/03	21/11/03	1/11/03	26/7/04	12/5/03	3/9/04
Due	15/6/05	Demand	$200/mo	$1000/mo	Demand	$400/mo
Face amount	5000<	3591<	13180<	25000<	2100<	12000<
Value of Security	none	none	24000	50000	none	10000
Notes:						
Beg. bal.	4000^{PWP}	3591^{PWP}	12780^{PWP}	—	2100^{PWP}	—
Additions				25000		12000
Payments	>(1000)	>(3591)	>(2400)	>(5000)	>(2100)	>(1600)
End bal.						
① Current	3000 ✓	—	2400 ✓	12000	—	4800
② Long term	—	—	7980	8000	—	5600
③ Total	3000 C	-0-	10380 C	20000 C	-0-	10400 C
	и	и	и	и	и	и
Interest						
Rate	5%	5%	5%	5%	5%	6%
Pd. to date	none	paid	31/12/04	30/9/04	paid	30/11/04
Beg. bal.	104^{PWP}	-0-^{PWP}	24^{PWP}	-0-	-0-^{PWP}	-0-
④ Earned	175 ✓	102 ✓	577 ✓	468 ✓	105 ✓	162 ✓
Received	-0-	>(102)	>(601)	>(200)	>(105)	>(108)
⑤ Accrued at 31/12/04	279	-0-	-0-	268	-0-	54
	и	и	и	и	и	и

✓- Tested
PWP-Agrees with prior year's working papers.
① Total of $22,200 agrees with working trial balance.
② Total of $21,580 agrees with working trial balance.
③ Total of $43,780 agrees with working trial balance.
④ Total of $1,589 agrees with miscellaneous income analysis in operations W/P.
⑤ Total of $601 agrees with A/R lead schedule.

7-22 Do the following with regard to the working paper for ABC Company Inc. shown on page 206.

a. List the deficiencies in the working paper.

b. For each deficiency, state how the working paper could be improved.

c. Prepare an improved working paper using an electronic spreadsheet software program. Include an indication of the audit work done as well as the analysis of the client data.

(Instructor's option)

PROFESSIONAL JUDGMENT PROBLEMS

7-23 The Internet has dramatically increased global e-commerce activities. Both traditional "brick and mortar" businesses and new dot-com businesses use the Internet to meet business objectives. For example, traditional retailer Toys "R" Us, Inc., also sells toys and other products through its web site, which is operated in partnership with Amazon.com.

a. Identify three specific business strategies that are likely reasons why Toys "R" Us is offering products for sale online.

b. Describe three business risks related to Toys "R" Us offering online sales.

c. Discuss possible reasons why Toys "R" Us decided to partner with Amazon.com to handle online sales.

d. Identify possible risks that could lead to material misstatements in the Toys "R" Us financial statements if its business risks related to online sales are not effectively managed.

7-24 You are engaged in the annual audit of the financial statements of Maulack Corp., a medium-sized wholesale company that manufactures light fixtures. The company has 25 shareholders. During your review of the minutes, you observe that the president's salary has been increased substantially over the preceding year by action of the board of directors. His present salary is much greater than salaries paid to presidents of companies of comparable size and is clearly excessive. You determine that the method of computing the president's salary was changed for the year under audit. In previous years, the president's salary was consistently based on sales. In the latest year, however, his salary was based on net income before income taxes. Maulack Corp. is in a cyclical industry and would have had an extremely profitable year except that the increase in the president's salary siphoned off much of the income that would have accrued to the shareholders. The president is a substantial shareholder.

Required

a. What is the implication of this condition on the fair presentation of the financial statements?

b. Discuss your responsibility for disclosing this situation.

c. Discuss the effect, if any, that the situation has on your auditor's opinion as to

(1) the fairness of the presentation of the financial statements.

(2) the consistency of the application of accounting principles.

(AICPA adapted)

CASE

7-25 Grande Stores is a large discount catalogue department store chain. The company has recently expanded from 6 to 43 stores by borrowing from several large financial institutions and from a public offering of common stock. A recent investigation has disclosed that Grande materially overstated net income. This was accomplished by understating accounts payable and recording fictitious supplier credits that further reduced accounts payable. An OSC investigation was critical of the evidence gathered by Grande's audit firm, Montgomery & Ross, in testing accounts payable and the supplier credits.

The following is a description of some of the fictitious supplier credits and unrecorded amounts in accounts payable, as well as the audit procedures.

1. McClure Advertising Credits—Grande had arrangements with some vendors to share the cost of advertising the vendor's product. The arrangements were usually agreed to in advance by the vendor and supported by evidence of the placing of the ad. Grande created a 114-page list of approximately 1,100 vendors, supporting advertising credits of $300,000. Grande's auditors selected a sample of 4 of the 1,100 items for direct confirmation. One item was confirmed by telephone, one traced to cash receipts, one to a vendor credit memo for part of the amount and cash receipts for the rest, and one to a vendor credit memo. Two of the amounts confirmed differed from the amount on the list, but the auditors did not seek an explanation for the differences because the amounts were not material.

The rest of the credits were tested by selecting 20 items (one or two from each page of the list). Twelve of the items were supported by examining the ads placed, and eight were supported by Grande debit memos charging the vendors for the promotional allowances.

2. Springbrook Credits—Grande created 28 fictitious credit memos totalling $257,000 from Springbrook Distributors, the main supplier of health and beauty aids to Grande. Grande's controller initially told the auditor that the credits were for returned goods, then said they were a volume discount, and finally stated they were a payment so that Grande would continue to use Springbrook as a supplier. One of the Montgomery & Ross staff auditors concluded that a $257,000 payment to retain Grande's business was too large to make economic sense.

The credit memos indicated that the credits were for damaged merchandise, volume rebates, and advertising allowances. The audit firm requested a confirmation of the credits. In response, Jon Steiner, the president of Grande Stores, placed a call to Mort Seagal, the president of Springbrook, and handed the phone to the staff auditor. In fact, the call had been placed to an officer of Grande. The Grande officer, posing as Seagal, orally confirmed the credits. Grande refused to allow Montgomery & Ross to obtain written confirmations supporting the credits. Although the staff auditor doubted the validity of the credits, the audit partner, Mark Franklin, accepted the credits based on the credit memoranda, telephone confirmation of the credits, and oral representations of Grande officers.

3. Ridolfi Credits—$130,000 in credits based on 35 credit memoranda from Ridolfi, Inc., were purportedly for the return of overstocked goods from several Grande stores. A Montgomery & Ross staff auditor noted the size of the credit and that the credit memos were dated subsequent to year-end. He further noticed that a sentence on the credit memos from Ridolfi had been obliterated by a felt-tip marker. When held to the light, the accountant could read that the marked-out sentence read, "Do not post until merchandise received." The staff auditor thereafter called Harold Ridolfi, treasurer of Ridolfi, Inc., and was informed that the $130,000 in goods had not been returned and Ridolfi did not owe Grande the money. Steiner advised Franklin, the audit partner, that he had talked to Harold Ridolfi, who claimed the staff auditor had misunderstood him. Steiner told Franklin not to have anyone call Ridolfi to verify the amount because of pending litigation between Grande and Ridolfi, Inc.

4. Accounts Payable Accrual—Montgomery & Ross assigned a senior with experience in the retail area to audit accounts payable. Although Grande had poor internal control, Montgomery & Ross selected a sample of 50 for confirmation of the several thousand vendors who did business with Grande. Twenty-seven responses were received, and 21 were reconciled to Grande's records. These tests indicated an unrecorded liability of approximately $290,000 when projected to the population of accounts payable. However, the investigation disclosed that Grande's president made telephone calls to some suppliers who had received confirmation requests from Montgomery & Ross and told them how to respond to the request.

Montgomery & Ross also performed a purchases cutoff test by vouching accounts payable invoices received for nine weeks after year-end. The purpose of this test was to identify invoices received after year-end that should have been recorded in accounts payable. Thirty percent of the sample ($160,000) was found to relate to the prior year, indicating a potential unrecorded liability of approximately $500,000. The audit firm and Grande eventually agreed on an adjustment to increase accounts payable by $260,000.

Required

Identify deficiencies in the sufficiency and competency of the evidence gathered in the audit of accounts payable of Grande Stores.

(AICPA adapted)

CHAPTER 8

MATERIALITY AND RISK

We have not "talked any numbers" yet. How does the auditor use the financial statements to decide what should be tested? How is information gathered during the planning stage and the client risk profile used to assess risk for each audit? In this chapter, you will be shown the relationship between the financial statements and a key concept that we addressed earlier, materiality. We will also explain the audit risk model and how it is used for planning.

LEARNING OBJECTIVES

After reading this chapter, you should be able to answer the following questions:

1. How is materiality used to assess the amount of work conducted during an audit engagement? What quantitative and qualitative factors does an auditor consider when setting materiality?

2. What is risk in auditing? What are the components of the audit risk model?

3. When assessing inherent risk, what does the auditor consider?

4. How do the components of the audit risk model relate to the amount of evidence that should be collected during an audit? How does materiality fit in with the audit risk model? What happens if risks change once the audit fieldwork has commenced?

EXPLAIN TO ME ONE MORE TIME THAT YOU DID A GOOD JOB, BUT THE COMPANY WENT BROKE

Maxwell Spencer is a senior partner in his firm, and one of his regular duties is to attend the firm's annual training session for newly hired auditors. He loves doing this because it gives him a chance to share his many years of experience with inexperienced people who have bright and receptive minds. He covers several topics formally during the day and then sits around and "shoots the breeze" with participants during the evening hours. Here we listen to what he is saying.

Suppose you are a retired 72-year-old man. You and your wife, Minnie, live on your retirement fund, which you elected to manage yourself, rather than receive income from an annuity. You concluded that your years in business gave you the ability to earn a better return than the annuity would provide.

So when you retired and got your bundle, you called your broker and discussed with him what you should do with it. He told you that the most important thing was to protect your principal, and recommended that you buy bonds. You settled on three issues that your broker and his firm believed were good ones, with solid balance sheets: (1) an entertainment company that was building a series of amusement parks across Canada, (2) a fast-growing alternative energy company, and (3) a major life insurance company. All you have to do is sit back and clip your coupons.

Ah, but the best made plans of mice and men... First, the entertainment company went broke and you can look forward to recovering only a few cents on the dollar over several years. Then, the alternative energy company failed, and you *might* get something back—eventually. Finally, the life insurance company is closed by the government and has to default on all of its outstanding bonds. A recovery plan is initiated, but don't hold your breath. Your best strategy is to apply for a job at McDonald's. They hire older people, don't they?

Now what could the auditors of these three entities ever say to you about how they planned and conducted their audits and decided to issue an unqualified opinion that would justify that opinion in your mind? You don't care about business failure versus audit failure, or risk assessment and reliability of audit evidence, or any of that technical mumbo jumbo. The auditors were supposed to be there for *you* when *you* needed them, and they weren't. And materiality? Anything that would have indicated a problem is material for you.

The message is, folks, that it's a lot easier to sweat over doing a tough audit right than it is to justify your judgments and decisions after it's too late. And God help you if you think that a harmed investor will ever see things from your point of view.

What does Maxwell's story tell you about the relevance of business risk? Think about the responsibilities of the auditor versus the responsibility of management. In the last chapter, we talked about the detailed audit planning process. How do the requirements to consider corporate governance and fraud during the audit process deal with the issues raised by Maxwell?

→8.1 THE IMPORTANCE OF MATERIALITY

The scope paragraph in an auditor's report includes two important phrases that are directly related to materiality and risk. These phrases are emphasized in the following two sentences of a standard scope paragraph.

> I conducted my audit in accordance with Canadian generally accepted auditing standards. Those standards require that I plan and perform an audit to obtain reasonable assurance whether the financial statements are free of material misstatement.

The phrase *obtain reasonable assurance* is intended to inform users that auditors do not guarantee or ensure the fair presentation of the financial statements. The phrase communicates that there is some *risk* that the financial statements are not fairly stated even when the opinion is unqualified.

The phrase *free of material misstatements* is intended to inform users that the auditor's responsibility is limited to *material* financial information. Materiality is important because it is impractical for auditors to provide assurances on immaterial amounts.

Thus, materiality and risk are fundamental concepts that are important to planning the audit and designing the audit approach. This chapter will show how these concepts fit into the planning phase of the audit.

Materiality

MATERIALITY—the magnitude of an omission or misstatement of accounting information that, in the light of surrounding circumstances, makes it *probable* that the judgment of a reasonable person relying on the information would have been changed or influenced by the omission or misstatement

Materiality was first discussed on pages 64–66 as a major consideration in determining the appropriate auditor's report to issue. The concepts of materiality discussed in this chapter are directly related to those in Chapter 3. We suggest you reread pages 64–66 before you study the following material.

Paragraph 5142.04 of the *CICA Assurance Handbook* defines materiality in the following way:

> A misstatement or the aggregate of all misstatements in financial statements is considered to be material if, in the light of surrounding circumstances, it is probable that the decision of a person who is relying on the financial statements, and who has a reasonable knowledge of business and economic activities (the user), would be changed or influenced by such misstatement or the aggregate of all misstatements.

The auditor's responsibility is to determine whether financial statements are materially misstated. If the auditor determines that there is a material misstatement, he or she will bring it to the client's attention so a correction can be made. If the client refuses to correct the statements, a qualified or an adverse opinion must be issued, depending on how material and pervasive the misstatement is. Auditors must, therefore, have a thorough knowledge of the application of materiality.

A careful reading of the *CICA Assurance Handbook* definition reveals the difficulty auditors have in applying materiality in practice. The definition emphasizes the decisions of users who have a reasonable knowledge of business and economic activities and who rely on the statements to make decisions. Auditors, therefore, must have knowledge of the likely users of their clients' statements and the decisions that are being made. For example, if an auditor knows financial statements will be relied on in a buy–sell agreement for the entire business, the amount that the auditor considers material may be smaller than for an otherwise similar audit. In practice, auditors often do not know who the users are or what decisions will be made.

There are four closely related steps in applying materiality. They are shown in Figure 8-1 and discussed in this section. The steps start with setting a preliminary judgment about materiality. Estimation of the amount of misstatements in each segment takes place throughout the audit. The final two steps are done near the end of the audit during the engagement completion phase.

CICA Assurance and Related Services Guideline AuG-41, "Applying the Concept of Materiality," suggests that an auditor be concerned with several levels of misstatement in assessing whether or not there is a material misstatement:

1. **Identified misstatements** (IM)—the actual misstatements discovered in the sample tested; they have not been corrected by management.
2. **Likely misstatements**—the projection of the actual misstatements in the sample to the population; the misstatements have not been corrected by management.
3. The sum of the identified misstatements and likely misstatements in the financial statements is called the *likely aggregate misstatement.*

IDENTIFIED MISSTATEMENTS—the actual misstatements discovered in the sample tested; the misstatements have not been corrected by management

LIKELY MISSTATEMENTS—the projection of the actual misstatements in the sample to the population; the misstatements have not been corrected by management; see also *direct projection method of estimating misstatement*

FIGURE 8-1   The Four Steps in Applying Materiality

4. **Further possible misstatements**—the misstatements over and above the likely aggregate misstatement that result from the imprecision in the sampling process. The sum of likely aggregate misstatement plus further possible misstatements is called the *maximum possible misstatement* (MPM).

The auditor is sure of an identified misstatement because it was determined to be the misstatement in the sample. The projection of that error to the population plus other actual identified misstatements—the likely misstatement—is based on the assumption that the sample is representative of the population. The auditor is fairly certain about the likely aggregate misstatement when he or she is talking to the client about making an adjustment; if the likely aggregate misstatement exceeds materiality, the auditor will require an adjustment.

Further possible misstatement is based on the imprecision in the sampling process. There are two risks: (1) the sample may not be representative, and (2) the auditor may misinterpret evidence.[1] The auditor recognizes that further possible misstatements are possible but not probable. It would not be appropriate to ask the client to make an adjustment for further possible misstatements by virtue of their very definition. The auditor may or may not require an adjustment when the maximum possible misstatement exceeds materiality.

Set Preliminary Judgment About Materiality

Ideally, an auditor decides early in the audit the combined amount of misstatements in the financial statements that would be considered material. Paragraph 5142.02 explains that the auditor considers materiality throughout the audit and states that "at the planning stage, materiality . . . [is] considered in determining the nature, timing and extent of the auditing procedures"; this is the preliminary judgment about materiality in step 1 of Figure 8.1. This judgment need not be quantified but often is. It is called a **preliminary judgment about materiality** because it is a professional judgment and may change during the engagement if circumstances change. Since materiality is defined in the context of users of financial statements, such a change would be unlikely unless additional information regarding users was obtained during the audit.

The preliminary judgment about materiality is thus the maximum amount by which the auditor believes the statements could be misstated and still *not* affect the decisions of reasonable users. This judgment is one of the most important decisions the auditor makes. It requires considerable professional judgment.

The reason for setting a preliminary judgment about materiality is to help the auditor plan the appropriate evidence to accumulate. If the auditor sets a low dollar amount, more evidence is required than for a high amount. Examine again the financial statements of Hillsburg Hardware Limited, on pages 136–151. What do you think is the combined amount of misstatements that would affect decisions of reasonable users? Do you believe a $100 misstatement would affect users' decisions? If so, the amount of evidence required for the audit is likely to be beyond that for which the management of Hillsburg Hardware can pay. Do you believe a $1 million misstatement would be material? Most experienced auditors would say that amount is far too large as a combined materiality amount.

The auditor may change the preliminary judgment about materiality during the audit if, for example, a new user of the financial statements is identified. Whenever that is done, the new judgment is called a **revised judgment about materiality**. Reasons for using a revised judgment can include a change in one of the factors used to determine the preliminary judgment or a decision by the auditor that the preliminary judgment was too small or, more likely, too large.

Preplan

Obtain background
information

Obtain information
about client's
legal obligations

Perform preliminary
analytical procedures

Set materiality, and
assess audit risk
and inherent risk

Understand
internal control
structure and
assess control risk

Develop overall audit
plan and audit program

---

[1]These two risks are called sampling risk and nonsampling risk respectively. They are discussed in detail in Chapter 12.

Factors Affecting Judgment Several factors affect setting a preliminary judgment about materiality for a given set of financial statements. The most important of these are discussed below.

MATERIALITY IS A RELATIVE RATHER THAN AN ABSOLUTE CONCEPT A misstatement of a given magnitude might be material for a small company, whereas the same dollar error could be immaterial for a large one. For example, a total error of $1 million would be extremely material for Hillsburg Hardware Limited because net income before tax is about $5.7 million. It would be immaterial for a company such as IBM, which has total assets and net income of several billion dollars. Hence, it is not possible to establish any dollar-value guidelines for a preliminary judgment about materiality applicable to all audit clients.

BASES ARE NEEDED FOR EVALUATING MATERIALITY Since materiality is relative, it is necessary to have bases for establishing whether misstatements are material. Common bases include the following:

1. 5 percent to 10 percent of net income before taxes. This number can be fairly volatile so most auditors use normalized net income (i.e., net income adjusted for unusual and non-recurring items such as a large inventory writedown) or average net income.
2. 1/2 percent to 5 percent of gross profit.
3. 1/2 percent to 1 percent of total assets.
4. 1/2 percent to 5 percent of shareholders' equity.
5. 1/2 percent to 1 percent of revenue.
6. The weighted average of methods 1 to 5.
7. A reducing percentage of the greater of revenue and assets.
8. 1/2 percent to 2 percent of expenses as suggested by the guideline for non-profit entities.

Current practice also includes exponential models, in which materiality starts low for small bases, rises exponentially, and then levels off. Also, scaled amounts are used that are larger than the percentages shown above. Those methods that use a range of percentages generally suggest that the largest percentage be used for smaller entities and the smallest percentage be used for larger entities. For example, under method 1, 10 percent would be used if the entity was small and 5 percent if it was very large; some percentage between 5 percent and 10 percent would be used for entities between the two extremes.

IMPACT OF QUALITATIVE FACTORS Certain types of misstatements are likely to be more important to users than others, even if the dollar amounts are the same. The auditors cannot plan to detect smaller amounts but must react if they are discovered. For example, amounts involving fraud and other irregularities are usually considered more important than unintentional errors of equal dollar amounts because fraud reflects on the honesty and reliability of the management or other personnel involved. To illustrate, most users would consider an intentional misstatement of inventory as being more important than clerical errors in inventory of the same dollar amount. In addition, while the amount of a fraud may be less than materiality, the impact of fraud on the entity may be much in excess of materiality. For example, assume materiality for an entity with worldwide operations was $200 million. An illegal payment in another country of $25,000 would be less than materiality but could lead, if the illegal payment were to be discovered by the authorities in the other country, to fines or seizure in that country of the entity's assets. The fines or seizures could be many times the amount of the illegal payment, resulting in loss of income or other damages that exceeded materiality.

Illustrative Guidelines The CICA currently does not provide specific materiality guidelines to practitioners. The concern is that such guidelines might be applied without considering all the complexities that should affect the auditor's final decision.

To show the application of materiality, illustrative guidelines are provided. They are intended only to help you better understand the concept of applying materiality in practice. The guidelines are stated in Figure 8-2 in the form of a policy guideline for a public accounting firm.

FIGURE 8-2 | **Illustrative Materiality Guidelines**

MCCUTCHEON & WILKINSON, CHARTERED ACCOUNTANTS
Edmonton, Alberta T6G 1N4
(780) 432-6900

POLICY STATEMENT
No. 32 IC
Title: Materiality Guidelines

Sally J. Wilkinson
Karen McCutcheon

Professional judgment is to be used at all times in setting and applying materiality guidelines. As a general guideline, the following policies are to be applied:

1. The combined total of misstatements in the financial statements exceeding 10 percent is normally considered material. A combined total of less than 5 percent is presumed to be immaterial in the absence of qualitative factors. Combined misstatements between 5 percent and 10 percent require the greatest amount of professional judgment to determine their materiality.
2. The 5 percent to 10 percent must be measured in relation to the appropriate base. Many times there is more than one base to which errors should be compared. The following guides are recommended in selecting the appropriate base:
   a. *Income statement.* Combined misstatements in the income statement should ordinarily be measured at 5 percent to 10 percent of operating income before taxes. A guideline of 5 percent to 10 percent may be inappropriate in a year in which income is unusually large or small. When operating income in a given year is not considered representative, it is desirable to substitute as a base a more representative income measure, such as normalized net income before taxes or average operating income for a three-year period.
   In the case of clients who operate in industries where operating income before taxes is not considered to be a useful base, ½ percent to 1 percent of revenue will be used as a guideline.
   b. *Balance sheet.* Combined misstatements in the balance sheet should originally be evaluated for total assets. For total assets, the guideline should be between ½ and 1 percent, applied in the same way as for the income statement. An alternative is to use ½ percent to 5 percent of shareholders' equity.
3. Qualitative factors should be carefully evaluated on all audits. In many instances they are more important than the guidelines applied to the income statement and balance sheet. The intended uses of the financial statements and the nature of the information on the statements, including footnotes, must be carefully evaluated.
4. If the guideline for the income statement is less than those selected for the balance sheet, the lesser amount should be used as a guideline for all misstatements that affect operating income before taxes. Misstatements such as misclassification errors would be evaluated using the greater amount.

Application to Hillsburg Hardware Limited Using the illustrative guidelines for McCutcheon & Wilkinson in Figure 8-2, it is now possible to decide on a preliminary judgment about materiality for Hillsburg Hardware Limited. The guidelines are as follows:

	Preliminary Judgment About Materiality			
	Minimum		Maximum	
	Percentage	Dollar Amount (in thousands)	Percentage	Dollar Amount (in thousands)
Net income before taxes	5	248	10	496
Gross profit	1/2	199	5	1,992
Total assets	1/2	307	1	614
Shareholders' equity	1/2	112	5	1,123
Revenue (net sales)	1/2	715	1	1,431

Assuming the auditor for Hillsburg Hardware decided that the general guidelines are reasonable, the first step would be to evaluate whether any qualitative factors significantly affect the materiality judgment. If not, considering the income statement base first, the auditor must decide that if combined misstatements on the income statement were less than $248,000, the statements would be considered fairly stated. If the combined misstatements exceeded $496,000, the statements would not be considered fairly stated. If the misstatements were between $248,000 and $496,000, a more careful consideration of all facts would be required. The auditor then applies the same process to the other three bases. Given the suggested guidelines calculated above and the fact that Hillsburg Hardware is a public company with a limited number of shareholders, the auditor would probably decide to use the larger of the bases, $496,000, as the preliminary judgment about materiality. Gross profit is also a base that fluctuates less from year to year than net income since companies may have fluctuating income levels.

The preliminary judgment about materiality should be adjusted for the effect of *net anticipated* misstatements to determine materiality available for unanticipated misstatements.

The illustration that follows is an example of adjusting for the effect of net anticipated misstatements:

Preliminary judgment about materiality, based on net income before extraordinary items		$496,000
Less		
Anticipated misstatements from specific tests	$50,000	
Carry forward misstatements from the previous year	80,000	
Anticipated client corrections	(75,000)	55,000
Materiality available for unanticipated misstatements		$441,000

The auditor, in the above example, is simply reducing the preliminary judgment of $496,000 for net anticipated misstatements of $55,000 to determine that $441,000 will be available for unanticipated misstatements. A useful analogy would be that of an individual going on a date who has $60 for dinner and a show but needs $10 for cab fare at the end of the evening. The amount available for spending for the evening is $50, not $60. Similarly, the amount available for unanticipated misstatements is really $441,000, not $496,000.

Some auditors allocate materiality to segments once they have determined materiality available for unanticipated misstatements. They use the amounts allocated to determine sample sizes and the amount of testing required. However, most auditors use total materiality available for unanticipated misstatements in audit planning on the grounds that the auditor is concerned about the aggregate misstatement in the financial statements as a whole and not in the misstatement in a particular account balance.

Estimate Misstatement and Compare

The first step in applying materiality involves planning, whereas the last three (steps 2, 3, and 4 in Figure 8-1) result from performing audit tests. The last three steps are discussed in greater detail in later chapters.

When the auditor performs audit procedures for each segment of the audit, a worksheet is kept of all misstatements found. For example, assume the auditor finds six client errors in a sample of 200 in testing inventory costs (identified misstatement). These misstatements are used to estimate the *total* misstatements in inventory (step 2). The total is referred to as an "estimate" or often a "projection" because only a sample, rather than the entire population, was audited. Estimation of projected misstatement is required by Section 5142. The projected misstatement amounts (likely misstatements) for each account are combined on the worksheet (step 3), and then the combined misstatement (likely aggregate misstatement) is compared to materiality (step 4).

Table 8-1 is used to illustrate the last three steps in applying materiality. For simplicity, only three accounts are included and the calculation of likely misstatements for accounts receivable and for inventory are shown. The preliminary judgment about materiality is $50,000. The likely misstatements are calculated based on actual audit tests. Assume, for example, that in auditing inventory, the auditor found $3,500 of net overstatement errors in a sample of $50,000 of the total population of $450,000. One way to calculate the estimate of the misstatements is to make a **direct projection** from the sample to the population and add

DIRECT PROJECTION METHOD OF ESTIMATING MISSTATEMENT—net misstatements in the sample, divided by the total sampled, multiplied by the total recorded population value; see also *likely misstatements*

SAMPLING ERROR—error that results because the auditor has sampled only a portion of the population

an estimate for **sampling error** (further possible misstatements). The calculation of the direct projection (likely misstatement) is:

$$\frac{\text{Net misstatements in the sample (\$3,500)}}{\text{Total sampled (\$50,000)}} \times \frac{\text{Total recorded population value (\$450,000)}}{} = \frac{\text{Direct projection estimate (\$31,500)}}{}$$

The estimate for sampling error results because the auditor has sampled only a portion of the population (this is discussed in detail in Chapters 12, 13, and 14). It is the amount by which a projected likely misstatement amount could be different from an actual (and unknown) total as a result of the sample not being representative. In this simplified example, the estimate for sampling error is assumed to be 50 percent of the direct projection of the misstatement amounts for the accounts where sampling was used (accounts receivable and inventory).

In combining the misstatements in Table 8-1, observe that the likely misstatements for the three accounts add to $43,500. The total sampling error (further possible misstatements) quite often is different from the sum of the sampling errors since varying levels of certainty must be incorporated and the total is usually calculated as a numeric range. It is shown here, adding up to the sum of the individual sampling errors for convenience. Sampling error represents the maximum error in account details not audited.

It is unlikely that this maximum error amount would exist in all accounts subjected to sampling. Thus, sampling methodology provides for determining a combined sampling error that takes this into consideration. Again, this is discussed in detail in Chapters 12, 13 and 14.

Table 8-1 shows that the maximum possible misstatement for the three accounts of $65,250 exceeds the preliminary judgment about materiality of $50,000. Furthermore, the major area of difficulty is inventory, where the maximum possible misstatement is $47,250. Because the estimated maximum possible misstatement exceeds the preliminary judgment, the financial statements are not acceptable. The auditor can either determine whether the estimated aggregate misstatement actually exceeds $50,000 by performing additional audit procedures or require the client to make an adjustment for likely misstatements. Assuming additional audit procedures are performed, they would be concentrated in the inventory area.

If the estimated maximum possible misstatement for inventory had been $24,000 ($16,000 plus $8,000 sampling error), the auditor probably would not need to expand audit tests, since the total maximum possible misstatement would be less ($18,000 + $24,000 = $42,000) than the $50,000 preliminary judgment. It is likely that the auditor would have accepted the balances in the three accounts.

TABLE 8-1	Illustration of Comparison of Maximum Possible Misstatement to Preliminary Judgment About Materiality

| | Maximum Possible Misstatement | | |
Account	Likely Misstatement	Sampling Error	Total
Cash	$ 0	N/A	$ 0
Accounts receivable	$12,000	$ 6,000[1]	$18,000
Inventory	$31,500	$15,750[2]	$47,250
Total estimated misstatement amount	$43,500	$21,750	$65,250
Preliminary judgment about materiality			$50,000

N/A = Not applicable; cash audited 100%. (1) 12,000 × 50% (assumed) (2) 31,500 × 50% (assumed)

8.2   RISK IN AUDITING AND THE AUDIT RISK MODEL

Risk

Risk in auditing means that the auditor accepts some level of uncertainty in performing the audit function. The auditor recognizes, for example, that there is uncertainty about the appropriateness of evidence, uncertainty about the effectiveness of a client's internal control, and uncertainty as to whether the financial statements are fairly stated when the audit is completed.

An effective auditor recognizes that risks exist and deals with those risks in an appropriate manner. Most risks that auditors encounter are difficult to measure and require careful thought for an appropriate response. For example, assume the auditor determines that the client's industry is undergoing significant technological changes, which affect both the client and the client's customers. This change may affect the obsolescence of the client's inventory, collectibility of accounts receivable, and perhaps even the ability of the client's business to continue. Responding to these risks properly is essential to achieving a quality audit.

The remainder of this chapter deals mostly with the risks that affect planning the engagement to determine the appropriate evidence to accumulate by applying the CICA's audit risk model. It concludes by showing the relationship between materiality and risk.

Illustration Concerning Risks and Evidence Before discussing the audit risk model, an illustration for a hypothetical company is provided in Table 8-2 as a frame of reference for the discussion. The illustration shows that the auditor has decided on a "medium" willingness to accept the risk that material misstatements exist after the audit is complete for all five cycles (A). It is common for auditors to want an equal likelihood of misstatements for each cycle after the audit is finished to permit the issuance of an unqualified opinion. Next, the table shows that there are differences among cycles in the frequency and size of expected misstatements (B). For example, there are almost no misstatements expected in the payroll and personnel cycle, but many in inventory and warehousing. The reason may be that the payroll transactions are highly routine, whereas there may be considerable complexities in recording inventory. Similarly, internal control is believed to differ in effectiveness among the five cycles (C). For example, internal controls in payroll and personnel are considered highly effective, whereas those in inventory and warehousing are considered ineffective.

The previous considerations (A, B, C) affect the auditor's decision about the appropriate extent of evidence to accumulate (D). For example, because the auditor expects few misstatements in payroll and personnel (B) and internal control is effective (C), the auditor plans for less evidence collection in the payroll and personnel cycle (D) than for inventory and warehousing. Recall that the auditor has the same (medium) level of willingness to accept material misstatements after the audit is finished for all five cycles (A), but a different extent of evidence is needed for various cycles. The difference is caused by differences in the auditor's expectations of misstatements and assessment of internal control.

Audit Approach The overall audit approach designed by most firms is strategic—overview tactical plans are developed that take into account the client's objectives and strategies considering the broader business environment within which the client operates. The previous chapter described the many steps involved in the audit planning process to help assess risks of client business failure and how well the business organization manages its own processes. This planning process helps the auditor gather the information needed to formulate conclusions for the audit risk model, which we discuss next. Then, the auditor decides upon a strategic approach for each cycle to plan the evidence mix. Throughout this process, the audit staff meet on an as needed basis, with full team meetings held at key decision points throughout the engagement.

Audit Risk Model for Planning

The primary way that auditors deal with risk in planning audit evidence is through the application of the **audit risk model**. The source of the audit risk model is the professional literature in the *CICA Assurance Handbook* in Section 5095, "Reasonable Assurance and

RISK—the acceptance by auditors that there is some level of uncertainty in performing the audit function

AUDIT RISK MODEL—a formal model reflecting the relationships among audit risk (*AR*), inherent risk (*IR*), control risk (*CR*), and planned detection risk (*PDR*); $AR = IR \times CR \times PDR$

TABLE 8-2 Illustration of Differing Evidence Among Cycles

	Sales and Collection Cycle	Acquisition and Payment Cycle	Payroll and Personnel Cycle	Inventory and Warehousing Cycle	Capital Acquisition and Repayment Cycle
A Auditor's willingness to permit material misstatements to exist after completing the audit (audit risk)	Low willingness (medium)	Low willingness (medium)	Low willingness (medium)	Low willingness (medium)	Low willingness (medium)
B Auditor's assessment of expectation of material misstatement before considering internal control (inherent risk)	Expect some misstatements (medium)	Expect many misstatements (high)	Expect few misstatements (low)	Expect many misstatements (high)	Expect few misstatements (low)
C Auditor's assessment of effectiveness of internal control to prevent or detect material misstatements (control risk)	Medium effectiveness (medium)	High effectiveness (low)	High effectiveness (low)	Low effectiveness (high)	Medium effectiveness (medium)
D Extent of evidence the auditor plans to accumulate (detection risk)	Medium level (medium)	Medium level (medium)	Low level (high)	High level (low)	Medium level (medium)

Audit Risk." A thorough understanding of the model is essential to effective auditing and to the study of the remaining chapters of this book.

The audit risk model is used primarily for planning purposes in deciding how much evidence to accumulate in each cycle. It is usually stated as follows: $AR = IR \times CR \times PDR$ where AR = audit risk, IR = inherent risk, CR = control risk, PDR = planned detection risk (Section 5095 refers to this as detection risk).

Audit Risk As stated in Chapter 7, **audit risk** is a measure of how willing the auditor is to accept that the financial statements may be materially misstated after the audit is completed and an unqualified opinion has been reached.[2] When the auditor decides on a lower audit risk, it means the auditor wants a higher level of assurance. Auditors sometimes refer to the terms "**audit assurance**," "overall assurance," or "level of assurance" instead of "audit risk." Audit assurance or any of the equivalent terms is the complement of audit risk, that is, one minus audit risk. For example, audit risk of 2 percent is the same as audit assurance of 98 percent. In other words, audit risk of 2 percent means the auditor is willing to accept a 2 percent risk that there are material errors in the financial statements. At the same time, a 98 percent level of assurance has been obtained that the financial statements are free of material errors. Zero risk would be certainty, and a 100 percent risk would be complete uncertainty. Complete assurance (zero risk) of the accuracy of financial statements is not economically practical. It has already been established in Chapter 5 that the auditor cannot guarantee the complete absence of material misstatements.

---

[2] "The Parable of Bert and Ernie" by Stephen Aldersley in *CAmagazine* (March 1988), pp. 60–61, illustrates two different audit situations where the risk of misstatements occurring is similar but where the consequences of failing to detect the misstatements are quite different. This is a classic tale. The author tells you that if you make a mistake with the small business, you must deal with Bert, who studied under Boris Karloff. "He's short, carries a long, mean-looking whip and wears boots with sharp studs ... but ... you can usually buy him a beer and convince him to ignore it." However, if you make the same kind of mistake with the big business, you have to deal with Ernie, "who wields an axe." But first, Ernie will call a public meeting, tell everyone what a lousy job you did, and that he'll "have your head for it." Both Bert and Ernie will end up going away as long as you have met "the Standard," but if you haven't, "you might wish Ernie had been able to use his equipment after all." It is an excellent discussion of audit risk in the context of a large versus small business.

Using the audit risk model, there is a direct relationship between audit risk and planned detection risk, and an inverse relationship between audit risk and planned evidence. For example, as the level of audit risk decreases (i.e., the auditor wants *more assurance*), more evidence needs to be gathered (planned detection risk is reduced, and *more assurance* is needed from audit evidence). As stated in Chapter 7, auditors also often assign more experienced staff or have an additional independent review of the working papers for a client with lower audit risk.

Inherent Risk As stated in Chapter 7, **inherent risk** is a measure of the auditor's assessment of the likelihood that a material misstatement might occur in the first place, that is, before considering the effectiveness of internal accounting controls. Inherent risk is the susceptibility of the financial statements to material misstatement, assuming no internal controls. If the auditor concludes that there is a high likelihood of misstatement, ignoring internal controls, the auditor would conclude that inherent risk is high. Internal controls are ignored in setting inherent risk because they are considered separately in the audit risk model as control risk. In Table 8-2, inherent risk (B) has been assessed high for inventory and lower for payroll and personnel and capital acquisitions and repayments. The assessment was likely based on discussions with management, knowledge of the company, and results in prior year audits. For example, there may be thousands of inventory transactions of many different types, with prior year files showing many errors. Payroll, personnel, and capital acquisition transactions could occur less frequently and be more frequently checked by outside parties (e.g., banks may process payroll and contracts may be reviewed externally for capital acquisitions). Factors to be examined when assessing inherent risk are discussed commencing on page 225. Inherent risk is normally assessed at the account balance assertion level.

Control Risk **Control risk** is a measure of the auditor's assessment of the likelihood that misstatements exceeding a tolerable amount in a segment will not be prevented or detected by the client's internal control. Control risk represents (1) an assessment of whether a client's internal control is effective for preventing or detecting misstatements and (2) the auditor's intention to rely on internal controls and thus assign a value to control risk below maximum (100 percent) as part of the audit plan. For example, assume the auditor concludes that internal control is completely ineffective to prevent or detect misstatements. This is the likely conclusion for inventory and warehousing in Table 8-2 (C). The auditor would therefore assign 100 percent risk factor to control risk. The more effective internal control, the lower the risk factor that *could* be assigned to control risk.

Before auditors can use a control risk of less than 100 percent, they must do three things: obtain an understanding of the client's internal control, evaluate how well it should function based on the understanding, and test internal control for effectiveness. The first of these is the *understanding* requirement that relates to all audits. The latter two are the *assessment of control risk* steps that are required when the auditor *chooses* to assess control risk at a level below maximum.

Understanding the corporate governance process, understanding internal control, assessing control risk, and their impact on evidence requirements are so important that the entire next chapter is devoted to that topic. However, it should be noted that the auditor can choose to place no reliance on internal controls after an understanding has been obtained. Then control risk must be set at 100 percent regardless of the actual effectiveness of the underlying internal control. Use of the audit risk model in this circumstance then causes the auditor to control audit risk entirely through a low level of planned detection risk (assuming inherent risk is high).

Planned Detection Risk **Planned detection risk** is a measure of the risk that audit evidence for a segment will fail to detect material misstatements, should such misstatements exist. There are two key points about planned detection risk. First, it is dependent on the other three factors in the model. Planned detection risk will change only if the auditor changes one of the other factors. Second, it determines the amount of evidence the auditor plans to accumulate inversely with the size of planned detection risk. Using the complement of

INHERENT RISK—a measure of the auditor's assessment of the likelihood that there are material misstatements in a segment before considering the effectiveness of internal controls

CONTROL RISK—a measure of the auditor's assessment of the likelihood that misstatements exceeding materiality in a segment will not be prevented or detected by the client's internal controls

PLANNED DETECTION RISK—a measure of the risk that audit evidence for a segment will fail to detect misstatements exceeding materiality, should such misstatements exist; $PDR = AR / (IR \times CR)$

detection risk, at 5 percent detection risk, the auditor needs to provide 95 percent assurance that the evidence collected will detect material errors. If planned detection risk is reduced to 2 percent, the auditor needs to accumulate more evidence (to obtain 98 percent assurance that evidence collected will detect material errors). For example, in Table 8-2 (D), planned detection risk is low for inventory and warehousing, which causes planned evidence to be high. The opposite is true for payroll and personnel, which has high planned detection risk, thus requiring less evidence gathering.

A numerical example is provided to solve for detection risk, even though it is not practical in practice to measure as precisely as these numbers imply. The numbers used are for the inventory and warehousing cycle in Table 8-2.

$$AR = 3.5\% \quad \text{(medium risk to be accepted)}$$
$$IR = 100\% \quad \text{(high risk of errors expected)}$$
$$CR = 100\% \quad \text{(low effectiveness of internal controls)}$$

$$AR = IR \times CR \times PDR \text{ or}$$

$$PDR = \frac{AR}{(IR \times CR)}$$

$$PDR = \frac{0.035}{1} \times 1 = 0.035 \text{ or } 3.5\%$$

(Auditor plans 3.5 percent risk of not detecting errors and seeks 96.5 percent assurance from substantive tests, as discussed in Chapter 14.)

Figure 8-3 shows how these audit risk model components interact. The inventory and warehousing cycle may have material errors present. This is represented by the material errors falling into the control risk tray, which has some holes in it and thus acts as a sieve. There may not be any material errors or there may be many. Since inherent risk for the inventory and warehousing cycle has been assessed as high, there are many material errors falling into the control risk tray, and inherent risk has been set at 100 percent. The purpose of internal controls is to prevent, detect, and correct material errors in the financial statements. The auditor has decided that in the inventory and warehousing cycle, there is low effectiveness in internal controls, so the control risk tray has holes in it, letting material errors escape, and thus control risk has been set at 100 percent (no reliance). For the auditor to obtain reasonable assurance that the financial statements are free of material error, these errors must be caught in the detection risk bowl, so that they can be brought to the attention of management for correction. The bowl is large enough so that 96.5 percent assurance of catching these errors through evidence gathering will occur (3.5 percent detection risk). When inherent risk is set at maximum and there is no reliance on internal controls (also set at maximum), then planned detection risk is equal to audit risk, here a 3.5 percent risk that misstatements will not be detected.

If control risk had been 0.50 instead of 1.0, planned detection risk would be 0.07 and planned evidence could therefore be reduced. Using Figure 8-3, this means that there would be fewer holes in the control risk tray (more errors would be detected by internal controls), and the size of the detection risk bowl could be smaller (less evidence would be required).

Relationships Between Audit Risk Model Components The audit risk desired affects the amount of evidence to be gathered. As audit risk decreases, assurance required increases and more evidence must be gathered, making the audit more costly. Think in terms of the number of audits conducted by all public accountants. What portion of these audits could include material misstatements without having an adverse effect on society? More undetected material misstatements could result in the audit being perceived as having less value.

Inherent risk and planned detection risk have an inverse relationship. Using Figure 8-3, we can see that when more material errors are likely to exist (inherent risk assessed as higher), if control risk stays the same, the detection risk bowl must be larger (more evidence to be gathered and lower detection risk).

Similarly, if inherent risk stays constant but control risk is higher (there are more holes in the control risk tray, letting more material errors through), then we again have to increase

FIGURE 8-3   Audit Risk Model Components

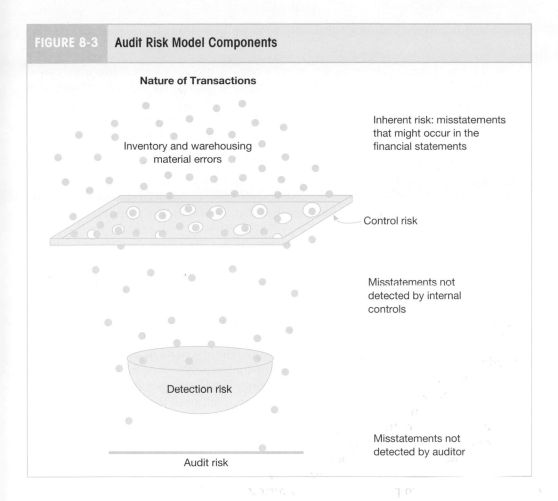

the size of our detection risk bowl (more evidence gathering needed and smaller detection risk). There is also an inverse relationship between the two types of risk.

Changing Audit Risk for Business Risk **Business risk** applies to both the PA firm and to clients. With respect to a client, Section 5141.030 explains how business risk arises from "significant conditions, events, circumstances, actions or inactions that could adversely affect the entity's ability to achieve its objectives and execute its strategies, or through the setting of inappropriate objectives and strategies." If a client decides to enter into a new product line that does poorly, and does not recognize that the line needs to be disposed of, such a decision could affect the entity's ability to continue as a going concern. The auditor assesses the entity's strategies as part of the development of a client risk profile. Business risk is also considered when setting audit risk and materiality.

With respect to the audit firm, if the audit firm acquires clients that do not pay their bills, are dishonest and result in significant litigation against the firm, then the PA firm itself will perhaps have a poor reputation and have going concern problems due to poor strategic decisions. The way firms handle business risk is through client continuance or acceptance reviews and with techniques such as quality assurance during the audit.

Research has indicated that several factors affect business risk. Only three of those are discussed here: the degree to which external users rely on the statements, the likelihood that a client will have financial difficulties after the auditor's report is issued, and the integrity of management. These factors also affect audit risk.

THE DEGREE TO WHICH EXTERNAL USERS RELY ON THE STATEMENTS When external users place heavy reliance on the financial statements, it is appropriate that audit risk be decreased. When the statements are heavily relied on, a great social harm could result if a material misstatement were to remain undetected in the financial statements. The cost of additional evidence can be more easily justified when the loss to users from material misstatements is substantial.

BUSINESS RISK—risk that the auditor or audit firm will suffer harm because of a client relationship, even though the auditor's report rendered for the client was correct

Several factors are good indicators of the degree to which statements are relied on by external users:

- *Client's size.* Generally speaking, the larger a client's operations, the more widely used the statements will be. The client's size, measured by total assets or total revenues, will have an effect on audit risk.
- *Distribution of ownership.* The statements of publicly held corporations are normally relied on by many more users than those of private or closely held corporations. For these companies, the interested parties include the provincial securities administrators such as the Alberta Securities Commission, perhaps even the SEC, financial analysts, creditors, suppliers, the government, and the general public. The availability of financial statements on the Internet allows for easy downloading of financial statement information for publicly traded companies. Therefore, distribution of these financial statements is potentially increasing due to technology.
- *Nature and amount of liabilities.* When statements include a large number of liabilities, they are more likely to be used extensively by actual and potential creditors than when there are few liabilities.

THE LIKELIHOOD THAT A CLIENT WILL HAVE FINANCIAL DIFFICULTIES AFTER THE AUDITOR'S REPORT IS ISSUED If a client is forced to file for bankruptcy or suffers a significant loss after completion of the audit, there is a greater chance of the auditor's being required to defend the quality of the audit than if the client were under no financial strain. The loss could be due to fraud, the loss of a major customer, or a computer disaster that cripples the company for a period of time. There is a natural tendency for those who lose money in a bankruptcy or because of a stock price reversal to file suit against the auditor. This can result from the honest belief that the auditor failed to conduct an adequate audit or from the users' desire to recover part of their loss regardless of the adequacy of the audit work.

In situations in which the auditor believes the chance of financial failure or loss is high, and there is a corresponding increase in business risk for the auditor, the level of audit risk should be reduced. If a subsequent challenge does occur, the auditor will then be in a better position to defend the audit results successfully. The total audit evidence and costs will increase, but this is justifiable because of the additional risk of lawsuits the auditor faces.

It is difficult for an auditor to predict financial failure before it occurs, but certain factors are good indicators of its increased probability:

- *Liquidity position.* If a client is constantly short of cash and working capital, it indicates a future problem in paying bills. The auditor must assess the likelihood and significance of a weak liquidity position getting worse.
- *Profits (losses) in previous years.* When a company has rapidly declining profits or increasing losses for several years, the auditor should recognize the future solvency problems the client is likely to encounter. It is also important to consider the changing profits relative to the balance remaining in retained earnings.
- *Method of financing growth.* The more a client relies on debt as a means of financing, the greater the risk of financial difficulty if the client's operations become less successful. It is also important to evaluate whether permanent assets are being financed with short-term or long-term loans. Large amounts of required cash outflows during a short period of time can force a company into bankruptcy.
- *Nature of the client's operations.* Certain types of businesses are inherently riskier than others. For example, other things being equal, there is a much greater likelihood of bankruptcy of a start-up technology company dependent on one product than a diversified food manufacturer.
- *Extent of reliance upon technology and quality of support strategies.* The more a client relies upon technology, the more important it is that the company have an adequate backup and disaster recovery plan in the event of hardware or software failure. Support strategies, such as maintenance in the event of minor hardware or software problems, need to be high quality so that relatively minor problems, such as failure in a communications processor, do not cause operational shut downs. Appendix C describes the phases of a typical disaster recovery plan.

- *Competence of management.* Competent management is constantly alert for potential financing difficulties and modifies its operating methods to minimize the effects of short-run problems. The ability of management must be assessed as a part of the evaluation of the likelihood of bankruptcy.

A major insurance company located in downtown Toronto on Bay Street occupied several floors of a high-rise building. On the tenth floor, there was a data centre housing mainframe computers, disk drives, printers, and telecommunications equipment for communicating with hundreds of insurance brokers and insurance offices. The data centre was physically segregated, with an automatic fire extinguishing system. On the ninth floor, immediately below the data centre, was an open area with microcomputers used by the actuaries (individuals who analyze mortality rates and thus determine how much the company should charge for life insurance). On the sixth floor was a tape vault, housing backup data and programs from the data centre.

On a Friday prior to a long weekend, the ninth floor open area caught fire. It was a massive fire, blackening the entire area and blowing out windows. Smoke filtered up to the tenth floor, where it seeped through holes in the data centre's walls (caused by previous movement of office partitions that had been attached to the data centre's walls). The operators (who had not been adequately trained) panicked and did not push the 15-cm wide red button beside the exit door that would have automatically shut off the power to all systems. Instead, they rapidly left the room. Although the fire extinguishing system was activated, smoke continued to seep in, and half of the disk drives crashed.

Large volumes of water poured onto the ninth floor, hitting the top of the tape vault and cracking it. (The tape vault was located in the building's "water well," the area to which water was supposed to flow so that it did not filter through the floors and ceilings of multiple floors.) Luckily, only about 5 cm of water settled in the bottom of the tape vault.

Saturday morning, a human chain of 300 people transferred backup media to Bay Street, where transport trucks loaded with mainframe computing equipment and peripherals waited, hooked up to the telephone cables at the front of the building. On Tuesday morning, the mainframe systems were up and running, as if nothing had happened to the tenth floor. The ninth floor actuaries were not so lucky. All of their backup media was kept in their desks on the ninth floor and had been destroyed.

However, one of the actuaries had gone on holiday one week prior to the fire. Thinking that he would do some work at home, he had taken a copy of the system with him when he left. Needless to say, he was a hero when he returned a week after the fire.

MANAGEMENT'S INTEGRITY As discussed in Chapter 7, as a part of new client investigation and continuing client evaluation, if a client has questionable integrity, the auditor is likely to assess audit risk lower or not accept or even resign from the audit. Companies with low integrity often conduct their business affairs in a manner that results in conflicts with their shareholders, regulators, and customers. These conflicts in turn often reflect on the users' perceived quality of the audit and can result in lawsuits and other disagreements. An obvious example of a situation in which management's integrity is questionable is prior criminal conviction of a key member of management. Other examples of questionable integrity might include frequent disagreements with previous auditors, the Canada Revenue Agency, the provincial securities commission, or the stock exchange where the company is listed. Frequent turnover of key financial and internal audit personnel and ongoing conflicts with labour unions and employees may also indicate integrity problems.

To assess audit risk, the auditor must first assess each of the factors affecting audit risk. Table 8-3 illustrates the methods used by auditors to assess each of the three factors already discussed. It is easy to see after examining Table 8-3 that the assessment of each of the factors is highly subjective, which means that the overall assessment is also highly subjective. A typical evaluation of audit risk is high, medium, or low, where a low audit risk assessment means a "risky" client requiring more extensive evidence, assignment of more experienced personnel, and/or a more extensive review of working papers. As the audit progresses, additional information about the client is obtained and audit risk may be modified.

Henry Rinsk, of Links, Rinsk & Rodman, Public Accountants, is the partner responsible for the audit of Hungry Food Restaurants Ltd., a chain of nine Manitoba family restaurants. The firm has audited Hungry Food for ten years and has always found management competent, cooperative, and easy to deal with. Hungry Food is family-owned with a business succession plan in place, profitable and liquid, and with little debt. Management has a reputation in the community for high integrity and good relationships with employees, customers, and suppliers.

After meeting with the other partners as part of the firm's annual client continuation meeting, Henry recommends that audit risk for Hungry Food be assessed as high. For Links, Rinsk & Rodman, this means no expansion of evidence, a "standard" review of working papers, and a "standard" assignment of personnel to the engagement.

→ ## 8.3 INHERENT RISK ASSESSMENT

Inherent Risk

The inclusion of inherent risk in the audit risk model is one of the most important concepts in auditing. It implies that auditors should attempt to predict where misstatements are most and least likely in the financial statement segments. This information affects the total amount of evidence the auditor is required to accumulate and influences how the auditor's efforts to gather the evidence are allocated among the segments of the audit.

There is always some risk that the client has made misstatements that are individually or collectively large enough to make the financial statements misleading. The misstatements can be intentional or unintentional, and they can affect the dollar balance in accounts or disclosure. Inherent risk can be low in some instances and extremely high in others.

The audit risk model shows the common impact that inherent and control risks have on detection risk. For example, an inherent risk of 40 percent and a control risk of 60 percent affect detection risk and planned evidence the same as an inherent risk of 60 percent and a control risk of 40 percent. In both cases, multiplying *IR* by *CR* results in a denominator in

TABLE 8-3	Methods Practitioners Use to Assess Audit Risk and Business Risk
Factors	**Methods Used by Practitioners to Assess Audit Risk and Business Risk**
External users' reliance on financial statements	• Examine the financial statements, including footnotes. • Read minutes of board of directors' meetings to determine future plans. • Examine filings with the provincial securities commission for a publicly held company. • Discuss financing plans with management.
Likelihood of financial difficulties	• Analyze the financial statements for financial difficulties using ratios and other analytical procedures. • Examine historical and projected cash flow statements for the nature of cash inflows and outflows. • Assess adequacy of disaster recovery plans.
Management integrity	• Follow the procedures discussed in Chapter 7 for client acceptance and continuance.

the audit risk model of 24 percent. The combination of inherent risk and control risk can be thought of as the *expectation of misstatements after considering the effect of internal controls.* Inherent risk is the expectation of misstatements before considering the effect of internal controls.

At the start of an audit, there is not much that can be done about changing inherent risk. Instead, the auditor must *assess the factors* that make up the risk and *modify audit evidence* to take them into consideration. The auditor should consider several major factors when assessing inherent risk:

- Nature of the client's business, including the nature of the client's products and services
- Nature of data processing systems and extent of use of data communications (see also Appendix D)
- Integrity of management
- Client motivation
- Results of previous audits
- Initial versus repeat engagement
- Related parties
- Nonroutine transactions
- Judgment required to record account balances and transactions correctly
- Assets that are susceptible to misappropriation
- Makeup of the population

Nature of the Client's Business Inherent risk for certain accounts is affected by the nature of the client's business. For example, there is a greater likelihood of obsolete inventory for an electronics manufacturer than for a steel fabricator. Similarly, loans receivable for a small loan company that makes unsecured loans are less likely to be collectible than those of a bank that makes only secured loans. Inherent risk is most likely to vary from business to business for accounts such as inventory, accounts and loans receivable, and property, plant, and equipment. The nature of the client's business should have little or no effect on inherent risk for accounts such as cash, notes, and mortgages payable. Information gained while obtaining knowledge about the client's industry and business, as discussed in Chapter 7, is useful for assessing this factor.

Focus Box 8-3

WHERE'S MY MONEY?

In Canada, as in other parts of the world, many people rely on debit card or automated banking services to pay for their purchases. Online payment systems such as PayPal are used to pay for electronic purchases. Many people carry only small amounts of cash.

On Saturday, October 27, 2001, for about 12 hours, starting at 11:00 A.M. Eastern Standard Time, there was a hardware failure at TD Canada Trust. Customers were unable to use online banking services (automated banking machines, Internet banking, and telephone banking). On November 10, 2004, Scotiabank services were similarly unavailable for up to two and a half hours. In October 2004, the PayPal online payment system was sporadically unavailable for almost a whole week.

Imagine how you would feel if you were standing in a grocery line and your debit card was refused and you had no cash to take your groceries home? Or if you were a merchant selling goods at an online auction and could not collect any of your cash from PayPal for a week, causing you to be late for supplier payments?

Hardware or software failures can cause a company to lose customers, as well as make it subject to lawsuits and other costs. The complexity of hardware and software systems are considered as part of inherent risks in the audit risk model—complex systems are harder to keep up and running (affecting the going concern concept, linked to audit risk) and are more likely to result in human errors during set up and maintenance (increasing inherent risks and control risks).

Sources: 1. *The Globe and Mail*, Monday, October 29, 2001, *[A TD Canada Trust advertisement]*, p. A15. 2. Flavelle, Dana, 2004, "Scotia banking machines hit by computer glitch," November 11, 2004, www.thestar.com. 3. Kandra, Anne, 2005, "The Problem with PayPal," *PCWorld*, February 2005, www.pcworld.com.

Nature of Data Processing Systems When programs are customized by an understaffed information systems group, there is a greater likelihood of programming errors than when an organization is using standard packaged software, thus increasing the likelihood of material error. (The system acquisition or development process is briefly summarized in Appendix D on page 234.)

The physical configuration of data processing systems affects the complexity of information systems. More complex systems are harder to understand and manage, thus increasing the likelihood of error. For example, a centralized data processing system with 15 data entry stations located on a single floor is easier to manage than a large financial institution's systems, where there are multiple central processing units, decentralized computing at minicomputers in regional centres, branches with microcomputers and automated teller machines processing transactions locally or transmitting to central locations, and electronic funds transfer transactions that are processed internationally. The scope of potential error is magnified a hundred fold in the more complex scenario. (The differences between centralized, decentralized, and distributed systems are summarized briefly in Appendix D on page 235.)

Integrity of Management When management is dominated by one or a few individuals who lack integrity, the likelihood of significantly misrepresented financial statements is greatly increased. For example, a lack of integrity of management has been found to exist in the great majority of significant accountants' liability cases. As stated in Chapter 7 and earlier in this chapter, management integrity affects the auditor's assessment of audit risk and, in extreme cases, may cause the auditor to reject the client.

When management has an adequate level of integrity for the auditor to accept the engagement, but cannot be regarded as completely honest in all dealings, auditors normally reduce audit risk and also increase inherent risk. For example, management may deduct capital items as repairs and maintenance expense on tax returns. The public accounting firm should first evaluate the cycles or accounts for which management is most likely to make misstatements. A higher level of inherent risk is appropriate wherever the auditor believes material misstatements may occur.

Client Motivation In many situations, management may believe it advantageous to misstate the financial statements. For example, if management receives a percentage of total profits as a bonus, there may be a tendency to overstate net income. Similarly, if a bond indenture requirement includes a specification that the current ratio must remain above a certain level, the client may be tempted to overstate current assets or to understate current liabilities by an amount sufficient to meet the requirement. Also, there may be considerable motivation for intentional understatement of income when management wants the company to pay less income tax. If management lacks integrity, some specific type of motivation may then lead management to misstate financial reports.

Results of Previous Audits Errors found in the previous year's audit have a high likelihood of occurring again in the current year's audit. This happens because many types of errors are systemic in nature, and organizations are often slow in making changes to eliminate them. Therefore, an auditor would be negligent if the results of the preceding year's examination were ignored during the development of the current year's audit program. For example, if the auditor found a significant number of errors in pricing inventory, inherent risk would likely be high, and extensive testing would have to be done in the current audit as a means of determining whether the deficiency in the client's system had been corrected. If, however, the auditor has found no errors for the past several years in conducting tests of an audit area, the auditor is justified in reducing inherent risk, provided that changes in relevant circumstances have not occurred.

Initial Versus Repeat Engagement Auditors gain experience and knowledge about the likelihood of misstatements after auditing a client for several years. The lack of previous years' audit results would cause most auditors to use a larger inherent risk for initial audits than for repeat engagements in which no material misstatements had been found. Most auditors set a high inherent risk in the first year of an audit and reduce it in subsequent years as they gain experience.

Related Parties Transactions between parent and subsidiary companies and those between management and the corporate entity are examples of related party transactions as defined by the *CICA Accounting Handbook's* Section 3840, "Related Party Transactions." These transactions do not occur between two independent parties dealing at "arm's length." Therefore, a greater likelihood exists of their misstatement, which should cause an increase in inherent risk. Determining the existence of related parties was discussed in Chapter 7.

Nonroutine Transactions Transactions that are unusual for the client are more likely to be incorrectly recorded by the client than routine transactions because the client lacks experience in recording them. Examples include fire losses, major property acquisitions, and lease agreements. Knowledge of the client's business and review of minutes of meetings, as discussed in Chapter 7, are useful to learn about nonroutine transactions.

Judgment Required to Record Account Balances and Transactions Correctly Many account balances require estimates and a great deal of management judgment. Examples are allowance for uncollectible accounts receivable, obsolete inventory, liability for warranty payments, and bank loan loss reserves. Similarly, transactions for major repairs or partial replacement of assets are examples requiring considerable judgment to record the information correctly.

Assets That Are Susceptible to Misappropriation The auditor should be concerned about the risk of possible defalcation in situations in which it is relatively easy to convert company assets to personal use. Such is the case when currency, marketable securities, or highly marketable inventory is not closely controlled. When the likelihood of defalcation is high, inherent risk is increased.

Makeup of the Population The individual items making up the total population also frequently affect the auditor's expectation of material misstatement. For example, most auditors would use a higher inherent risk for accounts receivable when most accounts are significantly overdue than when most accounts are current. Similarly, the potential for misstatements in inventory purchased several years ago would normally be greater than for inventory purchased in the past few months. Transactions with affiliated companies, amounts due from officers, cash disbursements made payable to cash, and accounts receivable outstanding for several months are examples of situations requiring a larger inherent risk and therefore greater investigation because there is usually a higher likelihood of misstatement than in more typical transactions.

Assessing Inherent Risk The auditor must evaluate the preceding factors and decide on an appropriate inherent risk factor for each cycle, account, and audit objective. Some factors, such as the integrity of management, will affect many or perhaps all cycles, whereas others, such as nonroutine transactions, will affect only specific accounts or audit objectives. Although the profession has not established standards or guidelines for setting inherent risk, the authors believe auditors are generally conservative in making such assessments. Most auditors would probably set inherent risk at well above 50 percent, even in the best of circumstances, and at 100 percent when there is any reasonable possibility of significant misstatements. For example, assume that in the audit of inventory, the auditor notes that (1) a large number of errors were found in the previous year and (2) inventory turnover has slowed in the current year. Many auditors would probably set inherent risk at a relatively high level (some would use 100 percent) for each audit objective for inventory in this situation.

→8.4 RELATING THE AUDIT RISK MODEL TO AUDIT PERFORMANCE

Summary of Risks

Figure 8-4 summarizes the factors that affect audit risk, inherent risk, and control risk. Based on the determined audit risk, the conclusion reached with respect to inherent risk, and both the conclusion and extent of reliance determined for control risk, the auditor determines the planned detection risk and the planned audit evidence to be accumulated.

Other Materiality and Risk Considerations

Audit Risk for Segments Both control risk and inherent risk are typically estimated for each cycle, each account, and each audit objective and are likely to vary from cycle to cycle, account to account, and objective to objective on the same audit. Internal controls may be more effective for inventory-related accounts than for those related to capital assets. Control risk would therefore also be different for different accounts depending on the effectiveness of the controls. Factors affecting inherent risk, such as susceptibility to defalcation and routineness of the transactions, are also likely to differ from account to account. For that reason, it is normal to have inherent risk vary for different accounts in the same audit unless there is some strong overriding factor of concern, such as management integrity.

Audit risk is ordinarily set by the auditor for the entire audit and held constant for each major cycle and account. Auditors normally use the same audit risk for each segment because the factors affecting audit risk are related to the entire audit, not individual accounts. For example, the extent to which financial statements are relied on for users' decisions is usually related to the overall financial statements, not just one or two accounts.

In the illustrations that follow in this and subsequent chapters, a common audit risk is used for segments and for the financial statements as a whole.

Because control risk and inherent risk may vary from cycle to cycle, account to account, or objective to objective, planned detection risk and required audit evidence will also vary.

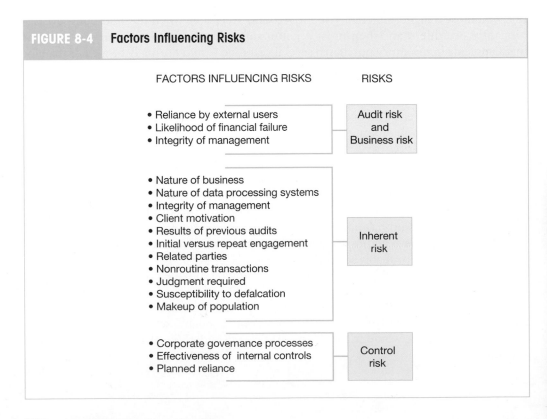

FIGURE 8-4   Factors Influencing Risks

The circumstances of each engagement are different, and the extent of evidence needed will depend on the unique circumstances. For example, inventory might require extensive testing on an engagement due to weak internal controls and concern about obsolescence due to technological changes in the industry. On the same engagement, accounts receivable may require little testing because of effective internal controls, fast collection of receivables, excellent relationships between the client and customers, and good audit results in previous years. Similarly, for a given audit of inventory, an auditor may assess that there is a higher inherent risk of a valuation misstatement because of the higher potential for obsolescence, but a low inherent risk of a classification misstatement because there is only purchased inventory.

Relating Risks to Balance-Related Audit Objectives It is common in practice to assess inherent and control risks for each audit objective. Auditors are able to effectively associate most risks with different objectives. It is reasonably easy to determine the relationship between a risk and one or two objectives. For example, obsolescence in inventory would be unlikely to affect any objective other than valuation.

Measurement Limitations One major limitation in the application of the audit risk model is the difficulty of measuring the components of the model. In spite of the auditor's best efforts in planning, the assessments of audit risk, inherent risk, control risk, and, therefore, planned detection risk are highly subjective and are approximations of reality at best. Imagine, for example, attempting to assess precisely inherent risk by determining the impact of factors such as the misstatements discovered in prior years' audits and technology changes in the client's industry.

To offset this measurement problem, many auditors use broad and subjective measurement terms, for example, "low," "medium," and "high." Audit firms have developed automated systems that help the auditor to ensure that the appropriate questions have been answered and assist in the documentation and tabulation of conclusions reached. Table 8-4 shows how auditors can use the information to decide on the appropriate amount of evidence to accumulate for a particular transaction cycle. For example, in situation 1, the auditor has decided to accept a high audit risk. The auditor has concluded that there is a low risk of misstatement in the cycle (inherent risk) and that internal controls are effective. Therefore, a high detection risk is appropriate. As a result, a low level of evidence is needed. Situation 3 is at the opposite extreme. If both inherent and control risks are high but the auditor wants a low audit risk, considerable evidence is required. The other three situations fall between the two extremes.

It is equally difficult to measure the amount of evidence implied by a given planned detection risk. A typical audit program that is intended to reduce detection risk to the planned level is a combination of several audit procedures, each using a different type of evidence that is applied to different audit objectives. Auditors' measurement methods are too imprecise to permit an accurate quantitative measure of the combined evidence. Instead, auditors subjectively evaluate whether sufficient evidence has been planned to satisfy a

TABLE 8-4	Relationships of Risk to Evidence				
Situation	Audit Risk	Inherent Risk	Control Risk	Planned Detection Risk	Amount of Evidence Required
1	High	Low	Low	High	Low
2	Low	Low	Low	Medium	Medium
3	Low	High	High	Low	High
4	Medium	Medium	Medium	Medium	Medium
5	High	Low	Medium	Medium	Medium

planned detection risk of low, medium, or high. Presumably, measurement methods are sufficient to permit an auditor to know that more evidence is needed to satisfy a low planned detection risk than for medium or high. Considerable professional judgment is needed to decide how much more. Continuing research in audit firms is used to help auditors to determine the mix of evidence required and to devise more effective means of gathering evidence as the nature of business transactions change. Some firms have an emphasis on controls reliance (where possible), while others decide that analytical review and tests of details should be emphasized instead.

In applying the audit risk model, auditors are concerned about both over- and under-auditing, but most auditors are more concerned about the latter. Under-auditing exposes the public accounting firm to legal liability and loss of professional reputation.

Because of the concern to avoid under-auditing, auditors typically assess risks conservatively. For example, an auditor might not assess either control risk or inherent risk below 0.5 even when the likelihood of misstatement is low. In these audits, a low control or inherent risk might be 0.5, medium 0.8, and high 1.0 if the risks are quantified.

Tests of Details of Balances Evidence Planning Worksheet Practising auditors develop various types of spreadsheets, templates, or computerized links to aid in relating the considerations affecting audit evidence to the appropriate evidence to accumulate. One such spreadsheet in printed form is included in Figure 8-5 for the audit of accounts receivable for Hillsburg Hardware Limited. The nine balance-related audit objectives introduced in Chapter 5 are included in the columns at the top of the spreadsheet. Rows one and two are audit risk and inherent risk, which were studied in this chapter. Materiality is included at the bottom of the worksheet. The engagement in-charge, Fran Moore, made the following decisions in the audit of Hillsburg Hardware Limited:

- *Materiality.* The preliminary judgment about materiality was set at $496,000 (10 percent of earnings before income taxes and extraordinary items of $4,961,000).
- *Audit risk.* Fran assessed audit risk as high because of the good financial condition of the company, high management integrity, and the relatively few public shareholders, about 1,000.
- *Inherent risk.* Fran assessed inherent risk as low for all balance-related audit objectives except valuation. In past years, there have been audit adjustments to the allowance for uncollectible accounts because it was found to be understated.

Planned detection risk would be approximately the same for each balance-related audit objective in the audit of accounts receivable for Hillsburg Hardware Limited if the only three factors the auditor needed to consider were audit risk, inherent risk, and materiality. The evidence planning spreadsheet shows that other factors must be considered before making the final evidence decisions. Control risk for the different transaction types is examined separately, as is the impact of analytical procedures. These are studied in subsequent chapters and will be integrated into the evidence planning spreadsheet at that time.

Relationship of Materiality and Risk and Audit Evidence The concepts of materiality and risk in auditing are closely related and inseparable. Materiality is a measure of magnitude or size while risk is a measure of uncertainty. Taken together they measure the uncertainty of amounts of a given magnitude. For example, the statement that the auditor plans to accumulate evidence such that there is only a 5 percent risk (audit risk) of failing to uncover misstatements exceeding materiality of $25,000 (materiality) is a precise and meaningful statement. If the statement eliminates either the risk or materiality portion, it would be meaningless. A 5 percent risk without a specific materiality measure could imply that a $100 or $1 million misstatement is acceptable. A $25,000 overstatement without a specific risk could imply that a 1 percent or 80 percent risk is acceptable.

As a general rule, there is a fixed relationship between materiality, risk, and audit evidence. If one of those components is changed, then one or both of the remaining components must also change to achieve the same audit risk. For example, if evidence is held

	Detail tie-in	Existence	Completeness	Accuracy	Classification	Cutoff	Valuation	Rights and Obligations	Presentation and Disclosure
Audit risk	high	high	high	high	high	high	high	high	high
Inherent risk	low	low	low	low	low	low	medium	low	low
Control risk–Sales									
Control risk–Cash receipts									
Control risk–Additional controls									
Analytical procedures									
Planned detection risk of tests of details of balances									
Planned audit evidence of tests of details of balances									

Materiality $496,000

constant and materiality is decreased, then the risk that a material but undiscovered misstatement could exist must increase. Similarly, if materiality were held constant and risk reduced, the required evidence would increase.

Refer again to Figure 8-3, where the different components of the audit risk model interact to achieve the specified audit risk. Planned evidence (the complement of planned detection risk) is used to offset any changes in inherent or control risks for a particular transaction cycle to achieve the targeted audit risk. Note that materiality is not present in the figure—materiality does not affect any of the four risks and the risks have no effect on materiality. Yet materiality is used in addition to the risks to determine the planned evidence required.

Evaluating Results

After the auditor plans the engagement and accumulates audit evidence, results of the audit can also be stated in terms of the audit risk model. However, research has shown that using the planning model to evaluate total audit results may result in an understatement of

achieved audit risk.[3] Achieved audit risk is the numeric value of audit risk using the assessed inherent risk; the value of control risk after documenting, evaluating, and testing internal controls (or the set value based on nonreliance); and the achieved detection risk.

During evaluation, the relationships can be used, but professional judgment is required to ensure that sufficient evidence has been collected rather than simple reliance on the formula.

The relationships show us that when insufficient evidence has been collected to achieve a specified audit risk, the following ways can be used to reduce achieved audit risk to the targeted level:

- *Reduce inherent risk.* Because inherent risk is assessed by the auditor based on the client's circumstances, this assessment is done during planning and is typically not changed unless new facts are uncovered as the audit progresses.
- *Reduce control risk.* Assessed control risk is affected by the client's internal controls and the auditor's tests of those controls. Auditors can reduce control risk by more extensive tests of controls if the client has effective controls.
- *Reduce achieved detection risk by increasing substantive audit tests.* Auditors reduce achieved detection risk by accumulating evidence using analytical procedures and tests of details of balances. Additional audit procedures, assuming that they are effective, and larger sample sizes both reduce achieved detection risk.

Subjectively combining these three factors to achieve an acceptably low audit risk requires considerable professional judgment. Some firms develop sophisticated approaches using computer modelling to help their auditors make those judgments, while other firms simply use automation to record the decisions made by each audit team.

Audit results are studied more extensively in later chapters.

Revising Risks and Evidence The audit risk model is a *planning* model, and it is therefore of limited use in evaluating results. Great care must be used in revising the risk factors when the actual results are not as favourable as planned.

No difficulties occur when the auditor accumulates planned evidence and concludes that the assessment of each of the risks was reasonable or better than originally thought. The auditor will conclude that sufficient appropriate audit evidence has been collected for that account or cycle.

Special care must be exercised when the auditor decides, on the basis of accumulated evidence, that the original assessment of control risk or inherent risk was understated or that audit risk was overstated. This is less problematic if the auditor has conducted inherent risk evaluation and completed tests of controls prior to commencing tests of details work. However, if work is being done concurrently, adjustments to the fieldwork process become more difficult.

In such a circumstance, the auditor should follow a two-step approach. First, the auditor must revise the original assessment of the appropriate risk. It would violate due care to leave the original assessment unchanged if the auditor knows it is inappropriate. Second, the auditor should consider the effect of the revision on evidence requirements, *without the use of the audit risk model*. Instead, the auditor should carefully evaluate the implications of the revision of the risk and modify evidence appropriately, so that sufficient evidence is collected.

For example, assume that the auditor confirms accounts receivable and, based on the misstatements found, concludes that the original control risk assessment as low was inappropriate. The auditor should revise the estimate of control risk upward and carefully consider the effect of the revision on the additional evidence needed in the sales and collection cycle.

---

[3]Research on U.S. Statement of Auditing Standards 47, which provides an evaluation form of the audit planning model, indicates that the formula can result in an understatement of achieved audit risk if the formula is used to evaluate total evidence collected.

APPENDIX C
DISASTER RECOVERY PLANNING

Disaster recovery planning is also known as "business continuity planning." The purpose of such a plan is to enable a business to continue operations in the event of failure of part or all of its information systems. Something as simple as a hard drive crash (in which the reading head of the hard drive fails, destroying the head, the disk, and the data on it) can cause enormous problems if a company has not given careful thought to contingency procedures. Think of your own personal computer. What would you do if this terrible event occurred? Focus Box 8-1, on page 223 describes how an insurance company fared when it had a fire that destroyed some microcomputers and disk drives.

Gary Baker provided a concise article in *CAmagazine*[4] several years ago that breaks down the disaster recovery process into five phases. The phases are as follows:

1. MANAGEMENT COMMITMENT TO THE CONCEPT OF DISASTER RECOVERY PLANNING Preparation of a disaster recovery plan (DRP) is time-consuming and requires the provision of funds and human resources. If management is not fully committed to this process, the resources will not be provided and the activity will falter.

2. RANKING OF BUSINESS PROCESSES The entity needs to ask, "What will happen if process X is not available?" Can the payroll be paid? Can goods be shipped out of the door? For organizations using paperless systems and electronic data interchange or electronic commerce, operations will likely cease if those systems are unavailable. Users need to identify what would happen if particular application processes were unavailable and the likely impact that this would have on the business. Baker suggests using one-day, three-day, and seven-day time frames when conducting this ranking.

3. IDENTIFYING MINIMUM RESOURCES REQUIRED From step 2, the entity will have identified applications that were critical to ongoing operations. Resources required to restore these operations (and perhaps some noncritical systems as well) now need to be identified and costed. Where multiple alternatives exist, they should be similarly identified and costed.

4. PREPARE A DATA CENTRE PLAN AND A USER PLAN The data centre plan addresses technical issues and procedures, such as obtaining hardware and software backup, and ensuring appropriate telecommunications access. The user plan identifies activities required to resume operations and can include manual alternative activities that would be completed if computing resources were unavailable.

5. TEST THE PLAN This trial run will help both data processing personnel and users identify any shortcomings in the DRP and provide a subsequent schedule for remedying those shortcomings.

There are a variety of technical publications and articles that can be used by organizations to prepare a disaster recovery plan or to obtain more detailed guidance on the components of planning.[5] In addition to those issues mentioned by Baker, it is important that an entity have current offsite backup of its systems, carry adequate appropriate insurance coverage, and continue to maintain its disaster recovery plans once the DRP has initially been developed.

Audit Impact The existence of an effective disaster recovery plan is linked to the auditor's assessment of the viability of the entity as a going concern. If an entity using integrated Electronic Data Interchange (EDI), Electronic Funds Transfers (EFTs), and automated shipping systems were to lose its systems and not have an effective DRP, the entity would likely fail if it could not recover its systems within a short period of time. Thus, the auditor might consider either lowering the numeric value of audit risk or asking the client to disclose the lack of appropriate disaster recovery plans in a note to the financial statement.

---

[4]Baker, G., "Quick Recoveries," *CAmagazine* (August 1995), pp. 49–50, 53.

[5]See, for example: Doughty, K., "Business Continuity: A Business Survival Strategy," *Information Systems Control Journal*, Vol. 1 (2002), pp. 28–36.

APPENDIX D

EFFECTS OF INFORMATION SYSTEMS SOFTWARE ACQUISITION AND HARDWARE CONFIGURATION ON EVIDENCE COLLECTION PROCESSES

Software Acquisition Organizations employ a wide variety of software, serving a broad range of purposes, such as providing the user interface, providing security, managing hardware and software, communicating information, and recording and processing transactions. Here, we focus on the process used to obtain software that serves the organization's needs.

Information Technology Control Guidelines[6] breaks down the software acquisition process into three general categories:

- In-house development (employees within the entity determine user requirements and build the software using one of many alternative development approaches)
- Systems acquisition (software is acquired from an outside vendor and implemented as is, or modified and implemented)
- Turnkey software development (custom software development is contracted to an outside party)

The type of process used will affect the nature of controls that need to be examined by the auditor.

Again, using the terminology of *Information Technology Control Guidelines*, the acquisition process is broken down into five phases:

1. *Investigation.* In this first phase, it is determined whether the proposed system should actually be obtained.
2. *Requirements analysis and initial design.* Then it is necessary to identify and document the overall functionality and purpose of the proposed system.
3. *Development [or acquisition] and system testing.* Specific functionality of the new system is identified and developed/acquired and tested.
4. *Conversion, implementation, and post-implementation review.* Data is converted from the old to the new system, live running of the system commences, and the system is evaluated to determine whether it satisfies the entity's needs.
5. *Ongoing maintenance.* Necessary changes to the system are undertaken as needed.

For the evidence gathering process, as part of the knowledge of business documentation, the auditor will determine what types of systems are in place, paying particular attention to those of financial or operational significance. The auditor will then make enquiries regarding the information systems change process: are information systems developed, modified, or acquired, and have there been any changes in the current year? Where changes have taken place, the auditor may be required to conduct a conversion audit (discussed in Chapter 17), as well as assess changes to controls due to the new or modified systems.

The complexity of the software development or acquisition process needs to be determined to assess inherent risks. Thus, an overview of the process would be gathered during the knowledge of business documentation for the client. Controls over the acquisition or development process are part of the control environment and general information systems controls. These general controls need to be documented and should reliance be placed in software programs during the audit, they would need to be tested, as discussed further in the next chapter.

---

[6]Canadian Institute of Chartered Accountants, *Information Technology Control Guidelines*, 3rd Edition, 1998, pp. 95–96.

Hardware Configuration[7] As part of the knowledge of business, the auditor would determine the type of equipment in use by the entity, where it was located, how it was interconnected, and whether data communications or Internet/Intranet access was occurring. This helps to determine the complexity and scope of further controls that need to be documented and evaluated.

The simpler hardware structures are a *centralized* system (where all processing is done from a single central system, requiring that users be logged onto that system to conduct business activity) and *decentralized* systems (where each location of a multiple location system has stand-alone, independent processing). Such pure systems exist in smaller businesses, but are otherwise rare. For centralized systems, the auditor must document controls primarily at that one location, while for decentralized systems, multi-location issues, such as commonality of software, need to be considered.

Most larger systems now are *distributed* systems, where computing or files are shared among users and computing facilities. For example, a *local area network* is a distributed system, since computing can be accomplished at the individual computer level or the common file server can be used. An organization with a head office computer and branch location computing systems that transmit information to the head office is using a distributed system. Financial institutions' automated teller machines and point-of-sale terminals can also be components of distributed systems. In such systems, controls over each category of software and hardware need to be documented. Frequently, specialist assistance will be required to conduct the control documentation and evaluation process.

SUMMARY

1. *How is materiality used to assess the amount of work conducted during an audit engagement?* Materiality is used to assess the impact that potential errors might have on users of the financial statements. The auditor needs to conduct the audit to a specified assurance level that the statements are free of material errors. Since materiality affects sample size, as materiality decreases, so does the need for increased audit testing.

   What quantitative and qualitative factors does an auditor consider when setting materiality? The auditor uses professional judgment to choose a base against which to calculate materiality. The numerical value decided upon is based upon factors such as the client risk profile, the extent of fluctuation of bases, and the amount of assurance required.

2. *What is risk in auditing?* Risk is used to describe the uncertainty associated with the conduct of the audit. Uncertainty is associated with different types of risks.

   What are the components of the audit risk model? Table 8-2 describes and illustrates audit risk, inherent risk, control risk, and [planned] detection risk.

3. *When assessing inherent risk, what does the auditor consider?* The text lists eleven major factors (p. 225) that are related to the nature of the client business, the integrity of its management, the types of transactions or processes, and the susceptibility of transactions to error or manipulation, as well as whether it is an initial or repeat engagement.

4. *How do the components of the audit risk model relate to the amount of evidence that should be collected during an audit?* Assessments are completed to the individual cycle, account, and audit objective level. These assessments are used, together with professional judgment, to decide upon the nature, quality, and quantity of evidence collected, resulting in a detailed audit program.

   How does materiality fit in with the audit risk model? The auditor decides upon materiality using professional judgment, with full awareness of the same information that is used to estimate the components of the audit risk model (Figure 8-6 on page 236). Then, materiality is used to help decide upon the amount of evidence that is collected on an assertion-by-assertion basis. Materiality and the components of the audit risk model do not directly affect each other, but both affect the amount of evidence collected.

   What happens if risks change once the audit fieldwork has commenced? In the end, the auditor must have sufficient evidence to state an audit opinion. If risk changes indicate that more evidence is required, the auditor needs to collect additional evidence.

   If the opposite occurs, then the auditor has collected too much evidence—however, auditors would tend to err in this direction rather than collecting too little evidence.

---

[7]For further explanations of hardware configuration, consult a management information systems text, for example: Kenneth C. Laudon, Jane P. Laudon, and Mary E. Brabston, 2005. "*Management Information Systems,*" Second Canadian Edition, Toronto, ON: Prentice Hall.

CICA ASSURANCE HANDBOOK SECTIONS REFERENCED IN THIS CHAPTER

Section 5095 – Reasonable assurance and audit risk.
Section 5141 – Understanding the entity and its environment and assessing the risks of material misstatement.

Section 5142 – Materiality.
AuG-41 – Applying the concept of materiality.

ESSENTIAL TERMS

Achieved audit risk—the numeric value of audit risk using the assessed inherent risk; the value of control risk after documenting, evaluating, and testing internal controls (or the set value based on nonreliance); and the achieved detection risk (p. 232).

Audit assurance—a complement to *audit risk*; an audit risk of 2 percent is the same as audit assurance of 98 percent; also called *overall assurance* and *level of assurance* (p. 218).

Audit risk—a measure of how willing the auditor is to accept that the financial statements may be materially misstated after the audit is completed and an unqualified audit opinion has been issued; see also *audit assurance* (p. 218).

Audit risk model—a formal model reflecting the relationships among audit risk (*AR*), inherent risk (*IR*), control risk (*CR*), and planned detection risk (*PDR*); $AR = IR \times CR \times PDR$ (p. 217).

Business risk—risk that the auditor or audit firm will suffer harm because of a client relationship, even though the auditor's report rendered for the client was correct (p. 221).

Control risk (CR)—a measure of the auditor's assessment of the likelihood that misstatements exceeding materiality in a segment

will not be prevented or detected by the client's internal controls (p. 219).

Direct projection method of estimating misstatement—net misstatements in the sample, divided by the total sampled, multiplied by the total recorded population value; see also *likely misstatements* (p. 216).

Further possible misstatements—the misstatements over and above the likely aggregate misstatement that result from the imprecision in the sampling process (p. 212).

Identified misstatements—the actual misstatements discovered in the sample tested; the misstatements have not been corrected by management (p. 211).

Inherent risk (IR)—a measure of the auditor's assessment of the likelihood that there are material misstatements in a segment before considering the effectiveness of internal controls (p. 219).

Likely misstatements—the projection of the actual misstatements in the sample to the population; the misstatements have not been corrected by management; see also *direct projection method of estimating misstatement* (p. 211).

Materiality—the magnitude of an omission or misstatement of accounting information that, in the light of surrounding circumstances, makes it *probable* that the judgment of a reasonable person relying on the information would have been changed or influenced by the omission or misstatement   (p. 210).

Planned detection risk (PDR)—a measure of the risk that audit evidence for a segment will fail to detect misstatements exceeding materiality, should such misstatements exist; $PDR = AR / (IR \times CR)$ (p. 219).

Preliminary judgment about materiality—the maximum amount by which the auditor believes that the statements could

be misstated and still *not* affect the decisions of reasonable users; used in audit planning   (p. 212).

Revised judgment about materiality—a change in the auditor's preliminary judgment made when the auditor determines that the preliminary judgment was too large or too small   (p. 212).

Risk—the acceptance by auditors that there is some level of uncertainty in performing the audit function   (p. 217).

Sampling error—error that results because the auditor has sampled only a portion of the population   (p. 216).

REVIEW QUESTIONS

8-1 Define the meaning of the term "materiality" as it is used in accounting and auditing. What is the relationship between materiality and the phrase "obtain reasonable assurance" used in the auditor's report?

8-2 Explain why materiality is important but difficult to apply in practice.

8-3 What is meant by "setting a preliminary judgment about materiality"? Identify the most important factors affecting the preliminary judgment.

8-4 Assume Rosanne Madden, a public accountant, is using 5 percent of net income before taxes as her major guideline for evaluating materiality. What qualitative factors should she also consider in deciding whether misstatements may be material?

8-5 Differentiate between identified misstatements, likely misstatements, and further possible misstatements. Explain why all three are important.

8-6 How would the conduct of an audit of a medium-sized company be affected by the company's being a small part of a large conglomerate as compared with its being a separate entity?

8-7 Define the "audit risk model" and explain each term in the model.

8-8 Explain the causes of an increased or decreased planned detection risk.

8-9 Explain why inherent risk is estimated for segments rather than for the overall audit. What is the effect on the amount of evidence the auditor must accumulate when inherent risk is increased from medium to high for a segment?

8-10 Explain the effect of extensive misstatements found in the prior year's audit on inherent risk, planned detection risk, and planned audit evidence.

8-11 Explain the relationship between audit risk and the legal liability of auditors.

8-12 State the categories of circumstances that affect audit risk, and list the factors that the auditor can use to indicate the degree to which each category exists.

8-13 Auditors have not been successful in measuring the components of the audit risk model. How is it possible to use the model in a meaningful way without a precise way of measuring the risk?

MULTIPLE CHOICE QUESTIONS

8-14 Choose the best response for the following questions:

a. Edison Corporation has a few large accounts receivable that total $1,400,000. Victor Corporation has a great number of small accounts receivable that also total $1,400,000. The importance of a misstatement in any one account is, therefore, greater for Edison than for Victor. This is an example of the auditor's concept of

(1) materiality.
(2) comparative analysis.
(3) reasonable assurance.
(4) relative risk.

b. Which of the following elements ultimately determines the specific auditing procedures that are necessary in the circumstances to afford a reasonable basis for an opinion?

(1) Auditor judgment
(2) Materiality
(3) Inherent risk
(4) Reasonable assurance

c. In considering materiality for planning purposes, an auditor believes that misstatements aggregating $10,000 would have a material effect on an entity's income statement, but that misstatements would have to aggregate $20,000 to materially affect the balance sheet. Ordinarily, it would be appropriate to design auditing procedures that would be expected to detect misstatements that aggregate

(1) $15,000
(2) $10,000
(3) $20,000
(4) $30,000

d. Inherent risk and control risk differ from planned detection risk in that they

    (1) arise from the misapplication of auditing procedures.
    (2) may be assessed in either quantitative or nonquantitative terms.
    (3) exist independently of the financial statement audit.
    (4) can be changed at the auditor's discretion.

e. The audit risk against which the auditor requires reasonable protection is a combination of two separate risks. The first of these is that material errors will occur in the accounting process by which the financial statements are developed and the second is that

    (1) a company's system of internal controls is not adequate to detect errors or frauds.
    (2) those errors that occur will not be detected in the auditor's examination.
    (3) management may possess an attitude that lacks integrity.
    (4) evidential matter is not competent enough for the auditor to form an opinion based on reasonable assurance.

DISCUSSION QUESTIONS AND PROBLEMS

8-15 The following are different types of misstatements that can be encountered on an audit:

    1.   A computer programming error that resulted in the use of a method of valuing inventory that is not in accordance with generally accepted accounting principles
    2.   Accidental failure to disclose a lawsuit for patent infringement when the amount of the liability is unknown
    3.   The recording as capital assets expenditures that should have been recorded as repairs and maintenance
    4.   The inclusion of invalid accounts in accounts receivable by preparing fictitious sales invoices to nonexisting customers.

Required

a. Assuming the amounts are equally material, rank the types of misstatements listed in terms of the difficulty of uncovering each one. (*Most difficult* is first.) Give reasons to support your answers.
b. Discuss whether auditors should have the same responsibility for uncovering the most difficult-to-find misstatement as for discovering the least difficult one. Consider this from the point of view of the auditors and the users of financial statements.

8-16 Statements of earnings and financial position for Prairie Stores Corporation are shown on page 239.

Required

a. Use professional judgment in reaching a preliminary judgment about materiality based on revenue, net income before taxes, total assets, and shareholders' equity. Your conclusions should be stated in terms of percentages and dollars.
b. Assume you complete the audit and conclude that your preliminary judgment about materiality has been exceeded. What should you do?
c. As discussed in part (b), likely net earnings from continuing operations *before* income taxes were used as a base for materiality when completing the audit. Discuss why most auditors use *before* tax net earnings instead of *after* tax net earnings when calculating materiality based on the income statement.

8-17 You are the in-charge auditor of the audit of the municipality of Sackville, New Brunswick. The municipality has a budget of about $65 million and has had a balanced budget for the last three years. There are about ten people in the accounting office and the rest of the employees are operational, dealing with supervision of roadwork, garbage collection, and similar matters. Many services are outsourced, minimizing the need for employees. The municipality has a chief executive officer and a controller, and reports to the council of elected representatives.

Required

For each of the following situations, state a preliminary conclusion for audit risk, inherent risk, control risk, and detection risk. Justify your conclusions. State any assumptions that are necessary for you to reach your conclusions.

    (1) This is the first year that you have been auditing Sackville. There has been extensive turnover after the recent election. Costs are out of control and it looks like it may be necessary to raise realty taxes by as much as 15 percent.
    (2) For four years now, you have been auditing Sackville. The employees are experienced and any control recommendations that you have suggested have been discussed, and where feasible, implemented. There is a tiny budget surplus this year, and it looks as if a balanced budget is in sight again for next year.
    (3) Sackville is being hit by bad press. It seems that one of the purchasing agents set up a fictitious company and was billing the municipality for goods that had not been received. To make it worse, the purchasing agent's wife was the assistant accountant. The office of the provincial Auditor General has sent a letter to the controller of Sackville stating that the municipality has been selected for audit by the provincial Auditor General's Office based on a random sample, and the provincial auditors will be arriving within two weeks of the completion of your audit.

Statement of Earnings
Prairie Stores Corporation

	For the 53 Weeks Ended April 5, 2004	For the 52 Weeks Ended March 31, 2003	April 1, 2002
Revenue			
Net sales	$8,351,149	$6,601,255	$5,959,587
Other income	59,675	43,186	52,418
	8,410,824	6,644,441	6,012,005
Costs and expenses			
Cost of sales	5,197,375	4,005,548	3,675,369
Marketing, general, and administrative expenses	2,590,080	2,119,590	1,828,169
Provision for loss on restructured operations	64,100	—	—
Interest expense	141,662	46,737	38,546
	7,993,217	6,171,875	5,542,084
Earnings from continuing operations before income taxes	417,607	472,566	469,921
Income taxes	196,700	217,200	214,100
Earnings from continuing operations	220,907	255,366	255,821
Provision for loss on discontinued operations, net of income taxes	20,700	—	—
Net earnings	$200,207	$255,366	$255,821

Statement of Financial Position
Prairie Stores Corporation

Assets		March 30, 2004		March 31, 2003
Current assets				
Cash		$39,683		$37,566
Temporary investments (at cost, which approximates market)		123,421		271,639
Receivables, less allowances of $16,808 in 2004 and $17,616 In 2003		899,752		759,001
Inventories				
Finished product	680,974		550,407	
Raw materials and supplies	443,175		353,795	
		1,124,149		904,202
Deferred income tax benefits		9,633		10,468
Prepaid expenses		57,468		35,911
Total current assets		2,254,106		2,018,787
Land, buildings, equipment at cost, less accumulated amortization		1,393,902		1,004,455
Investments in affiliated companies and sundry assets		112,938		83,455
Goodwill and other intangible assets		99,791		23,145
Total assets		$3,860,737		$3,129,842

Liabilities and Shareholders' Equity	March 30, 2004	March 31, 2003
Current liabilities		
Notes payable	$280,238	$113,411
Current portion of long-term debt	64,594	12,336
Accounts and drafts payable	359,511	380,395
Accrued salaries, wages, and vacations	112,200	63,557
Accrued income taxes	76,479	89,151
Other accrued liabilities including goods and services tax	321,871	269,672
Current liabilities	1,214,893	928,522
Long-term debt	730,987	390,687
Other noncurrent liabilities	146,687	80,586
Accrued income tax liability	142,344	119,715
Total liabilities	2,234,911	1,519,510
Shareholders' equity		
Common stock issued, 51,017 shares in 2005 and 50,992 in 2004	200,195	199,576
Retained earnings	1,425,631	1,410,756
Total shareholders' equity	1,625,826	1,610,332
Total liabilities and shareholders' equity	$3,860,737	$3,129,842

8-18 Six situations that involve the audit risk model as it is used for planning audit evidence requirements are listed. Numbers are used only to help you understand the relationships among factors in the risk model.

RISK	SITUATION					
	1	2	3	4	5	6
Audit risk	5%	5%	5%	5%	1%	1%
Inherent risk	100%	40%	60%	20%	100%	40%
Control risk	100%	60%	40%	30%	100%	60%
Planned detection risk	–	–	–	–	–	–

Required
a. Explain what each of the four risks mean.
b. Calculate planned detection risk for each situation.
c. Using your knowledge of the relationships among the foregoing factors, state the effect on planned detection risk (increase or decrease) of changing each of the following factors while the other two remain constant. Cite two situations from the table to support your comments.

 (1) A decrease in audit risk
 (2) A decrease in control risk
 (3) A decrease in inherent risk
 (4) An increase in control risk and a decrease in inherent risk of the same amount

d. Which situation requires the greatest amount of evidence and which requires the least?

8-19 Using the audit risk model, state the effect on control risk, inherent risk, audit risk, and planned evidence for each of the following independent events. In each of the events (a) to (j), circle one letter for each of the three independent variables and planned evidence: I = increase, D = decrease, N = no effect, and C = cannot determine from the information provided. Explain your reasoning.

a. The client's management materially increased long-term contractual debt:
Control risk   I D N C   Audit risk   I D N C
Inherent risk   I D N C   Planned evidence   I D N C

b. The company changed from a privately held company to a publicly held company
Control risk   I D N C   Audit risk   I D N C
Inherent risk   I D N C   Planned evidence   I D N C

c. The auditor decided to assess control risk at a level below maximum; it was previously assessed at maximum.
Control risk   I D N C   Audit risk   I D N C
Inherent risk   I D N C   Planned evidence   I D N C

d. The account balance increased materially from the preceding year without apparent reason:
Control risk   I D N C   Audit risk   I D N C
Inherent risk   I D N C   Planned evidence   I D N C

e. You determined through the planning phase that working capital, debt-to-equity ratio, and other indicators of financial condition had improved during the past year:
Control risk   I D N C   Audit risk   I D N C
Inherent risk   I D N C   Planned evidence   I D N C

f. The client purchased and installed new accounting software partway through the year:
Control risk   I D N C   Audit risk   I D N C
Inherent risk   I D N C   Planned evidence   I D N C

g. About halfway through the audit, you discover that the client is constructing its own building during idle periods, using factory personnel. This is the first time the client has done this and it is being done at your recommendation:
Control risk   I D N C   Audit risk   I D N C
Inherent risk   I D N C   Planned evidence   I D N C

h. In discussions with management, you conclude that management is planning to sell the business in the next few months. Because of the planned changes, several key accounting personnel quit several months ago for alternative employment. You also observe that the gross margin percent has significantly increased compared with that of the preceding year:
Control risk   I D N C   Audit risk   I D N C
Inherent risk   I D N C   Planned evidence   I D N C

i. There has been a change in several key management personnel. You believe that management is somewhat lacking in personal integrity, compared with the previous management. You believe it is still appropriate to do the audit:
Control risk   I D N C   Audit risk   I D N C
Inherent risk   I D N C   Planned evidence   I D N C

j. In auditing inventory, you obtain an understanding of internal control and perform tests of controls. You find it significantly improved compared with that of the preceding year. You also observe that due to technology changes in the industry, the client's inventory may be somewhat obsolete:
Control risk   I D N C   Audit risk   I D N C
Inherent risk   I D N C   Planned evidence   I D N C

8-20 The existence of risk is implicit in the phrase "in my opinion" that appears in the auditor's report. The auditor is indicating that he or she is accepting some risk that the opinion rendered may be incorrect. In planning and executing an audit, the auditor strives to reduce this risk to a level that is acceptable to the client, the users, and him- or herself.

Required
Discuss the steps that the auditor takes to reduce the risk to an acceptable level. What guidance do the professional standards provide to the auditor?

8-21 Some accountants have suggested that the auditor's report should include a statement of materiality level and audit risk that the auditor used in conducting the audit.

Required
a. The proponents of such disclosure believe that the information would be useful to users of the financial statements being reported on. Explain fully why you think they have this view.

b. Some accountants oppose such disclosure. Explain why you think they are not in favour of it.

c. What is your position on the issue?

PROFESSIONAL JUDGMENT PROBLEM

8-22 Excerpts from a court case appear below. The lawyer is in the process of examining his client, a public accountant, accused of negligence in the conduct of an audit.

Lawyer: Were you aware that the statements were being used by the creditor who was owed $100,000 that was secured by inventory?

Auditor: Yes, he was one of several users.

Lawyer: How did your audit strategy take into account the needs of this creditor?

Auditor: We assessed the engagement as being slightly riskier than usual.

Lawyer: And how did you determine materiality to be $250,000?

Auditor: We used principles in accordance with generally accepted auditing standards, namely:

- 5 percent to 10 percent of income before income taxes of $6 million, being $300,000 to $600,000
- 0.5 percent to 1 percent of total assets of $50 million, being $250,000 to $500,000

Because of the riskiness of this engagement, we adopted a conservative approach and took a lower materiality level than we would otherwise have chosen.

Required

In accordance with generally accepted auditing standards:
a. List the factors that you would consider in this situation. How would materiality affect the extent of audit testing? List any other matters that would be relevant.
b. Discuss the relationship between materiality and audit risk. Were these concepts appropriately considered in the situation described above?

(CICA adapted)

CASE

8-23 In the audit of Whirland Chemical Company, a large publicly traded company, you have been assigned the responsibility for obtaining background information for the audit. Your firm is auditing the client for the first time in the current year as a result of a dispute between Whirland and the previous auditor over the proper valuation of work-in-process inventory and the inclusion in sales of inventory that has not been delivered but has, for practical purposes, been completed and sold.

Whirland Chemical has been highly successful in its field in the past two decades, primarily because of many successful mergers negotiated by Bert Randolph, the president and chairman of the board. Even though the industry as a whole has suffered dramatic setbacks in recent years, Whirland continues to prosper, as evidenced by its constantly increasing earnings and growth. Only in the last 2 years have the company's profits turned downward. Randolph has a reputation for having been able to hire an aggressive group of young executives by the use of relatively low salaries combined with an unusually generous profit-sharing plan.

A major difficulty you face in the new audit is the lack of highly sophisticated accounting records for a company the size of Whirland. Randolph believes that profits come primarily from intelligent and aggressive action based on forecasts, not by relying on historical data that come after the fact. Most of the forecast data are generated by the sales and production department rather than by the accounting department. The personnel in the accounting department do seem competent but somewhat overworked and underpaid relative to other employees. One of the recent changes that will potentially improve the record-keeping is the installation of sophisticated computer equipment. All of the accounting records are not computerized yet, but such major areas as inventory and sales are included in the new system. Most of the computer time is being reserved for production and marketing because these areas are more essential to operations than record-keeping.

The first 6 months' financial statements for the current year include a profit of approximately only 10 percent less than the first 6 months of the preceding year, which is somewhat surprising, considering the reduced volume and the disposal of a segment of the business, Mercury Supply Co. The disposal of this segment was considered necessary because it had become increasingly unprofitable over the past 4 years. At the time of its acquisition from Roger Randolph, a brother of Bert Randolph, the company was highly profitable and was considered a highly desirable purchase. The major customer of Mercury Supply Co. was the Mercury Corporation, which is owned by Roger Randolph. Gradually, the market for its products declined as the Mercury Corporation began diversifying and phasing out its primary products in favour of more profitable business. Even though Mercury Corporation is no longer buying from Mercury Supply Co., it compensates for it by buying a large volume of other products from Whirland Chemical.

The only major difficulty Whirland faces right now, according to financial analysts, is underfinancing. There is an excessive amount of current debt and long-term debt because of the depressed capital markets. Management is reluctant to obtain equity capital at this point because the increased number of shares would decrease the earnings per share even more than 10 percent. At the present time, Randolph is negotiating with several cash-rich companies in the hope of being able to merge with them as a means of overcoming the capital problems.

Required

a. List the major concerns you should have in the audit of Whirland Chemical Company and explain why they are potential problems.
b. State the appropriate approach to investigating the significance of each item you listed in (a).

INTERNAL CONTROLS AND CONTROL RISK

"Why bother testing internal controls? We can just look at the numbers and the supporting documents, can't we?" Well, no! In a large organization with millions of transactions, ignoring internal controls would lead to a very expensive audit. For any sized organization, the ability to rely on the procedures performed by computer software (such as calculations) also reduces the amount of audit work required.

LEARNING OBJECTIVES

After reading this chapter, you should be able to address the following questions:

1. Why is the study of internal control important? What are the different perspectives of the client and the auditor?

2. What are the three basic concepts that enable an auditor's study of internal controls? List the four components of internal control. Why is the control environment the most important component of internal control?

3. How is management's risk assessment process relevant to the audit? Explain how accounting systems and control procedures together comprise control systems. What is the role of monitoring in supporting internal controls?

4. What does the auditor do to obtain an understanding of internal controls? How is control risk assessed, documented, and tested? Why is it important to link control risk to audit strategy and procedures?

5. What other types of internal control reports can an auditor issue? How is this relevant to the audit?

PHANTOM BOOKS

Senior executives at Livent Inc., the Toronto theatre owner and producer of Broadway-style shows including Show Boat, Ragtime, and Phantom of the Opera, took their theatrics to a new level when they allegedly engaged in a pervasive fraud to materially distort their financial statements over an eight-year period. According to charges filed by the Securities and Exchange Commission, the former chairman and CEO and former president together coaxed several of their longtime company associates, including the CFO and IT manager, to participate in a multifaceted scheme to manipulate profits.

In addition to orchestrating vendor kickback schemes to siphon off millions of dollars and numerous customer side-agreements to falsify revenues, senior management manipulated the accounting records to shift costs of shows to fixed assets from expenses. Their techniques included alteration of computer programs to lower expenses without a trace in order to hide the fraud from Livent auditors. In addition, they created "phantom" accounting records showing the adjustments so senior management could track the fraudulent entries and know the company's true financial condition. Ultimately, their distortions were revealed, and the executives faced charges both in the United States and Canada. Livent filed for bankruptcy and was subsequently sold to a team headed by a former Walt Disney Company executive.

Sources: 1. Securities and Exchange Commission, Litigation Release No. 16022, Washington, DC, January 1999. 2. Canadian Broadcasting Company, "Livent Founders Charged with Fraud," Arts Now, Toronto, October 10, 2002.

Collusion is extremely difficult to detect—if executive management, financial management, and information systems management all conspire to misstate the records, what can the auditor do? Chapter 10 will discuss risks associated with fraud. However, think about the basic ethical principles that we have discussed and rely upon. What indicators might exist within a business that violate these principles? How might such indicators be warning signals about internal control problems?

→9.1 DIFFERING PERSPECTIVES OF INTERNAL CONTROL

Chapter 9 is the third chapter dealing with planning the audit and designing an audit approach. The subject of internal control is sufficiently important in the audit process to merit inclusion in the generally accepted auditing standard (par. 5100.02(ii)):

> The auditor should obtain an understanding of the entity and its environment, including internal control, sufficient to identify and assess the risks...

The study of internal control, assessment of control risk, and related evidence gathering is a major component in the audit risk model studied in Chapter 8. Control risk is "*CR*" in the audit risk model. It was shown in Chapter 8 that planned audit evidence can be reduced when there are effective internal controls. This chapter shows why and how this can be done.

To understand how internal control is used in the audit risk model, knowledge of key internal control concepts is needed. Accordingly, this chapter focuses on the meaning and objectives of internal control from both the client's and the auditor's point of view, the components of internal control, and the auditor's methodology for fulfilling the requirements of the second examination standard. Professional guidance in considering internal control is found in Sections 5141 and 5143 of the *CICA Assurance Handbook*. Many practitioners consider it to be the most complex auditing standard in the literature.

Client and Auditor Concerns

In designing a system for control, management is likely to have some of the same concerns auditors have in evaluating the system, as well as additional or different concerns. This section examines the concerns of both clients and auditors.

Client Concerns As explained in Section 5141.042, "Internal control is the process designed and effected by those charged with governance, management, and other personnel to provide reasonable assurance about the achievement of the entity's objectives with regard to reliability of financial reporting, effectiveness and efficiency of operations, and compliance with applicable laws and regulations. It follows that internal control is designed and implemented to address identified business risks that threaten the achievement of any of these objectives."

The system consists of governance processes as well as many specific *policies and procedures* designed to provide management with reasonable assurance that the goals and objectives that it believes to be important to the entity will be met. These policies and procedures are often called *controls*, and collectively they comprise the entity's **internal control**.

Control systems must be *cost beneficial*. The controls adopted are selected by comparing the costs to the organization relative to the benefits expected. One benefit to management, but certainly not the most important, is the reduced cost of an audit when the auditor evaluates internal control as good or excellent and assesses control risk as much below maximum (i.e., as low).

Management typically has the following objectives in designing effective internal control.

MAINTAINING RELIABLE CONTROL SYSTEMS Management must have reliable control systems so that it will have accurate information for carrying out its operations and producing financial statements. A wide variety of information is used for making critical business decisions. For example, the price to charge for products is based in part on information about the cost of making the products. Information must be reliable and timely if it is to be useful to management for decision making.

INTERNAL CONTROL—the policies and procedures instituted and maintained by the management of an entity in order to (1) maintain reliable control systems, (2) safeguard assets including records, (3) optimize the use of entity resources, and (4) prevent and detect error and fraud. Internal control can provide only reasonable, not absolute, assurance that management's objectives are met

SAFEGUARDING ASSETS The physical assets of a company can be stolen, misused, or accidentally destroyed unless they are protected by adequate controls. The same is true of non-physical assets such as important records (e.g., confidential business proposals or research and development data) and accounting records (e.g., accounts receivable balances, financial details). Safeguarding certain assets and records has become increasingly important since the advent of computer systems. Large amounts of information stored on computer media such as a disk or cartridge tape can be destroyed or stolen if care is not taken to protect them. Management safeguards assets by controlling access and by comparisons of assets with records of those assets.

OPTIMIZING THE USE OF RESOURCES The controls within an organization are meant to optimize use of resources by preventing unnecessary duplication of effort and waste in all aspects of the business, and by discouraging other inefficient use of resources.

There may at times be a conflict between operational efficiency and safeguarding assets and records or providing reliable information. There is a cost attached to fulfilling these two objectives and, to the extent that the cost exceeds the benefits, the results may be operationally inefficient.

Management institutes procedures and rules to meet the goals of the company. Internal control is meant to provide reasonable assurance that these are followed by company personnel.

PREVENTING AND DETECTING ERROR AND FRAUD The internal controls of a company play an important role in the prevention and detection of error or fraud and other irregularities. Management must weigh cost versus benefit when considering this objective. The cost of preventing a particular misstatement should be balanced against the likelihood of the misstatement occurring and the amount of the misstatement that could occur. Risks associated with fraud are discussed further in Chapter 10.

COMPLIANCE WITH APPLICABLE LAWS AND REGULATIONS Canadian public companies that are listed on U.S. stock exchanges, or Canadian subsidiaries of such listed public companies, must comply with the *Sarbanes-Oxley Act of 2002*. This act requires companies to issue an internal control report that is examined by the auditor. Focus Box 9-1 explains how these rules may be implemented in Canada.

In addition, public, private, and not-for-profit organizations are required to follow many laws and regulations. Some are only indirectly related to accounting, such as environmental protection and human rights laws. Others are closely related to accounting, such as income tax regulations and fraud.

Focus Box 9-1

CANADIAN SECURITIES ADMINISTRATORS (CSA) HELP CREATE "SARBANES-OXLEY NORTH"

In October 2004, the Canadian Institute of Chartered Accountants issued an exposure draft titled "An Audit of Internal Control over Financial Reporting Performed in Conjunction with an Audit of Financial Statements." This exposure draft addressed the requirements of the U.S. *Sarbanes-Oxley Act of 2002* for all U.S. public companies to issue an "internal control report" that includes the following:

- A statement that management is responsible for establishing and maintaining an adequate internal control structure and procedures for financial reporting; and
- An assessment of the effectiveness of the internal control structure and procedures for financial reporting as of the end of the company's fiscal year.

This proposed standard was issued on the assumption that similar requirements would emerge for Canada. This assumption proved correct, as in February 2005, all members of the CSA, except British Columbia, released Multilateral Instrument 52-111 for comment. This Multilateral Instrument paralleled the requirements of Section 404 of the U.S. *Sarbanes-Oxley Act*.

In addition to the aforementioned points, these proposed rules require that management retains evidence supporting its evaluation of the effectiveness of internal control, that management's assessment be audited, and that material weaknesses in internal control over financial reporting be audited.

Auditor Concerns As discussed on page 243, the study of internal control and the resultant assessment of control risk are important to auditors and are specifically included as the second generally accepted auditing examination standard.

Management's internal control objectives go beyond financial statement objectives. In other words, there are aspects of internal control that are of interest to management but not to the auditor; consequently, the auditor does not concern himself or herself with those aspects of internal control in planning the audit. An example would be internal controls that have been set up by management to ensure that accurate information about the company's market share is collected and provided to the company's marketing department.

Paragraph 5141.044 explains that the auditor considers internal control only in the context of misstatement of transactions or account balances. The auditor examines whether internal controls prevent, detect, or correct material misstatements. The auditor can consider inherent risks together with control risks by assertion, or can consider inherent or control risks separately. This text generally considers them separately, although practice will vary.

CONTROLS RELATED TO THE RELIABILITY OF FINANCIAL REPORTING The auditor is interested primarily in controls that relate to the first of management's internal control objectives: maintaining reliable control systems. This is the area that directly impacts the reliability of the financial statements and their related assertions, and therefore impacts the auditor's objective of determining that the financial statements are fairly stated. The financial statements are not likely to reflect generally accepted accounting principles correctly if the controls affecting the reliability of financial reporting are inadequate. On the other hand, the statements can be fairly stated even if the controls do not promote efficiency and effectiveness in the company's operations.

As stated in Chapter 5, auditors have significant responsibility for the discovery of management and employee fraud and, to a lesser degree, certain types of illegal acts. Auditors are therefore also concerned with a client's controls over the safeguarding of assets and compliance with applicable laws and regulations if they affect the fairness of the financial statements. Internal controls, if properly designed and implemented, can be effective in preventing and detecting fraud.

It has already been stated that auditors should emphasize controls concerned with the reliability of data for *external reporting purposes*, but controls affecting internal management information, such as budgets and internal performance reports, should not be completely ignored. These types of information are often important sources for the auditor because they can be used to develop expectations for analytical procedures. If the controls over these internal reports are considered inadequate, the value of the reports as evidence diminishes.

EMPHASIS ON CONTROLS OVER CLASSES OF TRANSACTIONS The emphasis by auditors is on controls over classes of transactions rather than on account balances. The reason is that the accuracy of the output of the accounting system (account balances) is heavily dependent upon the accuracy of the inputs and processing (transactions). For example, if products sold, units shipped, or unit selling prices are incorrectly billed to customers for sales, both sales and accounts receivable will be misstated. If controls are adequate to ensure billings, cash receipts, sales returns and allowances, and charge-offs are correct, the ending balance in accounts receivable is likely to be correct.

In the study of internal control and assessment of control risk, therefore, auditors are primarily concerned with the **transaction-related audit objectives** discussed in Chapter 5. These objectives were discussed in detail on pages 122–123. Table 9-1 illustrates the development of transaction-related audit objectives for sales transactions.

During the study of internal control and assessment of control risk, the auditor does not, however, ignore internal controls over account balances. For example, transaction-related audit objectives typically have no effect on three balance-related audit objectives: valuation, rights and obligations, and presentation and disclosure. The auditor is likely to make a separate evaluation as to whether management has implemented internal controls for each of these three balance-related audit objectives.

TRANSACTION-RELATED AUDIT OBJECTIVES—six audit objectives that must be met before the auditor can conclude that the total for any given class of transactions is fairly stated. The general transaction-related audit objectives are occurrence, completeness, accuracy, classification, timing, and posting and summarization

TABLE 9-1	Sales Transaction-Related Audit Objectives
Transaction-Related Audit Objectives —General Form	Sales Transaction-Related Audit Objectives
Occurrence	Recorded sales are for shipments made to nonfictitious customers.
Completeness	Existing sales transactions are recorded.
Accuracy	Recorded sales are for the amount of goods shipped and are correctly billed and recorded.
Classification	Sales transactions are properly classified.
Timing	Sales are recorded on the correct dates.
Posting and Summarization	Sales transactions are properly included in the data files and are correctly summarized.

→9.2 STUDYING INTERNAL CONTROL

Key Concepts

There are three basic concepts underlying the study of internal control and assessment of control risk: management's responsibility, reasonable assurance, and inherent limitations.

Management's Responsibility Management, not the auditor, must establish and maintain the entity's controls. This concept is consistent with the requirement that management, not the auditor, is responsible for the preparation of financial statements in accordance with Canadian generally accepted accounting principles.

Reasonable Assurance A company should develop internal controls that provide reasonable, but not absolute, assurance that the financial statements are fairly stated. Internal controls are developed by management after considering both the costs and benefits of the controls. Management is often unwilling to implement an ideal system because the costs may be too high. For example, it is unreasonable for auditors to expect the management of a small company to hire several additional accounting personnel to bring about a small improvement in the reliability of accounting data. It is often less expensive to have auditors do more extensive auditing than to incur higher internal control costs.

Inherent Limitations Internal controls cannot be regarded as completely effective, regardless of the care followed in their design and implementation. Even if systems personnel could design an ideal system, effectiveness of the system would depend on the competency and dependability of the people using it. For example, assume that a procedure for counting inventory is carefully developed and requires two employees to count independently. If neither of the employees understands the instructions or if both are careless in doing the counts, the count of inventory is likely to be incorrect. Even if the count is right, management might override the procedure and instruct an employee to increase the count of quantities in order to improve reported earnings. Similarly, the employees might decide to overstate the counts intentionally to cover up a theft of inventory by one or both of them. This is called **collusion**.

Because of these inherent limitations of controls and because auditors cannot have more than reasonable assurance of the controls' effectiveness, there is almost always some level of control risk greater than zero. Therefore, even with the most effectively designed internal controls, the auditor must obtain audit evidence beyond testing the controls for every material financial statement account.

COLLUSION—a cooperative effort among employees to defraud a business of cash, inventory, or other assets

Method of Information Processing

The control concepts discussed in this chapter apply to all accounting systems regardless of complexity. There are major differences between a simple computerized accounting system using purchased software for a small service company and a complex distributed system for an international manufacturing business. Nevertheless, the control objectives are the same, and the methodology discussed in this chapter is applicable to both.

For simplicity, most illustrations in this chapter apply to simple computerized systems. These are considered to be batch-based systems or online data entry systems in centralized configurations, or using a local area network (LAN) with a single server. For a description of types of configurations, consult Appendix D to Chapter 8 on page 234. Unique considerations in more advanced systems are described in Appendix E of this chapter and in subsequent chapter examples.

Components of Internal Control

Internal control includes four categories of controls that management designs and implements to provide reasonable assurance that management's control objectives will be met. These are called the components of internal control and are (1) the control environment, (2) risk assessment, (3) control systems, and (4) monitoring. Figure 9-1 shows that the control environment is the umbrella for the other three components. Without an effective control environment, the other three components are unlikely to result in effective internal control, regardless of their quality.

Figure 9-2 on page 251 shows how automated information systems have *general computer controls* as part of control activities. General controls are those computer controls that can affect multiple transaction cycles and thus multiple classes of transactions. Controls for a particular transaction cycle are often called **application controls**. These can consist of manual control procedures, fully automated control procedures, or control procedures that are assisted by the computer systems, and are described in more detail later in the chapter. For convenience, the term "procedures" is often dropped during discussion, and the phrase "manual controls," for example, would be used to describe manual control procedures.

The components of internal control contain many control-related policies and procedures. The auditor is concerned primarily with those relating to preventing or detecting material misstatements in the financial statements. Those aspects will be the focus of the remainder of the chapter.

> **APPLICATION CONTROLS**—(synonymous with *control procedures*)—the set of manual, computer-assisted, or fully automated controls that comprise the controls for a particular transaction stream

The Control Environment

The essence of an effectively controlled organization lies in the attitude of its management. If top management believes control is important, others in the organization will sense that and respond by conscientiously observing the policies and procedures established. On the other hand, if it is clear to members of the organization that control is not an important concern to top management and is given "lip service" rather than meaningful support, it is almost certain that control objectives will not be effectively achieved.

The **control environment** consists of the actions, policies, and procedures that reflect the overall attitudes of top management, the directors, and the owners of an entity about

> **CONTROL ENVIRONMENT**—the actions, policies, and procedures that reflect the overall attitudes of top management, directors, and owners of an entity about control and its importance to the entity

---

FIGURE 9-1 | **Four Components of Internal Control**

Control Environment

Risk Assessment | Control Systems | Monitoring

---

control and its importance to the entity. For the purpose of understanding and assessing the control environment, the auditor should consider the factors discussed in Section 5141 of the *CICA Assurance Handbook*. The factors, which individually and collectively enhance or diminish internal control in an entity, are:

- Management philosophy and operating style (such as a commitment to quality and competence, and communication and enforcement of integrity and ethical values)
- Active participation by the board of directors or other individuals charged with governance
- Organizational structure
- Appropriate assignment of authority and responsibility (including management control methods, systems development methodology, and management reaction to external influences)
- Human resource policies and practices (including effective use of internal audit resources)

Management Philosophy and Operating Style Management should operate ethically and honestly and encourage like behaviour among employees. "Actions speak louder than words" is a saying that most of us have heard since childhood. Management, through its activities, provides clear signals to employees about the importance of control. For example, does management take significant risks or is it risk-averse? Do policies exist to protect information and ensure privacy and confidentiality? Are profit plans and budget data set as "best possible" plans or "most likely" targets? Can management be described as "fat and bureaucratic," "lean and mean," dominated by one or a few individuals, or "just right"? Does management use aggressive accounting to ensure budgets and goals are met? Understanding these and similar aspects of management's philosophy and operating style gives the auditor a sense of its attitude about control.

The Board of Directors and Audit Committee The board and its committees should take an active role in running the company and not simply rubber-stamp management's activities. Does the audit committee meet with the auditors, both external and internal, and support them in their activities? Can the external or internal auditors go to the audit committee with concerns about the company's operations knowing they will be heard? By understanding how the board and its committees, especially the audit committee, work, the auditor will be able to assess how active an oversight role they take with respect to the entity's accounting and financial reporting policies and practices.

Organizational Structure The entity's organizational structure defines the lines of responsibilities and authority that exist. Does the entity have an appropriate organizational structure for planning, directing, and controlling operations? Are authority and responsibility assignments within the organization structure clear? Is there an information systems steering committee that oversees the development and management of information systems? By understanding the client's organizational structure, the auditor can learn the management and functional elements of the business and perceive how control-related policies and procedures can be carried out.

Methods of Assigning Authority and Responsibility The methods of communicating assignment of authority and responsibility must take into account the reporting relationships and responsibilities existing within the entity and the entity's culture. Care must be taken that issues such as the entity's policy on ethical and social issues and organizational goals and objectives are considered. The communications might include such methods as memoranda from top management about the importance of control and control-related matters, formal organizational and operating plans, employee job descriptions and related policies, and policy documents covering employee behaviour such as conflicts of interest and formal codes of conduct, including policies forbidding software copyright violation.

Management Control Methods These are the methods that management uses to supervise the entity's activities. Do policies exist indicating the status of electronic communications?

Have logical access and monitoring methods (e.g., passwords and logging) been implemented that reinforce rights of usage as defined? Management methods that monitor the activities of others enhance the effectiveness of internal control in two ways. First, the conduct of such methods sends a clear message about the importance of control. Second, the methods serve to detect misstatements that may have occurred.

An example that illustrates management control methods is an effective *budgeting system* including subsequent periodic reports of the results of operations compared to budgets. An organization that has effective planning identifies material differences between actual results and the plan, and takes appropriate corrective action at the proper management level.

Systems Development Methodology Management has the responsibility for the development and implementation of the entity's systems and procedures. The auditor should know whether management has a methodology for developing and modifying automated and manual systems and procedures or whether change occurs on an *ad hoc* basis. Where custom program development is routinely undertaken, formal methodologies with appropriate checkpoints should exist, as well as a method of evaluating systems once they have been implemented. Policies to monitor ongoing program changes should also exist. When software systems are purchased, management should ensure that the software is consistent with organizational objectives.

Management Reaction to External Influences While external influences are beyond management's control, management should be aware of these influences and be prepared to react appropriately. For example, management (and its tax advisors) should be so knowledgeable of the tax laws in filing corporate tax returns that an audit by the Canada Revenue Agency would not uncover any surprises.

Management should be aware of changes in the economy and technology in the entity's industry. For example, a retailing company should be aware of a downturn in the economy that could lead to reduced sales. The company should probably reduce its level of inventory in such a situation.

Human Resource Policies and Practices An important aspect of any system of controls is personnel. If employees are competent and trustworthy, other controls can be absent and reliable financial statements will still result. Honest, efficient people are able to perform at a high level even when there are few other controls to support them. Even if there are numerous other controls, incompetent or dishonest people can reduce the system to a shambles. Even though personnel may be competent and trustworthy, people have certain innate shortcomings. They can, for example, become bored or dissatisfied, personal problems can disrupt their performance, or their goals may change.

Because of the importance of competent, trustworthy personnel in providing effective control, the method by which persons are hired, evaluated, and compensated is an important part of internal control.

Internal Audit An effective, competent, independent, and well-trained internal audit department, which reports to the audit committee of the board of directors, can greatly enhance the operations of an entity. Internal auditors are becoming more involved in planning and assessment activities, such as systems development audits, as well as monitoring the effectiveness of other control-related policies and procedures and by performing operational audits (discussed further in Chapter 24).

In addition to its role in the entity's control environment, an adequate internal audit staff can contribute to reduced external audit costs by providing direct assistance to the external auditor. Section 5050 defines the way internal auditors affect the external auditor's evidence accumulation. If the external auditor obtains evidence that supports the competence, integrity, and objectivity of internal auditors, then the external auditor can rely on the internal auditors' work in a number of ways.

Summary The auditor is interested in the control environment as a reflection of management's commitment to internal control for the entity. If the auditor concludes that management is actively attempting to develop strong internal control through some or all of the nine factors listed above, then the auditor can conclude that the entity's internal control can likely be relied on. On the other hand, if the auditor finds that management is not committed to a positive control environment, the information contained in the company's records is not likely to be very reliable.

→ 9.3 RISK ASSESSMENT, CONTROL SYSTEMS, AND MONITORING

Risk Assessment

RISK ASSESSMENT—management's identification and analysis of risks relevant to the preparation of financial statements in conformity with GAAP

Risk assessment for financial reporting is management's identification and analysis of risks relevant to the preparation of financial statements in conformity with GAAP. For example, if a company frequently sells products at a price below inventory cost because of rapid technology changes, it is essential for the company to incorporate adequate controls to overcome the risk of overstating inventory.

The auditor obtains knowledge about management's risk assessment process by determining how management identifies risk relevant to financial reporting, evaluating their significance and likelihood of occurrence, and deciding the actions needed to address the risks. Questionnaires and discussions with management are the most common ways to obtain this understanding.

All entities, regardless of size, structure, nature, or industry, face a variety of risks from external and internal sources that must be managed. Because economic, industry, regulatory, and operating conditions constantly change, management is challenged with developing mechanisms to identify and deal with risks associated with change. Internal control under one set of conditions will not necessarily be effective under another.

Identifying and analyzing risk is an ongoing process and a critical component of effective internal control. Management must focus on risks at all levels of the organization and take necessary actions to manage them. An important first step is for management to identify factors that may increase risk. Failure to meet prior objectives, quality of personnel, geographic dispersion of company operations, significance and complexity of core business processes, introduction of new information technologies, and entrance of new competitors all represent examples of factors that may lead to increased risk. Once a risk is identified, management estimates the significance of that risk, assesses the likelihood of the risk occurring, and develops specific actions that need to be taken to reduce the risk to an acceptable level. Of course, there is no cost-beneficial way to eliminate risk. However, management must assess how much risk is prudently acceptable and strive to maintain risk within this level.

Management's risk assessment differs from, but is closely related to, the auditor's risk assessment discussed in Chapter 8. Management assesses risks as a part of designing and operating internal controls to minimize errors and fraud. Auditors assess risks to decide the evidence needed in the audit. If management effectively assesses and responds to risks, the auditor will typically accumulate less evidence than when management fails to identify or respond to significant risks.

Control Systems

The *CICA Assurance Handbook* in paragraph 5141.043 lists control systems and in paragraphs 5141.067-5141.099 divides them into five components, where we have used four. These are (i) the control environment, (ii) the entity's risk assessment process, (iii) the information system (including communications), (iv) control activities, and (v) monitoring of controls. The *information system* or *accounting system* includes policies and procedures that management implements and supports that involve the collecting, transcribing, processing, and reporting of data; and the *control activities*, which include the policies and procedures that management implements and supports that enhance the reliability of the data. The data that are collected, transcribed, processed, and reported include financial data, production data, marketing data, and personnel data, as well as other information needed to operate the entity. The control procedures include segregation of duties, suitable authorization procedures, appropriate documents and records, adequate safeguards over assets and records, and independent verification of performance and recorded data.

When an organization uses automated information systems, *general control systems and procedures* are used to describe control systems and procedures that could affect multiple classes of transactions. This text has divided control systems into components. This division means that, for purposes of discussion in this text, there will be three elements of internal control systems: (1) general control systems and procedures, (2) the accounting system, and (3) the accounting system control procedures. Figure 9-2 places these elements in a hierarchy, showing how preceding elements of internal control affect following elements.

General (Computer) Control Systems **General (computer) control systems** affect multiple classes of transactions (also called *applications*) and are intended to establish a framework of overall control over information systems processing activities. As shown in Figure 9-2, they are grouped into the following types of control systems, containing policies and procedures:

GENERAL (COMPUTER) CONTROL SYSTEMS—internal controls for automated information systems pertaining to more than one transaction cycle that could be considered part of the control environment (pervasive) or are more detailed

- *Organization and management controls.* Policies and procedures related to controls should be established, and segregation of incompatible functions should exist.
- *Systems acquisition, development, and maintenance controls.* Application systems could be purchased, developed, or otherwise acquired. Once acquired, changes may need to be made. Established methodologies and control systems should be in place to provide reasonable assurance that the systems are authorized and efficient and function in a manner consistent with organizational objectives.
- *Operations and information systems support.* Systems should be available when needed and used for authorized purposes. This section covers employee operational training, adequate documentation of day-to-day procedures, business continuity planning and information systems recovery, and physical and logical security.

The actual activities used to implement the control systems are termed general (computer) control procedures. Table 9-2 on page 252 provides examples of specific objectives, and the general control procedures used to implement the objectives for each general control system. For the purposes of brevity, the examples are illustrative only, and do not include all of the procedures that an organization would require to achieve the specific objective.

General controls at Hillsburg Hardware Limited are included in Appendix E on pages 273–274. Examples of policies and procedures associated with automated systems have been included in the previously discussed control environment. Specific controls that affect transaction cycles are also discussed in the remainder of this chapter.

FIGURE 9-2	Manual and Automated Information Systems: Control Systems*
Manual Information System	**Automated Systems**
	General Control Systems and Procedures • Organization and management controls • Systems acquisitions, development, and maintenance controls • Operations and information systems support
Accounting System*	Application System*
Accounting System* Control Procedures • Manual controls	Application System* Control Procedures • Manual controls • Computer-assisted controls • Fully automated controls

*"Accounting systems" and "application systems" are used as synonymous terms.

| TABLE 9-2 | Examples of General Control Procedures for a Specific General Control Within Each Category of General Control System |

General Control System	Specific General Control Objective	General Control Policy or Procedure
Organization and management controls	Individuals using the organization's systems should have access to only those systems required to do their job effectively. (Segregation of duties)*	1. Managers are to describe necessary access rights by job description. 2. Unique user identification codes and passwords are to be assigned to each employee.
Systems acquisition, development, and maintenance controls	Current authorized versions of payroll programs are in use at all times. (Authorization of transactions and activities)*	1. Management is to monitor government budgets to understand the timing of payroll table changes. 2. The software supplier is to be contacted to ensure that updated payroll software is received on a timely basis.
Operations and information systems support	On-line systems should be fully operational between 8:00 a.m. and 6:00 p.m., Monday through Saturday. (Safeguards over use of assets)*	Duplicate hardware resources are to be kept functional for hardware systems.

*The phrase in parentheses shows the specific type of control procedure required, based on categories used with respect to accounting system control procedures. The difference is that general control procedures affect multiple classes of transactions. For example, functional allocation of access rights applies to sales, purchasing, and general ledger systems.

The Accounting System

ACCOUNTING SYSTEM—the set of manual and/or computerized procedures that collect, record, and process data and report the resulting information

An **accounting system** has several subcomponents, typically made up of classes of transactions such as sales, sales returns, collections, acquisitions, and so on. For each class of transactions, the accounting system must satisfy all six transaction-related audit objectives identified in Table 9-1 on page 246. For example, the sales accounting system should be designed to assure that all shipments of goods by a company are correctly recorded as sales (completeness and accuracy objectives) and reflected in the financial statements in the proper period (timing objective). The system must also avoid duplicate recording of sales and recording a sale if a shipment did not occur (occurrence objective).

For a small company with active involvement by the owner, a simple computerized accounting system involving primarily one honest, competent accountant may provide an adequate accounting system. A larger company requires a more complex system, which includes carefully defined responsibilities and written procedures.

The Control Procedures

CONTROL PROCEDURES—(synonymous with *application controls*) the set of manual and/or computerized procedures that enhance the reliability of information generated by the accounting system. They include segregation of duties, suitable authorization procedures, appropriate documents and records and controls over input, adequate safeguards over assets and records, and independent verification of performance and recorded data

SEPARATION OF DUTIES—segregation of the following activities in an organization: custody of assets, recording/data entry, systems development/acquisition and maintenance, computer operations, reconciliation, and authorization.

Control procedures are the policies and procedures that help ensure that necessary actions are taken to address risks in the achievement of the entity's objectives. There are potentially many policies and procedures in any entity that could be classified as control procedures. Major categories of controls are discussed below.

Appropriate Segregation of Duties Six general categories of activities should be separated from one another. These are custody of assets, recording or data entry of transactions, systems development or acquisition and maintenance, computer operations, reconciliation, and authorization of transactions and activities. The first five are discussed in this section, but, because of its importance, authorization of transactions and activities is discussed separately.

Naturally, the extent of **separation of duties** depends heavily on the size of the organization. In many small companies, it is not practical to segregate the duties to the extent suggested. In these cases, audit evidence may require modification.

SEPARATION OF CUSTODY OF ASSETS FROM ACCOUNTING The reason for not permitting the person who has temporary or permanent custody of an asset to account for that asset is to protect the firm against defalcation. Indirect access, such as access to cheque signature images, also must be separate. When one person performs both custody and accounting functions, there is an excessive risk of that person's disposing of or using the asset for personal gain and adjusting the records to relieve himself or herself of responsibility. If the cashier, for example, receives cash and is responsible for data entry of cash receipts and sales, it is possible for the cashier to take the cash received from a customer and adjust the customer's account by failing to record a sale or by recording a fictitious credit to the account.

SEPARATION OF OPERATIONAL RESPONSIBILITY FROM RECORDING OR DATA ENTRY OF TRANSACTIONS If each department or division in an organization were responsible for preparing its own records and reports, there would be a tendency to bias the results to improve its reported performance. In order to ensure unbiased information, record-keeping is typically included in a separate accounting department under the controller.

SEPARATION OF SYSTEMS DEVELOPMENT OR ACQUISITION AND MAINTENANCE FROM ACCOUNTING Systems development or acquisition comprises activities that create (or purchase) new methods of processing transactions, thus changing the way information is entered, displayed, reported, and posted against files or databases. Maintenance activities involve changes to these processes. These functions should be monitored to ensure that only authorized programs and systems consistent with management objectives are put into place. A programmer who could enter data could enter transactions (e.g., a wage rate increase) and then suppress the printout showing the transaction. Two job functions in this grouping are:

- *Systems analyst.* The systems analyst is responsible for the general design of the system. The analyst sets the objectives of the overall system and the specific design of particular applications.
- *Programmer.* Based on the individual objectives specified by the systems analyst, the programmer develops special flowcharts for the application, prepares computer instructions, tests the program, and documents the results.

If there is inadequate control over software systems or over individual programs, then the auditor would be unable to rely on activities handled by those systems. For example, imagine being unable to rely on interest calculations made by a bank or on the aging in the accounts receivable aged trial balance. These types of situations occur when the auditor is unable to rely on system or program changes. When the entity has systems development or maintenance functions, a *quality assurance function* tests the functioning of the new systems or changes, helping ensure that inadvertent errors or unauthorized functions have not been introduced.

SEPARATION OF COMPUTER OPERATIONS FROM PROGRAMMING AND ACCOUNTING These job functions include basic procedures such as handling output reports and taking backup copies of information, and more complex functions such as set-up of functional access rights in password systems or development of information systems recovery procedures. Help-desk or computer support personnel may also be included in this area. Personnel who have physical access to media or the capability to set access rights could steal confidential information or give themselves the right to do anything on the system. Separation from authorization, data entry of transactions, or the ability to change programs makes it harder for personnel to suppress a trail of their activities.

Some organizations have a librarian to provide physical custody of the media holding the computer programs, transaction files, and other important computer records. The librarian provides a means of important physical control over these records and releases them only to authorized personnel.

SEPARATION OF RECONCILIATION FROM DATA ENTRY Reconciliation involves comparing information from two or more sources, or independently verifying the work that has been completed by others. For example, independent preparation of a bank reconciliation by the accounting manager from the accounts receivable or accounts payable personnel would detect unauthorized use or disbursements of cash.

For batch-based computer systems, a *data control group* handles the flow of transactions from users, passing the transactions to data entry after logging the number of them, then matching output to logged details to help ensure that all transactions have been recorded, before passing the transactions and reports back to users. An *independent check* by someone other than the data entry person of key information entered, such as payroll rates or customer credit limits, also serves as a form of *data control function*.

Proper Authorization of Transactions and Activities If possible, it is desirable to prevent persons who authorize transactions from having control over the related assets. For example, the same person should not authorize the payment of a vendor's invoice and also sign the cheque in payment of the bill. The authorization of a transaction and the handling of the related asset by the same person increase the possibility of defalcation within the organization. A person who authorizes transactions and handles computer operations could suppress printouts documenting the transactions. Similarly, a programmer who could authorize transactions could set up a fictitious supplier, authorize payments to that supplier, then alter the accounts payable programs so that the transactions did not print on reports.

Authorization also includes authorization of new programs or changes to programs since this affects the way that transactions are processed.

Every transaction must be properly authorized if controls are to be satisfactory. If any person in an organization could acquire or expend assets at will, complete chaos would result. Authorization can be either *general* or *specific*. **General authorization** means that management establishes policies for the organization to follow. Subordinates are instructed to implement these general authorizations by approving all transactions within the limits set by the policy. Examples of general authorization are the issuance of fixed price lists for the sale of products, credit limits for customers, and fixed re-order points for making purchases. General authorization can be implemented manually or embedded within computer programs, for example, where computer systems check for and reject orders if they cause a customer's accounts receivable balance to exceed the established credit limit.

Specific authorization has to do with individual transactions. Management is often unwilling to establish a general policy of authorization for some transactions. Instead, it prefers to make authorizations on a case-by-case basis. One example is the authorization of a sales transaction by the sales manager for a used-car company. Another example is that grocery clerks are authorized to reverse only small dollar transactions; for larger transactions, a supervisor must insert a key or type a password before the transaction can be completed.

There is also a distinction between authorization and approval. Authorization is a policy decision for either a general class of transactions or specific transactions. Approval is the implementation of management's general authorization decisions. For example, assume management sets a policy authorizing the order of inventory when there is less than a three-week supply on hand. This is a general authorization. When a department orders inventory, the purchasing agent approves the order to indicate that the authorization policy has been met.

Adequate Documents and Records *Documents* and *records* are the physical objects (paper or electronic files) on which transactions are entered and summarized. They include such diverse items as sales invoices, purchase orders, subsidiary records, sales journals, and employee time cards. Both documents of original entry and records on which transactions are entered are important, but the inadequacy of documents normally causes greater control problems.

Documents and computer files perform the function of transmitting information throughout the client's organization and among different organizations. These records must be adequate to provide reasonable assurance that all assets are properly controlled and all transactions correctly recorded. For example, if the receiving department fills out a receiving report when material is obtained, the accounts payable department can verify the quantity and description on the vendor's invoice by comparing it with the information on the receiving report. Programming errors that result in inaccurate processing can result in inaccurate records.

Certain relevant principles dictate the proper design and use of documents, electronic transactions, and input screens. These should be:

GENERAL AUTHORIZATION—company-wide policies for the approval of all transactions within stated limits

SPECIFIC AUTHORIZATION—case-by-case approval of transactions not covered by company-wide policies

- Prenumbered or automatically numbered consecutively to facilitate control over missing records, and to aid in locating records when they are needed at a later date (significantly affects the transaction-related audit objective of completeness).
- Prepared at the time a transaction takes place, or as soon thereafter as possible. When there is a longer time interval, records are less credible and the chance for misstatement is increased (affects the transaction-related audit objective of timing).
- Sufficiently simple and described to ensure that they are clearly understood.
- Designed for multiple use whenever possible to minimize the number of different forms. For example, a properly designed and used shipping document can be the basis for releasing goods from storage to the shipping department, informing billing of the quantity of goods to bill the customer and the appropriate billing date, and updating the perpetual inventory records.
- Constructed in a manner that encourages correct preparation. This can be done by providing a degree of internal check within the form or record. For example, a document might include instructions for proper routing, blank spaces for authorizations and approvals, and designated column spaces for numerical data. Input screens would label fields that are to be entered, provide input entry edits (e.g., checking on valid date), and prevent users from proceeding until all relevant information has been completed.

CHART OF ACCOUNTS A control closely related to documents and records is the **chart of accounts,** which classifies transactions into individual balance sheet and income statement accounts. The chart of accounts is an important control because it provides the framework for determining the information presented to management and other financial statement users. The chart of accounts is helpful in preventing classification errors if it accurately and precisely describes which type of transactions should be in each account.

SYSTEMS MANUALS The procedures for proper record-keeping should be spelled out in systems manuals to encourage consistent application. The manuals should provide sufficient information to facilitate adequate record-keeping and the maintenance of proper control over assets. These could include procedural manuals, software user manuals, program documentation, and computer operations procedures.

Adequate Safeguards over Access to and Use of Assets and Records It is essential to have adequate internal control to protect assets and records. If assets are left unprotected, they can be stolen. If records are not adequately protected, they can be stolen, damaged, or lost.

CHART OF ACCOUNTS—a listing of all the entity's accounts, which classifies transactions into individual balance sheet and income statement accounts

In the event of such an occurrence, the accounting process as well as normal operations could be seriously disrupted. When a company is highly computerized, it is especially important to protect its computer equipment, programs, and data files. The equipment and programs are expensive and essential to operations. The data files are the records of the company and, if damaged, could be costly, or even impossible, to reconstruct.

The most important type of protective measure for safeguarding physical assets and records is the use of physical precautions. An example is the use of storerooms for inventory to guard against pilferage. When the storeroom is under the control of a competent and knowledgeable employee, there is also further assurance that obsolescence is minimized. Fireproof safes and safety deposit vaults for the protection of assets such as currency and securities are other important physical safeguards.

There are three categories of controls related to safeguarding data-processing equipment, programs, and data files. As with other types of assets, *physical controls* are used to protect the computer facilities. Examples are locks on doors to the computer room and terminals, adequate storage space for software and data files to protect them from loss, and proper fire-extinguishing systems. *Access controls* deal with ensuring that only authorized people can use the equipment and have access to software and data files. An example is an online access password system. *Backup* and *recovery procedures* are steps an organization can take in the event of a loss of equipment, programs, or data. For example, having a backup copy of programs and critical data files stored in a safe remote location together with information systems recovery procedures is important for maintaining business continuity.

INDEPENDENT CHECKS—internal control activities designed for the continuous internal verification of other controls

Independent Verification of Performance and the Accuracy of Recorded Amounts The last category of control procedures is the careful and continuous review of the other four, often referred to as *independent check on performance* or *internal verification*. The need for **independent checks** arises because internal control tends to change over time unless there is a mechanism for frequent review. Personnel are likely to forget or intentionally fail to follow procedures, or become careless unless someone observes and evaluates their performance. In addition, both fraudulent and unintentional misstatements are possible, regardless of the quality of the controls.

An essential characteristic of the persons performing internal verification procedures is independence from the individuals originally responsible for preparing the data. The least expensive means of internal verification is the separation of duties in the manner previously discussed. For example, when the bank reconciliation is performed by a person independent of the accounting records and handling of cash, there is an opportunity for verification without incurring significant additional costs.

Computerized accounting systems can be designed so that many internal verification procedures can be automated as part of the system, such as separate addition of subsidiary files for agreement to general ledger totals.

Monitoring

MONITORING—management's ongoing and periodic assessment of the quality of internal control performance to determine that controls are operating as intended and modified when needed

Monitoring activities deal with ongoing or periodic assessment of the quality of internal control performance by management to determine that controls are operating as intended and that they are modified as appropriate for changes in conditions. Information for assessment and modification comes from a variety of sources including studies of existing internal controls, internal auditor reports, exception reporting on control activities, reports by regulators such as the Office of the Superintendent of Financial Institutions, feedback from operating personnel, and complaints from customers about billing charges.

Internal Audit Function For many companies, especially larger ones, an internal audit department is essential to effective monitoring. For an internal audit function to be effective, it is important that the internal audit staff be independent of both the operating and accounting departments, and that it report directly to a high level of authority within the organization, usually the audit committee of the board of directors.

In addition to its role in monitoring an entity's internal controls, an adequate internal audit staff can contribute to reduced external audit costs by providing direct assistance to the external auditor, as was mentioned previously.

Size of Business and Internal Control The size of a company does have a significant effect on the nature of internal control and the specific controls. It is more difficult to establish adequate separation of duties in a small company. It would also be unreasonable to expect a small firm to have internal auditors. However, if the various components of internal control are examined, it becomes apparent that most are applicable to both large and small companies. Even though it may not be common to formalize policies in manuals, it is certainly possible for a small company to have competent, trustworthy personnel with clear lines of authority; proper procedures for authorization, execution, and recording of transactions; adequate documents, records, and reports; physical controls over assets and records; and, to a limited degree, checks on performance.

A major control available in a small company is the knowledge and concern of the top operating person, who is frequently an owner-manager. Knowledge about and personal interest in the organization and a close relationship with the personnel (often called "executive controls") make possible careful evaluation of the competence of the employees and the effectiveness of the overall system. For example, internal control can be significantly strengthened if the owner conscientiously performs such duties as signing all cheques after carefully reviewing supporting documents, reviewing bank reconciliations, examining accounts receivable statements sent to customers, approving credit, examining all correspondence from customers and vendors, and approving bad debts.

Summary of Internal Control A summary of the components of internal control discussed in the preceding sections (control environment, general controls, accounting systems, control procedures) is included in Table 9-3.

→9.4 INTERNAL CONTROLS AND THE AUDIT PROCESS

Overview of Understanding Internal Control for Audit Planning Purposes and Assessing Control Risk

The remainder of the chapter deals with how auditors obtain information about internal control and use that information as a basis for audit planning. To help understand how the auditor accomplishes this, an overview of the relevant parts of obtaining an understanding of internal control, assessing control risk, and relating the results to tests of financial statement balances are discussed. We also look at the impact of general controls and how controls

TABLE 9-3	Components of Internal Control		
	Internal Controls		
Control Environment	**General Control Systems and Procedures**	**Accounting Systems**	**Control Procedures**
Subelements of control environment: · management philosophy and operating style · active board participation · organizational structure · audit committee · methods of assigning authority and responsibility · management control methods · internal audit function · human resource policies and procedures · external influences · systems development methodology	Types of general controls: · organization and management · systems acquisition, development, and maintenance · operations and information systems support	Transaction-related audit objectives that must be satisfied: · occurrence · completeness · accuracy · classification · timing · posting and summarization	Categories of control procedures: · adequate separation of duties · proper authorization of transactions and activities · adequate documents and records · physical control over assets and records · independent checks on performance

are tested. Reporting on management's assessment of internal control is examined separately in the next section.

Reasons for Understanding Internal Control Sufficient to Plan the Examination The auditor must obtain sufficient understanding of the client's internal control to plan the examination for every audit and to assess risks. The extent of that understanding must, at a minimum, be sufficient to adequately plan the examination in terms of four specific planning matters.

AUDITABILITY The auditor must obtain information about the integrity of management and the nature and extent of the accounting records to be satisfied that sufficient appropriate audit evidence is available to support the financial statement balances and the auditor's report.

POTENTIAL MATERIAL MISSTATEMENTS The understanding should allow the auditor to identify the types of potential errors or fraud and other irregularities that might affect the financial statements, and to assess the risk that such misstatements might occur in amounts that are material to the financial statements.

PLANNED DETECTION RISK Control risk in the planning form of the audit risk model directly affects detection risk for each audit objective [$PDR = AR / (IR \times CR)$]. Information about internal control is used to assess control risk for each control objective, which in turn affects planned detection risk and planned audit evidence.

DESIGN OF TESTS The information obtained should allow the auditor to design effective tests of the financial statement balances for each audit assertion. Such tests include tests for monetary correctness of transactions and balances, as well as analytical procedures. These are discussed in more detail in Chapter 11.

Understanding Internal Control for Design and Implementation Each of the four components of internal control must be studied and understood. In obtaining that understanding, the auditor should consider two aspects: (1) the *design* of the various policies and procedures within each control element and (2) whether they have been implemented or placed in *operation.*

UNDERSTANDING THE CONTROL ENVIRONMENT Information is obtained about the control environment for each of the subcomponents discussed earlier in the chapter. The auditor then uses the understanding as a basis for assessing management's and the directors' attitudes and awareness about the importance of control. For example, the auditor might determine the nature of a client's budgeting system as a part of understanding the design of the control environment. The operation of the budgeting system might then be evaluated in part by (1) enquiry of budgeting personnel to determine budgeting procedures and (2) follow-up of differences between budget and actual amounts. The auditor might also examine client schedules comparing actual results to budgets.

UNDERSTANDING GENERAL CONTROLS The nature and level of complexity of automation in the information systems used at the organization will affect the amount of effort required by the auditor to understand general controls. The auditor obtains information about the organizational structure of the information systems processing department, the hardware and software configuration of computing systems, and a general description of the types of automated systems in use. This is used to plan the extent of work required to understand general controls. For example, if the organization has programmers on staff and many of its financial systems use customized software, then the auditor will need to spend time documenting the processes used to authorize, design, test, implement, and change such software. Appendix E on pages 273–274 provides a brief description of some general control systems and procedures at Hillsburg Hardware Limited. For further information on general controls, the reader should refer to the CICA's *Information Technology Control Guidelines*, 3rd edition.

UNDERSTANDING THE ACCOUNTING SYSTEM To understand the design of the accounting system, the auditor determines (1) the major classes of transactions of the entity; (2) how those transactions are initiated; (3) what accounting records and data files exist and their nature; (4) how transactions are processed from initiation to completion, including a description of processing handled by computer programs; and (5) the nature and details of the financial reporting process followed. Typically, this is accomplished and documented by a *narrative description* of the system or by *flowcharting*. (These are described later in the chapter.) The operation of the accounting system is often determined by tracing one or a few transactions through the accounting system (called a **transaction walk-through**).

TRANSACTION WALK-THROUGH— the tracing of selected transactions through the accounting system

UNDERSTANDING THE CONTROL PROCEDURES Auditors obtain an understanding of the control environment, general computer controls, and accounting system in a similar manner for most audits, but obtaining an understanding of control procedures varies considerably. For smaller clients, it is common to identify few or even no control procedures because controls are often ineffective due to limited personnel. In that case, a high assessed level of control risk is used; that is, control risk is assessed at maximum. For clients with extensive controls where the auditor believes controls are likely to be excellent, it is often appropriate to identify many controls during the controls understanding phase. In still other audits, the auditor may identify a limited number of controls during this phase and then identify additional controls later in the process. The extent to which controls are identified is a matter of audit judgment. The key part of this process is obtaining enough understanding so that controls can be understood for each audit assertion, allowing for design of audit tests. A methodology for identifying controls is studied later in the chapter.

Assessment and Decisions Once an understanding of internal control that is sufficient for audit planning is obtained, two major assessments must be made. The assessment of auditability is undertaken as part of the client acceptance or client continuance process.

ASSESS WHETHER THE FINANCIAL STATEMENTS ARE AUDITABLE The first assessment is whether the entity is auditable. Two primary factors determine auditability: the control environment, with an emphasis on the integrity of management, and the adequacy of accounting methods. Many audit procedures rely to some extent on the representations of management. For example, it is difficult for the auditor to evaluate whether inventory is obsolete without an honest assessment by management. If management lacks integrity, management may provide false representations causing the auditor to rely on unreliable evidence.

The accounting records serve as a direct source of audit evidence for most audit objectives. If the accounting records are deficient, necessary audit evidence may not be available. For example, if the client has not kept duplicate sales invoices and vendors' invoices, it would normally not be possible to do an audit. Unless the auditor can identify an alternative source of reliable evidence, or unless appropriate records can be constructed for the auditor's use, the only recourse may be to consider the entity unauditable.

When it is concluded that the entity is not auditable, the auditor discusses the circumstances with the client (usually at the highest level) and either withdraws from the engagement or issues a denial form of auditor's report.

DETERMINE THE LEVEL OF CONTROL RISK SUPPORTED BY THE UNDERSTANDING OBTAINED After obtaining an understanding of internal control, the auditor makes an initial assessment of control risk. Control risk is a measure of the auditor's expectation that internal controls *will neither prevent material misstatements* from occurring *nor detect and correct them* if they have occurred.

The initial assessment is made for each transaction-related audit objective for each major type of transaction. For example, the auditor makes an assessment of the existence objective for sales and a separate assessment for the completeness objective. There are different ways to express this expectation. Some auditors use a subjective expression such as high, moderate, or low. Others use numerical probabilities such as 1.0, 0.6, or 0.2.

The initial assessment usually starts with consideration of the control environment and then of general computer controls. If the attitude of management is that control is unimportant, it is doubtful that general controls or detailed control procedures will be reliable. If general controls are inadequate, then the individual automated systems affecting the transaction cycles will not be reliable. The best course of action in that case is to assume that control risk for all transaction-related audit objectives is at maximum (such as high or 1.0). On the other hand, if management's attitude is positive, the auditor then considers the specific policies and procedures within the control environment, the accounting system, and control procedures. Those policies and procedures are used as a basis for an assessment below maximum.

There are two important considerations about the assessment. First, the auditor does not have to make the assessment in a formal, detailed manner. In many audits, particularly of smaller companies, the auditor assumes that the control risk is at maximum whether or not it actually is. The auditor's reason for taking this approach is that he or she has concluded that it is more economical to audit the financial statement balances more extensively rather than to conduct tests of controls. Second, even though the auditor believes control risk is low, the level of control risk *assessed* is limited to that level supported by the evidence obtained. For example, suppose the auditor believes that control risk for unrecorded sales is low but has gathered little evidence in support of control procedures for the completeness objective. The auditor's assessment of control risk for unrecorded sales must either be moderate or high. It could be low only if additional evidence was obtained in support of the pertinent controls.

ASSESS WHETHER IT IS LIKELY THAT A LOWER ASSESSED CONTROL RISK COULD BE SUPPORTED When the auditor believes that actual control risk may be significantly lower than the initial assessment (i.e., actual controls in place are likely significantly better), he or she may decide to support a lower assessed control risk. The most likely case where this occurs is when the auditor has identified a limited number of controls during the understanding phase. Based on the results of the initial assessment, the auditor now believes that additional controls can be identified and tested to further reduce assessed control risk.

DECIDE ON THE APPROPRIATE ASSESSED CONTROL RISK After the auditor completes the initial assessment and considers whether a lower assessed control risk is likely, he or she is in a position to decide which assessed control risk should be used: either a level already supported in the initial assessment, or an even lower level that would need to be justified by further testing. The decision as to which level to use is essentially an economic one, recognizing the trade-off between the costs of testing relevant controls and the costs of substantive tests that would be avoided by reducing assessed control risk. Assume, for example, that for the existence and accuracy transaction-related audit objectives for sales, the auditor believes that the cost of confirming accounts receivable could be reduced by $5,000 by incurring $2,000 to support a lower assessed control risk. It would be cost effective to incur the $2,000 additional cost.

Where the client uses paperless systems or advanced automated processes such as electronic data interchange, Section 5141.116 explains that it may not be possible "to reduce the risks of material misstatement at the assertion level to an acceptably low level with audit evidence obtained only from substantive procedures." This is a roundabout way of saying that the auditor may be required to rely upon internal controls in such situations. Then, the cost-benefit decision is applied among alternative tests of controls rather than choosing between tests of controls and tests of details.

Tests of Controls Assessing control risk requires the auditor to consider the design of controls to evaluate whether they would be effective in meeting specific transaction-related audit objectives. In order to use specific controls as a basis for assessing control risk below maximum, specific evidence must be obtained about their *effectiveness* throughout all (or most) of the period under audit. The procedures to gather evidence about design and placement in operation during the understanding phase are called *procedures to obtain an understanding*. The procedures to test effectiveness of controls in support of assessing control risk below maximum are called **tests of controls**. Both are discussed in more detail later in the chapter.

TESTS OF CONTROLS—audit procedures to test the effectiveness of controls in support of control risk assessed below maximum

| Obtain understanding of internal control: design and operation | → | Assess control risk | → | Test controls | → | Decide planned detection risk and substantive tests |

Where the results of tests of controls support the design of controls as expected, the auditor proceeds to use the same assessed control risk. If, however, the tests of controls indicate the controls did not operate effectively, the assessed level of control risk must be reconsidered. For example, the tests may indicate that frequent program changes occurred during the year or that the person applying the control made frequent errors. In such situations, a higher assessed level of control risk would be used unless additional controls relating to the same transaction-related audit objectives could be identified and found effective.

Planned Detection Risk and Substantive Tests The result of the preceding steps is the determination of the assessed level of control risk, for each objective, for each of the entity's major transaction types. Where the assessed level of control risk is below maximum, it will be supported by specific tests of controls. These assessments are then related to the balance-related audit objectives for the accounts affected by the major transaction types. The appropriate level of detection risk for each balance-related audit objective is then determined using the audit risk model. The relationship of detection risk to audit objectives and the selection and design of audit procedures for substantive tests of financial statement balances are discussed and illustrated in Chapters 11 and 14.

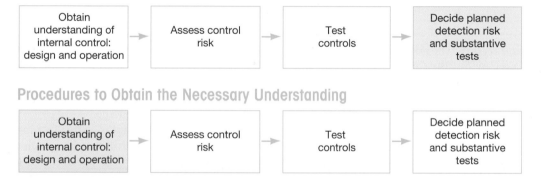

Procedures to Obtain the Necessary Understanding

In practice, the study of a client's internal control and assessment of control risk varies considerably from client to client. For smaller clients, many auditors obtain a level of understanding sufficient only to assess whether the statements are auditable, evaluate the control environment for management's attitude, and determine the adequacy of the client's accounting system. Often, for efficiency, control procedures are not tested, control risk is assumed to be maximum, and detection risk is therefore low. This approach is described as a substantive audit approach.

For many larger clients, especially for repeat engagements, the auditor plans on a low assessed level of control risk for most parts of the audit before the audit starts. This approach is a combined audit approach. Having determined that internal controls can be relied on, the auditor first obtains an understanding of the control environment and the accounting system at a fairly detailed level, then identifies specific controls that will reduce control risk and makes an assessment of control risk, then tests the controls for effectiveness. The auditor can conclude that control risk is low only after all three steps are completed. The three steps discussed above are now explained in more detail to illustrate further how the study of a client's internal control and assessment of control risk are done.

Procedures Relating to Design and Implementation The auditor's **procedures to obtain an understanding** of internal control attempt to find out about the elements of internal control, see that they have been implemented, and document the information obtained in a useful manner. The following are procedures relating to design and implementation.

PROCEDURES TO OBTAIN AN UNDERSTANDING—procedures used by the auditor to gather evidence about the design and implementation of specific controls

UPDATE AND EVALUATE AUDITOR'S PREVIOUS EXPERIENCE WITH THE ENTITY Most audits of a company are done annually by the same public accounting firm. Except for initial engagements, the auditor begins the audit with a great deal of information about the client's internal controls developed in prior years. Because systems and controls change infrequently, this information can be updated and carried forward to the current year's audit.

MAKE ENQUIRIES OF CLIENT PERSONNEL A logical starting place for updating information carried forward from the previous audit or for obtaining information initially is with appropriate client personnel. Enquiries of client personnel at the management, supervisory, and staff level will usually be conducted as part of obtaining an understanding of the design of internal control. Care must be taken to document the information collected.

READ CLIENT'S POLICY AND SYSTEMS MANUALS To design, implement, and maintain its internal controls, an entity must have extensive documentation of its own. This includes policy manuals and documents (e.g., a corporate code of conduct) and systems manuals and documents (e.g., an accounting manual and an organization chart). This information is studied by the auditor and discussed with company personnel to assure that it is properly interpreted and understood.

EXAMINE DOCUMENTS AND RECORDS The control environment, the details of the accounting system, and the application of control procedures will involve the creation of many documents and records. These will have been presented to some degree in the policy and systems manuals. By inspecting actual completed documents and records, the auditor can bring the contents of the manuals to life and better understand them. Inspection also provides evidence that the control policies and procedures have been placed in operation.

For businesses with large volumes (such as hundreds of thousands or millions of transactions) or paperless systems, the auditor is likely to use computer-assisted tests and online viewing of transactions as an alternative to viewing paper documents.

OBSERVE THE ENTITY'S ACTIVITIES AND OPERATIONS In addition to inspecting completed documents and records, the auditor can observe client personnel in the process of preparing them and carrying out their normal accounting and control activities. When the client uses paperless systems, this may require the running of test transactions through the system to verify the understanding, or specialist computer audit assistance. This further enhances understanding and verifies that control policies and procedures have been implemented.

Observation, documentation, and enquiry can be conveniently and effectively combined in the form of the transaction walk-through mentioned earlier. With that procedure, the auditor selects one or a few documents for the initiation of a transaction type and traces it (them) through the entire accounting process. At each stage of processing, the auditor makes enquiries and observes current activities, in addition to inspecting completed documentation for the transaction or transactions selected.

Documentation of the Understanding Three commonly used methods of documenting the understanding of internal control are narratives, flowcharts, and internal control questionnaires. These may be used separately or in combination, as discussed below.

NARRATIVE—a written description of a client's internal controls, including the origin, processing, and disposition of documents and records, and the relevant control procedures

NARRATIVE A **narrative** is a written description of a client's internal controls. A proper narrative of an accounting system and related controls includes four characteristics:

- The origin of every document and record in the system. For example, the description should state where customer orders come from and how sales invoices arise.
- All processing that takes place. For example, if sales amounts are determined by a computer program that multiplies quantities shipped by stored standard prices, that should be described.
- The disposition of every document and record in the system. The updating of computer files, method of storing of documents, and transferral to customers or discarding of documents should be described.
- An indication of controls relevant to the assessment of control risk. These typically include separation of duties (e.g., separating recording cash from handling cash), authorization and approvals (e.g., credit approvals), and internal verification (e.g., comparison of unit selling price to sales contracts).

FLOWCHART An internal control **flowchart** is a symbolic, diagrammatic representation of the client's documents and their sequential flow in the organization. An adequate flowchart includes the same four characteristics identified above for narratives.

Flowcharting is useful primarily because it can provide a concise overview of the client's system as an analytical tool in evaluation. A well-prepared flowchart aids in identifying inadequacies by facilitating a clear understanding of how the system operates. For most uses, it is superior to narrative descriptions as a method of communicating the characteristics of a system, especially to show adequate separation of duties. It is easier to follow a diagram than to read a description. It is also usually easier to update a flowchart, particularly one that is stored electronically, than a narrative. Most auditor flowcharting is now completed using automated working paper software. The auditor may also use the automatic program or automatic systems flowcharts that have been prepared by client software systems.

It would be unusual to use both a narrative and a flowchart to describe the same system, since both are intended to describe the flow of documents and records in an accounting system. Sometimes a combination of a narrative and flowchart is used. The decision to use one or the other or a combination of the two is dependent on two factors: relative ease of understanding by current- and subsequent-year auditors and relative cost of preparation.

INTERNAL CONTROL QUESTIONNAIRE An **internal control questionnaire** asks a series of questions about the controls in each audit area, including the control environment, as a means of indicating to the auditor aspects of internal control that may be inadequate. In most instances, it is designed to require a "yes" or "no" response, with "no" responses indicating potential internal control deficiencies. Where automated working paper software is used, the responses can be automatically linked and cross-referenced to supporting documentation and weakness investigation working papers.

The primary advantage of the questionnaire is the ability to cover each audit area thoroughly and reasonably quickly at the beginning of the audit. The primary disadvantage is that individual parts of the client's systems are examined without providing an overall view, although recently developed internal control documentation software overcomes this weakness. In addition, a standard questionnaire is often inapplicable to some audit clients, especially smaller ones.

Figure 9-3 on page 264 illustrates part of an internal control questionnaire for the sales and collection cycle of Hillsburg Hardware Limited. The questionnaire is also designed for use with the six transaction-related audit objectives. Notice that each objective (A through F) is a transaction-related objective as it applies to sales transactions (see shaded portions). The same is true for all other audit areas.

We believe the use of both questionnaires and flowcharts is highly desirable for understanding the client's system. Flowcharts provide an overview of the system, and questionnaires are useful checklists to remind the auditor of many different types of controls that should exist. When properly used, a combination of these two approaches should provide the auditor with an excellent description of the system.

It is often desirable to use the client's narratives or flowcharts and have the client fill out the internal control questionnaire, as long as any subsequent reliance on controls is adequately substantiated with testing. When understandable and reliable narratives, flowcharts, and questionnaires are not available from a client, which is frequently the case, the auditor must prepare them. Many auditors rely on electronic auditing tools, including industry-specific checklists and industry-specific flowcharting templates that can be completed and viewed electronically.

Assessing Control Risk

Once the auditor has obtained descriptive information and evidence in support of the design and operation of internal control, an **assessment of control risk** by transaction-

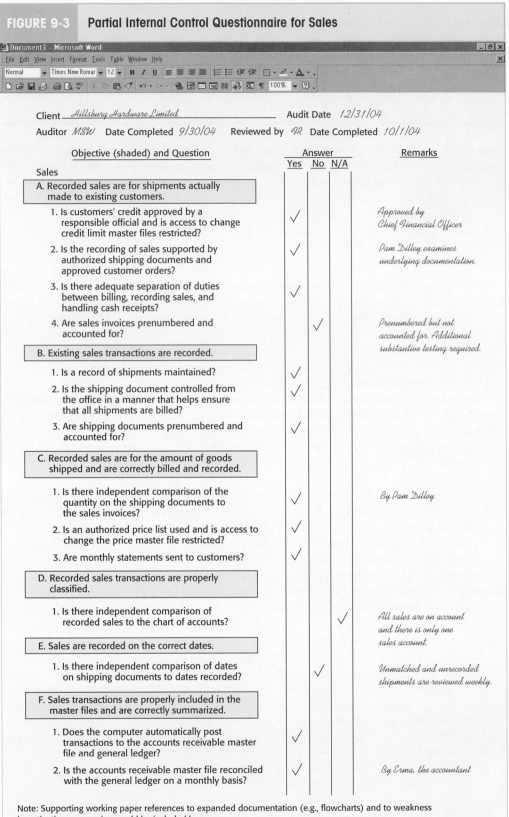

FIGURE 9-3 Partial Internal Control Questionnaire for Sales

Client _Hillsburg Hardware Limited_ _____ Audit Date _12/31/04_

Auditor _MSW_ Date Completed _9/30/04_ Reviewed by _AR_ Date Completed _10/1/04_

Objective (shaded) and Question	Yes	No	N/A	Remarks
Sales				
A. Recorded sales are for shipments actually made to existing customers.				
1. Is customers' credit approved by a responsible official and is access to change credit limit master files restricted?	✓			Approved by Chief Financial Officer
2. Is the recording of sales supported by authorized shipping documents and approved customer orders?	✓			Pam Dilley examines underlying documentation.
3. Is there adequate separation of duties between billing, recording sales, and handling cash receipts?	✓			
4. Are sales invoices prenumbered and accounted for?		✓		Prenumbered but not accounted for. Additional substantive testing required.
B. Existing sales transactions are recorded.				
1. Is a record of shipments maintained?	✓			
2. Is the shipping document controlled from the office in a manner that helps ensure that all shipments are billed?	✓			
3. Are shipping documents prenumbered and accounted for?	✓			
C. Recorded sales are for the amount of goods shipped and are correctly billed and recorded.				
1. Is there independent comparison of the quantity on the shipping documents to the sales invoices?	✓			By Pam Dilley
2. Is an authorized price list used and is access to change the price master file restricted?	✓			
3. Are monthly statements sent to customers?	✓			
D. Recorded sales transactions are properly classified.				
1. Is there independent comparison of recorded sales to the chart of accounts?			✓	All sales are on account and there is only one sales account.
E. Sales are recorded on the correct dates.				
1. Is there independent comparison of dates on shipping documents to dates recorded?		✓		Unmatched and unrecorded shipments are reviewed weekly.
F. Sales transactions are properly included in the master files and are correctly summarized.				
1. Does the computer automatically post transactions to the accounts receivable master file and general ledger?	✓			
2. Is the accounts receivable master file reconciled with the general ledger on a monthly basis?	✓			By Erma, the accountant

Note: Supporting working paper references to expanded documentation (e.g., flowcharts) and to weakness investigation summaries would be included here.

related audit objective can be made. This is normally done separately for each major type of transaction in each transaction cycle. For example, in the sales and collection cycle, the types of transactions usually involve sales, sales returns and allowances, cash receipts, and the provision for and write-off of uncollectible accounts.

Identify Transaction-Related Audit Objectives The first step in the assessment is to identify the transaction-related audit objectives to which the assessment applies. This is done by applying the transaction-related audit objectives introduced earlier, which are stated in general form, to each major type of transaction for the entity.

Identify Specific Controls The next step is to identify the specific controls that contribute to accomplishing each transaction-related audit objective. The auditor identifies pertinent controls by proceeding through the descriptive information about the client's system. Those policies and procedures that, in his or her judgment, provide control over the transaction involved are identified. In doing this, it is often helpful to refer back to the types of controls that *might* exist, and ask if they *do* exist. For example: Is there adequate segregation of duties and how is it achieved? Are the documents used well designed? Are there controls over inputting to the computer system?

The auditor should identify and include those controls that are expected to have the greatest impact on meeting the transaction-related audit objectives. These are often termed *key controls*. The reason for including only key controls is that they will be sufficient to achieve the transaction-related audit objectives and should provide audit efficiency.

Identify and Evaluate Weaknesses *Weaknesses* are defined as the *absence of adequate controls*, which increases the risk of misstatements existing in the financial statements. If, in the judgment of the auditor, there are inadequate controls to satisfy one of the transaction-related audit objectives, expectation of such a misstatement occurring increases. For example, if no internal verification of the valuation of payroll transactions is taking place, the auditor may conclude there is a weakness in internal control.

A four-step approach can be used for identifying significant **internal control weaknesses.**

IDENTIFY EXISTING CONTROLS Because weaknesses are the absence of adequate controls, the auditor must first know which controls exist. The methods for identifying existing controls have already been discussed.

IDENTIFY THE ABSENCE OF KEY CONTROLS Internal control questionnaires, narratives, and flowcharts are useful to identify areas in which key controls are lacking and the likelihood of misstatements is thereby increased. When control risk is assessed as moderate or high, there is usually an absence of controls.

DETERMINE POTENTIAL MATERIAL MISSTATEMENTS THAT COULD RESULT This step is intended to identify specific errors or fraud and other irregularities that are likely to result from the absence of controls. The importance of a weakness is proportionate to the magnitude of the errors or fraud and other irregularities that are likely to result from it.

CONSIDER THE POSSIBILITY OF COMPENSATING CONTROLS A compensating control is a control elsewhere in the system that offsets a weakness. A common example in a smaller company is active involvement of the owner. When a compensating control exists, the weakness is no longer a concern because the potential for misstatement has been sufficiently reduced.

Figure 9-4 on page 266 shows the documentation of weaknesses for the sales and collection cycle of Hillsburg Hardware Limited. The "Effect on Audit Evidence" column shows the effect of the weakness on the auditor's planned audit program.

The Control Risk Matrix

Many auditors use a *control matrix* to assist in the control-risk assessment process. Most controls affect more than one transaction-related audit objective, and often several different controls affect a given transaction-related audit objective. These complexities make a

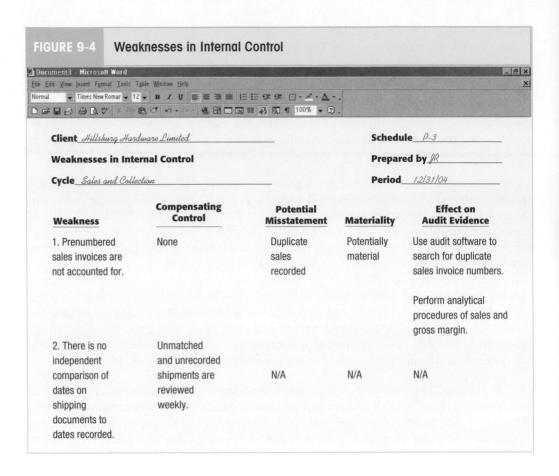

FIGURE 9-4 **Weaknesses in Internal Control**

Client *Hillsburg Hardware Limited* Schedule *P-3*

Weaknesses in Internal Control Prepared by *JR*

Cycle *Sales and Collection* Period *12/31/04*

Weakness	Compensating Control	Potential Misstatement	Materiality	Effect on Audit Evidence
1. Prenumbered sales invoices are not accounted for.	None	Duplicate sales recorded	Potentially material	Use audit software to search for duplicate sales invoice numbers. Perform analytical procedures of sales and gross margin.
2. There is no independent comparison of dates on shipping documents to dates recorded.	Unmatched and unrecorded shipments are reviewed weekly.	N/A	N/A	N/A

control risk matrix a useful way to help assess control risk. The control risk matrix is used to assist in identifying both controls and weaknesses and in assessing control risk.

Figure 9-5 illustrates the use of a control risk matrix for sales transactions of Hillsburg Hardware Limited. In constructing the matrix, the transaction-related audit objectives for sales were listed as column headings, and pertinent controls that were identified were listed as headings for the rows. In addition, where significant weaknesses were identified, they were also entered as row headings below the listing of key controls. The body of the matrix was then used to show how the controls contribute to the accomplishment of the transaction-related audit objectives and how weaknesses impact the objectives. In this illustration, a "C" was entered in each cell where a control partially or fully satisfied an objective, and a "W" was entered to show the impact of the weaknesses.

Assess Control Risk Once controls and weaknesses have been identified and related to transaction-related audit objectives, there can be an assessment of control risk. Again, the control risk matrix is a useful tool for that purpose. Referring to Figure 9-5, the auditor assessed control risk for Hillsburg's sales by reviewing each column for pertinent controls and weaknesses, and asking, "What is the likelihood that a material misstatement of the type to be controlled would not be prevented or detected and corrected by these controls, and what is the impact of the weaknesses?" If the likelihood is high, then control risk is high, and so forth.

Internal Control Letter and Related Matters During the course of obtaining an understanding of the client's internal control and assessing control risk, auditors obtain information that is of interest to the audit committee in fulfilling its responsibilities. Generally, such information concerns significant deficiencies in the design or operation of internal control (weaknesses).

AUDIT COMMITTEE COMMUNICATIONS The auditor is required to communicate internal control

Internal Control	Recorded sales are for shipments actually made to nonfictitious customers (occurrence).	Existing sales transactions are recorded (completeness).	Recorded sales are for the amount of goods shipped and are correctly billed and recorded (accuracy).	Sales transactions are properly classified (classification).	Sales are recorded on the correct dates (timing).	Sales transactions are properly included in the accounts receivable master file and are correctly summarized (posting and summarization).
Controls						
Credit is approved automatically by computer by comparison to authorized credit limits (C1).	C					
Recorded sales are supported by authorized shipping documents and approved customer orders (C2).	C		C			
Separation of duties between billing, recording of sales, and handling of cash receipts (C3).	C	C				C
Shipping documents are forwarded to billing daily and are billed the subsequent day (C4).	C				C	
Shipping documents are prenumbered and accounted for weekly (C5).		C			C	
Batch totals of quantities shipped are compared with quantities billed (C6).	C	C	C			
Unit selling prices are obtained from the price list master file of approved prices (C7).			C			
Sales transactions are internally verified (C8).				C		
Statements are mailed to customers each month (C9).	C		C			C
Computer automatically posts transactions to the accounts receivable subsidiary records and to the general ledger (C10).						C
Accounts receivable master file is reconciled to the general ledger on a monthly basis (C11).						C
Weaknesses						
There is a lack of internal verification for the possibility of sales invoices being recorded more than once (W1).	W					
There is a lack of control to test for timely recording (W2).					W	
Assessed control risk	Medium	Low	Low	Low*	High	Low

*Because there are no cash sales, classification is not a problem.

C = Control; W = Weakness.

Note: This matrix was developed using an internal control questionnaire, part of which is included in Figure 9-3 (p. 264), as well as flowcharts and other documentation of the auditor's understanding of internal control.

weaknesses to "the audit committee or equivalent." If the client does not have an audit committee, then the communication should go to the person (or persons) in the organization who has (have) overall responsibility for internal control, such as the board of directors or the owner-manager. The communication may be oral or written. An illustrative **internal-control-related-matters letter** is shown in Figure 9-6.

MANAGEMENT LETTERS   In addition to significant weaknesses in internal control, auditors often observe less significant internal control-related matters, as well as opportunities for the client to make operational improvements. These types of matters should also be communicated to the client. The form of communication is often a separate letter for that purpose, called a **management letter**. This letter needs to be clearly identified as a derivative report to indicate that the purpose of the engagement was not to determine weaknesses in internal control but that they were identified as a by-product of the audit. The letter would also indicate that the auditors may not have found all weaknesses.

Impact of General Controls

As described earlier and shown in Figure 9-2, general (computer) controls are controls over automated information systems with respect to organization and management; systems acquisition, development, and maintenance; and operations and information systems support. Table 9-2 provided examples of general (computer) control procedures.

Since general controls affect multiple transaction cycles, the quality of general controls should be assessed prior to the decision on whether reliance will be placed on controls or procedures in automated accounting systems. This occurs because there are three types of controls that can occur in automated accounting systems (see Figure 9-2). These are:

FIGURE 9-6   Internal-Control-Related-Matters Letter

CHESLEY & BEDARD
Chartered Accountants
2016 Village Boulevard
Ottawa, Ontario K1S 5B6

February 12, 2005

Audit Committee
Airtight Machine Inc.
1729 Athens Street
Ottawa, Ontario K1N 6N5

In planning and performing our audit of the financial statements of Airtight Machine Inc. for the year ended December 31, 2004, we considered its internal control in order to determine our auditing procedures for the purpose of expressing our opinion on the financial statements and not to provide assurance on internal control. However, we noted certain matters involving internal control and its operation that we consider to be of such significance that we believe they should be reported to you. The matters being reported involve circumstances coming to our attention relating to significant deficiencies in the design or operation of internal control that, in our judgment, could adversely affect the organization's ability to record, process, summarize, and report financial data consistent with the assertions of management in the financial statements.

The matter noted is that there is a lack of independent verification of the data entry of the customer's name, product number, and quantity shipped on sales invoices and credit memos. As a consequence, errors in these activities could occur and remain uncorrected, adversely affecting both recorded net sales and accounts receivable. This deficiency is particularly significant because of the large size of the average sale of Airtight Machine Inc.

This report is intended solely for the information and use of the audit committee, board of directors, management, and others in Airtight Machine Inc.

Very truly yours,

Chesley & Bedard

Chesley & Bedard

MANUAL CONTROL PROCEDURES These controls are performed by individuals that do not rely on reports or screens prepared by automated information systems. For example, goods received from a supplier are counted and recorded on a receiving report, then compared to the bill of lading that came with the shipment on the truck.

COMPUTER-ASSISTED CONTROL PROCEDURES **Computer-assisted controls** are performed by individuals with the assistance of a computer report or computer information. For example, inventory counts are recorded in the computer system. A report is printed identifying differences between the perpetual records and the inventory count so that a different count team can verify the discrepancy.

FULLY AUTOMATED CONTROL PROCEDURES **Fully automated controls** are performed using only automated information systems, with no manual or human intervention. For example, every morning, prior to commencing sales order processing, the accounts receivable subsystem automatically adds the accounts receivable open item file and transfers the total to a reconciliation file, where another program compares the total to the accounts receivable balance in the general ledger. If there is a difference, a warning message is sent to the accounts receivable data entry clerk. Normally, fully automated control procedures can best be tested with control tests. Computer assisted audit tests that would be suitable would include test data, integrated test facilities, or reperformance (using generalized audit software).

When identifying key controls in a system, the auditor may have identified a combination of manual, computer-assisted, or fully automated controls. For example, when considering credit approval prior to shipment, a manual control would require that each shipment be manually approved and initialled. A computer-assisted control would have the computer system print a report for the credit manager of questionable orders. The credit manager would review the report and release accepted orders for shipment. A fully automated control would have the computer system automatically reject all orders that caused customers to exceed their credit limit.

For an auditor to consider placing reliance upon either a computer-assisted or fully automated control, the auditor must have reasonable assurance that general controls over the computerized portion of the controls are effective. In particular, program change controls and access controls must be effective.

- *Program change controls.* There should be sufficient controls in place to ensure that programs throughout the year were adequately controlled. This provides reasonable assurance that there were no unauthorized program changes and that programs functioned consistently throughout the year.
- *Access controls.* Physical and logical access controls should exist to prevent unauthorized access to programs and data, and to document access so that accountability can be established. If unauthorized access to programs or data can be obtained, then the auditor would not be able to place reliance on the results of those programs or data throughout the year.

Should the auditor conclude that general controls are adequate, then the auditor has the choice of relying on any of the different types of controls in the accounting system that are identified as key controls (i.e., manual, computer-assisted, or fully automated). Should general controls be poor, then the auditor may be able to rely on only manual controls. Alternatively, the auditor may decide to assess control risk at maximum and not rely on any internal controls.

Tests of Controls

The controls that the auditor has identified in the assessment as reducing control risk (the key controls) must be supported by tests of controls to make sure they have been

COMPUTER-ASSISTED CONTROLS—controls that have a manual component and a computerized component, such as an individual using a computerized exception report to complete a task

FULLY AUTOMATED CONTROLS—a control that is undertaken without human intervention, such as a credit check where transactions are automatically rejected operating effectively throughout all, or most of, the audit period. For example, in Figure 9-5, each key control must be supported by sufficient tests of controls.

Procedures for Tests of Controls Four types of audit procedures are used to support the operation of key internal controls. They are as follows:

MAKE ENQUIRIES OF APPROPRIATE ENTITY PERSONNEL Although enquiry is not generally a strong source of evidence about the effective operation of controls, it is an appropriate form of evidence. For example, the auditor may determine that unauthorized personnel are not allowed access to computer files by making enquiries of the person who controls passwords.

EXAMINE DOCUMENTS, RECORDS, AND REPORTS Many controls leave a clear trail of documentary evidence. Suppose, for example, that when a customer order is received, it is used to update a customer accounts receivable record, which is approved for credit using the computer system. Orders that cause the customer to exceed the credit limit are printed and reviewed by the sales manager. The sales manager initials the listing for those orders that are to be accepted. (See the first and second key controls in Figure 9-5.) The auditor examines the credit exception report and ensures that required signatures or initials are present. Since this is a computer-assisted control (preparation of the exception report), the auditor reviews the general controls file to ensure that general controls are adequate prior to the conduct of this test. The auditor may examine a personal guarantee in a bank loan file if there is a need to increase credit, and this provides supporting evidence of the credit-granting process.

OBSERVE CONTROL-RELATED ACTIVITIES Other types of control-related activities do *not* leave an evidential trail. For example, separation of duties relies on specific persons performing specific tasks, and there is typically no documentation of the separate performance. (See the third key control listed in Figure 9-5.) For controls that leave no documentary evidence, the auditor generally observes them being applied. For computer-based controls, the auditor may consider the use of test data to determine whether the control is functioning. Test data are fictitious transactions entered in controlled circumstances, processed through the client systems. The auditor compares anticipated results to results that actually occurred from processing the transactions.

REPERFORM CLIENT PROCEDURES There are also control-related activities for which there are related documents and records, but their content is insufficient for the auditor's purpose of assessing whether controls are operating effectively. For example, assume prices on sales invoices are to be verified to a standard price list by client personnel as an internal verification procedure, but no indication of performance is entered on the sales invoices. (See the seventh key control in Figure 9-5.) In these cases, it is common for the auditor to actually reperform the control activity to see whether the proper results were obtained. For this example, the auditor can reperform the procedure by tracing the sales prices to the authorized price list in effect at the date of the transaction. Reperformance can also be automated. For example, if the company uses a complex algorithm to calculate its allowance for bad debts based on sales throughout the year, the algorithm could be duplicated and recalculated using **generalized audit software** (general purpose testing software with audit modules). If no misstatements are found, the auditor can conclude that the procedure is operating as intended.

GENERALIZED AUDIT SOFTWARE— general purpose software capable of reading and testing client data using special purpose modules such as extraction, sampling, and plotting

Extent of Procedures The extent to which tests of controls are applied depends on the intended assessed level of control risk. The lower the assessed level of control risk, the more extensive the tests of controls must be both in terms of the number of controls tested and the extent of tests of each control. For example, if the auditor wants to use a low assessed level of control risk, a larger sample size for documentation, observation, and reperformance procedures should be applied.

RELIANCE ON EVIDENCE FROM PRIOR YEAR'S AUDIT If evidence was obtained in the prior year's audit that indicates a key control was operating effectively, and the auditor determines that it is still in place, the extent of the tests of that control may be reduced substantially in the current year.

TESTING LESS THAN THE ENTIRE AUDIT PERIOD Ideally, tests of controls should be applied to transactions and controls for the entire period under audit. However, it is not always possible to do so. Where less than the entire period is tested, the auditor should determine whether changes in controls occurred in the period not tested and obtain evidential matter about the nature and extent of any changes.

Relationship of Tests of Controls to Procedures to Obtain an Understanding You will notice that there is a significant overlap between tests of controls and procedures to obtain an understanding. Both include enquiry, inspection, and observation. There are two primary differences in the application of these common procedures between phases. The auditor needs to understand internal control only as it applies to the financial statements as a whole and to relevant assertions relating to significant account balances or classes of transactions. In other words, the procedures to gain an understanding are applied only to certain control policies and procedures that have been instituted by the client. The auditor will obtain knowledge about the design of the relevant policies and procedures and determine whether or not they have been implemented. Tests of controls, on the other hand, are only applied when control risk has been assessed below maximum, and then only to key controls.

The second difference is that procedures to obtain an understanding are performed only on one or a few transactions or, in the case of observations, at a single point in time. Tests of controls are performed on larger samples of transactions (perhaps 20 to 100), and often observations are made at more than one point in time.

For key controls, tests of controls other than reperformance are essentially an *extension* of related procedures to obtain an understanding. For that reason, when auditors plan at the outset to obtain a low assessed level of control risk, they will combine both types of procedures and perform them simultaneously.

Table 9-4 illustrates this concept in more detail. Where only the required minimum study of internal control is planned, the auditor will conduct a transaction walk-through. In so doing, the auditor determines that the audit documentation is complete and accurate, and observes that the control-related activities described are in operation.

When the control risk is assessed below maximum, a transaction walk-through is performed and a larger sample of documents is inspected for indications of the effectiveness of the operation of controls. (The determination of appropriate sample size is discussed in Chapters 12 and 13.) Similarly, when observations are made, they will be more extensive and often at several points in time. Also, reperformance is an important test of some controls.

Two Audit Approaches

As we have explained, there are two approaches an auditor may take for a specific financial statement assertion: the *substantive* approach, where the auditor does not rely on internal controls; and the *combined* approach, where the auditor assesses control risk below maximum and does rely on internal controls.

A substantive approach is used when the auditor cannot rely on the internal controls with respect to a particular assertion or when it is not cost-effective to rely on the controls

TABLE 9-4	Relationship of Planned Assessed Level of Control Risks and Extent of Procedures	
	Planned Assessed Level of Control Risk	
Type of Procedure	High Level: Obtaining an Understanding Only	Lower Level: Tests of Controls
Enquiry	Yes—extensive	Yes—some
Inspection	Yes—with transaction walk-through	Yes—using sampling
Observation	Yes—with transaction walk-through	Yes—at multiple times
Reperformance	No	Yes—using sampling

for that assertion. Control risk is set at maximum for that assertion; planned detection risk will therefore be low and extent of evidence will be high. The auditor will obtain a sufficient understanding of the control environment and the accounting system to plan the audit and document the understanding and the control risk assessment; there would be no tests of controls.

A combined approach is used when the auditor can rely on the internal controls with respect to a particular assertion and control risk can be assessed at below maximum. Because control risk is set at below maximum for that assertion, planned detection risk will therefore be medium or high and extent of evidence will be medium or low respectively. The auditor will obtain a sufficient understanding of the control environment, the accounting system, and the control procedures to plan the audit and document the understanding and the control risk assessment; controls would be tested to support the assessment below maximum with the extent of testing varying inversely with the assessment as pointed out on page 270.

→9.5 EXPANSION OF INTERNAL CONTROL TESTING

In Chapter 3, we discussed a new report, where the auditor reports upon management's assessment of internal control. Such a report is required by Section 404(b) of the *Sarbanes-Oxley Act of 2002* in the U.S., affecting Canadian companies that are subsidiaries of American companies, or who register securities for sale in the United States. A sample report is shown in Figure 3-9 on page 71. Proposals by the Canadian Securities Administrators in Canada would have large Canadian companies (market capitalization over $500 million) provide such reports for years ending on or after June 30, 2006, with smaller companies phasing in over the subsequent three years.

Since management's assessment of internal control covers internal control over financial reporting, the scope of the internal control assessment is different than the scope of the financial statement audit. The auditor will need to assess whether additional testing is required (i.e., more testing than is needed for satisfaction of the audit assertions). Figure 9-7 describes potential differences in scope between the nature of internal control testing for an audit of internal control and an audit of financial statements. For this figure, management is concerned about additional controls that the auditor would not rely upon in the audit of the financial statements, requiring the auditor to do additional testing to be able to provide assurance upon management's assessment of internal control.

As of this writing, Canadian standards consist of an exposure draft issued in October 2004 titled, "An audit of internal control over financial reporting performed in conjunction with an audit of financial standards," that is substantially equivalent to the U.S. standard.

FIGURE 9-7 Potential Differences in Scope of Controls Tested in an Audit of Internal Control and an Audit of Financial Statements

Internal Controls Over Financial Reporting

Internal Controls Used to Assess Control Risk Below Maximum

Controls that must be tested in an audit of internal controls

Controls that must be tested in an audit of financial statements

This standard walks through the entire engagement, discussing planning, fieldwork, and reporting in detail. As with other engagements, management accepts responsibility for the internal control, and the same auditor who conducts the financial statement audit performs the audit of management's internal control assessment.

As part of the fieldwork, the auditor should test entity level controls (such as the control environment and general computer controls) as well as more specific preventative and detective controls. To assist in the risk assessment process, the auditor is required to segregate transactions into three categories: routine, non-routine, or estimation. Only those controls that achieve a control objective are tested, and testing varies from year to year. The testing extends past the end of the fiscal year to those periods that help ensure that the financial statements are properly completed, for example until February 15 for a December year end if that is the time when the final accrual journal entries are made for the fiscal year. Procedures are also described for the reporting and handling of weaknesses in internal control.

Chapter 3 provided an example of a combined audit report. The auditor could issue either a combined report or two separate reports, with the effective dates being the same as the dates for the financial statement audit.

Other special reports on internal control, such as reports on a service organization, are discussed in Chapter 23. Such special reports are normally conducted as separate engagements, and are not part of the annual financial statement audit.

APPENDIX E
GENERAL INFORMATION SYSTEMS CONTROLS

An Overview of General Control Systems at Hillsburg Hardware Limited

This appendix uses a historical perspective of Hillsburg Hardware Limited to show the change from a simple batch system to an online interactive database management system with Internet based capabilities.

The 1990s Back in 1990 when Hillsburg Hardware Limited only had 50 customers, the industry standard of a local area network with a single central server was more than adequate. All software consisted of standard packaged software. There were no onsite data processing personnel, and operating functions were shared among accounting and general staff. The receptionist was responsible for initiating backup before she left in the evening and the general manager kept a copy offsite at his home. The controller was responsible for maintaining password security profiles that controlled access rights. General controls were summarized as follows:

ORGANIZATION AND MANAGEMENT CONTROLS Management had a policy of establishing segregation of duties as much as possible with the existing personnel. Functions considered incompatible with respect to financial systems were separated.

SYSTEMS ACQUISITION, DEVELOPMENT, AND MAINTENANCE CONTROLS All software used was packaged software. The software was used in its original form (not modified). Software was obtained only in object code (machine language), so it could not be modified by Hillsburg Hardware personnel.

OPERATIONS AND INFORMATION SYSTEMS SUPPORT Company offices were open from 8:00 a.m. to 5:00 p.m. The network was left up and running 24 hours per day. A maintenance contract was kept with a major support organization to provide onsite support in the event of equipment failure. Staff were initially trained in the software packages used, and had software manuals to refer to in the event of queries. The controller prepared a set of instructions (about three pages) to be used in the event that a major disaster destroyed the building and the local area network. These instructions were intended to allow Hillsburg Hardware Limited personnel to resume operations at a local area network owned by their support organization for a fee of $500 per hour.

The Advanced Systems of 2005 Two years ago, Hillsburg finally updated its aging collection of systems to an integrated database management system running on a mid-range mini-computer. Packaged accounting software is still used, with support provided by the software supplier. Data in the database can be exported into spreadsheet files so that staff can prepare their own reports if needed.

With over 200 microcomputer work stations updating information and accessing the storage-area-network attached to the minicomputer, the company now has three full-time information systems personnel. The information systems manager works on and supervises a range of functions, such as technical support for staff and clients and updating the web site. The web site was custom developed, but maintenance is handled internally. Passwords are maintained by the controller's executive assistant.

To maintain security, data from the ONHAND (Online Niche-Hardware Availability Notification Database) customer database is ported across to a group of stand-alone high-end microcomputers every night, so that customers can enquire about the availability of products and the status of their orders via the Internet. Internet access for customers is handled via an ISP (Internet Service Provider). Hillsburg decided that there would be no direct data communications access from the minicomputer and from staff computers—a small group of machines are available for staff to check email. This machine configuration is used for electronic data interchange transactions between Hillsburg and ten key suppliers. Transactions are copied to and from the minicomputer systems three times per day.

ORGANIZATION AND MANAGEMENT CONTROLS There has been no change in policy. Duties are segregated as much as practical. Information systems support personnel do not have access to accounting data. A database administrator, who reports to the controller, is responsible for maintaining the data dictionary.

[*It is important that the database administration function be separated from other functions, such as data authorization. Each application will need to be examined to ensure that each data element has specified "owner" groups, with appropriate access controls, such as passwords.*]

SYSTEMS ACQUISITION, DEVELOPMENT, AND MAINTENANCE CONTROLS Accounting software is still packaged software, maintained externally. Information systems personnel cannot change the accounting software. The web site, and the electronic data interchange software, is maintained internally. Changes to these two pieces of software must be jointly approved by the Chief Financial Officer and the Vice President, Operations.

[*Those applications affected by EDI (electronic data interchange) will require greater reliance on programmed controls, as there will likely be less of a paper trail. This may require greater use of computer-assisted audit techniques, and will be discussed further in the audit of the acquisition and payment cycle. Controls in the data communications layer will need to be assessed (probably by a specialist).*]

OPERATIONS AND INFORMATION SYSTEMS SUPPORT All systems have current anti-virus software, and firewalls are in place for the group of Internet-accessible machines. Company offices are now open from 7:00 a.m. to 6:00 p.m. All systems are left up and running 24 hours per day. There is a more comprehensive backup and disaster recovery plan. Selected staff walk through this plan as a test every six months, to ensure that systems changes have been accounted for. There are maintenance plans for all purchased hardware and software.

[*Each application cycle will need to be considered separately to ensure adequate separation of duties are in place, using passwords or other techniques.*]

SUMMARY

1. *Why is the study of internal control important?* The second examination standard requires the auditor to understand the internal controls, as the quality of the internal controls directly impacts the financial statements and their related assertions.

   What are the different perspectives of the client and the auditor? The client is concerned about meeting organizational goals, which include having accurate information, safeguarding assets, optimizing the use of resources, and preventing and detecting error and fraud. The auditor needs to assess the overall risk of the engagement by considering the control environment and the controls over classes of transactions within the context of reasonable assurance.

2. *What are the three basic concepts that enable an auditor's study of internal controls?* These are management's responsibility for the establishment and maintenance of the entity's controls, that controls help provide reasonable assurance over the fairness of the financial statements, and that internal controls cannot be completely effective (inherent limitations).

   List the four components of internal control. They are the control environment, risk assessment, control systems, and monitoring.

   Why is the control environment the most important component of internal control? The control environment establishes the "tone at the top," including the extent of support that management gives to having high quality internal controls.

3. *How is management's risk assessment process relevant to the audit?* Management assesses risks as a part of designing internal controls to minimize errors and fraud. Without a risk assessment process, internal controls would be haphazard, rather than strategically addressing the needs of the organization.

   Explain how accounting systems and control procedures together comprise control systems. Accounting systems include the policies and procedures for collecting, transcribing, processing, and reporting data. Control procedures are those policies and procedures that support and enhance the reliability of the data.

   What is the role of monitoring in supporting internal controls? Monitoring is the ongoing or periodic assessment of the quality of internal control procedures. This will help the entity to confirm that controls are operating as intended or to modify internal controls for changes in business conditions.

4. *What does the auditor do to obtain an understanding of internal controls?* After assessing the integrity of management, the auditor uses enquiry, inspection, and observation to understand the control environment, and enquiry, inspection, observation, and reperformance to understand general controls, accounting systems, and control and monitoring procedures.

   How is control risk assessed, documented, and tested? After obtaining an understanding of internal control, the auditor considers whether the financial statements are auditable. Then, general controls are assessed for their impact upon the individual transaction cycles and audit objectives in the transaction cycles. Finally, each audit objective is examined for each transaction type to determine the potential risk of material misstatement based on potential reliance on internal controls for that audit objective. Normally, software is used in the documentation of this process.

   Why is it important to link control risk to audit strategy and procedures? The auditor is better able to design substantive procedures that compensate for risks during the audit engagement and thus conduct a better quality audit.

5. *What other types of internal control reports can an auditor issue?* The auditor can issue an opinion on management's assessment of internal control and also issue special reports on internal control.

   How is this relevant to the audit? An opinion on management's assessment of internal control is conducted at the same time as the financial statement audit and may include tests of additional controls, thus expanding the amount of work that would be completed during the financial statement audit engagement.

CICA ASSURANCE HANDBOOK SECTIONS REFERENCED IN THIS CHAPTER

Section 5050 – Using the work of internal audit.
Section 5100 – Generally accepted auditing standards.
Section 5141 – Understanding the entity and its environment and assessing the risks of material misstatement.

Section 5143 – The auditor's procedures in response to assessed risks.
Section 5220 – Internal Control in the Context of an Audit—Weaknesses in Internal Control

ESSENTIAL TERMS

Accounting system—the set of manual and/or computerized procedures that collect, record, and process data and report the resulting information   (p. 252).

Application controls—(synonymous with *control procedures*)—the set of manual, computer-assisted, or fully automated controls

that comprise the controls for a particular transaction stream (p. 247).

Assessment of control risk—a measure of the auditor's expectation that internal controls will neither prevent material misstatements from occurring nor detect and correct them if they have occurred; control risk is assessed for each transaction-related audit objective in a cycle or class of transactions   (p. 263).

Chart of accounts—a listing of all the entity's accounts, which classifies transactions into individual balance sheet and income statement accounts   (p. 255).

Collusion—a cooperative effort among employees to defraud a business of cash, inventory, or other assets   (p. 246).

Computer-assisted controls—controls that have a manual component and a computerized component, such as an individual using a computerized exception report to complete a task (p. 269).

Control environment—the actions, policies, and procedures that reflect the overall attitudes of top management, directors, and owners of an entity about control and its importance to the entity   (p. 247).

Control procedures—(synonymous with *application controls*) the set of manual and/or computerized procedures that enhance the reliability of information generated by the accounting system. They include segregation of duties, suitable authorization procedures, appropriate documents and records and controls over input, adequate safeguards over assets and records, and independent verification of performance and recorded data (p. 252).

Control risk—see *assessment of control risk.*

Control risk matrix—a methodology used to help the auditor assess control risk by matching key internal controls and internal control weaknesses with transaction-related audit objectives (p. 266).

Flow chart—a diagrammatic representation of the client's documents and records, and the sequence in which they are processed (p. 263).

Fully automated controls—controls that are undertaken without human intervention, such as a credit check where transactions are automatically rejected   (p. 269).

General authorization—company-wide policies for the approval of all transactions within stated limits   (p. 254).

General (computer) control systems—internal controls for automated information systems pertaining to more than one transaction cycle that could be considered part of the control environment (pervasive) or are more detailed   (p. 251).

Generalized audit software—general purpose software capable of reading and testing client data using special purpose modules such as extraction, sampling, and plotting   (p. 270).

Independent checks—internal control activities designed for the continuous internal verification of other controls   (p. 256).

Internal control—the policies and procedures instituted and maintained by the management of an entity in order to

(1) maintain reliable control systems, (2) safeguard assets including records, (3) optimize the use of entity resources, and (4) prevent and detect error and fraud. Internal control can provide only reasonable, not absolute, assurance that management's objectives are met   (p. 243).

Internal control questionnaire—a series of questions about the controls in each audit area used as a means of gaining an understanding of internal control   (p. 263).

Internal control letter—a letter from the auditor to the audit committee or senior management detailing significant weaknesses in internal control   (p. 268).

Internal control weaknesses—the absence of adequate controls; increases the risk of misstatements in the financial statements (p. 265).

Management letter—the auditor's written communication to management to point out less significant weaknesses in internal control and possibilities for operational improvements   (p. 268).

Monitoring—management's ongoing and periodic assessment of the quality of internal control performance to determine that controls are operating as intended and modified when needed (p. 256).

Narrative—a written description of a client's internal controls, including the origin, processing, and disposition of documents and records, and the relevant control procedures   (p. 262).

Procedures to obtain an understanding—procedures used by the auditor to gather evidence about the design and implementation of specific controls   (p. 261).

Risk assessment—management's identification and analysis of risks relevant to the preparation of financial statements in conformity with GAAP   (p. 250).

Separation of duties—segregation of the following activities in an organization: custody of assets, recording/data entry, systems development/acquisition and maintenance, computer operations, reconciliation, and authorization   (p. 252).

Specific authorization—case-by-case approval of transactions not covered by company-wide policies   (p. 254).

Tests of controls—audit procedures to test the effectiveness of controls in support of control risk assessed below maximum (p. 261).

Transaction-related audit objectives—six audit objectives that must be met before the auditor can conclude that the total for any given class of transactions is fairly stated. The general transaction-related audit objectives are occurrence, completeness, accuracy, classification, timing, and posting and summarization (p. 245).

Transaction walk-through—the tracing of selected transactions through the accounting system   (p. 259).

REVIEW QUESTIONS

9-1   Chapter 7 introduced the parts of the planning phase of audits. Which part is understanding internal control and assessing control risk? Which parts precede and follow that understanding and assessing?

9-2   Compare management's concerns about internal control with those of the auditor.

9-3   Frequently, management is more concerned about internal controls that promote operational efficiency than about those that result in reliable financial data. How can the independent auditor persuade management to devote more attention to controls affecting the reliability of accounting information when management has this attitude?

9-4 What is meant by the "control environment"? What are the factors the auditor must evaluate to understand it?

9-5 What is the relationship between the control environment and control systems?

9-6 The separation of operational responsibility from record keeping is meant to prevent different types of misstatements than the separation of the custody of assets from accounting. Explain the difference in the purposes of these two types of separation of duties.

9-7 Distinguish between general and specific authorization of transactions, and give one example of each type.

9-8 Explain what is meant by "independent checks on performance," and give five specific examples.

9-9 Distinguish between obtaining an understanding of internal control and assessing control risk. Also explain the methodology the auditor uses for each of them.

9-10 Define what is meant by a "control" and a "weakness in internal control." Give two examples of each in the sales and collection cycle.

9-11 Frank James, a highly competent employee of Brinkwater Sales Corporation, had been responsible for accounting-related matters for two decades. His devotion to the firm and his duties had always been exceptional, and over the years he had been given increased responsibility. Both the president of Brinkwater and the partner of an independent public accounting firm in charge of the audit were shocked and dismayed to discover that James had embezzled more than $500,000 over a 10-year period by not recording billings in the sales journal and subsequently diverting the cash receipts. What major factors permitted the defalcation to take place?

9-12 Distinguish between the objectives of an internal control questionnaire and the objectives of a flowchart for documenting information about a client's internal control. State the advantages and disadvantages of each of these two methods.

9-13 Explain what is meant by "significant deficiencies" as they relate to internal control. What should the auditor do when he or she has discovered significant deficiencies in internal control?

9-14 Explain what is meant by "tests of controls." Write one inspection of documents test of control and one reperformance test of control for the following internal control: hours of time cards are re-added by an independent payroll clerk and initialled to indicate performance.

9-15 Distinguish between a substantive approach and a combined approach in auditing a financial statement assertion.

MULTIPLE CHOICE QUESTIONS

9-16 The following are questions about internal control. Choose the best response.

a. When considering internal control, an auditor must be aware of the concept of reasonable assurance, which recognizes that the

(1) employment of competent personnel provides assurance that management's control objectives will be achieved.
(2) establishment and maintenance of internal control is an important responsibility of the management and *not* of the auditor.
(3) cost of internal control should *not* exceed the benefits expected to be derived therefrom.
(4) separation of incompatible functions is necessary to ascertain that the internal control is effective.

b. Taylor Sales Corp. maintains a large full-time internal audit staff that reports directly to the audit committee. Audit reports prepared by the internal auditors indicate that the system is functioning as it should and that the accounting records are reliable. The public accountant will probably

(1) eliminate tests of controls.
(2) increase the depth and study and evaluation of controls related to achievement of Taylor Sales Corp.'s corporate policies.
(3) avoid duplicating the work of the internal audit staff.
(4) place reliance on the work of the internal audit staff.

c. What is the independent auditor's principal purpose in obtaining an understanding of internal control and assessing control risk?

(1) To maintain a state of independence in mental attitude in all matters related to the audit.
(2) To comply with generally accepted accounting principles.
(3) To obtain a measure of assurance of management's efficiency.
(4) To determine the nature, timing, and extent of subsequent audit work.

(AICPA adapted)

d. An auditor uses assessed control risk to

(1) indicate whether materiality thresholds for planning and evaluation purposes are sufficiently high.
(2) evaluate the effectiveness of the entity's internal controls.
(3) identify transactions and account balances where inherent risk is at the maximum.
(4) determine the acceptable level of detection risk for financial statement assertions.

e. On the basis of audit evidence gathered and evaluated, an auditor decides to increase assessed control risk from that originally planned. To achieve an audit risk level that is substantially the same as the planned audit risk level, the auditor would

(1) increase inherent risk.
(2) increase materiality levels.
(3) decrease substantive testing.

(4) decrease planned detection risk.

(AICPA adapted)

DISCUSSION QUESTIONS AND PROBLEMS

9-17 The following are errors or fraud and other irregularities that have occurred in Fresh Foods Grocery Store Ltd., a wholesale and retail grocery company.

1. The incorrect price was used on sales invoices for billing shipments to customers because the incorrect price was entered into a computer file.
2. A vendor's invoice was paid twice for the same shipment. The second payment arose because the vendor sent a duplicate copy of the original two weeks after the payment was due.
3. Employees in the receiving department took sides of beef for their personal use. When a shipment of meat was received, the receiving department filled out a receiving report and forwarded it to the accounting department for the amount of goods actually received. At that time, two sides of beef were put in an employee's pickup truck rather than in the storage freezer.
4. During the physical count of inventory of the retail grocery, one counter wrote down the wrong description of several products and miscounted the quantity.
5. A salesperson sold an entire carload of lamb at a price below cost because she did not know the cost of lamb had increased in the past week.
6. On the last day of the year, a truckload of beef was set aside for shipment but was not shipped. Because it was still on hand, it was counted as inventory. The shipping document was dated the last day of the year, so it was also included as a current-year sale.

Required

a. For each error or fraud and other irregularity, identify one or more types of controls that were absent.

b. For each error or fraud and other irregularity, identify the objectives that have not been met.

c. For each error or fraud and other irregularity, suggest a control to correct the deficiency.

9-18 The division of the following duties is meant to provide the best possible controls for the Meridian Paint Company Ltd., a small wholesale store.

*1. Assemble supporting documents for general and payroll cash disbursements.
*2. Sign general disbursement cheques.
*3. Input information to prepare cheques for printing and signature, resulting in payments being recorded in the accounts payable, payments subsidiary system.
*4. Mail cheques to suppliers and deliver cheques to employees.
5. Cancel supporting documents to prevent their re-use.
*6. Update credit limit for customers in the order entry system.
*7. Input shipping and billing information to bill customers in the order entry system.
*8. Open the mail and prepare a prelisting of cash receipts.
*9. Enter cash receipts data in the accounts receivable subsystem used to prepare the cash receipts listing, and update the accounts receivable master file.
10. Prepare daily cash deposits.
*11. Deliver daily cash deposits to the bank.
*12. Assemble the payroll time cards and input the data into the payroll system to prepare payroll cheques.
*13. Sign payroll cheques.

14. Retrieve journal entries from all subsystems (i.e., order entry, accounts receivable, accounts payable and payments, payroll) to update the general ledger at the end of each month and review all accounts for unexpected balances.
15. Print the aged accounts receivable trial balance and review accounts outstanding more than 90 days.
*16. Print monthly statements for customers using the accounts receivable system, then mail the statements to customers.
17. Reconcile the monthly statements from vendors with the supplier balances according to the accounts payable system.
18. Reconcile the bank account.

Required

You are to divide the accounting-related duties 1 through 18 among Robert Smith, Karen Wong, and Barbara Chiu. All of the responsibilities marked with an asterisk are assumed to take about the same amount of time and must be divided equally between Smith and Wong. Both employees are equally competent. Chiu, who is president of the company, is not willing to perform any functions designated by an asterisk but is willing to perform a maximum of two of the other functions.

(AICPA adapted)

9-19 Recently, you had lunch with some friends at a new restaurant in your neighbourhood. After ordering, the server entered his password into a computer keyboard and punched in your order. The server continued taking orders and you noticed the cook removing a small printout and hanging it on the wall in front of him (presumably your order). When the food was ready, it was placed below your order. The server looked at the printout, put it in his pocket, and then brought your order to the table.

When you finished eating, the server again entered his password, and printed off two copies of your bill. One copy he attached to the order slip, while the second was brought to you. You decided to pay by credit card, so two copies of the credit card authorization were brought to the table for signature. You kept one and the signed copy was returned to the server.

Required
a. What internal controls (manual, computer-assisted, and automated) are present at the restaurant?

b. How could the manager of the restaurant evaluate the effectiveness of the controls?
c. What are the costs and benefits of the restaurant's controls?

9-20 Lew Pherson and Marie Violette are friends who are employed by different public accounting firms. One day during lunch they are discussing the importance of internal control in determining the amount of audit evidence required for an engagement. Pherson expresses the view that internal control must be carefully evaluated in all companies, regardless of their size, in basically the same manner. His public accounting firm requires a standard internal control questionnaire on every audit as well as a flowchart of every transaction area. In addition, he says the firm requires a careful evaluation of the system and a modification in the evidence accumulated based on the controls and weaknesses in the system. Violette responds by saying that she believes internal control cannot be adequate in many of the small companies she audits, although she recognizes that the *CICA Assurance Handbook* requires her to "obtain a sufficient understanding." She disagrees with the *Handbook* Recommendations and goes on to say, "Why should I spend a lot of time obtaining an understanding of internal control and assessing control risk when I know it has all kinds of weaknesses before I start? I would rather spend the time it takes to fill out all those forms in testing whether the statements are correct."

Required
a. Express in general terms the most important difference between the nature of the potential controls available for large and small companies.
b. Criticize the positions taken by Pherson and Violette, and express your own opinion about the similarities and differences that should exist in understanding internal control and assessing control risk for different-sized companies.

9-21 The following are partial descriptions of internal control for companies engaged in the manufacturing business:

1. Every day, hundreds of employees clock in using time cards at Generous Motors Corporation. The timekeepers collect these cards once a week and deliver them to the computer department. There the data on these time cards are entered into the computer. The information entered into the computer is used in the preparation of the labour cost distribution records, the payroll journal, and the payroll cheques. The treasurer, Mrs. Webber, compares the payroll journal with the payroll cheques, signs the cheques, and returns them to Mr. Strode, the supervisor of the computer department. The payroll cheques are distributed to the employees by Mr. Strode.

2. The smallest branch of Connor Cosmetics Inc. in Medicine Hat employs Mary Cooper, the branch manager, and her sales assistant, Jane Hendrix. The branch uses a bank account in Medicine Hat to pay expenses. The account is kept in the name of "Connor Cosmetics Inc.—Special Account." To pay expenses, cheques must be signed by Mary Cooper or by the treasurer of Connor Cosmetics, John Winters. Cooper receives the cancelled cheques and bank statements. She reconciles the branch account herself and files cancelled cheques and bank statements in her records. She also periodically prepares reports of disbursements and sends them to the home office.

Required
a. List the weaknesses in internal control for each of the above. To identify the weaknesses, use the methodology that was discussed in the chapter.
b. For each weakness, state the type of misstatement(s) that is (are) likely to result. Be as specific as possible.
c. How would you improve internal controls for each of the two companies?

(AICPA adapted)

9-22 You are a senior with a public accounting firm. In the course of reviewing a file prepared by a new staff accountant, you notice there is no letter to the client concerning weaknesses in internal control over purchases and payments. You also note that the staff person commented in the file that she had obtained the necessary understanding of internal control over purchases and payments to plan the audit and found internal control to be so weak that she planned to assess control risk at maximum. When you ask her about the apparent lack of communication, she says no letter was sent because she did not think the requirements of Section 5220 of the *CICA Assurance Handbook* applied.

Required
Prepare a response to the staff person explaining why you (and your firm) believe that such a letter is required by Section 5220 of the *Handbook*.

PROFESSIONAL JUDGMENT PROBLEM

9-23 Gaboria Paper Supplies Ltd. is one of your favourite clients. You started work there as a junior staff, and this year you will be the senior. The company is well organized and employees are friendly. Internal controls are good and procedures are highly automated with standard industry software.

You used standard sampling methods to select a sample to count for inventory. Items were traced from the warehouse floor to the count records and from the count records to the warehouse floor. There were only one or two minor count differences, and when employees recounted the items with audit staff, records were adjusted. All inventory tags were accounted for. You thanked your audit staff for their help, completed the inventory count file, then filed it in the filing cabinet at your office.

Three weeks later, when it was time to pull everything together to conduct the year end audit, to your horror, you could not find the inventory count file. You searched through all the files that started with G, and asked clerical staff at your office to help you look, but to no avail.

Required

a. What alternatives are available to you in the completion of the audit?
b. What role does the quality of internal control play in the actions available?
c. Can an audit of inventory still be completed? Why or why not?

CASE

9-24 Filmore and Gus, Chartered Accountants, are the auditors of Campbells' Toy Store (CTS), a local retail operation, and you, CA, are in charge of the audit. In January 2005, you completed the inventory count and internal control testing. All procedures ran smoothly and no discrepancies were found. It is now March 22, 2005, and you are at the CTS offices to start the February 28 year-end audit. The controller, Gina Cooper, is explaining an incident that occurred before year end.

"We lost control of our microcomputer system temporarily. At noon on February 14, 2005, our computer system shut down. A red heart then appeared on all the computer screens, with "Happy Valentine's Day" written under it. This went on for an hour, after which the computer system started working again.

"It appears that someone introduced a computer virus into our system that affected every program in the network. The virus program was activated by a time and date: noon on Valentine's Day. Once the program had run its course, our system returned to normal.

"We have no way of knowing just what else this program did. We still don't know how this virus got into the system. It could have been entered by one of our employees playing a joke or by someone breaking into our computer through our modem access, or the program could have come in through one of the purchased programs we use. We have spent a lot of time and money trying to remove this program and appear to have succeeded."

After you explained the virus incident to the audit partner, he asked you to provide him with a memo discussing the auditing implications of this event.

Required

Prepare the memo to the partner.

(CICA adapted)

CHAPTER 10

FRAUD AUDITING

Why do auditors fail to catch material frauds? Fraud is difficult to identify because it is intentional and an effort is made to cover it up. Nonetheless, if auditors plan and perform their audit giving consideration to the risk and red flags of fraud, the likelihood of identification is greatly increased.

LEARNING OBJECTIVES

After reading this chapter, you should be able to answer the following questions:

1. What is fraud and under what conditions is it most likely to exist? Explain the difference between fraudulent financial reporting and misappropriation of assets.

2. What is the auditor's responsibility for assessing the risk of fraud and detecting material misstatements due to fraud?

3. What features of corporate governance and of control environment would reduce fraud risks?

4. How should an auditor respond when there are identified fraud risks? What are some of the specific fraud risk areas and what is the auditor's responsibility once fraud is detected?

ACCOUNTING SCANDAL ROCKS PUBLIC TRUST

The profession was under fire and throughout the summer, newspapers were filled with details of a corporate accounting scandal. One of the largest, most respected companies in the United States had been caught inflating earnings and assets through blatant manipulation of the accounting rules. Thousands of investors and employees suffered. U.S. Congressional hearings were called to examine and understand the fraud, and everyone asked, "Where were the auditors?" The accounting profession was under immense political pressure from reform-minded lawmakers and the negative publicity surrounding the perceived audit failure cast all PAs in an unfavourable light.

The year was 1938. The corporate accounting scandal was McKesson-Robbins, and it arguably had a greater impact on the way audits are performed than any subsequent scandal, including those of Enron and WorldCom. McKesson-Robbins inflated assets and earnings by $19 million through the reporting of nonexistent inventory and fictitious sales.

In 1924, Philip Musica, a high school dropout with fraud convictions and a prison record, reinvented himself as F. Donald Coster and awarded himself a medical degree. "Dr. Coster" took control of McKesson-Robbins and embarked on a massive fraud to inflate its share price. Coster duped McKesson's auditors, and the investing public, into believing that the company had a huge drug inventory, worth multimillions of dollars. Coster created phony purchase orders, sales invoices, and other documents, all of which McKesson's auditors dutifully reviewed as evidence of the imaginary inventory. The fraud succeeded because the auditing standards of the day permitted auditors to confine themselves to reviewing documents and talking to management. They were not required to physically observe and verify inventories.

Contributions to this chapter were made by Linda A. Robinson, University of Waterloo.

Sources: Adapted from 1. Ramos, Michael, "SAS 99 Gives CPAs New Chance to Reclaim Reputation," December 2002 (www.CPA2biz.com/News/Viewpoint). 2. Presentation by PCAOB Board Member Daniel L. Goelzer at Investment Company Institute's 2003 Tax & Accounting Conference, September 15, 2003 (www.pcaobus.org/ transcripts/Goelzer_09-15-03.asp).

The story of McKesson-Robbins tells you that financial statement fraud is not a recent phenomenon. As many of the large financial statement frauds we read about take place in the U.S., Canadians may think themselves immune to such activity. However, this is not the case. Consider some significant Canadian financial reporting frauds include Livent, Nortel, Atlas Cold Storage, and Bre-X.

Even if the auditor counts inventory, misstatements can occur. What are the different ways that inventory could be misstated? How would you audit such misstatements?

→10.1   THE NATURE OF FRAUD

Types of Fraud

FRAUD—an intentional misstatement of the financial statements

Fraud is a broad legal concept, but in the context of auditing financial statements, it is defined as an intentional misrepresentation of a fact in the books of accounts and ultimately the financial statements. This misrepresentation may be directed against users of the financial statements such as shareholders or creditors, or against the organization itself by covering up or disguising embezzlement, misapplication of funds, or improper use of the organization's assets by officers, employees, and third parties. The two main categories of fraud are fraudulent financial reporting and misappropriation of assets, subjects that were introduced in Chapter 5.

FRAUDULENT FINANCIAL REPORTING—intentional misstatement or omission of amounts or disclosure in financial statements to deceive users

Fraudulent Financial Reporting **Fraudulent financial reporting** is an intentional misstatement or omission of amounts or disclosures with the intent to deceive users. Most cases of fraudulent financial reporting involve the intentional misstatement of amounts. For example, WorldCom is reported to have capitalized (as fixed assets) billions of dollars that should have been expensed. Omissions of amounts are less common, but a company can overstate income by omitting accounts payable and other liabilities. Fraudulent financial reporting is sometimes referred to as fraud "by the organization" as insiders perpetrate the fraud most often to boost share price or disguise losses.

Although most cases of fraudulent financial reporting involve overstatement of assets and income or omission of liabilities and expenses in an attempt to overstate income, it is important to note that companies occasionally deliberately understate income. For privately held companies, this may be done in an attempt to reduce income taxes. Companies may also intentionally understate income when earnings are high to create a reserve of earnings or "cookie jar reserves" that may be used to increase earnings in future periods. This practice is called *income smoothing* or *earnings management*. **Earnings management** involves deliberate actions taken by management to meet earnings objectives. It has been argued that many companies undertake some form of earnings management and that such activity is not necessarily fraudulent. For example, a company could choose to dispose of excess assets for a profit in a period when earnings are low to improve the reported net income. Such a management decision is not fraudulent if it is properly disclosed in the financial statements. It is the failure to disclose earnings management that makes the activity fraudulent. **Income smoothing** is a form of earnings management in which revenues and expenses are shifted between periods to reduce fluctuations in earnings. One technique to smooth income is to reduce the value of inventory and other assets of an acquired company at the time of

EARNINGS MANAGEMENT—deliberate actions taken by management to meet earnings objectives

INCOME SMOOTHING—form of earnings management in which revenues and expenses are shifted between periods to reduce fluctuations in earnings acquisition, resulting in higher earnings when the assets are later sold. Companies may also deliberately overstate inventory obsolescence reserves and allowances for doubtful accounts in periods of higher earnings.

Another common method of fraudulent financial reporting involves inadequate disclosure in the financial statements. A central issue in the Enron case was whether the company had adequately disclosed obligations to affiliates known as special-purpose entities. Also, Hollinger International Inc. failed to disclose payments made to Conrad Black as Chairman and CEO and other senior managers when newspaper assets were sold to third parties. Profits earned on the sale of newspapers that should have gone to the benefit of the shareholders of Hollinger were instead paid to senior management or related parties.

Misappropriation of Assets **Misappropriation of assets** is fraud that involves theft of an entity's assets. It is a fraud "against the organization" perpetrated most often by employees, customers, or suppliers. In many cases, the amounts involved are not material to the financial statements. However, the loss of company assets is an important management concern, and management's materiality threshold for fraud will likely be much lower than the materiality threshold used by the auditor for financial reporting purposes.

Misappropriation of assets is normally perpetrated at lower levels of the organization's hierarchy. In some notable cases, however, top management is involved in the theft of company assets. Because of management's greater authority and control over the organization's assets, defalcations involving top management can involve significant amounts. In one extreme example, the former CEO of Tyco International was charged by the SEC with stealing over $100 million in assets.

Examples of misappropriation of assets that could be perpetrated by an employee include theft of inventory where the records are altered to cover it up, skimming of cash, padding of expense accounts, and lapping of accounts receivable. A test to discover lapping is addressed on page 390. Examples of misappropriation of assets involving external parties include shoplifting, suppliers delivering lower quality goods than those for which the

MISAPPROPRIATION OF ASSETS
—a fraud involving the theft of an entity's assets

Focus Box 10-1

FRAUDULENT FINANCIAL REPORTING STATISTICS

The two most common techniques used by management to misstate financial statement information involve improper revenue recognition and overstatements of assets. According to a study commissioned by the Committee of Sponsoring Organizations of the Treadway Commission (COSO), 50 percent of U.S. companies committing financial statement fraud between 1987 and 1997 recorded revenues prematurely or created fictitious revenue transactions.

In addition to these revenue and receivable overstatements, 50 percent of the fraudulent companies overstated assets by overvaluing existing assets, recording fictitious assets or assets not owned, or capitalizing items that should have been expensed. Assets typically overstated included inventory, net accounts receivable due to understated allowances for doubtful accounts, and property, plant, and equipment. Only 18 percent of the fraudulent companies understated expenses or liabilities.

The median fraud was $4.1 million, which is relatively large given that the median company had total assets of $15.7 million. Eighty-three percent of the fraud cases were perpetrated by the chief executive officer (CEO) and/or the chief financial officer (CFO). These individuals allegedly engaged in the fraud to avoid reporting a pre-tax loss, to maintain requirements to continue trading company stock on one of the national stock exchanges, or to increase stock prices. The motivation to commit the fraud was high because, on average, company officers and members of the board of directors owned 32 percent of the company stock.

Consequences of the fraud were significant. More than 50 percent of the companies filed for bankruptcy or were under a substantially different form of ownership following the fraud period. Many of the individuals involved were forced to resign or were terminated as a result of the fraud. In some cases, those involved were jailed. Additionally, both the companies and individuals faced lawsuits filed by shareholders and the SEC.

Source: Adapted from *Fraudulent Financial Reporting: 1987–1997, An Analysis of U.S. Public Companies,* Committee of Sponsoring Organizations of the Treadway Commission, New York, 1999.

PROCUREMENT FRAUD—the manipulation of the contracting process

company was charged; and complex contract fraud through bid rigging. **Procurement fraud**, which is the manipulation of the contracting process, can be very expensive for an organization. The three main forms of procurement fraud are: a) bid rigging where the bidders for a contract collude to increase the price of the contract; b) bid fixing where a bidding party is provided with insider information, giving an unfair advantage; and c) bribery and kickbacks where the contract is awarded on the basis of a payment to a company insider involved in the contract-awarding decision. All three forms of procurement fraud are illegal and result in the company paying more for the goods or services than it should.

Misappropriation of assets is much more common than fraudulent financial reporting, but we don't often see it in the news. Because such fraud is often not material to the financial statements, it is usually dealt with internally. Such actions might range from filing a complaint with the police to a quick and quiet termination of the relationship.

Conditions for Fraud

Three conditions for fraud arising from fraudulent financial reporting and misappropriations of assets are described in Section 5135.012 of the *CICA Assurance Handbook* titled "The Auditor's Responsibility to Consider Fraud and Error." As shown in Figure 10-1, these three conditions are referred to as the **fraud triangle**.

FRAUD TRIANGLE—represents the three conditions of fraud: incentives/pressures, opportunities, and attitudes/rationalization

1. Incentives/Pressures. Management or other employees have incentives or pressures to commit fraud.
2. Opportunities. Circumstances provide opportunities for management or employees to commit fraud.
3. Attitudes/Rationalization. An attitude, character, or set of ethical values exists that allows management or employees to intentionally commit a dishonest act, or they are in an environment that imposes pressure sufficient to cause them to rationalize committing a dishonest act.

FRAUD RISK FACTORS—entity factors that increase the risk of fraud

Risk Factors for Fraudulent Financial Reporting An essential consideration by the auditor in uncovering fraud is identifying factors that increase the risk of fraud. These are referred to as fraud risk factors or red flags of fraud. Table 10-1 provides examples of **fraud risk factors** for each of the three conditions of fraud for fraudulent financial reporting. Even though the three conditions in the fraud triangle are the same for fraudulent financial reporting and misappropriation of assets, the risk factors are different. First, the risk factors for fraudulent financial reporting are discussed, followed by those for misappropriation of

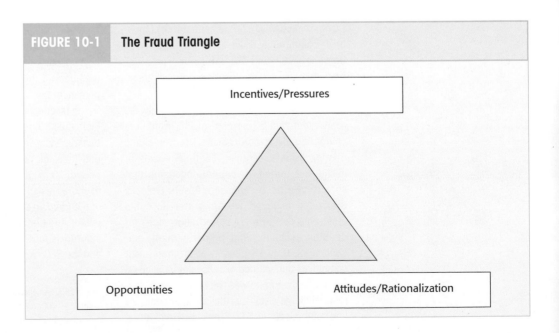

FIGURE 10-1   The Fraud Triangle

Incentives/Pressures

Opportunities

Attitudes/Rationalization

assets. Appendix A to section 5135 of the *CICA Assurance Handbook* provides further examples of fraud risk factors for both fraudulent financial reporting and misappropriation of assets. Later in the chapter, we discuss the auditor's use of the risk factors in uncovering fraud.

INCENTIVES/PRESSURES A common incentive for companies to manipulate financial statements is a decline in the company's financial prospects. A decline in earnings may threaten the company's ability to obtain financing and continue as a going concern. Companies may also manipulate earnings to meet analysts' forecasts of anticipated earnings for the quarter, to meet debt covenant restrictions, or to artificially maintain or inflate stock prices. In some cases, management may manipulate earnings just to preserve their reputation. Management with significant wealth tied up in stock options may have an incentive to inflate stock prices to increase the profits they earn personally when the options are exercised.

OPPORTUNITIES Financial statements of all companies are potentially subject to manipulation. However, the risk of fraudulent financial reporting is greater for companies in industries where significant judgments and estimates are involved. For example, valuation of inventories is subject to greater risk of misstatement for companies with diverse inventories in many locations. The risk of misstatement of inventories is further increased if those inventories are potentially obsolete.

TABLE 10-1	Examples of Risk Factors for Fraudulent Financial Reporting	
	Three Conditions of Fraud	
Incentives/Pressures	**Opportunities**	**Attitudes/Rationalization**
Management or other employees have incentives or pressures to materially misstate financial statements.	Circumstances provide an opportunity for management or employees to misstate financial statements.	An attitude, character, or set of ethical values exists that allows management or employees to intentionally commit a dishonest act, or they are in an environment that imposes pressure sufficient to cause them to rationalize committing a dishonest act.
Examples of Risk Factors	**Examples of Risk Factors**	**Examples of Risk Factors**
Financial stability or profitability is threatened by economic, industry, or entity operating conditions. Examples include significant declines in customer demand and increasing business failures in either the industry or overall economy. Excessive pressure for management to meet the requirements or expectations of third parties, such as the terms of debt covenant requirements. Management or the board of directors' personal net worth is materially threatened by the entity's financial performance.	Significant accounting estimates involve subjective judgments or uncertainties that are difficult to verify. Ineffective board of directors or audit committee oversight over financial reporting. High turnover or ineffective accounting, internal audit, or information technology staff.	Inappropriate or ineffective communication and support of the entity's values. Known history of violations of securities laws or other laws and regulations. Management's practice of making overly aggressive or unrealistic forecasts to analysts, creditors, and other third parties.

Opportunities for misstatement are greater if there is turnover in accounting personnel or other weaknesses in accounting and information processes. In many cases of fraudulent financial reporting, the company had an ineffective audit committee and board of director oversight of financial reporting.

ATTITUDES/RATIONALIZATION The attitude of top management toward financial reporting is a critical risk factor in assessing the likelihood of fraudulent financial statements. This attitude is commonly referred to as the "tone at the top" and will be discussed in more detail later in the chapter. If the CEO or other top managers display a significant disregard for the financial reporting process, for example, by consistently issuing overly optimistic forecasts or by being overly concerned about meeting analysts' earnings forecasts, fraudulent financial reporting is more likely. Also, management's character or set of ethical values may make it easier for them to rationalize a fraudulent act.

Risk Factors for Misappropriation of Assets The same three fraud triangle conditions apply to misappropriation of assets. However, in assessing risk factors, greater emphasis is placed on individual incentives and opportunities for theft. Table 10-2 provides examples of fraud risk factors for each of the three conditions of fraud for misappropriation of assets.

INCENTIVES/PRESSURES Financial pressures are a common incentive for employees who misappropriate assets. Employees with excessive financial obligations or with drug abuse or gambling problems may steal to meet their personal financial or other needs. Managers should be alert for signs of these problems in employees with access to assets or accounting records. While a background check should be performed for all potential employees, a credit check may be included for those who will have access to assets. Dissatisfied employees may steal from a sense of entitlement or as a form of attack against their employers. Companies can reduce fraud risk by dealing fairly with employees and monitoring employee morale.

OPPORTUNITIES Opportunities for theft exist in all companies. However, opportunities are greater in companies with accessible cash or with inventory or other valuable assets, especially if the assets are small or readily portable. For example, thefts of laptop computers are

TABLE 10-2	Examples of Risk Factors for Misappropriation of Assets	
	Three Conditions of Fraud	
Incentives/Pressures	Opportunities	Attitudes/Rationalization
Management or other employees have incentives or pressures to misappropriate material assets.	Circumstances provide an opportunity for management or employees to misappropriate assets.	An attitude, character, or set of ethical values exists that allows management or employees to intentionally commit a dishonest act, or they are in an environment that imposes pressure sufficient to cause them to rationalize a dishonest act.
Examples of Risk Factors	Examples of Risk Factors	Examples of Risk Factors
Personal financial obligations create pressure for those with access to cash or other assets susceptible to theft to misappropriate those assets. Adverse relationships between management and employees with access to assets susceptible to theft motivate employees to misappropriate those assets. Examples include the following: · Known or expected employee layoffs. · Promotions, compensation, or other rewards inconsistent with expectations.	Presence of large amounts of cash on hand or inventory items that are small, of high value, or are in high demand. Inadequate internal control over assets due to lack of the following: · Appropriate segregation of duties or independent checks. · Appropriate job applicant screening for employees performing key control functions. · Mandatory vacations for employees with access to assets.	Disregard for the need to monitor or reduce risk of misappropriating assets. Disregard for internal controls by overriding existing controls or failing to correct known internal control deficiencies.

fairly common and much more frequent than thefts of desktop systems. Retail establishments and other organizations that receive revenue in the form of cash are also susceptible to theft. Surveillance methods and inventory coding and tracking systems can reduce the potential for theft. For example, casinos handle extensive amounts of cash with little formal records of cash received. As a result, casinos make extensive use of video and human surveillance. On a more basic scale, one Canadian fast food chain has a small sign affixed to their cash registers advising patrons that if they don't receive a receipt, their meal is free. This simple control ensures that the sales are recorded in the cash register. Such a control costs the company nothing to implement and every patron becomes a watchdog.

Focus Box 10-3

OVERBEARING EMPLOYEE STEALS $2 MILLION OVER FIVE YEARS

Lucy Magda, 61, was the classified advertising manager of *The Standard* newspaper in St. Catharines, Ontario, from 1992 to 1997. During that time, *The Standard* went from a company that participated actively in the community, to a company in regression—firing employees and having a reduction in income. It seems that Lucy, an employee who had been with the company for 34 years, started pocketing advertising revenue rather than depositing it in the company bank accounts.

She kept detailed records of her thefts, which she thought were shredded. However, due to a cost-saving measure (the cancellation of the shredding contract), forensic investigators were able to document what she had taken.

How could such a theft remain undetected for five years? There was a lack of internal controls over cash, and Lucy's intimidation of her co-employees was tolerated. In June 2004, Lucy was sentenced to 34 months in jail.

Sources: 1. *The Globe and Mail*, 2004. "Lucy in the classified ad department with diamonds," July 6, sec. B. 2. R. v. Magda, (30 June 2004), 8808/03 (ON S.C.).

Weak internal controls create opportunities for theft. Inadequate separation of duties is practically a license for employees to steal. Whenever employees have custody or even temporary access to assets and maintain the accounting records for those assets, the potential for theft exists. As an example, if inventory storeroom employees also maintain inventory records, it is relatively easy for them to take inventory items and cover the theft by adjusting the accounting records.

Fraud is more prevalent in smaller businesses and not-for-profit organizations because it is more difficult for these entities to maintain adequate separation of duties. However, even large organizations may fail to maintain adequate separation in critical areas. As an illustration, Barings Bank incurred losses in excess of $1 billion from the activities of one trader because of inadequate separation of duties.

ATTITUDES/RATIONALIZATION Management's attitude toward controls and ethical conduct may allow employees and managers to rationalize the theft of assets. If management cheats customers through overcharging for goods or engaging in high-pressure sales tactics, employees may feel that it is acceptable for them to behave in the same fashion by cheating on expense or time reports.

→10.2 THE AUDITOR'S ROLE IN ASSESSING THE RISK OF FRAUD

Section 5135 provides guidance to auditors in assessing the risk of fraud. Auditors must maintain a level of professional skepticism as they consider a broad set of information, including fraud risk factors, to identify and respond to fraud risk. As discussed in Chapter 5, the auditor has a responsibility to respond to fraud risk by planning and performing the audit to obtain reasonable assurance that the financial statements are free from material misstatements, whether due to errors or fraud.

Professional Skepticism Section 5090.06 states that, in exercising **professional skepticism**, an auditor "is alert for evidence that contradicts or brings into question the reliability of

PROFESSIONAL SKEPTICISM—an attitude of the auditor that neither assumes management is dishonest nor assumes unquestioned honesty documents or representations of management or those charged with governance." In practice, maintaining this attitude of professional skepticism can be difficult because, despite some recent high-profile examples of fraudulent financial statements, material frauds are infrequent compared to the number of audits of financial statements conducted annually. Most auditors will never encounter a material fraud during their careers. Also, through client acceptance and continuance evaluation procedures, auditors reject most potential clients perceived as lacking honesty and integrity. Section 5135 emphasizes consideration of a client's susceptibility to fraud, regardless of the auditor's beliefs about the likelihood of fraud and management's honesty and integrity.

QUESTIONING MIND During audit planning for every audit, the engagement team must discuss the need to maintain a questioning mind throughout the audit in identifying fraud risks and critically evaluating audit evidence. In maintaining a questioning mind, auditors should set aside any prior beliefs about management's integrity and honesty and should consider the potential for management override of controls, given that fraud is possible in any audit.

CRITICAL EVALUATION OF AUDIT EVIDENCE Auditors should thoroughly probe the issues and acquire additional evidence as necessary. Auditors should be particularly careful when relying on the representations of management. Representation of management generally, in and of itself, does not represent sufficient audit evidence. Care should be taken to corroborate these representations.

Auditors should consult with other team members rather than rationalize or dismiss information or other conditions that indicate a material misstatement due to fraud may have occurred. For example, an auditor may uncover a current-year sale that should be properly reflected as a sale in the following year. Rather than conclude that the error is an isolated incident, the auditor should evaluate the reasons for the error, determine whether it was intentional or unintentional, and consider whether other such errors are likely to have occurred.

Sources of Information About Fraud Risks Information used to assess fraud risk is summarized in Figure 10-2. This information is considered in the context of the three conditions for fraud: incentives/pressures, opportunities, and attitudes/rationalization. Auditors should consider the following:

- Information obtained from communications among audit team members about their knowledge of the company and its industry, including how and where the company might be susceptible to material misstatements due to fraud.
- Responses to auditor enquiries of management about their views of the risks of fraud and about existing programs and controls to address specific identified fraud risks.
- Specific risk factors for fraudulent financial reporting and misappropriations of assets.
- Analytical procedures results obtained during planning that indicate possible, implausible, or unexpected analytical relationships.
- Knowledge obtained through other procedures, such as client acceptance and retention decisions, interim review of financial statements, and consideration of inherent or control risks.

COMMUNICATIONS AMONG AUDIT TEAM Section 5135 requires the audit team, including the engagement partner, to conduct discussions to share insights into the susceptibility of the entity to fraud and error. The results of the discussions, which should be documented, would address the following:

1. How and where they believe the entity's financial statements might be susceptible to material misstatement due to fraud
2. How management could perpetrate and conceal fraudulent financial reporting
3. How assets of the entity could be misappropriated
4. What circumstances exist that might be indicative of earnings management that could lead to fraudulent financial reporting
5. What known external and internal factors affecting the entity that might

    - create an incentive or pressure for management to commit fraud.

- provide the opportunity for fraud to be perpetrated.
- indicate a culture or environment that enables management to rationalize fraudulent acts.

6. How the auditor might respond to the susceptibility of material misstatements due to fraud

Discussions with the audit team should reinforce the importance of all members maintaining an independent state of mind throughout the audit and being attuned to potential new information that might change the original assessment of the risk of fraud.

ENQUIRIES OF MANAGEMENT AND AUDIT COMMITTEE Section 5135 requires the auditor to make specific enquiries about fraud in every audit. Enquiries of management and others within the company are important because the likelihood of fraud is often revealed through information received in response to the auditor's questions. Enquiries provide employees an opportunity to tell the auditor information that otherwise might not be communicated.

The auditor's enquiries of management should include whether management has knowledge of any fraud or suspected fraud within the company. Auditor enquiries about management's process of assessing and responding to fraud risks, the nature of fraud risks identified by management, and any internal controls implemented to address those risks provide useful information. The auditor should also enquire about any information reported by management to the audit committee about fraud risks and related controls.

The audit committee or equivalent often assumes an active role in overseeing management's fraud risk assessment and response processes. Section 5135 requires the auditor to enquire of the audit committee its views of the risks of fraud and whether the audit committee has knowledge of any fraud or suspected fraud. Part of the reason for these enquiries is to corroborate the evidence provided by management.

For entities with an internal audit function, the auditor should enquire about internal audit's views of fraud risks and whether they have any knowledge of actual or alleged fraud that was not corrected. They should also ask whether internal audit performed any procedures to identify or detect fraud during the year and if management has satisfactorily responded to their findings.

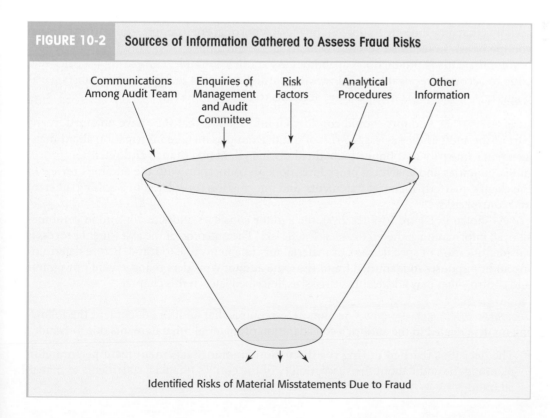

FIGURE 10-2   Sources of Information Gathered to Assess Fraud Risks

Communications Among Audit Team   Enquiries of Management and Audit Committee   Risk Factors   Analytical Procedures   Other Information

Identified Risks of Material Misstatements Due to Fraud

The auditor should also make enquiries of others within the entity whose duties lie outside the normal financial reporting lines of responsibility. When coming into contact with company personnel throughout the audit, such as the inventory warehouse manager or purchasing agents, the auditor may enquire about the existence or suspicion of fraud. Enquiries of executives and a wide variety of other employees with different levels of authority provide opportunities for the auditor to learn about risks of fraud. When responses are inconsistent, the auditor should obtain additional audit evidence to resolve the inconsistency and to support or refute the original risk assessment.

The auditor needs to take into account the oversight structure of the entity when assessing the risk of fraud. When the entity is smaller, without an audit committee, the owner-manager may be able to exercise effective oversight thus compensating for the absence of extensive internal controls. On the other hand, the auditor needs to keep in mind that the owner-manager may be more able to override controls.

RISK FACTORS Section 5135 requires the auditor to evaluate whether fraud risk factors exist that indicate incentives or pressures to perpetrate fraud, opportunities to carry out fraud, or attitudes or rationalizations used to justify a fraudulent action. Examples of fraud risk factors considered by auditors are included in Tables 10-1 (p. 285) and 10-2 (p. 286) and Appendix A of 5135. Professional judgment is required when determining whether a risk factor is present and, if so, the appropriate response. Fraud risk factors do not mean that fraud exists, only that the likelihood of fraud is higher. Auditors should consider these factors along with other information used to assess the risks of fraud.

ANALYTICAL PROCEDURES As discussed in Chapter 6, auditors should perform analytical procedures during the planning, testing, and completion phases of the audit. Analytical procedures help the auditor identify unusual or unexpected relationships that might indicate the presence of material misstatements in the financial statements.

Analytical procedures performed during planning may be helpful in identifying fraud risks. When results from analytical procedures differ from the auditor's expectations, the auditor evaluates those results along with other information to assess whether there is a heightened risk of fraud.

Because occurrences of fraudulent financial reporting often involve manipulation of revenue, Section 5135 requires the auditor to perform analytical procedures on revenue accounts. The objective is to identify unusual or unexpected relationships involving revenue accounts that may indicate fraudulent financial reporting. For example, comparing the sales volume based on recorded revenue with actual production capacity could reveal revenues beyond the entity's production capabilities. As another example, comparing the sales revenue to accounts receivable could reveal recorded sales that lack economic substance as bogus sales would remain unpaid and accounts receivable would grow.

OTHER INFORMATION Auditors should consider all information that they have obtained in any part of the audit as they assess the risk of fraud. Examples include information about management's integrity and honesty obtained during client acceptance and retention procedures, enquiries and analytical procedures done in connection with the auditor's review of the client's quarterly financial statements, and information considered in assessing inherent and control risks.

As shown in Figure 10-2 (p. 289), the auditor considers, individually and in combination, all information gathered to assess fraud risks. The outcome of the assessment process is the identification of specific risks of material misstatements due to fraud. Before determining audit responses to identified fraud risks, the auditor considers management's programs and controls that may address those risks, as described later in this chapter.

Documenting Fraud Assessment Section 5135 requires that auditors document the following matters related to the auditor's consideration of material misstatements due to fraud:

- The decisions reached during the discussion among engagement team personnel in planning the audit about the susceptibility of the entity's financial statements to material fraud.

- The assessed risk of material misstatement due to fraud.
- The response to the assessed risks of material fraud that were identified, including the impact on the nature, timing, and extent of audit procedures.
- Results of the procedures performed to address the risk of management override of controls.
- The nature of communications about fraud made to management, the audit committee, or others.
- Reasons supporting a conclusion that there is not a significant risk of material improper revenue recognition.

After fraud risks are identified and documented, the auditor should evaluate factors that reduce fraud risk before developing an appropriate response to the risk of fraud. Corporate governance and other control factors that reduce fraud risks are discussed in the next section.

→ 10.3 CORPORATE GOVERNANCE OVERSIGHT TO REDUCE FRAUD RISKS

The responsibility for implementing corporate governance and control procedures to minimize fraud lies with management and the board of directors or equivalent. Since the audit committee has oversight responsibility for the financial reporting process, the board often delegates responsibility for evaluating the risk of fraud to the audit committee as well. The risk of fraud can be reduced through a combination of prevention, deterrence, and detection measures. Because fraud is difficult to detect due to collusion and false documentation, a focus on fraud prevention and deterrence is often more effective and less costly. Programs and controls implemented by management to prevent fraud help reduce opportunities for it. Programs and controls implemented to deter fraud help persuade employees that they should not commit it because of the likelihood of detection and punishment.

There are three actions that an entity can take to prevent, deter, and detect fraud:

1. Create and maintain a culture of honesty and high ethics.
2. Evaluate fraud risks and implement programs and controls to mitigate identified fraud risks.
3. Develop an appropriate fraud oversight process.

We discuss the elements of these corporate governance and other control environment actions next. Understanding these actions is helpful to auditors in assessing the extent to which clients have implemented these fraud-reducing activities.

Creating a Culture of Honesty and High Ethics Research indicates that the most effective way to prevent and deter fraud is to implement programs and controls that are based on core values embraced by the company. These values create an environment that reinforces acceptable behaviour and expectations of each employee, which can be used to guide their actions. These values help create a culture of honesty and ethics that provides the foundation for employees in their job responsibilities. Creating a culture of honesty and high ethics includes six elements.

SETTING THE TONE AT THE TOP Management and the board of directors are responsible for setting the "tone at the top" for ethical behaviour in the company. Honesty and integrity by management reinforces honesty and integrity in employees throughout the organization.

Management cannot act one way and expect others in the company to behave differently. Through its actions and communications, management can show that dishonest and unethical behaviours are not tolerated, even if the results benefit the company. Statements by management about the absolute need to meet operating and financial targets create undue pressures that may lead employees to commit fraud to achieve them. In contrast, statements indicating management's desire to aggressively pursue entity goals and targets, while at the same time requiring honest and ethical actions to achieve those goals, clearly indicate to employees that integrity is a requirement. Such a message demonstrates that management and the board have zero tolerance for unethical behaviour.

Placer Dome Code of Conduct
www.placerdome.com/company/
corpgovernance/codeofconduct.
html

Bell Canada Enterprises Code of
Conduct
www.bce.ca/en/governance/
codeofconduct/index.php

RBC Financial Group Code of
Conduct
www.rbc.com/governance/pdf/
2005RBCCodeOfConduct.pdf

A tone at the top based on honesty and integrity provides the foundation upon which a more detailed code of conduct can be developed to provide more specific guidance about permitted and prohibited behaviour. Table 10-3 contains an example of the key contents of an effective code of conduct. The existence of a code of conduct is not adequate. To be effective, it must be communicated throughout the organization, employees must be educated on the code, and management and the board must lead by example. Examples of codes of conduct are available at the Placer Dome, Bell Canada Enterprises, and Royal Bank web sites, among others.

CREATING A POSITIVE WORKPLACE ENVIRONMENT Research shows that wrongdoing occurs less frequently when employees have positive feelings about their employer than when they feel abused, threatened, or ignored. In a positive workplace, there is improved employee morale, which may reduce employees' likelihood of committing fraud against the company.

Management should build a positive culture and work environment by implementing programs and initiatives to increase employee morale. Employees should be encouraged to contribute to that environment and support the entity's values and code of conduct. Employees should also have the ability to obtain advice internally before making decisions that appear to have legal or ethical implications.

Part of creating a positive workplace includes providing the employees with a process to report actual or suspected wrongdoing or potential violations of the code of conduct or ethics policy. Analysis of fraud cases often shows that employees were aware of improper activities by management, but they did not communicate their concerns, because they did not have a safe outlet. Organizations are now offering a complaint process in the form of a compliance or "whistle-blower" hotline that provides the employees with an opportunity to report their concerns anonymously. Some organizations outsource this service while others have a telephone "hotline" directed to or monitored by an ethics officer or General Counsel who is made responsible for investigating and reporting fraud or illegal acts. It is important that the organization have a protocol to inform the audit committee of complaints received. You can see an example of a complaint process at Barrick's web site.

Barrick
www.barrick.com

HIRING AND PROMOTING APPROPRIATE EMPLOYEES To be successful in preventing fraud, well-run companies implement effective screening policies to reduce the likelihood of hiring and promoting individuals with low levels of honesty, especially those who hold positions of trust. Effective hiring and promotion policies may include background checks on individuals being considered for employment or for promotion to positions of trust. Background checks verify a candidate's education, employment history, and personal references, including references about character and integrity. After an employee is hired, continuous evaluation of employee compliance with the company's values and code of conduct reduce the likelihood of fraud.

TRAINING All new employees should be trained about the company's expectations of employees' ethical conduct. Employees should be told of their duty to communicate actual or suspected fraud and the appropriate way to do so. Fraud awareness training should be tailored to employees' job responsibilities. For example, training for purchasing agents should be different than training for sales agents.

CONFIRMATION Companies should require employees to confirm annually their responsibilities for complying with the code of conduct. Employees should be asked to state that they understand the company's expectations and have complied with the code, and that they are unaware of any violations. These confirmations help reinforce the code of conduct policies and also help deter employees from committing fraud or other ethics violations. Most employees want to avoid making a false statement in writing and would rather disclose what they know. Follow-up by internal audit or others on disclosures and non-replies may uncover significant issues.

DISCIPLINE Employees must know that they are held accountable for failing to follow the company's code of conduct. Enforcement of violations of the code, regardless of the level of the employee committing the act, sends clear messages to all employees that compliance with the code of conduct and other ethical standards is important and expected. Thorough investigation of all violations and appropriate and consistent responses can be effective deterrents to fraud.

TABLE 10-3	Example Elements for a Code of Conduct
Code of Conduct Element	**Description**
Organizational Code of Conduct	The organization and its employees must at all times comply with all applicable laws and regulations, with all business conduct well above the minimum standards required by law.
General Employee Conduct	The organization expects its employees to conduct themselves in a businesslike manner and prohibits unprofessional activities, such as drinking, gambling, fighting, and swearing on the job.
Conflicts of Interest	The organization expects that employees will perform their duties conscientiously, honestly, and in accordance with the best interests of the organization and will not use their positions or knowledge gained for private or personal advantage.
Outside Activities, Employment, and Directorships	All employees share a responsibility for the organization's good public relations. Employees should avoid activities outside the organization that create an excessive demand on their time or create a conflict of interest.
Relationships with Clients and Suppliers	Employees should avoid investing in or acquiring a financial interest in any business organization that has a contractual relationship with the organization.
Gifts, Entertainment, and Favours	Employees must not accept entertainment, gifts, or personal favours that could influence or appear to influence business decisions in favour of any person with whom the organization has business dealings.
Kickbacks and Secret Commissions	Employees may not receive payment or compensation of any kind, except as authorized under organizational remuneration policies.
Organization Funds and Other Assets	Employees who have access to organization funds must follow prescribed procedures for recording, handling, and protecting money.
Organization Records and Communications	Employees responsible for accounting and record-keeping must not make or engage in any false record or communication of any kind, whether external or internal.
Information Systems	Employee usage guidelines require use of licensed software. Unauthorized software is prohibited. Emails and all electronic data are the property of the company. Offensive material may not be distributed. Policies for data usage and retention are clear.
Dealing with Outside People and Organizations	Employees must take care to separate their personal roles from their organizational positions when communicating on matters not involving the organization's business.
Prompt Communications	All employees must make every effort to achieve complete, accurate, and timely communications in all matters relevant to customers, suppliers, government authorities, the public, and others within the organization.
Privacy and Confidentiality	When handling financial and personal information about customers and others with whom the organization has dealings, employees should collect, use, and retain only the information necessary for the organization's business; internal access to information should be limited to those with a legitimate business reason for seeking that information.

Sources: 1. AICPA, "CPA's Handbook of Fraud and Commercial Crime Prevention." 2. Laudon, Kenneth C., Jane P. Laudon and Mary Elizabeth Brabston, 2005. "Management Information Systems," Second Canadian Edition, Toronto: Prentice Hall.

OTHER DECLARATIONS Some organizations have additional declarations that they require their employees to confirm agreement with annually. Similar to a code of conduct, these declarations set the behavioural tone of the organization. Declarations that might be found in a public accounting firm include:

- Confidentiality policy in which the employee and partner agree to maintain all client-related information in strict confidence.
- Independence policy in which the employee and partner agree to be free of any influence, interest, or relationship with a client and its affairs. Independence is a requirement under the rules of professional conduct as discussed in Chapter 2, but public accounting firms often require their employees to acknowledge their adherence to the rules.
- Electronic communication policy in which the employee and partner acknowledge that because email communications are unsecured, client matters should not be communicated over the Internet and the Internet should be used for business purposes only.
- Computer Software policy in which the employee and partner agree that all software on their company-provided computer complies with the laws and licensing agreements and that they have not taken copies of company licensed software for their own use.

Responsibility to Evaluate Risks of Fraud

Fraud cannot occur without a perceived opportunity to commit and conceal the act. The primary responsibility for identifying and measuring fraud risks, taking steps to mitigate identified risks, and monitoring internal controls that prevent and detect fraud lies with management and those charged with governance for the entity.

IDENTIFYING AND MEASURING FRAUD RISKS Effective fraud oversight begins with the recognition that fraud is possible and that almost any employee is capable of committing a dishonest act under the right circumstances. This recognition increases the likelihood that effective fraud prevention, deterrence, and detection programs and controls are implemented. Figure 10-3 summarizes factors that management should consider that may contribute to fraud in an organization.

In carrying out their responsibility, management and those charged with governance must assess fraud risks and establish corporate governance programs and controls to prevent, deter, and detect fraud. The assessment process should focus on the company's vulnerability to fraud. For example, the company's industry may create incentives or opportunities for employees to manipulate financial results, such as inventory reserves for a manufacturer, or to misappropriate cash for a bank. Assessing fraud risk may be part of management's overall enterprise risk management or it may be a separate process.

A fraud risk assessment, which may be conducted by internal audit, would begin by identifying all the areas in a company that are susceptible to fraud. These susceptibilities would include an assessment of areas of potential:

- fraudulent financial reporting such as improper revenue recognition, overstatement of assets, or understatement of liabilities;
- misappropriation of assets such as theft of cash or inventory;
- expenditures and liabilities for an improper purpose such as bribery or kickbacks;
- costs or expenditures avoided by fraud such as tax evasion or fraud against employees, which could include failure to pay insurance premiums; and
- improper financial conduct by senior management or the board, such as improper expense claims, regardless of their materiality.

MITIGATING FRAUD RISKS Management is responsible for designing and implementing programs and controls to mitigate fraud risks. Management can change business activities and processes prone to fraud in order to reduce incentives and opportunities for fraud. For example, management can outsource certain operations, such as transferring cash collections from company personnel to a bank lockbox system. Other programs and controls may be implemented at a company-wide level, such as the training of all employees about fraud risks and strengthening employment and promotion policies.

FIGURE 10-3 **Organizational Factors Contributing to Risk of Fraud**

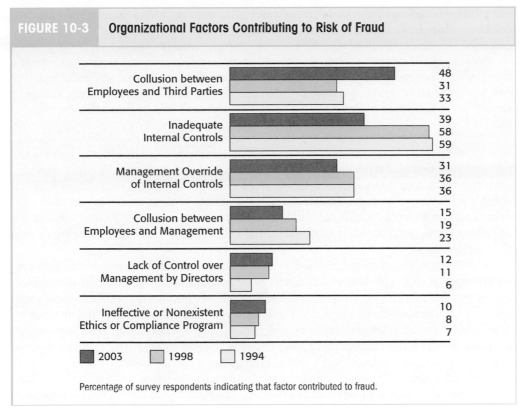

Collusion between Employees and Third Parties	48
	31
	33
Inadequate Internal Controls	39
	58
	59
Management Override of Internal Controls	31
	36
	36
Collusion between Employees and Management	15
	19
	23
Lack of Control over Management by Directors	12
	11
	6
Ineffective or Nonexistent Ethics or Compliance Program	10
	8
	7

■ 2003   ▧ 1998   ☐ 1994

Percentage of survey respondents indicating that factor contributed to fraud.

Source: Fraud Survey 2003, KPMG Forensics. Copyright © 2003 KPMG LLP. Reprinted with permission.

MONITORING FRAUD PREVENTION PROGRAMS AND CONTROLS For high fraud risk areas, management should periodically evaluate whether appropriate antifraud programs and controls have been implemented and are operating effectively. For example, management's review and evaluation of operating units' or subsidiaries' financial results increase the likelihood that manipulated results will be detected.

Internal audit plays a key role in monitoring activities to ensure that antifraud programs and controls are operating effectively. Internal audit activities can both detect and deter

---

Focus Box 10-4

ANTIFRAUD PROGRAMS AND CONTROLS: BEST PRACTICES

PricewaterhouseCoopers LLP issued a November 2003 white paper, "Key Elements of Antifraud Programs and Controls," to assist management and audit committees to design and implement effective antifraud programs and controls. The white paper places special emphasis on the control environment, emphasizing the importance of influencing the control consciousness of all employees.

The white paper calls for management and audit committee consideration of the potential for fraud as part of the company's enterprise risk assessment processes and lays out these essential elements of an effective company fraud risk assessment process. The assessment should include the following:

• A systematic, rather than haphazard, assessment process.

• Consideration of potential fraud schemes and scenarios.

• Assessment of company-wide, significant business units and significant accounts.

• Evaluation of the likelihood and significance of each risk to the company.

• Assessment of exposure arising from each of the categories of fraud risk.

• Testing of the effectiveness of the risk assessment process by internal audit.

• Documented oversight by the audit committee, including the consideration of the risk of override of controls by management.

Source: PricewaterhouseCoopers LLP, *Key Elements of Antifraud Programs and Controls*, November 2003 (www.pwc.com/antifraud).

fraud. Internal auditors assist in deterring fraud by examining and evaluating internal controls that reduce fraud risk. They assist in fraud detection by performing audit procedures to search for fraudulent financial reporting and misappropriation of assets.

Because management is often in a position to override internal controls, there is a strong need for corporate governance oversight for senior management actions. One of the strongest internal corporate governance mechanisms over senior management is the audit committee of the board of directors. The audit committee's role in fraud risk oversight is discussed next.

Audit Committee Oversight The audit committee has primary responsibility to oversee the organization's financial reporting and internal control processes. In fulfilling this responsibility, the audit committee considers the potential for management override of internal controls and oversees management's fraud risk assessment process, as well as antifraud programs and controls. The audit committee also assists in creating an effective "tone at the top" about the importance of honesty and ethical behaviour by reinforcing the entity's zero tolerance for fraud.

Audit committee oversight also serves as a deterrent to fraud by senior management. For example, direct reporting of key findings by internal audit to the audit committee, reports by ethics officers about calls to the whistle-blower hotline, and other reports about lack of ethical behaviour or suspected fraud increase the likelihood that any attempt by senior management to involve employees in committing or concealing fraud is promptly disclosed. An open line of communication between the audit committee and members of management one or two levels below senior management can also assist the audit committee in identifying fraud by senior management. Information received from external auditors can also help the audit committee in assessing the strength of the company's internal controls and the potential for fraudulent financial reporting.

Most audit committee charters authorize and provide adequate funding for the audit committee to investigate any matters within the scope of its financial reporting oversight responsibilities. Audit committees usually have the authority to retain legal, accounting, and other professional advisers to assist in any fraud investigation. Recent examples of where an

---

Focus Box 10-5

THE AUDIT COMMITTEE CHARTER

The Audit Committee Charter for many companies, such as Shell Canada Limited, assigns the audit committee responsibility to assist the board of directors. The committee fulfills its oversight responsibilities by reviewing financial information; systems of internal financial, business, and antifraud controls; and the audit process. The duties of the audit committee are to provide meaningful and effective oversight and counsel to the company's management. The audit committee is required to exercise constructive skepticism when relying on management and accounting professionals.

Auditors consider the ethical climate of an organization, which includes the audit committee, when assessing the risks of fraud within an organization. For example, they might consider the following factors:

- How the internal audit organization is organized, including whether the board, audit

committee, and senior management respect the functions and missions of each other and of the internal audit organization;

- The importance of ethical features in the organization, such as: unquestioned integrity at all levels, accountability and responsibility taken, openness, acceptance of mistakes as a learning vehicle, commitment to improving the organization, and internal collaboration; and

- The existence of formal policies that address: conflicts of interest, confidentiality, compliance with laws, rules and regulations, and the reporting of any illegal or unethical behaviour.

Sources: 1. Shell Canada, 2005. Audit Committee Charter. www.shell.ca/code/who/governance/audit_committee.pdf, Accessed May 2, 2005.
2. Verschoor, Curtis C., 2004. *"The Ethical Climate Barometer,"* The Internal Auditor, Vol. LXI:V.

audit committee has established a Special Committee to assist in the investigation of suspect financial reporting issues include Hollinger International Inc., Nortel Networks Corporation, Royal Group Technologies Limited, and Atlas Cold Storage Income Trust.

→10.4 THE AUDITOR'S ROLE IN RESPONDING TO THE RISK OF FRAUD

When risks of material misstatements due to fraud are identified, the auditor should first discuss these findings with management and obtain management's views of the potential fraud and existing controls designed to prevent or detect misstatements. As described in the previous section, management may have programs designed to prevent, deter, and detect fraud, as well as controls designed to mitigate specific risks of fraud. Auditors should then consider whether such programs and controls mitigate the identified risks of material misstatements due to fraud or whether control deficiencies increase the risk of fraud. Auditor responses to fraud risk include the following:

1. Change the overall conduct of the audit to respond to identified fraud risks.
2. Design and perform audit procedures to address identified risks.
3. Design and perform procedures to address the risk of management override of controls.

Change the Overall Conduct of the Audit There are several overall responses to an increased fraud risk. If the risk of misstatement due to fraud is increased, more experienced personnel may be assigned to the audit. Some PA firms assign a fraud specialist to the audit team for high-risk engagements.

Auditors should also consider management's choice of accounting principles. Careful attention should be placed on accounting principles that involve subjective measurements or complex transactions. Because there is a presumption of fraud risk in revenue recognition, auditors should also evaluate the company's revenue recognition policies.

Fraud perpetrators are often knowledgeable about audit procedures. For this reason, Section 5135 requires auditors to incorporate unpredictability in the audit plan. For example, auditors may visit inventory locations or test accounts that were not tested in prior periods. Auditors should also consider tests that address misappropriation of assets, even when the amounts are not typically material.

When the risk of fraud is increased, auditors should step outside their normal role of reviewing financial records and holding discussions with the entity's financial staff. They should gather information from as many sources as possible. For example, a review of the build-up of dust on inventory may be an indication of inventory valuation problems or the lack of organization around the premises may be an indication of an organization in crisis. Auditors need to look beyond the audit program for what is unusual and out of the norm. Consider the donut and the hole; in other words, both what is there and what is missing.

Design and Perform Audit Procedures to Address Fraud Risks The appropriate audit procedures used to address specific fraud risks depend on the account being audited and the type of fraud risk identified. For example, if concerns are raised about revenue recognition because of cutoff issues or channel stuffing, the auditor may review the sales journal for unusual activity near the end of the period and review the terms of sales. Specific procedures are described in the discussion of specific fraud risk areas later in this chapter. Appendix B to Section 5135 provides examples of audit procedures to address the risk of fraud. The auditor must exercise professional judgment when selecting the most appropriate procedure in the circumstances. The response will be unique depending upon the auditor's assessment of the type of fraud risk factors or conditions identified, and the account balance, class of transactions, and assertions affected.

Design and Perform Procedures to Address Management Override of Controls The risk of management override of controls exists in almost all audits. Because management is in a unique position to perpetrate fraud by overriding controls that are otherwise operating

The auditors of a public company successfully discovered an intentional misstatement when they stepped away from their standard audit program.

A manufacturing company whose products were shipped around the world showed a warranty provision to be consistent with past years' allowance and actual claims experienced. Vicky, the auditor assigned to that area of the engagement followed the audit program and confirmed with the VP Operations that nothing had changed since the previous year; she also reviewed the actual warranty claims' experience in the prior year. Both of these procedures supported the warranty provision as reported in the draft financial statements.

As a result, Vicky was initially prepared to sign off on the section concluding that the warranty provision was adequate. But was it? One afternoon she decided to take a walk through the back shop to talk to the warranty manager. The warranty manager enjoyed talking about his job and the challenges he experienced. He explained that some of the new products in the field were experiencing problems and he was anticipating all products of a particular class would be returned for repair at a significant cost.

Because Vicky was alerted to these potential problems, she performed an additional analysis after talking to the warranty manager. The warranty provision was subsequently increased to reflect the anticipated costs of repairs. The small profit the company was showing on the financial statements was quickly changed to a loss. Had Vicky simply followed the audit program, the misstatement would not have been identified.

effectively, auditors must perform procedures in every audit to address the risk of management override. Three procedures must be performed in every audit.

EXAMINE JOURNAL ENTRIES AND OTHER ADJUSTMENTS FOR EVIDENCE OF POSSIBLE MISSTATEMENTS DUE TO FRAUD Fraud often results from adjustments to amounts reported in the financial statements, even when there are effective internal controls in the rest of the recording processes. The auditor should first obtain an understanding of the entity's financial reporting process and internal controls over journal entries and other adjustments. Then, he or she should enquire of employees involved in the financial reporting process about inappropriate or unusual activity in processing journal entries and other adjustments. Section 5135 requires testing of journal entries and other financial statement adjustments. The extent of testing is affected by the effectiveness of controls and results of the enquiries. Fraudulent journal entries and other adjustments often occur at the end of a period, therefore the auditor would ordinarily select entries made at the beginning and end of the reporting period. However, because fraud can occur throughout the period, professional judgment should be used when considering whether to test journal entries throughout the period.

REVIEW ACCOUNTING ESTIMATES FOR BIASES Fraudulent financial reporting is often accomplished through intentional misstatement of accounting estimates. Section 5135 requires the auditor to consider the potential for management bias when reviewing current-year estimates. The auditor is required to "look back" at significant prior-year estimates to identify any changes in the company's processes or management's judgments and assumptions that might indicate a potential bias. For example, management's estimates may have been clustered at the high end of the range of acceptable amounts in the prior year and at the low end in the current year. If a possible bias by management in making accounting estimates is identified, the auditor should consider if the cumulative effect of the bias is designed to smooth earnings or achieve a desired earnings level.

EVALUATE THE BUSINESS RATIONALE FOR SIGNIFICANT UNUSUAL TRANSACTIONS Section 5135 places greater focus than was previously required on understanding the underlying business rationale for significant unusual transactions that might be outside the normal course of business for the company. The auditor should gain an understanding of the purposes of significant transactions to assess whether transactions have been entered into to engage in fraudulent financial reporting. For example, the company may engage in financing transactions to avoid reporting liabilities on the balance sheet. The auditor should determine whether the accounting treatment for any unusual transaction is appropriate in the circumstances, taking into account the substance of the transaction and not the form, and whether information about the transaction is adequately disclosed in the financial statements. For significant and unusual transactions, the auditor should consider investigating the possibility of related party transactions.

Update Risk Assessment Process The auditor's assessment of the risks of material misstatement due to fraud should be ongoing. Conditions may be identified during fieldwork that change or support a judgment about the initial assessment of fraud risks. Appendix C to Section 5135 includes examples of circumstances that indicate the possibility of fraud. While the list is not all encompassing, it is a good reference source of conditions. For example, the auditor should be alert during fieldwork for:

- Discrepancies in the accounting records, including problems concerning computer processing such as extensive errors that require manual corrections, last-minute adjustments that significantly affect financial results, or employees' access rights inconsistent with their authorized duties such as senior management preparation of journal entries.
- Conflicting or missing evidence including inconsistent, vague, or implausible responses to enquiries; unavailability of original documents, or inability to produce evidence of key systems development or program change testing in implementation activities.
- Problematic or unusual relationships between the auditor and management including unusual delays in providing requested information, undue time pressure imposed by management, unwillingness to facilitate auditor access to key electronic files for testing through computer-assisted audit techniques, or unwillingness to address identified weaknesses in internal controls on a timely basis.
- Other circumstances might include accounting policies inconsistent with industry norms, changes in accounting estimates not supported by a change in circumstances, or tolerance to violation of the entity's code of conduct.

Specific Fraud Risk Areas

Depending on the client's industry, certain accounts are especially susceptible to manipulation or theft. Figure 10-4 on page 300 indicates that rates of fraud are increasing, especially theft of assets. All the occurrences listed in Figure 10-4 are types of misappropriations of assets or fraud against the organization except for the final one, financial reporting fraud, which constituted only 7 percent in 2003. It is usually the financial reporting fraud that receives the most notice because of the magnitude of its impact on users of the financial statements. As mentioned previously, misappropriations of assets are usually immaterial to the financial statements; nonetheless, auditors should assess the risk. The following sections discuss specific high-risk accounts, including warning signs of fraud. Even with knowledge of these warning signs, fraud is extremely difficult to detect. However, awareness of these warning signs and fraud detection techniques increase the auditor's likelihood of identifying misstatements due to fraud.

Revenue and Accounts Receivable Fraud Risks Revenue and related accounts receivable and cash accounts are especially susceptible to manipulation and theft. A study sponsored by the Committee of Sponsoring Organizations (COSO) found that more than half of financial statement frauds involve revenues and accounts receivable. Similarly, when sales are made for cash or are quickly converted to cash, they are also highly susceptible to theft.

FRAUDULENT FINANCIAL REPORTING—RISKS FOR REVENUE As a result of the frequency of financial reporting frauds involving revenue recognition, Section 5135 requires auditors to identify revenue recognition as a fraud risk in most audits. Revenue is susceptible to manipulation for several reasons. Overstatement of revenues often increases net income by an equal amount because related costs of sales are often not recognized on fictitious or prematurely recognized revenues. Also, financial analysts and other market participants place increasing emphasis on revenue growth. There are three main types of revenue manipulations: fictitious revenues, premature revenue recognition, and manipulation of adjustments to revenues.

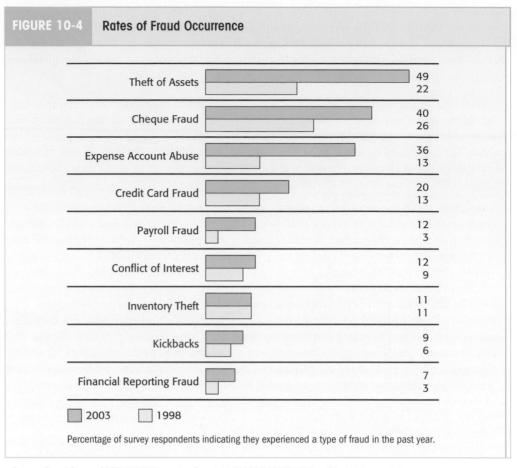

FIGURE 10-4 | **Rates of Fraud Occurrence**

	2003	1998
Theft of Assets	49	22
Cheque Fraud	40	26
Expense Account Abuse	36	13
Credit Card Fraud	20	13
Payroll Fraud	12	3
Conflict of Interest	12	9
Inventory Theft	11	11
Kickbacks	9	6
Financial Reporting Fraud	7	3

Percentage of survey respondents indicating they experienced a type of fraud in the past year.

Source: Fraud Survey 2003, KPMG Forensics. Copyright © 2003 KPMG LLP. Reprinted with permission.

Fictitious Revenues The most notorious forms of revenue fraud involve creating fictitious revenues. Although there have been several recent cases involving fictitious revenues, there are also many earlier examples. For example, the Ultramares case described in Chapter 4 (p. 91) involved fictitious revenue entries in the general ledger.

Financing arrangements are occasionally incorrectly recorded as revenue. In the Livent case, a number of transactions with third parties involved the assignment of certain intangible assets, such as the rights to stage a play, which Livent recorded as revenue. These transactions were accompanied by "side deals," which were not properly disclosed, requiring Livent to repurchase the assets in the future at amounts comparable to the consideration received by Livent on the "sale" of those assets. By failing to disclose the "side-deals," Livent improperly treated what were lending arrangements as revenue transactions.

Premature Revenue Recognition Companies often accelerate the timing of revenue recognition to meet earnings or sales forecasts. **Premature revenue recognition** is the recognition of revenue before GAAP requirements for recording revenue have been met. Premature revenue recognition should be distinguished from cutoff errors, in which transactions are inadvertently recorded in the incorrect period. In the simplest form of accelerated revenue recognition, sales that should have been recorded in the subsequent period are recorded as current period sales.

One method of fraudulently accelerating revenue is a "bill-and-hold" sale. Sales are normally recognized at the time goods are shipped. In a bill-and-hold sale, the goods are invoiced before they are shipped. Another method involves issuing side agreements that modify the terms of the sales transaction. For example, revenue recognition is likely to be inappropriate if a major customer agrees to take a significant amount of inventory at year-end, but a side agreement provides for more favourable pricing and unrestricted return of the goods if not sold by the customer. In some cases, as a result of the terms of the side agreement, the transaction does not qualify as a sale under generally accepted accounting principles.

Two notable recent examples of premature revenue recognition involve Bausch & Lomb Incorporated and Xerox Corporation. In the Bausch & Lomb case, items were shipped that were not ordered by customers, with unrestricted right of return and promises that the goods did not have to be paid for until sold. The revenue recognition issues at Xerox were more complex. Capital equipment leases include sales, financing, and service components. Because the sales component is recognized immediately, Xerox attempted to maximize the amount allocated to this aspect of the transaction.

Manipulation of Adjustments to Revenues The most common adjustment to revenue involves sales returns and allowances. A company may hide sales returns from the auditor to overstate net sales and income. If the returned goods are counted as part of physical inventory, the return may actually increase reported income. In this case, an asset increase is recognized through the counting of physical inventory, but the reduction in the related accounts receivable balance is not made. The completeness of sales returns can be verified by accounting for all receiving reports. However, if management has separate procedures for receiving returned goods, or if attempts are made to circumvent normal receiving procedures, other evidence may be necessary to verify the completeness of sales returns.

Bad debt expense is related to the revenue cycle but is normally treated as a sales expense, rather than as an adjustment to revenue. Companies may attempt to reduce bad debt expense by understating the allowance for doubtful accounts. Because the required allowance depends on the age and quality of accounts receivable, some companies have altered the aging of accounts receivable to make them appear more current. This can usually be readily verified by testing the accuracy of the aging, which is done by comparing the date on the original invoice to the aged accounts receivable trial balance.

WARNING SIGNS OF FRAUDULENT FINANCIAL REPORTING IN REVENUE There are many potential warning signals or symptoms of revenue fraud. Two of the most important are analytical procedures results and documentary discrepancies.

Analytical Procedures Analytical procedures, especially gross margin percentage and accounts receivable turnover, often signal revenue frauds. Fictitious revenue overstates the gross margin percentage and premature revenue recognition also overstates gross margin if the related cost of sales is not recognized. Fictitious revenues also lower accounts receivable turnover, because the fictitious revenues are not collected. Table 10-4 on page 302 includes comparative sales, cost of sales, and accounts receivable data for a company in which the financial statements included fictitious revenue. Notice how the accounts receivable increased, as there were no cash receipts to pay for the fictitious revenues. A higher gross profit percentage, which increased from 36 percent to 42 percent, and lower accounts receivable turnover ratio, which declined from 5.3 to 3.8, helped signal fictitious revenue and accounts receivable. When performing analytical procedures, the more years available to analyze, the more informative the trend analysis will be.

In some frauds, management generated fictitious revenues to make analytical procedures results, such as gross margin, similar to the prior year. In frauds like this, analytical procedures that compare client data with similar prior period data are typically not useful to signal the fraud. Analytical procedures should also compare client data to industry performance. Auditors should be aware of the risk of material misstatement related to revenue when the gross margin of the industry is declining while the entity under audit has remained stable.

Documentary Discrepancies Despite the best efforts of fraud perpetrators, fictitious transactions rarely have the same level of documentary evidence as legitimate transactions.

For example, in the well-known fraud at ZZZZ Best, insurance restoration contracts worth millions of dollars were supported by one- or two-page agreements and lacked many of the supporting details and evidence, such as permits, that are normally associated with such contracts. Some of the fraudulent journal entries at WorldCom for hundreds of millions of U.S. dollars were supported by nothing more than Post-it notes.

TABLE 10-4	Example of the Effect of Fictitious Receivables on Accounting Ratios		
	2005	2004	2003
Sales[a]	$265	$185	$105
Cost of sales	(155)	(115)	(67)
Gross profit	110	70	38
Gross profit percentage	42%	38%	36%
Year-end accounts receivable	70	38	20
Accounts receivable turnover[b]	3.8	4.9	5.3

[a]Dollar amounts in millions [b]Accounts receivable turnover calculated as Sales/Ending accounts receivable

Auditors should be aware of unusual markings and alterations on documents, and they should rely on originals rather than photocopies of documents. Because fraud perpetrators attempt to conceal fraud, even one unusual transaction in a sample should be considered a potential indicator of fraud that should be investigated.

MISAPPROPRIATION OF ASSETS—RECEIPTS INVOLVING REVENUE Although misappropriation of cash receipts is rarely as material as fraudulent reporting of revenues, such frauds can be costly to the organization because of the direct loss of assets. The objective of the misappropriation of assets is usually theft of cash. Many thefts of cash receipts are closely tied to the revenue cycle and are considered separately from other thefts of cash. A typical misappropriation of assets involves failure to record a sale or adjustments made to customer accounts to hide thefts of cash receipts.

Failure to Record a Sale One of the most difficult frauds to detect is when a sale is not recorded and the cash from the sale is stolen. Such frauds are somewhat easy to detect when goods are shipped on credit to customers. Tracing shipping documents to sales entries in the sales journal and accounting for all shipping documents can be used to verify that all sales have been recorded.

It is much more difficult to verify that all cash sales have been recorded, because there are no shipping documents to verify the completeness of sales, and there are no customer account receivable records supporting the sale. In such cases, other documentary evidence is necessary to verify that all sales are recorded. For example, a retail establishment may require that all sales be recorded on a cash register. Recorded sales can then be compared to the total amount of sales on the cash register tape.

Theft of Cash Receipts After a Sale Is Recorded It is much more difficult to hide the theft of cash receipts after a sale is recorded. If a customer's payment is stolen, regular reminder notices of unpaid accounts will quickly uncover the fraud. As a result, to hide the theft, the fraud perpetrator must reduce the customer's account in one of three ways: (1) record a sales return or allowance, (2) write off the customer's account, or (3) apply the payment from another customer to the customer's account, which is also known as lapping.

PREVENTING MISAPPROPRIATION OF ASSETS—REVENUES AND CASH RECEIPTS Thefts of sales and related cash receipts are normally best prevented and detected by internal controls designed to minimize the opportunity for fraud such as segregation of duties. Employees with access to cash receipts should not have access to accounting records that would allow them to manipulate customers' accounts to hide the theft. Analytical procedures and other comparisons may be useful in detecting larger frauds. Material misappropriation of cash receipts may be detected in cash flow analysis if revenues remain strong but cash shortfalls persist.

Sam Ralston was in charge of a university parking lot. He was supposed to place a parking receipt on the dash of the car when he received cash from the driver, but he would often collect the cash and wave the driver in without a receipt, particularly for sporting events. The university considered it too expensive to have two employees handle parking, and it was difficult to count the paid vehicles in a lot because some cars were parked by university employees with passes.

After several years, the university rotated Sam to another lot. An astute employee in the accounting office noticed that revenues collected from the lot seemed to increase after Sam's departure. Further investigation revealed that average revenues declined at the new lot to which Sam had been assigned. Confronted with the evidence, Sam confessed and was terminated from employment.

Inventory Fraud Risks Inventory is often the largest account on many companies' balance sheets and it is often difficult to verify the existence and valuation of inventories. As a result, inventory is susceptible to manipulation to achieve financial reporting objectives. Because inventory is also usually readily saleable, it is also susceptible to misappropriation.

FRAUDULENT FINANCIAL REPORTING—INVENTORY Fictitious inventory has been at the centre of several major cases of fraudulent financial reporting. Many large companies have varied and extensive inventory in multiple locations, making it relatively easy for the company to add fictitious inventory to accounting records.

Auditors are required to verify the existence of physical inventories. However, audit testing is done on a sample basis, and not all locations with inventory are typically tested. In some cases involving fictitious inventories, auditors informed the client in advance which inventory locations were to be tested. As a result, it was relatively easy for the client to transfer inventories to the locations being tested. In other cases, clients have added items to inventory after the count when auditors have failed to take copies of inventory count sheets.

WARNING SIGNS OF FRAUDULENT FINANCIAL REPORTING—INVENTORY As for accounts receivable, there are many potential warning signals or symptoms of inventory fraud. Analytical procedures are especially important for detecting inventory fraud.

Analytical Procedures Analytical procedures, especially gross margin percentage and inventory turnover, often signal inventory fraud. Fictitious inventory understates cost of goods sold and overstates the gross margin percentage. Fictitious inventory also lowers inventory turnover.

Purchases and Accounts Payable Fraud Risks Cases of fraudulent financial reporting involving accounts payable are relatively common, although less frequent than frauds involving inventory or accounts receivable. The deliberate understatement of accounts payable generally results in an understatement of purchases and cost of goods sold and an overstatement of net income. Significant misappropriations involving purchases can also occur in the form of payments to fictitious vendors, as well as kickbacks and other illegal arrangements with suppliers.

FRAUDULENT FINANCIAL REPORTING—ACCOUNTS PAYABLE Companies may engage in deliberate attempts to understate accounts payable and overstate income. This can be accomplished by not recording accounts payable until the subsequent period or by recording fictitious reductions to accounts payable.

All purchases received before the end of the year should be recorded as liabilities. This is relatively easy to verify if the company accounts for pre-numbered receiving reports. However, if the receiving reports are not pre-numbered or the company deliberately omits receiving reports from the accounting records, it may be difficult for the auditor to verify whether all liabilities have been recorded. In such cases, analytical evidence, such as unusual changes in ratios, may signal that accounts payable are understated.

Companies often have complex arrangements with suppliers that result in reductions to accounts payable for advertising credits and other allowances. These arrangements are often not as well documented as acquisition transactions. Some companies have used fictitious reductions to accounts payable to overstate net income. Auditors should read agreements with suppliers when amounts are material and make sure the financial statements reflect the substance of the agreements.

MISAPPROPRIATIONS OF ASSETS—ACQUISITION AND PAYMENT CYCLE The most common fraud in the acquisitions area is for the perpetrator to issue payments to fictitious vendors and deposit the cheques in a fictitious account. These frauds can be prevented by allowing payments to be made only to approved vendors and by carefully scrutinizing documentation supporting the acquisitions by authorized personnel before payments are made. In other misappropriation cases, the accounts payable clerk or other employee steals a cheque to a legitimate vendor. The purchases information is then resubmitted for payment to the vendor. Such fraud can be prevented by cancelling supporting documents to prevent their use as support for multiple payments.

Other Areas of Fraud Risk Almost every account is subject to manipulation. The following sections discuss other accounts with specific risks of fraudulent financial reporting or misappropriation.

FIXED ASSETS Fixed assets are a large balance sheet account for many companies and are often based on subjectively-determined valuations. As a result, fixed assets may be a target for manipulation, especially for companies without material receivables or inventories. For example, companies may capitalize repairs or other operating expenses as fixed assets. Such frauds are relatively easy to detect if the auditor examines evidence supporting fixed asset additions. Nevertheless, several recent cases of fraudulent financial reporting have involved improper capitalization of assets.

Because of their value and saleability, fixed assets are also targets for theft. This is especially true for fixed assets that are readily portable, such as laptop computers. To reduce the potential for theft, fixed assets should be physically protected whenever possible, engraved, or otherwise permanently labelled, and should be periodically inventoried.

Focus Box 10-8

CREATING INCOME BY CAPITALIZING EXPENSES

Atlas Cold Storage is an income trust based in Toronto offering temperature-controlled warehousing and distribution services. Between 2001 and 2003, Atlas entered into a series of significant acquisitions and new equity issues. By 2003, it had become North America's second largest cold storage facility. Atlas appeared to be performing well as cash distributions to the unit holders were stable and the price of units traded on the TSX were increasing. Then an anonymous letter was sent to the Ontario Securities Commission containing allegations with respect to the 2002 financial statements.

This was passed to the audit committee, who conducted an investigation with the assistance of forensic accountants. The report of the forensic accountants concluded that expenditures were inappropriately recorded as additions to capital assets. It is alleged that senior management instructed accounting staff to review invoices previously expensed for amounts that could be capitalized, thus increasing net income and capital assets.

The report also concluded that the purpose of the capitalizing of expenses was to overstate net income with the intent to improve the financial results. As a result of the findings, the auditors withdrew their audit report and reissued it on restated financial statements.

Sources: 1. Atlas Cold Storage, 2003. Press release—English, September 2. www.sedar.com/csfsprod/data40/filings/00570742/00000001/d%3A%5CWorkspace%5C08306145EB00004374.pdf, Accessed May 2, 2005. 2. The Securities Act, R.S.O. 1990, c. S-5, as amended and in the matter of Patrick Gouveia, Andrew Peters, Ronald Perryman and Paul Vickery. Statement of Allegations of Staff of the Ontario Securities Commission, June 2, 2004. www.osc.gov.on.ca/Enforcement/Proceedings/2004/soa_20040602_gouveia.jsp, Accessed May 2, 2005. 3. Hasselback, Drew, 2003. Atlas falls $100M on accounting errors. National Post, September 3, sec. IN.

PAYROLL EXPENSES Payroll is rarely a significant risk area for fraudulent financial reporting. However, companies may overstate inventories and net income by recording excess labour costs in inventory.

Company employees are sometimes used to construct fixed assets. Excess labour cost may be capitalized as fixed assets in these circumstances. Material fringe benefits, such as retirement benefits, are also subject to manipulation.

Payroll fraud involving misappropriation of assets is fairly common, but the amounts involved are often immaterial. The two most common areas of fraud are the creation of fictitious employees and overstatement of individual payroll hours. The existence of fictitious employees can usually be prevented by separation of the human resource and payroll functions. Overstatement of hours is typically prevented by use of time clocks or approval of payroll hours.

DETECTING COMPUTER FRAUD The use and increased complexity of computers in business make certain kinds of fraud easier to commit and harder to detect. Since data are not readily visible in paper form, computer systems can be used by management to prevent and detect fraud, by implementing adequate software controls, or by having data regularly checked for unusual patterns. For example, there are computer-assisted audit techniques used by auditors to look for post office box numbers for suppliers or customers.

The outcome of a fraud committed using a computer is no different than any fraud already discussed in this chapter: Assets are misappropriated or financial statements are fraudulently reported. To prevent such a fraud, management should ensure that there are access controls over the addition of new vendors or for changing addresses of existing vendors. They should also ensure that there is segregation of duties between employees who can add new vendors and employees who can process invoices or invoice payments.

Responsibilities When Fraud Is Suspected

Based upon a 2004 study, KPMG LLP reported that boards of directors look to their external auditors more than any other means of detecting financial reporting fraud.[1] However, an earlier survey, in 2003, discovered that more frauds are detected by internal controls or the internal audit function than by external auditors.[2] Internal auditors' primary focus is on controls and it is internal controls that will prevent and detect fraud. The existence of an effective internal audit group can act as a deterrent against fraud.

One spectacular example of an internal auditor identifying a financial reporting fraud was in the case of WorldCom. Cynthia Cooper, Vice-President—Internal Audit for WorldCom discovered that the company had been capitalizing over U.S. $3.5 billion of expenses. She was named by *Time* magazine as one of three "Persons of the Year" in 2002.

Responding to Misstatements That May Be the Result of Fraud Throughout an audit, the auditor continually evaluates whether evidence gathered and other observations made indicate material misstatement due to fraud. When fraud is suspected, the auditor gathers additional information to determine whether fraud actually exists. Often, the auditor begins by making additional enquiries of management and others. Such discussions should be corroborated either by reference to source documents or further analysis.

TYPES OF ENQUIRY TECHNIQUES As described in Chapter 6, enquiry can be an effective audit evidence gathering technique. Interviewing can help identify issues omitted from documentation or confirmations. The auditor can also modify questions during the interview based on the interviewee's responses.

Enquiry as an audit evidence technique should be tailored to the purpose for which it is being used. Depending on the purpose, the auditor may ask different types of questions and change the tone of the interview.

Informational Enquiry Auditors use **informational enquiry** to obtain information about facts and details that the auditor does not have. Usually the auditor wants information from the

[1]KPMG 2004. Survey on the Risk of Manipulation of Financial Statements, www.kpmg.ca
[2]Fraud Survey 2003, KPMG Forensics.

INFORMATIONAL ENQUIRY— enquiry to obtain information about facts and details the auditor does not have interviewee about past or current events or processes. The auditor poses open-ended questions that allow the respondent to provide details of events, processes, or circumstances. Auditors often use informational enquiry when gathering follow-up evidence about programs and controls or other evidence involving a misstatement or suspected fraud uncovered in the audit.

ASSESSMENT ENQUIRY—enquiry to corroborate or contradict prior information obtained

Assessment Enquiry Auditors also use enquiry to assess whether information already obtained is correct, factual, or truthful. The auditor uses **assessment enquiry** to corroborate or contradict prior information. The auditor often starts assessment enquiry with broad, open-ended questions that allow the interviewee to provide detailed responses, which can later be followed up with more specific questions. One common use of assessment enquiry is to corroborate management responses to earlier enquiries by asking questions of other employees.

Analysis Using Computers Computer-assisted audit techniques (CAATs) can be particularly useful when the risk of fraud is assessed as high and there are large volumes of data to analyze. CAATs are described in Appendix F to Chapter 13. Common computer assisted audit procedures that can be completed by generalized audit software include extraction (identifying transactions with certain characteristics, such as having a date outside the billing period or a high dollar amount), gap detection (looking for missing sequence numbers, such as receiving or shipping reports), duplicate detection (such as duplicate invoice numbers for the same supplier), recalculations (such as discounts or aging), stratification (grouping the transactions by a criteria such as amount or age), matching (comparing information from multiple data files, such as wage rate master files to payroll transactions), and statistical and trend analyses (graphing or tabulating trends over a period of time). Especially when there are hundreds of thousands or millions of transactions, these techniques are essential in assisting the auditor to identify which transactions are to be examined.

Focus Box 10-9

HIGH TECH FRAUD INVESTIGATION

A computer company with manufacturing facilities around the world discovered asset misappropriation through procurement fraud at one of its South American facilities. Fearing the fraud might be widespread, it initiated an investigation into its purchase/payment system. Given the high volume of transactions processed annually through the acquisition and payment cycle, the company chose to use computer-assisted techniques. This allowed the review of all transactions recorded in the system, easily identifying irregularities and patterns for further investigation. The first step in the investigation was to determine what would constitute an unusual transaction. A team, which included representatives from internal audit, procurement, and information technology, determined that a transaction with one or more of the following characteristics might be fraudulent:

- Purchase orders dated after invoices;
- Invoices dated after payments;
- Unusual patterns of payments to suppliers due to volume, timing, or amount;
- Addresses of suppliers the same as employee addresses; and
- Multiple suppliers with the same address.

The identified transactions were then manually reviewed to confirm or dispel the likelihood of further fraud.

Other Responsibilities When Fraud Is Suspected When an auditor suspects that fraud may be present, he is required to obtain additional evidence to determine whether material fraud has occurred. Auditors often use enquiry, as previously discussed, as part of that information gathering process. An auditor is also required to consider the implications for other aspects of the audit. For example, fraud involving the misappropriation of cash from a small petty cash fund normally is of little significance to the auditor, unless the matter involves higher-level management. In the latter situation, the petty cash fraud may indicate a more pervasive problem involving management's integrity. This may indicate to the auditor a need to re-evaluate the fraud risk assessment and the impact on the nature, timing, and extent of audit evidence.

Sometimes, auditors identify risks of material misstatements due to fraud that have internal control implications. There may also be cases where the auditor identifies deficiencies in management's antifraud programs and controls that will result in the programs' failure to mitigate the risk of fraud. In these situations, the auditor must communicate those items to the audit committee if they are considered significant deficiencies or material weaknesses. When auditing the financial statements, the auditor should consider those deficiencies while assessing internal controls over financial reporting, as described in Chapter 9.

RESPONSIBILITIES FOR REPORTING WHEN FRAUD IS SUSPECTED When the auditor suspects that fraud may be present, he should discuss the matter with an appropriate level of management, even if the matter might be considered inconsequential and should modify the audit approach for further investigation. The appropriate level of management should be at least one level above those involved. If the auditor believes that senior management may be involved in the fraud, the auditor should discuss the matter directly with the audit committee.

Focus Box 10-10

THE FORENSIC ACCOUNTANT

While all auditors need to understand what fraud is and how to respond when there is an identified fraud risk on an engagement, some accountants, called Forensic Accountants, specialize in fraud auditing. A fraud auditor is an accountant who, by virtue of his or her skills and experience, is an expert in detecting and documenting fraud in a company's books and records. Besides accounting and auditing knowledge, these specialists possess an investigative mentality, which is evidenced by skepticism and the ability to seek out alternative explanations and evidence.

Not all fraud auditors are forensic accountants. Forensic means "used in connection with the courts," so a forensic accountant's work would need to meet standards to be acceptable in court. Forensic accounting as a sub-discipline of accounting includes not only fraud auditing but also litigation support. It might involve testifying on the findings from an investigation. The CICA has the specialist designation of CA.IFA for Investigative and Forensic Accountants. This designation can be obtained after three years of post-qualification experience as a CA. Successful completion of a two year diploma program and 1,500 hours of experience in investigative and forensic accounting work are required.

Reporting to the Audit Committee or Equivalent Auditors should use professional judgment in determining which matters to report to the audit committee or equivalent. At a minimum, the auditor should communicate the following matters:

- questions the auditor might have regarding the honesty and integrity of management;
- any fraud involving management, no matter how trivial;
- fraud involving employees who play a significant role in the entity's financial reporting and internal controls process; or
- matters, while not material now, that may cause the financial statements to be materially misstated in the future.

Reporting Outside the Organization The disclosure of possible fraud to parties other than the client's senior management and its audit committee is ordinarily not part of the auditor's responsibility. As described in Chapter 2, the auditor has a professional duty to maintain the confidentiality of client information. In some limited circumstances, the auditor may have a statutory duty to communicate certain matters to regulators. This would be the case for financial institutions. If in doubt, the auditor should consider obtaining legal advice.

In exceptional circumstances, the results of the auditor's procedures may indicate such a significant risk of material misstatement due to fraud that the auditor should consider withdrawing from the audit. Such exceptional circumstances might include the entity's failure to take the appropriate actions that the auditor considers necessary, the discovery of false documentation, or significant concerns about management's or the audit committee's integrity.

SUMMARY

1. *What is fraud and under what conditions is it most likely to exist?* Fraud in an audit context refers to the intentional misrepresentation of facts that lead to a misstatement of the financial statements. It is more likely to exist in organizations with weak internal controls, a weak internal control environment, or an unethical business culture.

   Explain the difference between fraudulent financial reporting and misappropriation of assets. Fraudulent financial reporting occurs when there is an intentional misstatement of amounts or disclosures in the financial statements with the intent to deceive users of those statements. Misappropriation of assets involves the theft of assets, such as cash or inventory.

2. *What is the auditor's responsibility for assessing the risk of fraud and detecting material misstatements due to fraud?* The auditor must consider the risk of fraud and of financial statement fraud in every audit engagement to obtain reasonable assurance that the statements are free from material misstatement. This is part of the audit planning process and involves the use of professional skepticism.

3. *What features of corporate governance and of control environment would reduce fraud risks?* The three most important

things that an organization can do is: (i) create and maintain a culture of honesty and high ethics; (ii) evaluate fraud risks and implement controls and programs to mitigate identified risks; and (iii) develop a fraud risk oversight process.

4. *How should an auditor respond when there are identified fraud risks?* The auditor needs to communicate with the appropriate level of management. Then, the auditor needs to appropriately modify the audit process in response to the identified risks: change the overall conduct of the audit, and design and perform audit procedures to both address those risks and the risk of potential management override.

   What are some of the specific fraud risk areas and what is the auditor's responsibility once fraud is detected? Risks exist in every transaction cycle. Examples include theft of cash, fictitious suppliers or duplicate payments, unauthorized expenses, and overpaid or nonexistent employees. Once fraud is detected, the auditor has the responsibility to report to the appropriate level of management and the audit committee and to assess the effect on the audit and the financial statements.

CICA ASSURANCE HANDBOOK SECTIONS REFERENCED IN THIS CHAPTER

Section 5090 – Audit of financial statements—an introduction.
Section 5135 – The auditor's responsibility to consider fraud.

ESSENTIAL TERMS

Assessment enquiry—enquiry to corroborate or contradict prior information obtained   (p. 306).

Earnings management—deliberate actions taken by management to meet earnings objectives   (p. 282).

Fraud—an intentional misstatement of the financial statements (p. 282).

Fraud risk factors—entity factors that increase the risk of fraud (p. 284).

Fraud triangle—represents the three conditions of fraud: incentives/pressures, opportunities, and attitudes/rationalization (p. 284).

Fraudulent financial reporting—intentional misstatement or omission of amounts or disclosure in financial statements to deceive users   (p. 282).

Income smoothing—form of earnings management in which revenues and expenses are shifted between periods to reduce fluctuations in earnings   (p. 282).

Informational enquiry—enquiry to obtain information about facts and details the auditor does not have   (p. 305).

Misappropriation of assets—a fraud involving the theft of an entity's assets   (p. 283).

Premature revenue recognition—recognition of revenue before GAAP requirements for recording revenue have been met (p. 300).

Procurement fraud—the manipulation of the contracting process   (p. 284).

Professional skepticism—an attitude of the auditor that neither assumes management is dishonest nor assumes unquestioned honesty   (p. 287).

REVIEW QUESTIONS

10-1   Define fraudulent financial reporting and give two examples.

10-2   Define misappropriation of assets and give two examples.

10-3   Distinguish fraudulent financial reporting from misappropriation of assets.

10-4   What are the three conditions of fraud often referred to as "the fraud triangle?"

10-5 Give examples of risk factors for fraudulent financial reporting for each of the three fraud conditions: incentives/pressures, opportunities, and attitudes/rationalization.

10-6 Give examples of risk factors for misappropriation of assets for each of the three fraud conditions: incentives/pressures, opportunities, and attitudes/rationalization.

10-7 What sources are used by the auditor to gather information to assess fraud risks?

10-8 What should the audit team consider in its planning discussion about fraud risks?

10-9 Auditors are required to make enquiries of individuals in the company when gathering information to assess fraud risk. Identify those with whom the auditor must make enquiries.

10-10 Describe the purpose of corporate codes of conduct and identify three examples of items addressed in a typical code of conduct.

10-11 Discuss the importance of the control environment, or "setting the tone at the top," in establishing a culture of honesty and integrity in a company.

10-12 Distinguish management's responsibility from the audit committee's responsibility for designing and implementing antifraud programs and controls within a company.

10-13 What are the three categories of auditor responses to fraud risks?

10-14 What three auditor actions are required to address the potential for management override of controls?

10-15 Describe the three main techniques used to manipulate revenue.

10-16 You go through the drive-through window of a fast food restaurant and notice a sign that reads, "Your meal is free if we fail to give you a receipt." Why would the restaurant post this sign?

10-17 Name the two categories of enquiry and describe the purpose of each when used by an auditor to obtain additional information about a suspected fraud.

10-18 What matters related to fraud should be communicated with the audit committee?

10-19 You have identified a suspected fraud involving the company's controller. What must you do in response to this discovery?

MULTIPLE CHOICE QUESTIONS

10-20 Choose the best answer for the following questions:

a. Which of the following circumstances is most likely to cause an auditor to consider whether material misstatements due to fraud exist in an entity's financial statements?

(1) Management places little emphasis on meeting earnings projections of external parties.
(2) The board of directors oversees the financial reporting process and internal control.
(3) Significant deficiencies in internal control previously communicated to management have been corrected.
(4) Transactions selected for testing are not supported by proper documentation.

b. Which of the following circumstances is most likely to cause an auditor to increase the assessment of the risk of material misstatement of the financial statements due to fraud?

(1) Property and equipment are usually sold at a loss before being fully depreciated.
(2) Unusual discrepancies exist between the entity's records and confirmation replies.
(3) Monthly bank reconciliations usually include several in-transit items.
(4) Clerical errors are listed on a computer-generated exception report.

c. If an independent audit leading to an opinion on financial statements causes the auditor to believe that a material misstatement due to fraud exists, the auditor should first

(1) consider the implications for other aspects of the audit and discuss the matter with the appropriate levels of management.

(2) make the investigation necessary to determine whether fraud has actually occurred.
(3) request that management investigate to determine whether fraud has actually occurred.
(4) consider whether fraud was the result of a failure by employees to comply with existing controls.

d. An auditor discovers that a client's accounts receivable turnover is substantially lower for the current year than for the prior year. This trend may indicate that

(1) fictitious credit sales have been recorded during the year.
(2) employees have stolen inventory just before year end.
(3) the client recently tightened its credit-granting policies.
(4) an employee has been lapping receivables in both years.

e. Which of the following procedures will best detect the theft of valuable items from an inventory that consists of hundreds of different items selling for $1 to $10 and a few items selling for hundreds of dollars?

(1) Maintain a perpetual inventory of only the more valuable items, with frequent periodic verification of the validity of the perpetual inventory records.
(2) Have an independent auditing firm examine and report on management's assertion about the design and operating effectiveness of the control activities relevant to inventory.
(3) Have separate warehouse space for the more valuable items, with sequentially numbered tags.
(4) Require an authorized officer's signature on all requisitions for the more valuable items.

10-21 During audit planning, an auditor obtained the following information:

1. Management has a strong interest in employing inappropriate means to minimize reported earnings for tax-motivated reasons.
2. Assets and revenues are based on significant estimates that involve subjective judgments and uncertainties that are hard to corroborate.
3. The company is marginally able to meet exchange listing and debt covenant requirements.
4. Significant operations are located and conducted across international borders in jurisdictions where differing business environments and cultures exist.
5. There are recurring attempts by management to justify marginal or inappropriate accounting on the basis of materiality.
6. The company's financial performance is threatened by a high degree of competition and market saturation.

Required

Classify each of the six factors into one of these fraud conditions: incentives/pressures, opportunities, or attitudes/rationalization.

10-22 Recently, there has been a significant number of highly publicized cases of management fraud involving the misstatement of financial statements. Although most client managements possess unquestioned integrity, a very small number, given sufficient incentive and opportunity, may be predisposed to fraudulently misstate reported financial condition and operating results.

Required

a. What distinguishes management fraud from a defalcation?
b. What are an auditor's responsibilities, under generally accepted auditing standards, to detect management fraud?
c. What are the characteristics of management fraud that an auditor should consider to fulfill the auditor's responsibilities for detecting management fraud under generally accepted auditing standards?
d. Three factors that heighten an auditor's concern about the existence of management fraud include (1) an intended public placement of securities in the near future, (2) management compensation dependent on operating results, and (3) a weak internal control environment evidenced by lack of concern for basic controls and disregard of the auditor's recommendations. What other factors should heighten an auditor's concern about the existence of management fraud?

(AICPA adapted)

10-23 The Art Appreciation Society operates a museum for the benefit and enjoyment of the community.

When the museum is open to the public, two clerks, who are positioned at the entrance, collect a $5.00 admission fee from each nonmember patron. Members of the Art Appreciation Society are permitted to enter free of charge upon presentation of their membership cards.

At the end of each day, one of the clerks delivers the proceeds to the treasurer. The treasurer counts the cash in the presence of the clerk and places it in a safe. Each Friday afternoon, the treasurer and one of the clerks deliver all cash held in the safe to the bank and receive an authenticated deposit slip that provides the basis for the weekly entry in the accounting records.

The Art Appreciation Society board of directors has identified a need to improve its internal controls over cash admission fees. The board has determined that the cost of installing turnstiles, sales booths, or otherwise altering the physical layout of the museum will greatly exceed any benefits. However, the board has agreed that the sale of admission tickets must be an integral part of its improvement efforts.

Smith has been asked by the board of directors of the Art Appreciation Society to review the internal control over cash admission fees and provide suggestions for improvements.

Required

a. Indicate weaknesses in the existing internal controls over cash admission fees that Smith should identify. Recommend one improvement for each of the weaknesses identified. Organize the answer as indicated in the following illustrative example.

(AICPA adapted)

Weaknesses	Recommendation
1. There is no basis for establishing the number of paying patrons.	1. Prenumbered admission tickets should be issued upon payment of the admission fee.

b. Indicate which of the weaknesses, if any, increase the likelihood of misappropriation of assets.
c. Indicate which of the weaknesses, if any, increase the likelihood of fraudulent financial reporting.

(AICPA adapted)

10-24 The following misstatements are included in the accounting records of Joyce Manufacturing Company:

1. A sales invoice was incorrectly added by $1,000 as a result of a data entry error.
2. A material sale was unintentionally recorded for the second time on the last day of the year. The sale had originally been recorded 2 days earlier.
3. Cash paid on accounts receivable was stolen by the mail clerk when the mail was opened.
4. Cash paid on accounts receivable that had been prelisted by a secretary was stolen by the bookkeeper who

recorded cash receipts and accounts receivable. He failed to record the transactions.

5. A shipment to a customer was not billed because of the loss of the bill of lading.

6. Merchandise was shipped to a customer, but no bill of lading was prepared. Because billings are prepared from bills of lading, the customer was not billed.

7. A sale to a residential customer was unintentionally classified as a commercial sale.

8. Sales generated through the company's web site are recorded at the point the customers submit the orders online.

Required

a. Identify whether each situation is an error or fraud.

b. For each situation, list one or more controls that should have prevented it from occurring on a continuing basis.

c. For each situation, identify evidence the auditor could use to uncover it.

(AICPA adapted)

10-25 Appliances Repair and Service Company bills all customers rather than collecting in cash when services are provided. All mail is opened by Tom Gyders, treasurer. Gyders, a qualified accountant, is the most qualified person in the company who is in the office daily. Therefore, he can solve problems and respond to customers' needs quickly. Upon receipt of cash, he immediately prepares a listing of the cash and a duplicate deposit slip. Cash is deposited daily. Gyders uses the listing to enter the financial transactions in the computerized accounting records. He also contacts customers about uncollected accounts receivable. Because he is so knowledgeable about the business and each customer, he grants credit, authorizes all sales allowances, and charges off uncollectible accounts. The owner is extremely pleased with the efficiency of the company. He can run the business without spending much time there because of Gyders' effectiveness.

Imagine the owner's surprise when he discovers that Gyders has committed a major theft of the company's cash receipts. He did so by not recording sales, recording improper credits to recorded accounts receivable, and overstating receivables.

Required

a. Given that cash was prelisted, went only to the treasurer, and was deposited daily, what internal control deficiency permitted the fraud?

b. What are the benefits of a prelisting of cash? Who should prepare the prelisting and what duties should that person perform?

c. Assume that an appropriate person, as discussed in part (b) prepares a prelisting of cash. What is to prevent that person from taking the cash after it is prelisted but before it is deposited?

d. Who should deposit the cash, given your answer to part b?

10-26 Each year near the balance sheet date, when the president of Bargon Construction, Inc. takes a 3-week vacation to Mexico, she signs several cheques to pay major bills during the period she is absent. Jack Morgan, head bookkeeper for the company, uses this practice to his advantage. Morgan makes out a cheque to himself for the amount of a large vendor's invoice, and because there is no acquisitions journal, he records the amount in the cash disbursements journal as an acquisition from the supplier listed on the invoice. He holds the cheque until several weeks into the subsequent period to make sure that the auditors do not get an opportunity to examine the cancelled cheque. Shortly after the first of the year when the president returns, Morgan resubmits the invoice for payment and again records the cheque in the cash disbursements journal. At that point, he marks the invoice "paid" and files it with all other paid invoices. Morgan has been following this practice successfully for several years and feels confident that he has developed a foolproof method.

Required

a. What is the auditor's responsibility for discovering this type of embezzlement?

b. What weaknesses exist in the client's internal control?

c. What evidence could the auditor use to uncover the fraud?

(AICPA adapted)

10-27 The following are activities that occurred at Franklin Manufacturing, a private company.

1. Franklin's accountant did not record cheques written in the last few days of the year until the next accounting period to avoid a negative cash balance in the financial statements.

2. Franklin's controller prepared and mailed a cheque to a vendor for a carload of material that was not received. The vendor's chief accountant, who is a friend of Franklin's controller, mailed a vendor's invoice to Franklin, and the controller prepared a receiving report. The vendor's chief accountant deposited the cheque in an account he had set up with a name almost identical to the vendor's.

3. The accountant recorded cash received in the first few days of the next accounting period in the current accounting period to avoid a negative cash balance.

4. Discounts on cheques to Franklin's largest vendor are never taken, even though they are paid before the discount period expires. The president of the vendor's company provides free use of his ski lodge to the accountant who processes the cheques in exchange for the lost discounts.

5. Franklin shipped and billed goods to a customer in Winnipeg on December 23, and the sale was recorded on December 24, with the understanding that the goods would be returned on January 31 for a full refund plus a 5 percent handling fee.

6. Franklin's factory superintendent routinely takes scrap metal home in his pickup and sells it to a scrap dealer to make a few extra dollars.

7. Franklin's management decided not to include a footnote about a material uninsured lawsuit against the company on the grounds that the primary users of the statements, a small local bank, would probably not understand the footnote anyway.

Required

a. Identify which of these activities are frauds.
b. For each fraud, state whether it is a misappropriation of assets or fraudulent financial reporting.
c. For each fraud, identify a control that would have prevented or detected the fraud.

PROFESSIONAL JUDGMENT PROBLEM

10-28 The Kowal Manufacturing Company employs 50 production workers and has the following payroll procedures:

The factory foreman interviews applicants and, on the basis of the interview, either hires or rejects them. When applicants are hired, they prepare a TD1 (Employee's Withholding Exemption Certificate) and give it to the foreman. The foreman writes the hourly rate of pay for the new employee in the corner of the TD1 form and then gives the form to a payroll clerk as notice that the worker has been employed. The foreman verbally advises the payroll department of rate adjustments.

A supply of blank time cards is kept in a box near the entrance to the factory. Each worker takes a time card on Monday morning, fills in his or her name, and punches in their daily arrival and departure times at a time clock. At the end of the week, the workers drop the time cards in a box near the door to the factory.

On Monday morning, the completed time cards are taken from the box by a payroll clerk. One of the payroll clerks then records the payroll transactions using a computer system, which records all information for the payroll journal that was calculated by the clerk and automatically updates the employees' earnings records and general ledger. Employees do not receive a paycheque when they fail to turn in a time card.

The payroll cheques are manually signed by the chief accountant and given to the foreman. The foreman distributes the cheques to the workers in the factory and arranges for the delivery of the cheques to the workers who are absent. The payroll bank account is reconciled by the chief accountant, who also prepares the various quarterly and annual payroll tax reports.

Required

a. List the most important weaknesses in internal control and state the misstatements that are likely to result from the weakness. For each weakness, provide at least one control that could mitigate or prevent the weakness.
b. For each weakness that increases the likelihood of fraud, identify whether the likely fraud is misappropriation of assets or fraudulent financial reporting.

(AICPA adapted)

CASE

10-29 Smith is a junior on the financial statement audit of Super Computer Services Co. (SCS) for the year ended April 30, 2005. On May 6, 2005, Kent, the senior auditor assigned to the engagement, had the following conversation with Smith concerning the planning phase of the audit:*

Kent: Do you have all the audit programs updated yet for the SCS engagement?
Smith: Mostly. I still have work to do on the fraud risk assessment.
Kent: Why? Our "errors and irregularities" program from last year is still OK. It has passed peer review several times. Besides, we don't have specific duties regarding fraud. If we find it, we'll deal with it then.
Smith: I don't think so. That new CEO, Mint, has almost no salary, mostly bonuses and stock options. Doesn't that concern you?
Kent: No. Mint's employment contract was approved by the Board of Directors just three months ago. It was passed unanimously.
Smith: I guess so, but Mint told those stock analysts that SCS's earnings would increase 30 percent next year. Can Mint deliver numbers like that?
Kent: Who knows? We're auditing the '05 financial statements, not '06. Mint will probably amend that forecast every month between now and next May.
Smith: Sure, but all this may change our other audit programs.
Kent: No, it won't. The programs are fine as is. If you find fraud in any of your tests, just let me know. Maybe we'll have to extend the tests. Or maybe we'll just report it to the audit committee.
Smith: What would they do? Green is the audit committee's chair, and remember, Green hired Mint. They've been best friends for years. Besides, Mint is calling all the shots now. Brown, the old CEO, is still on the Board but Brown's never around. Brown's even been skipping the Board meetings. Nobody in management or on the Board would stand up to Mint.
Kent: That's nothing new. Brown was like that years ago. Brown caused frequent disputes with Jones, PA, the predecessor auditor. Three years ago, Jones told Brown how ineffective the internal audit department was then. Next thing you know, Jones is out and our firm is in. Why bother? I'm just as happy that those understaffed internal auditors don't get in our way. Just remember, the bottom line is . . . are the financial statements fairly presented? And they always have been. We don't provide any assurances about fraud. That's management's job.
Smith: But what about the lack of segregation of duties in the cash disbursements department? That clerk could write a cheque for anything.
Kent: Sure. That's a material weakness every year and probably will be again this year. But we're talking cost-effectiveness here, not fraud. We just have to do lots of testing on cash disbursements and report it again.
Smith: What about the big layoffs coming up next month? It's more than a rumour. Even the employees know it's going to happen, and they're real uptight about it.

Kent: I know, it's the worst kept secret at SCS, but we don't have to consider that now. Even if it happens, it will only improve next year's financial results. Brown should have let these people go years ago. Let's face it, how else can Mint even come close to the 30 percent earnings increase next year?

Required

a. Describe the fraud risk factors that are indicated in the preceding dialogue.

b. Describe Kent's misconceptions regarding the consideration of fraud in the audit of SCS's financial statements that are contained in the preceding dialogue, and explain why each is a misconception.

c. Describe an auditor's audit documentation requirements regarding the assessment of the risk of material misstatement due to fraud.

CHAPTER 11

OVERALL AUDIT PLAN AND AUDIT PROGRAM

There are so many different types of businesses—how can there be a common approach to the financial statement audit? Just like the architect of a multi-storey office tower, the auditor carefully plans his or her strategy, identifying the risks involved with the client and developing an audit approach known as an *audit strategy* to complete the engagement. This chapter looks at the development of the overall audit plan.

LEARNING OBJECTIVES

After reading this chapter, you should be able to answer the following questions:

1. What are the four different types of audit tests? Which type of test is a dual-purpose test?

2. What is *evidence mix*? How does the auditor choose the types of audit tests to be completed?

3. How are the different types of audit tests considered when designing an audit program?

4. What is an *audit strategy*? Describe the four phases of the financial statement audit.

CLIENTS HAVE CHANGED AND SO HAVE AUDITS

Jared and Gabrielle were comparing notes on two clients. Jared's client was implementing new enterprise-wide resource software—an integrated suite of programs that have a database core. Unfortunately, the implementation did not go well. There was a programming error in the new implementation that resulted in work in progress work orders being set to zero. Investigation of data errors resulted in the year-end results being delayed by almost two months. Jared and his staff spent numerous hours reviewing data conversion plans with the client and helping it compare information that was transferred from the old computer systems to the new data. The client was late filing its reports with the stock exchange and was threatened with de-listing of its stock.

Gabrielle waxed enthusiastic about mass customization. "My client is finally starting to make some money on their line of custom-made skirts and pants. Lower inventory overall meant that we only had to use two staff members on the inventory count and were able to reduce the fieldwork on inventory by over thirty percent." Her client found that customer loyalty for customized work was very high.

Jared was thankful that he had taken some extra information systems courses at university. His next step is to take the Certified Information Systems Auditor Examination and move into the information systems audit group at his firm.

Sources: 1. Schlosser, Julie, 2004. "A handful of companies are finally perfecting made-to-order for the masses. Here's how." Fortune, December 13. 2. Songini, Marc I., 2005. "Bungled ERP Installation Whacks Asyst," Computerworld, Vol. 39, Issue 2.

Think about the two businesses that Jared and Gabrielle discussed. How do information systems affect the way the business is run? What impact would this have on the audit planning processes? Most businesses, even small businesses, use technology in the execution of their transactions. It is important to understand how such technology is related to the business processes to adequately plan and execute the financial statement audit.

This chapter deals with the last step in the planning phase of an audit. This critical step results in the entire audit program, including audit procedures, sample sizes, items to select, and timing of the testing.

→11.1   PURPOSE OF DIFFERENT AUDIT TESTS

Types of Tests

Auditors use four basic **types of tests** to determine whether financial statements are fairly stated: procedures to obtain an understanding of internal control, tests of controls, analytical procedures, and tests of details of balances. The first two types of test are performed to assess control risk, whereas the last two are substantive tests. Substantive tests are used to reduce planned detection risk.

Procedures to Obtain an Understanding of Internal Control The methodology and **procedures used to obtain an understanding** of internal control were studied in Chapter 9. During that phase of an audit, the auditor must focus attention on both the design and the operation of aspects of internal control to the extent necessary to plan the rest of the audit effectively. A critical point made in Chapter 9 was that the understanding obtained must be supported with evidence. The purpose of the procedures performed, then, is to provide both understanding and evidence to support that understanding. Five types of audit procedures that relate to the auditor's understanding of internal control were identified in Chapter 9:

- Update and evaluate the auditor's previous experience with the entity.
- Make enquiries of client personnel.
- Read clients' policy and systems manuals.
- Examine documents and records.
- Observe entity activities and operations.

Tests of Controls A major use of the auditor's understanding of internal control is to assess control risk for each transaction-related audit objective. Examples are assessing the accuracy objective for sales transactions as low and the existence objective as moderate. Where the auditor believes control policies and procedures are effectively designed, and where it is efficient to do so, he or she will elect to assess control risk at a level that reflects that evaluation. This risk assessment is affected by the extent of automation of controls. In paperless systems or systems that rely fully upon automated controls, such as automatic re-ordering or electronic data interchange for document exchange, the auditor may be required to conduct tests of controls. This occurs as it may not be possible to reduce the risk of material misstatement for a specific transaction-related audit objective to an acceptably low level using only substantive tests. The procedures used to obtain such evidence are called **tests of controls**.

Tests of controls are performed to determine the effectiveness of both the design and operation of specific internal controls. These tests include the following types of procedures:

- Make enquiries of appropriate client personnel.
- Examine documents, records, and reports.
- Observe control-related activities.
- Reperform client procedures.

TYPES OF TESTS— the four categories of audit tests auditors use to determine whether financial statements are fairly stated: procedures to obtain an understanding of internal control, tests of controls, analytical procedures, and tests of details of balances

PROCEDURES USED TO OBTAIN AN UNDERSTANDING— procedures used by the auditor to gather evidence about the design and implementation of specific controls

TESTS OF CONTROLS— audit procedures to test the effectiveness of controls in support of a reduced assessed control risk

The first two procedures are the same as those used to obtain an understanding of internal control. Thus, performing tests of controls can be thought of as a continuation of the audit procedures used to obtain an understanding of internal control. The main difference is that with tests of controls, the objective is more specific and the tests are more extensive. For example, if the client's budgeting process is to be used as a basis for assessing a low level of risk that expenditures are misclassified, in addition to the procedures described in the example given for obtaining an understanding, the auditor might also select a recent budget report, trace its contents to source records, prove its mathematical accuracy, examine all variance reports and memos that flow from it, talk to responsible personnel about the follow-up actions they took, and examine documentation in support of those actions. In effect, when the auditor decides to assess control risk below maximum for any transaction-related audit objective, the procedures used to obtain an understanding of internal control are combined with the tests of controls. The amount of additional evidence required for tests of controls will depend on the amount and extensiveness of evidence obtained in gaining the understanding.

The purpose of tests of controls is to determine whether all six transaction-related audit objectives have been satisfied for each class of transactions. For example, the auditor will perform tests of controls to test whether recorded transactions occurred and actual transactions are recorded. The auditor also performs these tests to determine if recorded sales transactions are accurately recorded, recorded in the appropriate time period, correctly classified, and accurately summarized and posted to the general ledger and master files. If the auditor is confident that transactions were correctly recorded in the journals and correctly posted, he or she can be confident that general ledger totals are correct.

To illustrate typical tests of controls, it is useful to return to the control risk matrix for Hillsburg Hardware Limited in Figure 9-5, page 267. For each of the 11 controls included in Figure 9-5, Table 11-1 identifies a test of controls that might be performed to test its effectiveness. Notice that no test of control is performed for the weakness in Figure 9-5. It would make no sense to determine if the absence of a control is being adequately performed.

Dual-Purpose Tests A substantive test is a procedure designed to test for dollar amounts of errors or fraud and other irregularities directly affecting the correctness of financial statement balances. Such errors or fraud and other irregularities are a clear indication of misstatements of the accounts. The two main types of substantive procedures, analytical procedures and detailed tests of balances, are directed to significant account balances or classes of transactions because of the potential for a misstatement occurring (inherent risk) and because of the potential for a misstatement not being prevented or detected (control risk).

An auditor may perform auditing procedures that are both tests of controls and substantive procedures on the same sample of transactions or account balances for efficiency; such procedures are known as **dual-purpose tests**. Dual-purpose tests provide evidence of whether or not the controls being tested were operating effectively during the period and whether there are misstatements in the data produced by the accounting system. Reperformance always simultaneously provides evidence about both controls and monetary correctness.

DUAL-PURPOSE TESTS—the performing of auditing procedures that are both tests of controls and substantive procedures on the same sample of transactions or account balances for efficiency

Dual-purpose tests are often cost-effective when performed with the assistance of software, for example, generalized audit software. The auditor obtains a copy of the transaction file, for example, the detailed sales transaction history file. Substantive tests the auditor would do on such a transaction file include:

- Adding up the transactions, providing subtotals by month, and agreeing the subtotals to the general ledger (accuracy, posting, and summarization); and
- Adding up the individual lines of the invoice and comparing to the total for each invoice, printing exceptions (accuracy).

The latter test would also serve a control testing purpose. For example, differences between the auditor invoice total and the system invoice total could indicate a programming error, where invoices were not being added up correctly. Testing the accuracy of a program would be considered a control test.

TABLE 11-1	Illustration of Tests of Controls
Illustrative Key Controls	**Typical Tests of Controls**
Credit is approved automatically by the computer by comparison to authorized credit limits (C1).	Review exception report and ensure approval by credit manager (documentation).
Recorded sales are supported by authorized shipping documents and approved customer orders, which are attached to the duplicate sales invoice (C2).	Examine a sample of duplicate sales invoices to determine that each one is supported by an attached, authorized shipping document and approved customer order (documentation).
Separation of duties between billing, recording sales, and handling cash receipts (C3).	Observe whether personnel responsible for handling cash have no accounting responsibilities and enquire as to their duties (observation and enquiry).
Shipping documents are forwarded to billing daily and billed the subsequent day (C4).	Observe whether shipping documents are forwarded daily to billing and observe when they are billed (observation).
Shipping documents are issued in numerical order by the computer and are accounted for weekly (C5).	Account for a sequence of shipping documents and trace each to the sales journal (documentation and reperformance).
Shipping documents are batched daily and compared with quantities billed (C6).	Examine a sample of daily batches, recalculate the shipping quantities, and trace totals to reconciliation with input reports (reperformance).
Unit selling prices are obtained from the price list master file of approved prices (C7).	Examine a sample of sales invoices and agree prices to authorized computer price list. Review changes to price file throughout the year for proper approval (reperformance and documentation).
Sales transactions are internally verified (C8).	Examine document package for internal verification (classification).
Statements are mailed to all customers each month (C9).	Observe whether statements are mailed for 1 month and enquire about who is responsible for mailing the statements (observation and enquiry).
Once the batch of sales transactions is entered, the computer automatically posts transactions to the accounts receivable subsidiary records and to the general ledger (C10).	Trace postings from the batch of sales transactions to the subsidiary records and general ledger (reperformance).
Accounts receivable master file is reconciled to the general ledger on a monthly basis (C11).	Examine evidence of reconciliation for test month, and test accuracy of reconciliation (documentation and reperformance).

Analytical Procedures As discussed in Chapter 6, **analytical procedures** involve comparisons of recorded amounts to expectations developed by the auditor. They often involve the calculation of ratios by the auditor for comparison with previous years' ratios and other related data. For example, the auditor could compare sales, collections, and accounts receivable in the current year to amounts in previous years and calculate the gross margin percentage for comparison to previous years.

ANALYTICAL PROCEDURES—use of comparisons and relationships to determine whether account balances or other data appear reasonable

Focus Box 11-1

ADVANCED ANALYTICAL PROCEDURES HELP RUN BUSINESS PROCESSES

As businesses build systems that allow for up-to-the-minute details about sales and information, they need tools for understanding such large volumes of data. Those tools are analytical procedures supported by graphical displays, known as online analytical processing (OLAP), a common feature of centralized database systems.

For example, Cascade Designs is a maker of camping supplies. They use information about inventory at their customers' stores and internal gross margin information to help with produc-

tion planning. 7-Eleven stores use computer sales history data to help manage inventory: seasonal trends are taken into account to help minimize inventory while trying to avoid stock-outs of popular brands.

Sources: 1. Koenig, David, 2004. "7-Eleven goes wireless," *The Globe and Mail*, October 12, 2004.
2. Tedeschi, Bob, 2004. "With custom-built software, a manufacturer can take a retailer's orders in stride," *The New York Times*, October 11, 2004.

There are four purposes of analytical procedures, all of which were discussed in Chapter 6: understand the client's business, assess the entity's ability to continue as a going concern, indicate the presence of possible misstatements in the financial statements, and reduce detailed audit tests. All of these help the auditor decide the extent of other audit tests. To illustrate, if analytical procedures indicate there may be misstatements, more extensive investigation may be needed. An example is an unexpected change in the current year's gross margin percentage compared to the previous year's. Other tests may be needed to determine if there is a misstatement in sales or cost of goods sold that caused the change. On the other hand, if no material fluctuations are found using analytical procedures and the auditor concludes that fluctuations should not have occurred, other tests may be reduced. Analytical procedures are both a substantive procedure and a planning procedure to be used in designing the nature, extent, and timing of other audit procedures. When used as a substantive procedure, they would be performed at a more detailed level (Section 5301.10).

Tests of Details of Balances Section 5142.49 states that "substantive procedures are performed in order to detect material misstatements at the assertion level." In order to avoid confusion, this text will use the terms "analytical procedures" and "tests of details of balances" to describe the two components when they are considered as separate activities and the term "substantive procedures" to describe the aggregate testing for dollar misstatements directly affecting the correctness of financial statement balances.

Tests of details of balances focus on the ending general ledger balances for both balance sheet and income statement accounts, but the primary emphasis in most tests of details of balances is on the balance sheet. (Terms such as "detailed tests" and "direct tests of balances" may be used interchangeably with "tests of details of balances.") Examples include direct communication in writing with customers for accounts receivable, physical examination of inventory, and examination of vendors' statements for accounts payable. These tests of ending balances are essential to the conduct of the audit because, for the most part, the evidence is obtained from a source independent of the client and, thus, is considered to be highly reliable. The extent of these tests depends on the results of controls and analytical procedures.

Tests of details of balances have the objective of establishing the monetary correctness of the accounts they relate to and, therefore, are substantive tests. For example, confirmations test for monetary errors or fraud and other irregularities and are therefore substantive. Similarly, counts of inventory and cash on hand are also substantive tests.

Summary of Types of Tests Figure 11-1 summarizes the types of tests. Procedures to obtain an understanding of internal control and tests of controls are concerned with evaluating whether controls are sufficiently effective to justify reducing control risk and thereby reducing substantive audit tests. Analytical procedures emphasize the overall reasonableness of transactions and the general ledger balances, and tests of details of balances emphasize the ending balances in the general ledger. Together, the four types of audit tests enable the auditor to gather sufficient appropriate audit evidence to express an opinion on the financial statements.

Figure 11-1 also shows the relationships of the types of tests to the audit risk model. Observe that all four types of tests are used to satisfy sufficient appropriate audit evidence

FIGURE 11-1 Types of Audit Tests

$$AR = IR \times CR \times PDR$$

Procedures to obtain an understanding of internal control + Tests of controls + Analytical procedures + Tests of details of balances = Sufficient appropriate audit evidence per GAAS

FIGURE 11-2

FIGURE 11-2   Types of Audit Tests and Audit Assurance for Accounts Receivable

requirements. Also observe that procedures to obtain an understanding and tests of controls reduce control risk, whereas the two substantive tests are used to satisfy planned detection risk.

Figure 11-2 shows how the four types of tests are used to obtain assurance in the audit of one account, accounts receivable. It is apparent from examining Figure 11-2 that the auditor obtained a higher overall assurance for accounts receivable than the assurance obtained from any one test. The auditor can increase overall assurance by increasing the assurance obtained from any of the tests.

→11.2   EVIDENCE MIX DECISIONS

Relationship Between Tests and Evidence

Only certain types of evidence are obtained through each of the four types of tests. Table 11-2 on page 320 summarizes the relationship between types of tests and types of evidence. Several observations about Table 11-2 follow:

- Procedures to obtain an understanding of internal control and tests of controls involve only documentation, observation, enquiry, and reperformance.
- More types of evidence are obtained using tests of details of balances than by using any other type of test. Only tests of details of balances involve confirmation and physical examination.
- Enquiries of clients are made with every type of test.
- Documentation and reperformance are used for every type of test except analytical procedures.

Relative Costs The types of tests are listed in order of increasing cost as follows:

- Analytical procedures
- Procedures to obtain an understanding of internal control and tests of controls
- Tests of details of balances

The reason analytical procedures are least costly is the relative ease of making calculations and comparisons. Often, considerable information about potential misstatements can be obtained by simply comparing two or three numbers. Frequently, auditors calculate these ratios using computer software at minimal cost.

Tests of controls are also low in cost because the auditor is making enquiries and observations, examining such things as initials on documents and outward indications of other control procedures and performing reperformance, which includes recalculations and

TABLE 11-2	Relationship Between Types of Tests and Evidence							
	Type of Evidence							
Type of Test	Physical Examination	Confirmation	Documentation	Observation	Inquiries of the Client	Reperformance	Analytical Procedures
Procedures to obtain an understanding of internal control			✓	✓	✓	✓	
Tests of controls			✓	✓	✓	✓	
Analytical procedures					✓		✓
Tests of details of balances	✓	✓	✓		✓	✓	

tracings. Frequently, tests of controls can be done on a large number of items in a few minutes, especially if computer-based work, such as the use of test data, is included. Tests of details of balances are almost always considerably more costly than any of the other types of procedures. It is costly to send confirmations and to count assets. Because of the high cost of tests of details of balances, auditors usually try to plan the audit to minimize their use.

Naturally, the cost of each type of evidence varies in different situations. For example, the cost of an auditor's test counting inventory (a substantive test of the details of the inventory balance) frequently depends on the nature and dollar value of the inventory, its location, and the number of different items.

Relationship Between Tests of Controls and Substantive Tests To better understand the nature of tests of controls and substantive tests, an examination of how they differ is useful. An exception in a test of controls is only an indication of the likelihood of errors or fraud and other irregularities affecting the dollar value of the financial statements, whereas an exception in a substantive test is a financial statement misstatement. Exceptions in tests of controls are often referred to as "control test deviations." Thus, control test deviations are significant only if they occur with sufficient frequency to cause the auditor to believe there may be material dollar misstatements in the statements. Substantive tests should then be performed to determine whether dollar misstatements have actually occurred.

As an illustration, assume that the client's controls require an independent clerk to verify the quantity, price, and extension of each supplier's invoice, after which the clerk must initial the original invoice to indicate performance. A test of control audit procedure would be to examine a sample of suppliers' invoices for the initials of the person who verified the quantitative data. If there are a significant number of documents without a signature, the auditor should follow up with tests to determine if there are any monetary misstatements. This can be done by extending the tests of the suppliers' invoices to include verifying prices to purchase orders, extensions, and footings (reperformance) or by increasing the sample size for the confirmation of accounts payable (test of details of balances). Of course, even though the control is not operating effectively, the invoices may be correct. This will be the case if the persons originally preparing the supplier invoices did a conscientious and competent job. Similarly, even if there is an initial, there may be monetary misstatements due to initialling without performance or with careless performance of the internal control procedure. For these reasons, Section 5143.10 includes reperformance as one of the several auditing procedures performed. Some auditors prefer to reperform only when there is an indication of the need to do so.

Trade-off Between Tests of Controls and Substantive Tests As explained in Chapter 9, there is a trade-off between tests of controls and substantive tests. The auditor makes a decision during planning about whether to assess control risk below maximum. If control risk is assessed at maximum, the auditor would follow a substantive approach; if control risk is assessed below maximum, the auditor would follow a combined approach. Tests of controls must be performed to determine whether the assessed control risk is supported. If it is, planned detection risk in the audit risk model is increased and substantive procedures can therefore be reduced. Figure 11-3 shows the relationship between substantive tests and control risk assessment (including tests of controls) at differing levels of internal control effectiveness.

The shaded area in Figure 11-3 is the maximum assurance obtainable from control risk assessment and tests of controls. For example, at any point to the left of point A, assessed control risk is 1.0 because the auditor evaluates internal control as ineffective. Any point to the right of point B results in no further reduction of control risk because the public accounting firm has established the minimum assessed control risk that it will permit.

After the auditor decides the effectiveness of the client's internal controls, it is appropriate to select any point within the shaded area of Figure 11-3 consistent with the level of control risk the auditor decides is appropriate. To illustrate, assume that the auditor contends that internal control effectiveness is at point C. Tests of controls at the C_1 level would provide the minimum control risk, given internal control. The auditor could choose to perform no tests of controls (point C_3), which would support a control risk of 1.0. Any point between the two, such as C_2, would also be appropriate. If C_2 is selected, the audit assurance from tests of controls is $C_3 - C_2$ and from substantive tests is $C - C_2$. The auditor will likely select C_1, C_2, or C_3 based upon the relative cost of tests of controls and substantive tests.

Evidence Mix

There are significant variations in the extent to which the four types of tests can be used in different audits for differing levels of inherent risk and internal control effectiveness. There can also be variations from cycle to cycle within a given audit, from account balance to account balance within a particular cycle, and even between assertions for a particular account balance. Figure 11-4 shows the **audit evidence mix** for four different audits. In each case, considerable time was spent accumulating knowledge of business data, as well as completing analytical review for planning purposes. Assume sufficient appropriate audit

AUDIT EVIDENCE MIX—the combination of the four types of tests to obtain sufficient appropriate audit evidence for a cycle. There are likely to be variations in the mix from cycle to cycle depending on the circumstances of the audit

FIGURE 11-3 **Audit Assurance from Substantive Tests and Tests of Controls at Different Levels of Control Effectiveness**

C_3 No reliance on controls; not cost-effective.
C_2 Some reliance on controls.
C_1 Maximum reliance on controls.

FIGURE 11-4 | Variations in Evidence Mix

Audit 1—sophisticated internal controls	Extensive	Extensive	Extensive	Small
Audit 2—medium, some controls	Moderate	Moderate	Extensive	Moderate
Audit 3—medium, few controls	Moderate	Moderate	Extensive	
Audit 4—control testing planned, but controls not effective	Moderate	Moderate	Extensive	Extensive

Procedures to obtain an understanding of control

Test of controls

Substantive analytical procedures

Substantive tests of details of balances

Note: Auditors in all the audits have completed client risk profiles, have knowledge of the business, and have completed planning analytical procedures.

evidence was accumulated for all audits. Audit 1 is a large company, while Audits 2 through 4 are medium-sized companies. An analysis of each audit follows.

ANALYSIS OF AUDIT 1—SOPHISTICATED INTERNAL CONTROLS This client is a large company with sophisticated internal controls. The auditor, therefore, performs extensive tests of controls and relies heavily on the client's internal control to reduce substantive tests. Extensive analytical procedures are also performed to reduce tests of details of balances, which are, therefore, minimized. Because of the emphasis on tests of controls and analytical procedures, this audit can be done less expensively than other types of audits.

ANALYSIS OF AUDIT 2—MEDIUM, SOME CONTROLS This company is medium-sized, with some controls and some inherent risks. The auditor has, therefore, decided to do a medium amount of testing for all types of tests except analytical procedures, which will be done extensively.

ANALYSIS OF AUDIT 3—MEDIUM, FEW CONTROLS This company is medium-sized, but has few effective controls and significant inherent risks. Management has decided that it is not cost-effective to implement better internal controls. No tests of controls are done because reliance on internal control is inappropriate when controls are insufficient. The emphasis is on tests of details of balances, but some analytical procedures are also done. The reason for limiting analytical procedures is the auditor's expectations of misstatements in the account balances. The cost of the audit is likely to be relatively high because of the amount of detailed substantive testing.

ANALYSIS OF AUDIT 4—MEDIUM, INEFFECTIVE CONTROLS The original plan on this audit was to follow the approach used in Audit 2. However, the auditor found extensive control test deviations and significant misstatements using dual-purpose tests and analytical procedures. The auditor, therefore, concluded that the internal controls were not effective. Extensive tests of details of balances are performed to offset the unacceptable results of the other tests. The costs of this audit are higher because tests of controls and dual-purpose tests were performed but could not be used to reduce tests of details of balances.

Figure 11-4 shows the relative mix of audit evidence types. It does not reflect total audit cost since the costs associated with the tests will vary, depending on the specific test selected and the extent of computerized support used for conducting the tests.

→11.3   CREATING THE AUDIT PROGRAM

Design of the Audit Program

A combined audit approach is appropriate for most audits; such an approach includes both tests of controls and substantive procedures. The audit program for most audits is designed in three parts: tests of controls, analytical procedures, and tests of details of balances. There will likely be a separate set of audit programs for each transaction cycle. An example in the sales and collection cycle might be tests of controls audit programs for sales and cash receipts; an analytical procedures audit program for the entire cycle; and tests of details of balances audit programs for cash, accounts receivable, bad-debt expense, allowance for uncollectible accounts, and miscellaneous accounts receivable.

Tests of Controls The tests of controls audit program normally includes a descriptive section documenting the understanding obtained about internal control. It is also likely to include a description of the procedures performed to obtain an understanding of internal control and the assessed control risk. Both of these affect the tests of controls audit program. The methodology to design tests of controls is shown in Figure 11-5. The first three steps in the figure were described in Chapter 9. When controls are effective and planned control risk is low (i.e., the auditor chooses to rely on internal controls), a combined approach will be used and there will be tests of controls. Some dual-purpose tests may also be included. If control risk is assessed at maximum, the auditor will use a substantive audit approach (i.e., only substantive procedures will be used). The procedures already performed in obtaining an understanding of internal control may affect tests of controls.

AUDIT PROCEDURES The approach to designing tests of controls emphasizes satisfying the transaction-related audit objectives developed in Chapter 5. A three-step approach is followed when control risk is assessed below maximum:

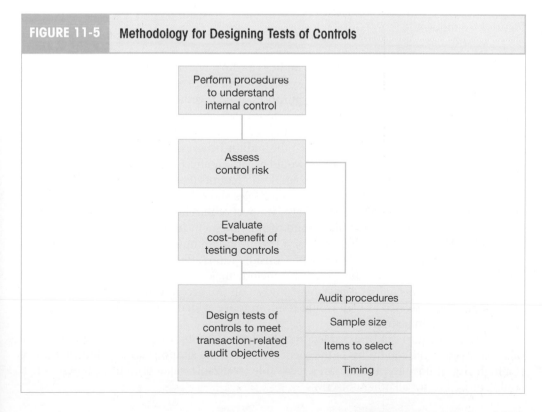

FIGURE 11-5   Methodology for Designing Tests of Controls

Perform procedures to understand internal control

Assess control risk

Evaluate cost-benefit of testing controls

Design tests of controls to meet transaction-related audit objectives

Audit procedures

Sample size

Items to select

Timing

1. Apply the transaction-related audit objectives to the class of transactions being tested, such as sales.
2. Identify specific controls to be relied upon that should reduce control risk for transaction-related audit objectives.
3. For all internal controls to which reduction in control risk is attributed (key controls), develop appropriate tests of controls. Where relevant, design appropriate dual-purpose tests (considering weakness in internal control and expected results of the tests of controls) for the potential types of errors or fraud and other irregularities related to those transaction-related audit objectives.

Analytical Procedures Many auditors perform extensive analytical procedures on all audits because they are relatively inexpensive. As stated in Chapter 6, analytical procedures are performed at three different stages of the audit: in the planning stage to help the auditor decide the other evidence needed to satisfy audit risk, during the audit in conjunction with tests of details of balances as part of substantive procedures, and near the end of the audit as a final test of reasonableness.

Section 5301, Analysis, requires the use of analytical procedures during both the planning phase and the completion phase of the audit; use of analytical procedures as a substantive procedure is optional.

Choosing the appropriate analytical procedures requires the auditor to use professional judgment. The appropriate use of analytical procedures and illustrative ratios are included in Chapter 6. There are also examples in several subsequent chapters. For example, page 434 illustrates several analytical procedures for the audit of accounts receivable.

Tests of Details of Balances The methodology for designing tests of details of balances is oriented to the balance-related audit objectives developed in Chapter 5 (pages 124–126). For example, if the auditor is verifying accounts receivable, the planned tests must be sufficient to satisfy each of the objectives. In planning tests of details of balances to satisfy those objectives, many auditors follow a methodology such as the one shown in Figure 11-6 (page 325) for accounts receivable. The design of these tests is normally the most difficult part of the entire planning process. Designing such procedures is subjective and requires considerable professional judgment.

A discussion of the key decisions in designing tests of details of balances as shown in Figure 11-6 follows.

SET MATERIALITY AND ASSESS AUDIT RISK AND INHERENT RISK FOR ACCOUNTS RECEIVABLE Setting the preliminary judgment about materiality for the audit as a whole is an auditor decision that was discussed in Chapter 8. A lower materiality would result in more testing of details than a higher amount. Analytical review for planning purposes, used together with a good knowledge of business and the industry, allows the auditor to identify obvious warning signals.

As discussed in Chapter 8, audit risk is normally decided for the audit as a whole, rather than by cycle. An exception might be when the auditor believes that a misstatement of a specific account, such as accounts receivable, would negatively affect users more than the same size misstatement of any other account. For example, if accounts receivable is pledged to a bank as security on a loan, audit risk may be set lower for sales and collections than for other cycles.

Inherent risk is assessed by identifying any aspect of the client's history, environment, or operations that indicates a high likelihood of misstatement in the current year's financial statements. This emphasizes the need for a broad-based knowledge of business that links risks to the external business environment. Considerations affecting inherent risk (discussed in Chapter 8) applied to accounts receivable include makeup of accounts receivable, nature of the client's business, initial engagement, and so on. An account balance for which inherent risk has been assessed as high would result in more evidence accumulation than for an account with low inherent risk.

Inherent risk also can be extended to individual audit objectives. For example, because of adverse economic conditions in the client's industry, the auditor may conclude that there is a high risk of uncollectible accounts receivable (realizable-value objective). Inherent risk could still be low for all other objectives.

FIGURE 11-6

Methodology for Designing Tests of Details of Financial Statement Balances—Accounts Receivable

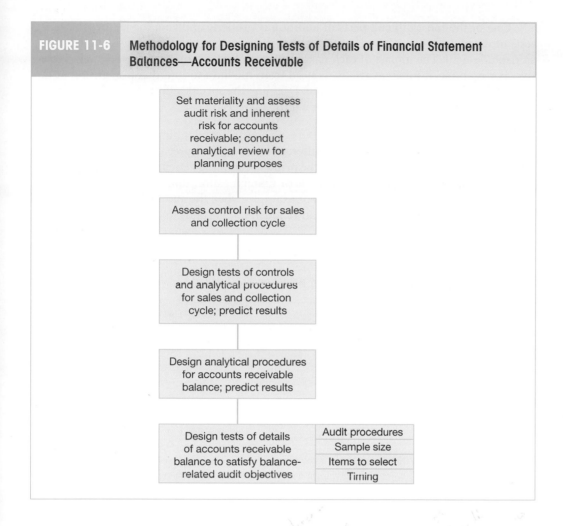

> Set materiality and assess audit risk and inherent risk for accounts receivable; conduct analytical review for planning purposes
>
> Assess control risk for sales and collection cycle
>
> Design tests of controls and analytical procedures for sales and collection cycle; predict results
>
> Design analytical procedures for accounts receivable balance; predict results
>
> Design tests of details of accounts receivable balance to satisfy balance-related audit objectives
>
> Audit procedures
> Sample size
> Items to select
> Timing

ASSESS CONTROL RISK Control risk is evaluated in the manner discussed in Chapter 9 and in earlier parts of this chapter. This methodology would be applied to both sales and collection in the audit of accounts receivable. Effective controls reduce control risk and therefore the evidence required for substantive procedures; inadequate controls increase the substantive evidence needed.

DESIGN TESTS OF CONTROLS AND ANALYTICAL PROCEDURES AND PREDICT RESULTS The methodology for designing tests of controls and analytical procedures was discussed earlier in this section and will be illustrated in subsequent chapters. The tests are designed with the expectation that certain results will be obtained. These predicted results affect the design of tests of details of balances as discussed below.

DESIGN TESTS OF DETAILS OF BALANCES TO SATISFY BALANCE-RELATED AUDIT OBJECTIVES The planned tests of details of balances include audit procedures, sample size, items to select, and timing. Procedures must be selected and designed for each account and each balance-related audit objective within each account. The balance-related audit objectives for accounts receivable are shown on page 436.

A difficulty the auditor faces in designing tests of details of balances is the need to predict the outcome of the tests of controls and analytical procedures before they are performed. This is necessary because the auditor should design tests of details of balances during the planning phase, but the appropriate design depends on the outcome of the other tests. In planning tests of details of balances, the auditor usually predicts that there will be few or no exceptions in tests of controls and analytical procedures, unless there are reasons to believe otherwise. If the results of the tests of controls and analytical procedures are not consistent with the predictions, the tests of details of balances will need to be changed as the audit progresses.

One of the most difficult parts of auditing is properly applying the factors that affect tests of details of balances. Each of the factors is subjective, requiring considerable professional judgment. The impact of each factor on tests of details of balances is equally subjective. For example, if inherent risk is reduced from medium to low, there is agreement that tests of details of balances can be reduced. Deciding the specific effect on audit procedures, sample size, timing, and items to select is a difficult decision.

Level of Disaggregation of Planning Activities The various planning activities discussed in Chapters 5 through 11 are applied at different levels of disaggregation, depending on the nature of the activity. Table 11-3 shows the primary planning activities and the levels of disaggregation normally applied. These levels of disaggregation range from the overall audit to the audit objective for each account. For example, when the auditor obtains background information about the client's business and industry, it pertains to the overall audit. As the

TABLE 11-3	Level to Which Planning Activities Are Applied					
		Level of Disaggregation				
Planning Activity		Overall Audit	Cycle	Account	Transaction-Related Audit Objective	Balance-Related Audit Objective
Preplan audit, develop client risk profile		P				
Conduct independence threat analysis		P				
Obtain background information		P				
Obtain information about client's legal obligations		P				
Conduct analytical procedures for planning purposes		P	P	P		
Set preliminary judgment about materiality		P				
Assess audit risk		P				
Assess inherent risk			P	P		
Understand internal control: Control environment and corporate governance / Accounting system / Control procedures		P	P P			
Identify key internal controls			P	P	P	
Identify internal control weaknesses		P			P	
Assess risks of fraud		P	P	P		
Assess planned control risk					P	
Design tests of controls					P	
Assess control risk achieved					P	
Design substantive analytical procedures				P		P
Design tests of details of balances						P

P = Primary level to which planning activity is applied. Where multiple columns are marked, the primary focus is the most detailed level.

audit progresses, the information will first be used in assessing audit risk and inherent risk and later is likely to affect tests of details of balances.

Illustrative Audit Program   Table 11-4 shows the tests of details of balances segment of an audit program for accounts receivable. The format used relates the audit procedures to the balance-related audit objectives. Notice that most procedures satisfy more than one objective. Also, more than one audit procedure is used for each objective. Audit procedures can be added or deleted as the auditor considers necessary. Sample size, items to select, and timing can also be changed for most procedures.

TABLE 11-4	Tests of Details of Balances Audit Program for Accounts Receivable

Accounts Receivable Balance-Related Audit Objectives

Sample Size	Items to Select	Timing*	Tests of Details of Balances Audit Procedures	Detail tie-in	Existence	Completeness	Accuracy	Classification	Cutoff	Realizable value	Rights	Presentation and disclosure
Trace 20 items; foot 2 pages and all subtotals	Random	I	1. Obtain an aged list of receivables: trace open items to supporting invoice detail, foot schedule, and trace to general ledger.	x								
All	All	Y	2. Obtain an analysis of the allowance for doubtful accounts and bad debt expense: test accuracy, examine authorization for write-offs, and trace to general ledger.	x	x	x	x			x		
100	30 largest 70 random	I	3. Obtain direct confirmation of accounts receivable and perform alternative procedures for nonresponses.		x	x	x	x	x		x	
NA	NA	Y	4. Review accounts receivable control account for the period. Investigate the nature of, and review support for, any large or unusual entries or any entries not arising from normal journal sources. Also investigate any significant increases or decreases in sales toward year end.		x		x	x	x		x	x
All	All	Y	5. Review receivables for any that have been assigned or discounted.								x	x
NA	NA	Y	6. Investigate collectibility of account balances.							x		
All	All	Y	7. Review lists of balances for amounts due from related parties or employees, credit balances, and unusual items, as well as notes receivable due after one year.		x			x				x
30 transactions for sales and cash receipts; 10 for credit memos	50% before and 50% after year end	Y	8. Determine that proper cutoff procedures were applied at the balance sheet date to ensure that sales, cash receipts, and credit memos have been recorded in the correct period.						x			

*I = Interim; Y = Year end; NA = Not applicable.

The audit program in Table 11-4 was developed after consideration of all the factors affecting tests of details of balances and is based on several assumptions about inherent risk, control risk, and the results of tests of controls and analytical procedures. As indicated, if those assumptions are materially incorrect, the planned audit program will require revision. For example, analytical procedures could indicate potential errors for several balance-related audit objectives, tests of controls results could indicate weak internal controls, or new facts could cause the auditor to change inherent risk.

Focus Box 11.2

AUDIT PROGRAMS USED IN PRACTICE

Professional Engagement Manual
www.cica.ca/cica

Most large public accounting firms develop their own standard audit programs, organized by industry, linked by audit objective often to data-bases including lists of expected controls and likely audit tests. Smaller firms often purchase similar audit programs from outside organizations. Standard audit programs are normally computerized and can easily be modified to meet the circumstances of individual audit engagements. One example of standard audit programs available for purchase is the CICA's *Professional Engagement Manual (PEM). PEM* is available in paper form, on diskette, or on CD-ROM and contains audit programs as well as general and industry-specific checklists that auditors can use and modify for individual engagements.

Standard audit programs, whether developed internally or purchased from an outside organization, can dramatically increase audit efficiency if they are used properly. They should *not* be used, however, as a substitute for an auditor's professional judgment. Because each audit is different, it is usually necessary to add, modify, or delete steps within a standard audit program in order to accumulate sufficient and competent evidence.

Relationship of Transaction-Related Audit Objectives to Balance-Related Audit Objectives It has already been shown that tests of details of balances must be designed to satisfy balance-related audit objectives for each account and the extent of these tests can be reduced when transaction-related audit objectives have been satisfied by tests of controls. It is, therefore, important to understand how each transaction-related audit objective relates to each balance-related audit objective. The following transaction-related audit objectives have a direct relationship with the balance-related audit objective:

Transaction-Related Audit Objective	Balance-Related Audit Objective
Occurrence	Existence or completeness
Completeness	Existence or completeness
Accuracy	Accuracy
Classification	Classification
Timing	Cutoff
Posting and summarization	Detail tie-in

This direct relationship can be illustrated by looking at sales transactions. If there are controls to ensure that all sales transactions that occur are recorded in the accounts receivable, then these controls can provide assurance with respect to the completeness balance-related audit objective.

However, even when all transaction-related audit objectives are met, the auditor will still rely primarily on substantive tests of balances to meet the following balance-related audit objectives: realizable value, rights and obligations, and presentation and disclosure, since few internal controls are related to these audit objectives. Some substantive tests of balances are also likely for the other balance-related audit objectives, depending on the results of the tests of controls.

The relationship of transaction-related audit objectives to balance-related audit objectives is shown in greater detail in Figure 14-3, page 420. This figure shows how transaction-related audit objectives for sales and cash receipts affect accounts receivable balance-related audit objectives. Notice in Figure 14-3 that the occurrence transaction-related audit objective for sales affects the existence balance-related audit objective for accounts receivable, whereas the occurrence transaction-related audit objective for cash receipts affects the completeness balance-related audit objective for accounts receivable. The reason is that sales increase accounts receivable, whereas cash receipts decrease accounts receivable.

→11.4 AUDIT PHASES
Summary of the Audit Process

The four phases of an audit were introduced at the end of Chapter 5. Considerable portions of Chapters 6 through 11 have discussed the different aspects of the process. Figure 11-7 on page 330 shows the four **phases for the entire audit process**. Table 11-5 on page 331 shows the timing of selected tests from each phase for an audit with a December 31 balance sheet date.

Phase I: Assess risk and plan the audit Chapters 6 through 11 have emphasized various aspects of planning the audit. At the end of phase I, the auditor should have a well-defined audit plan and a specific audit program for the entire audit. In this first phase, preplanning steps, development of a client risk profile, and assessment of control risk help the auditor decide on the strategic approach to the audit.

Obtaining information during preplanning, obtaining background information, obtaining information about the client's legal obligations, and performing preliminary analytical procedures help to assess audit risk and inherent risk. Excellent knowledge of business with linkages to the external environment assists in the evaluation of these risks. An understanding of internal control is required to provide a planned control risk. Assessments of materiality, audit risk, inherent risk, and control risk are used to develop an overall audit plan and audit program.

Phase II: Perform Tests of Controls Performance of the tests of controls occurs during this phase. The objectives of phase II are (1) to obtain evidence in support of the specific controls that contribute to the auditor's assessed control risk (i.e., where it is reduced below maximum) and (2) when dual-purpose tests are used, to obtain evidence in support of the monetary correctness of transactions. The former objective is met by performing tests of controls, and the latter by performing substantive procedures. Many of both types of tests are conducted simultaneously on the same transactions. When controls are not considered effective, or when control deviations are discovered, substantive tests can be expanded in phase III. An **audit strategy** consists of a planned approach to the mix between control tests and substantive tests, keeping in mind the assessed risks.

Since the results of tests of controls are a major determinant of the extent of substantive procedures (i.e., analytical procedures and tests of details of balances), they are often performed two or three months before the balance sheet date or during regular quarterly visits to the client. This helps the auditor plan for contingencies, revise the audit program for unexpected results, and complete the audit as soon as possible after the balance sheet date.

Phase III: Perform Analytical Procedures and Tests of Details of Balances The objective of phase III is to obtain sufficient additional evidence to determine whether the ending balances and footnotes in financial statements are fairly stated. The nature and extent of the work will depend heavily on the findings of the two previous phases.

There are two general categories of phase III procedures: analytical procedures and tests of details of balances. Analytical procedures are those that assess the overall reasonableness of transactions and balances. Tests of details of balances are specific procedures intended to test for monetary errors or fraud and other irregularities in the balances in the financial statements. Certain key transactions and amounts are so important that each one must be audited. Other items can be sampled.

PHASES OF THE AUDIT PROCESS—the four aspects of a complete audit: (1) assess risk and plan the audit, (2) perform tests of controls, (3) perform analytical procedures and tests of details of balances, and (4) complete the audit and issue the auditor's report

AUDIT STRATEGY—a planned approach to the conduct of audit testing, taking into account assessed risks

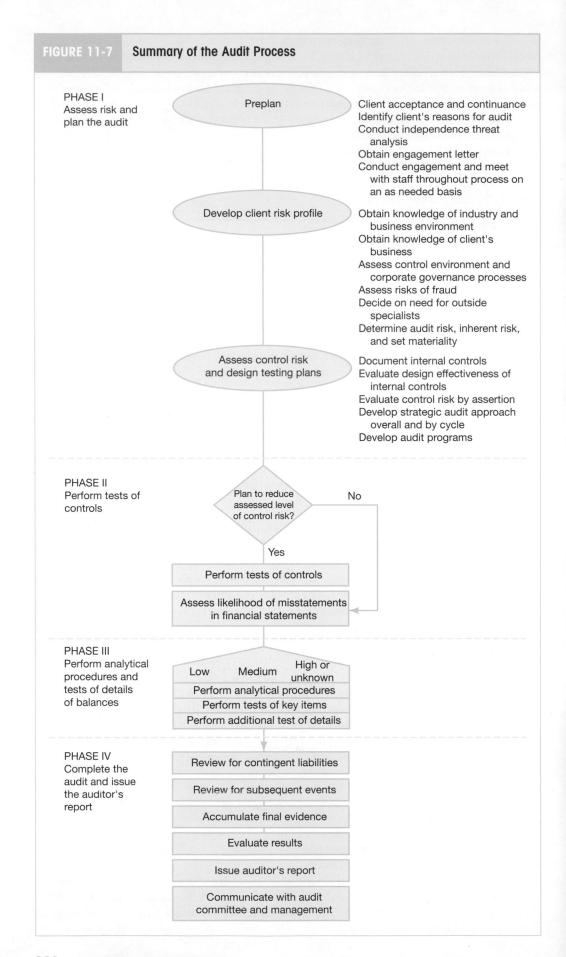

FIGURE 11-7 Summary of the Audit Process

PHASE I
Assess risk and
plan the audit

Preplan

Client acceptance and continuance
Identify client's reasons for audit
Conduct independence threat
   analysis
Obtain engagement letter
Conduct engagement and meet
   with staff throughout process on
   an as needed basis

Develop client risk profile

Obtain knowledge of industry and
   business environment
Obtain knowledge of client's
   business
Assess control environment and
   corporate governance processes
Assess risks of fraud
Decide on need for outside
   specialists
Determine audit risk, inherent risk,
   and set materiality

Assess control risk
and design testing plans

Document internal controls
Evaluate design effectiveness of
   internal controls
Evaluate control risk by assertion
Develop strategic audit approach
   overall and by cycle
Develop audit programs

PHASE II
Perform tests of
controls

Plan to reduce
assessed level
of control risk?

No

Yes

Perform tests of controls

Assess likelihood of misstatements
in financial statements

PHASE III
Perform analytical
procedures and
tests of details
of balances

Low   Medium   High or
                                  unknown

Perform analytical procedures

Perform tests of key items

Perform additional test of details

PHASE IV
Complete the
audit and issue
the auditor's
report

Review for contingent liabilities

Review for subsequent events

Accumulate final evidence

Evaluate results

Issue auditor's report

Communicate with audit
committee and management

Table 11-5 shows most analytical procedures being done both before and after the balance sheet date. Because of their low cost, it is common to use analytical procedures whenever they are relevant. They are frequently done early with preliminary data prior to year end as a means of planning and directing other audit tests to specific areas. The greatest benefit from calculating ratios and making comparisons occurs after the client has finished preparing its financial statements. Ideally, these analytical procedures are done before tests of details of balances so that they can then be used to determine how extensively to test balances. They are also used as a part of performing tests of balances and during the completion phase of the audit.

Table 11-5 also shows that tests of details of balances are normally done last. On some audits, all are done after the balance sheet date. When clients want to issue statements soon after the balance sheet date, however, the more time-consuming tests of details of balances will be done at interim dates prior to year end with additional work being done to "**roll forward**" the audited interim-date balances to year end. (This involves substantive work on journal entries and other activities during this period.) Substantive tests of balances performed before year end provide less assurance and are not normally done unless internal controls are effective.

ROLL FORWARD—substantive work on journal entries and transactions from a date prior to the balance sheet date to the year end

Phase IV: Complete the Audit and Issue the Auditor's Report After the first three phases are completed, it is necessary to accumulate some additional evidence for the financial statements, summarize the results, issue the auditor's report, and perform other forms of communication. This phase has several parts.

REVIEW FOR CONTINGENT LIABILITIES Contingent liabilities are potential liabilities that must be disclosed in the client's footnotes. Auditors must make sure the disclosure is adequate. A considerable portion of the search for contingent liabilities is done during the first three phases, but additional testing is done during phase IV. Contingent liabilities are studied in Chapter 21.

REVIEW FOR SUBSEQUENT EVENTS Occasionally, events occurring subsequent to the balance sheet date but before the issuance of the financial statements and auditor's report will have an effect on the information presented in the financial statements. Specific review procedures are designed to bring to the auditor's attention any subsequent events that may require recognition in the financial statements. Review for subsequent events is also studied in Chapter 21.

TABLE 11-5	Timing of Selected Tests		
Phase I	Plan and design audit approach. Update understanding of internal control. Update audit program. Perform preliminary analytical procedures.	31/8/04	
Phase II	Perform tests of controls for first 9 months of the year.	30/9/04	
Phase III	Confirm accounts receivable. Observe inventory.	31/10/04	
	Count cash. Perform cutoff tests. Request various other confirmations.	31/12/04	Balance sheet date
	Do analytical procedures, complete tests of controls, and do most tests of details of balances.	07/1/05	Books closed
Phase IV	Summarize results, review for contingent liabilities, review for subsequent events, accumulate final evidence including analytical procedures, and finalize audit.	08/3/05	Last date of fieldwork
	Issue auditor's report.	15/3/05	

ACCUMULATE FINAL EVIDENCE In addition to the evidence obtained for each cycle during phases I and II and for each account during phase III, it is also necessary to gather evidence for the financial statements as a whole during the completion phase. This evidence includes performing final analytical procedures; evaluating the going concern assumption; obtaining a client representation letter; and reading the annual report to make sure that the financial statements and the auditor's report have been accurately reproduced in the annual report, that the annual report is consistent with the financial statements, and that there are no material misstatements of fact in the annual report.

ISSUE AUDITOR'S REPORT The type of auditor's report issued depends on the evidence accumulated and the audit findings. The appropriate reports for differing circumstances were studied in Chapter 3.

COMMUNICATE WITH AUDIT COMMITTEE AND MANAGEMENT The auditor should communicate internal control-related matters to and discuss any problems encountered on the audit with the audit committee and senior management. In addition, paragraphs 5135.95, 5136.28, 5405.13, and Section 5751 require the auditor to communicate certain other matters to the audit committee or management upon completion of the audit or sooner. Although not required, auditors often also make suggestions to management to improve business performance.

SUMMARY

1. *What are the four different types of audit tests?* The four basic types of audit tests are: procedures to obtain an understanding of internal control, tests of controls, analytical procedures, and tests of details of balances.

   Which type of test is a dual-purpose test? A substantive test (remember that a substantive test comprises both analytical procedures and tests of details, used to quantify errors) can be used both to quantify errors and as a test of controls.

2. *What is evidence mix?* Evidence mix is the phrase used to explain the proportion of the different types of tests used in the audit engagement.

   How does the auditor choose the types of audit tests to be completed? Audit tests are selected based upon the level of assessed risks. For example, tests of control are conducted only if control risk is set below maximum and there is a potential of reliance upon internal controls.

3. *How are the different types of audit tests considered when designing an audit program?* The audit program is designed to ensure that sufficient competent evidence is gathered for each class of transaction (or account) for each relevant audit assertion. Audit tests are linked to the audit assertion in the context of assessed risks.

4. *What is an audit strategy?* An audit strategy is a planned approach to the conduct of the financial statement audit (or to audit testing), taking into account assessed risks.

   Describe the four phases of the financial statement audit. The four phases are: (I) plan and design an audit approach, (II) perform tests of controls, (III) perform analytical procedures and tests of details of balances, and (IV) complete the audit and issue the auditor's report.

CICA ASSURANCE HANDBOOK SECTIONS REFERENCED IN THIS CHAPTER:

Section 5135 – The auditor's responsibility to consider fraud.
Section 5136 – Misstatements—illegal acts.
Section 5142 – Materiality.
Section 5143 – The auditor's procedures in response to assessed risks.

Section 5301 – Analysis.
Section 5405 – Date of the auditor's report.
Section 5751 – Communications with those having oversight responsibility for the financial reporting process.

ESSENTIAL TERMS

Analytical procedures—use of comparisons and relationships to determine whether account balances or other data appear reasonable   (p. 317).

Audit evidence mix—the combination of the four types of tests to obtain sufficient appropriate audit evidence for a cycle. There are likely to be variations in the mix from cycle to cycle depending on the circumstances of the audit   (p. 321).

Audit strategy—a planned approach to the conduct of audit testing, taking into account assessed risks   (p. 329).

Dual-purpose tests—the performing of auditing procedures that are both tests of controls and substantive procedures on the same sample of transactions or account balances for efficiency (p. 316).

Phases of the audit process—the four aspects of a complete audit: (1) assess risk and plan the audit, (2) perform tests of controls, (3) perform analytical procedures and tests of details of balances, and (4) complete the audit and issue the auditor's report (p. 329).

Procedures used to obtain an understanding—procedures used by the auditor to gather evidence about the design and implementation of specific controls (p. 315).

Roll forward—substantive work on journal entries and transactions from a date prior to the balance sheet date to the year end (p. 331).

Tests of controls—audit procedures to test the effectiveness of controls in support of a reduced assessed control risk (p. 315).

Tests of details of balances—audit procedures testing for monetary errors or fraud and other irregularities to determine whether the nine balance-related audit objectives have been satisfied for each significant account balance (p. 318).

Types of tests—the four categories of audit tests auditors use to determine whether financial statements are fairly stated: procedures to obtain an understanding of internal control, tests of controls, analytical procedures, and tests of details of balances (p. 315).

REVIEW QUESTIONS

11-1 What are the four types of tests auditors use to determine whether financial statements are fairly stated? Identify which tests are performed to assess control risk and which tests are performed to achieve planned detection risk.

11-2 Distinguish between a test of controls and a substantive procedure. Give two examples of each.

11-3 Explain what is meant by "reperformance." Give an example. Why is reperformance often a dual-purpose test?

11-4 An auditor may perform tests of controls and substantive procedures simultaneously as a matter of audit convenience. However, the substantive procedures and sample size are, in part, dependent upon the results of the tests of controls. How can the auditor resolve this apparent inconsistency?

11-5 Explain how the calculation and comparison to previous years of the gross margin percentage and the ratio of accounts receivable to sales are related to the confirmation of accounts receivable and other tests of the accuracy of accounts receivable.

11-6 Distinguish between a combined audit approach and a substantive audit approach. Give one example of when each might be appropriate for the acquisition and payment cycle.

11-7 Assume that the client's internal controls over the recording and classifying of capital asset additions are considered weak because the individual responsible for recording new acquisitions has inadequate technical training and limited experience in accounting. How would this situation affect the evidence you should accumulate in auditing permanent assets as compared with another audit in which the controls are excellent? Be as specific as possible.

11-8 For each of the seven types of evidence discussed in Chapter 6, identify whether the evidence is applicable for procedures to obtain an understanding of internal control, tests of controls, analytical procedures, and tests of details of balances.

11-9 The following are three decision factors related to the assessed level of control risk: effectiveness of internal controls, cost-effectiveness of a reduced assessed level of control risk, and results of tests of controls. Identify the combination of conditions for these three factors that is required before a reduction in substantive procedures is permitted.

11-10 State the three-step approach to designing tests of controls.

11-11 Explain the relationship between the methodology for designing tests of transactions in Figure 11-5 (page 323) to the methodology for designing tests of details of balances in Figure 11-6 (page 325).

11-12 Why is it desirable to design tests of details of balances before performing tests of controls? State the assumptions the auditor must make in doing this. What does the auditor do if the assumptions prove to be incorrect?

11-13 Why do auditors frequently consider it desirable to perform audit tests throughout the year rather than wait until year end? List several examples of evidence that can be accumulated prior to year end.

MULTIPLE CHOICE QUESTIONS

11-14 Choose the best response for the following questions.

a. The auditor looks for an indication on duplicate sales invoices to see if the invoices have been verified. This is an example of

(1) a test of details of balances.

(2) an analytical procedure.
(3) a dual-purpose test.
(4) a test of controls.

b. Before reducing assessed control risk, the auditor obtains a reasonable degree of assurance that internal control is operating as planned. The auditor obtains this assurance by performing

(1) analytical procedures.
(2) substantive procedures.
(3) tests of controls.
(4) tests of trends and ratios.

c. Which of the following statements relating to tests of controls is most accurate?

(1) Auditing procedures cannot concurrently provide both evidence of the effectiveness of internal control and evidence required for substantive procedures.
(2) Tests of controls ordinarily should be performed as of the balance sheet date or during the period subsequent to that date.
(3) Tests of controls include observations of the proper segregation of duties that ordinarily may be limited to the normal audit period.
(4) Tests of controls should be based on proper application of an appropriate statistical sampling plan.

d. The two phases of the auditor's involvement with internal control are sometimes referred to as "understanding and assessment" and "tests of controls." In the tests of controls phase, the auditor attempts to obtain

(1) sufficient appropriate audit evidence to afford a reasonable basis for the auditor's opinion.
(2) assurances that informative disclosures in the financial statements are reasonably adequate.
(3) a reasonable degree of assurance that the client's controls are in use and are operating as planned.
(4) knowledge and understanding of the client's prescribed procedures and methods.

e. Which of the following is ordinarily considered a test of controls audit procedure?

(1) Send confirmation letters to banks.
(2) Obtain or prepare reconciliation of bank accounts as of the balance sheet date.
(3) Count and list cash on hand.
(4) Examine signatures on cheques.

(AICPA adapted)

DISCUSSION QUESTIONS AND PROBLEMS

11-15 The following are 11 audit procedures taken from an audit program:

1. Add the supplier balances in the accounts payable master file, and compare the total with the general ledger.
2. Examine vendors' invoices to verify the ending balance in accounts payable.
3. Compare the balance in employee benefits expense with previous years. The comparison takes the increase in employee benefits rates into account.
4. Discuss the duties of the cash disbursements bookkeeper with him or her, and observe whether he or she has responsibility for handling cash or preparing the bank reconciliation.
5. Confirm accounts payable balances directly with vendors.
6. Use generalized audit software to run a gap test on the cheques issued during the year. (Print a list of cheque numbers omitted from the normal cheque number sequencing.)

7. Examine the treasurer's initials on monthly bank reconciliations as an indication of whether they have been reviewed.
8. Examine vendors' invoices and other documentation in support of recorded transactions in the acquisitions journal.
9. Multiply the commission rate by total sales, and compare the result with commission expense.
10. Examine vendors' invoices and other supporting documents to determine whether large amounts in the repair and maintenance account should be capitalized.
11. Examine the initials of vendors' invoices that indicate internal verification of pricing, extending, and footing by a clerk.

Required

a. Indicate whether each procedure is a test of controls, an analytical procedure, or a test of details of balances.
b. Identify the type of evidence for each procedure.

11-16 Beds and Spreads, Inc. specializes in bed and bath furnishings. Its inventory system is linked through the Internet to key suppliers. The auditor identified the following internal controls in the inventory cycle:

1. The computer initiates an order only when perpetual inventory levels fall below prespecified inventory levels in the inventory master file.
2. The sales and purchasing department managers review inventory reorder points on a monthly basis for reasonableness. Approved changes to reorder points are entered into the master file by the purchasing department manager and an updated printout is generated for final review. Both managers verify that all changes were

entered correctly and initial the final printout indicating final approval. These printouts are maintained in the purchasing department.

3. The computer will initiate a purchase order only for inventory product numbers maintained in the inventory master file.
4. The purchasing department manager reviews a computer-generated exception report that highlights weekly purchases that exceed $10,000 per vendor.
5. Salesclerks send damaged merchandise on the store shelves to the back storage room. The sales department manager examines the damaged merchandise each month and prepares a listing showing the estimated

salvage value by product number. The accounting department uses the listing to prepare a monthly adjustment to recorded inventory values.

Required

a. Consider each of the preceding controls separately. State whether the control is manual, computer-assisted, or fully automated.

b. Describe how the extent of testing of each control would be affected in subsequent years if general controls are effective, particularly controls over program and master file changes.

c. For each control:
- provide an example of an audit procedure to test the control; and
- state the transaction-related audit objective associated with the audit procedure.

11-17 The following internal controls for the acquisition and payment cycle were selected from a standard internal control questionnaire.

1. Vendors' invoices are recalculated prior to payment.
2. Approved price lists are used for acquisitions.
3. Prenumbered receiving reports are prepared as support for purchases and are numerically accounted for.
4. Dates on receiving reports are compared with vendors' invoices before entry into the accounts payable system.
5. The accounts payable system is updated, balanced, and reconciled to the general ledger monthly.
6. Account classifications are reviewed by someone other than the preparer.
7. All cheques are signed by the owner or the manager.
8. The cheque signer compares data on supporting documents with cheques.
9. All supporting documents are cancelled after entry.
10. Cheques are mailed by the owner or manager, or a person under his or her supervision after signing.

Required

a. For each control, state which transaction-related audit objective(s) is (are) applicable.

b. For each control, write an audit procedure that could be used to test the control for effectiveness.

c. For each control, identify a likely misstatement, assuming the control does not exist or is not functioning.

d. For each likely misstatement, identify a substantive audit procedure to determine if the misstatement exists.

11-18 Jennifer Schaefer, a public accountant, follows the philosophy of performing interim tests of controls on every December 31 audit as a means of keeping overtime to a minimum. Typically, the interim tests are performed some time between August and November.

Required

a. Evaluate her decision to perform interim tests of controls.

b. Under what circumstances is it acceptable for her to perform no additional tests of controls work as part of the year-end audit tests?

c. If she decides to perform no additional testing, what is the effect on other tests she performs during the remainder of the engagement?

11-19 The following are three situations in which the auditor is required to develop an audit strategy:

1. The client has inventory at approximately 50 locations in the three Maritime provinces. The inventory is difficult to count and can be observed only by travelling by automobile. The internal controls over acquisitions, payments, and perpetual records are considered effective. This is the fifth year that you have done the audit, and audit results in past years have always been excellent.

2. This is the first year of an audit of a medium-sized company that is considering selling its business because of severe underfinancing. A review of the acquisition and payment cycle indicates that controls over disbursements are excellent, but controls over accounts payable cannot be considered effective. The client lacks receiving reports and a policy as to the proper timing to record acquisitions. When you review the general ledger, you observe that there are many adjusting entries to correct accounts payable.

3. You are doing the audit of a small loan company with extensive receivables from customers. Controls over granting loans, collections, and loans outstanding are considered effective, and there is extensive follow-up of all outstanding loans weekly. You have recommended a computer system for the past two years, but management believes the cost is too great, given the company's low profitability. Collections are an ongoing problem because many of the customers have severe financial problems. Because of adverse economic conditions, loans receivable have significantly increased and collections are less than normal. In previous years, you have had relatively few adjusting entries.

Required

a. For audit one, recommend an evidence mix for the four types of tests for the audit of inventory and cost of goods sold. Justify your answer.

b. For audit two, recommend an evidence mix for the audit of acquisitions and accounts payable. Justify your answer.

c. For audit three, recommend an evidence mix of the audit of outstanding loans. Justify your answer.

11-20 Kim Bryan, a new staff auditor, is confused by the inconsistency of the three audit partners to whom she has been assigned on her first three audit engagements. On the first engagement, she spent a considerable amount of time in the audit of cash disbursements by examining cancelled cheques and supporting documentation, but almost no time was spent on the verification of capital assets. On the second engagement, a different partner had her do less intensive tests in the cash disbursements area and take smaller sample sizes than in the first audit even though the company was much larger. On her most recent engagement under a third audit partner, there was a thorough test of cash disbursement transactions, far beyond that of the other two audits, and an extensive verification of capital assets. In fact, this partner insisted on a complete physical examination of all capital assets recorded on the books. The total audit time on the most recent audit was longer than that of either of the first two audits in spite of the smaller size of the company. Bryan's conclusion is that the amount of evidence to accumulate depends on the audit partner in charge of the engagement.

Required

a. State several factors that could explain the difference in the amount of evidence accumulated in each of the three audit engagements as well as the total time spent.
b. What could the audit partners have done to help Bryan understand the difference in the audit emphasis on the three audits?
c. Explain how these three audits are useful in developing Bryan's professional judgment. How could the quality of her judgment have been improved on the audits?

11-21 The following are parts of a typical audit for a company with a fiscal year end of July 31.

1. Confirm accounts payable.
2. Do tests of controls for acquisitions and payroll.
3. Do other tests of details of balances for accounts payable.
4. Do tests for review of subsequent events.
5. Preplan the audit.
6. Issue the auditor's report.
7. Understand internal control and assess control risk.
8. Do analytical procedures for accounts payable.
9. Set audit risk and decide preliminary judgment about materiality.
10. Summarize client risk profile.

Required

a. Put parts 1 through 10 of the audit in the sequential order in which you would expect them to be performed in a typical audit.
b. Identify those parts that would frequently be done before July 31.

PROFESSIONAL JUDGMENT PROBLEM

11-22 Gale Brewer, PA, has been the partner in charge of the audit of Merkle Manufacturing Company for 13 years. Merkle has had excellent growth and profits in the past decade, primarily as a result of the excellent leadership provided by Bill Merkle and other competent executives. Brewer has always enjoyed a close relationship with the company and prides himself on having made several constructive comments over the years that have aided in the success of the firm. Several times in the past few years, Brewer's PA firm has considered rotating a different audit team on the engagement, but this has been strongly resisted by both Brewer and Merkle.

For the first few years of the audit, internal controls were inadequate and the accounting personnel had inadequate qualifications for their responsibilities. Extensive audit evidence was required during the audit, and numerous adjusting entries were necessary. However, because of Brewer's constant prodding, internal controls improved gradually and competent personnel were hired. In recent years, there were normally no audit adjustments required, and the extent of the evidence accumulation was gradually reduced. During the past 3 years, Brewer was able to devote less time to the audit because of the relative ease of conducting the audit and the cooperation obtained throughout the engagement.

In the current year's audit, Brewer decided that the total time budget for the engagement should be kept approximately the same as in recent years. The senior in charge of the audit, Phil Warren, was new on the job and highly competent, and he had the reputation of being able to cut time off the budget. The fact that Merkle had recently acquired a new division through merger would probably add to the time, but Warren's efficiency would probably compensate for it.

The interim tests of controls took somewhat longer than expected because of the use of several new assistants, a change in the accounting system to computerize the inventory and other accounting records, a change in accounting personnel, and the existence of a few more errors in the tests of the system. Neither Brewer nor Warren was concerned about the budget deficit, however, because they could easily make up the difference at year end.

At year end, Warren assigned the responsibility for inventory to an assistant who also had not been on the audit before but was competent and extremely fast at his work. Even though the total value of inventory increased, he reduced the size of the sample from that of other years because there had been few errors in the preceding year. He found several items in the sample that were overstated as a result of errors in pricing and obsolescence, but the combination of all of the errors in the sample was immaterial. He completed the tests in 25 percent less time than the preceding year. The entire audit was completed on schedule and in slightly less time than the preceding year. There were only a few adjusting entries for the year, and only two of them were material. Brewer was extremely pleased with the results and wrote a special letter to Warren and the inventory assistant complimenting them on the audit.

Six months later, Brewer received a telephone call from Merkle and was informed that the company was in serious financial trouble. Subsequent investigation revealed that the inventory had been significantly overstated. The major cause of the misstatement was the inclusion of obsolete items in inventory (especially in the new division), errors in pricing as a result of the new computer system, and the inclusion of nonexistent inventory in the final inventory listing. Inventory had been intentionally overstated to compensate for the reduction in sales volume from the preceding year.

Required

a. List the major deficiencies in the audit and state why they took place.

b. What threats to independence had been ignored by Brewer?
c. What things should have been apparent to Brewer in the conduct of the audit?
d. If Brewer's firm is sued for negligence, what is the likely outcome?

CASE

11-23 Yope Plastics Limited (YPL) is a federally incorporated company that manufactures moulded plastics for household and some industrial uses. It has a large number of customers throughout Canada. Some items are custom-made but most are for stock. It is estimated that sales for the current year will be approximately $5,800,000 and net income $265,000. Major assets are accounts receivable ($1,400,00) and inventories ($1,700,000 of which $500,000 is raw materials, $200,000 work in process, and $1,000,000 finished goods). Major liabilities are bank debt amounting to $900,000 and accounts payable and accruals of $650,000. The year end is December 31.

The company has been managed by Mr. Yope, the owner, assisted by Mr. Grey, a competent but rather unimaginative treasurer/controller. The accounting systems have been adequate but not elaborate. No serious weaknesses in internal control have existed. The owner has had a rule-of-thumb method of calculating inventory balances in interim periods, which is based on his knowledge of the operations and a tour of the plant. The inventory computed in this way by the owner has always coincided fairly closely with the audited inventory figure at the year end. The general ledger inventory accounts have been updated annually at the December 31 year end.

The annual financial statements have been used for Mr. Yope's own purposes, for income tax purposes, and for the bank. The financial statements were basically prepared by the auditor, who also prepared a number of detailed back-up schedules.

Fairly, Small & Co. has been the auditor for many years, is very familiar with the company, and, among other services, carries out a statutory audit. Mrs. Keen, CA, has just been appointed partner responsible for the client as a result of the retirement of one of the five partners in the firm. She has been involved with the audit ever since joining the firm as a student a few years previously. The senior who will be in charge of the fieldwork this year has had two years' experience with the client and will have two assistants working for him from time to time.

The audit has always been routine and there has never been any trouble except for minor arguments over fees. Mr. Yope has always been very cooperative but is not at all knowledgeable on accounting and financial matters. His background is engineering and he is an inventor. In the past, the auditors have reviewed internal control and done some preliminary planning in the month of October. Minimum reliance has been placed on the internal control system because the work has been heavily concentrated on the year-end amounts. Tests of controls have not been necessary except in the sales system to obtain reasonable assurance that all sales were recorded. The inventory count, cash count, and cutoff information were taken at December 31 of each year, and the receivable, payable, and other confirmations were as at December 31 and mailed in mid- to late January. The year-end audit work was usually started in mid-February and finished in early March, which was the usual date of the auditor's report.

On March 31, 2004, Many Conglomerate Limited (MCL), also a federally incorporated company, purchased all the shares of YPL. Mr. Yope was retained as general manager, and Mr. Grey was also retained. In June 2004, MCL sent an accounting and systems person who

1. instructed Mr. Grey regarding a monthly and year-end reporting package and a new chart of accounts. No substantial changes were found to be necessary except as noted below with respect to inventories.
2. devised and installed a cost system, which enabled general ledger accounts to be updated on a monthly basis to account separately for raw materials, work in process, and finished goods.
3. prepared a budget for the coming year and instituted a budgeting system covering revenues and expenses and key balance sheet items.

Since then, Mrs. Keen has learned that Mr. Grey has adapted reasonably well to the monthly reporting and that the new inventory system does not seem to be causing major problems. However, Mr. Yope insists that it is too expensive and still relies on his rule of thumb. Mr. Grey has not yet come to grips with the budgeting system. Under the new system, the monthly trial balances (general ledger, accounts receivable, etc.) are usually ready by the 12th of the following month, and it takes about one additional day to prepare the reporting package for MCL. Mrs. Keen has also learned that YPL is planning to take its physical inventory at October 31, 2004, and then to rely on the general ledger entries between that date and the year end.

Fairly, Small & Co. has been informed that it will continue as auditor of YPL and that the company year end will remain at December 31. Mrs. Keen has also been informed of the following matters by Giant and Co., the auditor of MCL:

1. A normal scope statutory audit will be satisfactory for consolidation purposes. However, Fairly, Small & Co. is expected to ensure that the year-end reporting package provided by the company to MCL for consolidation purposes is reconciled to the audited financial statements prepared for shareholders. It will also be expected to initial each page of the package for identification purposes and ship it directly to Giant and Co.
2. Giant and Co. will be relying on Fairly, Small & Co.'s report.
3. The audit has to be completed and the report signed by January 31, 2005.

Required

a. What further information should Mrs. Keen obtain from Giant and Co. and for what reasons?
b. Prepare a memorandum from Mrs. Keen to her senior staff member who will be running the fieldwork, outlining for him, in point form, the nature of the changes that must be made to the previous year's auditing approach so that he can prepare a

detailed audit program. The memorandum should cover

(1) general matters of which the audit staff should be made aware;

(2) changes that will be necessary in the review and evaluation of internal controls;

(3) changes in the nature and timing of other auditing procedures, particularly those relating to major asset and liability accounts.

The memorandum should be comprehensive in describing the changes in the approach required but should not be a detailed list of auditing procedures, since the intention is that the senior prepare such a list. The memorandum should also point out areas where the change in approach would eliminate the necessity for work that was done in previous years.

(CICA adapted)

CHAPTER 12

AUDIT SAMPLING CONCEPTS

Since the auditor uses testing of transactions, there needs to be a means of choosing which items will be examined. Then, once the items have been chosen and audited, it is important to extrapolate the results to the population. In this chapter, you will look at the different types of sampling methods that an auditor is likely to use, and the role of judgment during the sampling process.

LEARNING OBJECTIVES

After reading this chapter, you should be able to answer the following questions:

1. **What is sampling? Why would an auditor use statistical rather than nonstatistical sampling? What are the different types of nonprobabilistic (nonstatistical) sampling methods used by auditors?**

2. **What are the three different ways that an auditor can select a statistical sample? List three common statistical sampling methodologies used by auditors.**

3. **Describe the 14 steps in planning, selecting, performing the tests, and evaluating a sample. What are four additional issues the auditor should consider during the sampling process?**

$1 BILLION IS A BIG NUMBER!

"How can they say that pensioners are underpaid by up to $1 billion? They only looked at about four thousand pensioners when there are two million people that are paid pensions," says Julie. Chang explained, "They must have taken a statistical sample. See—they say in the article that 15 percent of those audited had lower monthly payouts. This analysis of Canada's pension payments goes on to explain why those errors occurred."

The study above was conducted by the Retirement Planning Institute and illustrates how statistics are frequently quoted without clearly stating how numbers were developed. To help ensure that auditors properly document their use of statistics and the results, many audit software products are available. Such software is also used by internal auditors to extract data and analyze it in a variety of ways that could include statistical sampling and projection of error rates to the population from which the sample was selected.

Sources: 1. Campbell, Morgan, 2004. "Benefits errors cost pensioners up to $1 billion, study estimates," The Toronto Star, November 23, 2004. 2. Jackson, Russell A., 2004. "Get the most out of audit tools," Internal Auditor, Vol. LXI:IV, August 2004.

Do you think statements about testing should be carefully worded? What would you say to management if you found many errors of $1,000 that could be extrapolated to a potential misstatement of $15 million? How would you justify a correcting journal entry?

→12.1   THE NATURE OF SAMPLING

AICPA's Auditing Standards Board
www.aicpa.org/

The *CICA Assurance Handbook* in paragraph 5300.14 states that the auditor does not examine all the available evidence but rather examines samples from the available population, although sampling is not specifically defined. The AICPA's Auditing Standards Board in SAS 39 defines audit sampling as:

> The application of an audit procedure to less than 100 percent of the items within an audit balance or class of transactions for the purpose of evaluating some characteristics of the balance or class.

"Application of an audit procedure" in this definition means dealing with three aspects of audit sampling: (1) planning the sample, (2) selecting the sample and performing the tests, and (3) evaluating the results. As the chapter title implies, this chapter discusses sampling concepts, as applied to tests of controls or tests of details. The sales and collection cycle and its transactions are used as a frame of reference for discussing these concepts, but the concepts apply to any cycle. Chapter 13 applies these concepts to tests of controls, and Chapter 14 applies audit sampling to tests of details of balances. Figure 12-1, which uses the same information as Figure 11-1 on page 318, shows how audit sampling is related to the types of audit tests.

Chapter 13 and Chapter 14 are directly related to Chapter 12 in that the auditor must decide the audit procedures he or she plans to perform before applying audit sampling.

Representative Samples

REPRESENTATIVE SAMPLE—a sample with the same characteristics as those of the population

Whenever an auditor selects a sample from a population, the objective is to obtain a *representative* one. A **representative sample** is one in which the characteristics in the sample of audit interest are approximately the same as those of the population. This means that the sampled items are similar to the items not sampled. For example, assume that a client's internal controls require a clerk to attach a shipping document to every duplicate sales invoice, but the procedure is not followed exactly 3 percent of the time. If the auditor selects a sample of 100 duplicate sales invoices and finds 3 missing, the sample is highly representative. If two or four such items are found in the sample, the sample is reasonably representative. If many missing items or none are found, the sample is *nonrepresentative*.

In practice, auditors do not know whether a sample is representative, even after all testing is completed. Auditors can, however, increase the likelihood of a sample being

FIGURE 12-1   How Audit Sampling Is Related to the Types of Audit Tests

representative by using care in sample design, selection, and evaluation. Two things can cause a sample result to be nonrepresentative: nonsampling error and sampling error. The risk of these occurring is termed **nonsampling risk** and **sampling risk**; both can be controlled.

Nonsampling risk (nonsampling error) occurs when audit tests do not uncover existing exceptions in the sample. In the previous example in which three shipping documents were not attached to duplicate sales invoices, if the auditor concluded that no exceptions existed, there is a nonsampling error.

The two causes of nonsampling error are the auditor's failure to recognize exceptions and inappropriate or ineffective audit procedures. An auditor might fail to recognize an exception because of exhaustion, boredom, or lack of understanding of what constitutes an exception. Take for example the control of attaching a shipping document to the duplicate sales invoice. An exception would be defined as a missing document or a shipping document that does not agree to the sales invoice. An ineffective audit procedure for these exceptions would be the selection of a sample of shipping documents to determine if each is attached to a set of duplicate sales invoices. The auditor in this case would be unable to determine whether there were numerous sales invoices unsupported by shipping documents, since such sales invoices could not be selected. Careful design of audit procedures and proper supervision and instruction are ways to reduce nonsampling risk.

Sampling risk (sampling error) is an inherent part of sampling that results from testing less than the entire population. Even with zero nonsampling error, there is always a chance that a sample is not representative. For example, if a population has a 3 percent exception rate, the auditor could easily select a sample of 100 items containing no exceptions or many.

There are two ways to control sampling risk: increase sample size and use an appropriate method of selecting sample items from the population. Increasing sample size will reduce sampling risk, and vice versa. At the extreme, testing all the items of a population will have a zero sampling risk (since this is no longer sampling). Using an appropriate sampling method will reasonably assure representativeness. This does not eliminate or even reduce sampling risk, but it does allow the auditor to measure the sample risk associated with a given sample size in a reliable manner.

Statistical Versus Nonstatistical Sampling

Audit sampling methods can be divided into two broad categories: statistical and nonstatistical. These categories have important similarities and differences. They are similar in that they both involve the three steps identified in the introduction: (1) plan the sample, (2) select the sample and perform the tests, and (3) evaluate the results. The purpose of planning the sample is to make sure that the audit tests are performed in a manner that provides the desired sampling risk and minimizes the likelihood of nonsampling error. Selecting the sample involves deciding how to select sample items from the population. Performing the tests involves examining documents and performing other audit tests. Evaluating the results involves drawing conclusions based on the audit tests. To illustrate, assume that an auditor selects a sample of 100 duplicate sales invoices from a population, tests each to determine if a shipping document is attached, and determines that there are three exceptions. Deciding that a sample size of 100 is needed is a part of planning the sample. Deciding which 100 items to select from the population is a sample selection problem. Doing the audit procedure for each of the 100 items and determining that there were 3 exceptions constitutes performing the tests. Reaching conclusions about the likely exception rate in the total population when there is a sample exception rate of 3 percent is evaluating the results.

Statistical sampling differs from nonstatistical sampling in that, through the application of mathematical rules, it allows the quantification (measurement) of sampling risk in planning the sample (step 1) and evaluating the results (step 3). (You may remember calculating a statistical result at a 95 percent **confidence level** in a statistics course. The 95 percent confidence level provides a 5 percent sampling risk.) The quantification of sampling risk is appropriate only when the auditor selects the sample (step 2) using a *probabilistic* sample, which is discussed shortly.

In nonstatistical sampling, the auditor does not quantify sampling risk. Instead, the auditor selects those sample items that he or she believes will provide the most useful

NONSAMPLING RISK—the chance of exception when audit tests do not uncover existing exceptions in the sample; caused by failure to recognize exceptions and by inappropriate or ineffective audit procedures; synonymous with nonsampling error

SAMPLING RISK—the chance of exception inherent in tests of less than the entire population; may be reduced by using an increased sample size and using an appropriate method of selecting sample items from the population

STATISTICAL SAMPLING—the use of mathematical measurement techniques to calculate formal statistical results and quantify sampling risk

CONFIDENCE LEVEL—statement of probability

information in the circumstances (i.e., *nonprobabilistic* samples are chosen), and conclusions are reached about populations on a judgmental basis. For that reason, the selection of nonprobabilistic samples is often termed **judgmental sampling**.

It is equally acceptable under professional standards for auditors to use either statistical or nonstatistical sampling methods. However, it is essential that either method be applied with due care. All steps of the process must be followed carefully. When statistical sampling is used, the sample must be a probabilistic one, and appropriate statistical evaluation methods must be used with the sample results to make the sampling risk computations.

It is also acceptable to make nonstatistical evaluations by using probabilistic selection, but many practitioners prefer not to do so. They believe that statistical measurement of sampling risk is inherent in those samples and should not be ignored. It is *never* acceptable, however, to evaluate a nonprobabilistic sample as if it were a statistical sample. A summary of the relationship of probabilistic and nonprobabilistic selection to statistical and nonstatistical evaluation is shown in Table 12-1.

There are three types of sample selection methods commonly associated with nonstatistical audit sampling and three types of sample selection methods commonly associated with statistical audit sampling. These are listed below and discussed in the following sections.

The nonprobabilistic (judgmental) sample selection methods are:

- Directed sample selection
- Block sample selection
- Haphazard sample selection

Probabilistic sample selection methods are:

- Simple random sample selection
- Systematic sample selection
- Probability proportionate-to-size sample selection

Stratified sample selection can be applied to both nonprobabilistic and probabilistic sample selection methods.

Nonprobabilistic Sample Selection

Nonprobabilistic sample selection methods are those that do not meet the technical requirements for probabilistic sample selection. Since these methods are not based on strict mathematical probabilities, the representativeness of the sample may be difficult to determine. The information content of the sample, including its representativeness, will be based on the knowledge and skill of the auditor in applying his or her judgment in the circumstances.

Directed Sample Selection **Directed sample selection** is the selection of each item in the sample based on some judgmental criteria established by the auditor. The auditor does not rely on equal chances of selection, but, rather, deliberately selects items according to the criteria. Some auditors consider certain directed samples to be a form of analytical review. The important issue is ensuring that the test is clearly defined and its audit role identified. The criteria may relate to representativeness, or they may not. Commonly used criteria are the following:

ITEMS MOST LIKELY TO CONTAIN MISSTATEMENTS Frequently, auditors are able to identify which population items are most likely to be misstated. Examples are receivables outstanding for a long

TABLE 12-1	Relationship of Methods of Selecting Samples to Evaluating Results	
	Method of Evaluating Results	
Method of Selecting Sample	Statistical	Nonstatistical
Probabilistic	Preferable to use statistical	Acceptable to use nonstatistical
Nonprobabilistic	Not acceptable to use statistical	Mandatory to use nonstatistical

time, purchases from and sales to officers and affiliated companies, and unusually large or complex transactions. These kinds of items can be efficiently investigated by the auditor, and the results can be applied to the population on a judgmental basis. The reasoning underlying the evaluation of such samples is often that if none of the items selected contain misstatements, then it is highly unlikely that a material misstatement exists in the population.

ITEMS CONTAINING SELECTED POPULATION CHARACTERISTICS The auditor may be able to describe the various types and sources of items that make up the population and design the sample to be representative by selecting one or more items of each type. For example, a sample of cash disbursements might include some from each month, each bank account or location, and each major type of acquisition.

LARGE DOLLAR COVERAGE A sample can often be selected to cover such a large portion of total population dollars that the risk of drawing an improper conclusion by not examining small items is not a concern. For example, all transactions that have a value in excess of materiality could be examined. This is a practical approach on many audits, especially smaller ones. There are also statistical methods that are intended to accomplish the same effect.

Focus Box 12-1

PLAYING WITH NUMBERS?

You found a gorgeous second-hand desk on eBay for an unbelievable price—only $250! The eBay statistics said that the seller had completed over 600 transactions with a 99 percent positive feedback rate, so you decided to put up your credit card and pay. You waited and waited, and four weeks later you still had not received the desk. Checking eBay again, you found that there were at least 75 negative feedback comments about customers not receiving their products, all posted within a period of three weeks. It turned out that someone had hacked into the seller's accounts and was taking the money. The positive feedback statistics were no longer valid.

Health Connecticut is a consortium of 22 hospitals. The consortium recently implemented a web-based data warehouse that contains information about patients including illnesses and treatments provided. The hospitals are using online analytical processing (OLAP) to look at their entire patient population. They are examining healthcare trends and the costs of those trends. For example, if it seems that many patients are getting pneumonia, they will try to stock up on medication at bulk rates before the products are scarce and prices are driven up. With about 100,000 patients, they expect to save at least $8 million over two years. How do you measure these savings? What if prices do not go up on scarcity? Perhaps the costs would never have materialized.

These modern numerical analysis techniques rest upon classic selection methods. The eBay example is a haphazard sample (there was no distinguishing feature) while the Health Connecticut consortium is using directed sample selection (selecting items with specific population characteristics).

Sources: 1. Catrini, Vincent, 2003. "No catch-22 here: for 22 Connecticut hospitals, using a uniform web-based decision support system has cut operating costs and streamlined business," *Health Management Technology*, Vol. 23 (3), pp. 24–26. 2. Morochove, Richard, 2004. "Your online reputation is precious. Here's how to guard it," *The Toronto Star*, January 5, 2004, p. E2.

Block Sample Selection A **block sample** is the selection of several items in sequence. Once the first item in the block is selected, the remainder of the block is chosen automatically. One example of a block sample is the selection of a sequence of 100 sales transactions from the sales journal for the third week of March. A total sample of 100 could also be selected by taking 5 blocks of 20 items each, 10 blocks of 10, or 50 blocks of 2.

> BLOCK SAMPLE—a nonprobabilistic method of sample selection in which items are selected in measured sequences

It is ordinarily acceptable to use block samples only if a reasonable number of blocks are used. If few blocks are used, the probability of obtaining a nonrepresentative sample is too great, considering the possibility of such things as employee turnover, changes in the accounting system, and the seasonal nature of many businesses.

A common use of block testing is testing cutoff. The auditor would select a block of invoices, receiving documents, and shipping documents spanning both sides of the year-end date to ensure that the transactions were recorded in the proper period.

Haphazard Sample Selection When the auditor goes through a population and selects items for the sample without regard to their size, source, or other distinguishing characteristics, he or she is attempting to select without bias. This is called a **haphazard sample selection**.

The most serious shortcoming of haphazard sample selection is the difficulty of remaining completely unbiased in the selection. Because of the auditor's training and "cultural bias," certain population items are more likely than others to be included in the sample. For example, auditors may be inclined to select larger amounts or amounts from the middle of a period, or to avoid round dollar amounts.

Although haphazard and block sample selection appear to be less logical than directed sample selection, they are often useful as audit tools and should not be ignored. In some situations, the cost of more complex sample selection methods outweighs the benefits obtained from using them. For example, assume that the auditor wants to trace credits from the accounts receivable transaction history files to the duplicate bank deposit slips and other authorized sources as a test for fictitious credits in the data files. A haphazard or block approach is simpler and much less costly than other selection methods in this situation, and would be employed by many auditors.

→12.2 PROBABILISTIC AND STATISTICAL SAMPLES

Probabilistic Sample Selection

As previously indicated, to measure sampling risk, statistical sampling requires a **probabilistic sample**. There are three methods commonly used by auditors to obtain probabilistic samples: simple random sample selection, systematic sample selection, and stratified sample selection.

Simple Random Sample Selection A simple **random sample** is one in which every possible combination of elements in the population has an equal chance of constituting the sample. Simple random sampling is used to sample populations that are not segmented for audit purposes. For example, the auditor may wish to sample the client's cash disbursements for the year. A simple random sample of 60 items contained in the cash disbursements journal might be selected for that purpose. Appropriate auditing procedures would be applied to the 60 items selected, and conclusions would be drawn and applied to all cash disbursement transactions recorded for the year.

RANDOM NUMBER TABLES When a simple random sample is obtained, a method must be used that assures that all items in the population have an equal chance of selection. Suppose that in the above example there were a total of 12,000 cash disbursement transactions for the year. A simple random sample of one transaction would be such that each of the 12,000 transactions would have an equal chance of being selected. This would be done by obtaining a *random number* between 1 and 12,000. If the number were 3,895, the auditor would select and test the 3,895th cash disbursement transaction recorded in the cash disbursements journal.

Random numbers are a series of digits that have equal probabilities of occurring over long runs and that have no discernible pattern. An example of a commonly used **random number table** is the *Table of 105,000 Random Decimal Digits*, published by the U.S. Interstate Commerce Commission. A page from that table appears in Table 12-2. This table has numbered rows and columns, with five digits in each column. This format is convenient for reading the table and documenting the portion of the table used. The presentation of the digits as five-digit numbers is purely arbitrary.

It is easy, but time-consuming, to select samples using a random number table. For example, assume that the auditor is selecting a sample of 100 sales invoices from a file of prenumbered sales invoices beginning with document number 3,272 and ending with 8,825. Since the invoices use four digits, it is necessary to use four digits in the random number table. Assuming the first four digits of each five-digit set were used, and the arbitrary starting point in the random number table in Table 12-2 is row 1,009, column 2, then reading down, the first invoice for inclusion in the sample is 3,646. The next usable number is 6,186 since the next three numbers are all outside the population range.

COMPUTER GENERATION OF RANDOM NUMBERS It is useful to understand the use of random number tables as a means of understanding the concept of selecting simple random samples. However, most random samples obtained by auditors are obtained by using computer programs. There are three main types of these: electronic spreadsheet programs, random number generators, and generalized audit software programs.

The advantages of using computer programs in selecting random samples are time savings, reduced likelihood of auditor error in selecting the numbers, and automatic documentation. To illustrate computer generation of random numbers, Figure 12-2 shows a printout from a spreadsheet program. In the application illustrated, the auditor wishes to sample 30 items from a population of documents numbered from 140,672 to 283,294. The program requires only input parameters and the use of a predefined spreadsheet function by the auditor for a sample to be selected. The auditor can use the spreadsheet to generate random dates or ranges of sets of numbers (such as page and line numbers). It also provides output in both sorted and selection orders by means of the spreadsheet sort function.

REPLACEMENT VERSUS NONREPLACEMENT SAMPLING Random numbers may be obtained with replacement or without replacement. In *replacement sampling*, an element in the population can be included in the sample more than once, whereas in nonreplacement sampling, an element can be included only once. If the random number corresponding to an element is selected

TABLE 12-2	Random Number Table							
				Column				
Row	(1)	(2)	(3)	(4)	(5)	(6)	(7)	(8)
1000	37039	97547	64673	31546	99314	66854	97855	99965
1001	25145	84834	23009	51584	66754	77785	52357	25532
1002	98433	54725	18864	65866	76918	78825	58210	76835
1003	97965	68548	81545	82933	93545	85959	63282	61454
1004	78049	67830	14624	17563	25697	07734	48243	94318
1005	50203	25658	91478	08509	23308	48130	65047	77873
1006	40059	67825	18934	64998	49807	71126	77818	56893
1007	84350	67241	54031	34535	04093	35062	58163	14205
1008	30954	51637	91500	48722	60988	60029	60873	37423
1009	86723	36464	98305	08009	00666	29255	18514	49158
1010	50188	22554	86160	92250	14021	65859	16237	72296
1011	50014	00463	13906	35936	71761	95755	87002	71667
1012	66023	21428	14742	94874	23308	58533	26507	11208
1013	04458	61862	63119	09541	01715	87901	91260	03079
1014	57510	36314	30452	09712	37714	95482	30507	68475
1015	43373	58939	95848	28288	60341	52174	11879	18115
1016	61500	12763	64433	02268	57905	72347	49498	21871
1017	78938	71312	99705	71546	42274	23915	38405	18779
1018	64257	93218	35793	43671	64055	88729	11168	60260
1019	56864	21554	70445	24841	04779	56774	96129	73594
1020	35314	29631	06937	54545	04470	75463	77112	77126
1021	40704	48823	65963	39359	12717	56201	22811	24863
1022	07318	44623	02843	33299	59872	86774	06926	12672
1023	94550	23299	45557	07923	75126	00808	01312	46689
1024	34348	81191	21027	77087	10909	03676	97723	34469
1025	92277	57115	50789	68111	75305	53289	39751	45760
1026	56093	58302	52236	64756	50273	61566	61962	93280
1027	16623	17849	96701	94971	94758	08845	32260	59823
1028	50848	93982	66451	32143	05441	10399	17775	74169
1029	48006	58200	58367	66577	68583	21108	41361	20732
1030	56640	27890	28825	96509	21363	53657	60119	75385

more than once in nonreplacement sampling, it is not included in the sample a second time. Although both selection approaches are consistent with sound statistical theory, auditors rarely use replacement sampling.

Systematic Sample Selection In **systematic selection** (also known as *systematic sampling*), the auditor calculates an *interval* and then methodically selects the items for the sample based on the size of the interval. The interval is determined by dividing the population size by the number of sample items desired. For example, if a population of sales invoices ranges from 652 to 3,151 and the desired sample size is 125, the interval is 20 $[(3,151 - 651) \div 125]$. The auditor must now select a random number between 0 and 19 to determine the starting point for the sample. If the randomly selected number is 9, the first item in the sample is invoice number 661 (652 + 9). The remaining 124 items are 681 (661 + 20), 701 (681 + 20), and so on through item 3,141.

The advantage of systematic sampling is its *ease of use*. For most populations, the systematic sample can be drawn quickly, the approach automatically puts the numbers in sequence, and the appropriate documentation is easy to develop.

A major problem with systematic selection is the possibility of bias. Because of the way systematic selection works, once the first item in the sample is selected, all other items are chosen automatically. This causes no problem if the characteristic of interest, such as a possible control deviation, is distributed randomly throughout the population; however, in

FIGURE 12-2	Random Selection by Use of a Computer

RANGE

Lower	140,672
Upper	283,294

RANDOM NUMBERS

SELECTION ORDER		NUMERICAL ORDER	
		Sequence	Number
1	177,611	17	142,591
2	163,763	9	144,408
3	217,029	23	147,181
4	235,986	5	150,176
5	150,176	7	153,469
6	197,030	15	156,779
7	153,469	2	163,763
8	213,150	25	167,818
9	144,408	13	176,955
10	269,030	1	177,611
11	280,501	16	188,114
12	237,619	14	189,598
13	176,955	30	191,932
14	189,598	6	197,030
15	156,779	21	197,202
16	188,114	22	204,645
17	142,591	19	208,234
18	217,753	24	209,025
19	208,234	28	210,168
20	264,071	8	213,150
21	197,202	3	217,029
22	204,645	18	217,753
23	147,181	26	227,659
24	209,025	4	235,986
25	167,818	12	237,619
26	227,659	27	242,681
27	242,681	20	264,071
28	210,168	10	269,030
29	281,047	11	280,501
30	191,932	29	281,047

Source: Random selection prepared using @RAND function of spreadsheet software.

some cases, characteristics of interest may not be randomly distributed. For example, if a control deviation occurred at a certain time of the month or with certain types of documents, a systematic sample could have a higher likelihood of failing to be representative than a simple random sample. It is important, therefore, when systematic selection is used, to consider possible patterns in the population data that could cause sample bias.

A variation of systematic sample selection by unit of interest is used by the probability-proportionate-to-size (PPS) sampling methods, described in the next section. Here, the individual dollar is considered the unit of interest. The interval is determined based upon a statistical formula, and the transactions associated with that dollar interval are selected.

Stratified Sample Selection When a sample is *stratified,* it is split into smaller sets where each set has a similar characteristic. For example, stratification can occur by dollar amount (sales over $50,000, sales under that amount), by location (foreign vs. domestic), or by another criteria, such as whether commissions will be paid (sales from head office vs. made by travelling sales personnel). This can improve the efficiency of the audit by focusing work on transactions that may be more readily subject to material error. After data are stratified, the sample will be selected using one of the methods previously discussed (either probabilistic or nonprobabilistic).

Statistical Sampling Methodologies

Once the decision has been made to conduct statistical sampling, the auditor may choose from three broad categories of statistical sampling: attribute, probability-proportionate-to-size (PPS), and variables. (Discovery sampling is also described, but this is a subset of attribute sampling.) These methods are based upon underlying **sampling distributions**, such as binomial or normal distributions, which are beyond the scope of this text. Review your statistics text to examine these distributions. All three categories of sampling can be used for tests of controls or tests of details, although attribute sampling is normally used for controls testing while PPS and variables sampling are normally used for tests of details testing.

Attribute Sampling **Attribute sampling** is used to estimate the *proportion* of items in a population containing a characteristic or **attribute** of interest. This proportion is called the **occurrence rate** or **exception rate** and is the ratio of the items containing the specific attribute to the total number of population items. The occurrence rate is usually expressed as a percentage. For example, an auditor might conclude that the exception rate for the internal verification of sales invoices is approximately 3 percent, meaning that invoices are not properly verified 3 percent of the time. This methodology is designed to answer the question, How many items contain errors?

Auditors are interested in the occurrence of the following types of exceptions in populations of accounting data: (1) deviations from client's established controls, (2) monetary errors or fraud and other irregularities in populations of transaction data, and (3) monetary errors or fraud and other irregularities in populations of account balance details. Knowing the occurrence rate of such exceptions is particularly helpful for the first two types of exceptions, which relate to transactions. Therefore, auditors make extensive use of audit sampling that measures the occurrence or exception rate in performing tests of controls. With the third type of exception, the auditor usually needs to estimate the total dollar amount of the exceptions because a judgment must be made about whether the exceptions are material. When the auditor wants to know the total amount of a misstatement, he or she will use methods that measure dollars, not the exception or occurrence rate, such as PPS or variables methodologies.

The statistical sampling method most commonly used for tests of controls is *attribute sampling*. Whenever attribute sampling is used in this text, it refers to attribute statistical sampling for physical units. Both attribute sampling and nonstatistical sampling have attributes, which are the characteristics being tested for in the population, but attribute sampling is a statistical method. Attribute sampling is used primarily for tests of controls, but auditors also use attribute sampling for substantive procedures, particularly when performing dual purpose tests.

Attribute sampling may be based on physical units (e.g., invoices) or monetary units

SAMPLING DISTRIBUTION—a frequency distribution of the results of all possible samples of a specified size that could be obtained from a population containing some specific parameters

ATTRIBUTE SAMPLING—a statistical, probabilistic method of sample evaluation that results in an estimate of the proportion of items in a population containing a characteristic or attribute of interest

ATTRIBUTE—the characteristic being tested for in the population

OCCURRENCE RATE—the ratio of items in a population that contain a specific attribute to the total number of population items

EXCEPTION RATE—the percentage of items in a population that include exceptions in prescribed controls or monetary correctness (e.g., dollars). In the case of the former, the occurrence or exception rate would be a percentage; in the case of the latter, the exception would be a monetary amount.

An example of attribute sampling applied to tests of controls is shown in Chapter 13.

DISCOVERY SAMPLING This special type of attribute sampling is used when the auditor is looking for very few or near zero deviations. For example, if the auditor suspects that fraud or other irregularities exist in the data, the sample size needs to be designed to provide the assurance of finding at least one example of the fraud or other irregularity. This method can also be used for tests of detail in situations where few or no misstatements are expected, for example where calculations are performed by a computer program.

Proportionate-to-Size Sampling PPS sampling is also known as **monetary unit sampling** (MUS) or *dollar unit sampling* (DUS). PPS is a modified form of attribute sampling that focuses on a single unit of currency (in Canada, the dollar), rather than on a physical unit. In the balance of the text, the term monetary unit sampling (MUS) is used to refer to this form of sampling.

In physical unit sampling, the sampling unit is usually a document, such as a cheque, or a transaction, such as a sale. In monetary unit sampling, the sampling unit is the individual dollar. If sales for the year were made up of 15,000 transactions with a dollar value of $30,000,000, the sampling unit for physical unit attribute sampling would be an invoice, while the sampling unit for monetary unit sampling would be each of the 30,000,000 dollars. In the case of the former, each of the 15,000 invoices would have an equal chance of selection; in the case of the latter, each of the 30,000,000 dollars would have an equal chance of selection.

Monetary unit sampling allows the result of the testing to be stated in dollar terms. This allows the auditor to specify a dollar range of potential errors for a specified confidence level. It also increases the probability that larger invoices, totalling larger dollar amounts than smaller invoices, will be selected, since an invoice including 150,000 dollars will have a greater probability of being selected than one containing only 15 dollars. Monetary unit sampling is appropriate for tests of controls or for tests of details.

Variables Sampling Variables sampling is used when the auditor desires a dollar or quantitative conclusion with respect to the test conducted. The general class of methods called variables sampling includes several techniques. Those described in this section are difference estimation, ratio estimation, and mean-per-unit estimation.

DIFFERENCE ESTIMATION **Difference estimation** is used to measure the estimated total misstatement amount when there is both a recorded value and an audited value for each item in the sample. An example is confirming a sample of accounts receivable and determining the difference (misstatement) between the client's recorded amount and the amount the auditor considers correct for each selected account. The auditor makes an estimate of the population misstatement based on the number of misstatements, average misstatement size, and individual misstatement size in the sample. The result is stated as a point estimate plus or minus a computed precision interval at a stated confidence level.

Difference estimation frequently results in smaller sample sizes than any other method, and it is relatively easy to use. For that reason, difference estimation is used frequently by auditors.

RATIO ESTIMATION Ratio estimation is similar to difference estimation except that the point estimate of the population misstatement is determined by multiplying the portion of sample dollars misstated by the total recorded book value. The ratio estimate results in even smaller sample sizes than difference estimation if the size of the misstatements in the population is proportionate to the recorded value of the items. If the size of the individual misstatements is independent of the recorded value, the difference estimate also results in smaller sample sizes.

MEAN-PER-UNIT ESTIMATION In mean-per-unit estimation, the auditor is concerned with the audited value rather than the error amount of each item in the sample. Except for the definition of what is being measured, the mean-per-unit estimate is calculated in exactly the same manner as the difference estimate. The point estimate of the audited value is the average

DISCOVERY SAMPLING—a form of attribute sampling designed to look for one or very low occurrences

MONETARY UNIT SAMPLING (ALSO KNOWN AS PROBABILITY-PROPORTIONATE-TO-SIZE SAMPLING)—a modified form of attribute sampling that focuses on a single unit of currency (in Canada, the dollar), rather than on a physical unit

DIFFERENCE ESTIMATION—a form of sampling used to estimate the difference between the recorded value and the audited value audited value of items in the sample times the population size. The computed precision interval is computed on the basis of the audited value of the sample items rather than the misstatements. When the auditor has computed the upper and lower confidence limits, a decision is made about the acceptability of the population by comparing these amounts with the recorded book value.

→12.3   STEPS IN CONDUCTING THE SAMPLING PROCESS

Planning, Selecting, and Evaluating a Sample

Audit sampling is applied to tests of controls and tests of details through a set of 14 well-defined steps. The steps are divided into three sections: plan the sample, select the sample and perform the audit procedures, and evaluate the results. It is important to follow these steps carefully as a means of ensuring that both the auditing and the sampling aspects of the process are properly applied. The steps provide an outline of the discussion that follows. Table 12-7, shown at the end of the discussion on page 361, compares these steps for tests of controls (e.g., attribute sampling) and tests of details (e.g., MUS sampling).

PLAN THE SAMPLE

1. State the objectives of the audit test.
2. Decide if audit sampling applies.
3. Define attributes and exception or error conditions.
4. Define the population.
5. Define the sampling unit.
6. Specify tolerable exception rate or specify materiality.
7. Specify acceptable risk of assessing control risk too low or acceptable risk of incorrect acceptance.
8. Estimate the population exception rate or the misstatements in the population.
9. Determine the initial sample size.

SELECT THE SAMPLE AND PERFORM THE AUDIT PROCEDURES

10. Select the sample.
11. Perform the audit procedures.

EVALUATE THE RESULTS

12. Generalize from the sample to the population.
13. Analyze exceptions or misstatements.
14. Determine the acceptability of the population.

The general process of each step is described in this chapter, and related definitions are provided for new terms. Chapter 13 provides an example of tests of controls using nonstatistical and physical unit attribute sampling, while Chapter 14 does the same for tests of details using nonstatistical and MUS sampling.

1. State the Objectives of the Audit Test The overall objectives of the test must be stated in terms of the transaction cycle being tested. Typically, the overall objective of tests of controls is to test the application of controls and to determine whether the transactions contain monetary errors or fraud and other irregularities. For tests of details, the auditor determines the maximum amount of overstatement and understatement that could exist while still providing a sample with no misstatements (or for the number of misstatements that was found). The objectives of the audit test are normally decided as a part of designing the audit program in the context of risks by assertion.

2. Decide If Audit Sampling Applies In this section the term "**population**" is used. The population represents the body of data about which the auditor wishes to generalize.

Audit sampling applies whenever the auditor plans to reach conclusions about a population based on a sample. The auditor should examine the audit program and decide those

POPULATION—the body of data about which the auditor wishes to generalize audit procedures for which audit sampling applies. For example, in the following incomplete audit program (missing assertions), sampling could be used for procedures 3 through 5.

1. Review sales transactions for large and unusual amounts (analytical procedure or directed sample).
2. Observe whether the duties of the accounts receivable clerk are separate from the handling of cash (test of control).
3. Examine a sample of duplicate sales invoices for
   (a) credit approval by the credit manager (test of control)
   (b) the existence of an attached shipping document (test of control)
   (c) inclusion of a chart of accounts number (test of control)
4. Select a sample of shipping documents, and trace each to related duplicate sales invoices for existence (test of control).
5. Compare the quantity on each duplicate sales invoice with the quantity on related shipping documents (test of control).

Audit sampling is inappropriate for the first two procedures in this audit program. The first is an analytical procedure for which sampling is inappropriate. The second is an observation procedure for which no documentation exists to perform audit sampling.

For tests of details, while it is common to sample in many accounts, there are situations when sampling does not apply. For the population shown in the table below, the auditor may decide to audit only items over $5,000 and ignore all others because the total of the smaller ones is immaterial. In this case, the auditor has not sampled. Similarly, if the auditor is verifying capital asset additions and there are many small additions and one extremely large purchase of a building, the auditor may decide to ignore the small items entirely. Again the auditor has not sampled.

Population Item	Recorded Amount	Population item	Recorded Amount	Population Item	Recorded Amount	Population Item	Recorded Amount
1	$1,410	11	$2,270	21	$4,865	31	$ 935
2	9,130	12	50	22	770	32	5,595
3	660	13	5,785	23	2,305	33	930
4	3,355	14	940	24	2,665	34	4,045
5	5,725	15	1,820	25	1,000	35	9,480
6	8,210	16	3,380	26	6,225	36	360
7	580	17	530	27	3,675	37	1,145
8	44,110	18	955	28	6,250	38	6,400
9	825	19	4,490	29	1,890	39	100
10	1,155	20	17,140	30	27,705	40	8,435
							$207,295

3. Define Attributes and Exception or Error Conditions

Term Related to Planning	Test of Control (e.g., for Attribute Sample)	Test of Detail (e.g., for MUS Sample)
Define the item of interest.	Identify the characteristic or *attribute* of interest.	Individual dollars
Define exceptions or errors.	Define the control deviation (an *exception*)	Normally any monetary difference (an *error*)

Whenever audit sampling is used, the auditor must carefully define the characteristics (*attributes*) being tested and the exception conditions. Unless a precise statement of what constitutes an attribute is made in advance, the staff person who performs the audit procedure will have no guidelines for identifying exceptions.

Attributes of interest and exception conditions come directly from the audit procedures for which the auditor has decided to use audit sampling. For example, based on the portion of the partial test of control audit program described in step 2, the first attribute that can be tested by means of sampling is whether the duplicate sales invoice is approved for credit (procedure 3a). A deviation condition in a manual system would be lack of initials indicating credit approval. The absence of the defined attribute for any sample item will be an exception for that attribute.

Audit sampling for tests of details of balances measures monetary misstatements in the population. Thus, the misstatement conditions are any conditions that represent a monetary misstatement in a sample item. In auditing accounts receivable, for example, any client misstatement in a sample item is a misstatement.

4. Define the Population The auditor can define the population to include whatever data are desired, but he or she must sample from the entire population as it has been defined. The auditor may generalize *only* about that population that has been sampled. For example, in performing tests of controls of sales, the auditor generally defines the population as all recorded sales for the year. If the auditor samples from only one month's transactions, it is invalid to draw conclusions about the invoices for the entire year.

It is important that the auditor carefully define the population in advance, being consistent with the objectives of the audit tests. For different tests in the audit program of the same cycle, it may be necessary to define more than one population for a given set of audit procedures. For example, if the auditor intends to trace from sales invoices to shipping documents and from shipping documents to duplicate sales invoices, there are two populations (i.e., one population of shipping documents and another of duplicate sales invoices).

The population for tests of details using MUS or other dollar-based tests is defined as the *recorded dollar population*. The auditor then evaluates whether the recorded population is overstated or understated. For example, the population of accounts receivable shown above consists of 40 accounts totalling $207,295. Most accounting populations subject to audit would contain far more items totalling a much larger dollar amount.

STRATIFIED SAMPLING As mentioned earlier, the purpose of stratification is to permit the auditor to emphasize certain population items and de-emphasize others. In most audit sampling situations, auditors want to emphasize the larger recorded values; therefore, stratification is typically done on the basis of the size of recorded dollar values.

For example, examining the population in the table on page 350, there are many different ways to stratify the population. One such method follows:

Stratum	Stratum Criteria	Number Population	Dollars in Population
1	>$10,000	3	$88,955
2	$5,000 to $10,000	10	71,235
3	<$5,000	27	47,105
		40	$207,295

It is also important to test the population for completeness and detail tie-in before a sample is selected to ensure that all population items will be properly subjected to sample selection.

5. Define the Sampling Unit The major consideration in defining the physical sampling unit when conducting tests of controls is making it consistent with the objectives of the audit tests. Thus, the definition of the population and the planned audit procedures usually dictate the appropriate sampling unit. For example, if the auditor wants to determine how frequently the client fails to fill a customer's order, the sampling unit must be defined as the customer's order. If, however, the objective is to determine whether the proper quantity of the goods described on the customer's order is correctly shipped and billed, it is possible to define the sampling unit as the customer's order, the shipping document, or the duplicate sales invoice.

The sampling unit for nonstatistical audit sampling in tests of details of balances is almost always the item making up the account balance. For accounts receivable, it is the customer account name or number, or unpaid invoice, on the accounts receivable list. For statistical sampling, such as MUS, the definition of the sampling unit is an individual dollar.

Having the individual dollar as the sampling unit for MUS results in an automatic emphasis on physical units with larger recorded balances. Since the sample is selected on the basis of individual dollars, an account with a large balance has a greater chance of being included than an account with a small balance. For example, in accounts receivable confirmation, an account with a $5,000 balance has a 10 times greater probability of selection than one with a $500 balance, as it contains 10 times as many dollar units. As a result, there is no need to use stratified sampling with MUS. Stratification occurs automatically.

6. Specify Tolerable Exception Rate or Specify Materiality

Term Related to Planning	Test of Control (e.g., for Attribute Sample)	Test of Detail (e.g., for MUS Sample)
Specify tolerable exception rate (TER).	Specify the exception rate the auditor will permit in the population.	N/A
Specify materiality.	N/A	Use overall materiality available for the audit.

TOLERABLE EXCEPTION RATE (TER)—the exception rate that the auditor will permit in the population and still be willing to use the assessed control risk and/or the amount of monetary errors or fraud and other irregularities in the transactions established during planning

Establishing the **tolerable exception rate** (TER) requires *professional judgment* on the part of the auditor. TER represents the exception rate that the auditor will permit in the population and still be willing to use the assessed control risk and/or the amount of monetary errors or fraud and other irregularities in the transactions established during planning. For example, assume that the auditor decides that TER for the attribute of sales invoice credit approval is 6 percent. This means that the auditor has decided that even if 6 percent of the duplicate sales invoices are not approved for credit, the credit approval control is still effective in terms of the assessed control risk included in the audit plan.

TER is the result of an auditor's judgment. The suitable TER is a question of materiality and is therefore affected by both the definition and the importance of the attribute in the audit plan.

TER has a significant impact on sample size. A larger sample size is needed for a low TER than for a high TER. For example, a larger sample is required for a TER of 4 percent than for a TER of 6 percent.

For sampling for tests of details, materiality is used during the sampling process. It was stated in Chapter 8 that there were two methods for considering materiality: (1) materiality would *not* be allocated to individual accounts in planning the audit (the method adopted by the text); (2) materiality would be allocated to individual accounts at the planning stage. MUS uses method (1): the preliminary judgment about materiality is used to directly determine the tolerable misstatement amount for the audit of each account. Other sampling techniques (e.g., variables estimation) require method (2) and require the auditor to determine tolerable misstatement for each account by allocating the preliminary judgment about materiality over the accounts to be audited.

7. Specify Acceptable Risk of Assessing Control Risk Too Low or Acceptable Risk of Incorrect Acceptance

Term Related to Planning	Test of Control (e.g., for Attribute Sample)	Test of Detail (e.g., for MUS Sample)
Acceptable risk of assessing control risk too low (ARACR)	The risk that the auditor is willing to take of accepting a control as effective when the true population exception rate is greater	N/A
Acceptable risk of incorrect acceptance (ARIA)	N/A	The risk that the auditor is willing to take of accepting a balance as correct when the true misstatement is greater than materiality

Whenever a sample is taken, there is a risk that the quantitative conclusions about the population will be incorrect. This is always true unless 100 percent of the population is tested. As has already been stated, this is the case with both nonstatistical and statistical sampling.

For audit sampling in tests of controls, that risk is called the **acceptable risk of assessing control risk too low** (**ARACR**). ARACR is the risk that the auditor is willing to take of accepting a control as effective (or a rate of monetary errors or fraud and other irregularities as tolerable) when the true population exception rate is greater than the tolerable exception rate (TER). To illustrate, assume that TER is 6 percent, ARACR is 10 percent, and the true population exception rate is 8 percent. The control in this case is not acceptable because the true exception rate of 8 percent exceeds TER. The auditor, of course, does not know the true population exception rate. The ARACR of 10 percent means that the auditor is willing to take a 10 percent risk of concluding that the control is effective after all testing is completed, even when it is ineffective. If the auditor finds the control effective in this illustration, he or she will have over-relied on the system of internal control (used a lower assessed control risk than justified). ARACR is the auditor's measure of sampling risk.

In choosing the appropriate ARACR in a situation, the auditor must use his or her best judgment. Since ARACR is a measure of the risk that the auditor is willing to take, the main consideration is the extent to which the auditor plans to reduce assessed control risk as a basis for the extent of tests of details of balances. The lower the assessed control risk, the lower will be the ARACR chosen and the planned extent of tests of details of balances. The most common situation where audit sampling would be used for tests of controls is when the auditor decides to assess control risk at a lower level than can be supported by understanding internal control (alternative 3). If the auditor decides to assess control risk at maximum (alternative 1), tests of controls are not performed. If control risk is assessed at the level supported by understanding internal control (alternative 2), tests of controls are often restricted to enquiry and transaction walk-through tests.

For nonstatistical sampling, it is common for auditors to use ARACR of high, medium, or low instead of a percentage. A low ARACR implies that the tests of controls are important and corresponds to a low assessed control risk and reduced substantive tests of details of balances.

The auditor can establish different TER and ARACR levels for different attributes of an audit test. For example, auditors could use higher TER and ARACR levels for tests of credit approval than for tests of the existence of duplicate sales invoices and bills of lading.

Table 12-3 presents illustrative guidelines for establishing TER and ARACR. The guidelines should not be interpreted as representing broad professional standards; however, they are typical of the types of guidelines public accounting firms issue to their staff, or include embedded in software modules.

For tests of details, acceptable risk of incorrect acceptance (ARIA) is the risk that the auditor is willing to take of accepting a balance as correct when the true misstatement in the balance is greater than materiality. ARIA is the equivalent term to acceptable risk of assessing control risk too low (ARACR) for tests of controls.

There is an inverse relationship between ARIA and required sample size. If, for example, the auditor decides to reduce ARIA from 10 percent to 5 percent, the required sample size would increase. By reducing ARIA, we are increasing the required sampling assurance from 90 percent to 95 percent that the balance is correct, thus resulting in a larger sample size (i.e., the gathering of more evidence).

The primary factor affecting the auditor's decision about ARIA is assessed control risk in the audit risk model. When internal controls are effective, control risk can be reduced, permitting the auditor to increase ARIA. This, in turn, reduces the sample size required for the test of details of the related account balance.

A difficulty students often have is understanding how ARACR and ARIA affect evidence accumulation. In Chapter 11, it was shown that tests of details of balances for monetary errors or fraud and other irregularities can be reduced if internal controls are found to be effective through assessing control risk below maximum and performing tests of controls.

TABLE 12-3	Guidelines for ARACR and TER for Nonstatistical Sampling: Tests of Controls	
Factor	Judgment	Guideline

Assessed control risk. Consider:
  Nature, extent, and timing of substantive tests (extensive planned substantive tests relate to higher assessed control risk and vice versa).
  Quality of evidence available for tests of controls (a lower quality of evidence available results in a higher assessed control risk and vice versa).
	· Lowest assessed control risk
	· Moderate assessed control risk
	· Higher assessed control risk
	· Maximum control risk
		· ARACR of low
		· ARACR of medium
		· ARACR of high
		· ARACR is not applicable

Significance of the transactions and related account balances that the internal controls are intended to affect.	· Highly significant balances · Significant balances · Less significant balances	· TER of 4% · TER of 5% · TER of 6%

Note: The guidelines should recognize that there may be variations in ARACRs based on audit considerations. The guidelines above are the more conservative guidelines that could be followed.

The effects of ARACR and ARIA are consistent with that conclusion. If the auditor concludes that internal controls may be effective, control risk can be assessed at less than maximum. A lower control risk requires a lower ARACR in testing the controls, which in turn requires a larger sample size. If controls are found to be effective, control risk can remain low, which permits the auditor to increase ARIA (through use of the audit risk model), thereby requiring a smaller sample size in the related substantive tests of details of balances. The relationship between ARACR and ARIA is shown in Figure 12-3.

Besides control risk, ARIA is also directly affected by audit risk and inversely by other substantive tests already performed or planned for the account balance. For example, if audit risk is reduced, ARIA should also be reduced. If analytical procedures were performed and indicate that the account balance is fairly stated, ARIA should be increased. Stated differently, the analytical procedures are evidence in support of the account balance; therefore, less evidence from the detailed test of the balance using sampling is required to achieve audit risk. The same conclusion is appropriate for the relationship among dual purpose tests, ARIA, and sample size for tests of details of balances. The various relationships affecting ARIA are summarized in Table 12-4.

8. Estimate the Population Exception Rate or the Misstatements in the Population

Term Related to Planning	Test of Control (e.g., for Attribute Sample)	Test of Detail (e.g., for MUS Sample)
Estimated population exception rate (EPER)	The advance estimate of the percentage of exceptions in the population	N/A
Estimated misstatements in the population	N/A	The advance estimate of total dollar error in the population

When conducting tests of controls, an *advance estimate* of the **population exception rate (EPER)** should be made to plan the appropriate sample size. If the EPER is low, a relatively small sample size will satisfy the auditor's tolerable exception rate. When the expected exception rate is low, a less precise estimate of EPER can be used. To be more precise, an estimate of the population exception rate must be based on more data, that is, a larger sample.

FIGURE 12-3 **Effect of ARACR and ARIA on Required Evidence**

Controls Not Considered Effective	Controls Considered Effective
Control risk = 100%	Reduce control risk
ARACR = 100%	Reduce ARACR
Perform no tests of controls	Perform tests of controls
Use low ARIA	Increase ARIA*
Perform extensive substantive testing	Reduce planned substantive tests

*Assumes tests of controls were satisfactory, which permits control risk to remain low.

It is common to use the results of the preceding year's audit to make this estimate. If the prior year's results are not available, or if they are considered unreliable, the auditor can take a small *preliminary sample* of the current year's population for this purpose. It is not critical that the estimate be precise because the current year's sample exception rate is ultimately used to estimate the population characteristics.

Note that if a preliminary sample is used, it can be included in the final sample, as long as appropriate sample selection procedures are followed. For example, assume that an auditor takes a preliminary sample of 30 items to estimate the EPER that considers the entire

TABLE 12-4 **Relationship Among Factors Affecting ARIA, Effect on ARIA, and Required Sample Size for Audit Sampling**

Factor Affecting ARIA	Example	Effect on ARIA	Effect on Sample Size
Effectiveness of internal controls (control risk)	Internal controls are effective (reduced control risk)	Increase	Decrease
Audit risk	Likelihood of bankruptcy is low (increased audit risk)	Increase	Decrease
Analytical procedures	Analytical procedures performed with no indications of likely misstatements	Increase	Decrease

population. Later, if the auditor decides that a total sample size of 100 is needed, only 70 additional items will need to be properly selected and tested.

Similarly, for tests of details sampling, the auditor makes this estimate based on prior experience with the client and by assessing inherent risk, considering the results of tests of controls and of analytical procedures already performed.

9. Determine the Initial Sample Size Four factors determine the initial sample size for audit sampling for tests of controls: population size, TER, ARACR, and EPER. Population size is not nearly as significant a factor as the others and typically can be ignored.

An important characteristic of nonstatistical sampling compared to statistical methods is the need to decide the sample size using professional judgment for nonstatistical methods rather than by calculation using a statistical formula. Once the three major factors affecting sample size have been determined, it is possible for the auditor to determine an **initial sample size.**

The initial sample size is called that because the exceptions in the actual sample must be evaluated before it is possible to know whether the sample is sufficiently large to achieve the objectives of the tests.

SENSITIVITY OF SAMPLE SIZE TO A CHANGE IN THE FACTORS To properly understand the concepts underlying sampling in auditing, it is helpful to understand the effect of changing any of the four factors that determine sample size while the other factors are held constant. Table 12-5 illustrates the effect of increasing each of the four factors; a decrease will have the opposite effect.

A combination of two factors has the greatest effect on sample size: TER minus EPER. The difference is the *precision* of the planned sample estimate. For example, if TER (tolerable exception rate) is 5 percent and EPER (estimated population exception rate) is 2 percent, then precision is 3 percent. A smaller precision, which is called a more precise estimate, requires a larger sample.

Auditors using nonstatistical sampling for tests of details similarly determine the initial sample size judgmentally considering the factors discussed so far. Table 12-6 summarizes the primary factors that influence sample size for nonstatistical sampling of tests of details and how sample size is affected.

When the auditor uses stratified sampling, the sample size must be allocated among the strata. Typically, auditors allocate a higher portion of the sample items to larger population items. For example, using the data from Problem 14-22 on page 449, allocating a sample size of 15, the auditor might decide to select all three accounts from stratum 1, and six each from strata 2 and 3. Observe that audit sampling does not apply to stratum 1 because all population items are being audited.

For MUS sampling, sample size is determined using a statistical formula.

10. Select the Sample After the auditor has computed the initial sample size for the audit sampling application, he or she must choose the items in the population to be included in the sample. The sample can be chosen by using any of the probabilistic or nonprobabilistic methods discussed earlier in the chapter. It is important for the auditor to use a method that will permit meaningful conclusions about the sample results.

For stratified sampling, the auditor selects samples independently from each stratum.

TABLE 12-5	Effect on Sample Size of Changing Factors
Type of Change	Effect on Initial Sample Size
Increase acceptable risk of assessing control risk too low	Decrease
Increase tolerable exception rate	Decrease
Increase estimated population exception rate	Increase
Increase population size	Increase (minor effect)

Monetary unit samples are samples selected with probability proportionate to size (PPS). Such samples are of individual dollars in the population. Auditors cannot, however, audit individual dollars. Therefore, the auditor must determine the physical unit to perform the audit tests. For example, the auditor could select a random sample of population items and determine that dollar number 7,376 is to be selected. However, to perform the audit procedures, the auditor must identify the population item that corresponds to the 7,376th dollar, for example, the twelfth invoice transaction.

11. Perform the Audit Procedures The auditor performs the test of control audit procedures by examining each item in the sample to determine whether it is consistent with the definition of the attribute and maintains a record of all the exceptions found. When audit procedures have been completed for a test of control sampling application, there will be a sample size and a number of exceptions for each attribute.

To perform the test of detail audit procedures, the auditor applies the appropriate audit procedures to each item in the sample to determine whether it is correct or contains a misstatement. For example, in the confirmation of accounts receivable, the auditor mails the sample of confirmations in the manner described in Chapter 14 and determines the amount of misstatement in each account confirmed. For nonresponses, alternative procedures are used to determine the misstatements. The auditor tracks the recorded value and the audited value so that the aggregate client misstatement can be determined.

The auditor cannot expect meaningful results from using audit sampling unless the audit procedures are applied carefully.

12. Generalize from the Sample to the Population For tests of controls, the **sample exception rate** (SER) can be easily calculated from the actual sample results. SER equals the actual number of exceptions divided by the actual sample size.

It is improper for the auditor to conclude that the population exception rate is exactly the same as the sample exception rate; the chance that they are exactly the same is too

SAMPLE EXCEPTION RATE—the number of exceptions in the sample divided by the sample size

TABLE 12-6	Factors Influencing Sample Sizes for Tests of Details of Balances	
Factor	Conditions Leading to Smaller Sample Size	Conditions Leading to Larger Sample Size
a. **Control risk (ARACR).** Affects acceptable risk of Incorrect acceptance.	Low control risk	High control risk
b. **Risk for other substantive tests related to the same assertion** (including analytical procedures and other relevant substantive tests). Affects acceptable risk of incorrect acceptance.	Low risk associated with other relevant substantive tests	High risk associated with other relevant substantive tests
c. **Audit risk.** Affects acceptable risk of incorrect acceptance.	High audit risk	Low audit risk
d. **Materiality.**	Larger materiality	Smaller materiality
e. **Inherent risk.** Affects estimated misstatements in the population.	Low inherent risk	High inherent risk
f. **Expected size and frequency of misstatements.** Affects estimated misstatements in the population.	Smaller misstatements or lower frequency	Larger misstatements or higher frequency
g. **Number of items in the population.**	Almost no effect on sample size unless population is very small	Almost no effect on sample size unless population is very small

small. For nonstatistical methods, there are two ways to generalize from the sample to the population.

1. Add an estimate of sampling error to SER to arrive at a computed upper exception rate (CUER) for a given acceptable risk of assessing control risk too low. It is extremely difficult for auditors to make sampling error estimates using nonstatistical sampling because of the judgment required to do so; therefore, this approach is generally not used.
2. Subtract the sampling exception rate from the tolerable exception rate, which is calculated sampling error (TER – SER = calculated sampling error), and evaluate whether calculated sampling error is sufficiently large to indicate that the true population exception rate is acceptable. Most auditors using nonstatistical sampling follow this approach. For example, if an auditor takes a sample of 100 items for an attribute and finds no exceptions (SER = 0), and TER is 5 percent, calculated sampling error is 5 percent (TER of 5 percent – SER of 0 = 5 percent). On the other hand, if there had been four exceptions, calculated sampling error would have been 1 percent (TER of 5 percent – SER of 4 percent). It is much more likely that the true population exception rate is less than or equal to the tolerable exception rate in the first case than in the second one. Therefore, most auditors would probably find the population acceptable based on the first sample result and not acceptable based on the second.

In practice, auditors tend to test controls when they expect no exceptions. If no exceptions are found, then the control is considered to be reliable. However, when exceptions are found, it is more likely that the controls cannot be relied on, unless the situation(s) causing the control exception can be isolated (as discussed in the next section).

In addition, the auditor's consideration of whether sampling error is sufficiently large will depend on sample size. For example, if the sample size in the above example had been only 20 items, the auditor would have been much less confident that finding no exceptions was an indication that the true population exception rate did not exceed TER than finding no exceptions in a sample of 100 items. Note that under the second approach, the auditor does not make an estimate of the computed upper exception rate.

When generalizing tests of details, the auditor deals with dollar amounts rather than with exceptions. The auditor must generalize from the sample to the population by (1) projecting misstatements from the sample results to the population and (2) considering sampling error and sampling risk (ARIA). For example, assume that the auditor discovered three misstatements that netted to $389 overstatement. Can the auditor conclude that accounts receivable is overstated by $389? No, the auditor is interested in the *population* results (further possible misstatement is described in Chapter 8), not those for the sample (identified misstatement is defined in Chapter 8). It is therefore necessary to project from the sample to the population to estimate the population misstatement.

The first step is making a *point estimate*, which was defined as likely misstatement in Chapter 8. There are different ways to calculate the point estimate, but a common way is to assume that misstatements in the unaudited population are proportional to the misstatements in the sample. This calculation must be done for each stratum and then totalled, rather than for the total misstatements in the sample. Thus, the point estimate of the misstatement is determined by using a weighted-average method. For example, if the $389 total error were comprised as follows:

Stratum	Sample Size	Dollars Audited Recorded Value	Dollars Audited Audited Value	Client Misstatement
1	3	$ 88,955	$ 91,695	$(2,740)
2	6	43,995	43,024	971
3	6	13,105	10,947	2,158
	15	$146,055	$145,666	$ 389

then the point estimate would be calculated as shown:

Stratum	Client Misstatement + Recorded Value from Sample	×	Recorded Book Value for Stratum	=	Point Estimate of Misstatement
1	$(2,740) / $88,955		$88,955		$(2,740)
2	971 / 43,995		71,235		1,572
3	2,158 / 13,105		47,105		7,757
Total					$ 6,589

The point estimate of the error in the population is $6,589, indicating an overstatement. The point estimate, by itself, is not an adequate measure of the population misstatement, however, because of sampling error. In other words, because the estimate is based on a sample, it will be close to the true population misstatement, but it is unlikely that it is exactly the same. The auditor must consider the possibility that the true population misstatement is greater than the amount of misstatement that is tolerable in the circumstances whenever the point estimate is less than the tolerable misstatement amount. This must be done for both statistical and nonstatistical samples.

13. Analyze Exceptions or Misstatements In addition to determining the SER for each attribute control tested and evaluating whether the true but unknown exception rate is likely to exceed the tolerable exception rate, it is necessary to analyze individual exceptions to determine the breakdown in the internal controls that caused them. Exceptions could be caused by carelessness of employees, misunderstood instructions, intentional failure to perform procedures, or many other factors. The nature of an exception and its cause have a significant effect on the qualitative evaluation of the system. For example, if all the exceptions in the tests of internal verification of credit authorization for sales invoices occurred while the person normally responsible for performing the tests was on vacation, this would affect the auditor's evaluation of the internal controls and the subsequent investigation. The auditor could choose to test the period substantively when the employee was on vacation, and rely on internal controls for the remainder of the year.

Misstatements discovered during tests of details could be caused by control exceptions. For example, in confirming accounts receivable, suppose that all misstatements resulted from the client's failure to record returned goods. The auditor would determine why that type of misstatement occurred so often, the implications of the misstatements on other audit areas, the potential impact on the financial statements, and the effect on company operations.

An important part of misstatement analysis is deciding whether any modification of the audit risk model is needed. If the auditor concluded that the failure to record the returns discussed in the previous paragraph resulted from a breakdown of internal controls, it might be necessary to reassess control risk. That, in turn, would probably cause the auditor to reduce ARIA, which would increase planned sample size. As discussed in Chapter 8, revisions of the audit risk model must be done with extreme care because the model is intended primarily for planning, not evaluating results.

14. Determine the Acceptability of the Population For tests of controls, it was shown under "12. Generalize from the Sample to the Population" that most auditors subtract SER from TER when they use nonstatistical sampling and evaluate whether the difference, which is calculated sampling error, is sufficiently large. If the auditor concludes that the difference is sufficiently large, the control being tested can be used to reduce assessed control risk as planned, provided a careful analysis of the cause of exceptions does not indicate the possibility of other significant problems with internal controls.

When the auditor concludes that TER − SER is too small to conclude that the population is acceptable, the auditor must take specific action. Three courses of action can be followed.

REVISE TER OR ARACR This alternative should be followed only when the auditor has concluded that the original specifications were too conservative. Relaxing either TER or ARACR may be difficult to defend if the auditor is ever subject to review by a court or by peer review.

EXPAND THE SAMPLE SIZE An increase in the sample size has the effect of decreasing the sampling error if the actual sample exception rate does not increase. Of course, SER may also increase or decrease if additional items are selected.

REVISE ASSESSED CONTROL RISK If the results of the tests of controls do not support the planned assessed control risk, the auditor should revise assessed control risk upward. The effect of the revision is likely to increase tests of details of balances. For example, if tests of controls of credit approval indicate that those procedures are not being followed, the auditor may not be able to rely on the control and will therefore conduct additional substantive tests at year end. This is most likely to be done through tests of the bad debt allowance for accounts receivable and of bad debt expense for the year.

The decision whether to increase sample size until sampling error is sufficiently small or to revise assessed control risk must be made on the basis of cost versus benefit. If the sample is not expanded, it is necessary to revise assessed control risk upward and therefore perform additional substantive tests. The cost of additional tests of controls must be compared with the cost of additional substantive tests. If an expanded sample continues to produce unacceptable results, additional substantive tests will then be necessary.

If the original test performed is testing transactions for monetary errors or fraud and other irregularities, and an exception rate higher than that assumed is indicated, the response would generally be the same as for tests of controls.

For tests of details, an auditor using nonstatistical sampling cannot formally measure sampling error and therefore must subjectively consider the possibility that the true population misstatement aggregated with other misstatements exceeds materiality. This is done by considering (1) the difference between the point estimate and materiality, (2) the extent to which items in the population have been audited 100 percent, (3) whether misstatements tend to be offsetting or in only one direction, (4) the amounts of individual misstatements, and (5) sample size. To continue the example above, suppose that materiality is $40,000. In that case, the auditor may conclude that there is little chance, given the point estimate of $6,589, that the true population misstatement exceeds that amount.

Suppose that materiality is $12,000, only $5,411 greater than the point estimate. In that case, other factors would be considered. For example, if the larger items in the population were audited 100 percent (as was done here), any unidentified misstatements would be restricted to smaller items. If the misstatements tend to be offsetting and are relatively small in size, the auditor may conclude that the true population misstatement is likely to be less than materiality. Also, the larger the sample size, the more confident the auditor can be that the point estimate is close to the true population value. Therefore, the auditor would be more willing to accept that the true population misstatement is less than tolerable misstatement in this example, where the sample size is considered large, than where it is considered moderate or small. On the other hand, if one or more of these other conditions is different, the chance of a misstatement in excess of the tolerable amount may be judged to be high, and the recorded population unacceptable.

Even if the amount of likely misstatement is not considered material, the auditor must wait to make a final evaluation until the entire audit is completed. For example, the estimated total misstatement and estimated sampling error in accounts receivable must be combined with estimates of misstatements in all other parts of the audit to evaluate the effect of all misstatements on the financial statements as a whole.

For MUS and variables sampling, a formal decision rule is used for deciding the acceptability of the population. The decision rule used for MUS is similar to that used for nonstatistical sampling, but it is sufficiently different to merit discussion. The decision rule will be illustrated in Chapter 14, along with the illustration of a specific sample selection.

Summary of Sampling Steps Table 12-7 summarizes the steps used in sampling. It is apparent from the table that planning is an essential part of using any type of sampling. The purposes of planning are to make sure that the audit procedures are properly applied and that the sample size is appropriate for the circumstances. Sample selection is also important and must be done with care to avoid nonsampling errors. Performing the audit procedures must be done carefully to correctly determine the number of exceptions or the value of errors in the sample. It is the most time-consuming part of audit sampling.

Evaluating the results for tests of controls includes making an estimate of sampling error and comparing it to the tolerable exception rate, while for tests of details, dollar values must be extrapolated, with decision rules and methodologies varying depending upon the sampling method chosen. Exceptions or errors must be analyzed and, finally, acceptability of the population determined.

Other Considerations

For the sake of greater continuity, in the preceding discussion, we bypassed four important aspects of using sampling that are now discussed: random selection versus statistical measurement, adequate documentation, management letters, and the need for professional judgment.

Random Selection Versus Statistical Measurement Students often do not understand the distinction between random (probabilistic) selection and statistical measurement. It should now be clear that random selection is a part of statistical sampling but is not, by itself, statistical measurement. To have statistical measurement, it is necessary to generalize mathematically from the sample to the population.

It is acceptable to use random selection procedures without drawing statistical conclusions, but this practice is questionable if a reasonably large sample size has been selected. Whenever the auditor takes a random sample, regardless of his or her basis for determining its size, there is a *statistical measurement inherent in the sample*. Since there is little or no cost involved in computing the upper exception rate, we believe that it should be done whenever possible. It would, of course, be inappropriate to draw a statistical conclusion unless the sample were randomly selected or selected using a formal methodology, such as interval selection with a random start.

TABLE 12-7	Summary of Audit Sampling Steps

Steps—Audit Sampling for Tests of Controls	Steps—Audit Sampling for Tests of Details
Plan the Sample	**Plan the Sample**
1. State the objectives of the audit test.	1. State the objectives of the audit test.
2. Decide if audit sampling applies.	2. Decide if audit sampling applies.
3. Define attributes and exception conditions.	3. Define misstatement conditions.
4. Define the population.	4. Define the population.
5. Define the sampling unit.	5. Define the sampling unit.
6. Specify tolerable exception rate.	6. Specify materiality.
7. Specify acceptable risk of assessing control risk too low.	7. Specify acceptable risk of incorrect acceptance.
8. Estimate the population exception rate.	8. Estimate misstatements in the population.
9. Determine the initial sample size.	9. Determine the initial sample size.
Select the Sample and Perform the Audit Procedures	**Select the Sample and Perform the Audit Procedures**
10. Select the sample.	10. Select the sample.
11. Perform the audit procedures.	11. Perform the audit procedures.
Evaluate the Results	**Evaluate the Results**
12. Generalize from the sample to the population.	12. Generalize from the sample to the population.
13. Analyze the exceptions.	13. Analyze the misstatements.
14. Determine the acceptability of the population.	14. Determine the acceptability of the population.

Adequate Documentation It is important that the auditor retain adequate records of the procedures performed, the methods used to select the sample and perform the tests, the results found in the tests, and the conclusions drawn. This is necessary as a means of evaluating the combined results of all tests and as a basis for defending the audit if the need arises. Documentation is equally important for statistical and nonstatistical sampling. Examples of the type of documentation commonly found in practice are included in the case illustrations for Hillsburg Hardware Limited in Chapters 13 and 14.

Management Letters Documentation, evaluation, or testing of internal controls may lead to the discovery of a variety of internal control exceptions. These should be communicated to management and the audit committee regardless of the nature of the exceptions.

Need for Professional Judgment A criticism occasionally levelled against statistical sampling is that it reduces the use of professional judgment. A review of the 14 steps discussed in this chapter for sampling shows how unwarranted this criticism is. For proper application of sampling, it is necessary to use professional judgment in most of the steps. For example, selection of the initial sample size depends primarily on the TER, ARACR, and EPER. Choosing the first two requires the exercise of high-level professional judgment; the latter requires a careful estimate. Similarly, the final evaluation of the acceptability of the population for any form of sampling must also be based on high-level professional judgment.

SUMMARY

1. *What is sampling?* Sampling occurs when someone looks at less than 100 percent of the items in a population.

    Why would an auditor use statistical rather than nonstatistical sampling? With statistical sampling, the auditor can quantify sampling risk and also calculate a statistical result.

    What are the different types of nonprobabilistic (nonstatistical) sampling methods used by auditors? The three types are directed (items likely to contain misstatements, items containing selected population characteristics, or large dollar amounts), block, and haphazard.

2. *What are the three different ways that an auditor can select a statistical sample?* The auditor could use a random number table, generate random numbers using computer software, or use systematic selection with a random start.

    List three common statistical sampling methodologies used by auditors. These are attribute sampling, probability-proportionate-to-size sampling (also known as monetary unit sampling or dollar unit sampling), and variables sampling.

3. *Describe the 14 steps in planning, selecting, performing the tests, and evaluating a sample.* These steps are listed on page 349 and in Table 12-7 on page 361.

    What are four additional issues the auditor should consider during the sampling process? The auditor needs to ensure that random sampling occurs but that it is also important to generalize mathematically to provide for statistical measurement. The planning, selection, execution, and evaluation of the sampling process needs to be adequately documented. Any internal control exceptions or other errors found should be properly communicated to management and the audit committee. Both judgmental and statistical sampling require extensive use of professional judgment.

CICA ASSURANCE HANDBOOK SECTION REFERENCED IN THIS CHAPTER

Section 5300 – Audit evidence.

ESSENTIAL TERMS

Acceptable risk of assessing control risk too low (ARACR)— the risk that the auditor is willing to take of accepting a control as effective or a rate of monetary errors or fraud and other irregularities as tolerable, when the true population exception rate is greater than the tolerable exception rate   (p. 353).

Attribute—the characteristic being tested for in the population (p. 347).

Attribute sampling—a statistical, probabilistic method of sample evaluation that results in an estimate of the proportion of items in a population containing a characteristic or attribute of interest   (p. 347).

Block sample—a nonprobabilistic method of sample selection in which items are selected in measured sequences (p. 343).

Confidence level—statement of probability   (p. 341).

Difference estimation—a form of sampling used to estimate the difference between the recorded value and the audited value (p. 348).

Directed sample selection—a nonprobabilistic method of sample selection in which each item in the sample is selected based on some judgmental criteria established by the auditor (p. 342).

Discovery sampling—a form of attribute sampling designed to look for one or very low occurrences   (p. 348).

Estimated population exception rate (EPER)—exception rate the auditor expects to find in the population before testing begins   (p. 354).

Exception rate—the percentage of items in a population that include exceptions in prescribed controls or monetary correctness   (p. 347).

Haphazard sample selection—a nonprobabilistic method of sample selection in which items are chosen without regard to their size, source, or other distinguishing characteristics   (p. 344).

Initial sample size—sample size determined by professional judgment (nonstatistical sampling) or by statistical tables (attribute sampling)   (p. 356).

Judgmental sampling—use of professional judgment rather than statistical methods to select sample items for audit tests (p. 342).

Monetary unit sampling (MUS)—a modified form of attribute sampling that focuses on a single unit of currency (in Canada, the dollar), rather than on a physical unit   (p. 348).

Nonprobabilistic sample selection—a method of sample selection in which the auditor uses professional judgment to select items from the population   (p. 342).

Nonsampling risk—the chance of exception when audit tests do not uncover existing exceptions in the sample; caused by failure to recognize exceptions and by inappropriate or ineffective audit procedures; synonymous with nonsampling error   (p. 341).

Occurrence rate—the ratio of items in a population that contain a specific attribute to the total number of population items (p. 347).

Population—the body of data about which the auditor wishes to generalize   (p. 349).

Probabilistic sample selection—a method of sample selection in which it is possible to define the set of all possible samples, every possible sample has a known probability of being selected, and the sample is selected by a random process   (p. 344).

Probability-proportionate-to-size sampling—see *monetary unit sampling*   (p. 348).

Random number table—a listing of independent random digits conveniently arranged in tabular form to facilitate the selection of random numbers with multiple digits   (p. 344).

Random sample—a sample in which every possible combination of elements in the population has an equal chance of being selected   (p. 344).

Representative sample—a sample with the same characteristics as those of the population   (p. 340).

Sample exception rate (SER)—the number of exceptions in the sample divided by the sample size   (p. 357).

Sampling distribution—a frequency distribution of the results of all possible samples of a specified size that could be obtained from a population containing some specific parameters   (p. 347).

Sampling risk—the chance of exception inherent in tests of less than the entire population; may be reduced by using an increased sample size and using an appropriate method of selecting sample items from the population   (p. 341).

Statistical sampling—the use of mathematical measurement techniques to calculate formal statistical results and quantify sampling risk   (p. 341).

Systematic selection—a probabilistic method of sampling in which the auditor calculates an interval (the population size divided by the number of sample items desired) and selects the items for the sample based on the size of the interval and a randomly selected number between zero and the sample size (p. 346).

Tolerable exception rate (TER)—the exception rate that the auditor will permit in the population and still be willing to use the assessed control risk and/or the amount of monetary errors or fraud and other irregularities in the transactions established during planning   (p. 352).

REVIEW QUESTIONS

12-1   State what is meant by a "representative sample," and explain its importance in sampling audit populations.

12-2   Explain the major difference between statistical and non-statistical sampling. What are the three main parts of statistical and nonstatistical methods?

12-3   Explain the difference between replacement sampling and nonreplacement sampling. Which method do auditors usually follow? Why?

12-4   Describe systematic sample selection, and explain how an auditor would select 35 numbers from a population

of 1,750 items using this approach. What are the advantages and disadvantages of systematic sample selection?

12-5   Explain what is meant by "block sampling," and describe how an auditor could obtain 5 blocks of 20 sales invoices from a sales journal.

12-6   Describe what is meant by a "sampling unit." Explain why the sampling unit for verifying the existence of recorded sales differs from the sampling unit for testing for the possibility of omitted sales.

12-7 Distinguish between a sampling error and a nonsampling error. How can each be reduced?

12-8 What major difference between tests of controls and tests of details of balances makes attribute sampling inappropriate for tests of details of balances?

12-9 Explain the difference between an attribute and an exception condition. State the exception condition for the following audit procedure: the duplicate sales invoice has been initialled indicating the performance of internal verification.

12-10 Define "stratified sampling," and explain its importance in auditing. How could an auditor obtain a stratified sample of 30 items from each of 3 strata in the confirmation of accounts receivable?

12-11 Distinguish between the point estimate of the total misstatements (likely misstatement) and the true value of the misstatements in the population. How can each be determined?

12-12 State the relationship between the following:

  a. ARACR and sample size
  b. Population size and sample size
  c. TER and sample size
  d. EPER and sample size

12-13 Define what is meant by "sampling risk." Does sampling risk apply to nonstatistical sampling, MUS, attribute sampling, and variables sampling? Explain.

12-14 Explain what is meant by "analysis of exceptions," and discuss its importance.

12-15 Outline a situation for which discovery sampling would be used.

12-16 Distinguish between random selection and statistical measurement. State the circumstances under which one can be used without the other.

MULTIPLE CHOICE QUESTIONS

12-17 Select the most appropriate response for each question.

a. From a random sample of items listed from a client's inventory count, a public accountant estimates with a 10 percent ARACR that the CUER is between 4 percent and 6 percent. The accountant's major concern is that there is one chance in 10 that the true deviation rate in the population is

  (1) more than 6 percent.
  (2) less than 6 percent.
  (3) more than 4 percent.
  (4) less than 4 percent.

b. If all other factors specified in a sampling plan remain constant, changing the ARACR from 10 percent to 5 percent would cause the required sample size to

  (1) increase.
  (2) remain the same.
  (3) decrease.
  (4) become indeterminate.

c. In a random sample of 1,000 records, an auditor determines that the SER is 2 percent. The auditor can state that the exception rate in the population is

  (1) not more than 3 percent.
  (2) not less than 2 percent.

  (3) probably about 2 percent.
  (4) not less than 1 percent.

d. If an auditor wishes to select a random sample that must have a 10 percent ARACR and a TER of 10 percent, the size of the sample to be selected will decrease as the estimate of the

  (1) population exception rate increases.
  (2) population exception rate decreases.
  (3) population size increases.
  (4) ARACR increases.

(AICPA adapted)

e. From prior experience, a public accountant is aware that cash disbursements contain a few unusually large disbursements. In using statistical sampling, the public accountant's best course of action is to

  (1) increase the sample size to lessen the effect of the unusually large disbursements.
  (2) eliminate any unusually large disbursements that appear in the sample.
  (3) continue to draw new samples until no unusually large disbursements appear in the sample.
  (4) stratify the cash disbursements population so that the unusually large disbursements are reviewed separately.

DISCUSSION QUESTIONS AND PROBLEMS

12-18

a. For each of the following independent problems, design an unbiased random sampling plan using the random number table in Table 12-2. The plan should include defining the sampling unit, establishing a numbering system for the population, and establishing a correspondence between the random number table and the population. After the plan has been designed, select the first five sample items from the random number table for each problem. Use a starting point of row 1,009, column 1, for each problem. Read down the table using the left-most digits in the column. When you reach the last item in a column, go to the top of the next column.

  1. Prenumbered sales invoices in a sales journal where the

lowest invoice number is 1 and the highest is 6,211.
2. Prenumbered bills of lading where the lowest document number is 21,926 and the highest is 28,511.

b. Use an available random number generator in a spreadsheet or other source to obtain the above samples with the computer.

12-19 For the examination of the financial statements of Scotia Inc., Rosa Schellenberg, a public accountant, has decided to apply nonstatistical audit sampling in the tests of sales transactions. Based on her knowledge of Scotia's operations in the area of sales, she decides that the estimated population deviation rate is likely to be 3 percent and that she is willing to accept a 5 percent risk that the true population exception rate is not greater than 6 percent. Given this information, Schellenberg selects a random sample of 150 sales invoices from the 5,000 prepared during the year and examines them for exceptions. She notes the following exceptions in her working papers. There is no other documentation.

Required

a. Which of the following should be defined as an exception?
b. Explain why it is inappropriate to set a single acceptable TER and EPER for the combined exceptions.
c. State the appropriate analysis of exceptions for each of the exceptions in the sample.

Invoice No.	Comment
5028	Sales invoice had incorrect price but a subsequent credit note was sent out as a correction.

Invoice No.	Comment
6791	Voided sales invoice examined by auditor.
6810	Shipping document for a sale of merchandise could not be located.
7364	Sales invoice for $2,875 has not been collected and is six months past due.
7625	Client unable to locate the printed duplicate copy of the sales invoice.
8431	Invoice was dated three days later than the date of the shipping document.
8528	Customer purchase order is not attached to the duplicate sales invoice.
8566	Billing is for $100 less than it should be due to a pricing error.
8780	Client unable to locate the printed duplicate copy of the sales invoice.
9169	Credit not authorized, but the sale was for only $7.65.

12-20 An audit partner is developing an office training program to familiarize her professional staff with statistical decision models applicable to the audit of dollar-value balances. She wishes to demonstrate the relationship of sample sizes to population size and variability and the auditor's specifications as to tolerable misstatement and ARIA. The partner prepared the table below to show comparative population characteristics and audit specifications of the two populations.

Required

In items (1) through (5) below, you are to indicate for the specific case from the table that follows the required sample size to be selected from population 1 relative to the sample from population 2.

(1) In case 1 the required sample size from population 1 is _____.

(2) In case 2 the required sample size from population 1 is _____.

(3) In case 3 the required sample size from population 1 is _____.

(4) In case 4 the required sample size from population 1 is _____.

(5) In case 5 the required sample size from population 1 is _____.

Your answer should be selected from the following responses:

a. Larger than the required sample size from population 2.
b. Equal to the required sample size from population 2.
c. Smaller than the required sample size from population 2.
d. Indeterminate relative to the required sample size from population 2.

(AICPA adapted)

Table for Problem 12-20

	Characteristics of Population 1 Relative to Population 2		Audit Specifications as to a Sample from Population 1 Relative to a Sample from Population 2	
	Size	Estimated Population Exception Rate	Tolerable Misstatement	ARIA
Case 1	Equal	Equal	Equal	Lower
Case 2	Equal	Larger	Larger	Equal
Case 3	Larger	Equal	Smaller	Higher
Case 4	Smaller	Smaller	Equal	Higher
Case 5	Larger	Equal	Equal	Lower

12-21 You have just completed the accounts receivable confirmation process in the audit of Danforth Paper Company Ltd., a paper supplier to retail shops and commercial users.

Following are the data related to this process:

Accounts receivable recorded balance	$2,760,000
Number of accounts	7,320

A nonstatistical sample was taken as follows:

All accounts over $10,000 (23 accounts)	$465,000
77 accounts under $10,000	$81,500
Materiality	$100,000

Inherent and control risk are both high.
No relevant analytical procedures were performed.

The table at right gives the results of the confirmation procedures.

Required

Evaluate the results of the nonstatistical sample. Consider both the direct implications of the misstatements found and the effect of using a sample.

	Recorded Value	Audited Value
Items over $10,000	$465,000	$432,000
Items under $10,000	81,500	77,150
Individual misstatements for items under $10,000:		
Item 12	5,120	4,820
Item 19	485	385
Item 33	1,250	250
Item 35	3,975	3,875
Item 51	1,850	1,825
Item 59	4,200	3,780
Item 74	2,405	0
	19,285	14,935

12-22 Sampling, whether statistical or judgmental, is an integral part of the audit process. Its use raises fundamental auditing issues which have become the subject of professional literature and studies. A decision to use sampling involves a number of practical and conceptual considerations.

Required

Describe these considerations.

(CICA adapted)

PROFESSIONAL JUDGMENT PROBLEM

12-23 Diane, a computer audit technician, has been selecting payroll attribute samples for Soft Drink Distribution Systems (SDDS) Ltd. for several years. It took about a week to set up the computer-assisted audit test, and the client gave Diane a password to have read only access to the payroll files remotely. Every quarter, Diane spends less than half an hour selecting samples that she forwards to the audit team for their interim audit.

This year, the firm has assigned a new audit manager, Joe, to the SDDS audit. Joe has been assigned the task of trying to create a more efficient audit in order to maintain audit fees at the same level as the prior year. Joe has informed Diane that he will no longer require her services, that staff will use systematic sampling to select a sample from the 5,000 employees. They will ask the client to provide spreadsheet files in Excel for each weekly file, and then use an Excel macro to select the test. Joe believes it will take him an hour or two to set up the macro process, and then another hour or two to select the sample. Since his charge out rate is considerably less than Diane's, this will save some money on the audit.

When Diane asked Joe how he was going to evaluate the sample, he said he would use the firm's manual tables.

Required

What should Diane do? Discuss the advantages and disadvantages of the two sample selection methods described in the case.

CASE

12-24 CA's firm is joint auditor of the TC Bank and is responsible this year for the audit of securities. As in prior years, audit procedures have been carried out during the year on security transactions and balances recorded in the books. CA is planning the physical security count on October 31, the bank's fiscal year end. In prior years, this count had been carried out over a three-day period by a task force of auditors from both audit firms. The count continued 24 hours a day with teams of counters working 8-hour shifts until all the securities had been counted. During this period, the auditors took over control of the vaults so that the routine bank operations in the vault were effectively suspended (this suspension could range from one to three business days, depending on whether the count commenced Friday evening).

CA had discussed the forthcoming physical count with bank officials and some reservations had been expressed. First, the anticipated two-day disruption of the securities department in the current year was very inconvenient to the bank. Second, the audit fee was increasing each year and the officials questioned the justification of the cost of the count in sheer hours alone. And third, since the bank's computer department had complete records of all security transactions and certificates held on data files, it was suggested that a more modern approach to the count might be adopted. Further, CA knew that the count was inconvenient to his firm's staff planning as a large portion of the staff were needed to do this job during a busy time of the year.

After the meeting with bank officials, CA wondered whether the count might be done on a statistical sampling basis similar to sampling techniques used by his firm in verifying receivables. He sat down to draft a memorandum on this approach for consideration by his partners.

Required

Outline the points to be included in CA's memorandum under the following headings:

a. Audit objectives of the physical count.

b. Description and assessment of various statistical sampling techniques in terms of achieving the audit objectives.

c. Recommendations, taking into account any other considerations.

Note: For the purpose of your answer, ignore any statutory requirements of external bank auditors.

(CICA adapted)

APPLICATION OF THE AUDIT PROCESS TO THE SALES AND COLLECTION CYCLE

To understand how auditing is done in practice, it is important to understand how auditing concepts are applied to specific auditing areas. The sales and collection cycle is the first area we look at for a detailed application of auditing concepts because this cycle is an important part of every audit and because it is reasonably straightforward. The next two chapters apply the concepts you learned in Part 2 to the audit of sales, cash receipts, and the related income statement and balance sheet accounts in the cycle.

The objective of Chapter 13 is to help you learn the methodology for designing tests of controls for sales, cash receipts, and the other classes of transactions in the sales and collection cycle. Chapter 14 presents the methodology for designing audit procedures for the audit of account balances in the sales and collection cycle.

AUDIT OF THE SALES AND COLLECTION CYCLE: TESTS OF CONTROLS

Now that we have looked at the planning of the audit, including the risk assessment process, it is time to look at the execution phase—how do we actually do the testing? Which tests are conducted and for what purpose? In this chapter, we look at the testing of internal controls for the sales and collection cycle.

LEARNING OBJECTIVES

After reading this chapter, you should be able to answer the following questions:

1. What are typical records and transactions in the sales cycle?

2. How do general controls affect the audit of the sales and collection cycle? Describe the methodology for designing tests of controls for sales.

3. List the methodology for controls over: sales returns and allowances, cash receipts transactions, uncollectible accounts, and account balances. What is the effect of the results of tests of controls on the audit?

4. What is the typical audit process for tests of controls? How is an audit program of tests of controls of sales organized?

THE CHOICE IS SIMPLE—RELY ON INTERNAL CONTROL OR RESIGN

City Finance Inc. is one of the largest clients managed out of the Montreal office of a Big Four firm. It is a financial services conglomerate with almost 200 offices in Canada and the United States, as well as branch offices overseas. The company has over 200,000 accounts receivable and processes millions of sales and other transactions annually.

The company's computer centre is in a large environmentally controlled room containing several large mainframe computers and a great deal of ancillary equipment. There are two complete online systems, one serving as a backup for the other, as systems failure would preclude operations in all of the company's branches.

The company has an excellent system of checks and balances where branch office transaction totals are reconciled to head office data processing control totals daily, which in turn are reconciled to outside bank account records monthly. Whenever this regular reconciliation process indicates a significant out-of-balance condition, procedures are initiated to resolve the problem as quickly as possible. There is a large internal audit staff that oversees any special investigative efforts that are required.

Because City Finance Inc. is a public company, it must file its annual report with the Quebec and Ontario securities commissions within 90 days of its fiscal year end. In addition, the company likes to announce annual earnings and issue its annual report as soon after year end as

Very large organizations process millions of transactions and may have thousands (or even millions) of customers. The role of sampling, whether for tests of controls or tests of details, becomes important, as does the methodology used to conduct such sampling. What types of samples would you use for such large clients? Judgmental or statistical or both? Think about the different ways that you could use sampling for clients such as City Finance.

→13.1 THE TYPICAL SALES CYCLE

The overall objective in the audit of the sales and collection cycle is to evaluate whether the account balances affected by the cycle are fairly presented in accordance with generally accepted accounting principles. The following are typical accounts included in the sales and collection cycle:

- Sales
- Sales returns and allowances
- Bad-debt expense
- Cash discounts taken
- Trade accounts receivable
- Allowance for uncollectible accounts
- Cash in bank (debits from cash receipts)

The goods and services tax is collected by an entity and remitted to the federal government. Accordingly, in Figure 5-3 on page 117, the Hillsburg Hardware trial balance shows *goods and services tax payable* (the net liability) as being in the acquisitions and payment cycle, which is discussed in Chapter 18.

For example, look at the adjusted trial balance for Hillsburg Hardware Limited on page 117. Accounts on the trial balance affected by the sales and collection cycle are identified by the letter *S* in the left margin. Each of the above accounts is included, except cash discounts taken. For other audits, the names and the nature of the accounts may vary, of course, depending on the industry and client involved. There are differences in account titles for a service company, a retail company, and an insurance company, but the basic concepts are the same. To provide a frame of reference for understanding the material in this chapter, a retail outlet with consumers and commercial customers is assumed.

A brief summary of the way accounting information flows through the various accounts in the sales and collection cycle is illustrated in Figure 13-1 by the use of T-accounts. This figure shows that there are five **classes of transactions** included in **the sales and collection cycle**:

- Sales (cash and sales on account)
- Cash receipts
- Sales returns and allowances
- Charge-off of uncollectible accounts
- Bad-debt expense

CLASSES OF TRANSACTIONS IN THE SALES AND COLLECTION CYCLE—the categories of transactions for the sales and collection cycle in a typical company: sales, cash receipts, sales returns and allowances, charge-off of uncollectible accounts, and bad-debt expense

Figure 13-1 also shows that with the exception of cash sales, every transaction and amount ultimately is included in two balance sheet accounts, accounts receivable or allowance for uncollectible accounts.

For the most part, the audit of the sales and collection cycle can be performed independently of the audit of other cycles and subjectively combined with the other parts of the audit as the evidence accumulation process proceeds. Auditors must keep in mind that the concept of materiality requires them to consider the combination of misstatements in all parts of the audit before making a final judgment on the fair presentation of the financial statements. This is done by continuously summarizing errors and integrating regular file review throughout the engagement with the many parts of the audit.

The types of audit tests discussed in Chapter 11, and shown in Figure 11-1 on page 318, are all used extensively in the audit of the sales and collection cycle. Tests of controls are used primarily to test the effectiveness of internal controls over the five classes of transactions in the cycle and to test the dollar amounts of these same five classes of transactions. Analytical procedures are used to test the relationships among the account balances in the cycle, both to one another and to prior years' balances. Tests of details of balances are used to verify ending account balances, primarily accounts receivable. Tests of controls are studied in this chapter.

Nature of the Sales and Collection Cycle

The **sales and collection cycle** involves the decisions and processes necessary for the transfer of the ownership of goods and services to customers after they are made available for sale. It begins with a request by a customer and ends with the conversion of material or service into an account receivable, and ultimately into cash.

The cycle includes several classes of transactions, accounts, and business functions, as well as a number of documents, reports, and records. Information that could be included in computer data files is shown in Figure 13-2. The classes of transactions, accounts, business functions, and documents are shown in Table 13-1. Semi-permanent information and transaction information are updated during normal processing within the sales and collection cycle, as discussed in the remainder of this chapter.

SALES AND COLLECTION CYCLE— involves the decisions and processes necessary for the transfer of the ownership of goods and services to customers after they are made available for sale; begins with a request by a customer and ends with the conversion of material or service into an account receivable, and ultimately into cash

FIGURE 13-1	Accounts in the Sales and Collection Cycle

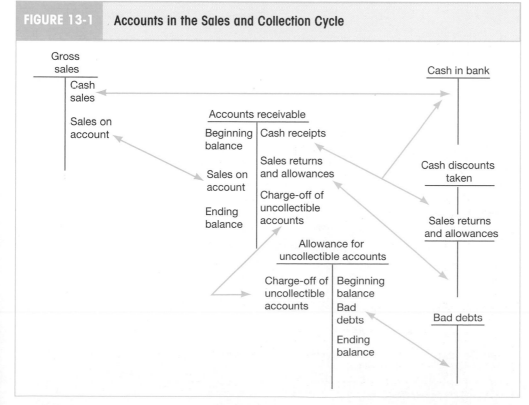

FIGURE 13-2	Typical Information Included in Accounts Receivable or Sales Computer Data Files

Semi-Permanent Information	Transaction Information
Semi-permanent information is often called **master file data**. It is established when a customer starts purchasing, and it is updated as customer information changes.	**Transaction information** is based on customer activity, and there is normally one transaction for each activity, such as a sale or cash payment.
Customer number or code	Customer number or code
Customer name	Customer name
Customer billing address	Transaction type (sale, credit, payment, adjustment)
Customer shipping address	
Customer phone number	Transaction date
Credit limit	Transaction amount
Payment terms (includes applicable discounts)	Transaction detail (item detail)
Year-to-date sales	Transaction tracking (the individual who entered the transaction)
Current balance outstanding	

TABLE 13-1	Classes of Transactions, Accounts, Business Functions, and Related Documents and Reports for the Sales and Collection Cycle

Classes of Transactions	Accounts	Business Functions	Documents and Reports
Sales	Sales Accounts receivable	Processing customer orders	Customer order
		Granting credit	Customer order
		Shipping goods	Shipping document
		Billing customers and recording sales	Sales invoice Sales journal/history report Summary sales report Accounts receivable trial balance Monthly statements
Cash receipts	Cash in bank (debits from cash receipts) Accounts receivable	Processing and recording cash receipts	Remittance advice Bank deposit detail Cash receipts journal
Sales returns and allowances	Sales returns and allowances Accounts receivable	Processing and recording sales returns and allowances	Credit memo Sales returns and allowances journal
Charge-off of uncollectible accounts	Accounts receivable Allowance for uncollectible accounts	Charging off uncollectible accounts receivable	Uncollectible account authorization form
Bad-debt expense	Bad-debt expense Allowance for uncollectible accounts	Providing for bad debts	Journal entry authorization
Master file change	Customer master file accounts	Maintaining semi-permanent data	Master file change form

Note: "Journal" and "history report" are synonymous terms.

The nature of computer processing used within a transaction cycle determines potential controls available in the system. For example, transactions can be processed using groups of transactions (also called **batch processing**), or they can be processed one at a time with immediate update against the data files (called **online processing**). Many companies use both methods. Payroll may be processed weekly in batch mode, while sales orders received over the telephone may be recorded as received. The nature of the controls available to monitor the transactions is thus different. A summary of these differences is shown in Table 13-2.

EFFECTS ON OTHER TRANSACTIONS OR ON OTHER SUBSYSTEMS For both batch and online systems, a transaction could cause other automatic transactions. For example, shipment of goods to customers could result in the automatic generation of a supplier purchase order if quantities fell below a certain level. Automatic postings to the general ledger could occur based on time or based on user initiation.

For both batch and online systems, it may be possible to identify who has entered transactions by associating user identification codes (user IDs) with the data entry person. This assists with segregation of duties.

Business Functions in the Cycle and Related Documents and Records

The business functions for a cycle are the key activities that an organization must complete to execute and record business transactions. Column three of Table 13-1 identifies the nine **business functions** in a typical **sales and collection cycle**. An understanding of these business functions for the sales and collection cycle promotes understanding of how an audit of the cycle is conducted. Students often also find it difficult to envision which documents and records exist in any given audit area and how they flow through the client's organization.

TABLE 13-2	Control Differences Between Batch and Online Systems	
Control Category	**Batch Systems**	**Online Systems**
Audit trails	Transactions can readily be traced from source transaction through to general ledger posting. Groups of documents are totalled and entered into the system, and reports are printed showing the document details and the totals. These totals can be traced to transaction history reports or transaction journals, and from there to the general ledger.	Transactions may be initiated and entered without source documents (e.g., be initiated by a telephone call and entered directly into a system). Paper will normally be produced when the goods are picked or shipped, with daily or weekly summaries printed. Controls such as document sequencing are used to ensure that all transactions are completed. A full audit trail may be available in electronic form only.
Error detection and correction	Since transactions are processed in groups, if one transaction is in error, the entire batch of transactions may be rejected from subsequent processing. Each transaction must be correct before all transactions can be processed.	The focus is on preventing incorrect transactions from being entered. For example, systems should check for invalid customer numbers and reasonableness of dates or amounts prior to processing individual transactions.
Segregation of duties	Segregation can be achieved by separating the functions of totalling and counting of source documents from data entry. A person other than the data entry person should verify that the control totals entered match the control totals prepared from source documents. This verification may be called **data control function**.	Decentralization to departments can result in individual users performing traditionally incompatible functions, such as entering and verifying cash receipts and sales and accounts receivable, and updating credit limits. Passwords could be used to separate some of these functions. Alternatively, independent preparation and review of exception reports could compensate for such segregation problems.

The business functions for the sales and collection cycle and the most common documents and records used in each function are examined in this section.

Processing Customer Orders The request for goods by a customer is the starting point for the entire cycle. Legally, it is an offer to buy goods under specified terms.

CUSTOMER ORDER This is a request for merchandise by a customer. It may be received by telephone, by letter, electronically, by a printed form that has been sent to prospective and existing customers, through salespeople, or in other ways.

Granting Credit Before goods are shipped, a properly authorized person or computer program must *approve credit* to the customer for sales on account. Weak practices in credit approval or in changing the credit limit in the master file frequently result in excessive bad debts and accounts receivable that may be uncollectible. For most firms, credit approval is handled by having credit limits established when the customer is set up in the customer master file. Sales are automatically authorized as long as the account receivable stays within the authorized credit limit. Once the balance approaches the credit limit, exception reports are printed for the credit manager, or other methods are used to determine whether credit limits should be extended or individual sales should continue to be approved.

Shipping Goods This critical function is the first point in the cycle where company assets are given up. Most companies recognize sales when goods are shipped. A shipping document is prepared at the time of shipment; this can be done automatically by the computer based on sales order information. The shipping document, which is frequently a multicopy bill of lading, is essential to the proper billing of shipments to customers. Companies that maintain perpetual inventory records also update them based on shipping information.

SHIPPING DOCUMENT This document is prepared to initiate the shipping of goods, indicating the description of the merchandise, the quantity shipped, and other relevant data. The original document is sent to the customer, and one or more copies are retained. It is also used as a signal to bill the customer. One type of shipping document is a bill of lading, which is a written contract between the carrier and the seller concerning the receipt and shipment of goods. Often bills of lading include only the number of boxes or kilograms shipped, rather than complete details of quantity and description. Throughout the text, we assume that complete details are included on bills of lading or on the internally generated shipping documents. Details of shipment are entered into the computer system so that perpetual inventory records can be updated and the billing process can commence.

Billing Customers and Recording Sales Since the billing of customers is the means by which the customer is informed of the amount due for the goods, it must be done correctly and on a timely basis. The most important aspects of billing are making sure that all shipments made have been billed, that no shipment has been billed more than once, and that each shipment is billed for the proper amount. Billing at the proper amount is dependent on charging the customer for the quantity shipped at the authorized price. The authorized price includes consideration of freight charges, insurance, and terms of payment.

In most systems, billing of the customer includes preparation of a multicopy sales invoice and updating of the sales transactions file, customer master file, and general ledger files for sales and accounts receivable. This information is used to generate the sales journal and, along with cash receipts and miscellaneous credits, allows preparation of the accounts receivable trial balance. Point-of-sale systems, such as those seen at many retail counters, often combine data entry and update for shipment, inventory, sales systems, and cash receipts with the entry of a single transaction.

SALES INVOICE This is a document indicating the description and quantity of goods sold, the price including freight, insurance, terms, and other relevant data. Typically, it is printed by the computer after the customer number, quantity, and destination of goods shipped are entered. The sales invoice is the method of indicating to the customer the amount of a sale and due date of a payment. The original invoice is sent to the customer, and one or more copies are retained.

SALES JOURNAL This is a listing of the sales history transaction file on a daily, weekly, monthly, or yearly basis. A detailed sales journal includes each sales transaction. It usually indicates gross sales for different classifications, such as product lines, the entry to accounts receivable, and miscellaneous debits and credits such as goods and services tax collected. The sales journal can also include sales returns and allowances transactions.

SUMMARY SALES REPORT This is a listing that summarizes sales for a period. The report typically includes information analyzed by key components such as customer, salesperson, product, and territory.

ACCOUNTS RECEIVABLE TRIAL BALANCE This is a listing of the amount owed by each customer at a point in time. It is prepared directly from the accounts receivable data files. It is most frequently an *aged* trial balance, showing how old the accounts receivable components of each customer's balance are as of the report date. This report can be printed showing only balances forward (i.e., the total owed by each customer) or on an open item basis (i.e., showing all sales invoices that have not been paid).

MONTHLY STATEMENT This is a document sent to each customer indicating the monthly beginning balance of accounts receivable, the amount and date of each sale, cash payments received, credit memos issued, and the ending balance due. It is, in essence, a copy of the customer's portion of the accounts receivable activity.

Processing and Recording Cash Receipts The preceding four functions are necessary for getting the goods into the hands of customers, properly billing them, and reflecting the information in the accounting records. The result of these four functions is sales transactions. The remaining five functions involve the collection and recording of cash, sales returns and allowances, charge-off of uncollectible accounts, providing for bad-debt expense, and maintenance of semi-permanent information contained in customer master files.

Processing and recording cash receipts includes receiving, depositing, and recording cash. Cash includes both currency and cheques. The most important concern is the possibility of theft. Theft can occur before receipts are entered in the records or later. The most important consideration in the handling of cash receipts is that all cash must be deposited in the bank at the proper amount on a timely basis and recorded in the cash receipts transaction file, which is used to prepare the cash receipts journal and update the customer master and general ledger files. Remittance advices are important for this purpose.

REMITTANCE ADVICE This is a document that accompanies the sales invoice mailed to the customer and can be returned to the seller with the cash payment. It is used to indicate the customer name, the sales invoice number, and the amount of the invoice when the payment is received. Often, a second copy of the sales invoice is used as a remittance advice. Alternatively, the customer may list the invoice numbers and amount paid on the cheque stub, which then serves as a remittance advice. If the customer fails to identify the invoices being paid with his or her payment, the data entry person must later allocate the payment to specific invoices. A remittance advice is used to permit the immediate deposit of cash and to improve control over the custody of assets.

BANK DEPOSIT DETAIL This is a list prepared by an independent person (someone who has no responsibility for recording sales or accounts receivable) when cash is received. This could take the form of a listing of cheques received or a duplicate bank deposit slip. It is used to verify whether cash received was recorded and deposited at the correct amounts and on a timely basis.

CASH RECEIPTS JOURNAL This is a listing of cash receipts from collections, cash sales, and all other cash receipts. It indicates total cash received, the credit to accounts receivable at the gross amount of the original sale, trade discounts taken, and other debits and credits. The daily entries in the cash receipts journal are supported by remittance advices. The journal is generated for any time period from the cash receipts transactions included in the computer files.

Processing and Recording Sales Returns and Allowances When a customer is dissatisfied with the goods purchased, the seller frequently accepts the return of goods or grants a reduction in the charges. The company normally prepares a receiving report for the returned goods and returns them to inventory. Returns and allowances must be correctly and promptly recorded. *Credit memos* are normally issued for returns and allowances to aid in maintaining control and to facilitate record keeping.

CREDIT MEMO This is a document indicating a reduction in the amount due from a customer because of returned goods or an allowance granted. It often takes the same general form as a sales invoice, but it supports reductions in accounts receivable rather than increases.

SALES RETURNS AND ALLOWANCES JOURNAL This is a listing of sales returns and allowances. It performs the same function as the sales journal. Many companies record these transactions using the same system as that used for the recording of sales. Transactions would thus be listed in the sales journal rather than a separate journal.

Charging Off Uncollectible Accounts Receivable

Despite the diligence of credit departments, it is not unusual for some customers not to pay their bills. When the company concludes that an amount is no longer collectible, it must be charged off. Typically, this occurs after a customer files bankruptcy or the account is turned over to a collection agency. Proper accounting requires an adjustment for these uncollectible amounts.

UNCOLLECTIBLE ACCOUNT AUTHORIZATION FORM This is an internal document, indicating authority to write off an account receivable as uncollectible.

Focus Box 13-1

LOCKBOX SYSTEMS AND ELECTRONIC FUNDS TRANSFER

Many companies engage a bank to assist in the processing of cash receipts from customers. Some companies use a lockbox system, whereby customers mail payments to an address maintained by bank personnel. The bank is responsible for opening all receipts, maintaining records of all payments by customers received at the lockbox address, and depositing receipts into the company's bank account on a timely basis. In other cases, receipts are submitted electronically from customers' bank accounts to a company bank account through the use of electronic funds transfer (EFT). For consumer purchases by credit card on web sites, the issuer of the credit card uses EFT to transfer funds into the company's bank account almost immediately after the sale. For both lockbox systems and EFT, the bank provides information to the company to prepare the cash receipt entries in the company's accounting records. The use of both lockboxes and EFT allows for faster deposit of cash receipts into company bank accounts and often reduces risks associated with company personnel handling cash receipts.

Providing for Bad Debts

The provision for bad debts must be sufficient to allow for the current period sales that the company will be unable to collect in the future. For most companies, the provision represents a residual, resulting from management's end-of-period adjustment of the allowances for uncollectible accounts. Period-end reports or journal entries are used to document this adjustment.

Customer Master File Change

The customer master file is a file for maintaining semi-permanent data used for processing sales, payments, and other transactions associated with customers. The master file information is provided by the customer, and reviewed and approved prior to set-up. Approval is necessary for the credit limit and payment terms in particular or for changes to these fields. It is also important that customers provide changes, such as shipping addresses, in writing, since an incorrect shipping address would result in goods being shipped to an incorrect (or unauthorized) location. This approval may be evidenced by a master file change form. The changes can then be authorized by an appropriate individual prior to entry.

The outstanding balance field in the customer master file is updated for sales, sales returns and allowances, and cash receipts. The total of the individual outstanding account balances in the customer master file equals the total balance of accounts receivable in the general ledger. A printout of the accounts receivable master file shows, by customer, the balance of accounts receivable at that time. It is also sometimes called "the accounts receivable subsidiary ledger" or "subledger." If the company has a database, then the master file data is directly linked to the transaction data. Other computer installations have separate transaction files for unpaid transactions, sales, sales returns and allowances, and cash receipts that are used to update individual accounts receivable balances in the master file as entered, daily or weekly. Figures 5-2A, B, and C (see pages 115–116) illustrate typical transaction flows for manual, batch, and database systems.

→13.2   GENERAL CONTROLS AND AUDIT METHODOLOGY FOR TESTS OF CONTROLS

Effect of General Controls

As described in Chapter 9, general controls can be part of the control environment and part of individual applications or transaction cycles. Prior to assessing the individual transaction cycle, the auditor documents general controls that are pervasive and that affect multiple transaction cycles. For example, access and control policies and program change control procedures affect multiple cycles. If unauthorized individuals could establish or change credit limits, this would cause problems with collectibility of accounts. Access controls could then be tested as general controls, providing some control assurance for each application cycle that is affected. Similarly, the existence of excellent program change controls that have been tested would allow the auditor to place reliance on programs within each of the transaction cycles. Poor program change controls would suggest that the auditor could potentially rely on only manual controls in the transaction cycle. If unauthorized individuals could change how the accounts receivable aging is calculated or how invoices are calculated, the transactions would be unreliable. Thus, prior to documenting controls and assessing control risk in an individual cycle, the auditor reviews the general controls working-paper file to determine the controls in place, and whether reliance can be placed on these controls. Frequently, this assessment is completed by a specialist within the auditor's firm and, in particular, is based on the auditor's risk assessment process.

Following are the key areas that the auditor would review as part of general controls:

- Organization structure and job responsibilities within the data processing department
- Program change controls
- Physical access and security
- Logical access and security
- Documentation of programs and operations

These categories of general controls can include complex areas, such as data communications, database management systems, Internet applications, electronic data interchange, and electronic funds transfer.

Methodology for Designing Tests of Controls for Sales

The methodology for obtaining an understanding of internal controls and designing tests of controls for sales is shown in Figure 13-3. This methodology was studied in general terms in Chapters 9 and 11. It is applied specifically to sales in this section. The bottom box in Figure 13-3 shows the four evidence decisions the auditor must make. This section deals with deciding the appropriate audit procedures. For the timing decision, the tests are usually performed at an interim date if internal controls are effective, but they can also be done after the balance sheet date. Decisions on the appropriate sample size and the items to select are studied on page 398.

Figure 13-3 is supported by Table 13-3, which summarizes the application of the methodology in the figure. Table 13-3 lists the specific transaction-related audit objectives for sales along with related key controls and common tests of controls for the objectives. Table 13-3 is referred to frequently throughout the section.

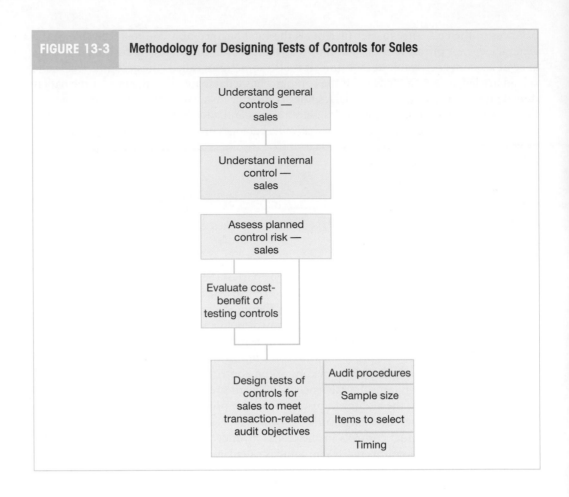

FIGURE 13-3 Methodology for Designing Tests of Controls for Sales

Understand general
controls —
sales

Understand internal
control —
sales

Assess planned
control risk —
sales

Evaluate cost-
benefit of
testing controls

Design tests of controls for sales to meet transaction-related audit objectives	Audit procedures
	Sample size
	Items to select
	Timing

Understand General Controls—Sales Certain general controls, such as access controls, will vary based upon the transaction cycle. The auditor needs to determine how password changes and other forms of security have been operationalized in the cycle. For example, some systems have passwords that allow entry into all functions of a cycle, while some systems have passwords that can be tailored to individual menu items. If a company has the latter type of system, it may be able to restrict master file changes and credit note generation. If these restrictions were not possible, then the auditor would look for other types of controls, such as the printing and review of reports that identify master file changes that have taken place.

The nature of programs in use affects the relevance of program change controls. When a company has purchased a software package and is unable to change the package, program change controls are considered excellent, since the programs cannot be changed. If the company has custom developed software with appropriate standards, documentation, and testing, controls over program changes are also likely to be assessed as good. When a company has informal program change procedures, poor testing, or no formal authorization of program changes, for example, program change controls are considered poor. This suggests that the auditor cannot rely on programs during the audit.

Problems with program change procedures or with access controls can have a strong impact on the auditor's assessment of control risk. The auditor may choose not to rely on any internal controls for clients with such control weaknesses.

Understand Internal Control—Sales Chapter 9 discussed how auditors obtain an understanding of internal control. A typical approach for sales is to conduct interviews, review internal audit working papers, study the clients' flowcharts, prepare an internal control questionnaire, and perform walk-through tests of sales. Figures 13-6 (page 393) and 13-7 (page 394) include an organization chart and a flowchart for Hillsburg Hardware Limited that are used to demonstrate the design of tests of controls for audit procedures.

TABLE 13-3 Summary of Transaction-Related Audit Objectives, Key Controls, and Tests of Controls for Sales

Transaction-Related Audit Objective	Key Internal Controls: Manual Systems	Key Internal Controls: Batch Systems	Key Internal Controls: Online Systems	Key Interdependent Internal Controls	Common Tests of Controls
Recorded sales are for shipments actually made to nonfictitious customers (occurrence).	• Recording of sales is supported by authorized shipping documents and approved customer purchase orders.	• Same as manual	• N/A. Likely no sales order documents.	• Review of exception reports that include unusual or large items extracted from transaction or master files.	• Examine copies of sales invoices for supporting bills of lading and customers' purchase orders. • Review the sales journal, general ledger, or trial balance for large or unusual items.*
	• Credit is approved before shipment takes place using manual review.	• Orders causing balances to exceed credit limits are printed on an exception report and are not processed for shipment.	• Orders causing balances to exceed credit limits require the entry of a supervisor password prior to shipment.††	• Orders causing balances to exceed credit limits are printed on an exception report and must be approved by a credit manager prior to shipment.	• Examine customer purchase order for credit approval. • Use test data to verify that orders causing balances to exceed credit limits are printed on exception reports. • Verify that password system has separate functionality for data entry and credit approval and that appropriate persons are assigned these functions. • Examine credit exception report for approval.
	• Sales invoices are prenumbered and properly accounted for (also satisfies completeness).	• Computer automatically generates sequential invoice numbers.	• Same as batch.	• Computer provides a report of missing invoice numbers, which are followed up by an independent person.	• Account for integrity of numerical sequence of sales invoices using block test. • Use generalized audit software to identify gaps in invoice numbers assigned.
	• N/A	• Only customer numbers existing in the customer master file are updated when they are entered.	• Sales invoices cannot be entered if the customer number is invalid.	• N/A	• Examine printouts of transactions rejected by the computer due to invalid customer numbers.† • Observe rejection of invalid customer numbers when entered by data entry staff into online system.
	• Approval is required to commence selling goods to a new customer or to change semi-permanent billing information.	• Approval is required to enter new customers or to change information for existing customers.	• A separate password is required to update customer master file information.	• Master file changes are printed on numerically controlled reports and reviewed by management.	• Examine master file change forms for authorization and compare to current master file information. • Review paper customer files for credit authorization forms and approval to accept customer.
	• Monthly statements are sent to customers; complaints receive independent follow-up (also satisfies posting and summarization).	• Same as manual.	• Same as manual.	• Same as manual.	• Observe whether statements are mailed, and examine customer correspondence files.

TABLE 13-3

Summary of Transaction-Related Audit Objectives, Key Controls, and Tests of Controls for Sales (continued)

Transaction-Related Audit Objective	Key Internal Controls: Manual Systems	Key Internal Controls: Batch Systems	Key Internal Controls: Online Systems	Key Interdependent Internal Controls	Common Tests of Controls
Existing sales transactions are recorded (completeness).	• Shipping documents (i.e., bills of lading or internal shipping documents) are prenumbered and accounted for.	• Same as manual.	• Same as manual.	• Computer checks for gaps in shipping document numbers and prints a report of missing numbers for independent follow-up.	• Account for integrity of numerical sequence of shipping documents using block test. • Trace shipping documents to resultant sales invoices and entry into sales history file and accounts receivable customer master file. • Verify independent follow-up of exception reports.
Recorded sales are for the amount of goods shipped and are correctly billed and recorded (accuracy).	• Determination that prices, terms, freight, and discounts are properly authorized.	• Invoices are prepared using prices, terms, freight, and discounts established in master files.	• Same as batch.	• Exception reports are reviewed by management.	• Recompute information on sales invoices. • Examine approved computer printout of unit selling prices and compare to invoice details.††
	• Shipping documents are matched to invoices. • Invoices are prepared using prices from an approved price list.	• Same as manual. • Approved unit selling prices are entered into the master files and used for all sales. • Batch totals are compared with computer summary reports.	• Shipping details are automatically used as the invoicing source. • Same as batch. • Invoice calculations (extensions, additions, taxes) are automatically calculated.		• Trace details on sales invoices to shipping documents, price lists, and customers' purchase orders. • Compare inventory selling prices in master files to approved master file change forms and invoice details. • Examine file of batch totals for initials of data control clerk; compare totals to summary reports.†† • Prepare test data and run through invoicing program to ensure program is functioning as required.
Sales transactions are classified to the correct account (classification).	• Adequate chart of accounts is used. • Internal review and verification is completed (also satisfies timing).	• Invoices can be posted only to valid customer accounts. • Posting is done automatically to sales account based upon batch totals.	• Invoices can only be prepared for valid customer accounts. • Posting is done automatically to sales account based upon periodic totals.	• Management reviews exception reports of unusual customer data.	• Review customer master file listing for adequacy. • Examine documents supporting sales transactions for proper classification. • Examine indication of internal verification on affected documents. • Use test data to verify that transactions are posted to correct general ledger accounts or conduct manual walk-through of transactions through programs.

TABLE 13-3 (continued)

Transaction-Related Audit Objective	Key Internal Controls: Manual Systems	Key Internal Controls: Batch Systems	Key Internal Controls: Online Systems	Key Interdependent Internal Controls	Common Tests of Controls
Sales are recorded on the correct dates (timing).	• Procedures requiring billing and recording of sales on a daily basis are performed as close to time of occurrence as possible.	• Same as manual. • System checks reasonableness of date entered.	• Same as manual. • System checks reasonableness of date entered.	• Management reviews sales and cost of sales analytical reports for reasonableness.	• Compare dates of recorded sales transactions with dates on shipping records. • Examine documents for unbilled shipments and unrecorded sales. • Verify management walk-through of analytical reports.
Sales transactions are updated correctly to the customer master file, and the posting to the general ledger summed these transactions correctly (posting and summarization).	• Transactions are summarized on a timely basis for posting to the general ledger. • Subsidiary accounts receivable records are periodically balanced to the general ledger.	• Customer master file is periodically printed for independent review. • Customer master file totals are compared with general ledger balance monthly and differences are investigated.	• Same as batch. • Same as batch.	• Aged accounts receivable trial balances are reviewed for reasonableness. • Run-to-run totals are compared and reconciled (i.e., previous monthly accounts receivable total plus transactions reconciles to current month totals).	• Examine initials on general ledger account reconciliation indicating comparison. • Trace sales journal entries to copies of sales orders, sales invoices, and shipping documents. • Foot journals and trace postings to general ledger and accounts receivable master files. • Use generalized audit software to add up the outstanding accounts receivable transactions and the balances in the accounts receivable master file. • Compare both independent totals to the accounts receivable general ledger balance.

* This analytical procedure can also apply to other objectives, including completeness, accuracy, and timing.

† This control would be tested on many audits by using the computer.

†† This control could also be considered an interdependent control, since both a computer-based and personal action are required.

Assess Planned Control Risk—Sales The auditor uses the information obtained in understanding internal control to assess control risk. There are four essential steps to this assessment, all of which were discussed in Chapter 9.

- First, the auditor needs a framework for assessing control risk. The framework for all classes of transactions is the six transaction-related audit objectives. For sales, these are shown for Hillsburg Hardware in Figure 13-8 on page 395. These six objectives are the same for every audit of sales.
- Second, the auditor must identify the key internal controls and weaknesses for sales. These are also shown in Figure 13-8. The controls and weaknesses will be different for every audit.
- After identifying the controls and weaknesses, the auditor relates them to the objectives and cross-references them to supporting working papers. This is also shown in Figure 13-8 with *W*s and *C*s in appropriate columns.
- Finally, the auditor assesses control risk for each objective by evaluating the controls and weaknesses for each objective. This step is a critical one because it affects the auditor's decisions about both tests of controls and substantive tests—it is a highly subjective decision. The bottom of Figure 13-8 shows the auditor's conclusions for Hillsburg Hardware Limited.

The section that follows discusses the key control activities for sales. A knowledge of these control activities is important for identifying the key controls and weaknesses for sales, which is the second step in assessing control risk.

ADEQUATE SEPARATION OF DUTIES Proper separation of duties helps to prevent various types of misstatements, both intentional and unintentional. To prevent fraud, it is important that anyone responsible for inputting sales and cash receipts transaction information into the computer be denied access to cash. It is also desirable to separate the credit-granting functions from the sales function, since credit checks are intended to offset the natural tendency of sales personnel to optimize volume even at the expense of high bad-debt write-offs. It is equally desirable that personnel responsible for doing internal comparisons are independent of those entering the original data. For example, comparison of batch control totals to summary reports and comparison of customer master file totals to the general ledger balance should be done by someone independent of those who input sales and cash receipt transactions.

PROPER AUTHORIZATION The auditor is concerned about authorization at *three key points*: credit must be properly authorized before a sale takes place; goods should be shipped only after proper authorization; and prices, including base terms, freight, and discounts, must be authorized. The first two controls are meant to prevent the loss of company assets by shipping to fictitious customers or those who will fail to pay for the goods. Price authorization is meant to make sure the sale is billed at the price set by company policy.

ADEQUATE DOCUMENTS AND RECORDS Since each company has a unique system of originating, processing, and recording transactions, it may be difficult to evaluate whether its procedures are designed for maximum control; nevertheless, adequate record-keeping procedures must exist before most of the transaction-related audit objectives can be met. Some companies, for example, automatically prepare a multicopy prenumbered sales invoice at the time a customer order is received. Copies of this document are used to approve credit, authorize shipment, record the number of units shipped, and bill customers. Under this system, there is almost no chance of the failure to bill a customer if all invoices are accounted for periodically. Under a different system, in which the sales invoice is prepared only after a shipment has been made, the likelihood of failure to bill a customer is high unless some compensating control exists.

PRENUMBERED DOCUMENTS An important characteristic of documents for sales is the use of prenumbering, which is meant to prevent both the failure to bill or record sales and the occurrence of duplicate billings and recording thereof. Of course, it does not do much good to have prenumbered documents unless they are properly accounted for. An example of the use of this control is the filing, by a billing clerk, of a copy of all shipping documents in sequential order after each shipment is billed, with someone else periodically accounting for all numbers and investigating the reason for any missing documents. Another example is programming the computer to prepare a listing of unused numbers at month's end with follow-up by appropriate personnel.

MAILING OF MONTHLY STATEMENTS The mailing of monthly statements by someone who has no responsibility for handling cash or preparing the sales and accounts receivable records is a useful control because it encourages a response from customers if the balance is improperly stated. For maximum effectiveness, all disagreements about the balance in the account should be directed to a designated official who has no responsibility for handling cash or recording sales or accounts receivable.

INTERNAL VERIFICATION PROCEDURES The use of independent persons for checking the processing and recording of sales transactions is essential for fulfilling each of the six transaction-related audit objectives. Examples of these procedures include accounting for the numerical sequence of prenumbered documents, checking the accuracy of document preparation, and reviewing reports for unusual or incorrect items. Examples include review of balances exceeding credit limits, approval of master file change reports, and examination of sales statistics.

Evaluate Cost Benefit of Testing Controls After the auditor has identified the key internal controls and weaknesses and assessed control risk, he or she decides whether substantive tests will be reduced sufficiently to justify the cost of performing tests of controls. Whenever it is practical, auditors make this decision before completing a matrix such as the one illustrated in Figure 13-8 on page 395. It makes little sense to incur the cost of identifying controls and assessing control risk below maximum if there will be no reduction of substantive tests.

Figure 13-3 and Table 13-3 are referred to during the subsequent discussion. Figure 13-3 (page 378) shows the methodology for designing tests of controls for sales. Table 13-3 (pages 379–381) provides detailed examples used throughout the chapter.

TRANSACTION-RELATED AUDIT OBJECTIVES (COLUMN 1) The **transaction-related audit objectives** included in Table 13-3 are derived from the framework developed in Chapters 5 and 9. Although certain internal controls satisfy more than one objective, it is desirable to consider each objective separately to facilitate a better assessment of control risk.

KEY INTERNAL CONTROLS (COLUMNS 2 THROUGH 5) The internal controls for sales are designed to achieve the six transaction-related audit objectives discussed in Chapters 5 and 9. If the controls necessary to satisfy any one of the objectives are inadequate, the likelihood of misstatements related to that objective is increased, regardless of the controls for the other objectives. The methodology for determining existing controls was studied in Chapter 9.

The source of the controls in these columns is a control risk matrix such as the one illustrated in Figure 13-8. A control may satisfy more than one audit objective if there is more than one *C* for that control on the control risk matrix.

COMMON TESTS OF CONTROLS (COLUMN 6) For each internal control on which the auditor chooses to rely, he or she designs a **test of control** to verify its effectiveness. Observe that the tests of controls in column 6 in Table 13-3 relate directly to the internal controls.

Design Tests of Controls for Sales For each control on which the auditor plans to rely to reduce assessed control risk, he or she must design one or more tests of controls to verify its effectiveness. In most audits, it is relatively easy to determine the nature of the test of the control from the nature of the control. For example, if the internal control is having the sales programs identify orders that cause customers to go over their credit limit and having the orders printed for subsequent approval, the test of control would include verifying that the program is functioning as designed and examining the credit exception report for approval.

The last column in Table 13-3 shows examples of tests of control for key internal controls in columns 2 through 5. For example, the first key internal control is "Recording of sales is supported by authorized shipping documents and approved customer purchase orders." The test of control is "Examine copies of sales invoices for supporting bills of lading and customers' purchase orders." For this test, it is important that the auditor start with sales invoices and examine documents in support of the sales invoices rather than go in the opposite direction. If the auditor traced from shipping documents to sales invoices, it would be a test of completeness. Direction of tests is discussed further on pages 385–386.

A common test of control for sales is accounting for a sequence of various types of documents, such as duplicate sales invoices selected from the sales journal, watching for omitted and duplicate numbers or invoices outside the normal sequence, called a "block test." This test simultaneously provides evidence of both the existence and completeness objectives. Should the auditor choose to use generalized audit software, then a gap test can be conducted by scanning the entire transaction history file and identifying any gaps in the numeric sequence. Types of computer-assisted audit tests (CAATs) are described in Appendix F on page 408.

The appropriate tests of controls for separation of duties are ordinarily restricted to the auditor's observations of activities and discussions with personnel. For example, it is possible to observe whether the billing clerk has access to cash when opening incoming mail or depositing cash. It is usually also necessary to ask personnel what their responsibilities are and if there are any circumstances where their responsibilities are different from the normal policy. For example, the employee responsible for billing customers may state that he or she does not have access to cash. Future discussion may elicit that when the cashier is on vacation, that person takes over the cashier's duties. Allocation of password functionality should also be reviewed to ensure that individuals have not been assigned functions that are incompatible.

Several of the tests of controls in Table 13-3 can be performed using the computer. For example, one of the key internal controls to prevent fraudulent or fictitious transactions is the inclusion of procedures to ensure that only approved information was entered into the customer master files. If a nonexistent customer number is entered into the computer, it would be rejected. A test of control for online data entry systems is for the auditor to attempt to enter nonexistent customer numbers into the computer to make sure that the computer control is in operation.

Dual-Purpose or Weakness Investigation Tests Some of the procedures listed in Table 13-3 are performed on every audit regardless of the circumstances, whereas others are dependent on the adequacy of the controls and the results of the tests of controls. Tests that can be used to quantify the extent of potential error can be used as dual-purpose tests (for assessing control risk and also as a substantive test; **weakness investigation tests**) or for quantifying the potential dollar effect of monetary errors or fraud and other irregularities due to control weaknesses.

The audit procedures used are affected by the internal controls and the nonquantitative tests of controls for that objective. Some of the tests are dual-purpose tests introduced in Chapter 11. In any event, the purpose of all tests in column 6 is to test the controls and assist the auditor in assessing control risk.

Materiality, results of the prior year, and the other factors discussed in Chapter 8 also affect the procedures used. Some of the audit procedures employed when internal controls are inadequate are discussed in a later section.

Determining the proper tests of controls procedures for sales is relatively difficult because the nature of client systems varies considerably.

In subsequent paragraphs, the procedures frequently *not* performed are emphasized, since they are the ones requiring an audit decision. The procedures are discussed in the same order in which they were included in Table 13-3. It should be noted that some procedures fulfill more than one objective.

RECORDED SALES OCCURRED For this objective, the auditor is concerned with the possibility of *three types of misstatements*: sales being included in the journals for which no shipment was made, sales recorded more than once, and shipments being made to nonexistent customers and recorded as sales. The first two types of misstatements can be intentional or unintentional; the last type is always intentional. As might be imagined, the inclusion of fraudulent sales is rare. The potential consequences are significant because they lead to an overstatement of assets and income.

WEAKNESS INVESTIGATION TESTS—tests conducted to determine whether a material error or material misstatement could occur due to a control weakness

There is an important difference between finding intentional and unintentional over-statements of sales. An unintentional overstatement normally also results in a clear over-statement of accounts receivable, which can often be easily found through confirmation procedures. For fraud, the perpetrator will attempt to conceal the overstatement, making it more difficult for auditors to find. Substantive tests of transactions may be necessary to discover overstated sales in these circumstances.

The appropriate tests of controls for testing the occurrence objective depends on where the auditor believes the misstatements are likely to take place. Many auditors do tests of controls for the occurrence objective only if they believe that a control weakness exists so that the potential error can be quantified; therefore, the nature of the tests depends on the nature of the potential misstatement as follows:

Recorded sale for which there was no shipment The auditor can trace from selected entries in the sales journal to make sure that related copies of the shipping and other supporting documents exist. If the auditor is concerned about the possibility of a fictitious duplicate copy of a shipping document, it may be necessary to trace the amounts to the perpetual inventory records as a test of whether inventory was reduced. This would not be possible for paperless systems, which require greater reliance on programmed controls.

Sale recorded more than once Duplicate sales can be determined by reviewing a numerically sorted list of recorded sales transactions for duplicate invoice or shipping document numbers or by running generalized audit software tests to identify all duplicated numbers.

Shipment made to nonexistent customers This type of fraud normally occurs only when the person recording sales is also in a position to authorize shipments or alter master file data. When internal controls are weak, it is difficult to detect fictitious shipments.

Another effective approach to detecting the three types of misstatements of sales transactions discussed above is to trace the *credit* in the accounts receivable master file to its source. If the receivable was actually collected in cash or the goods were returned, there must originally have been a sale. If the credit was for a bad-debt charge-off or a credit memo, or if the account was still unpaid at the time of the audit, intensive follow-up by examining shipping and customer order documents is required, since each of these could indicate an inappropriate sales transaction.

It should be kept in mind that *the ordinary audit is not primarily intended to detect fraud* unless the effect on the financial statements is material. Tests of controls to quantify potential errors should be necessary only if the auditor is concerned about the occurrence of fraud or material error due to inadequate controls.

EXISTING SALES TRANSACTIONS ARE RECORDED In many audits, the auditor is not as concerned about the completeness objective on the ground that overstatements of assets and income are a greater concern in the audit of sales transactions than their understatement. If there are inadequate controls, which is likely if the client does no independent internal matching between shipping documents and sales transactions to the sales journal, substantive procedures will be necessary.

An effective procedure to test for unbilled shipments is tracing selected shipping documents from a file in the shipping department to related duplicate sales invoices and the sales journal. To conduct a meaningful test using this procedure, the auditor must be confident that all shipping documents are included in the sample population. This can be done by accounting for a numerical sequence of the documents.

DIRECTION OF TESTS It is important that auditors understand the difference between tracing from source documents to the journals and tracing from the journals back to supporting documents. The former is a test for *omitted transactions* (completeness objective), whereas the latter is a test for *nonexistent transactions* (occurrence objective).

In testing for the occurrence objective, the starting point is the journal. A sample of invoice numbers is selected *from* the journal and traced *to* duplicate sales invoices, shipping documents, and customer orders. In testing for the completeness objective, the likely starting point is the shipping document. A sample of shipping documents is selected and traced *to* duplicate sales invoices and the sales journal as a test of omissions.

When designing audit procedures for the occurrence and completeness objectives, the starting point for tracing the document is essential. This is referred to as the *direction of tests*. For example, if the auditor is concerned about the occurrence objective but traces in the wrong direction (from shipping documents to the journals), a serious audit deficiency exists. The direction of the tests is illustrated in Figure 13-4.

When testing for the other five transaction-related audit objectives, the direction of tests is usually not relevant. For example, the accuracy of sales transactions can be tested by tracing from a duplicate sales invoice to a shipping document or vice versa.

RECORDED SALES ARE ACCURATELY RECORDED The accurate recording of sales transactions concerns shipping the amount of goods ordered, accurately billing for the amount of goods shipped, and accurately recording the amount billed in the accounting records.

Reperformance to ensure the accuracy of each of these aspects is ordinarily conducted in every audit.

Typical reperformance tests include recomputing information in the accounting records to verify whether it is proper. A common approach is to start with entries in the sales journal and compare the total of selected transactions with customer master file totals and duplicate sales invoices. Prices on the duplicate sales invoices are normally compared with an approved price list, extensions and footings are recomputed, and the details listed on the invoices are compared with shipping records for description, quantity, and customer identification. Where reliance is placed on computer-based systems to perform mathematical calculations, the auditor may use test data to ensure that these programs are functioning as described. Test data as an audit tool is described further in Appendix F on page 408. Frequently, customer purchase orders are also examined for the same information.

The comparison of tests of controls and substantive procedures for the accuracy objective is a good example of how audit time can be saved when effective internal controls exist. In manual systems, the test of controls for this objective takes minimal time because it involves examining only an initial or other evidence of internal verification. The test data approach can also be effective since only a small number of transactions need be processed to verify that programs are functioning correctly. Since the sample size for substantive procedures can be reduced if this control is effective, a significant saving will result from performing the test of controls due to its lower cost.

RECORDED SALES ARE PROPERLY CLASSIFIED Charging the correct general ledger account is less of a problem in sales than in some other transaction cycles, but it is still of some concern. When there are cash and credit sales, it is important not to debit accounts receivable for a cash sale or to credit sales for collection of a receivable. It is also important not to classify sales of operating assets, such as buildings, as sales. For those companies using more than one sales classification, such as companies issuing segmented earnings statements, proper classification is essential.

It is common to test sales for proper classification as part of testing for accuracy. The auditor examines supporting documents to determine the proper classification of a given transaction and compares this with the actual account in which it is recorded. Most

FIGURE 13-4   **Direction of Tests for Sales**

computer-based systems, whether batch or online, are set to post to the appropriate sales general ledger account automatically. The auditor then must determine the controls in place to ensure that unusual transactions are recorded to the correct account.

SALES ARE RECORDED ON THE CORRECT DATES It is important that sales be billed and recorded as soon after shipment takes place as possible to prevent the unintentional omission of transactions from the records and to make sure sales are recorded in the proper period. At the same time that tests of controls with respect to the accuracy objective are being performed, it is common to compare the date on selected bills of lading or other shipping documents with the date on related duplicate sales invoices and the sales journal or sales history file. Significant differences indicate a potential cutoff problem. Many computer systems require that the shipping date match the invoice date or that the invoice date be within a specified time period of the current date.

SALES TRANSACTIONS ARE PROPERLY UPDATED IN THE CUSTOMER MASTER FILE AND CORRECTLY SUMMARIZED The proper inclusion of all sales transactions in the customer master file is essential because the accuracy of these records affects the client's ability to collect outstanding receivables. Similarly, the sales transactions must be correctly totalled and posted to the general ledger if the financial statements are to be correct. In every audit, it is necessary to perform some clerical accuracy tests by footing the journals and tracing the totals and details to the general ledger and the master files to check whether there are intentional or unintentional misstatements in the processing of sales transactions. For most large systems, this is accomplished using generalized audit software, whereby the auditor obtains the client data files and performs mechanical accuracy testing (such as footings or other calculations) using computer software.

The extent of such tests is affected by the quality of the internal controls. Tracing individual transactions to a posting source is typically done as a part of fulfilling other transaction-related audit objectives, but footing the sales journal and tracing the totals to the general ledger is done as a separate procedure.

The distinction between posting and summarization and other transaction-related audit objectives is that posting and summarization includes footing journals, transaction or open item files, master file records, and ledgers and tracing from one to the other. Whenever footing and comparisons are restricted to these sources, the process is posting and summarization. In contrast, accuracy involves comparing documents with each other or with journals and data file records. To illustrate, comparing a duplicate sales invoice with either the sales journal or master file entry is an accuracy objective procedure. Tracing a sales transaction from a sales history file to an open item file and balancing the open item file to the customer master file is a posting and summarization procedure.

Summary of Methodology for Sales It is essential to understand the relationships among the columns in Table 13-3. The first column includes the six transaction-related audit objectives. The general objectives are the same for any class of transactions, but the specific objectives vary for sales, cash receipts, or any other classes of transactions. Columns 2 through 5 list one or more illustrative internal controls *for each transaction-related audit objective* for different types of systems, distinguishing between manual, batch, and online. The fifth column provides examples of **interdependent controls**. These controls require both a programmed and manual component to satisfy the audit objective. Many of these controls are supervisory controls, whereby a manager or supervisor would review an exception report or a monthly report for unusual information, and then conduct follow-up activities.

INTERDEPENDENT CONTROLS— controls that require both a programmed and manual component to satisfy an audit objective

It is essential that any given control be related to one or more specific objective(s). A test of control is meaningless unless it tests a specific objective. The table contains at least one test of control in column 6 for internal controls identified in columns 2 through 5.

Design and Performance Format Audit Procedures The information presented in Table 13-3 is intended to help auditors *design audit programs* that satisfy the transaction-related audit objectives in a given set of circumstances. If certain objectives are important in a given audit or when the controls are different for different clients, the methodology helps the auditor design an effective and efficient audit program.

DESIGN FORMAT AUDIT PROGRAM—the audit procedures resulting from the auditor's decisions about the appropriate audit procedures for each audit objective; this audit program is used to prepare a performance format audit program

PERFORMANCE FORMAT AUDIT PROGRAM—the audit procedures for a class of transactions organized in the format that they will be performed; prepared from a design format audit program

After the appropriate audit procedures for a given set of circumstances have been designed, they must be performed. It is likely to be inefficient to do the audit procedures as they are stated in the design format of Table 13-3. In converting from a **design** to a **performance format**, procedures are combined. This will

- eliminate duplicate procedures.
- make sure that when a given document is examined, all procedures to be performed on that document are done at that time.
- enable the auditor to do the procedures in the most effective order. For example, by footing the journal and reviewing the journal for unusual items first, the auditor gains a better perspective in doing the detailed tests.

The process of converting from a design to a performance format is illustrated for the Hillsburg Hardware Limited case application. The design format is shown in Table 13-5 on pages 397–398. The performance format is on pages 400–401 in Figure 13-10.

→ 13.3 METHODOLOGY FOR CONTROL TESTING IN THE REMAINDER OF THE CYCLE

Sales Returns and Allowances

The transaction-related audit objectives and the client's methods of controlling misstatements are essentially the same for processing credit memos as those described for sales, with two important differences. The first relates to materiality. In many instances, sales returns and allowances are so immaterial that they can be ignored in the audit altogether. The second major difference relates to emphasis on objectives. For sales returns and allowances, the primary emphasis is normally on testing the existence of recorded transactions as a means of uncovering any diversion of cash from the collection of accounts receivable that has been covered up by a fictitious sales return or allowance.

Although the emphasis for the audit of sales returns and allowances is often on testing the existence of recorded transactions, the *completeness* objective cannot be ignored. Unrecorded sales returns and allowances can be material and can be used by a company's management to overstate net income.

Naturally, the other objectives should not be ignored. However, because the objectives and methodology for auditing sales returns and allowances are essentially the same as for sales, we will not include a detailed study of the area.

FOCUS BOX 13-2

LOW-TECH AND HIGH-TECH BENEFITS

Resource-rich countries such as Azerbaijan (on the Caspian Sea) and Kyrgyzstan (in central Asia) are recording and publishing sales revenues (royalties) from resources. It is hoped that making the revenues public will encourage the governments to use the revenues to improve infrastructure and support for citizens, rather than having funds disappear. This low-tech disclosure method is an important antifraud tool.

International Truck and Engine implemented a costly data warehouse to enable aggregation of data by customers across its four divisions.

This enables the company to look at total sales by customer when considering the size of the discounts that will be given to customers for their purchases. This high-tech method of providing sales information allows the company to track the profitability of customers by division and provides better customer service.

Sources: 1. Barlas, Demir 2004. "Data Warehouse Success," www.line56.com/articles/default. asp?aricleid=6066. 2. Lemlerre, Jean. 2005. "Beating the 'resource curse' with transparency," *The Wall Street Journal*, March 18, 2005.

Internal Controls and Tests of Controls for Cash Receipts

The same methodology used for designing tests of controls over sales transactions is used for designing tests of controls over cash receipts. Similarly, cash receipts tests of controls audit procedures are developed around the same framework used for sales; that is, given the transaction-related audit objectives, key internal controls for each objective are determined and tests of controls are developed for each control to ensure the control is working and to determine monetary errors for each objective. As in all other audit areas, the tests of controls depend on the controls the auditor has identified to reduce the assessed level of control risk.

Key internal controls and common tests of controls to satisfy each of the internal control objectives for cash receipts are listed in Table 13-4 (page 391). This summary is similar to the previous one for sales. The differences are that key internal controls are shown in one column, rather then spread across four columns, and the tests of controls are split into two columns. The first column of tests of controls is controls that are used to detect whether controls have been followed (termed "general tests of controls"). The second column of tests of controls, used for quantification of potential errors, could serve as dual-purpose tests.

The detailed discussion of the internal controls and tests of controls that was included for the audit of sales is not included for cash receipts. Instead, the audit procedures that are most likely to be misunderstood are explained in more detail.

An essential part of the auditor's responsibility in auditing cash receipts is identification of weaknesses in internal control that increase the likelihood of fraud. In expanding on Table 13-4, the emphasis will be on those audit procedures that are designed primarily for the discovery of fraud. However, the reader should keep in mind throughout this discussion that the nonfraud procedures included in the table are the auditor's primary responsibility. Those procedures that are not discussed are omitted only because their purpose and the methodology for applying them should be apparent from their description.

Determine Whether Cash Received Was Recorded The most difficult type of cash defalcation for the auditor to detect is that which occurs *before the cash is recorded* in the cash receipts journal or other cash listing, especially if the sale and cash receipt are recorded simultaneously. For example, if a grocery store clerk takes cash and intentionally fails to register the receipt of cash on the cash register, it is extremely difficult to discover the theft. To prevent this type of fraud, internal controls such as those included in the third objective in Table 13-4 are implemented by many companies. The type of control will, of course, depend on the type of business. For example, the controls for a retail store in which the cash is received by the same person who sells the merchandise and rings up the cash receipts (termed "point-of-sale" or "POS" systems) should be different from the controls for a company in which all receipts are received through the mail several weeks after the sales have taken place. In a point-of-sale system, the sale must be recorded for the customer to receive a receipt. This may also remove the item from inventory, but, most important, it provides a control total that must be reconciled to the total cash (including credit card vouchers) that is received during the day.

It is normal practice to trace from *prenumbered remittance advices, prelists of cash receipts,* or the duplicate bank deposit slip to the cash receipts journal and subsidiary accounts receivable records as a test of the recording of actual cash received. This test will be effective only if the cash details were listed on a cash register tape or some other prelisting at the time the cash was received.

Prepare Proof of Cash Receipts A useful audit procedure to test whether all recorded cash receipts have been deposited in the bank account is a **proof of cash receipts**. In this test, the total cash receipts recorded in the cash receipts data files for a given period, such as a month, are reconciled with the actual deposits made to the bank during the same period. There may be a difference in the two due to deposits in transit and other items, but the amounts can be reconciled and compared. The procedure is not useful in discovering cash receipts that have not been recorded in the journals or time lags in making deposits, but it can help uncover recorded cash receipts that have not been deposited, unrecorded deposits, unrecorded loans, bank loans deposited directly into the bank account, and similar misstatements. A proof of cash receipts and cash disbursements is illustrated in Chapter 15 on page 466. This somewhat time-consuming procedure is ordinarily used only when controls are weak. In rare instances in which controls are extremely weak, the period covered by the proof of cash receipts may be the entire year.

PROOF OF CASH RECEIPTS—an audit procedure to test whether all recorded cash receipts have been deposited in the bank account by reconciling the total cash receipts recorded in the cash receipts journal for a given period with the actual deposits made to the bank

Test to Discover Lapping of Accounts Receivable **Lapping of accounts receivable**, which is a common type of defalcation, is the postponement of entries for the collection of receivables to *conceal an existing cash shortage*. The defalcation is perpetrated by a person who handles cash receipts and then enters them into the computer system. He or she takes the cash, defers recording the cash receipts from one customer, and covers the shortages with the receipts of another customer. These in turn are covered from the receipts of a third customer a few days later. The employee must continue to cover the shortage through repeated lapping, replace the stolen money, or find another way to conceal the shortage.

This defalcation can easily be prevented by separation of duties. It can be detected by comparing the name, amount, and dates shown on remittance advices with cash receipts journal entries and related duplicate deposit slips. Since the procedure is relatively time-consuming, it is ordinarily performed only when there is a specific concern with defalcation because of a weakness in internal control.

Audit Tests for Uncollectible Accounts

Occurrence of recorded write-offs is the most important transaction-related audit objective that the auditor should keep in mind in the verification of the write-off of individual uncollectible accounts. A major concern in testing accounts charged off as uncollectible is the possibility of the client covering up a defalcation by charging off accounts receivable that have already been collected. The major control for preventing this type of misstatement is proper authorization of the write-off of uncollectible accounts by a designated level of management only after a thorough investigation of the reason the customer has not paid.

Normally, verification of the accounts charged off takes relatively little time. A typical procedure is the examination of approvals by the appropriate person. For a sample of accounts charged off, it is also usually necessary for the auditor to examine correspondence in the client's files establishing the uncollectibility of the accounts. In some cases, the auditor will also examine credit reports such as those provided by Dun & Bradstreet Canada Limited or Creditel. After the auditor has concluded that the accounts charged off by general journal entries are proper, selected items should be traced to listings of the accounts receivable master file or to a transactions file as a test of the records.

Additional Internal Controls over Account Balances

The preceding discussion emphasized internal controls and tests of controls for the five classes of transactions that affect account balances in the sales and collection cycle. If the internal controls for these classes of transactions are determined to be effective and the related tests of controls support the conclusions, the likelihood of misstatements in the financial statements is reduced.

In addition, there may be internal controls directly related to account balances that have not been identified or tested as a part of tests of controls. For the sales and collection cycle, these are most likely to affect three balance-related audit objectives: valuation, rights and obligations, and presentation and disclosure.

Valuation is an essential balance-related audit objective for accounts receivable because collectibility of receivables is often a major financial statement item and has been an issue in a number of accountants' liability cases. It is, therefore, common for inherent risk to be high for the valuation objective.

Several controls are common for the valuation objective. One that has already been discussed is credit approval by an appropriate person. A second is the preparation of a periodic aged accounts receivable trial balance for review and follow-up by appropriate management personnel. A third control is a policy of charging off uncollectible accounts when they are no longer likely to be collected.

Rights and obligations and presentation and disclosure are rarely a significant problem for accounts receivable. Therefore, employing competent accounting personnel is usually sufficient control for these two balance-related audit objectives.

Transaction-Related Audit Objective	Key Internal Control	General Tests of Controls	Quantitative/Dual-Purpose Tests of Controls
Recorded cash receipts are for funds actually received by the company (occurrence).	Separation of duties between handling cash and record keeping or data entry.	Observe separation of duties.	Review the cash receipts journal, general ledger, and accounts receivable master file or trial balance for large and unusual amounts.*
	Independent reconciliation or review of bank accounts.	Observe independent reconciliation of bank account.	Trace from cash receipts listing to duplicate deposit slip and bank statements.
Cash received is recorded in the cash receipts journal (completeness).	Separation of duties between handling cash and record keeping. Use of remittance advices or a prelisting of cash. Immediate endorsement of incoming cheques. Internal verification of the recording of cash receipts. Regular monthly statements to customers.	Discussion with personnel and observation. As above. Observe immediate endorsement of incoming cheques. Examine indication of internal verification. Observe whether monthly statements are sent to customers.	Trace from remittances or prelisting to duplicate bank deposit slip and cash receipts journal. Review reconciliation reports of credit card or electronic funds transfer receipts.
Cash receipts are deposited and recorded at the amount received (accuracy).	Approval of cash discounts. Regular reconciliation of bank accounts. Comparison of batch totals to duplicate deposit slips and computer summary reports.	Examine remittance advices for proper approval. Review monthly bank reconciliations. Examine file of batch totals for initials of data control clerk; compare totals to summary reports.	Examine remittance advices and sales invoices to determine whether discounts allowed are consistent with company policy.
Cash receipts are properly classified (classification).	Use of adequate chart of accounts or automatic posting to specified accounts.	Review chart of accounts and computer-assigned posting accounts.	Examine documents supporting cash receipts for proper classification.
Cash receipts are recorded on correct dates (timing).	Procedure requiring recording of cash receipts on a daily basis.	Observe unrecorded cash at any point in time.	Compare dates of deposits with dates in the cash receipts journal.
Cash receipts are properly included in the customer master file and are correctly summarized (posting and summarization).	Regular monthly statements to customers. Use of properly approved master file change forms. Comparison of customer master file or aged accounts receivable trial balance totals with general ledger balance.	Observe whether statements are mailed. Examine master file change forms for proper authorization. Examine documentation verifying that comparison was completed.	Foot journals and trace postings to general ledger and accounts receivable master file.

* This analytical procedure can also apply to other objectives, including completeness, accuracy, and timing.

Effect of Results of Tests of Controls

The results of the tests of controls have a significant effect on the remainder of the audit, especially on the tests of details of balances part of substantive procedures. The parts of the audit most affected by the tests of controls for the sales and collection cycle are the balances in *accounts receivable, cash, bad-debt expense,* and *allowance for doubtful accounts.* Furthermore, if the results of the tests are unsatisfactory, it is necessary to do additional substantive testing for the propriety of sales, sales returns and allowances, charge-off of uncollectible accounts, and processing of cash receipts.

At the completion of the tests of controls, it is essential to *analyze each control test exception* to determine its cause and the implication of the exception on assessed control risk, which may affect the supported detection risk and thereby the substantive procedures.

The most significant effect of the results of the tests of controls in the sales and collection cycle is on the confirmation of accounts receivable. The type of confirmation, the size of the sample, and the timing of the test are all affected. The effect of the tests on accounts receivable, bad-debt expense, and allowance for uncollectible accounts is considered in Chapter 14.

Figure 13-5 illustrates the major accounts in the sales and collection cycle and the types of audit tests typically used to audit these accounts. This figure also shows how the audit risk model discussed in Chapter 8 relates to the audit of the sales and collection cycle.

→13.4   A REAL-LIFE EXAMPLE OF A SALES AUDIT
Case Illustration—Hillsburg Hardware Limited

The concepts for testing the sales and collection cycle presented in this chapter are now illustrated for Hillsburg Hardware Limited. The company's financial statements and the general ledger trial balance were shown in Chapter 5. Additional information was included in other chapters. A study of this case is intended to illustrate a methodology for designing audit procedures and integrating different parts of the audit.

Hillsburg Hardware Limited is a retail hardware company that focuses on selling high-quality power tools to individuals and the home improvement construction market. It is based in eastern Canada. Preliminary analytical review was conducted and shows continued maintenance of profit margins. This is the fourth year of the audit of this client, and there have never been any significant misstatements discovered in the tests. During the current year, a major change has occurred. The chief accountant left the firm and has been replaced by Erma Swanson. There has also been some turnover of other accounting personnel.

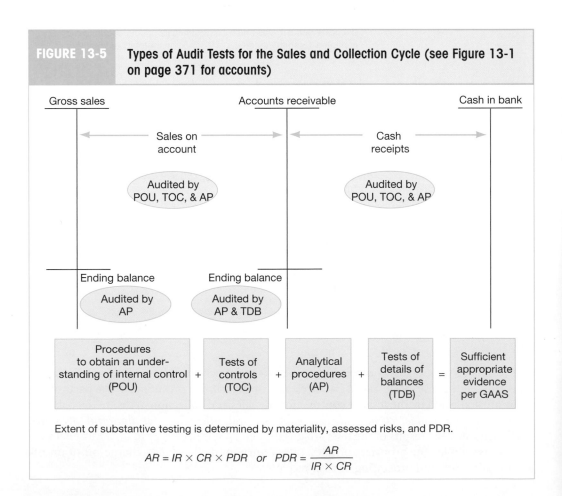

FIGURE 13-5   Types of Audit Tests for the Sales and Collection Cycle (see Figure 13-1 on page 371 for accounts)

Extent of substantive testing is determined by materiality, assessed risks, and PDR.

$$AR = IR \times CR \times PDR \quad or \quad PDR = \frac{AR}{IR \times CR}$$

The overall assessment by management is that the accounting personnel are reasonably competent and highly trustworthy. The president, Rick Chulick, has been the chief operating officer for approximately 10 years. He is regarded as a highly competent, honest individual who does a conscientious job. The following information is provided from the auditor's files:

- *The organization chart and flowchart of internal control prepared for the audit.* This information is included in Figures 13-6 and 13-7. Sales returns and allowances for this client are too immaterial to include in the flowchart or to verify in the audit.
- *Internal controls and weaknesses, and assessment of control risk for sales and cash receipts.* An appropriate approach to identifying and documenting internal controls and weaknesses and assessing control risk is included for sales in Figure 13-8 on page 395 and for cash receipts in Figure 13-9 on page 396. There are several things the auditor, Francine Martel, did to complete each matrix. First, she identified internal controls from flowcharts, internal control questionnaires, and discussions with client personnel. Only flowcharts are available in the Hillsburg case. Second, she identified weaknesses using the same sources. Third, she decided which transaction-related audit objectives are affected by the internal controls and weaknesses. Finally, she assessed control risk using the information obtained in the preceding three steps. The objective-by-objective matrices in Figures 13-8 and 13-9 were used primarily to help Francine Martel effectively assess control risk.
- *Tests of controls for each internal control.* The tests of controls for sales are included in the third and fifth columns of Table 13-5 (page 397) and for cash receipts in the same columns in Table 13-6 (page 399). The source of the internal controls is Figure 13-8 for sales and Figure 13-9 for cash receipts. Francine decided the appropriate tests for each control.

Notice that certain objectives in Tables 13-5 and 13-6 have only programmed controls (e.g., sales classification and timing and cash receipts classification), or existing controls are such that there are weaknesses (e.g., occurrence in Table 13-5; completeness in Table 13-6). The tests of controls listed in the fifth columns of Tables 13-5 and 13-6 are dual-purpose tests designed to determine if the client's accounting transactions exist, are complete, are accurate, are properly classified, are recorded on the correct dates, and are summarized in the journals and correctly posted to the appropriate ledger. Tests such as these, described in Chapter 11, are both tests of controls and substantive procedures. As was suggested earlier in this chapter, the purpose of such tests is to assist the auditor in assessing control risk and also in quantifying the potential amount of error when they are conducted as substantive tests.

FIGURE 13-6   **Hillsburg Hardware Partial Organization Chart: Personnel**

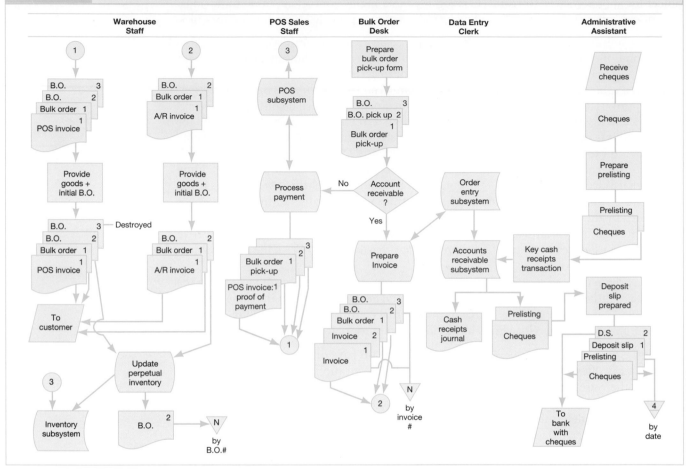

Notes

1. All correspondence is sent to the chief financial officer.
2. An exception report of missing bulk order numbers is printed weekly by the data entry clerk. The chief accountant discusses this with the warehouse staff supervisor to ensure that follow-up is undertaken.
3. All subsystems are posted to the general ledger on a daily basis after the close of business. The order-entry subsystem is also posted to the accounts receivable subsystem on a daily basis.
4. All prices in the point-of-sale (POS) system are based on prices in the master file. Should an override be necessary (e.g., due to damaged goods), the sales manager must enter his password to approve the price change. All such over-rides will be printed on an exception report by the data entry clerk on a weekly basis. These are reviewed by the chief accountant.
5. All prices used for accounts receivable are based on the same prices as the point-of-sale system, with the customer discount applied. Customer discounts are negotiated at the time of customer approval, and range from 10 percent to 25 percent, based on the customer's projected and actual sales volume. An authorized customer signature is required on all accounts receivable invoices that matches the signature on the in-house credit card.
6. Changes to the price master file and the customer master file for credit limits must be co-approved by the sales manager and the chief accountant on a master file change form. These are entered by the data entry clerk, and a sequentially numbered master file change report printed. This report is reviewed by the chief accountant for accuracy of data entry.
7. Payment at the POS desks can be made by cash, credit card, or debit card. Stand-alone credit card authorization and debit card entry machines are used to process non-cash payments. Daily totals (i.e., cash drawer, debit card totals, credit card totals) must equal the total sales recorded at each POS terminal.

8. There are two POS terminals for immediate payment and two bulk order desk terminals, where staff can enquire regarding inventory status and can prepare accounts receivable invoices using the order entry system for pre-authorized customers.
9. Warehouse staff compare bulk order quantities to amounts paid for or invoiced prior to providing goods, and initial the customer invoice. Customers sign copy 2 of the bulk order to indicate that goods have been taken.
10. An aged accounts receivable trial balance is printed weekly by the data entry clerk for follow-up by the chief accountant. At this time, the trial balance total is compared to the general ledger accounts receivable balance.
11. Statements are sent to customers monthly.
12. The administrative assistant stamps incoming cheques with a restrictive endorsement immediately upon receipt.
13. Deposits are made daily by the administrative assistant. Cash from the POS terminals is counted, recorded on the duplicate deposit slip, and added to the total of cheques received for the day.
14. Daily cash receipts postings from the POS system and the accounts receivable system are reconciled to the duplicate deposit slip by the data entry clerk.
15. The bank account is reconciled by the chief accountant on a monthly basis.
16. All bad-debt expenses and write-offs of bad debts are approved by the chief financial officer after being initiated by the chief accountant.
17. Financial statements are printed monthly by the data entry clerk and reviewed by the chief financial officer and the president.
18. All management (i.e., sales, purchasing and inventory control, accounting and the president) meet on a weekly basis to review exception reports and discuss weekly internal financial results. These meetings are not minuted.

Procedures for other locations are similar and not shown in this flow chart to simplify the discussion.

FIGURE 13-8   Control Risk Matrix for Hillsburg Hardware—Sales

	Sales Transaction–Related Objectives					
	Recorded sales are for shipments actually made to nonfictitious customers (occurrence).	Existing sales transactions are recorded (completeness).	Recorded sales are for the amount of goods shipped and are correctly billed and recorded (accuracy).	Sales transactions are properly classified (classification).	Sales are recorded on the correct dates (timing).	Sales transactions are updated correctly to the customer master file and the posting to the general ledger summed these transactions correctly (posting and summarization).
Internal Controls						
Scanned POS sales must be paid by cash, credit card, or debit card. (C1) **P**	C		C			
All external and internal credit card purchases require customer signature on the invoice. (C2)	C					
Bulk order pick-up form is matched to invoice and initialled. (C3)	C		C			
Credit is approved prior to customer account being established. (C4)	C					
Monthly statements are sent to accounts receivable customers. (C5)	C		C			C
Bulk order forms are prenumbered, and the number is entered on the invoice. Computer system flags missing numbers on an exception report. (C6) **P**		C	C			
POS invoices and accounts receivable invoices are automatically numbered by the computer. (C7) **P**		C	C			
All invoices are prepared using prices in the inventory master file. (C8) **P**			C			
Accounts receivable terms are based on the customer master file. (C9) **P**			C			
Price overrides must be approved by sales manager password. (C10) **P**			C			
Sales manager overrides are printed on an exception report and reviewed by the chief accountant. (C11) **P**			C			
Sales control account is coded into computer system, and all POS and bulk sales are posted to that account. (C12) **P**				C		
The invoice date is automatically the computer system date. (C13) **P**					C	
Posting to the data files is automatically handled by the computer system. (C14) **P**						C
Aged accounts receivable trial balance is compared to general ledger balance monthly. (C15)						C
weakness						
Evidence of follow-up on exception report of missing bulk order numbers is not documented. (W1)		W				
Assessed control risk	Low	Medium	Low	Low	Low	Low

Note: **P**—These controls are either programmed controls or interdependent controls (where part of the control is programmed and part of the control is handled by a person).

C = Control

W = Weakness

	Cash Receipts Transaction–Related Audit Objectives					
Internal Controls	Recorded cash receipts are for funds actually received by the company (occurrence).	Cash received is recorded in the cash receipts journal (completeness).	Cash receipts are deposited at the amount received (accuracy).	Cash receipts transactions are properly classified (classification).	Cash receipts are recorded on the correct dates (timing).	Cash receipts are properly included in the customer master file and are correctly summarized (posting and summarization).
Accountant reconciles bank account. (C1)	C		C			
Cheques are stamped with a restrictive endorsement. (C2)		C				
Statements are sent to customers monthly. (C3)		C	C			
Bank deposit slip reconciled to POS and accounts receivable postings. (C4)	C	C	C			
Cash is automatically posted to cash and accounts receivable accounts. (C5)				C		
System date is used for data entry. (C6)					C	
Cash receipts are deposited daily. (C7)					C	
Entry of correct customer number results in automatic posting to that customer master file record. (C8)						C
Accountant compares accounts receivable master file total with general ledger account. (C9)						C
Weaknesses — Prelisting of cash is not used to verify recorded cash receipts. (W1)		W				
Administrative assistant handles cheques after they are returned from cash receipts. (W2)		W				
Data entry clerk has access to cash receipts and maintains accounts receivable records. (W3)		W				
Assessed control risk	Low	High	Low	Low	Low	Low

C = Control
W = Weakness

Notice that certain objectives in Tables 13-5 and 13-6 have only programmed controls (e.g., sales classification and timing and cash receipts classification), or existing controls are such that there are weaknesses (e.g., occurrence in Table 13-5; completeness in Table 13-6). The tests of controls listed in the fifth columns of Tables 13-5 and 13-6 are dual-purpose tests designed to determine if the client's accounting transactions exist, are complete, are accurate, are properly classified, are recorded on the correct dates, and are summarized in the journals and correctly posted to the appropriate ledger. Tests such as these, described in Chapter 11, are both tests of controls and substantive procedures. As was suggested earlier in this chapter, the purpose of such tests is to assist the auditor in assessing control risk and also in quantifying the potential amount of error when conducted as substantive tests.

Francine decided on the tests of controls for each transaction-related audit objective listed in the third and fifth columns of Table 13-5 (sales) and Table 13-6 (cash receipts) for

TABLE 13-5 **Internal Controls and Tests of Controls for Hillsburg Hardware Limited—Sales* (Design Format)**

Transaction-Related Audit Objective	Existing Control†	Tests of Control, General	Weakness	Tests of Control, Dual-Purpose
Recorded sales are for shipments actually made to nonfictitious customers (occurrence).	Scanned POS sales must be paid by cash, credit card, or debit card. (C1) All external and internal credit card purchases require customer signature on the invoice. (C2) Bulk order pick-up form is matched to invoice and initialled. (C3) Credit is approved prior to customer account being established. (C4) Monthly statements are sent to accounts receivable customers. (C5)	Review POS procedures manual and discuss with POS staff. (6) Examine a sample of invoices for customer signature. (13.1) Examine a selection of invoices for matching bulk order form and initial. (13.3, 13.4) Examine a sample of master file change forms for evidence of approval. (14.1, 14.2) Observe whether monthly statements are mailed. (7)	Evidence of follow-up on exception report of missing bulk order numbers is not documented. (W1)	Use generalized audit software to print a list of customers exceeding their credit limit. (4.1)
Existing sales transactions are recorded (completeness).	Bulk order forms are prenumbered, and the number is entered on the invoice. Computer system flags missing numbers on an exception report. (C6) POS invoices and accounts receivable invoices are automatically numbered by the computer (C7)	Review a sample of sales invoices for bulk order form number. (13.2) Observe system in use, and observe incremental assignment of invoice numbers. (1.2, 2.1)		Use generalized audit software to print a report of all gaps in the bulk order forms. (4.2) Use generalized audit software to print a report of all gaps in the invoice numbers. (4.3, 4.4)
Recorded sales are for the amount of goods shipped and are correctly billed and recorded (accuracy).	All invoices are prepared using prices in the inventory master file. (C8) Accounts receivable terms are based on the customer master file. (C9) Price overrides must be approved by sales manager password. (C10) Sales manager overrides are printed on an exception report and reviewed by the chief accountant. (C11)	Observe invoice preparation process. (1.3, 2.2) Request bulk order staff to enter a different term, and see if computer rejects it. (2.3) Request staff to override a price, and observe whether sales manager password is required. (1.4, 2.4) Discuss disposition of exception reports with chief accountant and review report for evidence of review. (8)		Use generalized audit software to print a report of unusual credit terms, and trace to customer master file approval form. (4.5, 4.7)
Sales transactions are properly classified (classification).	Sales control account is coded into computer system, and all POS and bulk sales are posted to that account. (C12)	Examine a daily sales summary to verify account allocation. (5.1)		
Sales are recorded on the correct dates (timing).	The invoice date is automatically the computer system date. (C13)	Observe invoice preparation process. (1.5, 2.5)		

Transaction-Related Audit Objective	Existing Control†	Tests of Control, General	Weakness	Tests of Control, Dual-Purpose
Sales transactions are updated correctly to the customer master file, and the posting to the general ledger summed these transactions correctly (posting and summarization).	Posting to the data files is automatically handled by the computer system. (C14) Aged accounts receivable trial balance is compared to general ledger balance monthly. (C15)	Conduct walk-through testing to verify that posting process is functioning correctly for daily posting. (5.1, 5.2, 5.3)		Compare aged accounts receivable trial balance total to general ledger. (4.6)

* The procedures are summarized into a performance format in Figure 13-10. The number in parentheses after the procedure refers to Figure 13-10.
† Only the primary (key) control(s) for each objective is (are) shown. Most objectives are also affected by one or more additional controls.

the different objectives after considering assessed control risk, the tests of controls listed in the third column, and weaknesses of internal control for that objective.

Notice that the objective-by-objective format in Tables 13-5 and 13-6 is used to help Francine more effectively determine the appropriate tests. She could have chosen tests of controls just as easily by selecting tests of controls for each internal control included in Figures 13-8 and 13-9. Most audit firms use automated working-paper software that allows them to simultaneously work on audit objective assessment and the preparation of audit testing plans without the preparation of multiple lists, as shown in this text. The multiple lists are shown here to assist students in assimilation of the audit process.

- *Tests of controls audit program in a performance format.* The tests of controls in Table 13-5 and Table 13-6 are combined into one audit program in Figure 13-10 (pages 400–401). The cross-referencing of the numbers in parentheses shows that no procedures have been added to or deleted from Figure 13-10. The reasons Francine prepared the performance format audit program were to eliminate audit procedures that were included more than once in Tables 13-5 and 13-6 and to include them in an order that permits audit assistants to complete the procedures as efficiently as possible. Note the large number of programmed controls, walk-through tests, and general tests. These illustrate that in automated systems, where programmed controls can be relied on due to good general controls, the time spent on control testing can be reduced, since the effort required to conduct these tests is considerably less than the effort required to conduct sampling and tests of attributes through sampling. The generalized audit software tests are conducted at the same time as the substantive tests for accounts receivable (discussed further in Chapter 14).

Application of Attribute Sampling

To illustrate the sampling for the tests of controls concepts of Chapter 12, the sampling for the tests described in Figure 13-10 is now conducted. The only parts of the tests of the sales and collection cycle included here are the tests of payment approval by the customer, shipment verification of bulk orders, and approval of customer master file changes. It should be kept in mind that the procedures for Hillsburg Hardware Limited were developed specifically for that client and would probably not be applicable for a different audit. The audit procedures for these tests are taken from steps 13 and 14 of Figure 13-10.

Objectives, Deciding if Sampling Applies, Population, and Sampling Unit Most auditors use some type of preprinted form or software template to document each attribute's sampling application. An example of a commonly used form is given in Figure 13-11. The top part of the form includes a definition of the objective, the population, and the sampling unit.

TABLE 13-6	Internal Controls and Tests of Controls for Hillsburg Hardware Limited—Cash Receipts* (Design Format)				
Transaction-Related Audit Objective	Existing Control†	Tests of Control, General	Weakness	Tests of Control, Dual-Purpose
Recorded cash receipts are for funds actually received by the company (occurrence).	Accountant reconciles bank account. (C1) Bank deposit slip reconciled to POS and accounts receivable postings. (C4)**	Observe whether Swanson reconciles the bank account. (9)		Review the journals and transaction files for unusual transactions and amounts using GAS. (4.7) Summarize and prepare analysis of credits using GAS. (4.7, 4.8) Prepare a proof of cash receipts. (18) Examine a sample of daily reconciliations, verifying agreement to postings and to bank statement. (16)
Cash received is recorded in the cash receipts journal (completeness).	Cheques are stamped with a restrictive endorsement. (C2) Statements are sent to customers monthly. (C3)	Observe whether a restrictive endorsement is used on cash receipts. (10) Observe whether monthly statements are mailed. (7)	Prelisting of cash is not used to verify recorded cash receipts. (W1) Administrative assistant handles cheques after they are returned from data entry. (W2) Data entry clerk has access to cash receipts and maintains accounts receivable records. (W3)	Obtain the prelisting of cash receipts, and trace amounts to the cash receipts journal, testing for names, amounts, and dates. (19) Compare the prelisting of cash receipts with the duplicate deposit slip, testing for names, amounts, and dates. (16)
Recorded cash receipts are deposited at the amount received (accuracy).	Accountant reconciles bank account. (C1) Statements are sent to customers monthly. (C3)	Observe whether Swanson reconciles the bank account. (9) Observe whether monthly statements are mailed. (7)		The procedures for the occurrence objective also fulfill this objective.
Cash receipts are properly classified (classification).	Cash is automatically posted to cash and accounts receivable accounts. (C5)	Conduct walk-through. (5.4) Observe system use. (3.1)		Examine prelisting for proper account classification. (17)
Cash receipts are recorded on correct dates (timing).	System date is used for data entry. (C6) Cash receipts deposited daily. (C7)	Observe whether bank deposits are made daily. (11)		Trace the total from the cash receipts journal to the bank statement, testing for a delay in deposit. (16)
Cash receipts are properly included in the customer master file and are correctly summarized (posting and summarization).	Accountant compares aged accounts receivable trial balance total with general ledger account. (C9) Entry of correct customer number results in automatic posting to that customer master file record. (C8)	Observe whether Swanson compares total with general ledger account. (12) Observe data entry and conduct walk-through test. (3)		Foot and cross-foot the cash receipts journal using GAS, and trace totals to the general ledger on a test basis. (4.8)

GAS = generalized audit software.

* The procedures are summarized into a performance format in Figure 13-10. The number in parentheses after the procedure refers to Figure 13-10.

† Only the primary (key) control(s) for each objective is (are) shown. Most objectives are also affected by one or more additional controls.

** This control also satisfies completeness and accuracy.

TESTS OF CONTROLS AUDIT PROCEDURES FOR SALES AND CASH RECEIPTS
(Sample Size and the Items in the Sample Are Not Included)

Tests of Programs
1. Observe use of POS system to verify that
   1.1 POS sales must be paid by cash, credit card, or debit card.
   1.2 POS invoices are automatically numbered by the computer.
   1.3 Invoices are prepared using prices automatically pulled from the inventory master file.
   1.4 Price overrides must be approved using the sales manager password. (Request an attempt to enter an override.)
   1.5 Invoice date is equal to computer system date.
2. Observe use of bulk order desk and accounts receivable sales data entry to verify that
   2.1 Accounts receivable invoices are automatically numbered by the computer.
   2.2 Invoices are prepared using prices automatically pulled from the inventory master file.
   2.3 Credit terms are pulled automatically from the customer master file. (Request an attempt to enter an incorrect credit term.)
   2.4 Price overrides must be approved using the sales manager password. (Request an attempt to enter an override.)
   2.5 Invoice date is equal to computer system date.
3. Observe cash receipts data entry process to verify that
   3.1 System date is used for data entry.

Tests of Data Using Generalized Audit Software—Included with Substantive Field Work of Accounts Receivable
4. Obtain transaction history file, open item accounts receivable file and customer master file, and conduct the following tests:
   4.1 List customers with balances exceeding their credit limit.
   4.2 List gaps in bulk order form numbers.
   4.3 List gaps in POS invoice numbers.
   4.4 List gaps in accounts receivable invoice numbers.
   4.5 List customers with discount terms exceeding 25 percent.
   4.6 Foot open item file and customer master file and agree to general ledger.
   4.7 Summarize debits and credits by customer. Prepare graphs displaying analysis of debit and credit patterns.
   4.8 Summarize cash receipts and prepare totals by day and month.

Walk-through Tests
5. Conduct walk-through tests of three transactions for each of the following activities to verify that programs are functioning as described:
   5.1 POS daily sales summary is posted to correct general ledger accounts.
   5.2 Accounts receivable daily sales are posted to correct general ledger accounts.
   5.3 Sales transactions are posted to correct customer master file accounts.
   5.4 Cash receipts are posted to correct general ledger accounts.

General Tests
6. Review system procedures and discuss with personnel to verify that procedures are being followed as described.
7. Observe whether monthly statements are mailed.
8. Discuss disposition of exception reports with appropriate member of management independently to verify consistency of treatment.
9. Observe whether the accountant reconciles the bank account.
10. Observe whether a restrictive endorsement is used on cash receipts.
11. Observe whether bank deposits are made daily.
12. Observe whether the accountant compares the accounts receivable trial balance total with the general ledger account.

Tests for Billing of Customers and Recording of Sales in the Accounts
13. Select a sample of customer invoices using a random selection process and
   13.1 Ensure that the invoice copy has a customer signature.
      If the sale was for bulk goods:
   13.2 Verify that the bulk order form number was entered onto the invoice.
   13.3 Verify that the bulk order form product description and quantity matches the invoice details.
   13.4 Locate the warehouse copy of the bulk order form and verify that the customer signature on the warehouse copy of the bulk order form matches the signature on the invoice copy.
14. Select a sample of customer master file change forms using a random selection process, and
   14.1 Verify that appropriate approvals are present.
   14.2 Trace to printout, confirming data entry of the change and verifying presence of chief accountant's initials.

FIGURE 13-10   **(continued)**

Tests for Processing Cash Receipts and Recording the Amounts in the Records

15. Obtain the December prelistings of cash receipts, and trace amounts to the cash receipts journal, testing for names, amounts, and dates.
16. Compare the prelisting of cash receipts with the duplicate deposit slip, testing for names, amounts, and dates. Trace the total from the cash receipts journal to the duplicate bank deposit slip, and the total per the duplicate bank deposit slip to the bank statement, testing for a delay in deposit. For these dates, also trace the totals to the POS system and accounts receivable sales system totals.
17. Examine prelisting for proper account classification.
18. Prepare a proof of cash receipts.
19. Trace selected entries from the cash receipts journal to entries in the customer master file, and test for dates and amounts.
20. Trace selected credits from the accounts receivable master file to the cash receipts journal, and test for dates and amounts.

Define the Attributes of Interest The attributes used in this application are taken directly from the audit program. The procedures that can be used as attributes for a particular application of attributes sampling depend on the definition of the sampling unit. In this case, all the procedures in the billing function can be included. The attributes used for this case are listed in Figure 13-11.

The definition of the attribute is a critical part of attribute sampling. The decision as to which attributes to combine and which ones to keep separate is the most important aspect of the definition. If all possible types of attributes, such as customer name, date, price, and quantity, are separated for each procedure, the large number of attributes makes the problem unmanageable. However, if all the procedures are combined into one or two attributes, greatly dissimilar misstatements are evaluated together. Somewhere in between is a reasonable compromise.

Establish TER, ARACR, and EPER, and Determine Initial Sample Size The TER (tolerable exception rate) for each attribute is decided on the basis of the auditor's judgment of what exception rate is material. The failure to have a customer signature on an invoice would be highly significant since this could mean an inability to collect funds from a credit card organization or for a credit sale. Therefore, as indicated in Figure 13-11, the lowest TER (3 percent) is chosen for attribute 1. The incorrect billing of the customer for bulk sales represents potentially significant misstatements, but no misstatement is likely to apply to the full amount of the invoice. As a result, a 4 percent TER is chosen for matching of the bulk order form details and customer signature on that form. The second attribute has a higher TER since it is of less importance for the audit. The last item is also important, since it helps verify the authenticity of the customer.

An ARACR (acceptable risk of assessing control risk too low) of 10 percent is chosen because there are numerous other controls, such as programmed controls and management review of exception reports.

The estimated population exception rate (EPER) is based on previous years' results, modified upward slightly due to the change in personnel. Initial sample size for each attribute is determined from Table 13-7 on page 404 on the basis of the above considerations. This information is summarized for all attributes in Figure 13-14 on page 405. For convenience in selection and evaluation, the auditor decided to select a sample of 75 for attribute 1, 50 for attributes 2 and 3, 100 for attribute 5, and 75 for attribute 4. Based on past experience, the decision was made to select 30 samples from the POS invoices and the remainder from credit sales invoices, since these have a greater proportion of bulk sales orders.

Select the Sample The random selection for the case is straightforward except for the need for different sample sizes for different attributes. This problem can be overcome by selecting a random sample of 50 for use on all five attributes followed by another sample of 25 for attributes 1 and 5, and an additional 25 for attribute 4. Figure 12-2 on page 346

FIGURE 13-11   **Attribute Sampling Data Sheet**

Client	Hillsburg Hardware Limited	Year end	31/12/04
Audit Area	Tests of Controls—Billing Function and Recording of Sales	Pop. size	145,853

Define the objective(s) Examine duplicate sales invoices and related documents to determine if the system has functioned as intended and as described in the audit program.

Define the population precisely (including stratification, if any) POS invoices and credit sales invoices for the period 1/1/04 to 31/12/04. First POS number = 140672. Last POS number = 283294. First credit sales invoice number = 3600. Last credit sales invoice number = 6831

Define the sampling unit, organization of population items, and random selection procedures Sales invoice number, POS invoice numbers, and credit recorded in the sales files sequentially; random sampling.

Description of Attributes	Planned Audit				Actual Results			
	EPER	TER	ARACR	Initial sample size	Sample size	Number of exceptions	Sample exception rate	CUER
1. Invoice copy has customer signature. (13.1)	0	3	10	76				
For Bulk Sales: 2. Bulk order form number entered on invoice details. (13.2)	2	8	10	48				
3. Bulk order form details match invoice details. (13.3)	0	4	10	57				
4. Warehouse copy of bulk order form has customer signature. (13.4)	1	4	10	96				
5. Customer signature on warehouse copy of bulk order form matches signature on invoice. (13.4)	0	3	10	76				

Intended use of sampling results:

1. Effect on Audit Plan:

2. Recommendations to Management:

illustrates how the first 30 items were selected from the POS system using a spreadsheet template. The remaining items were selected in a similar manner.

Perform the Procedures and Generalize to the Population The audit procedures that are included in the audit program and summarized in the attribute sampling data sheet must be carefully performed for every item in the sample. As a means of documenting the tests and providing information for review, it is common to include a worksheet of the results. Some auditors prefer to include a worksheet containing a listing of all items in the sample; others prefer to limit the documentation to identifying the exceptions. This latter approach is followed in the example (Figure 13-12). Figure 13-13 summarizes the sampling process for the testing of master file change forms.

FIGURE 13-12 **Exceptions Found During Inspection of Sample Items for Attributes**

1. *Invoice copy has customer signature. (13.1)*

   Three exceptions found.

   POS invoices # 163763, 213150, and 237619 did not have customer signatures. These were all cash sales (i.e., not paid by credit card or debit card).

2. *Bulk order form number entered on invoice. (13.2)*

   Four exceptions found.

   POS invoice # 242681 missing bulk order number, although copy was attached.

   Credit sales invoice # 5802, 6137, and 8713 missing bulk order number, although copy was attached.

   No exceptions found for attributes 3, 4, and 5.

At the completion of the testing, the exceptions are tabulated to determine the number of exceptions in the sample for each attribute. This enables the auditor to compute the sample exception rate and determine the computed upper exception rate (CUER) using Table 13-8 on page 406. The exceptions for attribute 1 were considered not to be true exceptions since signatures are not required on invoices for purchases made by cash on POS invoices, although they are required for all other types of purchases. Exception information is summarized in Figure 13-14 (page 405) and Table 13-9 (page 408).

Exception Analysis The final part of the application consists of analyzing the deviations to determine their cause and drawing conclusions about each attribute tested. For every attribute for which CUER exceeds TER, it is essential that some conclusion concerning follow-up action be drawn and documented. The exception analysis and conclusions reached are illustrated in Table 13-9 (page 408) and summarized at the bottom of the data sheet in Figure 13-14 (page 405).

Determine the Acceptability of the Population The controls tested for attributes 1 through 5 of the billing function and recording of sales can be relied on, even though the bulk order invoice number was not recorded on the sales invoice, since there were no deviations in any of the other controls. Thus, the sales population is acceptable. Master file change forms and data entry verification reports were approved using existing policies, except where the designated individual was absent (see Figure 13-13 and Table 13-9). However, this enables a single individual to approve credit and customer master file changes, which could lead to

---

FIGURE 13-13 **Testing of Master File Change Forms**

Objectives: As defined in Figure 13-10 (14.1 and 14.2); authorization of master file change forms and proof of data entry verification.

Sampling: Applies to use of master file change forms throughout the year.

Population: Master file change forms used throughout the year. First form number used: 1201. Last form used: 2132.

TER: 5   **ARACR:** 10   **EPER:** 0   **Initial Sample Size:** 45

Results of Performing Procedures: Three exceptions found, on form # 1288, 1510, and 1599. In the first instance, signature of sales manager was missing. In the second and third, the signature of the chief accountant was missing. In all cases, the indicated person was on holiday. Also for the latter two forms, the data entry report was initialled by the sales manager, since the chief accountant was absent.

	No. of Exceptions	Sample Exception Rate	CUER
Attribute 1	3	6.7	14.2
Attribute 2	2	4.4	11.4

TABLE 13-7 — Determining Sample Size for Attribute Sampling

5 Percent ARACR

Estimated Population Exception Rate (in percentage)	Tolerable Exception Rate (in percentage)										
	2	3	4	5	6	7	8	9	10	15	20
0.00	149	99	74	59	49	42	36	32	29	19	14
0.25	236	157	117	93	78	66	58	51	46	30	22
0.50	*	157	117	93	78	66	58	51	46	30	22
0.75	*	208	117	93	78	66	58	51	46	30	22
1.00	*	*	156	93	78	66	58	51	46	30	22
1.25	*	*	156	124	78	66	58	51	46	30	22
1.50	*	*	192	124	103	66	58	51	46	30	22
1.75	*	*	227	153	103	88	77	51	46	30	22
2.00	*	*	*	181	127	88	77	68	46	30	22
2.25	*	*	*	208	127	88	77	68	61	30	22
2.50	*	*	*	*	150	109	77	68	61	30	22
2.75	*	*	*	*	173	109	95	68	61	30	22
3.00	*	*	*	*	195	129	95	84	61	30	22
3.25	*	*	*	*	*	148	112	84	61	30	22
3.50	*	*	*	*	*	167	112	84	76	40	22
3.75	*	*	*	*	*	185	129	100	76	40	22
4.00	*	*	*	*	*	*	146	100	89	40	22
5.00	*	*	*	*	*	*	*	158	116	40	30
6.00	*	*	*	*	*	*	*	*	179	50	30
7.00	*	*	*	*	*	*	*	*	*	68	37

10 Percent ARACR

Estimated Population Exception Rate (in percentage)	Tolerable Exception Rate (in percentage)										
	2	3	4	5	6	7	8	9	10	15	20
0.00	114	76	57	45	38	32	28	25	22	15	11
0.25	194	129	96	77	64	55	48	42	38	25	18
0.50	194	129	96	77	64	55	48	42	38	25	18
0.75	265	129	96	77	64	55	48	42	38	25	18
1.00	*	176	96	77	64	55	48	42	38	25	18
1.25	*	221	132	77	64	55	48	42	38	25	18
1.50	*	*	132	105	64	55	48	42	38	25	18
1.75	*	*	166	105	88	55	48	42	38	25	18
2.00	*	*	198	132	88	75	48	42	38	25	18
2.25	*	*	*	132	88	75	65	42	38	25	18
2.50	*	*	*	158	110	75	65	58	38	25	18
2.75	*	*	*	209	132	94	65	58	52	25	18
3.00	*	*	*	*	132	94	65	58	52	25	18
3.25	*	*	*	*	153	113	82	58	52	25	18
3.50	*	*	*	*	194	113	82	73	52	25	18
3.75	*	*	*	*	*	131	98	73	52	25	18
4.00	*	*	*	*	*	149	98	73	65	25	18
4.50	*	*	*	*	*	218	130	87	65	34	18
5.00	*	*	*	*	*	*	160	115	78	34	18
5.50	*	*	*	*	*	*	*	142	103	34	18
6.00	*	*	*	*	*	*	*	182	116	45	25
7.00	*	*	*	*	*	*	*	*	199	52	25
8.00	*	*	*	*	*	*	*	*	*	60	25

*Sample is too large to be cost-effective for most audit applications.

Notes: 1. This table assumes a large population. 2. Sample sizes are the same in certain columns even when expected population exception rates differ, because of the method of constructing the tables. Sample sizes are calculated for attributes sampling using the expected number of exceptions in the population, but auditors can deal more conveniently with expected population exception rates. For example, in the 15 percent column for tolerable exception rate, at an ARACR of 5 percent, initial sample size for most EPERs is 30.

FIGURE 13-14   **Attribute Sampling Data Sheet, Completed**

Client	Hillsburg Hardware Limited		Year End	31/12/04
Audit Area	Tests of Controls—Billing Function and Recording of Sales		Pop. Size	145,853

Define the objective(s) Examine duplicate sales invoices and related documents to determine if the system has functioned as intended and as described in the audit program.

Define the population precisely (including stratification, if any) POS invoices and credit sales invoices for the period 1/1/04 to 31/12/04. First POS number = 140672. Last POS number = 283294. First credit sales invoice number = 3600. Last credit sales invoice number = 6831.

Define the sampling unit, organization of population items, and random selection procedures Sales invoice number, POS invoice numbers, and credit recorded in the sales files sequentially; random sampling.

Description of Attributes	Planned Audit				Actual Results			
	EPER	TER	ARACR	Initial sample size	Sample size	Number of exceptions	Sample exception rate	CUER
1. Invoice copy has customer signature. (13.1)	0	3	10	76	75	0	0	3
For Bulk Sales: 2. Bulk order form number entered on invoice details. (13.2)	2	8	10	48	50	4	8	15.4
3. Bulk order form details match invoice details. (13.3)	0	4	10	57	50	0	0	4.5
4. Warehouse copy of bulk order form has customer signature. (13.4)	1	4	10	96	100	0	0	2.3
5. Customer signature on warehouse copy of bulk order form matches signature on invoice. (13.4)	0	3	10	76	75	0	0	3

Intended use of sampling results:

1. **Effect on Audit Plan:** Controls tested using attributes #1, 3–5 can be relied upon. Policies and procedures to remedy #2 should be discussed with management. No additional audit procedures required since no financial impact.

2. **Recommendations to Management:** See attached weakness investigation.

manipulation. The auditor should conduct additional testing by examining master file changes during the period when one of these two individuals was absent or on holiday. Assume that once additional testing was done, no unusual transactions were discovered. The auditor can then accept the population, although additional testing of the bad-debt allowance is still advisable.

Impact of Test of Controls Results on Audit Planning

After the tests of controls have been performed, it is essential to *analyze each test of control exception* to determine its cause and the implication of the exception on assessed control risk, which may affect the supported detection risk and thereby the substantive procedures.

Sample Size	Actual Number of Deviations Found										
	0	1	2	3	4	5	6	7	8	9	10
5 Percent ARACR											
25	11.3	17.6	*	*	*	*	*	*	*	*	*
30	9.5	14.9	19.5	*	*	*	*	*	*	*	*
35	8.2	12.9	16.9	*	*	*	*	*	*	*	*
40	7.2	11.3	14.9	18.3	*	*	*	*	*	*	*
45	6.4	10.1	13.3	16.3	19.2	*	*	*	*	*	*
50	5.8	9.1	12.1	14.8	17.4	19.9	*	*	*	*	*
55	5.3	8.3	11.0	13.5	15.9	18.1	*	*	*	*	*
60	4.9	7.7	10.1	12.4	14.6	16.7	18.8	*	*	*	*
65	4.5	7.1	9.4	11.5	13.5	15.5	17.4	19.3	*	*	*
70	4.2	6.6	8.7	10.7	12.6	14.4	16.2	18.0	19.7	*	*
75	3.9	6.2	8.2	10.0	11.8	13.5	15.2	16.9	18.4	20.0	*
80	3.7	5.8	7.7	9.4	11.1	12.7	14.3	15.8	17.3	18.8	*
90	3.3	5.2	6.8	8.4	9.9	11.3	12.7	14.1	15.5	16.8	18.1
100	3.0	4.7	6.2	7.6	8.9	10.2	11.5	12.7	14.0	15.2	16.4
125	2.4	3.7	4.9	6.1	7.2	8.2	9.3	10.3	11.3	12.2	13.2
150	2.0	3.1	4.1	5.1	6.0	6.9	7.7	8.6	9.4	10.2	11.0
200	1.5	2.3	3.1	3.8	4.5	5.2	5.8	6.5	7.1	7.7	8.3
10 Percent ARACR											
20	10.9	18.1	*	*	*	*	*	*	*	*	*
25	8.8	14.7	19.9	*	*	*	*	*	*	*	*
30	7.4	12.4	16.8	*	*	*	*	*	*	*	*
35	6.4	10.7	14.5	18.1	*	*	*	*	*	*	*
40	5.6	9.4	12.8	15.9	19.0	*	*	*	*	*	*
45	5.0	8.4	11.4	14.2	17.0	19.6	*	*	*	*	*
50	4.5	7.6	10.3	12.9	15.4	17.8	*	*	*	*	*
55	4.1	6.9	9.4	11.7	14.0	16.2	18.4	*	*	*	*
60	3.8	6.3	8.6	10.8	12.9	14.9	16.9	18.8	*	*	*
70	3.2	5.4	7.4	9.3	11.1	12.8	14.6	16.2	17.9	19.5	*
80	2.8	4.8	6.5	8.3	9.7	11.3	12.8	14.3	15.7	17.2	18.6
90	2.5	4.3	5.8	7.3	8.7	10.1	11.4	12.7	14.0	15.3	16.6
100	2.3	3.8	5.2	6.6	7.8	9.1	10.3	11.5	12.7	13.8	15.0
120	1.9	3.2	4.4	5.5	6.6	7.6	8.6	9.6	10.6	11.6	12.5
160	1.4	2.4	3.3	4.1	4.9	5.7	6.5	7.2	8.0	8.7	9.5
200	1.1	1.9	2.6	3.3	4.0	4.6	5.2	5.8	6.4	7.0	7.6

* Over 20 percent.

Note: This table presents computed upper deviation rates as percentages. Table assumes a large population.

For Hillsburg Hardware, assume that there were no other deviations beyond those described and analyzed in Table 13-9. This means that the auditor can accept the planned control risk in all areas except valuation (due to the exceptions found with master file changes).

Update the Evidence Planning Spreadsheet After completing tests of controls, the auditor should complete rows 3 through 5 of the evidence planning spreadsheet. Recall from Chapter 9 that the control risk rows could have been completed before the tests of controls

FIGURE 13-15		Evidence Planning Spreadsheet to Determine Tests of Details of Balances for Hillsburg Hardware Limited—Accounts Receivable							
	Detail tie-in	Existence (or occurrence)	Completeness	Accuracy	Classification	Cutoff	Valuation	Rights and obligations	Presentation and disclosure
Audit risk	high	high	high	high	high	high	high	high	high
Inherent risk	low	low	low	low	low	low	medium	low	low
Control risk – Sales	low	medium	low	low	low	low	high	not applicable	not applicable
Control risk – Cash receipts	low	high	low	low	low	low	not applicable	not applicable	not applicable
Control risk – Additional controls	none	none	none	none	none	none	none	low	low
Analytical procedures									
Planned detection risk for tests of details of balances									
Planned audit evidence for tests of details of balances									
			Materiality	$496,000					

were done, and then modified if the test results were not satisfactory. An updated evidence planning spreadsheet is shown in Figure 13-15. The spreadsheet is used to determine the extent of substantive tests required for the cycle.

The most significant effect of the results of the tests of controls in the sales and collection cycle is on the confirmation of accounts receivable. The type of confirmation, the size of the sample, and the timing of the test are all affected by the results of tests of controls. The effect of the tests on accounts receivable, bad-debt expense, and allowance for uncollectible accounts is further considered in Chapter 14.

Communication with Management In addition to adjusting the audit procedures, the auditor should ensure that management is informed of all exceptions and that the impact of the exceptions is appropriately discussed. In some instances, the auditor will conduct such a discussion verbally, but in many instances, a *management letter* will be issued, in which the exception is discussed, the implications of the exception explained, and recommendations for improvement in procedures identified. For the sales and collection cycle, the auditor might communicate in writing the exceptions with respect to master file change form approval, and recommend that another individual provide a second signature on these forms in the event of the sales manager's or chief accountant's absence. The likely individual recommended to do this would be the president of the organization. The management letter should be copied to the audit committee.

TABLE 13-9	Analysis of Exceptions		
Attribute	Number of Exceptions	Nature of Exceptions	Effect on the Audit and Other Comments
1, sales	3	Three POS invoices paid by cash did not have customer signatures. Each invoice was for less than $50.	No effect on the audit. Hillsburg policy has been clarified that cash purchase invoices do not require customer signature.
2, sales	4	One POS invoice and three credit sales invoices did not have the bulk order number on the face of the invoice, although the invoice copy was attached.	These omissions would show on the bulk order form exception report showing missing bulk order numbers. Management indicated that, unfortunately, new employees often forget to record this number, resulting in an excessive number of items on the exception report. This usually eases off. Since this does not have a financial effect on the audit (there were no errors in goods shipped), no further audit work is required.
1, master file changes	3	Three master file change forms for new credit accounts were approved by only the sales manager *or* the chief accountant.	Additional work on the bad-debt allowance should be completed in the event that bad credit risks have been approved. Master file changes submitted during the period of these managers' absence should be reviewed for unusual items.
2, master file changes	2	Two data entry verification reports of master file changes were verified by the sales manager rather than by the chief accountant.	See above.

APPENDIX F

COMPUTER-ASSISTED AUDIT TESTS

COMPUTER-ASSISTED AUDIT TESTS—tests that the auditor conducts using computer software or using the data or systems of the client

The general term **computer-assisted audit tests** (CAATs) is used to describe tests that the auditor conducts using computer software or using the data or systems of the client. The audit objectives of these tests do not change, but the actual form of the tests must change as the client system changes, just as other aspects of the audit change with a change in audit client.

The two most common forms of CAATs are test data and generalized audit software.

TEST DATA This includes the use of fictitious transactions to determine whether client programs are functioning as described. For Hillsburg Hardware, test data are used to determine whether the system rejects transactions that it should reject, such as invalid customer numbers, unapproved prices, unapproved credit terms, or invalid dates. This is the most common use of test data since the client data files need not be disrupted, and the testing can be performed quickly and efficiently.

Should the auditor wish to determine whether programs are calculating invoice extensions correctly, then test data would need to be prepared that show the expected result, and then the data entered into the client system. Such a test would result in an invoice being calculated and posted against a client account. A credit transaction would need to be created to reverse this invoice test from the client records (i.e., customer master file, transaction files, general ledger, and inventory files). Some of the inconvenience could be avoided by also establishing a fictitious client, but then the auditor has inserted deliberate fictitious transactions in the client's systems. This is the major drawback of test data. It is also a point-in-time test and verifies that the programs being tested are functioning as tested as of the time of the test. The auditor needs to conduct additional tests to determine that these same programs were used during the duration of the period under audit.

An integrated test facility overcomes the problems with test data by allowing the auditor to use test data in a test environment where it does not affect client accounting records. However, it can be used only with clients who have established such a capability during the initial set-up of their accounting systems.

GENERALIZED AUDIT SOFTWARE This consists of a software package that is used by the auditor to run routines against client data. Two common packages in Canada are Audit Command Language for Personal Computers (ACL-PC) and Interactive Data Extraction and Analysis (I.D.E.A.). The auditor obtains a copy of the client data files and runs one or more of the following types of activities against the data file. The examples shown are typical tests that would be run against the customer master file together with open item accounts:

Mathematical calculations: addition of debit and credit amounts, extensions
Aging functions: aging of the accounts to re-create figures in the aged accounts receivable trial balance
Comparisons: between the outstanding balance and the credit limit
Sampling: using random, dollar-unit, interval, or stratification

Certain functions of generalized audit software are often referred to as "parallel simulation," which is the reperformance of activities conducted by the client. For example, if the auditor re-creates the aged accounts receivable trial balance using client data, this is parallel simulation. This is a dual purpose test since it ensures the mechanical accuracy of the aging process (a substantive test), while also verifying that the client's aging program is functioning correctly (a controls test).

Examples of test data and generalized audit software are discussed in those chapters where transaction cycles are tested (primarily Chapters 16, 17, and 19), providing examples linked to specific audit objectives.

SUMMARY

1. *What are typical records and transactions in the sales cycle?* There are typically five classes of transactions included in the sales and collection cycle: sales, cash receipts, sales returns and allowances, charge-off of uncollectible accounts, and bad-debt expenses. Records include the customer master file and the transaction history file, with periodic listings such as sales journals and an aged accounts receivable trial balance.

2. *How do general controls affect the audit of the sales and collection cycle?* General controls affect multiple transaction cycles, so weaknesses in general controls, such as program change controls or access controls, would mean that the auditor might not be able to rely on programmed functions or segregation of duties. Strengths in general controls may allow the auditor to rely on those controls enforced by automated systems.

    Describe the methodology for designing tests of controls for sales. The auditor needs to understand general controls that apply to sales, as well as the application controls within the sales cycle to assess planned control risk for sales. Then, the cost benefit of testing controls is examined by assertion prior to designing tests of controls for the cycle. Where desired, dual purpose or weakness investigation tests are designed. An audit program in a performance format is used to conduct the tests.

3. *List the methodology for controls over: sales returns and allowances, cash receipts transactions, uncollectible accounts, and account balances.* The general methodology is the same for every transaction type. It depends upon the risk for the transaction type and associated assertions as well as the materiality of the transactions.

    What is the effect of the results of tests of controls on the audit? Where controls are functioning as described, the auditor may be able to reduce tests of details. As tests of controls tend to be less expensive to conduct than tests of details, this can result in an overall lower cost high-quality audit.

4. *What is the typical audit process for tests of controls?* Hillsburg Hardware Limited is used to illustrate how the many possible controls are narrowed down to the key controls in place at an organization for the audit assertions. Then, tests are designed and a sample selected. When testing is complete, the results are evaluated and the effect on the audit identified.

    How is an audit program of tests of controls of sales organized? When the audit program is developed, it is organized by audit assertion (audit objective). To conduct the testing, the audit steps are reorganized into a performance format that facilitates efficient completion of like audit procedures.

ESSENTIAL TERMS

In addition to these terms, see pages 374–376 for descriptions of the key documents and records used in the sales and collection cycle.

Batch processing—transaction processing using groups of transactions   (p. 373).

Business functions for the sales and collection cycle—the key activities that an organization must complete to execute and record business transactions for sales, cash receipts, sales returns and allowances, charge-off of uncollectible accounts, and bad debts   (p. 373).

Classes of transactions in the sales and collection cycle—the categories of transactions for the sales and collection cycle in a typical company: sales, cash receipts, sales returns and allowances, charge-off of uncollectible accounts, and bad-debt expense   (p. 370).

Computer-assisted audit tests—tests that the auditor conducts using computer software or using the data or systems of the client   (p. 408).

Data control function—independent verification of control total and source document detail to that keyed into the system by data entry   (p. 373).

Design format audit program—the audit procedures resulting from the auditor's decisions about the appropriate audit procedures for each audit objective; this audit program is used to prepare a performance format audit program   (p. 388).

Interdependent controls—controls that require both a programmed and manual component to satisfy an audit objective (p. 387).

Lapping of accounts receivable—the postponement of entries for the collection of receivables to conceal an existing cash shortage; a common type of defalcation   (p. 390).

Online processing—the processing of transactions one at a time with an immediate update against the data files   (p. 373)

Performance format audit program—the audit procedures for a class of transactions organized in the format that they will be performed; prepared from a design format audit program   (p. 388).

Proof of cash receipts—an audit procedure to test whether all recorded cash receipts have been deposited in the bank account by reconciling the total cash receipts recorded in the cash receipts journal for a given period with the actual deposits made to the bank   (p. 389).

Sales and collection cycle—involves the decisions and processes necessary for the transfer of the ownership of goods and services to customers after they are made available for sale; begins with a request by a customer and ends with the conversion of material or service into an account receivable, and ultimately into cash (p. 371).

Semi-permanent (or master file) data—in the sales and collection cycle, data that are established when a customer starts purchasing and updated as customer information changes; generally used for the processing of multiple transactions   (p. 372).

Tests of controls in the sales and collection cycle—audit procedures performed to determine the effectiveness of both the design and operations of specific internal controls. They include audit procedures testing for monetary errors or fraud and other irregularities to determine whether the six transaction-related audit objectives have been satisfied for each class of transactions in the sales and collection cycle   (p. 383).

Transaction information—information based on customer activity. There is normally one transaction for each activity. In the sales and collection cycle, examples include sale or cash payment transactions   (p. 372).

Transaction-related audit objectives in the sales and collection cycle—the six objectives that the auditor must satisfy for each class of transactions in the sales and collection cycle   (p. 383).

Weakness investigation tests—tests conducted to determine whether a material error or material misstatement could occur due to a control weakness   (p. 384).

REVIEW QUESTIONS

13-1   Describe the nature of the following documents and records, and explain their use in the sales and collection cycle: bill of lading, sales invoice, customer master file, credit memo, remittance advice, and monthly statement to customers.

13-2   Explain the importance of proper credit approval for sales. What effect do adequate controls in the credit function have on the auditor's evidence accumulation?

13-3   Distinguish between bad-debt expense and charge-off of uncollectible accounts. Explain why they are audited in completely different ways.

13-4   List the transaction-related audit objectives for the verification of sales transactions. For each objective, state one internal control that the client can use to reduce the likelihood of misstatements.

13-5   List the most important duties that should be segregated in the sales and collection cycle. Explain why it is desirable that each duty be segregated.

13-6   Explain how prenumbered shipping documents and sales invoices can be useful controls for preventing misstatements in sales.

13-7   What three types of authorizations are commonly used as internal controls for sales? For each authorization, state a test of controls that the auditor could use to verify whether the control was effective in preventing misstatements.

13-8   Explain the purpose of footing and cross-footing the sales journal and tracing the totals to the general ledger.

13-9   What is the difference between the auditor's approach in verifying sales returns and allowances and that for sales? Explain the reasons for the difference.

13-10 Explain why auditors usually emphasize the detection of fraud in the audit of cash. Is this consistent or inconsistent with the auditor's responsibility in the audit? Explain.

13-11 List the transaction-related audit objectives for the verification of cash receipts. For each objective, state one internal control that the client can use to reduce the likelihood of misstatements.

13-12 List several audit procedures the auditor can use to determine whether all cash received was recorded.

13-13 Explain what is meant by "proof of cash receipts," and state its purpose.

13-14 Explain what is meant by "lapping," and discuss how the auditor can uncover it. Under what circumstances should the auditor make a special effort to uncover lapping?

13-15 What audit procedures are most likely to be used to verify accounts receivable charged off as uncollectible? State the purpose of each of these procedures.

13-16 Under what circumstances is it acceptable to perform tests of controls for sales and cash receipts at an interim date?

13-17 Deirdre Brandt, a public accountant, tested sales transactions for the month of March in an audit of the financial statements for the year ended December 31, 2004. Based on the excellent results of the tests of controls, she decided to significantly reduce her substantive tests of details of balances at year end. Evaluate this decision.

13-18 BestSellers.com sells fiction and nonfiction books to customers through the company's web site. Customers place orders for books via the web site by providing their name, address, credit card number, and expiration date. What internal controls could BestSellers.com implement to ensure that shipments of books occur only for customers who have the ability to pay for those books? At what point would BestSellers.com be able to record the sale as revenue?

MULTIPLE CHOICE QUESTIONS

13-19 Choose the best response.

a. A company policy should clearly indicate that defective merchandise returned by customers is to be delivered to the

   (1) inventory control clerk.
   (2) sales clerk.
   (3) receiving clerk.
   (4) accounts receivable clerk.

b. For good internal control, the credit manager should be responsible to the

   (1) treasurer.
   (2) sales manager.
   (3) customer service manager.
   (4) operations manager.

c. A manufacturing company received a substantial sales return in the last month of the year, but the credit memorandum for the return was not prepared until after the auditors had completed their fieldwork. The returned merchandise was included in the physical inventory. The best control to ensure accurate recording is:

   (1) Receiving reports are prepared for all materials received, and such reports are numerically controlled.
   (2) Aging schedules of accounts receivable are prepared periodically.
   (3) Credit memoranda are prenumbered and all numbers are accounted for.

   (4) A reconciliation of the trial balance of customers' accounts with the general ledger control is prepared periodically.

d. Copies of sales invoices show different unit prices for apparently identical items. A control to prevent this would be:

   (1) Prices should be automatically placed on invoices from master file data.
   (2) Differences reported by customers are satisfactorily investigated.
   (3) All sales invoices are compared with shipping documents.
   (4) Statistical sales data are compiled and reconciled with recorded sales.

   (AICPA adapted)

e. To verify that all sales transactions have been recorded, a test of controls should be completed on a representative sample drawn from

   (1) the shipping clerk's file of duplicate copies of bills of lading.
   (2) the billing clerk's file of customer purchase orders.
   (3) a file of duplicate copies of sales invoices for which all prenumbered forms in the series have been accounted.
   (4) entries in the sales journal.

DISCUSSION QUESTIONS AND PROBLEMS

13-20 Items 1 through 8 are selected questions of the type generally found in internal control questionnaires used by auditors to obtain an understanding of internal control in the sales and collection cycle. In using the questionnaire for a particular client, a "yes" response to a question indicates a possible internal control, whereas a "no" indicates a potential weakness.

1. Are sales invoices independently compared with customers' orders for prices, quantities, extensions, and footings?
2. Are sales orders, invoices, and credit memoranda issued and filed in numerical sequence, and are the sequences accounted for periodically?
3. Are the selling function and cash register functions independent of the cash receipts, shipping, delivery, and billing functions?
4. Are all C.O.D., scrap, equipment, and cash sales accounted for in the same manner as charge sales, and is the record keeping independent of the collection procedure?
5. Is the collection function independent of, and does it constitute a check on, billing and recording sales?
6. Are customer master files balanced regularly to general ledger control accounts by an employee independent of billing functions?
7. Are cash receipts entered in the accounts receivable system by persons independent of the mail-opening and receipts-listing functions?
8. Are receipts deposited intact daily on a timely basis?

Required
a. For each of the questions above, state the transaction-related audit objectives being fulfilled if the control is in effect.
b. For each control, list a test of control to test its effectiveness.
c. For each of the questions above, identify the nature of the potential financial misstatements.
d. For each of the potential misstatements in part (c), list an audit procedure to determine whether a material error exists.

13-21 The following errors or fraud and other irregularities are included in the accounting records of Joyce Manufacturing Ltd.:

1. The credit limit for a new customer was entered as $20,000 rather than $2,000 into the customer master file.
2. A material sale was unintentionally recorded for the second time on the last day of the year. The sale had originally been recorded two days earlier.
3. Cash paid on accounts receivable was stolen by the mail clerk when the mail was opened.
4. Cash paid on accounts receivable that had been prelisted by a secretary was stolen by the bookkeeper who enters cash receipts and accounts receivable in the accounts receivable system. He failed to enter the transactions.
5. A shipment to a customer was not billed because of the loss of the bill of lading.
6. Merchandise was shipped to a customer, but no bill of lading was prepared. Since billings are prepared from bills of lading, the customer was not billed.
7. A sale to a residential customer was unintentionally classified as a commercial sale.

Required
a. Identify whether each misstatement is an error, or a fraud or other irregularity.
b. For each misstatement, state a control that should have prevented it from occurring on a continuing basis.
c. For each misstatement, state an audit procedure that could uncover it.

13-22 YourTeam.com is an online retailer of college and professional sports team memorabilia, such as hats, shirts, pennants and other sports logo products. Consumers select the university, college, or professional team from a pull-down menu on the company's web site. For each listed team, the web site provides a product description, picture, and price for all products sold online. Customers click on the product number of the items they wish to purchase. YourTeam.com has established the following internal controls for its online sales:

1. Only products shown on the web site can be purchased online. Other company products not shown on the web site listing are unavailable for online sale.
2. The online sales system is linked to the perpetual inventory system that verifies quantities on hand before processing the sale.
3. Before the sale is authorized, YourTeam.com obtains credit card authorization codes electronically from the credit card agency.
4. Online sales are rejected if the customer's shipping address does not match the credit card's billing address.
5. Before the sale is finalized, the online screen shows the product name, description, unit price, and total sales price for the online transaction. Customers must click on the Accept or Reject sales buttons to indicate approval or rejection of the online sale.
6. Once customers approve the online sale, the online sales system generates a Pending Sales file, which is an online data file that is used by warehouse personnel to process shipments. Online sales are not recorded in the sales journal until warehouse personnel enter the bill of lading number and date of shipment into the Pending Sales data file.

Required
a. For each control, identify the transaction-related audit objective(s) being fulfilled if each control is in effect.
b. For each control, describe potential financial misstatements that could occur if the control was not present.
c. For each control, identify an important general control that would affect the quality of the control.
d. For each control, list a test of control to test its effectiveness.

13-23 You were asked in February 2005 by the board of management of your church to review its accounting procedures. As part of this review, you have prepared the following comments relating to the collections made at weekly services and record-keeping for members' pledges and contributions:

1. The finance committee is responsible for preparing an annual budget based on the anticipated needs of the various church committees and for the annual fall "pledge campaign" during which most members make a commitment to contribute a certain amount to the church over the following year.
2. The financial records are maintained by the treasurer who has authority to sign cheques drawn on the church bank account.
3. The ushers take up the collection during the services each Sunday and place it uncounted in a deposit bag in the church safe.
4. The treasurer, who is retired, comes in Monday morning, counts the collection and deposits it into the church's bank account. Some members use predated numbered envelopes but most do not. The treasurer enters members' contributions into a spreadsheet for numbered envelopes.
5. The treasurer issues receipts to each member every January based on the spreadsheet amounts. The contributions up to 2003 had always exceeded the amounts pledged so that the value of receipts given out was less than total contributions; the excess was recorded as "loose" or "open" collection. In 2005, the total of the receipts given out by the treasurer exceeded the total funds received by the church.
6. The church is registered as a charity under the *Income Tax Act* and is required to file a return each year to comply with its rules. The chairperson of the finance committee is upset because the church has received a letter from the Canada Revenue Agency in connection with the return for 2005 because the return showed receipts given exceeded the funds actually received. The letter indicated that such differences could result in removal of the church's ability to issue income tax receipts.

Required

Identify the weaknesses and recommend improvements in procedures for
a. collections made at weekly services.
b. record keeping for members' pledges and contributions. Use the methodology for identifying weaknesses that was discussed in Chapter 9. Organize your answer sheets as follows:

Weakness	Recommended Improvement

(AICPA adapted)

13-24 Lenter Supply Corp. is a medium-sized distributor of wholesale hardware supplies in southern Manitoba. It has been a client of yours for several years and has instituted excellent internal control for sales at your recommendation.

In providing control over shipments, the client has prenumbered "warehouse removal slips" that are used for every sale. It is company policy never to remove goods from the warehouse without an authorized warehouse removal slip. After shipment, two copies of the warehouse removal slip are sent to billing for the computerized preparation of a sales invoice. One copy is stapled to the duplicate copy of a prenumbered sales invoice, and the other copy is filed numerically. In some cases, more than one warehouse removal slip is used for billing one sales invoice. The lowest warehouse removal slip number for the year is 14682 and the highest is 37521. The lowest sales invoice number is 47821 and the highest is 68507.

In the audit of sales, one of the major concerns is the effectiveness of the controls in making sure that all shipments are billed. You have decided to use audit sampling in testing internal controls.

Required

a. State an effective audit procedure for testing whether shipments have been billed. What is the sampling unit for the audit procedure?
b. Assuming that you expect no deviations in the sample but are willing to accept a TER of 3 percent, at a 10 percent ARACR, what is the appropriate sample size for the audit test? You may complete this assignment using nonstatistical sampling or attribute sampling.
c. Design a random selection plan for selecting the sample from the population using the random number table. Select the first 10 sample items using Table 12-2 on page 345. Use a starting point of row 1013, column 3.
d. Your supervisor suggests the possibility of performing other sales tests with the same sample as a means of efficiently using your audit time. List two other audit procedures that could conveniently be performed using the same sample, and state the purpose of each of the procedures.
e. Is it desirable to test the existence of sales with the random sample you have designed in part (c)? Why or why not?

13-25 The following is a partial audit program for the audit of cash receipts.

1. Review the cash receipts journal for large and unusual transactions.
2. Trace entries from the prelisting of cash receipts to the cash receipts journal to determine if each is recorded.
3. Compare customer name, date, and amount on the prelisting with the cash receipts journal.
4. Examine the related remittance advice for entries selected from the prelisting to determine if cash discounts were approved.
5. Trace entries from the prelisting to the deposit slip to determine if each has been deposited.

Required

a. Identify which audit procedures could be tested using attribute sampling.
b. What is the appropriate sampling unit for the tests in part (a)?
c. List the attributes for testing in part (a).
d. Assume an ARACR of 5 percent and a TER of 8 percent for tests of controls. The estimated population deviation rate for tests of controls is 2 percent. What is the initial sample size for each attribute?

13-26 The following questions concern the determination of the proper sample size in attributes sampling using the following table:

	1	2	3	4	5	6	7
ARACR (in percentage)	10	5	5	5	10	10	5
TER (in percentage)	6	6	5	6	20	20	2
EPER (in percentage)	2	2	2	2	8	2	0
Population size	1,000	100,000	6,000	1,000	500	500	1,000,000

Required

a. For each of the columns numbered 1 through 7, decide the initial sample size using nonstatistical methods.

b. For each of the columns numbered 1 through 7, determine the initial sample size needed to satisfy the auditor's requirements using attribute sampling from the appropriate parts of Tables 13-7 and 13-8 on pages 404 and 406.

c. Using your understanding of the relationship between the following factors and sample size, state the effect on the initial sample size (increase or decrease) of changing each of the following factors while the other three are held constant:

(1) An increase in ARACR
(2) An increase in the TER
(3) An increase in the EPER
(4) An increase in the population size

d. Explain why there is such a large difference in the sample sizes for columns 3 and 6.

e. Compare your answers in part (b) with the results you determined in part (a). Which of the four factors appears to have the greatest effect on the initial sample size? Which one appears to have the least effect?

f. Why is the sample size referred to as the initial sample size?

13-27 The following are auditor judgments and audit sampling results for six populations. Assume large population sizes.

	1	2	3	4	5	6
EPER (in percentage)	2	0	3	1	1	8
TER (in percentage)	6	3	8	5	20	15
ARACR (in percentage)	5	5	10	5	10	10
Actual sample size	100	100	60	100	20	60
Actual number of exceptions in the sample	2	0	1	4	1	8

Required

a. For each population, did the auditor select a smaller sample size than is indicated by using attribute sampling tables for determining sample size? Evaluate, selecting either a larger or smaller size than those determined in the tables.

b. Calculate the SER and CUER for each population.

c. For which of the six populations should the sample results be considered unacceptable? What options are available to the auditor?

d. Why is analysis of the deviations necessary even when the populations are considered acceptable?

e. For the following terms, identify which is an audit decision, a nonstatistical estimate made by the auditor, a sample result, and a statistical conclusion about the population:

(1) EPER
(2) TER
(3) ARACR
(4) Actual sample size
(5) Actual number of exceptions in the sample
(6) SER
(7) CUER

PROFESSIONAL JUDGMENT PROBLEM

13-28 Marvel Distributor Company receives orders by telephone, where they are entered into the online sales system. Twice a day, a report is sent to the credit department listing any accounts that have exceeded their credit limit. The credit supervisor initials those orders that are to be released, and returns the report to the order staff, who release the orders. Two copies of the sales invoices are then printed, with a different numeric series than the orders.

The customer copy of the sales invoice is held in a pending file awaiting notification that the order was shipped. The shipping copy of the sales invoice is routed through the warehouse. The shipping department personnel pack the order and manually prepare a two-copy bill of lading. They enter the bill of lading number into the computer system, which triggers the release of the sale to the order staff: a sales journal is printed, and sales staff pull these invoices for mailing. One copy of the bill of lading is attached to the shipping copy of the invoice, and the second copy is filed numerically in the shipping area.

Required

a. What weaknesses in internal control exist in this system? For each weakness, state the errors that could occur as a result of the weakness. For each weakness, provide a control that would prevent or detect the error.

b. What audit tests would the auditor conduct to determine whether the control weakness(es) resulted in a material error?

CASE

13-29 CA is the auditor of GR Ltd., the largest retailer of compact discs and cassette tapes in the city of Q. The company is a wholly-owned subsidiary of a nationwide wholesale music distributor. The ownership of the retail operation enables the parent company's management to keep abreast of changes in consumer buying patterns and tastes, thereby making the distributorship more quickly responsive to changes in demand than would otherwise be the case.

The merchandise inventory of GR Ltd. averages about 140,000 items of 15,000 different titles, 84 percent of which are CDs. In addition, there is a relatively small stock of peripheral items such as cleaners, catalogues, and ear plugs.

In order to provide current information on which CDs are selling, and to provide accurate inventory information for stock control, re-ordering, and financial statement preparation, GR uses point-of-sale computer terminals operating online with the parent company's computer.

All items are identifiable by the manufacturer's alphanumeric code, which identifies the manufacturer as well as the title. For the perpetual inventory system, GR Ltd. converts the alphanumeric code for each CD to a strictly numeric code. This code, which is fixed in length, is printed on labels by the staff and affixed to each CD when the CD is received and put into stock.

When a customer makes a purchase or returns merchandise, the sales clerk keys the following into the POS terminal:

1. A four-digit sales clerk identifier code
2. ENTER
3. A one-digit transaction code (sale or return)
4. CD stock number of first CD sold or returned, if a CD; a one-digit code for other items
5. ENTER
6. Quantity of the specific items being purchased or returned
7. ENTER
8. Unit price
9. ENTER
10. Repeats steps 4 through 9 for each item
11. TOTAL (POS terminal displays the merchandise total, adds the automatically computed sales tax and GST, and displays the amount due or refundable)
12. Amount tendered
13. ENTER (causing the computer to calculate and display the change due)
14. END

The transaction is held by the computer without processing until the transaction is terminated by pressing the END key. This delay permits the staff to void the transaction if an error has been made during entry. When the END key is depressed, the inventory information (items 3, 4, and 6 above) is used to update the inventory master file. While the transaction is being entered, the terminal prints a sales slip. The sales slip is not released by the terminal until the transaction is completed with the END key. Voided sales slips must be approved by the store manager or the assistant manager.

As part of his internal control review, CA has undertaken to assess the controls embodied in GR Ltd.'s sales and inventory systems. As part of this internal control review, CA proposed to use test transactions to determine which controls were operating in the computerized sales entry portion of the system, as described above.

Required

a. List the controls that should be programmed into the sales entry system described above. List only those programmed controls that relate to the processing of individual sale and return transactions.

b. Describe the transactions that you would include in your set of test transactions, and state which controls each transaction would test.

c. Explain procedures that CA could follow in conducting the above tests in order to protect the integrity of GR Ltd.'s inventory master file.

(CICA adapted)

CHAPTER 14

COMPLETING THE TESTS IN THE SALES AND COLLECTION CYCLE: ACCOUNTS RECEIVABLE

Substantive tests are considered the "finishing touch" for the audit of an account. The controls testing provides information about the quality of the client's systems so that the auditor has enough detail to design the tests of detail. In this chapter, we will look at one specific account—trade accounts receivable—and examine how the testing is designed, selected, executed, and evaluated.

LEARNING OBJECTIVES

After reading this chapter, you should be able to answer the following questions:

1. What is the process for designing tests of details of balances for accounts receivable? What is the relationship between the transaction-related and the balance-related audit objectives for the sales and collection cycle?

2. When and why are analytical review procedures completed as part of the audit of sales and accounts receivable? How is the amount of substantive testing related to the audit risk model?

3. Describe the audit tests that would be completed for each audit assertion. Why is confirmation one of the most important audit procedures?

4. Provide a description of an example test of detail. How is monetary unit sampling (MUS) executed and evaluated?

WHEN MORE ISN'T BETTER

On Cindy Veinot's first audit assignment, she is asked to handle the confirmation of accounts receivable. The audit client is a retailer with a large number of customer accounts. In previous years, Cindy's firm confirmed these accounts using negative confirmations. Last year, 200 negative confirmations were sent one month prior to year end. Those that were returned showed only timing differences; none represented a misstatement in the client's books.

Before the current year's planned confirmation date, Cindy performs a review of internal controls over sales and cash receipts transactions. She discovers that a new online system for sales transactions has been implemented, but the client is having considerable problems getting it to work properly. There are a significant number of misstatements in recording sales during the past few months. Cindy's tests of controls and substantive tests of sales transactions also identify similar misstatements.

When Cindy asks her supervisor what to do, she responds, "No problem, Cindy. Just send 300 confirmation requests instead of the usual 200." Cindy recalls from her auditing class that negative confirmation requests aren't considered to be good evidence when there are weak controls. Because customers are asked to respond only when there are differences, the auditor cannot be confident of the correct value for each misstatement in the sample. Cindy concludes that expanding the sample size is the wrong solution. When Cindy discusses her concerns with her supervisor, she responds, "You are absolutely right. I spoke too quickly. We need to sit down and think about a better strategy to find out if accounts receivable is materially misstated."

Cindy felt comfortable talking to her supervisor about her disagreement with the audit approach that had been used in the past. It is important to have the knowledge to ask questions like Cindy did. What other questions could she have asked to help her assess the audit approach for accounts receivable? What information would she require to select a sample for positive confirmations?

Figure 14-1 shows the relationship between analytical procedures and tests of detail and planned detection risk, using the audit risk model. We consider tests of controls for the sales and collection cycle, discussed in the previous chapter, to be part of phase II of the audit process (recall that phase I is planning). Tests of details of balances for the sales and collection cycle, studied in this chapter, are done in phase III.

→14.1   DESIGNING TESTS OF DETAILS OF BALANCES FOR ACCOUNTS RECEIVABLE

Methodology for Designing Tests of Details of Balances

Figure 14-2 shows the methodology that auditors follow in determining the appropriate tests of details of balances for accounts receivable. The methodology was introduced in Chapter 11 and is now applied to the audit of accounts receivable. This methodology integrates both the audit risk model and the types of audit tests that are shown in Figure 14-1.

Determining the appropriate tests of details of balances evidence is complicated because it must be decided on an objective-by-objective basis. There are several interactions that affect the evidence decision. For example, the auditor must consider inherent risk, which may differ by objective, and control risk, which also may vary by objective.

To help manage the decision-making process for the appropriate tests of details of balances, auditors often use an **evidence planning spreadsheet**. This spreadsheet was first introduced in Chapter 8 (Figure 8-5, page 231) and further amplified in Chapter 13 (Figure 13-15, page 407). The completed evidence planning spreadsheet is included as Figure 14-8 on page 438. This spreadsheet is directly related to the methodology in Figure 14-2. Both figures are discussed as we proceed.

EVIDENCE PLANNING SPREAD-SHEET—a working paper used to help the auditor decide whether planned audit evidence for tests of details of balances should be low, medium, or high for each balance-related audit objective

| FIGURE 14-1 | Relationship Between Analytical Procedures and Tests of Details of Balances to Planned Detection Risk |

Audit Risk Model

$$AR = IR \times CR \times PDR$$

Types of Audit Tests

Procedures to obtain an understanding of internal control + Tests of controls + Analytical procedures + Tests of details of balances = Sufficient appropriate audit evidence per GAAS

FIGURE 14-2 Methodology for Designing Tests of Details of Balances for Accounts Receivable

Set materiality. Assess audit risk and inherent risk for accounts receivable.

Assess control risk for sales and collection cycle.

Design and perform tests of controls for the sales and collection cycle.

Design and perform analytical procedures for accounts receivable balance.

Design tests of details of accounts receivable balance to satisfy balance-related audit objectives.

- Audit procedures
- Sample size
- Items to select
- Timing

Materiality Considerations

Accounts receivable is typically one of the most material accounts in the financial statements for companies that sell on credit. Even if the accounts receivable balance is not large, the transactions in the sales and collection cycle that affect the balance in accounts receivable are almost certain to be highly significant.

Inherent Risk

For most audits, inherent risk for accounts receivable assertions is moderate or low except for two objectives: accounts receivable is stated at realizable value, and sales and sales returns and allowances cutoff is correct. It is difficult, because of the judgments involved, for clients to evaluate realizable value and correctly adjust the allowance for uncollectible accounts. It is relatively easy for clients to intentionally misstate the allowance account because of the difficulty of the judgments. Similarly, it is common for clients to intentionally or unintentionally misstate cutoff.

Control Risk Considerations

Internal controls over sales and cash receipts and the related accounts receivable are at least reasonably effective for most companies because management is concerned with keeping accurate records as a means to good relations with customers. Auditors are often especially concerned with three aspects of internal controls: controls that prevent or detect defalcations, controls over cutoff, and controls related to the allowance for uncollectible accounts, such as aging of accounts receivable.

Accounts Receivable Balance-Related Audit Objectives

The nine general balance-related audit objectives are the same for every account balance and are applied to accounts receivable as **accounts receivable balance-related audit objectives**. The general objectives were first introduced in Chapter 5. These nine objectives applied to accounts receivable are:[1]

- Accounts receivable in the aged trial balance agree with related customer master file amounts, and the total is correctly added and agrees with the general ledger (detail tie-in).
- Recorded accounts receivable exist (existence).
- Existing accounts receivable are included (completeness).
- Accounts receivable are accurate (accuracy).
- Accounts receivable are properly classified (classification).
- Cutoff for accounts receivable is correct (cutoff).
- Accounts receivable are stated at realizable value (valuation).
- The client has rights to accounts receivable (rights and obligations).
- Accounts receivable presentation and disclosures are proper (presentation and disclosure).

The columns in the evidence planning spreadsheet in Figure 14-8 include the balance-related audit objectives. The auditor uses the factors in the rows to aid in assessing planned

ACCOUNTS RECEIVABLE BALANCE-RELATED AUDIT OBJECTIVES—the nine specific audit objectives used to help the auditor decide the appropriate audit evidence for accounts receivable

---

[1]Detail tie-in is included as the first objective here, as compared with being Objective 7 in Chapter 5, because tests for detail tie-in are normally done first.

detection risk for accounts receivable, by objective. All of these factors are decided during audit planning. They were studied in Chapters 8 through 13.

Set Materiality and Assess Audit Risk and Inherent Risk Setting materiality starts with the auditor making the preliminary judgment about materiality for the entire financial statements. Figure 14-8 shows that materiality was set at $496,000 for the Hillsburg Hardware audit by including the amount on the bottom of the evidence planning spreadsheet.

Audit risk is assessed for the financial statements as a whole and is not usually allocated to various accounts or objectives. Figure 14-8 shows an audit risk of high for every objective, which will permit a higher planned detection risk for accounts receivable than if audit risk were low.

Inherent risk is assessed for each objective for an account such as accounts receivable. It was assessed at low for all objectives except valuation for Hillsburg Hardware.

Assess Control Risk for the Sales and Collection Cycle The methodology for assessing control risk was studied in general in Chapter 9 and applied to sales and cash receipts transactions in Chapter 13. The framework used to identify control activities and internal control weaknesses was a control risk matrix. Examples are included in Figures 13-8 (page 395) and 13-9 (page 396).

The internal controls studied in Chapter 13 relate specifically to transaction-related audit objectives for classes of transactions. The two primary classes of transactions in the sales and collection cycle are sales and cash receipts.

The auditor must relate control risk for transaction-related audit objectives to balance-related audit objectives in deciding planned detection risk and planned evidence for tests of details of balances. For the most part, the relationship is straightforward. Figure 14-3 shows the relationship for the two primary classes of transactions in the sales and collection cycle. For example, assume that the auditor concluded that control risk for both sales and cash receipts transactions is low for the accuracy transaction-related audit objective. The auditor can, therefore, conclude that controls for the accuracy balance-related audit objective for accounts receivable are effective because the only transactions that affect accounts receivable are sales and cash receipts. Of course, if sales returns and allowances and charge-off of uncollectible accounts receivable are significant, assessed control risk must also be considered for these two classes of transactions.

Two aspects of the relationships in Figure 14-3 deserve special mention:

- For sales, the occurrence transaction-related audit objective affects the existence balance-related audit objective, but for cash receipts, the occurrence transaction-related audit objective affects the completeness balance-related audit objective.
- A similar relationship exists for the completeness transaction-related audit objective. The reason for this somewhat surprising conclusion is that an increase of sales increases accounts receivable, but an increase of cash receipts decreases accounts receivable. For example, recording a sale that did not occur violates the occurrence transaction-related audit objective and existence balance-related audit objective (both overstatements). Recording a cash receipt that did not occur violates the occurrence transaction-related audit objective, but it violates the completeness balance-related audit objective for accounts receivable because a receivable that is still outstanding is no longer included in the records.
- Three accounts receivable balance-related audit objectives are not affected by assessed control risk for classes of transactions. These are valuation, rights and obligations, and presentation and disclosure. When the auditor wants to reduce assessed control risk below maximum for these three objectives, separate controls are identified and tested. This was discussed in Chapter 9.

Figure 14-8 on page 438 includes three rows for assessed control risk: one for sales, one for cash receipts, and one for additional controls related to the accounts receivable balance. The source of each control risk for sales and cash receipts is the control risk matrix, assuming that the tests of controls results supported the original assessment. The auditor makes a separate assessment of control risk for objectives related only to the accounts receivable balance.

FIGURE 14-3

FIGURE 14-3 Relationship Between Transaction-Related and Balance-Related Audit Objectives for the Sales and Collection Cycle

Class of Transactions	Transaction-Related Audit Objectives	Accounts Receivable Balance-Related Audit Objectives								
		Detail tie-in	Existence	Completeness	Accuracy	Classification	Cutoff	Valuation	Rights and obligations	Presentation and disclosure
Sales	Occurrence		X							
	Completeness			X						
	Accuracy				X					
	Classification					X				
	Timing						X			
	Posting and summarization	X								
Cash receipts	Occurrence			X						
	Completeness		X							
	Accuracy				X					
	Classification					X				
	Timing						X			
	Posting and summarization	X								

Design and Perform Tests of Controls Chapter 13 dealt with deciding audit procedures and sample size for tests of controls and evaluating the results of those tests. The results of the tests of controls determine whether assessed control risk for sales and cash receipts needs to be revised. The evidence planning spreadsheet in Figure 14-8 shows three rows for control risk based on the completion and evaluation of those tests.

→14.2 THE IMPORTANCE OF ANALYTICAL PROCEDURES

Design and Perform Analytical Procedures

As discussed in Chapter 6, analytical procedures are done during three phases of the audit: during planning, when performing detailed tests in phase III, and as a part of completing the audit. Those affecting accounts receivable or the sales cycle that are done during planning and when performing detailed tests are discussed in this chapter.

Most year-end analytical procedures are done after the balance sheet date but before tests of details of balances. It makes little sense to perform extensive analytical procedures before the client has recorded all transactions for the year and finalized the financial statements. Where auditors also provide assurance on quarterly financial results, analytical review procedures are updated periodically throughout the year.

Table 14-1 presents examples of the major types of ratios and comparisons for the sales and collection cycle and potential misstatements that may be indicated by the analytical procedures. It is important to observe in the "Possible Misstatement" column that both balance sheet and income statement accounts are affected. For example, when the auditor performs

TABLE 14-1 | Analytical Procedures for Sales and Collections

Analytical Procedure	Possible Misstatement
Compare gross margin percentage with previous years (by product line).	Overstatement or understatement of sales and accounts receivable.
Compare sales by month (by product line) over time.	Overstatement or understatement of sales and accounts receivable.
Examine relationship between sales and cost of sales, for example, using regression analysis.	Understatement or overstatement of sales and accounts receivable.
Compare sales returns and allowances as a percentage of gross sales with previous years (by product line).	Understatement or overstatement of sales returns and allowances and accounts receivable.
Compare individual customer balances over a stated amount with previous years.	Misstatements in accounts receivable and related income statement accounts.
Compare bad debt expense as a percentage of gross sales with previous years.	Uncollectible accounts receivable that have not been provided for.
Compare number of days that accounts receivable are outstanding with previous years.	Overstatement or understatement of allowance for uncollectible accounts and bad-debt expense.
Compare aging categories as a percentage of accounts receivable with previous years.	Overstatement or understatement of allowance for uncollectible accounts and bad-debt expense.
Compare allowance for uncollectible accounts as a percentage of accounts receivable with previous years.	Overstatement or understatement of allowance for uncollectible accounts.

analytical procedures for sales, evidence is being obtained about both sales and accounts receivable.

In addition to the analytical procedures in Table 14-1, there should also be a review of accounts receivable for large and unusual amounts. Individual receivables that deserve special attention are large balances; accounts that have been outstanding for a long time; receivables from affiliated companies, officers, directors, and other related parties; and credit balances. The auditor should review the listing of accounts (aged trial balance) or run exception tests against the customer master file at the balance sheet date to determine which accounts should be investigated further.

The auditor's conclusion about analytical procedures for the sales and collection cycle is incorporated into the third row from the bottom on the evidence planning spreadsheet in Figure 14-8. Analytical procedures are substantive tests and therefore reduce the extent to which the auditor needs to test details of balances, if the analytical procedures' results are favourable.

Lesley Stopps, a public accountant, is the auditor for Great Western Lumber Company Ltd., a wholesale wood milling company. Lesley calculates the gross margin by three product lines and obtains industry information from published data listed at the end of this Focus Box.

In discussing the results, the controller states that Great Western has always had a higher gross margin on hardwood products than the industry because it focuses on the markets where it is able to sell at higher prices instead of emphasizing volume. The opposite is true of plywood where it has a reasonably small number of customers, each of which demands lower prices because of high volume. The controller states that competitive forces have caused reductions in plywood gross margin for both the industry and Great Western in 2003 and 2004. Great

Western has traditionally had a somewhat lower gross margin for softwood than the industry until 2005, when the gross margin went up significantly due to aggressive selling.

Stopps observed that most of what the controller said was reasonable given the facts. Hardwood gross margin for the industry was stable and approximately 3.5 to 4 percent lower than Great Western's every year. Industry gross margin for plywood has declined annually but is about 10 percentage points higher than Great Western's. Industry gross margin for softwood has been stable for the three years, but Great Western's has increased by a fairly large amount.

The change in Great Western's softwood gross margin from 20.3 percent to 23.9 percent is a concern to Stopps, so she goes through a three-step procedure.

1. Calculate the potential misstatement and evaluate the materiality of that amount. She calculates 23.9% − 20.3% × softwood sales and concludes the amount is potentially material.
2. Identify potential causes of the change:
   - overstatement of sales
   - overstatement of ending inventory (understatement of cost of goods sold)
   - understatement of purchases (understatement of cost of goods sold)
   - good results of aggressive selling
3. Indicate in the working papers a concern for the potential overstatement of sales and inventory and understatement of purchases of softwood. This may require an expansion of other substantive audit tests.

	2005 Gross Margin %		2004 Gross Margin %		2003 Gross Margin %	
	Great Western	Industry	Great Western	Industry	Great Western	Industry
Hardwood	36.3	32.4	36.4	32.5	36.0	32.3
Softwood	23.9	22.0	20.3	22.1	20.5	22.3
Plywood	40.3	50.1	44.2	54.3	45.4	55.6

Note: Industry figures are fictitious.

→14.3. THE RELATIONSHIP BETWEEN ASSERTIONS AND TESTS OF DETAIL

Design Tests of Details of Accounts Receivable The appropriate tests of details of balances depend upon the factors incorporated into the evidence planning spreadsheet in Figure 14-8. The second row from the bottom shows planned detection risk for each accounts receivable balance-related audit objective. Planned detection risk for each objective is an auditor decision, decided by subjectively combining the conclusions reached about each of the factors listed above that row.

Combining the factors that determine planned detection risk is complex because the measurement for each factor is imprecise and the appropriate weight to be given each factor is highly judgmental. On the other hand, the relationship between each factor and planned detection risk is well established. Figure 8-3 on page 221 illustrated these relationships. Figure 14-4 contrasts how changes in inherent and control risks affect detection risk and thus the planned audit evidence for tests of details of balances. For example, the left side of the diagram shows high inherent risk (many errors likely) and high control risk (the control risk "tray" has large holes in it). The right side shows low inherent risk (few errors likely) and low control risk (the control risk "tray" has only a few very small holes). The auditor knows that a high inherent risk or high control risk decreases planned detection risk and increases planned substantive tests, whereas good results from dual-purpose tests can lead to increased planned detection risk and decreased planned substantive tests.

The bottom row in Figure 14-8 shows the planned audit evidence for tests of details of balances for accounts receivable, by objective. As discussed in Chapters 8 and 11, planned audit evidence is the complement of planned detection risk.

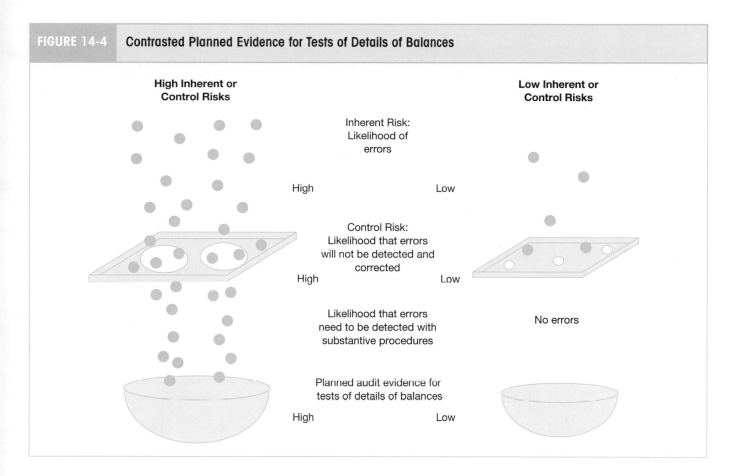

The conclusion that planned audit evidence for a given objective is high, medium, or low is implemented by the auditor deciding the appropriate audit procedures, sample size, items to select, and timing. The remainder of this chapter discusses these issues.

Tests of Details of Balances

Tests of details of balances for all cycles emphasize balance sheet accounts, but income statement accounts are not ignored because they are verified more as a byproduct of the balance sheet tests. For example, if the auditor confirms account receivable balances and finds overstatements due to mistakes in billing customers, there are overstatements of both accounts receivable and sales.

Confirmation of accounts receivable is the most important test of details of accounts receivable. Confirmation is discussed briefly in studying the appropriate tests for each of the balance-related audit objectives, then separately in more detail.

The discussion of tests of details of balances for accounts receivable that follows assumes that the auditor has completed an evidence planning spreadsheet similar to the one in Figure 14-8 and has decided planned detection risk for tests of details for each balance-related audit objective. The audit procedures selected and their sample size will depend heavily on whether planned evidence for a given objective is low, medium, or high. The discussion focuses on accounts receivable balance-related audit objectives.

Accounts Receivable Are Correctly Added and Agree with the Customer Master File and the General Ledger Most tests of accounts receivable and the allowance for uncollectible accounts are based on the **aged trial balance**. An aged trial balance is a listing of the balances in the accounts receivable customer master file at the balance sheet date. It includes the individual total balances outstanding and a breakdown of each balance by the time passed between the date of sale and the balance sheet date. An illustration of a typical aged trial balance summary, in this case for Hillsburg Hardware Limited, is given in Figure 14-5.

AGED TRIAL BALANCE—a listing of the balances in the accounts receivable master file at the balance sheet date broken down according to the amount of time passed between the date of sale and the balance sheet date

Notice that the total is the same as accounts receivable on the general ledger trial balance on page 117. This is an aged trial balance summary because it includes only totals for each customer. If the open item transactions were used to produce the aged trial balance, then the individual unpaid invoices would be listed to produce a detailed aged trial balance.

Testing the information on the aged trial balance for mechanical accuracy (reperformance) is a necessary audit procedure. It is ordinarily done before any other tests to assure the auditor that the population being tested agrees with the general ledger and accounts receivable master file. The total column and the columns depicting the aging must be test footed, and the total on the trial balance compared to the general ledger. In addition, a sample of individual balances should be traced to supporting documents, such as duplicate sales invoices, to verify the customer name, balance, and proper aging. The extent of the testing for detail tie-in depends on the number of accounts involved, the degree to which the customer master file data have been tested as a part of tests of controls, and the extent to which the schedule has been verified by an internal auditor or other independent person before it is given to the auditor.

For most large clients, this testing is most effectively completed using generalized audit software. The auditor obtains a copy of both the customer master file and the outstanding accounts receivable transactions. By performing the additions, aging, and subtotalling for each customer, the auditor conducts the dual purpose tests of verifying that the programs performing these functions are working correctly as well as quantifying any error. At the same time, samples for confirmation can be selected and unusual transactions identified using the auditor's criteria. For example, balances that exceed their credit limits, or outstanding transactions over a certain size, or extremely old outstanding transactions could be listed. These would be used during tests of the relevant audit objectives.

Recorded Accounts Receivable Exist The most important test of details of balances for determining the existence of recorded accounts receivable is the confirmation of customers' balances. When customers do not respond to confirmations, auditors also examine supporting documents to verify the shipment of goods and evidence of subsequent cash receipts to determine whether the accounts were collected. Normally, auditors do not examine shipping documents or evidence of subsequent cash receipts for any account in the sample that is confirmed, but these documents are used extensively as alternative evidence for nonresponses.

FIGURE 14-5	**Aged Trial Balance Summary for Hillsburg Hardware Limited**

Hillsburg Hardware Limited
Accounts Receivable
Aged Trial Balance
31/12/04

Schedule
Prepared by Client
Approved by

Date
5/1/05

				Aging, Based on Invoice Date			
Account Number	Customer	Balance 31/12/04	0–30 days	31–60 days	61–90 days	91–120 days	over 120 days
101011	Adams Supply Ltd.	73,290	57,966	15,324			
101044	Argonaut, Inc.	1,542	1,542				
101100	Atwater Brothers	85,518	85,518				
101191	Beekman Bearings Corp.	14,176	12,676		1,500		
101270	Brown and Phillips	13,952				13,952	
101301	Christopher Plumbing Ltd.	105,231	104,656	125	150	200	100
109733	Travellers Equipment Ltd.	29,765	29,765				
109742	Underhill Parts and Maintenance	8,963	8,963				
109810	UJW Co. Ltd.	15,832		9,832	6,000		
109907	Zephyr Plastics Corp.	74,300	60,085	14,215			
		20,196,800	10,334,169	5,598,762	2,598,746	1,589,654	75,469

Existing Accounts Receivable Are Included It is difficult to test for account balances omitted from the aged trial balance except by comparing the customer master file to the file of outstanding transactions and to the general ledger. For example, if the client accidentally excluded an account receivable from a manually prepared trial balance, the only way it would likely be discovered is by footing the accounts receivable trial balance and reconciling the balance with the control account in the general ledger.

If all sales to a customer were omitted from the sales journal or were not entered into the order entry system, the understatement of accounts receivable would be almost impossible to uncover by tests of details of balances. For example, auditors rarely send accounts receivable confirmations with zero balances, in part because research shows that customers are unlikely to respond to requests that indicate balances are understated. The understatement of sales and accounts receivable is best uncovered by tests of controls for shipments made but not recorded (completeness objective for tests of sales transactions) and by analytical procedures.

Accounts Receivable Are Accurate Confirmation of accounts selected from the accounts receivable trial balance is the most common test of details of balances for the accuracy of accounts receivable. When customers do not respond to confirmation requests, auditors examine supporting documents, in the same way as described for the existence objective. Tests of the debits and credits to particular customers' balances are done by examining supporting documentation for shipments and cash receipts.

Accounts Receivable Are Properly Classified It is normally relatively easy to evaluate the classification of accounts receivable by reviewing the aged trial balance for material receivables from affiliates, officers, directors, or other related parties. If notes receivable or accounts that should not be classified as a current asset are included with the regular accounts, these should also be segregated. Finally, if the credit balances in accounts receivable are significant, it is appropriate to reclassify them as accounts payable.

There is a close relationship between the classification objective as discussed here and the presentation and disclosure objective. Classification concerns determining whether the client has correctly separated different classifications of accounts receivable. Presentation and disclosure concern making sure the classifications are properly presented. For example, under the classification objective, the auditor determines if receivables from related parties have been separated on the aged trial balance. Under the presentation and disclosure objective, the auditor determines if related party transactions are correctly shown in the financial statements.

Cutoff for Accounts Receivable Is Correct **Cutoff misstatements** can occur for *sales, sales returns and allowances,* and *cash receipts.* They take place when current period transactions are recorded in the subsequent period or subsequent period transactions are recorded in the current period.

The objective of cutoff tests is the same regardless of the type of transaction, but the procedures vary. The objective is to verify whether transactions near the end of the accounting period are recorded in the proper period. The cutoff objective is one of the most important in the cycle because misstatements in cutoff can significantly affect current period income. For example, the intentional or unintentional inclusion of several large, subsequent period sales in the current period or the exclusion of several current-period sales returns and allowances can materially overstate net earnings.

In determining the reasonableness of cutoff, a threefold approach is needed: first, decide on the appropriate *criteria for cutoff*; second, evaluate whether the client has established *adequate procedures* to ensure a reasonable cutoff; and third, *test* whether a reasonable cutoff was obtained.

SALES CUTOFF The criterion used by most merchandising and manufacturing clients for determining when a sale takes place is the *shipment of goods*, but some companies record invoices at the time title passes. The passage of title can take place before shipment (as in the case of custom-manufactured goods), at the time of shipment, or subsequent to shipment. For the correct measurement of current-period income, the method must be in accordance with generally accepted accounting principles and consistently applied.

CUTOFF MISSTATEMENTS—misstatements that take place as a result of current period transactions being recorded in a subsequent period, or subsequent period transactions being recorded in the current period

The most important part of evaluating the client's method of obtaining a reliable cutoff is to determine the procedures in use. When a client issues prenumbered shipping documents sequentially, it is usually a simple matter to evaluate and test cutoff. Moreover, the segregation of duties between the shipping and the billing function also enhances the likelihood of recording transactions in the proper period. However, if shipments are made by company truck, the shipping records are not numbered, or shipping and billing department personnel are not independent of each other, it may be difficult, if not impossible, to be assured of an accurate cutoff.

When the client's internal controls are adequate, the cutoff can usually be verified by obtaining the shipping document number for the last shipment made at the end of the period and comparing this number with current and subsequent period recorded sales. As an illustration, assume the shipping document number for the last shipment in the current period is 1489. All recorded sales before the end of the period should bear a shipping document number preceding number 1490. There should also be no sales recorded in the subsequent period for a shipment with a shipping document numbered 1489 or lower. This can easily be tested by comparing recorded sales with the related shipping document for the last few days of the current period and the first few days of the subsequent period.

SALES RETURNS AND ALLOWANCES CUTOFF Generally accepted accounting principles require that sales returns and allowances be *matched with related sales* if the amounts are material. For example, if current period shipments are returned in the subsequent period, the proper treatment of the transactions is the inclusion of the sales return in the current period. (The returned goods would be treated as current period inventory.) For most companies, however, sales returns and allowances are recorded in the *accounting period in which they occur*, under the assumption of approximately equal, offsetting errors at the beginning and end of each accounting period. This is acceptable as long as the amounts are not significant.

When the auditor is confident that the client records all sales returns and allowances promptly, the cutoff tests are simple and straightforward. The auditor can examine supporting documentation for a sample of sales returns and allowances recorded during several weeks subsequent to the closing date to determine the date of the original sale. If the amounts recorded in the subsequent period are significantly different from unrecorded returns and allowances at the beginning of the period under audit, an adjustment must be considered. If internal controls for recording sales returns and allowances are evaluated as ineffective, a larger sample is needed to verify cutoff.

CASH RECEIPTS CUTOFF For most audits, a proper cash receipt cutoff is *less important* than either the sales or the sales returns and allowances cutoff because the improper cutoff of cash affects only the cash and the accounts receivable balances, not earnings. Nevertheless, if the misstatement is material, it could affect the fair presentation of these accounts, particularly when cash is a small or negative balance.

It is easy to test for a cash receipts cutoff misstatement (frequently referred to as "holding the cash receipts open") by tracing recorded cash receipts to subsequent period bank deposits on the bank statement. If there is a delay of several days, this could indicate a cutoff misstatement.

The confirmation of accounts receivable may also be relied on to some degree to uncover cutoff misstatements for sales, sales returns and allowances, and cash receipts, especially when there is a long interval between the date the transaction took place and the recording date. However, when the interval is only a few days, mail delivery delays may cause confusion of cutoff misstatements with normal reconciliation differences. For example, if a customer mails and records a cheque to a client for payment of an unpaid account on December 30 and the client receives and records the amount on January 5, the records of the two organizations will be different on December 31. This is not a cutoff misstatement, but a *reconcilable difference* due to the delivery time; it will be difficult for the auditor to evaluate whether a cutoff misstatement or a **timing difference** occurred when a confirmation reply is the source of information. This type of situation requires additional investigation such as inspection of underlying documents.

TIMING DIFFERENCE—a reported difference in a confirmation from a debtor that is determined to be a timing difference between the client's and debtor's records and therefore not a misstatement

Accounts Receivable Is Valued Correctly Tests of the **valuation** objective are performed to evaluate the account *allowance for uncollectible accounts*. Generally accepted accounting principles require that accounts receivable be stated at the amount that will ultimately be collected, which is gross accounts receivable less the allowance. The client's estimate of the total amount that is uncollectible is represented by the allowance for uncollectible accounts. Although it is not possible to predict the future precisely, it is necessary for the auditor to evaluate whether the allowance is reasonable considering all available facts.

VALUATION OF ACCOUNTS RECEIVABLE—the amount of the outstanding balances in accounts receivable that will ultimately be collected

The starting point for the evaluation of the allowance for uncollectible accounts is to review the results of the tests of controls that are concerned with the client's credit policy. If the client's credit policy has remained unchanged and the results of the tests of credit policy and credit approval are consistent with those of the preceding year, the change in the balance in the allowance for uncollectible accounts should reflect only changes in economic conditions and sales volume. However, if the client's credit policy or the degree to which it correctly functions have significantly changed, great care must be taken to consider the effects of these changes as well.

A common way to evaluate the adequacy of the allowance is to examine carefully the noncurrent accounts on the aged trial balance to determine which ones have not been paid subsequent to the balance sheet date. The size and age of unpaid balances can then be compared with similar information from previous years to evaluate whether the amount of noncurrent receivables is increasing or decreasing over time. The examination of credit files, discussions with the credit manager, and review of the client's correspondence file may also provide insights into the collectibility of the accounts. These procedures are especially important if a few large balances are noncurrent and are not being paid on a regular basis.

There are two pitfalls in evaluating the allowance by reviewing individual noncurrent balances on the aged trial balance. First, the current accounts are ignored in establishing the adequacy of the allowance even though some of these amounts will undoubtedly become uncollectible. Second, it is difficult to compare the results of the current year with those of previous years on such an unstructured basis. If the accounts are becoming progressively uncollectible over a period of several years, this fact could be overlooked. A way to avoid these difficulties is to establish the history of bad debt charge-offs over a period of time as a frame of reference for evaluating the current year's allowance. As an example, if historically a certain percentage of the total of each age category becomes uncollectible, it is relatively easy to compute whether the allowance is properly stated. If 2 percent of current accounts, 10 percent of 30- to 90-day accounts, and 35 percent of all balances over 90 days ultimately become uncollectible, these percentages could easily be applied to the current year's aged trial balance totals and the result compared with the balance in the allowance account. Of course, the auditor has to be careful to modify the calculations for changed conditions.

BAD-DEBT EXPENSE After the auditor is satisfied with the allowance for uncollectible accounts, it is easy to verify bad-debt expense. Assume that (1) the beginning balance was verified as a part of the previous audit, (2) the uncollectible accounts charged off were verified as a part of the tests of controls, and (3) the ending balance in the allowance account has been verified by various means. Then bad-debt expense is simply a residual balance that can be verified by a reperformance test.

The Client Has Rights to Accounts Receivable The client's rights to accounts receivable ordinarily cause no audit problems because the receivables usually belong to the client, but in some cases a portion of the receivables may have been pledged as collateral, assigned to someone else, factored, or sold at discount. Normally, the client's customers are not aware of the existence of such matters; therefore, the confirmation of receivables will not bring it to light. A review of the minutes, discussions with the client, confirmation with banks, and the examination of correspondence files are usually sufficient to uncover instances in which the client has limited rights to receivables.

Accounts Receivable Presentation and Disclosures Are Proper In addition to testing for the proper statement of the dollar amount in the general ledger, the auditor must also determine that information about the account balance resulting from the sales and collection cycle is properly presented and disclosed in the financial statements. The auditor must decide whether the client has properly combined amounts and disclosed related party information in the statements. To evaluate the adequacy of the presentation and disclosure, the auditor must have a thorough understanding of generally accepted accounting principles and presentation and disclosure requirements.

An important part of the evaluation involves deciding whether material amounts requiring separate disclosure have actually been separated in the statements. For example, paragraph 3020.01 and Section 3840 of the *CICA Accounting Handbook* require that receivables from officers and affiliated companies be segregated from accounts receivable from customers if the amounts are material. Similarly, under Section 1701, it is necessary for companies over a certain size to disclose information about revenues, operations, and assets for different segments of the business as well as information about export sales. The proper aggregation of general ledger balances in the financial statements also requires combining account balances that individually are not relevant for external users of the statements. If all accounts included in the general ledger were disclosed separately on the statements, most statement users would be more confused than enlightened.

As a part of proper disclosure, the auditor is also required to evaluate the adequacy of the *footnotes*. Required footnote disclosure includes information about the pledging, discounting, factoring, assignment of accounts receivable, and amounts due from related parties. Of course, in order to evaluate the adequacy of these disclosures, it is first necessary to know of their existence and to have complete information about their nature. This is generally obtained in other parts of the audit, as discussed in the previous section.

Confirmation of Accounts Receivable

One of the most important audit procedures is the *confirmation of accounts receivable*. This multi-purpose technique is used to satisfy the *existence, accuracy,* and *cutoff* objectives.

CICA Handbook Requirements Two major audit procedures are usually required by the *CICA Assurance Handbook*: the *confirmation of accounts receivable* and the *physical examination of inventory*. Both Canada and the U.S. require confirmation and physical examination.

Section 5303 defines a confirmation as "the process of obtaining and evaluating a direct communication from a third party in response to a request for information concerning one or more assertions underlying one or more financial statement items." Confirmations of receivables are required except in cases where the auditor has assessed the combined inherent risk and control risk as low or where the auditor concludes, in planning the audit, that confirmation would be ineffective. If the auditor did not confirm receivables, he or she would gain the required assurance by other means such as review of subsequent payments or examination of documentation supporting the receivable balance.

Although the remaining sections in this chapter refer specifically to the confirmation of accounts receivable from customers, the concepts apply equally to other receivables such as notes receivable, amounts due from officers, and employee advances.

Assumptions Underlying Confirmations An auditor makes two assumptions when accepting a confirmation as evidence. The first is that the person returning the confirmation is independent of the company and thus will provide an unbiased response. If this assumption is invalid, as would be the case if the confirmation of a fraudulent accounts receivable was sent to a company owned by an associate of the person committing the fraud, the value of the returned confirmation becomes zero. The second assumption is that the person returning the confirmation has knowledge of the account and the intent of the confirmation, and has carefully checked the balance to his or her books and records to ensure that the confirmation is in agreement. However, this second assumption may also not always be valid. Research has shown that some people return confirmations without really checking the balance; such a confirmation would have no value.

In many cases, the auditor is able to assess the independence of the person returning the confirmation, but sometimes a relationship may exist of which the auditor is not aware. Furthermore, it is almost always impossible for an auditor to know how much care was taken in checking the balance before the confirmation was signed and returned. Thus, weaknesses may exist in the confirmation of receivables. However, despite the possibility of weakness, confirmation is a procedure on which auditors rely.

In performing confirmation procedures, the auditor must decide the type of confirmation to use, timing of the procedures, sample size, and individual items to select. Each of these is discussed, along with the factors affecting the decision.

Confirmation Decisions

TYPE OF CONFIRMATION Two common types of confirmations are used for confirming accounts receivable: *positive* and *negative*. A **positive confirmation** is a communication addressed to the debtor requesting him or her to confirm directly whether the balance as stated on the confirmation request is correct or incorrect. Figure 14-6 illustrates a positive confirmation in the audit of Island Hardware Ltd. A variation of the first type of confirmation includes a listing of outstanding invoices making up the balance or a copy of the client customer statement attached by the auditor to the confirmation request. The listing of invoices is useful when the debtor uses a voucher system for accounts payable, while attaching the statement makes it easier for the debtor to respond.

A second type of positive confirmation, often called a **blank confirmation form**, does not state the amount on the confirmation but requests the recipient to fill in the balance or furnish other information. Because blank forms require the recipient to determine the information requested before signing and returning the confirmation, they are considered more reliable than confirmations that include the information. Research shows, however, that response rates are usually lower for blank confirmation forms. These forms are preferred for accounts payable confirmations when the auditor is searching for understatement of accounts payable.

A **negative confirmation** is also addressed to the debtor but requests a response only when the debtor disagrees with the stated amount. Figure 14-7 illustrates a negative confirmation in the audit of Island Hardware Ltd. that is a gummed label and would be attached to a customer's monthly statement. Often, the client can print the auditor's negative confirmation request directly onto the customer statements.

A positive confirmation is *more reliable* evidence because the auditor can perform follow-up procedures if a response is not received from the debtor. With a negative confirmation, failure to reply can only be regarded as a correct response even though the debtor may have ignored the confirmation request.

Offsetting the reliability disadvantage, negative confirmations are *less expensive* to send than positive confirmations, and thus more can be distributed for the same total cost. Negative confirmations cost less because there are no second requests and no follow-up of nonresponses. The determination of which type of confirmation to use is an auditor's decision, and it should be based on the facts in the audit. Positive confirmations are more effective in the following circumstances:

- When there are individual balances of relatively large amounts
- When there are few debtors
- When there is evidence or suspicion of fraud or serious error

When these conditions do not exist, it is appropriate to use negative confirmations.

Typically, when negative confirmations are used, the auditor puts considerable emphasis on the effectiveness of internal control as evidence of the fairness of accounts receivable, and assumes the large majority of the recipients will provide a conscientious reading and response to the confirmation request. Negative confirmations are often used for audits of municipalities, retail stores, banks, and other industries in which the receivables are due from the general public. In these cases, more weight is placed on tests of controls than on confirmations.

It is also common to use a combination of positive and negative confirmations by sending positive requests to accounts with large balances and negative requests to those with small balances.

The discussion of confirmations to this point shows that there is a continuum for the type of confirmation decision, starting with using no confirmation in some circumstances, to using only negatives, to using both negatives and positives, to using only positives. The

POSITIVE CONFIRMATION—a letter, addressed to the debtor, requesting that the recipient indicate directly on the letter whether the stated account balance is correct or incorrect and, if incorrect, by what amount

BLANK CONFIRMATION FORM—a letter, addressed to the debtor, requesting the recipient to fill in the amount of the accounts receivable balance; considered a positive confirmation

NEGATIVE CONFIRMATION—a letter, addressed to the debtor, requesting a response only if the recipient disagrees with the amount of the stated account balance

FIGURE 14-6   **Positive Confirmation**

Cockburn, Pedlar & Co.

Chartered Accountants
Cabot Bldg.
P.O. Box 123
3 King Street North
St. John's, Newfoundland A1C 3R5

Garner Hardware
80 Main Street
Cornerbrook, Newfoundland
A2H 1C8

August 15, 2005

To Whom It May Concern:

Re: Island Hardware Ltd.

    In connection with our audit of the financial statements of the above company, we would appreciate receiving from you confirmation of your account. The company's records show an amount receivable from you of $175.00 on June 30, 2005.

    Do you agree with this amount? If you do, please sign this letter in the space below. However, if you do not, please note at the foot of this letter or on the reverse side the details of any differences.

    Please return this letter directly to us in the envelope enclosed for your convenience.

Sincerely,

Cockburn, Pedlar & Co.

Cockburn, Pedlar & Co.

Per:

Please provide Cockburn, Pedlar & Co. with this information.

_____
J. Doe, Accountant, Island Hardware Ltd.

The above amount was owing by me (us) at the date mentioned.

_____

FIGURE 14-7   **Negative Confirmation**

AUDITOR'S ACCOUNT CONFIRMATION

Please examine this statement carefully. If it does NOT agree with your records, please report any exceptions directly to our auditors

    Cockburn, Pedlar & Co.
    Cabot Bldg.
    P.O. Box 123
    3 King Street North
    St. John's, Newfoundland
    A1C 3R5

who are making an examination of our financial statements. A stamped, addressed envelope is enclosed for your convenience in replying.

Do not send your remittance to our auditors.

primary factors affecting the decision are the materiality of total accounts receivable, the number and size of individual accounts, control risk, inherent risk, the effectiveness of confirmations as audit evidence, and the availability of other audit evidence.

TIMING The most reliable evidence from confirmations is obtained when they are sent as close to the balance sheet date as possible, as opposed to confirming the accounts several months before year end. This permits the auditor to test directly the accounts receivable balance on the financial statements without making any inferences about the transactions taking place between the confirmation date and the balance sheet date. However, as a means of completing the audit on a timely basis, it is frequently convenient to confirm the accounts at an interim date. This is permissible if internal controls are adequate and can provide reasonable assurance that sales, cash receipts, and other credits are properly recorded between the date of the confirmation and the end of the accounting period. Other factors the auditor is likely to consider in making the decision are the materiality of accounts receivable and the auditor's exposure to lawsuits because of the possibility of client bankruptcy and similar risks.

If the decision is made to confirm accounts receivable prior to year end, it may be necessary to test the transactions occurring between the confirmation date and the balance sheet date by examining such internal documents as duplicate sales invoices, shipping documents, and evidence of cash receipts, in addition to performing analytical procedures of the intervening period.

SAMPLE SIZE The main considerations affecting the number of confirmations to send are as follows:

- Materiality
- Inherent risk (relative size of total accounts receivable, number of accounts, prior year results, and expected misstatements)
- Control risk
- Achieved detection risk from other substantive tests (extent and results of analytical procedures and other tests of details)
- Type of confirmation (negatives normally require a larger sample size)

These factors are discussed further in the context of audit sampling for Hillsburg Hardware at the end of this chapter.

SELECTION OF THE ITEMS FOR TESTING Some type of *stratification is desirable* with most confirmations. A typical approach to stratification is to consider both the size of the outstanding balance and the length of time an account has been outstanding as a basis for selecting the balances for confirmation. In most audits, the emphasis should be on confirming larger and older balances, since these are most likely to include a significant misstatement. However, it is also important to sample some items from every material stratum of the population. In many cases, the auditor selects all accounts above a certain dollar amount and selects a statistical sample from the remainder.

Maintaining Control After the items for confirmation have been selected, the auditor must maintain control of the confirmations until they are returned from the debtor. If the client's assistance is obtained in preparing the confirmations, enclosing them in envelopes, or putting stamps on the envelopes, close supervision by the auditor is required. A return address must be included on all envelopes to make sure that undelivered mail is received by the public accounting firm. Similarly, self-addressed return envelopes accompanying the confirmations must be addressed for delivery to the public accounting firm's office. It is even important to mail the confirmations *outside* the client's office. All these steps are necessary to ensure independent communication between the auditor and the customer.

Follow-up on Nonresponses It is inappropriate to regard confirmations mailed but not returned by customers as significant audit evidence. For example, nonresponses to positive confirmations do not provide audit evidence. Similarly, for negative confirmations, the auditor should not conclude that the recipient received the confirmation request and verified the information requested. Negative confirmations do, however, provide some evidence of the existence assertion.

It is common when the auditor does not receive a response to a positive confirmation request to send a second and even a third request for confirmation. Even with these efforts, some debtors will not return the confirmation. Section 5303, "Confirmation," suggests two alternatives: (1) perform **alternative procedures**, or (2) treat the nonresponse as an error to be projected from the sample to the population in order to assess its materiality. The objective of alternative procedures is to determine by a means other than confirmation whether the nonconfirmed account existed and was properly stated at the confirmation date. The alternative procedures would include examining the following documentation to verify the validity and valuation of individual sales transactions making up the ending balance in accounts receivable.

SUBSEQUENT CASH RECEIPTS Evidence of the receipt of cash subsequent to the confirmation date includes examining remittance advices, entries in the cash receipts records, or perhaps even subsequent credits in the supporting records. On the one hand, the examination of evidence of subsequent cash receipts is a highly useful alternative procedure because it is reasonable to assume that a customer would not make a payment unless it was an existing receivable. On the other hand, the fact of payment does not establish whether there was an obligation on the date of the confirmation. In addition, care should be taken to specifically match each unpaid sales transaction with evidence of its payment as a test for disputes or disagreements over individual outstanding invoices.

DUPLICATE SALES INVOICES These are useful in verifying the actual issuance of a sales invoice and the actual date of the billing.

SHIPPING DOCUMENTS These are important in establishing whether the shipment was actually made and as a test of cutoff.

CORRESPONDENCE WITH THE CLIENT Usually, the auditor does not need to review correspondence as a part of alternative procedures, but correspondence can be used to disclose disputed and questionable receivables not uncovered by other means.

The extent and nature of the alternative procedures depend primarily upon the materiality of the nonresponses, the types of misstatements discovered in the confirmed responses, the subsequent cash receipts from the nonresponses, and the auditor's conclusions about internal control. It is normally desirable to account for all unconfirmed balances with alternative procedures even if the amounts are small, as a means of properly generalizing from the sample to the population.

Analysis of Differences When the confirmation requests are returned by the customer, it is necessary to determine the reason for any reported differences. In many cases, they are

ALTERNATIVE PROCEDURE—the follow-up of a positive confirmation not returned by the debtor with the use of documentation evidence to determine whether the recorded receivable exists and is collectible

FOCUS BOX 14-2

INCORRECT ALLOCATION OF CASH RECEIPTS LEADS TO SEC ACTIONS

Companies such as Xerox Corp. sell goods to customers outright, or provide financing, which includes leasing. A sales-type lease from Xerox results in periodic payments for customers that include repayment of the cost of the equipment (the "note receivable" portion of the lease) as well as financing costs and costs for services and supplies (perhaps for a maintenance contract). Thus, cash received needs to be carefully allocated to the appropriate asset and revenue accounts.

In June 2002, Xerox reduced its equipment revenue by U.S.$6.1 billion and its pre-tax earnings for 1997 through 2000 by U.S.$1.9 billion. Xerox had improperly recorded the timing and makeup of its sales in Latin America from 1997 to 2001. In addition, Xerox paid a U.S.$10 million fine to the SEC in April 2002.

The SEC sued the auditors of Xerox with respect to the 1997 through 2000 financial statements, naming both the firm and individual partners as defendants. The firm agreed to settle at U.S.$22 million in April 2005, which was still subject to court approval as of that date.

Sources: 1. Appleson, Gail. 2003. "SEC Sues KPMG over Xerox's financials," *The Financial Post*, January 30, 2003, FP14. 2. Gunsalus, Jim. 2002. " Xerox inflated sales by $1.9 billion U.S.," *The Toronto Star*, June 29, 2002, E4. 3. Priest, Andrew. 2005. "KPMG pays $22 million to settle SEC litigation relating to Xerox audits," accountingEducation.com, April 21, 2005, http://accountingeducation.com/news/news6095.html.

caused by timing differences between the client's and the customer's records. It is important to distinguish between these and exceptions, which represent misstatements of the accounts receivable balance. The most commonly reported types of differences in confirmations follow.

PAYMENT HAS ALREADY BEEN MADE Reported differences typically arise when the customer has made a payment prior to the confirmation date, but the client has not received the payment in time for recording before the confirmation date. Such instances should be carefully investigated to determine the possibility of a cash receipts cutoff misstatement, lapping, or a theft of cash.

GOODS HAVE NOT BEEN RECEIVED These differences typically result because the client records the sale at the date of shipment and the customer records the purchase when the goods are received. The time the goods are in transit is frequently the cause of differences reported on confirmations. These should be investigated to determine the possibility of the customer not receiving the goods at all or the existence of a cutoff misstatement on the client's records.

THE GOODS HAVE BEEN RETURNED The client's failure to record a credit memo could result from timing differences or the improper recording of sales returns and allowances. Like other differences, these must be investigated.

CLERICAL ERRORS AND DISPUTED AMOUNTS The most likely case of reported differences in a client's records occurs when the customer states that there is an error in the price charged for the goods, the goods are damaged, the proper quantity of goods was not received, and so forth. These differences must be investigated to determine whether the client is in error and what the amount of the error is.

In most instances, the auditor asks the client to reconcile the difference and, if necessary, communicates with the customer to resolve any audit disagreements. Naturally, the auditor must carefully verify the client's conclusions on each significant difference.

Drawing Conclusions When all differences have been resolved, including those discovered in performing alternative procedures, it is important to *re-evaluate internal control*. Each client misstatement must be analyzed to determine whether it was consistent or inconsistent with the original assessed level of control risk. If there is a significant number of misstatements that are inconsistent with the assessment of control risk, then it is necessary to revise the assessment and consider the effect of the revision on the audit.

It is also necessary to generalize from the sample to the entire population of accounts receivable. Even though the sum of the misstatements in the sample may not significantly affect the financial statements, the auditor must consider whether the population is likely to be materially misstated. This conclusion can be reached by using statistical sampling techniques or a nonstatistical basis. Projection of misstatements was discussed in Chapter 8 and is further explained in the example at the end of this chapter.

The auditor should always evaluate the *qualitative* nature of the misstatements found in the sample, regardless of the dollar amount of the projected misstatement. Even if the projected misstatement is less than materiality, the misstatements found in a sample can be symptomatic of a more serious problem.

The final decision about accounts receivable and sales is whether sufficient evidence has been obtained through analytical procedures, tests of controls, cutoff procedures, confirmation, and other substantive procedures to justify drawing conclusions about the correctness of the stated balance.

→14.4 AUDITING HILLSBURG HARDWARE ACCOUNTS RECEIVABLE

Case Illustration—Hillsburg Hardware Limited

The Hillsburg Hardware Limited case illustration used in Chapter 13 continues here to include the determination of the tests of details of balances audit procedures in the sales and collection cycle. Table 14-2 includes selected comparative trial balance information for the sales and collection cycle for Hillsburg Hardware Limited. Some of that information is used

TABLE 14-2 Selected Comparative Information for Hillsburg Hardware Limited—Sales and Collection Cycle

	Dollar Amounts (in thousands)		
	31-12-04	31-12-03	31-12-02
Gross sales	$144,328	$132,161	$123,438
Sales returns and allowances	1,242	935	753
Gross profit	39,845	36,350	33,961
Accounts receivable	20,197	17,521	13,852
Allowance for uncollectible accounts	1,240	1,311	1,283
Accounts receivable (net)	18,957	16,210	12,569
Bad-debt expense	3,323	2,496	2,796
Total current assets	51,027	49,895	49,157
Net earnings before taxes and extraordinary items	6,401	4,659	3,351
Number of accounts receivable	415	385	372
Number of accounts receivable with balances over $150,000	19	17	16

to illustrate several analytical procedures in Table 14-3. None of the analytical procedures indicated potential misstatements except the ratio of the allowance of uncollectible accounts to accounts receivable. The explanation at the bottom of Table 14-3 comments on the potential error.

Fran Moore prepared the evidence planning spreadsheet in Figure 14-8 as an aid to help her decide the extent of planned tests of details of balances. The source of each of the rows is as follows:

- *Materiality.* The preliminary judgment about materiality was set at $496,000.
- *Assessed audit risk.* Fran assessed audit risk as high (0.05) because of the good financial condition of the company, its financial stability, and the relatively few users of the financial statements. The company has a large working capital line of credit.
- *Inherent risk.* Fran assessed inherent risk as low for all objectives except valuation. In past years, there have been audit adjustments to the allowance for uncollectible accounts because it was found to be understated.

TABLE 14-3 Analytical Procedures for Hillsburg Hardware Limited—Sales and Collection Cycle

	31-12-04	31-12-03	31-12-02
Gross profit percent	27.8%	27.7%	27.7%
Sales returns and allowances/gross sales	0.9%	0.7%	0.6%
Bad debt expense/net sales	2.3%	1.9%	2.3%
Allowance for uncollectible accounts/accounts receivable	6.1%	7.5%	9.3%
Number of days receivables outstanding	48.1	43.6	39.6
Net accounts receivable/total current assets	37.2%	32.5%	25.6%

Note: Allowance as a percentage of accounts receivable has declined from 7.5 percent to 6.1 percent. Number of days receivable outstanding and economic conditions do not justify this change. Potential misstatement is approximately $282,758 ($20,197,000 × [0.075 − 0.061]).

- *Control risk.* Assessed control risk for sales and collections is taken from the assessment of control risk matrix for sales and cash receipts, modified by the results of the tests of controls. The control risk matrix is shown in Figures 13-8 and 13-9 on pages 395 and 396. The results of the tests of controls in Chapter 13 were consistent with the preliminary assessments of control, except for the completeness objective. The initial assessment was low, but tests of controls results changed the assessment to high.
- *Analytical procedures.* Fran chose to use analytical procedures to obtain medium levels of assurance from additional analytical procedures, as described in Table 14-3. These analytical procedures resulted in the detection of immaterial errors. All of these errors have been corrected in Hillsburg's accounts.
- *Planned detection risk and planned audit evidence.* These two rows are decided for each objective based on the conclusions in the other rows.

Table 14-4 shows the tests of details audit program for accounts receivable, by objective, and for the allowance for uncollectible accounts. The audit program reflects the conclusions for planned audit evidence on the planning spreadsheet in Figure 14-8. Table 14-5 (page 437) shows the audit program in a performance format. The audit procedures are identical to those in Table 14-4 except for procedure 2, which is an analytical procedure. The numbers in parentheses are a cross-reference between the two tables.

Using Monetary Unit Sampling to Select and Evaluate Confirmations

To illustrate the sampling for tests of details described in Chapter 12, monetary unit sampling is now conducted using accounts receivable data. Since Hillsburg Hardware has numerous accounts receivable, only portions of the population will be shown during this illustration.

The steps followed are based on the 14 steps in planning, selecting, and evaluating a sample, as shown in Chapter 12, starting on page 349.

Objectives, Deciding If Sampling Applies, Population, and Sampling Unit When auditors sample for tests of details of balances, the objective is to determine whether the account balance being audited is fairly stated. The audit objective here is to determine the amount of monetary error associated with the existence, accuracy, and cutoff of accounts receivable. This will be accomplished by sending and evaluating confirmations of the accounts receivable balance as of December 31. Sampling can be used to select the smaller items to be confirmed, since the auditor has decided that all amounts greater than $150,000 will be confirmed. Any monetary error between the recorded amount in the customer master file or the open item invoice amount and the confirmed amount is considered to be an error condition.

Hillsburg Hardware has total accounts receivable outstanding of $20,196,800. Since the sampling unit is defined as an individual dollar, the population size is equal to the total outstanding accounts receivable. However, the population is being divided into two strata. High dollar amounts over $150,000 are all being confirmed. A sample will thus be selected from the remainder.

The population for each stratum consists of the total of uncollected sales invoice amounts in that dollar range.

Specify Materiality and the Acceptable Risk of Incorrect Acceptance (ARIA), Provide an Estimate of Total Dollar Error in the Population, and Determine Sample Size

MATERIALITY The preliminary judgment about materiality is normally the basis for the tolerable misstatement amount used. If misstatements in non-dollar-unit-sampling tests (i.e., any other tests of details) were expected, tolerable misstatement would be materiality less those amounts. Tolerable misstatement may be different for overstatements or understatements. For this example, tolerable misstatement for both overstatements and understatements is $496,000, the materiality figure for Hillsburg Hardware for total accounts receivable.

ACCEPTABLE RISK OF INCORRECT ACCEPTANCE Setting ARIA is a matter of professional judgment and is often reached with the aid of the audit risk model. It is 5 percent for this example.

Balance-Related Audit Objective	Audit Procedure
Accounts receivable in the aged trial balance agree with related master file amounts, and the total is correctly added and agrees with the general ledger. (detail tie-in)	Foot open item file and customer master file and agree to general ledger. (1.1, 1.2)
The accounts receivable on the aged trial balance exist. (accuracy and existence)	Confirm accounts receivable using positive confirmations. Confirm all amounts over $150,000 and a statistical sample of the remainder. (7) Perform alternative procedures for all confirmations not returned on the first or second request. (8) Use generalized audit software (GAS) to provide reports of: · All customers with balances exceeding their credit limit (1.3) · All customers with discount terms exceeding 25 percent (1.4) · Debit and credit totals by customer (1.5) · Customers with balances over $150,000 (1.6) · A dollar-unit sample of the remainder (1.6)
Existing accounts receivable are included in the aged trial balance. (completeness)	Agree details of customers selected using GAS to the aged accounts receivable trial balance listing. (6)
Accounts receivable on the aged trial balance are properly classified. (classification)	Review the receivables listed on the aged trial balance for notes and related party receivables. (3) Enquire of management whether there are any related party notes or long-term receivables included in the trial balance. (4)
Transactions in the sales and collection cycle are recorded in the proper period. (cutoff)	Select the last 40 sales transactions from the current year's sales journal and the first 40 from the subsequent year's, and trace each to the related shipping documents, checking for the date of actual shipment and the correct recording. (11) Review large sales returns and allowances after the balance sheet date to determine whether any should be included in the current period. (12)
Accounts receivable is stated at realizable value. (valuation)	Use GAS to reperform aging for the aged accounts receivable trial balance. Agree totals by aging category to the trial balance listing. (1.7, 1.8) Discuss with the credit manager the likelihood of collecting older accounts. Examine subsequent cash receipts and the credit file on all accounts over 90 days, and evaluate whether the receivables are collectible. (9) Evaluate whether the allowance is adequate after performing other audit procedures relating to collectibility of receivables. (10)
The client has rights to the accounts receivable on the trial balance. (rights and obligations)	Review the minutes of the board of directors' meetings for any indication of pledged or factored accounts receivable. (5) Enquire of management whether any receivables are pledged or factored. (5)
Accounts in the sales and collection cycle and related information are properly presented and disclosed. (presentation and disclosure)	Review the minutes of the board of directors' meetings for any indication of pledged or factored accounts receivable. (5) Enquire of management whether any receivables are pledged or factored. (5)

Note: The procedures are summarized into a performance format in Table 14-5. The number in parentheses after the procedure refers to Table 14-5.

TABLE 14-5	Tests of Details of Balances Audit Program for Hillsburg Hardware Limited—Sales and Collection Cycle (Performance Format)

1. Obtain a copy of the customer master file and the accounts receivable open item transaction file as of December 31 and:
   1.1 Foot both the customer master file and the accounts receivable open item file.
   1.2 Agree the totals of the two files to each other and to the general ledger account balance.
   1.3 List all customers with balances exceeding their credit limit.
   1.4 List all customers with discount terms exceeding 25 percent.
   1.5 Provide a report that shows total debits and credit totals of open items by customer.
   1.6 List customer and transaction details for all customers exceeding $150,000, and a dollar unit sample of customers with balances below $150,000.
   1.7 Reperform the aging of the open items to derive the aged accounts receivable trial balance by customer.
   1.8 Agree the totals by aging category to the client-prepared aged accounts receivable trial balance.
2. Calculate analytical procedures indicated in carry-forward working papers (not included) and follow up any significant changes from prior years.
3. Review the receivables listed on the aged trial balance for notes and related party receivables.
4. Enquire of management whether there are any related party, notes, or long-term receivables included in the trial balance.
5. Review the minutes of the board of directors' meetings and enquire of management to determine whether any receivables are pledged or factored.
6. Agree details of customers selected using GAS to the aged accounts receivable trial balance listing.
7. Confirm accounts receivable using positive confirmations. Confirm all amounts over $150,000 and those selected in step 1.6.
8. Perform alternative procedures for all confirmations not returned on the first or second request.
9. Discuss with the credit manager the likelihood of collecting older accounts. Examine subsequent cash receipts and the credit file on all larger accounts over 90 days, and evaluate whether the receivables are collectible.
10. Evaluate whether the allowance is adequate after performing other audit procedures relating to collectibility of receivables.
11. Select the last 40 sales transactions from the current year's sales journal and the first 40 from the subsequent year's, and trace each to the related shipping documents, checking for the date of actual shipment and the correct recording.
12. Review large sales returns and allowances after the balance sheet date to determine whether any should be included in the current period.

ESTIMATE OF THE POPULATION EXCEPTION RATE Normally the estimate of the population exception rate for MUS is zero percent, as it is most appropriate to use MUS when no misstatements or only a few are expected. Where misstatements are expected, the total dollar amount of expected population misstatements is estimated and then expressed as a percentage of the population recorded value. In this example, some overstatement is expected. Based on past experience, a 0.5 percent expected exception rate is used.

ASSUMPTION OF THE AVERAGE PERCENT OF MISSTATEMENT FOR POPULATION ITEMS THAT CONTAIN A MISSTATEMENT
To determine the sample size, the auditor also needs to make assumptions about how much error there will be in items that contain a misstatement. This is termed **tainting** in *Dollar Unit Sampling: A Practical Guide for Auditors*.[2] Again there may be a separate assumption for the upper and lower bounds. This is also a matter of professional judgment. Assumptions should be based on the auditor's knowledge of the client and past experience, and if less than 100 percent is used, the assumptions must be clearly defensible. For this example, 50 percent is used for overstatements and 100 percent for understatements.

TAINTING—the average percent of misstatement for population dollars that contain a misstatement (used with MUS sampling)

These assumptions are summarized as follows:

Tolerable misstatement (same for upper and lower)	$496,000
Tolerable misstatement allocated to lower dollar strata	$300,000
Average percent of misstatement assumption, overstatements	50%

---

[2]See Leslie, Donald A., Albert D. Teitlebaum, and Rodney J. Anderson, *Dollar Unit Sampling: A Practical Guide for Auditors*, Toronto: Copp Clark Pitman, 1979, pp. 122–123 and 390.

FIGURE 14-8

Evidence Planning Spreadsheet to Determine Tests of Details of Balances for Hillsburg Hardware Limited—Accounts Receivable

	Detail tie-in	Existence (or occurrence)	Completeness	Accuracy	Classification	Cutoff	Valuation	Rights and obligations	Presentation and disclosure
Audit risk	high	high	high	high	high	high	high	high	high
Inherent risk	low	low	low	low	low	low	medium	low	low
Control risk – Sales	low	medium	low	low	low	low	high	not applicable	not applicable
Control risk – Cash receipts	low	high	low	low	low	low	not applicable	not applicable	not applicable
Control risk – Additional controls	none	none	none	none	none	none	none	low	low
Analytical procedures	good results	good results	good results	good results	good results	good results	unacceptable results	not applicable	not applicable
Planned detection risk for tests of details of balances	high	medium	high	high	high	high	low	high	high
Planned audit evidence for tests of details of balances	low	medium	low	low	low	low	high	low	low

Materiality $496,000

Average percent of misstatement assumption, understatements	100%
ARIA	5%
Accounts receivable—recorded value	$20.2 million
Accounts receivable—amounts less than $150,000	$13.1 million
Estimated misstatement in accounts receivable	0.5%

The *sample size* for the strata of amounts less than $150,000 is calculated as follows:

	Upper Bound	Lower Bound
Tolerable misstatement	300,000	300,000
Average percent of error assumption (divide by):	0.50	1.00
equals	600,000	300,000
Recorded population value (divide by):	13,100,000	13,100,000
Allowable percent error bound (TER)	4.6%	2.3%
Estimated population exception rate (EPER)	0.5%	0
Required sample size from the attributes table (Table 13-7, page 404) 5% ARACR, 5% and 3% TER, and 0.5% and 0 EPER	93	157

Since only one sample is taken for both overstatements and understatements, the *larger* of the two computed sample sizes would be used, in this case 157 items. Normally, generalized audit software is used to determine sample size and to actually select the sample items, once the auditor has determined the ARIA, ARACR, TER, and the EPER. The sample is selected using a statistical formula. High tolerable error rates for a specific procedure such as confirmations are acceptable where the auditor also relies on other audit procedures, such as tests of controls and analytical procedures.

In auditing the sample, finding any understatement amounts will cause the lower bound to exceed the tolerable limit because the sample size is based on no expected misstatements. On the other hand, several overstatement amounts might be found before the tolerable limit for the upper bound is exceeded. Where the auditor is concerned about unexpectedly finding a misstatement that would cause the population to be rejected, he or she can guard against it by arbitrarily increasing sample size above the amount determined by the tables. For example, in this illustration, the auditor might use a sample size of 190 instead of 157. Such a change would also result in a different CUER (computed upper exception rate).

Select the Sample and Perform the Audit Procedures The sample of items less than $150,000 is being selected using generalized audit software with monetary unit sampling. The software will use the ARACR, TER, and EPER to calculate a dollar interval, and then choose the accounts that correspond to that dollar interval. For example, if the dollar interval was $350,000 (the interval is normally less than materiality), with a random start of 6586, then the accounts would be summed. When the cumulative total reaches $6,586, this identifies the first account to be selected, and when it reaches $356,586 ($350,000 + $6,586) the second account will be selected. In this way, all 157 accounts will be selected. They will then be confirmed, the results audited, and the result for each physical unit (customer account) will be applied to the selected dollar that it contains.

The statistical methods used to evaluate monetary unit samples permit the inclusion of a physical unit in the sample more than once. For example, an item that was $700,000 or larger would be selected twice, since it is twice the size of the sample interval. This is handled at Hillsburg Hardware Limited by having the data divided into two strata—the larger amounts of greater than $150,000 are all being selected.

One problem using MUS (monetary unit sampling) selection is that population items with a zero recorded balance have no chance of being selected even though they could contain misstatements. Similarly, small balances that are significantly understated have little chance of being included in the sample. This problem can be overcome by doing specific audit tests for zero- and small-balance items, assuming that they are of concern.

Another problem is the inability to include negative balances, such as credit balances in accounts receivable, in the MUS sample. It is possible to ignore negative balances for MUS selection and test those amounts by some other means. An alternative is to treat them as positive balances (which is readily done with audit software by simply using absolute values) and add them to the total number of monetary units being tested; however, this complicates the evaluation process.

Fran determined from earlier generalized audit software tests that credit amounts were insignificant, and decided that no separate audit work would be done on those amounts.

Fran ensured that audit staff on the engagement properly handled the accounts receivable confirmation process. Confirmations were prepared and mailed, second requests were sent, discrepancies were reviewed, and alternative procedures were conducted for those items selected for which no replies were received.

Generalize from the Sample to the Population

Generalizing from the Sample to the Population When No Misstatements Are Found Using MUS Assume that during the audit, no misstatements were uncovered in the sample. The auditor next wants to determine the maximum amount of overstatement and understatement amounts that could exist in the population and still provide a sample with no misstatements. These are the upper misstatement bound and the lower misstatement bound, respectively. Assuming an ARIA of 5 percent, and using Table 13-8 on page 406, both the upper and lower bounds are determined by locating the intersection of the sample size (157) and the actual number of misstatements (0) in the same manner as for attribute sampling. The CUER of 2.0 percent on the table for 150 items represents both the upper and lower bound, *expressed as a percentage*.

Thus, based on the sample results and the misstatement bounds from the table, the auditor can conclude with a 5 percent sampling risk that no more than 2.0 percent of the dollar units in the population are misstated. To convert this percent into *dollars*, the auditor must make an assumption about the average percent of misstatement for population dollars that contain a misstatement. This assumption significantly affects the misstatement bounds. To illustrate this, first Fran's assumptions are shown, that is, a 50 percent misstatement assumption for overstatements and a 100 percent assumption for understatements, and a second assumption is shown with a 100 percent misstatement assumption for overstatements and a 200 percent assumption for understatements.

ASSUMPTION 1 (FRAN'S) Overstatement amounts equal 50 percent; understatement amounts equal 100 percent; misstatement bounds at a 5 percent ARIA are

Upper misstatement bound = $13,100,000 × 2% × 50% = $131,000
Lower misstatement bound = $13,100,000 × 2% × 100% = $262,000

The assumption is that, on the average, those population items that are misstated are misstated by the full dollar amount of the recorded value. Since the misstatement bound is 2.0 percent, the dollar value of the misstatement is not likely to exceed $131,000 (2.0 percent times 50 percent of the total recorded dollar units in the population). If all the amounts are overstated, there is an overstatement of $131,000. If they are all understated, there is an understatement of $262,000.

The assumption of 100 percent or 50 percent misstatements is very conservative, especially for overstatements. Assume that the actual population exception rate is 2.0 percent. The following two conditions both have to exist before the $131,000 properly reflects the true overstatement amount:

1. All amounts have to be overstatements. Offsetting amounts would have reduced the amount of the overstatement.
2. All population items misstated have to be 50 percent misstated. There could not, for example, be a misstatement such as a cheque written for $226 that was recorded as $262. This would be only a 13.7 percent misstatement (262 − 226 = 36 overstatement; 36/262 = 13.7%).

In the calculation of the misstatement bounds of $131,000 overstatement and $262,000 understatement, the auditor did not calculate a point estimate and precision amount as described in the next section on judgmental sampling. This is because the tables used include both a point estimate and a precision amount to derive the upper exception rate. Even though the point estimate and precision amount are not calculated for MUS, they are implicit in the determination of misstatement bounds and can be determined from the tables. For example, in this illustration, the point estimate is zero and the statistical precision is $131,000 for overstatement and $262,000 for understatement.

ASSUMPTION 2 Overstatement amounts equal 100 percent; understatement amounts equal 200 percent; misstatement bounds at a 5 percent ARIA are

Upper misstatement bound = $13,100,000 × 2% × 100% = $262,000
Lower misstatement bound = $13,100,000 × 2% × 200% = $524,000

The justification for a larger percent for understatements is the potential for a larger misstatement in percentage terms. For example, an accounts receivable recorded at $20 that should have been recorded at $200 is understated by 900 percent [(200 − 20)/20], whereas one that is recorded at $200 that should have been recorded at $20 is overstated by 90 percent [(200 − 20)/200].

Items containing large understatement amounts may have a small recorded value, due to those misstatements. As a consequence, because of the mechanics of MUS, few of them will have a chance of being selected in the sample. Because of this, some auditors select an additional sample of small items to supplement the monetary unit sample whenever understatement amounts are an important audit concern.

APPROPRIATE PERCENT OF MISSTATEMENT ASSUMPTION The appropriate assumption to make regarding the overall percent of misstatement in those population items containing a misstatement is an auditor's decision. The auditor must set these percentages based on personal judgment in the circumstances. In the absence of convincing information to the contrary, most auditors believe it is desirable to assume a 100 percent amount for both overstatements and understatements. This approach is considered highly conservative, but it is easier to justify than any other assumption. In fact, the reason upper and lower limits are referred to as misstatement bounds when MUS is used, rather than maximum likely misstatement or the commonly used statistical term "confidence limit," is due to widespread use of that conservative assumption. Unless stated otherwise, the 100 percent misstatement assumption is used in the chapter and problem materials when no misstatements are found.

Generalizing When Misstatements Are Found This section presents the evaluation method used when there are misstatements in the sample. The same illustration is continued; the only change is the assumption about the misstatements. The sample size remains at 157 and the recorded value is still $13,100,000, but now five misstatements in the sample are assumed. The misstatements are shown in Table 14-6.

The following changes to the process of generalizing need to be incorporated:

- *Overstatement and understatement amounts are dealt with separately and then combined.* First, initial upper and lower misstatement bounds are calculated separately for overstatement and understatement amounts. Next, a point estimate of overstatements and understatements is calculated. The point estimate of understatements is used to reduce the initial upper misstatement bound, and the point estimate of overstatements is used to reduce the initial lower misstatement bound. The method and rationale for these calculations will be illustrated by using the four overstatement and one understatement amounts in Table 14-6.
- *A different misstatement assumption is made for each misstatement, including the zero misstatements.* When there were no misstatements in the sample, an assumption was required as to the average percent of misstatement for the population items misstated. The misstatement bounds were calculated showing several different assumptions. Now that misstatements have been found, sample information is available to use in determining the misstatement bounds. The misstatement assumption is still required, but it can be modified based on this actual misstatement data.

Where misstatements are found, a 100 percent assumption for all misstatements is not only exceptionally conservative, it is inconsistent with the sample results. A common assumption in practice, and the one followed in this book, is that the actual sample misstatements are representative of the population misstatements. This assumption requires the auditor to calculate the percent that each sample item is misstated (misstatement ÷ recorded balance) and apply that percent to the population. The calculation

TABLE 14-6	Misstatements Found			
Customer No.	Recorded Accounts Receivable Amount	Audited Accounts Receivable Amount	Misstatement	Misstatement ÷ Recorded Amount
102073	$ 6,200	$ 6,100	$ 100	0.016
105111	12,910	12,000	910	0.070
105206	4,322	4,450	(128)	(0.030)
107642	23,000	22,995	5	0.0002
109816	8,947	5,947	3,000	0.335

of the percent for each misstatement is shown in the last column in Table 14-6. As will be explained shortly, a misstatement assumption is still needed for the zero misstatement portion of the computed results. For this example, a 50 percent misstatement assumption is used for the zero misstatement portion for overstatements and 100 percent for understatement misstatement bounds.

- *The auditor must deal with layers of the computed upper exception rate (CUER) from the attribute sampling table* (see Table 13-8, page 406). The reason for doing so is that there is a different misstatement assumption for each misstatement. Layers are calculated by first determining the CUER from the table for each misstatement and then calculating each layer. Table 14-7 shows the layers in the attribute sampling table for the example at hand. The layers were determined by reading across the table for a sample size of 150 from the 0 through 4 exception columns.
- *Misstatement assumptions must be associated with each layer.* The most common method of associating misstatement assumptions with layers is to be conservative by associating the largest dollar misstatement percents with the largest layers. Table 14-8 shows the association. For example, the largest percent misstatement was 0.335 for customer 109816. This misstatement is associated with the layer factor of 0.011, the largest layer where misstatements were found. The portion of the upper precision limit related to the zero misstatement layer has a misstatement assumption of 50 percent, which is still conservative. Table 14-8 shows the calculation of misstatement bounds before consideration of offsetting amounts.

The upper misstatement bound was calculated as if there were no understatement amounts, and the lower misstatement bound was calculated as if there were no overstatement amounts.

ADJUSTMENT FOR OFFSETTING AMOUNTS Most MUS users believe that the approach just discussed is overly conservative when there are offsetting amounts. If an understatement misstatement is found, it is logical and reasonable that the bound for overstatement amounts should be lower than it would be had no understatement amounts been found, and vice versa. The adjustment of bounds for offsetting amounts is made as follows: (1) a point estimate of misstatements is made for both understatement and overstatement amounts, and (2) each bound is reduced by the opposite point estimate.

The point estimate for overstatements is calculated by multiplying the average overstatement amount in the dollar units audited by the recorded value. The same approach is used for calculating the point estimate for understatements. In the example, there is one understatement amount of 3 cents per dollar unit in a sample of 150. The understatement point estimate is therefore $2,620 (0.03/150 × $13,100,000). Similarly, the overstatement point estimate is $36,785 [(0.335 + 0.07 + 0.016 + 0.0002)/150 × $13,100,000].

Table 14-9 shows the adjustment of the bounds that follow from this procedure. The initial upper bound of $190,564 is reduced by the estimated most likely understatement

TABLE 14-7	Percent Misstatement Bounds	
Number of Misstatements	Upper Precision Limit from Table	Increase in Precision Limit Resulting from Each Misstatement (Layers)
0	0.020	0.020
1	0.031	0.011
2	0.041	0.010
3	0.051	0.010
4	0.060	0.009

TABLE 14-8 — Illustration of Calculating Initial Upper and Lower Misstatement Bounds

Number of Misstatements (1)	Upper Precision Limit Portion* (2)	Recorded Value (3)	Misstatement Unit Error Assumption (4)	Bound Portion (Columns 2 × 3 × 4) (5)
Overstatements				
0	0.020	$13,100,000	0.50	$131,000
1	0.011	$13,100,000	0.335	48,274
2	0.010	$13,100,000	0.070	9,170
3	0.010	$13,100,000	0.016	2,096
4	0.009	$13,100,000	0.0002	24
Upper precision limit	0.06			
Initial misstatement bound				$190,564
Understatements				
0	0.020	$13,100,000	1.00	$262,000
1	0.011	$13,100,000	0.03	4,323
Lower precision limit	0.031			
Initial misstatement bound				$266,323

*ARIA of 5 percent. Sample size of 150.

error of $2,620 to an adjusted bound of $187,944. The initial lower bound of $266,323 is reduced by the estimated most likely overstatement amount of $36,785 to an adjusted bound of $229,538. Thus, given the methodology and assumptions followed, the auditor concludes that there is a 5 percent risk that accounts receivable is overstated by $187,944 or more, or understated by more than $229,538. It should be noted that if the misstatement assumptions were changed, the misstatement bounds would also change. The reader should be advised that the method used to adjust the bounds for offsetting amounts is but one of

TABLE 14-9 — Illustration of Calculating Adjusted Misstatement Bounds

Number of Misstatements	Unit Misstatement Assumption	Sample Size	Recorded Population	Point Estimate	Bounds
Initial overstatement bound					$190,564
Understatement misstatement					
1	0.030	150	$13,100,000	$ 2,620	(2,620)
Adjusted overstatement bound					$187,944
Initial understatement bound					$266,323
Overstatement misstatements					
1	0.335				
2	0.070				
3	0.016				
4	0.0002				
Sum	0.4212	150	$13,100,000	$36,785	(36,785)
Adjusted understatement bound					$229,538

Note: 150 is used as sample size for illustrative purposes.

several in current use. The method illustrated here is taken from Leslie, Teitlebaum, and Anderson.[3] All the methods in current use are reliable and somewhat conservative.

SUMMARY The following seven steps summarize the calculation of the adjusted misstatement bounds for monetary unit sampling when there are offsetting amounts. The calculation of the adjusted upper misstatement bound for the four overstatement amounts in Table 14-6 is used to illustrate. The evaluation process for MUS is complex and is best handled using computer software.

Steps to Calculate Adjusted Misstatement Bounds	Calculation for Misstatements in Table 14-6
1. Determine misstatement for each sample item, keeping overstatements and understatements separate.	Table 14-6 Four overstatements, one understatement
2. Calculate misstatement per dollar unit in each sample item (misstatement/recorded value).	Table 14-6 0.016, 0.07, 0.0002, 0.335
3. Layer misstatements per dollar unit from highest to lowest, including the percent misstatement assumption for sample items not misstated.	Table 14-8 0.5, 0.335, 0.07, 0.016, 0.0002
4. Determine upper precision limit using attribute sampling table, and determine the percent misstatement bound for each misstatement (layer).	Table 14-8 Total of 6 percent for four overstatements; calculate five layers. Total of 3.1 percent for one understatement; calculate two layers.
5. Calculate initial upper and lower misstatement bounds for each layer and total.	Table 14-8 Total of $190,564 and $266,323
6. Calculate point estimate for overstatements and understatements.	Table 14-9 $2,620 for overstatements $36,785 for understatements
7. Calculate adjusted upper and lower misstatement bounds.	$187,944 adjusted overstatement bound and $229,538 adjusted understatement bound

Analyze the Misstatements and Decide the Acceptability of the Population Fran and her staff analyzed the errors described in Table 14-6. The first two overstatement errors were due to accumulated discounts taken by customers that had not been properly removed from the accounts receivable. The understatement was due to a credit note that had accidentally been issued twice, and the large $3,000 difference was due to a change in discount rate. This customer had reached such a high volume of purchases that it was moved to a higher discount level, but Hillsburg staff did not implement the discount on a timely basis. In addition to calculating misstatement bounds, Fran will discuss with Hillsburg staff their management of discounts to ensure that these errors are corrected and to determine how future errors can be prevented. Fran could also have initiated additional substantive procedures to further quantify the extent of the dollar errors associated with discount differences.

Whenever a statistical method is used, a *decision rule* is needed to decide whether the population is acceptable. The decision rule for MUS is as follows:

If *both* the lower misstatement bound (LMB) and upper misstatement bound (UMB) fall between the understatement and overstatement tolerable misstatement amounts, accept the conclusion that the book value is not misstated by a material amount; otherwise, conclude that the book value is misstated by a material amount.

Since both lower and upper misstatement bounds are within $496,000, the set materiality level, the population book value is accepted.

---

[3]See Leslie, Teitlebaum, and Anderson, *op. cit.*

Action When a Population Is Rejected When one or both of the error bounds lie outside the tolerable misstatement limits and the population is not considered acceptable, the auditor has several options. Fran could wait until tests of other audit areas were completed to see if materiality of $496,000 was exceeded for the aggregated misstatements. Alternatively, she could perform expanded tests in other areas, increase the sample size (as explained on page 360), ask that the account balance be adjusted, or request the client correct the population (which would then have to be re-audited). If the aggregated errors exceed materiality and the client will not adjust the accounts, the auditor will have to consider refusing to give an unqualified opinion.

USE OF JUDGMENTAL SAMPLING Fran could have alternatively determined that judgmental sampling could be used to select the items to be confirmed below $150,000. She would then have followed 14 steps similar to those outlined in Chapter 12, as applied to nonstatistical rather than statistical sampling.

SUMMARY

1. *What is the process for designing tests of details of balances for accounts receivable?* Figure 14-2 provides a context: After setting materiality, assessing control risk, designing and testing internal control, the auditor designs tests of details for each audit assertion.

   What is the relationship between the transaction-related and the balance-related audit objectives for the sales and collection cycle? Figure 14-3 illustrates these relationships, showing that they are generally one-to-one except for occurrence/existence, occurrence/completeness, and completeness/existence.

2. *When and why are analytical review procedures completed as part of the audit of sales and accounts receivable?* Analytical procedures are completed during planning, as part of detailed testing, and as part of completing the audit. For the detailed testing, account specific ratios are calculated. Ratios could also be calculated for customers or products to provide more assurance.

   How is the amount of substantive testing related to the audit risk model? The extent of detailed testing is related to the value of planned detection risk. As planned detection risk decreases, the amount of assurance required from tests of detail increases, resulting in the need for more substantive testing.

3. *Describe the audit tests that would be completed for each audit assertion.* There are many different types of tests that could be conducted, but examples by assertion are detail tie-in—adding the accounts receivable master file and agreeing to the general ledger balance; existence—confirmation; completeness—comparison of customer master file to outstanding transaction file; accuracy—confirmation; classification—review of aged trial balance; cutoff—tracing transactions near the period end date; valuation—assessing fairness of bad-debt allowance; rights—review of bank confirmation; and presentation and disclosure—examining financial statement footnotes.

   Why is confirmation one of the most important audit procedures? It is a multi-purpose technique that addresses several audit assertions: existence, accuracy, and cutoff.

4. *Provide a description of an example test of detail.* Tables 14-4 and 14-5 list many audit procedures. For example, generalized audit software is used for parallel simulation—recreation of the aged accounts receivable trial balance totals by customer.

   How is monetary unit sampling (MUS) executed and evaluated? Based upon materiality, ARACR, TER, and EPER, software calculates a dollar interval. Then, that dollar interval is used together with a random start to select the sample. After audit tests are completed, the software can be used to calculate upper and lower precision limits, or these can be calculated manually.

CICA ASSURANCE HANDBOOK SECTION REFERENCED IN THIS CHAPTER

Section 5303 – Confirmation.

ESSENTIAL TERMS

Accounts receivable balance-related audit objectives—the nine specific audit objectives used to help the auditor decide the appropriate audit evidence for accounts receivable   (p. 418).

Aged trial balance—a listing of the balances in the accounts receivable master file at the balance sheet date broken down according to the amount of time passed between the date of sale and the balance sheet date   (p. 423).

Alternative procedure—the follow-up of a positive confirmation not returned by the debtor with the use of documentation evidence to determine whether the recorded receivable exists and is collectible   (p. 432).

Blank confirmation form—a letter, addressed to the debtor, requesting the recipient to fill in the amount of the accounts receivable balance; considered a positive confirmation   (p. 429).

Cutoff misstatements—misstatements that take place as a result of current period transactions being recorded in a subsequent period, or subsequent period transactions being recorded in the current period   (p. 425).

Evidence planning spreadsheet—a working paper used to help the auditor decide whether planned audit evidence for tests of details of balances should be low, medium, or high for each balance-related audit objective   (p. 417).

Negative confirmation—a letter, addressed to the debtor, requesting a response only if the recipient disagrees with the amount of the stated account balance   (p. 429).

Positive confirmation—a letter, addressed to the debtor, requesting that the recipient indicate directly on the letter whether the stated account balance is correct or incorrect and, if incorrect, by what amount   (p. 429).

Tainting—the average percent of misstatement for population dollars that contain a misstatement (used with MUS sampling)   (p. 437).

Timing difference (in an accounts receivable confirmation)—a reported difference in a confirmation from a debtor that is determined to be a timing difference between the client's and debtor's records and therefore not a misstatement   (p. 426).

Valuation of accounts receivable—the amount of the outstanding balances in accounts receivable that will ultimately be collected   (p. 427).

REVIEW QUESTIONS

14-1   Distinguish between tests of details of balances and tests of controls for the sales and collection cycle. Explain how the tests of controls affect the tests of details.

14-2   Cynthia Roberts, a public accountant, expresses the following viewpoint: "I do not believe in performing tests of controls for the sales and collection cycle. As an alternative, I send a lot of negative confirmations on every audit at an interim date. If I find a lot of misstatements, I analyze them to determine their cause. If internal controls are inadequate, I send positive confirmations at year end to evaluate the amount of the misstatements. If the negative confirmations result in minimal misstatements, which is often the case, I have found that internal controls are effective without bothering to perform tests of controls, and the CICA's confirmation requirement has been satisfied at the same time. In my opinion, the best test of internal controls is to go directly to third parties." Evaluate her point of view.

14-3   List five analytical procedures for the sales and collection cycle. For each test, describe a misstatement that could be identified.

14-4   Identify the nine accounts receivable balance-related audit objectives. For each objective, list one audit procedure.

14-5   Which of the nine accounts receivable balance-related audit objectives can be partially satisfied by confirmations with customers?

14-6   Distinguish between accuracy tests of gross accounts receivable and tests of the realizable value of receivables.

14-7   Explain why you agree or disagree with the following statement: "In most audits, it is more important to test carefully the cutoff for sales than for cash receipts."

Describe how you perform each type of test assuming the existence of prenumbered documents.

14-8   In what circumstances is it acceptable to confirm accounts receivable prior to the balance sheet date?

14-9   State the most important factors affecting the sample size in confirmations of accounts receivable.

14-10   In Chapter 12, one of the points brought out was the need to obtain a representative sample of the population. How can this concept be reconciled with the statement in this chapter that the emphasis should be on confirming larger and older balances since these are most likely to contain misstatements?

14-11   An auditor is determining the appropriate sample size for testing inventory valuation using MUS. The population has 2,620 items valued at $12,625,000. The tolerable misstatement for both understatements and overstatements is $500,000 at a 10 percent ARIA. No misstatements are expected in the population. Calculate the preliminary sample size using a 100 percent average misstatement assumption.

14-12   Define what is meant by "alternative procedures" and explain their purpose. Which alternative procedures are the most reliable? Why?

14-13   Explain why the analysis of differences is important in the confirmation of accounts receivable even if the misstatements in the sample are not material.

14-14   State three types of differences that might be observed in the confirmation of accounts receivable that do not constitute misstatements. For each, state an audit procedure that would verify the difference.

MULTIPLE CHOICE QUESTIONS

14-15 Choose the best response for the following questions:

a. As a result of analytical procedures, the independent auditor determines that the gross profit percentage has declined from 30 percent in the preceding year to 20 percent in the current year. The auditor should

(1) evaluate management's performance in causing this decline.
(2) investigate the credit manager's performance.
(3) require footnote disclosure.
(4) consider the possibility of a misstatement in the financial statements.

b. Once a public accountant has determined that accounts receivable have increased due to slow collections in a "tight money" environment, the public accountant would be likely to

(1) review the going concern ramifications.
(2) review the credit and collection policy.
(3) increase the balance in the allowance for uncollectible accounts.
(4) expand tests of collectibility.

c. In connection with his review of key ratios, the public accountant notes that Pyzi Inc. had accounts receivable equal to 30 days' sales at December 31, 2004, and to 45 days' sales at December 31, 2005. Assuming that there had been no changes in economic conditions, clientele, or sales mix, this change most likely would indicate

(1) a steady increase in sales in 2005.
(2) a steady decrease in sales in 2005.
(3) an easing of credit policies in 2005.
(4) a decrease in accounts receivable relative to sales in 2005.

(AICPA adapted)

d. In connection with her examination of Beke Supply Corp. for the year ended August 31, 2005, Sylvia Lowe, a public accountant, has mailed accounts receivable confirmations to three groups as follows:

Group Number	Type of Customer	Type of Confirmation
1	Wholesale	Positive
2	Current retail	Negative
3	Past-due retail	Positive

The confirmation responses from each group vary from 10 percent to 90 percent. The most likely response percentages are

(1) Group 1—90 percent; Group 2—50 percent; Group 3—10 percent
(2) Group 1—90 percent; Group 2—10 percent; Group 3—50 percent
(3) Group 1—50 percent; Group 2—90 percent; Group 3—10 percent
(4) Group 1—10 percent; Group 2—50 percent; Group 3—90 percent

e. In confirming a client's accounts receivable in prior years, an auditor found that there were many differences between the recorded account balances and the confirmation responses. These differences, which were not misstatements, required substantial time to resolve. In defining the sampling unit for the current year's audit, the auditor would most likely choose

(1) individual overdue balances.
(2) individual invoices.
(3) small account balances.
(4) large account balances.

DISCUSSION QUESTIONS AND PROBLEMS

14-16 The following are common tests of details of balances for the audit of accounts receivable.

1. Obtain a list of aged accounts receivable, foot the list, and trace the total to the general ledger.
2. Trace 35 accounts to the customer master file or open item transaction file for name, amount, and age categories.
3. Examine and document collections on accounts receivable for 20 days after the engagement date.
4. Request 25 positive and 65 negative confirmations of accounts receivable.
5. Perform alternative procedures on accounts not responding to second requests by examining subsequent collection documentation and shipping reports or sales invoices.
6. Test the sales cutoff by tracing entries in the sales journal for 15 days before and after the engagement date to shipping reports, if available, and/or sales invoices.
7. Determine and disclose accounts pledged, discounted, sold, assigned, or guaranteed by others.
8. Evaluate the materiality of credit balances in the aged trial balance.

Required

For each audit procedure, identify the balance-related audit objective or objectives it partially or fully satisfies.

- -

14-17 The following misstatements are sometimes found in the sales and collection account balances:

1. Cash received from collections of accounts receivable in the subsequent period are recorded as current period receipts.
2. The allowance for uncollectible accounts is inadequate due to the client's failure to reflect depressed economic

conditions in the allowance.

3. Several accounts receivable are in dispute due to claims of defective merchandise.
4. The pledging of accounts receivable to the bank for a loan is not disclosed in the financial statements.
5. Goods shipped and included in the current period sales were returned in the subsequent period.
6. Long-term interest-bearing notes receivable from affiliated companies are included in accounts receivable.

7. The aged accounts receivable trial balance total does not equal the amount in the general ledger.

Required

a. For each misstatement, identify the balance-related audit objective to which it pertains.
b. For each misstatement, list an internal control that should prevent it.
c. For each misstatement, list one test of details of balances audit procedure that the auditor can use to detect it.

14-18 André Auto Parts Inc. sells new parts for foreign automobiles to auto dealers. Company policy requires that a prenumbered shipping document be issued for each sale. At the time of pickup or shipment, the shipping clerk writes the date on the shipping document. The last shipment made in the fiscal year ended August 31, 2005, was recorded on document 2167. Shipments are billed in the order that the billing clerk receives the shipping documents.

For late August and early September, shipping documents are billed on sales invoices as follows:

Shipping Document No.	Sales Invoice No.
2163	4332
2164	4326
2165	4327
2166	4330
2167	4331
2168	4328
2169	4329
2170	4333
2171	4335
2172	4334

The August and September sales journals include the following information:

Sales Journal—August 2005

Day of Month	Sales Invoice No.	Amount of Sale
30	4326	$ 726.11
30	4329	1,914.30
31	4327	419.83
31	4328	620.22
31	4330	47.74

Sales Journal—September 2005

Day of Month	Sales Invoice No.	Amount of Sale
1	4332	$2,641.31
1	4331	106.39
1	4333	852.06
2	4335	1,250.50
2	4334	646.58

Required

a. What are the generally accepted accounting principles requirements for a correct sales cutoff?
b. Which sales invoices, if any, are recorded in the wrong accounting period, assuming a periodic inventory? Prepare an adjusting entry to correct the accounts for the year ended August 31, 2005.
c. Assume that the shipping clerk accidentally wrote August 31 on shipping documents 2168 through 2172. Explain how that would affect the correctness of the financial statements. How would you, as an auditor, discover that error?
d. Describe, in general terms, the audit procedures you would follow in making sure cutoff for sales is accurate at the balance sheet date.
e. Identify internal controls that would reduce the likelihood of cutoff errors. How would you test each control?

14-19 John Gossling, a public accountant, is examining the financial statements of a manufacturing company with a significant amount of trade accounts receivable. Gossling is satisfied that the accounts are properly summarized and classified and that allocations, reclassifications, and valuations are made in accordance with generally accepted accounting principles. He is planning to use accounts receivable confirmation requests to satisfy the third examination standard as to trade accounts receivable.

Required

a. Identify and describe the two forms of accounts receivable confirmation requests, and indicate the factors Gossling will consider in determining when to use each.
b. Assume that Gossling has received a satisfactory response to the confirmation requests. Describe how he could evaluate collectibility of the trade accounts receivable.
c. What are the implications to a public accountant if, during his or her examination of accounts receivable, some of a client's trade customers do not respond to the request for positive confirmation of their accounts?
d. What auditing steps should a public accountant perform if there is no response to a second request for a positive confirmation?

(AICPA adapted)

14-20 Johnson Clock Company sells specialty clocks, watches, and other timekeeping devices. Since its inception, the company has sold items through its home office store and at industry and collector trade shows around the country. To meet the demand from collectors around the world, the company began selling items through its Internet web site. Recent financial information about Johnson's sales is summarized in the following tables.

	Year Ended 12/31/04	Year Ended 12/31/03	Year Ended 12/31/02
Sales:			
Home office	$1,279,480	$1,218,552	$1,163,851
Trade show	773,265	739,259	704,391
Internet-based	147,772	122,462	52,884
Sales Returns:			
Home office	$ 25,589	$ 23,152	$ 25,605
Trade show	13,946	13,676	12,679
Internet-based	13,254	11,022	4,760

Required

Using the information given, design and perform analytical procedures for the sales and collection cycle at Johnson Clock Company. Based on the results of your analytical procedures, describe how the results related to the Internet-based sales differ from the home office and trade show sales.

	Year Ended 12/31/04	Year Ended 12/31/03	Year Ended 12/31/02
Cost of Goods Sold:			
Home office	$831,662	$816,429	$768,142
Trade show	491,023	480,518	454,332
Internet-based	81,275	66,129	28,822
Receivables Related to Sales from:			
Home office	$126,195	$123,524	$127,545
Trade show	74,149	68,862	67,544
Internet-based	3,239	3,020	1,159

Tolerable misstatement for sales and receivables is $12,000.

14-21 You have been assigned to the confirmation of aged accounts receivable for the Blank Paper Company Ltd. audit. You have tested the trial balance and selected the accounts for confirming. Before the confirmation requests are mailed, the controller asks to look at the accounts you intend to confirm to determine whether she will permit you to send them.

She reviews the list and informs you that she does not want you to confirm six of the accounts on your list. Two of them have credit balances, one has a zero balance, two of the other three have a fairly small balance, and the remaining balance is highly material. The reason she gives is that she feels the confirmations will upset these customers because "they are kind of hard to get along with." She does not want the credit balances confirmed because it may encourage the customers to ask for a refund.

In addition, the controller asks you to send an additional 20 confirmations to customers she has listed for you. She does this as a means of credit collection for "those who won't know the difference between a public accountant and a credit collection agency."

Required

a. Is it acceptable for the controller to review the list of accounts you intend to confirm? Discuss.
b. Discuss the appropriateness of sending the 20 additional confirmations to the customers.
c. Assuming the auditor complies with all the controller's requests, what is the effect on the auditor's opinion?

14-22 The following are the entire outstanding accounts receivable for Jake's Bookbinding Company Ltd. The population is smaller than would ordinarily be the case for statistical sampling, but an entire population is useful to show how to select samples by monetary unit sampling.

Required

a. Select a sample using systematic MUS sampling. Materiality is $50,000 and an appropriate MUS interval is $35,000. Use a starting point of 1857. Identify the physical units selected.
b. Why would an auditor use MUS?

Population Item	Recorded Amount	Population Item	Recorded Amount	Population Item	Recorded Amount	Population Item	Recorded Amount
1	$1,410	11	$ 2,270	21	$4,865	31	$ 935
2	9,130	12	50	22	770	32	5,595
3	660	13	5,785	23	2,305	33	930
4	3,355	14	940	24	2,665	34	4,045
5	5,725	15	1,820	25	1,000	35	9,480
6	8,210	16	3,380	26	6,225	36	360
7	580	17	530	27	3,675	37	1,145
8	44,110	18	955	28	6,250	38	6,400
9	825	19	4,490	29	1,890	39	100
10	1,155	20	17,140	30	27,705	40	8,435
							$207,295

14-23 You intend to use MUS as a part of the audit of several accounts for Roynpower Manufacturing Inc. You have done the audit for the past several years, and there has rarely been an adjusting entry of any kind. Your audit tests of all tests of controls for the transactions cycles were completed at an interim date, and control risk has been assessed as low. You therefore decide to use an ARIA of 10 percent for all tests of details of balances.

You intend to use MUS in the audit of the three most material asset balance sheet account balances: accounts receivable, inventory, and marketable securities. You feel justified in using the same ARIA for each audit area because of the low assessed control risk.

The recorded balances and related information for the three accounts are as follows:

	Recorded Value
Accounts receivable	$ 3,600,000
Inventory	4,800,000
Marketable securities	1,600,000
	$10,000,000

Net earnings before taxes for Roynpower are $2,000,000. You decide that materiality will be $100,000 for the client.

The audit approach will be to determine the total sample size needed for all three accounts. A sample will be selected from all $10 million, and the appropriate testing for a sample item will depend on whether the item is a receivable, inventory, or marketable security. The audit conclusions will pertain to the entire $10 million, and no conclusion will be made about the three individual accounts unless significant misstatements are found in the sample.

a. Evaluate the audit approach of testing all three account balances in one sample.
b. Calculate the required sample size for each of the three accounts assuming you decide that the tolerable misstatement in each account is $100,000. (Recall that tolerable misstatement equals preliminary judgment about materiality for MUS.)
c. How would you identify which sample item in the population to audit for the number 4,627,871? What audit procedures would be performed?
d. Assume you select a sample of 100 sample items for testing and you find one misstatement in inventory. The recorded value is $987.12, and the audit value is $887.12. Calculate the misstatement bounds for the three combined accounts, and reach appropriate audit conclusions.

14-24 You have been assigned to the first examination of the accounts of North Battleford Corp. for the year ending March 31, 2005. Accounts receivable were confirmed on December 31, 2004, and at that date the receivables consisted of approximately two hundred accounts with balances totalling $956,750. Seventy-five of these accounts with balances totalling $650,725 were selected for confirmation. All but 20 of the confirmation requests have been returned; 30 were signed without comments, 14 had minor differences which have been cleared satisfactorily, while 11 confirmations had the following comments:

1. We are sorry but we cannot answer your request for confirmation of our account as Duck Lake Inc. uses an accounts payable voucher system.
2. The balance of $1,050 was paid on December 13, 2004.
3. The balance of $7,750 was paid on January 5, 2005.
4. The balance noted above has been paid.
5. We do not owe you anything at December 31, 2004, as the goods, represented by your invoice dated December 30, 2004, number 25050, in the amount of $11,550, were received on January 5, 2005, on FOB destination terms.

6. An advance payment of $2,500 made by us in November 2004 should cover the two invoices totalling $1,350 shown on the statement attached.
7. We never received these goods.
8. We are contesting the propriety of this $12,525 charge. We think the charge is excessive.
9. Amount okay. As the goods have been shipped to us on consignment, we will remit payment upon selling the goods.
10. The $10,000, representing a deposit under a lease, will be applied against the rent due to us during 2005, the last year of the lease.
11. Your credit memo dated December 5, 2004, in the amount of $440 cancels the balance above.

What steps would you take to satisfactorily clear each of the above 11 comments?

(AICPA adapted)

14-25 During his interim audit visit, Charles Ai determined that one of the subsidiary companies of Mega Big Limited had experienced some very serious problems with respect to the credit management and collection of trade accounts receivable. During the first six months of the year, the accounts receivable of this subsidiary had almost doubled, the number of days' sales in accounts receivable had increased from 39 days to 64 days, and bad-debt expense had risen sharply.

Prepare an outline of the steps that should be taken to investigate the nature and causes of the credit and collection problems. (Do *not* consider the possibility of fraud.)

14-26 You are auditing the sales and collection cycle for the Smalltown Regional Hospital, a small not-for-profit hospital. The hospital has a reputation for excellent medical services and weak record keeping. The medical people have a tradition of doing all aspects of their job correctly, but because of a shortage of accounting personnel, there is not time for internal verification or careful performance. In previous years, your firm has found quite a few misstatements in billings, cash receipts, and accounts receivable. As in all hospitals, the two largest assets are accounts receivable and property, plant, and equipment.

The hospital has several large loans payable to local banks, and the two banks have told management that they are reluctant to extend more credit, especially considering the modern hospital that is being built in a nearby city.

In previous years, your response from patients to confirmation requests has been frustrating at best. The response rate has been extremely low, and those who did respond did not know the purpose of the confirmations or their correct outstanding balance. You have had the same experience in confirming receivables at other hospitals.

You conclude that control over cash is excellent and the likelihood of fraud is extremely small. You are less confident about unintentional errors in billing, recording sales, cash receipts, accounts receivable, and bad debts.

Required

a. Identify the major factors affecting client business risk and acceptable audit risk for this audit.
b. What inherent risks are you concerned about?
c. In this audit of the sales and collection cycle, which types of tests are you likely to emphasize?
d. For each of the following, explain whether you plan to emphasize the tests and give reasons:

(1) Tests of controls
(2) Substantive tests of transactions
(3) Analytical procedures
(4) Tests of details of balances

CASE

14-27 Loofa Limited is a dry goods chain selling mainly staples: practical clothing for the family, work clothes, shoes, notions, piece goods, and a relatively small amount of housewares. Its 170 stores are distributed across the country. Ten years ago, the president authorized the introduction of a credit card system, and within 2 years the company had issued 300,000 credit cards. In 2004, some 450,000 credit cards were in circulation with about 430,000 showing monthly activity. Seventy percent of the company's sales are made on credit, with some 75 percent of the credit sales made to company credit card holders and the other credit sales being made to holders of other credit cards.

The credit card system is one of several computerized systems processed on the company's computer. Relevant procedures for the computerized credit card system are as follows:

1. There are 140 stores located in areas other than the head office location. All credit card purchases are stored locally in the point of sales systems and then transmitted at night in a batch to head office, along with a header record that includes the number of transactions and a control total. The control totals and record counts are automatically verified by the head office computer system before the transactions are used to update individual customer records.
2. Cyclical billing is done at head office. Credit card holders have been divided into groups, the size of the group having been determined by dividing the number of customers (credit cards) by the number of working days in the month. Each group is billed once a month.
3. Remittances received by mail or in person at head office, write-offs, and other adjustments including service charges on overdue accounts are processed at head office.

4. The credit department at head office is responsible for the issue of credit cards and for a weekly advice to all stores of cards that have been inactive for 90 days and of delinquent credit cards. Credit cards are delinquent as soon as:
    (i) the customer exceeds his or her credit limit;
    (ii) the customer has made no payments for 60 days since the last billing;
    (iii) the credit card is reported stolen; or
    (iv) the customer has given notice of cancellation.

In addition to the above information, the auditor finds the following in the accounts:

Accounts receivable—credit cards	$8,218,374 Debit
Allowance for doubtful accounts (manually controlled)	1,221,000 Credit

During the discussion of the computerized system, the data processing manager indicated that he could have one of his programmers extract information from the credit card data files (i.e., customer master, transaction history, or open item transactions) according to the auditor's specifications.

Required

a. As auditor, assuming you accept the data processing manager's offer, describe with reasons the information you would ask to have extracted from the client data files.
b. How would you ensure that no credit card data would be excluded from the query programs prepared by the client programmer?

(CICA adapted)

PART 4 CHAPTERS 15-20

APPLICATION OF THE AUDIT PROCESS TO OTHER CYCLES

The chapters in Part 4 apply auditing concepts first presented in Chapters 5 through 12 and expanded in Chapters 13 and 14 to the other cycles in an audit. Although there are considerable similarities in auditing each cycle, there are also important differences that auditors need to understand.

Each of these chapters deals with a specific transaction cycle or part of a transaction cycle in much the same manner as Chapters 13 and 14 cover the sales and collection cycle. Each chapter in Part 4 demonstrates the relationship of internal controls, tests of controls, substantive tests of transactions, and analytical procedures to the related balance sheet and income statement accounts in the cycle and to tests of details of balances.

CHAPTER 15

AUDIT OF CASH BALANCES

"Cash" is available in many different ways—via cheque, credit card, debit card, or transferred electronically into your bank account. It is the way that we acquire assets and discharge our debts, so it has a pivotal role in the accounting process, being one side of many different types of transactions. Here, we will look at different types of cash accounts and how they are audited.

LEARNING OBJECTIVES

After reading this chapter, you should be able to answer the following questions:

1. What are the different types of cash accounts? Explain the relationship between cash and the transaction cycles.

2. Describe the steps in auditing the general cash account.

3. What additional procedures are conducted when there is suspicion of fraud? What is "kiting" and how is it audited?

4. How is an audit of the payroll cash account different from the audit of the general cash account? What special considerations exist for EFT (electronic funds transfer) transactions? How is petty cash audited?

SOCIETY EXPECTS A LOT FROM AUDITORS

Billing scam. Fake invoices. Overbilling. Funding fraud. What do these terms have in common? All of these illegal actions result in the theft of cash. Cash is tempting, it is often available in large amounts—and there is an expectation that when large amounts are stolen, the auditor will detect the activity. The following examples of fraud were all published in one month, March 2004.

The RCMP was investigating $160 million in apparently bogus software development or maintenance contracts, meaning that cash was paid for services not performed. The following week, an article claimed that retailers selling Canadian flags were asked to submit invoices for flags that were not shipped. The article speculated that the Canadian suppliers were paid large sums and inexpensive flags from China were purchased by the government offices instead—so a purchasing agent somewhere made a tidy profit.

The president of a pizza franchise was charged for taking money from potential franchisees, promising a complete business with support and training, but services were not delivered. A Burlington, Ontario man was charged and pleaded guilty to defrauding the Dufferin-Peel Catholic school board of over $800,000. Rather than providing services to the board via a limited company, invoices were submitted for services that were never provided.

These examples indicate the importance of auditing controls over cash and cash payments.

Sources: 1. Brennan, Richard, 2004. "Defence billing scam 'very sophisticated,'" The Toronto Star, March 12, 2004, p. A12. 2. Canadian Press, 2004. "Flag retailers claim government paid for fake invoices," The Toronto Star, March 19, 2004, p. A17. 3. Daw, James, 2004. "Pizza franchise chain founder charged," The Toronto Star, March 19, 2004, p. F1, F4. 4. Mitchell, Bob, 2004. "Educator guilty in school funding fraud," The Toronto Star, March 19, 2004, p. E5.

As an auditing student, you can understand the importance of paying for only those goods and services that a company receives. Yet, we need to remember that not all internal controls are perfect, and that harried employees may not carefully check all the documents pertaining to disbursements of cash. What kinds of questions would you ask about the processing of cash payments? To what extent would you examine detailed records? What would be the inherent risk associated with cash in most organizations?

Evidence accumulated for cash balances depends heavily on the results of the tests in the transaction cycles. Understanding the cash account is important because it links to all of those cycles. The auditor needs to consider the assessed risks from each cycle when auditing cash.

→15.1 CASH AND THE TRANSACTION CYCLES

Types of Cash Accounts

It is important to understand the different types of cash accounts because the auditing approach to each varies. The following are the major types of cash accounts.

General Cash Account The general account is the focal point of cash for most organizations because virtually all cash receipts and disbursements flow through this account at some time. The disbursements for the acquisition and payment cycle are normally paid from this account, and the receipts of cash in the sales and collection cycle are deposited in the account. In addition, the deposits and disbursements for all other cash accounts are normally made through the general account. Most small companies have only one bank account—the **general cash account**.

Imprest Payroll Account Some companies, as a means of improving internal control, establish a separate imprest bank account for making payroll payments to employees. In an **imprest payroll account**, a fixed balance, such as $1,000, is maintained in a separate bank account. Immediately before each pay period, one cheque is drawn on the general cash account to deposit the total amount of the net payroll in the payroll account. After all payroll cheques have cleared the imprest payroll account, the bank account should have a $1,000 balance. The only deposits into the account are of the periodic weekly (or semimonthly) payroll, and the only disbursements are payments to employees. For companies with many employees, the use of an imprest payroll account can improve internal control and reduce the time needed to reconcile bank accounts.

Branch Bank Account For a company operating in multiple locations, it is frequently desirable to have a separate bank balance at each location. **Branch bank accounts** are useful for building public relations in local communities and permitting the decentralization of operations to the branch level.

In some companies, the deposits and disbursements for each branch are made to a particular bank account, and the excess cash is periodically sent to the main office general bank account. The branch account in this instance is much like a general account, but at the branch level.

A somewhat different type of branch account consists of one bank account for receipts and a separate one for disbursements. All receipts are deposited in the branch bank, and the total is transferred to the general account periodically. The disbursement account is set up on an *imprest basis* but in a different manner from an imprest payroll account. A fixed balance is maintained in the imprest account, and the authorized branch personnel use these funds for disbursements at their own discretion as long as the payments are consistent with company policy. When the cash balance has been depleted, an accounting is made to the home office and a reimbursement is made to the branch account from the general account *after* the expenditures have been approved. The use of an imprest branch bank account improves controls over receipts and disbursements.

GENERAL CASH ACCOUNT—the primary bank account for most organizations; virtually all cash receipts and disbursements flow through this account at some time

IMPREST PAYROLL ACCOUNT—a bank account to which the exact amount of payroll for the pay period is transferred by cheque from the employer's general cash account

BRANCH BANK ACCOUNT—a separate bank account maintained at a local bank by a branch of a company

Imprest Petty Cash Fund A petty cash fund is actually not a bank account, but it is sufficiently similar to cash on deposit to merit inclusion in this section. It is used for small cash purchases that can be paid more conveniently and quickly by cash than by cheque. An **imprest petty cash fund** is set up on the same basis as an imprest branch bank account, but the expenditures are normally for a much smaller amount. Typical expenses include minor office supplies, stamps, and small contributions to local charities. Usually a petty cash account does not exceed a few hundred dollars and may not be reimbursed more than once or twice each month.

IMPREST PETTY CASH FUND—a fund of cash maintained within the company for small cash payments; its fixed balance is comparatively small, and it is periodically reimbursed

Cash Equivalents Excess cash accumulated during certain parts of the operating cycle that will be needed in the reasonably near future is often invested in short-term, highly liquid cash equivalents. Examples include term deposits, certificates of deposit, and money market funds. **Cash equivalents**, which can be highly material, are included in the financial statements as part of the cash account only if they are short-term investments that are readily convertible to known amounts of cash within a short time and there is little risk of a change in value from interest rate changes. Marketable securities and longer-term interest-bearing investments are not cash equivalents.

CASH EQUIVALENTS—excess cash invested in short-term, highly liquid investments, such as term deposits, certificates of deposit, and money market funds

Summary Figure 15-1 shows the relationship of general cash to the other cash accounts. All cash either originates from or is deposited in general cash. This chapter focuses on three types of accounts: the general cash account, the imprest payroll bank account, and the imprest petty cash fund. The others are similar to these.

Cash in the Bank and Transaction Cycles

A brief discussion of the relationship between cash in the bank and the other transaction cycles serves a dual function: it highlights the importance of the tests of various transaction cycles to the audit of cash, and it aids in further understanding the integration of the different transaction cycles. Figure 15-2 on page 456 illustrates the relationships of the various transaction cycles, the focal point being the general cash account.

An examination of Figure 15-2 indicates why the general cash account is considered significant in almost all audits, even when the ending balance is immaterial. The amount of cash flowing into and out of the cash account is frequently larger than for any other account in the financial statements. Furthermore, the susceptibility of cash to defalcation is greater than for other types of assets because most other assets must be converted to cash to make them usable.

FIGURE 15-1   Relationship of General Cash to Other Cash Accounts

FIGURE 15-2 | **Relationships of Cash in the Bank and Transaction Cycles**

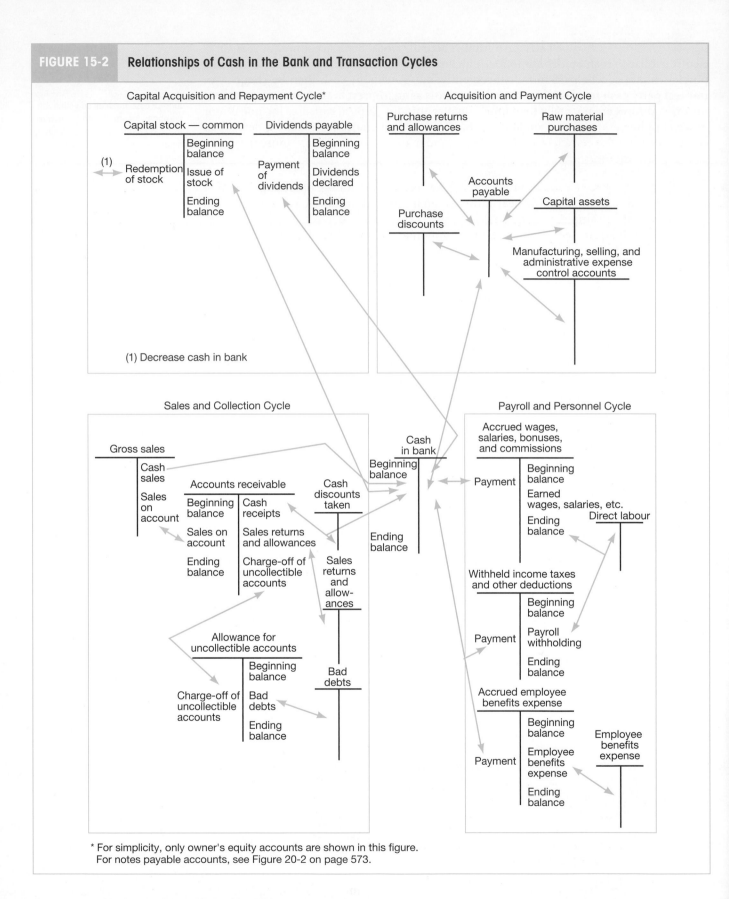

Capital Acquisition and Repayment Cycle*

Acquisition and Payment Cycle

Sales and Collection Cycle

Payroll and Personnel Cycle

(1) Decrease cash in bank

* For simplicity, only owner's equity accounts are shown in this figure.
For notes payable accounts, see Figure 20-2 on page 573.

In the audit of cash, an important distinction should be made between verifying the client's reconciliation of the balance on the bank statement to the balance in the general ledger and verifying whether recorded cash in the general ledger correctly reflects all cash transactions that took place during the year. It is relatively easy to verify the client's reconciliation of the balance in the bank account to the general ledger, which is the primary subject of this chapter, but a significant part of the total audit of a company involves verifying whether cash transactions are properly recorded. For example, each of the following misstatements ultimately results in the improper payment of or the failure to receive cash, but none will normally be discovered as a part of the audit of the bank reconciliation:

- Failure to bill a customer.
- Billing a customer at a lower price than called for by company policy.
- A defalcation of cash by interception of collections from customers before they are recorded. The account receivable is charged off as a bad debt.
- Duplicate payment of a vendor's invoice.
- Improper payments of officers' personal expenditures.
- Payment for raw materials that were not received.
- Payment to an employee for more hours than he or she worked.
- Payment of interest to a related party for an amount in excess of the going rate.

If these misstatements are to be uncovered in the audit, their discovery must come about through tests of controls. The first three misstatements could be discovered as part of the audit of the sales and collection cycle, the next three in the audit of the acquisitions and payment cycle, and the last two in the tests of the payroll and personnel cycle and the capital acquisition and repayment cycle, respectively.

Entirely different types of misstatements are normally discovered as part of the tests of a bank reconciliation. For example,

- Failure to include a cheque that has not cleared the bank on the outstanding cheque list, even though it has been recorded in the cash disbursements journal.
- Cash received by the client subsequent to the balance sheet date but recorded as cash receipts in the current year.
- Deposits recorded as cash receipts near the end of the year, deposited in the bank, and included in the bank reconciliation as a deposit in transit.
- Payments on notes payable that were debited directly to the bank balance by the bank but were not entered in the client's records.

The appropriate methods for discovering the preceding misstatements by testing the client's bank reconciliation will become apparent as we proceed. At this point, it is important that you distinguish between tests of controls that are related to the cash account and tests that determine whether the book balance reconciles to the bank balance.

→ 15.2 AUDIT OF THE GENERAL CASH ACCOUNT

On the trial balance of Hillsburg Hardware Limited, on page 117, there is only one cash account. Notice, however, that all cycles, except inventory and warehousing, affect cash in the bank.

In testing the year-end balance in the general cash account, the auditor must accumulate sufficient evidence to evaluate whether cash, as stated on the balance sheet, is fairly stated and properly disclosed in accordance with six of the nine balance-related audit objectives used for all tests of details of balances. Rights to general cash, its classification on the balance sheet, and the valuation of cash are not a problem.

The methodology for auditing year-end cash is essentially the same as for all other balance sheet accounts. This methodology is shown in Figure 15-3.

Internal Controls Internal controls over the year-end cash balances in the general account can be divided into two categories: *controls over the transaction cycles* affecting the recording of cash receipts and disbursements and *independent bank reconciliations*.

FIGURE 15-3   Methodology for Designing Tests of Details of Balances for Cash in the Bank

Set materiality and assess audit risk and inherent risk for cash in bank

Materiality Considerations
The cash balance is immaterial on most audits, but the cash transactions affecting the balance are almost always extremely material. There is therefore often potential for material misstatement of cash.

Assess control risk for cash in bank

Inherent Risk Considerations
Because cash is more susceptible to theft than other assets, there is high inherent risk for the existence objective. This objective is usually the focus in auditing cash balances. Typically, inherent risk is low for all other objectives.

Design and perform tests of controls for several cycles*

Control Risk Considerations
• Internal control effectiveness over cash balances varies significantly for different companies. The most important internal control is independent bank reconciliations.

Design and perform analytical procedures for cash in bank balance

• Internal controls over cash receipts and disbursements are important considerations in the audit and were discussed in earlier chapters.

Design tests of details of cash in bank balance to satisfy balance-related audit objectives

| Audit procedures |
| Sample size |
| Items to select |
| Timing |

*Cycles affected include sales and collection, acquisition and payment, payroll and personnel, and capital acquisition and repayment.

Controls affecting the recording of cash transactions are discussed in chapters pertaining to those cycles. For example, in the acquisition and payment cycle, major controls include the adequate segregation of duties between the cheque signing and the accounts payable functions, the signing of cheques by only a properly authorized person, the use of prenumbered cheques that are printed on special paper, adequate control of blank and voided cheques, careful review of supporting documentation by the cheque signer before cheques are signed, and adequate internal verification. If the controls affecting cash-related transactions are adequate, it is possible to reduce the audit tests of the year-end bank reconciliation.

A monthly **bank reconciliation** of the general bank account on a timely basis by someone independent of the handling or recording of cash receipts and disbursements is an essential control over the cash balance. The reconciliation is important to ensure that the books reflect the same cash balance as the actual amount of cash in the bank after consideration of reconciling items, but even more important, the *independent* reconciliation provides a unique opportunity for an internal verification of cash receipts and disbursements transactions. If the bank statements are received unopened by the reconciler and physical control is maintained over the statements until the reconciliations are complete, the cancelled cheques, duplicate deposit slips, and other documents included in the statement can be examined without concern for the possibility of alteration, deletions, or additions. A careful bank reconciliation by competent client personnel includes the following:

• Compare cancelled cheques with the cash disbursements journal for date, payee, and amount.
• Examine cancelled cheques for signature, endorsements, and cancellation.

BANK RECONCILIATION—the monthly reconciliation, usually prepared by client personnel, of the differences between the cash balance recorded in the general ledger and the amount in the bank account

- Compare deposits in the bank with recorded cash receipts for date, customer, and amount.
- Account for the numerical sequence of cheques, and investigate missing ones.
- Reconcile all items causing a difference between the book and bank balance, and verify their propriety.
- Reconcile total debits on the bank statement with the totals in the cash disbursements journal.
- Reconcile total credits on the bank statement with the totals in the cash receipts journal.
- Review month-end interbank transfers for propriety and proper recording.
- Follow up on outstanding cheques and stop-payment notices.

The first four of these internal procedures are directly related to the tests of controls of transaction cycles. The last five are directly related to the reconciliation of the book and bank balance and are discussed in greater detail later.

Because of the importance of monthly reconciliation of bank accounts, another common control for many companies is having a responsible employee review the monthly reconciliation as soon as possible after its completion.

Analytical Procedures In many audits, the year-end bank reconciliation is verified on a 100 percent basis. Testing the reasonableness of the cash balance is therefore less important than for most other audit areas.

It is common for auditors to compare the ending balance on the bank reconciliation, deposits in transit, outstanding cheques, and other reconciling items with the prior-year reconciliation. Similarly, auditors normally compare the ending balance in cash with previous months' balances. These analytical procedures may uncover misstatements in cash.

Audit Procedures for Year-End Cash A major consideration in the audit of the general cash balance is the possibility of fraud. The auditor must extend his or her procedures in the audit of year-end cash to determine the possibility of a material fraud when there are inadequate internal controls, especially the improper segregation of duties between the handling of cash and the recording of cash transactions in the journals. The study of cash in the following section assumes the existence of adequate controls over cash; therefore, fraud detection is not emphasized. At the completion of the study of typical audit procedures for the verification of year-end cash, procedures designed primarily for the detection of fraud are discussed.

The starting point for the verification of the balance in the general bank account is obtaining a bank reconciliation from the client for inclusion in the auditor's working papers. Figure 15-4 shows a bank reconciliation after adjustments. Notice that the bottom figure in the working paper is the adjusted balance in the general ledger. Although the bank reconciliation is normally prepared manually, or using a spreadsheet, many accounting systems allow the client to use computerized systems to prepare the list of outstanding cheques.

The frame of reference for the audit tests is the bank reconciliation. The balance-related audit objectives and common tests of details of balances are shown in Table 15-1. As in all other audit areas, the actual audit procedures depend on the risks and controls in the transaction cycles. Also, because of their close relationship in the audit of year-end cash, the existence of recorded cash in the bank, accuracy, and inclusion of existing cash (completeness) are combined. These three objectives are the most important ones for cash and therefore receive the greatest attention.

The following three procedures are discussed thoroughly because of their importance and complexity.

RECEIPT OF A BANK CONFIRMATION The direct receipt of a confirmation from every bank or other financial institution with which the client does business is necessary for every audit except when there are an unusually large number of inactive accounts. If the bank does not respond to a confirmation request, the auditor must send a second request or ask the client to telephone the bank. As a convenience to CAs as well as to bankers who are requested to fill out bank confirmations, the CICA has approved the use of a **standard bank confirmation form**. Figure 15-5 on page 462 is an illustration of such a completed standard bank

STANDARD BANK CONFIRMATION FORM—a form approved by the CICA and Canadian Bankers Association through which the bank responds to the auditor's request for information about the client's bank balances, loan information, and contingent liabilities

FIGURE 15-4   **Working Paper for a Bank Reconciliation**

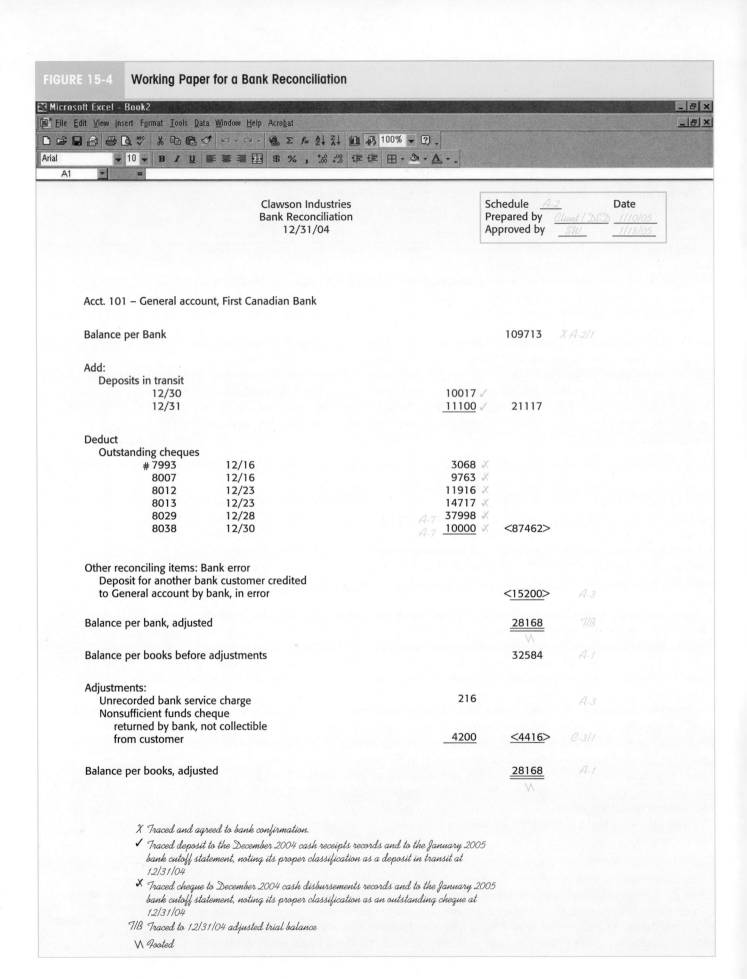

Clawson Industries
Bank Reconciliation
12/31/04

Schedule	A-2	Date
Prepared by	Client / DCD	1/10/05
Approved by	SW	1/18/05

Acct. 101 – General account, First Canadian Bank

Balance per Bank   109713   X A-2/1

Add:
   Deposits in transit
       12/30   10017 ✓
       12/31   11100 ✓   21117

Deduct
   Outstanding cheques
      # 7993   12/16   3068 X
       8007   12/16   9763 X
       8012   12/23   11916 X
       8013   12/23   14717 X
       8029   12/28   A-7   37998 X
       8038   12/30   A-7   10000 X   <87462>

Other reconciling items: Bank error
   Deposit for another bank customer credited
   to General account by bank, in error   <15200>   A-3

Balance per bank, adjusted   28168   T/B
                                                  W

Balance per books before adjustments   32584   A-1

Adjustments:
   Unrecorded bank service charge   216   A-3
   Nonsufficient funds cheque
     returned by bank, not collectible
     from customer   4200   <4416>   C-3/1

Balance per books, adjusted   28168   A-1
                                                   W

X Traced and agreed to bank confirmation.

✓ Traced deposit to the December 2004 cash receipts records and to the January 2005
   bank cutoff statement, noting its proper classification as a deposit in transit at
   12/31/04

X Traced cheque to December 2004 cash disbursements records and to the January 2005
   bank cutoff statement, noting its proper classification as an outstanding cheque at
   12/31/04

T/B Traced to 12/31/04 adjusted trial balance

W Footed

confirmation. This standard form has been agreed upon by the CICA and the Canadian Bankers Association. Similarly, CGAAC and the Canadian Bankers Association have approved a similar bank confirmation form for use by CGAs.

The importance of bank confirmations in the audit extends beyond the verification of the actual cash balance. It is typical for the bank to confirm loan information and bank balances on the same form. The confirmation in Figure 15-5 includes three outstanding loans and a contingent liability. Information on liabilities to the bank for notes, mortgages, or other debt typically includes the amount of the loan, the date of the loan, its due date, interest rate, and the existence of collateral.

The auditor completes the sections labelled "client," "chartered accountant," "financial institution," and "confirmation date"; a signing officer from the client signs in the "client" box authorizing the bank to provide the information; and the auditor sends the confirmation to the bank. While the bank should exercise due care in completing the confirmation, errors can occur. The auditor may wish to communicate with the bank if there is any information on the returned confirmation about which he or she is dubious or if any information that was expected is not reported.

TABLE 15-1	Balance-Related Audit Objectives and Tests of Details of Balances for General Cash in the Bank	
Balance-Related Audit Objective	**Common Tests of Details of Balances Procedures**	**Comments**
Cash in the bank as stated on the bank reconciliation foots correctly and agrees with the general ledger (detail tie-in).	Foot the outstanding cheque list and deposits in transit. Prove the bank reconciliation as to additions and subtractions, including all reconciling items. Trace the book balance on the reconciliation to the general ledger.	These tests are done entirely on the bank reconciliation, with no reference to documents or other records except the general ledger.
Cash in the bank as stated on the reconciliation exists (existence). Existing cash in the bank is included (completeness). Cash in the bank as stated on the reconciliation is accurate (accuracy).	(See extended discussion for each of these.) Obtain and test a bank confirmation. Obtain and test a cutoff bank statement. Test the bank reconciliation. Perform extended tests of the bank reconciliation. Prepare proof of cash. Test for kiting.	The first three procedures are the most important objectives for cash in the bank. The procedures are combined because of their close interdependence. The last three procedures should be done only when there are internal control weaknesses.
Cash receipts and cash disbursements transactions are recorded in the proper period (cutoff).	*Cash receipts* Count the cash on hand on the first day of the year and subsequently trace to deposits in transit and the cash receipts journal. Trace deposits in transit to subsequent period bank statement (cutoff bank statement). *Cash disbursements* Record the last cheque number used on the last day of the year and subsequently trace to the outstanding cheques and the cash disbursements journal. Trace outstanding cheques to subsequent period bank statement.	When cash receipts received after year end are included in the journal, a better cash position than actually exists is shown. It is called "holding open" the cash receipts journal. Holding open the cash disbursements journal reduces accounts payable and usually overstates the current ratio. The first procedure listed for receipts and disbursement cutoff tests requires the auditor's presence on the client's premises at the end of the last day of the year.
Cash in the bank is properly presented and disclosed (presentation and disclosure).	Examine minutes, loan agreements, and obtain confirmation for restrictions on the use of cash and compensating balances. Review financial statements to make sure (a) material savings accounts and guaranteed investment certificates, if access is restricted, are disclosed separately from cash in the bank, (b) cash restricted to certain uses and compensating balances are adequately disclosed, and (c) bank overdrafts are included as current liabilities.	An example of a restriction on the use of cash is cash deposited with a trustee for the payment of mortgage interest and taxes on the proceeds of a construction mortgage. A compensating balance is the client's agreement with a bank to maintain a specified minimum in its chequing account.

BANK CONFIRMATION

(Areas to be completed by client are marked §, while those to be completed by the financial institutions are marked †)

FINANCIAL INSTITUTION	CLIENT (Legal Name) §
(Name, branch, and full mailing address) §	Koa Foods Inc.
Bank of Columbia	St. Jacobs, Ontario
Westmount & Old Post Road	NOL 1KO
Waterloo, Ontario	The financial institution is authorized to provide the details requested herein to the below-noted firm of accountants
N2L 5M1	§ *J Koa*
CONFIRMATION DATE § December 31, 2004	Client's authorized signature
(All information to be provided as of this date)	Please supply copy of the most recent credit facility agreement (initial if required) § _____
(See Bank Confirmation Completion Instructions)	

1. LOANS AND OTHER DIRECT AND CONTINGENT LIABILITIES (If balances are nil, please state.)

NATURE OF LIABILITY/ CONTINGENT LIABILITY †	INTEREST (Note rate per contract) RATE † DATE PAID TO †		DUE DATE †	DATE OF CREDIT FACILITY AGREEMENT †	AMOUNT AND CURRENCY OUTSTANDING †
Loan	8%	31/12/04	Demand	5/5/99	$90,000
Loan	9%	30/11/04	30/5/06	1/4/98	$120,000
Loan	10%	31/12/04	Demand	1/6/00	$20,000
Guarantee	N/A		N/A	1/1/93	$8,000

ADDITIONAL CREDIT FACILITY AGREEMENT(S)

Note the date(s) of any credit facility agreement(s) not drawn upon and not referenced above †

2. DEPOSITS/OVERDRAFTS

TYPE OF ACCOUNT §	ACCOUNT NUMBER §	INTEREST RATE §	ISSUE DATE (if applicable) §	MATURITY DATE (if applicable) §	AMOUNT AND CURRENCY (Bracket if Overdraft) †
General	65422	—	—	—	$109,713
Payroll	65432	—	—	—	$4,000

EXCEPTIONS AND COMMENTS
(See Bank Confirmation Completion Instructions) †

STATEMENT OF PROCEDURES PERFORMED BY FINANCIAL INSTITUTION †
The above information was completed in accordance with the Bank Confirmation Completion Instructions.

Bill Brown   **Branch Contact**   W. Brown   (519) 884-1921
Authorized signature of financial institution   **Name and telephone number**

Please mail this form directly to our chartered accountant in the enclosed addressed envelope.

Name:	Kadous & Co.
Address:	P.O. Box 1939
	Waterloo, Ontario N2L 1G1
Telephone:	(519) 999-1234
Fax:	(519) 999-1235

Developed by the Canadian Bankers Association and the Canadian Institute of Chartered Accountants

After the bank confirmation has been received, the balance in the bank account confirmed by the bank should be traced to the amount stated on the bank reconciliation. Similarly, all other information on the reconciliation should be traced to the relevant audit working papers. In any case, if the information is not in agreement, an investigation must be made of the difference.

RECEIPT OF A CUTOFF BANK STATEMENT A **cutoff bank statement** includes a partial-period bank statement and the related cancelled cheques, duplicate deposit slips, and other documents included with bank statements, mailed by the bank directly to the public accounting firm's office. The purpose of the cutoff bank statement is to verify the reconciling items on the client's year-end bank reconciliation with evidence that is inaccessible to the client. To fulfill this purpose, the auditor requests that the client have the bank send directly to the auditor the statement for seven to ten days subsequent to the balance sheet date.

CUTOFF BANK STATEMENT—a partial-period bank statement and the related cancelled cheques, duplicate deposit slips, and other documents included in bank statements, mailed by the bank directly to the auditor. The auditor uses it to verify reconciling items on the client's year-end bank reconciliation

Many auditors prove the subsequent period bank statement if a cutoff statement is not received directly from the bank. The purpose of this proof is to test whether the client's employees have omitted, added, or altered any of the documents accompanying the statement. It is obviously a test for intentional misstatements. The auditor performs the proof in the month subsequent to the balance sheet date by (1) footing all the cancelled cheques, debit memos, deposits, and credit memos; (2) checking to see that the bank statement balances when the footed totals are used; and (3) reviewing the items included in the footings to make sure they were cancelled by the bank in the proper period and do not include any erasures or alterations.

TESTS OF THE BANK RECONCILIATION The reason for testing the bank reconciliation is to verify whether the client's recorded bank balance is the same amount as the actual cash in the bank except for deposits in transit, outstanding cheques, and other reconciling items. In testing the reconciliation, the cutoff bank statement provides the information for conducting the tests. Several major procedures are involved:

- Verify that the client's bank reconciliation is mathematically accurate.
- Trace the balance on the cutoff statement to the balance per bank on the bank reconciliation. A reconciliation is incomplete until these two are the same.
- Trace cheques included with the cutoff bank statement to the list of outstanding cheques on the bank reconciliation and to the cash disbursements journal. All cheques that cleared the bank after the balance sheet date and were included in the cash disbursements journal should also be included on the outstanding cheque list. If a cheque was included in the cash disbursements journal, it should be included as an outstanding cheque if it did not clear before the balance sheet date. Similarly, if a cheque cleared the bank prior to the balance sheet date, it should not be on the bank reconciliation.
- Investigate all significant cheques included on the outstanding cheque list that have not cleared the bank on the cutoff statement. The first step in the investigation should be tracing the amount of any items not clearing to the cash disbursements journal. The reason for the cheque not being cashed should be discussed with the client, and if the auditor is concerned about the possibility of fraud, the vendor's accounts payable balance should be confirmed to determine whether the vendor has recognized the receipt of the cash in its records. In addition, the cancelled cheque should be examined prior to the last day of the audit if it becomes available.
- Trace deposits in transit to the subsequent bank statement. All cash receipts not deposited in the bank at the end of the year should be traced to the cutoff bank statement to ensure they were deposited shortly after the beginning of the new year.
- Account for other reconciling items on the bank statement and bank reconciliation. These include such items as bank service charges, bank errors and corrections, and unrecorded note transactions debited or credited directly to the bank account by the bank. These reconciling items should be carefully investigated to ensure they have been treated properly by the client.

Summary of Audit Tests for the General Cash Account Figure 15-6 illustrates the types of audit tests used to audit the general cash account. This figure also shows how the audit risk model discussed in Chapter 8 relates to the audit of the general cash account.

FIGURE 15-6 Types of Audit Tests Used for General Cash

Cash in bank

| Beginning balance | |
| Cash receipts | Cash disbursements |

Audited by
POU-T, TOC-T, & AP

Audited by
POU-T, TOC-T, & AP

Ending balance

Audited by
POU-B, TOC-B,
AP, & TDB

| Procedures to obtain an understanding of internal control in transaction cycles* (POU-T) | + | Procedures to obtain an understanding of internal control over bank reconciliation process (POU-B) | + | Tests of controls in transaction cycles* (TOC-T) | + | Tests of controls over bank reconciliation process (TOC-B) | + | Analytical procedures* (AP) | + | Tests of details of balances (TDB) | = | Sufficient appropriate audit evidence per GAAS |

Extent of substantive testing is determined by assessed risks, materiality, and *PDR*. *PDR* is affected by factors in the audit risk model:

$$AR = IR \times CR \times PDR \quad or \quad PDR = \frac{AR}{IR \times CR}$$

* Procedures to obtain an understanding of internal control, tests of controls in transaction cycles, and analytical procedures are done for the four transaction cycles included in Figure 15-2. The primary tests of the ending cash balance are tests of details of balances.

→15.3 FRAUD-ORIENTED PROCEDURES

It is frequently necessary for auditors to extend their year-end audit procedures to test more extensively for the possibility of material fraud when there are material internal control weaknesses. Many fraudulent activities are difficult, if not impossible, to uncover; nevertheless, auditors are responsible for making a reasonable effort to detect fraud when they have reason to believe it may exist. The following procedures for uncovering fraud are discussed in this section: extended tests of the bank reconciliation, proofs of cash, and tests for kiting.

EXTENDED TESTS OF THE BANK RECONCILIATION When the auditor believes that the year-end bank reconciliation may be intentionally misstated, it is appropriate to perform extended tests of the year-end bank reconciliation. The purpose of the extended procedures is to verify whether all transactions included in the journals for the last month of the year were correctly included in or excluded from the bank reconciliation and to verify whether all items in the bank reconciliation were correctly included. Let us assume that there are material internal control weaknesses and that the client's year end is December 31. A common approach is to start with the bank reconciliation for November and compare all reconciling items with cancelled cheques and other documents in the December bank statement. In addition, all remaining cancelled cheques and deposit slips in the December bank statement should be compared with the December cash disbursements and receipts journals. All uncleared items in the November bank reconciliation and the December cash disbursements and receipts journals should be included in the client's December 31 bank reconciliation. Similarly, all reconciling items in the December 31 bank reconciliation should be items from the November bank reconciliation and December's journals that have not yet cleared the bank.

In addition to the tests just described, the auditor must also carry out procedures subsequent to the end of the year using the bank cutoff statement. These tests would be performed in the same manner as previously discussed.

PROOF OF CASH Auditors sometimes prepare a **proof of cash** when the client has material internal control weaknesses in cash. A proof of cash includes the following:

- A reconciliation of the balance on the bank statement with the general ledger balance at the beginning of the proof-of-cash period

PROOF OF CASH—a four-column working paper prepared by the auditor to reconcile the bank's record of the client's beginning balance, cash deposits, cleared cheques, and ending balance for the period with the client's records

- A reconciliation of cash receipts deposited with the cash receipts journal for a given period
- A reconciliation of cancelled cheques clearing the bank with the cash disbursements journal for a given period
- A reconciliation of the balance on the bank statement with the general ledger balance at the end of the proof-of-cash period

A proof of cash of this nature is commonly referred to as a four-column proof of cash—one column is used for each type of information listed above. A proof of cash can be performed for one or more interim months, the entire year, or the last month of the year. Figure 15-7 shows a four-column proof of cash for an interim month.

The auditor uses a proof of cash to determine whether

- All recorded cash receipts were deposited.
- All deposits in the bank were recorded in the accounting records.
- All recorded cash disbursements were paid by the bank.
- All amounts that were paid by the bank were recorded.

The concern in an interim-month proof of cash is not with adjusting account balances, but rather with reconciling the amounts per books and bank.

When the auditor does a proof of cash, he or she is combining tests of controls and tests of details of balances. For example, the proof of the cash receipts is a test of recorded transactions, whereas the bank reconciliation is a test of the balance in cash at a particular time. The proof of cash is an excellent method of comparing recorded cash receipts and disbursements with the bank account and with the bank reconciliation. However, the auditor must recognize that the proof of cash disbursements is not for discovering cheques written for an improper amount, fraudulent cheques, or other misstatements in which the dollar amount appearing on the cash disbursements records is incorrect. Similarly, the proof of cash receipts is not useful for uncovering the theft of cash receipts or the recording and deposit of an improper amount of cash.

TESTS FOR KITING Embezzlers occasionally cover a defalcation of cash by a practice known as **kiting**: transferring money from one bank to another and improperly recording the transaction. Near the balance sheet date, a cheque is drawn on one bank account and immediately deposited in a second account for credit before the end of the accounting period. In making this transfer, the embezzler is careful to make sure that the cheque is deposited at a late enough date so that it does not clear the first bank until after the end of the period. Assuming that the bank transfer is not recorded until after the balance sheet date, the amount of the transfer is recorded as an asset in both banks. Although there are other ways of perpetrating this fraud, each involves the basic device of increasing the bank balance to cover a shortage by the use of bank transfers.

KITING—the transfer of money from one bank account to another and improperly recording the transfer so that the amount is recorded as an asset in both accounts; used by embezzlers to cover a defalcation of cash

A useful approach to test for kiting, as well as for unintentional errors in recording bank transfers, is listing all bank transfers made a few days before and after the balance sheet date and tracing each to the accounting records for proper recording. An example of a bank transfer schedule is included in Figure 15-8. The working paper shows that there were four bank transfers shortly before and after the balance sheet date.

There are several things that should be audited on the bank transfer schedule.

- *The accuracy of the information on the bank transfer schedule should be verified.* The auditor should compare the disbursement and receipt information on the schedule to the cash disbursements and cash receipts journals to make sure that it is accurate. Similarly, the dates on the schedule for transfers that were received and disbursed should be compared to the bank statement. Finally, cash disbursements and receipts journals should be examined to ensure that all transfers a few days before and after the balance sheet date have been included on the schedule. The symbol explanations on the working paper in Figure 15-8 indicate that these steps have been taken.
- *The bank transfers must be recorded in both the receiving and disbursing banks.* If, for example, there was a $10,000 transfer from Bank A to Bank B, but only the disbursement was recorded, this would be evidence of an attempt to conceal a cash theft.

FIGURE 15-7   Interim Proof of Cash

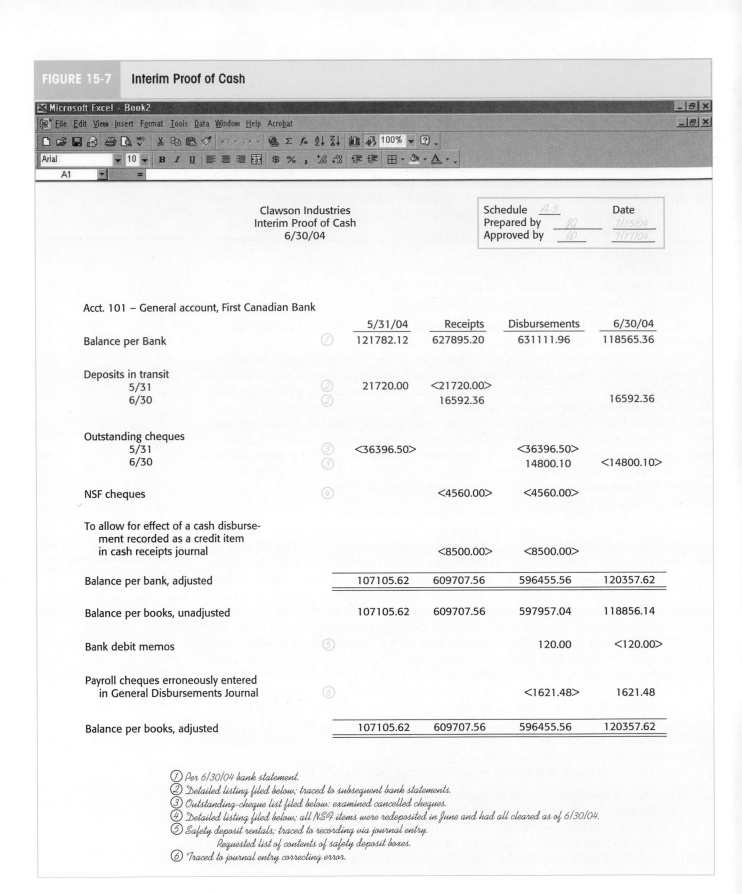

Clawson Industries
Interim Proof of Cash
6/30/04

Schedule _A-5_   Date
Prepared by _JG_   _7/15/04_
Approved by _RP_   _7/17/04_

Acct. 101 – General account, First Canadian Bank

		5/31/04	Receipts	Disbursements	6/30/04
Balance per Bank	①	121782.12	627895.20	631111.96	118565.36
Deposits in transit					
5/31	②	21720.00	<21720.00>		
6/30	②		16592.36		16592.36
Outstanding cheques					
5/31	③	<36396.50>		<36396.50>	
6/30	③			14800.10	<14800.10>
NSF cheques	④		<4560.00>	<4560.00>	
To allow for effect of a cash disbursement recorded as a credit item in cash receipts journal			<8500.00>	<8500.00>	
Balance per bank, adjusted		107105.62	609707.56	596455.56	120357.62
Balance per books, unadjusted		107105.62	609707.56	597957.04	118856.14
Bank debit memos	⑤			120.00	<120.00>
Payroll cheques erroneously entered in General Disbursements Journal	⑥			<1621.48>	1621.48
Balance per books, adjusted		107105.62	609707.56	596455.56	120357.62

① Per 6/30/04 bank statement.
② Detailed listing filed below; traced to subsequent bank statements.
③ Outstanding-cheque list filed below; examined cancelled cheques.
④ Detailed listing filed below; all NSF items were redeposited in June and had all cleared as of 6/30/04.
⑤ Safety deposit rentals; traced to recording via journal entry.
        Requested list of contents of safety deposit boxes.
⑥ Traced to journal entry correcting error.

- *The date of the recording of the disbursements and receipts for each transfer must be in the same fiscal year.* In Figure 15-8, the dates in the two "date recorded in books" columns [columns (4) and (7)] are in the same period for each transfer; therefore, they are

FIGURE 15-8 **Bank Transfer Working Paper**

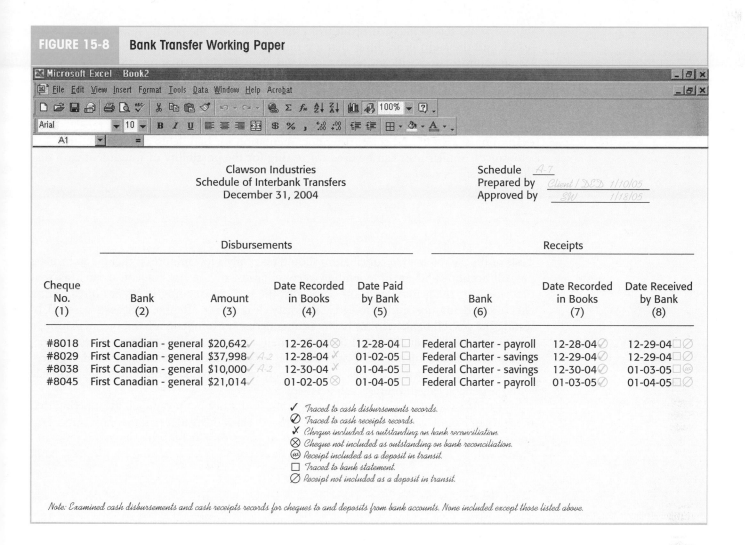

Clawson Industries
Schedule of Interbank Transfers
December 31, 2004

Schedule _A-7_
Prepared by _Client / DSD 1/10/05_
Approved by _SW   1/18/05_

			Disbursements			Receipts		
Cheque No. (1)	Bank (2)	Amount (3)	Date Recorded in Books (4)	Date Paid by Bank (5)	Bank (6)	Date Recorded in Books (7)	Date Received by Bank (8)
#8018	First Canadian - general	$20,642✓	12-26-04⊗	12-28-04☐	Federal Charter - payroll	12-28-04∅	12-29-04☐∅
#8029	First Canadian - general	$37,998✓ A-2	12-28-04✗	01-02-05☐	Federal Charter - savings	12-29-04∅	12-29-04☐∅
#8038	First Canadian - general	$10,000✓ A-2	12-30-04✗	01-04-05☐	Federal Charter - savings	12-30-04∅	01-03-05☐∅
#8045	First Canadian - general	$21,014✓	01-02-05⊗	01-04-05☐	Federal Charter - payroll	01-03-05∅	01-04-05☐∅

✓ Traced to cash disbursements records.
∅ Traced to cash receipts records.
✗ Cheque included as outstanding on bank reconciliation.
⊗ Cheque not included as outstanding on bank reconciliation.
ⓦ Receipt included as a deposit in transit.
☐ Traced to bank statement.
∅ Receipt not included as a deposit in transit.

Note: Examined cash disbursements and cash receipts records for cheques to and deposits from bank accounts. None included except those listed above.

correct. If a cash disbursement was recorded in the current fiscal year and the receipt in the subsequent fiscal year, it might be an attempt to cover a cash shortage.

- *Disbursements on the bank transfer schedule should be correctly included in or excluded from year-end bank reconciliations as outstanding cheques.* In Figure 15-8, the 12-31-04 bank reconciliation should include outstanding cheques for the second and third transfers but not the other two. [Compare the dates in columns (4) and (5).] Understating outstanding cheques on the bank reconciliation indicates the possibility of kiting.

- *Receipts on the bank transfer schedule should be correctly included in or excluded from year-end bank reconciliations as deposits in transit.* In Figure 15-8, the 12-31-04 bank reconciliation should indicate a deposit in transit for the third transfer but not for the other three. (Compare the dates for each transfer in the last two columns.) Overstating deposits in transit on the bank reconciliation indicates the possibility of kiting.

Even though audit tests of bank transfers are usually fraud-oriented, they are often performed on audits in which there are numerous bank transfers, regardless of the internal controls. When there are numerous intercompany transfers, it is difficult to be sure that each is correctly handled unless a schedule of transfers near the end of the year is prepared and each transfer is traced to the accounting records and bank statements. In addition to the possibility of kiting, inaccurate handling of transfers could result in a misclassification between cash and accounts payable. Due to the materiality of transfers and the relative ease of performing the tests, many auditors believe that the tests should always be performed.

SUMMARY OF FRAUD-ORIENTED PROCEDURES In designing audit procedures for uncovering fraud, careful consideration should be given to the nature of the weaknesses in internal control, the type of fraud that is likely to result from the weaknesses, the potential materiality of the fraud, and the audit procedures that are most effective in uncovering the misstatement. When auditors are specifically testing for fraud, they should keep in mind that audit procedures other than tests of details of cash balances may also be useful. Examples of procedures that may uncover fraud in the cash receipts area include the confirmation of accounts receivable, tests for lapping, reviewing the general ledger entries in the cash account for unusual items, tracing from customer orders to sales and subsequent cash receipts, and examining approvals and supporting documentation for bad debts and sales returns and allowances. Similar tests can be used for testing for the possibility of fraudulent cash disbursements.

→ 15.4 ADDITIONAL EXAMPLES OF CASH AUDITING

Audit of the Payroll Bank Account

Tests of the payroll bank reconciliation should take only a few minutes if there is an imprest payroll account and an independent reconciliation of the bank account such as that described for the general account. Typically, the only reconciling items are outstanding cheques, and, for most audits, the great majority clear shortly after the cheques are issued. In testing the payroll bank account balances, it is necessary to obtain a bank reconciliation, a bank confirmation, and a cutoff bank statement. The reconciliation procedures are performed in the same manner as those described for general cash. Naturally, extended procedures are necessary if the controls are inadequate or if the bank account does not reconcile with the general ledger imprest cash balance.

The discussion in the preceding paragraph should not be interpreted as implying that the audit of payroll is unimportant. Chapter 16 will show the reader that the most important audit procedures for verifying payroll are tests of controls. The most likely payroll misstatements will be discovered by those procedures rather than by checking the imprest bank account balance.

Audit of Electronic Cash Transactions

ELECTRONIC DATA INTERCHANGE (EDI)—the electronic transfer of business documents, such as invoices and purchase orders

ELECTRONIC FUNDS TRANSFER (EFT)—the electronic transfer of funds, either as payment or receipt (e.g., using a debit card)

As described in the focus box, many organizations are receiving cash or making cash payments electronically. For a typical small to medium-sized business, electronic cash receipts are used if the business sells to customers over the counter and accepts debit card payments from those customers. Electronic cash payments include automatic payments for loans, insurance, or payroll to employees. More sophisticated or larger businesses could use **electronic data interchange (EDI)** with their **electronic funds transfers (EFTs)**.

Control over Debit Card Cash Receipts When a business accepts debit card payments from its customers, the customer swipes his or her debit card and enters a personal identification number (PIN) to authorize the transfer of funds from the customer's bank account to the organization's bank account. At the same time, a two-part receipt is provided, with one copy going to the customer and the other to the organization.

Although most debit card transactions are processed accurately, a very small percentage are not. The organization should therefore continue its cash reconciliation functions as part of the bank reconciliation for these electronic transactions. Most organizations keep track of payment methods automatically using their point-of-sale (POS) systems. Thus, the daily sales are broken down by cash, debit card, credit card, cheque, and accounts receivable. When performing the bank reconciliation, the debit card total should agree to the amounts automatically deposited in the bank statement. This reconciliation should be handled by a person independent of the POS function. These receipts should be tested as part of the sales, receivables transaction cycle.

Control over Electronic Payments

AUTOMATIC PRE-AUTHORIZED MONTHLY PAYMENTS Loan payments, interest payments, and insurance payments made on a monthly or other regular interval are based on a loan agreement or regular invoice. When the bank statement is sent to an organization, likely the only evidence of this payment will be a line on the bank statement showing the amount, a reference number, and possibly the name of the company that was paid.

The organization under audit should have controls to ensure that only authorized amounts are set up for payment, and that all automatic withdrawals are recorded in the accounts in the period made. These payments should be tested as part of the purchases, payments cycle.

PAYROLL PAYMENTS As with a payroll paid by cheque, payroll payments made electronically should be paid using an imprest bank account.

Payment is usually initiated by the organization sending to the bank or other financial institution a set of forms or electronic data files specifying how much employees should be paid, what deductions should be made, the appropriate tax withholdings, and the bank accounts to which the funds should be transferred. The bank may (or may not) do the actual calculations, process payments, and send either a listing or a data file to the organization of payments made.

Again, there is a two-step authorization phase here. The first step covers master file information (e.g., wage rate, withholdings rate, bank account number), and the second covers the actual wages paid in a specific pay period. These controls should be documented, evaluated, and tested as part of the personnel and payroll cycle. As part of control over cash, a person independent of payroll should verify bank account numbers used for payments and should verify that payments from the imprest bank account match the payroll journal.

Audit of Electronic Receipts and Payments The extent of audit work conducted on the bank reconciliation depends on the assessed quality of internal controls. There are usually fewer outstanding bank transactions for electronic transactions than for paper transactions sent via mail since the timing difference between invoice and receipt is minimal.

When client personnel prepare the bank reconciliation, electronic payments should be agreed to an authorized schedule of such payments by date, payee account number, and amount. The auditor would review the authorized schedule of payments and controls over its preparation. Similarly, deposits would be traced to the client's POS system records.

For the imprest payroll account reconciliation, the auditor would review the documentation received from the bank and agree details to the reconciliation.

Summary For electronic receipts and payments, the discussion shows that there are changes in the types of controls required and the type of evidence available to the auditor. However, standard audit procedures are still used to verify existence, completeness, and accuracy.

Audit of Petty Cash

Petty cash is a unique account because it is frequently immaterial in amount, yet it is verified on most audits. The account is verified primarily because of the potential for defalcation and the client's expectation of an audit review even when the amount is immaterial.

Internal Controls over Petty Cash The most important internal control for petty cash is the use of an imprest fund that is the responsibility of *one individual*. In addition, petty cash funds should not be mingled with other receipts, and the fund should be kept separate from all other activities. There should also be limits on the amount of any expenditure from petty cash, as well as on the total amount of the fund. The type of expenditure that can be made from petty cash transactions should be well defined by company policy.

Whenever a disbursement is made from petty cash, adequate internal controls require a responsible official's approval on a prenumbered petty cash form. The total of the actual cash and cheques in the fund plus the total unreimbursed petty cash forms that represent actual expenditures should equal the total amount of the petty cash fund stated in the general ledger. Periodically, surprise counts and a reconciliation of the petty cash fund should be made by the internal auditor or another responsible official.

When the petty cash balance runs low, a cheque payable to the petty cash custodian should be written on the general cash account for the reimbursement of petty cash. The cheque should be for the exact amount of the prenumbered vouchers that are submitted as evidence of actual expenditures. These vouchers should be verified by the accounts payable clerk and cancelled to prevent their re-use.

Audit Tests for Petty Cash The emphasis in verifying petty cash should be on testing petty cash transactions rather than the ending balance in the account. Even if the amount of the petty cash fund is small, there is potential for numerous improper transactions if the fund is frequently reimbursed.

An important part of testing petty cash is first determining the client's procedures for handling the fund by discussing internal control with the custodian and examining the documentation of a few transactions. As a part of obtaining an understanding of internal control, it is necessary to identify internal controls and weaknesses. Even though most petty cash systems are not complex, it is often desirable to use a flowchart and an internal control questionnaire, primarily for documentation in subsequent audits. The tests of controls depend on the number and size of the petty cash reimbursements and the auditor's assessed level of control risk. When control risk is assessed at a low level and there are few reimbursement payments during the year, it is common for auditors not to test any further for reasons of immateriality. When the auditor decides to test petty cash, the two most common procedures are counting the petty cash balance and carrying out detailed tests of one or two reimbursement transactions. In such a case, the primary procedures should include footing the petty cash vouchers supporting the amount of the reimbursement, accounting for a sequence of petty cash vouchers, examining the petty cash vouchers for authorization and cancellation, and examining the attached documentation for reasonableness. Typical supporting documentation includes cash register tapes, invoices, and receipts.

Petty cash tests can ordinarily be performed at any time during the year, but as a matter of convenience, they are typically done on an interim date. If the balance in the petty cash fund is considered material, which is rarely the case, it should be counted at the end of the year. Unreimbursed expenditures should be examined as part of the count to determine whether the amount of unrecorded expenses is material.

SUMMARY

1. *What are the different types of cash accounts?* There are the general cash account, the imprest payroll account, branch bank accounts, an imprest petty cash fund, and cash equivalents.

    Explain the relationship between cash and the transaction cycles. Cash flows in and out of the cash account, with the other side of the accounting entry normally being in a different transaction cycle. For example, payroll payments, accounts payable payments, and receipts from sales all are recorded via the cash account.

2. *Describe the steps in auditing the general cash account.* Figure 15-3 describes the risk-based audit approach as it applies to cash. After assessing control risk on an assertion basis, tests of controls are designed and performed, followed by the design and completion of tests of details. Year-end procedures include obtaining a bank confirmation and a bank cutoff statement, as well as tests of the bank reconciliation.

3. *What additional procedures are conducted when there is sus-* picion of fraud? Extended tests of the bank reconciliation or a proof of cash could be completed.

    What is "kiting" and how is it audited? If kiting is suspected (taking advantage of timing differences between banks to inflate cash) then the auditor would prepare a bank transfer working paper.

4. *How is an audit of the payroll cash account different from the audit of the general cash account?* The payroll account may be an imprest account, containing only payroll cheques issued to employees. Having only a single transaction type means that it is easier to audit the account.

    What special considerations exist for EFT (electronic funds transfer) transactions? Such transactions could involve complex software and access controls, requiring an increased reliance on automated computer controls.

    How is petty cash audited? The auditor would likely examine controls over petty cash and conduct a petty cash count.

ESSENTIAL TERMS

Bank reconciliation—the monthly reconciliation, usually prepared by client personnel, of the differences between the cash balance recorded in the general ledger and the amount in the bank account   (p. 458).

Branch bank account—a separate bank account maintained at a local bank by a branch of a company   (p. 454).

Cash equivalents—excess cash invested in short-term, highly liquid investments, such as term deposits, certificates of deposit, and money market funds   (p. 455).

Cutoff bank statement—a partial-period bank statement and the related cancelled cheques, duplicate deposit slips, and other documents included in bank statements, mailed by the bank directly to the auditor. The auditor uses it to verify reconciling items on the client's year-end bank reconciliation   (p. 463).

Electronic data interchange (EDI)—the electronic transfer of business documents, such as invoices and purchase orders (p. 468).

Electronic funds transfer (EFT)—the electronic transfer of funds, either as payment or receipt (e.g., using a debit card) (p. 468).

General cash account—the primary bank account for most organizations; virtually all cash receipts and disbursements flow through this account at some time   (p. 454).

Imprest payroll account—a bank account to which the exact amount of payroll for the pay period is transferred by cheque from the employer's general cash account   (p. 454).

Imprest petty cash fund—a fund of cash maintained within the company for small cash payments; its fixed balance is comparatively small, and it is periodically reimbursed   (p. 455).

Kiting—the transfer of money from one bank account to another and improperly recording the transfer so that the amount is recorded as an asset in both accounts; used by embezzlers to cover a defalcation of cash   (p. 465).

Proof of cash—a four-column working paper prepared by the auditor to reconcile the bank's record of the client's beginning balance, cash deposits, cleared cheques, and ending balance for the period with the client's records   (p. 464).

Standard bank confirmation form—a form approved by the CICA and Canadian Bankers Association through which the bank responds to the auditor's request for information about the client's bank balances, loan information, and contingent liabilities   (p. 459).

REVIEW QUESTIONS

15-1 Explain the relationship between the initial assessed level of control risk, tests of controls for cash receipts, and tests of details of cash balances.

15-2 Explain the relationships between the initial assessed level of control risk, tests of controls for cash disbursements, and tests of details of cash balances. Give one example in which the conclusions reached about internal controls in cash disbursements would affect the tests of cash balances.

15-3 Why is the monthly reconciliation of bank accounts by an independent person an important internal control over cash balances? Which individuals would generally not be considered independent for this responsibility?

15-4 How do bank confirmations differ from positive confirmations of accounts receivable? Distinguish between them in terms of the nature of the information confirmed, the sample size, and the appropriate action when the confirmation is not returned after the second request. Explain the rationale for the differences between these two types of confirmations.

15-5 Why are auditors usually less concerned about the client's cash receipts cutoff than the cutoff for sales? Explain the procedure involved in testing for the cutoff for cash receipts.

15-6 What is meant by an "imprest bank account" for a branch operation? Explain the purpose of using this type of bank account.

15-7 When the auditor fails to obtain a cutoff bank statement, it is common to "prove" the entire statement for the month subsequent to the balance sheet date. How is this done and what is its purpose?

15-8 Distinguish between lapping and kiting. Describe audit procedures that can be used to uncover each.

15-9 Assume that a client with excellent internal controls uses an imprest payroll bank account. Explain why the verification of the payroll bank reconciliation ordinarily takes less time than the tests of the general bank account even if the number of cheques exceeds those written on the general account.

15-10 Distinguish between the verification of petty cash reimbursements and the verification of the balance in the fund. Explain how each is done. Which is more important?

15-11 Why is there a greater emphasis on the detection of fraud in tests of details of cash balances than for other balance sheet accounts? Give two specific examples that demonstrate how this emphasis affects the auditor's evidence accumulation in auditing year-end cash.

15-12 Explain why, in verifying bank reconciliations, most auditors emphasize the possibility of a nonexistent deposit in transit being included in the reconciliation and an outstanding cheque being omitted rather than the omission of a deposit in transit and the inclusion of a nonexistent outstanding cheque.

15-13 How would a company's bank reconciliation reflect an electronic deposit of cash received by the bank from credit card agencies making payments on behalf of customers purchasing products from the company's online web site, but not recorded in the company's records?

MULTIPLE CHOICE QUESTIONS

15-14 Choose the best response for the following:

a. A public accountant obtains a January 10 cutoff bank statement for a client directly from the bank. Very few of the outstanding cheques listed on the client's December 31 bank reconciliation cleared during the cutoff period. A probable cause for this is that the client

 (1) sent the cheques to the payees after year end.
 (2) has overstated its year-end bank balance.
 (3) is engaged in kiting.
 (4) is engaged in lapping.

b. The auditor should ordinarily mail confirmation requests to all banks with which the client has conducted any business during the year, regardless of the year-end balance, since

 (1) the mailing of confirmation forms to all such banks is required by generally accepted auditing standards.
 (2) the confirmation form also seeks information about indebtedness to the bank.
 (3) this procedure will detect kiting activities that would otherwise not be detected.
 (4) this procedure relieves the auditor of any responsibility with respect to nondetection of forged cheques.

c. On December 31, 2004, a company erroneously prepared an accounts payable transaction (debit cash, credit accounts payable) for a transfer of funds between banks. A cheque for the transfer was drawn January 3, 2005. This resulted in overstatements of cash and accounts payable at December 31, 2004. Of the following procedures, the most effective in disclosing this misstatement would be review of the

 (1) schedule of interbank transfers.
 (2) December 31, 2004, bank reconciliation for the two banks.
 (3) December 2004 cheque register.
 (4) support for accounts payable at December 31, 2004.

(AICPA adapted)

d. Which of the following is one of the better auditing techniques to detect kiting?

 (1) Prepare year-end bank reconciliations.
 (2) Prepare a schedule of bank transfers from the client's books.
 (3) Review composition of authenticated deposit slips.
 (4) Review subsequent bank statements and cancelled cheques received directly from the banks.

e. The cashier of Baker Company Ltd. in Yorkton, Saskatchewan, covered a shortage in the branch petty cash fund with cash obtained on December 31 from a bank in Yorkton by cashing an unrecorded cheque drawn on the Regina branch of another bank used by the company. The auditor would discover this manipulation by

 (1) preparing independent bank reconciliations as of December 31.
 (2) confirming the December 31 bank balances.
 (3) counting the petty cash fund at the close of business on December 31.
 (4) investigating items returned with the bank cutoff statements.

(AICPA adapted)

15-15 The following are fraud and other irregularities that might be found in the client's year-end cash balance. (Assume the balance sheet date is June 30.)

1. A cheque was omitted from the outstanding cheque list on the June 30 bank reconciliation. It cleared the bank July 7.
2. A cheque was omitted from the outstanding cheque list on the bank reconciliation. It cleared the bank September 6.
3. Cash receipts collected on accounts receivable from July 2 to July 5 were included as June 29 and 30 cash receipts.
4. A loan from the bank on June 26 was credited directly to the client's bank account. The loan was not entered in the books as of June 30.

5. A cheque that was dated June 26 and disbursed in June was not recorded in the cash disbursements journal, but it was included as an outstanding cheque on June 30.
6. A bank transfer recorded in the accounting records on July 2 was included as a deposit in transit on June 30.
7. The outstanding cheques on the June 30 bank reconciliation were underfooted by $2,000.

Required

a. Assuming that each of these misstatements was intentional, state the most likely motivation of the person responsible.
b. What control could be instituted for each intentional misstatement to reduce the likelihood of occurrence?
c. List an audit procedure that could be used to discover each misstatement.

15-16 You are auditing general cash for Trail Supply Corp. for the fiscal year ended July 31. The client has not prepared the July 31 bank reconciliation. After a brief discussion with the owner, you agree to prepare the reconciliation with assistance from one of Trail Supply's clerks. You obtain the following information:

	General Ledger	Bank Statement
Beginning balance	$ 4,611	$ 5,753
Deposits		25,056
Cash receipts journal	25,456	
Cheques cleared		(23,615)
Cash disbursements journal	(21,811)	
July bank service charge		(87)
Note paid directly		(6,100)
NSF cheque		(311)
Ending balance	$ 8,256	$ 696

June 30 Bank Reconciliation

Information in General Ledger and Bank Statement	
Balance per bank	$5,753
Deposits in transit	600
Outstanding cheques	1,742
Balance per books	4,611

In addition, the following information is obtained:

1. Cheques clearing that were outstanding on June 30 totalled $1,692.
2. Cheques clearing that were recorded in the July disbursements journal totalled $20,467.
3. A cheque for $1,060 cleared the bank but had not been recorded in the cash disbursements journal. It was for an acquisition of inventory. Trail Supply uses the periodic inventory method.
4. A cheque for $396 was charged to Trail Supply but had been written on a different associated company's bank account.
5. Deposits included $600 from June and $24,456 for July.
6. The bank charged Trail Supply's account for a nonsufficient funds (NSF) cheque totalling $311. The credit manager concluded that the customer intentionally closed its account and the owner left the city. The cheque was turned over to a collection agency.
7. The bank deducted $5,800 plus interest from Trail Supply's account for a loan made by the bank under an agreement signed four months ago. The note payable was recorded at $5,800 on Trail Supply's books.

Required

a. Prepare a bank reconciliation that shows both the unadjusted and adjusted balances as per the books.
b. Identify the nature of adjustments required.
c. What audit procedures would you use to verify each item in the bank reconciliation?

15-17 In the audit of the Regional Transport Company, a large branch that maintains its own bank account, cash is periodically transferred to the central account in Montreal. On the branch account's records, bank transfers are recorded as a debit to the home office clearing account and a credit to the branch bank account. Similarly, the home office account is recorded as a debit to the central bank account and a credit to the branch office clearing account. Gordon Light is the head bookkeeper for both the home office and the branch bank accounts. Because he also reconciles the bank account, the senior auditor, Cindy Marintette, is concerned about the internal control weakness.

As a part of the year-end audit of bank transfers, Marintette asks you to schedule the transfers for the last few days in 2004 and the first few days of 2005. You prepare the following list:

Amount of Transfer	Date Recorded in the Home Office Cash Receipts Journal	Date Recorded in the Branch Office Cash Disbursements Journal	Date Deposited in the Home Office Bank Account	Date Cleared the Branch Bank Account
$12,000	12-27-04	12-29-04	12-26-04	12-27-04
26,000	12-28-04	01-02-05	12-28-04	12-29-04
14,000	01-02-05	12-30-04	12-28-04	12-29-04
11,000	12-26-04	12-26-04	12-28-04	01-03-05
15,000	01-02-05	01-02-05	12-28-04	12-31-04
28,000	01-07-05	01-05-05	12-28-04	01-03-05
37,000	01-04-05	01-06-05	01-03-05	01-05-05

Required

a In verifying each bank transfer, state the appropriate audit procedures you should perform.

b. Prepare any adjusting entries required in the home office records.

c. Prepare any adjusting entries required in the branch bank records.

d. State how each bank transfer should be included in the December 31, 2004, bank reconciliation for the home office account after your adjustments in part b.

e. State how each bank transfer should be included in the December 31, 2004, bank reconciliation of the branch bank account after your adjustments in part c.

15-18 In connection with an audit you are given the following worksheet:

Bank Reconciliation, December 31, 2004

Balance per ledger December 31, 2004	$17,174.86
Add:	
Cash receipts received on the last day of December and charged to "cash in bank" on books but not deposited	2,662.25
Debit memo for customer's cheque returned unpaid (cheque is on hand but no entry has been made on the books)	200.00
Debit memo for bank service charge for December	5.50
	$20,142.61
Deduct:	
Cheques drawn but not paid by bank (see detailed list below)	$2,267.75
Credit memo for proceeds of a note receivable that had been left at the bank for collection but which has not been recorded as collected	400.00
Cheques for an account payable entered on books as $240.90 but drawn and paid by bank as $419.00	178.10	(2,945.85)
Computed balance	17,196.76
Unlocated difference	(200.00)
Balance per bank (checked to confirmation)	$16,996.76

Cheques Drawn but Not Paid by Bank

NO.	AMOUNT
573	$ 67.27
724	9.90
903	456.67
907	305.50
911	482.75
913	550.00
914	366.76
916	10.00
917	218.90
	$2,267.75

Required

a. Prepare a corrected reconciliation.

b. Prepare journal entries for items that should be adjusted prior to closing the books.

(AICPA adapted)

15-19 You are doing the first-year audit of Sherman School District and have been assigned responsibility for doing a four-column proof of cash for the month of October 2004. You obtain the following information:

1.	Balance per books	September 30	$8,106
		October 31	3,850
2.	Balance per bank	September 30	5,411
		October 31	6,730

3.	Outstanding cheques	September 30	$ 916
		October 31	1,278
4.	Cash receipts for October	per bank	26,536
		per books	19,711
5.	Deposits in transit	September 30	3,611
		October 31	693

6. Interest on a bank loan for the month of October, charged by the bank but not recorded, was $596.

7. Proceeds on a note of the Jones Company were collected

by the bank on October 28 but were not entered on the books:

Principal	$3,300
Interest	307
	$3,607

8. On October 26, a $407 cheque of the Billings Company was charged to Sherman School District's account by the bank in error.
9. Dishonoured cheques are not recorded on the books unless they permanently fail to clear the bank. The bank treats them as disbursements when they are dishonoured and deposits when they are redeposited. Cheques totalling $609 were dishonoured in October; $300 was redeposited in October and $309 in November.

Required

a. Prepare a four-column proof of cash for the month ended October 31. It should show both adjusted and unadjusted cash.
b. Prepare all adjusting entries.

PROFESSIONAL JUDGMENT PROBLEM

15-20 Yip-Chuk Inc. had weak internal control over its cash transactions. Facts about its cash position at November 30 were as follows:

The cashbooks showed a balance of $18,901.62, which included undeposited receipts. A credit of $100 on the bank's records did not appear on the books of the company. The balance per bank statement was $15,550. Outstanding cheques were no. 62 for $116.25, no. 183 for $150.00, no. 284 for $253.25, no. 8621 for $190.71, no. 8623 for $206.80, and no. 8632 for $145.28.

The cashier, Khalid Nasser, embezzled all undeposited receipts in excess of $3,794.41 and prepared the reconciliations appearing at right.

Required

a. Prepare a supporting schedule showing how much Khalid embezzled.
b. How did he attempt to conceal his theft?
c. Using only the information given, name two specific features of internal control that were apparently missing.

(AICPA adapted)

Balance, per books, November 30		$18,901.62
Add: Outstanding cheques		
8621	$190.71	
8623	206.80	
8632	145.28	
		442.79
		19,344.41
Less: Undeposited receipts		3,794.41
Balance per bank, November 30		15,550.00
Deduct: Unrecorded credit		100.00
True cash, November 30		$15,450.00

CASE

15-21 Julian Gomes is the auditor of Jahafra Hotel, a small independent hotel, which has a November 30 year end. In order to give written instructions to his staff regarding the verification of year-end cash on hand, Julian reviewed his working papers of last year and contacted the client to make sure there were no changes. From his review, he obtained the following information:

1. Cash on hand consisted of undeposited receipts, imprest change funds, and imprest petty cash funds.
2. The hotel had three point-of-sale cash terminals and eight cashiers. Each of the cashiers was responsible for an imprest change fund of $500.
3. The following funds were also used:
   (i) Auxiliary change funds of $1,000, controlled by the office manager

(ii) Three office petty cash funds of $50, each controlled by a different office staff member
(iii) Undeposited receipts, controlled by the assistant hotel manager
4. The hotel's policy was to deposit receipts daily and intact.
5. In order to avoid the hotel's busy times of day, the year-end cash count was made at about 6:00 a.m., December 1.
6. Internal control over cash was satisfactory.

Required

Prepare an audit program regarding verification of year-end cash on hand for the assistant.

(CICA adapted)

CHAPTER 16

AUDIT OF THE PAYROLL AND PERSONNEL CYCLE

A payroll payment helps us buy groceries, pay rent or a mortgage, and pay for tuition. For many workers, it may be the crucial reason why they show up for work every day. For a business, it can be the largest expense—if payroll is too high, gross margins are too low and the company could go into receivership. Good human resource policies help a business hire competent, honest employees who help provide for an effective and honest control environment.

LEARNING OBJECTIVES

After reading this chapter, you should be able to answer the following questions:

1. **Why is the payroll and personnel cycle important? What differentiates this cycle from other cycles? Describe the functions and records in this cycle.**

2. **List typical audit tests of controls by assertion.**

3. **What misstatements could a payroll analytical review process detect? Which liability and expense accounts in the payroll cycle are tested using tests of details?**

THE STAFF AUDITOR MUST NEVER "SIMPLY FOLLOW ORDERS"

Leslie, a recently qualified PA, has been assigned to the audit of Softnet, Inc., a software development company. Because it was the busy season, the engagement team was working 60 to 70 h per week.

Her immediate supervisor on the Softnet audit was Bob. Bob had been with the firm three years longer than Leslie, and worked on the Softnet audit the previous year. He was supervising Leslie's work on capitalized software development costs. In preparing herself, Leslie had read *CICA Accounting Handbook* Section 3450 ("Research and Development Costs") and had a good understanding of the accounting rules concerning the capitalization of such costs. She understood, for example, that costs could not be capitalized until after technological feasibility was established either through detail program design or product design and the completion of a working model, confirmed by testing.

Bob drafted an audit program for capitalized software development costs. The steps were fairly general, but Bob added several oral instructions. He told Leslie to verify the payroll costs, which were a significant part of the development cost, and to talk to Joe, Softnet's controller, about whether the projects with capitalized costs had reached the technological feasibility stage. Leslie tested the payroll costs and found no misstatements. She also made enquiries of Joe and was told that the appropriate stage of completion was reached. Leslie documented Joe's representation in the working papers and went on to the next area assigned to her.

Later, Leslie began to have second thoughts. She understood that management's representations were a weak form of audit evidence, and she was concerned about whether Joe was the most knowledgeable person about the technical status of software projects. To resolve her concerns, she decided to talk to the responsible software engineers about one of the projects. She intended to clear this with Bob, but he was at another client's office that morning, so she proceeded on her own initiative. The engineer she talked to on the first project told her that he was almost finished with a working model but hadn't tested it yet. She decided to enquire about another project and discovered the same thing. Leslie documented these findings on a working paper and planned to discuss the situation with Bob as soon as he returned to the job.

When Leslie (somewhat proud of herself) told Bob of her findings and showed him the working paper, he told her the following:

> Listen Leslie, I told you just to talk to Joe. You shouldn't do procedures that you're not instructed to do. I want you to destroy this working paper and don't record the wasted time. We're under a lot of time pressure, and we can't bill Softnet for procedures that aren't necessary. Joe knows what he's talking about. There's nothing wrong with the capitalized software development costs. The fact that Softnet has working products that it's selling indicates that technological feasibility was reached.

Leslie was extremely distressed with this reaction from Bob but followed his instructions. She later talked to the audit partner about the situation during her annual counselling session. He mollified her concerns by pointing out that Bob was an experienced senior and probably had a broader perspective of the situation than she had as the staff assistant. Rather than worry, she should try and learn as much from working with the senior as she could.

The following fall, the OSC conducted an investigation of Softnet and found, among other things, that it had overstated capitalized software development costs. The OSC brought an action against both the management of Softnet and its auditors.

What quality control standards were violated during the Softnet audit engagement? What procedures should Leslie's firm have had in place to prevent this type of auditing error? Would you want to work for this firm? Current auditing standards should prevent this type of judgment error on audit engagements.

→16.1 THE NATURE AND IMPORTANCE OF THE PAYROLL AND PERSONNEL CYCLE

The **payroll and personnel cycle** involves the employment and payment of all employees, regardless of classification or method of determining compensation. The employees include executives on straight salary plus bonus, office workers on monthly salary with or without overtime, salespeople on a commission basis, and factory and unionized personnel paid on an hourly basis.

The cycle is important for several reasons. First, the salaries, wages, employee benefits (e.g., Canada Pension, employment insurance, health and dental care), and other employer costs (e.g., workplace safety insurance) are a major expense in all companies. Second, labour is such an important consideration in the valuation of inventory in manufacturing and construction companies that the improper classification and allocation of labour can result in a material misstatement of net income. Finally, payroll is an area in which large amounts of company resources can be wasted through inefficiency or stolen through fraud.

The Hillsburg Hardware Limited trial balance on page 117 in Chapter 5 includes typical general ledger accounts affected by the payroll and personnel cycle. They are identified as

PAYROLL AND PERSONNEL CYCLE—the transaction cycle that begins with the hiring of personnel, includes obtaining and accounting for services from the employees, and ends with payment to the employees for the services performed and to the government and other institutions for withheld and accrued employee benefits payroll and personnel accounts by the letter *P* in the left column. In larger companies, many general ledger accounts are often affected by payroll. It is common, for example, for large companies to have 50 or more payroll expense accounts. Payroll also affects work-in-process and finished goods inventory accounts for manufacturing companies.

As with the sales and collection cycle, the audit of the payroll and personnel cycle includes obtaining an understanding of internal control, assessment of control risk, tests of controls, analytical procedures, and tests of details of balances.

There are several important differences between the payroll and personnel cycle and other cycles in a typical audit.

- *There is only one class of transactions for payroll.* Most cycles include at least two classes of transactions. For example, the sales and collection cycle includes both sales and cash receipts transactions and often sales returns and charge-off of uncollectibles. Payroll has only one class because the receipt of services from employees and the payment for those services through payroll occur within a short time period.
- *Transactions are far more significant than related balance sheet accounts.* Payroll-related accounts such as accrued payroll and withheld taxes are usually small compared to the total amount of transactions for the year.
- *Internal controls over payroll are effective for almost all companies, even small ones.* The reasons for effective controls are harsh federal and provincial penalties for errors in withholding and paying payroll taxes, and employee morale problems if employees are not paid or are underpaid.

Because of these three characteristics, auditors typically emphasize tests of controls and analytical procedures in the audit of payroll.

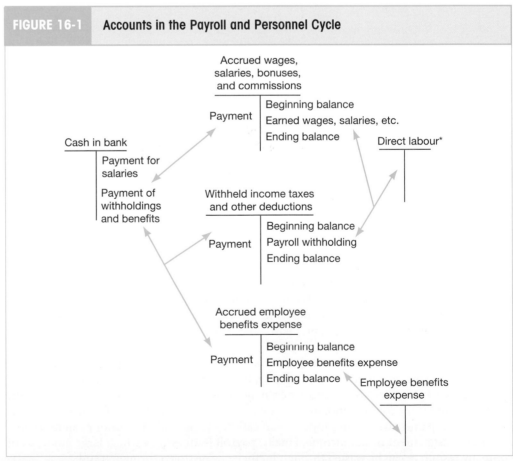

FIGURE 16-1   Accounts in the Payroll and Personnel Cycle

*Separate operating accounts for payroll also normally include officers' salaries and bonuses, office salaries, sales salaries and commissions, and indirect manufacturing labour. These accounts have the same relationship to accrued wages and withheld taxes and other deductions that is shown for direct labour. Some companies use a payroll service that performs all of the above functions.

The way in which accounting information flows through the various accounts in the payroll and personnel cycle is illustrated by T-accounts in Figure 16-1. In most systems, the accrued wages and salaries account is used only at the end of an accounting period. Throughout the period, expenses are charged when the employees are actually paid rather than when the labour costs are incurred. The accruals for labour are recorded by adjusting entries at the end of the period for any earned but unpaid labour costs.

Functions in the Cycle, Related Documents and Records, and Internal Controls

The payroll and personnel cycle begins with the hiring of personnel and ends with payment to the employees for the services performed and to the government and other institutions for employee withholdings (i.e., income tax, Canada [or Quebec] Pension Plan, employment insurance), and employee benefits (i.e., required contributions by the employer for the Canada [or Quebec] Pension Plan, employment insurance, workplace safety insurance, hospital insurance plans, provincial health and education taxes; and voluntary or negotiated employer contributions to company pension, medical, or dental plans). In between, the cycle involves obtaining services from the employees consistent with the objectives of the company and accounting for the services in a proper manner.

Column 3 of Table 16-1 identifies the five business functions in a typical payroll and personnel cycle. The table also shows the relationships among the business functions, classes of transactions, accounts, and documents and records. The business functions and related documents are discussed in this section. In addition, there is a discussion of key internal controls to prevent errors or fraud and irregularities in providing data and to ensure the safety of assets.

Personnel and Employment The personnel (or human resources) department provides an independent source for interviewing and hiring qualified personnel. The department is also an independent source of records for the internal verification of wage information.

TABLE 16-1	Classes of Transactions, Accounts, Business Functions, and Related Documents and Records for the Payroll and Personnel Cycle		
Class of Transactions	Accounts	Business Functions	Documents and Records
Payroll	Payroll cash Payroll expense accounts	Personnel and employment	Personnel records Deduction authorization form
	Payroll withholding accounts Payroll accrual accounts	Master file change	Rate authorization form
		Timekeeping and payroll preparation	Time card Job time ticket Summary payroll report Payroll journal Payroll master file Payroll transaction and history files
		Payment of payroll	Payroll cheque
		Preparation of employee withholdings and benefit remittance forms and payment of taxes	Form T-4 Employee withholdings and benefit remittance forms

PERSONNEL RECORDS **Personnel records** include such data as the date of employment, personnel investigations, approval of rates of pay, authorized deductions, performance evaluations, and termination of employment.

DEDUCTION AUTHORIZATION FORMS These are forms authorizing payroll deductions, including the number of exemptions for withholding of income taxes (TD-1), Canada Savings Bonds, charitable contributions, union dues, government or private insurance, and pension, medical, or dental plans.

RATE AUTHORIZATION FORM This is a form authorizing the rate of pay. The source of the information is a labour contract, authorization by management, or, in the case of officers, authorization from the board of directors.

INTERNAL CONTROLS From an audit point of view, the most important internal controls in personnel involve formal methods of informing the timekeeping and payroll preparation personnel of new employees, the authorization of initial and periodic changes in pay rates, and the termination date of employees no longer working for the company. As a part of these controls, segregation of duties is extremely important. No individual with access to time cards, payroll records, or cheques should also be permitted access to personnel records. A second important control is the adequate investigation of the competence and trustworthiness of new employees.

Timekeeping and Payroll Preparation This function is of major importance in the audit of payroll because it directly affects payroll expense for the period. It includes the preparation of time cards or time records by employees; the summarization and calculation of gross pay, deductions, and net pay; the preparation of payroll cheques; and the preparation of payroll records. There must be adequate controls to prevent misstatement in each of these activities.

TIME CARD OR TIME RECORD A **time card** is a document indicating the time an employee started and stopped working each day and the number of hours the employee worked. For many employees, the time card is prepared automatically by time clocks. Time cards are usually submitted weekly. Alternatively, many companies assign each employee a magnetic stripe card. Each employee "swipes" the card through a time clock, and a computer system tracks the employee's time, producing electronic records and printed reports of the time worked.

JOB TIME TICKET This document indicates particular jobs on which a factory employee worked during a given time period. This form is used only when an employee works on different jobs or in different departments. Use of electronic systems and magnetic stripe cards allows companies to track time spent on specific jobs using computer systems rather than by handling job tickets for each job.

SUMMARY PAYROLL REPORT This computer-generated document summarizes payroll for a period in various forms. One summary lists the totals debited to each general ledger account for payroll charges. These will equal gross payroll for the period. Another common summary for a manufacturing company lists the totals charged to various jobs in a job cost accounting system. Similarly, commissions earned by each salesperson may be summarized.

PAYROLL JOURNAL This is a journal for recording payroll cheques. It typically indicates gross pay, withholdings, and net pay. The payroll journal is generated for any time period from the payroll transactions included in the computer files. The totals from the journal are also included in the payroll master file by employee. Journal totals are posted to the general ledger by the computer.

PAYROLL MASTER FILE This file summarizes each payroll transaction by employee and maintains total employee wages paid for the year to date. The **payroll master file** is updated from payroll computer transaction files. The total of the individual employee earnings in the master file equals the total balance of gross payroll in various general ledger accounts.

PAYROLL TRANSACTION AND HISTORY FILES The transaction record for each employee includes gross pay for each payroll period, deductions from gross pay, net pay, cheque number, and date. This information is used to update the payroll master file.

INTERNAL CONTROLS Adequate control over the time in the time records includes the use of a time clock or other method of making certain that employees are paid for the number of hours they worked. There should also be controls to prevent anyone from checking in for several employees or submitting a fraudulent time record.

The summarization and calculation of the payroll can be controlled by well-defined policies for the payroll department, separation of duties to provide automatic cross-checks, reconciliation of payroll hours with independent production records, and independent internal verification of all important data. For example, payroll policies should require a competent, independent person to recalculate actual hours worked, review for the proper approval of all overtime, and examine time records for erasures and alterations or for unusually long hours. Similarly, batch control totals over hours worked can be calculated when payroll time cards are used and compared to the actual hours entered by the computer. Finally, a printout of wage and withholding rates included in the computer files can be obtained and compared to authorized rates in the personnel files.

Controls over the preparation of payroll cheques include preventing those responsible for preparing the cheques from having access to time records, signing or distributing cheques, or independently verifying payroll output. In addition, the cheques should be prenumbered and verified through independent bank reconciliation procedures.

When manufacturing labour affects inventory valuation, special emphasis should be put on controls to make sure labour is distributed to proper account classifications. There must also be adequate internal controls for recording job time records and other relevant payroll information in the cost accounting records. Independent internal verification of this information is an essential control.

Payment of Payroll The actual signing and distribution of the cheques must be properly handled to prevent their theft.

PAYROLL CHEQUE This is a cheque written to the employee for services performed. The cheque is prepared as a part of the payroll preparation function, but the authorized signature makes the cheque an asset. The amount of the cheque is the gross pay less taxes and other deductions withheld. After the cheque is cashed and returned to the company from the bank, it is referred to as a cancelled cheque. It is now common for paycheques to be directly deposited into employees' bank accounts.

INTERNAL CONTROLS Controls over cheques should include limiting the authorization for signing the cheques to a responsible employee who does not have access to timekeeping or the preparation of the payroll, the distribution of payroll by someone who is not involved in the other payroll functions, and the immediate return of unclaimed cheques for redeposit. If a cheque-signing machine is used to replace a manual signature, the same controls are required; in addition, the cheque-signing machine must be carefully controlled.

Most companies use an **imprest payroll account** to prevent the payment of unauthorized payroll transactions. An imprest payroll account is a separate payroll account in which a small balance is maintained. A cheque for the exact amount of each net payroll is transferred from the general account to the imprest account immediately before the distribution of the payroll. The advantages of an imprest account are that it limits the client's exposure to payroll fraud, allows the delegation of payroll cheque-signing duties, separates routine payroll expenditures from irregular expenditures, and facilitates cash management. It also simplifies the reconciliation of the payroll bank account if it is done at the low point in the payment cycle.

Where employee payments are made directly into their bank account, independent verification of the reports produced by the bank or payroll service provider should occur in lieu of the independent cheque-signature process.

Preparation of T-4s and Employee Withholdings and Benefits Remittance Forms The timely preparation and mailing of T-4s and employee withholdings and benefits remittance forms is required by federal and provincial laws.

T-4 FORM The **T-4 form** is issued for each employee summarizing the earnings record for the calendar year. The information includes gross pay, income taxes withheld, other withholdings, and taxable benefits such as employer contributions to government or privately sponsored medical plans. The same information is also submitted to the Canada Revenue Agency and, if appropriate, provincial tax authorities. This information is prepared from the payroll master file and is normally prepared by computer.

EMPLOYEE WITHHOLDINGS AND BENEFITS REMITTANCE FORMS The **employee withholdings and benefits remittance forms** are submitted to the federal government and to other organizations for the payment of withholdings and employee benefits. The nature and due date of the forms vary depending on the type of withholding or benefit and the size of the organization (e.g., weekly, monthly, or quarterly). These forms are prepared from information in the payroll master file or payroll history file. As dollar volume increases, more frequent remittances are required.

INTERNAL CONTROLS The most important control in the preparation of these returns is a well-defined set of policies that carefully indicate when each form must be filed. Most computerized payroll systems include the preparation of payroll tax returns using the information on the payroll transaction and master files. The independent verification of the output by a competent individual is an important control to prevent misstatements and potential liability for taxes and penalties.

→ 16.2 INTERNAL CONTROL TESTING

Figure 16-2 shows the methodology for designing tests of controls for the payroll and personnel cycle. It is the same methodology used in Chapter 13 for the sales and collection cycle.

Internal control for payroll is normally highly structured and well controlled in order to control cash disbursed and to minimize employee complaints and dissatisfaction. It is common to use electronic data-processing techniques to prepare all journals and payroll cheques. In-house systems are often used, as are outside service centre systems such as banks or financial institutions. Thus, general controls such as control over program changes or program updates and over access to data files must be evaluated. It is usually not difficult to establish good control in the payroll and personnel cycle. For factory and office employees, there are usually a large number of relatively homogeneous, small-amount transactions. There are fewer executive payroll transactions, but they are ordinarily consistent in timing, content, and amount. Because of relatively consistent payroll concerns from company to company, high-quality computer software packages are available, resulting in good controls over program changes. Consequently, auditors seldom expect to find exceptions in testing payroll transactions. Occasionally control test deviations occur, but most monetary errors or fraud and other irregularities are corrected by internal verification controls or in response to employee complaints.

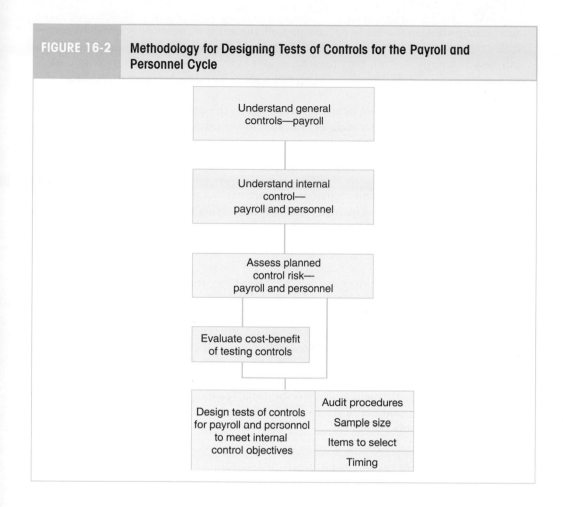

FIGURE 16-2 Methodology for Designing Tests of Controls for the Payroll and Personnel Cycle

Understand general controls—payroll

Understand internal control— payroll and personnel

Assess planned control risk— payroll and personnel

Evaluate cost-benefit of testing controls

Design tests of controls for payroll and personnel to meet internal control objectives

| Audit procedures |
| Sample size |
| Items to select |
| Timing |

Internal Controls and Tests of Controls

Tests of control procedures are the *most important* means of verifying account balances in the payroll and personnel cycle. The emphasis on tests of controls is due to the lack of independent third-party evidence, such as confirmation for verifying accrued wages, withholdings, accrued benefits payable, and other balance sheet accounts. Furthermore, in most audits, the amounts in the balance sheet accounts are small and can be verified with relative ease if the auditor is confident that payroll transactions are correctly entered into the computer and that withholding and benefit remittance forms are properly prepared.

Even though the tests of controls are the most important part of testing payroll, many auditors spend little time in this area. In many audits, there is a minimal risk of material misstatements even though payroll is frequently a significant part of total expenses. There are three reasons for this: employees are likely to complain to management if they are underpaid, all payroll transactions are typically uniform and uncomplicated, and payroll transactions are extensively audited by federal and provincial governments for income tax withholding and for pension, employment insurance, and health care payments.

Following the same approach used in Chapter 13 for tests of sales and cash receipts transactions, the internal controls and tests of controls for each objective and related monetary misstatements are summarized in Table 16-2. Again, the reader should recognize that

- The internal controls will vary from company to company; therefore, the auditor must identify the controls and weaknesses for each organization.
- Controls the auditor intends to use for reducing assessed control risk must be tested with tests of controls.
- The tests of controls will vary depending on the assessed control risk and the other considerations of the audit, such as the effect of payroll on inventory. Where an outside

service organization is used to process payroll, the auditor must consider whether controls at the client are sufficient to ensure that the transaction-related audit objectives are satisfied. If not, the auditor may need to request evidence regarding controls at the service organization, including the existence of a service auditor's report on controls, discussed in Chapter 22.

- The tests of controls are not actually performed in the order given in Table 16-2. The tests of controls are performed in as convenient a manner as possible, using a performance format audit program.

Payroll Withholdings and Benefits Remittance Forms and Payments Payroll withholdings and benefits are an important consideration in many companies, both because the amounts are often material and because the potential liability for failure to file timely forms can be severe.

PREPARATION OF PAYROLL WITHHOLDINGS AND BENEFITS REMITTANCE FORMS As a part of understanding the internal control structure, the auditor should review the preparation of at least one of each type of employee withholding and benefits remittance form that the client is responsible for filing. There is a potential liability for unpaid balances and penalty and interest if the client fails to prepare the forms properly.

A detailed reconciliation of the information on the remittance forms and the payroll records may be necessary when the auditor believes that there is a reasonable chance the remittance forms may be improperly prepared. Indications of potential errors in the forms include the payment of penalties and interest in the past for improper payments, new personnel in the payroll department who are responsible for the preparation of the remittance forms, the lack of internal verification of the information, and the existence of serious liquidity problems for the client.

PAYMENT OF THE TAXES WITHHELD AND OTHER WITHHOLDINGS AND BENEFITS ON A TIMELY BASIS It is desirable to test whether the client has fulfilled its legal obligation in submitting payments for all payroll withholdings and benefits as a part of the payroll tests even though the payments are usually made from general cash disbursements. The withholdings of concern in these tests are such items as taxes, Canada (or Quebec) Pension Plan, employment insurance, union dues, insurance, and Canada Savings Bonds. The auditor must first determine the client's requirements for submitting the payments. The requirements are determined by reference to such sources as tax laws, Canada Pension Plan rules, employment insurance rules, union contracts, and agreements with employees. After the auditor knows the requirements, it is easy to determine whether the client has paid the proper amount on a timely basis by comparing the subsequent payment with the payroll records.

Inventory and Fraudulent Payroll Considerations Auditors often extend their procedures considerably in the audit of payroll under the following circumstances: (1) when payroll significantly affects the valuation of inventory and (2) when the auditor is concerned about the possibility of material fraudulent payroll transactions.

RELATIONSHIP BETWEEN PAYROLL AND INVENTORY VALUATION In audits in which payroll is a significant portion of inventory, a frequent occurrence for manufacturing and construction companies, the improper account classification of payroll can significantly affect asset valuation for accounts such as work in process, finished goods, or construction in process.

For example, the overhead charged to inventory at the balance sheet date can be overstated if the salaries of administrative personnel are inadvertently or intentionally charged to indirect manufacturing overhead. Similarly, the valuation of inventory is affected if the direct labour cost of individual employees is improperly charged to the wrong job or process. When some jobs are billed on a cost-plus basis, revenue and the valuation of inventory are both affected by charging labour to incorrect jobs.

When labour is a material factor in inventory valuation, there should be special emphasis on testing the internal controls over proper classification of payroll transactions. Consistency from period to period, which is essential for classification, can be tested by reviewing the chart of accounts and procedures manuals. It is also desirable to trace job

Transaction-Related Audit Objective	Key Internal Control	Common Tests of Controls	
Recorded payroll payments are for work actually performed by existing employees (occurrence).	Time records are approved by supervisors. Time clock is used to record time. Adequate personnel files. Separation of duties between personnel, timekeeping, and payroll disbursements. Only employees existing in the computer data files are accepted when they are entered. Authorization to issue cheques.	Examine the cards or listings for indication of approvals. Examine time records. Review personnel policies. Review organization chart, discuss with employees, and observe duties being performed. Examine printouts of transactions rejected by the computer as having nonexistent employee numbers, or determine whether invalid entries are accepted at point of entry.[†] Examine payroll records for evidence of approval.	Review the payroll journal, general ledger, and payroll earnings records for large or unusual amounts.*[†] Compare cancelled cheques with payroll journal for name, amount, and date. Examine cancelled cheques for proper endorsement. Compare cancelled cheques with personnel records.
Existing payroll transactions are recorded (completeness).	Payroll cheques are prenumbered and accounted for. Independent preparation of bank reconciliation.	Account for a sequence of payroll cheques, or conduct gap testing.[†] Discuss with employees and observe reconciliation.	Reconcile the disbursements in the payroll journal with the disbursements on the payroll bank statement. Prove the bank reconciliation.
Recorded payroll transactions are for the amount of time actually worked and at the proper pay rate; withholdings are properly calculated (accuracy).	Internal verification of calculations and amounts. Batch totals are compared with computer summary reports. Authorization of wage rate, salary, or commission rate. Authorization of withholdings, including amounts for insurance and Canada Savings Bonds.	Examine indication of internal verification. Examine file of batch totals for initials of data control clerk; compare totals to summary reports.[†] Examine payroll records for indication of internal verification. Examine authorizations in personnel file.	Recompute hours worked from time records. Compare pay rates with union contract, approval by board of directors, or other source. Recompute gross pay.[†] Check withholdings by reference to appropriate tables[†] and authorization forms in personnel file. Recompute net pay.[†] Compare cancelled cheque with payroll journal for amount.
Payroll transactions are properly classified (classification).	Adequate chart of accounts. Internal verification of classification.	Review chart of accounts. Examine indication of internal verification; determine that software posts to correct accounts.[†]	Compare classification with chart of accounts or procedures manual. Review time records for employee department and job records for job assignment, and trace through to labour distribution.
Payroll transactions are recorded on the correct dates (timing).	Procedures require recording transactions as soon as possible after the payroll is paid. Internal verification.	Examine the procedures manual and observe when recording takes place. Examine indication of internal verification.	Compare date of recorded cheque in the payroll journal with date on cancelled cheques and time records. Compare date on cheque with date the cheque cleared the bank.
Payroll transactions are properly included in the payroll master file and transaction files; they are properly summarized (posting and summarization).	Internal verification of payroll file contents. Comparison of payroll master file with payroll general ledger totals.	Examine indication of internal verification. Examine initialled summary total reports indicating comparisons have been made.	Test clerical accuracy by footing the payroll journal and tracing postings to general ledger and the payroll master file.[†]

* This analytical procedure can also apply to other objectives, including completeness, valuation, and timeliness.

† This control would be tested on many audits by using the computer, possibly with generalized audit software.

records or other evidence that an employee has worked on a particular job or process to the accounting records that affect inventory valuation. For example, if each employee must account for all of his or her time on a weekly basis by allocating individual job numbers, a useful test is to trace the recorded hours of several employees for a week to the related job-cost records to make sure each has been properly recorded. It may also be desirable to trace from the job-cost records to employee summaries as a test for nonexistent payroll charges being included in inventory.

Tests for Nonexistent Payroll Although auditors are not primarily responsible for the detection of fraud, they must extend audit procedures when internal controls over payroll are inadequate. There are several ways employees can significantly defraud a company in the payroll area. This discussion is limited to tests for the two most common types—nonexistent employees and fraudulent hours.

The issuance of payroll cheques to individuals who do not work for the company (nonexistent employees) frequently results from the continuance of an employee's remuneration after his or her employment has been terminated. Usually, the person committing this type of defalcation is a payroll clerk, supervisor, fellow employee, or perhaps the former employee. For example, under some systems, a supervisor could clock in daily for an employee and approve the time record at the end of the time period. If the supervisor also distributes paycheques, considerable opportunity for defalcation exists.

Certain procedures can be performed on cancelled cheques as a means of detecting defalcation. A procedure used on payroll audits is comparing the names on cancelled cheques with time cards and other records for authorized signatures and reasonableness of the endorsements. It is also common to scan endorsements on cancelled cheques for unusual or recurring second endorsements as an indication of a possible fraudulent cheque. The examination of cheques that are recorded as voided is also desirable to make sure they have not been fraudulently used. Where employees are paid automatically by bank deposits to the employees' accounts, the auditor can look for duplicated bank account numbers, post office boxes, or for common employee addresses.

A test for nonexistent employees is tracing selected transactions recorded in the payroll journal to the personnel department to determine whether the employees were actually employed during the payroll period. The endorsement on the cancelled cheque written out to an employee can be compared with the authorized signature on the employee's withholding authorization forms.

A procedure that tests for proper handling of terminated employees is selecting several files from the personnel records for employees who were terminated in the current year to determine whether each received his or her termination pay in accordance with company policy. Continuing payments to terminated employees is tested by examining the payroll records in the subsequent period to ascertain that the employee is no longer being paid. Naturally, this procedure is not effective if the personnel department is not informed of terminations.

In some cases, where employees are paid by cheque, the auditor may request a surprise payroll payoff. This is a procedure in which each employee must pick up and sign for his or her cheque in the presence of a supervisor and the auditor. Any cheques that have not been claimed must be subject to an extensive investigation to determine whether an unclaimed cheque is fraudulent. Surprise payoff is frequently expensive and in some cases may even cause problems with a labour union, but it may be the only means of detecting a defalcation.

Fraudulent hours exist when an employee reports more time than was actually worked. Because of the lack of available evidence, it is usually difficult for an auditor to determine whether an employee records more time on his or her time card or time record than was actually worked. One procedure is reconciling the total hours paid according to the payroll records with an independent record of the hours worked, such as those often maintained by production control. Alternatively, it may be possible to observe an employee clocking in more than one time card under a buddy approach. However, it is ordinarily easier for the client to prevent this type of defalcation by adequate controls than for the auditor to detect it.

Analysis of Exceptions and Conclusions As mentioned previously, most internal controls for payroll are highly structured and well controlled. It is common to use electronic data-processing techniques. In-house systems are often used, as are outside service centre systems and electronic funds transfers. It is usually not difficult to establish good control in payroll. For factory and office employees, there are usually a large number of relatively homogeneous, small amount transactions. There are fewer executive payroll transactions, but they are ordinarily consistent in timing, content, and amount. Because of relatively consistent payroll concerns from company to company, high-quality computer software packages are available. Consequently, auditors seldom expect to find exceptions in testing payroll transactions. Occasionally control test deviations occur, but most monetary errors are corrected by internal verification controls or in response to employee complaints. There are, however, specific types of errors that give the auditor particular concern in auditing payroll transactions:

- Classification errors in charging labour to inventory and job cost accounts. As previously indicated, these can result in misstated earnings.
- Computational errors when a computerized system is used. Recall that one of the primary characteristics of the computer is processing consistency. If a calculation error is made for one item, it is probably made on every other similar item. As indicated, these errors are rare due to the high quality of most software packages.
- Any errors that indicate possible fraud, particularly relating to the executive payroll.

Generally, the tests of controls performed in the payroll cycle will use *attribute sampling* under a plan that assumes a zero deviation rate. Sampling size should be large enough to give the auditor a reasonable chance of finding at least one deviation if an intolerable number of deviations exists.

If classification errors are found through this procedure, the sample selected for attributes will often then be used to make an estimate of the total monetary error involved. Sample expansion is usually necessary, however, to achieve a precise enough estimate to conclude whether the total error is material in amount.

If a computational error or one indicating possible fraud is found, specific investigation will be required to determine what allowed such an error to occur. Generally, further sampling and estimation are not done; rather, a nonstatistical approach based on the circumstances is taken.

If no exceptions are found, or if those found are not alarming or unexpected, the auditor will conclude that assessed control risk can be reduced as planned, and he or she will proceed with the tests of details of balances of the affected accounts without modification.

→ 16.3 ANALYTICAL REVIEW AND TESTS OF DETAIL

Analytical Procedures

The use of analytical procedures is as important in the payroll and personnel cycle as it is in every other cycle. Table 16-3 illustrates analytical procedures for the balance sheet and income statement accounts in the payroll and personnel cycle. Most of the relationships included in Table 16-3 are highly predictable and are therefore useful for uncovering areas in which additional investigation is desirable. The auditor should consider any changes in business policies or business practices when conducting the analytical procedures.

Tests of Details of Balances for Liability and Expense Accounts

Figure 16-3 on page 489 summarizes the methodology for deciding the appropriate tests of details of balances for payroll liability accounts. The methodology is the same as that followed in Chapter 14 for accounts receivable. Normally, however, payroll-related liabilities are less material than accounts receivable; therefore, there is less inherent risk.

The verification of the liability accounts associated with payroll, often termed **accrued payroll expenses**, ordinarily is straightforward if internal controls are operating effectively. When the auditor is satisfied that payroll transactions are being properly recorded in the payroll journal and the related employee withholding and benefits remittance forms are being accurately prepared and promptly paid, the tests of details of balances should not be time-consuming.

ACCRUED PAYROLL EXPENSES— the liability accounts associated with payroll including accounts for accrued salaries and wages, accrued commissions, accrued bonuses, accrued benefits, and accrued employee benefits

TABLE 16-3	Analytical Procedures for the Payroll and Personnel Cycle
Analytical Procedure	**Possible Misstatement Detected in**
Compare payroll expense account balance with previous years (adjusted for pay rate increases and increases in volume).	Payroll expense accounts
Compare direct labour as a percentage of sales with previous years.	Direct labour
Compare commission expense as a percentage of sales with previous years.	Commission expense
Compare payroll benefits expense as a percentage of salaries and wages with previous years (adjusted for changes in the benefits rates)	Payroll benefits expense and payroll benefits liability
Compare accrued payroll benefits accounts with previous years.	Accrued payroll benefits and payroll benefits expense

The objectives in testing payroll-related liabilities are to determine whether accruals in the trial balance are stated at correct amounts (accuracy) for all payroll accounts (completeness), and transactions in the payroll and personnel cycle are recorded in the proper period (cutoff). The primary concern in both objectives is to make sure there are no understated or omitted accruals. The major liability accounts in the payroll and personnel cycle are now discussed.

Amounts Withheld from Employees' Pay Income taxes withheld, but not yet disbursed, can be tested by comparing the balance with the payroll journal, the withholding remittance form prepared in the subsequent period, and the subsequent period cash disbursements. Other withheld items such as the Canada (or Quebec) Pension Plan, employment insurance, union dues, Canada Savings Bonds, and insurance can be verified in the same manner. If internal controls are operating effectively, cutoff and accuracy can easily be tested at the same time by these procedures.

Accrued Salaries and Wages The accrual for salaries and wages arises whenever employees are not paid for the last few days or hours of earned wages until the subsequent period. Salaried personnel may receive all of their pay except overtime on the last day of the month, but frequently several days of wages for hourly employees are unpaid at the end of the year.

The correct cutoff and valuation of accrued salaries and wages depend on company policy, which should be followed consistently from year to year. Some companies calculate the exact hours of pay that were earned in the current period and paid in the subsequent period, whereas others compute an approximate proportion. For example, if the subsequent payroll results from three days' employment during the current year and two days' employment during the subsequent year, the use of 60 percent of the subsequent period's gross pay as the accrual is an example of an approximation.

Once the auditor has determined the company's policy for accruing wages and ensures it is consistent with that of previous years, the appropriate audit procedure to test for cutoff and valuation is evaluating the reasonableness of the method and then recalculating the client's accrual. The most likely error of any significance in the balance is the failure to include the proper number of days of earned but unpaid wages.

Accrued Commissions The same concepts used in verifying accrued salaries and wages are applicable to accrued commissions, but the accrual is often more difficult to verify because companies frequently have several different types of agreements with salespeople and other commissioned employees. For example, some salespeople might be paid a commission

FIGURE 16-3 **Methodology for Designing Tests of Details of Balances for Payroll Liabilities**

Set materiality and assess audit risk and inherent risk for payroll liability accounts

Assess control risk for the payroll and personnel cycle

Design and perform tests of controls for the payroll and personnel cycle

Design and perform analytical procedures for the payroll and personnel cycle

Design tests of details of payroll accounts balances to satisfy balance-related audit objectives

| Audit procedures |
| Sample size |
| Items to select |
| Timing |

Materiality Considerations

Most companies have a large number of transactions involving payroll, often involving large total amounts. However, balance sheet accounts are normally insignificant, except for labour charged to inventory.

Inherent Risk Considerations

- There is inherent risk of payroll fraud because most transactions involve cash. The occurrence objective is therefore often considered to be important.
- For manufacturing companies with significant labour charged to inventory, there is potential for misclassification between payroll expense and inventory or among categories of inventory.

Control Risk Considerations

- Internal controls are normally good for payroll transactions because of the potential effect on employee morale and strict federal and provincial tax laws.
- Many companies use outside service centres for processing payroll. The auditor should not assume that the controls of an outside service centre are good.

every month and earn no salary, while others will get a monthly salary plus a commission paid quarterly. In some cases, the commission varies for different products and may not be paid until several months after the end of the year. In verifying accrued commissions, it is necessary first to determine the nature of the commission agreement and then to test the calculations based on the agreement. It is important to compare the method of accruing commissions with previous years for purposes of consistency. If the amounts are material, it is also common to confirm the amount that is due directly with the employees.

Accrued Bonuses In many companies, the year-end unpaid bonuses to officers and employees are such a major item that the failure to record them would result in a material misstatement. The verification of the recorded accrual can usually be accomplished by comparing it with the amount authorized in the minutes of the board of directors.

Accrued Vacation Pay, Sick Pay, or Other Benefits The consistent accrual of these liabilities relative to those of the preceding year is the most important consideration in evaluating the fairness of the amounts. The company policy for recording the liability must first be determined, followed by the recalculation of the recorded amounts.

Accrued Employee Benefits This account will include the employer's share of Canada (or Quebec) Pension Plan payments and employment insurance payments as well as workplace safety insurance. The employer's share can be verified by examining remittance forms prepared in the subsequent period to determine the amount that should have been recorded as a liability at the balance sheet date.

Tests of Details of Balances for Expense Accounts Several accounts in the income statement are affected by payroll transactions. The most important are officers' salaries and bonuses, office salaries, sales salaries and commissions, and direct manufacturing labour. There is frequently a further breakdown of costs by division, product, or branch. Fringe benefits such as dental insurance may also be included in the expenses.

There should be relatively little additional testing of the income statement accounts in most audits beyond the analytical procedures, tests of controls, and related tests of liability accounts, which have already been discussed. Extensive additional testing should only be necessary when weaknesses are found in internal control, significant errors are discovered in the liability tests, or major unexplained variances are found in the analytical procedures. Nevertheless, some income statement accounts are often tested in the personnel and payroll cycle. These include officers' compensation, commissions, and total payroll.

OFFICERS' COMPENSATION It is common to verify whether the total compensation of officers is the amount authorized by the board of directors because disclosure of the salaries and other compensation of the top five officers is required by certain provincial securities commissions. Verification of the officers' compensation is also warranted because some individuals may be in a position to pay themselves more than the authorized amount. The usual audit test is to obtain the authorized salary of each officer from the minutes of the board of directors' meetings and compare it with the related earnings record.

COMMISSIONS Commission expense can be verified with relative ease if the commission rate is the same for each type of sale and the necessary sales information is available in the accounting records. The total commission expense can be verified by multiplying the commission rate for each type of sale by the amount of sales in that category. If the calculations are complex, the auditor may decide that these calculations should be tested using generalized audit software or automated audit techniques. If the desired information is not available, it may be necessary to test the annual or monthly commission payments for selected salespeople and trace those to the total commission payments. When the auditor believes it is necessary to perform these tests, they are normally done in conjunction with tests of accrued liabilities.

EMPLOYEE BENEFITS EXPENSE Employee benefits expense for the year can be tested by first reconciling the total payroll on each employee benefits remittance form with the total payroll for the entire year. Total employee benefits expense can then be recomputed by multiplying the appropriate rate by the payroll. The calculation is frequently time-consuming because the benefits are usually applicable on only a portion of the payroll and the rate may change part way through the year if the taxpayer's financial statements are not on a calendar-year basis. On most audits, the calculation is costly and is unnecessary unless analytical procedures indicate a problem that cannot be resolved through other procedures. When the auditor believes that the test is necessary, it is ordinarily done in conjunction with tests of employee benefits accruals.

TOTAL PAYROLL A closely related test to the one for employee benefits is the reconciliation of total payroll expense in the general ledger with the T-4 Summary that the company must send in to the Canada Revenue Agency by the end of February each year. The objectives of the test are to determine whether payroll transactions were charged to a non-payroll account or not recorded in the payroll journal at all. The audit objectives are certainly relevant, but it is questionable whether the procedure is useful in uncovering the type of error for which it was intended. Since the T-4 Summary and the payroll are usually both prepared directly from the payroll master file, the errors, if any, are likely to be in both records. The procedure may be worthwhile in rare situations, but it is usually unnecessary. Tests of controls are a better means of uncovering these two types of errors in most audits.

Summary

Figure 16-4 illustrates the major accounts in the payroll and personnel cycle and the types of audit tests used to audit these accounts. This figure also shows how the audit risk model discussed in Chapter 8 relates to the audit of the payroll and personnel cycle.

FIGURE 16-4   Types of Audit Tests for the Payroll and Personnel Cycle

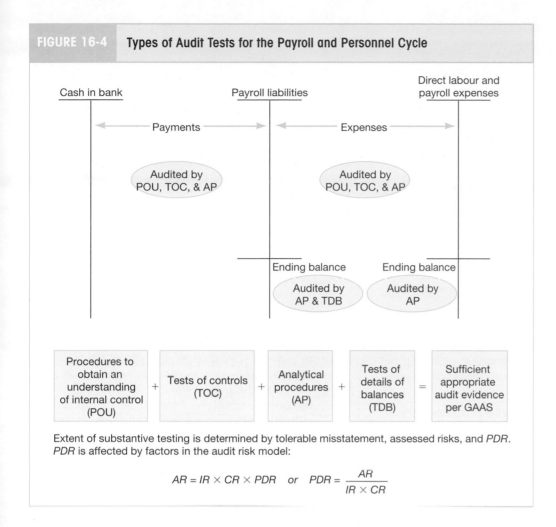

Extent of substantive testing is determined by tolerable misstatement, assessed risks, and *PDR*. *PDR* is affected by factors in the audit risk model:

$$AR = IR \times CR \times PDR \quad or \quad PDR = \frac{AR}{IR \times CR}$$

SUMMARY

1. *Why is the payroll and personnel cycle important?* This cycle involves the employment and payment of all employees. Salaries, wages, and associated benefits are a major expense; labour is an important cost component for manufacturing and construction companies and, if improperly managed, could result in wasted resources.

    What differentiates this cycle from other cycles? There is only one class of transaction. The total transaction value can be far more significant than balance sheet accounts. Internal control over payroll tends to be effective for most companies due to harsh federal and provincial penalties for errors in withholdings and taxes.

    Describe the functions and records in this cycle. Table 16-1 lists each of the business functions (personnel and employment, master file change, timekeeping and payroll preparation, payment, preparation of withholding and tax remittances) with the associated documents and records.

2. *List typical audit tests of controls by assertion.* Table 16-2 lists transaction-related audit objectives, key internal controls, and common tests of controls for payroll. For example, a test of occurrence is examining payroll records for evidence of approval.

3. *What misstatements could a payroll analytical review process detect?* Table 16-3 lists several analytical procedures that could detect potential errors in the following accounts: payroll expense, direct labour, commission expense, payroll benefits expenses, and liabilities.

    Which liability and expense accounts in the payroll cycle are tested using tests of details? The auditor would test the following accounts: withholding benefits and taxes, accrued salaries and wages, accrued commissions, accrued vacation pay, accrued sick benefits, officers' compensation, commissions, employee benefits, and payroll costs.

ESSENTIAL TERMS

Accrued payroll expenses—the liability accounts associated with payroll including accounts for accrued salaries and wages, accrued commissions, accrued bonuses, accrued benefits, and accrued employee benefits   (p. 487).

Employee withholdings and benefits remittance forms—forms that the employer submits to federal and provincial authorities for the payment of withholdings and employee benefits   (p. 482).

Imprest payroll account—a bank account to which the exact amount of payroll for the pay period is transferred by cheque from the employer's general cash account   (p. 482).

Payroll and personnel cycle—the transaction cycle that begins with the hiring of personnel, includes obtaining and accounting for services from the employees, and ends with payment to the employees for the services performed and to the government and other institutions for withheld and accrued employee benefits (p. 477).

Payroll master file—a computer file for recording each payroll transaction for each employee and maintaining total employee wages paid and related data for the year to date   (p. 480).

Personnel records—records that include such data as the date of employment, personnel investigations, rates of pay, authorized deductions, performance evaluations, and termination of employment   (p. 480).

T-4 form—a form issued to each employee summarizing the earnings record for the calendar year   (p. 482).

Time card—a document indicating the time that the employee started and stopped working each day and the number of hours worked   (p. 480).

REVIEW QUESTIONS

16-1 Identify five general ledger accounts that are likely to be affected by the payroll and personnel cycle in most audits.

16-2 Explain the relationship between the payroll and personnel cycle and inventory valuation.

16-3 List five tests of controls that can be performed for the payroll cycle, and state the purpose of each control being tested.

16-4 Explain why the percentage of total audit time in the cycle devoted to performing tests of controls is usually far greater for the payroll and personnel cycle than for the sales and collection cycle.

16-5 Evaluate the following comment by an auditor: "My job is to determine whether the payroll records are fairly stated in accordance with generally accepted accounting principles, not to find out whether the client is following proper hiring and termination procedures. When I conduct an audit of payroll, I keep out of the personnel department and stick to the time cards, journals, and payroll cheques. I don't care whom the client hires and whom it fires, as long as it properly pays the employees it has."

16-6 Distinguish between the following payroll audit procedures and state the purpose of each: (1) Trace a random sample of prenumbered time cards to the related payroll cheques in the payroll register, and compare the hours worked with the hours paid, and (2) trace a random sample of payroll cheques from the payroll register to the related time cards, and compare the hours worked with the hours paid. Which of these two procedures is typically more important in the audit of payroll? Why?

16-7 In auditing payroll withholding and payroll benefits expense, explain why emphasis should normally be on evaluating the adequacy of the employee withholding and benefits remittance forms preparation procedures rather than on the employee withholding and benefits liability. If the preparation procedures are inadequate, explain the effect that this will have on the remainder of the audit.

16-8 List several analytical procedures for the payroll and personnel cycle, and explain the type of error that might be indicated when there is a significant difference in the comparison of the current year with previous years' results for each of the tests.

16-9 Explain the circumstances under which an auditor should perform audit tests primarily designed to uncover fraud in the payroll and personnel cycle. List three audit procedures that are primarily for the detection of fraud, and state the type of fraud that the procedure is meant to uncover.

16-10 List the types of authorizations in the payroll and personnel cycle, and state the type of misstatement that is enhanced when each authorization is lacking.

16-11 Explain why it is common to verify total officers' compensation even when the tests of controls results in payroll are excellent. What audit procedures can be used to verify officers' compensation?

16-12 Explain what is meant by an "imprest payroll account." What is its purpose as a control over payroll?

16-13 List several audit procedures that the auditor can use to determine whether recorded payroll transactions are recorded at the proper amount.

MULTIPLE CHOICE QUESTIONS

16-14 Choose the best response for the following questions:

a. A factory supervisor at Steblecki Corporation discharged an hourly worker but did *not* notify the payroll department. The supervisor then forged the worker's signature on time cards and work tickets and, when giving out the cheques, diverted the payroll cheques drawn from the discharged worker to his own use. The most effective procedure for preventing this activity is to

(1) have a paymaster who has *no* other payroll responsibility distribute the payroll cheques.
(2) have someone other than persons who prepare or distribute the payroll obtain custody of unclaimed payroll cheques.
(3) require written authorization for all employees added to or removed from the payroll.
(4) from time to time, rotate persons distributing the payroll.

b. A public accountant reviews Shah Ltd.'s payroll procedures. An example of an internal control weakness is to assign to a department supervisor the responsibility for

(1) initiating requests for salary adjustments for subordinate employees.
(2) distributing payroll cheques to subordinate employees.
(3) reviewing and approving time reports for subordinates.
(4) interviewing applicants for subordinate positions prior to hiring by the personnel department.

c. A computer operator perpetrated a theft by preparing erroneous T-4 forms. The operator's income tax withheld was overstated by $2,000 and the income tax withheld from all other employees was understated. Which of the following audit procedures would detect such a fraud?

(1) Multiplication of the applicable rate by the individual's gross taxable earnings.
(2) Using employees' TD-1 forms and withholding tables to determine whether deductions authorized per pay period agree with amounts deducted per pay period.
(3) Footing and crossfooting of the payroll register followed by tracing postings to the general ledger.
(4) Vouching cancelled cheques to income tax withholding remittance forms.

d. In the audit of which of the following types of profit-oriented enterprises would the auditor be most likely to place special emphasis on tests of controls for proper classifications of payroll transactions?

(1) A service organization
(2) A wholesaling organization
(3) A retailing organization
(4) A manufacturing organization

e. A common audit procedure in the audit of payroll transactions involves tracing selected items from the payroll journal to employee time cards that have been approved by supervisory personnel. This procedure is designed to provide evidence in support of the audit proposition that

(1) only proper employees worked and their pay was properly computed.
(2) all employees worked the number of hours for which their pay was computed.
(3) jobs on which employees worked were charged with the appropriate labour cost.
(4) internal controls relating to payroll disbursements are operating effectively.

(AICPA adapted)

DISCUSSION QUESTIONS AND PROBLEMS

16-15 The following misstatements are included in the accounting records of Lathen Manufacturing Ltd.:

1. Direct labour was unintentionally charged to job 620 instead of job 602 by the payroll clerk when he entered the job tickets. Job 602 was completed and the costs were expensed in the current year, whereas job 620 was included in work in process.
2. Jane Block and Frank Demery take turns "punching in" for each other every few days. The absent employee comes in at noon and tells the supervisor that he or she had car trouble or some other problem. The supervisor does not know the employee is getting paid for the time.
3. The supervisor submits a fraudulent time card for a former employee each week and delivers the related payroll cheque to the employee's house on the way home from work. They split the amount of the paycheque.
4. Employees frequently overlook recording their hours worked on job-cost tickets as required by the system. Many of the client's contracts are on a cost-plus basis.
5. The payroll clerk prepares a cheque to the same nonexistent person every week when entering payroll transactions in the microcomputer system, which also records the amount in the payroll journal. The clerk submits it along with all other payroll cheques for signature. When the cheques are returned to the clerk for distribution, the clerk takes the cheque and deposits it in a special bank account bearing that person's name.
6. In withholding income taxes from employees, the computer operator overrides the standard tax calculation, taking $2.00 extra from dozens of employees each week and crediting the amount to the operator's own employee earnings record.

Required
a. For each misstatement, state a control that should have prevented it from occurring on a continuing basis.
b. For each misstatement, state a test of control audit procedure that could uncover it.

16-16 In comparing total employee benefits expense with the preceding year, Marilyn Brendin, public accountant, observed a significant increase, even though the total number of employees had only increased from 175 to 195. To investigate the difference, she selected a large sample of payroll disbursement transactions and carefully tested the withholdings for each employee in the sample by referring to Canada Pension Plan, employment insurance, and other benefits withholding tables. In her test, she found no exceptions; therefore, she concluded that employee benefits expense was fairly stated.

Required

a. Evaluate Brendin's approach to testing employee benefits expense.
b. Discuss a more suitable approach for determining whether employee benefits expense was properly stated in the current year.

16-17 As part of the audit of McGree Plumbing and Heating Ltd., you have responsibility for testing the payroll and personnel cycle. Payroll is the largest single expense in the client's trial balance, and hourly wages make up most of the payroll total. Employees are paid every two weeks. A unique aspect of the business is the extensive overtime incurred by employees on some days. It is common for employees to work only three or four days during the week but to work long hours while they are on the job. McGree's management has found that this actually saves money, in spite of the large amount of overtime, because the union contract requires payment for all travel time. Since many of the employees' jobs require long travel times and extensive startup costs, this policy is supported by both McGree and the employees.

You have already carefully evaluated and tested the payroll and personnel cycle's internal control and concluded that it contains no significant weaknesses. Your tests included tests of the time cards, withholdings, pay rates, the filing of all required employee withholding and benefits remittance forms, payroll cheques, and all other aspects of payroll.

As part of the year-end tests of payroll, you are responsible for verifying all accrued payroll as well as the company's liability for withholdings and accrued benefits. The accrued factory payroll includes the last six working days of the current year. The client has calculated accrued wages by taking 60 percent of the subsequent period's gross payroll and has recorded it as an adjusting entry to be reversed in the subsequent period.

Required

List all audit procedures, organized by assertion, you would follow in verifying accrued payroll and the liability for withholdings and accrued employee benefits.

16-18 In the audit of Larnet Manufacturing Corp., the auditor concluded that internal controls were inadequate because of the lack of segregation of duties. As a result, the decision was made to have a surprise payroll payoff one month before the client's balance sheet date. Since the auditor had never been involved in a payroll payoff, she did not know how to proceed.

Required

a. What is the purpose of a surprise payroll payoff?

b. What other audit procedures can the auditor perform that may fulfill the same objectives?
c. Discuss the procedures that the auditor should require the client to observe when the surprise payroll payoff is taking place.
d. At the completion of the payroll payoff, there are frequently several unclaimed cheques. What procedures should be followed for these?

16-19 During the first-year audit of Omato Wholesale Stationery Ltd., you observe that commissions amount to almost 25 percent of total sales, which is somewhat higher than in previous years. Further investigation reveals that the industry typically has larger sales commissions than Omato and that there is significant variation in rates depending on the product sold.

At the time a sale is made, the salesperson records his or her commission rate and the total amount of the commissions on the office copy of the sales invoice. When sales are entered into the microcomputer system for the recording of sales, the debit to sales commission expense and credit to accrued sales commission are also recorded. As part of recording the sales and sales commission expense, the accounts receivable clerk verifies the prices, quantities, commission rates, and all calculations on the sales invoices. Both the customer master and the salespersons' commission master files are updated when the sale and sales commission are recorded. On the fifteenth day after the end of the month, the salesperson is paid for the preceding month's sales commissions.

Required

a. Develop an audit program, by assertion, to verify sales commission expense assuming that no audit tests have been conducted in any audit area to this point.
b. Develop an audit program, by assertion, to verify accrued sales commissions at the end of the year assuming that the tests you designed in part (a) resulted in no significant misstatements.

16-20 Dunlop Ltd., a property management company, has a subsidiary, Riber Ltd., that is constructing an office building to be operated as a rental property by Dunlop. The building is being constructed by an independent contractor on the basis of direct costs plus 20 percent. Direct costs are defined as material used and labour costs incurred in the construction. The 20 percent is intended to cover overhead and profit.

At August 31, 2005, the degree of completion is estimated at 75 percent. Brett Dunlop, president of Dunlop, has just asked you as Dunlop's and Riber's internal auditor to conduct an investigation of the labour costs that are about $1 million over estimates. Dunlop has some concerns about the contractor's honesty. He says that he is satisfied with the material costs, however.

A review of the contract between Riber and the contractor and a talk with Dunlop reveal the following:

1. Wage rates, specified in the contract, are based on union contracts. The rates vary with the trade and worker's experience.
2. Employees are paid by the contractor. The payroll records are kept by an independent computer service bureau. The contractor sends a monthly payroll summary by employee to Riber to support her invoice.

3. Brett Dunlop explained that construction workers' mobility made it very difficult to verify that employees listed on the monthly summary actually worked on the site. He added that he had no confidence in the timekeeping system used on the site.
4. The contract provides Riber with the right to examine the books of the contractor.

Required

List the procedures, by assertion, you would perform to carry out the investigation requested by Dunlop. State why you would perform each procedure.

(CICA adapted)

PROFESSIONAL JUDGMENT PROBLEM

16-21 Archer Uniforms, Inc., is a distributor of professional uniforms to retail stores that sell work clothing to professionals, such as doctors, nurses, and security guards. Traditionally, most of the sales are to retail stores throughout Canada and the United States. Most shipments are processed in bulk for delivery directly to retail stores or to the corporate office warehouse distribution facilities for retail store chains. In early 2004, Archer Uniforms began offering the sale of uniforms directly to professionals through its company web site. Professionals can access online information about uniform styles, sizes, and prices. Purchases are applied to the customer's personal credit card, and the credit card agencies wire funds to Archer's bank account periodically throughout the month. Management made this decision based on its conclusion that the online sales would tap a new market of professionals who do not have easy access to retail stores. Thus, the volume of shipments to retail stores is expected to remain consistent.

Given that Archer's IT staff lacked the necessary experience to create and support the online sales system, management engaged an information technology consulting firm to design and maintain the online sales system.

Required

a. Before performing analytical procedures related to the payroll and personnel cycle accounts, develop expectations of how these recent events at Archer Uniforms, Inc., will affect payroll expense for the following departments during 2004 compared to prior years. Indicate the degree (extensive, moderate, little) to which you expect the payroll expense account balance to increase or decrease during 2004, with reasons supported by the facts of the case.

1. Warehouse and Shipping Department
2. IT Department
3. Accounts Receivable Department
4. Accounts Payable Department
5. Receiving Department
6. Executive Management
7. Marketing

b. Provide additional audit procedures (by assertion) that might be required.

CASES

16-22 Carrie Ahwahli is the auditor of Abbolah Ltd., a large manufacturing company with several plants across Canada. All accounting records are automated using a combination of software packages and customized programming.

In prior years, Abbolah had never recorded accrued vacation pay in its accounts but instead had recognized the expense when vacations were taken by the employees. This was considered reasonable since employees took their vacation throughout the year. For the year ended December 31, 2005, however, the company decided to set up the liability at that date for accrued vacation pay. This coincided with changes in personnel policies requiring employees to take their holidays in specified time periods during the year.

The company employs approximately 2,400 employees, each of whom belongs to one of four unions. Employees' entitlement to vacation pay is based on length of service (calculated from the month of employment) and varies according to the terms of each union contract. Some specific variations in calculations are required based on sick-leave entitlements as well.

Complete personnel information for all employees is maintained on a payroll master file, which is updated weekly. An "Employee Status Report" containing all master file details for specified employees is produced on request.

A specially written computer program was prepared to determine the amount of accrued vacation pay, since the standard software packages used by the company could not handle the calculations. This program extracted the relevant data from the payroll master file as at December 31, 2005, calculated the amount of accrued vacation pay for each employee, recorded the details in a separate data file, and printed a summarized report showing only the grand total of the accrued vacation pay.

Required

a. How could an audit trail be provided to enable Carrie to perform tests of details of the accrued vacation pay? What practical difficulties may arise?
b. Explain briefly how Carrie could use either test data or generalized audit software to check the accuracy of the computer program.

(CICA adapted)

16-23 In many companies, labour costs represent a substantial percentage of total dollars expended in any one accounting period. One of the auditor's primary means of verifying payroll transactions is by a detailed payroll test.

You are making an annual examination of Lethbridge Inc., a medium-sized manufacturing company. You have selected a number of hourly employees for a detailed payroll test. The worksheet outline at right has been prepared.

Required

a. What factors should the auditor consider in selecting his or her sample of employees to be included in any payroll test?

b. Using the column numbers as a reference, state the principal way(s) that the information for each heading would be verified.

c. In addition to the payroll test, the auditor employs a number of other audit procedures in the verification of payroll transactions. List five additional procedures that may be employed and the corresponding audit objective.

Column Number	Heading
1	Employee number
2	Employee name
3	Job classification
	Hours worked:
4	Straight time
5	Premium time
6	Hourly rate
7	Gross earnings
	Deductions:
8	Income tax withheld
9	Canada Pension Plan withheld
10	Employment insurance withheld
11	Union dues
12	Amount of cheque
13	Cheque number
14	Account number charged
15	Description of account

(AICPA adapted)

CHAPTER 17

AUDIT OF THE ACQUISITION AND PAYMENT CYCLE

How do you pay your bills? Do you have a credit card statement that is paid monthly? Do you have any payments that you pay by cheque or via electronic banking? Profit-oriented and other businesses also have many different ways that they pay their bills. As auditors, we need to be concerned, first of all, that only appropriate bills are recorded in the financial statements, and also that none are omitted. Then, we also audit the payment process.

LEARNING OBJECTIVES

After reading this chapter, you should be able to answer the following questions:

1. What are the major business functions, documents, and records in the acquisition and payment cycle?

2. How are tests of controls designed for the acquisition and payment cycle?

3. Why is accounts payable considered separately from acquisitions or payments? Why is the auditor more concerned about understatement of accounts payable rather than overstatement?

4. What is a system conversion? What issues does the auditor need to address during a conversion audit?

FALSE PURCHASES CAMOUFLAGE OVERSTATED PROFITS

Comptronix Corporation announced that senior members of its management team had overstated profits and there would be material adjustments to the prior years' audited financial statements. Central to the fraud was the use of fictitious accounts payable purchases for large equipment items to overstate fixed assets and hide fictitious sales.

The senior executives circumvented Comptronix's existing internal controls by bypassing the purchasing and receiving departments so that no one at Comptronix could discover the scheme. Comptronix employees usually created a fairly extensive paper trail for equipment purchases. Company internal controls over acquisition and cash disbursement transactions typically required a purchase order, receiving report, and vendor invoice before payment could be authorized by the Chief Operating Officer or the controller/treasurer, who were both participants in the fraud. As a result, the executives were able to bypass controls related to cash disbursements and authorize payment for nonexistent purchases without creating any documents for the fictitious transactions.

The company also created fictitious sales and related receivables. The company issued cheques to pay for the false purchase transactions. The cheques were then redeposited into the company's account and recorded as collections on the fictitious receivables. As a result, it appeared that the fictitious sales were collected, and that payment was made to support the false fixed asset purchases.

Sources: 1. Accounting and Auditing Enforcement Release No. 543, Commerce Clearing House, Inc., Chicago. 2. Beasley, Mark S., Frank A. Buckless, Steven M. Glover, Douglas F. Prawitt. 2003. "Comptronix Corporation: Identifying Inherent Risk and Control Risk Factors," Case 11 in Auditing Cases, an Interactive Learning Approach, Second Edition, Toronto: Prentice Hall.

What types of audit tests would detect fictitious purchases? Or fictitious customers? This case illustrates how inherent and control risks associated with financial statement fraud have an impact on two specific transaction cycles—purchases and sales. The audit needs to be an integrated process that considers the effect of risks at each cycle.

→17.1 THE NATURE OF THE ACQUISITION AND PAYMENT CYCLE

The acquisition of goods and services includes such items as the purchase of raw materials, equipment, supplies, utilities, repairs and maintenance, and research and development. The cycle does not include the acquisition and payment of employees' services or the internal transfers and allocations of costs within the organization. The former are a part of the payroll and personnel function, and the latter are audited as part of the verification of individual assets or liabilities. The acquisition and payment cycle also excludes the acquisition and repayment of capital (interest-bearing debt and owners' equity), which are considered separately in Chapter 20.

The audit of the acquisition and payment cycle is studied in Chapters 17 and 18. In this chapter, the format for discussing internal control introduced in earlier chapters is repeated. In Chapter 18, several other important balance sheet accounts that are a part of the acquisition and payment cycle are examined. These are manufacturing equipment, prepaid insurance, and accrued liabilities. The chapter also discusses tests of details of income statement accounts included in the acquisition and payment cycle.

ACQUISITION AND PAYMENT CYCLE—the transaction cycle that includes the acquisition of and payment for goods and services from suppliers outside the organization

The **acquisition and payment cycle** includes two distinct classes of transactions— acquisitions of goods and services and cash disbursements for those acquisitions. Purchases returns and allowances is also a class of transactions, but, for most companies, the amounts are immaterial.

There are a larger number and variety of accounts in the acquisition and payment cycle in a typical company than for any other cycle. Examine the trial balance for Hillsburg Hardware Limited on page 117. Accounts affected by the acquisition and payment cycle are identified by the letter "*A*" in the left column. Notice first that accounts affected by the cycle include asset, liability, expense, and miscellaneous income accounts, and second, the large number of accounts affected. It is not surprising, therefore, that it often takes more time to audit the acquisition and payment cycle than any other cycle.

The way the accounting information flows through the various accounts in the acquisition and payment cycle is illustrated by T-accounts in Figure 17-1. To keep the illustration manageable, only the control accounts are shown for the three major categories of expenses used by most companies. For each control account, examples of the subsidiary expense accounts are also given.

Figure 17-1 shows that every transaction is either debited or credited to accounts payable. Because many companies make some purchases directly by cheque or through petty cash, the figure is an oversimplification. We assume that cash transactions are processed in the same manner as transactions flowing through accounts payable.

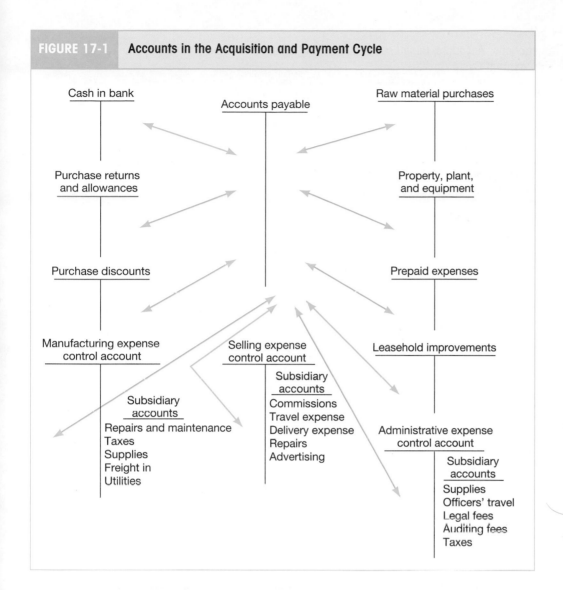

| FIGURE 17-1 | Accounts in the Acquisition and Payment Cycle |

The acquisition and payment cycle involves the decisions and processes necessary for obtaining the goods and services for operating a business. The cycle typically begins with the initiation of a purchase requisition by an authorized employee who needs the goods or services and ends with payment for the benefits received. Although the discussion that follows deals with a small manufacturing company that makes tangible products for sale to third parties, the same principles apply to a service company, a government unit, or any other type of organization.

Column 3 of Table 17-1 identifies the five business functions in a typical acquisition and payment cycle. The table shows the relationships among the classes of transactions, accounts, business functions, and documents and records. The business functions and related documents are discussed in this section. In addition, there is a discussion of key internal controls to prevent misstatements and to ensure the safety of assets.

Processing Purchase Orders The request for goods or services by the client's personnel is the starting point for the cycle. The exact form of the request and the required approval depend on the nature of the goods and services and company policy.

PURCHASE REQUISITION A **purchase requisition** is a request for goods and services by an authorized employee. It may take the form of a request for such acquisitions as materials by a shop supervisor or the storeroom supervisor, outside repairs by office or factory personnel, or insurance by the vice-president in charge of property and equipment.

PURCHASE REQUISITION—request by an authorized employee to the purchasing department to place an order for inventory and other items used by an entity

Classes of Transactions	Accounts	Business Functions	Documents and Records
Acquisitions	Inventory Property, plant, and equipment Prepaid expenses Leasehold improvements Accounts payable Manufacturing expenses Selling expenses Administrative expenses	Processing purchase orders	Purchase requisition Purchase order Vendor master file Purchase transaction file
		Receiving goods and services Recognizing the liability Vendor master file changes	Receiving report Acquisitions journal Summary acquisitions report Vendor's invoice Debit memo Vendor transaction file Voucher Vendor master file Accounts payable trial balance Vendor's statement
Cash disbursements	Cash in bank (from cash disbursements) Accounts payable Purchase discounts	Processing and recording cash disbursements	Cheque Cheque transaction file Cash disbursements journal

PURCHASE ORDER—a document prepared by the purchasing department indicating the description, quantity, and related information for goods and services that the company intends to purchase

PURCHASE ORDER A **purchase order** document records the description, quantity, and related information for goods and services that the company intends to purchase. This document is frequently used to indicate authorization to procure goods and services. Purchase order details are retained in a *purchase order transaction file.*

VENDOR MASTER FILE This file sums individual acquisitions, cash disbursements, and acquisition returns and allowances for each vendor. Those companies that have automated purchasing systems ensure that authorized vendor information, such as credit terms, contact name, and shipping terms, is established and recorded in the vendor master file. The file also keeps track of total purchase commitments and total liabilities (unpaid invoices) by vendor.

PURCHASE ORDER TRANSACTION FILE As purchase commitments are made, transaction details are recorded in the purchase order file. Automated systems automatically number the purchase orders sequentially and assist in tracking purchase commitments, expected delivery dates, and items that have been back-ordered (i.e., when the vendor currently does not have stock, but shipments are expected later).

INTERNAL CONTROLS Proper *authorization* for acquisitions and changes to the vendor master file is an essential part of this function because it ensures that the goods and services acquired are for authorized company purposes, and it avoids the acquisition of excessive or unnecessary items. Most companies permit general authorization for the acquisition of regular operating needs, such as inventory at one level and acquisitions of capital assets or similar items at another. For example, acquisitions of capital assets in excess of a specified dollar limit may require board of directors' action; items acquired relatively infrequently, such as insurance policies and long-term service contracts, are approved by certain officers; supplies and services costing less than a designated amount are approved by supervisors and department heads; and some types of raw materials and supplies are re-ordered automatically whenever they fall to a predetermined level, often by direct communication with vendors' computers. Where automatic purchase orders are generated, care must be taken to ensure that re-order points are monitored so that only those goods still required by the company are purchased.

After an acquisition has been approved, an order to acquire the goods and services must be initiated. An order is issued to a vendor for a specified item at a certain price to be delivered at or by a designated time. The order is usually in writing and is a legal document that is an offer to buy. For most routine items, a purchase order is used to indicate the offer.

It is common for companies to establish purchasing departments to ensure an adequate quality of goods and services at a minimum price. For good internal control, the purchasing department should not be responsible for authorizing the acquisition or receiving the goods. All purchase orders should be prenumbered and should include sufficient columns and spaces to minimize the likelihood of unintentional omissions on the form when goods are ordered.

Receiving Goods and Services The receipt by the company of goods and services from the vendor is a critical point in the cycle because it is the point at which most companies first recognize the acquisition and related liability on their records. When goods are received, adequate control requires examination for description, quantity, timely arrival, and condition.

RECEIVING REPORT A **receiving report** document is prepared at the time tangible goods are received and indicates the description of goods, the quantity received, the date received, and other relevant data. The receipt of goods and services in the normal course of business represents the date that clients normally recognize the liability for an acquisition. Where an organization has automated purchase order systems, the receipt needs to be entered into the computer system to signal that the goods have been received. This information would also be used to update perpetual inventory systems.

INTERNAL CONTROLS Most companies have the receiving department initiate a receiving report as evidence of the receipt and examination of goods. One copy is normally sent to the storeroom, where it is used to update the quantity fields of the computer records, and another to the accounts payable department for its information needs. To prevent theft and misuse, it is

RECEIVING REPORT—a document prepared by the receiving department at the time tangible goods are received, indicating the description of the goods, the quantity received, the date received, and other relevant data; part of the documentation necessary for payment to be made important that the goods be *physically controlled* from the time of their receipt until their disposal. The personnel in the receiving department should be independent of the storeroom personnel and the accounting department. Finally, the accounting records should transfer responsibility for the goods as they are transferred from receiving to storage and from storage to manufacturing.

Recognizing the Liability The proper recognition of the liability for the receipt of goods and services requires *prompt and accurate* recording. The initial recording has a significant effect on the recorded financial statements and the actual cash disbursement; therefore, great care must be taken to include only existing company acquisitions at the correct amounts.

ACQUISITIONS JOURNAL This journal lists acquisition transactions. A detailed acquisitions journal includes each acquisition transaction. It usually includes several classifications for the most significant types of acquisitions, such as the purchase of inventory, repairs and maintenance, supplies, the entry to accounts payable, and miscellaneous debits and credits. The acquisitions journal can also include acquisition returns and allowances transactions if a separate journal is not used. The acquisitions journal is generated for any time period from the acquisition transactions included in the computer files. Individual transaction amounts are posted to the vendor master file and journal totals are posted to the general ledger.

SUMMARY ACQUISITIONS REPORT This report summarizes acquisitions for a period. The report typically includes information analyzed by key components such as account classification, type of inventory, and division.

VENDOR'S INVOICE The **vendor's invoice** indicates such things as the description and quantity of goods and services received, price including freight, cash discount terms, and date of the billing. It is an essential document because it specifies the amount of money owed to the vendor for an acquisition.

DEBIT MEMO The **debit memo** indicates a reduction in the amount owed to a vendor because of returned goods or an allowance granted. It often takes the same general form as a vendor's invoice, but it supports reductions in accounts payable rather than increases.

VENDOR TRANSACTION FILE This file, detailing transactions of individual vendors, indicates both the details of the vendor's invoice and debit memo details from accounts payable. Payments to vendors are deducted from outstanding transactions and recorded in a cheque transaction file. Unpaid transactions are used to prepare the *accounts payable trial balance*. The sum of the unpaid transactions should always agree to the sum of liabilities in the vendor master file and to the general ledger accounts payable total.

VOUCHER This document is frequently used by organizations to establish a formal means of recording and controlling acquisitions. Vouchers include a cover sheet or folder for containing documents and a package of relevant documents such as the purchase order, copy of the packing slip, receiving report, and vendor's invoice. After payment, a copy of the cheque is added to the voucher package.

VENDOR MASTER FILE As described earlier, the **vendor master file** sums individual acquisitions, cash disbursements, and acquisition returns and allowances for each vendor. The master file is updated from the purchase order, receiving report, invoice, returns and allowances, and cash disbursements transaction files. The total of the individual account balances in the master file equals the total balance of accounts payable in the general ledger.

ACCOUNTS PAYABLE TRIAL BALANCE The **accounts payable trial balance** is a listing by each vendor of the amount owed at a point in time. It is prepared directly from the accounts payable master file and open item transaction files. It can be prepared in summary form (showing totals only by vendor) or in detail (showing the current month's transactions plus any unpaid transactions making up the opening balance).

VENDOR'S STATEMENT The **vendor's statement**, prepared monthly by the vendor, indicates a customer's beginning balance, acquisitions, returns and allowances, payments, and ending balance. These balances and activities are the vendor's representations of the transactions for the period and not the client's. Except for disputed amounts and timing differences, the client's accounts payable transaction file details and vendor master file totals should be the same as the vendor's statement.

INTERNAL CONTROLS In some companies, the recording of the liability for acquisitions is made on the basis of the receipt of goods and services, and in other companies, it is deferred until the vendor's invoice is received. In either case, the accounts payable department typically has responsibility for verifying the propriety of acquisitions. This is done by comparing the details on the purchase order, the receiving report, and the vendor's invoice to determine that the descriptions, prices, quantities, terms, and freight on the vendor's invoice are correct. Typically, extensions, footings, and account distribution are also verified.

The level of automation of the accounts payable system varies. Some organizations simply record the total amount of the vendor invoice into the accounts payable system. In that case, it is important that all of the above steps, including recalculation of the vendor invoice, are completed before the invoice is entered into the system. For highly integrated computer systems, the vendor invoice details entered manually or received electronically include each line of the invoice (i.e., the item number, description, quantity, price, and terms). The computer systems can then make the comparison to the purchase order details and recalculate the vendor invoice. Accurate and authorized entry by the organization's personnel of receiving order details is important so that the system can confirm that the quantity received is equal to the quantity ordered and the quantity billed by the vendor.

An important control in the accounts payable and information processing departments is requiring that those personnel who record acquisitions *do not have access* to cash, marketable securities, and other assets. Adequate documents and records, proper procedures for record keeping, and independent checks on performance are also necessary controls in the accounts payable function.

Processing and Recording Cash Disbursements For most companies, payment is made by computer-prepared cheques from information included in the acquisition transactions file at the time goods and services are received. Cheques are typically prepared in a multi-copy format, with the original going to the payee, one copy being filed with the vendor's invoice and other supporting documents, and another copy being filed numerically. In most cases, individual cheques are recorded in a cash disbursements (cheque) transactions file.

CHEQUE This is the means of paying for the acquisition when payment is due. After the cheque is signed by an authorized person, it is an asset. Therefore, signed cheques should be mailed by the signer or a person under his or her control. When cashed by the vendor and cleared by the client's bank, it is referred to as a "cancelled cheque."

CASH DISBURSEMENTS JOURNAL This journal is for recording cash disbursement transactions. The cash disbursements journal is generated for any time period from the cash disbursement (cheque) transactions included in the computer files. Details from the transaction file are posted to the vendor transaction file and vendor master file. Transaction totals are posted to the general ledger.

INTERNAL CONTROLS The most important controls in the cash disbursements function include the signing of cheques by an individual with proper authority, separation of responsibilities for signing the cheques and performing the accounts payable function, and careful examination of the supporting documents by the cheque signer at the time the cheque is signed.

The cheques should be prenumbered and printed on special paper that makes it difficult to alter the payee or amount. Care should be taken to provide physical control over blank, voided, and signed cheques. It is also important to have a method of cancelling the supporting documents to prevent their re-use as support for another cheque at a later time. A common method is to mark the documents as "entered" when recorded in the computer system and to write the cheque number on the supporting documents when cheques are issued or documents are paid (e.g., electronic bank transfer).

→17.2   TESTS OF CONTROLS

In a typical audit, the most time-consuming accounts to verify by tests of details of balances are accounts receivable, inventory, capital assets, accounts payable, and expense accounts. Of these five, four are directly related to the acquisition and payment cycle. The net time saved can be dramatic if the auditor can reduce the tests of details of the accounts by using tests of controls to verify the effectiveness of internal controls for acquisitions and cash disbursements. It should not be surprising, therefore, that tests of controls for the acquisition and payment cycle receive a considerable amount of attention in well-conducted audits, especially when the client has effective internal controls.

Tests of controls for the acquisition and payment cycle are divided into two broad areas: *tests of acquisitions* and *tests of payments*. Acquisition tests concern four of the five functions discussed earlier in the chapter: processing purchase orders, vendor master file changes, receiving goods and services, and recognizing the liability. Tests of payments concern the fifth function, processing and recording cash disbursements.

The six transaction-related audit objectives developed in Chapters 5 and 9 are again used as the frame of reference for designing tests of controls for acquisition and cash disbursement transactions. For each objective, the auditor must go through the same logical process that has been discussed in previous chapters. First, the auditor must understand the general controls applicable to the cycle and the cycle's internal controls to determine which controls exist. After the auditor has identified existing controls and weaknesses for each objective, an initial assessment of control risk can be made for each objective. At this point, the auditor must decide which controls he or she plans to test to satisfy the initial assessment of control risk. After the auditor has developed the audit procedures for each objective, the procedures can be combined into an audit program that can be efficiently performed. Figure 17-2 summarizes that methodology. It is the same one used in Chapter 13 for sales and cash receipts. Again, the emphasis in the methodology is on determining the appropriate audit procedures, sample size, items to select, and timing.

Verifying Acquisitions   Key internal controls and common tests of controls for each transaction-related audit objective are summarized in Table 17-2. An assumption underlying the internal controls and audit procedures is the existence of a separate acquisitions process for recording all acquisitions.

In studying Table 17-2, it is important to relate internal controls to objectives and to relate tests of controls to both internal controls and monetary misstatements that would be absent or present due to controls and weaknesses in the system. It should be kept in mind that a set of audit procedures for a particular audit engagement will vary with the internal controls and other circumstances.

Four of the objectives for acquisitions deserve special attention. A discussion of each of these objectives follows.

RECORDED ACQUISITIONS ARE FOR GOODS AND SERVICES RECEIVED, CONSISTENT WITH THE BEST INTERESTS OF THE CLIENT (OCCURRENCE)   If the auditor is satisfied that the controls are adequate for this objective, tests for improper and nonexistent transactions can be greatly reduced. Adequate controls are likely to prevent the client from including as a business expense or asset those transactions that primarily benefit management or other employees rather than the entity being audited. In some instances, improper transactions are obvious, such as the acquisition of unauthorized personal items by employees or the actual embezzlement of cash by recording a fraudulent purchase in the purchases journal. In other instances, the propriety of a transaction is more difficult to evaluate, such as the payment of officers' memberships to country clubs, expense-paid vacations to foreign countries for members of management and their families, and management-approved illegal payments to officials of foreign countries. If the controls over improper or nonexistent transactions are inadequate, extensive examination of supporting documentation is necessary.

EXISTING ACQUISITIONS ARE RECORDED (COMPLETENESS)   Failure to record the acquisition of goods and services received directly affects the balance in accounts payable and may result in an overstatement of net income and owners' equity. Because of this, auditors are usually very

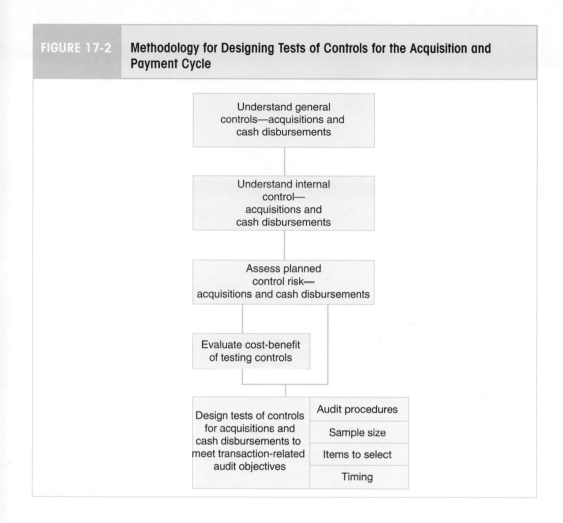

concerned with the completeness objective. In some instances, it may be difficult to perform tests of details to determine whether there are unrecorded transactions, and the auditor must rely on controls for this purpose. In addition, since the audit of accounts payable generally takes a considerable amount of audit time, effective internal control, properly tested, can significantly reduce audit costs.

ACQUISITIONS ARE ACCURATELY RECORDED (ACCURACY) Since the accuracy of many asset, liability, and expense accounts depends on the correct recording of transactions in the acquisitions journal, the extent of tests of details of many balance sheet and expense accounts depends on the auditor's evaluation of the effectiveness of the internal controls over the accuracy of recorded acquisitions transactions. For example, if the auditor believes the capital assets are correctly recorded in the books of original entry, it is acceptable to vouch fewer current period acquisitions than if the controls are inadequate.

When a client uses perpetual inventory records, the tests of details of inventory can also be significantly reduced if the auditor believes the perpetuals are accurate. The controls over the acquisitions included in the perpetuals are normally tested as a part of the tests of controls for acquisitions, and the controls over this objective play a key role in the audit. The inclusion of both quantity and unit costs in the inventory perpetual records permits a reduction in the tests of the physical count and the unit costs of inventory if the controls are operating effectively.

ACQUISITIONS ARE CORRECTLY CLASSIFIED (CLASSIFICATION) The auditor can reduce the tests of details of certain individual accounts if he or she believes internal control is adequate to provide reasonable assurance of correct classification in the acquisitions journal. Although all accounts are affected to some degree by effective controls over classification, the two areas most affected are current period acquisitions of capital assets and all expense accounts, such

Transaction-Related Audit Objective	Key Internal Control	Common Tests of Controls	
Recorded acquisitions are for goods and services received, consistent with the best interests of the client (occurrence).	Existence of purchase requisition, purchase order, receiving report, and vendor's invoice attached to the voucher.[†]	Examine documents in voucher for existence.	Review the acquisitions journal, general ledger, and transaction files for large or unusual amounts.[*]
	Approval of acquisitions at the proper level. Cancellation of documents to prevent their re-use.	Examine indication of approval. Examine indication of cancellation.	Examine underlying documents for reasonableness and authenticity (vendors' invoices, receiving reports, purchase orders, and requisitions).
	Internal verification of vendors' invoices, receiving reports, purchase orders, and purchase requisitions.[†]	Examine indication of internal verification.[‡]	Trace inventory purchases to inventory files. Examine capital assets acquired.
	New vendors and changes to vendor file approved. Vendor master file independently examined periodically.	Examine master file change forms, and trace details to vendor master file. Discuss review process with management.	Review vendor master file for unusual credit terms, prices, or P.O. box addresses.[‡]
Existing acquisition transactions are recorded (completeness).	Purchase orders are prenumbered and accounted for.	Account for a sequence of purchase orders.[‡]	Trace from a file of receiving reports to the acquisitions journal.[†]
	Receiving reports are prenumbered and accounted for.[†] Vouchers are prenumbered and accounted for. Internal verification of calculations and amounts.	Account for a sequence of receiving reports.[‡] Account for a sequence of vouchers.[‡]	Trace from a file of vendors' invoices to the acquisitions journal.
Recorded acquisition transactions are accurate (accuracy).	Batch totals are compared with computer summary reports. Approval of acquisitions for prices and discounts.	Examine indication of internal verification.[‡] Examine file of batch totals for initials of data control clerk; compare totals to summary reports.[‡] Examine indication of approval.	Compare recorded transactions in the acquisitions journal with the vendor's invoice, receiving report, and other supporting documentation.[†‡] Recompute the clerical accuracy on the vendors' invoices, including discounts and freight.[‡]
Acquisition transactions are properly classified (classification).	Adequate chart of accounts. Automatic updates and posting.	Examine procedures manual and chart of accounts. Enter test transactions or observe entry, and trace to correct file.	Compare classification with chart of accounts by reference to vendors' invoices.
Acquisition transactions are recorded on the correct dates (timing).	Procedures require recording transactions as soon as possible after the goods and services have been received. Transaction date must be system date (today's date) or a reasonable date.	Examine procedures manual and observe whether unrecorded vendors' invoices exist. Observe data entry process.	Compare dates of receiving reports and vendors' invoices with dates in the acquisitions journal.[†]
Acquisition transactions are properly included in the vendor and inventory master files, and are properly summarized (posting and summarization).	Comparison of accounts payable master file or trial balance totals with general ledger balance.	Examine initials on general ledger accounts indicating comparison.	Test clerical accuracy by footing the journals and tracing postings to general ledger and accounts payable and inventory master files.

[*] This analytical procedure can also apply to other objectives including completeness, valuation, and timing.

[†] Receiving reports are used only for tangible goods and are therefore not available for services, such as utilities and repairs and maintenance. Frequently, vendors' invoices are the only documentation available.

[‡] This control would be tested on many audits by using the computer.

as repairs and maintenance, utilities, and advertising. Since performing documentation tests of current period capital asset acquisitions and expense accounts for accuracy are relatively time-consuming audit procedures, the saving in audit time can be significant.

Verifying Cash Disbursements The same format used in Table 17-2 for acquisitions is also used in Table 17-3 for cash disbursements. The assumption underlying these controls and audit procedures is the existence of separate cash disbursements and acquisitions processes. The comments made about the methodology and process for developing audit procedures for acquisitions apply equally to cash disbursements.

Once the auditor has decided on procedures, the acquisitions and cash disbursements tests are typically performed concurrently. For example, for a transaction selected for examination from the acquisitions journal, the vendor's invoice and the receiving report are examined at the same time as the related cancelled cheque. Thus, the verification is speeded up without reducing the effectiveness of the tests.

Attribute Sampling for Tests of Controls Because of the importance of tests of controls for acquisitions and cash disbursements, the use of attribute sampling is common in this audit area. The approach is basically the same as for the tests of controls of sales discussed in Chapter 13. It should be noted, however, with particular reference to the most essential transaction-related audit objectives presented earlier, that most of the important attributes in the acquisition and payment cycle have a direct monetary effect on the accounts. Furthermore, many of the types of errors or fraud and other irregularities that may be found represent a misstatement of earnings and are of significant concern to the auditor. For example, there may be inventory cutoff misstatements or an incorrect recording of an expense amount. Because of this, the tolerable exception rate selected by the auditor in tests of many of the attributes in this cycle is relatively low. Since the dollar amounts of individual transactions in the cycle cover a wide range, it is also common to segregate very large and unusual items and to test them on a 100 percent basis.

→17.3 AUDIT OF ACCOUNTS PAYABLE

Accounts payable are unpaid obligations for goods and services received in the ordinary course of business. It is sometimes difficult to distinguish between accounts payable and accrued liabilities, but it is useful to define a liability as an account payable if the total amount of the obligation is known and owed at the balance sheet date. The accounts payable account therefore includes obligations for the acquisition of raw materials, equipment, utilities, repairs, and many other types of goods and services that were received before the end of the year. The great majority of accounts payable can also be recognized by the existence of vendors' invoices for the obligation. Accounts payable should also be distinguished from interest-bearing obligations. If an obligation includes the payment of interest, it should be recorded properly as a note payable, contract payable, mortgage payable, or bond payable.

The methodology for designing tests of details for accounts payable is summarized in Figure 17-3. This methodology is the same as that used for accounts receivable in Chapter 14. It is common for accounts payable to be material and thus there may be several inherent risks. Internal controls are often ineffective for accounts payable because many companies depend on the vendors to bill them and remind them of unpaid bills. Tests of details for accounts payable, therefore, often need to be extensive.

Internal Controls The effects of the client's internal controls on accounts payable tests can be illustrated by two examples. In the first, assume that the client has highly effective internal controls over recording and paying for acquisitions. The receipt of goods is promptly documented by prenumbered receiving reports; prenumbered vouchers are promptly and efficiently prepared and recorded in the acquisition transactions file and thus in the vendor master file. Cash disbursements are also made promptly when due, and the disbursements are immediately recorded in the cash disbursements transactions file and the vendor master file. On a monthly basis, individual accounts payable balances in the vendor master file are reconciled with vendors' statements, and the total is compared with the general ledger

Transaction-Related Audit Objective	Key Internal Control	Common Tests of Controls	
Recorded cash disbursements are for goods and services actually received (occurrence).	Adequate segregation of duties between accounts payable and custody of signed cheques. Examination of supporting documentation before signing of cheques by an authorized person. Approval of payment on supporting documents at the time cheques are signed.	Discuss with personnel and observe activities. Discuss with personnel and observe activities. Examine indication of approval.	Review the cash disbursements journal, general ledger, and vendor master file for large or unusual amounts.* Trace the cancelled cheque to the related acquisitions journal entry and examine for payee name and amount. Examine cancelled cheque for authorized signature, proper endorsement, and cancellation by the bank. Examine supporting documents as a part of the tests of acquisitions.
Existing cash disbursement transactions are recorded (completeness).	Cheques are prenumbered and accounted for. A bank reconciliation is prepared monthly by an employee independent of recording cash disbursements or custody of assets.	Account for a sequence of cheques.† Examine bank reconciliations and observe their preparation.	Reconcile recorded cash disbursements with the cash disbursements on the bank statement (proof of cash disbursements).
Recorded cash disbursement transactions are accurate (accuracy).	Internal verification of calculations and amounts. Monthly preparation of a bank reconciliation by an independent person.	Examine indication of internal verification.† Examine bank reconciliations and observe their preparation.	Compare cancelled cheques with the related acquisitions journal and cash disbursements journal entries.† Recompute cash discounts.† Prepare a proof of cash disbursements.
Cash disbursement transactions are properly classified (classification).	Adequate chart of accounts. Internal verification of classification.	Examine procedures manual and chart of accounts. Examine indication of internal verification.	Compare classification with chart of accounts by reference to vendors' invoices and acquisitions journal.
Cash disbursement transactions are recorded on the correct dates (timing).	Procedures require recording of transactions as soon as possible after the cheque has been signed. Transaction date must be system date.	Examine procedures manual and observe whether unrecorded cheques exist. Observe data entry process.	Compare dates on cancelled cheques with the cash disbursements journal. Compare dates on cancelled cheques with the bank cancellation date.
Cash disbursement transactions are properly included in the vendor master file and properly summarized (posting and summarization).	Internal verification of vendor master file contents. Comparison of vendor master file or trial balance totals with general ledger balance.	Examine indication of internal verification.† Examine initials on general ledger accounts indicating comparison.	Test clerical accuracy by footing journals and tracing postings to general ledger and vendor master file.†

*This analytical procedure can also apply to other objectives including completeness, accuracy, and timing.
† This control would be tested on many audits by using the computer.

by an independent person. Under these circumstances, the verification of accounts payable should require little audit effort once the auditor concludes that internal controls are operating effectively.

In the second example, assume that receiving reports are not used, the client defers recording acquisitions until cash disbursements are made, and, because of a weak cash

FIGURE 17-3

Methodology for Designing Tests of Details of Balances of Accounts Payable

Set materiality and assess audit risk and inherent risk for accounts payable

Assess control risk for accounts payable

Design and perform tests of controls for the acquisition and payment cycle

Design and perform analytical procedures for the acquisition and payment cycle

Design tests of details of accounts payable balance to satisfy balance-related audit objectives

| Audit procedures |
| Sample size |
| Items to select |
| Timing |

Materiality Considerations
Most companies have a large number of acquisition and cash disbursement transactions and one or more material balance sheet accounts such as accounts payable and property, plant, and equipment. There are also likely to be several immaterial accounts such as prepaid expenses and certain accruals.

Inherent Risk Considerations
Inherent risks are likely to vary widely from company to company for this cycle. Examples of potentially high inherent risk circumstances follow:

- Extensive trade-ins of property, plant, and equipment
- Significant related party transactions
- Purchases of goods and services for construction of buildings or equipment

Control Risk Considerations
Internal controls vary widely from company to company for this cycle. Many smaller companies often lack separation of duties and other controls. Larger companies typically, but not always, have highly effective internal controls over acquisitions and cash disbursements.

position, bills are frequently paid several months after their due date. When an auditor faces such a situation, there is a high likelihood of an understatement of accounts payable; therefore, under these circumstances, extensive tests of details of accounts payable are necessary to determine whether accounts payable are properly stated at the balance sheet date.

The most important controls over accounts payable have already been discussed as part of the control and recording of acquisitions and cash disbursements. In addition to these controls, it is important to have a monthly reconciliation of vendors' statements with recorded liabilities and of the outstanding transaction file with the vendor master file and the general ledger. This should be done by an independent person, or by computer software.

Analytical Procedures The use of analytical procedures is as important in the acquisition and payment cycle as it is in every other cycle. Table 17-4 illustrates analytical procedures for the balance sheet and income statement accounts in the acquisition and payment cycle that are useful for uncovering areas in which additional investigation is desirable. Frequently, these ratios are calculated using the auditor's generalized audit software.

One of the most important analytical procedures for uncovering misstatements of accounts payable is comparing current-year expense totals to prior years. For example, by comparing current utilities expense to the prior year, the auditor may determine that the last utilities bill for the year was not recorded. Comparing expenses to prior years is an effective analytical procedure for accounts payable because expenses from year to year are relatively stable if income is stable. Examples include rent, utilities, and other expenses billed on a regular basis.

Balance-Related Audit Objectives for Tests of Details The overall objective in the audit of accounts payable is to determine whether accounts payable are fairly stated and properly disclosed. Eight of the nine balance-related audit objectives discussed in Chapter 5 are applicable to accounts payable. Valuation is not applicable to liabilities.

TABLE 17-4	Analytical Procedures for Acquisition and Payment Cycle

Analytical Procedure	Possible Misstatement
Compare acquisition-related expense account balances with prior years.	Misstatement of accounts payable and expenses.
Review list of accounts payable for unusual, nonvendor, and interest-bearing payables.	Classification misstatement for nontrade liabilities.
Compare individual accounts payable with previous years.	Unrecorded or nonexistent accounts, or misstatements.
Calculate ratios such as purchases divided by accounts payable, and accounts payable divided by current liabilities.	Unrecorded or nonexistent accounts, or misstatements.

The auditor should recognize the difference in emphasis between the audit of liabilities and the audit of assets. When assets are being verified, attention is focused on ensuring that the balance in the account is not overstated. The validity of recorded assets is constantly questioned and verified by confirmation, physical examination, and examination of supporting documents. The auditor should certainly not ignore the possibility of assets being understated, but the fact remains that the auditor is more concerned about the possibility of overstatement than understatement. The opposite approach is taken in verifying liability balances, that is, the main focus is on the discovery of understated or omitted liabilities.

The difference in emphasis in auditing assets and liabilities results directly from the *legal liability of public accountants*. If equity investors, creditors, and other users determine subsequent to the issuance of the audited financial statements that owners' equity was materially overstated, a lawsuit against the public accounting firm is fairly likely. Since an overstatement of owners' equity can arise either from an overstatement of assets or from an understatement of liabilities, it is natural for public accountants to emphasize those two types of misstatements. The probability of a successful lawsuit against a public accountant for failing to discover an understatement of owners' equity is far less likely.

Nevertheless, the auditing profession must avoid too much emphasis on protecting users from overstatements of owners' equity at the expense of ignoring understatements. If assets are consistently understated and liabilities are consistently overstated for large numbers of audited companies, the decision-making value of financial statement information is likely to decline. Therefore, even though it is natural for auditors to emphasize the possibility of overstating assets and understating liabilities, uncovering the opposite types of misstatement is also a significant responsibility.

Tests of Details of Accounts Payable The same balance-related audit objectives that were used as a frame of reference for verifying accounts receivable in Chapter 14 are also applicable to liabilities with three minor modifications. The most obvious difference in verifying liabilities is the nonapplicability of the ownership objective. The second difference is in the rights and obligations objective. For assets, the auditor is concerned with the client's rights to the use and disposal of assets. For liabilities, the auditor is concerned with the client's obligations for the payment of the liability. If the client has no obligation to pay a liability, it should not be included as a liability. The third difference was discussed above: in auditing liabilities, the emphasis is on the search for understatements rather than for overstatements.

Table 17-5 includes the balance-related audit objectives and common tests of details of balances procedures for accounts payable. The actual audit procedures will vary considerably depending on the nature of the entity, the materiality of accounts payable, the nature and effectiveness of internal controls, and inherent risk.

Out-of-Period Liability Tests Because of the emphasis on understatements in liability accounts, out-of-period liability tests are important for accounts payable. The extent of

Balance-Related Audit Objective	Common Tests of Details of Balances Procedures	Comments
Accounts payable in the accounts payable list agree with related master file, and the total is correctly added and agrees with the general ledger (detail tie-in).	Foot the accounts payable list.[†] Trace the total to the general ledger. Trace individual vendor's invoices to transaction file for names and amounts.	All pages need not ordinarily be footed if done manually. Unless controls are weak, tracing to transaction file should be limited.
Accounts payable in the accounts payable list exist (existence).	Trace from accounts payable list to vendors' invoices and statements. Confirm accounts payable, emphasizing large and unusual amounts.	Ordinarily receives little attention because the primary concern is with understatements.
Existing accounts payable are in the accounts payable list (completeness).	Perform out-of-period liability tests (see discussion).	These are essential audit tests for accounts payable.
Accounts payable in the accounts payable list are accurate (accuracy).	Perform same procedures as those used for existence objective and out-of-period liability tests.	Ordinarily, the emphasis in these procedures for accuracy is understatement rather than omission.
Accounts payable in the accounts payable list are properly classified (classification).	Review the list and master file for related parties, notes or other interest-bearing liabilities, long-term payables, and debit balances.	Knowledge of the client's business is essential for these tests.
Transactions in the acquisition and payment cycle are recorded in the proper period (cutoff).	Perform out-of-period liability tests (see discussion). Perform detailed tests as a part of physical observation of inventory (see discussion). Test for inventory in transit (see discussion).	These are essential audit tests for accounts payable. These are referred to as *cutoff tests*.
The company has an obligation to pay the liabilities included in accounts payable (obligations).	Examine vendors' statements and confirm accounts payable.	Normally not a concern in the audit of accounts payable because all accounts payable are obligations.
Accounts in the acquisition and payment cycle are properly presented and disclosed (disclosure).	Review financial statements to make sure material related-party, long-term, and interest-bearing liabilities are segregated.	Ordinarily not a problem.

[†]This test of details would be conducted on many audits by using the computer.

tests to uncover unrecorded accounts payable, frequently referred to as "the search for unrecorded accounts payable," depends heavily on assessed control risk and the materiality of the potential balance in the account. The same audit procedures used to uncover unrecorded payables are applicable to the accuracy objective. The audit procedures that follow are typical tests.

EXAMINE UNDERLYING DOCUMENTATION FOR SUBSEQUENT CASH DISBURSEMENTS The purpose of this audit procedure is to uncover payments made in the subsequent accounting period that represent liabilities at the balance sheet date. The supporting documentation is examined to determine whether a payment was for a current period obligation. For example, if inventory was received prior to the balance sheet date, it will be so indicated on the receiving report. Frequently, documentation for payments made in the subsequent period are examined for several weeks, especially when the client does not pay its bills on a timely basis. Any payment that is for a current period obligation should be traced to the accounts payable trial balance to make sure it has been included as a liability.

EXAMINE UNDERLYING DOCUMENTATION FOR BILLS NOT PAID SEVERAL WEEKS AFTER THE YEAR END This procedure is carried out in the same manner as the preceding one and serves the same purpose. The only difference is that it is done for unpaid obligations near the end of the examination include a request for information about notes and acceptances payable, as well as consigned inventory that is owned by the vendor but stored on the client's premises. An illustration of a typical accounts payable confirmation request is given in Figure 17-4.

Due to the availability of vendors' statements and vendors' invoices, which are both relatively reliable evidence because they originate from a third party, the confirmation of accounts payable is less common than confirmation of accounts receivable. If the client has adequate internal controls and vendors' statements are available for examination, then confirmations are normally not sent. However, when the client's internal controls are weak, when statements are not available, or when the auditor questions the client's integrity, then it is desirable to send confirmation requests to vendors. Because of the emphasis on understatements of liability accounts, the accounts confirmed should include large accounts, active accounts, accounts with a zero balance, and a representative sample of all others.

In most instances in which accounts payable are confirmed, it is done shortly after the balance sheet date. However, if assessed control risk is low, it may be possible to confirm accounts payable at an interim date as a test of the effectiveness of internal controls. Then if the confirmation indicates that the internal controls are ineffective, it is possible to design other audit procedures to test accounts payable at year end.

When vendors' statements are examined or confirmations are received, there must be a *reconciliation* of the statement or confirmation with the accounts payable list. Frequently, differences are caused by inventory in transit, cheques mailed by the client but not received by the vendor at the statement date, and delays in processing the accounting records. The reconciliation is of the same general nature as that discussed in Chapter 14 for accounts receivable. The documents typically used to reconcile the balances on the accounts payable list with the confirmation or vendor's statement include receiving reports, vendors' invoices, and cancelled cheques.

FIGURE 17-4	**Accounts Payable Confirmation Request**

Roger Mead Ltd.
1600 Westmount Ave. N.
Kenora, Ontario
P9N 1X7

January 15, 2005

Szabo Sales Co. Ltd.
2116 King Street
Kenora, Ontario
P9N 1G3

To Whom It May Concern:

Our auditors, Adams and Lelik, LLP, are conducting an audit of our financial statements. For this purpose, please furnish directly to them, at their address noted below, the following information as of December 31, 2004.

    (1) Itemized statements of our accounts payable to you showing all unpaid items;
    (2) A complete list of any notes and acceptances payable to you (including any which have been discounted) showing the original date, dates due, original amount, unpaid balance, collateral and endorsers; and
    (3) An itemized list of your merchandise consigned to us.

Your prompt attention to this request will be appreciated. A stamped, addressed envelope is enclosed for your reply.

Yours truly,

Sally Palm

Roger Mead Ltd.
per Sally Palm

Adams and Lelik, LLP
215 Tecumseh Crescent
Kenora, Ontario
P9N 2K5

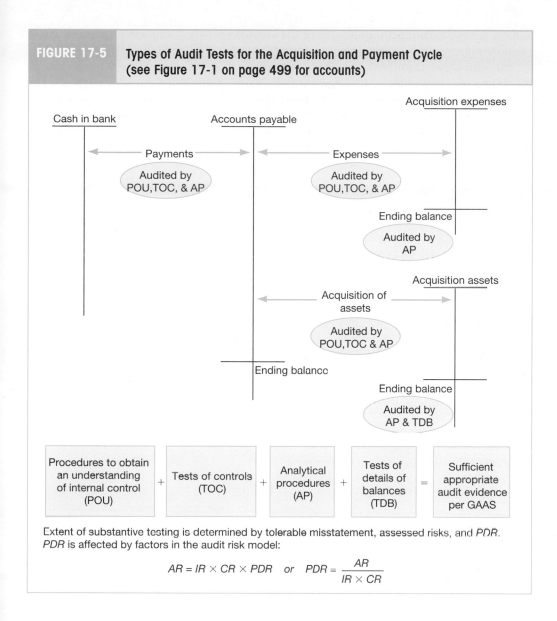

FIGURE 17-5 Types of Audit Tests for the Acquisition and Payment Cycle (see Figure 17-1 on page 499 for accounts)

$$AR = IR \times CR \times PDR \quad or \quad PDR = \frac{AR}{IR \times CR}$$

Sample Size Sample sizes for accounts payable tests vary considerably depending on such factors as the materiality of accounts payable, number of accounts outstanding, assessed control risk, and results of the prior year. When a client's internal controls are weak, which is not uncommon for accounts payable, almost all population items must be verified. In other situations, minimal testing is needed.

Statistical sampling is less commonly used for the audit of accounts payable than for accounts receivable. It is more difficult to define the population and determine the population size in accounts payable. Since the emphasis is on omitted accounts payable, it is essential that the population include all potential payables.

Summary

Figure 17-5 illustrates the major accounts in the acquisition and payment cycle and the types of audit tests used to audit these accounts. This figure also shows how the audit risk model discussed in Chapter 8 relates to the audit of the acquisition and payment cycle.

→17.4 AUDIT OF SYSTEM CONVERSIONS

Organizations are not static. With time, as an organization grows or shrinks, or changes its business objectives, the procedures within an organization also change. Often, when the auditor returns to conduct the audit, he or she identifies minor changes in procedures, causing minor changes in risk assessments, internal control testing, and tests of details.

At other times, the organization has undertaken a major change in its systems by implementing a new computer system or has made major changes to a particular system. For example, a client that previously processed its accounts payable and cash disbursements manually could use a standard accounting software package. A large client could change a batch-processing accounts payable and cash disbursements system to an online processing system, as described in the following focus box.

Focus Box 17-2

CONVERSION TO NEW SYSTEM HIDES $5 MILLION ERROR

A large pharmaceutical company had been using complex data processing methods for many years. It had custom programmed accounting systems and used data communications to send and receive orders and other business documents. The accounts payable system was falling behind—it was batch processing-based and not integrated with the purchasing system. Accordingly, the information systems personnel designed and tested many new programs for updating the accounts payable and purchasing systems. These systems were put in place at the company's year-end date, January 31. Systems were run parallel (i.e., both the old and new systems were used) for the month of January, with the new system used exclusively effective February 1. The auditors relied on the equiva-

lency of the two systems and on the fact that the company normally had excellent controls in accounts payable and cash disbursements. However, due to excessive workload, goods received on January 31 were not recorded until February 1, and, *therefore, were recorded only in the new system.* Thus, accounts payable and purchases were understated by $5 million, resulting in an overstatement of income—a highly significant cutoff error.

This error was detected by the auditors *in the following year's audit,* resulting in a restatement of the prior financial statements. The client was very understanding but commented, "We knew the financial results last year were too good to be true!"

When an organization changes an entire system or set of systems, there are three issues that the auditor needs to address:

- A new system of internal controls will need to be documented and evaluated.
- The auditor will need to audit the actual data conversion process.
- The auditor will need to determine whether accounting policies have been changed.

New System of Internal Controls When new computer programs are put in place, the controls that are part of those programs will change. For example, if the system changes from batch to online, then controls to help ensure data entry accuracy will likely occur as information is entered, rather than be checked for a group of transactions. If a system changes from manual to automated, then new controls will be present in the programs, such as automatic calculation of invoice extensions, which previously needed to be completed manually. Also, activities done by persons handling these systems may change.

The auditor needs to document the new procedures, evaluate these procedures, and determine the effect on control risk. Should reliance on the programmed controls be tested, the auditor may have the option of using the same audit procedures as in prior years or may need to design new audit procedures, such as the creation of test transactions to determine that programs are functioning as intended. If the client has run its systems in parallel (i.e., run both the old and the new systems for a period of time), then the auditor can evaluate the new system by examining the records kept during this parallel process.

Auditing the Data Conversion Process When computer systems are established for the first time, a major task is the creation of master files. For example, purchase orders cannot be processed nor accounts payable vendor invoices entered if the vendor and information such as name, address, and terms are not established in the vendor master file. Quantities ordered or received cannot be entered if the inventory item, description, and price do not exist in the inventory master file. The number of vendors could be in the hundreds, while the number of inventory items could number in the thousands.

Determining the audit procedures required involves a risk assessment process. Inherent risk may increase because these are new systems in place and employees may not be aware of the actions required. By determining the extent of employee training and the rigour of the implementation process, the auditor can assess whether inherent risk is affected. The rigour of the implementation process also affects control risk. If the implementation process is properly planned, conducted, and supervised, the auditor can rely on these controls. Conversely, if controls over the conversion process are poor or are not documented, the auditor must conduct tests of details. Table 17-6 combines the features of Tables 17-2 and 17-5 to describe audit objectives for the conversion of a batch system to an online system. Table 17-6 shows possible key controls, tests of controls, and tests of details that would be required should controls be absent.

Notice that two audit objectives are not included. Classification is not included since accuracy and agreement between the two systems ensures that classification is satisfied. The same is true for posting and summarization: if individual and total vendor amounts are correct and details from the old system agree to the new system, then posting and summarization are also satisfied.

Careful review of Table 17-6 shows that the tests can be simplified to the following three types:

- Tests comparing details from the new system to the old system (to verify that only accurate, authorized information has been established)
- Tests comparing details from the old system to the new system (to ensure accuracy and that no transactions have been omitted)
- Cutoff testing to ensure that transactions are included in only the proper system and have not been omitted

TABLE 17-6	Audit Objectives, Key Controls, Tests of Controls, and Tests of Details for System Conversion of Accounts Payable		
Audit Objective	**Key Internal Control**	**Common Tests of Controls**	**Common Tests of Details**
Only authorized vendors are established with balances for goods and services actually received (existence).	Agree vendor file details for each vendor from the new (online) system to the old (batch) system.	Review vendor file listings for evidence of agreement.	On a test basis, agree vendor file details for each vendor from the new (online) system to the old (batch) system.
All vendor balances as of the date of conversion are included (completeness).	Agree aged accounts payable trial balance details from the old (batch) system to the new (online) system for each vendor and in total. Agree the total to the general ledger.	Review aged accounts payable trial balance listings for evidence of comparison.	On a test basis, agree aged accounts payable trial balance details from the old (batch) system to the new (online) system for each vendor and in total. Agree total to general ledger.
Details in the new system agree to details from the old system. New information is accurate (accuracy).	Same as for completeness.	Same as for completeness.	Same as for completeness.
Information is recorded in the appropriate system and is not omitted (cutoff).	Procedures exist to ensure appropriate cutoff of transactions (i.e., transactions are recorded only once in the proper system and are not omitted).	Conduct cutoff tests, as described on page 512, for receiving reports and vendor invoices.	Same as for tests of controls.

CONVERSION AUDIT—the audit procedures required when an organization changes its system to a different automated system

Thus, a **conversion audit** uses audit tests that we have used in other portions of our audit. The emphasis is on the accurate and authorized establishment of new master files and on the cutoff of transactions in the appropriate system.

Determining Whether Accounting Policies Have Changed This could be done concurrently with inventory costing. For example, if inventory is counted only at year end (a periodic system), it would be costed on a FIFO (first-in, first-out) basis, whereas most computer systems use average costing or weighted average costing. Should the method of inventory costing change, the auditor would need to gather and include sufficient evidence that there is adequate disclosure on the financial statements for this change in accounting policy.

SUMMARY

1. *What are the major business functions, documents, and records in the acquisition and payment cycle?* Table 17-1 states that the business functions for acquisitions are: processing purchase orders, receiving goods and services, recognizing liabilities, and vendor master file changes, while the business function for cash disbursements (payments) is the processing and recording of cash disbursements. The table also lists documents, records, and accounts.

2. *How are tests of controls designed for the acquisition and payment cycle?* We follow the same methodology for the acquisition and payment cycle as for other cycles—after assessing risks at the organization level, we move to understanding controls at the cycle level so that risks can be assessed and tested by assertion. Then, tests of controls are designed for those assertions where the auditor chooses to place reliance upon the control.

3. *Why is accounts payable considered separately from acquisitions or payments?* Accounts payable is the ending balance

sheet obligation, whereas acquisitions and payments are the transactions that occur throughout the year.

Why is the auditor more concerned about understatement of accounts payable rather than overstatement? Should accounts payable be understated, income would be overstated. There is likely to be a greater legal liability to an auditor if a potential investor relies on overstated income than understated income.

4. *What is a system conversion?* A system conversion occurs when an organization replaces or makes major changes to its existing systems (whether manual or automated).

What issues does the auditor need to address during a conversion audit? The auditor needs to consider that there is likely a new system of internal controls that will need to be documented and evaluated. The auditor will also need to audit the actual data conversion process, and determine whether there have been any changes in accounting policies.

ESSENTIAL TERMS

Accounts payable trial balance—a listing by each vendor of the amount owed at a point in time; prepared directly from the accounts payable master file (p. 502).

Acquisition and payment cycle—the transaction cycle that includes the acquisition of and payment for goods and services from suppliers outside the organization (p. 498).

Conversion audit—the audit procedures required when an organization changes its system to a different automated system (p. 518).

Debit memo—a document indicating a reduction in the amount owed to a vendor because of returned goods or an allowance granted (p. 502).

FOB destination—shipping contract in which title to the goods passes to the buyer when the goods are received (p. 513).

FOB origin—shipping contract in which title to the goods passes to the buyer at the time that the goods are shipped (p. 513).

Purchase order—a document prepared by the purchasing department indicating the description, quantity, and related information for goods and services that the company intends to

purchase (p. 500).

Purchase requisition—request by an authorized employee to the purchasing department to place an order for inventory and other items used by an entity (p. 499).

Receiving report—a document prepared by the receiving department at the time tangible goods are received, indicating the description of the goods, the quantity received, the date received, and other relevant data; part of the documentation necessary for payment to be made (p. 501).

Vendor master file—a computer file for maintaining a record for each vendor of individual acquisitions, cash disbursements, and acquisition returns and allowances, and vendor balances (p. 502).

Vendor's invoice—a document that specifies the details of an acquisition transaction and amount of money owed to the vendor for an acquisition (p. 502).

Vendor's statement—a statement prepared monthly by the vendor, which indicates the customer's beginning balance, acquisitions, payments, and ending balance (p. 502).

17-1 List five asset accounts, three liability accounts, and five expense accounts included in the acquisition and payment cycle for a typical manufacturing company.

17-2 List one possible internal control for each of the six transaction-related audit objectives for cash disbursements. For each control, list a test of controls to test its effectiveness.

17-3 List one possible control for each of the six transaction-related audit objectives for acquisitions. For each control, list a test of controls to test its effectiveness.

17-4 What is the importance of cash discounts to the client, and how can the auditor verify whether they are being used in accordance with company policy?

17-5 What are the similarities and differences in the objectives of the following two procedures?

1. Select a random sample of receiving reports and trace them to related vendors' invoices and acquisitions journal entries, comparing the vendor's name, type of material and quantity acquired, and total amount of the acquisition.
2. Select a random sample of acquisitions journal entries and trace them to related vendors' invoices and receiving reports, comparing the vendor's name, type of material and quantity acquired, and total amount of the acquisition.

17-6 What is meant by a "voucher"? Explain how its use can improve an organization's internal controls.

17-7 Explain why most auditors consider the receipt of goods and services the most important point in the acquisition and payment cycle.

17-8 Explain the relationship between tests of the acquisition and payment cycle and tests of inventory. Give specific examples of how these two types of tests affect each other.

17-9 Explain the relationship between tests of the acquisition and payment cycle and tests of accounts payable. Give specific examples of how these two types of tests affect each other.

17-10 Explain why it is common for auditors to send confirmation requests to vendors with "zero balances" on the client's accounts payable listing but uncommon to follow the same approach in verifying accounts receivable.

17-11 Distinguish between a vendor's invoice and a vendor's statement. Which document should ideally be used as evidence in auditing acquisition transactions and which for directly verifying accounts payable balances? Why?

17-12 It is less common to confirm accounts payable at an interim date than accounts receivable. Explain why.

17-13 In testing the cutoff of accounts payable at the balance sheet date, explain why it is important that auditors coordinate their tests with the physical observation of inventory. What can the auditor do during the physical inventory to enhance the likelihood of an accurate cutoff?

17-14 Distinguish between FOB destination and FOB origin. What procedures should the auditor follow concerning acquisitions of inventory on an FOB origin basis near year end?

17-15 John has discovered that his client converted to an integrated set of software packages one month prior to the year end. During the last month of the fiscal year, the client ran systems parallel. John decides that he can do the audit as usual because the old system is still in operation. Next year, he will have to audit only the new system because the old system will no longer be in use. Evaluate John's decision regarding the audit.

MULTIPLE CHOICE QUESTIONS

17-16 Choose the best response to the following questions:

a. Budd, the purchasing agent of Lake Hardware Wholesalers Ltd., has a relative who owns a retail hardware store. Budd arranged for hardware to be delivered by manufacturers to the retail store on a COD basis, thereby enabling his relative to buy at Lake's wholesale prices. Budd was probably able to accomplish this because of Lake's poor internal control over

  (1) purchase orders.
  (2) purchase requisitions.
  (3) cash receipts.
  (4) perpetual inventory records.

b. Which of the following is an internal control that would prevent paid disbursement documents from being presented for payment a second time?

  (1) The date on cash disbursement documents should be within a few days of the date that the document is presented for payment.

  (2) Unsigned cheques should be prepared by individuals who are responsible for signing cheques.
  (3) Cash disbursement documents should be approved by at least two responsible management officials.
  (4) The official signing the cheque should compare the cheque with the documents and should deface the documents.

(AICPA adapted)

c. Which of the following audit procedures is best for identifying unrecorded trade accounts payable?

  (1) Examining unusual relationships between monthly accounts payable balances and recorded cash payments
  (2) Reconciling vendors' statements to the file of receiving reports to identify items received just prior to the balance sheet date
  (3) Reviewing cash disbursements recorded subsequent to the balance sheet date to determine whether the related payables apply to the prior period

(4) Investigating payables recorded just prior to and just subsequent to the balance sheet date to determine whether they are supported by receiving reports

d. In auditing accounts payable, an auditor's procedures most likely would focus primarily on management's assertion of

(1) existence or occurrence.
(2) completeness.
(3) presentation and disclosure.
(4) valuation or allocation.

e. When using confirmations to provide evidence about the completeness assertion for accounts payable, the appropriate population most likely is

(1) vendors with whom the entity has previously done business.
(2) amounts recorded in the accounts payable subsidiary ledger.
(3) payees of cheques drawn in the month after year-end.
(4) invoices filed in the entity's open invoice file.

DISCUSSION QUESTIONS AND PROBLEMS

17-17 The following misstatements are included in the accounting records of Westgate Manufacturing Corp.

1. Telephone expense (account 2112) was unintentionally charged to repairs and maintenance (account 2121).
2. Acquisitions of raw materials are frequently not recorded until several weeks after the goods are received due to the failure of the receiving personnel to forward receiving reports to accounting. When pressure from a vendor's credit department is put on Westgate's accounting department, it searches for the receiving report, records the transactions in the acquisitions journal, and pays the bill.
3. The accounts payable clerk prepares a monthly cheque to Story Supply Ltd. for the amount of an invoice owed and submits the unsigned cheque to the treasurer for payment along with related supporting documents that have already been approved. When she receives the signed cheque from the treasurer, she records it as a debit to accounts payable and deposits the cheque in a personal bank account for a company named Story Ltd. A few days later she records the invoice in the acquisitions journal again, resubmits the documents and a new cheque to the treasurer, and sends the cheque to the vendor after it has been signed.

4. The amount of a supplier invoice is entered as $6,412.87 instead of $4,612.87. The cheque is also issued and mailed for this amount.
5. The accounts payable clerk intentionally held onto and did not mail seven large cheques written on December 26 to prevent cash in the bank from having a negative balance. They were mailed on January 2 of the subsequent year.
6. Each month a fraudulent receiving report is submitted to accounting by an employee in the receiving department. A few days later he sends Westgate an invoice for the quantity of goods ordered from a small company he owns and operates in the evening. A cheque is prepared, and the amount is paid when the receiving report and the vendor's invoice are matched by the accounts payable clerk.

Required

a. For each misstatement, identify the transaction-related audit objective that was not met.
b. For each misstatement, state a control that should have prevented it from occurring on a continuing basis.
c. For each misstatement, state a substantive audit procedure that could uncover it.

17-18 The following auditing procedures were performed in the audit of accounts payable:

1. Examine supporting documents for cash disbursements several days before and after year end.
2. Examine the acquisition and payment journals for the last few days of the current period and first few days of the succeeding period, looking for large or unusual transactions.
3. Trace from the general ledger trial balance and supporting working papers to determine if accounts payable, related parties, and other related assets and liabilities are properly included on the financial statements.
4. For liabilities that are payable in a foreign currency, determine the exchange rate and check calculations.
5. Discuss with the controller whether any amounts included on the accounts payable list are due to related parties, debit balances, or notes payable.

6. Obtain vendors' statements from the controller, and reconcile to a listing of accounts payable.
7. Obtain vendors' statements directly from vendors, and reconcile to the listing of accounts payable.
8. Obtain the accounts payable aged trial balance listing and the accounts payable open transaction file. Re-add the data file, and agree totals to the listing and to the general ledger.

Required

a. For each procedure, identify the type of audit evidence used.
b. For each procedure, use the matrix on page 521 to identify which balance-related audit objective(s) was (were) satisfied. (Procedure 1 is completed as an illustration.)
c. Evaluate the need to have certain objectives satisfied by more than one audit procedure.

Audit Procedure	Balance-Related Audit Objective							
	Detail tie-in	Existence	Completeness	Accuracy	Classification	Cutoff	Obligations	Presentation and disclosure
1			X			X		
2								
3								
4								
5								
6								
7								
8								

17-19 You are the staff auditor testing the combined purchase and cash disbursements journal for a small audit client. Internal control is regarded as reasonably effective, considering the number of personnel.

The in-charge auditor has decided that a sample of 80 items should be sufficient for this audit because of the excellent controls and gives you the following instructions:

1. All transactions selected must exceed $100.
2. At least 50 of the transactions must be for purchases of raw materials because these transactions are typically material.
3. It is not acceptable to include the same vendor in the sample more than once.
4. All vendors' invoices that cannot be located must be replaced with a new sample item.
5. Both cheques and supporting documents are to be examined for the same transactions.
6. The sample must be random, after modifications for instructions 1 through 5.

Required

a. Evaluate each of these instructions for testing acquisition and cash disbursements transactions.
b. Explain the difficulties of applying each of these instructions to attributes sampling.

17-20 You were in the final stages of your examination of the financial statements of Ozine Corporation for the year ended December 31, 2004, when you were consulted by the corporation's president. He believes that there is no point to your examining the 2005 acquisitions data files and testing data in support of 2005 entries. He stated that: (1) bills pertaining to 2004 that were received too late to be included in the December acquisitions data files were recorded as of the year end by the corporation by journal entry, (2) the internal auditor made tests after the year end, and (3) he would furnish you with a letter confirming that there were no unrecorded liabilities.

Required

a. Should a public accountant's test for unrecorded liabilities be affected by the fact that the client made a journal entry to record 2004 bills that were received late? Explain.
b. Should a public accountant's test for unrecorded liabilities be affected by the fact that a letter is obtained in which a responsible management official confirms that, to the best of his or her knowledge, all liabilities have been recorded? Explain.
c. Should a public accountant's test for unrecorded liabilities be eliminated or reduced because of the internal audit tests? Explain.
d. Assume that the corporation, which handled some government contracts, had no internal auditor but that an auditor from the Auditor General's office spent three weeks auditing the records and was just completing her work at this time. How would the public accountant's unrecorded liability test be affected by the work of the auditor from the Auditor General's office?
e. What sources in addition to the 2004 acquisitions data files should the public accountant consider to locate possible unrecorded liabilities?

(AICPA adapted)

17-21 Because of the small size of the company and the limited number of accounting personnel, the Dry Goods Wholesale Company Ltd. initially records all acquisitions of goods and services at the time that cash disbursements are made. At the end of each quarter when financial statements for internal purposes are prepared, accounts payable are recorded by adjusting journal entries. The entries are reversed at the beginning of the subsequent period. Except for the lack of a purchasing system, the controls over acquisitions are excellent for a small company. (There are adequate prenumbered documents for all receipt of goods, proper approvals, and adequate internal verification wherever possible.)

Before the auditor arrives for the year-end audit, the bookkeeper prepares adjusting entries to record the accounts payable as of the balance sheet date. The aged trial balance is listed as of the year end, and a manual schedule is prepared adding the amounts that were entered in the following month. Thus, the accounts payable balance equals the aged trial balance plus the following month's journal entry for invoices received after the year end. All vendors' invoices supporting the journal entry are retained in a separate file for the auditor's use.

In the current year, the accounts payable balance has increased dramatically because of a severe cash shortage. (The cash shortage apparently arose from expansion of inventory and facilities rather than lack of sales.) Many accounts have remained unpaid for several months and the client is getting pressure from several vendors to pay the bills. Since the company had a relatively profitable year, management is anxious to complete the audit as early as possible so that the audited statements can be used to obtain a large bank loan.

Required
a. Explain how the lack of a complete aged accounts payable trial balance will affect the auditor's tests of controls for acquisitions and cash disbursements.
b. What should the auditor use as a sampling unit in performing tests of acquisitions?
c. Assuming that no misstatements are discovered in the auditor's tests of controls for acquisitions and cash disbursements, how will that result affect the verification of accounts payable?
d. Discuss the reasonableness of the client's request for an early completion of the audit and the implications of the request from the auditor's point of view.
e. List the audit procedures that should be performed in the year-end audit of accounts payable to meet the cutoff objective.
f. State your opinion as to whether it is possible to conduct an adequate audit in these circumstances.

17-22 Donnen Designs, Inc. is a small manufacturer of women's casual-wear jewellery, including bracelets, necklaces, earrings, and other moderately priced accessory items. Most of its products are made from silver, various low-cost stones, beads, and other decorative jewellery pieces. Donnen Designs is not involved in the manufacturing of high-end jewellery items, such as those made of gold and semiprecious or precious stones.

Personnel responsible for purchasing raw material jewellery items for Donnen Designs would like to place orders directly with suppliers who offer their products for sale through Internet web sites. Most suppliers provide pictures of all jewellery components on their web sites, along with pricing and other sales-term information. Customers who have valid business licenses are able to purchase the products at wholesale, rather than retail prices. Customers can place orders online and pay for those goods immediately by using a valid credit card. Purchases made by credit card are shipped by the suppliers once the credit approval is received from the credit card agency, which usually occurs the same day. Customers can also place orders online with payment being later made by cheque. However, in that event, purchases are not shipped until the cheque is received and cashed by the supplier. Some of the suppliers allow a 30-day full-payment refund policy, whereas other suppliers accept returns but only grant credit toward future purchases from that supplier.

Required
a. Identify advantages for Donnen Designs if management allows purchasing personnel to order goods online through supplier web sites.
b. Identify potential risks associated with Donnen Designs' purchase of jewellery pieces through supplier Internet web sites.
c. Describe advantages of allowing purchasing agents to purchase products online using a Donnen Designs credit card.
d. Describe advantages of allowing purchasing agents to purchase products online with payment made only by cheque.
e. What internal controls could be implemented to ensure that

(1) purchasing agents do not use Donnen credit cards to purchase non-jewellery items for their own purposes, if Donnen allows purchasing agents to purchase jewellery using Donnen credit cards?
(2) purchasing agents do not order jewellery items from the suppliers and ship those items to addresses other than Donnen addresses?
(3) Donnen does not end up with unused credits with jewellery suppliers as a result of returning unacceptable jewellery items to suppliers who only grant credit toward future purchases?

PROFESSIONAL JUDGMENT PROBLEM

17-23 In testing cash disbursements for Immanuel Klein Ltd., you perform minimum tests of 15 transactions as a means of assessing control risk. In your tests, you discover the following exceptions:

1. Two items in the acquisitions journal have been misclassified.

2. Three invoices had not been initialled by the controller, but there were no dollar misstatements evident in the transactions.
3. Five receiving reports were recorded in the acquisitions journal at least two weeks later than their date on the receiving report.
4. One invoice had been paid twice. The second payment

was supported by a duplicate copy of the invoice. Both copies of the invoice had been marked "paid."

5. One cheque amount in the cash disbursements journal was for $100 less than the amount stated on the vendor's invoice.
6. One voided cheque was missing.
7. Two receiving reports for vendors' invoices were missing from the transaction packet. One vendor's invoice had an extension error, and the invoice had been initialled to verify that the amount had been checked.

Required

a. Identify whether each of exceptions 1 through 7 was a control test deviation, a monetary error or fraud and other irregularities, or both.
b. For each exception, identify which transaction-related audit objective was not met.
c. What is the audit importance of each of these exceptions?
d. What follow-up procedures would you use to determine more about the nature of each exception?
e. How would each of these exceptions affect the balance of your audit? Be specific.
f. Identify internal controls that should have prevented each misstatement.

CASE

17-24 You have been assigned to the audit of Compu Co. (CC), a new client of your firm, Neer & Farr, Chartered Accountants. You are responsible for the accounts payable section of this year's audit. You have prepared the following description of the accounts payable system from discussions with CC staff.

Head office of CC processes the accounts payable for its branch offices. When a new branch is set up on the automated accounts payable system, it is requested to send to head office a detailed accounts payable trial balance and an accounts payable vendor list, approved by the manager of the branch. The accounts payable vendor list includes vendor name, address, discount terms, and other descriptive information, such as telephone number and personal contact.

The head office accounts payable department consists of an accounts payable supervisor and three clerks.

The accounts payable supervisor assigns and records vendor codes on the original vendor list provided by the branch manager. Vendor codes are assigned alphanumerically, based on the vendor's name. This list is used as a source of input to the computer system, and a photocopy of the list is returned to the branch for its reference.

The branch manager approves the invoices and codes them as to general ledger allocation prior to sending them to head office for payment. The supervisor reviews the allocation of the invoices and passes them on to one of the clerks. Each clerk is responsible for specific branches. The clerks scan the vendor list, call up the vendor file on the screen, and enter the invoice details into the system. If the vendor is not on the vendor list, the clerks check for similar names on the screen to verify that the vendor

has not been set up since the vendor list was printed and then add a new vendor using the standard method. The clerks then record the invoice against this new vendor.

By means of an error message, the system identifies invoices that have already been entered for payment so that invoices that have inadvertently been entered twice are detected. However, the accounts payable clerks are able to override this error message since it is sometimes necessary for an invoice to be entered twice (e.g., if partial payment was made earlier and the balance is now being paid in full). Once an invoice has been entered for payment, the accounts payable clerk files the invoice alphabetically by vendor name.

Cheques are run Mondays and Thursdays, based on due dates. Because of the high volume of cheques processed, the accounts payable supervisor signs all cheques. However, cheques for amounts greater than $50,000 must also be signed by the head office controller. The cheques are mailed directly to suppliers from head office. A copy of the cheque register, showing which invoices have been paid, is sent to the branch.

The partner on the CC engagement has requested that you prepare a memo that identifies the control strengths and weaknesses in CC's accounts payable system and analyzes their impact on this year's audit (i.e., identifying tests of controls and compensating audit procedures needed). The memo should also provide practical recommendations for the resolution of the accounts payable system weaknesses.

Required

Prepare the memo requested by the partner.

(CICA adapted)

CHAPTER 18

COMPLETING THE TESTS IN THE ACQUISITION AND PAYMENT CYCLE: VERIFICATION OF SELECTED ACCOUNTS

There are many different types of organizations with different types of accounts. A restaurant will have food costs, a clothing store will buy fashion goods, and a department store will have a range of products delivered by many different suppliers, normally to a central warehouse.

LEARNING OBJECTIVES

After reading this chapter, you should be able to answer the following questions:

1. In addition to inventory, what are the other accounts that need to be audited? What process should be followed in the audit of manufacturing equipment?

2. Why is the audit of prepaid expenses important? How are prepaid expenses audited? Why are intangible assets difficult to audit?

3. What are some examples of typical accrued liabilities? How are accrued property taxes audited?

4. What is the process for auditing income and expense accounts? Why is analytical review an important technique in the audit of operations?

WHY DON'T OUR CUSTOMERS WANT TO RECEIVE THEIR BILLS ELECTRONICALLY?

Business to business document exchanges are booming, with the use of electronic data interchange and the Internet. Many businesses would like to cut their costs even further by sending electronic bills to individuals. You can obtain your telephone bill and your bank balance electronically—why not others? According to Forrester Research Inc., it seems that customers would be interested if the bills could go to a central location.

There is a free Canada Post service that transmits bills, company statements, and payroll information to employees electronically rather than by mail. This service is a dedicated secure transmission at www.epost.ca. If many consumers end up using this service, they would have a webdox rather than a mailbox, which would be particularly convenient for individuals who travel frequently.

Sources: 1. Buckler, Grant, 2004. "Webdoxs-epost union creates big e-biller," The Globe and Mail, September 30, 2004. 2. Langton, Jerry, 2004. "Cheque's not in the mail—it's in epost," The Toronto Star, November 11, 2004.

Would you use an electronic mailbox? What controls would you want to have in place before using such a service? Would you still want a paper copy as well as an electronic copy? How would the absence of paper invoices affect the audit of a business that sent its customer invoices out in only electronic form?

These are the questions that we need to ask as the nature of documentation shifts from paper to electronic form. As we rely upon electronic rather than paper documents, we will need to assess the functioning of computer programs, and possibly create test data or examine the stored information using generalized audit software.

→18.1   EXAMINING OTHER ACCOUNTS: AUDITING MANUFACTURING ASSET ACQUISITIONS

An important characteristic of the acquisition and payment cycle is the large number of accounts involved. These include the following:

- Accounts payable
- Accrued professional fees
- Accrued property taxes
- Buildings
- Cash in the bank
- Commercial franchises
- Cost of goods sold
- Goods and Services Tax payable
- Income tax expense

- Income taxes payable
- Insurance expense
- Inventory
- Land
- Leases and leasehold improvements
- Manufacturing equipment
- Organization costs
- Patents, trademarks, and copyrights

- Prepaid insurance
- Prepaid rent
- Prepaid taxes
- Professional fees
- Property taxes
- Rent expense
- Supplies
- Travel expense
- Utilities

Since the audit procedures for many of these accounts are similar, an understanding of the appropriate methodology for each can be obtained by studying the following selected account balances:

- Cash in bank—affected by all transaction cycles (Chapter 15)
- Inventory—represents tangible assets and is typically used up in one year (Chapter 19)
- Prepaid insurance—represents prepaid expenses (Chapter 18)
- Manufacturing equipment—represents long-lived tangible assets (Chapter 18)
- Accounts payable—represents specific liabilities for which the amounts and the dates of the future payments are known (Chapter 17)
- Accrued property taxes—represents estimated liabilities (Chapter 18)
- Operations accounts—include several methods of verifying all accounts in this category (Chapter 18).

The methodology for designing tests of details of balances for the above accounts is the same as that shown in Figure 17-3 on page 509 for accounts payable. Each account is a part of the acquisition and payment cycle. Therefore, the only change required in the figure is the replacement of accounts payable with the account being audited. For example, if the account being discussed is accrued property taxes, simply substitute accrued property taxes for accounts payable in the first, second, and last boxes in the figure.

The types of audit tests used to audit the above accounts are the same as those shown in Figure 17-5 on page 515. Figure 17-5 also illustrates how the audit risk model discussed in Chapter 8 relates to the audit of these accounts.

Capital assets are assets that have expected lives of more than one year, are used in the business, and are not acquired for resale. The intention to use the assets as a part of the operation of the client's business and their expected life of more than one year are the significant characteristics that distinguish these assets from inventory, prepaid expenses, and investments.

Capital assets can be classified as follows:

- Land and land improvements
- Buildings and building improvements
- Manufacturing equipment
- Furniture and fixtures
- Autos and trucks
- Leasehold improvements
- Construction of property, plant, and equipment in process

Audit of Manufacturing Equipment

In this section, the audit of manufacturing equipment is discussed as an illustration of an appropriate approach to the audit of all capital asset accounts. When there are significant differences in the verification of other types of capital assets, they are briefly examined.

Overview of the Accounts The accounts commonly used for manufacturing equipment are illustrated in Figure 18-1. The relationship of manufacturing equipment to the acquisition and payment cycle is apparent by examining the debits to the asset account. Since the source of debits in the asset account is the acquisitions journal, the accounting system has already been tested for recording the current period's additions to manufacturing equipment as part of the test of the acquisition and payment cycle. Because equipment additions are infrequent and may be subject to special controls, such as board of directors' approval, the auditor may decide not to rely heavily on these tests.

The primary accounting record for manufacturing equipment and other capital asset accounts is generally a property or **capital asset master file** with supporting purchase, disposal, and amortization[1] transactions. The contents of the data files must be understood for a meaningful study of the audit of manufacturing equipment. The files will be composed of a set of records, one for each piece of equipment and other types of property owned. In turn, each record will include descriptive information, date of acquisition, original cost, current-year amortization, and accumulated amortization for the property. The totals of detailed transactions for each property item will equal the total in the master file for that piece of property, and the total of the master file for all items of property will equal the general ledger balances for the related accounts.

The files will also contain information about property acquired and disposed of during the year. Proceeds, gains, and losses will be included for disposals.

Auditing Manufacturing Equipment Manufacturing equipment is normally audited differently from current asset accounts for three reasons: (1) there are usually fewer current-period acquisitions of manufacturing equipment, (2) the amount of any given acquisition is often material, and (3) the equipment is likely to be kept and maintained in the accounting records for several years. Because of these differences, the emphasis in auditing manufacturing equipment is on the verification of current-period acquisitions rather than on the balance in the account carried forward from the preceding year. In addition, the expected life of assets over one year requires amortization and accumulated amortization accounts, which are verified as part of the audit of the assets. Additions should be traced to the capital cost allowance section of the tax working papers.

Although the approach to verifying manufacturing equipment is dissimilar from that used for current assets, several other accounts are verified in much the same manner. These include patents, copyrights, catalogue costs, and all capital asset accounts.

In the audit of manufacturing equipment, it is helpful to separate the tests into the following categories:

- Analytical procedures
- Verification of current-year acquisitions

---

[1]The term "amortization" is used in *CICA Assurance Handbook* Section 3061, "Property, Plant and Equipment," to describe the process of charging the cost of a capital asset to expense over its useful life. However, many organizations and accountants refer to the process as "depreciation," especially when using the term in connection with property, plant, and equipment. The text will use the term "amortization."

CAPITAL ASSET MASTER FILE—a computer file containing records for each piece of equipment and other types of property owned; the primary accounting record for manufacturing equipment and other capital asset accounts

FIGURE 18-1 **Manufacturing Equipment and Related Accounts**

(1) Acquisitions of manufacturing equipment arise from the acquisition and payment cycle. See Figure 17-1 on page 499.

- Verification of current-year disposals
- Verification of the ending balance in the asset account
- Verification of amortization expense
- Verification of the ending balance in accumulated amortization

Analytical Procedures As in all audit areas, the nature of the analytical procedures depends on the nature of the client's operations. Table 18-1 illustrates the type of ratio and trend analysis frequently performed for manufacturing equipment.

Verification of Current-Year Acquisitions The proper recording of current-year additions is important because of the long-term effect the assets have on the financial statements. The failure to capitalize a capital asset, or the recording of an acquisition at the improper amount, affects the balance sheet until the firm disposes of the asset. The income statement is affected until the asset is fully amortized.

Because of the importance of current-period acquisitions in the audit of manufacturing equipment, seven of the nine balance-related audit objectives for tests of details of balances are used as a frame of reference. (Valuation and presentation and disclosure are discussed on page 531 in connection with the verification of ending balances.)

The balance-related audit objectives and common audit tests are shown in Table 18-2. As in all other audit areas, the actual audit tests and sample size depend heavily on materiality,

TABLE 18-1 **Analytical Procedures for Manufacturing Equipment**

Analytical Procedure	Possible Misstatement
Compare amortization expense divided by gross manufacturing equipment cost with previous years.	Misstatement in amortization expense and accumulated amortization.
Compare accumulated amortization divided by gross manufacturing equipment cost with previous years.	Misstatement in accumulated amortization.
Compare monthly or annual repairs and maintenance, supplies expense, small tools expense, and similar accounts with previous years.	Expensing amounts that should be capital items.
Compare gross manufacturing cost divided by some measure of production with previous years.	Idle equipment or equipment that has been disposed of but not written off.

assessed risks, and the results of prior-year tests. Materiality is of special importance for verifying current-year additions. They vary from immaterial amounts in some years to a large number of significant acquisitions in others. Accuracy and classification are usually the major objectives for this part of the audit.

The starting point for the verification of current-year acquisitions is normally a schedule obtained from the client of all acquisitions recorded in the general ledger during the year. A typical schedule lists each addition separately and includes the date of the acquisition, vendor, description, notation of new or used, life of the asset for amortization purposes, amortization method, cost, and any relevant income tax information such as capital cost allowance rates and the investment tax credit if applicable. The client obtains this information from the capital asset master file.

In studying Table 18-2, one should recognize the importance of examining vendors' invoices and related documents in verifying acquisitions of manufacturing equipment. This subject is discussed in the next section.

Examination of Supporting Documentation The most common audit test to verify additions is examination of vendors' invoices and receiving reports. Additional testing besides that which is done as a part of the tests of controls is frequently considered necessary to verify the current-period additions because of the complexity of many equipment transactions and the materiality of the amounts. It is ordinarily unnecessary to examine supporting documentation for each addition, but it is normal to verify large and unusual transactions for the entire year as well as a representative sample of typical additions. The extent of the verification depends on the auditor's assessed control risk for acquisitions and the materiality of the additions.

Tests for acquisitions are accomplished by comparing the charges on vendors' invoices with recorded amounts. The auditor must be aware of the client's capitalization policies to determine whether acquisitions are valued in accordance with generally accepted accounting principles and are treated consistently with those of the preceding year. For example, many clients automatically expense items that are less than a certain amount, such as $100. The auditor should be alert for the possibility of material transportation and installation costs, as well as the trade-in of existing equipment.

The auditor should also ensure that government grants for fixed assets are properly accounted for as required by Section 3800 of the *CICA Accounting Handbook*, "Government Assistance."

TABLE 18-2	Balance-Related Audit Objectives and Tests of Details of Balances for Manufacturing Equipment Additions	
Balance-Related Audit Objective	**Common Tests of Details of Balances Procedures**	**Comments**
Current-year acquisitions in the acquisitions schedule agree with related data file amounts, and the total agrees with the general ledger (detail tie-in).	Foot the acquisitions schedule. Trace the total to the general ledger. Trace the individual acquisitions to the data files for amounts and descriptions.	These tests should be limited unless controls are weak. All increases in the general ledger balance for the year should reconcile to the schedule.
Current-year acquisitions as listed exist (existence).	Examine vendors' invoices and receiving reports. Physically examine assets.	It is uncommon to physically examine additions unless controls are weak or amounts are material.
Existing acquisitions are recorded (completeness).	Examine vendors' invoices of closely related accounts such as repairs and maintenance to uncover items that should be manufacturing equipment. Review lease and rental agreements.	This objective is one of the most important ones for manufacturing equipment.
Current-year acquisitions as listed are owned (ownership).	Examine vendors' invoices.	Ordinarily no problem for equipment. Property deeds, abstracts, and tax bills are frequently examined for land or major buildings.
Current-year acquisitions as listed are accurate (accuracy).	Examine vendors' invoices.	Extent depends on inherent risk and effectiveness of internal controls.
Current-year acquisitions as listed are properly classified (classification).	Examine vendors' invoices in manufacturing equipment account to uncover items that should be classified as office equipment, part of the buildings, or repairs. Examine vendors' invoices of closely related accounts such as repairs to uncover items that should be manufacturing equipment. Examine rent and lease expense for capitalizable leases.	The objective is closely related to tests for completeness. It is done in conjunction with that objective and tests for accuracy.
Current-year acquisitions are recorded in the proper period (cutoff).	Review transactions near the balance sheet date for proper period.	Usually done as a part of accounts payable cutoff tests.
The client has rights to current-year acquisitions (rights).	Examine vendors' invoices.	Ordinarily no problem for equipment. Property deeds and tax bills are frequently examined for land or major buildings.

In conjunction with testing current-period additions for existence and valuation, the auditor should also review recorded transactions for proper classification. In some cases, amounts recorded as manufacturing equipment should be classified as office equipment or as a part of the building. There is also the possibility that the client has improperly capitalized repairs, rents, or similar expenses.

The inclusion of transactions that should properly be recorded as assets in repairs and maintenance expense, lease expense, supplies, small tools, and similar accounts is a common client error. The error results from lack of understanding of generally accepted accounting principles and some clients' desire to avoid income taxes. The likelihood of these types of misclassifications should be evaluated in conjunction with obtaining an understanding of internal controls in the acquisition and payment cycle. If the auditor concludes that material misstatements are likely, it may be necessary to vouch the larger amounts debited to the expense accounts. It is a common practice to do this as a regular part of the audit of the capital asset accounts.

Verification of Current-Year Disposals

INTERNAL CONTROLS The most important internal control over the disposal of manufacturing equipment is the existence of a formal method to inform management of the sale, trade-in, abandonment, or theft of recorded machinery and equipment. If the client fails to record disposals, the original cost of the manufacturing equipment account will be overstated indefinitely, and the net book value will be overstated until the asset is fully amortized. Another important control to protect assets from unauthorized disposal is the requirement for authorization for the sale or other disposal of manufacturing equipment. Finally, there should be adequate internal verification of recorded disposals to make sure assets are correctly removed from the accounting records.

AUDIT TESTS The two major objectives in the verification of the sale, trade-in, or abandonment of manufacturing equipment are that *existing disposals are recorded* and *recorded disposals are accurately valued.*

The starting point for verifying disposals is the client's schedule of recorded disposals or an extract of disposals from the fixed asset data files. The schedule typically includes the date at which the asset was disposed of, the name of the person or firm acquiring the asset, the selling price, the original cost of the asset, the acquisition date, the accumulated amortization of the asset, and the capital cost allowance recapture, if any. Mechanical accuracy tests of the schedule are necessary, including footing the schedule, tracing the totals on the schedule to the recorded disposals, and tracing the cost and accumulated amortization of the disposals to the property master file. The proceeds from disposal should be traced to the capital cost section of the tax working papers. Where there is significant activity in these accounts, the auditor may use audit software to reperform the calculations. It is more effective to use spreadsheet software to reperform calculations than to do them by hand.

Because the failure to record disposals of manufacturing equipment no longer used in the business can significantly affect the financial statements, *the search for unrecorded disposals is essential.* The nature and adequacy of the controls over disposals affect the extent of the search. The following procedures are frequently used for verifying disposals:

- Review whether newly acquired assets replace existing assets.
- Analyze gains on the disposal of assets and miscellaneous income for receipts from the disposal of assets.
- Review plant modifications and changes in product line, taxes, or insurance coverage for indications of deletions of equipment.
- Make enquiries of management and production personnel about the possibility of the disposal of assets.

When an asset is sold or disposed of without having been traded in for a replacement asset, the *valuation* of the transaction can be verified by examining the related sales invoice and property master file. The auditor should compare the cost and accumulated amortization in the master file with the recorded entry in the general journal and recompute the gain or loss on the disposal of the asset for comparison with the accounting records.

Two areas deserve special attention in the valuation objective. The first is the *trade-in of an asset for a replacement.* When trade-ins occur, the auditor should ensure that the new asset is properly capitalized and that the replaced asset is properly eliminated from the records, considering the book value of the asset traded in and the additional cost of the new asset. The second area of special concern is the disposal of assets affected by *capital cost allowance recapture.* Since the recapture affects the current year's income tax expense and liability, the auditor must evaluate its significance. While discussion of the tax implications is beyond the scope of this text, the auditor should ensure that the proceeds on disposal are properly recorded in the tax working papers.

Verification of Asset Balance

INTERNAL CONTROLS The nature of the internal controls over existing assets determines whether it is necessary to verify manufacturing equipment acquired in prior years. Important controls include the use of a master file for individual capital assets, adequate physical controls over assets that are easily movable (e.g., tools, vehicles), assignment of identification numbers to each plant asset, and periodic physical count of capital assets and their reconciliation by accounting personnel. A formal method of informing the accounting department of all disposals of permanent assets is also an important control over the balance of assets carried forward into the current year.

AUDIT TESTS Usually, the auditor does not obtain a list from the client of all assets included in the ending balance of manufacturing equipment. Instead, audit tests are determined on the basis of the master file.

Typically, the first audit step concerns the detail tie-in objective: manufacturing equipment as listed in the master file agrees with the general ledger. Examining a printout of the master file that totals to the general ledger balance is ordinarily sufficient. The auditor may choose to test foot a few pages or use generalized audit software to reconcile balances in the data files.

After assessing control risk for the existence objective, the auditor must decide whether it is necessary to verify the existence of individual items of manufacturing equipment included in the master file. If the auditor believes there is a high likelihood of significant disposed capital assets that are still recorded in the accounting records, an appropriate procedure is selecting a sample from the master file and examining the actual assets. In rare cases, the auditor may believe that it is necessary that the client take a complete physical inventory of capital assets to make sure they actually exist. If a physical inventory is taken, the auditor normally observes the count.

Ordinarily, it is unnecessary to test the valuation of capital assets recorded in prior periods because presumably they were verified in previous audits at the time they were acquired. However, the auditor should be aware that companies might occasionally have on hand manufacturing equipment that is no longer used in operations. If the amounts are material, the auditor should evaluate whether they should be written down to net realizable value or at least be disclosed separately as "nonoperating equipment."

A major consideration in verifying the ending balance in capital assets is the possibility of existing *legal encumbrances* (presentation and disclosure objective). A number of methods are available to determine if manufacturing equipment is encumbered. These include reading the terms of loan and credit agreements and mailing loan confirmation requests to banks and other lending institutions. Information with respect to encumbered assets may also be obtained through discussions with the client or confirmations with company lawyers. In Ontario, the auditor may obtain information from the Department of Corporate and Consumer Affairs, for a small fee, about the existence of encumbrances under the *Personal Property Security Act*. Other provinces have similar procedures for checking on liens and encumbrances.

The *proper presentation and disclosure* of manufacturing equipment in the financial statements must be carefully evaluated to ensure that generally accepted accounting principles are followed. Manufacturing equipment should include the gross cost and should ordinarily be separated from other permanent assets. Leased property should also be disclosed separately, and all liens on property must be included in the footnotes.

Verification of Amortization Expense Amortization expense is one of the few expense accounts that is not verified as a part of tests of controls. The recorded amounts are determined by *internal* **allocations** rather than by exchange transactions with outside parties. When amortization expense is material, more tests of details of amortization expense are required than for an account that has already been verified through tests of controls.

ALLOCATION—the division of certain expenses, such as amortization and manufacturing overhead, among several expense accounts

The most important objectives for amortization expense are proper valuation and accuracy. These involve determining whether the client is following a *consistent amortization policy* from period to period and whether the client's *calculations are accurate*. In determining the former, there are four considerations: the useful life of current period acquisitions, the method of amortization, the estimated salvage value, and the policy of amortizing assets in the year of acquisition and disposition. The client's policies can be determined by having discussions with the client and comparing the responses with the information in the auditor's permanent files.

In deciding on the reasonableness of the useful lives assigned to newly acquired assets, the auditor must consider a number of factors: the actual physical life of the asset, the expected useful life (taking into account obsolescence and the company's normal policy of upgrading equipment), and established company policies on trading in equipment. Occasionally, changing circumstances may necessitate a re-evaluation of the useful life of an asset. When this occurs, a change in accounting estimate rather than a change in accounting principle is involved. The effect of this on amortization must be carefully evaluated.

A useful method of testing amortization is to make a calculation of its overall reasonableness. The calculation is made by multiplying the unamortized capital assets by the amortization rate for the year. In making these calculations, the auditor must make adjustments for current-year additions and disposals, assets with different lengths of life, and assets with different methods of amortization. The calculations can be made fairly easily if the public accounting firm includes in the permanent file a breakdown of the capital assets by method of amortization and length of life. If the overall calculations are reasonably close to the client's totals and if assessed control risk for amortization expense is low, tests of details for amortization can be minimized.

In many audits, it is also desirable to check the mechanical accuracy of amortization calculations. This is done by recomputing amortization expense for selected assets to determine whether the client is following a proper and consistent amortization policy. To be relevant, the detailed calculations should be tied in to the total amortization calculations by footing the amortization expense on the property master file and reconciling the total with the general ledger. Assuming the client maintains computerized amortization and amortization records, it may be advantageous to use the computer in testing the calculations.

Verification of Accumulated Amortization The debits to accumulated amortization are normally tested as a part of the audit of disposals of assets, whereas the credits are verified as a part of amortization expense. If the auditor traces selected transactions to the accumulated amortization records in the property master file as a part of these tests, little additional testing should be required.

Two objectives are usually emphasized in the audit of accumulated amortization:

- Accumulated amortization as stated in the asset master file agrees with the general ledger. This objective can be satisfied by test footing the accumulated amortization on the asset master file and tracing the total to the general ledger.
- Accumulated amortization in the master file is properly valued.

In some cases, the life of manufacturing equipment may be significantly reduced because of such changes as reductions in customer demands for products, unexpected physical deterioration, or a modification in operations. Because of these possibilities and if the decline in asset value is permanent, it may be appropriate to write the asset down to net realizable value.

→ 18.2 PREPAID ASSETS AND INTANGIBLES
Audit of Prepaid Expenses, Deferred Charges, and Intangibles

Prepaid expenses, deferred charges, and intangibles are assets that vary in life from several months to several years. Their inclusion as assets results more from the concept of matching expenses with revenues than from their resale or liquidation value. The following are examples:

- Prepaid rent
- Organization costs
- Prepaid taxes
- Patents

- Prepaid insurance
- Trademarks
- Deferred charges
- Copyrights

There is a major difference in audit approach between tangible assets and intangible assets. Intangible assets include goodwill, copyrights and trademarks, deferred expenses (such as research and development), and may even include capitalized charges for brand names that have a good reputation in the market. Such assets can be extremely difficult to value, as they do not have a ready market, and could plummet in value overnight. For example, the value of a trade name could drop if there are production problems with the brand, or if the brand is targeted in a terrorist activity. The auditor needs to ensure that there is an audit staff member on the team who is expert in dealing with such intangible assets so that management's assessment of the value of the asset and of any amortization can be fairly judged. Independent expert valuation may also be required.

In this section, the audit of prepaid insurance is discussed as an account representative of this group because (1) it is found in most audits—virtually every company has some type of insurance, (2) it is typical of the problems frequently encountered in the audit of this class of accounts, and (3) the auditor's responsibility for the review of insurance coverage is an additional consideration not encountered in the other accounts in this category.

Overview of Prepaid Insurance The accounts typically used for prepaid insurance are illustrated in Figure 18-2. The relationship between prepaid insurance and the acquisition and payment cycle is apparent in examining the debits to the asset account. Since the source of the debits in the asset account is the purchase journal, the payments of insurance premiums have already been partially tested by means of the acquisition and cash disbursement transactions.

Internal Controls The internal controls for prepaid insurance and insurance expense can be divided into three categories: controls over the acquisition and recording of insurance, controls over insurance coverage, and controls over the charge-off of insurance expense.

Controls over the acquisition and recording of insurance are a part of the acquisition and payment cycle. These should include proper authorization for new insurance policies and payment of insurance premiums consistent with the procedures discussed in that cycle.

A record of insurance policies in force and the due date of each policy (**insurance register** or spreadsheet) is an essential control to make sure the company has adequate insurance at all times. The control should include a provision for periodic review of the adequacy of the insurance coverage by an independent qualified person.

INSURANCE REGISTER—a record of insurance policies in force and the due date of each policy

The detailed records of the information in the prepaid insurance register should be verified by someone independent of the person preparing them. A closely related control is the use of monthly "standard journal entries" for insurance expense. If a significant entry is required to adjust the balance in prepaid insurance at the end of the year, it indicates a potential misstatement in the recording of insurance expense throughout the year or in the calculation of the year-end balance in prepaid insurance.

Audit Tests Throughout the audit of prepaid insurance and insurance expense, the auditor should keep in mind that the amount in insurance expense is a residual based on the beginning balance in prepaid insurance, the payment of premiums during the year, and the ending balance. The only verifications of the balance in the expense account that are ordinarily necessary are analytical procedures and a brief test to be sure that the charges to insurance expense arose from credits to prepaid insurance. Since the payments of premiums are tested as part of the tests of controls and analytical procedures, the emphasis in the tests of details of balances is on prepaid insurance and on examining the adequacy of insurance coverage.

FIGURE 18-2	Prepaid Insurance and Related Accounts

(1) Acquisitions of insurance premiums arise from the acquisition and payment cycle. This can be observed by examining Figure 17-1 on page 499.

In the audit of prepaid insurance, a schedule is obtained from the client or prepared by the auditor that includes each insurance policy in force, policy number, insurance coverage for each policy, premium amount, premium period, insurance expense for the year, and prepaid insurance at the end of the year. An example of a schedule obtained from the client for the auditor's working papers is given in Figure 18-3. The auditor's tests of prepaid insurance are normally indicated on the schedule.

ANALYTICAL PROCEDURES A major consideration in the audit of prepaid insurance is the frequent *immateriality* of the beginning and ending balances. Furthermore, few transactions are debited and credited to the balance during the year, most of which are small and simple to understand. Therefore, the auditor can generally spend a short time verifying the balance. Analytical procedures are important as a means of identifying potentially significant misstatements. The following are commonly performed analytical procedures of prepaid insurance and insurance expense:

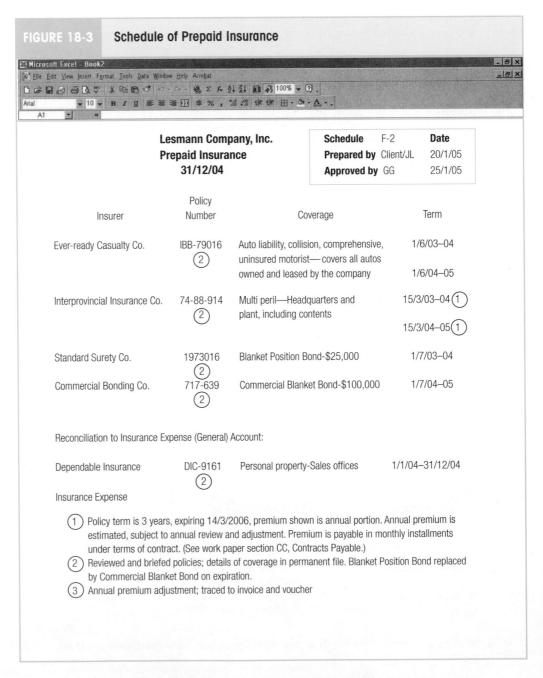

FIGURE 18-3 Schedule of Prepaid Insurance

- Compare total prepaid insurance and insurance expense with previous years as a test of reasonableness.
- Compute the ratio of prepaid insurance to insurance expense, and compare it with previous years.
- Compare the individual insurance policy coverage on the schedule obtained from the client with the preceding year's schedule as a test of the elimination of certain policies or a change in insurance coverage.
- Compare the computed prepaid insurance balance for the current year on a policy-by-policy basis with that of the preceding year as a test of an error in calculation.
- Review the *insurance coverage* listed on the prepaid insurance schedule with an appropriate client official or insurance broker for adequacy of coverage. The auditor cannot be an expert on insurance matters, but his or her understanding of accounting and the valuation of assets is important in making certain a company is not underinsured.

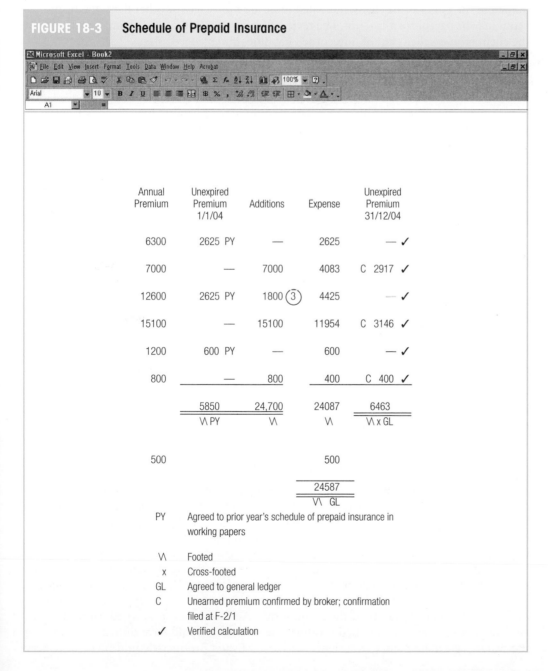

FIGURE 18-3   **Schedule of Prepaid Insurance**

Annual Premium	Unexpired Premium 1/1/04	Additions	Expense	Unexpired Premium 31/12/04
6300	2625 PY	—	2625	— ✓
7000	—	7000	4083	C 2917 ✓
12600	2625 PY	1800 ③	4425	— ✓
15100	—	15100	11954	C 3146 ✓
1200	600 PY	—	600	— ✓
800	—	800	400	C 400 ✓
	5850	24,700	24087	6463
	Ⅴ PY	Ⅴ	Ⅴ	Ⅴ x GL
500			500	
			24587	
			Ⅴ GL	

PY	Agreed to prior year's schedule of prepaid insurance in working papers
Ⅴ	Footed
x	Cross-footed
GL	Agreed to general ledger
C	Unearned premium confirmed by broker; confirmation filed at F-2/1
✓	Verified calculation

For many audits, no additional tests need be performed beyond the review for overall reasonableness unless the tests indicate a high likelihood of a significant misstatement or assessed control risk is high. The discussion of these high risk tests is organized around the balance-related audit objectives for performing tests of details of asset balances. Valuation is not applicable.

INSURANCE POLICIES IN THE PREPAID SCHEDULE ARE VALID, AND ALL EXISTING POLICIES ARE LISTED (EXISTENCE AND COMPLETENESS) The verification of existence and tests for omissions of the insurance policies in force can be tested in one of two ways: by referring to supporting documentation or by obtaining a confirmation of insurance information from the company's insurance agent. The first approach entails examining insurance invoices and policies in force. If these tests are performed, they should be done on a limited test basis. Sending a confirmation to the client's insurance agent is preferable because it is usually less time-consuming than vouching tests, and it provides 100 percent verification.

THE CLIENT HAS RIGHTS TO ALL INSURANCE POLICIES IN THE PREPAID SCHEDULE (RIGHTS) The party who will receive the benefit if an insurance claim is filed has the rights. Ordinarily, the recipient named in the policy is the client, but when there are mortgages or other liens, the insurance claim may be payable to a creditor. The review of insurance policies for claimants other than the client is an excellent test of unrecorded liabilities and pledged assets.

PREPAID AMOUNTS ON THE SCHEDULE ARE ACCURATE, AND THE TOTAL IS CORRECTLY ADDED AND AGREES WITH THE GENERAL LEDGER (ACCURACY AND DETAIL TIE-IN) The accuracy of prepaid insurance involves verifying the total amount of the insurance premium, the length of the policy period, and the allocation of the premium to unexpired insurance. The amount of the premium for a given policy and its time period can be verified simultaneously by examining the premium invoice or the confirmation from an insurance agent. Once these two have been verified, the client's calculations of unexpired insurance can be tested by recalculation. The schedule of prepaid insurance can then be footed and the totals traced to the general ledger to complete the detail tie-in tests.

THE INSURANCE EXPENSE RELATED TO PREPAID INSURANCE IS PROPERLY CLASSIFIED (CLASSIFICATION) The proper classification of debits to different insurance expense accounts should be reviewed as a test of the income statement. In some cases, the appropriate expense account is obvious because of the type of insurance (e.g., insurance on a piece of equipment), but in other cases, allocations are necessary. For example, fire insurance on the building may require allocation to several accounts, including manufacturing overhead. Consistency with previous years is the major consideration in evaluating classification.

INSURANCE TRANSACTIONS ARE RECORDED IN THE PROPER PERIOD (CUTOFF) Cutoff for insurance expense is normally not a significant problem because of the small number of policies and the immateriality of the amount. If the cutoff is checked, it is reviewed as part of accounts payable cutoff tests.

PREPAID INSURANCE IS PROPERLY DISCLOSED (PRESENTATION AND DISCLOSURE) In most audits, prepaid insurance is combined with other prepaid expenses and included as a current asset. The amount is usually small and not a significant consideration to statement users.

→18.3 AUDIT OF ACCRUED LIABILITIES

ACCRUED LIABILITIES—estimated unpaid obligations for services or benefits that have been received prior to the balance sheet date; include accrued commissions, accrued income taxes, accrued payroll, and accrued rent

Accrued liabilities are estimated unpaid obligations for services or benefits that have been received prior to the balance sheet date. Many accrued liabilities represent future obligations for unpaid services resulting from the passage of time but are not payable at the balance sheet date. For example, the benefits of property rental accrue throughout the year; therefore, at the balance sheet date, a certain portion of the total rent cost that has not been paid should be accrued. If the balance sheet date and the date of the termination of the rent agreement are the same, any unpaid rent is more appropriately called "rent payable" than an "accrued liability."

A second type of accrual is one in which the amount of the obligation must be estimated due to the uncertainty of the amount due. An illustration is accrued warranty costs with respect to a new or modified product: the company would have difficulty estimating the warranty expense since experience with established products would be of only very limited assistance. The following are common accrued liabilities, including payroll-related accruals discussed as a part of Chapter 16.

- Accrued officers' bonuses
- Accrued commissions
- Accrued income taxes
- Accrued interest
- Accrued payroll

- Accrued payroll taxes
- Accrued pension costs
- Accrued professional fees
- Accrued rent
- Accrued warranty costs

The verification of accrued expenses varies depending on the nature of the accrual and the circumstances of the client. For most audits, accruals take little audit time, but, in some instances, accounts such as accrued income taxes, warranty costs, and pension costs are material and require considerable audit effort. To illustrate, the audit of accrued property taxes is discussed in the next section.

Auditing Accrued Property Taxes The accounts typically used by companies for accrued property taxes are illustrated in Figure 18-4. The relationship between accrued property taxes and the acquisition and payment cycle is the same as for prepaid insurance and is apparent from examining the debits to the liability account. Since the source of the debits is the cash disbursement journal, the payments of property taxes have already been partially tested by means of the tests of the acquisition and payment cycle.

The balance in property tax expense is a residual amount that results from the beginning and ending balances in accrued property taxes and the payments of property taxes. Therefore, the emphasis in the tests should be on the ending property tax liability and payments. In verifying accrued property taxes, all nine balance-related audit objectives except realizable value are relevant, but two are of special significance:

1. Existing properties for which accrual of taxes is appropriate are on the accrual schedule. The failure to include properties for which taxes should be accrued would understate the liability (completeness). A material misstatement could occur, for example, if taxes on property were not paid before the balance sheet date and were not included as accrued property taxes.
2. Accrued property taxes are accurately recorded. The greatest concern in accuracy is the consistent treatment of the accrual from year to year (accuracy).

The primary methods of testing for the inclusion of all accruals are (1) to perform the accrual tests in conjunction with the audit of current-year property tax payments and (2) to compare the accruals with those of previous years. In most audits, there are few property tax payments, but each payment is often material and therefore it is common to verify each one.

First, the auditor should obtain a schedule of property tax payments from the client and compare each payment with the preceding year's schedule to determine whether all payments have been included in the client-prepared schedule. It is also necessary to examine the permanent asset working papers for major additions and disposals of assets that may affect the property taxes accrual. If the client is expanding its operations, all property affected by local property tax regulations should be included in the schedule even if the first tax payment has not yet been made.

FIGURE 18-4 | **Accrued Property Taxes and Related Accounts**

(1) Payments of property taxes arise from the acquisition and payment cycle. This can be observed by examining Figure 17-1 on page 499.

After the auditor is satisfied that all taxable property has been included in the client-prepared schedule, it is necessary to evaluate the reasonableness of the total amount of property taxes on each property being used as a basis to estimate the accrual. In some instances, the total amount has already been set by the taxing authority, and it is possible to verify the total by comparing the amount on the schedule with the tax bill in the client's possession. In other instances, the preceding year's total payments must be adjusted for the expected increase in property tax rates.

The auditor can verify the accrued property tax by recomputing the portion of the total tax applicable to the current year for each piece of property. In making this calculation, it is essential to use the same portion of each tax payment as the accrual that was used in the preceding year unless justifiable conditions exist for a change. After the accrual and property tax expense for each piece of property have been recomputed, the totals should be added and compared with the general ledger. In many cases, property taxes are charged to more than one expense account. When this happens, the auditor should test for proper classification by evaluating whether the proper amount was charged to each account.

→18.4 AUDIT OF OPERATIONS

The audit of operations is meant to determine whether the income and expense accounts in the financial statements are fairly presented in accordance with generally accepted accounting principles. The auditor must be satisfied that each of the income and expense totals included in the income statement, as well as net earnings, is not materially misstated.

In conducting audit tests of the financial statements, the auditor must always be aware of the importance of the income statement to users of the statements. Many users rely more heavily on the income statement than on the balance sheet for making decisions. Equity investors, long-term creditors, union representatives, and frequently even short-term creditors are more interested in the ability of a firm to generate profit than in the liquidity value or book value of the individual assets.

Considering the purposes of the statement of earnings, the following two concepts are essential in the audit of operations:

1. The matching of periodic expense to periodic income is necessary for a proper determination of operating results.
2. The consistent application of accounting principles for different periods is necessary for comparability.

These concepts must be applied to the recording of individual transactions and to the combining of accounts in the general ledger for statement presentation.

Approach to Auditing Operations The audit of operations cannot be regarded as a separate part of the total audit process. A misstatement of an income statement account will most often equally affect a balance sheet account, and vice versa. The audit of operations is so intertwined with the other parts of the audit that it is necessary to interrelate different aspects of testing operations with the different types of tests previously discussed. A brief description of these tests serves as a review of material covered in other chapters; but more important, it shows the interrelationship of different parts of the audit with operations testing. The parts of the audit directly affecting operations are

- Analytical procedures
- Tests of controls
- Analysis of account balances
- Tests of details of balance sheet accounts
- Tests of allocations

This section emphasizes the operations accounts directly related to the acquisition and payment cycle, but the same basic concepts apply to the operations accounts in all other cycles.

Analytical Procedures Analytical procedures were first discussed in Chapter 6 as a general concept and have been referred to in subsequent chapters as a part of particular audit areas.

Analytical procedures should be considered a part of the test of the fairness of the presentation of both balance sheet and income statement accounts. A few analytical procedures and their effect on operations in the acquisition and payment cycle are shown in Table 18-3.

Tests of Controls Tests of controls have the effect of simultaneously verifying balance sheet and operations accounts. For example, when an auditor concludes that internal controls provide reasonable assurance that transactions in the acquisitions journal exist and are accurately recorded, correctly classified, and recorded in a timely manner, then evidence exists as to the correctness of individual balance sheet accounts (e.g., accounts payable, capital assets) and income statement accounts (e.g., advertising, repairs). Conversely, inadequate controls and misstatements discovered through tests of controls are an indication of the likelihood of misstatements in both the income statement and the balance sheet.

Understanding internal control and the related tests of controls to determine the appropriate assessed control risk is the most important means of verifying many of the operations accounts in each of the transaction cycles. For example, if the auditor concludes after adequate tests that assessed control risk can be reduced to low, the only additional verification of operating accounts such as utilities, advertising, and purchases should be analytical procedures and cutoff tests. However, certain income and expense accounts are not verified at all by tests of controls, and others must be tested more extensively by other means. These are discussed as we proceed.

Analysis of Account Balances For some accounts, the amounts included in the operations accounts must be analyzed even though the two previously mentioned tests have been performed. The meaning and methodology of analysis of accounts will be described first, followed by a discussion of when expense account analysis is appropriate.

Expense account analysis is the examination of underlying documentation of the individual transactions and amounts making up the total particular expense account. The underlying documents are similar in nature to those used for examining transactions as a part of tests of acquisitions transactions and include invoices, receiving reports, purchase

EXPENSE ACCOUNT ANALYSIS— the examination of underlying documentation of individual transactions and amounts making up the total of an expense account

TABLE 18-3	Typical Analytical Procedures for Operations
Analytical Procedure	**Possible Misstatement**
Compare individual expenses with previous years.	Overstatement or understatement of a balance in an expense account.
Compare individual asset and liability balances with previous years.	Overstatement or understatement of a balance sheet account that would also affect an income statement account (i.e., a misstatement of inventory affects cost of goods sold).
Compare individual expenses with budgets.	Misstatement of expenses and related balance sheet accounts.
Compare gross margin percentage with previous years.	Misstatement of cost of goods sold and inventory.
Compare inventory turnover ratio with previous years.	Misstatement of cost of goods sold and inventory.
Compare prepaid insurance and insurance expense with previous years.	Misstatement of insurance expense and prepaid insurance.
Compare commission expense divided by sales with previous years.	Misstatement of commission expense and accrued commissions.
Compare individual manufacturing expenses divided by total manufacturing expenses with previous years.	Misstatement of individual manufacturing expenses and related balance sheet accounts.

orders, and contracts. Figure 18-5 illustrates a typical working paper showing expense analysis for legal expenses.

The major difference between expense account analysis and internal control testing is the degree of concentration on an individual account. Since the tests of controls are meant to assess the appropriate level of control risk, they constitute a general review that usually includes the verification of many different accounts. The analysis of expense and other operations accounts consists of the examination of the transactions in specific accounts to

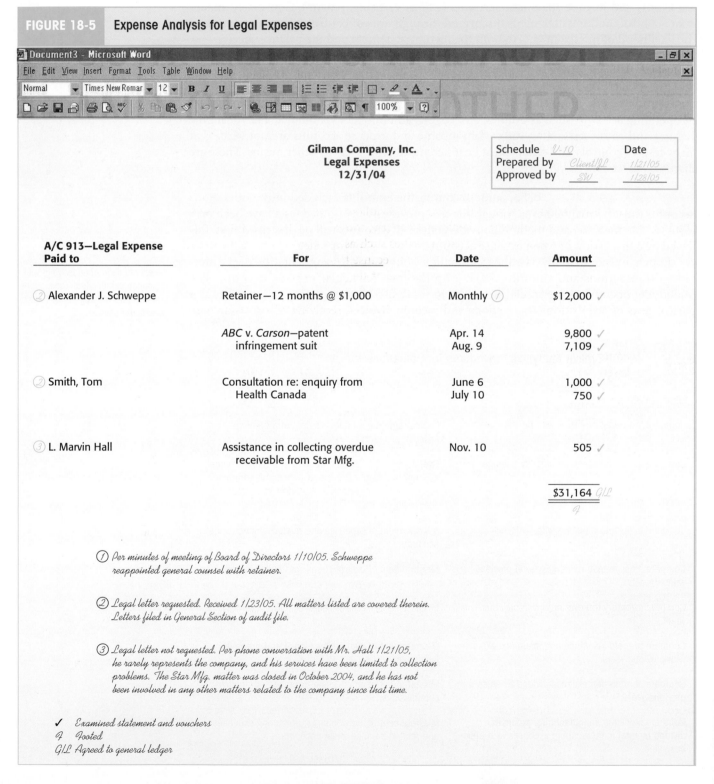

FIGURE 18-5   Expense Analysis for Legal Expenses

Gilman Company, Inc.
Legal Expenses
12/31/04

Schedule _V-10_   Date
Prepared by _Client/JL_ _1/21/05_
Approved by _SW_   _1/28/05_

A/C 913—Legal Expense

Paid to	For	Date	Amount
② Alexander J. Schweppe	Retainer—12 months @ $1,000	Monthly ①	$12,000 ✓
	ABC v. Carson—patent infringement suit	Apr. 14 Aug. 9	9,800 ✓ 7,109 ✓
② Smith, Tom	Consultation re: enquiry from Health Canada	June 6 July 10	1,000 ✓ 750 ✓
③ L. Marvin Hall	Assistance in collecting overdue receivable from Star Mfg.	Nov. 10	505 ✓
			$31,164 _G/L_ F

① Per minutes of meeting of Board of Directors 1/10/05. Schweppe reappointed general counsel with retainer.

② Legal letter requested. Received 1/23/05. All matters listed are covered therein. Letters filed in General Section of audit file.

③ Legal letter not requested. Per phone conversation with Mr. Hall 1/21/05, he rarely represents the company, and his services have been limited to collection problems. The Star Mfg. matter was closed in October 2004, and he has not been involved in any other matters related to the company since that time.

✓ Examined statement and vouchers
F Footed
G/L Agreed to general ledger

determine the propriety, classification, valuation, and other specific information about each account analyzed.

Assuming satisfactory classification results are found in tests of controls and substantive tests of transactions, auditors normally restrict expense analysis to those accounts with a relatively high likelihood of material misstatement. For example, auditors often analyze repairs and maintenance expense accounts to determine if they erroneously include property, plant, and equipment transactions; rent and lease expense are analyzed to determine the need to capitalize leases; and legal expense is analyzed to determine whether there are potential contingent liabilities, disputes, illegal acts, or other legal issues that may affect the financial statements. Accounts such as utilities, travel expense, and advertising are rarely analyzed unless analytical procedures indicate high potential for material misstatement.

Frequently, the expense account analysis is done as a part of the verification of the related asset. For example, it is common to analyze repairs and maintenance as a part of verifying capital assets, rent expense as a part of verifying prepaid or accrued rent, and insurance expense as a part of testing prepaid insurance.

Tests of Allocations Several expense accounts that have not yet been discussed arise from the internal allocation of accounting data. These include expenses such as the amortization of capital assets and the amortization of copyrights and catalogue costs. The allocation of manufacturing overhead between inventory and cost of goods sold is an example of a different type of allocation that affects the expenses.

Allocations are important because they determine whether a particular expenditure is an asset or a current-period expense. If the client fails to follow generally accepted accounting principles or fails to calculate the allocation properly, the financial statements can be materially misstated. The allocation of many expenses such as the amortization of capital assets and the amortization of copyrights is required because the life of the asset is greater than one year. The original cost of the asset is verified at the time of acquisition, but the charge-off takes place over several years. Other types of allocations directly affecting the financial statements arise because the life of a short-lived asset does not expire on the balance sheet date. Examples include prepaid rent and insurance. Finally, the allocation of costs between current-period manufacturing expenses and inventory is required by generally accepted accounting principles as a means of reflecting all the costs of making a product. Intangible assets with an indefinite life are not written off. The auditor needs to assess whether the life of the asset is still indefinite, and whether there has been an impairment of value of any of the intangibles.

Income statement accounts resulting from allocations are typically not verified as a part of tests of controls or tests of details of balance sheet accounts. Analytical procedures are used extensively for verifying allocations, but additional detailed testing is frequently needed.

In testing the allocation of expenditures such as prepaid insurance and manufacturing overhead, the two most important considerations are adherence to generally accepted accounting principles and consistency with the preceding period. The two most important audit procedures for allocations are tests for overall reasonableness and recalculation of the client's results. It is common to perform these tests as a part of the audit of the related asset or liability accounts. For example, amortization expense is usually verified as part of the audit of capital assets; the amortization of patents is tested as part of verifying new patents or the disposal of existing ones; and the allocations between inventory and cost of goods sold are verified as part of the audit of inventory.

Review of Related Party Transactions

While the examination of underlying documents in the tests of controls is designed primarily to verify transactions with third parties, related transactions with affiliates and subdivisions within the client's organization are also included in the examination. The possibility of improper recording and disclosure of transactions between independent entities was discussed in Chapter 7 in the section dealing with related party transactions.

Section 6010, "Audit of Related Party Transactions," adopts a risk-based approach and provides guidance to the auditor for assessing inherent and control risks and ultimately determining the extent of substantive testing for related party transactions. An Appendix to Section 6010 lists examples of audit procedures and how related party transactions could be measured.

When a client deals with related parties, Section 3840 of the *CICA Accounting Handbook* requires that the nature of the relationship, the nature and extent of transactions, and amounts due to and from the related parties, including contractual obligations and contingencies, be properly disclosed for the financial statements to be in conformity with GAAP. Services and inventory acquired from related parties must be properly valued, and other exchange transactions must be carefully evaluated for propriety and reasonableness. Related party transactions must be audited more extensively than those with third parties.

SUMMARY

1. *In addition to inventory, what are the other expense accounts that need to be audited?* Any expense accounts that have the potential to be misstated by a material amount should be audited. The auditor could use analytical review to target those accounts that need further testing.

   What process should be followed in the audit of manufacturing equipment, an asset? The auditor needs to consider the risk of misstatement by audit objective to target testing. Analytical procedures (Table 18-1) can assist. Then, a sample of transactions would be selected for verification to supporting acquisitions documentation (e.g., invoices or purchase contracts), and tests of details conducted for relevant audit objectives (Table 18-2).

2. *Why is the audit of prepaid expenses important?* Prepaid expenses are important in the process of matching expenses with revenues. Misstatements in prepaid expenses would also result in misstatements in revenue.

   How are prepaid expenses audited? Risks and internal controls are assessed before designing audit tests that include determination of the period covered by the prepaid assets and calculation of the portion that is to be expensed.

   Why are intangible assets difficult to audit? Intangible assets are difficult to value if they were not acquired at arms length. There may be limited evidence establishing useful life, making it difficult to assess management's valuation or the amount of amortization for the year.

3. *What are some examples of typical accrued liabilities?* Accruals include management bonuses, interest, payroll costs, property taxes, and insurance.

   How are accrued property taxes audited? Assuming amounts are material, the auditor will normally look at current year payments, recalculate the amount to be recorded in the current year, and compare treatment to prior years.

4. *What is the process for auditing income and expense accounts?* Based upon risk assessment and the quality of internal controls, the primary techniques include analytical review and tracing to source documents for selected accounts or sampled items.

   Why is analytical review an important technique in the audit of operations? Analytical review allows the auditor to test the fairness of presentation of both the balance sheet and income statement amounts.

CICA ASSURANCE HANDBOOK SECTION REFERENCED IN THIS CHAPTER

Section 6010 – Audit of related party transactions.

ESSENTIAL TERMS

Accrued liabilities—estimated unpaid obligations for services or benefits that have been received prior to the balance sheet date; include accrued commissions, accrued income taxes, accrued payroll, and accrued rent   (p. 536).

Allocation—the division of certain expenses, such as amortization and manufacturing overhead, among several expense accounts   (p. 531).

Capital asset master file—a computer file containing records for each piece of equipment and other types of property owned; the primary accounting record for manufacturing equipment and other capital asset accounts   (p. 526).

Expense account analysis—the examination of underlying documentation of individual transactions and amounts making up the total of an expense account   (p. 539).

Insurance register—a record of insurance policies in force and the due date of each policy   (p. 533).

REVIEW QUESTIONS

18-1 Explain the relationship between tests of controls for the acquisition and payment cycle and tests of details of balances for the verification of capital assets. Which aspects of capital assets are directly affected by the tests of controls, and which are not?

18-2 Explain why the emphasis in auditing capital assets is on the current-period acquisitions and disposals rather than on the balances in the account carried forward from the preceding year. Under what circumstances would the emphasis be on the balances carried forward?

18-3 What is the relationship between the audit of property accounts and the audit of repair and maintenance accounts? Explain how the auditor organizes the audit to take this relationship into consideration.

18-4 List and briefly state the purpose of all audit procedures that might reasonably be applied by an auditor to determine that all capital asset retirements have been recorded on the books.

18-5 In auditing amortization expense, what major considerations should the auditor keep in mind? Explain how each can be verified.

18-6 Explain the relationship between the tests of controls for the acquisition and payment cycle and the tests of details of balances for verification of prepaid insurance.

18-7 Explain why the audit of prepaid insurance should ordinarily take a relatively small amount of audit time if the client's assessed control risk for acquisitions is low.

18-8 Distinguish between the evaluation of the adequacy of insurance coverage and the verification of prepaid insurance. Explain which is more important in a typical audit.

18-9 Explain the relationship between accrued rent and the tests of controls for the acquisition and payment cycle. Which aspects of accrued rent are not verified as a part of the tests of controls?

18-10 In verifying accounts payable, it is common to restrict the audit sample to a small portion of the population items, whereas in auditing accrued property taxes it is common to verify all transactions for the year. Explain the reason for the difference.

18-11 What is meant by "the analysis of expense accounts"? Explain how expense account analysis relates to the tests of controls that the auditor has already completed for the acquisition and payment cycle.

18-12 How would the approach for verifying repair expense differ from that used to audit amortization expense? Why would the approach be different?

18-13 List the factors that should affect the auditor's decision whether or not to analyze a particular account balance. Considering these factors, list four expense accounts that are commonly analyzed in audit engagements.

18-14 Why does the auditor examine transaction detail for subsidiaries, affiliates, officers, and directors?

MULTIPLE CHOICE QUESTIONS

18-15 Choose the best response for the following questions:

a. Which of the following is an internal control weakness related to factory equipment?

   (1) Cheques issued in payment of purchases of equipment are signed by the production supervisor.
   (2) Proceeds from sales of fully amortized equipment are credited to other income.
   (3) All acquisitions of factory equipment must be made by the department in need of the equipment.
   (4) Factory equipment replacements are generally made when estimated useful lives, as indicated in amortization schedules, have expired.

b. With respect to an internal control measure that will assure accountability for capital asset retirements, management should implement controls that include

   (1) continuous analysis of miscellaneous revenue to locate any cash proceeds from sale of capital assets.
   (2) periodic enquiry of plant executives by internal auditors as to whether any capital assets have been retired.
   (3) continuous use of serially numbered retirement work orders.

   (4) periodic observation of capital assets by the internal auditors.

                        (AICPA adapted)

c. The controller of Eigram Manufacturing, Inc. wants to use ratio analysis to identify the possible existence of idle equipment or the possibility that equipment has been disposed of without having been written off. Which of the following ratios would best accomplish this objective?

   (1) Amortization expense/book value of manufacturing equipment
   (2) Repairs and maintenance cost/direct labour costs
   (3) Gross manufacturing equipment cost/units produced
   (4) Accumulated amortization/book value of manufacturing equipment

d. Which of the following best describes the independent auditor's approach to obtaining satisfaction concerning amortization expense in the income statement?

   (1) Determine the method for computing amortization expense, and ascertain that it is in accordance with generally accepted accounting principles.
   (2) Verify the mathematical accuracy of the amounts

charged to income as a result of amortization expense.

(3) Reconcile the amount of amortization expense to those amounts credited to accumulated amortization accounts.

(4) Establish the basis for amortizable assets, and verify the amortization expense.

e. Before expressing an opinion concerning the results of operations, the auditor should proceed with the examination of the income statement by

(1) making net income comparisons to published industry trends and ratios.

(2) applying a rigid measurement standard designed to test for understatement of net income.

(3) analyzing the beginning and ending balance sheet inventory amounts.

(4) examining income statement accounts concurrently with the related balance sheet accounts.

(AICPA adapted)

DISCUSSION QUESTIONS AND PROBLEMS

18-16 For each of the following misstatements in property, plant, and equipment accounts, state an internal control that the client could implement to prevent the misstatement from occurring and a substantive audit procedure that the auditor could use to discover the misstatement.

1. The asset lives used to amortize equipment are less than reasonable, expected useful lives.
2. Capitalizable assets are routinely expensed as repairs and maintenance, perishable tools, or supplies expense.
3. Computer equipment that is abandoned or traded for replacement equipment is not removed from the accounting records.
4. Amortization expense for manufacturing operations is charged to administrative expenses.
5. Tools necessary for the maintenance of equipment are stolen by company employees for their personal use.
6. Acquisitions of property are recorded at an improper amount.
7. A loan against existing equipment is not recorded in the accounting records. The cash receipts from the loan never reached the company because they were used for the down payment on a piece of equipment now being used as an operating asset. The equipment is also not recorded in the records.

18-17 The following types of internal controls are commonly employed by organizations for property, plant, and equipment:

1. A capital asset master file is maintained with a separate record for each capital asset.
2. Written policies exist and are known by accounting personnel to differentiate between capitalizable additions, freight, installation costs, replacements, and maintenance expenditures.
3. Purchases of capital assets in excess of $20,000 are approved by the board of directors.
4. Whenever practical, equipment is labelled with metal tags and is inventoried on a systematic basis.
5. Amortization charges for individual assets are calculated

for each asset; recorded in a capital asset master file that includes cost, amortization, and accumulated amortization for each asset; and verified periodically by an independent clerk.

Required

a. State the purpose of each of the internal controls listed. Your answer should refer to the type of misstatement that is likely to be reduced because of the control.

b. For each internal control, list one test of controls that the auditor can use to test for its existence.

c. List one test of controls for determining whether the control is actually preventing misstatements in property, plant, and equipment.

18-18 Hardware Manufacturing Company Limited, a closely held corporation, has operated since 1994 but has not had its financial statements audited. The company now plans to issue additional capital stock to be sold to outsiders and wishes to engage you to examine its 2004 transactions and render an opinion on the financial statements for the year ended December 31, 2004.

The company has expanded from one plant to three and has frequently acquired, modified, and disposed of all types of equipment. Capital assets have a net book value of 70 percent of total assets and consist of land and buildings, diversified machinery and equipment, and furniture and fixtures. Some property was acquired by donation from shareholders. Amortization was recorded by several methods using various estimated lives.

Required

a. May you confine your examination solely to 2004 transactions as requested by this prospective client whose financial statements have not previously been examined? Why or why not?

b. Prepare an audit program for the January 1, 2004, opening balances of the land, building, and equipment and accumulated amortization accounts of Hardware Manufacturing Company Limited, organized by audit objective.

(AICPA adapted)

18-19 As part of the audit of different audit areas, it is important to be alert for the possibility of unrecorded liabilities. For each of the following audit areas or accounts, describe a liability that could be uncovered and the audit procedures that could uncover it.

a. Minutes of the board of directors' meetings

b. Land and buildings
c. Rent expense
d. Interest expense
e. Cash surrender value of life insurance
f. Cash in the bank
g. Officers' travel and entertainment expense

18-20 Eugene Fikursky, a staff assistant, was asked to analyze interest and legal expense as a part of the first-year audit of Chinook Manufacturing Corp. In searching for a model to follow, Fikursky looked at other completed working papers in the current audit file and concluded that the closest thing to what he was looking for was a working paper for repair and maintenance expense account analysis. Following the approach used in analyzing repairs and maintenance, he made a schedule of all interest and legal expenses in excess of $500 and verified them by examining supporting documentation.

Required

a. Evaluate Fikursky's approach to verifying interest and legal expense.
b. Suggest a better approach to verifying these two account balances.

18-21 In performing tests of the acquisition and payment cycle for Oakville Manufacturing, Inc., the staff assistant did a careful and complete job. Since internal controls were evaluated as excellent before tests of controls were performed and were determined to be operating effectively on the basis of the lack of exceptions in the tests of controls, the decision was made to reduce significantly the tests of expense account analysis. The in-charge auditor decided to reduce, but not eliminate, the acquisition-related expense account analysis for repair expense, legal and other professional expense, miscellaneous expense, and utilities expense on the grounds that they should always be verified more extensively than normal accounts. The decision was also made to eliminate all account analysis for the purchase of raw materials, amortization expense, supplies expense, insurance expense, and the current-period additions to capital assets.

Required

a. List considerations in the audit other than the quality of internal controls that should affect the auditor's selection of accounts to be analyzed.
b. Assuming no significant problems were identified on the basis of the other considerations in part (a), evaluate the auditor's decision to reduce but not eliminate expense account analysis for each account involved. Justify your conclusions.
c. Assuming no significant problems were identified on the basis of the other considerations in part (a), evaluate the auditor's decision to eliminate expense account analysis for each account involved. Justify your conclusions.

PROFESSIONAL JUDGMENT PROBLEM

18-22 Huge Software House Limited (HSH) employs several hundred people writing software for several specific industries and has general purpose software for all accounting applications (such as sales, accounts receivable, general ledger). HSH sells both functional software and integrated database systems. The balance sheet contains accounts receivable ($101 million), inventory ($25 million), and deferred development costs ($250 million).

Accounts receivable consists of trade accounts receivable for purchases of software, and current amounts due on leases of software and maintenance contracts. Inventory includes raw materials (blank CD-ROMs and DVDs media) and finished goods (software that has been completed and has not yet been marketed, as well as software that has been transferred onto the media, at a cost that consists of a prorated portion of deferred development costs). Deferred development costs contain costs of labour over the last three years pertaining to the software that is being developed and that the company believes is a clearly marketable product.

Required

a. Identify the audit objectives associated with the audit of accounts receivable, inventory, and deferred development costs that are likely at high risk of material misstatement. Justify your assessment.
b. For each high risk identified in part (a), state at least one substantive audit procedure that you could conduct to test the assertion for that account.

CASE

18-23 As the manager of the audit of Vernal Manufacturing Inc., you are investigating the operations accounts. The in-charge auditor assessed control risk for all cycles as low, supported by tests of controls. There are no major inherent risks affecting operations. Accordingly, in auditing the operations accounts, you decide to emphasize analytical procedures. The in-charge auditor prepared a schedule of the key income statement accounts that compares the prior year totals to the current year's and includes explanations of variances obtained from discussions with client personnel. This schedule is included in Exhibit I on page 546.

a. Evaluate the explanations for variances provided by client personnel. List any alternative explanations to those given.

b. Indicate which variances are of special significance to the audit and how they should affect additional audit procedures.

EXHIBIT I — Vernal Manufacturing Inc. Operations Accounts 31/12/04

ACCOUNT	PER G/L 31/12/03	PER G/L 31/12/04	CHANGE AMOUNT	PERCENT	EXPLANATIONS BY CLIENT
Sales*	$8,467,312	$9,845,231	$1,377,919	16.3	Sales increase due to two new customers who account for 20% of volume. Larger
Sales returns and allowances	(64,895)	(243,561)	(178,666)	275.3	returns due to need to cement relations with these customers.
Gain (loss) on sale of assets	43,222	(143,200)	(186,422)	-431.3	
Interest income	243	223	(20)	-8.2	Trade-in of several sales cars that needed replacement.
Miscellaneous income	6,365	25,478	19,113	300.3	
	8,452,247	9,484,171	1,031,924	12.2	
Cost of goods sold:					
Beginning inventory	1,487,666	1,389,034	(98,632)	-6.6	Increase in these accounts due to increased volume with new customers as indi-
Purchases	2,564,451	3,430,865	866,414	33.8	cated above.
Freight in	45,332	65,782	20,450	45.1	
Purchase returns	(76,310)	(57,643)	18,667	-24.5	
Factory wages	986,755	1,145,467	158,712	16.1	
Factory benefits	197,652	201,343	3,691	1.9	
Factory overhead	478,659	490,765	12,106	2.5	
Factory amortization	344,112	314,553	(29,559)	-8.6	
Ending inventory	(1,389,034)	(2,156,003)	(766,969)	55.2	Inventory being held for new customers.
	4,639,283	4,824,163	184,880	4.0	
Selling, general and administrative:					
Executive salaries	167,459	174,562	7,103	4.2	Normal salary increases.
Executive benefits	32,321	34,488	2,167	6.7	
Office salaries	95,675	98,540	2,865	3.0	
Office benefits	19,888	21,778	1,890	9.5	
Travel and entertainment	56,845	75,583	18,738	33.0	Sales and promotional expenses increased in an attempt to obtain new major
Advertising	130,878	156,680	25,802	19.7	customers. Two obtained and program will continue.
Other sales expense	34,880	42,334	7,454	21.4	
Stationery and supplies	38,221	21,554	(16,667)	-43.6	Probably a misclassification; will investigate.
Postage	14,657	18,756	4,099	28.0	Normal increase.
Telephone	36,551	67,822	31,271	85.6	Normal increase.
Dues and memberships	3,644	4,522	878	24.1	Normal increase.
Rent	15,607	15,607	0	0.0	
Legal fees	14,154	35,460	21,306	150.5	Timing of billing for fees.
Accounting fees	16,700	18,650	1,950	11.7	Normal increase.
Amortization	73,450	69,500	(3,950)	-5.4	Normal change.
Bad-debt expense	166,454	143,871	(22,583)	-13.6	Haven't reviewed yet for the current year.
Insurance	44,321	45,702	1,381	3.1	Normal change.
Interest expense	120,432	137,922	17,490	14.5	Normal change.
Other expense	5,455	28,762	23,307	427.3	Amount not material.
	1,087,592	1,212,093	124,501	11.4	
	5,726,875	6,036,256	309,381	5.4	
Income before taxes	2,725,372	3,447,915	722,543	26.5	Increase due to increased income before tax.
Income taxes	926,626	1,020,600	93,974	10.1	
Net income	$1,798,746	$2,427,315	$628,569	34.9	

*Sales are shown net of Goods and Services Taxes.

CHAPTER 19

AUDIT OF THE INVENTORY AND WAREHOUSING CYCLE

Look around your room. What is in it—bookshelves, a desk, carpeting, books, pens, pencils, paper supplies? All of these items are produced by companies, stored, and sold to businesses that distribute or sell to consumers. The diversity of organizations involved in the manufacture, distribution, and sales of products is reflected in the many different types of accounting systems to track the costs and routing of inventory.

LEARNING OBJECTIVES

After reading this chapter, you should be able to answer the following questions:

1. What are the components of the inventory and warehousing cycle?

2. What are the five different parts of the inventory and warehousing cycle that are audited? Provide an overview of the process used to audit the inventory and warehousing cycle.

3. What role does each of the following types of tests play in the audit of inventory? (i) analytical review, (ii) physical observation of inventory, (iii) pricing and compilation tests.

4. Describe how the relationship between the tests of different cycles affects the audit of inventory.

EFFECTIVE SUPPLY CHAIN MANAGEMENT REDUCES INVENTORY

From the store shelves through to the replenishment system, The Bay and Zellers have implemented current technology to reduce stock outs on the shelves and receive products faster from suppliers, resulting in better customer service and lower inventory. Wireless technology is used to scan products on the shelf and in the stockroom, helping to confirm the accuracy of the perpetual inventory system.

Zellers has 300 stores, all using point-of-sale (POS) systems that update inventory as goods leave the store. An integrated inventory database allows inventory to be managed centrally for purchasing, while still providing for twice-daily reports so that stores can manage their stock. Purchasing staff and suppliers exchange information and electronic documents via an Internet portal—an easy to use web-based menu that provides a standard interface.

Sources: 1. Langton, Jerry, 2004. "Portals open doors to sales," The Toronto Star, October 21. 2. Patrick, Ryan B., 2004. "HBC puts LID technology on Zellers inventory," ComputerWorld Canada, Vol. 20 (19).

One of the key advantages of automated inventory management is that it enables organizations to provide expanded descriptions of their inventory products on a real-time basis to key business partners such as suppliers and customers, perhaps via the Internet. Information about quantities on hand, the location of products, and other key inventory data helps inventory suppliers work with management to monitor the flow of goods. Expanded access to information may increase business risks, such as the risk that sensitive proprietary information may unintentionally be made available to unauthorized users. Think about our control framework: the control environment, general controls, and application controls. What are some examples of controls that Zellers and The Bay would need to have to minimize risks of unauthorized access to their inventory data?

→19.1 THE NATURE OF THE INVENTORY AND WAREHOUSING CYCLE

Inventory takes many different forms, depending on the nature of the business. For retail or wholesale businesses, the most important inventory is merchandise on hand that is available for sale. For hospitals, it includes food, drugs, and medical supplies. A manufacturing company has raw materials, purchased parts, and supplies for use in production; goods in the process of being manufactured; and finished goods available for sale. We have selected manufacturing company inventories for presentation in this text. However, most of the principles discussed apply to other types of businesses as well.

For the reasons that follow, the audit of inventories is often the most complex and time-consuming part of the audit:

- Inventory is generally a major item on the balance sheet, and it is often the largest item making up the accounts included in working capital.
- The inventory items are often in different locations, which makes physical control and counting difficult. Companies must have their inventory accessible for the efficient manufacture and sale of the product, but this dispersal creates significant audit problems.
- The diversity of the items in inventories creates difficulties for the auditor. Such items as jewels, chemicals, and electronic parts present problems of observation and valuation.
- The valuation of inventory is difficult due to such factors as obsolescence and the need to allocate manufacturing costs to inventory.
- There are several acceptable inventory valuation methods, but any given client must apply a method consistently from year to year. Moreover, an organization may prefer to use different valuation methods for different parts of the inventory, which is acceptable under GAAP.

The trial balance for Hillsburg Hardware Limited on page 117 shows that only two accounts are affected by inventories and warehousing: inventory and cost of goods sold. However, both accounts are highly material. For a manufacturing company, a great many accounts are affected because labour, acquisitions of raw materials, and all indirect manufacturing costs affect inventory.

The physical flow of goods and the flow of costs in the **inventory and warehousing cycle** for a manufacturing company are shown in Figure 19-1. The direct tie-in of the inventory and warehousing cycle to the acquisition and payment cycle and to the payroll and personnel cycle can be seen by examining the debits to the raw materials, direct labour, and manufacturing overhead T-accounts. The direct tie-in to the sales and collection cycle occurs at the point where finished goods are relieved (credited) and a charge is made to cost of goods sold. This close relationship to other transaction cycles in the organization is a basic characteristic of the audit of the inventory and warehousing cycle.

INVENTORY AND WAREHOUSING CYCLE—the transaction cycle that involves the physical flow of goods through the organization, as well as related costs

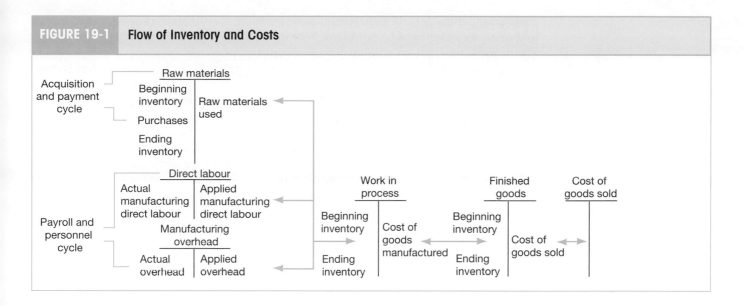

FIGURE 19-1   Flow of Inventory and Costs

Functions in the Cycle and Internal Controls

The inventory and warehousing cycle can be thought of as comprising two separate but closely related systems: one involving the actual *physical flow of goods* and the other the *related costs*. As inventories move through the company, there must be adequate controls over both their physical movement and their related costs. A brief examination of the six functions making up the inventory and warehousing cycle will help you to understand these controls and the audit evidence needed to test their effectiveness.

Process Purchase Orders *Purchase requisitions* are used to inform the purchasing department for which inventory items to place orders. Requisitions may be initiated by stockroom personnel when inventory reaches a predetermined level, orders may be placed for the materials required to produce a particular customer order, or orders may be initiated on the basis of a periodic inventory count by a responsible person. Regardless of the method followed, the controls over purchase requisitions and the related purchase orders are evaluated and tested as part of the acquisition and payment cycle. Many organizations use only purchase orders, relying on automated systems to identify the need to obtain materials or products.

Receive New Materials Receipt of the ordered materials is also part of the acquisition and payment cycle. Materials received should be inspected for quantity and quality. The receiving department produces a *receiving report* that becomes a part of the necessary documentation before payment is made. After inspection, the materials are sent to the storeroom and the receiving documents are typically sent to purchasing, the storeroom, and accounts payable. Control and accountability are necessary for all transfers.

Store Raw Materials When materials are received, they are stored in the stockroom until needed for production. Materials are issued out of stock to production upon presentation of a properly approved materials requisition, work order, or similar document that indicates the type and quantity of materials needed. This requisition document is used to update the perpetual inventory master files and to make book transfers from the raw materials to work-in-process accounts.

Process Goods The processing portion of the inventory and warehousing cycle varies greatly from company to company. The determination of the items and quantities to be produced is generally based on specific orders from customers, sales forecasts, predetermined finished goods inventory levels, or economic production runs. Frequently, a separate production control department is responsible for the determination of the type and quantity of items to be produced. Within the various production departments, provision must be made to account for the quantities produced, control of scrap, quality controls, and physical protection of the material in process. The production department must generate production and scrap reports so that the accounting department can reflect the movement of materials in the books and determine accurate costs of production.

In any company involved in manufacturing, an adequate *cost accounting system* is an important part of the processing of goods function. The system is necessary to indicate the relative profitability of the various products for management planning and control and to value inventories for financial statement purposes. There are two types of cost systems (although many variations and combinations of these systems are employed): **job cost** and **process cost**. The main difference is whether costs are accumulated by individual jobs when material is issued and labour costs incurred (job cost), or whether they are accumulated by particular processes, with unit costs for each process assigned to the products passing through the process (process cost).

Cost accounting records consist of master files, worksheets, and reports that accumulate material, labour, and overhead costs by job or process as the costs are incurred. When jobs or products are completed, the related costs are transferred from work in process to finished goods on the basis of production department reports.

Store Finished Goods As finished goods are completed by the production department, they are placed in the stockroom awaiting shipment. In companies with good internal controls, finished goods are kept under physical control in a separate limited access area. The control of finished goods is often considered part of the sales and collection cycle.

Ship Finished Goods Shipping of completed goods is an integral part of the sales and collection cycle. Any shipment or transfer of finished goods must be authorized by a properly approved shipping document. The controls for shipment have already been studied in previous chapters.

Perpetual Inventory Files One of the records for inventory that has not been previously discussed is **perpetual inventory data files**. Separate perpetual records are normally kept for raw materials and finished goods. Most companies do not use perpetuals for work in process.

The perpetual inventory master file normally includes only information such as item number, description, unit cost, quantity on hand, and quantity on order. The supporting transaction files contain supporting records of the units of inventory purchased and sold. Sales price information and vendor information could also be included in data files.

For acquisitions of raw materials, the perpetual inventory master file is updated automatically when acquisitions of inventory are processed as part of recording acquisitions. For example, when the computer system enters the number of units and unit cost for each raw material purchase, this information is used to update perpetual inventory master files along with the acquisitions journal and accounts payable master file. Chapter 17 described the recording of acquisition transactions.

Transfers of raw materials from the storeroom must be separately entered into the computer to update the perpetual records. Typically, only the units transferred need to be entered because the computer can determine the unit costs from the master file. Raw materials perpetual inventory data files that have unit costs include, for each raw material, beginning and ending units on hand, units and unit cost of each purchase, and units and unit cost of each transfer into production.

Finished goods perpetual inventory data files include the same type of information as raw materials perpetuals, but are considerably more complex if costs are included along with units. Finished goods costs include raw materials, direct labour, and manufacturing overhead, which often requires allocations and detailed record keeping. When finished goods perpetuals include unit costs, the cost accounting records must be integrated into the computer system.

JOB COST SYSTEM—the system of cost accounting in which costs are accumulated by individual jobs when material is used and labour costs are incurred

PROCESS COST SYSTEM—the system of cost accounting in which costs are accumulated for a process, with unit costs for each process assigned to the products passing through the process

PERPETUAL INVENTORY DATA FILES—continuously updated computerized records of inventory items purchased, used, sold, and on hand for merchandise, raw materials, and finished goods. The master file normally contains the balance of quantity on hand, as well as prices and description of items. The transaction files contain activity details, such as shipments (items sold) and receipts (goods purchased)

Summary of Inventory Documentation The physical movement and related documentation in a basic inventory and warehousing cycle is shown in Figure 19-2. The figure re-emphasizes the important point that the recording of costs and movement of inventory as shown in the books must correspond to the physical movements and processes.

→19.2 PARTS OF THE AUDIT OF INVENTORY

The overall objective in the audit of the inventory and warehousing cycle is to determine that raw materials, work in process, finished goods inventory, and cost of goods sold are fairly stated on the financial statements. The basic inventory and warehousing cycle can be divided into five distinct parts.

Acquire and Record Raw Materials, Labour, and Overhead This part of the inventory and warehousing cycle includes the first three functions in Figure 19-2: processing of purchase orders, receipt of raw materials, and storage of raw materials. The internal controls over these three functions are first studied then tested as part of performing tests of controls in the acquisition and payment cycle and the payroll and personnel cycle. At the completion of the acquisition and payment cycle, the auditor is likely to be satisfied that acquisitions of raw materials and manufacturing costs are correctly stated. Samples should be designed to ensure that these systems are adequately tested. Similarly, when labour is a significant part of inventory, the payroll and personnel cycle tests should verify the proper accounting for these costs.

Transfer Assets and Costs Internal transfers include the fourth and fifth functions in Figure 19-2: processing the goods and storing finished goods. These two activities are not related to any other transaction cycles and therefore must be studied and tested as part of the inventory and warehousing cycle. The accounting records concerned with these functions are referred to as the **cost accounting records**.

COST ACCOUNTING RECORDS— the accounting records concerned with the manufacture and processing of the goods and storing finished goods

Ship Goods and Record Revenue and Costs The recording of shipments and related costs, the last function in Figure 19-2, is part of the sales and collection cycle. Thus, the internal controls over this function are studied and tested as part of auditing the sales and collection cycle. The tests of controls should include procedures to verify the accuracy of the perpetual inventory master files.

FIGURE 19-2	Functions in the Inventory and Warehousing Cycle

Functions

	Process purchase orders	Receive raw materials	Store raw materials*	Process the goods	Store finished goods*	Ship finished goods
Flow of Inventory		Receive raw materials	Put materials in storage	Put materials in production	Put completed goods in storage	Ship finished goods
Related Documentation	Purchase requisition	Receiving report	Raw materials perpetual inventory master file	Raw materials requisition	Finished goods perpetual inventory master file	Shipping document
	Purchase order	Vendor's invoice		Cost accounting records**	Cost accounting records**	Finished goods perpetual inventory master file
						Cost accounting records**

* Inventory counts are taken and compared with perpetual inventory master files at any stage of the cycle. The auditor must determine that cutoff for recording documents corresponds to the physical location of the items in the process. A count must ordinarily be taken at least once a year. If the perpetual system is operating well, this can be done on a cycle basis throughout the year.

** Includes cost information for materials, direct labour, and overhead.

Physically Observe Inventory Observing the client taking a physical inventory count is necessary to determine whether recorded inventory actually exists at the balance sheet date and is properly counted by the client. Inventory is the first audit area for which physical examination is an essential type of evidence used to verify the balance in an account. Physical observation is discussed further in this chapter.

Price and Compile Inventory Costs used to value the physical inventory must be tested to determine whether the client has correctly followed an inventory method that is in accordance with generally accepted accounting principles and is consistent with previous years. Audit procedures used to verify these costs are referred to as "**price tests**." In addition, the auditor must verify whether the physical counts were correctly summarized, the inventory quantities and prices were correctly extended, and the extended inventory was correctly footed. These tests are called "**compilation tests**."

Figure 19-3 summarizes the five parts of the audit of the inventory and warehousing cycle and shows the cycle in which each is audited. The first and third parts of the audit of the inventory and warehousing cycle have already been discussed in connection with other cycles. The importance of the tests of these other cycles should be kept in mind throughout the remaining sections of this chapter.

Audit of Cost Accounting

The cost accounting systems and controls of different companies vary more than most other areas because of the wide variety of items of inventory and the level of sophistication desired by management. For example, a company that manufactures an entire line of farm machines would have completely different kinds of cost records and internal controls than a steel fabricating shop that makes and installs custom-made metal cabinets. Not surprisingly, small companies with owners who are actively involved in the manufacturing process need less sophisticated records than do large multi-product companies.

Cost Accounting Controls **Cost accounting controls** are those related to the physical inventory and the consequent costs from the point at which raw materials are requisitioned to the point at which the manufactured product is completed and transferred to storage. It is convenient to divide these controls into two broad categories: (1) physical controls over raw materials, work in process, and finished goods inventory; and (2) controls over the related costs.

INVENTORY PRICE TESTS—audit procedures used to verify the costs used to value physical inventory

INVENTORY COMPILATION TESTS—audit procedures used to verify whether physical counts of inventory were correctly summarized, inventory quantities and prices were correctly extended, and extended inventory was correctly footed

COST ACCOUNTING CONTROLS—controls over physical inventory and the related costs from the point at which raw materials are requisitioned to the point at which the manufactured product is completed and transferred to storage

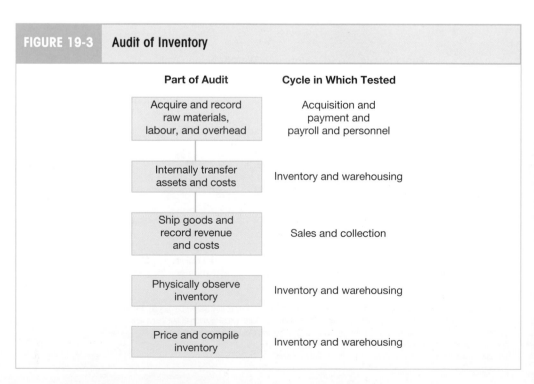

FIGURE 19-3	Audit of Inventory

Part of Audit	Cycle in Which Tested
Acquire and record raw materials, labour, and overhead	Acquisition and payment and payroll and personnel
Internally transfer assets and costs	Inventory and warehousing
Ship goods and record revenue and costs	Sales and collection
Physically observe inventory	Inventory and warehousing
Price and compile inventory	Inventory and warehousing

Almost all companies need physical controls over their assets to prevent loss from misuse and theft. The use of physically segregated, limited access storage areas for raw materials, work in process, and finished goods is one major control to protect assets. In some instances, the assignment of custody of inventory to specific responsible individuals may be necessary to protect the assets. Approved prenumbered documents for authorizing movement of inventory also protect the assets from improper use. Copies of these documents should be sent directly to accounting by the persons issuing them, bypassing people with custodial responsibilities. An example of an effective document of this type is an approved materials requisition for obtaining raw materials from the storeroom.

Perpetual inventory data files maintained by persons who do not have custody of or access to assets are another useful cost accounting control. Perpetual inventory data files are important for a number of reasons: they provide a record of items on hand, which is used to initiate production or purchase of additional materials or goods; they provide a record of the use of raw materials and the sale of finished goods, which can be reviewed for obsolete or slow-moving items; and they provide a record that can be used to pinpoint responsibility for custody as part of the investigation of differences between physical counts and the amounts shown on the records.

Another important consideration in cost accounting is the existence of adequate internal controls that integrate production and accounting records for the purpose of obtaining accurate costs for all products. The existence of adequate cost records aids management in pricing, controlling costs, and costing inventory.

Tests of Cost Accounting The concepts in auditing cost accounting are no different from those discussed for any other transaction cycle. Figure 19-4 shows the methodology that the auditor should follow in determining which tests to perform. In auditing cost accounting, the auditor is concerned with four aspects: physical controls over inventory,

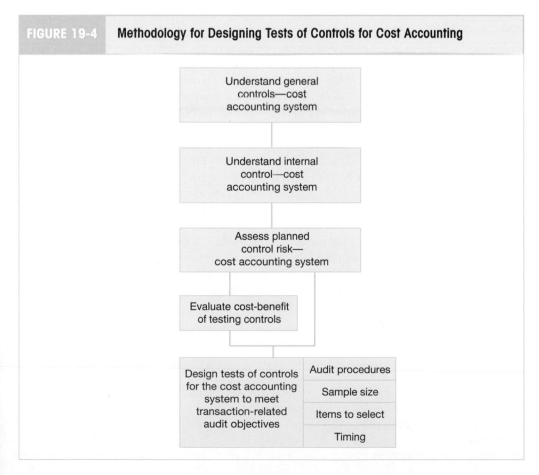

FIGURE 19-4   Methodology for Designing Tests of Controls for Cost Accounting

documents and records for transferring inventory, perpetual inventory master files and transaction files, and unit cost records.

PHYSICAL CONTROLS The auditor's tests of the adequacy of the physical controls over raw materials, work in process, and finished goods must be restricted to observation and enquiry. For example, the auditor can examine the raw materials storage area to determine whether the inventory is protected from theft and misuse by the existence of a locked storeroom. The existence of an adequate storeroom with a competent custodian in charge also ordinarily results in the orderly storage of inventory. If the auditor concludes that the physical controls are so inadequate that the inventory will be difficult to count, the auditor should expand his or her observation of physical inventory tests to ensure that an adequate count is carried out.

DOCUMENTS AND RECORDS FOR TRANSFERRING INVENTORY The auditor's primary concerns in verifying the transfer of inventory from one location to another are that the recorded transfers are valid (the inventory exists), the transfers that have actually taken place are recorded, and the quantity, description, and date of all recorded transfers are accurate. First, it is necessary to understand the client's internal controls for recording transfers before relevant tests can be performed. Once the internal controls are understood, the tests can easily be performed by examining documents and records. For example, a procedure to test the existence and accuracy of the transfer of goods from the raw materials storeroom to the manufacturing assembly line is accounting for a sequence of raw material requisitions, examining the requisitions for proper approval, and comparing the quantity, description, and date with the information on the raw material perpetual inventory transaction files. Similarly, completed production records can be compared with perpetual inventory files to be sure all manufactured goods were physically delivered to the finished goods storeroom.

Technology has improved the ability to track the movement of goods throughout production. For example, products are labelled with standardized bar codes that can be scanned by laser to track the movement of inventory items.

PERPETUAL INVENTORY MASTER AND TRANSACTION FILES The existence of adequate perpetual inventory master files has a major effect on the *timing and extent* of the auditor's physical examination of inventory. For one thing, when there are accurate perpetual inventory master files, it is frequently possible to test the physical inventory prior to the balance sheet date. An interim physical inventory can result in significant cost savings for both the client and the auditor, and enables the client to receive the audited statements earlier. Perpetual inventory master files also enable the auditor to reduce the extent of the tests of physical inventory when the assessed level of control risk related to physical observation of inventory is low.

Tests of the perpetual inventory master files and supporting detail transaction files for the purpose of reducing the tests of physical inventory or changing their timing are done through the use of documentation. Documents to verify the purchase of raw materials can be examined when the auditor is verifying acquisitions as part of the tests of the acquisition and payment cycle. Documents supporting the reduction of raw materials inventory for use in production and the increase in the quantity of finished goods inventory when goods have been manufactured are examined as part of the tests of the cost accounting documents and records in the manner discussed in the preceding section. Support for the reduction in the finished goods inventory through the sale of goods to customers is ordinarily tested as part of the sales and collection cycle. Usually, it is relatively easy to test the accuracy of the perpetuals after the auditor determines how internal controls are designed and decides to what degree assessed control risk should be reduced.

UNIT COST RECORDS Obtaining accurate cost data for raw materials, direct labour, and manufacturing overhead is an essential part of cost accounting. Adequate cost accounting records must be integrated with production and other accounting records in order to produce accurate costs of all products. Cost accounting records are pertinent to the auditor in that the valuation of ending inventory depends on the proper design and use of these records.

In testing the inventory cost records, the auditor must first develop an understanding of general controls applicable to this cycle and of internal control. This is frequently somewhat time-consuming because the flow of costs is usually integrated with other accounting records, and it may not be obvious how internal control provides for the internal transfers of raw materials and for direct labour and manufacturing overhead as production is carried out.

Once the auditor understands internal control, the approach to internal verification involves the same concepts that were discussed in the verification of sales and acquisition transactions. Whenever possible, it is desirable to test the cost accounting records as part of the acquisition, payroll, and sales tests to avoid testing the records more than once. For example, when the auditor is testing acquisition transactions as part of the acquisition and payment cycle, it is desirable to trace the units and unit costs of raw materials to the perpetual inventory data files and the total cost to the cost accounting records. Similarly, when payroll cost data are maintained for different jobs, it is desirable to trace data from the payroll summary directly to the job cost record as a part of testing the payroll and personnel cycle.

A major difficulty in the verification of inventory cost records is determining the reasonableness of cost allocations. For example, the assignment of manufacturing overhead costs to individual products entails certain assumptions that can significantly affect the unit costs of inventory and therefore the fairness of the inventory valuation. In evaluating these allocations, the auditor must consider the reasonableness of both the numerator and the denominator that result in the unit costs. For example, in testing overhead applied to inventory on the basis of direct labour dollars, the overhead rate should approximate total actual direct labour dollars. Since total manufacturing overhead is tested as part of the tests of the acquisition and payment cycle and direct labour is tested as part of the payroll and personnel cycle, determining the reasonableness of the rate is not difficult. However, if manufacturing overhead is applied on the basis of machine hours, the auditor must verify the reasonableness of the machine hours by separate tests of the client's machine records. The major consideration in evaluating the reasonableness of all cost allocations, including manufacturing overhead, is consistency with previous years.

→19.3   CONDUCTING THE AUDIT TESTS
Analytical Procedures

Analytical procedures are as important in auditing inventory and warehousing as in any other cycle. Table 19-1 includes several common analytical procedures and possible misstatements that may be indicated when fluctuations exist. Several of those analytical procedures have also been included in other cycles. An example is the gross margin percent.

Tests of Details for Inventory

The methodology for deciding which tests of details of balances to do for inventory and warehousing is essentially the same as that discussed for accounts receivable, accounts

TABLE 19-1	Analytical Procedures for the Inventory and Warehousing Cycle
Analytical Procedure	**Possible Misstatement**
Compare gross margin percentage with previous years.	Overstatement or understatement of inventory and cost of goods sold.
Compare inventory turnover (costs of goods sold divided by average inventory) with previous years.	Obsolete inventory, which affects inventory and cost of goods sold.
Compare unit costs of inventory with previous years.	Overstatement or understatement of inventory. Overstatement or understatement of unit costs.
Compare extended inventory value with previous years.	Misstatements in compilation, unit costs, or extensions that affect inventory and cost of goods sold.
Compare current-year manufacturing costs with previous years (variable costs should be adjusted for changes in volume).	Misstatement of unit costs of inventory, especially direct labour and manufacturing overhead, which affect inventory and cost of goods sold.

payable, and all other balance sheet accounts. It is shown in Figure 19-5. Notice that test results of several other cycles besides inventory and warehousing affect tests of details of balances for inventory.

Because of the complexity of auditing inventory, two aspects of tests of details of balances are discussed separately: (1) physical observation and (2) pricing and compilation. These topics are studied in the next two sections.

Physical Observation of Inventory

Prior to the late 1930s, auditors generally avoided responsibility for determining either the physical existence of or the accuracy of the count of inventory. Audit evidence for inventory quantities was usually restricted to obtaining a certificate from management as to the correctness of the stated amount. In 1938, the discovery of major fraud in the McKesson & Robbins Company in the United States caused a re-appraisal by the accounting profession of its responsibilities relating to inventory. In brief, the financial statements for McKesson & Robbins at December 31, 1937, which were "certified" by a major accounting firm, reported total consolidated assets of $87 million. Of this amount, approximately $19 million was subsequently determined to be fictitious ($10 million in inventory and $9 million in receivables). Due primarily to its adherence to generally accepted auditing practices of that period, the auditing firm was not held directly at fault in the inventory area. However, it was noted that if certain procedures, such as observation of the physical inventory, had been carried out, the fraud would probably have been detected.

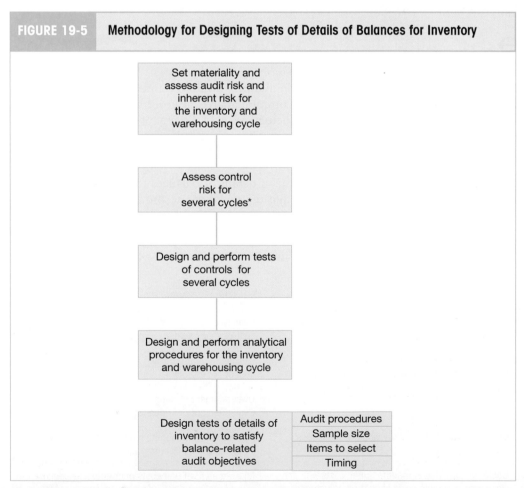

| FIGURE 19-5 | Methodology for Designing Tests of Details of Balances for Inventory |

Set materiality and assess audit risk and inherent risk for the inventory and warehousing cycle

Assess control risk for several cycles*

Design and perform tests of controls for several cycles

Design and perform analytical procedures for the inventory and warehousing cycle

Design tests of details of inventory to satisfy balance-related audit objectives

Audit procedures
Sample size
Items to select
Timing

*Cycles affecting tests of balances for inventory include inventory and warehousing cycle (cost accounting system), sales and collection cycle (sales only), acquisition and payment cycle (acquisitions only), and payroll and personnel cycle.

Paragraph 6030.05 of the *CICA Assurance Handbook* states:

Observation of the client's physical stocktaking, whether this is at the end of the financial period or at some other date, is considered a most useful auditing procedure in assessing the degree of care which management exercises in establishing the existence and condition of inventories.

This notion of physical attendance is reinforced by paragraph 6030.09:

Generally accepted auditing procedures in respect of inventories should include:... attendance by the auditors at the stocktaking, whether this is at the end of the financial period or at other times...

"If attendance at the stocktaking is not practicable in the circumstances," paragraph 6030.10 permits the auditor to apply "other satisfactory procedures." The phrase "not practicable" is taken to mean not feasible in the circumstances and not merely inconvenient or difficult. For example, an auditor who was appointed after a company's year end would find it not practicable to count inventory; driving 100 km to attend an inventory count at a remote location may be neither practical nor convenient. If precluded, for any reason, from attending the physical stocktaking, the auditor must exercise judgment in deciding whether or not attendance was "practicable."

An essential point in the Section 6030 requirements is the distinction between the observation of the physical count and the responsibility for taking the count. The client has responsibility for setting up the procedures for taking an accurate physical inventory and actually making and recording the counts. The auditor's responsibility is to evaluate and observe the client's physical procedures and draw conclusions about the adequacy of those procedures and about the quantity and condition of the physical inventory.

Paragraph 6030.07 does permit the auditor to count the inventory at a time other than the client's stocktaking "if there is a good internal control over inventories."

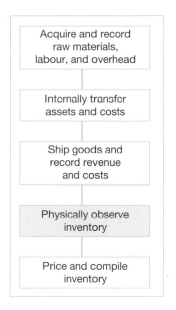

Acquire and record raw materials, labour, and overhead

Internally transfer assets and costs

Ship goods and record revenue and costs

Physically observe inventory

Price and compile inventory

Controls Regardless of the client's inventory record-keeping method, there must be a periodic physical count of the inventory items on hand. The client can take the physical count at or near the balance sheet date, at a preliminary date, or on a cycle basis throughout the year. The last two approaches are appropriate only if there are adequate perpetual inventory master files and transaction files.

In connection with the client's physical count of inventory, adequate controls include proper instructions for the physical count, supervision by responsible personnel, independent internal verification of the counts, independent reconciliations of the physical counts with perpetual inventory master files, and adequate control over count tags, sheets, or computerized records.

An important aspect of the auditor's understanding of the client's physical inventory controls is complete familiarity with them before the inventory-taking begins. This is necessary to evaluate the effectiveness of the client's procedures, but it also enables the auditor to make constructive suggestions beforehand. If the inventory instructions do not provide adequate controls, the auditor must spend more time ensuring that the physical count is accurate.

Audit Decisions The auditor's decisions in the physical observation of inventory are of the same general nature as in any other audit area: selection of audit procedures, timing, determination of sample size, and selection of the items for testing. The selection of the audit procedures is discussed throughout the section; the other three decisions are discussed briefly at this time.

TIMING The auditor decides whether the physical count can be taken prior to year end primarily on the basis of the accuracy of the perpetual inventory files. When an interim physical count is permitted, the auditor observes it at that time and also tests the perpetuals for transactions from the date of the count to year end. When the perpetuals are accurate, it may be unnecessary for the client to count the inventory every year. Instead, the auditor can compare the perpetuals with the actual inventory on a sample basis at a convenient time. When there are no perpetuals and the inventory is material, a complete physical inventory must be taken by the client near the end of the accounting period and tested by the auditor at the same time.

SAMPLE SIZE Sample size in physical observation is usually difficult to specify in terms of the number of items because the emphasis during the tests is on observing the client's procedures rather than on selecting particular items for testing. A convenient way to think of sample size in physical observation is in terms of the total number of hours spent rather than the number of inventory items counted. The most important determinants of the amount of time needed to test the inventory are the adequacy of the internal controls over the physical counts, the accuracy of the perpetual inventory files, the total dollar amount and the type of inventory, the number of different significant inventory locations, and the nature and extent of misstatements discovered in previous years and other inherent risks. In some situations, inventory is such a significant item that dozens of auditors are necessary to observe the physical count, whereas in other situations, one person can complete the observation in a short time. Special care is warranted in the observation of inventory because of the difficulty of expanding sample size or reperforming tests after the physical inventory has been taken.

SELECTION OF ITEMS The selection of the particular items for testing is an important part of the audit decision in inventory observation. Care should be taken to observe the counting of the most significant items and a representative sample of typical inventory items, to enquire about items that are likely to be obsolete or damaged, and to discuss with management the reasons for excluding any material items.

Physical Observation Tests The same balance-related audit objectives that have been used in previous sections for tests of details of balances provide the frame of reference for discussing the physical observation tests. However, before the specific objectives are discussed, some comments that apply to all the objectives are appropriate.

The most important part of the observation of inventory is determining whether the physical count is being taken in accordance with the client's instructions. To do this effectively, *it is essential that the auditor be present* while the physical count is taking place. When the client's employees are not following the inventory instructions, the auditor must either contact the supervisor to correct the problem or modify the physical observation procedures. For example, if the procedures require one team to count the inventory and a second team to recount it as a test of accuracy, the auditor should inform management if he or she observes both teams counting together.

Obtaining an adequate understanding of the client's business is even more important in physical observation of inventory than for most aspects of the audit because inventory varies so significantly for different companies. A proper understanding of the client's business and its industry enables the auditor to ask about and discuss such problems as inventory valuation, potential obsolescence, and existence of consignment inventory intermingled with owned inventory. A useful starting point for the auditor to become familiar with the client's inventory is a tour of the client's facilities, including receiving, storage, production, planning, and record-keeping areas. The tour should be led by a supervisor who can answer questions about production, especially about any changes in the past year.

Common tests of details audit procedures for physical inventory observation are shown in Table 19-2. Detail tie-in and presentation and disclosure are the only balance-related audit objectives not included in the table. These objectives are discussed under compilation of inventory. The assumption throughout is that the client records inventory on prenumbered tags on the balance sheet date. In reality, smaller businesses may use inventory sheets rather than inventory tags. Larger businesses with heavily automated systems will not use tags at all. Rather, individuals will use hand-held scanners to scan each inventory location and item code, then manually enter the amount counted.

In addition to the detailed procedures included in Table 19-2, the auditor should walk through all areas where inventory is warehoused to make sure that all inventory has been counted and properly tagged. When inventory is in boxes or other containers, these should be opened during test counts. It is desirable to compare high dollar value inventory to counts in the previous year and inventory master files as a test of reasonableness. These two procedures should not be done until the client has completed its physical counts.

TABLE 19-2	Balance-Related Audit Objectives and Tests of Details of Balances for Physical Inventory Observation	
Balance-Related Audit Objective	**Common Inventory Observation Procedures**	**Comments**
Inventory as recorded on tags exists (existence).	Select a random sample of tag numbers and identify the tag with that number attached to the actual inventory. Observe whether movement of inventory takes place during the count.	The purpose is to uncover the inclusion of nonexistent items as inventory.
Existing inventory is counted and tagged and tags are accounted for to make sure none are missing (completeness).	Examine inventory to make sure it is tagged. Observe whether movement of inventory takes place during the count. Enquire as to inventory in other locations. Account for all used and unused tags to make sure none are lost or intentionally omitted. Record the tag numbers for those used and unused for subsequent follow-up.	Special concern should be directed to omission of large sections of inventory. This test should be done at the completion of the physical count. This test should be done at the completion of the physical count.
Inventory is counted accurately (accuracy).	Recount client's counts to make sure the recorded counts are accurate on the tags (also check descriptions and unit of count, such as dozen or gross). Compare physical counts with perpetual inventory master file. Record client's counts for subsequent testing.	Recording client counts in the working papers on *inventory count sheets* is done for two reasons: to obtain documentation that an adequate physical examination was made, and to test for the possibility that the client might change the recorded counts after the auditor leaves the premises.
Inventory is classified correctly on the tags (classification).	Examine inventory descriptions on the tags and compare with the actual inventory for raw material, work in process, and finished goods. Evaluate whether the percent of completion recorded on the tags for work in process is reasonable.	These tests would be done as a part of the first procedure in the valuation objective.
Information is obtained to make sure sales and inventory purchases are recorded in the proper period (cutoff).	Record in the working papers for subsequent follow-up the last shipping document number used at year end. Make sure the inventory for that item was excluded from the physical count. Review shipping area for inventory set aside for shipment but not counted. Record in the working papers for subsequent follow-up the last receiving report number used at year end. Make sure the inventory for that item was included in the physical count. Review receiving area for inventory that should be included in the physical count.	Obtaining proper cutoff information for sales and purchases is an essential part of inventory observation. The appropriate tests during the fieldwork were discussed for sales in Chapter 13 and for purchases in Chapter 17.
Obsolete and unusable inventory are excluded or noted (valuation).	Test for obsolete inventory by enquiry of factory employees and management, and be alert for items that are damaged, rust- or dust-covered, or located in inappropriate places.	
The client has right to inventory recorded on tags (rights and obligations).	Enquire as to consignment or customer inventory included on client's premises. Be alert for inventory that is set aside or specially marked as indications of non-ownership.	

Acquire and record
raw materials,
labour, and overhead

Internally transfer
assets and costs

Ship goods and
record revenue
and costs

Physically observe
inventory

Price and compile
inventory

STANDARD COST RECORDS—
records that indicate variances
between projected material, labour,
and overhead costs, and the actual
costs

Audit of Pricing and Compilation

An important part of the audit of inventory is performing all the procedures necessary to make certain the physical counts were properly priced and compiled. *Pricing* includes all the tests of the client's unit prices to determine whether they are correct. *Compilation* includes all the tests of the summarization of the physical counts, the extension of price times quantity, footing the inventory summary, and tracing the totals to the general ledger.

Pricing and Compilation Controls The existence of adequate internal control for unit costs that is integrated with production and other accounting records is important to ensure that reasonable costs are used for valuing ending inventory. One important internal control is the use of **standard cost records** that indicate variances in material, labour, and overhead costs and can be used to evaluate production. When standard costs are used, procedures must be designed to keep the standards updated for changes in production processes and costs. The review of unit costs for reasonableness by someone independent of the department responsible for developing the costs is also a useful control over valuation.

An internal control designed to prevent the overstatement of inventory through the inclusion of obsolete inventory is a formal review and reporting of obsolete, slow-moving, damaged, and overstated inventory items. The review, which should be done by a competent employee, includes reviewing perpetual inventory master files for inventory turnover, possibly using generalized audit software, and holding discussions with engineering or production personnel.

Compilation internal controls are needed to provide a means of ensuring that the physical counts are properly summarized, priced at the same amount as the unit perpetual records, correctly extended and totalled, and included in the general ledger at the proper amount. Important compilation internal controls are adequate documents and records for taking the physical count, adequate controls over program changes, and proper internal verification. If the physical inventory is taken on prenumbered tags and carefully reviewed before the personnel are released from the physical examination of inventory, there should be little risk of misstatement in summarizing the tags. The most important internal control over accurate determination of prices, extensions, and footings is adequate controls over the programs that perform these calculations, with internal verification or review of output reports by a competent, independent person.

Pricing and Compilation Procedures Balance-related audit objectives for tests of details of balances are also useful in discussing pricing and compilation procedures. The objectives and related tests are shown in Table 19-3, except for the cutoff objective. Physical observation, which was previously discussed, is a major source of cutoff information for sales and purchases. The tests of the accounting records for cutoff are done as part of sales (sales and collection cycle) and purchases (acquisition and payment cycle).

The frame of reference for applying the objectives is a listing of inventory obtained from the client that includes each inventory item's description, quantity, unit price, and extended value. The inventory listing is in inventory item description order with raw material, work in process, and finished goods separated. The total equals the general ledger balance.

The proper valuation (pricing) of inventory is often one of the most important and time-consuming parts of the audit. In performing pricing tests, three things about the client's method of pricing are extremely important: the method must be in accordance with generally accepted accounting principles, the application of the method must be consistent from year to year, and cost versus market value (replacement cost or net realizable value) must be considered. Because the method of verifying the pricing of inventory depends on whether items are purchased or manufactured, these two categories are discussed separately.

PRICING PURCHASED INVENTORY The primary types of inventory included in this category are raw materials, purchased parts, and supplies. As a first step in verifying the valuation of purchased inventory, it is necessary to establish clearly whether FIFO, LIFO, weighted average, or some other valuation method is being used. It is also necessary to determine which costs should be included in the valuation of a particular item of inventory. For example, the auditor must find out whether freight, storage, discounts, and other costs are included and

TABLE 19-3	Balance-Related Audit Objectives and Tests of Details of Balances for Inventory Pricing and Compilation	
Balance-Related Audit Objective	Common Tests of Details of Balances Procedures	Comments
Inventory in the inventory listing schedule agrees with the physical inventory counts, the extensions are correct, and the total is correctly added and agrees with the general ledger (detail tie-in).	Perform compilation tests (see existence, completeness, and accuracy objectives). Extend the quantity times the price on selected items. Foot the inventory listing schedules for raw materials, work in process, and finished goods. Trace the totals to the general ledger.	Unless controls are weak, extending and footing tests should be limited. For large inventories, these tests should be conducted using generalized audit software.
Inventory items in the inventory listing schedule exist (existence).	Trace inventory listed in the schedule to inventory tags and auditor's recorded counts for existence and description.	The next six objectives are affected by the results of the physical inventory observation. The tag numbers and counts verified as a part of physical inventory observation are traced to the inventory listing schedule as a part of these tests.
Existing inventory items are included in the inventory listing schedule (completeness).	Account for unused tag numbers shown in the auditor's working papers to make sure no tags have been added. Trace from inventory tags to the inventory listing schedules, and make sure inventory on tags is included. Account for tag numbers to make sure none have been deleted.	
Inventory items in the inventory listing schedule are accurate (accuracy).	Trace inventory listed in the schedule to inventory tags and auditor's recorded counts for quantity and description. Perform price tests of inventory. For a discussion of price tests, see text material on pages 560–563.	
Inventory items in the inventory listing schedule are properly classified (classification).	Compare the classification into raw materials, work in process, and finished goods by comparing the descriptions on inventory tags and auditor's recorded test counts with the inventory listing schedule.	
Inventory items in the inventory listing are stated at realizable value (valuation).	Perform test of lower of cost or market, selling price, and obsolescence.	
The client has rights to inventory items in the inventory listing schedule (rights and obligations).	Trace inventory tags identified as non-owned during the physical observation to the inventory listing schedule to make sure these have not been included. Review contracts with suppliers and customers and enquire of management for the possibility of the inclusion of consigned or other non-owned inventory, or the exclusion of owned inventory.	
Inventory and related accounts in the inventory and warehousing cycle are properly disclosed (presentation and disclosure).	Examine financial statements for proper presentation and disclosure, including: • Separate disclosure of raw materials, work in process, and finished goods. • Proper description of the inventory costing method. • Description of pledged inventory. • Inclusion of significant sales and purchase commitments.	Pledging of inventory and sales and purchase commitments are usually uncovered as a part of other audit tests.

compare the findings with the preceding year's audit working papers to ensure that the methods are consistent.

In selecting specific inventory items for pricing, emphasis should be put on the larger dollar amounts and on products that are known to have wide fluctuations in price, but a representative sample of all types of inventory and departments should be included as well. Stratified variable or monetary unit sampling is commonly used in these tests.

The auditor should list the inventory items he or she intends to verify for pricing and request that the client locate the appropriate vendors' invoices. It is important that a sufficient number of invoices be examined to account for the entire quantity of inventory for the particular item being tested, especially for the FIFO valuation method. Examining a sufficient number of invoices is useful in uncovering situations in which clients value their inventory on the basis of the most recent invoice only and, in some cases, in discovering obsolete inventory. As an illustration, assume that the client's valuation of a particular inventory item is $12.00 per unit for 1,000 units, using FIFO. The auditor should examine the most recent invoices for acquisitions of that inventory item made in the year under audit until the valuation of all of the 1,000 units is accounted for. If the most recent acquisition of the inventory item were for 700 units at $12.00 per unit and the immediately preceding acquisition were for 600 units at $11.30 per unit, then the inventory item in question was overstated by $210.00 (300 × $0.70).

When the client has perpetual inventory master files that include unit costs of acquisitions, it is usually desirable to test the pricing by tracing the unit costs to the perpetuals rather than to vendors' invoices. In most cases, the effect is to reduce the cost of verifying inventory valuation significantly. Naturally, when the perpetuals are used to verify unit costs, it is essential to test the unit costs on the perpetuals to vendors' invoices as a part of the tests of the acquisition and payment cycle.

PRICING MANUFACTURED INVENTORY The auditor must consider the cost of raw materials, direct labour, and manufacturing overhead in pricing work in process and finished goods. The need to verify each of these has the effect of making the audit of work-in-process and finished goods inventory more complex than the audit of purchased inventory. Nevertheless, such considerations as selecting the items to be tested, testing for whether cost or market value is lower, and evaluating the possibility of obsolescence also apply.

In pricing raw materials in manufactured products, it is necessary to consider both the unit cost of the raw materials and the number of units required to manufacture a unit of output. The unit cost can be verified in the same manner as that used for other purchased inventory—by examining vendors' invoices or perpetual inventory master files. Then it is necessary to examine engineering specifications, inspect the finished product, or find a similar method to determine the number of units it takes to manufacture a particular product.

Similarly, the hourly costs of direct labour and the number of hours it takes to manufacture a unit of output must be verified while testing direct labour. Hourly labour costs can be verified by comparison with labour payroll or union contracts. The number of hours needed to manufacture the product can be determined from engineering specifications or similar sources.

The proper manufacturing overhead in work in process and finished goods is dependent on the approach being used by the client. It is necessary to evaluate the method being used for consistency and reasonableness and to recompute the costs to determine whether the overhead is correct. For example, if the rate is based on direct labour dollars, the auditor can divide the total manufacturing overhead by the total direct labour dollars to determine the actual overhead rate. This rate can then be compared with the overhead rate used by the client to determine unit costs.

When the client has *standard cost records*, an efficient and useful method of determining valuation is the review and analysis of variances. If the variances in material, labour, and manufacturing overhead are small, this is evidence of reliable cost records.

COST OR MARKET In pricing inventory, it is necessary to consider whether replacement cost or net realizable value is lower than historical cost. For purchased finished goods and raw materials, the most recent cost of an inventory item as indicated on a vendor's invoice of the subsequent period is a useful way to test for replacement cost. All manufacturing costs must be considered for work in process and finished goods for manufactured inventory. It is also necessary to consider the sales value of inventory items and the possible effect of rapid fluctuation of prices to determine net realizable value. Finally, it is necessary to consider the possibility of obsolescence in the evaluation process.

→19.4 INTEGRATION OF THE TESTS

The most difficult part of understanding the audit of the inventory and warehousing cycle is grasping the interrelationship of the many different tests the auditor makes to evaluate whether inventory and cost of goods sold are fairly stated. Figure 19-6 and the discussion that follows are designed to aid the reader in perceiving the audit of the inventory and warehousing cycle as a series of integrated tests.

Tests of the Acquisition and Payment Cycle Whenever the auditor verifies acquisitions as part of the tests of the acquisition and payment cycle, evidence is being obtained about the accuracy of raw materials purchased and all manufacturing overhead costs except labour. These acquisition costs either flow directly into cost of goods sold or become the most significant part of the ending inventory of raw material, work in process, and finished goods. In audits involving perpetual inventory master files, it is common to test these as a part of tests of controls procedures in the acquisition and payment cycle. Similarly, if manufacturing costs are assigned to individual jobs or processes, they are usually tested as part of the same cycle.

FIGURE 19-6	Interrelationship of Various Audit Tests

Tests of the Payroll and Personnel Cycle When the auditor verifies labour costs, the same comments apply as for acquisitions. In most cases, the cost accounting records for direct and indirect labour costs can be tested as part of the audit of the payroll and personnel cycle if there is adequate advance planning.

Tests of the Sales and Collection Cycle Although the relationship is less close between the sales and collection cycle and the inventory and warehousing cycle than between the two cycles previously discussed, it is still important. Most of the audit testing in the storage of finished goods as well as the shipment and recording of sales takes place when the sales and collection cycle is tested. In addition, if standard cost records are used, it may be possible to test the standard cost of goods sold at the same time that sales tests are performed.

Tests of Cost Accounting Tests of cost accounting are meant to verify the controls affecting inventory that were not verified as part of the three previously discussed cycles. Tests are made of the physical controls, transfers of raw material costs to work in process, transfers of costs of completed goods to finished goods, perpetual inventory master files, and unit cost records.

Physical Inventory, Compilation, and Pricing In most audits, the underlying assumption in testing the inventory and warehousing cycle is that cost of goods sold is a residual of beginning inventory plus acquisitions of raw materials, direct labour, and other manufacturing costs minus ending inventory. When the audit of inventory and cost of goods sold is approached with this idea in mind, the importance of ending inventory becomes obvious. Physical inventory, compilation, and pricing are each equally important in the audit because a misstatement in any one results in misstated inventory and cost of goods sold.

In testing the physical inventory, it is possible to rely heavily on the perpetual inventory master files if they have been tested as part of one or more of the previously discussed tests. In fact, if the perpetual inventory master files are considered reliable, the auditor can observe and test the physical count at some time during the year and rely on the perpetuals to keep adequate records of the quantities.

When testing the unit costs, it is also possible to rely, to some degree, on the tests of the cost records made during the tests of transaction cycles. The existence of standard cost records is also useful for the purpose of comparison with the actual unit costs. If the standard costs are used to represent historical cost, they must be tested for reliability.

SUMMARY

1. *What are the components of the inventory and warehousing cycle?* The inventory and warehousing cycle normally has the following functions: processing of purchase orders, receiving of material, storage of raw materials, processing of products, storage of work in process and finished goods, shipment of finished goods, and update of inventory records.

2. *What are the five different parts of the inventory and warehousing cycle that are audited?* For the purposes of auditing the cycle, it is divided into the following parts: (i) acquisition and recording of raw materials, labour, and overhead; (ii) transferring assets and costs among inventory types (to work in process and to finished goods); (iii) shipment of goods and recording of associated revenue and costs; (iv) physically observing the inventory count process; and (v) conducting pricing and compilation tests of inventory.

   Provide an overview of the process used to audit the inventory and warehousing cycle. In the context of the overall risk of the engagement and the cycle, the auditor docu-

ments general and application level controls, assesses control risks, and tests those controls, by assertion, where there is intended reliance. After assessing the results of the tests of controls, analytical procedures and tests of detail are conducted.

3. *What role does each of the following types of tests play in the audit of inventory?* (i) *analytical review*—to assess the likelihood of potential misstatements and to target tests of detail; (ii) *physical observation of inventory*—this is a set of procedures that provides assurance for the following assertions: existence, completeness, accuracy, classification, cutoff, valuation, and rights and obligations; see Table 19-2; (iii) *pricing and compilation tests*—using Table 19-3, we can see that these tests provide assurance with respect to detail tie-in, existence, completeness, accuracy, classification, valuation, rights and obligations, and presentation and disclosure.

4. *Describe how the relationship between the tests of different cycles affects the audit of inventory.* Tests of the acquisition and payment cycle provide evidence about the accuracy of

raw materials purchases and all manufacturing overhead costs except labour. Tests of the payroll and personnel cycle provide assurance with respect to the labour cost components of inventory. Tests of both of these cycles, as well as of the sales and collection cycle, provide assurance with respect to the cutoff assertion for all of these cycles, as well as the inventory and warehousing cycle.

CICA ASSURANCE HANDBOOK SECTION REFERENCED IN THIS CHAPTER

Section 6030 – Inventories.

ESSENTIAL TERMS

Cost accounting controls—controls over physical inventory and the related costs from the point at which raw materials are requisitioned to the point at which the manufactured product is completed and transferred to storage   (p. 552).

Cost accounting records—the accounting records concerned with the manufacture and processing of the goods and storing finished goods   (p. 551).

Inventory and warehousing cycle—the transaction cycle that involves the physical flow of goods through the organization, as well as related costs   (p. 548).

Inventory compilation tests—audit procedures used to verify whether physical counts of inventory were correctly summarized, inventory quantities and prices were correctly extended, and extended inventory was correctly footed   (p. 552).

Inventory price tests—audit procedures used to verify the costs used to value physical inventory   (p. 552).

Job cost system—the system of cost accounting in which costs are accumulated by individual jobs when material is used and labour costs are incurred   (p. 550).

Perpetual inventory data files—continuously updated computerized records of inventory items purchased, used, sold, and on hand for merchandise, raw materials, and finished goods. The master file normally contains the balance of quantity on hand, as well as prices and description of items. The transaction files contain activity details, such as shipments (items sold) and receipts (goods purchased)   (p. 550).

Process cost system—the system of cost accounting in which costs are accumulated for a process, with unit costs for each process assigned to the products passing through the process (p. 550).

Standard cost records—records that indicate variances between projected material, labour, and overhead costs, and the actual costs   (p. 560).

REVIEW QUESTIONS

19-1   Give the reasons why inventory is often the most difficult and time-consuming part of many audit engagements.

19-2   Explain the relationship between the acquisition and payment cycle and the inventory and warehousing cycle in the audit of a manufacturing company. List several audit procedures in the acquisition and payment cycle that support your explanation.

19-3   What is meant by "cost accounting records," and what is their importance in the conduct of an audit?

19-4   Many auditors assert that certain audit tests can be significantly reduced for clients with adequate perpetual records that include both unit and cost data. What are the most important tests of the perpetual records that the auditor must make before he or she can reduce the assessed level of control risk? Assuming the perpetuals are determined to be accurate, which tests can be reduced?

19-5   Before the physical examination, the auditor obtains a copy of the client's inventory instructions and reviews them with the controller. In obtaining an understanding of inventory procedures for a small manufacturing company, these deficiencies are identified: shipping operations will not be completely halted during the physical examination, and there will be no independent verification of the original inventory count by a second counting team. Evaluate the importance of each of these deficiencies, and state its effect on the auditor's observation of inventory.

19-6   At the completion of an inventory observation, the controller requested a copy of all recorded test counts from the auditor to facilitate the correction of all discrepancies between the client's and the auditor's counts. Should the auditor comply with the request? Why or why not?

19-7   What major audit procedures are involved in testing for the ownership of inventory during the observation of the physical counts and as part of subsequent valuation tests?

19-8   In the verification of the amount of the inventory, the auditor should identify slow-moving and obsolete items. List the auditing procedures that could be employed to determine whether slow-moving or obsolete items have been included in inventory.

19-9   During the taking of physical inventory, the controller intentionally withheld several inventory tags from the employees responsible for the physical count. After the auditor left the client's premises at the completion of the inventory observation, the controller recorded nonexistent inventory on the tags and thereby significantly overstated earnings. How could the auditor have uncovered the misstatement assuming there are no perpetual records?

19-10 Explain why a proper cutoff of purchases and sales is heavily dependent on the physical inventory observation. What information should be obtained during the physical count to make sure cutoff is accurate?

19-11 Define what is meant by "compilation tests." List several examples of audit procedures to verify compilation.

19-12 Included in the December 31, 2004, inventory of Kupitz Supply Ltd. are 2,600 deluxe ring binders in the amount of $5,902. An examination of the most recent purchases of binders showed the following costs: January 26, 2005, 2,300 at $2.42 each; December 6, 2004, 1,900 at $2.28 each; and November 26, 2004, 2,400 at $2.07 each. What is the misstatement in valuation of the December 31, 2004, inventory for deluxe ring binders assuming FIFO inventory valuation? What would your answer be if the January 26, 2005, purchase were for 2,300 binders at $2.12 each?

19-13 Ruswell Manufacturing Ltd. applied manufacturing overhead to inventory at December 31, 2004, on the basis of $3.47 per direct labour hour. Explain how you would evaluate the reasonableness of total direct labour hours and manufacturing overhead in the ending inventory of finished goods.

19-14 Each employee for Gedding Manufacturing Corp., a firm using a job-cost inventory costing method, must reconcile his or her total hours worked to the hours worked on individual jobs using a job time sheet at the time weekly payroll time cards are prepared. The job time sheet is then stapled to the time card. Explain how you could test the direct labour dollars included in inventory as part of the payroll and personnel tests.

19-15 Assuming that the auditor properly documents receiving report numbers as part of the physical inventory observation procedures, explain how he or she should verify the proper cutoff of purchases, including tests for the possibility of raw materials in transit, later in the audit.

MULTIPLE CHOICE QUESTIONS

19-16 Choose the best response for the following questions:

a. In a company whose materials and supplies include a great number of items, a fundamental deficiency in control requirements would be indicated if

  (1) the cycle basis for physical inventory-taking had been used.

  (2) a perpetual inventory master file had not been maintained for items of small value.

  (3) the storekeeping function had been combined with production and record keeping.

  (4) minor supply items had been expensed when acquired.

b. When an auditor tests a client's cost accounting records, the auditor's tests are *primarily* designed to determine that

  (1) the internal controls are in accordance with generally accepted accounting principles and are functioning as planned.

  (2) quantities on hand have been determined based on acceptable cost accounting techniques that reasonably approximate actual quantities on hand.

  (3) physical inventories are in substantial agreement with book inventories.

  (4) costs have been properly assigned to finished goods, work in process, and cost of goods sold.

c. The accuracy of perpetual inventory transaction files may be established, in part, by comparing perpetual inventory records with

  (1) purchase orders.

  (2) purchase requisitions.

  (3) receiving reports.

  (4) vendor payments.

d. An auditor would *most* likely learn of slow-moving inventory through

  (1) enquiry of store personnel.

  (2) enquiry of sales personnel.

  (3) physical observation of inventory.

  (4) review of perpetual inventory data files.

e. An inventory turnover analysis is useful to the auditor because it may detect

  (1) inadequacies in inventory pricing.

  (2) the optimum automatic re-order points.

  (3) the existence of obsolete merchandise.

  (4) methods of avoiding cyclical holding costs.

DISCUSSION QUESTIONS AND PROBLEMS

19-17 Items 1 through 8 are selected questions typically found in questionnaires used by auditors to obtain an understanding of internal controls in the inventory and warehousing cycle. In using the questionnaire for a particular client, a "yes" response to a question indicates a possible internal control, whereas a "no" indicates a potential weakness.

  1. Does the receiving department prepare prenumbered receiving reports and account for the numbers periodically for all inventory received, showing the description and quantity of materials?

  2. Is all inventory stored under the control of a custodian in areas where access is limited?

  3. Are all shipments to customers authorized by prenumbered shipping documents?

4. Is a detailed perpetual inventory master file maintained for raw materials inventory?
5. Are physical inventory counts made by someone other than storekeepers and those responsible for maintaining the perpetual inventory master file?
6. Are standard cost records used for raw materials, direct labour, and manufacturing overhead?
7. Is there a stated policy with specific criteria for writing off obsolete or slow-moving goods?
8. Is the clerical accuracy of the final inventory compilation checked by a person independent of those responsible for preparing it?

a. For each of the preceding questions, state the purpose of the internal control.
b. For each internal control, list a test of controls to test its effectiveness.
c. For each of the preceding questions, identify the nature of the potential financial misstatement(s) if the control is not in effect.
d. For each of the potential misstatements in part (c), list a substantive audit procedure to determine whether a material misstatement exists.

19-18 The following errors or omissions are included in the inventory and related records of Westbox Manufacturing Company Ltd.

1. An inventory item was priced at $12 each instead of at the correct cost of $12 per dozen.
2. During the physical inventory-taking, the last shipments for the day were excluded from inventory and were not included as a sale until the subsequent year.
3. The clerk in charge of the perpetual inventory master file altered the quantity on an inventory tag to cover up the shortage of inventory caused by his theft during the year.
4. After the auditor left the premises, several inventory tags were lost and were not included in the final inventory summary.
5. In recording raw materials purchases, the improper unit price was included in the perpetual inventory transaction file and master file. Therefore, the inventory valuation was misstated because the physical inventory was priced by referring to the perpetual records.
6. During the physical count, several obsolete inventory items were included.
7. Because of a significant increase in volume during the current year and excellent control over manufacturing overhead costs, the manufacturing overhead rate applied to inventory was far greater than actual cost.

a. For each misstatement, state an internal control that should have prevented it from occurring.
b. For each misstatement, state a substantive audit procedure that could be used to uncover it.

19-19 You encountered the following situations during the December 31, 2004, physical inventory of Latner Shoe Distributing Corp.
a. Latner maintains a large portion of the shoe merchandise in 10 warehouses throughout eastern and central Canada. This ensures swift delivery service for its chain of stores. You are assigned alone to the Halifax warehouse to observe the physical inventory process. During the inventory count, several express trucks pulled in for loading. Although infrequent, express shipments must be attended to immediately. As a result, the employees who were counting the inventory stopped to assist in loading the express trucks. What should you do?
b. (1) In one storeroom of 10,000 items, you have test counted about 200 items of high value and a few items of low value. You found no misstatements. You also note that the employees are diligently following the inventory instructions. Do you think you have tested enough items? Explain.
(2) What would you do if you counted 150 items and found a substantial number of counting errors?
c. In observing an inventory of liquid shoe polish, you note that a particular lot is five years old. From inspection of some bottles in an open box, you find that the liquid has solidified in most of the bottles. What action should you take?
d. During your observation of the inventory count in the main warehouse, you found that most of the prenumbered tags that had been incorrectly filled out are being destroyed and thrown away. What is the significance of this procedure and what action should you take?

19-20 In connection with her examination of the financial statements of Knutson Products Co. Ltd., an assembler of home appliances, for the year ended May 31, 2005, Raymonde Mathieu, public accountant, is reviewing with Knutson's controller the plans for a physical inventory at the company warehouse on May 31, 2005.

Finished appliances, unassembled parts, and supplies are stored in the warehouse, which is attached to Knutson's assembly plant. The plant will operate during the count. On May 30, the warehouse will deliver to the plant the estimated quantities of unassembled parts and supplies required for May 31 production, but there may be emergency requisitions on May 31. During the count, the warehouse will continue to receive parts and supplies and to ship finished appliances. However, appliances completed on May 31 will be held in the plant until after the physical inventory.

What procedures should the company establish to ensure that the inventory count includes all items that should be included and that nothing is counted twice?

(AICPA adapted)

19-21 The table below shows sales, cost of sales, and inventory data for Aladdin Products Supply Inc., a wholesale distributor of cleaning supplies. All amounts are in thousands.

	2005	2004	2003	2002
Sales	$23.2	$21.7	$19.6	$17.4
Cost of sales	17.1	16.8	15.2	13.5
Beginning inventory	2.3	2.1	1.9	1.5
Ending inventory	2.9	2.3	2.1	1.9

Required
a. Calculate the following ratios:
   (1) Gross margin as a percentage of sales
   (2) Inventory turnover
b. List several logical causes of the changes in the two ratios.
c. Assume that $500,000 is considered material for audit planning purposes for 2005. Could any of the fluctuations in the computed ratios indicate a possible material misstatement? Demonstrate this by performing a sensitivity analysis.
d. What should the auditor do to determine the actual cause of the changes?

19-22 Often, an important aspect of a PA's audit of financial statements is observation of the taking of physical inventory.

Required
a. What are the general objectives or purposes of the PA's observation of the taking of the physical inventory? (Do not discuss the procedures or techniques involved in making the observation.)
b. For what purposes does the PA make and record test counts of inventory quantities during observation of the taking of the physical inventory? Discuss.
c. A number of companies employ outside service companies that specialize in counting, pricing, extending, and footing inventories. These service companies usually furnish a certificate attesting to the value of the inventory. Assuming that the service company took the inventory on the balance sheet date:
   (1) How much reliance, if any, can the PA place on the inventory certificate of outside specialists? Discuss.
   (2) What effect, if any, would the inventory certificate of outside specialists have upon the type of report the PA would render? Discuss.
   (3) What reference, if any, would the PA make to the certificate of outside specialists in the standard audit report?

19-23 You are testing the summarization and cost of raw materials and purchased part inventories as part of the audit of Rubber Products and Supply Corp. There are 2,000 inventory items with a total recorded value of $648,500.

Your audit tests will compare recorded descriptions and counts with the final inventory listing, compare unit costs with vendors' invoices, and extend unit costs times quantity. A misstatement in any of those is defined as a difference. You plan to use monetary unit sampling.

You make the following decisions about the audit of inventory:

Tolerable misstatement (same for upper as for lower)	$24,000
Average percent of error assumption—overstatements	50%
Average percent of error assumption—understatements	100%
Acceptable risk of incorrect acceptance	5%
Estimated error rate in the population.	5%

Required
a. What are the advantages of using monetary unit sampling in this situation?
b. What is the sample size necessary to achieve your audit objectives using monetary unit sampling?
c. Disregarding your answer to part (b), assume that a sample of 125 items is selected and that the following differences between book and audited values are identified (understatements are in parentheses). The book or recorded amounts are also shown.

Item No.	Difference	Book Amount
1	$19	$700
2	11	136
3	(19)	820
4	40	250
5	90	300
6	38	210
7	(90)	2,150
8	70	300
9	(85)	950
Total	$74	

For each of the other 116 items in the sample, there was no difference between the book and the audited values.

Based on this sample, calculate the adjusted overstatement and understatement error bounds.

d. Is the book value misstated?

PROFESSIONAL JUDGMENT PROBLEM

19-24 Technology Parts, Inc., is a retailer of computer hardware components. The company purchases inventory items in bulk directly from parts manufacturers and sells the parts to computer and other technology equipment manufacturers that use them as components in their products. Technology Parts, Inc., grants suppliers access to its inventory management system through its Internet web site. Suppliers have real-time access to information about the parts inventory, including information about quantities held, storage locations, and forecasted product demand. In addition, customers have online access through the web site to information containing product descriptions, price, delivery estimates, availability status, and quality and reliability ratings. Customers can also access information to assess the compatibility of selected parts with other components used in their production processes.

Required

a. Identify business objectives that Technology Parts' management may be able to achieve by providing this information online to key suppliers and customers.

b. How might the availability of the information to suppliers and customers increase Technology Parts' business risk?

c. What processes should Technology Parts' management implement to minimize business risks?

d. How might the availability of the information increase the risk of material misstatements in the financial statements?

e. How are the components of the audit risk model affected by the Internet access?

CASE

19-25 Rakhi Grande has been assigned to the audit of Produce Distributors Inc. (PDI), a new client with his firm, Beaver & Jones, Chartered Accountants. The company is a wholesale distributor of produce, groceries, dry goods, and other related products to grocery store chains and independent grocers.

Rakhi's assistant, Charlie, who has limited experience with automated systems, has asked him for assistance in preparing a plan for the audit of PDI's year-end inventory. He specifically wants advice on which computer controls and what computer-generated information may be relied on and the audit procedures necessary to justify that reliance.

Charlie has prepared the following notes on the client's system and planned count procedures:

System Notes

1. The financial inventory system is automated and fully integrated with other financial accounting systems (e.g., order entry, general ledger). Automatic updates to the inventory records occur at the same time as the shipping documents are printed. The computer system recalculates average cost of inventory items when receipt of goods is recorded.

2. Stock-out reports are printed daily. Because the incidence of negative quantities has significantly decreased over the last year, the client believes a small book-to-physical adjustment will be required.

3. The warehouse supervisor has a special password, allowing him to access and change inventory information to take into account expired, broken, and damaged goods. An expired, broken, and damaged goods report is printed monthly.

4. Fresh produce is shipped directly from suppliers to grocers based on direct shipping instructions that PDI has transmitted to suppliers over telephone lines. All accounting records are updated by the computer system. A numeric control sequence is automatically assigned by the computer system and is used by accounting to control paper flow.

5. PDI ships to several large grocery chains in response to purchase orders received over telephone lines. These orders are listed on a transfer report, and the shipping documents are then printed.

Count Procedures

1. Prenumbered count tags will be used. Product stock number, description, and location will be preprinted on the tags by the computer in both human-readable and machine-readable form. To record quantities counted, warehouse personnel will use optical scanning devices to read the preprinted information, and then manually enter the quantity counted into the computer system. Any changes to preprinted information such as change in location will also be entered manually.

2. Two discrepancy reports will be generated by the system: one identifying differences between quantities counted and perpetual records, and one listing missing count tags. The information will be followed up, and any changes to inventory records will be authorized by the warehouse supervisor.

Required

What advice should Rakhi give to Charlie?

(CICA adapted)

CHAPTER 20

AUDIT OF THE CAPITAL ACQUISITION AND REPAYMENT CYCLE

Owners' equity may be considered a residual account for corporations—this is where the result of current operations is posted. However, other large transactions, such as dividend payments and the equity portion of financial instruments, also flow through this account. The auditor needs to carefully examine each of these potentially large transactions.

LEARNING OBJECTIVES

After reading this chapter, you should be able to answer the following questions:

1. What are the four key characteristics of the capital acquisition and repayment cycle? What is the methodology for designing tests of balances for notes payable? What is the purpose of conducting analytical procedures for notes payable?

2. What is the difference in equity between public and closely held corporations? Provide examples of common internal controls over owners' equity transactions. What are the main concerns when auditing capital stock?

"OFF-BALANCE SHEET" FINANCING THE CENTRE OF ATTENTION AT ENRON

In late 2001, Enron Corp. filed for bankruptcy in the U.S. More than U.S. $60 billion in shareholder value was wiped out. *The Toronto Star* called Enron's financial statements an "elaborate fiction." The main cause of restatement was losses not previously disclosed due to lack of consolidation. This problem also "hid" many partnerships containing off-balance sheet financing.

The public was first made aware of these losses when Enron reported a quarterly loss of U.S. $618 million on October 16, 2001. The following month, the company restated financial results back to 1997, removing another U.S. $600 million in profit.

The Globe and Mail indicated that "Enron kept hundreds of millions of dollars in debt off the balance sheet for several years." Unfortunately, many Enron employees had their pensions loaded with Enron stock, now worthless.

Due to the massive scale of this corporate failure, as of January 18, 2002, there were 12 U.S. government committees and agencies conducting investigations. These included the Senate Banking Committee, the Senate Finance Committee, and the Department of Justice.

The recommendations of these committees led to the July 2002 *Sarbanes-Oxley Act* and the formation of the PCAOB (Public Company Accounting Oversight Board) to provide oversight and quality control over CPAs performing public company audits in the United States. As discussed in the first three chapters of this text, numerous changes occurred in Canada as well.

Sources: 1. Yost, Pete, "Enron Auditor Says Andersen Shares Blame," The Globe and Mail (January 22, 2002), p. B12. 2. Wells, Jennifer, "From Gas Company to Wheeler-Dealer to Bust," The Toronto Star (January 19, 2002), pp. C1, C4, C5. 3. Olive, David, "Time to Rewrite the Book on Accounting Practices," The Toronto Star (January 26, 2002), pp. E1, E4, E16.

Enron had established complex relationships with other companies allowing the creation of profits by exchanging stock with related companies as Enron's stock prices increased in the market. Then, as partner stock prices plunged, Enron was unable to sustain growth and did not have the cash to continue operations. Other methods were also used to overstate income. As an auditor of a large client, what could you do to maintain your independence? What would you say to an existing client with an audit fee in the millions that engaged in irregular accounting practices?

→20.1 THE NATURE OF THE CAPITAL ACQUISITION AND REPAYMENT CYCLE

The final transaction cycle discussed in this text relates to the acquisition of capital resources in the form of interest-bearing debt and owners' equity and the repayment of the capital. The capital acquisition and repayment cycle also includes the payment of interest and dividends. The following are the major accounts in the cycle:

- Notes payable
- Contracts payable
- Mortgages payable
- Capital stock—preferred
- Capital stock—common
- Retained earnings
- Bonds payable

- Interest expense and accruals
- Dividends declared
- Dividends payable
- Proprietorship—capital account
- Partnership—capital accounts
- Options, foreign exchange contracts
- Other financial instruments

Four characteristics of the **capital acquisition and repayment cycle** significantly influence the audit of these accounts:

1. *Relatively few transactions affect the account balances, but each transaction is often highly material in amount.* For example, bonds are infrequently issued by most companies, but the amount of a bond issue is normally large. Due to the large size of most bond issues, it is common to verify each transaction taking place in the cycle for the entire year as a part of verifying the balance sheet accounts. Audit working papers include the beginning balance of every account in the capital acquisition and repayment cycle and document every transaction that occurred during the year.
2. *The exclusion of a single transaction could be material in itself.* Considering the effect of understatements of liabilities and owners' equity, which was discussed in Chapter 17, omission is a major audit concern.
3. *There is a legal relationship between the client entity and the holder of the stock, bond, or similar ownership document.* In the audit of the transactions and amounts in the cycle, the auditor must ensure that the significant legal requirements affecting the financial statements have been properly fulfilled and adequately disclosed in the statements.
4. *There is a direct relationship between the interest and dividends accounts and debt and equity.* In the audit of interest-bearing debt, it is desirable to simultaneously verify the related interest expense and interest payable. This holds true for owners' equity, dividends declared, and dividends payable.

CAPITAL ACQUISITION AND REPAYMENT CYCLE—the transaction cycle involving the acquisition of capital resources in the form of interest-bearing debt and owners' equity, and the repayment of the capital

The audit procedures for many of the accounts in the capital acquisition and repayment cycle can best be understood by selecting representative accounts for study. Therefore, this chapter discusses (1) the audit of notes payable and the related interest expense and interest payable to illustrate interest-bearing capital and (2) common stock, retained earnings, and dividends.

The methodology for determining tests of details of balances for capital acquisition accounts is the same as that followed for all other accounts. For example, the methodology for notes payable is shown in Figure 20-1.

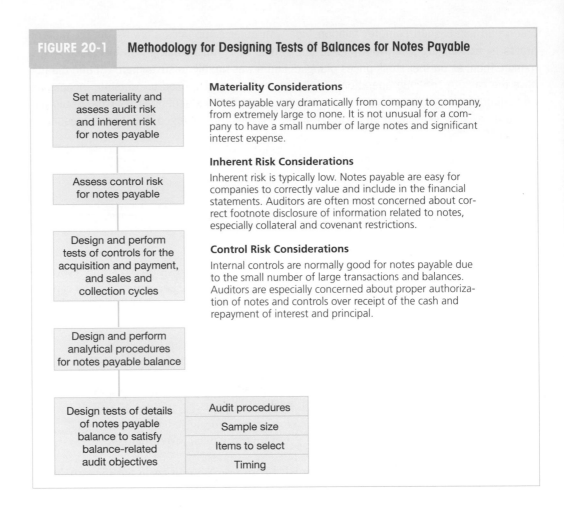

FIGURE 20-1 Methodology for Designing Tests of Balances for Notes Payable

Set materiality and assess audit risk and inherent risk for notes payable

Materiality Considerations

Notes payable vary dramatically from company to company, from extremely large to none. It is not unusual for a company to have a small number of large notes and significant interest expense.

Assess control risk for notes payable

Inherent Risk Considerations

Inherent risk is typically low. Notes payable are easy for companies to correctly value and include in the financial statements. Auditors are often most concerned about correct footnote disclosure of information related to notes, especially collateral and covenant restrictions.

Design and perform tests of controls for the acquisition and payment, and sales and collection cycles

Control Risk Considerations

Internal controls are normally good for notes payable due to the small number of large transactions and balances. Auditors are especially concerned about proper authorization of notes and controls over receipt of the cash and repayment of interest and principal.

Design and perform analytical procedures for notes payable balance

Design tests of details of notes payable balance to satisfy balance-related audit objectives

| Audit procedures |
| Sample size |
| Items to select |
| Timing |

Jane Wong was the audit senior for the audit of a real estate management company. The company frequently purchased and sold buildings of various sizes. As part of her audit, Jane read the purchase and sale agreements for all of the properties purchased and sold during the current year. One small apartment building had an unusual clause—the vendor agreed to take back a mortgage, rather than having the mortgage financed by a bank. However, the client had only recorded the down payment of $900,000 in the books.

Jane pointed out the error to the client, resulting in the set up of an additional $3 million in fixed assets and in mortgages payable.

Notes Payable

NOTE PAYABLE—a legal obligation to a creditor, which may be unsecured or secured by assets

A **note payable** is a legal obligation to a creditor, which may be unsecured or secured by assets. Typically, a note is issued for a period somewhere between one month and one year, but there are also long-term notes of over a year. Notes are issued for many different purposes, and the pledged property includes a wide variety of assets, such as securities, inventory, and capital assets. The principal and interest payments on the notes must be made in accordance with the terms of the loan agreement. For short-term loans, a principal and interest payment is usually required only when the loan becomes due; but for loans over 90 days, the note usually calls for monthly or quarterly interest payments.

Overview of Accounts The accounts used for notes payable and related interest are shown in Figure 20-2. It is common to include tests of principal and interest payments as a part of the audit of the acquisition and payment cycle because the payments are recorded in the cash disbursement journal. However, due to their relative infrequency, in many cases no capital

FIGURE 20-2   Notes Payable and the Related Interest Accounts

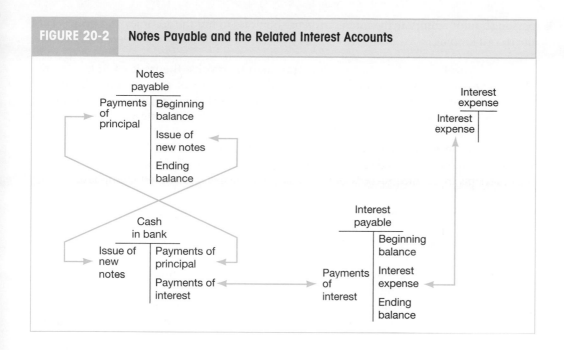

transactions are included in the tests of controls sample. Therefore, it is also normal to test these transactions as a part of the capital acquisition and repayment cycle.

Objectives The objectives of the auditor's examination of notes payable are to determine whether

- The internal controls over notes payable are adequate.
- Transactions for principal and interest involving notes are properly authorized and recorded as defined by the six transaction-related audit objectives.
- The liability for notes payable and the related interest expense and accrued liability are properly stated as defined by eight of the nine balance-related audit objectives. (Realizable value is not applicable to liability accounts.)

Internal Controls There are four important controls over notes payable:

PROPER AUTHORIZATION FOR THE ISSUE OF NEW NOTES Responsibility for the issuance of new notes should be vested in the board of directors or high-level management personnel. Generally, two signatures of properly authorized officials are required for all loan agreements. The amount of the loan, the interest rate, the repayment terms, and the particular assets pledged are all part of the approved agreement. Whenever notes are renewed, it is important that they be subject to the same authorization procedures as those for the issuance of new notes.

ADEQUATE CONTROLS OVER THE REPAYMENT OF PRINCIPAL AND INTEREST The periodic payments of interest and principal should be controlled as part of the acquisition and payment cycle. At the time the note was issued, the accounting department should have received a copy in the same manner in which it receives vendors' invoices and receiving reports. The accounts payable department should automatically issue cheques for the notes when they fall due, again in the same manner in which it prepares cheques for acquisitions of goods and services. The copy of the note is the supporting documentation for payment.

PROPER DOCUMENTS AND RECORDS These include the maintenance of subsidiary records and control over blank and paid notes by a responsible person. Paid notes should be cancelled and retained under the custody of an authorized official.

PERIODIC, INDEPENDENT VERIFICATION Periodically, the detailed note records should be reconciled with the general ledger and compared with the note holders' records by an employee who is not responsible for maintaining the detailed records. At the same time, an independent person should recompute the interest expense on notes to test the accuracy and propriety of the record keeping.

Tests of Controls Tests of notes payable transactions involve the issue of notes and the repayment of principal and interest. The audit tests are part of tests of controls for cash receipts (Chapter 13) and cash disbursements (Chapter 17). Additional tests of controls are often performed as part of tests of details of balances due to the materiality of individual transactions.

Tests of controls for notes payable and related interest should emphasize testing the four important internal controls discussed in the previous section. In addition, the accurate recording of receipts from note proceeds and payments of principal and interest is emphasized.

Analytical Procedures Analytical procedures are essential for notes payable because tests of details for interest expense and accrued interest can frequently be eliminated when results are favourable. Table 20-1 illustrates typical analytical procedures for notes payable and related interest accounts.

The auditor's independent estimate of interest expense, using average notes payable outstanding and average interest rates, tests the reasonableness of interest expense but also tests for omitted notes payable. If actual interest expense is materially larger than the auditor's estimate, one possible cause could be interest payments on unrecorded notes payable.

Tests of Details of Balances The normal starting point for the audit of notes payable is a *schedule of notes payable and accrued interest* obtained from the client. A typical schedule is shown in Figure 20-3 on pages 576 and 577. The usual schedule includes detailed information of all transactions that took place during the entire year for principal and interest, the beginning and ending balances for notes and interest payable, and descriptive information about the notes, such as the due date, the interest rate, and the assets pledged as collateral.

When there are numerous transactions involving notes during the year, it may not be practical to obtain a schedule of the type shown in Figure 20-3. In that situation, the auditor is likely to request that the client prepare a schedule or computer spreadsheet of only those notes with unpaid balances at the end of the year. This would show a description of each note, its ending balance, and the interest payable at the end of the year, including the collateral and interest rate.

The objectives and common audit procedures are summarized in Table 20-2. Realizable value is not included in the table because it is not applicable to notes payable. The schedule of notes payable is the frame of reference for the procedures. The amount of testing depends heavily on materiality of notes payable and the effectiveness of internal controls.

The three most important balance-related audit objectives in notes payable are as follows:

- Existing notes payable are included (completeness).
- Notes payable in the schedule are accurately recorded (accuracy).
- Notes payable are properly presented and disclosed (presentation and disclosure).

TABLE 20-1	Analytical Procedures for Notes Payable
Analytical Procedure	**Possible Misstatement**
Recalculate approximate interest expense on the basis of average interest rates and overall monthly notes payable.	Misstatement of interest expense or accrued interest, or omission of an outstanding note payable.
Compare individual notes outstanding with the prior year.	Omission or misstatement of a note payable.
Compare total balance in notes payable, interest expense, and accrued interest with prior year.	Misstatement of notes payable, interest expense, or accrued interest.

TABLE 20-2 **Objectives and Tests of Details of Balances for Notes Payable and Interest**

Balance-Related Audit Objectives	Common Tests of Details of Balances Procedures	Comments
Notes payable in the notes payable schedule agree with the client's notes payable register or master file (detail tie-in).	Foot the notes payable list for notes payable and accrued interest.† Trace the totals to the general ledger. Trace the individual notes payable to the master file.	Frequently, these are done on a 100 percent basis because of the small population size.
Notes payable in the schedule exist (existence).	Confirm notes payable. Examine duplicate copy of notes for authorization. Examine corporate minutes for loan approval.	
Existing notes payable are included in the notes payable schedule (completeness).	Examine notes paid after year end to determine whether they were liabilities at the balance sheet date. Obtain a *standard bank confirmation* that includes specific reference to the existence of notes payable from all financial institutions with which the client does business. (Bank confirmations are discussed more fully in Chapter 15.) Review the *bank reconciliation* for new notes credited directly to the bank account by the bank. (Bank reconciliations are also discussed more fully in Chapter 15.) Obtain confirmations from creditors who have held notes from the client in the past and are not currently included in the notes payable schedule. This is the same concept as a "zero balance" confirmation in accounts payable. Analyze interest expense to uncover a payment to a creditor who is not included in the notes payable schedule. This procedure is automatically done if the schedule is similar to the one in Figure 20-3 because all interest payments are reconciled with the general ledger. Examine paid notes for cancellation to make sure they are not still outstanding. They should be maintained in the client's files. Review the minutes of the board of directors for authorized but unrecorded notes.	This objective is important for uncovering both errors and fraud and other irregularities. The first three of these procedures are done on most audits. The others are frequently done only when internal controls are weak.
Notes payable and accrued interest on the schedule are accurate (accuracy).	Examine duplicate copies of notes for principal and interest rates. Confirm notes payable, interest rates, and last date for which interest has been paid with holders of notes. Recalculate accrued interest.†	In some cases, it may be necessary to calculate, using present-value techniques, the imputed interest rates, or the principal amount of the note. An example is when equipment is acquired for a note.†
Notes payable in the schedule are properly classified (classification).	Examine due dates on duplicate copies of notes to determine whether all or part of the notes are a noncurrent liability. Review notes to determine whether any are related-party notes or accounts payable.	
Notes payable are included in the proper period (cutoff).	Examine duplicate copies of notes to determine whether notes were dated on or before the balance sheet date.	Notes should be included as current-period liabilities when dated on or before the balance sheet date.
The company has an obligation to pay the notes payable (rights and obligations).	Examine notes to determine whether the company has obligations for payment.	
Notes payable, interest expense, and accrued interest are properly presented and disclosed (presentation and disclosure).	Examine duplicate copies of notes. Confirm notes payable. Examine notes, minutes, and bank confirmations for restrictions. Examine balance sheet for proper disclosure of noncurrent portions, related parties, assets pledged as security for notes, and restrictions resulting from notes payable.	Proper financial statement presentation, including footnote disclosure, is an important consideration for notes payable.

†This test could be completed using spreadsheet software or other computerized methods in audits where volume is high.

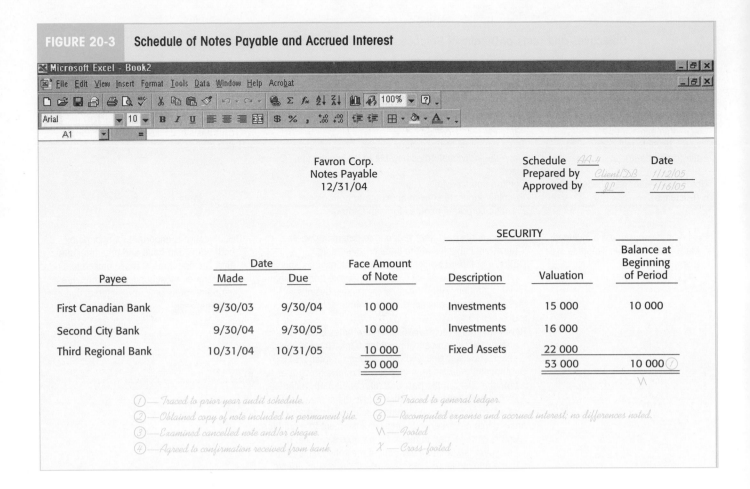

Favron Corp.
Notes Payable
12/31/04

Schedule _AA-4_ Date
Prepared by _Client/DB_ _1/12/05_
Approved by _JP_ _1/16/05_

Payee	Date Made	Date Due	Face Amount of Note	SECURITY Description	SECURITY Valuation	Balance at Beginning of Period
First Canadian Bank	9/30/03	9/30/04	10 000	Investments	15 000	10 000
Second City Bank	9/30/04	9/30/05	10 000	Investments	16 000	
Third Regional Bank	10/31/04	10/31/05	10 000	Fixed Assets	22 000	
			30 000		53 000	10 000 ①

① — Traced to prior year audit schedule.
② — Obtained copy of note included in permanent file.
③ — Examined cancelled note and/or cheque.
④ — Agreed to confirmation received from bank.
⑤ — Traced to general ledger.
⑥ — Recomputed expense and accrued interest; no differences noted.
∧ — Footed
✗ — Cross-footed

The first two objectives are important because a misstatement could be material if even one note is omitted or incorrect. Presentation and disclosure are important because generally accepted accounting principles require that the footnotes adequately describe the terms of notes payable outstanding and the assets pledged as collateral for the loans. If there are significant restrictions on the activities of the company required by the loans, such as compensating balance provisions or restrictions on the payment of dividends, these must also be disclosed in the footnotes.

→20.2 OWNERS' EQUITY

PUBLICLY HELD CORPORATION—a corporation whose stock is publicly traded; typically, there are many shareholders and frequent changes in the ownership of the stock

CLOSELY HELD CORPORATION—a corporation whose stock is not publicly traded; typically, there are only a few shareholders and few, if any, capital stock account transactions during the year; also known as a private corporation

A major distinction must be made in the audit of owners' equity between **publicly** and **closely held corporations** (also known as *private corporations*). Public companies are permitted by their articles of incorporation to issue shares to the public; closely held companies tend to be private companies with restricted share ownership. In most closely held corporations, there are few if any transactions during the year for capital stock accounts, and there are typically only a few shareholders. The only transactions entered in the owners' equity section are likely to be the change in owners' equity for the annual earnings or loss and the declaration of dividends, if any. The amount of time spent verifying owners' equity is frequently minimal for closely held corporations even though the auditor must test the existing corporate records.

For publicly held corporations, the verification of owners' equity is more complex due to the larger numbers of shareholders and frequent changes in the individuals holding the stock. In this section, the appropriate tests for verifying the major accounts—capital stock, retained earnings, and the related dividends—in a publicly held corporation are discussed. The other accounts in owners' equity are verified in much the same way as these.

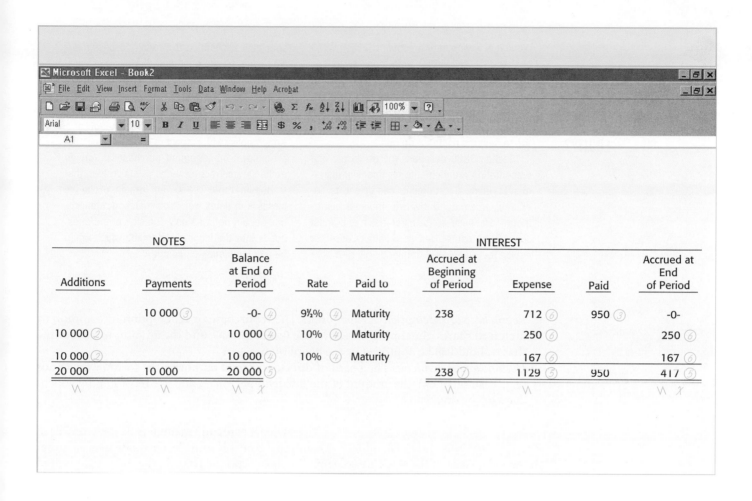

	NOTES				INTEREST			
Additions	Payments	Balance at End of Period	Rate	Paid to	Accrued at Beginning of Period	Expense	Paid	Accrued at End of Period
	10 000 ③	-0- ④	9½% ④	Maturity	238	712 ⑥	950 ③	-0-
10 000 ②		10 000 ④	10% ④	Maturity		250 ⑥		250 ⑥
10 000 ②		10 000 ④	10% ④	Maturity		167 ⑥		167 ⑥
20 000	10 000	20 000 ⑤			238 ⑦	1129 ⑤	950	417 ⑤
⋀	⋀	⋀ ✗			⋀	⋀		⋀ ✗

Overview of Accounts An overview of the specific owners' equity accounts discussed in this section is given in Figure 20-4.

Objectives The objectives of the auditor's examination of owners' equity are to determine whether

- The internal controls over capital stock and related dividends are adequate.
- Owners' equity transactions are recorded properly as defined by the six transaction-related audit objectives.
- Owners' equity balances are properly presented and disclosed as defined by the balance-related audit objectives for owners' equity accounts. (Rights/obligations and realizable value are not applicable.)

Internal Controls Several important internal controls are of concern to the independent auditor in owners' equity: proper authorization of transactions, proper record keeping, adequate segregation of duties between maintaining owners' equity records and handling cash and stock certificates, and the use of an independent registrar and stock transfer agent.

PROPER AUTHORIZATION OF TRANSACTIONS Since each owners' equity transaction is typically material, many of these transactions must be approved by the board of directors. The following types of owners' equity transactions usually require specific authorization.

- *Issuance of capital stock* The authorization includes the type of the equity to issue (e.g., preferred or common stock), number of shares to issue, issue price (also known as the stated value), privileges or conditions that attach to the stock, and date of the issue.

- *Repurchase or redemption of capital stock* The repurchase or redemption of common or preferred shares, the timing of repurchase (redemption), and the amount to pay for the shares should all be approved by the board of directors.
- *Declaration of dividends* The board of directors should authorize the form of dividends (e.g., cash or stock), the amount of the dividend per share, and the record and payment dates of the dividends.

PROPER RECORD KEEPING AND SEGREGATION OF DUTIES When a company maintains its own records of stock transactions and outstanding stock, internal controls must be adequate to ensure that the actual owners of the stock are recognized in the corporate records, the correct amount of dividends is paid to the shareholders owning the stock as of the dividend record date, and the potential for employee fraud is minimized. The proper assignment of personnel and adequate record-keeping procedures are useful controls for these purposes.

FIGURE 20-4	Owners' Equity and Dividends Accounts

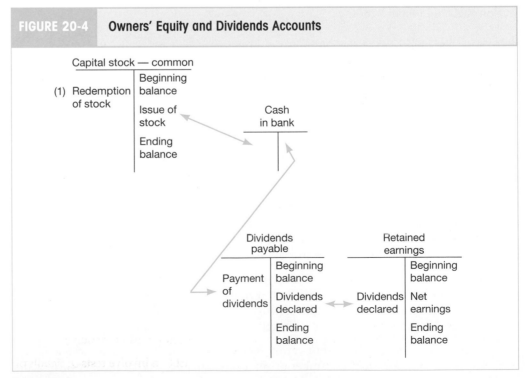

(1) Decrease cash

The most important procedures for preventing misstatements in owners' equity are (1) well-defined policies for preparing stock certificates and recording capital stock transactions and (2) independent internal verification of information in the records. The client must be certain when issuing and recording capital stock that there is compliance with the relevant federal (for federally incorporated companies) or provincial (for provincially incorporated companies) laws governing corporations and the requirements in the articles of incorporation. For example, the classes of shares and the number of shares that the company is authorized to issue affect issuance and recording.

A control over capital stock used by most companies is the maintenance of stock certificate books and shareholders' capital stock master and transaction files. A **capital stock certificate book** is a record of the issuance and repurchase of capital stock for the life of the corporation. For large public corporations, these records would be automated rather than kept manually. There would normally be a book or file for each type (preferred or common) and each class (common, class A; common, class B; etc.). The record for a particular capital stock transaction includes such information as the certificate number, the number of shares issued, the name of the person to whom it was issued, and the issue date. When shares are repurchased, the capital stock certificate book should include the cancelled certificates and the date of their cancellation. A shareholders' capital stock master file is the record of the outstanding shares at any given time. The master file acts as a check on the accuracy of the capital stock certificate book or transaction details and the preferred and common stock balances in the general ledger. It is also used as the basis for the payment of dividends.

CAPITAL STOCK CERTIFICATE BOOK OR RECORDS—a record of the issuance and repurchase of capital stock for the life of the corporation

The disbursement of cash for the payment of dividends should be controlled in much the same manner as was described in Chapter 16 for the preparation and payment of payroll. Dividend cheques should be prepared from the capital stock certificate book by someone who is not responsible for maintaining the capital stock records. After the cheques are prepared, it is desirable to have an independent verification of the shareholders' names and the amount of the cheques and a reconciliation of the total amount of the dividend cheques with the total dividends authorized in the minutes. The use of a separate imprest dividend account is desirable to prevent the payment of a larger amount of dividends than was authorized.

INDEPENDENT REGISTRAR AND STOCK TRANSFER AGENT Some companies engage an **independent registrar** and **stock transfer agent** (usually one organization such as a trust company performs both tasks, but the job may be split between two such organizations) as a control to prevent the improper issue of share certificates and to maintain shareholder records. The function of an independent registrar is to ensure that stock is issued by a corporation in accordance with the capital stock provisions in the articles of incorporation and the authorization of the board of directors. The registrar is responsible for signing all newly issued share certificates and making sure old certificates are received and cancelled before a replacement certificate is issued when there is a change in the ownership of the stock.

INDEPENDENT REGISTRAR—an outside person or organization engaged by a corporation to ensure that its stock is issued in accordance with capital stock provisions in the corporate charter and authorizations by the board of directors

STOCK TRANSFER AGENT—an outside person or organization engaged by a corporation to maintain the shareholder records and often to disburse cash dividends

Most large corporations also employ the services of a stock transfer agent for the purpose of maintaining the shareholder records, including those documenting transfers of share ownership. The employment of a transfer agent not only serves as a control over the share records by putting them in the hands of an independent organization but reduces the cost of record keeping. Many companies also have the transfer agent disburse cash dividends to shareholders, thereby further transferring internal control. Corporations should have adequate procedures to verify on a periodic basis that transfer agents perform only authorized transactions.

Audit of Capital Stock There are four main concerns in auditing capital stock:

- Existing capital stock transactions are recorded (completeness).
- Recorded capital stock transactions exist and are accurately recorded (occurrence and accuracy).
- Capital stock is accurately recorded (accuracy).
- Capital stock is properly presented and disclosed (presentation and disclosure).

The first two concerns involve tests of controls, and the last two involve tests of details of balances.

EXISTING CAPITAL STOCK TRANSACTIONS ARE RECORDED This objective is easily satisfied when a registrar or transfer agent is used. The auditor can confirm with him or her whether any capital stock transactions occurred and the valuation of existing transactions. Review of the minutes of the board of directors' meetings, especially near the balance sheet date, and examination of client-held stock records are also useful to uncover issuances and repurchases of capital stock.

RECORDED CAPITAL STOCK TRANSACTIONS EXIST AND ARE ACCURATELY RECORDED The issuance of new capital stock for cash, the merger with another company through an exchange of stock, the donation of shares, and the repurchase of shares each require extensive auditing. Regardless of the controls in existence, it is normal practice to verify all capital stock transactions because of their materiality and permanence in the records. Existence can ordinarily be tested by examining the minutes of the board of directors' meetings for proper authorization.

Accurate recording of capital stock transactions for cash can be readily verified by confirming the amount with the transfer agent and tracing the amount of the recorded capital stock transactions to cash receipts. (In the case of repurchased shares, the amounts are traced to the cash disbursements journal.) In addition, the auditor must verify whether the correct amounts were credited to capital stock by referring to the articles of incorporation to determine the stated value of the capital stock.

When capital stock transactions involve stock dividends, acquisition of property for stock, mergers, or similar non-cash transfers, the verification of valuation may be considerably more difficult. For these types of transactions, the auditor must be certain that the client has correctly computed the amount of the capital stock issue in accordance with generally accepted accounting principles. For example, in the audit of a major merger transaction, the auditor has to evaluate whether the transaction is a purchase or, in very rare instances, a pooling of interests. Frequently, considerable research is necessary to determine which accounting treatment is correct for the existing circumstances. After the auditor reaches a conclusion as to the appropriate method, it is necessary to verify that the amounts were correctly computed.

CAPITAL STOCK IS ACCURATELY RECORDED The ending balance in the capital stock account is verified by first determining the number of shares outstanding at the balance sheet date. A confirmation from the transfer agent is the simplest way to obtain this information. When no transfer agent exists, the auditor must rely on examining the stock records and accounting for all shares outstanding in the stock certificate records, examining all cancelled certificates, and accounting for blank certificates. After the auditor is satisfied that the number of shares outstanding is correct, the recorded value in the capital account can be verified by multiplying the number of shares by the stated value of the stock. It is audited by verifying the share amounts of recorded transactions during the year and adding them to or subtracting them from the beginning balance in the account.

A major consideration in the accuracy of capital stock is verifying whether the number of shares used in the calculation of earnings per share is accurate. It is easy to determine the correct number of shares to use in the calculation when there is only one class of stock and a small number of capital stock transactions. The problem becomes much more complex when there are convertible securities, stock options, or stock warrants outstanding. It is important for the auditor to have a thorough understanding of Section 3500, "Earnings Per Share," in the *CICA Accounting Handbook* before verifying the number of basic and diluted shares.

CAPITAL STOCK IS PROPERLY PRESENTED AND DISCLOSED The most important sources of information for determining proper presentation and disclosure are the articles of incorporation, the minutes of board of directors' meetings, and the auditor's analysis of capital stock transactions. The auditor should determine that there is a proper description of each class of stock, including such information as the number of shares issued and outstanding and any special rights of an individual class. The proper disclosure of stock options, stock warrants, and convertible securities should also be verified by examining legal documents or other evidence of the provision of these agreements.

Audit of Dividends The emphasis in the audit of dividends is on the transactions rather than the ending balance. The exception is when there are dividends payable.

The six transaction-related audit objectives for transactions are relevant for dividends. Dividends are usually audited on a 100-percent basis and cause few problems. The following are the most important objectives, including those concerning dividends payable:

- Recorded dividends occurred (occurrence).
- Existing dividends are recorded (completeness).
- Dividends are accurately recorded (accuracy).
- Dividends that exist are paid to shareholders (existence).
- Dividends payable are recorded (completeness).
- Dividends payable are accurately recorded (accuracy).

Existence of recorded dividends can be checked by examining the minutes of board of directors' meetings for the amount of the dividend per share and the dividend date. When the auditor examines the board of directors' minutes for dividends declared, the auditor should be alert to the possibility of unrecorded dividends declared, particularly shortly before the balance sheet date. A closely related audit procedure is reviewing the permanent audit working-paper file to determine if there are restrictions on the payment of dividends in bond indenture agreements or preferred stock provisions.

The accuracy of a dividend declaration can be audited by recomputing the amount on the basis of the dividend per share and the number of shares outstanding. If the client uses a transfer agent to disburse dividends, the total can be traced to a cash disbursement entry to the agent and also confirmed.

When a client keeps its own dividend records and pays the dividend itself, the auditor can verify the total amount of the dividend by recalculation and reference to cash disbursed. In addition, it is necessary to verify whether the payment was made to the shareholders who owned the stock at the dividend record date. The auditor can test this by selecting a sample of recorded dividend payments and tracing the payee's name on the cancelled cheque to the dividend records to ensure the payee was entitled to the dividend. At the same time, the amount and the authenticity of the dividend cheque can be verified.

Tests of dividends payable should be done in conjunction with declared dividends. Any unpaid dividend should be included as a liability.

Audit of Retained Earnings For most companies, the only transactions involving retained earnings are net earnings for the year and dividends declared. But there may also be corrections of prior-period earnings, prior-period adjustments charged or credited directly to retained earnings, and the setting up or elimination of appropriations of retained earnings.

The starting point for the audit of retained earnings is an analysis of retained earnings for the entire year. The audit schedule showing the analysis, which is usually part of the permanent file, includes a description of every transaction affecting the account.

The audit of the credit to retained earnings for net income for the year (or the debit for a loss) is accomplished by simply tracing the entry in retained earnings to the net earnings figure on the income statement. The performance of this procedure must, of course, take place fairly late in the audit after all adjusting entries affecting net earnings have been completed.

An important consideration in auditing debits and credits to retained earnings other than net earnings and dividends is determining whether the transactions should have been included. For example, prior-period adjustments can be included in retained earnings only if they result from a change in accounting policy or are intended to correct an error in prior-period financial statements. The auditor should ensure that the accounting is in accordance with "Accounting Changes," Section 1506 of the *CICA Accounting Handbook*.

Once the auditor is satisfied that the recorded transactions are appropriately classified as retained earnings transactions, the next step is to decide whether they are accurately recorded. The audit evidence necessary to determine accuracy depends on the nature of the transactions. If there is a requirement for an appropriation of retained earnings for a bond sinking fund, the correct amount of the appropriation can be determined by examining the bond indenture agreement.

Another important consideration in the audit of retained earnings is evaluating whether there are any transactions that should have been included but were not. If a stock dividend was declared, for instance, the market value of the securities issued should be capitalized by a debit to retained earnings and a credit to capital stock. Similarly, if the financial statements include appropriations of retained earnings, the auditor should evaluate whether it is still necessary to have the appropriation as of the balance sheet date. As an example, an appropriation of retained earnings for a bond sinking fund should be eliminated by crediting retained earnings after the bond has been paid off.

Of primary concern in determining whether retained earnings are correctly disclosed on the balance sheet is the existence of any restrictions on the payment of dividends. Frequently, agreements with bankers, shareholders, and other creditors prohibit or limit the amount of dividends the client can pay. These restrictions must be disclosed in the footnotes to the financial statements.

SUMMARY

1. *What are the four key characteristics of the capital acquisition and repayment cycle?* (i) There are relatively few transactions, but these are often highly material. (ii) The exclusion of a single transaction could result in a material misstatement. (iii) A legal relationship exists between the client and the holder of the capital instrument. (iv) There is a direct relationship between interest or dividends paid and the corresponding debt or equity amount.

   What is the methodology for designing tests of balances for notes payable? After assessing risks and allocating materiality, tests of controls (if appropriate) are designed, tested, and evaluated. Then, analytical procedures are performed, followed by the design and execution of tests of details of balances.

   What is the purpose of conducting analytical procedures for notes payable? These calculations are designed to detect potential misstatements in interest expense, accrued interest, or notes payable, including the detection of the potential omission of a note.

2. *What is the difference in equity between public and closely held corporations?* Publicly held companies tend to have a more complex share structure than closely held corporations, resulting in a greater variety of transactions. Also, as there are more shareholders, there tends to be more changes in ownership of share capital.

   Provide examples of common internal controls over owners' equity transactions. To ensure proper authorization, transactions such as declaration of dividends, purchase, redemption, or issuance of capital stock should be approved by the board of directors. Adequate records should be kept of changes in share ownership to ensure payment of dividends to owners of shares. An independent registrar and stock transfer agent may be used to help ensure adequate segregation of duties.

   What are the main concerns when auditing capital stock? The auditor is concerned about the following assertions: completeness of all capital stock transactions, accurate recording of capital stock transactions, accurate recording of issued capital, and proper presentation and disclosure of capital stock.

ESSENTIAL TERMS

Capital acquisition and repayment cycle—the transaction cycle involving the acquisition of capital resources in the form of interest-bearing debt and owners' equity, and the repayment of the capital (p. 571).

Capital stock certificate book or records—a record of the issuance and repurchase of capital stock for the life of the corporation (p. 579).

Closely held corporation—a corporation whose stock is not publicly traded; typically, there are only a few shareholders and few, if any, capital stock account transactions during the year; also known as a private corporation (p. 576).

Independent registrar—an outside person or organization engaged by a corporation to ensure that its stock is issued in accordance with capital stock provisions in the corporate charter and authorizations by the board of directors (p. 579).

Note payable—a legal obligation to a creditor, which may be unsecured or secured by assets (p. 572).

Publicly held corporation—a corporation whose stock is publicly traded; typically, there are many shareholders and frequent changes in the ownership of the stock (p. 576).

Stock transfer agent—an outside person or organization engaged by a corporation to maintain the shareholder records and often to disburse cash dividends (p. 579).

20-1 List four examples of interest-bearing liability accounts commonly found in balance sheets. What characteristics do these liabilities have in common? How do they differ?

20-2 Why are liability accounts that are included in the capital acquisition and repayment cycle audited differently from accounts payable?

20-3 It is common practice to audit the balance in notes payable in conjunction with the audit of interest expense and interest payable. Explain the advantages of this approach.

20-4 With which internal controls should the auditor be most concerned in the audit of notes payable? Explain the importance of each.

20-5 Which analytical procedures are most important in verifying notes payable? Which types of misstatements can the auditor uncover by the use of these tests?

20-6 Why is it more important to search for unrecorded notes payable than for unrecorded notes receivable? List several audit procedures the auditor can use to uncover unrecorded notes payable.

20-7 What is the primary purpose of analyzing interest expense? Given this purpose, what primary considerations should the auditor keep in mind when doing the analysis?

20-8 Distinguish between the tests of controls and tests of details of balances for liability accounts in the capital acquisition and repayment cycle.

20-9 List four types of restrictions that long-term creditors often put on companies when granting them a loan. How can the auditor find out about each of these restrictions?

20-10 What are the major internal controls over owners' equity?

20-11 How does the audit of owners' equity for a closely held corporation differ from that for a publicly held corporation? In what respects are there no significant differences?

20-12 Describe the duties of a stock registrar and a transfer agent. How does the use of their services affect the client's internal controls?

20-13 What kinds of information can be confirmed with a transfer agent?

20-14 What should be the major emphasis in auditing the retained earnings account? Explain your answer.

20-15 Explain the relationship between the audit of owners' equity and the calculations of earnings per share. What are the main auditing considerations in verifying the earnings per share figure?

MULTIPLE CHOICE QUESTIONS

20-16 Choose the best response for the following questions:

a. The auditor's program for the examination of long-term debt should include steps that require the

   (1) examination of any bond trust indenture.
   (2) inspection of the accounts payable master file.
   (3) verification of the existence of the bondholders.
   (4) investigation of credits to the bond interest income account.

b. During the year under audit, a company has completed a private placement of a substantial number of bonds. Which of the following is the most important step in the auditor's examination of bonds payable?

   (1) Examining the bond records maintained by the transfer agent.
   (2) Confirming the amount issued with the bond trustee.
   (3) Tracing the cash received from the issue to the accounting records.
   (4) Recomputing the annual interest cost and the effective yield.

c. Several years ago, Conway, Inc., secured a conventional real estate mortgage loan. Which of the following audit procedures would most likely be performed by an auditor examining the mortgage balance?

   (1) Recomputing mortgage interest expense.

   (2) Examining the current year's cancelled cheques.
   (3) Reviewing the mortgage amortization schedule.
   (4) Inspecting public records of registered mortgages.

d. An audit program for the examination of the retained earnings account should include verification of

   (1) authorization for both cash and stock dividends.
   (2) market value used to charge retained earnings to account for a 2-for-1 stock split.
   (3) approval of the adjustment to the beginning balance as a result of a write-down of an account receivable.
   (4) approval of the adjustment to the beginning balance as a result of a change in the estimated life of certain fixed assets.

e. Where no independent stock transfer agents are employed and the corporation issues its own shares and maintains share records, cancelled stock certificates should

   (1) be defaced to prevent re-issuance and attached to their corresponding stubs.
   (2) be destroyed to prevent fraudulent re-issuance.
   (3) be defaced and sent to the Ministry of Consumer and Business Services.
   (4) not be defaced but segregated from other stock certificates and retained in a cancelled certificates file.

(AICPA adapted)

DISCUSSION QUESTIONS AND PROBLEMS

20-17 Items 1 through 6 are questions typically found in a standard internal control questionnaire used by auditors to obtain an understanding of internal control for notes payable. In using the questionnaire for a particular client, a "yes" response indicates a possible internal control, whereas a "no" indicates a potential weakness.

1. Are liabilities for notes payable incurred only after written authorization by a proper company official?
2. Is a notes payable master file maintained?
3. Is the individual who maintains the notes payable master file someone other than the person who approves the issue of new notes or handles cash?
4. Are paid notes cancelled and retained in the company files?
5. Is a periodic reconciliation made of the notes payable master file with the actual notes outstanding by an individual who does not maintain the master file?
6. Are interest expense and accrued interest recomputed periodically by an individual who does not record interest transactions?

Required

a. For each of the preceding questions, state the purpose of the control.
b. For each of the preceding questions, identify the type of financial statement misstatement that could occur if the control were not in effect.
c. For each of the potential misstatements in part (b), list an audit procedure that could be used to determine whether a material misstatement existed.

20-18 The following are frequently performed audit procedures for the verification of bonds payable issued in previous years.

1. Obtain a copy of the bond indenture agreement and review its important provisions.
2. Determine that each of the bond indenture provisions has been met.
3. Analyze the general ledger account for bonds payable, interest expense, and unamortized bond discount or premium.
4. Test the client's calculations of interest expense, unamortized bond discount or premium, accrued interest, and bonds payable.
5. Obtain a confirmation from the bondholder.

Required

a. State the purpose of each of the five audit procedures listed.
b. List the provisions for which the auditor should be alert in examining the bond indenture agreement.
c. For each provision listed in part (b), explain how the auditor can determine whether its terms have been met.
d. Explain how the auditor should verify the unamortized bond discount or premium.
e. List the information that should be requested in the confirmation of bonds payable with the bondholder.

20-19 The ending general ledger balance of $186,000 in notes payable for Sisam Manufacturing Inc. is made up of 20 notes to 8 different payees. The notes vary in duration anywhere from 30 days to 2 years and in amount from $1,000 to $10,000. In some cases, the notes were issued for cash loans; in other cases, the notes were issued directly to vendors for the purchase of inventory or equipment. The use of relatively short-term financing is necessary because all existing properties are pledged for mortgages. Nevertheless, there is still a serious cash shortage.

Record-keeping procedures for notes payable are not good, considering the large number of loan transactions. There is neither a notes payable master file nor an independent verification of ending balances; however, the notes payable records are maintained by a secretary who does not have access to cash.

The audit has been done by the same public accounting firm for several years. In the current year, the following procedures were performed to verify notes payable:

1. Obtain a list of notes payable from the client, foot the notes payable balances on the list, and trace the total to the general ledger.
2. Examine duplicate copies of notes for all outstanding notes included on the listing. Compare the name of the lender, amount, and due date on the duplicate copy with the list.
3. Obtain a confirmation from lenders for all listed notes payable. The confirmation should include the due date of the loan, the amount, and interest payable at the balance sheet date.
4. Recompute accrued interest on the list for all notes. The information for determining the correct accrued interest is to be obtained from the duplicate copy of the note. Foot the accrued interest amounts and trace the balance to the general ledger.

Required

a. What should be the emphasis in the verification of notes payable in this situation? Explain.
b. State the purpose of each of the four audit procedures listed.
c. Evaluate whether each of the four audit procedures was necessary. Evaluate the sample size for each procedure.
d. List other audit procedures that should be performed in the audit of notes payable in these circumstances.

20-20 The following covenants are extracted from the indenture of a bond issue outstanding from McMullen Corp. The indenture provides that failure to comply with its terms in any respect automatically advances the due date of the loan to the date of noncompliance (the regular date is 20 years from now).

List any audit steps or reporting requirements that you feel should be taken or recognized in connection with each one of the following with respect to your audit of McMullen Corp.

a. The debtor company shall endeavour to maintain a working capital ratio of 2:1 at all times, and, in any fiscal year following a failure to maintain said ratio, the company shall restrict compensation of officers to a total of $750,000. Officers for this purpose shall include a chair of the board of directors, a president, all vice-presidents, a secretary, and a treasurer.

b. The debtor company shall keep all property that is security

for this debt insured against loss by fire to the extent of 100 percent of its actual value. Policies of insurance comprising this protection shall be filed with the trustee.

c. The debtor company shall pay all taxes legally assessed against the property that is security for this debt within the time provided by law for payment without penalty, and shall deposit receipted tax bills or equally acceptable evidence of payment of same with the trustee.

d. A sinking fund shall be deposited with the trustee by semi-annual payments of $300,000, from which the trustee shall, in his or her discretion, purchase bonds of this issue.

(AICPA adapted)

20-21 Evangeline Ltd. took out a 20-year mortgage on June 15, 2005, for $2,600,000 and pledged its only manufacturing building and the land on which the building stands as collateral. Each month subsequent to the issue of the mortgage, a monthly payment of $20,000 is paid to the mortgagor. You are in charge of the current-year audit for Evangeline, which has a balance sheet date of December 31, 2005. The client has been audited previously by your public accounting firm, but this is the first time Evangeline Ltd. has had a mortgage.

Required

a. Explain why it is desirable to prepare a working paper for the permanent file for the mortgage. What type of information should be included in the working paper?

b. Explain why the audits of mortgage payable, interest expense, and interest payable should all be done together.

c. List the audit procedures that should ordinarily be performed to verify the issue of the mortgage, the balance in the mortgage and interest payable accounts at December 31, 2005, and the balance in interest expense for the year 2005.

20-22 The following audit procedures are commonly performed by auditors in the verification of owners' equity:

1. Review the articles of incorporation and bylaws for provisions about owners' equity.
2. Review the minutes of the board of directors' meetings for the year for approvals related to owners' equity.
3. Analyze all owners' equity accounts for the year and document the nature of any recorded change in each account.
4. Account for all certificate numbers in the capital stock book for all shares outstanding.
5. Examine the stock certificate book for any stock that was cancelled.

6. Recompute earnings per share.
7. Review debt provisions and senior securities with respect to liquidation preferences, dividends in arrears, and restrictions on the payment of dividends or the issue of stock.

Required

a. State the purpose of each of these seven audit procedures, including the audit assertion(s).

b. List the type of misstatements the auditors could uncover by the use of each audit procedure.

20-23 The Bergonzi Corporation is a medium-sized wholesaler of grocery products with 4,000 shares of stock outstanding to approximately 25 shareholders. Because of the age of several retired shareholders and the success of the company, management has decided to pay dividends six times a year. The amount of the bimonthly dividend per share varies depending on the profits, but it is ordinarily between $5 and $7 per share. The chief accountant, who is also a shareholder, prepares the dividend cheques, records the cheques in the dividend journal, and reconciles the bank account. Important controls include manual cheque signing by the president and the use of an imprest dividend bank account.

The auditor verifies the dividends by maintaining a schedule of the total shares of stock issued and outstanding in the permanent working papers. The total amount of stock outstanding is

multiplied by the dividends per share authorized in the minutes to arrive at the current total dividend. This total is compared with the deposit that has been made to the imprest dividend account. Since the transfer of stock is infrequent, it is possible to verify dividends paid for the entire year in a comparatively short time.

Required

a. Evaluate the usefulness of the approach followed by the auditor in verifying dividends in this situation. Include both the strengths and the weaknesses of the approach.

b. List other audit procedures that should be performed in verifying dividends in this situation. Explain the purpose of each procedure.

20-24 Xiel Limited is a Canadian manufacturing company with a June 30 fiscal year end. Until recently, the company had financed its operations with equity capital, supplemented by bank loans and other current indebtedness.

On August 31, 2004, the company issued $10 million of 20-year, $8\frac{1}{2}$ percent first mortgage sinking fund bonds, secured by a specific charge against certain company properties. The bonds were distributed to the public through a group of investment dealers for a fee equalling 2 percent of the par value of the issue. The bonds were sold to the public at $99.

A trust company agreed to act as a trustee under the bond indenture and was also appointed transfer agent and interest-paying agent. The company paid fees totalling $25,000 for legal, audit, printing, and other costs in connection with the issue.

The company's auditor of long standing retired in March of 2005. You were then appointed auditor. You have reviewed the company's accounting system and internal controls but have not yet performed any further audit procedures.

List the audit procedures you should perform in order to form an opinion on the bond indebtedness and interest expense shown in the June 30, 2005, financial statements.

(CICA adapted)

PROFESSIONAL JUDGMENT PROBLEM

20-25 E-Antiques Inc. is an Internet-based market maker for buyers and sellers of antique furniture and jewellery. The company allows sellers of antique items to list descriptions of those items on the E-Antiques web site. Interested buyers review the web site for antique items and then enter into negotiations directly with the seller for purchase. E-Antiques receives a commission for each transaction.

The company, founded in 2000, initially obtained capital through equity funding provided by the founders and through loan proceeds from financial institutions. In early 2003, E-Antiques became a publicly held company when it began selling shares on a national stock exchange. Although the company had never generated profits, the stock offering generated huge proceeds based on favourable expectations for the company, and the stock quickly increased to above $100 per share.

Management used the proceeds to pay off loans to financial institutions and to reacquire shares issued to the company founders. Proceeds were also used to fund purchases of hardware and software to support the online market. The balance of unused proceeds is currently held in the company's bank accounts.

Required

a. Before performing analytical procedures related to the capital acquisition and repayment cycle accounts, consider how the process of becoming publicly held would affect accounts at E-Antiques Inc. Describe whether each of the following balances would increase, decrease, or experience no change between 2002 and 2003 because of the public offering:

(1) Cash
(2) Accounts receivable
(3) Property, plant, and equipment
(4) Accounts payable
(5) Long-term debt
(6) Common stock
(7) Retained earnings
(8) Dividends
(9) Revenues

b. During 2004, the stock price for E-Antiques plummeted to around $19 per share. No new shares were issued during 2004. Describe the impact of this drop in stock price on the following accounts for the year ended December 31, 2004:

(1) Common stock
(2) Retained earnings

c. How does the decline in stock price affect your assessment of client business risk and acceptable audit risk?

20-26 The controller of Abracadabra Limited has presented Joan Smylowsky, the company's auditor, with the financial statements for the year ended June 30, 2005. The statements include the statement of contributed surplus and retained earnings for the year (below, left).

Required

a. Outline audit procedures that Joan would apply to verify the items presented in the statement of contributed surplus and retained earnings. (Note: Ignore procedures related to "Net income for the year.")

b. Evaluate the financial statement presentation, and comment on alternatives recommended in the *CICA Handbooks*.

(CICA adapted)

Abracadabra Limited
Statement of Contributed Surplus and Retained Earnings
For the Year Ended June 30

	2005	2004
Contributed surplus		
Incentive grants (note 4)	$94,200	
Deduct:		
Cost of redemption of preferred shares in excess of their issued values	40,000	
Balance at end of year	$54,200	
Retained earnings		
Balance, beginning of year	$1,025,000	$ 980,000
Net income for the year	128,000	105,000
	$1,153,000	$1,085,000
Deduct:		
Dividend on preferred shares	$30,000	$60,000
Extraordinary adjustments to company pension plan (note 5)	73,000	
	103,000	
Balance at end of year	$1,050,000	$1,025,000

Abracadabra Limited
Notes to Financial Statements
For the Year Ended June 30, 2005

Note 4

During the year, the company received the following grants from the Government of Canada: Grant received relating to wage expenses of the year and future year for new jobs created by plant expansion — $44,200

Grant received relating to the acquisition of fixed assets for plant expansion — $50,000

Note 5

During the year, the benefits payable under the company's pension plan were modified. Accordingly, the company made past service payments to the trustees of the plan totalling $53,000.

The consulting actuaries carried out the normal biennial actuarial revaluation, which is required by the company's pension plan. Accordingly, the company made payments to the trustees of the plan totalling $20,000.

PART 5 CHAPTERS 21 TO 24

COMPLETING THE AUDIT AND OFFERING OTHER SERVICES

Chapter 1 introduced the many different types of accountants and the types of services they provide. The chapters in this part expand on this discussion. The provision of special skills during audit engagements, assurance services other than audits, and nonassurance services constitutes an important contribution by accountants to the business community, as long as the audit engagements are performed in conformity with the professional rules of conduct, while maintaining objectivity and independence.

The last of the four phases of an audit is completing the audit, which is covered in Chapter 21. Even when the other phases of the audit are done well, if the completion phase is done poorly, the quality of the audit will be low. If the planning phase and the two testing phases are done well, the completion phase is typically relatively easy.

Chapter 22 focuses on small business, both non-profit and for-profit enterprises. Review and compilation engagements are the primary focus of this chapter. Chapter 22 also discusses the standards for assurance engagements, including compilation and review engagements, as well as providing a framework for the conduct of such engagements. There is also a discussion of interim financial information and future-oriented information, useful for businesses acquiring debt or share capital.

Chapter 23 looks at engagements where accountants require advanced skills. These are specialized assurance engagements such as environmental audits, WebTrust and SysTrust, and business valuations. The need for expertise in the financial statement audit, including each of the transactions cycles, is discussed by examining advanced information systems, service centre audits, and tax complexities.

Chapter 24 covers services performed most often by governmental and internal auditors, including risk assessment and systems control design, training and education on risk management and internal controls, specialized audits such as operational audits, and financial statement audits.

CHAPTER 21

COMPLETING THE AUDIT

As the audit progresses, the auditor continues to assess results, to determine whether planned risks match actual risks. When all cycle, account, and assertion testing has been completed, the evidence as a whole needs to be examined, together with some additional tests that are non-cycle specific. Then, the auditor can decide whether sufficient evidence has been collected to provide an audit opinion.

LEARNING OBJECTIVES

After reading this chapter, you should be able to answer the following questions:

1. How does the auditor search for contingent liabilities? What is the purpose of obtaining a confirmation from the client's law firms? Why must these "legal letters" be in a specified format? Describe examples of procedures conducted during a review for subsequent events.

2. Provide examples of work completed as part of the final evidence gathering process.

3. What does the auditor do to evaluate the adequacy of accumulated evidence?

4. What communications is the auditor required to send after the completion of the audit? What can the auditor do if a misstatement is discovered after the audit report is issued?

GOOD REVIEW REQUIRES MORE THAN LOOKING AT WORKING PAPERS

Larry Bedard, an audit senior of Messier, Nixon & Royce, assigned staff assistant Clawson Lum the audit of accounts payable for Westside Industries Ltd., a large equipment manufacturer. Accounts payable is a major liability account for a manufacturing company, and testing accounts payable cutoff is an important audit area. Testing primarily involves reviewing the liability recorded by the client by examining subsequent payments to suppliers and other creditors to assure that they were properly recorded.

Bedard observed that Lum was spending a lot of time on the phone, apparently on personal matters. Shortly before the audit was completed, Lum announced that he was leaving the firm. In spite of Lum's distractions due to his personal affairs, he completed the audit work he was assigned within the budgeted time.

Because of Bedard's concern about Lum's work habits, he decided to review the working papers with extreme care. Every schedule he reviewed was properly prepared, with tick marks entered and explained by Lum, indicating that he had made an extensive examination of underlying data and documents and had found the client's balance to be adequate as stated. Specifically, there were no payments subsequent to year end for inventory purchases received during the audit period that had not been accrued by Westside.

When Bedard finished the audit, he turned the working papers over to Kelsey Mayburn, an audit manager on the engagement, for her review. She had considerable knowledge about equipment manufacturers and about Westside Industries. Mayburn reviewed all the working papers, including analytical procedures performed during the audit. After performing additional analytical procedures during her review, she contacted Bedard to inform him that accounts payable did not seem reasonable to her. She asked him to do some additional checking. Bedard went back and looked at all the documents that Lum had indicated in the working papers that he had inspected. It was quickly apparent that Lum had either not looked at the documents or did not know what he was doing when he inspected them. Almost $1 million of documents applicable to the December 31, 2004 audit period had not been included as liabilities. Mayburn's review likely saved Messier, Nixon & Royce significant embarrassment or worse consequences.

The Westside Industries situation illustrates the positive elements of quality control—a manager who understood the client and was able to point out an area where additional audit work needed to be done. What are some other aspects of quality control that could have identified the potential cutoff error? What audit procedures would have detected the cutoff error in accounts payable? This review process indicates the importance of analytical procedures in the final stage of the audit.

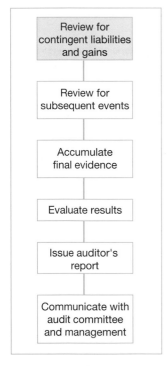

CONTINGENT LIABILITY—a potential future obligation to an outside party for an unknown amount resulting from activities that have already taken place

→21.1 SELECTED FINAL AUDIT PROCEDURES

Review for Contingent Liabilities

Paragraph 3290.02 of the *CICA Accounting Handbook* defines a contingency as

... an existing condition or situation involving uncertainty as to possible gain or loss to an enterprise that will ultimately be resolved when one or more future events occur or fail to occur.

The auditor is concerned both with the nature of the future event and with the amount involved. Just as he or she is concerned with recognizing a contingent liability, the auditor must also be able to recognize a recorded asset that is really a contingent asset and that has the effect of overstating the net worth of the business.

Three conditions indicate the existence of a **contingent liability**: (1) there is a potential future payment to an outside party that resulted from an existing condition, (2) there is uncertainty about the amount of the future payment, and (3) the outcome will be resolved by some future event or events. For example, contingencies include lawsuits that have been filed but not yet resolved.

This uncertainty of the future payment can vary from extremely likely to highly unlikely. Section 3290 of the *CICA Accounting Handbook* describes three levels of likelihood of occurrence and the appropriate financial statement treatment for each likelihood; the three levels are likely, unlikely, and not determinable. The ability to estimate the amount of the loss is also a factor that must be considered. Table 21-1 describes the various alternatives. Although the *Handbook* does not require disclosure of "unlikely" events, if such a potential event could have a significant adverse effect, disclosure should be considered.

The decision as to the appropriate treatment requires considerable professional judgment. (A contingent gain should never be accrued, but rather, if its future confirmation is very likely, it should be disclosed in the notes.)

When the proper disclosure in the financial statements of material contingencies is through footnotes, the footnote should describe the nature of the contingency to the extent it is known, an estimate of the amount, or a statement that the amount cannot be estimated. The following is an illustration of a footnote related to pending litigation:

The Company is a defendant in a legal action instituted in the Alberta Court of the Queen's Bench by Mountain Supply Ltd. for alleged product defect. The amount claimed is $792,000 and the Company is vigorously contesting the claim. The Company's legal counsel is unable,

TABLE 21-1	Likelihood of Occurrence of Contingencies and Financial Statement Treatment	
Likelihood of Occurrence of Event	**Financial Statement Treatment**
Unlikely to occur	No disclosure is necessary.
Not determinable	Footnote disclosure is necessary.
Likely to occur and the amount can be estimated	Financial statement accounts are adjusted.
Likely to occur and the amount cannot be estimated	Footnote disclosure is necessary.

at the present time, to give any opinion with respect to the merits of this action. Settlement, if any, that may be made with respect to these actions is expected to be accounted for as a charge against income for the period in which settlement is made.

Certain contingent liabilities are of considerable concern to the auditor:

- Pending litigation for patent infringement, product liability, or other actions
- Income tax disputes
- Product warranties
- Notes receivable discounted
- Guarantees of obligations of others
- Unused balances in outstanding letters of credit

Auditing standards make it clear that management, not the auditor, is responsible for identifying and deciding the appropriate accounting treatment for contingent liabilities. In many audits, it is impractical for auditors to uncover contingencies without management's cooperation.

The auditor's objectives in verifying contingent liabilities are to evaluate the accounting treatment of known contingent liabilities and to identify, to the extent practical, any contingencies not already identified by management.

Audit Procedures Many of these potential obligations are ordinarily verified as an integral part of various segments of the engagement rather than as a separate activity near the end of the audit. For example, guarantees of obligations of others may be tested as part of confirming bank balances and loans from banks. Similarly, income tax disputes can be checked as part of analyzing income tax expense, reviewing the general correspondence file, and examining Canada Revenue Agency reports and statements. Even if the contingencies are verified separately, it is common to perform the tests well before the last few days of completing the engagement to ensure their proper verification. The tests of contingent liabilities near the end of the engagement are more a review than an initial search.

The appropriate audit procedures for testing contingencies are less well defined than those already discussed in other audit areas because the primary objective at the initial stage of the tests is to determine the *existence* of contingencies. As the reader knows from the study of other audit areas, it is more difficult to discover unrecorded transactions or events than to verify recorded information. Once the auditor is aware that contingencies exist, the evaluation of their materiality and the disclosure required can ordinarily be satisfactorily resolved.

The following are some audit procedures commonly used to search for contingent liabilities. The list is not all-inclusive, and each procedure is not necessarily performed on every audit.

- Enquire of management (orally and in writing) regarding the possibility of unrecorded contingencies. In these enquiries, the auditor must be specific in describing the different kinds of contingencies that may require disclosure. Naturally, enquiries of management are not useful in uncovering the intentional failure to disclose existing contingencies, but if management has overlooked a particular type of contingency or does not fully comprehend accounting disclosure requirements, the enquiry can be fruitful. At the completion of the audit, management is typically asked to make a written statement as part of the letter of representation that it is aware of no undisclosed contingent liabilities.

- Review current and previous years' Canada Revenue Agency notices of assessment. The reports may indicate areas in which disagreement over unsettled years is likely to arise. If an audit by the Canada Revenue Agency has been in progress for a long time, there is an increased likelihood of an existing tax dispute.
- Review the minutes of directors' and shareholders' meetings for indications of lawsuits or other contingencies.
- Analyze legal expense for the period under audit, and review invoices and statements from the client's law firms for indications of contingent liabilities, especially lawsuits and pending tax assessments.
- Obtain a confirmation from all major law firms performing legal services for the client as to the status of pending litigation or other contingent liabilities. This procedure is discussed in more depth shortly.
- Review existing working papers for any information that may indicate a potential contingency. For example, bank confirmations may indicate notes receivable discounted or guarantees of loans.
- Obtain letters of credit in force as of the balance sheet date, and obtain a confirmation of the used and unused balances.
- Read contracts, agreements, and related correspondence and documents.

Evaluation of Known Contingent Liabilities If the auditor concludes that there are contingent liabilities, he or she must evaluate the significance of the potential liability and the nature of the disclosure that is necessary in the financial statements. The potential liability is sufficiently well known in some instances to be included in the statements as an actual liability. In other instances, disclosure may be unnecessary if the contingency is highly remote or immaterial. The public accounting firm may obtain a separate evaluation of the potential liability from its own law firm rather than relying on management or management's lawyers. The client's law firm is an advocate for the client and frequently loses perspective in evaluating the likelihood of losing the case and the amount of the potential judgment.

COMMITMENTS—agreements that the entity will hold to a fixed set of conditions, such as the purchase or sale of merchandise at a stated price, at a future date, regardless of what happens to profits or to the economy as a whole

Commitments Closely related to contingent liabilities are **commitments** to purchase raw materials or to lease facilities at a certain price, agreements to sell merchandise at a fixed price, bonus plans, profit-sharing and pension plans, royalty agreements, and similar items. For a commitment, the most important characteristic is the *agreement to commit the firm to a set of fixed conditions* in the future, regardless of what happens to profits or the economy as a whole. In a free economy, presumably the entity agrees to commitments as a means of bettering its own interests, but these commitments may turn out to be less or more advantageous than originally anticipated.

Section 3280.01 of the *CICA Accounting Handbook* requires disclosure of the details of any contractual obligation that is significant to a client's current financial position or future operations. All commitments are ordinarily either described together in a separate footnote or combined in a footnote related to contingencies.

The search for unknown commitments is usually performed as part of the audit of each audit area. For example, in verifying sales transactions, the auditor should be alert for sales commitments. Similarly, commitments for the purchase of raw materials or equipment can be identified as part of the audit of each of these accounts. The auditor should also be aware of the possibility of commitments as he or she is reading contracts and correspondence files, and should therefore query management.

Obtain Confirmation from Client's Law Firms

ENQUIRY OF THE CLIENT'S LAW FIRMS—a letter from the client's legal counsel informing the auditor of pending litigation or any other information involving legal counsel that is relevant to financial statement disclosure

OUTSTANDING CLAIM—a lawsuit that has been brought against a client; also known as an *asserted claim*

A major procedure on which auditors rely for evaluating known litigation or other claims against the client and identifying additional ones is sending a **letter of enquiry to the client's law firms**. There are two categories of lawsuits: an **outstanding** (or *asserted*) **claim** exists when a suit has been brought or when the client has been notified that a suit will be brought; a **possible** or **unasserted claim** exists when no suit has been filed but is possible. An example of the latter is a situation in which the lawyer is aware of a violation of a patent agreement that could be damaging to the client.

POSSIBLE OR UNASSERTED CLAIM—a potential legal claim against a client where the condition for a claim exists but no claim has been filed

The auditor relies on the lawyer's expertise and knowledge of the client's legal affairs to provide a professional opinion about the expected outcome of existing lawsuits and the likely amount of the liability, including court costs. The lawyer is also likely to know of pending litigation and claims that management may have overlooked.

Many public accounting firms analyze legal expense for the entire year and have the client send a standard lawyer's letter to every law firm with which it has been involved in the current or preceding year, plus any law firm that it occasionally engages. In some cases, this involves a large number of law firms, including some dealing in aspects of law that are far removed from potential lawsuits.

The standard letter of confirmation to the client's law firm, which should be prepared on the client's letterhead and signed by one of the company's officials, should include the following:

- A list, prepared by management, of outstanding and possible claims with which the lawyer has had significant involvement
- A description of the nature and the current status of each claim and possible claim
- An indication of management's evaluation of the amount and likelihood of loss or gain for each listed claim and possible claim
- A request that the lawyer reply to the client, with a signed copy going to the public accounting firm, advising whether management's descriptions and evaluations of the outstanding and possible claims are reasonable

Lawyers are not required to mention any omission of possible claims in their response to the enquiry letter, and thus do not directly notify the auditor of them. Instead, lawyers discuss these possible claims with the client separately and inform management of its responsibility to inform the auditor.

Whether management does so or not is its decision; Paragraph 6560.19 requires the auditor to obtain a letter of representation from management that it has disclosed *all* outstanding and possible claims. In short, unless management discloses the existence of possible claims to the auditor, the auditor has no means of discovering whether or not any such claims exist.

Focus Box 21-1

WILL IT TAKE DEATH OR DISASTER FOR THE CLIENT TO ACT?

As an auditor, assessing corporate governance includes assessing the organization's responsibility for the health and well-being of employees and other individuals. For example, the Basel Convention prohibits the exporting of electronic waste (e.g. computers, screens), yet it seems that many organizations are violating this convention.

In a more vivid example, employees of a Canadian waste management company complained about the speed and reckless manner in which a driver was operating a front-end loader in the plant. Subsequently, an employee who was acting as a "spotter" for a backward driving task was killed by this same driver. The company was fined $300,000 for health and safety violations for failing to ensure that the front-end loader was driven by a competent person. The U.S. parent company refused to book correcting journal entries advised by its auditors. The auditors made a 'deal' for the parent company to book these entries over a period of ten years, which they did not do. The auditors were fined U.S. $7 million for participating in this side deal.

It is important that auditors consider the behaviour of management with respect to known laws, regulations, and the health and safety of their employees, as this may be an indicator of management's attitude toward the integrity of the financial statements. Such behaviour could also lead to contingent liabilities such as fines for consequences of violations, or for costs such as clean-up of environmentally polluted areas.

Sources: 1. Beasley, Mark S., Frank A. Buckless, Steven M. Glover, and Douglas F. Prawitt, Toronto: 2003. *Auditing Cases, an Interactive Learning Approach*, Second Edition, Prentice-Hall. 2. Ministry of Labour, 2004. "Canadian Waste Services Inc. fined $300,000 for health and safety violation," Government of Ontario, Canada. 3. Ross, Rachel, 2005. "Toxic exportation," *The Toronto Star*, January 3, 2005, pp. D1, D3.

Any differences between management's identification and assessment of outstanding and possible claims and the law firm's would be resolved, if possible, in a meeting of the law firm, the auditor, and management. Failure to resolve the differences would force the auditor to consider a reservation of opinion on the auditor's report.

- A request for information regarding any unlisted outstanding or potential legal actions or a statement that the client's list was complete

An example of a typical standard enquiry letter sent to a lawyer's office is shown in Figure 21-1. The letter should be sent toward the end of the audit so that the lawyer is communicating about contingencies up to approximately the date of the auditor's report.

FIGURE 21-1 **Typical Enquiry of Lawyer**

PEPPERTREE PRODUCE INC.
293 rue Crécy
Montréal, Québec

January 26, 2005

Rowan and Gunz
Barristers and Solicitors,
412 Côte des Neiges,
Montréal, Québec
H3C 1J7

To Whom It May Concern:

In connection with the preparation and audit of our financial statements for the fiscal period ended December 31, 2004, we have made the following evaluations of claims and possible claims with respect to which your firm's advice or representation has been sought:

Description	Evaluation
Calvert Growers vs. Peppertree Produce Inc., nonpayment of debt in the amount of $16,000, trial date not set.	Peppertree Produce Inc. disputes this billing on the grounds that the produce was spoiled and expects to successfully defend this action.
Desjardins, Inc. vs. Peppertree Produce Inc., damages for breach of contract in the amount of $40,000, trial date not set.	It is probable that this action will be successfully defended.
Foodex Ltd. has a possible claim in connection with apples sold to them by Peppertree Produce Inc. The apples apparently had not been properly washed by the growers to remove insect spray, and a number of Foodex Ltd.'s customers became ill after eating said apples.	No claim has yet been made, and we are unable to estimate possible ultimate loss.

Would you please advise us, as of February 28, 2005, on the following points:
a. Are the claims and possible claims properly described?
b. Do you consider that our evaluations are reasonable?
c. Are you aware of any claims not listed above that are outstanding? If so, please include in your response letter the names of the parties and the amount claimed.

This inquiry is made in accordance with the Joint Policy Statement of January, 1978, approved by the Canadian Bar Association and the Auditing Standards Committee of the Canadian Institute of Chartered Accountants.

Please address your reply, marked "Privileged and Confidential," to this company and send a signed copy of the reply directly to our auditors, Jeannerette & Cie, Comptables Agrées, 1133 rue Sherbrooke, Montréal, Québec, H3C 1M8.

Yours truly,

Charles D. Peppertree

Charles D. Peppertree, President

c.c. Jeannerette & Cie

Limited or Nonresponses from Law Firms Law firms in recent years have become reluctant to provide certain information to auditors because of their own exposure to legal liability for providing incorrect or confidential information. The nature of the refusal of law firms to provide auditors with complete information about contingent liabilities falls into two categories: the refusal to respond due to a lack of knowledge about matters involving contingent liabilities, and the refusal to disclose information that the lawyer regards as confidential. As an example of the latter, the lawyer might be aware of a violation of a patent agreement that could result in a significant loss to the client if it were known (possible claim). The inclusion of the information in a footnote could actually cause the lawsuit and, therefore, be damaging to the client.

When the nature of the lawyer's legal practice does not involve contingent liabilities, the lawyer's refusal to respond causes no audit problems. It is certainly reasonable for lawyers to refuse to make statements about contingent liabilities when they are not involved with lawsuits or similar aspects of the practice of law that directly affect financial statements.

A serious audit problem does arise, however, when a lawyer refuses to provide information that is within the lawyer's jurisdiction and may directly affect the fair presentation of financial statements. If a lawyer refuses to provide the auditor with information about material existing lawsuits (outstanding claims) or possible claims, *the auditor's report would have to be modified to reflect the lack of available evidence.* The "Joint Policy Statement concerning communications with law firms regarding claims and possible claims in connection with the preparation and audit of financial statements," an appendix to Section 6560 of the *CICA Assurance Handbook*, has the effect of encouraging lawyers to cooperate with auditors in obtaining information about contingencies, as the law firm's confidential relationship with its clients will not be violated. The Joint Policy Statement was approved by the Canadian Bar Association, the Council of the Bermuda Bar Association, and the Auditing Standards Committee (now the Auditing and Assurance Standards Board) of the CICA.

Review for Subsequent Events

The auditor must review transactions and events occurring after the balance sheet date to determine whether anything occurred that might affect the fair presentation or disclosure of the statements being audited. The auditing procedures required by Section 6550 "Subsequent Events" to verify these transactions and events are often referred to as the **review for subsequent events** or *post-balance sheet review.*

The auditor's responsibility for reviewing for subsequent events is normally limited to the period beginning with the balance sheet date and ending with the date of the auditor's report. Since the date of the auditor's report usually corresponds with the completion of the important auditing procedures in the client's office, the subsequent events review should be completed near the end of the engagement. Figure 21-2 shows the period covered by a subsequent events review and the timing of that review.

REVIEW FOR SUBSEQUENT EVENTS—the auditing procedures performed by auditors to identify and evaluate subsequent events

FIGURE 21-2 Period Covered by Subsequent Events Review

- The auditor is responsible for subsequent events occurring between 31/12/04 and 10/4/05.
- Most subsequent events audit procedures are performed between approximately 11/3/05 and 10/4/05.

Types of Subsequent Events Two types of **subsequent events** require consideration by management and evaluation by the auditor: those that have a direct effect on the financial statements and require adjustment and those that have no direct effect on the financial statements but for which disclosure is advisable.

THOSE THAT HAVE A DIRECT EFFECT ON THE FINANCIAL STATEMENTS AND REQUIRE ADJUSTMENT These events or transactions provide additional information to management in determining the valuation of account balances as of the balance sheet date and to auditors in verifying the balances. For example, if the auditor is having difficulty determining the correct valuation of inventory because of obsolescence, the sale of raw material inventory as scrap in the subsequent period should be used as a means of determining the correct valuation of the inventory as of the balance sheet date.

Such subsequent period events as the following require an adjustment of account balances in the current year's financial statements if the amounts are material:

- The declaration of bankruptcy due to the deteriorating financial condition of a customer with an outstanding accounts receivable balance
- The settlement of litigation at an amount different from the amount recorded on the books
- The disposal of equipment not being used in operations at a price below the current book value
- The sale of investments at a price below recorded cost

Whenever subsequent events are used to evaluate the amounts included in the statements, care must be taken to distinguish between conditions that existed at the balance sheet date and those that came into being after the end of the year. The subsequent information should not be incorporated directly into the statements if the conditions causing the change in valuation did not take place until after year end. For example, the sale of scrap in the subsequent period would not be relevant in the valuation of inventory for obsolescence if the obsolescence took place after the end of the year. Also, an amount outstanding from a customer who declared bankruptcy after year end, due to uninsured fire damage to its premises, should not be removed from the accounts receivable balance until the year the damage took place.

THOSE THAT HAVE NO DIRECT EFFECT ON THE FINANCIAL STATEMENTS BUT FOR WHICH DISCLOSURE IS ADVISABLE Subsequent events of this type provide evidence of conditions that did not exist at the date of the balance sheet being reported on but are so significant that they require disclosure even though they do not require adjustment. Ordinarily, these events can be adequately disclosed by the use of footnotes, but occasionally one event may be so significant as to require supplementing the historical statements with statements that include the effect of the event as if it had occurred on the balance sheet date (i.e., *pro forma* statements).

Following are examples of events or transactions occurring in the subsequent period that may require disclosure rather than an adjustment in the financial statements:

- Decline in market value of investments
- Issuance of bonds or shares
- Decline in market value of inventory as a consequence of government action barring further sale of a product
- Uninsured loss of inventories as a result of fire or other disaster
- Purchase of a business or trademark

Audit Tests Audit procedures for the subsequent events review can be conveniently divided into two categories: procedures normally integrated as part of the verification of year-end account balances and those performed specifically for the purpose of discovering events or transactions that must be recognized as subsequent events.

The first category includes cutoff and valuation tests that are done as part of the tests of details of balances. For example, subsequent period sales and acquisition transactions are examined to determine whether the cutoff is accurate. Similarly, many valuation tests involving subsequent events are also performed as part of the verification of account balances. As an example, it is common to test the collectibility of accounts receivable by reviewing subsequent period cash receipts. It is also a normal audit procedure to compare the subsequent period purchase price of inventory with the recorded cost as a test of lower of cost or market valuation. The procedures for cutoff and valuation have been discussed sufficiently in preceding chapters and are not repeated here.

The second category of tests is performed specifically for the purpose of obtaining information that must be incorporated into the current year's account balances or footnotes. These tests include the following:

ENQUIRE OF MANAGEMENT Enquiries vary from client to client but normally are about the existence of potential contingent liabilities or commitments, significant changes in the assets or capital structure of the company, the current status of items that were not completely resolved at the balance sheet date, and the existence of unusual adjustments made subsequent to the balance sheet date.

Enquiries of management about subsequent events must be held with the proper client personnel to obtain meaningful answers. For example, discussing tax or union matters with the accounts receivable supervisor would not be appropriate. Most enquiries should be made of the controller, the vice-presidents, or the president, depending on the information desired.

CORRESPOND WITH LAW FIRMS Correspondence with law firms, which was previously discussed, takes place as part of the search for contingent liabilities. In obtaining confirmation letters from law firms, the auditor must remember his or her responsibility for testing for subsequent events up to the date of the auditor's report. A common approach is to request that the law firm date and mail the letter as of the expected completion date for fieldwork.

REVIEW INTERNAL STATEMENTS PREPARED SUBSEQUENT TO THE BALANCE SHEET DATE The emphasis in the review should be on (1) changes in the business relative to results for the same period in the year under audit and (2) changes after year end. The auditor should pay particular attention to major changes in the business or environment in which the client is operating. The statements should be discussed with management to determine whether they are prepared on the same basis as the current period statements, and there should be enquiries about significant changes in operating results.

REVIEW RECORDS PREPARED SUBSEQUENT TO THE BALANCE SHEET DATE Journals, data files, and ledgers should be reviewed to determine the existence and nature of any transaction related to the current year. If the journals are not kept up to date, the documents relating to the journals should be reviewed.

EXAMINE MINUTES PREPARED SUBSEQUENT TO THE BALANCE SHEET DATE The minutes of shareholders' and directors' meetings subsequent to the balance sheet date must be examined for important subsequent events affecting the current period financial statements.

OBTAIN A LETTER OF REPRESENTATION The letter of representation written by the client to the auditor formalizes statements the client has made about different matters throughout the audit, including discussions about subsequent events.

Dual Dating Chapter 3 discussed dating the auditor's report and introduced the notion of **dual dating**, or *double dating*, from Section 5405 of the *CICA Assurance Handbook*. Occasionally, the auditor determines that an important subsequent event occurred after the fieldwork was completed but before the auditor's report was issued. The source of such information is typically management or the press. An example is the acquisition of another company by the audit client on April 23, when the last day of fieldwork was April 11. In such a situation, section 6550.06 of the *CICA Assurance Handbook* requires the auditor to extend audit tests for the newly discovered subsequent event to ensure that the client has correctly accounted for it (i.e., either adjusted the statements or disclosed the event). The auditor has two equally acceptable options for expanding subsequent event tests: expand the period of all subsequent events tests to the date at which the auditor is satisfied that the newly determined subsequent event is correctly stated, or restrict the review to matters related to the new subsequent event. For the first option, the

DUAL-DATED AUDITOR'S REPORT—the use of one auditor's report date for normal subsequent events and a later date for one or more subsequent events that come to the auditor's attention after the fieldwork has been completed auditor's report date would be changed, whereas for the second, the auditor's report would be *dual dated*. In the previous example of the acquisition, assume that the auditor returned to the client's premises and completed audit tests on April 30 pertaining only to the acquisition. The auditor's report would be dual dated as follows: April 11, 2005, except for note 17, for which the date is April 30, 2005.

→ 21.2   ACCUMULATE FINAL EVIDENCE

The auditor has a few final accumulation responsibilities that apply to all cycles besides the search for contingent liabilities and the review for subsequent events. The four most important ones, as well as management discussion and analysis, are discussed in this section. All four are done late in the engagement.

Final Analytical Procedures Analytical procedures were introduced in Chapter 6 and applied to specific cycles in several chapters. Analytical procedures are normally used as part of planning the audit, during the performance of detailed tests in each cycle as part of substantive procedures, and at the completion of the audit.

Analytical procedures done during the completion of the audit are useful as a final review for material misstatements or financial problems not noted during other testing, and to help the auditor take a final objective look at the financial statements. It is common for a partner to closely review the analytical procedures during the final review of working papers and financial statements. Typically, a partner has a good understanding of the client and its business because of ongoing relationships. Knowledge of the client's business and its business environment combined with effective analytical procedures help identify possible oversights in an audit. Section 5301 requires the auditor to use analytical procedures as part of the completion phase of the audit.

Evaluation of Going Concern Assumption The Commission to Study the Public's Expectation of Audits (Macdonald Commission) suggested in Recommendation 10 that management should disclose in the financial statements if "there is significant danger that [the company] may not be able to continue as [a going concern] throughout the foreseeable future."[1] The implication of this and other recommendations is that the auditor should pay particular attention to the going concern assumption during the audit but especially when performing the final review of the disclosures in the financial statements.

J.E. Boritz, in the CICA research study *The "Going Concern" Assumption: Accounting and Auditing Implications*, suggests, "Auditors, as part of every audit, should independently examine the support for management's implicit or explicit assertion about the validity of the 'going concern' assumption."[2] He also suggests that the auditor should modify the auditor's report to reflect his or her concern about the client's ability to operate when the "degree of doubt" about the validity of the going concern assumption exceeds 50 percent.[3]

U.S. standards (SAS 59) require the auditor to evaluate whether there is a substantial doubt about a client's ability to continue as a going concern for at least one year beyond the balance sheet date. If the auditor concludes that there is substantial doubt, the auditor's report should include an explanatory paragraph following the opinion paragraph to describe that conclusion. International Standard on Auditing 570, "Going Concern," also requires the auditor to consider the appropriateness of the going concern assumption.

It is the conclusion of the authors that the auditor should follow the suggestions with respect to the going concern assumption proposed by Macdonald and Boritz.

---

[1]"50 Ways to Change Our Ways," *CAmagazine* (July 1988), p. 42. The July issue of *CAmagazine* includes several articles dealing with the report of the Commission to Study the Public's Expectations of Audits (Macdonald Commission).

[2]Boritz, J.E., *The "Going Concern" Assumption: Accounting and Auditing Implications*, Toronto: Canadian Institute of Chartered Accountants, 1991, p. xiv, 102–104.

[3]Ibid., pages xiv–xv and 104–106.

Client Representation Letter *CICA Assurance Handbook* section 5370, titled "Management Representations," takes effect for periods beginning on or after August 1, 2005. The section requires that the auditor obtain a written management representation letter from management to confirm information that has been provided to the auditor during the audit engagement. There are four other situations where assurance recommendations discuss the auditor obtaining written representations:

1. Section 5136.21 requires written representation from management regarding awareness or disclosure of illegal acts;
2. Section 6010.27 indicates the auditor should have written disclosure with respect to related party transactions and their disclosure;
3. Section 6550.04 (f) states that the auditor would normally include as part of a subsequent events review, written confirmation from management of any verbal representations; and
4. Section 6560.19 requires written representation from the client that outstanding and possible legal claims have been disclosed.

Section 5370 explains that the **management representation letter** is required to document management's representations (normally oral information) that have been provided during the audit. The client representation letter is prepared on the client's letterhead, addressed to the public accounting firm, and signed by high-level corporate officials, usually the president and chief financial officer.

There are two purposes of the management representation letter:

- *To impress upon management its responsibility for the assertions in the financial statements.* For example, if the letter of representation includes a reference to pledged assets and contingent liabilities, honest management may be reminded of its unintentional failure to disclose the information adequately. To fulfill this objective, the letter of representation should be sufficiently detailed to act as a reminder to management.
- *To document the responses from management to enquiries about various aspects of the audit.* This provides written documentation of client representations in the event of disagreement or a lawsuit between the auditor and the client.

The letter should be dated as of the auditor's report date to make sure there are representations related to the subsequent events review. To prevent surprises, the auditor should discuss the type of representations with the client during the planning of the audit, and as needed throughout the engagement. The letter implies that it has originated with the client, but it is common practice for the auditor to prepare the letter and request the client to type it on the company's letterhead and sign it. Refusal by a client to prepare and sign the letter should probably cause the auditor to consider a qualified opinion or denial of opinion.

Many specific matters should be included, when applicable, in a client representation letter. A few of these follow:

- Management's acknowledgment of its responsibility for the fair presentation in the statements... in conformity with generally accepted accounting principles or [an appropriate disclosed] basis of accounting
- Availability of all financial records and related data
- Completeness and availability of all minutes of meetings of shareholders, directors, and committees of directors
- Information concerning related party transactions and related amounts receivable or payable
- Plans or intentions that may affect the carrying value or classification of assets or liabilities
- Disclosure of compensating balances or other arrangements involving restrictions on cash balances and disclosure of lines of credit or similar arrangements

A client representation letter is a written statement from a non-independent source and therefore *cannot be regarded as reliable evidence.* Accordingly, where possible, the auditor should seek evidence to substantiate management's assertions. The letter does provide minimal evidence that management has been asked certain questions, but its primary purpose is

MANAGEMENT REPRESENTATION LETTER—a written communication from the client to the auditor formalizing statements that the client has made about matters pertinent to the audit

psychological and to protect the auditor from potential claims by management that it was unaware of its responsibilities. There are occasions, though, when written representations may be the only source of audit evidence (for example, management intends to launch a new product line).

Other Information in Annual Reports Section 7500 of the *CICA Assurance Handbook* details the auditor's responsibility for **information in the annual report** of a company. The primary responsibility is to ensure that the financial statements and auditor's report are accurately reproduced in the annual report. If the company's annual report has not been issued, correcting any misstatement is relatively easy; the auditor can simply ask management to correct the misstatement in the report. On the other hand, if the financial statements and annual report have already been issued when the misstatement is discovered, the auditor must be satisfied that management will take "reasonable steps" to notify users about the misstatement. If the auditor is not so satisfied, notice should be given to the board of directors and consideration should be given to what further action should be taken.

The auditor should also read the entire annual report to ascertain if any of the other information in the annual report is inconsistent with the financial statements. For example, assume that the president's letter in the annual report refers to an increase in earnings per share from $2.60 to $2.93. The auditor is required to compare that information to the financial statements to make sure that it corresponds. If an error exists in the financial statements and they have not been issued, the auditor should have them corrected or issue a reservation of opinion; if they have been issued, the auditor should treat the error as a subsequent discovery of a misstatement (Section 5405) and notify management. If it is the annual report that requires revision, the auditor should notify management. If the auditor cannot gain satisfaction from management, including the audit committee and the board of directors, the auditor should consider what further action is warranted.

The auditor has responsibilities beyond searching for misstatements in the financial statements in the annual report or for inconsistencies between the financial statements and other material in the annual report; section 7500.30 requires the auditor to advise management of any material misstatements of fact that are contained in the annual report (or as posted on the company web site or on SEDAR.com). The annual report may include, for instance, information about a fictitious lucrative contract with the company, which would affect the following years' business and profits significantly. If management refuses to correct the misstatements, the auditor should advise the audit committee and the board of directors. If satisfaction is still not obtained by the auditor, further action should be considered.

Management Discussion and Analysis The academic and professional literature include descriptions of research and articles that indicate that users of financial statements and annual reports are interested in an entity's future as well as its past and present. While an entity's financial statements, including the notes to those statements, present information about the entity's financial position and financial history, until recently, there was little information to inform users of expectations of the entity's management for the foreseeable future. In addition, there was a belief that it would be helpful to users if management were to provide a narrative expressing its interpretation of the entity's financial position and operations.

Section 4250, "Future-Oriented Financial Information (FOFI)," was added to the *CICA Accounting Handbook* in 1989 to provide guidance on preparing such information with the financial statements but did not require that FOFI be provided. To date, few companies are providing information under Section 4250. There is an Assurance and Related Services Guideline AuG-6, "Examination of a Financial Forecast or Projection Included in a Prospectus or Other Public Offering Document" that provides guidance on handling FOFI included in a prospectus but does not deal with the auditor's involvement when such information is included in an annual report.

In Canada and the United States, securities regulators, recognizing that there is a limit to the amount of information that can be communicated by the financial statements, including the notes, are requiring companies that borrow money from or sell stock to the public to provide a comment from management in the annual report; the comment would be supplementary to the financial statements and provide information about management's expectations. Such a report has come to be known as **management discussion and analysis** (MD&A).

MD&A is generally required by securities administrators in Canada. For example, the Ontario Securities Commission (OSC) requires most of its larger registrants to provide MD&A in their annual reports and with interim financial statements. There is also a series of prescribed questions that must be answered by management in the MD&A filed with the securities commissions. The general purpose of MD&A is to describe the performance of the company and the risks within which it operates. To assist boards of directors and senior management, the CICA established the Canadian Performance Reporting Board, which authorizes the CICA to publish guidance documents, issue papers, and research reports. An important guidance document issued is titled "Management's Discussion and Analysis: Guidance on Preparation and Disclosure." The guidance provides general disclosure principles, a disclosure framework, and a framework for overseeing the reliability and timeliness of disclosure. The intention is that the guidance be used by management, the board of directors, and the audit committee throughout the financial oversight process.

The auditor's role with respect to MD&A arises from the fact that MD&A is included in the annual report and thus falls under the auditor's review pursuant to Section 7500.

→21.3 EVALUATE RESULTS

After performing all audit procedures in each audit area, the auditor must integrate the results into *one overall conclusion*. Ultimately, the auditor must decide whether sufficient appropriate audit evidence has been accumulated to warrant the conclusion that the financial statements are stated in accordance with generally accepted accounting principles.

Figure 21-3 summarizes the parts of the audit that must be reviewed in the evaluation of results. The emphasis is on the conclusions reached through tests of controls, analytical procedures, and tests of details of balances for each of the five cycles shown in the figure. Five aspects of evaluating the results are discussed below.

Sufficiency of Evidence The final summarization of the adequacy of the evidence is a review by the auditor of the entire audit to determine whether all important aspects have been adequately tested considering the risks of the engagement. A major step in this process is reviewing the audit programs to make sure that all parts have been accurately completed and documented and that all audit objectives have been met. An important part of the review is deciding whether the audit program is adequate considering the problem areas that were discovered as the audit progressed. For example, if misstatements were discovered as part of the tests of sales, the initial plans for the tests of details of accounts receivable balances may have been insufficient. The final review should evaluate whether the revised audit program is adequate.

As an aid in drawing final conclusions about the adequacy of the audit evidence, auditors frequently use **completing the engagement checklists**. These are reminders of aspects of the audit that must not be overlooked. An illustration of part of a completing the engagement checklist is given in Figure 21-4 on page 603.

If the auditor concludes that he or she has *not* obtained sufficient evidence to draw a conclusion about the fairness of the client's representations, there are two choices: additional evidence must be obtained, or either a qualified opinion or a denial of opinion must be issued. The former is the more common choice as a client is not likely to agree to have a qualified auditor's report because of the auditor's failure to do sufficient work.

Evidence Supporting Auditor's Opinion An important part of evaluating whether the financial statements are fairly stated is summarizing the misstatements uncovered in the audit. Whenever the auditor uncovers misstatements that are in themselves material, entries should be proposed to the client to correct the statements. It may be difficult to determine the appropriate amount of adjustment because the true value of the misstatement is unknown; nevertheless, it is the auditor's responsibility to determine the required adjustment. In addition to the material misstatements, there are often a large number of

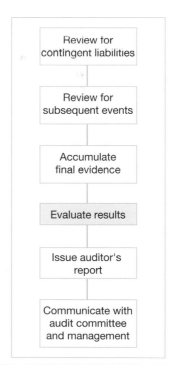

Review for contingent liabilities

Review for subsequent events

Accumulate final evidence

Evaluate results

Issue auditor's report

Communicate with audit committee and management

FIGURE 21-3   **Evaluating Engagement Results**

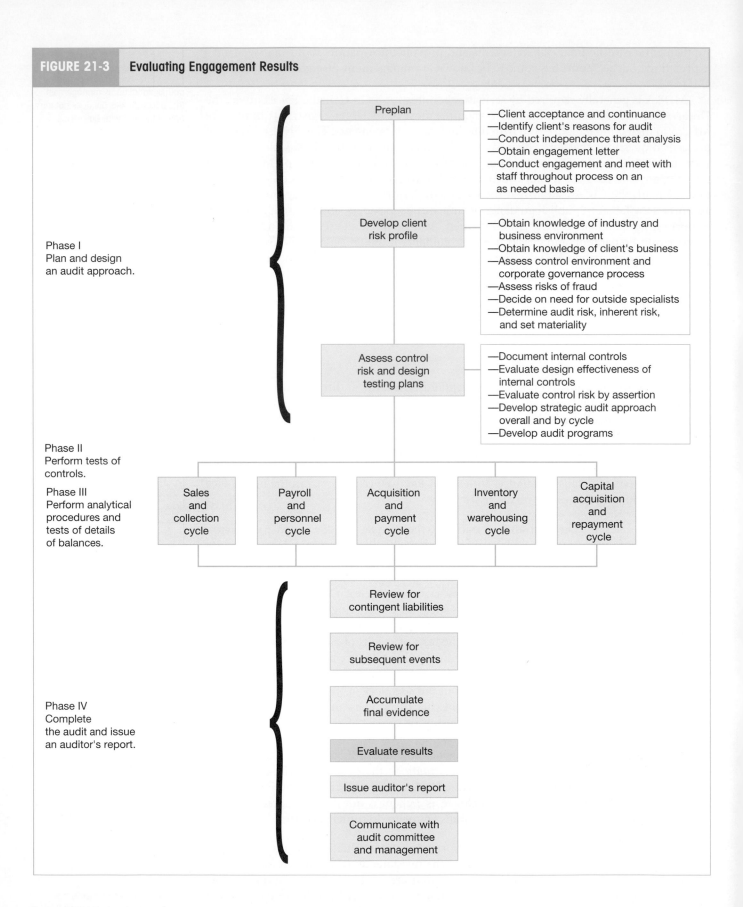

FIGURE 21-4   Completing the Engagement Checklist

	YES	NO	W/P Ref.
1. *Examination of prior year's working papers*			
a. Were last year's working papers and review notes examined for areas of emphasis in the current-year audit?	____	____	____
b. Was the permanent file reviewed for items that affect the current year?	____	____	____
2. *Internal control*			
a. Has internal control been adequately understood and reviewed?	____	____	____
b. Is the scope of the audit adequate in light of the assessed level of control risk?	____	____	____
c. Have all major weaknesses been included in a management letter and material weaknesses in a letter to the audit committee or senior management?	____	____	____
3. *General documents*			
a. Were all current-year minutes and resolutions reviewed, abstracted, and followed up?	____	____	____
b. Has the permanent file been updated?	____	____	____
c. Have all major contracts and agreements been reviewed and abstracted or copied to ascertain that the client complies with all existing legal requirements?	____	____	____

immaterial misstatements discovered that are not adjusted at the time they are found. It is necessary to combine individually immaterial misstatements to evaluate whether the combined amount is material. The auditor can keep track of the misstatements and combine them in several different ways, but many auditors use a convenient method known as an **unadjusted misstatement worksheet** or *summary of possible adjustments*. It is relatively easy to evaluate the overall significance of several immaterial misstatements with this type of working paper.

The auditor should consider carry-forward misstatements from the previous year in analyzing misstatements and the need for adjustment. For example, if closing inventory was understated by $15,000 in 2004 and overstated by $10,000 in 2005, the effect on income in 2005 would be $25,000. Although the individual misstatements may be immaterial, the combined effect might well be material and require adjustment.

If the auditor believes that he or she *has* sufficient evidence but that it does not warrant a conclusion of fairly presented financial statements, the auditor again has two choices: the statements must be revised to the auditor's satisfaction, or either a qualified or an adverse opinion must be issued. Notice that the options here are different from those in the case of obtaining insufficient evidence.

Financial Statement Disclosures A major consideration in completing the audit is determining whether the disclosures in the financial statements are adequate. Throughout the audit, the emphasis in most examinations is on verifying the accuracy of the balances in the general ledger by testing the most important accounts on the auditor's trial balance. Another important task is to ensure that the account balances on the trial balance are correctly aggregated and disclosed on the financial statements. Naturally, adequate disclosure includes consideration of all of the statements including related footnotes.

Review for adequate disclosure in the financial statements at the completion of the audit is not the only time the auditor is interested in proper disclosure. Unless the auditor is constantly alert for disclosure problems, it is impossible to perform the final disclosure review adequately. For example, as part of the examination of accounts receivable, the auditor must be aware of the need to separate accounts receivable, notes receivable, and other amounts due from affiliates and those due from customers. Similarly, there must be a segregation of current from noncurrent receivables and a disclosure of the factoring or discounting of notes receivable if such is the case. An important part of verifying all account balances is determining whether generally accepted accounting principles were properly applied on a basis consistent with that of the preceding year. The auditor must carefully document this information in the working papers to facilitate the final review.

UNADJUSTED MISSTATEMENT WORKSHEET—a summary of immaterial misstatements not adjusted at the time they were found, used to help the auditor assess whether the combined amount is material; also known as a *summary of possible adjustments*

As part of the final review for financial statement disclosure, many public accounting firms require the completion of a **financial statement disclosure checklist** for every engagement. This questionnaire is designed to remind the auditor of common disclosure problems encountered on audits and to facilitate the final review of the entire audit by an independent partner. An illustration of a partial financial statement disclosure checklist is given in Figure 21-5. Naturally, reliance on a checklist should not replace the auditor's own knowledge of generally accepted accounting principles. In any given audit, some aspects of the engagement require much greater expertise in accounting than can be obtained from such a checklist.

Working Paper Review There are three main reasons why it is essential that the working papers be thoroughly reviewed by another member of the audit firm at the completion of the audit:

- *To evaluate the performance of inexperienced personnel.* A considerable portion of most audits is performed by audit personnel with less than four or five years of experience. These people may have sufficient technical training to conduct an adequate audit, but their lack of experience affects their ability to make sound professional judgments in complex situations.
- *To make sure that the audit meets the public accounting firm's standard of performance.* Within any organization, the performance quality of individuals varies considerably, but careful review by top-level personnel in the firm assists in maintaining a uniform quality of auditing.
- *To counteract the bias that frequently enters into the auditor's judgment.* Auditors may attempt to remain objective throughout the audit, but it is easy to lose proper perspective on a long audit when there are complex problems to solve.

Except for a final independent review, which is discussed shortly, the review of the working papers should be conducted by someone who is knowledgeable about the client and the unique circumstances in the audit. Therefore, the initial review of the working papers prepared by any given auditor is normally done by the auditor's immediate supervisor. For example, the least experienced auditor's work is ordinarily reviewed by the audit

FIGURE 21-5	Financial Statement Disclosure Checklist: Property, Plant, and Equipment

	YES	NO	W/P Ref.
1. Are the following disclosures in the financial statements or notes:			
a. Cost for each major category of capital assets?	____	____	____
b. The amount of amortization for the period?	____	____	____
c. Accumulated amortization, including the amount of any write-downs, for each major category of capital assets at the balance sheet date?			
d. The amount of any writedowns during the period?	____	____	____
e. The amortization method used, including the amortization period or rate, for each major category of capital assets including leased assets?	____	____	____
f. The net carrying amount of a capital asset not being amortized because it is under construction or development, or has been removed from service for an extended period?	____		
2. Are the nature, basis of measurement, amount, and related gains and losses of nonmonetary transactions disclosed?	____	____	____
3. Has consideration been given to disclosure of fully amortized capital assets still in use?	____	____	____
4. Are carrying amounts of property mortgaged and encumbered by indebtedness disclosed?	____	____	____
5. Is the carrying amount of property that is not a part of operations and is idle or held for investment or sale segregated?	____	____	____

senior; the senior's immediate supervisor, who is normally a supervisor or manager, reviews the senior's work and also reviews less thoroughly the papers of the inexperienced auditor. When several staff are working together at an engagement, team review by means of interview is used. The senior meets with staff on a daily basis, discusses the nature of findings, and ensures that these are appropriately recorded in the electronic working papers before the actual client documents are returned to the client. Finally, the partner assigned to the audit must ultimately review all working papers, but the partner reviews those prepared by the supervisor or manager more thoroughly than the others. Except for the final independent review, most of the **working paper review** is done as each segment of the audit is completed.

WORKING PAPER REVIEW—a review of the completed audit working papers by another member of the audit firm to ensure quality and counteract bias

Independent Review At the completion of larger audits, the financial statements and the entire set of working papers are often reviewed by a completely **independent reviewer** who has not participated in the engagement. This reviewer, usually a partner, frequently takes an adversarial position to ensure the adequacy of the conduct of the audit. The audit team must be able to justify the evidence they have accumulated and the conclusions they have reached on the basis of the unique circumstances of the engagement.

INDEPENDENT REVIEW—a review of the financial statements and the entire set of working papers by a completely independent reviewer to whom the audit team must justify the evidence accumulated and the conclusions reached

Summary of Evidence Evaluation Figure 21-6 summarizes the evaluation of the sufficiency of the evidence and the decision as to whether the evidence supports the opinion. The top portion of the figure shows the planning decisions that determine the planned audit evidence. It was taken from Figure 8-6 on page 236. The bottom portion shows how the auditor evaluates the sufficiency of the actual evidence by first evaluating whether the evidence gathered using substantive procedures was adequate to achieve the audit risk set for the audit given the auditor's assessment of inherent risk and control risk for the account and cycle and then making the same evaluation for the overall financial statements. The auditor also evaluates whether the evidence supports the audit opinion by first estimating misstatements in each account and then for the overall financial statements. In practice, both sets of evaluations are made at the same time. On the basis of these evaluations, the auditor's report is issued for the financial statements.

→ 21.4 AUDITOR COMMUNICATIONS AND SUBSEQUENT FACTS

Communicate with the Audit Committee and Management

After the audit is completed, there are several potential communications from the auditor to client personnel. Most of these are directed to the audit committee or senior management, but communications with operating management are also common. Section 5750, "Communication with Management of Matters Identified During the Financial Statement Audit," and Section 5751, "Communications with Those Having Oversight Responsibility for the Financial Reporting Process," are the framework sections for reporting matters discovered during the course of the audit.

Communicate Misstatements and Illegal Acts Section 5135 of the *CICA Assurance Handbook* requires the auditor to ensure that the appropriate level of management is informed of existing misstatements that are other than trivial. In addition, the auditor must ensure that the audit committee or similarly designated group (e.g., board of directors, board of trustees) is informed of all significant misstatements, whether or not they are adjusted. Misstatements include intentional (fraud or other irregularities) or unintentional (errors) misstatements. The audit committee can be informed by either the auditor or management, and this should be done on a timely basis. This requirement indicates the increased concern over the auditor's responsibility for the detection and prevention of misstatements.

Illegal acts are violations of laws or government regulations. Section 5136 requires the auditor to communicate illegal or possibly illegal acts, such as noncompliance with waste disposal regulations, to the audit committee or equivalent group on a timely basis. The audit committee may also expect the auditor to communicate such matters as unusual actions that increase the risk of loss to the company; actions that could cause serious embarrassment to the entity, such as breaches of the company's code of conduct; significant transactions that appear to be inconsistent with the ordinary course of business; or other matters. The audit committee's wishes should be discussed and clarified with the audit committee prior to the auditor's undertaking of the audit fieldwork.

Communicate Reportable Internal Control Conditions As discussed in Chapter 5, Section 5135 includes misstatements that indicate significant deficiencies in the design or operation of internal control in its definition of significant misstatements that must be reported to the audit committee. Although the auditor has no duty to report less significant internal control weaknesses identified during the audit to the client, he or she commonly does so as a client service. In addition, some auditors provide suggestions for improvements in internal control. In larger companies, this communication is made to the audit committee, and in smaller companies, to the owners or senior management. The nature and form of this communication were discussed in Chapter 9. The auditor is required to report to both management and the audit committee any weakness in internal control that could lead to material errors.

Other Communication with Audit Committee The auditor should communicate certain additional information obtained during the audit for audits where there is an audit committee or similarly designated body. Like all communications with the audit committee, the purpose is to keep the committee informed of auditing issues and findings that will assist it in performing its supervisory role for financial statements.

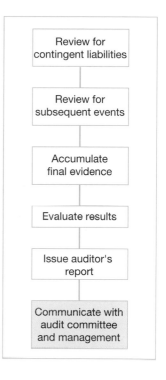

Audit committees were introduced in Chapter 2. The audit committee has an important oversight role for many companies. The following are issues that should be discussed or communicated with the audit committee, or a similarly designated body, by the auditor with the intent of keeping the audit committee informed:

- The auditor's responsibilities under generally accepted auditing standards, including responsibility for understanding and evaluating internal control and the concept of reasonable rather than absolute assurance
- Confirmation of the auditor's independence, including a breakdown of the fees billed between audit and other services, and a disclosure of any relationships between the auditor and the client (or its related entities or directors, officers, or employees)
- Planning of the current audit, including such matters as the general approach, areas of perceived high risk, materiality and risk levels selected, planned reliance on other auditors (including the internal audit department), and timing of the audit
- The significant accounting principles and policies selected and applied to the financial statements, the existence of acceptable alternatives, and the acceptability of those selected by management
- Management's judgments and estimates of sensitive accounting-related issues and the auditor's conclusions about the reasonableness of them
- Disagreements with management about the scope of the audit, applicability of accounting principles, and wording of the auditor's report, whether or not satisfactorily resolved
- Difficulties encountered in performing the audit, such as lack of availability of client personnel, failure to obtain necessary information, and an unreasonable timetable in which to complete the audit
- Any unresolved matters arising from review of the entire annual report and identification of misstatements in reproducing the financial statements or the auditor's report, or of inconsistencies between the statements and other information in the report
- If the auditor becomes aware of any consultation with other accountants about accounting or auditing matters, the auditor's opinions about the subjects of these consultations
- Any major issues discussed with management in connection with the appointment of the auditor, including those related to the application of accounting principles, auditing standards, and fees

Communication with the audit committee normally takes place more than once during each audit and can be oral, written, or both, although certain communications, such as the independence letter and possible material misstatements, must be in writing. For example, issues dealing with the auditor's responsibilities and significant accounting policies are usually discussed early in the audit, preferably during the planning phase. Disagreements with management and difficulties encountered in performing the audit would be communicated after the audit is completed or earlier if the problems hinder the auditor's ability to complete the audit. The most important matters are communicated in writing to minimize misunderstanding and to provide documentation in the event of subsequent disagreement.

Management Letters The purpose of a management letter (letter of recommendation) is to inform the client of the public accountant's recommendations for improving the client's business. The recommendations focus on suggestions for more efficient operations. The combination of the auditor's experience in various businesses and a thorough understanding gained in conducting the audit place the auditor in a unique position to provide management with assistance.

A management letter is different from a required communication on matters related to internal control discussed in Chapter 9. The latter is required whenever there are significant internal control weaknesses. A management letter is optional and is intended to help the client operate its business more effectively. Auditors write management letters for two reasons: to encourage a better relationship between the public accounting firm and management and to suggest additional tax and management advisory services that the public accounting firm can provide.

There is no standard format or approach for writing management letters. Each letter should be developed to meet the style of the auditor and the needs of the client, consistent with the public accounting firm's concept of management letters. It should be noted that many auditors combine the management letter with the required communication on internal control-related matters.

Subsequent Discovery of Facts[4]

If the auditor becomes aware *after the audited financial statements have been released* that some information included in the statements is materially misleading, the auditor has an obligation under Section 5405 of the *CICA Assurance Handbook* to make certain that users who are relying on the financial statements are informed about the misstatements.

The *CICA Assurance Handbook* requires the auditor first to discuss the matter with management and, if required or appropriate, with the board of directors or the audit committee. The auditor also has an obligation, under the *Canada Business Corporations Act* (Section 171(7)) to notify each of the directors. The directors are required to prepare and issue revised financial statements or otherwise inform the shareholders. The directors must also inform the director of the Corporations Branch of the Department of Consumer and Corporate Affairs and may have to inform other regulatory agencies.

If a director or officer discovers a misstatement of any size, he or she is required to notify the audit committee *and* the auditor. The responsibilities of the former are not specified, but presumably the director would notify his fellow directors. The auditor would first decide if the misstatement is material and, if so, notify each director.

The most likely case in which the auditor is faced with this problem occurs when the financial statements are determined to include a material misstatement subsequent to the issuance of an unqualified report. Possible causes of misstatements are the inclusion of material fictitious sales, the failure to write off obsolete inventory, or the omission of an essential footnote. Regardless of whether the failure to discover the misstatement was the fault of the auditor or the client, the auditor's responsibility remains the same.

The most desirable approach to follow if the auditor discovers that the statements are misleading is to request that the client issue an immediate revision of the financial statements containing an explanation of the reasons for the revision. The auditor may decide, after consideration of the misstatement, to revise the financial statements and issue a double dated auditor's report with respect to the misstatement. On the other hand, the auditor may decide that further work is required and a new auditor's report, with the current date, is necessary. The auditor's report, in any event, should clearly indicate that the previous statements were withdrawn and that they have been revised. This information would normally be in a paragraph following the opinion paragraph. If a subsequent period's financial statements were completed before the revised statements could be issued, it is acceptable to disclose the misstatements in the subsequent period's statements.

---

[4]The discussion in this section is more closely related to the auditor's report, which is the subject of Chapter 3, than it is to completing the audit. However, many students of auditing confuse the examination of subsequent period events as a part of post-balance sheet review with the subsequent discovery of facts existing at the balance sheet date. The latter is studied at this point to eliminate the confusion.

If the client refuses to cooperate in disclosing the misstated information, the auditor should inform the board of directors of this fact. In addition, the auditor should seek legal advice as to what he or she should do to discharge his or her responsibilities and consider resigning from the engagement.

It is important to understand that the subsequent discovery of facts requiring the recall or re-issuance of financial statements *does not arise from developments occurring after the date of the auditor's report*. For example, if an auditor believes that an accounts receivable is collectible after an adequate review of the facts at the date of the auditor's report but the customer subsequently files for bankruptcy, a revision of the financial statements is not required. The statements must be recalled or re-issued only when information that would indicate that the statements were not fairly presented *already existed at the auditor's report date*. If, in the previous example, the customer had filed for bankruptcy before the audit report date, there would be a subsequent discovery of facts.

In an earlier section, it was shown that the auditor's responsibility for subsequent events review begins on the balance sheet date and ends on the date of the completion of the fieldwork. Any pertinent information discovered as part of the review can be incorporated in the financial statements before they are issued. Note that the auditor has no responsibility to search for subsequent facts of the nature discussed in this section, but if the auditor discovers that issued financial statements are improperly stated, he or she must take action to correct them. The auditor's responsibility for reporting on improperly issued financial statements does not start until the date of the auditor's report. Typically, an existing material misstatement is found as part of the subsequent year's audit, or it may be reported to the auditor by the client.

Figure 21-7 shows the difference in the period covered by the review for subsequent events and that for the discovery of facts after the auditor's report date. If the auditor discovers subsequent facts after the audit report date, but before the financial statements are issued, he or she would require that the financial statements be revised before they are issued.

| FIGURE 21-7 | Review for Subsequent Events and Subsequent Discovery of Facts |

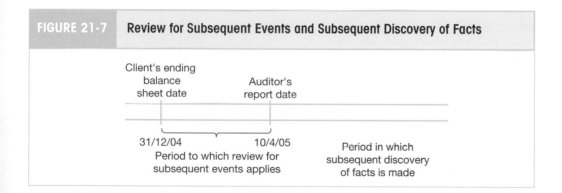

SUMMARY

1. *How does the auditor search for contingent liabilities?* Toward the end of the engagement, it is called a "review" for contingent liabilities, since each cycle has procedures that are intended to search for contingent liabilities (e.g., review of bank confirmations). At this stage, the auditor conducts final enquiries with management, reviews the working papers for comments about tax assessments, directors' and shareholders' meetings, and legal expenses and ensures that legal documents such as contracts have been examined. Legal letters (discussed as follows) are reviewed for the responses received.

   What is the purpose of obtaining a confirmation from the client's law firms? These confirmations are used to evaluate known litigation or other claims against clients for potential contingent liabilities.

   Why must these "legal letters" be in a specified format? In order to protect their client's confidentiality, lawyers indicate whether they agree or disagree with the information that is provided by the client, in a format that has been approved by Bar Associations and the CICA.

   Describe examples of procedures conducted during a review for subsequent events. Testing is done in each transaction cycle (e.g., during cutoff testing of documents). Other procedures include procedures listed in (1) above. In addition, the auditor reviews internal financial statements or budgets completed after the year end and reviews minutes and records prepared after the balance sheet date.

2. *Provide examples of work completed as part of the final evidence gathering process.* The auditor will calculate final analytical procedures and again evaluate the going concern assumption. The client will be asked to prepare and sign a representation letter. The auditor will review information that management plans to include in the annual report and the management discussion and analysis.

3. *What does the auditor do to evaluate the adequacy of accumulated evidence?* Figure 21-3 reiterates the many steps and phases of the audit process. The partner and the engagement review team, in consultation with the audit team, will review the quality and sufficiency of evidence for all cycles, assertions, and end of engagement processes in the context of audit risk and the client risk profile.

4. *What communications is the auditor required to send after the completion of the audit?* The following communications are sent throughout the engagement (they could be sent throughout the engagement, or on a timely basis after the engagement is completed): any reportable internal controls that could lead to material weaknesses, management letter, and independence letter. In addition, any other matters that need to be communicated, such as suspicion of fraud or illegal acts, would also be sent.

What can the auditor do if a misstatement is discovered after the audit report is issued? If a subsequent material misstatement is discovered, it is management's responsibility to adjust the financial statements. The auditor may need to contact the director(s), the audit committee, or regulatory agencies. The auditor's report will need to be revised to state that the previous financial statements have been withdrawn and that they have been revised.

CICA ASSURANCE HANDBOOK SECTIONS REFERENCED IN THIS CHAPTER

Section 5135 – The auditor's responsibility to consider fraud.
Section 5136 – Misstatements—illegal acts.
Section 5301 – Analysis.
Section 5370 – Management representations.
Section 5405 – Date of the auditor's report.
Section 5750 – Communication with management of matters identified during the financial statement audit.
Section 5751 – Communications with those having oversight responsibility for the financial reporting process.

Section 6010 – Audit of related party transactions.
Section 6550 – Subsequent events.
Section 6560 – Communications with law firms regarding claims and possible claims.
Section 7500 – Auditor association with annual reports, interim reports and other public documents.
AuG-6 – Examination of a financial forecast or projection included in a prospectus or other public offering document.

ESSENTIAL TERMS

Commitments—agreements that the entity will hold to a fixed set of conditions, such as the purchase or sale of merchandise at a stated price, at a future date, regardless of what happens to profits or to the economy as a whole (p. 592).

Completing the engagement checklist—a reminder to the auditor of aspects of the audit that may have been overlooked (p. 601).

Contingent liability—a potential future obligation to an outside party for an unknown amount resulting from activities that have already taken place (p. 590).

Dual-dated auditor's report—the use of one auditor's report date for normal subsequent events and a later date for one or more subsequent events that come to the auditor's attention after the fieldwork has been completed (p. 597).

Enquiry of the client's law firms—a letter from the client's legal counsel informing the auditor of pending litigation or any other information involving legal counsel that is relevant to financial statement disclosure (p. 592).

Financial statement disclosure checklist—a questionnaire that reminds the auditor of disclosure problems commonly encountered in audits and that facilitates the final review of the entire audit by an independent partner (p. 604).

Independent review—a review of the financial statements and the entire set of working papers by a completely independent

reviewer to whom the audit team must justify the evidence accumulated and the conclusions reached (p. 605).

Management discussion and analysis (MD&A)—supplemental analysis and explanation by management that accompanies but does not form part of the financial statements (p. 601).

Management representation letter—a written communication from the client to the auditor formalizing statements that the client has made about matters pertinent to the audit (p. 599).

Other information in annual reports—information that is not a part of published financial statements but is published with them; must be read by auditors for inconsistencies with the financial statements and misleading information (p. 600).

Outstanding claim—a lawsuit that has been brought against a client; also known as an *asserted claim* (p. 592).

Possible claim—*see* unasserted claim.

Review for subsequent events—the auditing procedures performed by auditors to identify and evaluate subsequent events (p. 595).

Subsequent events—transactions and other pertinent events that occurred after the balance sheet date that affect the fair presentation or disclosure of the statements being audited (p. 596).

Unadjusted misstatement worksheet—a summary of immaterial misstatements not adjusted at the time they were found, used to help the auditor assess whether the combined amount is material; also known as a *summary of possible adjustments* (p. 603).

Unasserted claim—a potential legal claim against a client where the condition for a claim exists but no claim has been filed (p. 593).

Working paper review—a review of the completed audit working papers by another member of the audit firm to ensure quality and counteract bias (p. 605).

REVIEW QUESTIONS

21-1 Distinguish between a contingent liability and an actual liability, and give three examples of each.

21-2 In the audit of James Mobley Ltd., you are concerned about the possibility of contingent liabilities resulting in income tax disputes. Discuss the procedures you could use for an extensive investigation in this area.

21-3 Explain why the analysis of legal expense is an essential part of every audit engagement.

21-4 During the audit of Merrill Manufacturing Corp., Ralph Pyson, a public accountant, has become aware of four lawsuits against the client through discussions with the client, reading corporate minutes, and reviewing correspondence files. How should Pyson determine the materiality of the lawsuits and the proper disclosure in the financial statements?

21-5 Describe the action that an auditor should take if a law firm refuses to provide information that is within its jurisdiction and may directly affect the fair presentation of the financial statements.

21-6 Distinguish between subsequent events requiring adjustment and those requiring disclosure. Give two examples of each type.

21-7 In obtaining confirmations from law firms, Betty Chui's aim is to receive the confirmation letters as early as possible after the balance sheet date. This provides her with a signed letter from every law firm in time to investigate properly any exceptions. It also eliminates the problem of a lot of unresolved loose ends near the end of the audit. Evaluate Chui's approach.

21-8 Explain why an auditor would be interested in a client's future commitments to purchase raw materials at a fixed price.

21-9 What major considerations should the auditor take into account in determining how extensive the review of subsequent events should be?

21-10 Distinguish between subsequent events occurring between the balance sheet date and the date of the auditor's report, and subsequent discovery of facts existing at the date of the auditor's report. Give two examples of each, and explain the appropriate action by the auditor in each instance.

21-11 Compare and contrast the accumulation of audit evidence and the evaluation of the adequacy of the disclosures in the financial statements. Give two examples in which adequate disclosure could depend heavily on the accumulation of evidence and two others in which audit evidence does not normally affect the adequacy of the disclosure significantly.

21-12 Explain the meaning of the following: The auditor should actively evaluate whether there is substantial doubt about the client's ability to continue as a going concern.

21-13 Distinguish between a management representation letter and a management letter, and state the primary purpose of each. List some items that might be included in each letter.

21-14 What is meant by "reading other financial information" in annual reports? Give an example of the type of information that the auditor would be examining.

21-15 Explain why you think securities regulators in certain jurisdictions require public companies to provide MD&A in their annual reports.

21-16 Distinguish between regular working-paper review and independent review, and state the purpose of each. Give two examples of important potential findings in each of these two types of review.

MULTIPLE CHOICE QUESTIONS

21-17 Choose the best response for the following questions:

a. The audit step most likely to reveal the existence of contingent liabilities is

(1) accounts payable confirmations.
(2) an enquiry directed to law firms.
(3) mortgage-note confirmation.
(4) a review of vouchers paid during the month following the year end.

b. A purpose of the management representation letter is to

(1) serve as an introduction to company personnel and an authorization to examine the records.
(2) remind management of its primary responsibility for financial statements.
(3) discharge the auditor from legal liability for his or her examination.
(4) confirm in writing management's approval of limitations on the scope of the audit.

(AICPA adapted)

c. An example of an event occurring in the period of the auditor's fieldwork subsequent to the end of the year being audited that normally would not require disclosure in the financial statements or the auditor's report would be

   (1) issuance of a widely advertised capital stock issue with restrictive covenants.
   (2) decreased sales volume resulting from a general business recession.
   (3) serious damage to the company's plant from a widespread flood.
   (4) settlement of a large liability for considerably less than the amount recorded.

d. With respect to issuance of an auditor's report that is dual dated for a subsequent event occurring after the completion of fieldwork but before issuance of the auditor's report, the auditor's responsibility for events occurring subsequent to the completion of fieldwork is

   (1) limited to the specific event referred to in the auditor's report.
   (2) limited to all events occurring up to the date of issuance of the report.
   (3) extended to include all events occurring until the date of the last subsequent event referred to in the auditor's report.
   (4) extended to include all events occurring up to the date of submission of the report to the client.

e. Shona Karr has examined the financial statements of Lurch Corporation for the year ended December 31, 2004. Although Karr's fieldwork was completed on February 27, 2005, Karr's auditor's report was dated February 28, 2005, and was received by the management of Lurch on March 5, 2005. On April 4, 2005, the management of Lurch asked that Karr approve inclusion of this report in its annual report to shareholders, which will include unaudited financial statements for the first quarter ended March 31, 2005. Karr approved the inclusion of this auditor's report in the annual report to shareholders. Under the circumstances, Karr is responsible for enquiring as to subsequent events occurring through

   (1) February 27, 2005.
   (2) February 28, 2005.
   (3) March 31, 2005.
   (4) April 4, 2005.

(AICPA adapted)

DISCUSSION QUESTIONS AND PROBLEMS

21-18 Kathy Choi, a public accountant, has completed the audit of notes payable and other liabilities for Valley River Electrical Services Ltd. and now plans to audit contingent liabilities and commitments.

Required

a. Distinguish between contingent liabilities and commitments, and explain why both are important in an audit.

b. Identify three useful audit procedures for uncovering contingent liabilities that Choi would likely perform in the normal conduct of the audit even if she had no responsibility for uncovering contingencies.

c. Identify three other procedures Choi would likely perform specifically for the purpose of identifying undisclosed contingencies.

21-19 In an examination of Marco Corporation as of December 31, 2004, the following situations exist. No related entries have been made in the accounting records.

1. Marco Corporation has guaranteed the payment of interest on the 10-year, first mortgage bonds of Chen Corp., an affiliate. Outstanding bonds of Chen Corp. amount to $150,000 with interest payable at 8 percent per annum, due June 1 and December 1 each year. The bonds were issued by Chen on December 31, 2002, and all interest payments have been met by that company with the exception of the payment due December 1, 2004. Marco Corporation states that it will pay the defaulted interest to the bondholders on January 15, 2005.

2. During the year 2004, Marco Corporation was named as a defendant in a suit for damages by Dalton Inc. for breach of contract. A decision adverse to Marco Corporation was rendered, and Dalton Inc. was awarded $40,000 in damages. At the time of the audit, the case was under appeal to a higher court.

3. On December 23, 2004, Marco Corporation declared a common share dividend of 1,000 shares with a stated value of $100,000 of its common shares, payable February 2, 2005, to the common shareholders of record on December 30, 2004.

Required

a. Describe the audit procedures that you would use to learn about each of the above situations.

b. Describe the nature of the adjusting entries or disclosure, if any, that you would require for each of these situations.

(AICPA adapted)

21-20 The fieldwork for the June 30, 2004, audit of Tracy Brewing Ltd. was finished August 19, 2004, and the completed financial statements, accompanied by the signed auditor's reports, were mailed September 6, 2004. In each of the highly material events (a through i), state the appropriate action (1 through 4) for the situation, and justify your response. Possible actions are as follows:

1. Adjust the June 30, 2004, financial statements.
2. Disclose the information in a footnote in the June 30, 2004, financial statements.

3. Request the client to recall the June 30, 2004, statements for revision.
4. No action is required.

The events are as follows:

a. On December 14, 2004, the auditor discovered that a debtor of Tracy Brewing went bankrupt on October 2, 2004. The sale of goods took place April 15, 2004, but the amount appeared to be collectible on June 30, 2004, and August 19, 2004.

b. On August 15, 2004, the auditor discovered that a debtor of Tracy Brewing went bankrupt on August 1, 2004. The most recent sale had taken place April 2, 2003, and no cash receipts had been received since that date.

c. On December 14, 2004, the auditor discovered that a debtor of Tracy Brewing went bankrupt on July 15, 2004, due to declining financial health. The sale of goods had taken place January 15, 2004.

d. On August 6, 2004, the auditor discovered that a debtor of Tracy Brewing went bankrupt on July 30, 2004. The cause of the bankruptcy was an unexpected loss of a major lawsuit on July 15, 2004, resulting from a product deficiency suit by a different customer.

e. On August 6, 2004, the auditor discovered that a debtor of Tracy Brewing went bankrupt on July 30, 2004, for a sale that took place on July 3, 2004. The cause of the bankruptcy was a major uninsured fire on July 20, 2004.

f. On May 31, 2004, the auditor discovered an uninsured lawsuit against Tracy Brewing that had originated on February 28, 2004.

g. On July 20, 2004, Tracy Brewing settled a lawsuit out of court that had originated in 2001 and is currently listed as a contingent liability.

h. On September 14, 2004, Tracy Brewing lost a court case that had originated in 2001 for an amount equal to the lawsuit. The June 30, 2004, footnotes state that, in the opinion of legal counsel, there will be a favourable settlement.

i. On July 20, 2004, a lawsuit was filed against Tracy Brewing for a patent infringement action that allegedly took place in early 2004. In the opinion of legal counsel, there is a danger of a significant loss to the client.

21-21 Melanie Adams is a partner in a medium-sized public accounting firm and takes an active part in the conduct of every audit she supervises. She follows the practice of reviewing all working papers of subordinates as soon as it is convenient, rather than waiting until the end of the audit.

When the audit is nearly finished, Adams reviews the working papers again to make sure she has not missed anything significant. Since she makes most of the major decisions on the audit, there is rarely anything that requires further investigation. When she completes the review, she prepares a draft of the financial statements, gets them approved by management, and has them assembled in her firm's office. No other partner reviews the working papers because Adams is responsible for signing the auditor's reports.

Required

a. Evaluate the practice of reviewing the working papers of subordinates on a continuing basis rather than when the audit is completed.

b. Is it acceptable for Adams to prepare the financial statements rather than make the client assume the responsibility?

c. Evaluate the practice of not having a review of the working papers by another partner in the firm.

21-22 Ruben Chavez, public accountant, has prepared a management representation letter for the president and controller to sign. It contains references to the following items:

1. Inventory is fairly stated at the lower of cost or market and includes no obsolete items.
2. All actual and contingent liabilities are properly included in the statements.
3. All subsequent events of relevance to the financial statements have been disclosed.

Required

a. Why is it desirable to have a letter of representation from the client concerning the above matters when the audit evidence accumulated during the course of the engagement is meant to verify the same information?

b. To what extent is the letter of representation useful as audit evidence? Explain.

c. List several other types of information commonly included in a letter of representation.

21-23 In connection with your examination of the financial statements of Olars Mfg. Corporation for the year ended December 31, 2004, your review of subsequent events disclosed the following items:

1. January 3, 2005: The provincial government approved a plan for the construction of an express highway. The plan will result in the expropriation of a portion of land owned by Olars Mfg. Corporation. Construction will begin in late 2005. No estimate of the condemnation (expropriation) award is available.

2. January 4, 2005: The funds for a $25,000 loan to the corporation made by Mr. Olars, the president, on July 15, 2004, were obtained by him by a loan on his personal life insurance policy. The loan was recorded in the account "loan from officers." Mr. Olars' source of the funds was not disclosed in the company records. The corporation pays the premiums on the life insurance policy, and Mrs. Olars, wife of the president, is the beneficiary.

3. January 7, 2005: The mineral content of a shipment of ore, which was en route on December 31, 2004, was determined to be 72 percent. The shipment was recorded at year end at an estimated content of 50 percent by a debit to raw material inventory and a credit to accounts

payable in the amount of $20,600. The final liability to the vendor is based on the actual mineral content of the shipment.

4. January 15, 2005: As a result of a series of personal disagreements between Mr. Olars and his brother-in-law, the treasurer, the latter resigned, effective immediately, under an agreement whereby the corporation would purchase his 10 percent stock ownership at book value as of December 31, 2004. Payment is to be made in two equal amounts in cash on April 1, 2005, and October 1, 2005. In December 2004, the treasurer obtained a divorce from his wife, who was Mr. Olars' sister.

5. January 31, 2005: As a result of reduced sales, production was curtailed in mid-January and some workers were laid off. On February 5, 2005, all the remaining workers went on strike. To date, the strike is unsettled.

6. February 10, 2005: A contract was signed whereby Mammoth Enterprises purchases from Olars Mfg. Corporation all of the latter's capital assets (including rights to receive the proceeds of any property condemnation), inventories, and the right to conduct business under the name "Olars Mfg. Division." The effective date of the transfer will be March 1, 2005. The sale price was

$500,000, subject to adjustment following the taking of a physical inventory. Important factors contributing to the decision to enter into the contract were the policy of the board of directors of Mammoth Enterprises to diversify the firm's activities and the report of a survey conducted by an independent market appraisal firm that revealed a declining market for Olars products.

Required

Assume that the items described came to your attention prior to completion of your audit work on February 15, 2005. For *each* item:

a. Give the audit procedures, if any, that would have brought the item to your attention. Indicate other sources of information that may have revealed the item.

b. Discuss the disclosure that you would recommend for the item, listing all details that you would suggest should be disclosed. Indicate those items or details, if any, that should not be disclosed. Give your reasons for recommending or not recommending disclosure of the items or details.

(AICPA adapted)

21-24 In a letter to the audit committee of Cline Wholesale Company, Jerry Schwartz, PA, informed them of weaknesses in the control of inventory. In a separate letter to senior management, he elaborated on how the weaknesses could result in a significant misstatement of inventory by the failure to recognize the existence of obsolete items. In addition, Schwartz made specific recommendations in the management letter on how to improve internal control and save clerical time by installing a computer system for the company's perpetual records. Management accepted the recommendations and installed the system under Schwartz's direction. For several months, the system worked beautifully, but unforeseen problems developed when a master file was erased. The cost of reproducing and processing the

inventory records to correct the error was significant, and management decided to scrap the entire project. The company sued Schwartz for failure to use adequate professional judgment in making the recommendations.

Required

a. What is Schwartz's legal and professional responsibility in the issuance of management letters?

b. Discuss the major considerations that will determine whether he is liable in this situation.

c. Did Schwartz abide by the Professional Rules of Conduct? Explain your reasoning.

21-25 In analyzing legal expense for Boastman Bottle Company, Bart Little, public accountant, observes that the company has paid legal fees to three different law firms during the current year. In accordance with his accounting firm's normal operating practice, Little requests standard confirmation letters as of the balance sheet date from each of the three law firms.

On the last day of fieldwork, Little notes that one of the confirmations has not yet been received. The confirmation from the second law firm contains a statement to the effect that the law firm deals exclusively in registering patents and refuses to com-

ment on any lawsuits or other legal affairs of the client. The confirmation letter from the third law firm states that there is an outstanding unpaid bill due from the client and recognizes the existence of a potentially material lawsuit against the client but refuses to comment further to protect the legal rights of the client.

Required

a. Evaluate Little's approach to requesting the confirmations and his follow-up on the responses.

b. What should Little do about each of the confirmations?

21-26 Betty Ann Jarrett, CA, was reading the annual report of Watgold Ltd. and noticed that the president's report contradicted several items in the audited financial statements included in the report.

Required

What are Betty Ann's responsibilities in this instance?

21-27 You are a partner in the public accounting firm of Lind and Hemming. One of your larger clients is Yukon Corp., a company incorporated under the *Canada Business Corporations Act*,

which has a December 31 year end. Yukon's 2004 audit was completed in January 2005; the auditor's report was dated January 28, 2005.

It is now August 2005 and professional staff from your office are working at Yukon doing interim work on the December 31, 2005, audit. Yesterday, the senior in charge of the audit gave you a memo dated August 4, 2005, revealing that the staff have discovered that several large blocks of inventory were materially overpriced at December 31, 2004, and have since been written down to reflect their true value.

You have just finished reviewing again the 2004 working papers and have determined that the error was a sampling error; your firm does not appear to have been negligent.

Required

What action would you take and why? Support your answer.

PROFESSIONAL JUDGMENT PROBLEM

21-28 You are in charge of the audit fieldwork of a multinational public company with subsidiaries in Europe, Asia, and South America, which has expanded very rapidly over the last few years. Your firm has recognized that public accounting firms perform audit examinations in those countries in which subsidiaries are located. The following paragraphs are extracted from a letter received from one of these public accounting firms just prior to the issuance of your audit opinion on the consolidated financial statements. As in past years, your planned audit opinion contained no qualifications. The subsidiary audited by the public accounting firm that sent you the letter accounts for approximately 20 percent of consolidated sales, net income, and assets.

> Our review of cash expenditures revealed a number of payments to senior government officials amounting to approximately 50 percent of net income before taxes. These payments have been recorded as promotional expenses. We were unable to obtain documentary evidence to support the nature of these payments, but client management personnel claim that these payments were necessary in order to obtain government approval for some client sales contracts. We were informed that these payments represent donations to political campaign funds.

> Although we have no direct evidence, we believe that these payments have been instrumental in obtaining a number of very profitable contracts that contributed over 50 percent of sales.

> Finally, our discussions with client personnel, all of whom are citizens of this country, lead us to believe that they took it upon themselves to authorize these payments. We found no evidence to suggest that the payments were made known in advance to head office management. However, we cannot state whether head office management was subsequently informed of these payments.

Required

Discuss your professional responsibilities in this situation assuming the two following situations:

a. Donations to political campaign funds are legal in the subsidiary's country.
b. Donations to political campaign funds are illegal in the subsidiary's country.

(CICA adapted)

CASE

21-29 In your audit of Aviary Industries for calendar year 2004, you found a number of matters that you believe represent possible adjustments to the company's books. These matters are described below. Management's attitude is that "once the books are closed, they're closed," and management does not want to make any adjustments. Planning materiality for the engagement was $100,000, determined by computing 5 percent of expected income before taxes. Actual income before taxes on the financial statements prior to any adjustments is $1,652,867.

Possible adjustments:

1. Several credit memos that were processed and recorded after year end relate to sales and accounts receivable for 2004. These total $23,529.
2. Inventory cutoff tests indicate that $22,357 of inventory received on December 30, 2004, was recorded as purchases and accounts payable in 2005. These items were included in the inventory count at year end and therefore were included in ending inventory.
3. Inventory cutoff tests also indicate several sales invoices recorded in 2004 for goods that were shipped in early 2005. The goods were not included in inventory but were set aside in a separate shipping area. The total amount of these shipments was $36,022. (Ignore cost of sales for this item.)

4. The company wrote several cheques at the end of 2004 for accounts payable that were held and not mailed until January 15, 2005. These totalled $48,336. Recorded cash and accounts payable at December 31, 2004, are $2,356,553 and $2,666,290, respectively.
5. The company has not established a reserve for obsolescence of inventories. Your tests indicate that such a reserve is appropriate in an amount somewhere between $20,000 and $40,000.
6. Your review of the allowance for uncollectible accounts indicates that it may be understated by between $25,000 and $50,000.

Required

a. Determine the adjustments that you believe must be made for Aviary's financial statements to be fairly presented. Include the amounts and accounts affected by each adjustment.
b. Why may Aviary Industries' management resist making these adjustments?
c. Explain what you consider the most positive way of approaching management personnel to convince them to make your proposed changes.
d. Describe your responsibilities related to unadjusted misstatements that management has determined are immaterial individually and in the aggregate.

CHAPTER 22

ASSURANCE SERVICES: REVIEW AND COMPILATION ENGAGEMENTS

In addition to financial statement audits, a public accountant performs a variety of services for clients with respect to financial information or business operations. This chapter begins by reviewing the nature of assurance engagements, then describes examples of specific engagements.

LEARNING OBJECTIVES

After reading this chapter, you should be able to answer the following questions:

1. How is the assurance engagement general standard different from the audit standard? How is it similar? Provide an example of a special report that provides (i) high assurance and (ii) no assurance.

2. Why are review and compilation services important? Explain how the evidence collection procedures are related to the assurance level provided for audits, reviews, and compilations.

3. What type of report does the PA provide for interim financial information? How does the PA report on future-oriented information?

SKEPTICISM APPLIES TO ALL TYPES OF ENGAGEMENTS

Menard Construction Ltd. was a contractor specializing in apartment complexes in Alberta. The owner of the construction company, Tony Menard, reached an agreement with a promoter named Alice Mayberry to serve as contractor on three projects that Mayberry was currently marketing. One problem with the agreement was that Menard would not receive final payment for the construction work until all partnership units were sold.

The first partnership offering was completely sold and Menard was paid. Unfortunately, the next two partnerships were not completely sold. To solve this problem, Menard loaned money to relatives and key employees who bought the necessary interests for the partnerships to close so that Menard would receive the final payment.

When Menard Construction Ltd. had a review service performed by Renée Fortin, a public accountant and sole practitioner, the accounting records showed loans receivable from a number of employees and individuals named Menard. Fortin observed that the loans were made just before the second and third partnerships closed, and they were for amounts that were multiples of $15,000, the amount of a partnership unit. Fortin asked Menard to explain what happened. Menard told her, "When I received the money from the first partnership escrow, I wanted to do something nice for relatives and employees who had been loyal to me over the years. This is just my way of sharing my good fortune with the ones I love. The equality of the amounts is just a coincidence."

When Fortin considered the reasonableness of this scenario, she found it hard to believe. First, the timing was odd. Second, the amounts seemed to be an unusual coincidence. Third, if he really had

It is difficult to resign from an engagement. As a professional accountant, to maintain your professional integrity and protect your business, you may have to do this at some time in your professional career. Think about difficult decisions that you have made in your life. How have they enhanced your ability to act with integrity?

→22.1 ATTEST AND ASSURANCE ENGAGEMENTS

In addition to being involved with audits of historical financial statements prepared in accordance with generally accepted accounting principles, public accountants commonly deal with situations involving other types of information, varying levels of assurance, and other types of reports.

This chapter describes the wide range of services that a public accountant can provide. It is very important that the public accountant properly communicate to users of information with which he or she is associated both the nature and extent of the association as described in *CICA Assurance Handbook* Section 5020. There are a number of figures in this chapter that illustrate the various forms of communication that the public accountant may issue. In studying them, you should note similarities and differences between the auditor's report discussed in Chapter 3 and the communications in this chapter.

Engagement letters were discussed in Chapter 7; an illustration of an engagement letter appears in Figure 7-2 on page 188. The various topics discussed below suggest the need for an engagement letter describing exactly what work the public accountant, acting as auditor or accountant, will do for the client and the proposed communication that will describe the work done (e.g., Figure 22-2 on page 620). The need for an engagement letter that is tailored to reflect the circumstances of the engagement cannot be overemphasized.

Assurance Engagements

Public accountants have increasingly been asked to perform a variety of audit-like or assurance services for different purposes. For example, a public accountant might be asked to provide assurance on the reliability of computer software or with respect to the meeting of environmental standards by an entity. Existing standards dealt primarily with historical financial statements prepared according to generally accepted accounting principles, whereas the new services often dealt with other types of information. Accordingly, the guidance provided to accountants became difficult to formulate and communicate effectively without disrupting the cohesiveness of the existing standards in the *Accounting and Assurance Handbooks*.

The problem is addressed by the profession through the issuance of *CICA Assurance Handbook* Section 5025, "Standards for Assurance Engagements." The development of the section was a cooperative venture between the CICA's Auditing and Assurance Standards Board and the Public Sector Accounting and Auditing Board (now the Public Sector Accounting Board). The section establishes the standards for all assurance engagements and applies to:

- Public and private sector engagements
- Attest engagements and direct reporting engagements
- Engagements such as audits that provide a high level of assurance and engagements such as reviews that provide a lower level of assurance

The section defines an **assurance engagement** as "an engagement where, pursuant to an accountability relationship between two or more parties, a practitioner is engaged to issue a written communication expressing a conclusion concerning a subject matter for which the accountable party is responsible." There are three parties to the relationship: (1) the practitioner, (2) the user(s), and (3) the person who is accountable (usually management). Figure 22-1 (based on Section 5025.07) illustrates this relationship. The user could be any stakeholder who will use the information on which the assurance is provided.

The section was designed to provide guidance for a broader range of services than the existing standards in the *Handbooks*. For example, the new section considers both attest engagements and direct reporting engagements. **Attest engagements** are engagements where the auditor expresses a conclusion on a written assertion about a subject prepared by a party accountable for the assertion, such as management. The assertion measures the subject matter using appropriate criteria. The special reports discussed in the remainder of this chapter are all attest engagements.

A **direct reporting engagement** is an engagement where the auditor *directly* expresses a conclusion on his or her evaluation of subject matter using certain criteria; management does not report in a direct reporting engagement. Perhaps the best example of a direct reporting engagement is the communication by the Auditor General to Parliament. In her report, the Auditor General, Sheila Fraser, describes what was found as a result of audits performed by her office. Public sector auditing is discussed further in Chapter 24. Other types of direct reporting engagements are also discussed in Chapter 23.

The *criteria* referred to in the previous paragraph are the benchmark or standard against which the subject matter is measured. For example, the criteria in a financial statement audit are GAAP.

The general standard states, "Before undertaking an assurance engagement, the practitioner should have a reasonable basis for believing the engagement can be completed in accordance with the assurance standards." The practitioner and all others involved with the assurance engagement should have adequate proficiency to perform the engagement and should collectively possess adequate knowledge of the subject matter. In addition, the engagement should be performed with due care and an objective state of mind.

The practitioner should obtain some form of evidence that an accountability relationship exists (i.e., that management is responsible for the subject matter). The evidence will normally be an acknowledgment from management but may be in some other form.

The section requires the practitioner to identify or develop criteria that can be used to evaluate the subject matter. The importance of this requirement cannot be overemphasized. If the criteria are not suitable, the value of the assurance engagement is doubtful. The section suggests that the necessary characteristics are relevance, reliability, neutrality,

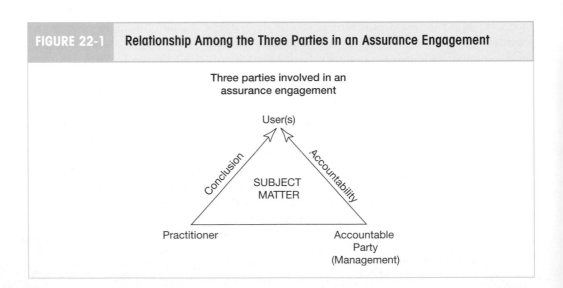

FIGURE 22-1   Relationship Among the Three Parties in an Assurance Engagement

Three parties involved in an assurance engagement

User(s)

Conclusion

Accountability

SUBJECT MATTER

Practitioner

Accountable Party (Management)

understandability, and completeness. The section lists sources of criteria that may be considered generally accepted and suggests that they are preferred. Other sources are acceptable subject to certain conditions. Criteria that could result in the report being misleading should not be used.

There are three performance standards outlined in Section 5025:

- The work should be adequately planned, and there should be proper supervision.
- The practitioner should consider both significance (similar to materiality) and engagement risk (similar to audit risk) when planning and performing the engagement.
- Sufficient evidence should be gathered to support the conclusion the practitioner expresses in his or her report.

The reporting standards for Section 5025 indicate that, as a minimum, the report should:

1. Identify to whom the report is directed.
2. Describe the objective of the engagement.
3. Identify management's assertion in an attest engagement.
4. Distinguish between the responsibilities of management and the practitioner.
5. Identify the applicable standards in accordance with which the engagement was conducted.
6. Identify the criteria against which the subject matter was evaluated.
7. Provide a conclusion that states the level of assurance being conveyed and/or any reservation that the practitioner may have.
8. State the date of the report.
9. Identify the practitioner.
10. Identify the place of issue.

Note that the reporting standards are much like those of GAAS found in Section 5400 and discussed in Chapter 3.

There can be scope limitations leading to a qualification or a denial of opinion with an assurance engagement. There can also be a qualification or an adverse opinion with an assurance engagement when:

- In a direct reporting engagement, the subject matter does not conform to the criteria.
- In an attest engagement, the assertion made by management does not present fairly the criteria used or conformity of the subject matter with the criteria, or if essential information has not been presented or is presented in an inappropriate manner.

Figure 22-2 illustrates the form of communication that would be issued under Section 5025. The report is an attest report providing a high level of assurance. The criteria for the engagement are described in an appendix to the report not provided with this example. Note the extra paragraph following the opinion paragraph; it is an example of additional information that the practitioner may wish to include to make the auditor's report more informative.

You should compare Figure 22-2 to Figure 3-1 on page 58 in order to understand the differences and similarities between a standard auditor's report and a report issued in connection with an assurance engagement.

This example auditor's report is the current Canadian standard with respect to reporting on the effectiveness of the system of internal control over financial reporting. The Canadian Securities Administrators (CSA) have proposed that management of certain Canadian public companies be required to report on the effectiveness of internal control over financial reporting. Auditors will report on management's assessment for those companies. This mirrors the U.S. *Sarbanes-Oxley Act* requirements under Section 404. In Canada, the new regulations would be phased in for the largest companies (i.e., those with market capitalization over $500 million) and commence with financial years ended on or after June 30, 2006. This type of report would become part of the financial statement audit, as illustrated with the Hillsburg Hardware Limited financial statements in Chapter 5. Figure 22-2 is included here as an example of a typical assurance report.

AUDITOR'S REPORT CONCERNING EFFECTIVENESS OF THE SYSTEM OF INTERNAL CONTROL OVER FINANCIAL REPORTING

To the Shareholders of Gaa Corp.

We have audited management's assertion that Gaa Corp. maintained an effective system of internal control over financial reporting as of December 31, 2004, in relation to the criteria described in the appendix to this report. Management's assertion is included in the accompanying report "Report on Effectiveness of Internal Control at Gaa Corp." as of December 31, 2004. The maintenance of an effective system of internal control over financial reporting is the responsibility of management. Our responsibility is to express an opinion on management's assertion about the effectiveness of the internal control system based on our audit.

We conducted our audit in accordance with Canadian generally accepted auditing standards. Those standards require that we plan and perform an audit to obtain reasonable assurance that management's assertion is free from significant misstatements. An audit includes examining, on a test basis, evidence supporting the content and disclosures in management's assertion. An audit also includes assessing the criteria used and the significant judgments made by management, as well as evaluating the overall presentation of management's assertion.

In our opinion, management's assertion presents fairly, in all significant respects, the effectiveness of the system of internal control over financial reporting of Gaa Corp. as of December 31, 2004, based on the criteria referred to above.

Because of the inherent limitations in any internal control system, errors or fraud and other irregularities may occur and not be detected. Also, projections of any evaluation of the internal control system over financial reporting to future periods are subject to the risk that the internal control system may become inadequate because of changes in conditions, or that the degree of compliance with the policies or procedures may deteriorate.

Edmonton, Alberta
February 7, 2005

Brunkof & Makepeace

Chartered Accountants

Reports on the Results of Applying Specified Auditing Procedures to Financial Information Other Than Financial Statements (Section 9100) At the opposite end of the assurance spectrum, we have an engagement that includes audit procedures but provides no assurance, covered by Section 9100. This section is concerned with an accountant's application of prespecified auditing procedures to financial information. The engagement is not an assurance engagement and an expression of an opinion is not expected. Since the client specifies what auditing procedures are to be applied and the form of report that is to be issued, distribution of the report is normally restricted. The accountant reaches an agreement with the client with respect to all three issues before beginning the engagement. In this situation, the accountant should comply both with the general standard and the first examination standard.

The report should specify

- The financial information to which the procedures were applied.
- The procedures applied.
- The factual results of the procedures; negative assurance should not be expressed.
- That an audit was not performed; there should be a disclaimer of opinion.
- Any restrictions on circulation of the report.

Figure 22-3 is an illustration of such a report. It was prepared in the situation where the financial statements were audited, but gross sales were not audited on a store-by-store basis.

→22.2   REVIEW AND COMPILATION SERVICES

Many public accountants are involved with nonpublic clients that do not have audits. A company may believe an audit is unnecessary due to the active involvement of the owners in the business, lack of significant debt, or absence of regulations requiring the company to have one. Common examples are smaller companies and professional organizations such as partnerships of physicians and lawyers.

FIGURE 22-3   Example of a Report Under Section 9100

ACCOUNTANTS' REPORT IN CONNECTION WITH GROSS SALES

To Garner Limited

As requested by Okanagan Stores Limited, we report that the gross sales of the company's store at King Street, Kelowna, B.C. for the year ended June 30, 2005, are recorded in the amount of $790,000 in the general ledger sales account of the company and form part of the company's gross sales in its financial statements for the year then ended, on which we reported on August 3, 2005.

Our examination of the company's financial statements for the year ended June 30, 2005, was not directed to the determination of gross sales or other financial information of individual stores. We have not performed an audit of and accordingly do not express an opinion on the amount of gross sales referred to in the preceding paragraph.

It is understood that this report is to be used solely for computing percentage rental and is not to be referred to or distributed to any person who is not a member of management of Garner Limited or Okanagan Stores Limited.

Kelowna, B.C.
August 8, 2005

Carter & Wilhelm

Certified General Accountants

These organizations often engage a public accountant to provide tax services and to assist in the preparation of accurate financial information without an audit. Providing these services is a significant part of the practice of many smaller public accounting firms. When a public accountant provides any services involving financial statements, certain requirements exist. The requirements for review engagements are covered in *CICA Assurance Handbook* Sections 8100, 8200, 8500, and 8600. Requirements for compilation engagements appear in Section 9200.

The assurance provided by reviews and compilations is considerably below audits, and the practitioners' reports are intended to convey that difference. Similarly, the extent of evidence accumulation differs among the three types of engagements (i.e., audit, review, and compilation). Figure 22-4 illustrates the difference in both the evidence accumulation and the level of assurance provided. The amount of assurance and extent of evidence accumulation, shown in Figure 22-4, are not well defined by the profession. This is because both evidence accumulation and assurance are subjective. Only a practitioner in the circumstances of an engagement can judge how much evidence is sufficient and what level of assurance has actually been attained.

Table 22-1 compares audits, reviews, and compilations on a number of dimensions and, as such, is helpful in understanding the differences among the three types of engagement.

Terms of Engagement While the *Assurance Handbook* sections covering review and compilation engagements do not require an engagement letter, they do require that the public accountant and the client reach an understanding and agreement regarding the services to be provided. A *written* agreement as to the nature and extent of services is most appropriate. The engagement letter would include such items as follows:

- A description of the services to be provided.
- A discussion of the client's responsibility for providing complete and accurate information.
- A statement that an audit is not to be performed and that, consequently, no opinion will be expressed. In the case of a compilation engagement, the fact that no assurance results should be stated.
- A note on any restrictions on the distribution of the statements.
- A statement that each page of the statements should be clearly marked "unaudited."
- The probable content of the communication to be appended by the accountant.

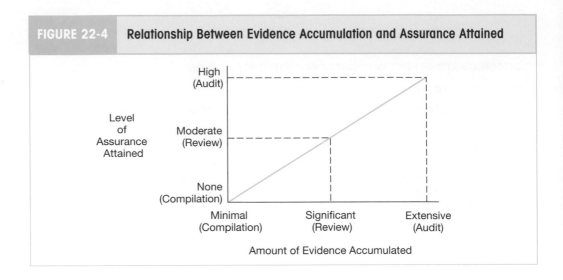

- The fact that the engagement cannot be relied on to detect error or fraud and other irregularities.
- Possibly a comment to the effect that the statements do not satisfy any statutory requirements.

Figure 22-5 on page 624 provides an example of an engagement letter for a review of annual financial statements.

Focus Box 22-1

INDEPENDENCE REPORTING MAY BE REQUIRED FOR A REVIEW ENGAGEMENT

Section 5751.02 of the *CICA Assurance Handbook* defines organizations with public accountability. In addition to public enterprises and regulated enterprises such as financial institutions, the following organizations are also considered to have public accountability:

- Co-operative business (for example, a housing co-op);
- Not-for-profit organizations (this would include registered and unregistered charities, associations, condominiums, clubs);
- Pension plans; and
- Government and public sector entities.

Many of the organizations listed, such as registered charities and condominiums, are required to have audits. However, non-registered charities and clubs may not be required to have an audit, and thus could have a review or compilation.

Yet, because these organizations have public accountability, the PA would be required to communicate with the audit committee about various matters described in Section 5701, including independence, specifying audit and non-audit fees, and disclosing any relationships between the public accountant and the entity.

REVIEW ENGAGEMENT—one that consists primarily of enquiry, analytical procedures, and discussion with the limited objectives of assessing whether the information being reported on is plausible within the framework of appropriate criteria

Review **Review engagement** is defined by *CICA Assurance Handbook* paragraph 8100.05 as consisting primarily of "enquiry, analytical procedures and discussion.... with the limited objective of assessing whether the information being reported on is plausible within the framework of appropriate criteria." *Plausible* can be defined as being worthy of belief.

General Review Standards Section 8100, "General Review Standards," discusses the acceptance of an engagement and the standards applicable to review engagements. These include knowledge of the client's business, review procedures, documentation, and reporting. Review engagements should be accepted by a public accountant only if the accountant believes that he or she has the necessary competence in the subject matter to be reported on.

TABLE 22-1 Comparison of Audit, Review, and Compilation Engagements

	Amount of Evidence to Be Collected	Procedures Used to Collect Evidence	Levels of Assurance Provided	Relative Cost of Engagement	Communication Title	Engagement Letter Desired	Area Proficiency Required In	Public Accountant Required to Be Objective?	Knowledge of Business Required?	Understanding of Internal Control Required?	Documentation Required?
Audit	Extensive	Inspection, Observation, Enquiry, Confirmation, Computation, Analysis	High	High	Auditor's Report	Yes	Auditing	Yes	Yes	Yes	Yes
Review	Significant	Enquiry, Analysis, Discussion, Others if necessary	Moderate	Moderate	Review Engagement Report	Yes	Review	Yes	Yes	No	Yes
Compilation	Minor	Computation	None	Low	Notice to Reader	Yes	Accounting	No	No	No	Not specifically stated but desirable

FIGURE 22-5   **Example of an Engagement Letter for a Review Engagement**

September 23, 2004

JOSEPHINE LIMITED
677 PETER STREET
WINNIPEG, MANITOBA
R3Y 1Z6

Attention: Josephine Collins, President

Dear Ms. Collins:

The purpose of this letter is to outline the nature of our involvement with the financial statements of Josephine Limited for the year ending December 31, 2004. As agreed, we will conduct a review, consisting primarily of enquiry, analytical procedures, and discussion in accordance with the generally accepted standards for review engagements.

Unless unanticipated difficulties are encountered, our report will be substantially in the following form:

> We have reviewed the balance sheet of Josephine Limited as at December 31, 2004, and the statements of income, retained earnings, and cash flows for the year then ended. Our review was made in accordance with Canadian generally accepted standards for review engagements and accordingly consisted primarily of enquiry, analytical procedures, and discussion related to information supplied to us by the company.

> A review does not constitute an audit, and consequently, we do not express an opinion on these financial statements.

> Based on our review, nothing has come to our attention that causes us to believe that these financial statements are not, in all material respects, in accordance with Canadian generally accepted accounting principles.

This review does not constitute an audit. For example, it does not contemplate a study and evaluation of internal control, tests of accounting records, and responses to enquiries by obtaining audit evidence through inspection, observation, or confirmation and other procedures ordinarily performed during an audit. Accordingly, this review is not intended to, and will not, result in the expression of an audit opinion or the fulfilling of any statutory or other audit requirement. Since we are not accepting this engagement as auditor, we request that you do not record this as an auditing engagement in the minutes of your shareholders' meetings. You may wish to obtain legal advice concerning statutory auditing requirements.

It is understood that:

(a) you will provide the information required for us to complete this review;
(b) the responsibility for the accuracy and completeness of the representations in the financial statements remains with you;
(c) if our name is to be used in connection with the financial statements, you will attach our review engagement report when distributing the financial statements to third parties; and
(d) each page of the financial statements will be conspicuously marked "Unaudited."

This engagement cannot be relied on to prevent or detect error or fraud and other irregularities. We wish to emphasize that control over and responsibility for the prevention and detection of error or fraud and other irregularities remains with management.

The arrangements outlined in this letter will continue in effect from year to year unless evidenced by a new engagement letter.

If you have any questions about the contents of this letter, please raise them with us. If the services outlined are in accordance with your requirements and if the above terms are acceptable to you, please sign the copy of this letter in the space provided and return it to us. We appreciate the opportunity of continuing to be of service to your company.

Yours very truly,

Simunic & Stein
Chartered Accountants

The services and terms set out are as agreed.
Josephine Limited
Per

Valerie Mann

PROCEDURES SUGGESTED FOR REVIEWS Reviews imply a level of assurance somewhere between that of an audit and the absence of assurance provided by a compilation. A review does not include obtaining an understanding of internal controls or tests of controls, independent confirmation, or physical examination. The emphasis in reviews is on four broad areas:

- *Obtain knowledge of the client's business.* The information should be about the nature of the client's organization and business transactions; its accounting records and employees; the basis, form, and content of the financial statements; and accounting matters peculiar to the client's business and industry.
- *Make enquiries of client personnel.* The objective of these enquiries is to determine whether the financial statements are fairly presented, assuming that management does not intend to deceive the accountant. The CICA Assurance and Related Services Guideline AuG-20, entitled "Performance of a Review of Financial Statements in Accordance with Sections 8100 and 8200," lists illustrative enquiries. It has been substantially reproduced in Table 22-2.
- *Perform analytical procedures.* These are meant to identify relationships and individual items that appear to be unusual. Analytical procedures performed during a review engagement would normally be less extensive than during an audit. The appropriate analytical procedures are the same as the ones already studied in Chapter 6 and in those chapters dealing with substantive procedures. Explanations for relationships and items that appear to be unusual would be obtained by enquiry of appropriate client personnel.
- *Have discussions with management concerning information received and the information being reported on.*

TABLE 22-2	Partial List of Example Enquiries for Review Engagements

Preliminary Considerations

1. Are the services to be provided mutually agreed upon? Has desirability of obtaining an engagement letter been considered?
2. Is it clear that an auditor has not been appointed with respect to the financial statements that are the subject of this engagement?
3. Are generally accepted accounting principles being used? If not, is the basis of accounting being used appropriate in the circumstances?

Knowledge of Business

1. What is the nature of the business?
2. What are the major assets and liabilities, costs and expenses, and sources of revenue? Who are the major customers and suppliers?
3. Has a knowledge of the accounting system been obtained sufficient to understand the manner in which transactions are recorded, classified, and summarized?
4. What books and records are kept?
5. Has appropriate consideration been given to:
   (a) prior period financial statements?
   (b) prior period working paper and related files?
   (c) prior period accounting problems?
   (d) reservations in the previous report?

Financial Statement Items

A series of questions are suggested about the various financial statement items.

Overall Review

1. Has appropriate consideration been given to:
   (a) the inter-relationship of financial statement items?
   (b) a comparison of significant components of the statement of income (in light of current operating and economic conditions) with budgets and figures for preceding periods?

   (c) significant operating ratios?
   (d) identification of related parties and related party transactions?
   (e) whether or not the enterprise is economically dependent on any one?
   (f) the need to obtain bank confirmation of specific matters?
2. Have enquiries been made concerning matters discussed at meetings, if any, of shareholders and directors and committees thereof that may affect the financial statements?
3. Has there been communication with other public accountants who have reviewed or audited the financial statements of significant components of the reporting enterprise?
4. Have there been any changes in accounting principles and, if so, have these changes been adequately disclosed?
5. Are there any events that occurred after the end of the financial period that would have significant effect on the financial statements or would be significant to readers of the financial statements?
6. Have all matters that in your professional judgment are important to support the content of your report been documented?
7. Do the financial statements agree with the records of the enterprise?

Final Considerations

1. Have the financial statements and the review engagement report been discussed with the client?
2. Is the client satisfied that the financial statements are complete and accurate?
3. Has a letter of representation been obtained? Does it contain all representations by the client that should be documented?
4. Based on the review performed, do the financial statements appear to be plausible in the circumstances within the framework of generally accepted accounting principles?
5. Is the form and content of the review engagement report appropriate to this engagement and is it dated to correspond with the date of substantial completion of the review?

The standards for review engagements are similar to generally accepted auditing standards, except that they deal with reviews and not audits. They are as follows, Section 8100.15:

General standard

The review should be performed and the review engagement report prepared by a person or persons having adequate technical training and proficiency in conducting reviews, with due care and an objective state of mind.

Review standards

(i) The work should be adequately planned and properly executed. If assistants are employed, they should be properly supervised.

(ii) The public accountant should possess or acquire sufficient knowledge of the business carried on by the enterprise so that intelligent enquiry and assessment of information obtained can be made.

(iii) The public accountant should perform a review with the limited objective of assessing whether the information being reported on is plausible in the circumstances within the framework of appropriate criteria. Such a review should consist of:

(a) enquiry, analytical procedures and discussion; and

(b) additional or more extensive procedures when the public accountant's knowledge of the business carried on by the enterprise and the results of the enquiry, and analytical procedures and discussion cause him or her to doubt the plausibility of such information.

Reporting standards

(i) The review engagement report should indicate the scope of the review. The nature of the review engagement should be made evident and be clearly distinguished from an audit.

(ii) The report should indicate, based on the review:

(a) whether anything has come to the public accountant's attention that causes him or her to believe that the information being reported on is not, in all material respects, in accordance with appropriate criteria; or

(b) that no assurance can be provided.

The report should provide an explanation of the nature of any reservations contained therein and, if readily determinable, their effect.

The requirement that the accountant have sufficient knowledge of the client's enterprise and type of business is made so that the accountant can assess whether the information to be reported on is plausible in the circumstances. The accountant would not be able to make the required enquiry and assessment of the information obtained without such knowledge. For

Focus Box 22-2

WE WOULD LIKE TO HAVE NON-GAAP FINANCIAL STATEMENTS PLEASE . . .

What would you say if your client requested financial statements that were not in accordance with GAAP? After coughing discreetly, you might say "Okay."

Section 8200.46 permits "differential reporting options" if the organization is not publicly accountable and the owners unanimously consent. There are additional restrictions in Section 8200.55, though: this differential reporting needs to be in accordance with regulatory or legislative requirements or in accordance with written contractual agreements such as in a buy/sell agreement.

These restrictions may change in the future. Private companies without external users may be allowed to "opt out" of GAAP, according to Paul Cherry, chair of the Accounting Standards Board (effective May 2005). Mr. Cherry made the above observation as part of a discussion with respect to the five-year plan of the Accounting Standards Board (AcSB). The plan described an intention to move Canadian GAAP toward International GAAP, with variations likely permitted for companies that need to list on American stock exchanges, and for other users such as small business and non-profit enterprises.

Sources: 1. *CICA Assurance Handbook*, Section 8200.
2. Colapinto, Robert, 2005. "The future direction of accounting standards," *CAmagazine*, May 2005, pp. 20–22.

instance, the accountant would not be able to assess the plausibility of manufactured inventory unless he or she had knowledge of the company's product and manufacturing processes.

The review standards should be appropriate to the particular engagement; for example, it is likely that procedures would differ between a review of financial statements and financial information. The review procedures do not preclude audit procedures if the accountant believes that more extensive procedures are required to assess plausibility. However, once the accountant decides to use more extensive procedures, such as audit procedures, the particular procedure must be carried out to completion. The accountant should not carry out an audit procedure to partial completion simply because the engagement is a review.

Materiality would be measured in the same manner as with an audit.

Negative assurance should be expressed only when the standards applicable to a review engagement described above have been met.

In addition to the reporting standards listed above, the communication should identify the information presented, state that a review does not constitute an audit, and state that the review, which consisted primarily of enquiry, analytical procedures, and discussion, was made in accordance with generally accepted standards for review engagements. The purpose of stating that a review does not constitute an audit is to ensure that financial statement users are aware that a review provides a lower level of assurance than an audit. The accountant should also state, except when a reservation is required, that nothing has come to his or her attention as a result of his or her review that causes him or her to believe that the information is not, in all material respects, in accordance with an appropriate disclosed basis of accounting, which, except in special circumstances, should be generally accepted accounting principles, or in the case of nonfinancial information, other appropriate criteria. In addition, each page of information reported on should be marked "unaudited."

Reservations may be required in the accountant's report when the review cannot be completed, when there is a departure from the appropriate criteria, or when the accountant concludes that the client's interpretation of an agreement or regulation is not reasonable. The reservation would be disclosed in a reservation paragraph in the review engagement report, which would appear immediately preceding the negative assurance paragraph. The reason for the reservation and the effect of the reservation on the information reported on should also be disclosed.

The discovery of a misstatement after the release of the report by the accountant should be treated in the same way as the discovery of a misstatement by an auditor after the release of audited financial statements.

Focus Box 22-3

REVIEW ENQUIRY RELEVANT TO NOT-FOR-PROFIT ORGANIZATIONS

Not-for-profit organizations (NPOs) do not have shareholders, but they do have a Board of Directors. These directors are elected by members, rather than shareholders, so the accountant needs to find out how membership is determined. If the accountant is a member (such as a golf club), his or her independence might be questioned. One possibility is to ask for a bylaw stating that the accountant cannot vote for Board members. This is particularly relevant since the accountant must report a number of issues to the audit committee (a subcommittee of the Board). Important issues for NPOs include the following:

- Completeness of revenues: Are numeric receipts issued? How is fund raising handled? What is the mix between government grants and fundraising?

- Valuation of donated assets or services: How are donated services or donated assets valued? Are charitable donation receipts given for these items and services? Are valued amounts defensible for tax purposes? Is volunteer time recorded at NIL?

- Existence of donated assets: Are these items added to a capital asset ledger, even if they were donated and have been recorded at a NIL value?

- Compliance with regulations: Are funds dispersed in accordance with their intended purpose? Is an accounting system in place that properly tracks and distributes restricted funds? How does the NPO ensure that directors do not receive any funds or benefits?

REVIEWS OF FINANCIAL STATEMENTS Section 8200 provides guidelines that apply to a review of financial statements in addition to those in Section 8100 when the accountant is reporting on interim or annual financial statements. An example of a report that the accountant would issue is shown in Figure 22-6.

FINANCIAL INFORMATION OTHER THAN FINANCIAL STATEMENTS Section 8500 describes the sorts of financial information that might be included under this grouping. This section is parallel to Section 5805 and refers the accountant to Section 5805 for further guidance in this matter. When the information is prepared in accordance with an agreement or a regulation and that agreement requires interpretations, the report should refer to such interpretations. Figure 22-7 shows the form a communication might take when the auditor is reporting on financial information other than financial statements.

REVIEWS OF COMPLIANCE WITH AGREEMENTS AND REGULATIONS Section 8600 is parallel to Section 5815. The accountant should read the relevant provisions of the agreement or regulation, enquire about how the client monitors its compliance with the provisions, and consider whether the provisions have been consistently applied. In the review engagement report, the public accountant should identify the provisions of the agreement or regulation that establish the criteria on which his or her assessment of compliance is based. As well, any significant interpretations of the criteria made by the accountant when the criteria were nonspecific and any significant changes in interpretations from the previous year should be identified. Figure 22-8 presents an example of a report that the accountant might issue.

Compilation Compilation services are bookkeeping services that lead to the completion of financial statements. It is common for smaller public accounting firms to own one or more microcomputers and provide bookkeeping services, monthly or quarterly financial statements, and tax services for smaller clients.

In **compilation engagements**, discussed in Section 9200, the public accountant provides assistance in compiling financial statements but is not required to provide any assurance about the statements; the engagement is not an assurance engagement. The statements may be complete (i.e., include balance sheet, income statement, and statement of cash flows); they may be part of a complete set of financial statements; or they may be for the whole enterprise or for a part of the enterprise. The accountant assembles the information supplied by the client and ensures that it is arithmetically correct; the accountant is

> **COMPILATION ENGAGEMENT—** non-audit engagement in which the public accountant provides assistance in compiling financial statements but is not expected to provide assurance about the statements

---

FIGURE 22-6	Example of a Report Under Section 8200

REVIEW ENGAGEMENT REPORT

To R. Fortin

I have reviewed the balance sheet of Leger Inc. as at December 31, 2004, and the statements of income, retained earnings, and cash flows for the year then ended. My review was made in accordance with Canadian generally accepted standards established for review engagements and accordingly consisted primarily of enquiry, analytical procedures, and discussion related to information supplied to me by the company.

A review does not constitute an audit, and consequently, I do not express an audit opinion on these financial statements.

Based on my review, nothing has come to my attention that causes me to believe that these financial statements are not, in all material respects, in accordance with Canadian generally accepted accounting principles.

Montréal, Québec
February 18, 2005

a. Vachon

Certified General Accountant

FIGURE 22-7   Example of a Report Under Section 8500

REVIEW ENGAGEMENT REPORT

To Kamloops Limited

At the request of Pacific Limited, I have reviewed the plant and equipment of Pacific Limited as at March 31, 2005 (calculated in accordance with the provisions of section 10 of the mortgage agreement with Kamloops Limited dated May 5, 2002, and the interpretations set out in note 1). My review was made in accordance with Canadian generally accepted standards for review engagements and accordingly consisted primarily of enquiry, analytical procedures, and discussion related to information supplied to me by the company.

A review does not constitute an audit, and consequently, I do not express an audit opinion on this plant and equipment.

Based on my review, nothing has come to my attention that causes me to believe that this plant and equipment are not presented fairly in accordance with the provisions of section 10 of the mortgage agreement with Kamloops Limited dated May 5, 2002, and the interpretations set out in note 1.

Vancouver, B.C.
June 7, 2005

L. Daryl
Chartered Accountant

FIGURE 22-8   Example of a Report Under Section 8600

REVIEW ENGAGEMENT REPORT

To J. O'Sullivan

I have reviewed Separate Limited's compliance as at December 31, 2004, with covenants to be complied with described in sections 8 to 10 inclusive of the agreement dated November 3, 2002, with Waterloo Inc. My review was made in accordance with Canadian generally accepted standards for review engagements and accordingly consisted primarily of enquiry, analytical procedures, and discussion related to information supplied to me by the company.

A review does not constitute an audit, and consequently, I do not express an audit opinion on this matter.

Based on my review, nothing has come to my attention that causes me to believe that the company is not in compliance with covenants to be complied with described in sections 8 to 10 inclusive of this agreement.

Calgary, Alberta
January 18, 2005

G. Ou
Certified General Accountant

concerned with neither the accuracy or completeness of the information nor whether the financial statements comply with GAAP. Although the accountant should not be associated with false or misleading financial statements, determining whether the statements are false or misleading can be difficult because of his or her limited involvement.

Section 9200.10 sets out criteria for accepting a compilation engagement:

(a) there is no reason to believe that the financial statements the public accountant has been engaged to compile are false or misleading; and

(b) the public accountant believes that the client understands that:
   (i) such statements may not be appropriate for general purpose use; and
   (ii) uninformed readers could be misled unless they are aware of the possible limitations of the statements, and of the public accountant's very limited involvement.

PROFESSIONAL STANDARDS There are standards that the public accountant must follow in performing a compilation engagement:

- The services should be performed and the communication should be prepared by a person or persons having adequate technical training and proficiency in accounting, and with due care.
- The work should be adequately planned and properly executed. If assistants are employed, they should be properly supervised.

If the public accountant ascertains that the financial statements may be false or misleading, he or she must obtain additional information and amend the statements or resign from the engagement.

FORM OF REPORT The communication from the public accountant in a compilation engagement is entitled "Notice to Reader." Each page of the statements should either include the "Notice to Reader" heading itself or the statement "Unaudited—See Notice to Reader." The communication should

(a) state that the public accountant compiled the statement from information provided by management;

(b) state that the public accountant did not audit, review or otherwise attempt to verify the accuracy or completeness of such information;

(c) caution readers that the statement may not be appropriate for their purposes; and

(d) not express any form of opinion or negative assurance.

An example of a "Notice to Reader" appears in Figure 22-9.

Departures from generally accepted accounting principles should not be referred to in the report as this may suggest that the public accountant has a responsibility to detect and report all such departures.

Compilation standards also apply to the information actually included in a client's tax return. The Institute of Chartered Accountants of Ontario issued in its December 1998/January 1999 issue of *Checkmark* (a regular newsletter to members) a technical news services release concerning tax returns. The release stated, "members must attach a Notice to Reader to the financial information that they have compiled regardless of whether the information is prepared separately or included as part of a tax schedule." Thus, accountants should include a "Notice to Reader" with personal tax returns prepared on behalf of clients.

→22.3 INTERIM FINANCIAL INFORMATION AND FUTURE-ORIENTED INFORMATION

Interim Financial Information

Interim financial information may be audited, reviewed, or compiled by a public accountant. The decision depends on how much assurance is desired from the accountant's

---

FIGURE 22-9	Example of Report Under Section 9200

NOTICE TO READER

I have compiled the balance sheet of New B Ltd. as at March 31, 2005, and the statements of income, retained earnings, and cash flows for the year then ended from information provided by management. I have not audited, reviewed, or otherwise attempted to verify the accuracy or completeness of such information. Readers are cautioned that this statement may not be appropriate for their purposes.

Halifax, N.S.
June 12, 2005

R. Fundy

Chartered Accountant

---

involvement and how timely the information must be. Estimates normally have to be made in order to prepare the information on a timely basis. Therefore, the information may not be as reliable as annual financial information. Since the objective of producing interim financial information is to provide up-to-date information to users of the statements, such information is usually not audited. Section 7050, "Auditor Review of Interim Financial Statements," provides thorough guidance for review of financial statements for a financial reporting period that is shorter than the fiscal year. Sections 8100, 8200, 8500, and 8600 can also be consulted when interim financial information is reviewed. If it is compiled, Section 9200 is relevant.

Future-Oriented Financial Information

Section 4250, "**Future-Oriented Financial Information (FOFI)**," establishes accounting standards for such information. The CICA also issued Assurance and Related Services Guideline AuG-6, titled "Examination of a Financial Forecast or Projection Included in a Prospectus or Other Public Offering Document." This Guideline is directed at prospective information included in offering documents.

Assurance and Related Services Guideline AuG-16, "Compilation of a Financial Forcast or Projection," indicates the standards that the public accountant should follow when compiling a forecast or projection for a client who does not require the public accountant to provide any assurance.

Chapter 1 points out that Assurance and Related Services Guidelines do not have the force of Recommendations. Their intent is to provide guidance in the absence of Recommendations.

Forecasts and Projections Future-oriented financial information deals with the future, not with the past. Section 4250 describes two general types of future-oriented financial information: forecasts and projections. A **forecast** is prospective financial information prepared using assumptions reflecting management's judgment as to the most probable courses of action for the entity. The information is presented to the best of management's knowledge and belief. A **projection** is prepared using one or more assumptions (hypotheses) that do not necessarily reflect the most likely course of action in management's judgment.

Use of Prospective Financial Statements **Prospective financial statements** are for either *general* use or *special* use. General use refers to use by any third party. An example of general use would be inclusion of a financial forecast in a prospectus for the sale of shares of a large public company. Special use refers to use by third parties with whom the responsible party is negotiating directly. An example of special purpose future-oriented financial information would be the inclusion of a financial projection in a takeover bid circular aimed at current shareholders of the company, or for a business applying for a bank loan.

Acceptance of the Engagement The following discussion pertains to Assurance and Related Service Guideline AuG-6. As with other types of engagements performed by the public accountant, it is important to ensure that the nature and terms of involvement with future-oriented financial information are understood and agreed to by management, preferably in writing. Management should also acknowledge its responsibilities related to the financial information. AuG-6 identifies a number of matters that should be agreed to by management and the public accountant:

- The anticipated form of the financial forecast
- The period of time to be covered
- The fact that management will prepare and present the forecast in accordance with accounting standards established by the CICA and in accordance with any applicable securities requirements
- The fact that management is responsible for the forecast: its presentation, the process of preparation, and the assumptions used
- The fact that management is responsible for obtaining or developing appropriate support for the assumptions sufficient to enable the public accountant to report without reservation

FUTURE-ORIENTED FINANCIAL INFORMATION (FOFI)—information about prospective results of operations, financial position, and/or changes in financial position based on assumptions about future economic conditions and courses of action; may be presented either as a forecast or projection

FORECAST—prospective financial information prepared using assumptions as to the most probable courses of action for the entity

PROJECTION—prospective financial information prepared using assumptions reflecting management's judgment as to the most probable course of action for the entity; prepared using one or more assumptions (hypotheses) that do not necessarily reflect the most likely course of action in management's judgment

PROSPECTIVE FINANCIAL STATEMENTS—financial statements that deal with expected future data rather than with historical data

- The need for the public accountant to have access to outside specialists and third party reports obtained by management (e.g., a feasibility study)
- The anticipated form and content of the public accountant's report
- The fact that the public accountant has no responsibility to update his or her report for events and circumstances occurring after the date of that report

PROFESSIONAL STANDARDS There are standards that the public accountant should follow in examining prospective information. The services should be performed by someone with adequate technical training and proficiency in auditing, and the examination should be performed and the report prepared with due care. The work should be adequately planned and any assistants should be properly supervised. Sufficient evidence should be obtained to provide a reasonable basis for the report. Important matters should be documented to indicate that sufficient appropriate evidence has been obtained.

Before accepting such an engagement, the public accountant should ensure the following:

- There is adequate support for the assumptions used to prepare the financial information. For example, management of a new company may not be able to provide such support.
- Any hypotheses used do not significantly impair the quality of the financial information.
- Management is willing to disclose all significant assumptions.
- The period to be covered by the forecast or projection does not extend beyond the point where future results can be reasonably estimated.
- Any hypotheses are not false or misleading. If they are, the public accountant cannot be involved with the financial information.

Examination of Prospective Financial Statements An examination of future-oriented financial information involves evaluating the preparation of the future-oriented financial information and the underlying assumptions and assessing the plausibility of hypotheses. In addition, the public accountant would evaluate the presentation of the financial information for conformity with CICA presentation and disclosure guidelines (Section 4250) and ensure that accounting policies are consistent with those used in the historical financial statements. The public accountant would obtain a written letter of representation from management acknowledging its responsibility for preparing the forecast or projection and indicating that forecast figures are management's best estimate of the forecast results. Finally, the accountant would issue an examination report.

These evaluations are based primarily on accumulating evidence about the completeness and reasonableness of the underlying assumptions as disclosed in the prospective financial information. This requires the accountant to become familiar with the client's business and industry, to identify the significant matters on which the client's future results are expected to depend ("key factors"), and to determine that appropriate assumptions have been included with respect to these.

In developing a knowledge of the industry and business, the public accountant should focus on areas such as:

- The availability and cost of resources that the client needs for continuing operations
- The nature and condition of markets in which the client operates
- Specific industry factors such as competition, sensitivity to economic conditions, accounting principles and practices, regulatory requirements, and technology
- Past performance by the client and its competitors

Reporting The accountant's report on an examination of financial statements should include:

- An identification of the financial information presented
- A description of the nature of the examination
- A statement that the examination of the financial information was made in accordance with AuG-6
- A statement that the public accountant assumes no responsibility to update the report for events and circumstances occurring after the report date
- The accountant's opinion as to whether the assumptions are suitably supported, consistent with the client's plans, and provide a reasonable basis for the information; the forecast or projection reflects these assumptions; and the information is prepared in conformity with the CICA's presentation and disclosure standards
- A caveat that the prospective results may not be achieved
- A disclaimer of opinion as to the achievability of the forecast or projection

For projections, the report would also:

- State that the assumptions used include a hypothesis.
- State that since a hypothesis need not be supported, procedures were limited to ensuring it was consistent with the purpose of the projection.
- Provide an opinion regarding the consistency of the hypothesis with the purpose of the projection.

Figure 22-10 is an example of a report on a financial forecast. The date of the report would be the date of the completion of the fieldwork by the public accountant.

FIGURE 22-10 **Example of a Report on a Financial Forecast**

AUDITOR'S REPORT ON FINANCIAL FORECAST

To the Directors of Nomad Corp.

The accompanying financial forecast of Nomad Corp. consisting of a balance sheet as at June 30, 2006, and the statements of income, retained earnings, and changes in financial position for the period then ending has been prepared by management using assumptions with an effective date of June 30, 2005. We have examined the support provided by management for the assumptions, and the preparation and presentation of this forecast. Our examination was made in accordance with Auditing Guideline AuG-6 issued by the Canadian Institute of Chartered Accountants. We have no responsibility to update this report for events and circumstances occurring after the date of our report.

In our opinion, as of the date of this report, the assumptions developed by management are suitably supported and consistent with the plans of the Company, and provide a reasonable basis for the forecast; this forecast reflects such assumptions; and the financial forecast complies with the presentation and disclosure standards for forecasts established by the Canadian Institute of Chartered Accountants.

Since this forecast is based on assumptions regarding future events, actual results will vary from the information presented and the variations may be material. Accordingly, we express no opinion as to whether this forecast will be achieved.

Toronto, Ontario
August 15, 2005

McWhite & Kedwell

Chartered Accountants

SUMMARY

1. *How is the assurance engagement general standard different from the audit standard?* The assurance standard requires that the PA believe it is possible to complete the engagement. The equivalent statement (i.e., having a reasonable basis to conduct an audit), is not present in the audit standard.

    How is it similar? Both general standards require adequate proficiency to perform the engagement, having knowledge of the business or subject matter, and that the engagement be completed with due care and an objective state of mind.

    Provide an example of a special report that provides

    (i) *high assurance*—an auditor's report concerning the effectiveness of the system of internal control over financial reporting; *and*

    (ii) *no assurance*—an accountant's report on gross sales that were not audited.

2. *Why are review and compilation services important?* Many businesses and other organizations do not require the assurance level that is provided by an audit. Even some banks require only moderate assurance (i.e., a review engagement) for bank loans. A key service that may not require assurance is the preparation of information included with a tax return.

    Explain how the evidence collection procedures are related to the assurance level provided for audits, reviews, and compilations. Audits require the greatest amount of evidence collection, with the requirement that objective evidence be collected, where possible. This results in the audit providing the greatest assurance level of the three engagements. Reviews require less evidence, and the procedures are normally limited to enquiry, analysis, and discussion, while compilations provide no assurance—the accountant does not gather any evidence.

3. *What type of report does the PA provide for interim financial information?* Interim financial information can be audited, reviewed, or compiled. The type of report depends on the type of engagement.

    How does the PA report on future-oriented information? The PA evaluates the assumptions used by management and confirms that the information has been compiled correctly (compilation engagement).

CICA ASSURANCE HANDBOOK SECTIONS REFERENCED IN THIS CHAPTER

Section 4250 – Future-oriented financial information.
Section 5020 – Association.
Section 5025 – Standards for assurance engagements.
Section 5400 – The auditor's standard report.
Section 5701 – Other reporting matters.
Section 5751 – Communications with those having oversight responsibility for the financial reporting process.
Section 5805 – Special reports–audit reports on financial information other than financial statements.
Section 5815 – Special reports–audit reports on compliance with agreements, statutes and regulations.
Section 7050 – Auditor review of interim financial statements.
Section 8100 – General review standards.
Section 8200 - Public accountant's review of financial statements.

Section 8500 – Reviews of financial information other than financial statements.
Section 8600 – Reviews of compliance with agreements and regulations.
Section 9100 – Reports on the results of applying specified auditing procedures to financial information other than financial statements.
Section 9200 – Compilation engagements.
AuG-6 – Examination of a financial forecast or projection included in a prospectus or other public offering document.
AuG-16 – Compilation of a financial forecast or projection.
AuG-20 – Performance of a review of financial statements in accordance with sections 8100 and 8200.

ESSENTIAL TERMS

Assurance engagement—one where, pursuant to an accountability relationship between two or more parties, a practitioner is engaged to issue a written communication expressing a conclusion concerning a subject matter for which the accountable party is responsible   (p. 618).

Attest engagement—one where the auditor expresses a conclusion on a written assertion about subject matter prepared by a party accountable for the assertion, such as management; the assertion measures the subject matter using appropriate criteria (p. 618).

Compilation engagement—non-audit engagement in which the public accountant provides assistance in compiling financial statements but is not expected to provide assurance about the statements   (p. 628).

Direct reporting engagement—one where the auditor directly expresses a conclusion on his or her evaluation of the subject matter using certain criteria and where the accountable party is responsible for the subject matter   (p. 618).

Forecast—prospective financial information prepared using assumptions as to the most probable courses of action for the entity   (p. 631).

Future-oriented financial information (FOFI)—information about prospective results of operations, financial position, and/or changes in financial position based on assumptions about future economic conditions and courses of action; may be presented either as a forecast or projection   (p. 631).

Projection—prospective financial information prepared using assumptions reflecting management's judgment as to the most probable course of action for the entity; prepared using one or more assumptions (hypotheses) that do not necessarily reflect the most likely course of action in management's judgment   (p. 631).

Prospective financial statements—financial statements that deal with expected future data rather than with historical data (p. 631).

Review engagement—one that consists primarily of enquiry, analytical procedures, and discussion with the limited objectives of assessing whether the information being reported on is plausible within the framework of appropriate criteria (p. 622).

REVIEW QUESTIONS

22-1   Distinguish between an "attest engagement" and a "direct reporting engagement."

22-2   Explain why criteria are so important with respect to assurance engagements.

22-3   Identify the three parties to an accountability relationship, and explain each of their roles.

22-4   Give three examples of the special reports that a public accountant may be asked to issue. Explain why these reports would be requested.

22-5   Why are reports on the results of applying specified auditing procedures to financial information other than financial statements prepared by public accountants?

22-6   How do the general standards applicable to review engagements differ from generally accepted auditing standards?

22-7   Contrast the level of assurance provided by negative assurance discussed in Sections 8100, 8200, 8500, and 8600 of the *CICA Assurance Handbook* with the level of assurance provided by the opinion given in the auditor's report.

22-8   What is the intent of Section 9200, "Compilation Engagements," in the *CICA Assurance Handbook*?

22-9   Discuss the standards for compilation engagements, and explain why they differ from those for review engagements and audits.

22-10   The financial statements prepared for a compilation engagement may not be complete according to GAAP. Why is this exception permitted? Provide examples of information that might be excluded.

22-11   Explain how the review engagement for an NPO differs from the review engagement for a profit-oriented entity.

22-12   On what does the auditor comment in his or her comments on financial forecasts? On what does the auditor disclaim an opinion and why?

MULTIPLE CHOICE QUESTIONS

22-13   Choose the best response for the following questions:

a. A public accountant normally performs enquiry, analytical procedures, and discussion in order to assess whether or not the information being reported on is plausible. If those procedures cause him or her to doubt the plausibility, the public accountant should

   (1)   provide a reservation in the review engagement report.
   (2)   resign.
   (3)   perform a compilation engagement.
   (4)   perform procedures similar to audit procedures.

b. A compilation is described as a "related service" because

   (1)   the public accountant has no liability for errors.
   (2)   the compilation is a form of consulting service.
   (3)   no assurance is provided by the public accountant.
   (4)   only the general standard of GAAS applies to compilations.

c. For a compilation engagement the accountant needs to ensure that:

   (1)   The compiled statements comply with GAAP.
   (2)   The statements are not false or misleading.

   (3)   He/She has an objective state of mind.
   (4)   The statements are mathematically accurate.

d. The greatest concern to the public accountant in a future-oriented financial information (FOFI) engagement is

   (1)   that management's projections may not be met.
   (2)   that users may believe that the public accountant's involvement ensures that the prospective results will be achieved.
   (3)   that management assumptions are not reasonable.
   (4)   that the appropriate standards were followed in preparing the FOFI.

e. Which of the following statements best describes negative assurance?

   (1)   The public accountant states that in his/her opinion the plausibility of the financial statements is not in doubt.
   (2)   The public accountant states that there is no reason to not accept the plausibility of the financial statements.
   (3)   The public accountant states that in his/her opinion the financial statements are plausible.
   (4)   The public accountant states that there is a low probability the financial statements are not plausible.

22-14 Prentice Manufacturing Limited is a Canadian-controlled public company that issued shares to the public for the first time in 1980. The shares are listed on both Canadian and U.S. stock exchanges. Al Prentice, the president of the company, approaches Don Migwam, a public accountant, who is currently performing the interim audit of the company. The company has decided to have their interim financial statements reviewed by the auditors for the first time.

Mr. Prentice would like to publish the interim results following Migwam's review and has asked him to do whatever is necessary to give his "certification" and suggest whatever changes are necessary to present these interim statements in accordance with generally accepted accounting principles. He informs Migwam that the three-month statement of earnings will also be circulated to minority shareholders in the United States and will therefore likely have to conform to the American accounting pronouncements (AICPA, FASB) as well as Canadian ones.

Required

Assume the role of Don Migwam, a public accountant. Outline the following:
a. The points you would include in a letter to Mr. Prentice on your responsibility with respect to the interim financial statements
b. The nature of any work you would have to perform in this regard

(CICA adapted)

22-15 Your firm has just accepted the audit appointment of Floss Ltd., a major confectionery retailer with more than 60 leased stores in shopping malls across Canada. Every lease calls for a base rent plus a percentage of the store's sales. The "sales escalation" clause in each lease requires Floss Ltd. to have its auditor issue a report to the lessor on the sales of the store covered by the lease. However, the leases do not specify the nature and extent of the audit effort or the form of the report.

The audited financial statements show only the aggregate figure for sales at all stores, and the previous audits had involved visiting only some of the locations each year on a rotating basis. The former auditors had not extended their procedures for the purposes of reporting to lessors but had simply reported to individual lessors the following:

> As requested by Floss Ltd., we report that the sales of the corporation's store in Penticton Plaza for the year ended September 30, 2004, are recorded in the amount of $ _____ in the general ledger sales account of the corporation.
>
> Our examination of the corporation's financial statements for the year ended June 30, 2004, was not directed to the determination of sales of individual stores, nor have we examined the corporation's financial statements for the three-month period subsequent to June 30, 2004. We have not performed an audit of, and accordingly do not express an opinion on, the amount of sales referred to in the preceding paragraph.

This year several lessors, including one that owns nine malls containing Floss Ltd. stores, have objected to this report, stating that it provides them with no assurance that sales at individual store locations are fairly stated. You, as a representative of your firm, have explained to the management of Floss Ltd. that it would cost considerably more in time and audit effort to provide an audit opinion on sales at each particular store location.

The management of Floss Ltd. is very unhappy with the prospect of paying the extra costs for an individual audit of sales at each location. The chief financial officer has observed that "it seems to us that your firm should be able to give some reasonable intermediate level of assurance between nothing, which is what the former auditors' reports seem to indicate, and a full scope audit opinion." In particular, the officer has asked why your firm cannot simply report, solely on the basis of your financial statement audit, as follows:

> As requested by Floss Ltd., we report that, in our opinion, the sales of the corporation's store at Hilltop Plaza (Hamilton, Ontario) for the year ended September 30, 2005, in the amount of $ _____ are fairly stated in all respects material to the financial statements taken as a whole.

Required

Discuss the three reporting approaches identified by the chief financial officer of Floss Ltd. and any other reporting approaches that could satisfy both Floss Ltd. management and the lessors.

(CICA adapted)

22-16 Joseph, a PA, has been keeping the books for his father's business, JoPar Tech Ltd. in the evenings, while working with other clients during the day. Yesterday, Joseph's father proudly announced that he had negotiated a loan with the Federal Business Development Bank at favourable rates so that he could purchase $120,000 in new machinery and equipment. Upon reviewing the loan agreement, Joseph discovered that one of the requirements of the loan agreement is that JoPar Tech Ltd. submits financial statements that have been reviewed by a PA within 90 days of the fiscal year end.

Required

a. Can Joseph complete a review engagement report for JoPar Tech Ltd.? Why or why not?
b. What type of engagement can Joseph complete with respect to the financial statements of JoPar Tech Ltd.?
c. What would you advise Joseph to do? Why?

22-17 You are doing a review engagement and the related tax work for Regency Tools, Inc., a tool and die company with $2,000,000 in sales. Inventory is recorded at $125,000. Prior year unaudited statements, prepared by the company without assistance from a public accounting firm, disclose that the inventory is based on "historical cost estimated by management." You obtain the following facts:

1. The company has been growing steadily for the past five years.
2. The unit cost of typical material used by Regency Tools has increased dramatically for several years.
3. The inventory cost has been approximately $125,000 for five years.
4. Management intends to use a value of $125,000 again for the current year-end financial statements.

When you discuss with management the need to get a physical count and an accurate inventory, the response is negative. Management is concerned about the effects on income taxes of a more realistic inventory. The company has never been audited and has always estimated the historical cost of inventory. You are convinced, based upon enquiry and ratio analysis, that a conservative evaluation would be $500,000 at historical cost.

Required

a. What are the generally accepted accounting principle requirements for valuation and disclosure of inventory for unaudited financial statements with a review report?
b. Identify the potential legal and professional problems that you face in this situation.
c. What procedures would you normally follow for a review engagement when the inventory is a material amount? Be as specific as possible.
d. How should you resolve the problem in this situation? Identify alternatives, and evaluate the costs and benefits of each.

22-18 The following items represent a series of unrelated procedures that an accountant may consider performing in an engagement to review or compile the financial statements of a nonpublic entity. Procedures may apply to only one, both, or neither type of engagement.

1. The accountant should establish an understanding with the entity regarding the nature and limitations of the services to be performed.
2. The accountant should make enquiries concerning actions taken at the board of directors meetings.
3. The accountant should obtain a level of knowledge of the accounting principles and practices of the entity's industry.
4. The accountant should obtain an understanding of the entity's internal control.
5. The accountant should perform analytical procedures designed to identify relationships that appear to be unusual.

6. The accountant should send a letter of enquiry to the entity's attorney to corroborate the information furnished by management concerning litigation.
7. The accountant should obtain a management representation letter from the entity.
8. The accountant should make enquiries about events subsequent to the date of the financial statements that would have a material effect on the financial statements.
9. The accountant should perform a physical examination of inventory.

Required

a. Indicate which procedures are required to be performed on a review engagement.
b. Indicate which procedures are required to be performed on a compilation engagement.

22-19 Your public accounting firm is the auditor of Taylor Fruit Farms, Inc., a company located in Penticton, B.C., and incorporated under the laws of British Columbia. You have been requested by the management of Taylor to issue an opinion under Section 5815 of the *CICA Assurance Handbook* with respect to Taylor's compliance under the terms of a chattel mortgage issued by J.L. Lockwood Corp. as part of your audit of Taylor Fruit Farms, Inc. J.L. Lockwood Corp. is a supplier of irrigation equipment. Much of the equipment, including that supplied to Taylor, is sold on a secured contract basis. Unlike Taylor Fruit Farms, Lockwood is not an audit client of yours.

In addition to the present equipment, Taylor informs you that Lockwood is evaluating whether it should sell another $500,000 of equipment to Taylor Fruit Farms.

You have been requested to send Taylor the report under Section 5815 concerning the following matters:

1. The current ratio has exceeded 2.0 in each quarter of the unaudited statements prepared by management and in the annual audited statements.
2. Total owners' equity is more than $800,000.
3. The company has not violated any of the legal requirements of British Columbia's fruit-growing regulations.
4. Management is competent and has made reasonable business decisions in the past three years.
5. Management owns an option to buy additional fruit land adjacent to its present property.

Required

a. Define the purpose of a report under Section 5815.
b. Is it necessary to conduct an audit of a company before issuing a report on compliance under Section 5815?
c. Would you include all five matters listed above in your report? If not, explain why you would exclude any from the report.

22-20 It is now March 2006. Margaret Monson, the owner of Major Products Manufacturing Inc., a small successful long-time audit client of your firm, has requested you to work with Major in preparing three-year forecasted information for the year ending December 31, 2006, and two subsequent years. Monson informs you that she intends to use the forecasts, together with the audited financial statements, to seek additional financing to expand the business. Monson has had little experience in formal forecast preparation and counts on you to assist her in any way possible. She wants the most supportive opinion possible from your firm to add to the credibility of the forecast. She informs you that she is willing to do anything necessary to help you prepare the forecast.

First, she wants projections of sales and revenues and earnings from the existing business, which she believes could continue to be financed from existing capital.

Second, she intends to buy a company in a closely related business that is currently operating unsuccessfully. Monson states that she wants to sell some of the operating assets of the business and replace them with others. She believes that this will make the company highly successful. She has made an offer on the new business, subject to obtaining proper financing. She also informs you that she has received an offer on the assets that she intends to sell.

Required

a. Explain circumstances under which it would and would not be acceptable to undertake the engagement.
b. Why is it important that Monson understand the nature of your reporting requirements before the engagement proceeds?
c. What information will Monson have to provide you before you can complete the forecasted statements? Be as specific as possible.
d. Discuss, in as specific terms as possible, the nature of the report you will issue with the forecasts, assuming that you are able to properly complete them.

22-21 O'Sullivan, a public accountant, has completed the audit of Sarawak Lumber Supply Co. Ltd. and has issued a standard unqualified report. In addition to a report on the overall financial statements, the company needs a special audit report on three specific accounts: sales, net fixed assets, and inventory valued at FIFO. The report is to be issued to Sarawak's lessor, who bases annual rentals on these three accounts. O'Sullivan was not aware of the need for the special report until after the overall audit was completed.

Required

a. Explain why O'Sullivan is unlikely to be able to issue the special audit report without additional audit tests.
b. What additional tests are likely to be needed before the special report can be issued?
c. Assume that O'Sullivan is able to satisfy all the requirements needed to issue the special report, and write the report. Make any necessary assumptions.

PROFESSIONAL JUDGMENT PROBLEM

22-22 Ballantine Church has been located on a central downtown street in Toronto for over 120 years. Originally, the church was in the middle of farmland but is now surrounded by high rises. The church has an active parish community that engages in fund raising in the neighbourhood, assisting the homeless, and providing drop-in housing during the winter. Francine, the parish priest, and the church board have decided it is time to have a review engagement completed for the church finances. In the past, this work has been completed by church members on a part-time basis.

The church organizes its finances based on five funds: operating, endowment, youth, homeless, and music scholarship. Any transfers from the endowment fund to the operating fund must be approved by the board. The church has about $1.2 million in cash and marketable securities in the bank. The church is valued at zero on the balance sheet.

The church also owns a large house. Francine lives in a section and the rest of the property is used for storage, as office space for three permanent church staff, and as meeting space.

Required

a. What should you do before you accept the review engagement?
b. Outline the process for conducting the review engagement and describe any analytical review procedures that you would conduct specific to the church. What types of questions would you ask that are specific to the church to address plausibility of financial information?

CASE

22-23 Quality Review is the franchisor of a national accounting review course for candidates taking CA, CGA, and CMA examinations. Quality Review is responsible for providing all materials, including cassettes and video material, doing all national and local advertising, and giving assistance in effectively organizing and operating local franchises. The fee to the participant is $1,500 for the full course if all parts of the examination are taken. Quality Review gets 50 percent of the total fee.

The materials for the review course are purchased by Quality Review from Ronnie Johnson, a highly qualified writer of review materials. Quality Review receives one copy of those materials from Johnson and reproduces them for candidates.

Quality Review must pay Johnson a $60 royalty for each full set of materials used and 12 percent of the participant fee for partial candidates. The contract between Johnson and Quality Review requires an audited report to be provided by Quality Review on royalties due to Johnson. Recorded gross fees for the 2004 review course are $1,500,000.

Even before the audit is started, there is a dispute between Quality Review and Johnson. Quality Review does not intend to pay royalties on certain materials. Johnson disagrees with that conclusion but the contract does not specify anything about it. The following are the disputed sales on which Quality Review refuses to pay royalties:

1. Materials sent to instructors
   for promotion $31,000
2. Uncollected fees due to bad debts 6,000
3. Candidates who paid no fee because
   they performed administrative duties
   during the course 16,000
4. Refunds to customers who were
   dissatisfied with the course 22,000
   Total $75,000

a. Assume that you are engaged to do the ordinary audit of Quality Review and the special audit of royalties for Johnson. What additional audit testing beyond the normal tests of royalties is required because of the special audit?
b. Assume that the financial statements of Quality Review are found to be fairly stated except for the unresolved dispute between Johnson and Quality Review. Write the appropriate audit report.
c. Write the report for total royalties to Johnson, assuming that the information as stated in the case is correct and the dispute is not resolved.

CHAPTER 23

USING ADVANCED SKILLS

Accountants work with many different clients, in a broad spectrum of settings from small to large and complex businesses. Many different types of services are required for these clients. Accountants can provide advisory services and address the complexities of engagements during the financial statement audit.

LEARNING OBJECTIVES

After reading this chapter, you should be able to answer the following questions:

1. Explain how WebTrust and SysTrust help provide assurance over information systems. Describe services provided by environmental auditing. What is a business valuation?

2. What are the characteristics of advanced information systems? How do customized systems increase going concern risks? What internal controls should be implemented for database management systems? What is an example of a multiple information processing location risk?

3. What is the most important control in a small business that affects information technology?

4. Why would an auditor need information about controls at a client's computer service organization? How can a tax specialist contribute during a financial statement audit?

5. Where can one find information about proposed changes in audit standards?

AN ACCOUNTANT'S EDUCATION SHOULDN'T STOP WITH AN ACCOUNTING DESIGNATION

Bob, Joanne, Brigitte, and Tom all went to university together, and each received his or her accounting designation about 10 years ago. They get together for lunch regularly. Recently, Joanne announced that she had successfully obtained her CBV (Chartered Business Valuator) designation. As a tax practitioner, Joanne believed this would help her clients immensely with respect to tax planning. Groans (from Tom) and cheers (from the others) greeted her.

"Pretty late for you to do something like this. It's so hard to get back into studying, especially for the CBV program," commented Brigitte, who had obtained her CISA (Certified Information Systems Auditor) designation five years previously. Bob agreed. Bob is a CFA (Certified Financial Analyst) who practises in the Mergers and Acquisitions Department of a large public accounting firm.

Tom smiled and said, "You couldn't get me to write another exam! It's difficult enough keeping up to date in tax and accounting and auditing standards, as well as learning how to use all the different accounting software packages on the market. Getting some designation wouldn't help my clients with their software and accounting needs."

Bob, Joanne, Brigitte, and Tom reflect the changing face of accounting professionals. Having met the challenge of obtaining an accounting designation and working with a diversity of clients, Bob, Joanne, and Brigitte updated their educational qualifications and business experience to help them satisfy the needs of their clients. However, some practitioners, like Tom, feel that while ongoing education and experience are important, additional designations may not be appropriate for them.

Do you have a special interest in tax, valuations, or a particular industry group, such as non-profit organizations? As a public accountant, you would have the opportunity to use your accounting designation as an important base for moving forward in the business community.

→23.1 THE NEED FOR ADVANCED SKILLS: SPECIALIZED ASSURANCE ENGAGEMENTS

Professional accounting organizations understand the need for specialization, and have decided it is time to officially recognize these realities. For example, the CICA has approved several "CA-Designated Specialists":

- CA•IFA (Investigative and Forensic Accounting);
- CA•IT (Information Technology);
- CA•CBV (Corporate Finance Business Valuation);
- CA•CIA (Internal Auditing);
- CA•CISA (Information Systems Auditing); and
- CA•CIRP (Insolvency and Restructuring).

There is a world of opportunity awaiting interested, qualified professionals. Accounting firms are expanding in the business advisory and consulting areas.

Special Engagements

Chapter 22 explained that assurance engagements could be either attest engagements or direct reporting engagements. The following discussion uses direct reporting as a basis, although attest engagements could also be appropriate in certain situations. The previous chapter defined a direct reporting engagement as an engagement in which the auditor directly expresses a conclusion on his or her evaluation of a subject matter using certain criteria and for which management does not report. For example, an auditor could be asked to evaluate the controls surrounding the use of electronic commerce in connection with purchases made using a company's web page. Management provides a list of its business activities and business objectives, not a list of controls. Should the controls be of adequate quality, the auditor would be able to issue a WebTrust seal (see next section for more details) for placement on the web page. The seal confirms to users of the web page that acceptable control quality was achieved. The auditor uses published criteria when making the assessment of control quality.

Criteria used for a direct reporting engagement could be externally available, provided by a specific user, or established by agreement between the auditor and management. In a direct reporting engagement, the auditor is adding value by providing (or denying) assurance that the criteria have (or have not) been met.

Remember, these special engagements can be provided only if they do not jeopardize the auditor's independence with respect to the financial statement audit, or, for a listed company, if the PA firm is not the client's financial statement auditor. Chapter 2 explains the threats that could arise from providing prohibited services: self-interest threat (if special service fees are large in proportion to the audit fee), self-review threat (should the auditor design a system and then subsequently audit it), or advocacy threat (when the PA acts as an advocate for the client). For example, we discuss business valuation services later in the chapter—these services could not be provided by the PA firm that conducts the financial statement audit for a listed entity. Even for a non-listed entity, the PA should ensure that there is no threat to perceived independence.

Many organizations have voluntarily registered the entity as adhering to specific **ISO** (International Organization for Standardization) standards, such as **ISO-9000** (quality assurance standards) and ISO-14000 (environmental management standards). The auditor uses the criteria associated with the international standards to confirm that the entity has met the ISO standards.

ISO—International Organization for Standardization, a worldwide federation of national standards bodies from some 130 countries

ISO-9000—standards provided by the International Organization for Standardization (ISO) with respect to quality assurance management

The International Organization for Standardization or ISO is a worldwide federation of national standards bodies from some 130 countries, having one body from each country.

The ISO is a nongovernmental organization established in 1947. Its stated mission is to promote the development of standardization to facilitate the international exchange of goods and services and to develop cooperation in intellectual, scientific, technological, and economic activity.

The ISO web site notes that ISO is not an acronym but rather derived from the Greek word *isos*, meaning "equal." This international name was chosen so that acronyms would not change with the language used. Whatever the country, the short form is always ISO.

The organization indicates that international standards exist for the following reasons:

- To improve worldwide progress in trade liberalization

- To assist interpenetration of industry sectors
- To facilitate worldwide communications systems
- To provide global standards for emerging technologies
- To assist developing countries in creating infrastructures

One area where Canadian accountants could provide criteria and measurement for businesses is the assessment of greenhouse gas (GHG) emissions. This would help in the potential trading of GHG credits, in the context of the Kyoto Protocol, an agreement signed in 1998 with the goal of reducing emissions of six greenhouse gases. Such assessment is also useful for understanding the local environmental impact of businesses.

Sources: 1. Glenn, Shannon and John Beech, 2002. "Emissions trading: are you ready?" *CAmagazine*, August 2002, pp. 24–29. 2. The International Organization for Standardization, www.iso.org.

International Organization for Standardization (ISO)
www.iso.org

The distinction between assurance services and business advisory services can be blurred. Some firms would call the above ISO standards examination business advisory services. Other firms reserve the term "business advisory services" for the completion of work that may not have any predetermined criteria. Some examples follow:

- The management of a manufacturing company observes that its gross profits are declining but is not sure why. An accountant is called in to identify what can be done: should quality control be improved or does overtime need to be reduced?
- The internal auditor is asked to assist in the selection and implementation of software and hardware for a new accounting system.
- During the annual financial statement audit, the auditor notices that there are significant weaknesses in general computer controls (perhaps program development controls or access controls are poor). The auditor will discuss with management how further assistance can be contracted to provide detailed guidance for general controls and a specific application cycle indicating how controls should be improved.

BUSINESS ADVISORY SERVICES—services agreed on by an accountant and a client for the completion of a specific task (or set of tasks)

In theory, direct reporting engagements and attest engagements are those engagements that require specified standards (or criteria) to be used, while **business advisory services** relate to the completion of a specified task (or set of tasks) agreed upon by the accountant and the client. In practice, the term "business advisory services" may be used loosely to encompass almost any type of work that assists a client.

WebTrust

EDI and EFTs (electronic funds transfers) have related hazards (e.g., stolen credit card numbers, amounts taken from or deposited to the wrong account, and duplicate payments charged to a customer). One of the reasons consumers might not purchase items via an Internet web site is fear of credit card numbers being misused, either during the transaction or by the entity that is storing the information. Another reason could be that since the consumer cannot walk into a store and touch the goods, he or she may have doubts as to the goods' existence or whether they will really be shipped. These fears led to the idea for WebTrust.

WebTrust was successfully launched in the fall of 1997 with a joint press release issued by the CICA and the AICPA. Information about WebTrust is available on the CICA web

CICA
www.cica.ca

page. The WebTrust principles (extracted from this web site) specifically address the potential concerns of consumers:

- *Business practice disclosure*: The entity is to disclose its business practices for e-commerce transactions and execute those transactions using these disclosed business practices.
- *Transaction integrity*: Effective controls are maintained to ensure that customers' orders placed using e-commerce are completed and billed as agreed.
- *Information protection*: Effective controls are maintained to ensure that private customer information is protected.

The WebTrust auditor's report is linked to the CICA web site where criteria for WebTrust are displayed. The report is addressed to management and has the following paragraphs:

- An introductory paragraph indicating that an audit was conducted, defining criteria, and specifying a time period. It is explained that it is management's responsibility to provide the controls; the auditor is expressing an opinion on those controls.
- A scope paragraph further defining the standards and explaining the type of work required.
- An opinion paragraph indicating that the standards were met.
- Additional explanatory and disclaimer paragraphs. The first indicates that fraud or errors may not be detected and that controls may change in the future. The second indicates that the WebTrust seal is symbolic of the contents of the report but does not provide assurance in itself. The third states that there is no representation regarding the quality of goods and services provided.

Reference to Chapter 22 will show that this is a standard format followed by special reports. The controls used by businesses may be highly technical and may involve encryption, the use of firewalls, or other controls that the entity considers necessary. The **WebTrust seal** is initially obtained by an organization when those principles have been met using specified criteria. An electronic seal is placed upon the client's web page, which is linked to the CICA (or AICPA) web site so that consumers can obtain information about WebTrust and establish the seal's authenticity as well as find out about the standards associated with the seal. The seal must be periodically renewed by having an audit confirm that the standards are still in place and operating effectively.

WEBTRUST SEAL—a seal placed on a web site upon completion of an auditor's report, verifying compliance with standards with respect to business practices and controls over electronic commerce transactions

SysTrust As more organizations become dependent on information technology, the security, availability, and accuracy of computer systems are critical. An unreliable system can trigger a chain of business events that negatively affect the company, its customers, suppliers, and other business partners. The AICPA and CICA jointly developed the *SysTrust* service to provide assurance that a system is reliable.

In a *SysTrust* engagement, the *SysTrust* licensed accountant evaluates a company's computer system using *Trust Services* principles and criteria, as shown in Table 23-1, and determines whether controls over the system exist. The accountant then performs tests to determine whether those controls were operating effectively during a specified period. If the system meets the requirements of the *Trust Services* principles and criteria, an examination-level unqualified attestation report is issued. A licensed *SysTrust* accountant may report on only one *Trust Services* principle or any combination of *Trust Services* principles.

An organization may request a *SysTrust* engagement for a system that is in the pre-implementation phase. For this type of engagement, the accountant reports on the suitability of the design of controls, and the report is at a point in time rather than for a period of time.

SYSTRUST—an engagement where the PA evaluates a company's computer system

ISO-14000 Audits and Environmental Auditing

An auditor would be concerned with environmental issues in the audited financial statements because of possible contingent liabilities. What if the client is not complying with specific environmental legislation? There could be fines for violating the legislation. There could also be clean-up costs associated with inappropriately handling waste or dangerous substances. The public may prefer purchasing products from or investing in those companies that run their businesses responsibly, taking the environment into account.

TABLE 23-1	Five Trust Services Principles
Principle	**The entity discloses and maintains compliance with its**
Security	security practices, ensuring that the system is protected against unauthorized access (both physical and logical).
Availability	availability practices, ensuring that the system is available for operation and use as committed or agreed.
Processing Integrity	processing integrity, ensuring that system processing is complete, accurate, timely, and authorized.
Online Privacy	online privacy practices, ensuring that personal information obtained as a result of e-commerce is collected, used, disclosed, and retained as committed or agreed.
Confidentiality	confidentiality practices, ensuring that information designated as confidential is protected as committed or agreed.

With respect to the financial statement audit, Assurance and Related Services Guideline AuG-19, "Audit of Financial Statements Affected by Environmental Matters," released in January 1994, provides guidance. Audit of the actions undertaken by management with respect to specific legislation is a compliance audit (discussed in the next chapter) that is also a direct reporting engagement and requires significant expertise on the part of the auditor.

The ISO standards, set by the Geneva-based International Organization for Standardization, require that registered entities adhere to the published standards. Standards are lengthy and require that organizations establish policies and procedures associated with the standards, have internal processes that ensure that the standards are met, and submit to an independent review by an outside organization that is qualified to inspect that standard. The audit team that conducts an **ISO-14000** audit must have expertise in auditing, in the ISO standards, and in the practice of environmental management and/or auditing; have adequate knowledge of the business processes to plan the audit; and adhere to the standards of assurance engagements.

ISO-14000—standards provided by the International Organization for Standardization (ISO) with respect to environmental management

In addition to conducting ISO-14000 audits, professional accounting firms could conduct audits with respect to specific environmental legislation, assist organizations in improving their management of environmental pollutants, or perform other specified consulting assignments. Such work helps both the organization and the legislators to verify that appropriate actions are being taken in this area that affects us all.

Business Valuations "Obtaining the highest price in an open and unrestricted market is the goal of any business that's up for sale."[1] Qualified accountants are trained in **business valuation**, using methods such as net present value of projected cash flows to provide a value for the shares or assets of a business. The following focus box provides one example of why business valuations are needed.

BUSINESS VALUATION—provision of a value for the shares or assets of a business

In addition to providing an estimated value for the business, qualified accountants can, in their capacity as advisors to the vendors, arrange an auction process to sell a business. Cole describes the process of arranging an auction from potential purchaser identification through to negotiations and closing of a sale.[2]

Business valuations are required for numerous reasons. These could include marital breakdown, estate planning, or business mergers. The public accountant's analytical skills and professional judgment assist clients in this process.

---

[1]Cole, S., "Going Once, Going Twice...," *CAmagazine* (January/February 1999), pp. 41–42, 50.
[2]Ibid, p. 42.

Helen's husband died suddenly of a heart attack, leaving her the majority shareholder of a specialized manufacturing business with revenues of $2 million. The managers did not listen to her, and she didn't understand the business very well, so the business suffered. After several years of losses, Helen started using a variety of consultants.

Finally, an acquaintance recommended a qualified accountant. The accountant, Diane, started with a business review, identifying efficiency problems and the need to trim excess management. Then quality control procedures were improved. A building was sold to bring in necessary capital. Helen was gradually building up her expertise, working with both the accountant and selected individuals in the business. An unprofitable segment was disposed of. The company became profitable, and profit sharing was implemented with key employees.

Helen had proven herself capable. After talking about selling the business for three years, she started getting serious in her talks with the general manager of the business, who was interested in taking it over. Diane called Bob, a qualified accountant who specialized in business valuations, and Helen engaged Bob to conduct a business valuation. The valuation would be used during negotiations between herself and her general manager.

→23.2 ADVANCED INFORMATION SYSTEMS

What Are Advanced Information Systems?

An organization is likely to have advanced automated systems when its systems have one or more of the following characteristics:

- Custom-designed operational or strategic information systems
- Use of database management systems
- Use of data communications (including Internet)
- Use of paperless systems such as electronic data interchange or electronic funds transfer
- A complex hardware or software processing configuration

The existence of each of these characteristics affects the nature of information systems processing at the organization and thus also affects the audit process. This section describes the characteristics, while subsequent sections describe the effects on internal controls.

Extent of Custom-Designed Operational and Strategic Information Systems[3] The Appendix to Chapter 8 described the forms of software acquisition as being in-house development, acquisition from an outside vendor, or turnkey software development (where an outsider prepares custom software). Here, we discuss the type of custom software as opposed to standard packaged software. Figure 23-1 summarizes the advantages and disadvantages of these two types of software.

Increased use of customization can improve a business entity's competitive advantage or efficiency of operations. However, should **strategic information systems** fail or have errors, they increase costs and risks to the business. During the audit planning process, the auditor identifies the nature of such systems and the type of development process. In highly automated or integrated systems, auditors prefer to rely on the computer systems since it is more efficient to test programmed controls than to conduct tests of details. Where the system development process is complex or error prone, the auditor may assess the risk of program errors occurring as high, leading to an increased assessment of inherent risk and control risk.

When systems are so strategic that they could affect the ability of the entity to continue as a going concern if they fail, then the auditor takes a closer look at the disaster recovery planning process, as discussed in Chapter 8. For example, if a bank's teller functions and automated teller machines could not function for a lengthy period of time, banks would be

STRATEGIC INFORMATION SYSTEM—a system that provides a competitive advantage or improves efficiency within an entity

---

[3]See also Laudon, K. C., J.P. Laudon, and M. E. Brabston, *Management Information Systems*, Second Canadian Edition, 2005, p. 342.

FIGURE 23-1 — Advantages and Disadvantages of Custom Software and Packaged Software

	Custom Software	Packaged Software
Advantages	Tailored to meet company's exact needs.	Less costly than custom programming.
	The company conducts operations in its own often unique way.	Implementation can commence immediately after the package has been selected.
	Can more likely be used to gain strategic advantage than a software package.	Risk of system error and incorrect choice can be reduced by testing the software before purchase is made.
		Depending on the area, there are likely to be many packages available.
		Annual maintenance costs are low.
		Usually comes with user and other operating documentation.
		In-house technical analysis and programming personnel are likely not needed.
DisAdvantages	Very costly to develop.	The package may not "fit" the way the company does business or may be less efficient than customized systems.
	Lengthy program development times are common, from several months to several years.	Package evaluation process is costly and time-consuming.
	Rigorous testing program required to ensure that systems are error free.	In-house resources may be insufficient to resolve problems with system use or operations.
	Significant employee time is required for development, testing, and standard setting.	
	An iterative process that requires a high level of user and management involvement is needed to ensure greater likelihood of successful implementation.	

unable to provide basic services. Similarly, grocery stores with point-of-sale terminals would be unable to sell goods when their systems were down.

Use of Database Management Systems[4] A database system consists of two parts:

DATABASE—a collection of data that is shared and used by different users for different purposes

DATABASE MANAGEMENT SYSTEM—a system consisting of software used to create, maintain, and operate a database

- The **database**: the collection of data that is shared and used by different users for different purposes
- The **database management system**: the software that is used to create, maintain, and operate the database

Many software packages now sold use a database as an underlying file structure, and automatically maintain the profile of the database as part of the system. The use of such a software package does not normally indicate complexity or advanced automated information systems.

Complexity is introduced where a separate database management system is acquired, and the client is required to set up a separate *database administration* function to maintain the *data dictionary*.[5] With such systems, separate custom programs must be written to access and work with the data in the database. Thus, the database management system is separate from the application programs. Figure 23-2 illustrates how the data dictionary would be

---

[4]Ibid., p. 233.

[5]Ibid., p. 234.

FIGURE 23-2   Database Components

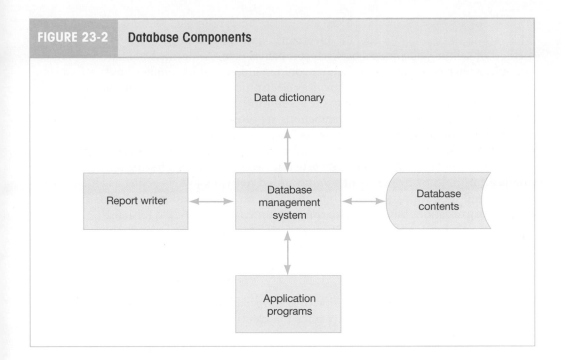

used to maintain the profile of the database contents, while access to the database through applications or a report writer is also handled by the database management system.

Effects of Database Management Systems on Internal Controls

It is important for the auditor to be aware of the existence of a database management system, since it affects all areas of general controls. These general controls include the following:

ORGANIZATION AND MANAGEMENT CONTROLS The database administrator requires specialized skills to establish and maintain the database. He or she should be segregated from other functions, such as data authorization. Typical responsibilities of the database administrator include creation and maintenance of the data dictionary, assistance with development of logical views of the data, allocation of physical storage for the database, provision for backup, and security and privacy of the data elements.

SYSTEMS ACQUISITION, DEVELOPMENT, AND MAINTENANCE CONTROLS The systems development life cycle necessitates added controls to ensure that (1) the database is developed in accordance with business needs and (2) programs accessing the database are accurate and authorized and control concurrent options (to ensure that several individuals do not attempt to change the same data element at the same time).

OPERATIONS AND INFORMATION SYSTEMS SUPPORT This includes the need for security over the data dictionary and over access to the database. The person in charge of this area works together with the database administrator.

Each application cycle needs to be examined to ensure that the appropriate controls are in place:

- Since many departments may need to access key information, such as customer name and address, a single data "owner" should be assigned responsibility for defining access and security rules, such as who can use the data (access) and what functions they can perform (security).
- Passwords should be used to restrict access to the database based on the security rules defined above.
- Segregation of duties should occur with respect to system design, database design, database administration, system operation, and authorization of data placed into the database.

Use of Paperless Systems Such as Electronic Data Interchange[6] or Electronic Funds Transfer[7] in Data Communications **Electronic data interchange** (EDI) is an electronic method of sending documents between companies using a specified standard format. For example, a pharmaceutical manufacturer could mandate that its suppliers must accept standard purchase orders and submit invoices electronically. EDI is either implemented as a stand-alone system or integrated into the accounting systems. Stand-alone systems are used as receiving and sending stations: transactions are often printed out, reviewed, and rekeyed into the appropriate application system. In integrated systems, the EDI transaction is automatically translated into a format that can be read by the application system. EDI transactions can be sent and received directly between two organizations having direct data communications links or by means of a **value added network** (**VAN**) acting as an electronic mailbox and forwarding service. Thus, there are no longer paper documents that move between organizations but rather electronic documents in a standard format.

Electronic funds transfer (EFT), also referred to as *electronic commerce* or *E-commerce*, is the transmission of cash equivalents using **data communications**. Examples include:

- Use of a debit card by a consumer to authorize the transfer of funds from the consumer's account to a merchant's account
- (As an extension of EDI) submission of appropriate transactions for the electronic payment of the invoice by the entity once the electronic invoice has been received and approved for payment
- Automatic payment of employee payroll from the company's bank account to the employee's bank account

Effects of Data Communications and Multiple Locations on Internal Controls

Figure 23-3 shows a business with a head office, a branch office, and an Internet home page that is used by customers for ordering goods. At point (1), head office initiates data communications to connect with the branch at point (2) using a **communications channel** (3) such as a public telephone line. Customers use Internet service providers to connect to the head office Internet home page at (4). The Internet home page is linked to the head office order entry software. The following unauthorized activities could occur at the numeric points of Figure 23-3:

1. A hacker could dial into the head office system, penetrating the systems and copying, altering, or removing data or programs.
2. A hacker could similarly dial into the branch office system, penetrating the systems and copying, altering, or removing data or programs.
3. The line could be tapped and data copied.
4. Orders could be placed using fraudulent credit cards. A hacker could penetrate the web site and alter it by placing inappropriate material on the site. A hacker could penetrate the web site and gain access to the accounting systems, with the same result as (2). Viruses could be transmitted and placed on the head office or branch office systems.

Table 23-2 summarizes the data communications risks and provides examples of control procedures that would be used to deal with each risk. When conducting the audit of entities that use data communications, the auditor needs to extend the assessment of general and application controls to the data communications process. Table 23-2 shows that controls previously discussed, such as the use of passwords and physical segregation, can be used to effectively deal with data communications risks.

Related to data communications is the risk associated with multiple information processing locations. Table 23-3 on page 650 describes examples of these risks and provides examples of control procedures that would reduce the risks.

---

[6]See *Audit Implications of EDI*, The Canadian Institute of Chartered Accountants, 1996; and Splettstoesser, I. B., "Managing and Auditing Electronic Data Interchange," *The CPA Journal* (November 1997), pp. 26–32.

[7]See Powell, R., "Auditing Electronic Funds Transfer," *IS Audit and Control Journal*, Vol. II (1994), pp. 48–51; and Perry, J. T. and G. P. Schneider, *New Perspectives on E-Commerce,* Toronto, Ontario: Thomson Learning, 2001.

FIGURE 23-3 **Potential Data Communications Risk Points**

Internet home page
(4)

Head office
(1)

(3)

(2)

Customers

Branch office

(1) Data communications connection at head office

(2) Data communications connection at branch office

(3) Communications medium

(4) Internet connection

TABLE 23-2 **Examples of Data Communications Risks and Controls**[8]

Data Communications Risk	Examples of Control Procedures to Deal with the Risk
Inappropriate access to the accounting or other systems via data communications, with resulting loss of confidentiality or damage (see (1) and (2) on Figure 23-3).	Create multiple levels of passwords; change passwords regularly.
Data intercepted or copied during data communications (see (3) on Figure 23-3).	Ensure that confidential data undergoes **encryption** (scrambling) during transmission.
Inappropriate access to the accounting or other systems via the Internet, with resulting loss of confidentiality or damage (see (4) on Figure 23-3).	Physically segregate Internet home page equipment and software from other systems. Use **firewalls** (software and/or hardware that restricts access to and from Internet sites).
Viruses could be placed onto the head office or branch office systems, causing destruction of data or programs or disruption of service (see (4) on Figure 23-3).	Same as above. Also, acquire current anti-virus software, and keep the software current.

ENCRYPTION—the process of scrambling data so that they cannot be read directly

FIREWALL—software and/or hardware that is used to restrict access to and from Internet sites

[8]See also Schwartau, W., "Creating Boundaries: Protecting Companies and Employees on the Information Superhighway," *IS Audit and Control Journal*, vol. I (1996), pp. 28–32; and Ramakrishnan, G., "Risk Management for Internet Banking," *Information Systems Control Journal*, vol. 6 (2001), pp. 48–50.

TABLE 23-3

TABLE 23-3 | **Examples of Risks from Multiple Information Processing Locations and Control Procedures**

Multiple Information Processing Locations Risk	Examples of Control Procedures to Reduce the Risk
Data processed in multiple locations could become inconsistent (e.g., inventory prices).	One location has primary responsibility for updating the information. Exception reports are printed and differences between locations followed up.
Programs could be inaccurate or unauthorized at one or more locations.	Head office controls all program changes. Branch offices are sent only the object code.
Branches could have unauthorized access to head office programs and data or vice versa.	Clear responsibilities are assigned for data and program ownership and change rights. Adequate access control systems are used to enforce these rights (e.g., confidential passwords).
Some data sent from one location to another might not be received (i.e., incomplete or inaccurate transmissions).	Use control totals, record counts, and sequential numbering of transactions and follow up any missing or out-of-sequence data.

As part of the knowledge of business, the auditor would have obtained system hardware and software configuration diagrams. These would inform the auditor about the extent of the complexity associated with data communications or multiple locations. General controls over data communications software and passwords are critical when assessing control risks associated with data communications. The auditor must be assured that controls are in place for:

- Accurate functioning of data communications software
- Custody of and periodic changes to **encryption keys** (codes used to scramble and unscramble data)
- Effective functioning of firewalls
- Effective controls over issuance, maintenance, and removal of passwords

ENCRYPTION KEYS—codes used to scramble and unscramble data

Once these technical areas have been assessed, the auditor would then consider each application cycle.

→23.3 SMALL BUSINESS INFORMATION TECHNOLOGY CONTROLS

Our discussions of internal control have indicated that small businesses frequently rely on owner/manager supervision. This is true whether a business uses manual or automated information systems. In this section, we examine the likely characteristics of a small business using the control framework of Figure 9-1 (page 247), Four Components of Internal Control.

Control Environment

The quality of the control environment depends on the attitudes of the owner/manager. If the owner/manager adequately supervises employees, hires only competent employees, and encourages practices such as the use of confidential passwords, then the organization will have a more positive control environment than a situation in which the owner is an absentee one and encourages the use of illegal copies of software.

General Control Systems and Procedures

ORGANIZATION AND MANAGEMENT CONTROLS There are often fewer people in the accounting department, perhaps even only one person; thus, segregation of duties may not be possible.

Controls are often informal, lacking written authorization procedures. The owner/manager can readily override controls by personally performing clerical or operating functions.

SYSTEMS ACQUISITION, DEVELOPMENT, AND MAINTENANCE CONTROLS Use of packaged software is common in the accounting systems. A variety of software packages are available; they range in quality. Where programming is undertaken, controls over changes may be poor since an informal process will likely be used rather than a structured approach.

OPERATIONS AND INFORMATION SYSTEMS SUPPORT Primarily because of the small size of the organization, the information systems are likely to be simpler systems, using a centralized form of processing. The entity is unlikely to have in-house expertise on systems and would normally place reliance on software and hardware suppliers for system support and maintenance. Passwords may be in use but are in a simple form (i.e., the accounting personnel may have a single password that allows access to all systems and all functions).

Application Control Procedures When a software package is used and the entity is not capable of making changes to the software (since most software packages are provided only in machine code), certain controls in the software become important. For example, calculations in invoicing and inventory costing (mechanical accuracy), posting of transactions to subsidiary systems and to the general ledger (detail tie-in), and aging of accounts receivable (valuation) are all functions normally present in software packages, which assist the business and on which the auditor can rely.

Practical Controls to Be Exercised by the Owner/Manager For controls to be practical in a small business, they need to be activities that can be performed in a short period of time; otherwise it is unlikely that an owner/manager will implement them.

SYSTEMS ACQUISITION, DEVELOPMENT, AND MAINTENANCE CONTROLS It is important that the owner/manager understand the nature of software used by the business and how business needs might change. This includes software maintenance needs. For example, if the company uses a payroll package, then the company should expect to receive an upgrade whenever tax rates change. The owner should ensure that authorized programs are implemented (i.e., only valid, copyrighted materials should be implemented). If program changes are implemented, an employee should be assigned to test and keep a record of changes.

OPERATIONS AND INFORMATION SYSTEMS SUPPORT Backups should be made daily, with at least two copies of recent data kept offsite. Although a formal disaster recovery plan may not be contemplated, the entity should have a current contact for hardware and software support in the event of system problems. As a minimum, documentation to provide for ongoing operations should be present, such as a list of the procedures that are normally completed on a daily, weekly, and monthly basis.

APPLICATION CONTROL PROCEDURES These procedures include *controls to prevent fraud*. The most important control concept here is the separation of authorization from the recording of transactions. As in other sizes of business, the owner/manager needs to remain vigilant to prevent computer fraud or other types of fraud. Chapters 13 through 20 indicate that the owner should perform certain key activities, such as signing payroll cheques with a supporting payroll journal, signing accounts payable cheques with supporting documentation, and reviewing master file information.

Summary When a small business has automated information systems, the required key controls are the same as those required in a small business using manual procedures. These are owner/manager controls. In addition, reliance on the computer programs may be useful. Activities to maintain ongoing operations, such as backup and operational documentation, should also be present.

Most small businesses have a lack of expertise in the selection, design, or operation of their automated information systems and frequently call on their accountant as a business advisor to help in these areas.

Some clients still have certain types of data processed at an independent computer service organization. For example, many companies have banks process their payrolls or have trust companies maintain their share and dividend records.

In a **computer service organization** operation, the client submits input data, either on paper forms or by means of data communications. The service organization processes it for a fee and provides the output transactions to the client along with the agreed-upon output. Generally, the service organization is responsible for designing the computer system and providing adequate controls to ensure that the processing is reliable.

The difficulty that the independent auditor faces when a computer organization is used is in determining the adequacy of the service organization's internal controls. The auditor cannot automatically assume that the controls are adequate simply because the service organization is an independent enterprise. If the client's service organization application involves the processing of significant financial data, the auditor must consider the need to understand and test the service organization's controls.

The extent of obtaining an understanding and testing of the service organization should be based on the same criteria that the auditor uses in evaluating a client's own internal controls. The depth of the understanding depends on the complexity of the system and the extent to which the auditor intends to assess control risk below maximum to reduce other audit tests. If the auditor concludes that active involvement with the service organization is the only feasible way to conduct the audit, it may be necessary to obtain an extensive understanding of the service organization's internal controls, test them by the use of test data and other tests of controls, and use the computer to perform computer-assisted audit tests. Extensive testing of this nature is unlikely in most audits because such traditional service organization applications are reasonably simple. When the client has controls that involve comparing the input details provided by the client to the output details provided by the service provider, reference to controls at the service provider may not be necessary. (This is known as the "black box" approach.) However, some review of the service centre is usually done.

In recent years, it has become increasingly common to have *one* independent auditor obtain an understanding of and test the service organization's internal control for the use of *all* customers and their independent auditors. The purpose of these independent reviews is to provide customers with a reasonable level of assurance of the adequacy of the service organization's internal controls and to eliminate the need for redundant audits by the service organization's customers' auditors. If the service organization has many customers and each one requires an understanding of the service organization's internal controls by its own independent auditor, the inconvenience to the service organization can be substantial. An independent auditor can complete a special report for service organizations under Section 5970, "Auditor's Report on Controls at a Service Organization." The report would describe the scope of the audit and the conclusions. It is then the responsibility of the customer's auditor to decide the extent to which he or she wants to rely on the service organization's auditor's report. Section 5310, "Audit Evidence Considerations When an Enterprise Uses a Service Organization," is instructive in that regard.

Service Organizations and Outsourcing

The Auditing and Assurance Standards Board released Section 5970, "Auditor's Report on Controls at a Service Organization" in 2005 in response to the many different types of service organizations and outsourcing that have occurred in recent years. For example, you can have your computer programming done in Pakistan, your programming in Russia, and your architectural design work in Bulgaria. The Internet and high-speed data communications capabilities have enabled businesses to move these functions to remote parts of the world.

The new section uses the basis that service auditor reports would be used primarily by other auditors, not by clients or users of service organizations. This is in conformity with International Standard on Auditing 402, "Audit Considerations Relating to Entities Using Service Organizations," and the American AICPA SAS 70, "Service Organizations."

COMPUTER SERVICE ORGANIZATION—an external organization that processes transactions or performs other information systems processing services

Potential Tax Issues During a Financial Statement Audit

It is important during the conduct of the financial statement audit that the audit team have the expertise necessary to adequately conduct the audit. We have discussed the need for specialists in auditing inventory, information systems, and accounts involving estimates, such as actuarial calculations. Another specialist that can contribute during all phases of the audit is the tax specialist. Tax is such a broad area that individuals may specialize by industry, by country (e.g., the PA firm could have individuals who work with American or European taxes), or by type of tax (e.g., commodity and excise versus income taxes). Following are just a few areas where the auditor needs to ensure that the assistance of such specialists is readily available.

Corporate Tax Payable Calculations With mergers and acquisitions and different types of taxes, the auditor needs to take care that balances forward and special tax treatments are handled properly. For example, a company may have research and development applications, which allow for preferential tax credits. Other credits are available for specific industries and certain parts of Canada, depending on where the provincial or federal government is encouraging job creation. The calculation of the actual tax rate may also be complex.

It is important that the tax specialist review the tax payable provision, as an error in the tax payable provision could result in the misstatement of income. Many firms require that a senior audit team member prepare the corporate tax returns and that a tax specialist review the audit report before it is finalized. This will help prevent misstatements in the income tax provision.

Sales Cycle—Goods and Services Tax (GST) Collectible As a consumer, you may believe that goods and services tax is a 7 percent tax on most items. However, for a business, it is not quite so simple. In food service, for example, there may not be any tax due if you purchase a single item (such as a Danish), but there might be tax due if you purchase a package of six. This means that computer software needs to be carefully designed to ensure that point-of-sale systems accurately charge the tax.

Non-profit organizations that are registered charities do not need to collect GST for their charitable purpose, but they might need to collect GST for products that they sell, such as t-shirts with logos. It is important that all organizations, including non-profit organizations and charities collect GST when required, or they could be liable to the government for the uncollected taxes. Tax specialists help organizations review their procedures to ensure that they are collecting taxes on the appropriate products.

Purchases and Payments Cycle—Goods and Services Tax (GST) Recoverable Organizations can claim rebates against GST collected for GST paid on purchases used to produce goods and services sold. However, they must pay GST on products for their own use. Some organizations can claim only partial rebates. Non-profit and educational organizations have different rebate levels, depending on the type of organization. Tax specialists can help the auditor review the tax rate that is being used by non-profit organizations for accuracy.

Payroll and Personnel Cycle—Taxable Benefits There are many different taxable benefits, such as housing, vehicle expenses, and benefits related to use of meal facilities. A PA with tax expertise can help the client review the methods used for calculating benefits. This could include reviewing procedures embedded in payroll software.

→23.5 WHAT'S NEW IN RESEARCH?

As the business world constantly changes, new types of businesses emerge and business practices change. Thus, accountants must also change in the way audits are conducted for such businesses.

All professional associations have some form of research activity. For example, the Certified General Accountants Association has a federal Research Foundation, chartered in 1913, that sponsors research. The results of the research are published in articles or books

Certified General Accountants Association
www.cga-online.org

and are available for purchase. The CISA (Certified Information Systems Auditor) designation is provided by the Information Systems Audit and Control Association, which also has a Research Foundation. Research grants are provided to academics, and the association itself conducts research into topics that are technology-related, such as controls in electronic commerce.

The CICA provides regular status reports on its web page of the activities being undertaken by a variety of task forces and committees. Check this web site for a list of the outstanding exposure drafts. Most exposure drafts are resolved and either removed or implemented within a relatively short period of time, so they are not listed here. At the CICA web site, you can also find links to the International Auditing and Assurance Standard Board (IAASB), where international auditing standards for comment are posted.

SUMMARY

1. *Explain how WebTrust and SysTrust help provide assurance over information systems.* With WebTrust, the independent auditor examines controls at a client web site with respect to business practice disclosure, transaction integrity, and information protection. SysTrust evaluates controls over specific information system processing systems.

   Describe services provided by environmental auditing. The auditor could attest to compliance with environmental standards such as ISO-14000, conduct audits with respect to specific environmental legislation, or assist organizations in improving their management of environmental pollutants.

   What is a business valuation? This is a financial assessment to provide a value for the shares or assets of a business.

2. *What are the characteristics of advanced information systems?* Advanced systems will likely have one or more of the following characteristics: complex custom-designed software, database management system implementations, a variety of data communications methods, paperless systems or e-commerce, or a complex hardware or software processing configuration.

   How do customized systems increase going concern risks? With complex systems, the risk of program errors increases, affecting the likelihood of system failure. If the risk of program error is high, there is an increase in the likelihood of business failure.

   What internal controls should be implemented for database management systems? Important internal controls include segregation from programming and data authorization, clear definition of data ownership, and well managed password access.

   What is an example of a multiple information processing location risk? Table 23-3 lists several risks. One example would be the risk that a program differs at multiple locations, perhaps due to unauthorized access to programs.

3. *What is the most important control in a small business that affects information technology?* The most important control for a small business is the quality of the control environment provided by the owner/manager. This affects all systems, whether manual or automated.

4. *Why would an auditor need information about controls at a client's computer service organization?* If the service organization provides services that are not managed or controlled by client staff, then the auditor may need assurance with respect to the activities performed at the service organization.

   How can a tax specialist contribute during a financial statement audit? The tax specialist can provide assistance with the calculation of income taxes payable, income tax provision, GST collectible and recoverable, employee benefits, and can verify that the client is calculating these amounts correctly.

5. *Where can one find information about proposed changes in audit standards?* For proposed changes to the *CICA Assurance Handbook*, check out the CICA web site at www.cica.ca.

CICA ASSURANCE HANDBOOK SECTIONS REFERENCED IN THIS CHAPTER

Section 5310 - Audit evidence considerations when an entity uses a service organization.

Section 5970 - Auditor's report on controls at a service organization.

AuG-19 – Audit of financial statements affected by environmental matters.

ESSENTIAL TERMS

Business advisory services—services agreed on by an accountant and a client for the completion of a specific task (or set of tasks) (p. 642).

Business valuation—provision of a value for the shares or assets of a business (p. 644).

Communications channel—the medium used to transmit data from one location to another (e.g., microwave, satellite, telephone line) (p. 648).

Computer service organization—an external organization that processes transactions or performs other information systems processing services (p. 652).

Database—a collection of data that is shared and used by different users for different purposes (p. 646).

Database management system—a system consisting of software used to create, maintain, and operate a database (p. 646).

Data communications—the process of sending data electronically from one physical location to another (p. 648).

E-commerce—*see* Electronic funds transfers.

Electronic commerce— *see* Electronic funds transfers.

Electronic data interchange—an electronic method of sending documents between companies using a specified standard format (p. 648).

Electronic funds transfers (EFTs)—the transmission of cash equivalents using data communications (also known as *electronic commerce* or *E-commerce*) (p. 648).

Encryption—the process of scrambling data so that they cannot be read directly (p. 649).

Encryption keys—codes used to scramble and unscramble data (p. 650).

Firewall—software and/or hardware that is used to restrict access to and from Internet sites (p. 649).

ISO—International Organization for Standardization, a worldwide federation of national standards bodies from some 130 countries (p. 641).

ISO-14000—standards provided by the International Organization for Standardization (ISO) with respect to environmental management (p. 644).

ISO-9000—standards provided by the International Organization for Standardization (ISO) with respect to quality assurance management (p. 641).

Strategic information system—a system that provides a competitive advantage or improves efficiency within an entity (p. 645).

SysTrust—an engagement where the PA evaluates a company's computer system (p. 643).

Value added network (VAN)—an intermediary for an organization using EDI; translates, stores, and forwards EDI transactions (p. 648).

WebTrust seal—a seal placed on a web site upon completion of an auditor's report, verifying compliance with standards with respect to business practices and controls over electronic commerce transactions (p. 643).

REVIEW QUESTIONS

23-1 What are the distinguishing characteristics of a direct reporting engagement?

23-2 Provide three examples of business advisory services.

23-3 What is the theoretical difference between an assurance engagement and a business advisory service?

23-4 List three reasons why consumers might not want to pay for goods electronically using the Internet. Explain how the WebTrust principles address these concerns.

23-5 Explain why international standards such as ISO-14000 are important. Why would an entity voluntarily register for ISO-14000?

23-6 Identify the different categories of expertise required to conduct an ISO-14000 audit.

23-7 List the services that a business valuator can provide to a client.

23-8 List the phases of the systems development life cycle (refer to an MIS textbook), and identify at least one activity that the accountant could undertake in each phase.

23-9 List five characteristics of advanced automated information systems. Define each characteristic and provide an example.

23-10 Explain why the use of customized software is more likely to increase the complexity of information systems than the use of packaged software.

23-11 What is the difference between a software package that uses database file structures and one that uses a database management system? Why is the latter more likely to increase system complexity?

23-12 Identify the types of controls that are affected by the implementation of database management systems. For each type of control, provide an example of the effects.

23-13 List four risks that face entities using data communications. Provide at least one example of how the risk could be mitigated.

23-14 Describe the risks associated with entities that process information using multiple locations. For each risk, provide a potential control.

23-15 Describe five important characteristics of EDI systems that are significant to the auditor.

23-16 Identify audit and control issues associated with EDI and EFTs.

23-17 Explain why a PA might require specialist tax assistance during a financial statement audit.

MULTIPLE CHOICE QUESTIONS

23-18 Choose the best response for the following questions:

a. A WebTrust engagement requires an auditor to provide assurance with respect to

(1) the accuracy and authorization of electronic commerce transactions.
(2) the controls over electronic data interchange transactions.
(3) security over the data communications and data retrieval process.
(4) controls over business practices and related controls over electronic commerce.

b. One of the reasons that consumers may not purchase items using an electronic web site is due to concern over having their credit card numbers compromised. The WebTrust principle that addresses this concern is

(1) business practice disclosure: the entity is to disclose its business practices for e-commerce transactions and execute the transactions using those disclosed business practices.
(2) transaction integrity: effective controls are maintained to ensure that customers' orders placed using e-commerce are completed and billed as agreed.
(3) information protection: effective controls are maintained to ensure that private customer information is protected.
(4) firewall usage: hardware and software firewalls are used to coordinate and manage Internet traffic.

c. Medium Financial Corporation has a complex hardware configuration. There is a central computer, as well as branch computers and automated teller machines. An Internet banking interface is being considered. Several thousand transactions are processed each day. Given good internal controls, the likely audit approach would be

(1) a test of details approach only, due to the uniqueness of the system.
(2) controls testing only, due to the high volume of transactions processed.
(3) a combined audit approach, with reliance on specialist assistance.
(4) primary reliance on a service auditor's report, due to the outsourced software.

d. Small Manufacturing Company has only two staff members that get involved in accounting: the owner and a full-time bookkeeper/receptionist. Which of the following functions is it most important that the owner do, rather than the receptionist?

(1) Review of master file changes
(2) Transferral of backup tapes offsite
(3) Approval of programming standards
(4) Printing of accounts receivable aging report

e. JKM Company is an on-line Internet-based bookstore. Customers place orders, inputting their credit card numbers. All Internet electronic traffic is encrypted, but passwords are not required for customers. To prevent hackers from accessing JKM's accounting systems, JKM should

(1) use firewalls to restrict access of known problem web sites.
(2) use dial-back methods to connect with all customers who want to place an order.
(3) use a dedicated, stand-alone computer for web site systems.
(4) have detection software to prevent junk e-mail and other abuses.

DISCUSSION QUESTIONS AND PROBLEMS

23-19 Farmco Limited (Farmco), a privately owned apple farm, is highly debt leveraged. Two loans from XYZ Bank are currently outstanding: a long-term loan that is secured by the farm's land, building structure, and equipment; and, a short-term demand loan that is secured by unharvested apples valued at net realizable value. Farmco also leases some of the farming equipment from a local supplier. It is now one month before the harvesting of the apples. The bank has given you a special assignment to assess the adequacy of the security for Farmco's loans.

Required
Discuss which audit procedures you would carry out in completing this assignment and why.

(CICA adapted)

23-20 Turner Valley Hospital plans to install a database management system, Hosp Info, that will maintain patient histories including tests performed and their results, vital statistics, and medical diagnoses. The system also will manage personnel and payroll, medical and non-medical supplies, and patient and provincial health care billings. The decision was taken by the board of the hospital on the advice of a consultant who was a former employee of Medical Data Services Inc., the developer of Hosp Info.

Turner Valley Hospital's chief information officer has come to your accounting firm to ask for advice on what general controls she should ask Medical Data Services Inc. to install to preserve the integrity of the information in the system and to deal with privacy issues.

The system would permit data about patients to be entered by doctors, nurses, and medical technologists.

Required

a. Describe in general terms the controls you would suggest for the system as a whole.

b. Considering the nature of Turner Valley Hospital, describe potential risks the hospital should be concerned about with respect to Hosp Info.

c. What are the advantages of such a database management system?

23-21 During the past six months, your company has consistently been losing competitive bids to a nearby company whose bids always seem to be slightly lower. Subsequent investigation reveals that an employee of your company in the payroll department has been stealing your bid data and selling it to the competitor for $5,000 per bid. Your company has offices in five buildings. Computing services are provided using five local area networks connected by a common carrier.

Required

a. Identify methods that the employee could be using to obtain the data.

b. For each method, identify at least one control that could have been used to detect or prevent the data theft.

23-22 It was a typical madhouse time on the night before a payroll run. Some employees were entering time cards; other employees were checking data entry lists to time cards and calling supervisors about employee numbers that they couldn't read. The system started slowing down, and then staff started getting ABORT—RETRY messages when they tried to execute programs. Initially, technical support staff suspected a cable break or an operating system failure. Diagnostics were run, revealing nothing. Finally, a staff member began running the SCAN virus detection program and uncovered a new virus that seemed to have originated from the central server. The virus cost the company about 25 person-hours in technical support and about 70 hours in overtime for payroll clerks, who stayed until 4 a.m.

The company has one local area network with 250 stations using linked central servers. Some stations have hard disks up to 20 gigabytes in size; some stations have no disk drives at all. Salespeople have laptop computers that they use to dial in from remote locations to conduct customer enquiries and place customer orders.

Required

a. Identify the potential sources of the virus infection.

b. How could this virus infection have been prevented?

c. What elements of a disaster recovery plan are required for recovery from a virus infection?

PROFESSIONAL JUDGMENT PROBLEM

23-23 Frank is the owner of Frankincents Machining Limited, a custom machining centre with 10 full-time employees and a part-time bookkeeper, Norma, who comes in two days a week. Norma convinced Frank to purchase a small business suite of accounting packages and a microcomputer with a laser printer. Norma has set up the records on the computer, and all accounting work is now handled using the accounting packages (i.e., order entry, accounts receivable, cash disbursements, general ledger, payroll). It took Norma about three months, and she initially had some difficulty balancing the subsystems, but everything seems to be functioning properly now. Frank did not consult with you, his accountant, prior to implementing the systems.

Required

a. Identify the risks associated with the current method of handling accounting records at Frankincents Machining Limited.

b. Identify those activities that Frank should handle in sales, accounts receivable, cash disbursements, and payroll. Explain why.

CASES

23-24 Acme Manufacturing Limited (AML) consists of two operating divisions: Acme Plastics, which produces various plastic consumer products, and Acme Chemicals, which uses a by-product of Acme Plastics to produce various resins for sale to other companies for further processing. A summary process chart of the operations and additional comments are included in Figure I.

As a result of increasing public concern about environmental issues, Donna Rideout, the president of AML, has asked the audit engagement partner for AML to provide her with a proposal to conduct an environmental audit of the Acme Plastics division. The results will be used to provide an environmental

"report card" for the division and will be included in the company's next annual report to its shareholders.

The partner has asked you to provide him with a memo that discusses the unique issues in accepting this type of engagement. Your memo should include a discussion of the audit approach for this engagement and the nature and content of the report that would be issued as a result of the environmental audit.

Required

Prepare the memo requested by the partner.

(CICA adapted)

FIGURE I   Acme Plastics, Summary Process Chart and Additional Comments

Summary Process Chart—Acme Plastics Division

Additional Comments

Polymer resins used for the process are purchased from U.S. suppliers and shipped to the plant in specially built tanker trucks used by AML. To avoid contamination of the various resins in transit, it is necessary to rinse the inside of each tank with water after each shipment.

Water, obtained from the nearby river, is also used in the process as both an ingredient and a coolant. The coolant water returning to the river is tested regularly to ensure compliance with local regulations.

The process requires considerable heat, which is produced by thermal generators that burn natural gas. The gas arrives by pipeline from the local gas company. Some of the excess heat is recycled throughout the plant to reduce heating costs in winter.

The process produces two highly flammable liquid by-products, known as Oxy-1 and Oxy-2. Oxy-1 is packaged into 200 L drums and stored until sold to the Acme Chemical Division. Acme Chemical further processes it into a varnish resin and sells this product to various paint manufacturers.

At present, there is no commercially viable use for Oxy-2, which is also stored in 200 L drums and kept in a storage area at the back of the property. When necessary (about twice a year), Acme Plastics contracts We-Take-All Ltd., an independent waste disposal company, to have the drums removed.

23-25 Miles Jones has been assigned as the audit senior responsible for a new client, Starfire Electric Limited (SEL). The engagement partner, Ms. Rogers, explained that SEL is a reputable private corporation located in Vancouver. It manufactures electrical components for residential and industrial uses. Major product lines include electrical fuses and circuit breakers for residential uses and heavy-duty breakers and transformers for industrial uses. During the current year, SEL also began producing electrical heating units for commercial applications.

SEL has been growing steadily over the past 10 years and has plants located in Vancouver, Calgary, and Winnipeg. It started with 10 employees and now employs over 200. Transformers are manufactured at the Vancouver plant, circuit breakers at the Calgary plant, and electrical fuses and heating units at the Winnipeg plant. In total, SEL produces about 600 products.

SEL has been experiencing some difficulty in obtaining supplies of plastics used as raw material in the production of circuit breakers. It is investigating the purchase of a plastics company located in the United States to ensure an adequate supply. SEL is considering a public offering after the year end to raise the estimated $10 million required to purchase this company.

Because SEL is considering a public offering, the directors decided that SEL should have its financial statements audited. A local chartered accounting firm had issued Notice to Readers for SEL since its incorporation. SEL looked for a larger accounting firm that could better serve its expanding operations and appointed your firm as auditors for the year ending September 30, 2005. Ms. Rogers has communicated with the previous accountants and has obtained an engagement letter from SEL.

Ms. Rogers asks you to prepare a planning memo for her review regarding the audit and accounting and other issues pertaining to this new assignment, along with your recommendations on how to deal with each of them.

After your meeting with Ms. Rogers, you visit SEL's head office and obtain the most recent financial statements (see Figure II) and other information about the client's operations as shown:

- Each plant operates as a separate profit centre, maintaining its own accounting system on a local area network. Each plant uses a copy of the head office programs. These programs are stored in object code (machine language) on the plant's server.
- Each plant is responsible for the control of its own computer operations, and each produces special-purpose reports for its own use using a general-purpose report writer as the need arises. The five accounting personnel at each location handle computer operations and the use of the report writer. File layouts are used to decide which data fields to access. Copies of new report formats are sent to head office as attachments to electronic mail messages when completed. Since these reports and new programs are produced as required, no formal testing procedures exist.
- Each plant also submits to head office a set of accounting reports and supplementary information. These are submitted in a standard format, electronically, for use in the preparation of combined corporate financial statements. The statements are prepared by the controller using a spreadsheet package.

- SEL's inventory consists of raw materials, work in progress, and finished goods. Raw materials include copper, used as a conductor in almost all of the components; silver, used for contacts in the electrical breakers; and plastic and steel, used in the casings for breakers and transformers. Most of the raw materials are purchased from suppliers in the United States.
- SEL uses a standard costing system to account for its inventory. A standard cost is prepared for each product by each plant based on its own production capacity, time and motion studies, and engineering estimates. Each standard cost consists of a raw material component, a direct labour component, and an overhead component that is based on direct labour hours. The costing and perpetual inventory systems were custom written by head office programmers.
- New standards are established once a year on April 1. The standard costs are entered in a standard cost master file and used to value inventories. Only two people at each plant have the password that allows them to change the standard cost master file. Password changes are controlled by the computer operators, who are informed orally of the need for change. The revaluation allowance resulting from the annual conversion of March 31 inventories to the new standard is amortized over the inventory turnover period. Normally, sales prices are updated at the same time by the sales supervisor using a separate password.
- The Vancouver plant's standard cost master file had been inadvertently changed during the performance of some computer program maintenance. The programs had been transmitted to the plant server from the head office systems by the head office's programming department. The head office programmers are attempting to determine the cause of the data changes to ensure that the problem does not recur. As a result of the inadvertent change, the books in Vancouver had been showing favourable variances in the direct labour and overhead components of $50,000 and $100,000 respectively. As of August 31, $60,000 of these variances has been allocated to cost of sales.
- The company web page is maintained by head office personnel, with information on all of the different types of products and services. Since the web page provides information only (customers cannot place orders), it is located directly on the head office server. Customers can view product information and send e-mail queries to anyone at the company using the web page.

Required

Prepare the memo requested by the partner.

(CICA adapted)

FIGURE II **Starfire Electric Limited Extracts**

Starfire Electric Limited Extracts from Unaudited Balance Sheet

	(In thousands of dollars) As at	
	August 31, 2005	**September 30, 2004**
Assets		
Current		
Cash	$ 244	$ 54
Accounts receivable, net	4,771	4,601
Inventories	9,256	7,922
	14,271	12,577
Fixed assets, net	6,707	5,547
	$20,978	$18,124
Liabilities		
Current		
Accounts payable and accrued liabilities	$ 6,779	$ 5,892
Income taxes payable	45	54
Current portion of long-term debt	312	255
	7,136	6,201
Long-term debt	4,258	3,595
Deferred income taxes	1,401	1,274
Shareholders' Equity		
Share capital	2	2
Retained earnings	8,181	7,052
	8,183	7,054
	$20,978	$18,124

Starfire Electric Limited
Extracts from Unaudited Statements of Income and Retained Earnings

	(In thousands of dollars) As at	
	August 31, 2005 (11 months)	**September 30, 2004 (12 months)**
Net sales	$35,846	$31,454
Income before the following:	$ 3,017	$ 2,511
Amortization	954	750
Interest on long-term debt	350	386
Other interest	12	20
	1,316	1,156
Income before income taxes	1,701	1,355
Income taxes		
— current	445	574
— deferred	127	(115)
	572	459
Net income	1,129	896
Retained earnings at beginning of the period	7,052	6,156
Retained earnings at end of the period	$ 8,181	$ 7,052

CHAPTER 24

ASSURANCE SERVICES: INTERNAL AUDITING AND GOVERNMENT AUDITING

Many PAs work in industry, in internal audit departments, or in government. Government auditors in the Auditor General's offices play important roles in providing accountability for government departments and programs.

LEARNING OBJECTIVES

After reading this chapter, you should be able to answer the following questions:

1. What is the role of internal auditing in many organizations? What are the key differences between operational auditing and financial auditing? Provide an example of an audit criterion of effectiveness and efficiency associated with each.

2. How are the functions of an Auditor General office different from an internal audit office? How is independence facilitated for government and internal auditors? What are some sources of criteria for conducting an operational audit?

3. List the phases in operational auditing. Where can one find sample reports of value-for-money audits?

APPLYING THE COSO MODEL TO CUSTOMER RELATIONSHIP MANAGEMENT

The Committee of Sponsoring Organizations of the Treadway Commission's (COSO's) internal control model uses five components: the control environment, risk assessment, control activities, information and communication, and monitoring. [In this text, we have combined the last two components—see Chapter 9.] We can use this model in many ways—for organizing our analysis, for creating a process to audit, and for developing a quantitative assessment process, as proposed by Perry and Warner in the April 2005 issue of the *Internal Auditor*.

Let's take a look at a call centre, a key component of customer relationship management (a process used to serve customers and increase sales). Call centres can be used to process orders, handle customer complaints, and deal with maintenance of products—a variety of important services.

A good *control environment* results in clearly articulated compensation and hiring policies, as well as identifies the importance of computer access controls where management recognizes the importance of its people and its data. The *risk assessment process* identifies data input risks (where software is not integrated) or service risks (if employees are put under time pressures in dealing with customers). *Control activities* would include programmed controls to ensure that data are consistent across customer relationships and accounting (such as common customer names and addresses), and limit tests (to prevent common errors such as a transaction for $300 being recorded as $3,000).

Information and communication with *monitoring* result from the review of customer complaints and customer statistics with feedback to staff for changing their practices. Using a control model allows for the examination of processes strategically, helping businesses assess whether their goals are being met and customers are being served.

Sources: 1. Aldhizer, III, George R., and James D. Cashell, 2004. "Customer relationship management: risks and controls," Internal Auditor, Vol. LXI:VI. 2. Perry, William E., and H. C. "Pete" Warner, 2005. "A quantitative assessment of internal controls," Internal Auditor, Vol. LXII:II.

What kind of work would you like to do once you have received your accounting designation? Are you interested in public accounting or working in industry? You could become a financial officer, an internal auditor, or a public sector auditor—all of these positions provide the opportunity to get to know particular entities very well.

→24.1   INTERNAL AUDITING

As discussed in Chapter 1, internal auditors are employed by entities to help improve the organization's operations. Internal auditors typically use a risk-based approach in consultation with the audit committee to determine the type of work that they will complete. This could include operational auditing, systems development auditing, fraud auditing, and providing assistance with the financial statement audit conducted by the external auditors. Their role in auditing has increased dramatically in the past two decades, primarily because of the increased size and complexity of many corporations.

In financial auditing, internal auditors are responsible for evaluating whether their company's internal controls are designed and operate effectively and whether the financial statements are fairly presented. Because internal auditors spend all of their time with one company, their knowledge about the company's operations and internal controls is much greater than the external auditors' knowledge.

Guidelines for performing internal audits for companies are not as well defined as for external audits. This occurs because of the wide variety of internal audits. Based on user requirements, the audit purpose, audit methods, and audit reports must be customized. Management of different companies may have widely varying expectations of the type and extent of financial auditing to be done by internal auditors. For example, management of one company may decide that internal auditors should be extensively involved in systems development, whereas others may decide that their work should focus primarily on financial controls and fraud audits.

The Institute of Internal Auditors (IIA)
www.theiia.org

THE INSTITUTE OF INTERNAL AUDITORS (IIA)—an organization for internal auditors that establishes ethical and practice standards; provides education, a professional exam, and a professional designation; and encourages professionalism for its members

STANDARDS FOR THE PRACTICE OF INTERNAL AUDITING—guidelines issued by the Institute of Internal Auditors, covering the activities and conduct of internal auditors

The Institute of Internal Auditors Internal auditors look to **The Institute of Internal Auditors (IIA)** for professional guidance. The IIA is an organization that functions for internal auditors much as the CICA does for CAs, the CGAAC for CGAs, and the SMAC for CMAs; it establishes ethical standards and **standards for the practice of internal auditing**, provides education, and encourages professionalism for its approximately 103,000 members. The IIA has played a major role in the increasing influence of internal auditing. For example, the IIA has established a highly regarded certification program resulting in the designation of Certified Internal Auditor (CIA) for those who meet the testing and experience requirements.

The IIA standards include attribute standards, performance standards, and implementation standards (Figure 24-1).

Relationship of Internal and External Auditors There are both differences and similarities between the responsibilities and conduct of audits by internal and external auditors. The primary difference is to whom each party is responsible. The external auditor is responsible to financial statement users who rely on the auditor to add credibility to the statements. The internal auditors are responsible to management, although, to improve independence, they should report to the audit committee. Even with this important difference, there are

ATTRIBUTE STANDARDS

1000 Purpose, Authority, and Responsibility. The purpose, authority, and responsibility of the internal audit activity should be formally defined in a charter, consistent with the *Standards*, and approved by the board.

1100 Independence and Objectivity. The internal audit activity should be independent, and internal auditors should be objective in performing their work.

1200 Proficiency and Due Professional Care. Engagements should be performed with proficiency and due professional care.

1300 Quality Assurance and Improvement Program. The chief audit executive should develop and maintain a quality assurance and improvement program that covers all aspects of the internal audit activity and continuously monitors its effectiveness. The program should be designed to help the internal auditing activity add value and improve the organization's operations and to provide assurance that the internal audit activity is in conformity with the *Standards* and the *Code of Ethics*.

PERFORMANCE STANDARDS

2000 Managing the Internal Audit Activity. The chief audit executive should effectively manage the internal audit activity to ensure it adds value to the organization.

2100 Nature of Work. The internal audit activity evaluates and contributes to the improvement of risk management, control, and governance systems.

2200 Engagement Planning. Internal auditors should develop and record a plan for each engagement.

2300 Performing the Engagement. Internal auditors should identify, analyze, evaluate, and record sufficient information to achieve the engagement's objectives.

2400 Communicating Results. Internal auditors should communicate the engagement results promptly.

2500 Monitoring Progress. The chief audit executive should establish and maintain a system to monitor the disposition of results communicated to management.

2600 Management's Acceptance of Risks. When the chief audit executive believes that senior management has accepted a level of residual risk that is unacceptable to the organization, the chief audit executive should discuss the matter with senior management. If the decision regarding residual risk is not resolved, the chief audit executive and senior management should report the matter to the board for resolution.

Source: From *The International Standards for the Professional Practice of Auditing*, Copyright © 2004 by The Institute of Internal Auditors, Inc., 247 Maitland Avenue, Altamonte Springs, FL 32701-4201. Reprinted with permission.

many similarities between the two groups. Both must be competent as auditors and remain objective in performing their work and reporting their results. They both, for example, follow a similar methodology in performing their audits, including planning and performing tests of controls and substantive tests. Similarly, they both use the audit risk model and materiality in deciding the extent of their tests and evaluating results. Their decisions about materiality and risks may differ, however, because external users may have different needs from management's.

External auditors rely on internal auditors through the use of the audit risk model. Auditors significantly reduce control risk and thereby reduce substantive testing if internal auditors are effective. The fee reduction of the external auditor is typically substantial when there is a highly regarded internal audit function. External auditors typically consider internal auditors effective if they are independent of the operating units being evaluated, competent and well trained, and have performed relevant audit tests of the internal controls and financial statements.

Section 5050, "Using the Work of Internal Audit," permits the external auditor to use the internal auditor for direct assistance on the audit. This means that the external auditor is permitted to treat internal auditors much like his or her own audit staff. The incentive for management is a reduced audit fee, whereas the incentive for the public accounting firm is retaining the client. The risk to the external auditor is the lack of competent and independent performance by the internal auditors. Before using internal auditors, the external auditor must be confident of their competence, independence, and objectivity. In addition, external auditors typically review the internal auditor's work to make certain that it was done correctly.

Operational Auditing

Although **operational auditing** is generally understood to deal with efficiency and effectiveness, there is less agreement on the use of that term than one might expect. Many people prefer to use the terms "**value-for-money auditing**" or "performance auditing" instead of

> OPERATIONAL AUDITING—the review of an organization for efficiency and effectiveness. The terms management auditing, performance auditing, and operational auditing are often used synonymously

> VALUE-FOR-MONEY AUDITING—a public sector audit that considers the economy, efficiency, and effectiveness with which an entity's operations are conducted; see also operational auditing

"operational auditing" to describe the review of organizations for efficiency and effectiveness. Those people typically describe operational auditing broadly, including evaluating internal controls and even testing those controls for effectiveness (tests of controls). Others do not distinguish among the terms "performance auditing," "management auditing," and "operational auditing."

Differences Between Operational and Financial Auditing

Three major differences exist between operational auditing and financial auditing: the purpose of the audit, the distribution of the reports, and the inclusion of nonfinancial areas in operational auditing. Due to the breadth of the services offered, many internal auditors provide internal consulting. They thus perform work similar to that described in the previous chapter as business advisory services.

PURPOSE OF THE AUDIT The major distinction between financial and operational auditing is the purpose of the tests. Financial auditing emphasizes whether historical information was correctly recorded. Operational auditing emphasizes effectiveness and efficiency. The financial audit is oriented to the past, whereas an operational audit concerns operating performance for the future. An operational auditor, for example, may evaluate whether a type of new material is being purchased at the lowest cost to save money on future raw-material purchases.

DISTRIBUTION OF THE REPORTS For financial auditing, the report typically goes to many users of financial statements, such as shareholders and bankers, whereas operational auditing reports are intended primarily for management. As indicated in Chapter 3, well-defined wording is needed for financial auditing reports as a result of the widespread distribution of the reports. Because of the limited distribution of operational reports and the diverse nature of audits for efficiency and effectiveness, operational auditing reports vary considerably from audit to audit.

INCLUSION OF NONFINANCIAL AREAS Operational audits cover any aspect of efficiency and effectiveness in an organization and can therefore involve a wide variety of activities. For example, evaluating the effectiveness of an advertising program or the efficiency of factory employees would be part of an operational audit. Financial audits are limited to matters that directly affect the fairness of financial statement presentation. Operational audits also differ from financial audits in that financial audits are done on an annual basis. Operational audits are done cyclically in that parts of the organization are audited each year based upon a risk assessment process.

Effectiveness Versus Efficiency

EFFECTIVENESS—the degree to which the organization's objectives are achieved

EFFICIENCY—the degree to which costs are reduced without reducing effectiveness

ECONOMY—the degree to which goods and services of suitable quality are acquired at the lowest price

Effectiveness refers to the accomplishment of objectives, whereas efficiency refers to the resources used to achieve those objectives. An example of effectiveness is the production of parts without defects. **Efficiency** concerns whether those parts are produced at minimum cost. **Economy**, which may be defined as acquiring goods or services of suitable quality at the best price, is often included with efficiency.

Effectiveness Before an operational audit for effectiveness can be performed, there must be specific criteria for what is meant by effectiveness. An example of an operational audit for effectiveness would be to assess whether the elevator maintenance department of a hotel chain has met its assigned objective of achieving elevator safety in the chain's many hotels. Before the operational auditor can reach a conclusion about the department's effectiveness, criteria for elevator safety must be set. For example, is the objective to see that all elevators in the chain's hotels are inspected at least once a year? Is the objective to ensure that no fatalities occurred due to elevator breakdowns, or that no breakdowns occurred?

Efficiency As with effectiveness, there must be defined criteria for what is meant by doing things more efficiently before operational auditing can be meaningful. It is often easier to set efficiency than effectiveness criteria if efficiency is defined as reducing cost without reducing effectiveness. For example, if two different production processes manufacture a product of identical quality, the process with the lower cost is considered more efficient.

Table 24-1 outlines several types of inefficiencies that frequently occur and often are uncovered through operational auditing.

Relationship Between Operational Auditing and Internal Controls In Chapter 9, it was stated that management establishes internal controls to help it meet its own goals. Certainly, two important goals of all organizations are efficiency and effectiveness. The following four concerns in setting up good internal controls were identified and discussed in Chapter 9:

- To maintain reliable systems
- To safeguard assets including records
- To optimize the use of resources
- To prevent and detect error and fraud

Each of those four concerns can be part of operational auditing if the purpose is to achieve efficient and effective operations. For example, reliable cost accounting information is important to management in deciding such things as which products to continue and the selling price of products. Similarly, failure to safeguard assets such as accounts receivable files on a computer could result in the company being unable to collect money owing when it is due.

There are two significant differences in internal control evaluation and testing for financial and operational auditing: the purpose of the evaluation and testing of internal controls, and the normal scope of internal control evaluation.

The primary purpose of internal control evaluation for financial auditing is to determine the extent of substantive audit testing required. The purpose of operational auditing is to evaluate efficiency and effectiveness of internal control and make recommendations to management. Although control procedures might be evaluated in the same way for both financial and operational auditing, their purpose differs. To illustrate, an operational auditor might determine if internal verification procedures for duplicate sales invoices are effective to ensure that the company does not offend customers but also receives all money owed. A financial auditor often does the same internal control evaluation, but the primary purpose is to reduce confirmation of accounts receivable or other substantive procedures. A secondary purpose, however, of many financial audits is to make operational recommendations to management.

The scope of internal control evaluation for financial audits is restricted to matters affecting the financial statements, whereas operational auditing concerns any control affecting efficiency or effectiveness based on risks. Therefore, for example, an operational audit could be concerned with policies and procedures established in the marketing department to determine the effectiveness of catalogues used to market products.

TABLE 24-1	Types of Inefficiencies
Types of Inefficiency	**Example**
Acquisition of goods and services is excessively costly.	Bids for purchases of materials are not required.
Raw materials are not available for production when needed.	An entire assembly line must be shut down because necessary materials were not ordered.
There is duplication of effort by employees.	Identical production records are kept by both the accounting and production departments because they are unaware of each other's activities.
Work is done that serves no purpose.	Copies of vendor's invoices and receiving reports are sent to the production department where they are filed without ever being used.

Who Performs Operational Audits?

Operational audits are usually performed by one of three groups: internal auditors, government auditors, or consulting firms.

Internal Auditors Many internal audit departments do both operational and financial audits as well as compliance audits. Often, operational and financial audits are done simultaneously. An advantage that internal auditors have in doing operational audits is that they spend all their time working for the company they are auditing. They thereby develop considerable knowledge about the company and its business, which is essential to effective operational auditing.

To maximize their effectiveness, the internal audit department staff should report to the audit committee of the board of directors. This organizational structure helps internal auditors remain independent. For example, if internal auditors report to the controller, it is difficult for them to evaluate independently and make recommendations to senior management about inefficiencies in the controller's operations.

Focus Box 24-1

STRATEGIC INTERNAL AUDITING WORKS WITH THE ORGANIZATIONAL UNITS TO ENHANCE CORPORATE GOVERNANCE

The risk-based approach of internal auditing considers the existence of quality programs in the organization, such as ISO-9000 production quality standards, and the existence of legal compliance review functions. Units considered low risk are not audited. Consultation with corporate governance (addressing conformance) and business governance (addressing performance) help the internal auditor consider organizational risks and priorities, key control systems, and internal audit skills and resources when designing the work to be completed.

An important audit that can assist the external auditors is an assessment of the ethical climate at an organization. The ethical climate is a barometer of the well-being of an entity. Regulations and guidelines within the organization are a valuable indicator. The internal auditors will look at the following in conducting such an audit:

*   How the internal audit function is structured, considering its level of respect, resources, and planning methods;

*   Formal assessment of ethical culture, examining whether there is integrity at all levels, accountability processes, openness, whether mistakes are learning tools, existence of commitment to best practices, and the extent of collaboration and holistic rather than parochial thinking;

*   Ethics and compliance programs, their quality, level of monitoring, and consideration of governmental laws and regulations, including the presence of a whistle-blowing program.

Tools for auditing the corporate climate include employee interviews, focus groups, and attitude surveys that are administered to ensure the confidentiality of responses. Modern internal auditors are trained in auditing and research methods and have the ability to hire specialists to help them audit the multiple types of operational units in organizations.

Sources: 1. Parkinson, Michael, 2004. "A strategy for providing assurance," *Internal Auditor*, Vol. LXI:VI.
2. Verschoor, Curtis, 2004. "The ethical climate barometer," *Internal Auditor*, Vol. LXI:V.

→ 24.2 GOVERNMENT AUDITORS

The Auditor General offices conduct both financial statement audits where mandated by legislation (e.g., crown corporations and government financial statements) and program (or operational) audits at government departments, universities, and school boards. They are also given resources to subcontract the financial or program audits to public accounting firms.

There are other auditors employed by governments such as Canada Revenue Agency auditors and provincial tax auditors. However, the discussion in this chapter focuses on government auditors who do operational and financial statement audits.

The Auditor General of Canada reported in 2004 with respect to various initiatives that affected Canada's national security. One of the points raised in the report was the inability of the passport office to provide accurate and timely data in "watch lists," lists of individuals who were suspected terrorists or who were wanted for criminal activities.

The 2005 report expanded on these findings. The passport office does meet targeted performance levels for its clients, balancing cost, service, and security of new passports issued. The issuance of passports is a large part of the service provided by this office (98 percent). However, reliable cost information is absent, which makes it difficult to assess the cost of the new security demands (e.g., digital photographs). This 2005 report repeated that the watch lists were out of date because the passport office is unable to obtain data in electronic form from other government offices.

Audit objectives included determining whether the passport office had effective and reasonable cost controls over the issuance of passports and whether it established and achieved reasonable levels of service. The 11-member audit team conducted fieldwork at 15 offices and at the national headquarters. Documentation was reviewed (background, procedural, and passport case files), sampling procedures used, and both personal and e-mail interviews conducted.

Sources: 1. "National Security in Canada—The 2001 Anti-Terrorism Initiative," Report of the Auditor General of Canada to the House of Commons, 2004, Chapter 3. 2. "Passport office—passport services," Report of the Auditor General of Canada to the House of Commons, 2005, Chapter 3.

Public Accounting Firms When public accounting firms do an audit of historical financial statements, part of the audit usually consists of identifying operational problems and making recommendations that may benefit the audit client. The recommendations can be made orally, but they are typically made by use of a *management letter*. Management letters were discussed in Chapter 21.

The background knowledge about a client's business that an external auditor must obtain in doing an audit often provides useful information for giving operational recommendations. For example, suppose the auditor determined that inventory turnover for a client slowed considerably during the current year. The auditor is likely to determine the cause of the reduction to evaluate the possibility of obsolete inventory that would misstate the financial statements. In determining the cause of the reduced inventory turnover, the auditor may identify operational causes, such as ineffective inventory acquisition policies, that can be brought to the attention of management. An auditor who has a broad business background and experience with similar businesses is more likely to be effective at providing clients with relevant operational recommendations than a person who lacks those qualities.

Independence and Competence of Operational Auditors

The two most important qualities for an operational auditor are *independence* and *competence*.

To ensure that investigation and recommendations are made without bias, who the auditor reports to is important. Independence is seldom a problem for public accounting firm auditors because they are not employed by the company being audited. As stated earlier, independence of internal auditors is enhanced by having the internal audit department report to the audit committee or president. Similarly, government auditors should report to a level above the operating departments. The Auditor General of Canada, for example, reports to an all-party committee of Parliament as a means of enhancing independence.

The responsibilities of operational auditors can also affect their independence. The auditor should not be responsible for performing operating functions in a company or for correcting deficiencies when ineffective or inefficient operations are found. For example, it would negatively affect their independence if auditors were responsible for designing an automated information system for acquisitions or for correcting it if deficiencies were found during an audit of the acquisitions system.

It is acceptable for auditors to recommend changes in operations, but operating personnel must have the authority to accept or reject the recommendations. If auditors had the authority to require implementation of their recommendations, they would actually have the responsibility for auditing their own work the next time an audit was conducted. Independence would therefore be reduced.

The Institute of Internal Auditors considers independence of internal auditors critical and has guidelines for independence as part of its attribute standards.

Competence is, of course, necessary to determine the cause of operational problems and to make appropriate recommendations. Competence is a major problem when operational auditing deals with wide-ranging operating problems. For example, imagine the difficulties of finding qualified internal auditors who can evaluate both the effectiveness of an advertising program and the efficiency of a production assembly process. The internal audit staff doing that type of operational auditing would presumably have to include some personnel with backgrounds in marketing and others with backgrounds in production.

Criteria for Evaluating Efficiency and Effectiveness

A major difficulty found in operational auditing, as with assurance services discussed in Chapters 22 and 23, is determining specific criteria for evaluating whether operations have been efficient and effective. In auditing historical financial statements, GAAP are the broad criteria for evaluating fair presentation. Audit objectives are used to set more specific criteria in deciding whether GAAP have been followed. In operational auditing, no such well-defined criteria exist.

One approach to setting criteria for operational auditing is stating that the objectives are to determine whether some aspect of the entity could be made more effective or efficient and to recommend improvements. While perhaps adequate for experienced and well-trained auditors, this poorly defined approach would be difficult for most auditors to follow.

Specific Criteria More specific criteria are usually desirable before operational auditing is started. The auditor considers risks when setting criteria. For example, suppose you are doing an operational audit of the equipment layout in plants for a company to address the issues of quality control and efficient production. The following are some specific criteria, stated in the form of questions, that might be used to evaluate plant layouts:

- Were all plant layouts approved by home office engineering at the time of original design?
- Has home office engineering done a re-evaluation study of plant layout in the past five years?
- Is each piece of equipment operating at 60 percent of capacity or more for at least three months each year?
- Does the layout facilitate the movement of new materials to the production flow?
- Does the layout facilitate the production of finished goods?
- Does the layout facilitate the movement of finished goods to distribution centres?
- Does the plant layout effectively utilize existing equipment?
- Is the safety of employees endangered by the plant layout?

Sources of Criteria There are several sources that the operational auditor can utilize in developing specific evaluation criteria. These include the following:

HISTORICAL PERFORMANCE A simple set of criteria can be based on actual results from prior periods (or audits). The idea behind using these criteria is to determine whether things have become better or worse in comparison. The advantage of these criteria is that they are easy to derive; however, they may not provide much insight into how well or poorly the audited entity is really doing.

BENCHMARKING Most entities subject to an operational audit are not unique; there are many similar entities within the overall organization or outside it. In those cases, the performance data of comparable entities are an excellent source for developing criteria for benchmarking. For internal comparable entities, the data are usually readily available. When the comparable entities are outside the organization, they are often willing to make such information available. It is also often available through industry groups and governmental regulatory agencies.

ENGINEERED STANDARDS In many types of operational auditing engagements, it may be possible and appropriate to develop criteria based on engineered standards—for example, time and motion studies to determine production output rates. These criteria are often time-consuming and costly to develop as they require considerable expertise; however, they may be very effective in solving a major operational problem and well worth the cost. It is also possible that some standards can be developed by industry groups for use by all their members, thereby spreading the cost and reducing it for each participant. These groups may be within the industry of the subject organization or may be functional such as an application system's users' organization.

PUBLISHED STANDARDS OR CRITERIA As discussed in the previous chapter, there are ISO (International Organization for Standardization) standards for a variety of management processes, such as quality control management and environmental management. Published best practices for the development of automated information systems are available from the Software Engineering Institute (SEI) at Carnegie Mellon University, which was initially funded by the U.S. Department of Defence.

Software Engineering Institute (SEI)
www.sei.cmu.edu

DISCUSSION AND AGREEMENT Sometimes objective criteria are difficult or costly to obtain, and criteria are developed through simple discussion and agreement. The parties involved in this process should include management of the entity to be audited, the operational auditor, and the entity or persons to whom the findings will be reported.

→24.3 THE OPERATIONAL AUDIT PROCESS

Phases in Operational Auditing

There are three phases in an operational audit: planning, evidence accumulation and evaluation, and reporting and follow-up.

Planning The planning in an operational audit is similar to that discussed in earlier chapters for an audit of historical financial statements. Like audits of financial statements, the operational auditor must determine the scope of the engagement, assess risks, and communicate with the organizational unit. It is also necessary to staff the engagement properly, obtain background information about the organizational unit, understand internal control, and decide on the appropriate evidence to accumulate.

The major difference between planning an operational audit and planning a financial audit is the extreme diversity in operational audits. Because of this diversity, it is often difficult to determine specific objectives of an operational audit. The objectives will be based on the criteria developed for the engagement. As discussed in the preceding sections, these will depend on the specific circumstances at hand. For example, the objectives for an operational audit of the effectiveness of internal controls over petty cash would be dramatically different from those of an operational audit of the efficiency of a research and development department.

Another difference is that staffing is often more complicated in an operational audit than in a financial audit. This again is because of the breadth of the engagements. Not only are the areas diverse—for example, production control, advertising, and strategy planning—but also the objectives within those areas often require special technical skills. For example, the auditor may need an engineering background to evaluate performance on a major construction project.

Finally, it is important to spend more time with the interested parties reaching consensus on the terms of the engagement and the criteria for evaluation in an operational audit than in a financial audit. This was alluded to in the preceding section for criteria developed through discussion. Regardless of the source of the criteria for evaluation, it is essential that the auditee, the auditor, and the sponsor of the engagement (e.g., the audit committee) be in clear and complete agreement on the objectives and criteria involved. This agreement will facilitate effective and successful completion of the operational audit.

Evidence Accumulation and Evaluation The seven types of evidence studied in Chapter 6 and used throughout the book are equally applicable for operational auditing. Because internal controls and operating procedures are a critical part of operational auditing, it is common to extensively use documentation, client enquiry, and observation. Confirmation and reperformance are used less extensively for most operational audits.

To illustrate evidence accumulation in operational auditing, we return to the example discussed earlier about evaluating the safety of elevators for a chain of hotels. Assume there is agreement that the objective is to determine whether an inspection is made annually of each elevator in every hotel in the chain by a competent inspector. To satisfy the completeness objective, the auditor would, for example, examine blueprints of the hotel buildings and elevator locations and trace them to the head office's master list to ensure that all elevators are included in the population. Additional tests on newly constructed hotels would be appropriate to assess the timeliness with which the central listing is updated.

Assuming that the head office list is determined to be complete, the auditor can select a sample of elevator locations and evidence can be collected as to the timing and frequency of inspections. The auditor may want to consider inherent risk by doing heavier sampling of older elevators with previous safety defects. The auditor may also want to examine evidence to determine whether the elevator inspectors were competent to evaluate elevator safety. The auditor may, for example, evaluate inspectors' qualifications by reviewing résumés, training programs, competency exams, and performance reports.

It is also likely that the auditor would want to reperform the inspection procedures for a sample of elevators to obtain evidence of inconsistencies in reported and actual conditions.

In the same manner as for financial audits, operational auditors must accumulate sufficient appropriate evidence to afford a reasonable basis for a conclusion about the objectives being tested. In the elevator example, the auditor must accumulate sufficient evidence about elevator safety inspections. After the evidence is accumulated, the auditor must decide whether it is reasonable to conclude that an inspection is made annually of each elevator in each hotel owned by the chain by a competent inspector.

Reporting and Follow-up Two major differences between operational and financial auditing reports affect operational auditing reports. First, in operational audits, the report is usually sent only to management and the audit committee, with a copy to the unit being audited. The lack of third-party users reduces the need for standardized wording in operational auditing reports. Second, the diversity of operational audits requires a tailoring of each report to address the scope and objectives of the audit, findings, and recommendations.

The combination of these two factors results in major differences in operational auditing reports. Report writing often takes a significant amount of time to communicate audit findings and recommendations clearly.

Follow-up is important in operational auditing when recommendations are made to management. The purpose is to determine whether the recommended changes were made, and if not, why.

Examples of Operational Audit Findings

A broad variety of documents discussing existing internal audits and operational audits is generally available. Often, these articles show up as "how to" articles where internal auditors take the experience gained during audits and share this experience with the broader community.

The *Internal Auditor* is a bimonthly publication of the Institute of Internal Auditors. Following is a selection of recent articles:

- *RFID Risk Management,* by J. Kopalchick III and Christopher Monk (April 2005). This article looks at the benefits and risks of RFID (radio frequency identification) with a study of risks at Gillette Co.
- *Fraud Resistant P-cards,* by Donald Holdegraver (April 2005). Holdegraver describes P-cards (procurement cards) and itemizes controls, policies, and procedures that can help reduce the risk of fraud associated with these cards.
- *ERM: A Status Report,* by Mark S. Beasley, Richard Clune, and Dana R. Hermanson (February 2005). The IIA Research Foundation funded a study to examine internal auditing's role in the implementation of ERM (enterprise resource management) systems. This article describes the respondents, the stage of development of ERM at various

organizations, and whether the organizations involved have a Chief Risk Officer or equivalent. Internal auditors were involved in coordinating roles, identifying risk, suggesting control activities, monitoring the process, providing leadership and education, and identifying responses to risks.

- *A 10-Step Sarbanes-Oxley Solution*, by Kristina Kendall (December 2004). Kendall describes the steps undertaken by a pilot program to help ensure Sarbanes-Oxley compliance for Anthem Blue Cross and Blue Shield, a large health-care company in the United States.
- *Customer Relationship Management: Risks and Controls,* by George R. Aldhizer III and James D. Cashell (December 2004). Risks and controls for customer relationship management are described in general and for a specific call centre that was audited. Risk categories include: data input, discount policy, access, and security.

Auditor General reports are available at the following web sites:

- Canada: www.oag-bvg.gc.ca (Also the Auditor General for Northwest, Nunavut, and Yukon Territories, 2004 report available at www.oag-bvg.gc.ca/domino/reports.nsf/html/01nunavut_e.html)
- Alberta: www.oag.ab.ca
- British Columbia: www.bcauditor.com/AuditorGeneral.htm
- Manitoba: www.oag.mb.ca
- New Brunswick: www.gnb.ca/oag-bvg/index-e.asp
- Newfoundland and Labrador: www.ag.gov.nl.ca/ag/
- Nova Scotia: www.gov.ns.ca/audg/
- Ontario: www.auditor.on.ca
- Prince Edward Island: www.assembly.pe.ca/auditorgeneral/index.php
- Quebec: www.vgq.gouv.qc.ca
- Saskatchewan: www.auditor.sk.ca

The Auditor General reports cover a broad range of diverse audits. As these reports are public, you can see the risk assessments, objectives of the audit, how the audit was conducted, and the findings in great detail. For example, the printed version of the 2004 Annual Report of the Office of the Provincial Auditor of Ontario (now the Auditor General of Ontario) to the Legislature is 519 pages long. Fourteen value-for-money (operational or program) audits were discussed in this report. The Office of the Public Guardian and Trustee, a government office, was audited. The Ontario Disability Support Program was audited, as were community-based services and the employment rights and responsibilities program. The Ontario audit report also includes follow-up recommendations from the 2002 annual report, providing a public accountability—have previous recommendations been implemented?

This follow-up is important for all types of auditors. Management, the audit committee, or the legislature are concerned that operations are handled effectively.

SUMMARY

1. *What is the role of internal auditing in many organizations?* Internal auditors help improve an organization's operations—they perform operational auditing, systems development auditing, and fraud auditing, and provide assistance with the financial statement audit.

    What are the key differences between operational auditing and financial auditing? The differences are driven by the objectives. The results of a financial statement audit are an opinion on the financial statements, whereas operational audits are based upon the risks and criteria for that particular audit, normally related to effectiveness or efficiency.

    Provide an example of an audit criterion associated with each of effectiveness and efficiency. Effectiveness: Are the elevators adequately maintained to ensure safety of passengers? Efficiency: Are raw materials purchased at the best quality for the best possible price?

2. *How are the functions of an Auditor General office different from an internal audit office?* An Auditor General office also conducts financial statement audits, which are outside the scope of an internal audit office.

    How is independence facilitated for government and internal auditors? Government auditors report to an all-party legislative group or to the legislature. Internal auditors report to the audit committee to help improve independence.

What are some sources of criteria for conducting an operational audit? Criteria can be obtained based upon historical performance, from benchmarking with comparable organizations, from engineered or published standards, or from discussion and agreement with the clients.

3. *List the phases in operational auditing.* The phases are planning, evidence accumulation and evaluation, and reporting and follow-up.

Where can one find sample reports of value-for-money audits? Publicly available operational audit reports (also known as value-for-money reports) can be obtained from the web sites of the Auditor Generals for Canada and the provinces. Information about results of operational audits can also be obtained from written publications such as the *Internal Auditor* journal.

CICA ASSURANCE HANDBOOK SECTION REFERENCED IN THIS CHAPTER

Section 5050 – Using the work of internal audit.

ESSENTIAL TERMS

Economy—the degree to which goods and services of suitable quality are acquired at the lowest price (p. 664).

Effectiveness—the degree to which the organization's objectives are achieved (p. 664).

Efficiency—the degree to which costs are reduced without reducing effectiveness (p. 664).

The Institute of Internal Auditors (IIA)—an organization for internal auditors that establishes ethical and practice standards; provides education, a professional exam, and a professional designation; and encourages professionalism for its members (p. 662).

Operational auditing—the review of an organization for efficiency and effectiveness. The terms *management auditing, performance auditing*, and *operational auditing* are often used synonymously (p. 663).

Standards for the Practice of Internal Auditing—guidelines issued by the Institute of Internal Auditors, covering the activities and conduct of internal auditors (p. 662).

Value-for-money auditing—a public sector audit that considers the economy, efficiency, and effectiveness with which an entity's operations are conducted; *see also* operational auditing (p. 663).

REVIEW QUESTIONS

24-1 Explain the role of internal auditors for financial auditing. How is it similar to and different from the role of external auditors?

24-2 Explain the difference in the independence of internal auditors and external auditors in the audit of historical financial statements. How can internal auditors best achieve independence?

24-3 Describe what is meant by an "operational audit."

24-4 Identify the three major differences between financial and operational auditing.

24-5 Distinguish between efficiency and effectiveness in operational audits. State one example of an operational audit examining efficiency and another examining effectiveness.

24-6 Identify the four concerns that management has in establishing internal controls. Explain how each of those four concerns can be part of operational auditing.

24-7 Explain why many people think of internal auditors as the primary group responsible for conducting operational audits.

24-8 Explain the role of public accountants in operational auditing. How is this similar to and different from the role of internal auditors?

24-9 Under what circumstances are external auditors likely to be involved in operational auditing? Give one example of operational auditing by a public accounting firm.

24-10 Explain what is meant by the "criteria for evaluating efficiency and effectiveness." Provide five possible specific criteria for evaluating effectiveness of an automated information system for payroll.

24-11 Identify the three phases of an operational audit.

24-12 Explain how planning for operational auditing is similar to and different from financial auditing.

24-13 What are the major differences between reporting for operational auditing and financial auditing?

24-14 Explain why the Auditor General of Canada performs value-for-money audits rather than simply performing financial audits of the various government departments.

24-15 Choose the best response for the following questions:

a. The independence of the internal audit department will most likely be assured if it reports to the

(1) president.
(2) vice-president of finance.
(3) treasurer.
(4) audit committee of the board of directors.

b. Which of the following may compromise the independence of an internal auditor?

(1) Performing an audit where the auditor recently had operating responsibilities
(2) Failing to review the auditor's report with the auditee prior to distribution
(3) Reviewing automated systems prior to implementation
(4) Following up on corrective action in response to audit findings

c. Internal auditors should be objective in performing audits. Which of the following situations violates standards concerning objectivity?

(1) The auditor reviews a department in which the auditor has the responsibility for cosigning cheques.
(2) The auditor who reviews accounts receivable worked in that department for three months as a trainee two years ago.
(3) The auditor reviews a department that continues to use procedures recommended by that auditor when the department was established.
(4) The auditor reviews the same department for two years in succession.

d. The first step an operational auditor should take in performing a management study to help the director of marketing determine the optimum allocation of the advertising budget for company products is to

(1) establish and discuss with the director the key objectives of the study.
(2) analyze prior years' advertising costs.
(3) hold discussions with media personnel.
(4) determine the amount of projected sales for the purpose of establishing the proposed sales budget.

e. A preliminary survey of the human resources in a data-processing function includes a review of personnel records and practices. When the audit objective is to ascertain the economy of operation of the data-processing function, the internal auditor would seek evidence with respect to

(1) training programs that are in conformity with company policies and procedures.
(2) backup procedures relative to absenteeism, disability, and retirement.
(3) adequacy of the company's information dissemination procedures regarding personnel policies.
(4) assignment of personnel to tasks for which their education and training are appropriate.

DISCUSSION QUESTIONS AND PROBLEMS

24-16 Lajod Ltd. has an internal audit department consisting of a manager and three staff auditors. The manager of internal audit reports to the corporate controller. Copies of audit reports are routinely sent to the audit committee of the board of directors as well as to the corporate controller and the individual responsible for the area or activity being audited.

The manager of internal audit is aware that the external auditors have relied on the internal audit function to a substantial degree in the past. However, in recent months, the external auditors have suggested that there may be a problem related to objectivity of the internal audit function. This objectivity problem may result in more extensive testing and analysis by the external auditors.

The external auditors are concerned about the amount of nonaudit work performed by the internal audit department. The percentage of nonaudit work performed by the internal auditors in recent years has increased to about 25 percent of their total hours worked. A sample of five recent nonaudit activities are as follows:

1. One of the internal auditors assisted in the preparation of policy statements on internal control. These statements included such things as policies regarding sensitive payments and standards of internal controls.

2. The bank statements of the corporation are reconciled each month as a regular assignment for one of the internal auditors. The corporate controller believes that this strengthens internal controls because the internal auditor is not involved in the receipt and disbursement of cash.

3. The internal auditors are asked to review the budget data in every area each year for relevance and reasonableness before the budget is approved. In addition, an internal auditor examines the variances each month, along with the associated explanations. These variance analyses are prepared by the corporate controller's staff after consultation with the individuals involved.

4. One of the internal auditors has recently been involved in the design, installation, and initial operation of a new computer system. The auditor was primarily concerned with the design and implementation of internal accounting controls and the computer application controls for the new system. The auditor also conducted the testing of the controls during the test runs.

5. The internal auditors are frequently asked to make accounting entries for complex transactions before the transactions are recorded. The employees in the accounting department are not adequately trained to handle such transactions. In addition, this serves as a means of maintaining internal control over complex transactions.

Required

a. Define "objectivity" as it relates to the internal audit function.
b. For each of the five situations outlined, explain whether the objectivity of Lajod Ltd.'s internal audit department has been materially impaired. Consider each situation independently.
c. The manager of internal audit reports to the corporate controller.

(1) Does this reporting relationship result in a problem of objectivity? Explain your answer.
(2) Would your answer to any of the five situations in requirement (b) have changed if the manager of internal audit reported to the audit committee of the board of directors? Explain your answer.

(CMA adapted)

24-17 Superior Co. manufactures automobile parts for sale to the major U.S. automakers. Superior's internal audit staff is to review the internal controls over machinery and equipment and make recommendations for improvements when appropriate. The internal auditors obtained the following information during the assignment:

- Requests for purchase of machinery and equipment are normally initiated by the supervisor in need of the asset. The supervisor discusses the proposed acquisition with the plant manager. A purchase requisition is submitted to the purchasing department when the plant manager is satisfied that the request is reasonable and that there is a remaining balance in the plant's share of the total corporate budget for capital acquisitions.
- Upon receiving a purchase requisition for machinery or equipment, the purchasing department manager looks through the records for an appropriate supplier. A formal purchase order is then completed and mailed. When the machine or equipment is received, it is immediately sent to the user department for installation. This allows the economic benefits from the acquisition to be realized at the earliest possible date.
- The property, plant, and equipment ledger control accounts are supported by lapse schedules organized by year of acqui-

sition. These lapse schedules are used to compute depreciation as a unit for all assets of a given type that are acquired in the same year. Standard rates, amortization methods, and salvage values are used for each major type of capital assets. These rates, methods, and salvage values were set 10 years ago during the company's initial year of operation.
- When machinery or equipment is retired, the plant manager notifies the accounting department so that the appropriate entries can be made in the accounting records.
- There has been no reconciliation since the company began operations between the accounting records and the machinery and equipment on hand.

Required

Identify the internal control weaknesses and recommend improvements that the internal audit staff of Superior Co. should include in its report regarding the internal controls over capital assets. Use the following format in preparing your answer:

Weaknesses	Recommendations
1.	1.

24-18 Haskin Inc. was founded 40 years ago and now has several manufacturing plants in Central and Western Canada. The evaluation of proposed capital expenditures became increasingly difficult for management as the company became geographically dispersed and diversified its product line. Thus, the Capital Budgeting Group was organized in 2000 to review all capital expenditure proposals in excess of $50,000.

The Capital Budgeting Group conducts its annual planning and budget meeting each September for the upcoming calendar year. The group establishes a minimum return for investments (hurdle rate) and estimates a target level of capital expenditures for the next year based on the expected available funds. The group then reviews the capital expenditure proposals that have been submitted by the various operating segments. Proposals that meet either the return on investment criterion or a critical need criterion are approved to the extent of available funds.

The Capital Budgeting Group also meets monthly, as necessary, to consider any projects of a critical nature that were not expected or requested in the annual budget review. These monthly meetings allow the Capital Budgeting Group to make adjustments during the year as new developments occur.

Haskin's profits have been decreasing slightly for the past two years in spite of a small but steady sales growth, a sales growth that is expected to continue through 2006. As a result of the profit stagnation, top management is emphasizing cost control, and all aspects of Haskin's operations are being reviewed for cost reduction opportunities.

Haskin's internal audit department has become involved in the company-wide cost reduction effort. The department has already identified several areas where cost reductions could be realized and has made recommendations to implement the necessary procedures to effect the cost savings. Tom Watson, internal audit director, is now focusing on the activities of the Capital Budgeting Group in an attempt to determine the efficiency and effectiveness of the capital budgeting process.

In an attempt to gain a better understanding of the capital budgeting process, Watson decided to examine the history of one capital project in detail. A capital expenditure proposal of Haskin's Regina plant that was approved by the Capital Budgeting Group in 2004 was selected randomly from a population of all proposals approved by the group at its 2003 and 2004 annual planning and budget meetings.

The Regina proposal consisted of a request for five new machines to replace equipment that was 20 years old and for which preventive maintenance had become very expensive. Four of the machines were for replacement purposes, and the fifth was for planned growth in demand. Each of the four replacement machines was expected to result in annual maintenance cost savings of $10,000. The fifth machine was exactly like the other four and was expected to generate an annual contribution of $15,000 through increased output. Each machine cost $50,000 and had an estimated useful life of eight years.

Required

a. Identify and discuss the issues that Haskin Inc.'s internal audit department must address in its examination and evaluation of the Regina plant's 2004 capital expenditure project.

b. Recommend procedures to be used by Haskin's internal audit department in the audit review of the Regina plant's 2004 capital expenditure project.

(CMA adapted)

PROFESSIONAL JUDGMENT PROBLEM

24-19 Projections indicated that there would be record numbers of homeless over the next few years, so the city decided that it was important to have shelters available. Accordingly, contracts were signed with two hotels in the downtown area over a three-year period. The hotels and motels committed to have rooms available in the two coldest months of the year, and the city agreed to pay for the rooms at the rate of $40 per night. The hotel rooms were intended for homeless families.

At the same time, local churches got together and arranged to have volunteers staff the churches and provide hot meals so that the churches could be used as shelters by single individuals. The result was that the hotel rooms were not used, and over a period of three years, the city paid almost $850,000 for empty rooms. This was publicized when the Auditor General for the city published his annual report.

Required

a. What objectives and criteria would the city Auditor General have used when conducting his audit of expenditures for the homeless?

b. Draft a section of the value-for-money report that would explain how the audit was conducted as well as the findings.

c. What recommendations for improvement might be included in the audit report?

CASE

24-20 Mont Louis Hospital, which is affiliated with a leading university, has an extremely reputable research department that employs several renowned scientists. The research department operates on a project basis. The department consists of a pool of scientists and technicians who can be called on to participate in a given project. Assignments are made for the duration of the project, and a project manager is given responsibility for the work.

All major projects undertaken by the research department must be approved by the hospital's administrative board. Approval is obtained by submitting a proposal to the board outlining the project, the expected amount of time required to complete the work, and the anticipated benefits. The board also must be informed of major projects that are terminated because of potential failure or technological changes that have occurred since the time of project approval. An overall review of the status of open projects is submitted to the board annually.

In many respects, profit-making techniques utilized by business firms are applied to the management of the research department. For example, the department conducts preliminary research work on potential major projects that it has selected prior to requesting the board to approve the project and commit large amounts of time and money. The department also assesses the potential for grants and future revenues of the project. Financial reports for the department and each project are prepared periodically and reviewed with the administrative board.

Over 75 percent of the cost of operating the department is for labour. The remaining costs are for materials utilized during research. Materials used for experimentation are purchased by the hospital's central purchasing department. Once these materials are delivered, the research department is held accountable for their storage, their utilization, and the assignment of their costs to the projects.

In order to protect the hospital's right to discoveries made by the research department, staff members are required to sign waiver agreements at the time of hire and at certain intervals thereafter. The agreements relinquish the employees' rights to patent and royalty fees relating to hospital work.

Mont Louis's excellent reputation is due in part to the success of the research department. The research department has produced quality research in the health-care field and has always been able to generate revenues in excess of its costs. Mont Louis's administrative board believes that the hospital's continued reputation depends on a strong research department, and therefore, the board has requested that the university's internal auditors perform an operational audit of the department. As part of its request for the operational audit, the board has presented the following set of objectives that the internal audit is to achieve.

The operational audit to be conducted by the university's internal audit department should provide assurances that

- the research department has assessed the revenues and cost aspects of each project to confirm that the revenue potential is equal to or greater than estimated costs.
- appropriate controls exist to provide a means to measure how projects are progressing and to identify if corrective actions are required.
- financial reports prepared by the research department for presentation to the administrative board properly reflect all revenues (both endowment and royalty sources and appropriated funding) and all costs.

Required

a. Evaluate the objectives presented by the administrative board to the university's internal audit department in terms of their appropriateness as objectives for an operational audit. Discuss fully:
   (1) the strengths of the objectives.
   (2) the modifications and/or additions needed to improve the set of objectives.

b. Outline, in general terms, the basic procedures that would be suitable for performing the audit of the research department.

c. Identify three documents that members of the university's internal auditing staff would be expected to review during the audit, and describe the purpose that the review of each document serves in carrying out the audit.

(CMA adapted)

INDEX

The suffix -*f* indicates a figure, -*t* indicates a table, and –*n* indicates a note.

C

CA-Designated Specialists, 641
CAmagazine, 16
Cameron v. Piers, Conrod & Allen, 90, 90*f*
Campbell, Morgan, 339*n*
Canada Business Corporations Act, 16, 20, 46, 48, 49
Canada Post, 8
Canada Revenue Agency, 5
  see also tax return audit
Canada Revenue Agency auditors, 13
Canada–U.S. reporting differences, 61
Canadian Bar Association, 595
Canadian cheque processing systems, 255
Canadian Comprehensive Auditing Foundation, 12*n*
Canadian Council of Better Business Bureaus (CCBBB), 8
Canadian Depository for Securities Limited, 9
Canadian Institute of Chartered Accountants (CICA)
  see also CICA Assurance Handbook
  assurance on Internet transactions, 10
  auditing recommendations, 17
  continuing education, 16
  described, 3, 12
  exposure drafts, 654
  internal control report, 244
  management discussion and analysis (MD&A) standards, 62
  research and publications, 16, 654
  standards and rules, establishment of, 16–17
Canadian Payments Association, 255
Canadian Performance Reporting Board, 601
Canadian Public Accountability Board (CPAB), 14, 22, 24
Canadian Securities Administrators (CSA), 9, 24, 25, 48, 111, 244, 619
capital acquisition and repayment cycle
  accounts in, 571
  characteristics, 571
  defined, 571
  nature of, 571–576
  notes payable, 572–576
  owners' equity, 576–582
capital asset master file, 526
capital assets, 525
capital cost allowance recapture, 530
capital stock audit, 579–580
capital stock certificate book, 579
capitalization of expenses, 304
Cascade Designs, 317
case law, 86–87
cash accounts
  branch bank accounts, 454
  cash equivalents, 455
  general cash account, 454, 457–463
  imprest payroll account, 454
  imprest petty cash fund, 455
  relationship of general cash to other cash

accounts, 455, 455*f*
  types of, 454–455
cash and transaction cycles
  bank reconciliation, 457, 459, 464
  bank transfer working papers, 459–467, 467*f*
  cash accounts, types of, 454–455
  cash in the bank and, 455–457, 456*f*
  electronic cash transactions, 468–469
  fraud-oriented procedures, 464–468
  general cash account audit, 457–463
    see also general cash account
  kiting, 465–467
  payroll bank account, 468
  petty cash, 470
  proof of cash, 464–465, 466*f*
  verification of reconciliation *vs.* verification of recorded cash, 457
cash auditing. *See* cash and transaction cycles
cash disbursements, 503, 508*t*
  see also acquisition and payment cycle
cash disbursements journal, 503
cash equivalents, 455
cash in the bank. *See* general cash account
cash ratio, 172
cash receipts
  cutoff, 426
  debit card cash receipts, 469
  failure to record, 389
  incorrect allocation, 432
  internal controls, 388–390
  key controls, 391*t*
  lapping of accounts receivable, 390
  prelists of cash receipts, 389
  processing and recording, 375
  proof of cash receipts, 389
  subsequent, and confirmation of accounts receivable, 432
  tests of controls, 388–390, 390*t*
  transaction-related audit objectives, 390*t*
cash receipts journal, 375
Cashell, James D., 662*n*, 671
Catrini, Vincent, 343*n*
causal connection, absence of, 91, 95
CDS Inc., 9
centralized systems, 235
Certified Fraud Examiner (CFE), 110
certified general accountant (CGA), 3
Certified General Accountants Association of Canada (CGAAC), 3, 12, 16, 653
Certified Information Systems Auditor (CISA), 4, 654
certified internal auditor (CIA), 4
Certified Management Accountant (CMA), 3
Certified Public Accountants (CPAs), 10
CGA Magazine, 16
chart of accounts, 255
chartered accountants (CAs)
  audit attest function, 12
  described, 3
cheque processing systems, 255, 503

Cherry, Paul, 626
chief executive officer, 25, 111, 283
chief financial officer, 25, 283
CIBC Amicus, 158
CICA Accounting Handbook
  accounting changes, 581
  commitments, disclosure of, 592
  contingent liabilities, 590
  disclosure of segment information, 191
  earnings per share, 580
  financial instruments, 578
  fraud risk factors, 194
  future-oriented financial information (FOFI), 600
  government assistance, 528
  management representation letter, 599
  options, 578
  related party, 191, 542
  related-party transactions, 227
  warrants, 578
CICA Assurance Handbook
  accounting principles, application of, 46, 51
  adequacy of planning, 184
  agreement terms, 111
  amortization, 526*n*
  analysis, 166, 167, 598
  analytical procedures, 162–163, 290, 318
  annual reports, information in, 600
  association, 84, 617
  assurance engagement, 9, 26
  assurance engagement standards, 617–618, 619
  Assurance Recommendations, 17
  audit evidence, 155, 158, 340, 652
  audit evidence collection methods, 158
  audit objective, 110
  audit planning, 184
  audit procedures, 153
  audit risk, 217–218
  audit risk model and, 217–218
  auditor's report, 48, 58, 59
  auditor's responsibilities, 111, 112, 113
  auditor's standard report, 21, 26, 619
  audit environment, understanding of, 128
  authority of auditing assurance standards, 26
  business risk, 221
  change in accounting principle, 61
  communication of reportable internal control conditions, 606–607
  communication with audit committee, 332
  communication with management, 332, 605
  communication with those with oversight responsibility, 605
  communications with law firms, 595
  compilation engagement, 621, 628–629, 630*f*, 631
  completion phase, 167
  compliance with agreements, statutes

F

familiarity threat, 42, 43, 43*t*
fictitious receivables, 302*t*
fictitious revenues, 300
fiduciary duty, 82
final audit procedures
    accumulation of final
        evidence, 598–601
    analytical procedures, 598
    auditor communications, 605–608
    commitments, 592
    completing the engagement
        checklists, 601, 603*f*
    confirmation from client's law
        firms, 592–595
    contingent liabilities, review
        for, 590–592, 591*t*
    evaluation of results, 601–605, 602*f*
    evidence supporting auditor's
        opinion, 601–603
    financial statement
        disclosures, 603–604
    going concern assumption, 598
    independent reviewer, 605
    information in the annual report, 600
    management discussion and analysis
        (MD&A), 600–601
    management letter, 608
    management representation letter, 599
    subsequent discovery of
        factors, 608–609
    subsequent events, 595–597
    sufficiency of evidence, 601
    unadjusted misstatement
        worksheet, 605
    working paper review, 604–605
Financial Administration Act, 12
Financial Post Company, 169
financial ratios
    average accounts receivable
        turnover, 173
    average days to collect, 173
    average days to convert inventory to
        cash, 173
    average days to sell, 173
    average inventory turnover, 173
    book value per common share, 174
    cash ratio, 172
    computation of various ratios, 175–176
    current ratio, 172
    debt-to-equity ratio, 173
    dividend obligations, ability to
        meet, 173–174
    earnings per share, 174
    efficiency ratio, 174
    leverage ratios, 174
    long-term debt obligations, ability to
        meet, 173–174
    operating ratios, 174–175
    performance ratios, 174–175
    profit margin ratio, 174
    profitability ratio, 174
    quick ratio, 172
    return on common equity ratio, 174

    return on total assets ratio, 174
    short-term debt-paying ability, 172
    short-term liquidity, 172–173
    solvency ratios, 173–174
    tangible net assets to equity ratio, 173
    times interest and preferred dividends
        earned, 173
    times interest earned, 173
Financial Reporting in Canada, 16
financial statement audit
    as assurance engagement, 9
    described, 7
    historical cost financial statements, 9
financial statement cycles, 114–118
financial statement disclosure
    checklist, 604, 604*f*
financial statements
    assertions about presentation and
        disclosure, 122
    comparative financial statements, 61
    differential reporting options, 626
    disclosures, 603–604
    external users' reliance on, 221–222
    indication of possible
        misstatements, 166–167
    prospective financial statements, 631,
        632
    reasonable assurance, 246
    review of, 628, 628*f*
    unusual uncertainties, 62
    working papers, relationship to, 199*f*
finished goods
    physical controls, 554
    shipping, 550
    storage, 550
firewall, 650
firm, 41
    see also public accounting firms
fixed assets, 304
Flavelle, Dana, 225*n*
flowchart, 263
FOB destination, 513
FOB origin, 513
FOB shipping point, 513
foot, 165*t*
forecasts, 631, 633*f*
    see also future-oriented financial
        information (FOFI)
Foreign Corrupt Practices Act of 1977, 102
forensic accountant, 307
forensic auditors, 109–110
Forum of Firms (FOF), 99
Fraser, Bruce W., 3*n*
Fraser, Sheila, 2–3, 618
fraud
    antifraud programs and controls, 295
    computer-assisted audit techniques
        (CAATs), 306
    computer fraud, 113, 305
    conditions for, 284–287
    constructive fraud, 86
    corporate governance and, 291–296
    and criminal liability, 95–96
    defined, 86, 282

    earnings management, 282
    employee fraud. *See* defalcation
    forensic auditors, 110
    fraudulent financial
        reporting, 282–283, 284–286,
        285*t*
    and general cash balance, 459
    income smoothing, 282
    kiting, 465–467
    management fraud, 84, 112
    misappropriation of assets, 283–284,
        286–287, 286*t*
    motivation for, 285
    and other irregularities, 112
    payroll, 484–486
    prevention and detection of, 244
    procurement card fraud, 528
    procurement fraud, 284
    rates of occurrence, 300*f*
    recorded sale, no shipment, 385
    responsibilities when fraud
        suspected, 305–307
    risk factors, 284–287
    sale recorded more than once, 385
    shipment to nonexistent customers, 385
    types of, 282–284
fraud and other irregularities, 112
fraud assessment
    analytical procedures, 290
    audit team discussions, 288–289
    auditor's role, 287–291
    critical evaluation of audit
        evidence, 288
    documentation of, 290–291
    enquiry of management and audit
        committee, 289–290
    fraud risk factors, evaluation of, 290
    information sources about fraud
        risks, 288–289, 289*f*
    professional skepticism, 287–288
    questioning mind, 288
fraud prevention
    additional declarations, 294
    antifraud programs and controls, 295
    audit committee oversight, 296
    code of conduct, elements of, 293*t*
    confirmation, 292
    culture of honesty, 291–294
    discipline, 292–293
    ethics, 291–294
    fraud prevention programs and
        controls, 295–296
    hiring and promotion of appropriate
        employees, 292
    positive workplace environment, 292
    reduction of fraud risks, 291–297
    responsibility to evaluate fraud
        risks, 294–296
    tone at the top, 291–292
    training, 292
fraud prevention programs and
    controls, 295–296
Fraud Resistant P-cards
    (Holdegraver), 670